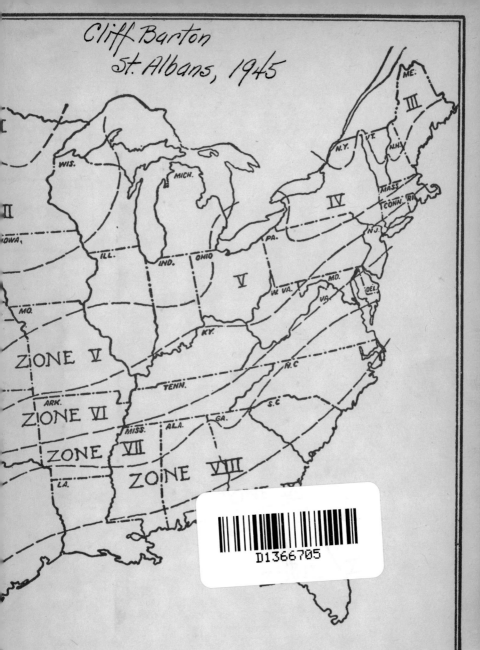

Each zone represents an area in which similar climatic conditions prevail. The zones are based on average annual minimum winter temperatures for the years 1895 to 1935, but rainfall and soil are factors not taken into consideration.

Foreword

Gardening is a craft, a science, and an art. To practise it well requires the enthusiasm of the true amateur and the understanding of the true student.

A garden is sensitive to the will of the gardener. For this reason it reflects the taste of the present, and it changes from generation to generation with changing ideals. Gardening is an art close to the hearts of the American people; and unlike most other works of art, a garden requires of its owner something more than mere appreciation. He must care for it, renew it, and put his thought and handiwork into its very life. Within recent years the interest in gardening has become ever more widespread, and among the home owners of America there is a growing appreciation of the fact that it is the doing of the practical tasks in an artistic way which gives lasting satisfaction and which will raise the craft of gardening to the status of an art.

In the preparation of AMERICA'S GARDEN BOOK, the authors have endeavored to meet the needs of those living in suburban and country communities for accurate information on all phases of garden-making. The subject matter is not confined to flower and vegetable gardening, but includes all the activities within the meaning of the word. Throughout the book it has been the aim of the authors not only to present the latest and most approved methods and practices of gardening, but also to emphasize the importance of the results as judged from the artistic standpoint. No attempt has been made to write an all-inclusive encyclopedia. Although practically every phase of gardening is discussed, there is evident an element of selection, dictated by matters of taste. The lists of garden flowers, trees, and shrubs are not complete catalogues, but contain a selection of those varieties which have merit as materials for planting compositions.

With the exception of a few cases, the International Rules of Botanical Nomenclature have been followed, so that the names agree with those used in Bailey's *Standard Cyclopedia of Horticulture* and in Rehder's *Manual of Cultivated Trees and Shrubs.* The exceptions have been made in recognizing habitual usage, and in such cases *Standardized Plant Names* by the American Joint Committee on Horticultural Nomenclature has been the authority. For example, the authors have preferred to retain the use of Azalea, which is everywhere understood, rather than to be botanically correct and to call all Azaleas, Rhododendrons. Common names of plants are those given in *Standardized Plant Names.*

In designating the relative hardiness of trees, shrubs, and vines, the map published by the United States Department of Agriculture in the *Atlas of American Agriculture* has been used. Each zone represents an area in which similar climatic conditions prevail. The data are based on average annual minimum winter temperatures, but rainfall and soil have not been taken into consideration. The zone of hardiness of the various species has been derived largely from Rehder's *Manual of Cultivated Trees and Shrubs.*

The authors are indebted to Doctor Ruth Patrick, head of the Department of Botany at the School of Horticulture, for her valuable contribution of the chapter on "The Culture of Plants in Nutrient Solutions," and for her aid in the preparation of the material on the propagation of ferns and on certain plant diseases. The authors also wish to express their appreciation to Mr. John A. Andrew, Jr., of the School of Horticulture, for contributing the chapters on Fruits and Vegetables, and to Miss June E. Schroth for her faithful help in the preparation of the plants lists and her aid in many other details.

LOUISE BUSH-BROWN
The School of Horticulture
Ambler, Pennsylvania
JAMES BUSH-BROWN

Contents

ix

CONTENTS

CONTENTS

xi

CONTENTS

CONTENTS

xiii

CONTENTS

CONTENTS

xv

CONTENTS

Illustrations

xvii

ILLUSTRATIONS

ILLUSTRATIONS

ILLUSTRATIONS

America's
Garden Book

>>×<<

Soils and Soil Improvement

There is no subject of more fundamental importance to the gardener than that of soil management. In order to handle garden soils intelligently, and to maintain or increase the fertility of the soil, it is necessary to have a thorough knowledge not only of the soil itself, but also of the manner in which plants receive their nutrients from the soil.

There are comparatively few soils which provide ideal conditions for plant growth, but if a wise program of soil management is put into effect, much may be accomplished in improving the structure, the fertility, and the water-holding capacity of soils of widely varying types.

There are certain factors affecting plant growth over which a gardener has very little control, such as climate, rainfall, sunshine and humidity; but over the various factors of soil management he has very definite control. The soil is a heritage which has come to us from the past—a heritage which we in turn will pass on, and it is the privilege of those who work with it to regard it as a trust. Not only for our own immediate benefit should we strive to conserve, and to maintain, and to increase its fertility—it is our obligation to the generations of gardeners who are to follow us.

SOIL FORMATION

The formation of the soil is a process which has continued since earliest geologic times when the surface of the earth was composed entirely of rock. The action of sun and frost, air and water upon these rock surfaces of the earth has resulted in a gradual process of disintegration and the consequent slow formation of soils. Æons ago the first plants grew in the hollows and crevices of the rocks where this newly formed mineral soil had found lodgement. And as these primitive plants died, they decayed and formed food for other plants, and gradually, as the millenniums passed, this decaying organic matter became mixed with the mineral soil, thus enriching it, and increasing the earth's vegetation. In sections where primeval forest growth abounds we find deep, porous soils, rich in humus, which are classed as peaty soils. Such soils are also found in peat bogs and are composed almost entirely of decayed organic matter. In other sections we find soils which are classed as mineral soils, being composed largely of mineral matter. And in between these two extreme types, the peaty soils and the mineral soils, we find many soils of widely varying character.

Most soils, as we find them in our gardens today, are comprised of five intermingled components: the mineral substances obtained from the slow disintegration of rock surfaces; humus or decaying organic matter; minute living organisms such as the bacteria, protozoa and fungi which are present in large quantities in most soils; water, which holds in solution the dissolved mineral salts; and air. In sections where the soil has been under cultivation for many years or where the program of soil management has been poor we find soils which have lost much of their humus content and which, in many cases, have become depleted of their mineral elements. It is these soils which present the greatest problems.

TYPES OF SOIL

Soils are generally grouped into three classes according to structure: sand, silt, or clay. These classes are determined by the size of the soil particles. Sand contains 20 particles or less to a millimeter, silt 20 to 200 particles to a millimeter, and clay 200 or more. A soil of ideal texture is a mixture of sand, silt and clay, being classed as a good garden loam. The structure of the soil has a very direct bearing upon its water-holding capacity, upon its warmth in early spring, upon the ease with which it can be worked or handled, and upon the penetration of plant roots and the consequent nutrition of the plant.

Clay Soils. A clay soil has a water-holding capacity many times higher than that of a sandy soil because each soil particle is capable of holding a film of water upon its surface. Therefore a clay soil possessing 200 particles per millimeter is capable of holding ten times as much water as sand which possesses only 20 particles to the same area. The water-holding capacity of clay soils may be an asset in seasons of extreme drought, but it is, on the whole, almost as much of a liability as it is an asset. Heavy clay soils are very slow in drying out in the spring, and all planting operations and general cultural practices must therefore be delayed. It does not absorb the sun's rays as readily as does a soil of lighter texture and, therefore, does not warm up as quickly in the spring, thus delaying the normally eager spring growth of plants. If left uncultivated too long after a rain, a clay soil will form a hard, baked crust which makes it impossible for either air or moisture to reach the roots of the plants, and in some cases it will form deep cracks. On the other hand, if it is plowed or cultivated or otherwise handled when it is too wet, it will form hard lumps which are exceedingly difficult to break down. A clay soil is one of the most difficult of all soil types to handle wisely, and every effort should be made to improve its structure. Much may be accomplished by the addition of sand, humus, and compost, and even sifted coal ashes will be of some benefit. It is also an advantage to spade or plow clay soils in the autumn, leaving them in a very rough condition throughout the winter. The action of the frost will have a beneficial effect on the close texture of the soil, making it somewhat more mellow and friable.

Sandy Soils possess many of the advantages which are lacking in soils of a decidedly heavy texture. They warm up quickly in the spring, they are easy to work. On the other hand, sandy soils are not retentive of moisture and many of the soluble plant foods may be lost through leaching. It is quite as important, therefore, to improve the structure of sandy soils as it is to improve the structure of heavy clay soils. This may be accomplished most successfully by the addition of liberal quantities of organic matter.

Loam Soils. The ideal soil for most garden operations is a fertile loam, which is a mixture of sand, clay, and humus. It should be porous enough in texture to provide good drainage and adequate aeration; it should be spongy enough to retain an ample supply of moisture; it should contain sufficient humus to provide favorable conditions for the growth of the soil bacteria, which play such an important part in plant nutrition; and it should contain all the mineral elements necessary for the healthy, normal growth of plant life. A soil of this type is the desideratum of every gardener, and with a good program of soil management and an intelligent understanding of the needs of growing plants, much may be accomplished in building a soil which will very nearly approximate the ideal.

HUMUS

An adequate supply of humus in the soil is one of the most important factors in a program of good soil management.

Humus serves many functions in improving the structure and character of the soil. It increases the water-holding capacity of soils; it modifies the soil structure; it readily absorbs the sun's rays and consequently increases and stimulates plant growth in early spring; it prevents the leaching of soluble plant foods; it liberates compounds which, in turn, act upon the chemical elements in the soil, thus making available to the plants mineral nutrients which would otherwise remain in insoluble form; and it promotes the bacterial action in the soil to a very marked degree.

The value of humus in increasing the water-holding capacities of soils can hardly be overemphasized. It is unlike the particles of mineral soils in that it does not merely hold the water on its surface; it soaks it in like a sponge. In a series of recent experiments to test the water-holding capacities of soils of varying types, it was found that 100 pounds of sand will hold 25 pounds of water; 100 pounds of clay will hold 50 pounds of water, and 100 pounds of humus will hold 190 pounds of water. From 20 to 40 per cent of the water-holding capacity of soils is due to their humus content, and in seasons of prolonged drought soils high in humus content will remain moist in both the upper and lower soil horizons far longer than soils which are deficient in humus, and plant growth is correspondingly greater.

Humus is also of great value in improving the texture of soils, as it has the ability to modify the soil structure to a very marked degree. A soil which is of mellow, friable texture, the kind which we class as an ideal garden loam, is made up of crumbs of soil held together in a granule, and it is the humus which furnishes the binding material for these soil particles. A soil of this texture permits the rapid renewal of moisture and food nutrients. It also permits easy root penetration, which is an important factor, as the roots travel to the water and food in the soil, not vice versa. When a clay soil is deficient in humus it becomes tight and compact in structure. The penetration of the roots is therefore restricted and the nutrition of the plant is often seriously limited in consequence. Such a soil has a tendency to become hard and baked when it is dry, and is far less permeable to water than soil of a more open structure. Not only does the water penetrate the soil less readily but it is also more quickly evaporated. Soils of this type may be greatly improved in texture by the application of liberal amounts of humus. When sandy soils are deficient in humus, many valuable plant nutrients are lost through leaching and plant growth also suffers seriously from lack of moisture in times of drought. It is, therefore, quite as important to see that sandy soils are well supplied with humus as it is to maintain an adequate humus supply in clay soils.

Humus and Mineral Fertilizers. Mineral fertilizers supplement, but in no way do they replace, humus. Recent experiments have proved that mineral fertilizers are much more effective if they are applied either with, or immediately following, an application of humus, than if they are applied alone. At the Maryland Experiment Station, crop yields have shown an increase varying from $\frac{1}{5}$ to $\frac{1}{3}$ more when manure and mineral fertilizers were applied together than when double the amount of either was applied alone. This same principle would apply to the building up of soil fertility in the garden.

5

SOURCES OF HUMUS

Peat. The various forms of peat provide an excellent source of humus. Technically, peat may be defined as the partially carbonized organic residue of plants, the decomposition of which has taken place under standing water. The peats may be classed into several groups: those of deep water, marsh, swamp, and bog origin. When the process of decay of such substances as tree trunks, mosses, sedges, and grasses takes place under water, the decomposition is greatly retarded because of the exclusion of air, and the resulting product, known as peat, differs considerably from the humus which is found in upland forests.

Peat is rich in organic matter, is highly absorbent and retentive of moisture, and has the added advantage of being comparatively free from weed seeds and harmful fungi. Peat is usually somewhat acid in its reaction and it must, therefore, be used with discrimination. It is of particular value for use in connection with the planting of broad-leaved evergreens, such as rhododendrons, laurel, azaleas, and many of the acid-loving woodland plants, but it should not be used too liberally in connection with plants which are not acid tolerant. The actual fertilizing value of peat is comparatively low. It contains some nitrogen, the amount varying from 1 to 3.5 per cent, depending upon the source of the peat, and it is extremely low in phosphorus and potash.

The two kinds of peat most readily obtainable are imported peat and domestic peat. The imported peat comes in tightly packed bales, weighing about 200 pounds. It is largely of bog origin, being a sphagnum type of peat, and it is very low in nitrogen content. When it is to be incorporated in the soil, or used as a mulch, the handling of it will be greatly facilitated if the bale is thoroughly soaked before it is opened. When dry it is rather difficult to handle because of its light, somewhat fluffy texture.

Domestic peat has a higher moisture content, is darker in color and finer in texture. In general it is considered a better source of humus than the imported peat, as it may be more thoroughly incorporated with the soil and its effect is more lasting.

Leaf Mold is an excellent and usually a readily available source of humus. It is highly retentive of moisture, is rich in organic matter, and has the ability to change into a more readily available form various nitrogenous materials in the soil. Leaf mold varies considerably in its reaction upon the soil. Oak leaves and pine needles, when decayed, form a leaf mold which is definitely acid in its reaction. However, the majority of our deciduous trees form a leaf mold which is very mildly acid or entirely neutral in reaction. The best and most abundant source of leaf mold is the natural forest floor. A small but readily available supply may be kept at hand by making a compost of leaves each autumn. If the pile is kept moist and if an occasional handful of a complete fertilizer* is spread over the leaves as the pile is being made, the process of decay will be hastened and the resulting product will be of greater value.

The Compost Pile. A compost pile is a valuable adjunct to every garden. It provides an excellent source of soil which is relatively rich in plant food and high in organic content. Such soils are of particular value as potting soils for house plants, and for use in the greenhouse. They are of value also in the preparation of perennial borders and rose beds, and as a top-dressing for lawns. Indeed, there are so many uses for a good compost that the supply seems never to be quite sufficient to meet one's needs.

The ingredients which go into the making of a compost pile will vary considerably, depending to a large extent upon the materials which one has at hand. Sod, grass clippings, weeds, manure, leaves, hay, straw, ground-up cornstalks, or any other form of quickly decaying vegetable matter may be used. The pile may vary in width from 4 to 6 feet and it may be of any desired length. The top of the pile should be slightly concave in order to catch as much rain as possible. The usual procedure is to have a basic layer of inverted sods, or some coarse material. Alternating layers of soil and vegetable matter are then built up. Manure may be used to excellent advantage if it is available,

*See page 22.

7

but it is not an essential ingredient. The decomposition of the organic material will be hastened if a commercial fertilizer is sprinkled liberally over it when the pile is being constructed. A mixture of 75 pounds of sulphate of ammonia, 50 pounds of superphosphate, and 100 pounds of ground limestone per ton of material is recommended. If manure is used it should not come into contact with any of the ground limestone as it will cause the ammonia to be liberated and much of the fertility will be lost. The compost pile should be kept moist, and it is well to turn it at intervals of every few months, restacking it so that

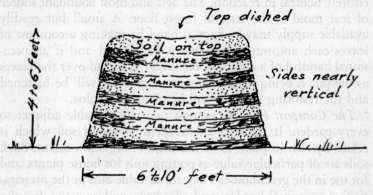

Cross Section of Compost Pile

the outer portion is placed in the center of the new pile. The rate of decomposition will depend upon the materials used and whether or not a commercial fertilizer is added to hasten the bacterial action.

Cover Crops. Cover crops are often spoken of as "green manures." The term is applied to crops which are grown for the sole purpose of being plowed or spaded under, in order to improve the physical texture of the soil, to increase its organic content, and to increase its fertility. Such a procedure is one of the best and also one of the least expensive methods of improving poor, worn out soils. It is, on the whole, more suitable for large-scale operations than for use on small areas. It may play a very important part, however, in the initial preparation of the soil for a vegetable garden or a fruit orchard, or for a lawn area of any considerable extent.

The most valuable cover crops, from the standpoint of increasing the fertility of the soil, are the legumes, such as soybeans, alfalfa, the clovers, and the vetches. The legumes actually increase the nitrogen content of the soil through the aid of the nitrogen-fixing bacteria. These highly specialized bacteria, which have the ability to take nitrogen from the air, are minute, rod-shaped bodies which are found in the soil under certain favorable conditions. When these bacteria come into contact with the roots of certain legume plants, they enter the root hairs, causing a slight irritation which results in the growth of a tiny, round ball called a nodule. These bacteria take nitrogen from the air and supply it to the plant. The plant, in return, furnishes other food matter to the bacteria which enables them to multiply rapidly. This relationship is called symbiosis. There is a slight difference in the forms of bacteria found on different types of legumes—one form living on one group of legumes, another living only on certain other types. Some legumes, such as alfalfa, are very dependent upon the nitrogen-fixing bacteria and the plants are unable to make vigorous, normal growth, or to survive at all, unless these bacteria are present in the soil. Other legumes, such as soybeans, are considerably less dependent and will make reasonably good growth on soil where no bacteria are present. When grown under such conditions, however, these crops are no more valuable than a non-leguminous crop, as they do not increase the nitrogen content of the soil unless the bacteria are present. In order to insure the presence of these nitrogen-fixing bacteria in the soil all legume crops should be inoculated, previous to planting, with an especially prepared inoculant, carrying the exact type of bacteria needed for the particular legume which is to be grown. Such inoculants are obtainable from any commercial seed house and are accompanied by full instructions.

The value of legumes as cover crops can hardly be over-emphasized. A well-grown leguminous crop which is plowed under at the proper stage of growth will frequently add from 100 to 150 pounds of actual nitrogen to the soil per acre. This would be practically the equivalent of 10 to 15 tons of good animal manure.

The stage of growth at which cover crops are plowed under has a very direct influence upon the value of the crop. The nitrogen and mineral content are highest shortly before maturity. Therefore, the crop should be plowed under when it is in a slightly immature stage.

If cover crops are to be grown on soils of very low fertility, the eventual value of the crop as a soil improver will be greatly increased if the cover crop receives the benefit of an application of commercial fertilizer, and if conditions are made generally favorable for good growth. There is little to be gained from growing a cover crop on land which is so poor that it can support little in the way of plant growth. Under such conditions, the resulting benefits will hardly justify the cost of seed and labor.

It is a generally accepted fact that the crops which are planted immediately following the plowing under of a cover crop (particularly a non-leguminous crop) will thrive infinitely better if a fairly liberal application of a commercial fertilizer is made at the time that the crop is turned under. The same principle applies to the plowing under of a heavy growth of sod. This is due to the fact that the process of decomposition is carried on by certain of the bacteria in the soil. These bacteria need to use the nitrogen in the soil in order to carry on their activities, and unless a surplus of nitrogen is present the plants suffer in consequence. By applying a high nitrogenous fertilizer such a surplus may be assured and there will be a readily available supply both for the bacteria and for the plants.

DESIRABLE COVER CROPS*

LEGUMINOUS CROPS

Alfalfa is a perennial crop and consequently requires a longer time to become established than the annual and biennial crops, but there

*Dates recommended for plowing under are applicable to the latitude of Pennsylvania and Ohio. In any locality, cover crops should be turned under when slightly immature.

are instances when its use as a cover crop is justified. In a case where a country property is purchased and there are open fields which will eventually be put into lawns, no better use can be made of the land than to put it into alfalfa.

Time and Rate of Seeding: The seed may be sown in early spring or late summer at the rate of 10 to 12 pounds per acre and it should be inoculated. If the field is weedy late summer sowing is preferable.

Soil Requirements: A well-drained soil of reasonably good fertility with a pH. of 6.5 or above. (See page 24 for an explanation of pH.)

Time of Plowing Under: Hay may be harvested for a number of years and the crop may be plowed under in the fall or in the spring when the ground is desired for some other purpose, such as a lawn area, garden or orchard. When plowed under, the tops and roots contain approximately 2.65 per cent nitrogen and as much as 150 pounds per acre of actual nitrogen may be added to the soil.

Hairy Vetch is a winter annual and is one of the most valuable of all soil builders.

Time and Rate of Seeding: May be sown early in September at the rate of 3 to 4 pecks per acre. The seed should be inoculated.

Soil Requirements: It thrives best on a sandy, well-drained soil with a pH. of 6.5 or slightly above.

Time of Plowing Under: Should be plowed under about the middle of May. If turned under at this season the top growth and roots will contain approximately 3.75 per cent nitrogen.

Mammoth Red Clover. Being a biennial, it is necessary for red clover to occupy the ground for a considerable length of time and it is therefore not as well suited for a cover crop as are some of the other legumes, although it is rated as a splendid soil builder.

Time and Rate of Seeding: It should be sown very early in the spring, preferably with a small grain crop such as oats, or on a wheat crop sown the previous fall. Rate of seeding—8–12 pounds per acre. Inoculate seed.

Soil Requirements: A soil of at least moderate fertility with a pH. above 5.5.

Time of Plowing Under: Should be plowed under just before full bloom the year after sowing.

Soybeans are one of the most valuable of all cover crops as they are a summer annual and make rapid growth.

Time and Rate of Seeding: Soybeans should be sown in May or early June at the rate of 2 bushels per acre.

Soil Requirements: If grown on very poor soil a complete fertilizer should be added. Soil should have a pH. above 5.

Time of Plowing Under: It is very important that soybeans be plowed under before the vines have become too mature. The most generally accepted practice is to turn them under when the beans in the pods are about half grown. At this stage, the tops and roots will contain approximately 2.65 per cent nitrogen.

Sweet Clover is a biennial which possesses tremendous soil building potentialities.

Time and Rate of Seeding: Sweet clover should be sown early in the spring either on, or with, a small grain crop. The usual rate of seeding is 10 to 12 pounds per acre.

Soil Requirements: Sweet clover is one of the few legumes which will grow well on very poor soil. It thrives reasonably well on washed clay land. Its one definite requirement is a soil high in lime content with a pH. of 6.5 or above.

Time of Plowing Under: The crop may be plowed under the spring following seeding. In order to secure good results it is essential that it be turned under before it reaches maturity. If plowed under between April 15 and May 1 the maximum percentage of nitrogen will be secured, often running as high as 3.75 per cent.

NON-LEGUMINOUS CROPS

Rye is considered the most valuable of all the non-legumes as a cover crop. Although it does not increase the actual nitrogen content of the soil, it adds a considerable amount of organic matter.

Time and Rate of Seeding: Rye should be sown during early September, being seeded at the rate of 1½ to 2 bushels per acre.

Soil Requirements: Rye succeeds reasonably well on a soil of average fertility and is almost entirely indifferent to the matter of soil acidity, thriving well on decidedly acid soil.

Time of Plowing Under: Rye should be plowed under in the spring when it has reached a height of approximately 10 inches. At this time the plant contains a greater percentage of nitrogen than at any other stage of its development, sometimes running as high as 1.75 per cent.

Rye and Hairy Vetch may be sown in combination, and make a very excellent cover crop.

Time and Rate of Seeding: They should be seeded early in September at the rate of 5 pecks per acre, the mixture containing 60 pounds of rye to 20 pounds of hairy vetch.

Soil Requirements: Soil pH. above 6.5 because of the vetch.

Time of Plowing Under: About the middle of May.

ANIMAL MANURES

Long before commercial fertilizers were thought of, the good qualities of animal manures in improving and maintaining soil fertility were known and appreciated. Not only does animal manure increase the fertility of the soil, but it also serves other important functions as well. It increases the organic content of the soil; it improves the physical structure of the soil; it increases the bacterial activity to a very appreciable degree; and it has, in general, a very beneficial effect upon the soil.

Contrary to popular belief, the actual elements of fertility contained in animal manures are very meager when compared with those contained in most inorganic commercial fertilizers. The following table indicates the usual percentages found in various types of manure.

	Nitrogen	*Phosphorus*	*Potassium*
Poultry Manure	1.0	0.8	0.4
Sheep Manure	0.95	0.35	1.0
Horse Manure	0.7	0.25	0.55
Cow Manure	0.6	0.15	0.45
Pig Manure	0.5	0.35	0.4

It is even more startling to realize that, low as the above percentages may seem, only one-half of the nitrogen, one-half of the potassium and one-sixth of the phosphorus are readily available for use by the plants. It can, therefore, be seen that the actual fertility added to the soil by an application of animal manure is very slight, and that the benefits derived from such an application are those which are more directly concerned with the physical character of the soil.

The value of animal manure, from a standpoint of fertility,

depends to a considerable extent upon the method of handling. If a high percentage of the nutrients which it contains as fresh manure is to be conserved it must be handled with care. The most generally accepted practice is to store manure under cover, to keep it piled in watertight pits and to keep the stack constantly moist, never allowing it to dry out or to become firefanged through overheating. If manure is not properly handled it may lose a very large percentage of its nutrients and it may become practically valueless from a standpoint of increasing the actual fertility of the soil.

The rate of application of stable manure varies from what is considered a moderate application of 15 tons per acre to an extremely heavy application of 40 tons per acre; or from 70 pounds per 1000 square feet to 2000 pounds per 1000 square feet.

Fresh manure should never be used where it will come into direct contact with the root formation of the plants as it is liable to cause severe burning. Most gardeners prefer to use manure after it has become partially rotted. In this form the nutrients are more readily available and the danger of any harmful effects is largely mitigated. On large-scale operations manure is usually spread upon the surface of the soil and is then plowed in. On smaller areas it is forked or spaded into the soil.

Dehydrated Manures. There are various forms of dry, shredded and pulverized manures on the market. From the standpoint of economy, such manures are a poor investment. During the process of dehydrating, some of the nitrogen is lost, and comparatively little actual fertility is added to the soil. For the same expenditure, far better results may be obtained from the use of domestic humus and commercial fertilizers.

Liquid Manures. The type of liquid manure formerly used to a considerable extent by gardeners was made by immersing a bushel of manure in a barrel of water. The modern method which consists of dissolving a highly concentrated nitrogenous fertilizer, such as nitrate of soda, urea, or ammonium sulphate, or a well-balanced complete fertilizer, in water and thus applying it to the plant is far superior both from a standpoint of economy, ease of application, and the reliability of the results.

ARTIFICIAL MANURE

In these days when manure is often difficult to obtain, it is a source of satisfaction to the gardener to be able to make an artificial manure which is very similar in every way to the natural product. This may be done by mixing commercial fertilizers and lime with straw, hay, weeds, grass clippings, leaves or any other garden refuse. It is essential that this work be undertaken in the late spring or early summer as the decomposition of the material is dependent upon bacterial action, and correct temperature and abundant moisture are factors of vital importance. To each ton of straw or other litter, the following ingredients should be added—

                60 pounds sulphate of ammonia
                30 pounds superphosphate
                25 pounds potassium chloride
                50 pounds ground limestone

The method of making artificial manure resembles that for making compost, previously outlined, but for convenience it is repeated here. The pile should be approximately 4 to 6 feet wide, 4 feet high and any desired length. A 4-inch layer of composting material should be placed upon the surface of the ground. This should be liberally sprinkled with the fertilizing ingredients and it should then be thoroughly soaked with water. This process should be repeated until the pile has reached the desired height. The top of the pile should be slightly hollow, or concave, so that it will retain as much water as possible. Unless the rainfall is unusually heavy, the pile should be soaked daily for the period of a week or more in order that the bacterial action may be promoted as rapidly as possible. After the process of decomposition has started, a thorough weekly soaking will usually be sufficient. The sides as well as the top of the pile should be soaked, and the pile should be kept moist at all times. Within three or four months the material should have become sufficiently decomposed, and it will have a composition very similar to a good quality barnyard manure. One ton of straw will produce approximately three tons of organic material.

PLANT NUTRITION

In order to provide for an adequate supply of nutrients in the soil it is essential to understand something of the method by which plants manufacture their food from the elements obtained from the soil and the air.

Plants obtain carbon dioxide from the air, and their mineral nutrients from the soil, these being absorbed in solution form by the root hairs. From these elements a plant is able, in the presence of light, to manufacture sugars, proteins, and other complex organic substances which are used by the plant in the production of new tissue, or for the maintenance of existing tissues. As long as all the essential elements are present in sufficient amounts, the plant is able, in the presence of light, to continue this process of food manufacture throughout its life. If one or more of the elements obtained from the soil, or if the carbon dioxide of the air, is not present in sufficient quantities, the production of food becomes limited and the growth of the plant is seriously affected.

There are eleven mineral elements which are essential for the normal growth of plants: nitrogen, phosphorus, potassium, magnesium, calcium, manganese, aluminum, iron, copper, boron and zinc. Some of these, such as boron, zinc, copper and several others, are spoken of as trace elements and are usually present in the soil in sufficient amounts to supply the needs of the plants. The three elements which are most likely to be deficient in soils which have been brought under cultivation are nitrogen, phosphorus, and potassium. Each of these elements has an important function to fulfill in promoting healthy plant growth.

NITROGEN

Nitrogen is an essential element for plant growth. Its most important function is to stimulate vegetative development and it is, therefore, particularly necessary in the production of leaves and stems. If an excess of nitrogen is applied, the effects are decidedly harmful, as it will result in an overluxuriant growth of foliage at the expense of flowers and fruit, and maturity will consequently be delayed. The cell walls of the stems will also become weakened and the plant's resistance to disease will be appreciably lowered.

Nitrogen is seldom found in the soil in a free state, it being almost invariably found in combination with other elements. Soils are usually lowest in available nitrogen during the early spring months and it is at this season that quickly available nitrogenous fertilizers are of particular value. It also sometimes happens that in prolonged periods of heavy rains during the summer much of the available nitrogen is leached out of the soil, and when such a condition occurs an immediate application of nitrogen should be made.

SOURCES OF INORGANIC NITROGEN

When applying nitrogen in any of the inorganic forms, the material should not come into direct contact with the foliage of the plant as it may cause severe burning. If it is accidentally dropped onto the foliage it should be washed off immediately with a strong spray of water.

Nitrate of Soda. The most quickly available form of nitrogen is nitrate of soda which contains approximately 15 per cent nitrogen. Upon application it is almost immediately available to the plant. It is more quickly available in acid soils than in alkaline soils. It should be used only on well-established plants which are making active growth and the soil should be moist when an application is made. Nitrate of soda may be applied in the dry form, the substance being scattered upon the surface of the soil at the rate of 1 pound to 100 square feet, or it may be applied in the form of a solution, being dissolved in water at the rate of 1 ounce to 2 gallons of water. In soils where lime is not present, the long-continued use of nitrate of soda may cause a toxic condition, because of an undue accumulation of sodium carbonate.

Calcium Nitrate contains 15 per cent nitrogen. It is readily available, but leaves a decidedly alkaline residue in the soil and it is, therefore, not as generally used as nitrate of soda. The rate of application is approximately the same.

Ammonium Sulphate is a by-product obtained in the manufacture of coal-gas, and it contains approximately 20 per cent or more of nitrogen in a readily available form. In warm soils it is often as quickly available as is nitrate of soda, and it has been proven that in alkaline soils its availability is even quicker and greater than nitrate of soda. When it is used over a period of many years it has a tendency to develop an acid reaction in the soil, but any difficulty of this nature may be readily overcome by the use of lime. When ammonium sulphate is applied to acid soils the results will be more satisfactory if it is used in combination with superphosphate, than if it is used alone. The usual rate of application varies from 1 to 2 pounds per 100 square feet, or, in the form of a solution, 1 ounce to 2 gallons of water.

Urea is a synthetic form of nitrogen, being a combination of ammonia and carbon dioxide. It contains 46 per cent nitrogen in a form which is quickly soluble, but it is not as quick in its action as nitrate of soda. Being a highly concentrated form of nitrogen, urea must be used with care and discretion. When applied dry it should be mixed with sand, in order that an even distribution may be secured. It is usually applied at the rate of ½ pound per 100 square feet. In the liquid form it is used at the rate of 1 ounce to 7 gallons of water.

Ammonium Phosphate is obtainable in two forms—as mono-ammonium phosphate which contains 10 per cent nitrogen and 48 per cent phosphoric acid; and as di-ammonium phosphate, which is more highly concentrated and contains 21 per cent nitrogen and 53 per cent phosphoric acid. A similar material is put out under the trade name of ammophos. The usual rate of application of ammonium phosphate varies from 1 to 2 pounds per 100 square feet.

Cyanamid is another synthetic product of fairly high concentration, being composed of calcium cyanamid and calcium hydroxide. It contains from 20 to 25 per cent of nitrogen and it is highly alkaline in its reaction. The usual rate of application is approximately 1 pound per 100 square feet.

Nitrophoska. A series of highly concentrated complete fertilizers have been put out under the trade name of Nitrophoska, and these furnish an excellent source of nitrogen. Several combinations are available, analyzing 15–30–15, 15.5–15.5–19 and 15–11–26. (See page 22 for explanation of this ratio.) The rate of application varies from 1 to 2 pounds per 100 square feet.

SOURCES OF ORGANIC NITROGEN

In general the organic forms of nitrogen are less highly concentrated than the inorganic forms and are more slowly available to the plants.

Cottonseed Meal contains approximately 7 per cent of nitrogen which becomes slowly available over a long period of time. It is more readily available in warm soils than in cold soils. The usual rate of application varies from 2 to 5 pounds per 100 square feet. There is practically no danger of overstimulation of the plants or of burning when cottonseed meal is used, and in addition to nitrogen it supplies other elements of fertility in small amounts. The usual analysis is 7 per cent nitrogen, 2 to 3 per cent phosphorus, 2 per cent potash.

Castor Pomace is very similar to cottonseed meal in general composition, containing slightly less nitrogen. The nitrogen content usually averages about 5 per cent and a somewhat heavier application is therefore made.

Dried Blood is an excellent organic source of nitrogen, containing from 9 to 14 per cent. The nitrogen is in a form which is readily soluble and therefore quickly available to the plant. The usual rate of application varies from 2 to 3 pounds per 100 square feet.

PHOSPHORUS

Phosphorus is an essential element in all functions of plant growth and it is particularly associated with the production of fruits and seeds. It also induces good root development, contributes towards the formation of strong cell walls and, in general, hastens maturity. Phosphorus also helps to balance an overabundance of nitrogen in the soil. Phosphorus is fixed in the soil soon after it is applied and it does not leach out. As it does not travel in the soil it must be absorbed by the plant at the point where it falls. There is practically no danger from excessive applications. The acidity of the soil determines to some extent the availability of phosphorus, it being more available in slightly acid soils than in definitely alkaline soils. The presence of ammonium sulphate increases its availability, while the presence of calcium carbonate, sodium nitrate, and iron salts decreases it.

SOURCES OF PHOSPHORUS

Superphosphate is the most commonly used source of phosphorus, and it is obtainable in various grades—16, 20, or 45 per cent. It is the product which results from treating raw phosphate rock with sulphuric acid. The rate of application varies from 3 to 10 pounds per 100 square feet, according to the needs of the soil.

When superphosphate is applied as a top dressing, its penetration is very slow. It is wise, therefore, to work it thoroughly into the soil whenever it is possible to do so, either by lightly forking it in, or by cultivating it in with a hand weeder.

Basic Slag, a by-product in the manufacture of steel, is sometimes used as a source of phosphorus. It usually contains from 10 to 25 per cent phosphoric acid and from 40 to 50 per cent lime. The phosphorus in basic slag is practically all available, as it becomes water soluble as soon as it is acted upon by carbon dioxide. The rate of application is approximately the same as for superphosphate.

Bone Meal. Raw bone meal is made from finely ground bone and contains from 3 to 4 per cent nitrogen and from 20 to 25 per cent phosphoric acid. Although the phosphorus content may seem high, it is held in a tricalcium form, and is very, very slowly available. The small percentage of nitrogen is quickly available but the phosphorus becomes available so slowly that, in many instances, the use of bone meal is of doubtful value. It is true that it is one of the safest and most fool-proof fertilizers which one can use—but unless it is applied many months before it is needed, the plants will derive practically no benefit from it. Steamed bone meal is of even less value than raw bone meal as during the process of steaming some of the nitrogen is lost. The fineness of bone meal has a very direct effect upon its availability, and weather conditions also have some influence, as, regardless of the time of year when it is applied, it seldom becomes available until warm weather. On the whole, when plants are in need of phosphorus, it is wiser to apply it in the form of superphosphate than in the form of bone meal.

Rock Phosphate is the material which is used in the manufacture of superphosphate. While it usually contains from 66 to 80 per cent calcium phosphate, its availability is very low and its use is not recommended.

POTASSIUM

Potassium is of particular value in promoting the general vigor of the plant and it increases the resistance of the plant to certain diseases. Potassium also plays an important part in sturdy root formation. In general, it has a balancing influence on other plant nutrients.

SOURCES OF POTASSIUM

Potassium chloride is one of the most commonly used sources of potash. It contains from 48 to 50 per cent in a readily available form, as it is immediately soluble. The usual rate of application is 1 pound to 100 square feet.

Muriate of Potash contains approximately 45 per cent potash and is applied at the same rate.

Potassium sulphate is another inorganic source of potash, containing approximately 48 per cent potash. It is readily soluble, and therefore quickly available to the plant.

Wood Ashes are also a valuable source of potash, although much less highly concentrated than the inorganic forms. Wood ashes vary tremendously in composition. Ash produced from hardwood trees, and which has not been leached by exposure to rain, often runs as high as 10 per cent available potash, while wood ashes produced from softwood trees, or wood ashes which have been exposed to rain may contain less than 2 per cent potash. Wood ashes also run high in lime content, sometimes containing as much as 40 per cent lime. The type of wood ashes most readily available on the market is a high-grade, unleached hardwood ash. Wood ashes are usually applied at the rate of 50 to 75 pounds per 1000 square feet.

COMPLETE FERTILIZERS

For general garden use, for lawns, for the vegetable and fruit garden, for the flower border, and for trees and shrubs, an application of a well-balanced complete fertilizer is the most satisfactory method of supplying the needed plant nutrients. Such fertilizers are usually based on a ratio of 1 per cent nitrogen, 2 per cent phosphorus and 1 per cent potash, or 1 per cent nitrogen, 3 per cent phosphorus and 1 per cent potash, or any desired multiple of these ratios:—such as 2-6-2, 4-12-4; 5-10-5; 15-30-15. Whenever the analysis of a complete commercial fertilizer is stated in such a way as is outlined above, the first numeral denotes the percentage of *nitrogen,* the second numeral the percentage of *phosphorus,* and the third numeral the percentage of *potash.* In addition to these three essential elements of fertility which are always present in any "complete" fertilizer, there are also usually present some of the minor, or trace, elements which are needed in very small amounts, such as manganese, iron, and sulphur. In the preparation of commercial fertilizers most reliable firms make it a practice to supply the required amount of nitrogen in two, sometimes three, forms; in a quickly available inorganic form, in a somewhat more slowly available form, and in a very slowly available organic form. Such a practice greatly increases the value of any fertilizer from the standpoint of the gardener, as it means that the nitrogen becomes available for the use of the plant over a long period of time.

The time and rate of application of complete commercial fertilizers vary considerably with the individual requirements of the plant and the purpose of the application. The most approved fertilizer practices are discussed in detail in the various chapters on Lawns, Roses, Perennials, Greenhouse Crops, etc.

SOIL TESTS

Since it is sometimes difficult to determine deficiencies which are not pronounced, yet which may be of considerable importance, it is well to have an occasional soil analysis made. Soil samples may be sent to any of the State Agriculture Experiment Stations for analysis.

OBTAINING SOIL SAMPLES

The season when the sample is taken, the method of obtaining the sample, and the preparation of the sample are all factors of importance.

Time of Sampling. The most reliable information concerning the need for fertilization and for the application of lime may be obtained from samples taken either in the early spring or in late fall. During the active growing season the nutrient level of the soil is affected to some extent by the growth of the plants which occupy the area. Heavy rainfalls also very definitely affect the nutrient level and low tests are frequently secured after periods of prolonged leaching. Nitrates and ammonia nitrogen are the most variable, as they are the elements which are the most easily lost by leaching.

Method of Sampling. A trowel or spade may be used to make a V-shaped hole, 6 or 7 inches deep. Remove the loose dirt from the hole and then cut a thin, uniform slice off the straight side of the hole from top to bottom. If the sample is being taken from a lawn area it should represent the zone of the feeding roots, which will vary from 3 to 6 inches. If the area to be tested is of considerable size, or if it varies in texture to any marked degree, it will be necessary to obtain several samples. If there is a decided variance in the general character of the soil, one section being of a sandy texture and another section having a more dense structure, the samples should be kept separate. If the soil is uniform in character, the samples may be mixed together, forming a composite sample.

Preparing the Sample. After the sample has been obtained, the soil should be spread out to dry on a clean sheet of paper. Care should be taken to prevent the soil from becoming contaminated with dust, fumes or chemicals of any kind.

After the soil is thoroughly dry it should be packed for shipment.

SOIL ACIDITY

The relative acidity or alkalinity of the soil is commonly expressed in terms of the symbol pH. The neutral point in the scale is 7. Soil testing below a pH. 7 is acid; soil testing above pH. 7 is alkaline.

SOIL-TESTING SCALE

pH. 9.5	intensely alkaline
pH. 9.	strongly alkaline
pH. 8.5	definitely alkaline
pH. 8.	moderately alkaline
pH. 7.5	slightly alkaline
pH. 7.	neutral
pH. 6.5	very slightly acid
pH. 6.	slightly acid
pH. 5.5	moderately acid
pH. 5.	moderately acid
pH. 4.5	definitely acid
pH. 4.	strongly acid
pH. 3.5	intensely acid

The pH. values are based on logarithms, 10 being the base. Therefore, a soil testing pH. 5 is 10 times as acid as soil testing pH. 6; while a soil testing pH. 4 is 100 times as acid as soil testing pH. 6. (In going either up or down the pH. scale from the neutral point of pH. 7, the value of the unit is 10 times greater than the next one approaching 7.)

Most herbaceous plants and the majority of our commonly grown trees and shrubs prefer a soil that is very nearly neutral in its reaction. A few plants seem to be entirely indifferent to soil conditions and will thrive equally well in soil with either a neutral, acid, or alkaline reaction, while some plants definitely prefer a strongly acid soil, or a soil of pronounced alkalinity. In general garden practice, it is well to maintain a soil reaction as nearly neutral as possible, ranging between a pH. 6 and a pH. 7. Many woodland plants prefer definitely acid soil (see Chapter XVII). Among the herbaceous perennials, Japanese anemones and a few others prefer a definitely alkaline soil, but the majority thrive best when the soil has a neutral reaction.

The reaction of the soil is not a stable factor, as there is a tendency for soils, except in very arid regions, to become, slowly, more and more acid. This is due to the fact that, with the gradual seepage of rainwater through the soil, the elements such as calcium and sodium are dissolved more rapidly than the more strongly acid elements such as carbon and silicon. An increase in soil acidity is also brought about by the application of such fertilizers as ammonium sulphate, ammonium phosphate and urea, which have a definitely acid reaction.

Every gardener should know how to make simple, rapid tests to determine the pH. of the soil. There are now many very excellent and yet inexpensive soil-testing outfits on the market, and such a kit should be considered an essential part of one's equipment. Complete directions will accompany each outfit and these should be followed with exactitude.

After the degree of soil acidity has been determined, a satisfactory program may be worked out. It is a comparatively simple matter to bring an acid soil to a more nearly neutral state, provided a few simple rules are followed.

LIME

Lime serves several important functions. It is of particular value in correcting the acidity of the soil, and, in addition to this function, it also changes the structure of the soil, hastens bacterial action in the soil, aids in the liberation of plant foods which would otherwise remain in the soil in unavailable form, hastens the decomposition of organic matter, and supplies a small amount of calcium, which is one of the essential plant foods.

Lime is usually applied either in the form of ground limestone or as hydrated lime. Hydrated lime is quicker in its action but it is not as lasting in its effect.

Lime should never be used in combination with animal manures or with nitrogenous fertilizers, as it causes the rapid release of ammonia.

When lime is applied it should be spread over the surface of the ground and should then be thoroughly mixed with the upper few inches of soil. It should not be plowed or spaded deeply into the soil.

The rate of application depends entirely upon the forms in which the lime is applied, and the texture of the soil. The accompanying table will serve as a general guide.

DANGER OF EXCESSIVE APPLICATIONS

An excessive application of lime has a very injurious effect upon some plants, causing a condition known as lime-induced chlorosis. This is regarded as a physiological disease, and it is due directly to a deficiency of iron in the plant tissues. The symptoms are very marked in most plants, and are most apt to appear on young growth in the early spring, although they may be noticed at almost any time during the growing season. The leaves present a characteristically mottled appearance, being either yellow or whitish in color. The mid-rib of the leaf and the veins remain a very dark green, and the mottling takes place in the areas between the veins.

Iron is absolutely essential for the production of chlorophyll, which is the green coloring matter of the leaf, and when iron is not present in sufficient quantities, the chlorophyll fails to develop. This deficiency of iron in the plant is very closely associated with the lime content of the soil, as the solubility of iron in the soil is dependent, to a large extent, upon the degree of soil acidity. Iron is readily soluble in a definitely acid soil, but as the pH. of the soil approaches the neutral point, the iron becomes less and less soluble. In soils which are decidedly alkaline, comparatively little iron, or, in extreme cases, no iron at all is available for the plant. Therefore, the long-continued

RATE OF APPLICATION OF LIME*

SOIL ACIDITY	LIGHT SANDY SOIL				MEDIUM SANDY SOIL			
	HYDRATED LIME		GROUND LIMESTONE		HYDRATED LIME		GROUND LIMESTONE	
	per 1000 sq. ft.	per acre	per 1000 sq. ft.	per acre	per 1000 sq. ft.	per acre	per 1000 sq. ft.	per acre
pH 4.0	60 lbs.	2610 lbs.	90 lbs.	3915 lbs.	80 lbs.	3480 lbs.	120 lbs.	5220 lbs.
pH 4.5	55 lbs.	2392 lbs.	82 lbs.	3567 lbs.	75 lbs.	3480 lbs.	112 lbs.	4872 lbs.
pH 5.0	45 lbs.	1957 lbs.	67 lbs.	2914 lbs.	60 lbs.	2610 lbs.	90 lbs.	3915 lbs.
pH 5.5	35 lbs.	1522 lbs.	52 lbs.	2262 lbs.	45 lbs.	1957 lbs.	67 lbs.	2914 lbs.
pH 6.0	None	None	None	None	None	None	None	None

SOIL ACIDITY	LOAM AND SILT LOAM				CLAY LOAM			
	HYDRATED LIME		GROUND LIMESTONE		HYDRATED LIME		GROUND LIMESTONE	
	per 1000 sq. ft.	per acre	per 1000 sq. ft.	per acre	per 1000 sq. ft.	per acre	per 1000 sq. ft.	per acre
pH 4.0	115 lbs.	5002 lbs.	172 lbs.	7482 lbs.	145 lbs.	6307 lbs.	217 lbs.	9439 lbs.
pH 4.5	105 lbs.	4567 lbs.	157 lbs.	6827 lbs.	135 lbs.	5872 lbs.	202 lbs.	8787 lbs.
pH 5.0	85 lbs.	3697 lbs.	127 lbs.	5524 lbs.	100 lbs.	4356 lbs.	150 lbs.	6525 lbs.
pH 5.5	65 lbs.	2827 lbs.	97 lbs.	4219 lbs.	80 lbs.	3480 lbs.	120 lbs.	5220 lbs.
pH 6.0	None	None	None	None	None	None	None	None

NOTE: A light application of lime at the rate of 25 lbs. per 1000 sq. ft. has proved beneficial on certain soils, even though the soil has a pH value of 6.0.

* As it is not advisable to apply more than 50 lbs. of hydrated lime or 75 lbs. of ground limestone per 1000 sq. ft. at any one time, it will be necessary to make several successive applications on strongly acid soils and raise the pH gradually. It is often detrimental to plant growth to make an excessively heavy application of lime at one time.

use, or excessive applications, of lime, bone meal, wood ashes, and certain inorganic fertilizers tend to increase the alkalinity of the soil to a point where it is not favorable for certain forms of plant growth, due to this precipitation of iron, which consequently becomes unavailable to the plant.

In general garden practice, it is well to maintain the soil at a pH. slightly below the neutral point, and not to increase its alkalinity beyond a pH. of 7.5, which seems to be the point of safety for many plants. There are, of course, special plant groups which are definitely more acid or alkaline tolerant, and some which prefer a decidedly acid soil, but for the majority of garden plants a pH. slightly below neutral is the safest.

If a condition of lime-induced chlorosis occurs, it may be corrected by the use of iron sulphate (ferrous sulphate) used in a finely powdered form at the rate of 2½ to 3 pounds per 100 square feet. The iron sulphate should be sprinkled evenly over the surface of the soil, cultivated lightly in, and the soil should then be watered. Care must be taken not to allow the material to come into any contact with the foliage of the plants, as its effect is decidedly injurious.

II

Design

Landscape design differs in several respects from the other arts. The designer works with materials such as land form, which is comparatively immobile, and plant form which is undergoing constant change. A work of sculpture or an oil painting represents something which is expressed through the medium of the artist. But a work of landscape art is, itself, still a landscape; it is more than an artist's representation of a landscape on a piece of canvas. A landscape can be very radically changed, in fact it is constantly changing, and it is the function of the designer to guide these natural changes and to instigate artificial change in the appearance of the scene, in order to produce more convenient facilities and a more artistic composition.

Every site has pictorial assets and liabilities. Some are apparent, some are latent. The creative designer must be able to see through the actual conditions to a number of possible compositions and to a number of solutions of the practical problems. The first step in designing is the evaluating of these possibilities, and the second is the summing up of the practical facilities which much be provided. In the preliminary study of a design, one must endeavor to plan for every practical facility in such a way as to preserve the picturesque qualities of the site.

With the practical requirements for modern living and the physical conditions of the property made familiar, design, as such, may be considered. Landscape designing is a method of reaching decisions in regard to the arrangement of various parts to make a unified and harmonious whole which is fitted to its site and purposes. Major decisions come first, details later.

A designed landscape is a work of art and not a copy of

nature. The fact that a garden is achieved by working in harmony with natural laws, does not excuse us from recognizing that it is capable of being a beautiful composition. Because it takes mental effort to think of these abstractions of artistic composition and to make them realities as the attributes of a specific plan, some gardeners seem to prefer to remove the garden from the realm of art and to make it merely a collection of horticultural perfections. Such a garden may become an excellent museum, but it is not a thing of beauty in itself.

CREATING A DESIGN

The process of creating a design is a method of making decisions between many possible arrangements. Without a design nothing can be decided in advance. Without design there is no opportunity, until it is too late, to decide between several alternatives. The creation of a design is a means of sifting out all possible solutions of the problem in order to reach satisfactory decisions regarding function, form, materials and æsthetic quality. The process of designing crystallizes and makes clearer the image of the composition. It is a systematic method of foreseeing results. By a series of preliminary sketches the design is evolved, out of the practical requirements of the case, out of the restrictions and opportunities of the site, out of the imagination of the designer. In a sense, the early sketches for a design are experiments to test the practicability, and the pictorial possibilities of ideas. These early sketches may be discarded, as better arrangements supersede less adequate ones. The best elements of several schemes may be combined to make a more satisfactory composition, and ultimately the design will be a scheme which incorporates the most practical and more desirable ideas of the owner and the designer. The first purpose of creating a design is, therefore, to clarify ideas, to make them definite and to improve upon them by a process of experimentation in pictorial form.

THE FUNDAMENTAL QUALITIES OF GOOD DESIGN

There are certain fundamental qualities inherent in all good design, and a landscape composition should have the same

Photograph by F. S. Lincoln

A Landscape in the Naturalistic Manner

qualities which are found in other forms of art. It should have unity, harmony, and fitness to use.

By separating a composition from its surroundings with a hedge or fence we may enhance its unity, in the same way that a frame separates the picture from the wall and thus emphasizes its completeness. A dominant focal point, or center of interest, a consistency of style, and the rhythmic repetition of minor details will also contribute to the unity of the composition.

A well-designed landscape must have harmony of scale in its parts and details; harmony of line and form, giving it balance; harmony in color combinations; and it must be in harmony with its surroundings. Each of these subtle relationships has its bearing on the resulting composition. Each must be studied before a satisfying composition is possible.

Scale is one of the most difficult qualities to maintain. It is so easy for some detail to become too large and over-dominant, or too small, "out of proportion." Harmony of relation to the site begins with harmony of form. The new must blend comfortably with the existing conditions. The placing of a structure with one long side against the hill; a narrow flat terrace between the façade and the hillside sloping into the foreground will result in a harmonious composition. Harmony with the surroundings includes harmony of plant forms. That is the real reason why exotic plants look out of place. Foreign architecture seems inappropriate partly because it does not have forms significant of our climate, partly because it does not relate closely to our racial heritage.

Color harmony is too intricate a subject to treat adequately in a brief discussion. But suffice it to say that bright colors in close relation and strong contrasts are more difficult to combine satisfactorily than softer tints of those same colors. White will tend to make less conflicting the more brilliant colors. A safe scheme to adopt is to have only one really bright color in a composition. For example, bright blue should be combined with pale tones of yellow, orange or pink. The warm colors, red, orange and yellow, are best used in small quantities, or in flowers of small scale. That is why Heuchera sanguinea is more pleasing and more adaptable to use in combination with other flowers than is Salvia officinalis.

PRACTICAL CONSIDERATIONS

In considering the design of a particular property, there are bound to be local restrictions and practical conditions which must be met in order to secure the greatest convenience in an economical way. For instance, for a flower garden, the practical requirements include rich deep soil, sufficient exposure to sunshine and air, protection from strong winds, water supply, rapid drainage of surface water, accessibility to the work area. All these things must be provided in the plan before we can consider design from the æsthetic standpoint. Similarly, there are sets of conditions imposed on the design of roads, lawns and all the utilities which connect the house with means of modern convenience. These practical conditions must be met, and must be planned for in advance, so that each can function without interference and without detracting from the final pictorial effect of the composition. A successful design is one which meets them all, fulfills all practical requirements, and does it gracefully and economically. No amount of good composition in the æsthetic aspect of a place can compensate for failure to make the place as a whole, and its separate parts, functional.

From a completed plan detailed working drawings may be prepared which make possible exact estimates of quantities, and estimates of cost of construction. These detailed plans are also the basis for organizing the construction work. Often different kinds of work, such as grading, construction and planting, must be carried on simultaneously, in different parts of the place. Because much of this is seasonal, a careful time-schedule is important. None of this would be possible without a plan on which are designated the limits and location of the work.

Finally, in considering the place as a whole as a setting for gracious living over a period of years, the annual cost of maintenance in terms of dollars and of hours of effort should be predicted with reasonable accuracy.

Gardens of the Governor's Palace, Williamsburg, Virginia

STYLE IN LANDSCAPE DESIGN

Style in architecture and in landscape design is intimately connected with the social customs, the economics, and the political structure of the times in which it is produced. Indeed, the various stylistic expressions of design, and the evolution of design itself, have come about more as a result of economic trends and the social history of peoples than by a narrow development within the arts.

Every race or generation which has developed a recognizable architectural style has done so partly out of its environment and partly out of its own peculiar culture, as well as out of its sense of beauty and order. Habit and tradition tend to fix existing styles, while changing social customs tend to bring about new styles.

The influence of one country upon another has been tremendous at times, but seldom has a style been transplanted without some modification in expression, due to local standards of worth. This is particularly true of architecture and of landscape design. When the Gothic style which flourished in western Europe penetrated Italy, it did not reach a full expression there. It was applied as a sort of veneer to buildings not at all Gothic in form and resulted in such compromises as are expressed by the Doge's Palace in Venice. Later, when the classic style of Renaissance Italy was adopted by other countries of Europe, it became not so purely classic as it had been in the country of its revival. Roofs were steeper and contained dormer windows, a hold-over from the Gothic tradition. In the stoneless regions of eastern England and in Holland, it became necessary to substitute brick for the stone of classic Rome. This warmer material gave the designer much freedom, and an opportunity for variety in texture not heretofore associated with the austerity of the ancient precedent. The resulting Georgian style of England and the Dutch renaissance style were, therefore, quite different in character from the precedent which inspired them.

Landscape design, because of the very nature of its material, is even more limited by local conditions than is architecture.

Plant materials can be used only in climatic zones which are somewhat similar to those of their place of origin. While an Italian villa can be built in New England and its structure may be archeologically correct, it cannot be embellished by the traditional cypresses, the stone pines and the olive trees.

Style in gardens is as recognizable as style in houses. The precedents most often followed in this country are the graceful architectural designs of Italy and the verdant masses of vegetation and the abundant bloom of the English landscape; the one formal and the other informal. As the informal style blends imperceptibly with the surrounding free landscape it should be used in the larger areas away from the house. In restricted areas, and in the immediate surroundings of the house, some expression of formality is appropriate as the setting for architecture. The degree of formality will depend to a considerable extent upon the architectural character of the house. A brick Georgian house will require a very definite expression of formality, such as trees in balanced symmetry, straight paths, paved and precisely edged, and a flat terrace with a clipped hedge at the outer rim to provide a satisfactory transition between the artificiality of the structure and the naturalness of the outer landscape; whereas a thatched cottage, or a picturesque half-timbered Elizabethan house, would permit only the most quaint expression of formality in small-scale pattern with an abundance of foliage softening the straight lines.

There are many degrees of formality, and indeed there may, and often should, be varying degrees of formality on the same property, each harmonious to its setting. Formality of plan does not always mean a strictly formal appearance. A straight avenue flanked by trees of the same kind and size at equal intervals is formal. But the natural outline of those trees softens the formality. On the other hand, formality may be carried to such an extreme that exact margins and artificial plant forms must be maintained by constant trimming. Not all formality is harsh; in fact, as it is used in this country, most formal design is greatly mitigated by the very nature of the material.

Flowering Magnolias and Boxwood

PLACING THE HOUSE ON THE SITE

Among the first decisions in developing the landscape surroundings for a home is that of the position of the house, its orientation in respect to view, sunshine and prevailing wind; its relation to the land form, and, what is still more important, its relation to the other units of the design. Far too often one sees a house which was built before any clear idea was formed of its relation to adjoining units. When, later, the grounds are developed, it is found that there is insufficient space for something of major importance. The forecourt may be too small for the comfortable turning of automobiles. A slight difference in the location of the house would have been sufficient for the proper planning of all adjacent parts. As it is, a compromise is fixed which can never be properly removed, and the whole design suffers.

If various portions of the property offer possible house sites, a series of sketch plans should be drawn showing the house on each of these sites and its relation to the necessary functional units such as the approach, the living area and the service area. Each of these three units constitutes a major element in the design. Each is important and must be carefully studied. In hilly country it often happens that only one house site is at all possible for proper development. This tends to limit the chances for experiment and often makes necessary a few compromises.

Where, as so often happens, a rigid straight-line street system has been imposed on irregular topography, we may expect to find properties which cannot be developed satisfactorily except by devising the most ingenious design.

On small places, the nearness of property lines makes orientation of the house parallel to them almost obligatory. Diagonal placing of a structure on a small lot results in awkward triangles of land. On the position of the house will depend the arrangement of entrance and service area. In relating the house to the street, as distance increases, privacy is augmented, but usable area is reduced. Distance from the street is not the only, or the best, way to insure the privacy of the home. A more logical solution and the most effective on small properties is to arrange the house so that the entrance hall and the service rooms are toward the front and the living rooms open their windows away from the street and toward the gardens.

The design of the house and the design of the grounds about it are interdependent. A modification in the design of one part to increase its convenience or harmony, is likely to necessitate a change in the design of the other part. Thus site and house design have a very close interrelationship. In fact the site may impose very grave restrictions on the size and shape of the house. From the very beginning of the development of the design, the house and the plan of its site should be studied together. Only in this way is it possible to solve the various problems satisfactorily, and to make the house fit comfortably into its surroundings.

THE DESIGN OF THE ESTATE

Thus far, we have considered design in its general aspect; what it is, and what is accomplished by it. When we consider design as applied to a certain type of problem, the estate, we find that the principal requirements are similar in most cases. The three major functional units of the estate are the approach, the service area, and the area devoted to living and recreational pursuits. In general, the approach should be reasonably direct, the service area·convenient and accessible, and the living area ample, secluded and attractive. Each of these units should be contiguous with the corresponding portion of the house, each should be as complete and as segregated from the others as is practical. Local topographic conditions may dictate compromises in this scheme but wherever it is possible to adhere to this program the plan should result in a convenient, economical and functional arrangement.

Since most houses have four major façades, it is a logical plan to assign to each a different function in its relation to the grounds. For instance, one long side usually flanks the approach (forecourt or front yard), while the opposite long side may be arranged with a terrace as a foreground to the view.

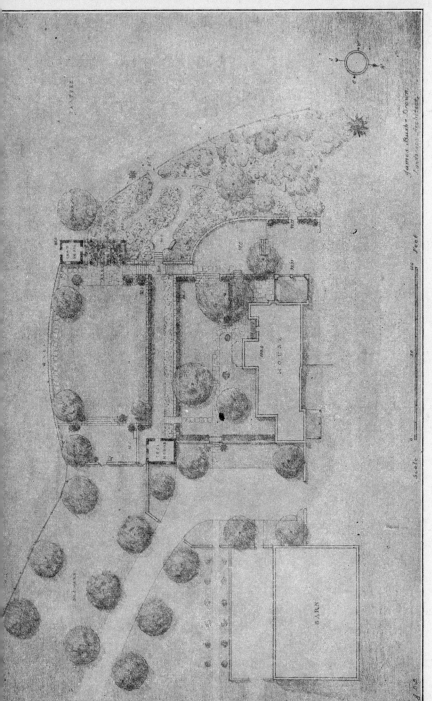

Plan of a Small Estate

One short side may face the service yard or service court and the other the flower garden. Variations from this simple scheme are possible as the house plan becomes more intricate, but it is a fairly typical model.

After assigning different areas of the ground to different uses, one of the next important steps is to separate these areas from one another and connect them logically. This is best done by masses of foliage, trees, shrubs, hedges, fences, or walls. The designer should indicate on the plan the position of open lawn and of trees; the position of screen plantings to hide unsatisfactory views; the positions of viewpoints, and the directions of distant views. There is an element of the practical and an element of the æsthetic in each of these decisions.

In the light of these major decisions, we can decide which portions of the grounds should be designed in a formal way and which should be developed informally.

Different individuals and different conditions of site and usage will require varying expressions of design, which on the one hand may be an extremely formal style as a setting for conventional living, or on the other hand a naturalistic style for the more simple life. The site of the estate imposes restrictions on the design, and it often presents possibilities peculiar to itself. The designer's success will depend largely upon how well these restrictions and possibilities have been realized and utilized. Not only that, but sometimes liabilities may be turned into assets, by clever planning. A certain site may be developed in any one of a number of ways, but the more closely the design follows the dictates of the site, the more satisfactory will be the results, the more economical will be the construction, and the more convenient the maintenance.

The component parts of an estate on a modest scale may include only such features as lawn, grove of trees, an enclosure of shrubs about the boundary, means of access to the entrance and service areas. Or for a larger establishment there may be these plus many others, such as flower and vegetable gardens, play areas, orchards, and stables. Whatever units may be included, they should be arranged in a sequence that will make them

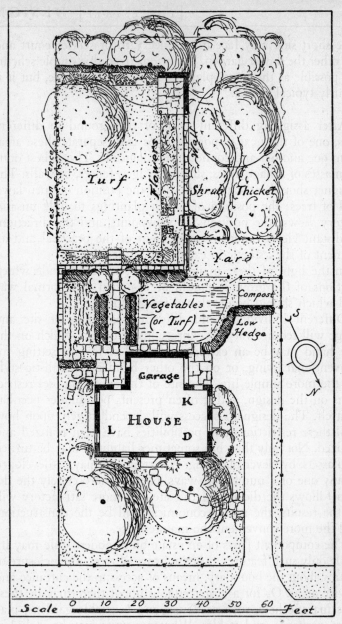

A Suburban Home

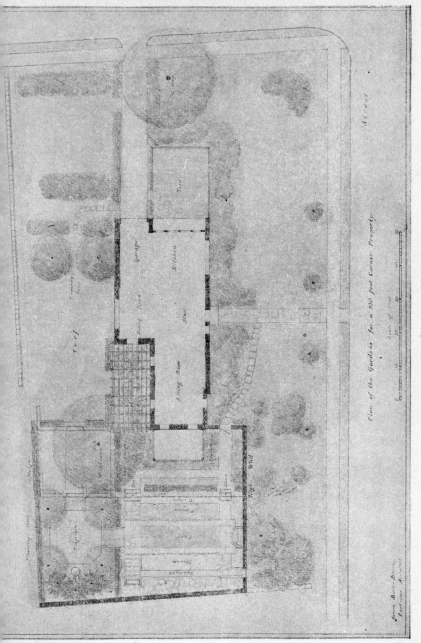

Plan of a 100-foot Corner Property

readily accessible and easily maintained and, if possible, capable of future expansion.

No two owners are apt to have the same combination of personal desires for their homes, and sites vary in their capacity for development. But in general the successful estate is one which is designed for the proper and economic functioning of its various parts; which has a distinction and individuality arising either from the nature of the site or from the artistry of the design (or both); and which reflects the taste of the owners, and satisfies their desires most completely.

Every problem in estate design is an individual problem, the terms of which are dictated by the wishes of the owner. It is influenced by the nature of the site, and, very often, by the amount of money available for development and maintenance.

THE DESIGN OF SMALL PROPERTIES

The principles of good design for a small property do not differ from those of larger areas. The beauty of the design is dependent, to a large extent, upon these same qualities—unity, harmony, and utility. Whereas in large estates, spaciousness is everywhere apparent, in small properties spaces must be very carefully planned, and economically used. No amount of embellishment can overcome the inconvenience of an ill-adapted plan, or make up for the loss of available space caused by an illogical arrangement of parts.

In the planning of a small lot, a half acre or less, the economy of space is of the utmost importance and this should begin with the placing and arrangement of the house. This subject is often sadly neglected, however, and most suburban houses are placed on the lot which they occupy with utter disregard for the general design of the property. The house is frequently placed very nearly in the center of the lot and the garage at the extreme rear, in the vain hope that it will be less conspicuous. But such a position for the garage often appropriates for the driveway 20 per cent of all the land not occupied by the house, and, if repeated by the neighbors, results in a panorama of many garages as well. The delivery of goods is frequently by a circuitous route, making semipublic that section of the home grounds which is traversed by the delivery man.

The most functional arrangement and the one most economical of space is that in which the service door, the kitchen and the purely utilitarian part of the grounds and house are grouped together near the street. The living quarters would then occupy the more remote part of the house and would look out over a secluded yard which would be unencumbered by garage, kitchen-door and clothes line. It is needless to point out that this plan gives the most direct route for deliveries and for the family car, while the main approach is adequate and attractive and the living rooms private. The notion that a garage is ugly, *ipso facto,* has been entirely exploded. By building it of the same material and joining it to the house, the interests of convenience and economy of space are better served. Whatever the arrangement, the three major functional units of the home grounds, approach, living quarters and service area, should be separated from one another. This theory is entirely contrary to the old and absurd notion of "front" and "back," so habitually practiced in American suburbs. That theory results in placing the service area away from the street and the living quarters next to the street where the life of the household will be as much as possible in the public gaze, an obvious absurdity. There is much to favor the reorientation of the modern house along the lines of seclusion from the street. An enclosed yard with the major windows of the house opening upon it is vastly more livable than an open front yard with windows toward the restless street. (Page 47 shows such a plan.)

On the small lot every square foot of ground must be utilized to the best advantage, either for the growing of fruits and vegetables and flowers, for lawn, for service area or for children's play. And here, let us say that even in enlightened and progressive communities where playgrounds exist, nothing quite takes the place of a sand pile or a favorite tree to climb in a child's own home yard.

On a very small lot, bounded as it is by straight property lines and the straight lines of the house, a formal or rectilinear design is usually the most logical and most effective. This does

Photograph by Richard Averill Smith   *Beatrice Morgan Goodrich, Landscape Architect*

A Corner of a Flower Garden

Here the fence marks a definite separation of the formal and the informal.

not imply that the design must necessarily be symmetrical. The placing of a few well-chosen trees in a formal way, and the developing of one or two axes will be enough to make the plan harmonize with its semi-artificial site. The planting of the shrubs and flowers may be more incidental as long as their placing preserves the major lines. Unity of design may be obtained by emphasizing the boundaries, by definitely separating the property from its adjoining neighbors, and by concentrating interest within the area. The boundary may take the form of a hedge, a fence, or a wall, and it sets off and enhances the composition within.

One sees so many examples of efforts wasted because of the lack of a definite plan. Trees, shrubs and flowers are so often planted in haphazard fashion without regard for the beauty of the composition as a whole, or the eventual size of the plants. The same amount of diligent effort and money applied to carrying out a well-conceived plan would result in a much more satisfying and beautiful picture. It is not a matter of expense, but rather the exercise of forethought and good taste, which is necessary to create beautiful home surroundings, and the small property deserves as much consideration as the large estate.

FOUNDATION PLANTING

"Foundation Planting" has been given altogether too much emphasis in this country. It all came about, and the habit became fixed, several decades ago, when the foundations of houses were made, as they still so often are, of ugly material such as concrete block, while the house itself was a self-respecting frame structure. Bushes and low evergreens were called upon to mask the existence of this regrettable, but apparently unavoidable, condition. The nursery catalogs were filled with pictures of various combinations of dwarf evergreens. Variety of form, and color, and texture seemed to be the great aim in this type of planting. It never occurred to people that the array of tall and short croquets, round and oval globes, and the green and yellow and blue pincushions, with a pair of stiff blue toy trees, had

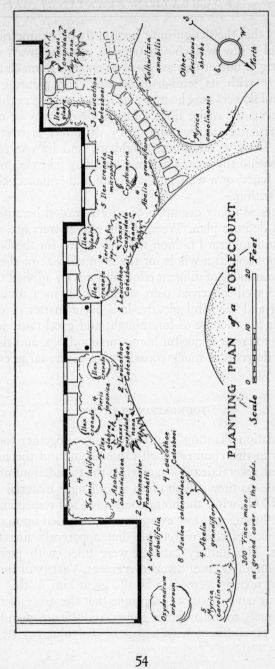

PLANTING PLAN of a FORECOURT

Scale

0   10   20

Feet

The Plants Used Here Are Largely Evergreen Shrubs Which Are Hardy on the Northern Exposure

A Good Example of Foundation Planting

Simple, dignified, and restrained.

only covered up one type of ugliness with another. The only difference was that for monotony there was substituted a restlessness; for frank utility, a discordant decoration.

Now foundation planting has persisted, even where house walls are built of brick or stone from ground to cornice, and it has been practiced with the often expressed purpose of fitting the house to the surrounding area, harmonizing its vertical surfaces with the horizontal of the ground, compromising the artificiality of architecture with the naturalness of the landscape. These purposes are worthy, and they should be accomplished by some such device as planting, but how much *harmony* is there in some of these stiffly spotted little evergreens? Does a building *fit* into its site better if it is surrounded by a mantle of greenery, and will those little artificial trees really harmonize a dignified piece of architecture with a gracious sweep of lawn? A finely designed house that has charm arising from its own design has more in common with a simple, dignified landscape of trees and graceful lawn than it has with what we have come to mean by typical "foundation planting." It is time that we stopped thinking about foundation planting altogether, and allowed ourselves to think about the whole setting of the house, its background and foreground, the ground forms, and the play of lights and shadows upon its walls. Then we would let the planting at the base of the walls be as unobtrusive as possible, and so moderate would we be in the use of both quantity and variety of plants that the attention would remain on the structure, where it should rightly be. The planting in the foreground of the house should contain only such plants as harmonize with each other. A few varieties in greater number are more easily harmonized than are many varieties. Yet variety is a quality which enriches, and makes possible a succession of interest as the season advances. With care in the selection, it is possible to use variety and yet keep to a fixed general character. This may be accomplished to a considerable extent by avoiding the use of plants which are conspicuous because they are unique in form or color. A beautiful house needs a beautifully designed setting, one which embraces the whole house as a dominant element in the composition, and subordinates the details to their proper places. A planting which is simple and dignified, such as that shown on page 54, will always remain satisfying.

TREES AND SHRUBS AS PART OF THE LANDSCAPE COMPOSITION

Plantings of trees and shrubs form the masses in the land-scape plan. Not only are they important objects in themselves, interesting in outline, texture, and color, but they are the best means of marking the boundaries of the place, and separating the various functional areas from each other. A mass of flowering shrubs, a hedge, or a vine-covered fence, each makes an excellent screen about the service yard. Where a view is to be kept open, the most effective means of relating it to the foreground is to frame it within the branches of trees in the middle distance. This separates it from every other scene, fixes the attention upon the distance, and contrasts the shadowy foreground with the light-filled countryside. At the same time, the trees afford shade which makes the house and its adjoining lawn or terrace more livable in summer. Trees and shrubs determine, by their position, the shapes of open areas in the design, contrast the solids and masses with the open spaces, the shade with the sunlight. The designers of the Italian villas were masters of the use of this kind of dramatic contrast.

It is a matter of great importance that care be taken to protect the existing trees upon a piece of property which is to be developed. In this connection, it is well to remember what the building of a house is apt to do to trees standing close about. Foundations cut through the root system, the excavations lower the water level of the sub-soil, thus reducing the tree's available water supply, and paved areas of drive, or terrace, deprive the soil of its normal supply of water and air. In many instances, trees become so encumbered with adverse conditions, as a result of building operations, that they die after several years of struggle. Prompt and adequate feeding of the tree may save it, but the chances are against it. It is an obvious absurdity to compromise a house plan to save a worthy tree and then have it die from lack of consideration of its needs. A new structure should be kept at such a distance from any tree which is to be

Terrace Steps and Wall Fountain

saved, that only a very small fraction of the roots is disturbed.

Each tree should be selected for a variety of purposes—shade, flower, fruit, or picturesque outline. To fulfill most completely the exacting requirements of the home property, trees should have the following characteristics. They should be in scale with

Photograph by Philip B. Wallace   *Thomas W. Sears, Landscape Architect*

A Gracious Setting of a House

their surroundings; they should have good habits, that is, they should never drop sections of bark (Sycamore) or unpleasant fruit (Ginkgo) on the terrace; or be the habitual home of insects (Wild Cherry), or require much spraying and attention to protect them from insects. They should not produce flowers with a disagreeable odor, like the Hawthorns and Privets; they should not be brittle and lose great branches in the storms; and they should not disperse their seedlings in too great a quantity. If, besides these negative qualities, they possess well-shaped, symmetrical heads or picturesque outlines, if they produce beautiful flowers or fruits, or if they turn to gorgeous hues in autumn, then they are especially desirable.

For the small suburban property the choice is necessarily more limited than it is for the large estate, as the matter of scale must be given consideration. In most designs, a sense of proper scale is one of the most difficult qualities to preserve. A small house may be made to seem still smaller by giving it a big chimney. We say then that the chimney is "out of scale." The same thing applies to the design of a residential property. A small yard may seem even smaller because of the presence of very large trees. This changing of the apparent scale may be just what we wish to accomplish. Certainly there is no more home-like picture than a little New England farmhouse standing in the shelter of a great elm tree. But some houses do not belong to this type of setting. In the suburbs there is not the open countryside to make the elm tree seem at home and appropriate. Everywhere is evident that saving of space, forced by the high price of land. The lots are narrow, usually too narrow for the houses upon them; the street, if it is a local residential street, is narrow in proportion with the amount of traffic it is to carry. The elm tree in such a situation may very well be too large—much as we love the elm. The fact is that where the small suburban lot is the subject of the planting scheme, smaller trees are better adapted.

An adequate expenditure on trees and shrubs which require comparatively little care is an excellent investment. The plants continue to increase in value as the years pass, and to contribute, as nothing else can, to the value of the property.

THE DESIGN OF THE FLOWER GARDEN

The formal flower garden offers a great opportunity for beautiful expression in landscape design. Within the flower garden is concentrated the greatest wealth of plant material, and upon its maintenance is lavished the most meticulous care. Gardens

Tulips and Box Bushes

A Walled Garden

General Plan of a Garden (Type 1). Open Interior

James Bush-Brown, Landscape Architect

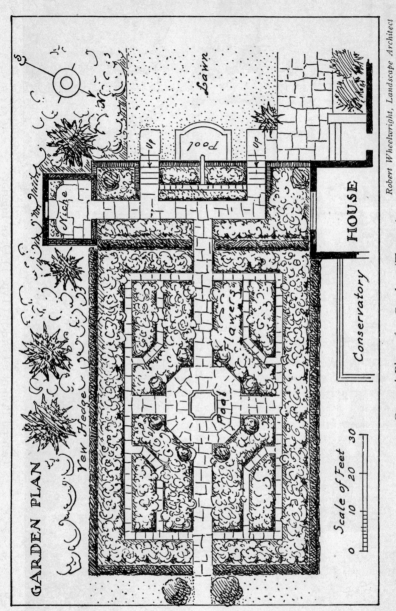

General Plan of a Garden (Type 2)
Pattern of pavement and flower beds.

Robert Wheelwright, Landscape Architect

need not be large or lavish in order to capture that charm and loveliness which is justly theirs. Beauty of proportion, harmony of line and mass, contrast of light and shade, the subtle and beautiful combinations of color, all these combine to make a garden a work of art.

The design for a flower garden may usually be classified into any one of four general types—the garden with an open interior, comprised largely of lawn or pavement with the flower borders about the edges; the garden in which the flower beds occupy a large proportion of the entire area and are separated by a pattern of pathways, the whole design resembling a geometric pattern; the garden which combines these two arrangements with a central panel of turf; and the garden which covers a large area, the pathways dividing the garden into a number of large quadrangles. The four types are shown on pages 65, 66, 68 and 69.

The first type is one of the most simple, and yet one of the most pleasant expressions of design, and is appropriate for the small intimate garden, being particularly well adapted for the garden which, of necessity, must be long and narrow in shape. The second type is appropriate for the garden in which pattern is important, and it is most effective when placed so that the pattern may be seen from an upper level. It is the style most frequently used for boxwood gardens, rose gardens and the stylistic gardens of Dutch and French character. The third type requires space and an ample use of the open area to offset the concentrated flower masses in the patterned beds. The fourth is typically Tudor or Elizabethan in origin, but its style has persisted until the present day. It requires an ample area to provide the long vistas, the allées of overshadowing trees, and the effect of spaciousness.

Proportion in garden design is a subtle, yet a very important thing. In general, the proportions of areas, the dimensions of which are commensurate, are more pleasing than those which are unrelated. For instance, a turf panel surrounded by flower beds and pavement which is exactly half or two thirds as wide as it is long is in good proportion. The same principle applies to other dimensions of the garden, especially to the distances between axes. The size of the flower beds should be propor-

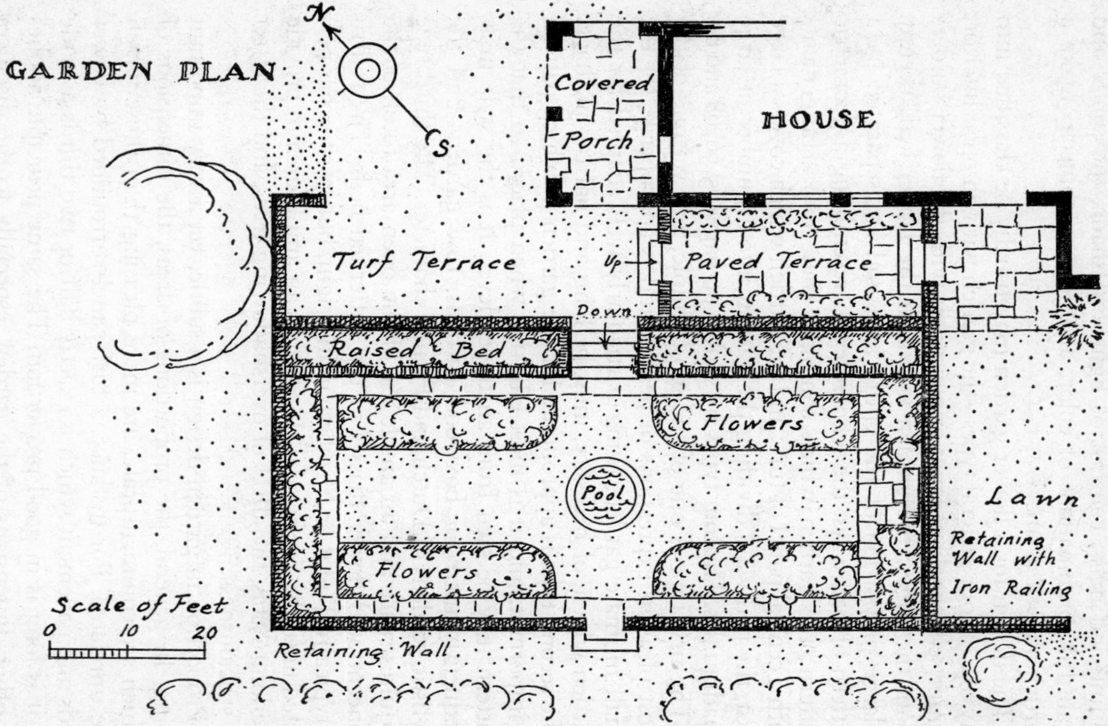

GARDEN PLAN

HOUSE

Covered Porch

Paved Terrace

Up

Down

Turf Terrace

Raised Bed

Flowers

Flowers

Pool

Flowers

Lawn

Retaining Wall with Iron Railing

Retaining Wall

N

S

Scale of Feet
0   10   20

General Plan of a Garden (Type 3)

James Bush-Brown, Landscape Architect

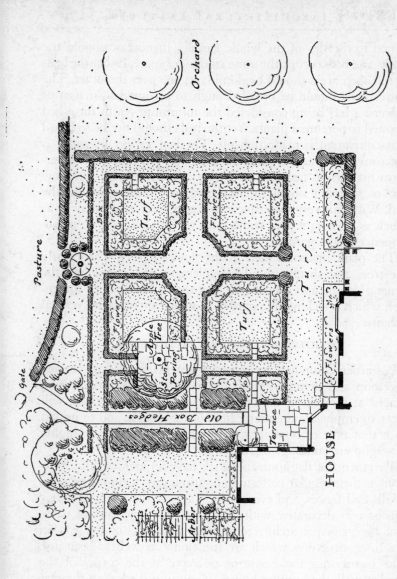

General Plan of a Garden (Type 4)

James Bush-Brown, Landscape Architect

Orchard

Pasture

Gate

Box

Box

Flowers

Turf

Turf

Turf

Turf

Flowers

Apple Tree

Stone Paving

Old Box Hedges

Terrace

Flowers

HOUSE

Arbor

tioned to the size of the whole garden. In no case should the walks and beds occupy the same amount of space. Either the beds or the open areas should be dominant, one over the other. The flower beds should be broad enough to accomodate masses of flowers, 4 feet being considered the minimum width for a bed devoted to perennial plants. Yet the beds should not be so broad that cultivation is made difficult. The bed 12 feet in width is not convenient, as the gardener must step into the bed to perform his various tasks. If a very wide bed is desired a narrow line of stepping stones should be placed midway within the bed. With this very inconspicuous passageway a bed may be as much as 12 or 14 feet in width, and yet be a cause of no inconvenience to the gardener.

The plant materials used in the flower garden, particularly the trees and shrubs, should supplement and strengthen the general design, and should give to it that valuable third dimension which is lacking in a garden in which there are no vertical accents.

ARCHITECTURAL FEATURES IN THE GARDEN

A garden composed entirely of plant material is apt to lack precision and definiteness of design. An architectural feature placed at the end of an axis, or used as a central motif, will serve to emphasize the major lines of the design, and to impart to it that note of regularity, so important in the more highly wrought surroundings of the house.

Pavements of flagstone and brick have an architectural function, as their regular pattern and outline give form to the plan. Walls and fences, and even hedges, are architectural, and they can be very decorative with their rhythmic repetition of parts. But the principal architectural embellishments of the garden are those structures which are functional as well as beautiful. The picturesque tool-house or dovecote at the corner of the garden wall, the summer house, the potting shed, even the rear of the garage, all offer infinite possibilities for pleasant architectural treatment. Lattices, arbors, trellises and pergolas not only provide practical support for vines but also contribute to the architectural embellishment of the garden. Fountains, sun-

Photograph by Philip B. Wallace

The Flower Garden

Beatrice Farrand, Landscape Architect

dials, statues, seats and benches may be treated as incidental ornaments or as dominant features, but in either case they are architectural in character and give permanence to scenes made up largely of changing plant forms.

The architectural features in a garden should be in complete harmony with the architecture of the house and its surroundings. If the house is informal in character, the summer house in the garden may be of a somewhat rustic design. If, on the other hand, the architecture of the house is distinctly formal, the architectural features in the garden must carry out the formality of the general scheme. If the house is colonial in character, the dominant features in the garden should be of the same period and in like character.

THE USE OF PLANT MATERIAL IN DESIGN

By arranging plants in harmonious compositions it is possible to change an ordinary scene which has no distinction and no natural advantages to one of rare beauty and charm. The wide variety of form, color, and texture found in plant materials offers infinite possibilities both for harmony and for contrast.

Harmony is one of the principal elements of good design and it is interesting to note that the forces of nature are constantly at work to harmonize the landscape scene, and that they are capable of slowly restoring it to orderliness after man's intrusion. In windy places the plants remain close to the ground, and develop tough stems and tenacious leaves. Even trees which normally grow tall and straight in the forest will adapt themselves to the wind by growing broad and low. On steep banks where the rain at first washes the soil away, vines will begin to spread out over the bare ground, dead leaves will collect under the tangle, and presently all manner of plants spring up from seeds and reclothe the earth with verdure. These are examples of nature's methods of harmonizing life forces with the elements. The result is usually a harmonious composition because the very plant forms have had to adapt themselves to the conditions of the site. Any one working with plants must understand the forces of nature to which the plants are exposed, and the ability of the plants to thrive under varying conditions.

One of the most important considerations in the arrangement of plants in the landscape composition is the point of view from which the plants will be seen. So important is it that unless the viewpoint is well chosen the beauty of the plants may be greatly diminished, or lost entirely. For example—many small, delicate rock plants are best seen at close range and should preferably be planted on a bank above the path, whereas the best effect produced by other rock plants is that of a broad carpet of color which should be viewed from a distance of many feet. The blossoms of the red maple in early spring are far more beautiful when viewed from a distance with the gray winter forest behind them than they are when seen at close range. Sugar maples in their autumn brilliance are finer when seen in masses at a distance than they are in the foreground. Rhododendrons are far more magnificent when viewed at a distance of forty feet than they are at three feet. And so one could recall example after example of the effect of viewpoint upon the appearance and beauty of plants. Therefore, in creating a landscape composition with plants the point of view should be one of the first considerations, for the interrelation of viewpoint, foreground, objects of principal interest and background is nowhere more important than in the art of landscape architecture. Each has its effect upon the other. Together they make up the conditions under which the picture is made.

The simplest aspect of a plant is its silhouette. In some situations the shadowy stems of trees contrasted with a sunny meadow or against an open sea beyond produce a picturesque composition in line, as, for instance, the twisted trunks of sassafras along a shore line. In other instances trees make a silhouette by spreading dark masses of foliage against the sky, the pines being distinguished for their bold outlines. Another dramatic silhouette is made by white birch seen against a background of hemlocks. Any tree of distinctive outline, such as the American elm, the white oak, or the Lombardy poplar, is excellent in silhouette. Often a mist or a winter's snowstorm will bring into silhouette trees which at other times merge with those about them. Different species of native trees have typically character-

A Garden House

Robert Wheelwright, Landscape Architect

A Summer House in Georgian Style

Climbing Roses on an Old Springhouse

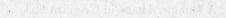

istic outlines which make them recognizable by their silhouette alone. Hickory, sugar maple, black walnut, tulip trees, the white ash and the Kentucky coffee tree are among the most easily distinguished native trees.

The three most outstanding aspects of plants are form, texture, and color. The outline of a tree seen as a silhouette is a print of its form, but the more subtle modelling is better appreciated by the play of light on the surface of the foliage masses. The importance of form in design can hardly be overemphasized, as it gives balance and substance to the composition. And form is much more than outline. Whereas the outline of Juniperus chinensis Pfitzeriana and the outline of Taxus cuspidata are very similar, their forms are quite different, because the branches of the yew are in somewhat flat planes, while the many, fine branches of the juniper are grouped in thick masses.

Texture is a matter of leaf size and distribution. The contribution which some trees and shrubs make to a landscape composition is largely in the texture of their foliage. Notable for this rather subtle beauty are the Katsura tree (Cercidiphyllum japonicum), the birches, the locusts, the English maple and the English oak. Many of the azaleas have leaves grouped in rosettes at the end of the branches which make beautiful patterns. The same effect at a larger scale is produced by the compound leaves of the horse chestnut. Trees and shrubs with compound leaves are apt to have finer textures than those with simple leaves. This is not true in all cases, however, because the ash and cherry are about the same in texture. The leaves of some plants are so large that it is difficult to adjust them to the textures of other plants. In this group we find such plants as the castor oil bean, elephant ears, and in some instances, Magnolia macrophylla.

As elements in a landscape composition, plants are the pigments in a color scheme, and every plant contributes its facet of color to the whole mosaic of colors. Some of the colors, in fact many of them, change with the seasons, the gray of winter merging into the green of spring, with a short period of brilliance at blossom time or at the time of fruiting. Outline, form, mass, and texture are all important elements in the design, but in many compositions, particularly in the flower garden, it is color which has the strongest appeal. The arrangement of plants to produce harmonious color compositions is one of the most fascinating and thrilling accomplishments of the designer, and it is one of the most joyous expressions of garden art.

SUGGESTIONS FOR PLANTING COMPOSITIONS

Cornelian Cherry (Cornus mas) and Spice Bush (Benzoin æstivale) against a background of hemlocks, with spring bulbs in the foreground.

Winter Jasmine (Jasminum nudiflorum) trained against a stone wall with Lonicera fragrantissima growing beside it.

Magnolia stellata with drifts of Narcissus, variety Seagull, beneath it.

Brilliant orange-yellow Crocus blooming beneath the bronzy winter foliage of Leucothoë Catesbæi.

Magnolia soulangeana and Magnolia Kobus against a background of evergreens, with Mertensia and Muscari in the foreground.

Silver Bell Tree (Halesia carolina) with masses of Mertensia blooming beneath it.

Daphne cneorum with Iris azurea blooming beneath its branches.

Pink Columbine, pale blue bulbous Iris (variety Wedgewood), pink Heuchera, lavender Viola (variety Maggie Mott).

Tall yellow Tulips (variety Moonlight), orange Iceland Poppies, white Columbine, yellow Pansies.

Anchusa italica (variety Dropmore) with oriental Poppy (variety Princess Ena or Mrs. Perry).

Viola (variety Arkwright Ruby) with Antirrhinum (variety Bonfire) and Delphinium chinense.

Artemisia lactiflora with pale pink Gladioli of the Primulinus type, and Salvia farinacea.

Japanese Anemone (variety Queen Charlotte) with Salvia azurea.

Linum perenne with Iceland Poppy (variety Coonara pink).

Foxgloves (variety Sutton's apricot) blooming in the background with Antirrhinum (variety Sutton's apricot) in the foreground.

Single, pink Canterbury Bells, Sweet William (variety Fairy and Newport Pink), Candidum Lilies and Delphinium.

Single early Tulip (variety General De Wet), Narcissus (variety White Lady), Mertensia, Siberian Wallflower, Primroses (Munstead Strain), and Phlox divaricata.

A Garden House

A Shaded Terrace with Wellhead and Seat

III

Construction Problems

GRADING

The process of converting land to more intensified use is very apt to make necessary changes in the grades of ground surfaces. Such constructions as roadways and the immediate surroundings of house and play areas need to conform to certain standards of practicality and use. Sloping surfaces, too steep for convenient travel, must be brought down to more gentle grades in order to accommodate new roads. The formality appropriate for the terraces of a house usually demands flat surfaces of ground. The games of tennis, bowls, baseball, etc., require carefully levelled areas. These operations of changing the levels of ground are classed as grading.

GRADING FOR A NEW HOUSE

The subject of grading about a new house usually receives scant attention on the part of the owner. There are so many questions of furnishings and fixtures to be decided that problems of landscape design are sometimes postponed until these are disposed of. Meanwhile, often the earth from the cellar excavation has been dumped and spread over a considerable area, thus covering up much valuable top-soil, and the floor levels are fixed, regardless of the design of the ground areas round about.

GRADING REQUIREMENTS INFLUENCE DESIGN

Adjusting a house to its site is not an easy problem at best. When it has been complicated by postponing its consideration until the house has imposed a new set of conditions, it is rendered even more difficult of satisfactory solution. However, when a house and the surrounding areas have been designed together, it is possible to compromise each to accommodate the other. The raising of floor grades by a few inches above the level originally planned may be enough to save several hundred dollars in the grading item alone, or will make possible an easier transition between architecture and landscape. The shifting of the house several feet from the site originally selected may make possible a better grade and an easier curve in the driveway. These results are worth attaining, and can be had by taking pains to make at least a general landscape plan of the property, with a grading plan of the house site, *before* the house is built. All these things may be considered a part of design and, of course, they are. But because there are certain factors such as maximum grade and minimum curve which limit road forms, the problems of grading in many cases determine what the design may be.

TOPOGRAPHY

Planning changes in ground form requires careful measurement and the recording of existing grades as a basis for studies. Such a record of the site is called a topographic plan because it represents the ground slopes. By a series of lines called contour lines, each connecting all points on the earth's surface that are at an equal elevation, the plan very readily expresses the configuration of the ground. Where the lines are close together, the ground is steep; where they are far apart, the ground is nearly level.

GRADING PLAN

The finished plan representing the original ground form and the ground levels after they have been adjusted to new requirements, is called a grading plan. It is the working drawing controlling the excavating and filling operations. From this plan earthwork quantities are computed and the new levels staked out.

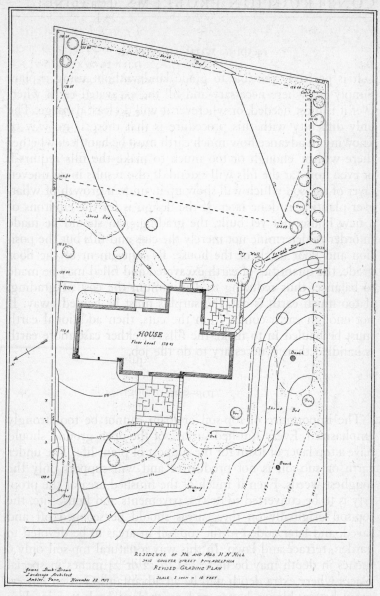

A Grading Plan of a Suburban Property

Contour lines indicate slopes.

GRADING WITHOUT A PLAN

It is perfectly possible to grade land without using a plan. Simply cut where necessary and fill the excavated earth wherever it is most needed, or wherever it will do least damage. The only difficulty with this procedure is that there is no way of knowing in advance how much earth must be handled, whether there will be enough or too much to make the fills required, or even how far the fills will extend. It also results in an uneven layer of top-soil which will show up in uneven growth of whatever planting is done later. If the design is for the environs of a new house, not yet built, the grading plan should be made in order to determine not merely the cuts and fills but the position and floor levels of the house. By adjustment of the floor grade, the quantities of earth excavated and filled may be made to balance, thus reducing to a minimum the cost of grading. If too much earth is cut, the surplus must be hauled away. If not enough earth comes from the cuts, then additional earth must be hauled in to make the fills. In either case more earth is handled than is necessary to do the job.

TOP–SOIL

The importance of top-soil or loam cannot be too strongly emphasized. Every finished surface of the open ground should have a top layer of loam for the support of plant life. The under earth or sub-soil is not productive and will support only the toughest weeds. Even if much of the finished area of the property is to be converted to drives, pavements and house site, the top-soil originally on these areas should be scooped off and saved, and later added to the top-soil in areas to be devoted to garden, terrace and lawn. In this way a natural top-soil only 6 inches in depth may be increased to 12 or 24 inches in special places where extra depth will be an advantage. Garden flowers grow better, bloom better and resist drought better in deep loam than they do in shallow soil. Fertilizer may be used to make up for the lack of proper depth in soil, but its effect is temporary at best, whereas a rich top-soil 15 inches deep is a permanent asset.

When grading begins, all the top-soil should be removed with a scoop from the whole area to be graded and dumped conveniently near, but outside, the field of operations. It is wise to save all available top-soil. If some is left over, the surplus will help make compost, and top-dressing, and renew the soil in the greenhouse and coldframes for several years to come.

EXCAVATION

The next step is to excavate for the foundations and for the areas to be lowered. The earth thus removed should be placed, whenever possible, in its final position, handling the earth only once. The spreading of earth in areas of fill should be done in layers not deeper than 6 inches and each layer should be rolled before the next is spread. This method compacts the earth so firmly that there will be practically no settling of sub-soil during subsequent years.

SETTLING OF FILLED SOIL

Failure to compact the earth while it is being filled will cause a gradual settling of the earth during three or four years. In some places this settling is no detriment, but in others, adjacent to terrace steps, the settling will cause the steps to appear above their normal position, sometimes as much as several inches, a very awkward condition in a finished landscape.

SUB-GRADES

The grades of the sub-soil should be brought to levels below the proposed final grade equal to the thickness of top-soil or paving required in these various areas. Thus, if it is intended that a terrace should be furnished with 15 inches of top-soil, the sub-soil should be smoothed off at a level 15 inches below final grades.

MINIMUM SLOPE

No area of turf or of pavement should be absolutely level or be so shaped that a concave surface will collect water. Though they should look level, actually terraces should slope away from the building with a fall of at least one foot (preferably more) to a hundred feet.

LAWNS FOR TENNIS OR CROQUET

Lawns for tennis or croquet should be graded to an even, smooth surface, but they should not be absolutely level. One method is to slope the ground away from the net to the back-stop fence at the minimum degree of slope. This has the effect of making the top of the net actually higher than it should be in relation to players on the base line. Another method is to slope the whole court evenly from end to end. Another is to slope it from the center foul lines towards the sides and from the base lines out to the end fences. Croquet lawns may be graded similarly, from the middle out to the edges.

DRAINAGE OF SURFACE WATER

Catch basins and drain inlets are important adjuncts to the drive, court, terrace and flower garden. Properly placed and connected with a drain, they will remove surface water before it has a chance to flood flower beds or wash out banks. The drains should extend in straight lines from one basin to the next and should be at least a foot below the surface. The smallest size practicable for drains is 6 inches in diameter. Drains which take the outflow of three or more basins should be 8 inches or more in diameter. Unless the town has separate storm water sewers, the outlet of drains usually must be taken care of on the property, either by being brought to the surface, distributed through a tile field, or emptied into a dry well, or into a stream.

A Tile Field is a series of tile pipes branching off from the main drain in parallel lines, 10 or 15 feet apart and about 15 inches below the surface. The pipes are laid in trenches and are filled about with crushed stone. The upper few inches of the trench are filled with top-soil. The water flowing through the pipes seeps out into the crushed stone, saturates the soil, and the grass roots absorb the water. It is important to locate the tile field in open ground away from trees. Sunshine keeps the soil in condition to absorb the water. Tree roots are likely to find their way into the drain and clog it. Also important is the grade of the pipe. It should fall at the rate of ½ of 1 per cent ($\frac{1}{16}$-inch to the foot). A steep pitch in the pipes will cause the water to run to the end.

A Dry Well is an excavation into the sub-soil, usually 6 or 8 feet deep and 4 or 6 feet in diameter, the sides of which are walled with stone. It is covered by a stone or concrete slab. It fills up in a storm and the water seeps away slowly into the sub-soil.

FILLING TRENCHES

The back-filling of the trenches must be done with the greatest of care. The earth should be filled in layers of 6 inches and each layer sprinkled and tamped into place. This method will avoid future settling. A trench ought to accommodate the pipe and all the soil which came out of it, even if this means a slight mounding up of earth along the trench line. The mound will probably disappear after the first winter.

TOP–SOIL AND FINISHED GRADING

After the sub-soil has been brought by excavating and filling to the proper grades, and after the trenches have been refilled, the top-soil may be brought back and spread. If the grading has been in process for several months and the top-soil has been piled up during the house-building operation, many of the old grass roots should be pretty well decomposed, but the pile may be covered with weeds, and the soil will be full of weed seeds. Spreading it out in its final position will give the weeds a chance to germinate. Then if the ground is cultivated before grass seed is sown, many of the weeds may be eliminated. If time permits, it is an advantage to let three or four weeks elapse between finished grading and sowing. Whether such a program can be followed will depend on the time of year the grading is completed. The most favorable time for starting a lawn is August or early September, and the next best is early spring. If top-soil has been spread in the autumn too late for starting a lawn, then the ground should go through the winter with a cover crop of rye which can be sown in October and turned under in the spring. Rye should be sown at the rate of a bushel and a half per acre.

WATER SUPPLY SYSTEMS, AND UNDERGROUND PIPE LINES

After sub-grades are finished, and if possible, before the top-soil has been spread, the utility lines may be laid. House water supply pipes must be in trenches at a depth greater than the maximum frost penetration for the region. House sewers and drains from catch basins and from the roofs need not be as deep, although 15 inches or 18 inches of dirt over the pipes is advisable to keep them out of the way of planting operations.

Water supply pipes leading to garden-hose connections need not be below frost line, if they are constructed in such a way as to permit the emptying of the pipe when the water is shut off for the winter. For this reason the pipes should slope to an outlet at the cut-off valve or at the spigot. An all-season outdoor water supply system must have pipes below the frost line and self-draining hydrants rather than faucets.

Gas pipes may be shallow but they must be so graded that there is a moisture outlet at each low point in the line.

Catch basins are so constructed that the outlet is well above the bottom. The sediment which collects should be removed periodically before it reaches the level of the outlet drain. Neglected catch basins are the principal cause of stoppages in the drainage system.

The size of the drain from the catch basin is dependent on the area of land which it is to drain. The table opposite gives the pipe sizes and grades for draining areas of turf under conditions of rainfall prevailing in eastern North America.

The minimum grade for 6-inch tile drains is 1 per cent but 2 per cent or more is better because the faster flowing water keeps the pipe clear. Increase in the grade of the pipe increases the flow and capacity.

UNDER–DRAINING WET LAND

Land which contains too much moisture, or which is so slow to dry out in early spring that spring operations are retarded,

TABLE TO DETERMINE SIZE OF DRAIN PIPE REQUIRED

SIZE OF PIPE	GRADE OF PIPE	AREA TO BE DRAINED	
		IN TURF	IN PAVEMENT
6″ Tile	2%	7,000 sq. ft.	3,500 sq. ft.
8″ Tile	2%	12,000 " "	6,000 " "
10″ Tile	2%	19,000 " "	9,500 " "
6″ Tile	4%	10,000 " "	5,000 " "
8″ Tile	4%	18,000 " "	9,000 " "
10″ Tile	4%	28,000 " "	14,000 " "

may be greatly improved by drainage lines. The tile pipes for draining land should be laid about 18 to 24 inches below the surface, and the ditch should be filled with crushed stone or gravel to within 8 inches of the surface. Strips of roofing paper should be spread over the stone ballast and then covered with top-soil to bring the trench to an even grade. The pipes should be laid at a grade of about 2 per cent in parallel lines 15 or 20 feet apart, and the outlet should be carried to a stream. The pipes most often used for this purpose are 3-inch agricultural tile drain pipes, but the main carrying off the outlet from several laterals should be 4- or 6-inch vitrified tile drain pipe.

TERRACES

The terrace is an important feature of the modern home. It is a transition between house and garden and is often the foreground of an open view. In the great Italian villas the terraces commanded views over the countryside. They often extended across the whole garden scheme, and by the architectural treat-

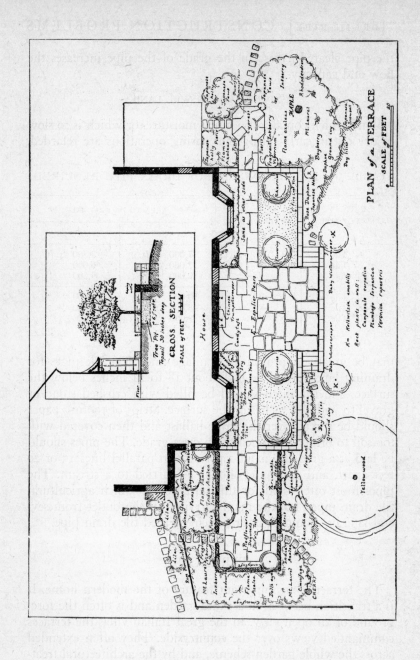

PLAN of a TERRACE

SCALE of FEET

CROSS SECTION
SCALE of FEET

Tree Pit. 4.5 feet
Topsoil 30 inches deep

House

K = Kolkwitzia amabilis

Rock plants in wall:
Campanula carpatica
Plumbago larpentae
Veronica rupestris

MAPLE

92

Photograph by Philip B. Wallace

An Informal House Terrace

Photograph by Sylvia Saunders

A House Terrace

ment of their outlines with balustrades they pleasantly combined architecture with plant forms. Often they were embellished with sculpture, fountains, potted plants and patterned pavements, and usually they were shaded by large trees. Wherever garden art has felt the Italian influence, terraces have formed an important element in the landscape design.

ARCHITECTURAL FUNCTIONS OF THE TERRACE

Because of its architectural form, almost every house requires some degree of formality in its immediate surroundings, and the terrace, with its precise outline of clipped hedge, parapet, or balustrade, may well mark the limit of the formal area. The terrace makes a platform for the house and thereby adjusts it to its site in a graceful and easy transition. Furthermore, the terrace is another room to the house, useful whenever it is pleasant enough to sit out-of-doors. In this respect the terrace must be arranged for various weathers, part of it being open to the breezes of summer and part hemmed in by the house so that it is exposed to the warm sunlight of early spring mornings.

SCALE AND PROPORTION

The size and proportions of a terrace are a matter of scale. The bulk of the house, the size of the property and the extent of the lawn are factors, and function is also to be considered. It is safe to say that one is more apt to make a terrace too narrow than too broad. The broad terrace has an air of spaciousness and makes a good foreground to a distant view. A narrow terrace is only appropriate on a restricted site where other elements, such as the lawn, are also compact, or where a broader terrace would cut off a pleasant view down into a valley. Unless conditions of the site dictate otherwise, the terrace should be at least as broad as the height of the house façade flanking it.

THE RAISED TERRACE

The house terrace may be raised above surrounding land by a wall or bank; it may be level with the lawn, the separation being made merely by the edge of the pavement; or it may be sunk below the adjacent ground. The grading will be suggested by the conditions of the site. The terrace floor should slope slightly away from the house and the surface water should be collected in drain inlets at the outer rim. The terrace floor may be treated in a number of ways; pavement to accommodate the furniture, smooth turf, small pebble surface, or, what is usually better, a combination of these materials. A broad expanse of stone paving just outside the house can be uncomfortably hot. If only a small part of the terrace is paved and if it is shaded by large trees, summer heat will be greatly mitigated. The various paving materials described for garden paths are suitable for terraces.

THE SUNKEN TERRACE

Built upon the side of a hill, the terrace floor is maintained by a masonry wall or by a smoothly graded bank. If the hill ascends above the terrace it, too, must be retained, and the treatment of this wall may be made an interesting feature of the design. A long, unbroken masonry wall may be monotonous; but divided into bays by buttresses or pilasters, or surmounted by a balustrade, it becomes architectural, something in harmony with the artificiality of the place. Vines clinging to the wall or hanging down over it from above, or fruit trees pleached against it, impart a softness of texture in pleasing contrast to the rugged masonry.

DRAINING THE TERRACE

Because of the importance of ridding the terrace of rainwater promptly, drain inlets should be placed at frequent intervals. On a terrace eighty or a hundred feet long, four drain inlets at the outer margin are sufficient to carry off the surplus water of a storm. The ground surface should slope toward the drain inlets. The inlet gratings may be small and inconspicuous, 8 inches x 12 inches being ample. For the construction of drains and inlets see Drainage of Surface Water on page 88.

A House Terrace Beneath Maples

The flagstone paving is not raised above the lawn.

PLANTS IN THE STONE PAVING

A very pleasant effect of stone paving is produced by planting between the flagstones little flowering plants or herbs. Such a paving is not laid on a concrete base but on a cushion of sand and pockets of soil for the plants are prepared beneath the crevices.

PLANTS APPROPRIATE FOR PLANTING IN SOIL BETWEEN PAVING STONES

Ajuga reptans	Sempervivum atlanticum
Arabis alpina	Silene acaulis
Arenaria montana	Statice Armeria
Arenaria verna	Statice alpina
Campanula glomerata acaulis	Thymus citriodorus
Gypsophila repens	Thymus Serpyllum vulgaris
Herniaria glabra	Thymus Serpyllum lanuginosus
Mazus rugosus	Veronica repens
Sedum acre	Veronica rupestris
Sedum sexangulare	Veronica Serpyllifolia
Sempervivum arachnoideum	

BANKS

In many cases an evenly sloping bank, simply treated, will be appropriate and will function as well as a retaining wall. The advantages of the wall are its architectural character, its economy of space, and its permanence. The advantages of the bank are its more natural character and economy of construction costs. The bank sloping down from a terrace or up from the terrace may be planted with interesting ground cover plants to prevent erosion and to reduce maintenance costs. The bank may rise from the top of a low retaining wall. This arrangement of form and material imparts a note of precision which harmonizes with the formality of the terrace.

THE TURF BANK

Turf clad banks have been used since olden times and nothing else can present such a finished effect as an accurately graded and well maintained turf terrace bank. Turf banks should not be graded to a steeper slope than one foot of rise to two feet of horizontal dimension. Starting turf on a slope is more difficult than on level land. A heavy rain coming before the turf has formed will erode the soil and will make necessary patching, regrading, and reseeding. Laying turf over the whole bank is the most certain method of starting grass on a bank. If the surface water from the hillside above the bank is diverted by turf gutters, the bank grass may be started with seed sowing. In this case, strips of turf placed in horizontal lines along the banks at intervals of 4 or 6 feet will arrest the washing away of soil. This precaution is worth the additional cost.

THE PLANTED BANK

A bank well furnished with top-soil and covered with densely spreading plants is, perhaps, the most satisfactory and economical treatment of the change in levels. The slope should be 1 foot of rise to 2½ feet of horizontal dimension, or it may be even less steep. By a careful selection of plants the bank may be made very beautiful. Conditions of soil and exposure may affect or even dictate a choice of plants. Such a great variety of plants is suitable for covering a bank that a wide range of choice is possible.

For a bank in sunshine sloping down from the terrace a satisfactory combination is jasmine and Rosa Wichuraiana, with Cotoneaster horizontalis at the margins. For a shady or partially shaded bank periwinkle (Vinca minor), with narcissus coming up among it, is charming in the spring and green throughout the season. A terrace with a planted bank below it should be outlined with a low hedge.

GROUND COVER PLANTS FOR BANKS

Woody Plants
    Akebia quinata
    Arctostaphylos uva-ursi (Bearberry)
    Calluna vulgaris (Heather)
    Comptonia asplenifolia (Sweetfern)

Cotoneaster horizontalis (Rock Cotoneaster)
Euonymus radicans (Wintercreeper)
Euonymus radicans coloratus
Euonymus radicans minimus
Hedera helix (English Ivy)
Jasminum nudiflorum (Winter Jasmine)
Juniperus communis depressa (Spreading Juniper)
Juniperus horizontalis (Creeping Juniper)
Juniperus Sabina (Savin)
Lonicera japonica Halliana (Hall's Honeysuckle)
Lycium chinense (Chinese Matrimony Vine)
Pachysandra terminalis (Japanese Spurge)
Rhus canadensis (Fragrant Sumac)
Rosa humilis (Pasture Rose)
Rosa lucida (Virginia Rose)
Rosa multiflora (Japanese Rose)
Rosa Wichuraiana (Wichurian Rose)
Spiræa tomentosa (Hardhack)
Vinca minor (Periwinkle)

Hardy Perennial Plants

Ajuga reptans (Bugle)
Arabis alpina (Alpine Rockcress)
Arenaria montana (Mountain Sandwort)
Cerastium tomentosum (Snow-in-Summer)
Convallaria majalis (Lily-of-the-Valley)
Hemerocallis fulva (Tawny Daylily)
Lysimachia nummularia (Moneywort)
Nepeta Mussini
Phlox subulata (Moss Phlox)
Plumbago larpentæ
Sedum acre (Goldmoss)
Thymus Serpyllum (Thyme)

GARDEN WALLS

FREE—STANDING WALLS

In olden times, high walls were built around gardens to protect them. Often a moat also surrounded the garden. In some cases the walls were reared as much for shelter against winds as for protection, and they provided supports for fruit trees, trained against them. A southern wall surface stimulated spring growth in the espalier trees and induced earlier flowering and earlier fruiting. Besides these practical functions of garden walls, there is the unescapable charm of the wall as a background for flowers and foliage or as a beautiful evidence of the seclusion which they help to create.

A broad, unbroken surface of masonry is not always interesting, but a wall divided into panels or interrupted by projecting buttresses, or one built with a combination of materials pleasantly blended, has an architectural significance. It is the link which unites the garden and the house as parts of one composition.

It is essential that the top of the wall be protected from the weather. One of the most practical means of preventing the moisture from entering the masonry from above is to cover the wall with a coping of flagstones set in cement mortar joints. This definite edge also gives a finish to the structure. A sharp-pitched roof of slate, brick, shingles or painted boards is sometimes used, the latter being common in Pennsylvania. A brick coping is also frequently used and a wedge-shaped top built of brick courses in diminishing thicknesses is very picturesque. Molded brick set on edge is a favorite wall finish in Virginia.

In the South, walls are sometimes built with some of the bricks omitted, leaving holes in the wall to allow for the passage of air currents. It is important in the South not to exclude all the breezes and the perforated wall is a screen but not an absolute barrier. An unusual wall found in Virginia and supposed to be the invention of Thomas Jefferson is the serpentine wall of brick. Because of its constantly changing direction, it is stronger against wind pressure than a straight wall of the same thickness. Therefore, it may be built only one brick thick and is more economical of material, and far more picturesque than the straight wall. A modern version of the thin wall, one brick thick, is a wall braced at intervals by vertical iron rods built to clasp the brick masonry. It is less expensive than the usual 8-inch brick wall.

Photograph by James Bush-Brown

Retaining Walls and Flower Beds

A wall typical of South Carolina is a brick wall with arched panels of stucco. The piers are thick and the panels only one brick in thickness.

In crowded suburban areas, the high wall is sometimes employed to secure the privacy of the garden. This type of suburban yard is more in use now than it was two decades ago, but the walled yard has long been common in England.

RETAINING WALLS

A retaining wall must hold its position against the pressure of the earth behind it. At seasons of alternate freezing and thawing, ground pressure is considerable. We see its effect when paved roads heave in early spring. If the wall is not adequate to hold, the pressure thus exerted may be translated into one of four kinds of movement in the wall. (1) The wall may be forced to bulge out of shape, opening cracks in the masonry. This is apt to happen in dry walls in which there is no mortar to hold the stones together. The pressure and strain is there in all walls. (2) The whole wall may slide away from the hill. This can happen if the footings of the wall are not deep enough to have a firm hold in the soil. (3) The wall can be forced to revolve about its base line and thus made to lean forward out of position. (4) The wall may be lifted up vertically by the action of frost beneath the footings. This can happen when the foundations do not extend below the frost line of the region.

DIMENSION OF RETAINING WALLS

It has been found by long practice that the proportions shown in the sectional sketch are adequate to withstand the pressures in the soil. The footings are below frost line and slope down toward the rear. The thickness of the wall at the base equals one third of the height measured from the lower ground level. The top of the wall is 18 inches thick. Special conditions, such as heavy moving traffic along the top of the wall, will make necessary a greater bulk of masonry than for normal conditions.

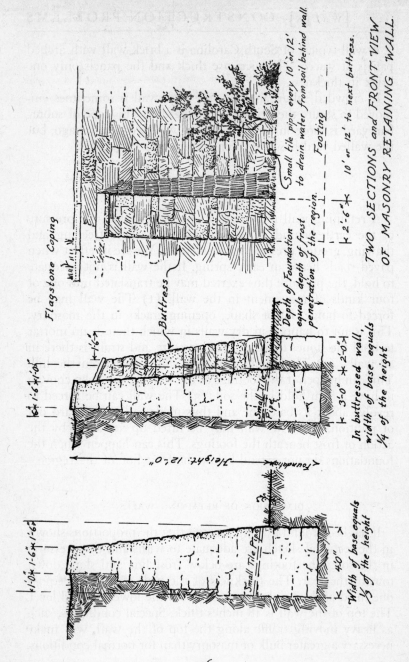

Flagstone Coping

Buttress

Small tile pipe every 10' or 12' to drain water from soil behind wall.

Footing

10' or 12' to next buttress.

2'-6"

Depth of Foundation equals depth of frost penetration of the region.

TWO SECTIONS and FRONT VIEW OF MASONRY RETAINING WALL.

1'-0" 1'-6" 1'-6"

3'-0" 2'-0"

Small Tile Pipe

In buttressed wall, width of base equals ¼ of the height

Height 12'-0"

Foundation

1'-0" 1'-6" 1'-6"

4'-0"

Small Tile Pipe

Width of base equals ⅓ of the height

BUTTRESSES

By building projections or buttresses into the face of the wall at intervals of 10 or 12 feet, the effective base of the wall is widened, thus making the structure more resistant to the tendency to revolve about its base, and hence more secure. Any revolving of the wall would have to become a lifting of the center of gravity as is shown in the sketch section. The buttresses must be built with the wall as part of the structure. The wider the projection of the base of the buttresses the greater is the resistance to pressure. A buttressed wall may be built thinner and still be as strong as a plain wall of the same height. Buttresses may be made a decorative element, dividing a long wall into bays.

DRAINAGE HOLES

Pressure from wet soil is greater than pressure from dry soil. To prevent the soil behind a retaining wall from becoming saturated, or simply to permit the normal flow of water through the sub-soil to continue, uninterrupted by the wall, small holes should be left in the masonry near the base of the wall at intervals of 10 or 12 feet.

BONDING STONES

Stones should be laid into the wall in such a way as to form a strong bond. That is, the long dimension of the stone should be horizontal and each stone should bridge over the joint between the two stones in the course below. In this way no long vertical joint will appear. In any retaining wall some stones should run from the front to the back face across the wall to tie the masonry more firmly together.

MIXTURE FOR MASONRY WALLS

The mortar should be a mixture of one part Portland cement and two parts sand.

The masonry wall, well built, is a structure of great strength, a permanent installation. The retaining walls of the great Italian villas have remained intact for four or five hundred years.

DRY RETAINING WALLS

Less expensive to build, but also less secure, is the dry retaining wall, built without mortar. A special construction of the dry wall is described in Chapter XVI. Both of these are called "gravity" walls because they hold their place by reason of their own weight.

REINFORCED CONCRETE WALL

Another type, known as the "cantilever" wall, holds partly by the weight of earth upon a broad projecting footing. This is built of reinforced concrete, and is therefore a monolith. It is much lighter and thinner in construction than the gravity wall, and is used in regions where sand is common and stone is scarce. The concrete is poured between temporary forms built of lumber. Steel reinforcing rods form a mesh of 12- or 15-inch squares, which gives the concrete great rigidity, and prevents it from cracking under unequal pressure. The inner surface of a concrete wall should be sealed with an application of a waterproofing compound. Tar is the basis of most waterproof material, and it should be applied when hot. Unless this is done the concrete is likely to become porous and to crack. With this protection from ground water, a concrete retaining wall may be faced with a coat of stucco or with brick. But unless the wall has been waterproofed, the stucco will peel off and the brick will blossom out with rosettes of lime deposited by moisture coming through the bricks and then evaporating.

GARDEN PATHS

A garden path—the very words bring to memory old brick walks bordered with boxwood, strips of turf between long flower borders; flagstones set about by tiny herbs and overarched with spreading branches of magnolias. One could as easily imagine a garden without flowers, as a garden without paths. The path is one of the components of the garden plan which gives expression to the design; in some cases by making a pattern among the flower beds, in some by accenting the lines

Photograph by James Bush-Brown

A High Garden Wall Clothed in Vines

of symmetry, and in still others by the use of subtle turn and graceful curve.

In considering the construction of paths there are a number of matters which should be given careful thought—the selection of the materials to be used, the suitability, the original cost, and the expense of upkeep.

In many cases, the suitability of one material over another will be the deciding factor. On an area where there is much travel back and forth, turf would not be desirable as it would lack the greatly needed quality of durability. Within the confines of a garden, however, where there is comparatively little passing to and fro, grass paths are entirely satisfactory. On the other hand, if one has a wooded tract, and has consequently developed the place along informal or naturalistic lines, a path of tanbark would undoubtedly be the most suitable. In a setting of this sort paths of brick or gravel would be out of harmony with the surroundings. For a pathway leading from the sidewalk to the door where there is constant passing, some durable material such as gravel, brick, or flagstones should be used.

Costs will vary considerably in different parts of the country. In sections where there are natural outcroppings of rock, and stone is plentiful, flagstone paths might be the most economical, while in other sections they might be almost prohibitive in price, due to the expense of shipping the materials. In the case of turf and tanbark paths, much of the work may be done by unskilled labor and the costs may consequently be kept low. On the other hand, a turf path requires more upkeep than do most of the other types. It must be kept mowed and it must be kept edged, for nothing detracts more from the trim and pleasing appearance of a garden than straggly grass and frowzy edges. This question of upkeep is one that should be taken into careful consideration before the final decision is made.

LINES AND GRADES

In a formal garden, the lines and dimensions of paths must be laid out with great care. The best way to establish a straight line is to stretch a cord between two stakes. A steel tape or a heavy cloth tape is essential, and a surveyor's transit is a great aid. Lacking a transit, right angles may be marked off on the ground by the 3-4-5 method. This is most easily done by three persons, using a tape and three stakes.

Taking three sections of tape, the lengths of which are proportioned to one another as 3 is to 4 and as 4 is to 5, and placing them end to end in a triangle, the angle between the "3" section and the "4" section will be a square angle or 90 degrees. The reason for this is the old geometric theorem, "The square of the hypotenuse of a right-angled triangle is equal to the sum of the squares of the other two sides." Thus, $3^2 + 4^2 = 5^2$ or $9 + 16 = 25$. If the lengths of the two lines are to extend some distance it is best to use longer pieces of tape than 3, 4, and 5 feet, because a slight error in holding the tapes together would increase proportionately with the distance to the end of the line. Sections 9 feet, 12 feet and 15 feet are convenient.

The most direct and satisfactory way of marking a "free-hand" curve is to fling a section of garden hose or heavy rope on the ground. The hose may be adjusted until the desired alignment is reached and it may then be marked by frequent stakes.

Grades are important in path building. Surface water must be induced to run off promptly, and this can best be done by making the center of the paths slightly higher than the sides. (On a 6-foot brick path, ¾ of an inch; on a 6-foot flagstone, ½ inch; on a 6-foot gravel, 1 inch.) Also, the path must slope slightly lengthwise (at least 1 foot in 100 feet) and there should be catch basins or drain inlets at points where water may be collected and carried off by under ground pipes. These subjects have been more fully treated under Grading in this chapter.

BRICK

Brick walks are usually very pleasant in character and obtain a mellowness and charm with age which makes strong appeal. The initial cost is comparatively high but if a good quality of brick is used and if the walk is carefully laid it should give service for many years. In some of our old colonial gardens

A Garden Path of Brick

we find paths laid two centuries or more ago which are still in good condition and attest to the worth of the fine craftsmanship of our forefathers.

In sections of the country where there is but light frost action and where there is a natural layer of sandy or gravelly soil, no additional foundation is needed for the path. If frost seldom penetrates more than 2 or 3 inches into the ground it is possible to lay the bricks directly upon a cushion of sand after the subgrades have been determined. In the North, however, it is necessary to do a much more expensive and laborious piece of work and a foundation course must be carefully prepared before the bricks are laid. Unless this is done the action of the frost will gradually heave the bricks out of place, causing some to be cracked and broken, and before many years have elapsed one will have an unsightly and entirely unsatisfactory piece of paving. Bricks may be laid either upon a concrete base with a cinder foundation or upon a cushion of sand above a cinder foundation. Where the bricks are to be laid with mortar joints, the concrete base should be used. After the grades have been established and the earth has been excavated to a depth of 12 inches below the finished grade, a 6-inch layer of cinders should be put in place. A 3-inch layer should first be spread, watered thoroughly and then rolled or tamped. The second layer should be handled in the same manner. The base course of concrete should then be prepared and spread over the cinders to a depth of 3 inches. A mixture of one part cement, three parts sand and five parts gravel is recommended for this purpose. After this concrete foundation has set for twenty-four hours, the bricks should be laid according to the desired pattern upon a thin coat of mortar, one part cement to three parts sand. When the mortar has set and the bricks are firmly in place the joints should be filled. This may be done in one of two different ways. If the joints are small, a quarter of an inch or less in width, a dry mixture of cement and sand in the proportion of one cement to two of sand may be swept into the joints. After the bricks have been swept entirely free of cement, the walk should be watered with a fine, gentle spray until the cement in the joints has become thoroughly wet. Where the joints are large it is advisable to make a very wet mixture of the same proportions and pour it carefully between the bricks until the joints are filled.

When a brick walk is to be laid upon a sand cushion a similar foundation course of cinders is used. Upon the surface of the

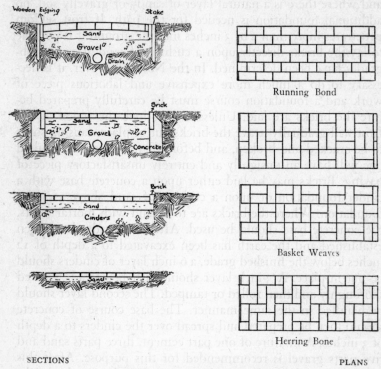

SECTIONS

PLANS

Construction of Brick Paths

cinders a 2-inch layer of fine sand should be spread and it should be thoroughly rolled or tamped before the bricks are set in place. After the bricks are laid, the joints should be filled with sand. As the bricks are being laid, the surface of the walk should be kept at an even and uniform level. This may easily be done by placing a wide board crosswise with the path and tamping it until the surface is even. As brick walks which are laid in sand have a tendency to creep, the joints becoming gradually wider and wider, a curb should always be used.

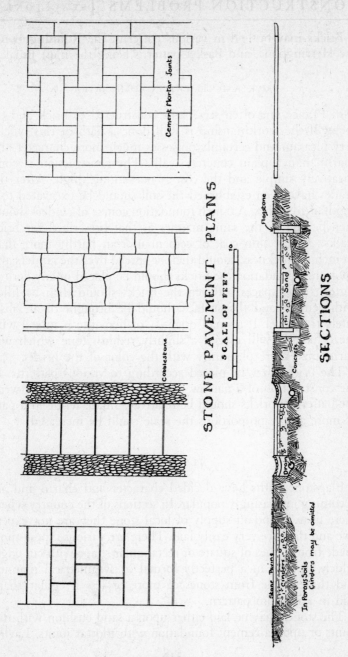

STONE PAVEMENT PLANS

SCALE OF FEET

Cement Mortar Joints

Cobblestone

Stone Paving

SECTIONS

Flagstone

Sand

Concrete

Drain

Cinders

In Porous Soils
Cinders may be omitted

Bricks may be laid in various patterns, the Running Bond, the Herringbone, and Basket patterns being the most usual.

BRICK AND CEMENT IN COMBINATION

In France one often sees paths constructed of brick and cement. If the workmanship is well done a path of this type is very pleasant and certainly possesses much more character and charm than a plain concrete walk. The construction is comparatively simple and the cost is not unduly high. After the grades have been established the soil should be excavated to a depth of 10 inches. A 6-inch foundation course of cinders should then be laid in the same manner as that prescribed for brick walks. A very thin coat of cement mortar, hardly more than an inch in thickness, should then be spread over the cinders and upon this foundation the bricks should be placed in any desired pattern. The spaces between the bricks should then be filled with cement and the surface should be brought to an absolutely true level. If a small quantity of hematite is mixed with the cement it will give it a slightly reddish tone which will harmonize more pleasantly with the color of the bricks.

The bricks may be placed according to various patterns. In the construction of a narrow path, the area of cement between the patterned bricks should be relatively small, while in a path of more ample proportions the scale could be increased.

FLAGSTONE

Flagstone paths have decided character and charm and are becoming increasingly popular. In sections of the country where there is an abundant supply of local stone they are not expensive and they are very easily laid. There are various types—those made from stones of square or rectangular shape with cut edges which are laid in a perfectly formal or symmetrical manner, and those made from stones of more or less irregular shape laid in a random pattern.

The stones may be laid either upon a sand cushion with dirt joints or upon a cement foundation with mortar joints. Laying

A Garden Path of Flagstones

Photograph by Jessie Tarbox Beals

them with earth joints makes possible the growing of turf or low-creeping plants between the stones, a feature greatly to be desired. The laying of a flagstone path on a sand cushion is a very simple matter and does not require a great amount of skill. The ground should be excavated to a depth which will bring the stones to the desired level and a layer of fine sand about ½ inch in depth should be spread over the surface of the soil. The stones may then be put in place and care should be taken to see that they are very firm, with no tendency to wobble or teeter. If the lower surface of the stone is uneven it will be necessary to remove a portion of the soil directly under the protruding point in order that it may settle firmly into its bed. The surface of the path should be true to the desired grade, and as the stones are set in place a carpenter's level should be used to check up on the surface. After the stones are in place, good top-soil should be spread over the surface of the path and swept into the joints or, if desired, the joints may be filled with small strips of turf. There are a number of rock plants which are of very low-creeping habit and are particularly suitable for planting between flagstones. Creeping thyme is a dainty little thing and when crushed under foot it emits a sweet, pungent fragrance. Gypsophila repens and Veronica repens are also excellent.

When flagstones are to be laid with mortar joints they must be set in cement. The soil should be excavated to a depth of 10 inches and a 6-inch layer of cinders should be spread in two layers 3 inches thick, each layer being watered, rolled or tamped. A 3-inch layer of cement should be spread upon this foundation course of cinders, being mixed in the proportions of one part cement, three parts sand and five parts gravel. After the cement has set for twenty-four hours a thin coat of cement mortar should be spread over it and the flagstones set in the mortar. After the stones have become firm, mortar should be poured into the joints.

GRAVEL

Gravel walks were very often used during colonial times and they have maintained their popularity throughout the years. There are numerous methods of construction. If the walk is to have but little travel upon it and if the ground is naturally well drained the gravel may be laid directly upon the soil after the sub-grade has been established. Constructed in this manner, however, a walk will not withstand hard wear and during wet weather it will have a tendency to become very soft and springy. A much better walk will result if an under-course of slag or crushed stone is used. In the construction of a walk of this type, the soil should be excavated to a depth of 7 inches below the finished grade. A 5½-inch layer of slag or crushed stone of a size which will pass a 2½-inch screen should then be spread and thoroughly tamped or rolled. The gravel should be spread upon this surface and should be well watered and rolled. Gravel known as "pit gravel" is greatly to be pre-ferred to washed gravel for the surfacing of walks and should be obtained whenever it is possible. If it is necessary to use washed gravel, limestone dust to the amount of approximately 15 per cent should be mixed with it in order to help bind the surface. Gravel used for the wearing surface of paths should be of a size which will pass a ½-inch mesh.

STEPPING STONES

Stepping stones laid in turf make a very pleasant path. Be-cause of their rather informal character they are, perhaps, more suitable for a casual or incidental path than for a walk which is anything in the way of a thoroughfare.

The stones selected for a path of this type should be of com-fortable size, at least 12 to 15 inches square, and the upper sur-face should be reasonably smooth. It is not necessary that the stones be of absolutely regular shape as very pleasant effects may be obtained with stones of slightly irregular outline. The stones should be placed at even intervals and spaced far enough apart to permit a pleasant, easy step from one stone to the next, 18 inches being the usual distance.

The setting of the stones is a very simple matter. If a new walk is being made they may be set at the same time that the surrounding area of grass is sown or they may be easily set in

Garden Steps

Informal Stone Steps

a piece of established turf. The stones should be placed upon the surface of the ground and their final position determined. The outline of each stone should then be marked with the edge of a trowel and after the stone has been lifted to one side the soil within the prescribed area should be removed to the proper depth. A light layer of fine sand should be placed at the bottom of the excavation, as this makes a better bed upon which to rest the stone and settle it into its final position. When placing the stones, care should be taken to see that they are perfectly firm and that they do not teeter from side to side. If the bottom of the stone is uneven it may be necessary to remove it several times and cut one portion of the excavation or build up another until the stone is absolutely firm. The surface of the stone should be level with the area of turf about it. Not only does this make a difference in the general appearance of the path but it greatly facilitates the use of the lawn mower. The soil should be rammed in close around the edges, after the stones have been set in place.

TANBARK

Tanbark is particularly suitable for woodland walks and is also frequently used in gardens of formal design. It has much to recommend it as a material for the surfacing of paths. It is comparatively inexpensive; its mellow, reddish-brown color forms a pleasing contrast with the areas of turf and foliage about it; it is easy to handle and under ordinary conditions no elaborate system of underdrainage is necessary; it offers an unusually pleasant and springy surface; and it dries almost immediately after a rain. Even during the heaviest rains tanbark never becomes muddy and it is of such a porous nature that it seldom retains standing pools of water.

A good quality of tanbark should be procured for the construction of paths. A poor grade is not cheap at any price as it is apt to contain large, lumpy pieces and various foreign substances. The best grades usually are obtained from oak and hemlock barks. Unless the path is to be constructed in a very low, swampy area, no underdrainage is necessary. In a case of this sort either a foundation course of cinders or a tile drain may be used. Ordinarily, however, all that is necessary is to see that the ground is levelled to the desired grade before the tan-bark is spread. A layer 3 inches in depth makes an excellent and very durable path. Immediately after spreading, the tan-bark should be thoroughly soaked and rolled. One ton of tan-bark will provide a 3-inch layer for a path 3 feet wide and 60 feet long.

TURF

A turf path has a number of advantages. The initial cost of materials is comparatively low, and the construction requires no great degree of skill. And undoubtedly an area of green, luxuriant turf possesses a beauty and a charm which are difficult to equal in other materials.

Turf paths may be readily established from seeding or, if immediate effect is desired, sod may be laid. In either case the preliminary preparation of the ground is very much the same. If the soil is a medium or light loam no under-drainage will be necessary. If, however, the soil is of heavy clay texture or if the path is to be constructed in a low area which has poor natural drainage some means of artificial drainage should be provided. A 6-inch vitrified tile drain laid 2 feet below the surface of the soil directly under the middle line of the path will usually prove entirely adequate and will add greatly to the enjoyment of a turf walk which might otherwise be soggy and practically unusable after heavy rains or in the early spring when the frost is coming out of the ground. Instead of using tile drains the soil may be excavated to a depth of 12 inches and a 6-inch layer of cinders placed over the sub-soil. A 6-inch layer of good top-soil should be placed above the cinders. This should be levelled off to the proper grade and should then be raked until it is finely pulverized. The first rolling will show up any slight unevenness which may be corrected by subsequent rakings. Where the path is to be seeded approximately one pound of seed will be required per thirty square yards. Only seed of the very highest quality should be used and it is wise to obtain a mixture which does not contain any clover as it will make a turf of much finer texture. Clover also has the unfortunate ten-

Terrace Steps

Ramped Steps

dency to become rather slippery when it is wet which is a decided disadvantage. The various Bent grasses are excellent, and mixtures containing Kentucky Blue Grass, Chewings New Zealand Fescue and Red Top are very desirable. The seed should be sown both lengthwise and crosswise with the path in order to get an even distribution. The ground should be rolled immediately after the seed is sown as a firm seed bed is one of the secrets of success in obtaining a good area of turf.

If the walk is sodded great care should be taken to obtain sod of the best possible quality. Nothing is more disappointing than to go to the trouble and expense of sodding only to find, later on, that one has a lot of poor, coarse grass that will never make a really good turf. The sod, which usually comes in long rolls, should be laid lengthwise with the path and care should be taken to see that the joints are broken. After it is laid, the sod should be rolled and then thoroughly soaked. It should not be allowed to dry out until it has become well established.

EDGINGS

The best method of keeping the margins of garden paths permanently neat is to build edgings or small curbs. Many materials may be used for marking the path and separating it from the garden beds. Bricks on edge, or on end, are appropriate for brick or gravel paths. The use of planks dipped in creosote and held at intervals by stakes is an old colonial method, and is appropriate in an old-fashioned garden with gravel paths. It is also good with tanbark. Flagstones set on edge is good with flagstone paving or gravel. Tile is interesting in an architectural garden. In recent years metal has become more generally used. After a period of experiment with iron, it has been found that zinc is more durable and unobtrusive. It is excellent for use between the driveway and the lawn, and also in the geometric patterns of garden beds and paths.

GARDEN STEPS

As a change in levels in a garden necessitates a pleasant and easy transition from one level to another, garden steps may become an important feature. Unless the steps are rustic in character, such as split logs, hewn railroad ties, or long heavy stones, they should rest upon a foundation with footings below the frost line. The steps should be in harmony with the sur-

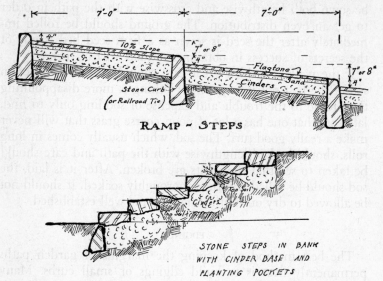

RAMP - STEPS

STONE STEPS IN BANK
WITH CINDER BASE AND
PLANTING POCKETS

rounding area, and should be as broad as the path that leads to them.

The angle of ascent of outdoor steps should be less steep than that of interior stairways. In general, the broader the tread, the lower should be the riser. A good formula for proportions in determining the size of individual steps is as follows: one tread plus two risers should equal 27 inches. Thus, steps 6 inches high will require 15-inch treads, while steps 5 inches high should have 17-inch treads. The treads should be constructed so that they pitch slightly towards the front, about ¼ of an inch, in order that the water may drain off readily after a rain.

FOUNDATIONS

Foundations for stone or brick steps may be built of rubble masonry. Any irregular pieces that are not easily used in fin-

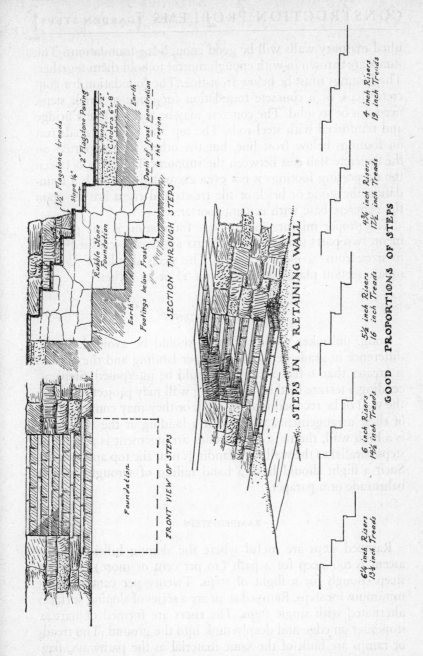

SECTION THROUGH STEPS

FRONT VIEW OF STEPS

STEPS IN A RETAINING WALL

GOOD PROPORTIONS OF STEPS

ished masonry walls will be good enough for foundations. The stones are thrown in with enough mortar to hold them together. The footings must be below frost line. The foundation for concrete steps, or a concrete foundation for stone or brick steps, need not be so solid. The concrete may be formed like a bridge and reinforced with steel rods. The top and bottom treads rest on footings below frost line, but the others are supported on the concrete slab cast between the supports. The earth between the supporting footings is not even excavated. On such a foundation the stone or brick or tile treads and risers are set upon the concrete base with cement mortar.

The proper mixture for concrete foundation is one part cement, two parts sand and three parts aggregate—crushed stone in sizes from ¾ inch to 1 inch. The steels should be ⅝-inch square section placed at intervals of 12 or 15 inches.

STEP ARRANGEMENTS

Long, unbroken flights of steps should be avoided. If the difference in grade between the upper landing and the bottom is greater than 6 feet a landing should be interposed. Steps ascending a terrace held by a retaining wall may project out from the wall or be recessed into the wall, or they may combine both of these arrangements, often with a landing at the wall. If it is a high wall, the most harmonious arrangement is a flight of steps parallel to the wall with landings near the top and bottom. Such a flight should have a hand railing of wrought iron, a balustrade or a parapet.

RAMPED STEPS

Ramped steps are useful where the sloping hillside of the ascent is too steep for a path (10 per cent or more), and not steep enough for a flight of steps. Twenty per cent is about minimum for steps. Ramped steps are a series of sloping surfaces alternated with single steps. The risers are formed of narrow stones set on edge and deeply sunk into the ground. The treads or ramps are built of the same material as the pathways, flagstone or brick being the materials most frequently used in this country. The narrow streets of hillside towns in Europe are frequently made into ramped steps, with stone risers and cobblestone ramps. A rustic path in a woodland is frequently stepped by placing logs across the path for the risers. Railroad ties are also good for this purpose.

The proper dimensions for ramped steps may be determined by establishing the distance between the risers at three normal paces, between 6'-3" and 8'-0", and the height of the riser as from 3 to 5 inches. The slope of the ramp should be not greater than 12 per cent. Obviously the steeper the ramp and the higher the tread, the shorter should be the length of the ramp.

GARDEN POOLS

Water is the symbol of life. It is that which makes all life possible. In Persia and in Northern Africa where a garden is a highly developed oasis in an arid land and is considered a paradise, water is indispensable. The sound of a trickling fountain is pleasant indeed to those whose senses are accustomed to the barren dryness of the outer world.

While garden pools had their origin in warm countries and their primary purpose was to cool the atmosphere, the almost universal appeal of sparkling water has made them equally appreciated in Northern climes. The idea of a fountain or pool as a garden feature was first brought to Europe by the Crusaders, after their contacts with the older and more highly developed culture of the East. And even in the comparatively damp climate of England and Scotland the fountain idea has persisted, although with somewhat less elaboration and emphasis than it has received in Italy and Spain.

Besides its original function of providing refreshment in hot weather by cooling the surrounding air, the garden pool fulfills a distinctly decorative purpose. Set in a frame of stone, the gleaming mirror of its surface becomes an object of admiration and attention. It may be used as the central feature of the garden, or it may be used as a terminal motive for a major or minor axis. It often provides a fitting foreground for a piece of sculpture, and, moreover, its usefulness and charm can be heightened by making it the habitation of fish and water-loving plants.

In the design of a garden pool the major decisions are the size, the shape, the material to be used for the coping, the depth of the water, and the color of the bottom.

It is important that the pool should be in harmony with its surroundings, and that it should be in scale as a detail of the garden design. Its setting, in patterned paving or in turf, should be carefully studied. The shape will depend very largely upon the general plan of the garden and, to a limited extent perhaps, upon the personal preference of the owner. In some gardens a round pool would be the most logical and pleasing from a standpoint of design; while in other gardens a square or oblong pool would be more in keeping with the general scheme.

The material to be used in the construction of the coping is largely a matter of personal choice. A simple flagstone coping is always pleasant and is particularly suitable if the garden is small or of somewhat informal character. For gardens of more formal and elaborate design a coping of cut stone might be preferred. Colored tiles are very decorative and lovely, and they may be used both as a coping and as a complete lining for the pool. While concrete may be used as a coping it is decidedly less attractive and less interesting than most other materials.

Within recent years it has become quite the vogue to paint the bottom, and sometimes both the bottom and sides, of garden pools. If the bottom is painted black it gives an appearance of much greater depth. Blue is the most popular color, as it gives a reflection of the sky, but care must be taken not to choose too harsh a tone.

When considering the construction of a pool it must be borne in mind that the first cost is usually the last. A pool is a very permanent feature of the garden, requiring little or no upkeep. When once its construction has been completed, it will be a source of satisfaction for years to come. Fortunately for the home owner, a garden pool need not be an elaborate or an expensive thing. A pool of simple design and small in size may be constructed for a very modest sum and much of the labor can often be done by the owner of the garden.

A Formal Pool and Box Hedges

CONSTRUCTION OF CONCRETE POOLS

In constructing a garden pool the major considerations are: absolute watertightness; drainage; and water supply, including the control of inlet, outlet and overflow. The walls of the pool are, essentially, retaining walls, and as such they must be strong enough to withstand the soil pressure against them and to resist the pressure of frost. There must be no heaving, due to the action of frost, as this will crack the walls and throw the coping out of level. A pool which has been poorly constructed, and which consequently is cracked by frost year after year, can become a source of constant annoyance. It is a difficult undertaking to repair a pool that has developed a leak, and it is therefore a matter of sound economy to see that the pool is well constructed in the beginning.

The ground surrounding the pool should be absolutely level. This is a matter of vital importance, which is sometimes overlooked in the construction of a home-made pool. If a pool is constructed on ground that is only slightly uneven the result will be unsatisfactory. If there is no other alternative, and if a pool must be constructed on ground which is slightly sloping, it will be necessary to raise the coping on one side. If this is not done, the surface will have the appearance of a tilted dish.

Concrete is one of the best materials to be used for the construction of garden pools. For a pool of average size, the bottom should be 5 inches thick and the walls 8 inches thick. For very large pools these figures should be slightly increased, while for very small pools they may be somewhat reduced, although it is not wise to reduce them to any appreciable extent. In the construction of the small pool it is not necessary to reinforce the sides. In the construction of a pool which is more than 15 feet in length, however, the sides should be reinforced with steel rods in order to maintain the concrete in a monolith against varying pressures.

The soil should be excavated to a depth of from 12 to 18 inches below the proposed floor level of the pool. The sides of the excavation should be vertical and in line with the

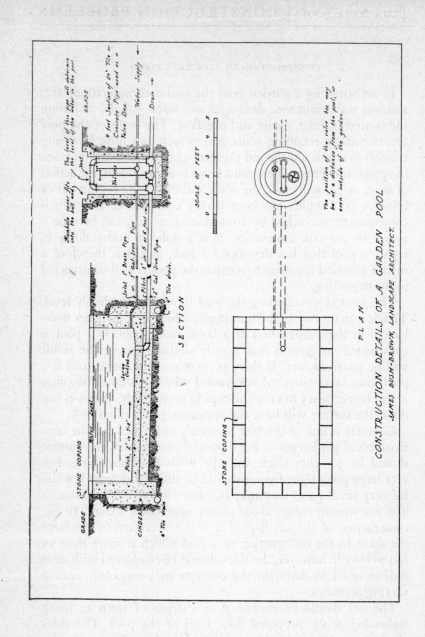

SECTION

PLAN

SCALE OF FEET

CONSTRUCTION DETAILS OF A GARDEN POOL

JAMES BUSH-BROWN, LANDSCAPE ARCHITECT.

outside wall of the pool. A layer of cinders should be spread over the bottom of the excavation and should be tamped firmly into place. If the cinders are sprinkled with water it will help the mass to settle into place. This layer of cinders will act as a drain and will keep the ground-water away from the under-surface of the concrete, thus reducing the danger of heaving, due to the action of the frost. The actual depth of the layer of cinders will depend somewhat upon the character of the soil. In light sandy soils a layer only a few inches in depth will be satisfactory, while in soils of a heavy clay texture a layer 12 inches in depth is advisable.

Forms. After the excavation has been completed the wooden forms should be constructed. They must be built in such a way that no part of the form is in contact with either the sides or the floor of the pit. This is accomplished by suspending the frame-work from beams extending across the excavation, the beams being held in place at each end by stout stakes driven into the ground well beyond the outside of the pit. The boards used in the construction of the form should be capable of making tight joints, in order to prevent the concrete from leaking through when it is poured. The form should be vertical, and true to the line of the inner edge of the pool. The earth sides of the excavation serve as the form on the outer side, the space between earth and wood being filled with concrete.

Pipes. The piping should be put in place at the time the forms are built as it will be necessary for some of the pipes to extend through the concrete. Wherever a pipe is to pass through the concrete it should be fitted with a flange in order to make a tight joint and to prevent it from working loose. Brass pipes are undoubtedly the most satisfactory for use in the construction of a pool, as they are not subject to rust. Wrought-iron piping is sometimes used and is not as expensive as brass, but it is far less durable and is subject to the corroding effect of cinders when it comes into direct contact with them. The inlet pipe may be brought in below the surface of the water, if desired, or it may be used in the form of a dripping fountain, or as a jet of water rising above the surface of the pool. For a dripping fountain a ¼-inch lead pipe, reduced at the end, is the most satisfactory and most easily handled. For a jet, the pipe should be fitted with a brass nozzle reducer. One pipe may serve both as an outlet and as an overflow if it is fitted with a branch pipe, or gooseneck, which will rise to the height of the water surface and return to the main pipe again. In the portion of the main pipe between the point of branching and the return of the gooseneck there is a valve which, when closed, makes the gooseneck the overflow of the pool. By merely opening the valve the water may be drained entirely out of the pool. A small detail which is of considerable importance, however, is that there should be a small hole in the top of the gooseneck in order to prevent it from becoming a syphon.

Reinforcing. If the walls of the pool are to be reinforced, the steel rods should be put into place before the concrete is poured. The rods should be suspended in such a position that they are two or three inches within the concrete wall. Each rod should extend up into the walls of the pool at either end and the rods should be fastened together with wire at points where they cross, thus forming a network. Five-eighths-inch rods are the usual size.

Concrete. The concrete should be poured in one operation in order to form a monolith. A reliable grade of cement should be used and it should be mixed in the proportions of one part cement, two parts sand and three parts crushed stone or trap rock. Slag, which is very often used for concrete work, should never be used in the construction of a pool because of its porous nature. Soft stones such as limestone and sandstone should also be avoided. The concrete should be mixed in an open box or mixing trough. The required quantity of sand should be measured first and placed in the bottom of the trough. The cement should then be measured and poured on the sand. The dry sand and cement should be thoroughly mixed, being shovelled back and forth, before the crushed stone is added. After all the dry ingredients have been mixed, sufficient water should be added to make a rather mobile mixture, approximately five gallons to every sack of cement. Only enough water should be used to make the mixture flow easily into the forms, but not enough water to make it sloppy or soupy. The quantity of water used has a very direct influence upon the strength and water-tightness of the finished concrete. The floor, or bottom, of the pool should be poured first, and before it has finished setting, certainly before twenty-four hours have elapsed, the walls should be poured. The pouring of the walls should be done in one operation in order to alleviate any danger of subsequent cracks. The forms should be left in place for several days while the concrete is hardening. Soon after the forms have been removed, and before the concrete has become thoroughly dry, the surface coating of cement mortar should be applied. A mixture of one part cement to two parts of sand should be used and it should be spread smoothly over the entire surface with a plasterer's trowel and a straightedge template. Since it requires two or three weeks for all the moisture to evaporate out of the concrete, and since the curing process continues during this period, some time should elapse before the pool is filled with water. If the pool is filled before the concrete has been properly cured and while it is still porous, there will be a gradual seepage of water through the concrete and it may never become thoroughly watertight.

CONSTRUCTION OF LEAD POOLS

For a naturalistic pool with an irregular outline, or for a formal pool with a stone coping, the adaptability of sheet lead is becoming more generally appreciated. Lead is pliable, durable, practically indestructible. The advantages of its use as compared with concrete for the construction of pools are many. In concrete construction, every precaution is taken to prevent the freezing and thawing of the soil from cracking the concrete by exerting irregular pressures. Steel reinforcing rods are necessary in making an immobile structure in all but small pools. With lead the pressure merely bulges the metal but does not open cracks in it. No forms are necessary. The excavation for the lead pool need be no deeper than the required water depth, the metal being only 1/16-inch thick instead of 6 or 8 inches as with concrete. The methods of construction are simple, so that the labor cost is moderate. Lead has no damaging effect on fish or plants, it cannot corrode, and since lead pipes used by the Romans in the age of Augustus are still in good condition, it may be considered permanent.

Excavation and Grades. The work of constructing a lead pool may be done in the following manner: Excavate the soil to the required depth and shape, saving the top-soil for use in making compost or for similar purposes, and disposing of sub-soil by making a fill or trucking it away. The outline of the pool may be determined by levelling. If a surveyor's level is obtainable, this will be the quickest and most accurate help in establishing grades. Otherwise, a line level, which is a spirit level provided with a hook at each end, may be used. A stake is driven into the ground and the water level marked on the stake. A cord attached to the stake at this mark and stretched out tightly may be made horizontal by hanging the line level at its middle and raising or lowering the outer end of the cord until the bubble comes to rest in the middle of the tube. If the level is placed in the middle of the string, the sag will be equalized, the two ends being at the same height.

In portions of the pool margin along which there is to be a bog garden, the excavation should continue out beyond the apparent shore line for whatever width the bog is to have and for a depth of six inches. The same treatment is used on a rocky shore, the shelf being made as wide as the first row of rocks. Where the turf is to come down to the water's edge, the shelf is not necessary.

Material and Its Handling. The sheet lead comes in various thicknesses and widths up to twelve feet wide. The thickness known as "four pound," that is, four pounds to the square foot, or 1/16-inch thick, is pliable enough to bend easily into shape and firm enough to withstand a good deal of pounding. Before it is spread on the floor of the excavation, sharp rocks should be removed so as to eliminate the possibility of puncture. Rocks used along a bank should not have sharp edges which might wear holes through the lead. If the pool is to have a drain, which is a great convenience, the pipe should be laid before the lead lining is spread and it can be soldered to the lead at the lowest point of the floor. The lead is rolled out across the excavation. If the pool is to be broader than the width of the sheet,

A Pool as a Central Feature

A Small Garden Pool

then two or more sheets may be spliced together. This is done by folding the edges together in a lock joint, the same method used by tinsmiths in joining two pieces of roofing tin. One edge is folded up against a plank so that one inch of metal stands at right angles to the sheet. The edge of the piece adjoining is folded so that two inches of metal are upright, and the two pieces are brought together. Then the longer edge is folded down and around the shorter edge, and the two thus joined are flattened out on the side of the short edge, by blows of a wooden mallet. A strip of solder is then run along the crease to fill the voids in the fold. The solder should be half lead and half tin. A metal worker's tools, torch, solder pot and soldering iron are required for this part of the work, and it would be an advantage to have the services of a tinsmith. The rim of the metal should extend to a level an inch or more above the water and in such a way that it is buried in the bank. The outlet overflow should be arranged over a lip of the lead at the exact level required for the surface of the water. The rim of the formal pool should be arranged with the lead extending under and across the back of the coping stones. The lead may be cut into the sizes required and the edges may be trimmed to the margin line by cutting part way through the sheet lead with a strong knife blade, and all the way through for the first few inches. Then the sheet may be torn in two.

The pool floor may be painted with a white lead base paint. However, there is no real advantage in painting because the bare lead will soon take on a dark tone quite natural in appearance. In a naturalistic pool a certain amount of sediment collecting on the bottom may be expected.

The pool may remain full of water all winter, and if the depth of water is two and a half feet or more the goldfish may spend the winter under the ice, without danger.

CONSTRUCTION OF COPPER POOLS

Sheet copper is sometimes used as the lining of wall fountains or small garden pools. The metal is put together by lock joints which are then sealed with solder in the same method described for lead pools. Pools which are raised above the ground level by masonry walls or by a cut stone coping may be fitted with a copper lining. The advantage of this method is the avoidance of the necessity of a foundation under the whole area of the pool and the removal of the risk of cracked concrete. Large copper kettles are excellent as garden pools. With a stone coping a kettle makes a very good round raised pool or it may be sunk into the ground so that the rim is flush with the surface.

Water plants are not adversely affected by copper, but goldfish are made sick or are killed by copper impurities in the water.

CONSTRUCTION OF STONE POOLS

For dripping fountains, no material is more satisfactory than stone. A broad stone, 6 inches thick and slightly concave, makes an excellent shallow pool from the lip of which the water can trickle to a larger basin. The inlet for such a fountain can be a little lead pipe a quarter inch in diameter concealed under a protruding stone at the back of the great stone.

CONSTRUCTION OF CLAY-LINED POOLS

A modification of the concrete pool is the pool with a clay bottom. The clay pool is very like a natural pond in its formation because the bottom is a layer of clay. Spread evenly two or three inches thick and worked into the consistency of a mud pie, it will hold water remarkably well. In regions where clay is obtainable it has many advantages as a material for a large pool. No serious injury can come to the clay floor. No forms are required for building, and the actual labor of handling the material in construction is less than for concrete.

MAINTENANCE

With adequate facilities for maintaining a flow of water through the pool, and for emptying it, the care and general upkeep are made easy. An occasional cleaning out of sediment and fallen leaves is practically all that is necessary. In northern regions the concrete pool should be protected from the action of the frost during the winter months. The water should be drained off before freezing weather, and a few sticks or boards should be placed in the bottom to absorb the thrust of any small amount of ice which may form after snow has melted.

A concrete pool may be arranged for winter with the water level just a little below normal by placing in the water a few large floating logs. The logs will absorb the thrust from the ice, thus relieving the pressure on the concrete walls. Another device is to build the pool with such sharply sloping sides that when the ice forms it merely slides up the sides as it expands, and no pressure is transmitted to the structure.

WAYS OF REDUCING COSTS

Those who desire a garden pool and are deterred by the apparently high cost of installation may be interested in methods of reducing the costs. Plumbing is a big item. Its need may be eliminated by using the garden hose to fill and empty the pool. Reinforcing rods comprise a big item. They may be omitted if the pool is small and of simple shape.

Emptying a pool with fifty feet or one hundred feet of garden hose is a simple trick, requiring only a place lower than the pool floor within reach of the hose, whence the water may flow off. To start the working of a syphon, place one end of the hose down the slope at this low point. Hold the other end near the edge of the pool and pour water into it out of a watering can. When the water begins to flow out of the lower end of the hose and while still pouring water into the upper end, plunge the end of the hose, together with the watering can, into the pool. The flow thus started will continue until the pool is practically empty. The watering-can may be removed as soon as the flow from the pool has been established. The flow will continue until the water level reaches the end of the hose.

FOUNTAINS

In centuries past the fountain was the most highly-wrought and most decorative feature of the garden. In dry climates where the presence of water was always highly prized, the garden fountain symbolized the life-giving power of water. At great expense water was piped to the fountains and from the fountains it flowed in little canals throughout the garden to irrigate the soil and make possible the growing of the plants.

During the Italian Renaissance the fountain became an elaborate work of art, combining spouting jets of water with architectural and sculptural forms. The Italian noblemen vied with one another in the display of animated water features in their villas. The water was often piped from streams several miles away to supply a series of fountains which were so arranged that the overflow of one fountain supplied the next fountain on a lower terrace.

The fountain in most American gardens of today is a much less complicated feature, but it is none the less important, and it is often the one note of architectural embellishment. The simplest type is the pool fountain with a single stream rising in a vertical jet from the center. The structure of such a fountain consists merely of a brass nozzle on the supply pipe at the water level. An elaboration of this arrangement is a central pedestal supporting a shallow basin, from the rim of which the water drips into the pool. In such a fountain the central jet is sometimes replaced by a sculptured figure. Greater elaboration occasionally takes the form of minor jets of water near the rim. There is the danger of a fountain design becoming overornamented and fussy, thus loosing both dignity and unity. As with so many other subjects, simplicity and beauty of proportion are the attributes of good design.

The wall fountain as a terminal feature at the end of an axis possesses infinite possibilities for artistic expression. Water coming from a modelled lead spout or through a trough-shaped stone and falling in a narrow stream to the pool below is one of the most satisfactory arrangements for the inlet.

Fountains are definitely architectural in character and they may be used as the dominating motif in the design or as a more incidental feature.

A Wall Fountain

FENCES

In colonial villages of New England, the houses and public buildings were usually grouped about the village green, which was the center of community life. A gravel road, shaded by elms, skirted the rim of the green, and the dignified white clapboard houses were set back in ample yards.

In those days it was the custom to let cows and horses wander at will, finding pasture where they could, and the dooryards about the dwellings were, therefore, enclosed by picket fences. In fact, in some sections of the country, each householder was required by law to fence his property. Within these enclosures flourished pleasant little dooryard gardens similar to the gardens which our forefathers had known and loved in their native England. As with other architectural details of the house, especially the doorway and cornice, the fence posts were beautifully designed, and the fence expressed those great qualities of fitness and precision. Such a fence served the double purpose of protecting the flowers and herbs and giving architectural expression to the setting of the house. We may be sure that the cultured townsfolk of those days were not unaware of this latter function.

Fences are built to accomplish these certain purposes: to protect crops and gardens against animals, to enclose pastures, to mark property lines, to hide unpleasant vistas, to secure greater seclusion, to support vines, and to embellish places with architectural frames. This diversity of purpose, combined with a diversity of available material, has given to fences a wide range in appearance. Some of the most practical fences are also picturesque, and, because of the good materials built into them by careful workmanship, add much in beauty and dignity. Whatever its primary purpose, a fence should be made a thing of architectural beauty.

Materials and methods have brought about the designs of several distinctive types of fences. In certain regions the abundance of some good material has made a special type of fence structure typical of that locality. Thus the stone wall and the picket fence express New England; the zigzag rail fence, Virginia and Kentucky; the post and rail fence, Virginia; and the post and board fence, Pennsylvania.

Today transportation makes available materials other than those from local sources, and has opened markets for the best

Photograph by James Bush-Brown

A Nantucket Picket Fence with English Ivy

materials which in earlier times were used only in the regions of their origin. Thus we can have for posts not merely the red cedar of the neighboring pastures, but cypress as well, which will outlast it. Also available are fence materials assembled in manageable units made in Virginia, Michigan, New Jersey, and France, and shipped all over the country.

As with so many other products of modern manufacture and distribution, local tradition in fence design is no longer dominant. The decision as to the type of fence for a certain place should be based on the consideration of strength, durability, appearance and cost.

The practical attributes of a good fence are strength sufficient to hold its place against wind; durability, that is, soundness after many years of exposure to weather; good appearance, the ability to remain neat and trim without much attention to maintenance; economy of construction costs in relation to the life of the fence.

REQUISITES OF A GOOD FENCE

One of the severest tests of a fence comes from the action of rot. It is at the ground line where the material of the post is subject to alternating wet and dry conditions that rot acts most rapidly. (In desert country this is negligible.) Only such material as will withstand rot should be used for posts. Among the best woods for this purpose are Southern Cypress and California Redwood. The true White Cedar of the swamps and the Red Cedar are the best eastern native trees for posts, and Chestnut, Locust and Arborvitæ (often incorrectly called White Cedar) are also much used. Besides the resisting quality of the wood itself, further life may be imparted to the wood tissue by filling it with creosote. This oily substance fills the pores of the wood and poisons the food supply of the fungus. Painting creosote on the surface of the wood avails little. It should be applied under pressure by a machine, so that the whole post absorbs it. This is the method employed by electric companies to preserve their poles.

Not merely the posts but all wood of carpentry fences is subject to rot, and this is most apt to begin wherever two pieces are nailed together. The moisture gets into the crevice and is absorbed by the wood. Gradual drying of the wood again makes conditions ideal for the growth of decay fungi, providing the combination of wood, water and air. Periodic painting will preserve a fence by preventing moisture from entering the surface of the wood, but these crevices are hard to fill, and their inner surfaces impossible to reach. As a precaution to be taken at the time of construction, the surfaces of the pickets and rails where they join one another, and the surfaces of the rails and posts where they in turn join, should be painted before the fence is put together. It may not be so convenient to give the rails two coats of paint after they are cut and the pickets one coat before they are nailed on, but the extra labor entailed will be well repaid in the increased life of the fence. In all, three coats of paint should be applied to a new fence.

Another test of fences is the force of wind. All types of fence should have posts set into the ground deep enough to hold firm against the wind pressure. For most fences 2 feet, 6 inches, and for some, 2 feet will be deep enough. The backfilling of dirt about the posts must be accompanied by firm tamping of the soil. Any tendency of the posts to wiggle will be increased rather than diminished by the force of wind and weather. Fence corners should be cross-braced. Solid board fences, if placed as windbreaks, should have additional side bracing.

Rust is another damaging process. To retard its action, steel and iron posts and rails should be galvanized. Wrought-iron and cast-iron railings and grills should be painted with a special rust-resisting paint and repainted every few years. Concrete posts cast on a reinforced steel frame are very satisfactory, because the metal is enclosed in the concrete and such a post requires no attention. In the construction of wooden fences, only galvanized nails and galvanized staples should be used. Screws should be of brass. The wire fences and wire supports for vines should be galvanized iron or copper.

TYPES OF FENCES

The most satisfactory types of fences are here listed with an appraisal of their advantages and limitations.

Split Rail Fence. The "Snake fence" or split rail fence is one of the most picturesque for open farm lands. It originated in Virginia in colonial times, and is often called Virginia rail fence, though more properly the Kentucky rail fence, because of its frequent use in that state. It is made of rails split from poles cut in the woods close at hand. Chestnut and Ash were the favorite trees because their wood splits most easily. The rails were put together without nails or wire and were only anchored at the junctions by two slanting rails leaned against the junction of horizontal rails. A great deal of wood is required for the construction of this fence, but no other tool except the axe, and no

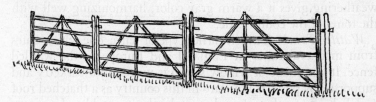

English Hurdle Fence

Post and Board Fence   Post and Rail Fence

other materials, are required. It is, therefore, the fence of the pioneer. As forests became depleted, a modification of this fence, which requires less wood, was developed, the Virginia rail fence, strictly speaking. With this the rails are laid end overlapping end in a straight line, their points of junction being kept upright by two posts set in the ground, one on each side, and wired together at the top. A more modern version of this is the post and rail fence with three slots cut in the single post to receive the ends of the rails.

The Post and Rail Fence is a very handsome pasture enclosure, and is suitable for the property lines of country residences. White Cedar posts with large slots cut in them are erected at intervals of 10 feet. The rails, half-round arborvitæ poles 11 feet long, are tapered to flat ends which are thrust through the slots in the posts. There are three sizes of posts, making three-rail, four-rail or five-rail fences. It is an easy type of fence to erect and is most satisfactory for its rugged appearance and durability. The weathering gives it a warm gray color, harmonizing well with the tones of the countryside.

Wattled Fence. A much earlier type of fence, one which dates from mediæval times in England and Europe, is the wattled fence. It was made of willow saplings woven into basketry and supported by posts. It is as rare in this country as a thatched roof and belongs to that era when only the vegetable plots were fenced and animals roamed. It is picturesque, rustic and humble.

The English Hurdle Fence is a very useful type and it has been in use for many centuries. Split Chestnut rails are built into a braced frame and nailed together. The end pieces of each panel extend 2 feet below the lower rail to become the posts. Each panel is a unit 8 feet long which is easily handled. The posts are driven into the ground with a sledge hammer and then the adjacent posts are pegged together. This is the most convenient form for temporary fences to enclose pastures and yards. It is picturesque, easily erected and easily moved. It is made in two sizes, for horses and sheep.

Post and Board Fence is framed on Red Cedar or Cypress posts erected at 10- or 12-foot intervals. Three or four horizontal rough boards 1 inch x 8 inches, or 1 inch x 6 inches are nailed to the posts with wide spaces between them. A vertical 6-inch board covers the board ends against each post and a 6-inch square board caps the post like a shed roof. Rough sawed Pine boards are usually used. Whitewashed or sometimes painted white, this makes a very neat type of farm fence and it is occasionally used for suburban property, especially with a house of colonial architecture.

The Board Fence, or board fence with lattice top, has rustic posts 10 feet apart and three horizontal connecting rails of 3-inch x 4-inch joists. Many variances in design and proportions are

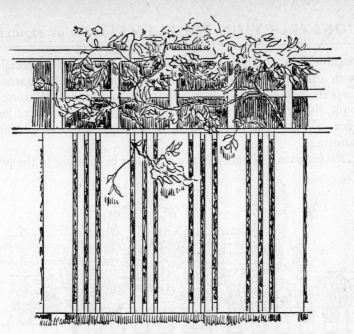

Board Fence with Lattice Top

Spindle Fence

possible. It is appropriate for gardens and town yards, especially with a house of colonial tradition, and for enclosing a garden. Cypress, Yellow Pine or White Pine are usually used. If strongly built, the lattice may support such vines as clematis, silver lace vine, akebia, but not wisteria. This type requires periodic painting.

Basket-weave Hickory Fence is similar in framing to the pre-

Picket Gate

ceding type, and suggests the wattled fence of mediæval times.

The Woven Split Sapling Arborvitæ Fence is rustic in character and makes an opaque screen. The construction is simple and strong. Red Cedar posts are set at 10-foot intervals and are connected with two or three Cedar rails. Panels of split Aborvitæ rods about 1½ inches wide are woven together with wire and are nailed on to the rails, so that the finished fence is a continuous wall of rustic vertical lines. With the bark still on, the fence immediately has an old appearance, but with the bark stripped off, a year of mellowing will be required. This fence

Picket Fence

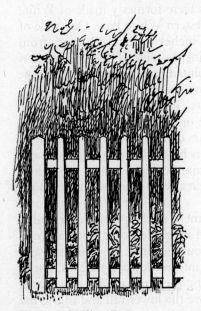

Paling Fence   Paling Fence with Hand Rail

may be whitewashed, but it is more attractive in the rough. The fence is somewhat transparent because of the small spaces between the rods. A solid screen results from putting the fence material on both sides of the frame and such a fence 6½ or 7 feet high makes an adequate opaque barrier on the property line or about a service yard. The lower sizes are effective protection for dooryard gardens. Mellowing to soft tones of brown-gray, this rustic fence is appropriate with houses of the English Tudor or French Norman tradition, but is out of place with Georgian and Colonial architecture.

The Picket Fence or paling fence has long been the customary enclosure for town yards. It is very common in New England, less so in Pennsylvania, and rare in Virginia. In some parts of New England the posts are single pieces of granite, but usually Cedar posts, kept painted, are the supports at intervals from 8 to 12 feet. The rails are rather stout, 2 inches x 4 inches being minimum, but larger sizes, 3 inches x 4 inches, are more usual. Fir is preferred for rails. Pickets were formerly made of White Pine, and are still available in western White Pine. One style of this fence has narrow palings 2 inches wide which taper from the bottom to a blunt top, 1¼ inches wide. The wider pickets 2½ inches to 3½ inches wide, pointed or cut into a simple shape at the top, are nailed to the rails with spaces between them about equal to the width of the pickets. They extend well above the top rail to a height 3 feet more or less from the ground. The lower end should be about 2 inches off the ground. It is advisable to paint the frame and the pickets before the pickets are put on. Two or three coats of white paint will put a new fence into condition to last three or four years. Repainting should be done about every three years.

The Spindle Fence is a refinement of the picket fence and is suitable for the formal dooryard or garden of a colonial mansion. The spindles are round, about 1¼ inches in diameter, and pass through holes in the rails at intervals of 5 to 7 inches. Variations from this are made by giving the fence a solid board base, or even a third rail 16 inches above the lower rail and filling the space with a lattice of square bars in diamond pattern, the round spindles extending from the intermediate rail through the upper rail. Such a fence with graceful fenceposts is in keeping with the careful carpentry of modillioned cornices and a carved broken pediment above the door.

"Snow Fences" consist of pickets woven by horizontal wires and fastened to metal posts driven into the ground. Used as a

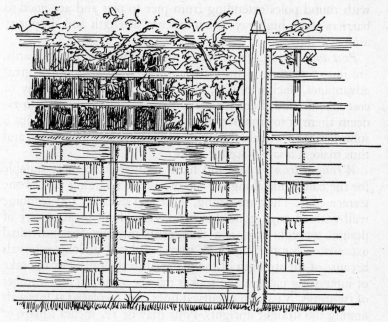

Basket Weave Hickory Fence

winter precaution, they are erected at a distance of 50 or 75 feet from the road, toward the prevailing wind; they create enough obstacles to cause snow to form drifts in the lee close to the fence and not in the road. They may be used for any other temporary purpose, to surround play yards or dog runs. The life of the fence is usually about ten years.

Lattice Fences are most closely associated with the French style of garden art for the French developed the lattice to intricate patterns. But very simple lattices were used in colonial gardens as supports for vines, particularly climbing roses.

Painted white to harmonize with the frame house or the white trim of brick or stone structure, the lattice is an adjunct of formal design.

Fences of Stone Pier Posts and Wood Rail construction are best suited to such places as automobile parking lots or the brink of a view in a public park. Variations of this may be even heavier with round poles extending from pier to pier and are good as barriers along highway embankments. Strength and simplicity are needed here.

Post and Woven Wire Fences, such as surround factory yards, are out of place in a finished landscape, but their three great advantages, unclimbability, absolute rigidity, and economy of cost recommend them for certain places. The only way to redeem them is to smother them in vines. Such a fence about a suburban yard will absolutely exclude animals and children, and thus make it a safe place for birds.

Wrought-Iron Fences and hand railings seem most suitable for the balustrade along the top of a stone retaining wall at the terrace edge. They are strong, light and durable, and combine well with massive stone structures. Capable of great variety of design, wrought iron is a wonderful medium for individual expression. Supporting posts may be placed at long intervals because of the strength of the material in the rails. For the sake of interesting pattern, the spokes may be varied in any number of twistings. A pattern of curved lines may be placed at intervals among the straight uprights. Posts may be $1\frac{1}{4}$ inches square or even only $\frac{7}{8}$ inch square, while the spokes at $\frac{1}{2}$ inch will look and will actually be strong enough. Occasional braces, rods running from near the top to a few inches off the line of fence, will keep it firm. The iron railing is fastened to the stone by drilling holes 4 inches deep in the coping of the wall and fastening the post into the hole by melted lead.

A rust-resisting paint should be applied to the iron work before it is erected, and it should be repainted every three years.

The advantages of such a grill along the terrace or above the garden steps is that views down into garden or glen are not obstructed as they would be by a parapet wall, and the iron work makes a pleasing patterned silhouette against the distance.

A wrought-iron grill fence is expensive in original cost, but is practically indestructible and requires very little care.

The Cast-Iron Fence or grill has much the same qualities as the wrought iron. However, it is not as strong and the pattern is made not so much by a series of narrow pieces making lines, as by a series of flat pieces making masses. The pattern repeats itself in rhythm, like wallpaper, and for this reason it is not as versatile as wrought iron.

IV

Lawns

When one plants a tree one does so with the full realization that one may be planting for posterity—that it will increase in dignity as the years pass, and that a century or more hence it may still cast welcome shade for those who linger beneath its branches.

It is difficult to realize, however, that a lawn may be as permanent a planting as the trees that cast their shade upon it. Many of the lawns which surround the beautiful manor houses of England were planted more than five hundred years ago and today the fine quality of this English turf is an inspiration to gardeners throughout the world.

In sharp contrast to the luxuriant, verdant greensward of the English countryside we have the shabby, weed-infested areas which surround so many of our American homes—areas which hardly deserve to have the title of lawn bestowed upon them. It would seem that we are all too willing to accept defeat when it comes to the establishment of a good lawn. We fail to recognize the fact that a lawn is not a temporary planting—that, on the contrary, it is one of the most permanent of plantings, and that the first step is to make a careful study of the factors which contribute towards the establishment and maintenance of a fine piece of turf.

ESTABLISHMENT OF NEW LAWNS

In a program of successful lawn making the essential factors are: adequate preparation of the soil before planting; selection of the proper seed; method and time of sowing; watering, rolling, and subsequent treatment until the lawn has become well established.

PREPARATION OF THE SOIL

It is a far easier task to improve the condition of the soil before planting than it is to improve either the texture or the fertility of the soil after planting. The importance of adequate preparation of the soil before the seed is sown can hardly be over-emphasized. The establishment of proper grades, the need for more adequate drainage, the physical texture of the soil, the fertility of the soil, and the degree of soil acidity must all be taken into consideration.

If grading is to be done the top-soil should be carefully removed, and after the grading has been completed it·should be replaced. This procedure will increase the cost of the grading but will prove to be a matter of sound economy in the end. (Refer to instructions in regard to grading in the preceding chapter.)

Unless the area which is to be sown to grass seed possesses low spots which are apt to be soggy at some seasons of the year, under-drainage will not be necessary. Frequently such low spots can be improved with proper grading but if this is not possible they may be effectively drained with agricultural tile. Four-inch tile drains should be used, the trenches being from 15 to 24 inches deep and approximately 20 feet apart. There should be a fall of at least three inches in every 50 feet. The tile should be laid end to end and the joints covered with strips of tar paper in order to keep the soil out of the tile while the trench is being refilled.

Organic Matter. The physical texture of the soil plays a very important part in the establishment of a fine turf. It may be improved to a very marked degree by the addition of organic matter. Most soils, with the exception of woodland soils, are deficient in humus. Soils with a marked deficiency of organic matter present very serious problems as they are low in water-holding capacity, are poorly aerated, become too readily compacted, tend to be less fertile, and, in general, provide a very poor medium for the healthy, vigorous growth of lawn grasses. It is a well accepted fact that practically all of our better lawn grasses thrive best on a soil which is well supplied with organic matter.

Organic matter may be supplied in the form of well rotted manure, spent mushroom soil, compost, cover crops, raw native peat, and the peat moss of commerce.* Manure has the disadvantage of introducing weed seeds into the lawn area and in many communities it is not readily available at a reasonable price. The great point in its favor is that it increases the fertility of the soil as well as adding organic matter. If it is applied several months previous to planting, the weed seeds will germinate and can be controlled by cultivation before the grass seed is sown. Spent mushroom soil is a mixture of rotted manure and soil and is of particular value in improving the texture of sandy and shaly soils. In sections of the country where mushrooms are grown commercially it is readily available at a very reasonable price and it is one of the most satisfactory forms in which organic matter can be supplied. Good garden compost is somewhat similar to mushroom soil and is also an excellent source of organic matter. If it is possible to plan the program of work well in advance and to devote several months to the preparation of the soil one or more cover crops may be grown and the organic content of the soil may be increased in this way with comparatively little expense. When a new home is being built it is frequently possible to do this during the process of construction. The following cover crops are recommended:

Fall Sowing—per acre, 1 bushel rye and 1 peck winter vetch; per 1000 square feet, 1½ quarts rye and ½ pint vetch. Sow in September or early October. Plow or spade the crop under in the spring when it has attained a height of 12 inches.

Early Spring Sowing—per acre, 2 bushels oats and 1 peck Canada field peas; per 1000 square feet, 1½ quarts oats and ½ pint Canada field peas. Sow as early in the spring as possible and plow or spade under about the middle of June.

Late Spring Sowing—per acre, 1 bushel soybeans, 1 peck of millet; per 1000 square feet, 1 quart soybeans, 1 cup of millet. Sow between the middle of May and the middle of June. Inoculate the soybeans before planting in order to gain the full benefit of their nitrogen fix-

*Obtainable under various trade names.

ing abilities. Plow or spade under at least one month before the time of lawn seeding.

Peat moss is a less desirable source of organic matter than some of the other forms of peat, as it supplies practically no plant food, decomposes more rapidly than any other form, and leaves the smallest supply of permanent humus in the soil. Raw native peat decomposes more slowly than peat moss and is consequently of more value. It is advisable to apply both peat moss and the raw native peat sometime previous to planting in order to allow them to become partially decomposed, as the benefits will be decidedly greater. Cultivated peat decomposes more slowly than any of the other forms of peat and the beneficial effects are consequently more lasting.

The rate of application of organic matter will depend upon the character of the soil. Light sandy soils will require liberal applications in order that they may become more retentive of moisture. Soils of a dense, heavy texture will also be greatly improved and the drainage of the surface water will be facilitated if liberal quantities are applied. Manure should be applied at the rate of 1000 to 1500 pounds per 1000 square feet of lawn area, or 20 to 30 tons per acre. Peat moss should be applied at the rate of 4 bales per 1000 square feet of lawn area, or approximately 170 bales per acre. Native moist peat should be applied at the rate of 2 cubic yards per 1000 square feet of area, 86 cubic yards per acre.

It is essential that the organic matter, in whatever form it may be applied, be thoroughly incorporated with the upper five or six inches of top-soil. The organic matter, particularly when it is applied in the form of peat moss, should never be allowed to form a definite layer, either upon the surface of the soil or below the surface, as such a layer has a very undesirable effect on plant growth. The organic matter should be thoroughly plowed, forked, or spaded into the upper five or six inches of top-soil. A rototiller is excellent for this purpose and leaves the soil in fine tilth.

Fertilizers. The fertility of the soil is one of the most important factors in the establishment of a new lawn. It is a widely accepted premise that all of our most desirable lawn grasses require a soil of fairly high fertility if they are to produce a fine quality of turf. It is well, therefore, to see that adequate nutrients are supplied before planting. The application of a well balanced complete fertilizer will usually give the most satisfactory results, the amount required depending upon the natural fertility of the soil. On soils of medium fertility an application of 15 pounds per 1000 square feet will usually be sufficient, or approximately 650 pounds per acre. On soils of low fertility the application should be increased to 25 to 30 pounds per 1000 square feet or 1000 to 1200 pounds per acre. A complete commercial fertilizer containing 5 per cent nitrogen, 10 per cent phosphorus, and 5 per cent potash (designated as a 5-10-5) will prove to be a well balanced fertilizer for average soils. The analysis of the fertilizer may be changed to meet various soil requirements. If clover is to be used in the seed mixture less nitrogen need be applied in the form of commercial fertilizer. A heavier application of potash is needed on sandy soils than on heavy clay soils. The commercial fertilizer should be thoroughly mixed with the upper five inches of top soil before the grass seed is sown.

Soil Acidity. The majority of our better lawn grasses prefer an almost neutral or very slightly acid soil. A few types, such as the bent grasses and the fescues, while tolerant of rather strong soil acidity, will make better, healthier growth on soils which are more nearly neutral. For practically all types of desirable lawn grasses it is therefore advisable to have an acidity which does not fall below a pH. value of 5.5* and which preferably ranges between pH. 6 and pH. 7. Soil tests should be made to determine the existing degree of acidity. If the tests show that the soil is too acid the condition may be readily corrected by an adequate application of lime.

Lime may be applied in the form of hydrated lime, ground limestone or finely ground oyster shells. Hydrated lime is more rapid in its action than either of the other forms. One pound of a good quality of hydrated lime is equal in value to 1½ pounds of ground limestone. When the application is made it is important that the lime be distributed very uniformly over

*See page 24 on Soil Acidity and pH. values.

the surface of the soil and worked lightly into the upper few inches of top soil. The lime will move downward in the soil but not laterally and, therefore, any soil areas which are not directly covered by the lime will receive no benefit from the application. There are various outfits on the market for the distribution of lime but on very small areas where the use of machinery is not justified one of the most satisfactory methods of application is to place the hydrated lime in a coarse, loosely woven burlap bag and to drag it back and forth over the area. If one prefers, the bag may be held a few inches above the soil and the lime shaken out onto the surface.

The importance of applying lime at the time that the seed bed is prepared can hardly be overstressed. If applications are delayed until after the sod has become established it will require several years to entirely correct any marked degree of acidity, whereas this condition may be rapidly and thoroughly overcome if an adequate application is made at the time of planting, provided that the lime is worked well into the soil to a depth which will correspond to the ultimate penetration of the grass roots.

The rate of application will depend entirely upon the degree of soil acidity. On soils of extremely high acidity it is advisable to make several applications as it has been found that the heavy liming of strongly acid soils is detrimental to normal plant growth. This extreme condition would be met only very occasionally. Soils testing over pH. 6 will require no application of lime. Soils testing between pH. 5 and pH. 6 should receive an application of 50 pounds of hydrated lime or 75 pounds of finely ground limestone per 1000 square feet, or 1 ton of hydrated lime per acre and 1½ tons of ground limestone. Soils testing between pH. 4 and pH. 5 or below should receive two or more applications, the total amount varying from 60 pounds to 145 pounds per 1000 square feet of hydrated lime, or 2¼ to 3 tons per acre. Only in very extreme cases would as much as 145 pounds per 1000 square feet be necessary. In general, sandy soils of a given degree of acidity require lighter applications of lime than do heavy clay soils of the same pH. value. Applications should therefore be slightly adjusted to meet the various soil types. Not more than 50 or 60 pounds of hydrated lime or its equivalent in ground limestone should be applied at one time to 1000 square feet. If heavier applications are necessary the amount should be divided. It must be borne in mind that not only does lime correct conditions of soil acidity, but it serves other functions as well. It helps to improve the physical structure of the soil, and consequently increases its water-absorbing capacity, and it also provides both calcium and magnesium, which are essential elements for normal plant growth.

PREPARATION OF THE SEED BED

After the organic matter, fertilizer and lime have been thoroughly incorporated with the soil, the seed bed may be prepared for planting. On large areas this is done with the use of spike tooth and drag harrows and a smoothing board. On small areas it may be very easily accomplished with an iron hand rake. The surface should be reasonably firm and it should be absolutely even with no hollows or small depressions.

SELECTION OF SEED

The selection of the proper seed is one of the most vitally important decisions in the establishment of a new lawn, and upon this decision may rest success or failure. The first point to consider is the type of lawn which one wishes to have.

GENERAL PURPOSE LAWNS

The majority of home owners wish to have a lawn of luxuriant green turf which will withstand a reasonable amount of wear and which may be maintained with a minimum expenditure of time and money. If the soil, site and climate are favorable, Kentucky blue grass will meet these requirements more completely than any other type of lawn grass. There is no other grass which can equal Kentucky blue grass in its ability to produce a fine, dense turf under average conditions of care and maintenance. Kentucky blue grass has, however, a few very definite requirements for satisfactory growth. It prefers a moderately cool, humid climate; it requires a fairly fertile soil; it thrives best on a good garden loam with a tendency towards heaviness; and it requires a soil that is very nearly neutral in reaction, a pH. ranging between 6 and 7.5 being considered ideal. Kentucky blue grass is not tolerant of dense shade, and it does not thrive well on soil of low fertility, as, under such conditions, it soon develops into a thin, weedy, and unsatisfactory turf and is eventually crowded out by inferior grasses. It is not as well adapted to extremely sandy types of soil as are some of the other lawn grasses; it does not do well under conditions of intense heat, and it is not tolerant of any great degree of acidity.

Kentucky blue grass germinates more slowly than many other lawn grasses and also requires a longer time to become established, and does not begin to form a dense, springy turf until the second year. The results will therefore be most satisfactory if Kentucky blue grass is sown in combination with other grasses, but, for the general purpose lawn, it should form at least 50 per cent of the seed mixture. It is a very long-lived, persistent grass and in time, if conditions are favorable for its growth, it will usually crowd out the more inferior grasses and will become completely dominant.

Several very excellent formulas for grass seed mixtures have been worked out by the various Agricultural Experiment Stations and these mixtures are now offered by some of the more reliable seed firms. For the general purpose lawn the following mixtures are recommended.

Mixture No. 1 (Cornell University Mixture)

Kentucky Blue Grass	50%
Rough-stalked Meadow Grass	15%
Rhode Island Bent	10%
True Creeping Red Fescue or Chewings Fescue	10%
Welsh Pasture Timothy No. S 50	10%
Kent Wild White Clover	5%

(Clover may be omitted if desired.)

Mixture No. 2 (N. J. Agricultural Experiment Station)

Kentucky Blue Grass	50%
Red Top (recleaned)	25%
German Mixed Bent	10%
Rye Grass	10%
White Clover (if desired)	5%

LAWNS FOR POOR SOILS

In establishing a lawn on soil which is definitely low in fertility and which cannot be immediately improved to a point where it will be able to support the better types of lawn grasses, it is wise to use some of the varieties which are less exacting in their demands. The fescues are the most satisfactory grasses for this purpose as they thrive well on poor, sandy soils, are tolerant of acidity, will endure considerable shade, and will withstand long periods of drought. The leaves of the fescues are tough and wire-like, and in habit of growth the plants are low and inclined to be somewhat bunchy. It is advisable, therefore, to sow the fescues in mixture with other grasses in order to obtain a better quality of turf. Of the many varieties Chewings Fescue and True Creeping Red Fescue are the most desirable for lawn purposes. The seeds of the fescues lose their vitality rapidly and as a poor percentage of germination is frequently secured it is necessary to make rather heavy seedings. For a lawn on poor, sandy soil or on extremely acid soil the following mixture is recommended:

Chewings Red Fescue	35%
Red Top (recleaned)	20%
Colonial Bent	15%
Kentucky Blue Grass	10%
Rye Grass	15%
White Clover	5%

(N. J. Agricultural Experiment Station)

PUTTING-GREEN TYPE OF LAWN

If one does not have to take into consideration the cost of development or of maintenance, it is possible to establish a lawn with turf of such supremely fine quality that it will resemble a putting green. It is sometimes possible to develop such a lawn area on a small terrace or as a turf panel in a garden, even although it might not prove practicable to attempt it on a larger area. For this purpose the bent grasses are the most desirable.

They are of low-growing, semi-creeping habit and, if given proper care, they produce a turf of superior quality and beauty. The three most desirable types of bent grass are Colonial Bent, Creeping Bent, and Velvet Bent.

Colonial Bent. The two most widely used strains of Colonial Bent are known as New Zealand Bent and Rhode Island Bent. These strains are frequently sown alone and are also used very generally in grass mixtures. They do not form as dense or compact a sod as do some of the other bent grasses but they will thrive under less favorable conditions.

Creeping Bent. Creeping bent may also be sown alone or in mixture with other grasses. When creeping bent is grown from seed it spreads rapidly, forming a dense mat of creeping stems at the surface of the soil which requires frequent mowing and top-dressing. The two most popular strains of creeping bent are Metropolitan and Washington. These two strains are always propagated by stolons rather than by seed. Stolons are the prostrate shoots, characteristic of the bent grasses. These shoots creep along the surface of the ground, forming roots at frequent intervals. The stolons are usually sold in sections of sod, 1 square foot of nursery sod being sufficient to plant from 5 to 10 square feet of lawn. The ground must be thoroughly prepared before the stolons are planted. The sod is cut into small pieces and scattered over the surface of the ground at the rate of 100 pounds per 1000 square feet. The stolons should be covered immediately with ½ inch of sifted top-soil and they should never be allowed to dry out, either before or after planting. These two strains of creeping bent, Washington and Metropolitan, are used extensively on golf courses and produce a fine quality of turf.

Velvet Bent. Velvet bent is the true aristocrat among lawn grasses and is, without exception, considered the most desirable of all the bent grasses. Velvet bent possesses all the qualities necessary for the production of a perfect piece of turf. When once well established it is persistent, vigorous and hardy, and it produces a remarkably fine-textured turf with an almost velvet-like quality. Velvet bent may be propagated either by seed or by stolons, and as there is a great difference in the various strains which are obtainable it is essential to procure seed or stolons of some strain which is known to be superior. The seed is expensive, but as it is extremely fine only a very small quantity is required. Velvet bent should not be sown in mixture with other bent grasses or in general mixtures as it does not do well.

All of the bent grasses are tolerant of considerable soil acidity but will thrive equally well on nearly neutral soils. They will withstand light shade, they do well on moist soils and they are extremely well adapted to close mowing, it being desirable to keep a bent lawn mown to a height of $\frac{1}{4}$ to $\frac{1}{2}$ inch. In general the bent grasses are much more exacting in their demands than are most of the other lawn grasses. In addition to an adequate program of fertilization it is necessary to apply frequent top dressings of rich compost in order to provide ideal conditions for vigorous growth. The bent grasses are also more subject to attacks from various fungous diseases than are most other grasses. It is wise, therefore, not to attempt to develop a bent lawn unless one is fully prepared to meet the additional requirements of labor and expense which are involved.

LAWNS FOR SHADY AREAS

For shady areas it is necessary to choose grasses which are tolerant of such conditions. It must be borne in mind that all grasses require some sunlight for satisfactory growth, and if the shade is too dense it is well to resort to some evergreen ground cover rather than to attempt to produce a lawn. A careful program of pruning will frequently mitigate the density of the shade sufficiently to make it possible to grow lawn grasses under large trees. If the pruning program is carried out over a period of several years it may be done without injuring the form or beauty of the trees. The program consists of gradually removing the lower branches of the trees so that the morning and afternoon sun may reach the grass. The tree will put on additional growth at the top to compensate for what has been cut away and will continue to maintain its natural form. Two or three feet of the lower branches may be cut away entirely each year and at the end of five years the foliage level will have been raised as much as 10 feet.

The following grass mixtures are recommended for shady areas.

No. 1 (Cornell Mixture)

Rough-stalked Meadow Grass	50%
Chewings Fescue	20%
Kentucky Blue Grass	20%
Rhode Island Bent	10%

No. 2 (N. J. Agricultural Exp. Station)

Chewings Fescue	20%
Rough-stalked Meadow Grass	30%
German Mixed Bent	10%
Red Top (recleaned)	10%
Kentucky Blue Grass	20%
Meadow Fescue	10%

TEMPORARY LAWNS

It occasionally happens that one desires to plant a purely temporary lawn. In moving into a new home late in the spring it would be folly to attempt to plant a permanent lawn at a season of the year when it is most difficult for the better types of lawn grasses to establish themselves, and under such conditions it is wise to resort to temporary measures. Within the space of a few brief weeks it is possible to obtain a rich and almost luxuriant growth of turf if the correct type of seed is used. Either the perennial rye grass or the domestic rye grass should be selected for this purpose. The growth is somewhat coarse and rank, but at least the grass will form a welcome covering of green on ground that might otherwise be bare. Before planting, a complete fertilizer (6–8–4 analysis) should be worked into the soil at the rate of 10 pounds per 1000 square feet in order to stimulate growth. The seed should be sown at the rate of 6 pounds per 1000 square feet. The soil should be kept moist until the seed has germinated and the grass should be mown when it has reached a height of 2 inches. This temporary grass may be plowed or spaded under when the time approaches to prepare the seed bed for the permanent lawn, and it will benefit the soil by adding a small amount of organic matter.

TIME OF SOWING GRASS SEED

The one point upon which all authorities seem to agree is that the most desirable time for sowing lawn grasses is in late August or early September. If it is not possible to do the work at this season of the year, seed may be sown in *early* spring. Late spring and summer sowings are not recommended except in the case of purely temporary lawns. Early autumn sowing has several advantages over spring sowing. Practically all of the lawn grasses make their best growth during cool, moist weather and the autumn months usually provide very favorable conditions for good germination of the seed and for the sturdy, vigorous growth of the young grass. There is comparatively little competition from weeds at this season of the year and by the following summer the autumn-sown turf should be so well established that it will not suffer seriously from drought or other adversities.

METHOD OF SOWING

In sowing grass seed the chief aim is to provide for an even distribution of seed over the lawn area. Sowing should always be done on a calm day when there is practically no wind, as it is otherwise impossible to make an even sowing. It is well to divide the quantity of seed in half and to sow in two directions, covering the area twice, walking first north and south, and the second time east and west. The seed should be raked into the soil very lightly to a depth of not more than $\frac{1}{8}$ of an inch, and the area should then be lightly rolled. If there is not sufficient rainfall after sowing to keep the area moist it is advisable to resort to artificial watering. Water should be applied in the form of a very light, mist-like spray. Heavy watering is apt to cause a hard crust to form on the surface of the soil which will severely interfere with germination. Unless it is possible to water thoroughly it is wiser not to water at all. Light, insufficient watering will do infinitely more harm than good.

RATE OF SOWING

The quantity of seed required will depend to some extent upon the type of grass seed which is being used.

General Purpose Lawn Mixture, Shady Lawn Mixture, Poor Soil Mixture. 4 pounds per 1000 square feet; 150 pounds per acre.
Velvet Bent. 2 pounds per 1000 square feet; 85 pounds per acre.

MOWING NEW GRASS

Young, newly sown grass (with the exception of the bent grasses) should not be cut until the blades have reached a height of 2 inches. The mower blades should be carefully set so that the final cut will not be closer than 1½ inches. If young grass is mown too closely it will prevent the formation of a vigorous root system and will seriously injure the quality of the turf.

SODDING NEW AREAS

Undoubtedly, the most rapid method of establishing turf is sodding. It consists of cutting strips of sod from an existing lawn, laying them carefully together on the new area and encouraging the grass roots to re-establish themselves in the soil. Under certain conditions, this method may be preferable to starting grass from seeds or stolons, because it has the advantage of being so quickly accomplished that there will be no opportunity for a hard rain to wash away the soil and ruin the surface of the newly prepared ground. On banks or steep slopes this is an advantage. It is seldom possible to make as fine a lawn by this method as it is with the slower processes. However, where an immediate effect is desired, sodding is the only sure way.

Turf selected for cutting and transplanting should be well-established grass growing in open ground and free from crab grass and weeds. The best source is a lawn that has been grown from seed and is composed of a mixture, blue grass predominating over red top and fescue, with little or no clover.

Sodding should be done at a time when there will be four or five or more weeks of good growing weather before the beginning of winter or summer. Root growth is almost stationary at these seasons of drought or freezing. Unless the roots become established well enough to supply moisture and nourishment to the blades, the summer sun or the winter frosts will kill the grass altogether.

Before cutting sod, the lawn should be mown closely. The edges of the sod strips are then cut by a rotary blade or by a spade held in a vertical position. The sod is thus divided by these vertical cuts into strips 12 or 15 inches wide and 10 feet or more long. If the job is a small one, cutting sod into squares may be more convenient. A specially built sod spade with its handle at an angle with the blade is forced under the sod, cutting off the lower roots and lifting up a mat of upper roots about 1½ inches thick. The strips are then rolled up and loaded into a truck or wheelbarrow. It is important to keep the edges of the strips straight and parallel and at a uniform distance apart. To facilitate this, a wide plank is laid on the sod with its edge at the last cut, and the new cut is made along the opposite side. This regularity will make more easy the task of laying the sod.

The ground on which the sod is to be laid must be graded to an even surface, cultivated, raked, and rolled, and any irregularities smoothed out. The turf is then laid, the strip being unrolled into place, firmed with blows of the back of the spade. Any irregularities caused by an uneven thickness of the sod should be adjusted at this time by rolling back the strip and filling or cutting the soil below as required. This is the part of the work in which skill and patience are important and which will make the difference between an uneven turf and a smooth one. After rolling with a hand roller, the whole area should be watered until it is thoroughly soaked, and it should not be allowed to dry out until it has become well established.

MAINTENANCE OF EXISTING LAWNS

It is advisable for every home owner to work out a careful program of lawn maintenance and to adhere faithfully to the schedule. The majority of the lawns in this country suffer sadly from neglect. After a lawn is once established the owner is all too apt to assume that the only subsequent care which it requires is that of periodic mowing. Under such conditions of neglect, however, it does not take many years for a good lawn to deteriorate into a poor lawn. The fertility of the soil becomes gradually depleted to the point where it can no longer support the better types of lawn grasses, and the inferior grasses consequently become more and more dominant; the soil becomes increasingly more acid in its reaction and therefore more impervious to water; the lawn becomes less resistant to injury from drought and from insect attacks; and weeds gradually creep in and will, in time, almost entirely crowd out the grasses. It is therefore a matter of sound economy to follow a carefully planned program of lawn maintenance.

The most important considerations in such a program are: rolling, fertilization, liming, cutting, weed control, and disease and insect-pest control.

ROLLING

The question of lawn rolling is a much debated one and one upon which authorities fail to agree. It is undoubtedly true that rolling is an operation which has been much overdone in the past, and the present consensus of opinion seems to be in favor of one or two light rollings in the spring. Rolling should not be done until all possibility of alternate thawing and freezing is past. It should be done when the soil is moderately moist— never when it is soggy. Too frequent rolling is apt to cause an undesirable compaction of the soil which tends to interfere with the normal, thrifty growth of the turf. This danger is much greater on heavy soils than on soils of a more sandy character. A water-ballast roller is the most desirable type for lawn use as the weight may be adjusted to meet varying conditions. The roller should be just heavy enough to press the crowns back into the soil without making the soil unduly compact.

FERTILIZATION

The maintenance of soil fertility is one of the major considerations in any program of lawn management. All of our most desirable lawn grasses require a soil of reasonably good fertility for satisfactory development. It is far wiser, and far better economy, to maintain this fertility from year to year by periodic applications of commercial fertilizers and composts than it is to allow the soil to become depleted.

The three most important elements of fertility needed by lawn grasses for satisfactory growth are nitrogen, phosphorus, and potash. Nitrogen produces a vigorous growth of leaves and stems, phosphorus is needed for good root development, and potash is valuable in promoting general vigor and resistance to disease. A complete commercial fertilizer contains these three essential elements. The true value of a commercial fertilizer, however, depends not only upon the actual content of plant food, but also upon the form in which the nutrients are supplied. This point is of particular importance in the fertilization of lawn grasses.

Nitrogen may be supplied in the form of ammonia compounds, nitrate compounds, or organic compounds. The ammonia compounds, such as sulphate of ammonia and urea, are quickly available but have a decided tendency to leave the soil more acid. This disadvantage is not as serious as it might seem, however, as it may be readily overcome by a sufficient application of lime. Nitrate compounds, such as nitrate of soda, are also quickly available and do not tend to increase the acidity of the soil. They are, therefore, to be preferred on soils that are strongly acid. The various organic forms of nitrogen, such as bone meal, tankage, cottonseed meal and soybean meal, decompose much more slowly than the inorganic forms and are not active in releasing plant nutrients except under conditions of warmth and moisture. Even though they may be applied in the fall or early spring they supply very little in the way of plant food until the beginning of summer. They are more valuable for use on sandy soils than on heavy clay soils as they are not lost through leaching as are some of the more readily available organic forms. The ideal fertilizer for lawn grasses contains all three forms of nitrogen compounds, in the proportion of approximately ⅓ from nitrate compounds, ⅓ from ammonia compounds, and ⅓ from organic compounds. An excess of nitrogen should be avoided as it will stimulate an overluxuriant leaf growth at the expense of vigorous root development. From 4 to 6 per cent of nitrogen in a complete fertilizer is usually sufficient, and if clover is used in the seed mixture the percentage may be somewhat reduced or, in some cases, entirely omitted, as the nitrogen-fixing bacteria on the roots of the clover will supply sufficient nitrogen to meet the needs of the grasses.

Phosphorus may be supplied most effectively in the form of superphosphate. As most soils are deficient in phosphorus it usually constitutes from 8 to 10 per cent of the complete fertilizer mixture. There is no danger in applying it in too large a quantity as it does not produce any harmful effect on the turf.

Potash is usually supplied in the form of muriate of potash.

Lawn fertilizers should be applied early in the spring and again in the autumn. It is not advisable to apply fertilizers during the summer months as the effects are apt to be definitely harmful rather than beneficial.

Even distribution of the fertilizer is essential as areas not covered will receive no direct benefit from the application. If the application is made when the grass is dry there will be no danger of burning the turf.

The rate of application will depend, to a large extent, upon the natural fertility of the soil. On soils of medium to poor fertility a yearly application of from 20 to 30 pounds of a well balanced complete fertilizer (5–8–5, 5–10–5, or 4–8–4 analysis) per 1000 square feet will give excellent results. This is at the rate of approximately 1000 pounds per acre. Half the amount should be applied in early spring and half in the autumn. For soils of reasonably high fertility the application may be reduced to about half this amount.

If well rotted, composted manure or spent mushroom soil is available it may be used as a top dressing on the lawn, either to supplement or to entirely take the place of the commercial fertilizer.

USE OF LIME ON LAWNS

In order to promote a vigorous, healthy growth of the lawn grasses the soil reaction should be kept as nearly neutral as possible. While it is true that the bent grasses and the fescues are decidedly tolerant of acid soil, they will make better growth on more nearly neutral soils.

Normally, grasses produce a new crop of roots each year. The old roots die, adding humus to the soil. On extremely acid soil, however, these old roots fail to decay and the soil tends to become seriously sod bound.

Another point in favor of maintaining a neutral soil reaction is the recently discovered fact that on highly acid soils the grasses are unable to use nitrogen in the form of ammonium compounds. Under such conditions the grass apparently absorbs the nitrogen but cannot assimilate it, and a toxic reaction occurs. It is also a well-known fact that when soils become highly acid something happens to the structure of the soil itself, and it gradually becomes less and less permeable to water. An adequate application of lime therefore not only overcomes the acidity of the soil, but also improves the structure of the soil and increases its water-absorbing capacity, as well as supplying small quantities of plant food in the form of calcium and magnesium.

If soil tests indicate a degree of acidity below a pH. of 6, an application of lime should be made, either in the form of hydrated lime or in the form of finely ground limestone. The most favorable seasons for applying lime are autumn, winter and very early spring, when the alternate freezing and thawing of the ground will enable the lime to penetrate more deeply into the soil. It may, however, be applied at any season of the year. Lime is slow in its reaction and no appreciable benefits will be noticed until five or six months after the application has been made. However, the eventual beneficial effects of lime are of long duration and will be apparent for several years. Unless the soil is intensely acid, which occurs infrequently, an application of lime once every two or three years will be sufficient to maintain the correct soil reaction. (For the rate of application refer to the table on page 27.)

CUTTING

The height at which turf should be cut depends entirely upon the type of grass which is being grown. Velvet bent, Creeping bent and Colonial bent require very close mowing and should be kept at a height of ¼ to ½ inch. Lawns which are predominantly Kentucky blue grass should never be cut more closely than 1 inch, and 1¼ inches is considered the ideal height. The lawn mower should be checked periodically and adjusted whenever necessary. In order to adjust a mower so that it will cut at a given height, set the roller which is on the back of the mower so that the bedknife, which is the long flat blade against which the blades on the revolving reel cut, is at the desired height.

Frequent and wisely regulated mowing tends to produce a fine-textured turf, as new leaf growth is stimulated. If a lawn is neglected and the grass is allowed to become too tall before it is cut the results are very unfortunate, as the growth becomes coarse and tough and the leaves lose their healthy, deep green color.

Extremely early mowing should be avoided on lawns which are predominantly Kentucky blue grass. The root system of most of our lawn grasses is entirely renewed each spring and if the grass is closely mown early in the season there will be a decided reduction in root development. The quality of the turf will suffer considerably in consequence, and the grass will be less able to withstand the vicissitudes of summer droughts. In order to insure vigorous root growth, the first spring mowing should not be done until the grass has reached a height of two inches.

Under normal conditions the grass clippings should be allowed to remain on the lawn, thus helping to maintain the humus supply in the soil. If, because of a long period of wet weather or for some other unavoidable cause, the grass has become unusually long and rank in growth the clippings will have a tendency to form a mat on the surface of the newly mown lawn and will have a very detrimental effect on the growth of the turf. In some cases, where the clippings are not too heavily matted they may be scattered by whipping them back and forth over the lawn with a long bamboo pole held in a low, almost horizontal position. If the clippings are so heavy that such a procedure would not be effective, they should be raked up with a light bamboo rake and removed. If the lawn mower is equipped with a grass catch the necessity of raking will be eliminated.

In selecting lawn mowers of the motor type it is advisable to avoid those which are equipped with heavy rollers, as they have a tendency to make the soil too compact. The danger of soil compaction is far greater on heavy soils than on light, sandy soils.

RENOVATION OF OLD LAWNS

The renovation of old lawns presents a very special problem. If a lawn has become shabby, and if the better grasses have been crowded out by grasses of inferior character or by encroaching weeds, one must decide whether it is wise to attempt to improve the existing sod, or whether it would be better to plow or spade the entire area and make a fresh start. Much may be accomplished by a program of fertilization, top-dressing, and reseeding, and it is usually the most economical practice, unless the area is in exceptionally bad condition. A good complete fertilizer (5–10–5 or 10–6–4) should be applied either in very early spring or in the early autumn at the rate of 15 to 30 pounds per 1000 square feet. The surface of such areas as may require reseeding should be loosened with an iron rake or with a spiker. It is futile to sow grass seed on hard, firmly compacted soil. A good top-dressing of rich garden loam and humus (preferably cultivated peat) should be applied to these areas, and after the seed has been sown the soil should be lightly firmed with the back of the rake or with a very light roller. If a light covering of salt hay is spread over the area which has been sown it will help to conserve the moisture in the soil and will hasten germination. The salt hay should be removed as soon as the seed has germinated, as it will encourage damping off if allowed to remain too long.

LAWNS FOR THE SOUTH

The establishment and maintenance of lawns in the South present very special problems. Blue grass, which is the chief ingredient of most lawn-grass mixtures in the North, will not thrive under conditions of extreme heat or drought, and it is therefore necessary to find as a substitute a grass which is able to endure southern conditions. The grass which meets these requirements more completely than any other is Bermuda grass. Although it does not produce the luxuriant green turf obtainable with a seeding of blue grass, it makes a fairly satisfactory lawn. The great disadvantage of Bermuda grass is that it is liable to become a serious pest in garden and field, as it spreads rapidly after it is well established, and unless effort is made to keep it within bounds it will encroach upon the garden. Bermuda grass is a long-lived, persistent perennial grass which spreads by strong, underground root stalks, and it will grow on almost any type of soil. It may be established either by seeding or by planting small pieces of broken sod. A firm and well-prepared seed bed is desirable.

A winter lawn may be obtained by sowing annual Italian Rye grass on the Bermuda grass sod in the autumn. The rye grass germinates quickly and will produce an effect of green turf during the winter months, but will die out entirely upon the approach of warm weather.

GRASS SUBSTITUTES

A substitute for grass which has proved fairly satisfactory under certain conditions is the little, low-growing herb camomile (Anthemis nobilis). It thrives well in full sun, prefers a light, well-drained soil, and is particularly well adapted to planting on sunny banks where it is difficult to secure or maintain a stand of grass. It retains its beautiful deep green color throughout the winter months. Camomile is occasionally used on paths in herb gardens and it is delightfully in harmony with the quaint character of such a garden. It is not well adapted to areas that are subjected to constant wear, as it has a tendency to become shabby and die out, leaving bare, brown patches which require frequent renovation.

CONTROL OF LAWN PESTS

Injury from Grubs. The grubs of the Japanese beetle and those of the Asiatic beetle cause considerable damage to lawns in certain sections of the country. The grubs feed upon the grass roots in the spring and if they are present in sufficient numbers they may seriously injure the growth of the turf, and, in extreme cases, may actually kill the grass. The adult beetles lay their eggs in the green turf during the summer months. After hatching the small grubs feed upon the grass roots during the autumn, burrowing more deeply into the soil to pass the winter in an inactive stage. In the spring they work their way up to the surface again and resume their feeding for a few weeks before they pass into the adult stage. The most satisfactory measure of control is the application of arsenate of lead powder at the rate of from 10 to 15 pounds per 1000 square feet; approximately 400 to 500 pounds per acre. In order to provide for an even distribution, the arsenate of lead should be mixed with ten times its own volume of sand or fine loam. It should be spread over the surface of the lawn when the grass is dry and should then be watered in with a fine spray. It may be applied at any time of the year, provided that the ground is not frozen. Applications in early spring or in the autumn are the most effective, as it is at this time that the grubs are actively at work. Neither lime nor inorganic fertilizers should be applied with the arsenate of lead. It is wise to allow several weeks to elapse between the application of one chemical and another. The arsenate of lead powder may be applied in the form of a solution instead of in the dry state, if preferred. One pound of arsenate of lead powder may be dissolved in two gallons of water and applied at the rate of 20 gallons of the solution to 1000 square feet of turf. On small areas it may be applied with a watering can. The precaution must be taken, however, to wash the arsenate solution into the soil before it dries on the grass. This may be done most effectively with a garden hose. When a new lawn is being established it is not advisable to apply arsenate of lead until several months after the turf has been sown. Grass seed germinates more slowly and requires a longer time to become established in soil that has been treated with arsenate of lead than it does in soil which has not been treated. If arsenate of lead is watered in, there is practically no danger to dogs or other small animals.

Chinch Bug Injury. Within recent years Chinch bugs have caused very serious damage to many lawns in the vicinity of New York and Philadelphia and they are spreading rapidly to other sections. They are particularly destructive on bent turf, being less injurious on lawns composed largely of Kentucky blue grass, or the fescues. Chinch bugs injure the lawn by puncturing the stem of the grasses and sucking the juices of the plant, causing a very characteristic browning of the turf. If the infestation is particularly severe the grass may be killed out entirely. Attacks are most likely to occur where the grass is fully exposed to the sun, shaded areas being almost immune from trouble of this nature. When fully grown, Chinch bugs are about 1/8 of an inch in length; the body is black, and the wings, which are white with black markings, lie folded flat upon the back. The newly hatched young are wingless. Chinch bugs pass the winter in the adult stage, either in the turf or in tall grasses near by. The eggs are deposited by the females on the stems of the lawn grasses in early spring, the first generation hatching in May or early June and becoming full grown in July. The second generation hatches in July or August and reaches maturity in late September. Lawn injury is usually most severe in July and September when the bugs are feeding most actively as they approach maturity.

There are two measures of control which have given fairly satisfactory results, although it is generally conceded that

Chinch bugs are hard to eradicate entirely after they have once established themselves on a lawn area. Finely ground tobacco dust with a nicotine content of 1 per cent may be applied at the rate of 25 pounds per 1000 square feet of turf; approximately 1000 pounds per acre. As soon as the application has been made, the dust should be worked well into the crowns of the plants either with a grass broom or with the back of a garden rake. Rotenone dust may also be used, being applied in the same manner at the rate of 25 pounds per 1000 square feet of turf. It is, however, somewhat more expensive than tobacco dust. As soon as the presence of Chinch bugs is detected an immediate application should be made. In areas where they are known to be prevalent lawns may be protected by giving two applications of tobacco dust or rotenone during the season, one about the middle of June and one about the middle of August.

Sod Webworms. Lawns are occasionally injured by various small caterpillars known as sod webworms. The injury is first evident in the appearance of small, irregular, brownish patches in the grass, caused by the feeding of the young caterpillars. If the webworms are present in sufficient numbers the lawn may become very ragged in appearance and large areas may be entirely killed out. It is important that measures of control should be undertaken before any great amount of damage occurs. Turf injury due to sod webworms is readily distinguishable from any other type of injury by the very characteristic, silk-lined burrows of the caterpillars which may be detected upon the crowns of the grass at the surface of the ground. One of the most satisfactory measures of control is the use of arsenate of lead, applied either as a dust or as a spray. When applied in the form of a spray it should be used at the rate of 2 pounds of arsenate of lead to 20 gallons of water for every 1000 square feet of turf. After the spray has been applied the grass should be watered lightly. When applied in the form of a powder it is used at the rate of 7½ pounds per 1000 square feet. In this form it may be applied very easily with a rotary hand duster. The area to be treated should be clipped rather short and the grass should be dry when the application is made. The dust should be worked into the crowns with a grass broom or with the back of a rake and the grass should then be watered thoroughly with a strong spray. No further watering should be given for forty-eight hours.

LAWN DISEASES

Brownpatch. Brownpatch is a fungous disease caused by Rhizoctonia solani. Many species of lawn grasses are affected, the bent grasses being particularly susceptible to injury. Some soils seem to be comparatively free from the fungus causing brownpatch, while other soils are badly infected. The disease is particularly prevalent during long periods of hot, humid weather. An excessive supply of nitrogen, overwatering, poor drainage conditions, and high soil acidity are contributing factors in the spread of the disease.

When the turf first becomes affected it turns a very dark green in color, and then gradually becomes a light brown, having the appearance of dead, dried grass. The patches are somewhat circular in outline, although very irregular in shape, and they vary in size from a diameter of a few inches to a diameter of several feet.

The most effective measure of control for brownpatch consists of the application of a mercury compound. Either the organic or inorganic forms may be used. Both corrosive sublimate and calomel have proved very effective, and they may be applied either in the form of a solution, or in a dry state, being mixed with sand or with soil. Either of the following methods of application may be used.

Method No. 1

Dissolve 3 ounces of corrosive sublimate in 50 gallons of water and apply with a sprinkling can or with a sprayer. It is important that a very even application be made, and the lawn should be watered thoroughly as soon as the fungicide has been applied. The above quantity is sufficient to effectively treat 1000 square feet of turf. Either calomel or mercuric oxide may be substituted for the corrosive sublimate if desired. In extremely hot, humid weather there is greater danger of injury to the turf, and the quantity of the mercuric compound should be reduced to 1 ounce.

Method No. 2

Mix 3 ounces of corrosive sublimate, calomel or mercuric oxide (reduce the amount to 1 ounce in very hot, humid weather) with 6 or 8 quarts of sand or finely sifted compost, and distribute it evenly over the turf. The lawn should be watered thoroughly as soon as the application has been made.

The usual practice is to treat a lawn only upon the appearance of the disease. In sections where it is prevalent, periodic treatments are advised as a preventive measure, being applied before the disease actually appears.

Dollarspot is a form of brownpatch, causing small, circular patches hardly more than 2 inches in diameter. The patches are of a somewhat lighter color than those which are typical of brownpatch. The measures of control are identical.

CONTROL OF LAWN WEEDS

On areas where a sound program of turf management is faithfully carried out, there will be comparatively little trouble with weeds. Vigorous, rapidly growing grass is capable of crowding out many of the existing weeds and is also capable of preventing new weeds from gaining a foothold. Many excellent lawns which are entirely free from weeds have been established and are maintained solely through the application of the fundamental practices of good lawn management.

If, however, these practices have been neglected and if a lawn area has become badly infested with weeds, very definite measures of weed eradication should be adopted, along with a general improvement in the management program for the lawn.

On very small areas hand weeding may be practised with excellent results. It is of vital importance, however, that the weeds be removed before seed has formed. After the hand weeding has been completed, all bare areas should be prepared for reseeding in accordance with the general principles involved in the seeding of new lawns.

While hand weeding may be practical on small areas or

where the infestation is very slight, it is not a feasible practice for large areas, as it is far too tedious and costly a method. On large areas effective weed control may best be obtained through the use of various chemicals. Within recent years a great deal of research has been carried on by the various experiment stations in regard to the chemical control of weeds and it has been proved conclusively that practically all of our common lawn weeds may be entirely eradicated through the proper and timely use of various chemicals. The factors contributing to the success of this method are: the selection of the chemical which has been found to be most effective for the control of each particular weed or group of weeds; the method and time of application; the rate of application; and the subsequent method of the re-establishment of the turf.

Most lawn weeds may be divided into three classes according to their general habit of growth. It has been found that for each of these groups some one method of chemical control will give the best results. It is, therefore, important to select the chemical which is most effective for the particular type of weed to be eradicated.

ANNUAL GRASSES—CRAB-GRASS, GOOSE-GRASS, POA ANNUA

Of these three weed-like grasses which infest lawn areas, crab-grass is by far the most troublesome. In order to eradicate it or to keep it under control, it is well to know something of its habit of growth. Crab-grass is a tender annual, thriving in full sun and unable to endure shade. The seed germinates late in the spring, the plants make slow growth during early summer, grow rapidly during late July and August, reseed most prolifically, and are killed by the first light frost. In controlling crab-grass, we have three points of attack: to hand-weed the young plants if the area is small; to provide for such a luxuriant growth of the better lawn grasses and to maintain the lawn at a sufficient height (1½ inches) so that the young crab-grass seedlings cannot gain a foothold; or to use some chemical measure of control, which will either kill the crab-grass or will prevent it from reseeding.

The chemical which has been proved most effective in the control of crab-grass is Sodium Chlorate.

METHOD OF TREATMENT FOR CRAB-GRASS

Between July 10 and July 20, treat infested areas with Sodium Chlorate in accordance with either of the following methods:

1. Mix 2 pounds of Sodium Chlorate with 14 quarts of dry sand or soil. Sift the mixture onto the infested area, using an ordinary kitchen sifter. Apply at the rate of 2 pounds of Sodium Chlorate (plus the sand as a carrier) to every 1000 square feet of lawn area.

2. Dissolve 2 pounds of Sodium Chlorate in 10 gallons of water and apply in the form of a fine, mistlike spray. A knapsack or bucket sprayer may be used for small lawns; a barrel or power sprayer for larger lawns. A garden hose fitted with an aspirator nozzle is also satisfactory. This solution should cover an area of 1000 square feet.

Precautions. It is matter of vital importance to apply the Sodium Chlorate at the prescribed rate. If applied at the rate of 5 pounds per 1000 square feet, Sodium Chlorate will kill the desirable turf grasses as well as the weedy grasses. Some grasses are much more susceptible to the injurious effects of Sodium Chlorate than are other grasses. Fortunately crab-grass is one of the most sensitive of all grasses and its growth is seriously checked by a light application of Sodium Chlorate which does no permanent injury to the lawn. It is, therefore, possible to kill or prevent the seeding of crab-grass without injury to the more desirable lawn grasses. A lawn that has been treated with Sodium Chlorate will have a yellowish or brownish cast for a short period as the growth of all the grasses is temporarily checked. The treatment is not recommended for lawns less than one year old.

When using Sodium Chlorate the following precautions should be observed. Keep Sodium Chlorate in a metal container. Sodium Chlorate itself is not combustible but when it is mixed with dry organic matter or with other combustible materials, the mixture is highly inflammable and is as dangerous as gasoline. Any clothing or shoes which have become saturated with Sodium Chlorate should be thoroughly washed with clear water before they are allowed to dry. It is wise to wear rubbers when applying Sodium Chlorate. Do not smoke when using it.

After the crab-grass has been killed or its growth has been

seriously checked, it is essential to re-establish good turf on the infested areas. The crab-grass should be raked or hoed out and the area should be prepared for reseeding.

MAT–FORMING WEEDS: CHICKWEED, SPEEDWELL, GROUND IVY, KNOTWEED, SELF–HEAL, LAWN PENNYWORT (HYDROCOTYLE ROTUNDIFOLIA)

In this group we find several weeds which are sometimes very troublesome on lawns and which, if no control measures are undertaken, may, in time, entirely ruin a lawn area.

Sodium Arsenite has proved to be the most effective chemical for the control of weeds in this group. As it is a dangerous poison it should be handled with care and animals should not have access to any herbage which has been treated.

METHOD OF TREATMENT

Treatments may be made at any time during the growing season. The lawn area which has been treated will become uniformly brown for a period of 5–6 days, but will fully recover within the following few weeks.

1. Mix 6 ounces of Sodium Arsenite with 12 quarts of dry sand and sift over the infested area. An ordinary kitchen sifter is very satisfactory. Apply at the rate of 6 ounces of Sodium Arsenite to every 1000 square feet of lawn area, and it is important that an even application be made. At the time that the application is made the soil should be moderately moist and the grass should be in good, growing condition.

2. Dissolve 4 ounces of Sodium Arsenite in 20 gallons of water and apply as a spray. This quantity is sufficient for 1000 square feet (10 pounds per acre).

Sodium Chlorate and Sodium Arsenite may be used together as a combination spray for crab-grass and the various mat-forming weeds. Two pounds of Sodium Chlorate and 2 ounces of Sodium Arsenite per 1000 square feet of area applied as a fine, mist-like spray has proved very effective.

ROSETTE-FORMING WEEDS

Dandelions, Buckhorn, and Plantain are the most common weeds in this group. If the infestation is light, the spot method may be used, each individual weed being treated, either by applying the chemical by hand or with a weed cane. A weed cane is a very handy implement which has been devised for this purpose and it is capable of delivering a small amount of the chemical upon the pressure of a lever. Larger areas where the weeds are growing in patches may be treated very effectively by sifting the chemical onto the leaves using a kitchen sifter for this purpose.

A combination of three parts Sulphate of Ammonia and one part Sulphate of Iron, known as SA-SI, has proved to be one of the most effective measures of control for the broad-leaved, rosette-forming weeds in this group.

SA–SI kills the weeds by changing the chemical composition of the cell sap. The combined action of these two sulphates is much more effective than when either one is used alone.

Method of Application

On small areas when the weeds are to be spotted, ¼ teaspoonful of SA–SI should be dropped into the crown of each plant either by hand or with a weed cane. For larger areas the material may be mixed with sand at the rate of 1 pound of SA–SI to 10 quarts of sand. The material should be sifted lightly over the weeds in the early morning while they are still wet with dew, the above proportions being sufficient for an area of 1000 square feet. Several light applications of this nature are preferable to one heavy application as there is less danger of injury to the surrounding turf. Applications of SA–SI should be made during the spring and autumn when the ground is well supplied with moisture and when the lawn grasses are making rapid growth. It should not be applied during a period of drought or during the heat of midsummer.

Ground Covers

In many situations ground cover plants are more appropriate and more satisfactory than turf. Small areas of grass are a continual chore to keep mown and trimmed, but the ground covers require almost no care. On steep banks where mowing is difficult, ground covers are much more satisfactory and less labor to maintain. They hold the soil just as well as turf and the texture is far more interesting. The ground about and under shrubs, particularly broad-leaved evergreens, should be covered with ground covers rather than remain bare. Cultivation of the soil disturbs the roots of Rhododendron and Laurel, but Japanese Spurge and Periwinkle are excellent protection and soil conditioners. Not only do they make the place tidy but they hold the fallen leaves from blowing away, thus helping to add annually to the humus content. Some ground cover plants, such as Periwinkle, are excellent in company with Narcissus which grows up through it delightfully. When the leaves of the Narcissus droop down after the blooming season and become unsightly, they should not be cut back for this is detrimental to the plants; they may be tucked under the Periwinkle.

It sometimes takes a year or more for a bed of ground cover to become established, but once established it is permanent. Periwinkle looks well at the end of the first season. English Ivy, if planted at wide intervals, requires two seasons to fill a space, but more immediate results come from putting in many small plants placed at 6-inch intervals. In every case the advantages of rapid results should be weighed against those of economy. Often planting costs have a very wide range when a sparse planting for a three-year program is compared with a close planting for results the first season. Like all good things a perfect ground cover takes time to produce.

For the open sunny places, for banks, wherever a large high ground cover is in scale with other things, nothing surpasses Rosa Wichuraiana, the wild Trailing Rose with white blossoms. Its long arching stems make a thick mat of foliage standing less than two feet off the ground and spreading by long stems. The edge of such a bank planting could be made tidy by a line of Cotoneaster horizontalis, which is another excellent bank cover. Its flat arching sprays form planes of verdure enriched in September by quantities of small, bright red berries.

Rosa Max Graf, a recent hybrid of R. Wichuraiana and R. rugosa, has the hardiness, freedom from disease, the crinkly leaves and deep pink blossoms of R. rugosa, and the trailing disposition of R. Wichuraiana. It is truly a worthy ground cover for the sunny bank.

For an utterly wild situation in soil too sandy for most shrubs, Scotch Broom (Cytisus scoparius), is a worthy choice. Its long stems remain green all winter. In May and June, it bears quantities of bright yellow pea-like blossoms which are very effective in masses.

Nothing quite equals the spreading Junipers. Juniperus communis depressa forms a mat 18–24 inches high with ascending but ever-spreading branches, and foliage of interesting texture. J. horizontalis is lower, more prostrate and reaches out with long wandering stems. It is best associated with other ground covers such as Snow-in-Summer (Cerastium tomentosum). Its variety, Douglasii, the Waukegan Juniper, has bluish foliage which in winter turns a clear purple and is one of the most beautiful of the prostrate evergreens. Juniperus Sabina, and J. Sabina camariscifolia, its blue-leaved form, are also good vigorous growers which form dense mats 18 inches high.

Among ground covers that are smaller in scale than the foregoing and suitable for sunny places in the more sophisticated areas (next to the terrace or on banks beside the garden) the following are most appropriate: Aster Mauve Cushion, Dianthus deltoides, Gypsophila repens, Helianthemum, Iberis

Photograph by Samuel H. Gottscho Armand R. Tibbits, Landscape Architect

Spreading Junipers in a Naturalistic Composition

sempervirens, Nepeta Mussini, Cerastium tomentosum, and Phlox subulata. These may be used in combination with each other and most of them are excellent on banks. Thymus citriodorus, T. lanuginosus, and T. Serpyllum are very low to the ground and need to have the place to themselves. They are also good as inhabitants of the crevices in flagstone pavings because they do not at all mind being stepped on.

For the partially shaded areas there is a wealth of material. Here belong the Cotoneasters, Hemerocallis, Euonymus vines, Phlox divaricata and many others. Among the best ground covers for this partially shaded place is Phlox divaricata. Its lavender-blue flowers in May sprinkled over great areas of ground are a wonderful sight. Likewise, the Forget-me-nots make a good ground cover in shady and moist places and their bright little blue blossoms keep appearing for months. The dwarf Veronicas, V. repens and V. rupestris also form dense masses of foliage in semi-shade and produce blue flowers in spikes.

Mazus reptans is a lovely little plant, 2 inches high, with tiny lavender lobelia-like blossoms. It prefers partial shade, spreads into dense mats and even becomes established in the lawn where it can be mown like grass.

For the really shady places there are Periwinkle and Japanese Spurge (Pachysandra), both excellent and long-lived and thriving in the deep shade. Even the shade of the Norway Maple will not prevent them from forming a thick mat of foliage if given a start in new soil spread above the root-filled existing soil. Indeed, Periwinkle and Japanese Spurge also do well in partial shade and are not unhappy in the sun if given plenty of water. One of the most delightful of all ground covers is the combination of Periwinkle and Plumbago larpentæ (Ceratostigma plumbaginoides). The soft lavender-blue blossoms of the Periwinkle come in May and June and the brilliant blue flowers of the Plumbago carry the period of bloom well into the autumn. During the spring months one is hardly aware that the Plumbago forms a part of the planting, but in late summer it begins to assume a more important role and by September it has become completely dominant.

English Ivy and Lily-of-the-valley probably stand the con-

BEST GROUND COVER PLANTS

Scientific Name	Common Name	Height	Number of Plants per sq. yd.	Color of Flowers	Season	Best Exposure	Soil
Ajuga genevensis	Geneva Bugle	8"	15–25	Bright blue	June	Dense shade	Rich
reptans	Carpet Bugle	4"	18–30	Blue	May	Dense shade	Rich
Arctostaphylos uva-ursi	Bear-berry	6"	4	White flowers Red berries	May	Part shade	Acid
Arenaria montana	Mt. Sandwort	4"	18–30	White	May–Aug.	Light or med. shade	Light, porous
Aster Mauve Cushion		9"	5–9	Mauve	October	Sun or half shade	Any
Calluna vulgaris	Scotch Heather	2–3'	4	Purplish	August	Sun	Acid
Cerastium tomentosum	Snow-in-summer	10"	8–10	White	June	Sun or light shade	Any
Convallaria majalis	Lily-of-the-valley	8"	9–18	White	May	Dense or part. shade	Rich, manure mulch
Cornus canadensis	Bunchberry	5"	18–20	White	June	Shade	Rich and acid
Cotoneaster horizontalis microphylla	Rock Spray	18"	2–4	Pink	June	Partial shade	Rich
		2'	2–4	White. Red berries	May	Part shade	Acid
Cytisus scoparius	Scotch Broom	4'	1	Yellow	May–June	Sun	Banks, dry sandy
Dianthus deltoides	Maiden Pink	12"	6–9	Pink	June–July	Sun or half shade	Any
Euonymus radicans	Wintercreeper	3'	1			Light shade	Rich
radicans acutus		2½'	1–2			Light shade	Rich
radicans coloratus		2½'	1–2			Light shade	Rich
radicans kewensis		2'	1–2			Light shade	Rich
Dicksonia punctilobula	Hay-scented Fern	15"	6–9			Sun, shade or dry woods	Rich
Galax aphylla	Galax	6"	10	White	July	Dense shade	Acid
Gaultheria procumbens	Wintergreen	4"	9	White		Dry open woods	Acid
Gypsophila repens	Creeping Chalk-plant	10"	1–6	White	July–Sept.	Sun	Dry, poor
Hedera helix	English Ivy	10"	6–9			Dense or part. shade	Rich
Helianthemum varieties	Sun Rose	6"		Yellow, orange, red, pink	July	Sun	Lime, porous
Hemerocallis flava	Tawny Daylily	2½'	4	Yellow	June	Sun or part. shade	Any
fulva	Lemon Daylily	3'	2	Deep orange	July	Sun or part. shade	Any

Botanical name	Common name	Height	No.	Color	Bloom	Exposure	Soil
Hypericum Moserianum	St. Johnswort	1½'	4-6	Yellow	July-Aug.	Sun or part. shade	Light, sandy
Iberis sempervirens	Candytuft	6"	4-6	White	May	Sun	Rich
Juniperus horizontalis	Prostrate Juniper	10"	1-2			Sun	Light
hor. Douglasii	Douglas Juniper	10"	1-2			Sun	Light
Sabina tamariscifolia		2'	1			Sun	Light
communis depressa		2'-3'	1				Any
Leiophyllum buxifolium	Sand Myrtle	15"	4	White	May	Part shade	Light, acid
Mazus reptans		4"	9-18	Lavender	May	Sun or part. shade	Any
Myosotis palustris, var. semperflorens	Forget-me-not	8"	9	Pale blue	June-Aug.	Part. shade	Low wet places
Nepeta Mussini		15"	4-6	Lavender	May	Sun or part. shade	Any
Pachysandra terminalis	Jap. Spurge	8"	9-36	White (Inconspicuous)	May	Dense or part. shade	Rich
Phlox divaricata	Blue Phlox	12"	9	Lavender-blue	May-June	Partial shade	Rich
Phlox subulata	Moss Pink	6"	6-9	Pink	April	Sun	Any
Plumbago larpentae	Leadwort	9"	9	Deep blue	Aug.-Sept.	Partial shade	Rich
Polypodium vulgare	Polypody Fern	6"	6-18			Dense or part. shade	Rich
Rosa Max Graf		2'	1	Deep pink	June	Sun	Rich
Wichuraiana		1½'	9	White	June	Sun	Rich
Sedum acre	Stone crop	4"	9	Yellow	June		
album			9	White	July-Aug.		
Fosterianum			9	Yellow	June	Sun or partial shade	Sandy
lydium		3"	9	White			
sarmentosum		3"	9	Yellow	June-July		
stoloniferum			9	Rose	April-May		
ternatum			9	White			
Thymus citriodorus	Lemon Thyme	4"	18-36	Purplish	June-Sept.	Sun or part. shade	Rich
lanuginosus	Woolly Thyme	3"	18-36	Deep pink	June-Sept.	Sun or part. shade	Rich
Serpyllum	Wild Thyme	4"	6-9	Dark red	June-Sept.	Sun or part. shade	Rich
Tradescantia virginiana	Spiderwort	12-15"		Blue	May-July	Dense or part. shade	Rich
Veronica repens		2"	18	Light blue	May-June	Light or med. shade	Rich
rupestris		3"	18	Blue	May	Light shade	Rich
filiformis				Blue	May-July	Dense or part. shade	Rich
Vinca minor	Periwinkle ("Myrtle")	8"	9-27	Blue, purple white	May-June	Dense or part. shade	Rich
Zanthorhiza apiifolia	Yellow root	15"	9-18	Red	May	Dense or part. shade	Rich in humus

tinual shade of the north side of buildings better than any other
ground cover. Bugle (Ajuga reptans) also is absolutely at home
in such a place, producing a thick mat of dark foliage and deep
blue spikes of flowers. It is a vigorous plant with habits of
spreading.

Ground Cover Plants Which Are Good but Expensive, and Require a Longer Time to Become Established

Arctostaphylos uva-ursi, Bear-berry, is an ericaceous trailing vine
with red berries in autumn. Excellent on steep banks and rock
gardens, it is slow to become established. It requires acid soil and
partial shade.

Leiophyllum buxifolium, Sand Myrtle, is good for partially shady
places in light acid soil. It is an evergreen shrub about 15 inches
high.

Cotoneaster microphylla enjoys partial shade and acid soil. It is
an evergreen shrub forming dense masses and grows 2 feet high.

Calluna vulgaris, Scotch Heather, is good in sunny places in acid
soil.

Ground Cover Plants Which Are Inexpensive but Troublesome

(They become weeds and are difficult to restrain or exterminate.)

Lonicera japonica, Japanese Honeysuckle.
Lonicera japonica Halliana, Hall's Climbing Honeysuckle.
Lycium chinense, Chinese Matrimony Vine.
Lycium halimifolium, Matrimony Vine.
Lysimachia nummularia, Moneywort, Creeping Charlie.
Nepeta Glechoma, Ground Ivy, Gill-over-the-ground.

Vines

In a garden design vines have a number of important uses, for they are both decorative and functional. Probably the earliest use of vines was for fruit and wine production, but the decorative value of grape vines was so apparent that the garden builders of Italy occasionally used grape arbors as part of the scheme of the formal garden. The arbor in the Villa Medici at Fiesole is a good example. The arbor was simply a practical means of spreading the grape vines overhead in such a way as to fully expose the vine to the sun. That the interior of the arbor was cool and shady was only a result, not a purpose, of good vine culture. The famous arbors at Amalfi were not architecturally designed. They consisted of round masonry piers, supporting poles, and a mesh of smaller sticks for the vines to cover. It would seem a waste of effort to build elaborate architectural pergolas, as the vines will obliterate the support in a few years and the trouble of keeping the woodwork painted increases as the vines take possession. E. H. Wilson in his *Aristocrats of the Garden* points out a somewhat obvious, though forgotten, truth. "Now it is the Rambler Roses we admire and it is intended that we should admire them, and not the structure on which they cling, no matter how costly or architecturally beautiful this structure may happen to be."

Nevertheless, most vines must have support. And since the various vines differ according to their habits of growth and climbing equipment, the support must be suitable to the type of vine selected. Those which climb by stems, twining around the support, as the Wisteria, and those which have tendrils which reach out and grasp small objects in the manner of the grape vine, need the lattice, arbor or fence type of support. Those which cling to things by means of roots or modified fruit stems need brick or stone masonry walls or great boulders as support. Boston Ivy and Ficus repens are examples.

Some vines will grow without supports, but the amazing fact about many of them is that when grown in this manner they lose their vine characteristics and become shrub-like in form. Euonymus radicans is an outstanding example of this modification. In some cases such vines will send out quantities of long, straight stems along the surface in an effort to find a support. Such are the tactics of Wisteria. Many others, like Virginia Creeper and Rosa Wichuraiana, Lycium halimifolium, and English Ivy are quite content to scramble on the ground and often make good ground covers. However, when they reach a support, up they go, for vines are essentially outlaws. They are opportunists in the plant kingdom. If they did not grow rapidly up and over their neighbors they would not reach the light. All nature seems to be a vast competition for existence. Each species of plant, animal, and insect has survived the struggle by adapting itself to its surroundings and by developing special traits or abilities which give it an advantage over its competitors. The vine's self-preservation comes from its capacity to grow up rapidly without taking time to produce wood strong enough to support itself. It depends on its neighbors for support, and eventually it may even kill the very tree which offers it support by smothering its foliage. Furthermore, vine roots range as widely and freely as their stems. This makes them bad neighbors for many plants.

A gardener should understand these tendencies in vines and make provision for them. Vines are exceedingly valuable for their dense foliage, for the beauty of their flower and for their fruit, and they justly have a place in the garden scheme. The difficulty is to keep them in their place.

SOIL PREPARATION FOR VINES

As a general rule vines are not fussy about soil. The usual preparation for shrub beds will be adequate for vines. However, flowering vines, especially clematis, respond to additional richness in the soil, and they will well repay the gardener who pre-

Vines on a Connecticut House

pares beds of deep top-soil and manure. In preparation of beds for flowering vines, dig down to a foot below the grade, removing the sub-soil and add a 6-inch layer of a mixture of one part well-rotted manure and three parts top-soil, then spread a layer of 6 inches of top-soil. The rapidly growing vines such as Wisteria and Trumpet Creeper do better with fertilizer, and Wisteria requires a great deal of moisture. English Ivy dislikes lime and does better in slightly acid soil.

SUPPORTS

The best type of support for vines is the one which gives the required structural strength and stability, and at the same time makes a neat appearance. Slender, reinforced concrete posts at intervals of 15 feet with stout copper wires run between them offer excellent and permanent support. This construction will form a high fence, to spread the vines into a vertical wall. The southern Italians used sturdy stone piers, round and tapering, with a deep groove across the top to receive the poles which extended across from post to post. The piers were in two rows and the connecting poles supported many lateral poles which extended from side to side.

In a sophisticated garden, the more architectural arbor has its place, but in many cases the growth of the vines will so completely cover all but the posts that such embellishment seems unwarranted.

Vines which clamber up a trellis on a frame house are a serious obstacle to the periodic painting which the house requires. If rambler roses are trained on the trellis, the painting is both difficult and uncomfortable. To overcome this trouble, the trellis should be built so that, together with the vines, it may be detached from the building. One of the best ways to accomplish this is to hinge the trellis at the bottom and fasten the top to a cleat on the house wall by means of a bolt. When the painting begins, the bolt may be removed, the trellis swung out and held in a slanting position by a strut. There will be sufficient pliancy in the stems of the vine to bend along with the hinge.

For the support of rather small twining vines or shrubs against a stone or brick wall, a special nail is manufactured. From the head projects a strip of soft metal, which is bent around the vine stem to hold it in place. The nails are driven into the cement mortar joint and, because of the rough surface of the metal, hold firmly in the mortar. This is a most satisfactory device for training jasmine, forsythia or firethorn against a masonry wall.

For the support of large, stem-twining vines against a masonry wall metal frame lattices are good. Less expensive is a large mesh network of wire cables fastened to expansion bolts which project out about 8 inches from the face of the wall. The wires are made tight by turn buckles. This is suitable for such strong vines as wisteria and actinidia and if the wires are placed 3 feet apart, forming squares, a very pleasing pattern of greenery and masonry is produced. This is a satisfactory means of covering a large bare wall surface flanking a city garden.

MAINTENANCE

Pruning vines to produce better bloom or to keep the plants within bounds is an annual task requiring patience and skill. Vine prunings and the removal of the old wood may require several cuts to each stem so that they can be untangled. The same principles of pruning apply to flowering vines as to fruit trees. Prune to guide future growth.

Vines like wisteria produce quantities of large stems which tangle in grotesque knots. As the stems grow and expand, the knots become tighter, and in this way the vine is apt to strangle itself. This may be avoided in part by reducing the number of major stems when the vine is still young, and by training the early growth in such a way as not to form heavy twisted ropes made up of several stems. If the central part of the plant is well branched, the formation of tangles in the outer parts is not so serious. They can be removed without spoiling the vine.

Spraying against insects should be done as part of the general spraying program for the place.

THE MORE IMPORTANT VINES

Actinidia polygama (Silver Vine) is a vigorous and tall-growing vine with handsome foliage which is remarkably free from insect pests and diseases. It produces small white flowers in cymes of three blossoms at the axils of the leaf in June, and the fruit, which ripens in September or October, is a greenish-yellow berry about an inch long. As the plants are sometimes diœcious there occasionally occurs a vine which does not bear fruit.

Support: Trellis or wires on a wall.
Exposure: Sun or shade.
Soil: Rich garden.loam.
Propagation: Seed and layering.
Culture: Occasional thinning out of the mass of stems to improve appearance.

Akebia quinata is a charming, slender vine, with beautiful foliage made up of five-parted leaves. The flowers are deep rosy purple, waxy in texture, opening valve-like into three parts. They are not conspicuous or fragrant but as cut flowers they are delightful. The vine is rather low growing and is excellent on a trellis or for covering a low wall. They need the support of a wall or wires.

Support: Trellis or wires on a wall.
Exposure: Sun or shade.
Soil: Rich garden loam.
Propagation: Seed and layering.
Culture: Occasional thinning out of the mass of stems to improve appearance.

Aristolochia durior (A. sipho) (Dutchman's Pipe) is an old-fashioned favorite, not often seen nowadays. It is a foliage vine, with large heart-shaped leaves thickly overlapping one another. If grown on a series of horizontal slats or wires it will form an opaque wall of green, which is very effective as a barrier or screen. The flowers, though not conspicuous, are very entertaining. They resemble a Dutchman's pipe, and from this comes its common name. It is native to the woodlands of the eastern United States from Pennsylvania and Minnesota southward to Georgia and has long been in cultivation.

Support: Arbor, trellis, or wires. (Excellent to screen a porch.)
Exposure: Sun or partial shade.
Soil: Loam with lime.

Propagation: Layering.
Culture: Water well in dry weather.

Campsis chinensis, the Chinese Trumpet Creeper, has very few aerial rootlets and, therefore, requires the support of a trellis. It may be distinguished from its relative by the fact that it has fewer leaflets, seven or nine. The flowers are larger, bright scarlet and open in August and September. By many, it is considered superior to the native trumpet creeper.

Support: Trellis.
Exposure:
Soil:
Propagation: } Similar to C. radicans.
Culture:

Campsis radicans. The Trumpet Creeper, variously named *Campsis radicans, Tecoma radicans* and *Bignonia radicans,* is a wonderful vine with orange and scarlet tubular blossoms in terminal clusters in July, each blossom 3 or 4 inches long. The rich foliage is very dense and consists of compound leaves of nine or eleven leaflets. It is native to the forests from Pennsylvania to Texas and has been in cultivation since colonial times. Several varieties exist, some with deeper red blossoms, some blooming earlier.

Support: Masonry wall or tree trunk. Clings by rootlets.
Exposure: Sunshine.
Soil: Rich garden loam.
Propagation: Seed, hardwood cuttings.
Culture: Requires no attention.

Celastrus orbiculatus (or C. articulatus), an oriental species, is even more vigorous than the native Bittersweet and produces an abundance of brilliant orange and scarlet fruit. The flowers being in axillary clusters are somewhat hidden in the leaves and the fruit is not really conspicuous until the leaves fall. Conditions and requirements are similar to those of C. scandens.

Celastrus scandens (Waxwork or Climbing Bittersweet), another native of our forests, is an old favorite and still very popular. It is closely related to Euonymus, which it resembles in its fruit formation. This vigorous, high-climbing vine with rich foliage in a great variety of shapes has strong, twisty stems. The orange and red fruit which ripens in October lasts all winter even when brought into the house to decorate the mantel or table. Indeed the fruit is so persistent that bunches of it may be kept over for a second winter season of decorations. The fruit is borne on terminal panicles, which fact makes it conspicuous. Its chief value is as a vine for covering an arbor and casting shade. It will ascend to the top of any deciduous tree, and is at home in the shadiest forest glade. This vine is diœcious, the pistillate and staminate flowers being on separate plants.

Support: Tree, arbor, fence or trellis.
Exposure: Shade or sunshine.
Soil: Loam rich in humus.
Propagation: Seed or by cuttings from fruiting plants.
Culture: Requires no attention.

Clematis paniculata (Sweet Autumn Clematis). The Clematis is probably the most varied of vines. The color range of the flowers runs through white, pink, scarlet, red, yellow, blue and purple. *Clematis paniculata* is undoubtedly the most popular. It grows rapidly, covers arbor or fence with a thick mat of foliage, and blooms with an abundance of white, fragrant flowers in September and October, the flowers being followed by a profusion of feathery, twisted seed pods. So light and airy are the fruits that they create an illusion of a mass of flowers of a different sort, and this fantastic effect lasts for many weeks.

Support: Trellis, fence or arbor.
Exposure: Full sunshine.
Soil: Rich garden loam.
Propagation: Layering.
Culture: Requires no attention.

Clematis montana and **Clematis montana rubens** are old favorites. The blossoms, 3 inches across, are much larger than those of C. paniculata and cover the whole vine as completely. The flowers of C. montana are white and those of C. montana rubens are rose. *C. Jackmani* has large purple flowers of four petals which open from August to October. Within recent years many very beautiful new varieties of large flowering Clematis have been introduced. Among the most outstanding varieties are *Romana,* which bears huge, lavender-blue flower; *La France,* a beautiful shade of deep lavender; *Prince Hendrick,* with magnificent flowers of a soft lavender hue; *W. E. Gladstone,* with flowers of a pale lavender; *C. Henryi,* with large white blooms and *C. lanuginosa candida,* a beautiful pure white.

These new, large-flowered hybrid Clematis are both the joy and despair of many a gardener. They are so gloriously beautiful that one longs to be able to grow them to perfection, yet they are temperamental in the extreme and perfection is hard to obtain. The essentials of success may be outlined as follows:

Support: Some form of support as soon as the vines have been planted.

Exposure: Morning sun, afternoon shade. Roots in shade, foliage in sunshine.

Soil: A cool, moist, yet well-drained soil, deeply prepared and adequately enriched with well-rotted manure, and top-dressed with lime.

Propagation: Layering.

Culture: The root mass should be planted at least 2 or 3 inches below the surface. A good mulch or some form of shade over the roots throughout the season is important.

Pruning: Early in the spring.

Fertilizer and Mulch: A mulch of well-rotted manure applied to the beds every autumn and an occasional top-dressing of lime in the spring.

Euonymus radicans and its varieties *vegetus* and *Carrieri* are vigorous growers. They are the best evergreen vines in the vicinity of Boston and other regions which are too far north for English Ivy. Carrieri is a little less hardy than the other two. *E. radicans coloratus* is still not well known though it was introduced in 1914. This handsome evergreen vine has thinner leaves which turn a bright crimson in the autumn and bronze in the winter. It makes one of the best ground covers for banks because it spreads so readily. Spaced at 6-foot intervals or wider, in a few years the whole bank will be clothed with the vine. In this prostrate position the top of the vine is about 2 feet high. Like other forms of Euonymus, these varieties are subject to oystershell scale and require spraying with miscible oil.

Support: Walls.

Exposure: Sunshine.

Soil: Good garden loam.

Propagation: Seed, stratified until spring. Cuttings in July and August. Layers.

Culture: Spray for scale in February or March with miscible oil.

Hedera helix is the most satisfactory evergreen vine. Known as English Ivy, it is really native throughout central Europe, and has been in cultivation since ancient times. It is doubtfully hardy in Boston where it is best protected by being grown on a wall with a northern exposure where it will receive no winter sunshine. In Philadelphia it attains a luxuriant height, often reaching to a chimney top, although always the yearly growth is slow. Many forms of this Ivy have been discovered, varying largely in leaf form and habit of growth. Variety *baltica* has smaller leaves and is hardier. Variety *conglomerata* has very crowded foliage on dwarf and slow-growing stems. About seventy-five varieties of Hedera helix are obtainable.

Support: Walls, especially old walls. It seems to dislike new mortar.

Exposure: In the northern part of its range, winter shadow is essential to prevent winter-killing of foliage. A north wall is preferred.

Soil: Rich garden soil with humus. Acid reaction.

Propagation: Layering and cuttings.

Lonicera Henryi was introduced from China in 1908. It also is a half-evergreen climber and, like sempervirens, bears its red and yellow or purplish red tubular blossoms in clusters at the end of the branches. The fruit is purple.

Support: Arbor, trellis.

Exposure: Sunshine or partial shade.

Soil: Rich loam.

Propagation: Cuttings, layering.

Culture: Prune in early spring.

Lonicera japonica Halliana (Hall's Climbing Honeysuckle) is another half-evergreen vine, which grows rampantly over the ground and over trellises. It is capable of smothering anything, making a wild tangle where it is undisturbed. The axillary flowers are borne in pairs and are white at first, changing to yellow as they mature, and they give continuous bloom from June to September. This has become naturalized throughout the eastern states, and where it is well established it is difficult to weed out. It is recommended only for rough, wild places.

Lonicera sempervirens (Scarlet Trumpet Honeysuckle) is one of the finest climbing honeysuckles and one of the first to be cultivated. The scarlet flowers have very long tubes and are borne in long clusters of six, from May until August. The leaves, especially those beneath the flower clusters, have a curious way of being united about the stem. It is native from Connecticut to Texas and is half evergreen in its northern range, evergreen farther south. It is subject to attack of insects (plant lice) and requires spraying for protection.

Support: Arbor, trellis.
Exposure: Sunshine or partial shade.
Soil: Rich loam.
Propagation: Cuttings, layering.
Culture: Prune in early spring.

Parthenocissus quinquefolia (Ampelopsis virginiana) (Virginia Creeper) is a well-known native vine, which clambers over stone walls and fences, clinging by rootlets with disk-like ends. This special equipment for climbing, which is really a modified fruit cluster, enables it to ascend masonry walls as readily as does English Ivy. It has been much used since colonial times as a background or as an arbor shelter. It also makes a ground cover. Its compound leaves make a beautiful pattern and turn a brilliant crimson in the autumn. The bluish black fruit ripens in September. It is a very useful foliage plant, grows well in shade or sun, is hardy as far north as Ottawa and is a common native from Maine to Florida.

Support: Trees, trellis, arbor, masonry or field-stone walls or fences.
Exposure: Sunshine, shade or partial shade.
Soil: Loam rich in humus.
Propagation: Layering and cuttings.
Culture: Prune in early spring.

Parthenocissus tricuspidata (Ampelopsis Veitchii) known as Boston Ivy, really comes from Japan and China, and was introduced by Veitch in 1862. It is the strongest and one of the fastest growing of vines, being able to cover the entire façade of a large public building in a few years. Its petioles are long, and thus the leaves project out from the wall, often more than a foot. It fastens itself firmly to brick or stone wall surfaces and is able to bear much weight besides itself.

Support: Masonry wall.
Other Requirements: Similar to P. quinquefolia.

Polygonum Auberti (Chinese Fleece-vine). The Polygonums are rapidly growing vines which bloom abundantly for a long period. The most common species in cultivation is P. Auberti. In general disposition, it resembles Clematis paniculata, blooms earlier and lasts longer. The flowers are cream-white and are borne in long thread-like panicles in vast quantities which completely cover the top of the vine. It is excellent on arbors or for covering fences and buildings or merely as a tangle in a thicket. The one disadvantage of this vine is its prolific production of seedlings which spring up readily. It is related to P. Sieboldi which has become such a difficult weed to eradicate. Polygonum should be planted only where its vigorous growth will not become a threat to other plants.

Support: Trellis, arbor or fence.
Exposure: Sunshine.
Soil: Any soil.
Propagation: Cuttings, layering and seed.
Culture: Cut back too rampant growth.

Pueraria hirsuta (P. Thunbergiana) (Kudsu Vine) is a tall-growing vine. It bears purple, pea-like blossoms followed by pods. The leaves are dark green and the flowers somewhat hidden among them. The bloom is not particularly showy but lasts for a long time, from July to September.

Support: Arbor or trellis; high wall with fasteners to hold the stems or several horizontal wires.

Exposure: Sun or partial shade.
Soil: Rich loam.
Propagation: Seed or cuttings.
Culture: No special care.

Wisteria (sometimes spelled Wistaria). To many people, there is but one Wisteria, Wisteria sinensis, that superbly beautiful vine with great hanging panicles of lavender-purple flowers of delightful fragrance. However, there are six distinct species of Wisteria and several varieties. While *Wisteria sinensis* is beautiful, *W. floribunda* and *W. japonica* are both highly desirable, the one because it is hardier than sinensis and the other for its late season of bloom in June and July. W. frutescens, not at present on the market, is a native American species and is most attractive because of its very small blossoms borne in small panicles not more than 4 inches long. It is suitable for planting beside a colonial cottage. There are white forms of W. sinensis and W. floribunda and a very lovely long-panicled variety of floribunda, W. floribunda macrobotrys (or W. multijuga). This bears purple blossom clusters which hang 3 or 4 feet long from the arbor.

215

Wisteria is a vigorous, high-climbing vine and is remarkably long-lived. The stems are particularly strong and tough. Left alone it will completely cover a house, wrestle the posts loose from the porch, pry the shingles off of the roof and entangle the shutters. It must be planted where its capacity for doing damage is minimized. A metal support is to be preferred to a wooden structure. Though picturesque in a tree, wisteria may eventually kill its host.

Sometimes people are disappointed with wisteria because it never blooms. This condition is easily understood when we consider that it is a very long-lived vine and for this reason requires fifteen years or so to mature. However, there are strains which mature at a younger age. The most satisfactory practice is to secure "grafted stock," scions from blooming plants grafted upon roots. These grafted vines are apt to bloom the first or second year. Although wisteria is a vigorous grower it sometimes takes several years to establish itself after being transplanted.

Support: The strongest kind of beams in arbor or trellis or strong metal frame. Never let it climb over a roof or among shutters.

Exposure: Sunshine on foliage, shadow on roots.

Soil: Porous garden loam, rich in manure and humus.

Propagation: Grafts on wisteria roots for early bloom. Layering. Seeds for long-postponed results.

Culture: Just as we prune fruit trees for better production, pruning a vine will often result in greater quantity of bloom. Wisteria which so easily outgrows its situation and has great vitality, may be severely pruned to induce better bloom and to keep it within bounds. Vines which have failed to bloom should be pruned in summer, removing new growth to about six buds. Annual pruning in the dormant season may be more severe, leaving only two buds. Remove all runners which travel along the ground in search of other supports. Cut off and disentangle the interfering branches, cutting back to a main stem.

Water liberally, especially in the dry seasons and during blooming period.

ANNUAL VINES

Because of their rapid growth and their flowering capacities annual vines are very useful in the garden and about the house. To cover the bareness of a new house, annual vines on the porch lattice are very welcome. They can be planted along with the more permanent woody vines which in a few years will take their places on fence or arbor.

Among the best annual vines are:

Cobæa scandens (Cup-and-saucer vine). Purple or white in July.

Cucurbita ovifera (Ornamental Gourd). Fruit in great variety of shape and marking.

Dolichos Lablab (Hyacinth-bean). Reddish violet flowers in racemes.

Ipomœa purpurea (Convolvulus) (Morning Glory). Lavender blue tubular flowers; variety *tricolor*, "Heavenly blue," has large clear blue blossoms.

Ipomœa Bona-Nox (Moon flower). White flowers opening in the evening. Soak the hard seeds of the Ipomœas in warm water for two hours or notch them slightly on the side to hasten germination.

Phaseolus coccineus (Scarlet runner). Rapid climber.

Tropæolum majus (Nasturtium). Variety of bright colors all summer.

The annual vines are of easy culture; they may be sown out of doors in any good garden loam as soon as danger of frost is past and may be trained on any convenient type of support or trellis.

VINES FOR SOUTHERN GARDENS

Allamanda Hendersoni

Rosa Banksiæ (Banksian Rose)

Campsis radicans

Rosa lævigata (Cherokee Rose)

Clematis texensis

Jasminum nudiflorum

Lonicera sempervirens

TABULAR LIST OF PERENNIAL VINES

KEY:
I.—Inconspicuous flowers.
The climbing habit is indicated by: A.—Aerial roots, clinging to support. T.—Coiling tendrils. S.—Twining stems.

Scientific Name	Common Name	Height in Feet	Zone of Hardiness*	Color	Bloom Season	Climbing Habit	Remarks and Best Type of Support
Actinidia arguta	Actinidia	50	V	White	June	S	Fruit green-yellow—Sept.
A. polygama	Silver Vine	15	VI	White	June	S	Fruit yellow in Sept.
Akebia quinata		30	V	Purplish-brown	May	S	Clambers over walls
Allamanda Hendersoni		Clambering	IX	Yellow	Feb.–Nov.	S	For Southern gardens and greenhouse
Ampelopsis aconitifolia		30	V	Greenish	August	T	Arbor or fence
A. heterophylla		30	V or VI	Greenish	July–Aug.	T	Arbor or fence; fruit bright red
Aristolochia durior	Dutchman's Pipe	30	V	Yellow-green		S	Trellis or wires
Campsis radicans (Tecoma r.) (Bignonia r.)	Trumpet Creeper	30	V	Orange and scarlet	July–Sept.	A	Walls or tree trunks (clings firmly)
C. chinensis	Chinese Trumpet Creeper	30	VI or VII	Scarlet	Aug.–Sept.	S	Needs trellis support
Celastrus orbiculatus	Oriental Bittersweet	36	V	Greenish-white	June	S	Fruit orange-yellow, seed scarlet
C. scandens	American Bittersweet	20	IV	White	June	S	Fruit, yellow, vermillion seeds, Oct. (Fences or trees)
Clematis Henryi		6	VI	White	May–June	T	Flowers 5" across
C. Jackmani		10	V or VI	Purple	July–Oct.	T	Flowers 5" or 6" across
C. lanuginosa		6	VI	White to pale lilac	July–Sept.	T	Flowers 4" across
C. montana		25	VI	White	July	T	Flowers 3" across
C. montana rubens		25	VI	Pink	May–June	T	
C. paniculata	Virgin's Bower	25	V	White	Aug.–Oct.	T	Large clusters of small flowers
C. texensis	Scarlet Clematis	6	VII	Scarlet	July–Sept.	T	For southern gardens
Euonymus radicans	Spindle Vine	25	V	Green-white	June	A	Evergreen

Botanical name	Common name	Ht.	Mo.	Color	Season	H.*	Remarks
Ficus repens (F. pumila)	Climbing Fig	Creeping	VIII			A	For the South
Hedera helix	English Ivy	80	VI (V)	Green	June	A	Masonry wall
Hydrangea petiolaris	Climbing Hydrangea	75	V	White	June–July	A	Clings firmly to walls
Lonicera japonica Halliana	Hall's Honeysuckle	30	V	White	June–Sept.	S	Becomes dominant weed
L. Henryi		20	V	Red	June–Aug.	S	Trellis. Half evergreen
L. sempervirens	Trumpet Honeysuckle	30	V	Orange and scarlet	May–August	S	Trellis. Very showy flowers. (Evergreen)
Parthenocissus quinquefolia	Virginia creeper	50		I.		A & S	Fruit blue, wall or arbor
P. tricuspidata	Boston Ivy	100		I.		A	Masonry walls
Polygonum Auberti	Chinese Fleece-vine	20	VII	White	July–Sept.	S	Trellis and arbor
Pueraria Thunbergiana	Kudzu Bean	60	VI	Violet-purple	July–Aug.	S	Wires. In North, perennial. In South, a woody vine
Rosa Banksiae	Banksia Rose	20	VII	White or yellow	June–Aug.	S	For the South
R. laevigata	Cherokee Rose	15		White		S	For the South
Schizophragma hydrangeoides	Climbing Hydrangea	30	VII	White	July	A	Good in shade
Vitis aestivalis	Summer Grape	Strong		I.		T	Fruit not edible
V. cordifolia	Frost Grape	Vigorous		I.		T	Fruit edible after frost
Wisteria floribunda	Japanese Wisteria	25	VI	Violet-blue	June	S	Basal flowers open first
W. frutescens	American Wisteria	40	VI	Lilac-purple	June	S	Flower clusters small
W. sinensis	Chinese Wisteria	25	VI	Violet-blue	June	S	All flowers open at once

* *See Zone Map of Hardiness on inside of front and back covers.*

VII

Trees

Ever since the dawn of civilization the forest and its products have been natural resources affecting the economics of human life, and man has come to understand the importance of trees in relation to his welfare and happiness. Like so many fundamental truths, we are aware of it long before we can ascribe reasons for it. Our love of trees is one of these instinctive affections which has its origin in racial history, and it finds expression in our urge to plant and care for them. The benefits, both physical and æsthetic, derived from trees are so many and so obvious that homes in the country and in the suburbs are invariably sheltered by trees. In the great arid regions of the Southwest where summer suns and desert sands combine to develop terrific heat every ranch homestead and watering place for cattle has a few Cottonwood trees for shade.

USES AND USEFULNESS

Trees may be grown for many purposes. They may be grown for the sheer beauty of their form, foliage or flowers. They may be grown to provide shelter from the wind or to provide shade; they may be grown for the production of fruits, nuts, timber, sugar, turpentine or other products which may be derived from the forests. And in addition to these many uses trees fulfill other important functions. There are many degrees of usefulness among trees. Some must be considered as weeds or pests, but the good far outnumber the unworthy. We can encourage one group and diminish the other, thus bringing about a gradual change toward a better environment.

IMPORTANCE OF FORESTS

It is becoming increasingly evident that the presence of forests, or their absence, is an important factor in determining

Photograph by Walter Beebe Wilder

Ancient Trees

climate. In a country well furnished with forests the climate is more even, and the seasonal changes more gradual than in a comparatively treeless region. It is now well recognized that there is a direct connection between the severity of floods in the Ohio Valley and the condition of the mountainsides of the Alleghenies. The absorbing power of a natural forest floor is so great that there is practically no runoff of surface water, whereas in cornfields and denuded hillsides the runoff during a heavy rain is 80 per cent or more. The reduction of forest area by the cutting of timber has permitted the rapid funnelling of rain water and melting snow into the valleys, and the consequent increase in the frequency and severity of floods. This water, moving over the land, carries with it the surface soil, the only soil which has any nourishment for plant growth. Thus the forest is not merely a source of lumber but an equalizer of water-flow, a preventer of floods and a conserver of soil fertility.

As civilization and its demands for forest products spread over southern Europe, one country after another has used up its forests. Every country in which civilization has flourished for many centuries has become deforested in the process, and the exhaustion of the soil has been one of the factors in the cycle of changing fortunes of those nations. China, Mesopotamia, Palestine, Greece, Italy, and Spain, have all experienced this change toward a drier climate, and a less productive soil.

It is believed that Columbus was sent westward not so much to discover new sources of gold, as to find a country abounding in forest land. Probably the reason that the Spaniards began colonizing the new world a hundred years before the English did, was that their country had become at an earlier date unable to support the people, and this was due in part to the loss of the Spanish forests.

NATIVE TREES

In a landscape composition the trees native to a region are usually to be preferred to exotic trees. In New England and the northern states, the Elm, Sugar Maple, White Oak, and White Pine are typical trees dominant in the landscape, and their use in plantings here is appropriate and satisfying. On the other hand, on the coastal plains where Spruce trees are not native, Norway Spruces and Blue Spruces will always look artificial and out of place.

FOREIGN TREES

This does not mean that no foreign trees should be used. In formal designs there is no such restriction. But if a naturalistic scene is desired, then the trees selected should be either native or kinds the appearance of which has much in common with the native trees. For instance, the Scholar-Tree, Sophora japonica, though it comes from the Orient, blends agreeably with the foliage of native deciduous trees, and will be pleasing as a specimen flowering tree or as a member of a grove. But Sciadopitys verticillata, the Umbrella-Pine, another oriental, being unlike anything we have in this country, would seem an intrusion if placed in a naturalistic setting.

TREES IN A LANDSCAPE DESIGN

As an element in landscape composition, trees are very important and they are used for various purposes in design. Groups of them form the masses in the design as contrasted with the open area, as for example, the bosques and tapis-verts of France. Many trees together make a background for the structure and for the more intimate details of the design. Individual trees may be accents in the design or incidental notes of the picturesque. By their shapes trees express line as well as mass in the composition. Thus the famous group of Cypresses at Villa Falconieri gives dominant vertical line to the composition. The wind-swept Monterey Cypresses of California make horizontal lines against the sky and sea.

Many trees produce flowers in profusion, thus giving the garden picture greater scale and variety and more richness of color. Many trees are adorned with ornamental fruit, and with some the foliage turns a glorious color in autumn. Still others have picturesque branching forms which are particularly interesting in winter.

Trees, especially ornamental trees, should be considered as

a long-time, though continuous, crop. The mature trees about the house will eventually become aged and subject to decay, and home-owners with forethought will plant young trees to take their place, long before the old trees go. In this way the general form of the composition and the essential shade will be maintained, although individual members of the group may change. Seedling trees come up constantly in places not requiring them. If they are not removed while young, they may spoil the appearance of the hedge or shrub border or rob the soil in the flower bed.

DISTANCE APART

In planting new trees, their eventual proportions should be considered. Nothing is more futile than the planting of many trees on a small place. Within a few years, the inevitable crowding will have an unfavorable effect upon the beauty of the individual trees and upon the general arrangements. It is sometimes hard to cut down trees we enjoy, and the crowding is allowed to continue. It is an advantage to plant woodland trees closely because young trees benefit by mutual protection. A young forest thus started may be thinned out with an axe later. But there is no justification for crowding specimen lawn trees.

PLANTING MATURE AND YOUNG TREES

Sometimes it is a great advantage to transplant mature trees and to place them where they are most needed. Thus is avoided many years of waiting for the trees to develop, but in most cases, especially when economy of investment must be considered, smaller trees are better. On the other hand, it is a great mistake for an owner to postpone planting trees for several years. The money invested in small trees the first year of his possession of a new home will enhance its value more certainly than it could were it put to any other use. The trees themselves will increase in value. A twenty-five-dollar tree may be worth fifty dollars after six years of growing.

SELECTION OF TREES

In selecting trees for a place, there are many points which should be considered. Not merely the size of the tree when mature, but its hardiness in the climate, its resistance to wind, its adaptability to soil conditions, its habits and rapidity of growth, its production of flowers and fruit, its undesirable habits such as shedding bark or poisonous fruit—these points should all be taken into account.

From a list of fairly dependable trees a great variety may be selected which together will produce bloom over a period from April to August, then a succession of ornamental fruit and rich autumn coloration. There are trees which are suitable for unusual conditions, such as wet soil, dry gravelly soil, city atmosphere, wind, heat, and drought, and there are trees which for one reason or another are not dependable or satisfactory.

PREPARATION OF SOIL FOR PLANTING

Trees growing in the woods have a soil rich in humus, porous but moist, all the conditions most favorable to growth. Trees growing in lawn or field have a soil usually less rich in humus, less porous and more full of grass roots. Preparing the soil before trees are transplanted is one of the essentials to success. Rich soil stimulates the vigor of trees, thereby equipping them with abundant vitality that will make them less subject to disease and less vulnerable to attack by insects. Undernourished trees start with a handicap in the battle for existence. The proper preparation of soil for tree planting will include plowing and harrowing to eliminate turf roots, or deep hand-digging if on a small scale; addition of humus or peat moss to lighten the soil and make it porous but moisture-conserving; adding sand to a soil that is too heavy with clay; and breaking up the clay sub-soil with deep plowing. Well-rotted manure may be added to improve the soil texture and increase the available nourishment.

In preparing soil for the planting of large deciduous trees, the top-soil should be removed, sub-soil excavated to a depth of 18 inches or 2 feet below the final grade, and the hole filled with additional top-soil. The shock of transplanting is more severe with a mature tree than with a young tree and the added depth of rich soil will be a wonderful help in re-establishing the root system. The planting bed should be round and 3 feet wider than the diameter of the ball of earth that will come with the roots. If possible, this preparation should be done six months or a year in advance of planting to allow the soil to settle.

In preparing the soil for tree planting, if rock is encountered at a depth too shallow to permit the proper soil preparation, one of three alternative procedures must be chosen. In some situations, the grade of the ground may be raised by filling in top-soil over a wide area to a depth that will cover the rock by 18 inches of earth. In other cases, the position of the tree may be changed, without seriously affecting the pictorial composition, to a place where the underlying rock is deeper. But if a tree must be planted at a certain position where rock is near the surface, the rock will have to be removed. Blasting a hole in the rock, removing the pieces and filling the place with soil is the best method. But if blasting cannot be performed, the rock may be broken by an old method. On a cold day, build a wood fire on the rock, heating it. Rake away the ashes and pour water on the rock. The rapid change of temperature will crack the rock and the pieces can be pried up with a crowbar and wedge.

PREPARATION OF TREES FOR TRANSPLANTING

Wax Sprays. After many experiments, beginning in 1932, Doctor E. J. Miller and his colleagues at the Michigan State Experiment Station have devised an emulsified wax capable of being dissolved in water. It can be sprayed over the entire tree so that not only the trunk but the whole tree is covered with a thin film of wax which is flexible, colorless and lasting. While it retards evaporation it does not completely arrest transpiration. It can be applied to large trees with a power sprayer or to small trees and bushes by a hand spray. So satisfactory are the results that when this method is used on deciduous stock in a dormant state, pruning is not always necessary; and it makes a better bark protection than wrapping the trunk with burlap. (See Moisture Requirements.) It should be sprayed during a temperature of 45 degrees F. or warmer. For deciduous stock, one spraying is usually enough. In transplanting evergreen trees, the spraying of wax emulsion before digging and after setting is an enormous help in retarding evaporation and, in the case of the more rapidly growing evergreens such as Norway spruce, it may obviate the necessity of lifting the tree with ball and burlap, the method heretofore considered essential in handling evergreens.

While the transplanting of deciduous trees in full leaf is not recommended, if such a procedure is necessary it may be done with a high percentage of success if the whole plant is sprayed with wax to cover both surfaces of the leaves. In July, 1934, when temperatures ranged around 90 and 95 degrees, a nursery transplanted 22 Moline elms, 11 of which were sprayed with wax and 11 were untreated. Of the 11 wax-sprayed trees, only one died, while of the 11 trees untreated, only one survived the transplanting.

If a tree has been transplanted from the woods to a sunny position it is likely to suffer somewhat from sun scorch and too rapid evaporation. This can be obviated by the use of wax emulsion spray.

Wax sprays have been used for the preservation of fruits and vegetables for the market or to prolong their period of storage, to retard the wilting of cut flowers, to protect annual and perennial plants from wilting after transplanting, to protect cuttings and grafts from evaporation, and for similar purposes in many other horticultural processes. The use of spray to coat whole trees with a protective film is quite new, and it is likely that if this method is developed and becomes more generally practised, it will make radical changes in planting programs, prolonging the planting season into the late spring and commencing it earlier in the autumn, reducing the severity of pruning, or eliminating it altogether.

Defoliation. Another method of preparing trees for transplanting is called defoliation. This consists of cutting with shears (not pulling off from the twigs) all of the leaves of the tree, or all but one-fourth of the leaves. This method is used particularly on the hollies, both American and English, when they are being transplanted in northern regions. New leaves will grow out in due time and meanwhile the tree will not be losing moisture. Nurserymen report that they have never lost a holly from transplanting if it has been defoliated.

METHODS OF TRANSPLANTING

(A) *Bare Root Transplanting*. Bare root transplanting, the method used in moving most deciduous shrubs and young deciduous trees from the nursery to their permanent location, depends for success on taking up a large proportion of the root system, placing it in the ground again as soon as possible, and removing enough of the top (branches and foliage) to compensate for the temporary reduction of activity in the roots. This operation is best accomplished in early spring when the twigs are bare or in the autumn when the plant is losing its leaves.

In digging up a tree, the plantsman begins by digging into the ground in a circle at the outer ends of the roots, and works in toward the trunk, spading and forking the earth from the roots. Thus, practically all the important main roots and a large portion of the fibrous roots remain intact. What earth clings to the roots is carried with them, and is a great benefit to the plant while it is reestablishing itself in the new place. These little particles of soil held by the fine roots keep the contact and hence capillary action uninterrupted during transportation and they continue to function unless they become very dry while out of the ground.

The time which elapses between digging in the nursery and planting in the new position should be reduced to a minimum. The roots should never be exposed to the sun or wind during this interval. If a group of plants must be kept waiting for several hours, as is usual on a large planting job, they should at least be in the shade of a tree or building and their roots

should be covered with burlap. A better precaution against
drying of the roots is to heel the trees in at once in a convenient
place. Then if planting work is interrupted or delayed, the
trees can wait until all is ready. To heel in trees·or shrubs, dig
a trench large enough to accommodate the roots, throwing the
soil to one side. Place the roots of the plants in the trench in
such a way that the stems are inclined at an angle of 45 degrees
or lower, and cover the roots with the loose soil. If the roots

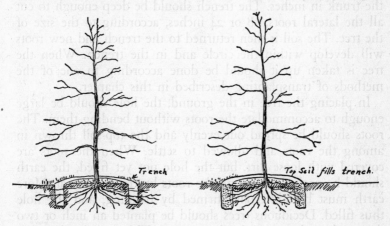

The Effect of Root Pruning is to Concentrate the Roots in the Ball

are very dry when the plants are received, they should be
soaked in a barrel of water for a half hour before being heeled
in. And the soil covering the roots should be kept wet. In
such a situation trees and shrubs may be kept safely for several
weeks.

When the trees are dug in the nursery, they are bundled,
labelled, and gathered for shipment. The risk of injury from
chafing of the bark on the side of the truck may be minimized
by the placing of a wad of burlap bagging where the trunk
rests on the brim. An injury to the bark at this time is apt to
cause a lowering of vitality in the plant and consequent failure.

Transplanting trees from the woods or from your own
grounds entails more risk than transplanting from the nursery,

because in the nursery each tree has been transplanted or root-pruned once or twice to induce the growth of fibrous roots in a concentrated mass. The roots of forest-grown seedlings are rangy and it is difficult to dig them up and make them stay together. If a tree is to be transplanted from the woods it should be prepared for the journey by pruning its roots a year in advance. This is done by digging a trench around the tree at a distance from the trunk equal in feet to the diameter of the trunk in inches. The trench should be deep enough to cut all the lateral roots, 18 or 24 inches, according to the size of the tree. The soil is then returned to the trench and new roots will develop within the circle and in the trench. When the tree is taken up it should be done according to one of the methods of transplanting described in this chapter.

In placing the tree in the ground, the hole should be large enough to accommodate the roots without bending them. The roots should be spread out evenly and the top-soil thrown in among the roots and allowed to settle. When the roots are covered with loose dirt, but the hole not yet filled, the earth should be packed in among the roots by treading on it. More earth must be added and firmed by treading, and the hole thus filled. Deciduous trees should be planted an inch or two deeper than they were in the nursery. This permits the roots to be better protected from drying, pending the establishment of the plant. Evergreens should be planted at the same level, never deeper than their former position. Deep planting of evergreens may result in depriving the roots of adequate air in the soil.

The top of the tree should be cut back quite severely, to equalize the rate of evaporation with the ability of the reduced root system to supply water. This is particularly true of oaks and other slow-growing trees. The top should be pruned the same day that the tree is planted. Postponement of this part of the work permits the plant to lose moisture and vitality. When the tree is pruned later, the pruning will need to be even more severe and the results will not be so satisfactory. The amount of pruning required will depend on the kind of tree, and on the season, *early* spring planting needing less pruning than later planting. (See page 247 for pruning.)

The ground about the newly planted tree should be shaped like a saucer to receive a generous supply of water the first day and on succeeding days. The function of the water is not so much at first to give the plant the extra water which it needs but to firm the soil about its feeding roots and to drive out the air pockets which inevitably remain in newly turned soil. The roots can take up only so much water, no matter how much is put on the soil, but the air in the soil can dry out the little roots before they become established. Water should be frequently given after planting and for the remainder of the growing season. But watering should be intermittent with intervals of several days between for drying and aëration of the soil.

Trees which are 12 feet or more high should be held in place by three or five guy wires fastened to stakes radiating from the trunk. The upper end of the wire should be looped through a piece of old garden hose and passed around a lower crotch. The wires are tightened by twisting two strands about a stick. Loose guy wires are of no use at all, because they will not prevent the tree trunk from shaking and the roots from being loosened in the soil.

Use of Peat Moss. In a series of recent experiments conducted at the New York State Agricultural Experiment Station, the value of peat moss in planting trees has been proven. Two-year-old apple trees were planted in clay loam. In one row a pail of damp granulated peat moss was mixed with the soil used to fill each tree hole in planting. In the other row the trees were planted as usual with no peat moss. At the end of the growing season, during which there was adequate rainfall, the peat-treated trees had made an average terminal growth of 82 inches as compared with 14 inches for the other trees. This superiority of the trees planted with peat moss continued during the three succeeding seasons as shown by larger top growth, larger trunk diameter, and greater root development. At the end of this time the roots of the peat-treated trees were found to be extended far beyond the limits of the peat in the soil, while the roots of the untreated trees were meager and restricted. The following year a similar test was started using dry peat moss unmixed with soil spread in the hole before planting. During this season a continued drought made growing conditions far from ideal and in this case the peat-treated trees showed little superiority over the untreated trees. Further tests showed the superiority of damp peat moss mixed with soil over the dry peat moss unmixed.

The conclusion reached from these trials is that in a clay loam the peat moss improves aëration in the soil and gives it a more constant water-holding capacity.

In a wet season aëration in the clay loam soil is decidedly diminished, and it is assumed that the presence of peat in the soil is a means of adequate circulation of oxygen to the roots. This may be the principal function of the peat moss in the soil. Certain it is that great benefits to root development and top-growth result from its use, and that these benefits are evident year after year.

(B) *Transplanting with a Ball of Earth.* Most evergreen trees, some deciduous trees and some large shrubs require a more painstaking method of transplanting. The slowness of growth of the evergreens prevents them from becoming established after transplanting with bare roots. For this class of trees and for a few species of shrubs transplanting is done with a ball of earth, wrapped tightly about with burlap. The roots of such plants as Box and Hemlock form a dense mass in the soil and it is easy to keep the earth together with burlap and hemp cord, but in moving plants with more loosely arranged roots, such as many of the Junipers, it is more difficult to prevent the ball from cracking. A broken ball or crumbling earth is apt to mean a dead tree. The ground must be in good condition before the trees are dug. If it is too dry the earth will crack away from the roots in balling or while moving. This condition may be remedied by a thorough watering several days before transplanting. If it is too wet, the earth will cling and cannot be worked.

The method used by nurserymen in transplanting evergreens which are to be handled in this way is to dig a trench around the specimen at a distance outside the ends of the fibrous roots

and as deep as the roots may penetrate. When carefully done
the side of the trench is beyond the root ends and the earth

Transplanting a Large Elm

is then gradually cut away until the roots are encountered.
In digging deciduous trees, the outer roots are cut off and the
ball made smaller. The trench is usually wide enough for a

man to work in, and this space enables him to get his pick and spade well under the rim of the ball. By digging a gallery under and all around the rim, he carves out the undersurface of the ball, leaving it perched on a pedestal in the center. An

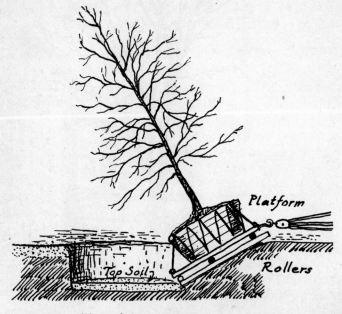

Transplanting a Tree with a Ball

1. The tree is lowered into the hole on skids, by block and tackle

incline is dug at one side to the floor of the hole up which the ball is to be dragged. Burlap bagging is wrapped about the sides and bottom of the ball and laced with hemp twine very tightly to the ball. When all is in readiness to take the tree out of the ground, a chain is passed around the ball, the end of the chain is hooked on to one of its links at a point about one-third or one-fourth of the circumference from the direction of pull. In other words the pulling chains start to work tangent to the edge of the ball. The pull twists the ball

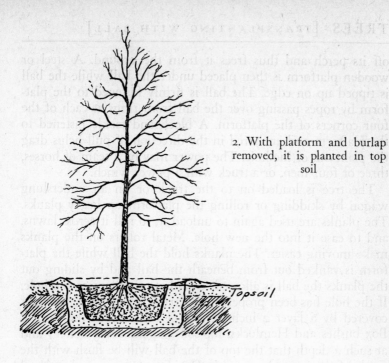

2. With platform and burlap removed, it is planted in top soil

Topsoil

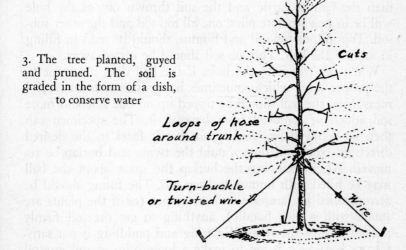

3. The tree planted, guyed and pruned. The soil is graded in the form of a dish, to conserve water

Cuts

Loops of hose around trunk

Turn-buckle or twisted wire

Wire

off its perch and thus frees it from the ground. A steel or wooden platform is then placed under the ball while the ball is tipped up on edge. The ball is firmly fastened to the platform by ropes passing over the ball from rings at each of the four corners of the platform. A block and tackle fastened to the platform and anchored in the direction of pull helps drag the plant out of the hole. The power may be a team of horses, three or four men, or a truck with a power winch.

The tree is loaded on to the truck or on an underslung wagon by skidding or rolling the platform up heavy planks. The planks are used again to unload it, to roll it across lawns, and to ease it into the new hole. Metal rollers on the planks make moving easier. The planks hold the ball while the platform is yanked out from beneath the ball and by sliding out the planks the ball is allowed to settle to the floor of the hole. If the hole has been properly prepared it will have a flat floor covered by a layer 2 inches thick of top-soil (in the case of Box bushes and Hemlocks, top-soil and humus is better) and at such a depth that the top of the ball will be flush with the grade of the ground around it. Deciduous trees may be placed 2 inches lower. The hole will be about 2 feet wider in diameter than the ball of earth, and the soil thrown out of the hole will be in two separate piles, one all top-soil and the other sub-soil. Top-soil, or top-soil and humus, should be used in filling in around the ball. The sub-soil should be carted away.

When the tree is in the hole, if the ball does not come to the proper level, which sometimes happens in spite of careful measuring, the ball should be tipped up on one side and more soil added or removed from beneath it. The specimen can then be revolved by winding so that it faces in the desired direction. Not until then should the twine and burlap be removed. After removing the burlap the space about the ball may be filled with humus and top-soil. The filling should be accompanied by tamping with a tamper (or if the plants are small, with a pick handle), anything to get the soil firmly packed against the roots. Watering and puddling is not satisfactory because it is apt to make a loose soup of soil around the tree in which the tree and its ball may be moved and tipped over by the wind. Water may be applied later after the hole is almost filled with firm soil, but not during the filling. If the outer surface of the ball has become dry and caked during transportation then this condition should be remedied by soaking the ball in water before the earth is filled in. The plantsman must in this case decide between two risks, that of having unstable soil about the ball saturated with water, or of permitting the tree roots to suffer from being encased in a hard crust of dry clay soil.

After placing the ball in the hole the burlap is carefully removed. If the earth has not held well and the ball is about to crack, one is tempted to avoid the broken ball by not removing the bagging, cutting away the burlap at the base and leaving a circle of burlap beneath the ball, to rot during the two or three succeeding years. If this expedient is adopted the lateral roots will not be affected and the down-growing roots will eventually find their way through the bagging. This practice is not favored by plantsmen because of the interference with root growth. Recent experiments show that the rotting bag forms a solvent that is poisonous to the plant.

Placing top-soil about the ball must be done in such a way as to assure firmness of the plant in the ground and the exclusion of air pockets in the soil. A layer of soil should be thrown in and trodden and tamped until it is firm. Then another layer should be added and made compact, the process repeated until the hole is filled. If the soil is all tossed in to fill the hole and then tamped, the lower soil cannot be firmly packed and there will be too much air remaining in the soil.

After planting is finished, the precautions and technique described for planting with bare roots should be employed. Evergreen trees and broad-leaved evergreen shrubs will benefit by a permanent mulch of peat moss or a carpet of rotting leaves to retain moisture and retard evaporation from the soil.

TREES WHICH SHOULD BE TRANSPLANTED WITH BALL OF EARTH

Any tree with a trunk larger than 6 inches in diameter should be transplanted with ball and burlap. Smaller sizes of the following trees also should be transplanted by this method.

Japanese Maples	Birch
Hickories	Magnolia
Persimmon	Sourwood
Beech	Sassafras
Sour gum	Sugar Maple
Walnut	Dogwood
Tulip tree	Oaks (nearly all)
Sweet gum	Evergreens (nearly all)

Trees which should be moved only when they are very young, three or four years old, are Tulip tree and Sour gum. The Sour gum especially is difficult to re-establish after transplanting.

TRANSPLANTING VERY LARGE TREES

Transplanting large mature trees is a job to be undertaken only by experienced men with adequate equipment. The same precautions must be taken with large trees as with shrubs. The roots must be kept moist during the time when they are out of the ground, and they must be carefully placed and firmly packed about with soil. The amount of leafage (evaporation surface) must be reduced in proportion to the loss of feeding roots. The task is made more difficult by the great weight of soil that must be moved with the roots, and by the longer period of time that the tree is out of the ground, but the principles remain the same. The size of the ball of earth required for proper transplanting is proportionate to the tree. It is out of the question to take all the roots of a large deciduous tree, but for most species the diameter of the ball in feet should at least equal the diameter of the trunk in inches.

Transplanting is a shock to the tree but a shock that may be reduced by preparing the tree for its removal. A year in advance of the transplanting, the circle of the ball is marked out and a trench is dug to a depth of two feet, cutting through the existing roots. The trench is then filled entirely with top-soil. During the year, the tree will form a dense mat of fibrous roots in the top-soil, which will be ready to grow out into a new layer of top-soil in the new location. When the tree is lifted, the new fibrous roots will hold the soil firmly together. The transplanting may be done in early autumn or in spring. It has also been found possible and satisfactory to transplant trees in winter with the ground frozen solid. This is best done in a series of operations beginning the previous year by preparing the ball as described. In the late autumn the trench is dug and the tree ball twisted off its ground base. There it is left with the open trench around it, until the ground is frozen. During the winter the tree can be bound up with burlaps and cord, tilted up and placed on a platform and removed to the new position, put into the hole and left there still unplanted until spring weather thaws the ground. Then the space about the tree is filled with good top-soil.

In handling trees of large size, all the sliding, lifting, rolling on rollers, and skidding of the ball down into the hole should be done without sudden jostling or bumping. A block and tackle anchored to a "dead-man" will transmit the power of the winch and motor or the pull of a gang of men to a slow steady motion. The descent into the hole by an inclined plane is the part which is most apt to bring disaster. Unless the power is strong enough to hold it back, the tree ball may roll with great force down the sloping planks and strike the earth side of the excavation, thus cracking the ball. If the platform is on rollers, it may be gently eased down into the hole by slacking up slowly on the rope of the block and tackle.

TRANSPLANTING SEASONS

The best times for transplanting trees, shrubs and vines are early spring and early autumn. Because of severe winters in Canada, northern New England, Michigan, Wisconsin and west of Omaha, spring planting is preferred. The spring planting season cannot be fixed by calendar. It begins as soon as the ground is dry enough to work, and continues until the buds of deciduous trees have sent forth their young leaves to ½ or 1 inch long. Thus, oaks, which leaf out late, may be transplanted later than horse chestnuts. The evergreen planting season continues longer. The autumn season begins in late August for evergreens, and with the turning color of the leaves for deciduous plants, and continues until freezing weather, except for evergreen trees and broad-leaved evergreens which should not be moved after the middle of October. Many evergreen trees and most deciduous trees may be transplanted with a frozen ball of earth during the winter as described for transplanting large trees.

Some trees can be transplanted safely only at one season; notably magnolias, which should be moved only in very early spring. The magnolia roots are very easily broken, and since loss of root activity is to be expected after transplanting it is wise to move them when root growth is most active, before flowering in spring. Other trees for which early spring planting is preferred to autumn planting are flowering dogwood (Cornus florida), canoe birch (Betula papyrifera), sweet gum (Liquidambar Styraciflua), tupelo (Nyssa sylvatica), black walnut (Juglans nigra), bald cypress (Taxodium distichum), tulip tree (Liriodendron tulipifera).

GRADING AROUND A TREE

If the grades about a tree are to be altered by filling soil over the original ground level, then special precautions should be taken to prevent the smothering of the roots. A fill of 4 inches of good top-soil over the roots of deciduous trees will do no damage, although it might affect evergreens unfavorably. A fill of a foot or more would be very harmful. The quantity of air and also of water in the soil diminishes in accordance with the depth. Thus, when roots growing at a depth of 18 inches are covered so that they are 36 inches from the surface, they are deprived of their normal oxygen and water rations. To overcome this handicap it is advisable to construct some device for maintaining a contact between the air and the root-containing soil. It is important to do this before the fill is made. First, the original soil is loosened by forking. Then a dry stone wall is built up around the tree, if possible at a distance of several feet from the base of the trunk and to the level of the

Photograph by Richard Averill Smith

Entrance Drive with Dogwood Trees in Bloom

new grade. Several 4-inch agricultural tile drains are laid in lines radiating from the inner surface of this wall. Over the whole area is spread a course of crushed slag, or coarse crushed stone, or large gravel. This material is put on to a depth of 6 inches or to within 12 or 15 inches of the final grades. Above this is spread a layer of straw or preferably manure to prevent the soil above from sifting down through the stones or slag. Finally a layer of top-soil is spread to a depth of 6 or 8 inches. This construction should cover the whole area of tree roots. The tile pipes may be used to conduct water to the roots and may be filled by a hose.

If soil has been washed away from the roots of large trees, as sometimes happens on steep slopes, or if the ground is worn down by passing feet, the damage to the trees may eventually be fatal. Restoration of the natural grade by filling a layer of top-soil to cover the roots and establishing a turf or a ground cover crop to retain the soil is the only permanent remedy.

CARE OF TREES AFTER TRANSPLANTING

Transplanting is a shock to a plant. It necessarily interrupts or somewhat retards the life processes. The diminished vitality of the tree renders it more open to attack by insects and diseases, and less able to withstand the effects of unusual weather conditions, which may ensue.

Moisture Requirements. The greatest danger during transplanting and the subsequent weeks is from desiccation, or excessive loss of moisture through natural transpiration of foliage while the disturbed roots are unable to replace water and thus maintain a normal moisture content in the tissues. The function of pruning is to diminish the area of foliage and hence reduce the rate of evaporation.

Watering the tree at intervals is a very important part of after-care. The soil should be thoroughly soaked once a week if rain is insufficient, because the soil should never be allowed to become really dry. On the other hand, in a soil kept constantly saturated, the water will exclude the air from the roots. Proper watering will enable the roots to take up the soil-moisture rapidly and will encourage root growth. Evaporation through the bark is another outlet of plant moisture. A method long in use by plantsmen to retard this evaporation during the first year after transplanting is to wrap the trunk and larger branches with burlap. It is effective, especially against winter drying, but has the disadvantage of harboring insects, and in some positions the objection of unsightliness.

Cultivation and Mulch. To keep the soil about newly planted trees in condition and to eliminate the competition of grass roots, the soil may be cultivated, and a mulch of well-rotted manure, straw, leaves, or peat moss may be spread to a depth of 2 or 3 inches over the area occupied by the roots.

After spring planting the mulch may remain on the ground for two or three months and then should be worked into the ground by shallow spading, taking care not to reach the tree roots. After autumn planting the mulch should remain on the surface all winter to minimize the effect of alternate freezing and thawing, and should be worked into the soil in the spring. A lasting benefit to the trees will result from applying a mulch each autumn for several years after transplanting. Then when the trees are well started, and the ground is in good condition, these circles under the trees may be sown to grass.

For any tree or shrub which is growing in a region colder than its normal zone of hardiness, a mulch every winter is an essential protection. For instance at Philadelphia, Crape Myrtle and Fig may be wintered over year after year by proper mulching and sheltering from wind. The Holly is another tree which benefits from a mulch.

Ground Covers as Root Protection. A treatment more beneficial to the trees, however, and one which may be used in certain situations where lawn is not essential, is a planting of pachysandra, periwinkle or English ivy. These plants have the ability to thrive in even dense shade, in many places doing better than grass, and what is most important for the tree, they will collect fallen leaves, thus adding annually to the leaf mold in the soil. This subject has been more fully discussed in the chapter on Ground Covers.

FERTILIZING TREES

In their natural habitat in the forest, trees are nourished by a soil rich in organic material which is being constantly replenished by the humus from the decaying leaves. The carpet of decaying leaves on the ground conserves moisture in the soil. In the artificial situation in the suburbs or on the lawn no such renewal of the soil takes place. On the contrary the turf prevents much of the moisture from penetrating the soil, and uses much of the available nutrients. Leaves are raked up, seldom rot on the ground under the trees.

To make up for the deficiency of soil fertility it has been found beneficial to the trees to put into the soil solutions of nitrates, phosphates and potash. This feeding should be done every two or three years.

Time of Application. Applications of fertilizer may be made at any time from early spring until midsummer and from the middle of September until late November. No applications should be made between July 15 and September 15 as there is danger of stimulating a late, succulent growth which will be subject to winter-killing. Tree roots take in nutrients most readily during the period of early spring growth and they continue to absorb nutrients in the autumn long after the leaves have been shed.

Method of Application. The feeding roots of most trees extend from the trunk to a considerable distance beyond the ends of the overhead branches, and the fertilizer should be applied over this entire area. Holes, varying in depth from 12 to 15 inches, should be drilled, being spaced from 15 to 18 inches apart. A mature tree will need about a hundred holes. Into each of these holes is put from one-tenth to one-fourth of a pound of complete fertilizer, and the holes are then filled with water to dissolve the fertilizer.

Kind and Amount of Fertilizer. A 10–6–4 complete fertilizer is recommended as a good general fertilizer for the feeding of trees and it should be applied at the rate of 5 pounds for each inch of trunk diameter. For the average soil, deficient in all three major elements, this fertilizer containing 10 per cent nitrogen, 6 per cent phosphorus, and 4 per cent potash is very satisfactory. Special soil conditions may suggest a different proportion of these elements, as for instance, 4–8–7 in a soil more markedly lacking in phosphorus and potash than in nitrogen. A test of the soil is a help in determining what fertilizer mixture to use. To the student of trees, the trouble is often evident from the symptoms, and the trees may be treated accordingly with success.

Doctor Carl G. Deuber gives the following table of symptoms and their causes:

Symptoms	Causes
1. Poor leaf growth which causes:	
a. Dwarf plants, yellowish color	lack of nitrogen
" " grayish color	lack of phosphorus or potash
b. Tall, spindly plants	lack of light
2. Chlorosis or yellowing of leaf	
a. Uniform all over leaf	lack of iron, excess of lime, magnesium, sodium, potash, carbonates, manganese
b. Patchy, spreading from midrib outward	lack of magnesium
c. Mottled	lack of lime
d. Spotty	lack of potash
e. Leaf yellowing, then drying at tip and from edges inward	lack of potash
f. Leaf yellowing, then drying from midrib outward	lack of nitrogen
3. Patches on leaf	
a. Brown patches like "scorching"	lack of potash
b. Brown patches chiefly in center	lack of magnesium
4. Rich green leaves and large thick stems	large supply of nitrogen
5. Dark colored leaves, tendency to crinkle	lack of potash in relation to nitrogen
6. Patchy appearance of foliage, some dark green, others lighter	acidity of soil

No commercial fertilizer should be placed in the hole in which a tree is to be planted, as the risk of burning the roots is too great.

WATERING

Lack of adequate water in the soil is a very frequent cause of trees' distress. On a warm summer day a mature tree often loses by evaporation through its foliage, as much as 10 barrels of water. To make up this loss during dry weather, trees should be watered thoroughly at intervals of about 10 days. Frequent light watering accomplishes no good because the water does not sink deeply into the soil.

SPRAYING TO DIMINISH EFFECT OF CITY SOOT AND GAS

Sulphur dioxid and other gases often present in the air in cities are detrimental to many of our finest trees. The accumulation of soot on the surface of leaves clogs the pores and retards respiration. These conditions are particularly hard on the evergreen trees, the leaves of which remain active for several years. To minimize the damage to the trees from these atmospheric impurities, the foliage may be washed with hose spray about once a week during the growing season. This treatment will be helpful with such evergreens as Arborvitæ and Chamæcyparis as well as with deciduous trees.

PRUNING

Shade trees require comparatively little pruning. The removal of dead or diseased wood and the cutting out of crowded or interfering branches is usually all that is necessary. Pruning of small dead branches will often prevent the rotting of large branches or of the trunk. The cut should be made through live wood and close to the junction with the larger stem. In removing small branches cut from below, part way through, then from above. This lower cut will prevent the weight of the branch, in falling, from ripping off a section of bark below the branch just before the saw cuts through. Larger and heavier branches need even more precaution to prevent this splitting of the bark. (See sketch Chapter XXVI.)

First cut part way through from below in the position of the final cut. Then cut through from above at a distance of a few inches out from the crotch. After the limb is cut off leaving this stump, cut the stump to a flat surface and paint it with pruning paint. Small cuts may be protected either by grafting wax or by pruning paint. The purpose of the painting is to avert decay by preventing the entrance of fungi or any other damaging organisms.

Trees which have been injured by storm or which have begun to decay will require more attention than mere pruning. The rotted wood should be removed in the cavity down to the live wood. A hammer and chisel may be used to cut away the decayed wood. The surface of the sound wood thus exposed should be painted with pruning paint, or the whole cavity should be filled with prepared cavity cement, a plastic substance which remains flexible and never becomes absolutely hard. Most authorities strongly favor the filling of the cavity, because they believe that it is the best way to protect the wood from reinfection and from moisture.

Forked branches of such trees as the American Elm are apt to split below the fork. Bolting the branches together is the best way to strengthen the structure of the tree. The bolt should pass through the center of each branch and be fastened by a nut on thread at each end.

For control of insect pests and diseases, see Chapter XXXII.

TREES FOR DRY, SANDY SOIL*

Deciduous

Acer campestre	Hedge Maple
Ginnala	Amur Maple
Negundo	Box Elder
tataricum	Tatarian Maple
Ailanthus glandulosa	Tree of Heaven

*In the lists of trees which follow, scientific names appear in the left-hand column and the corresponding common names in the right-hand column.

248

Deciduous (continued)

Betula alba	European White Birch
Maximowicziana	Monarch Birch
populifolia	Gray Birch
Carya glabra	Pignut
Populus alba	White Poplar
grandidentata	Largetooth Aspen
tremuloides	Quaking Aspen
Prunus cerasus	Sour Cherry
serotina	Black Cherry
Ptelea trifoliata	Wafer Ash, Hop Tree
Quercus coccinea	Scarlet Oak
Robinia Pseudoacacia	Black Locust

Evergreen

Juniperus chinensis	Chinese Juniper
virginiana	Red Cedar
Picea alba	Canadian Spruce
excelsa	Norway Spruce
Pinus montana	Swiss Mountain Pine
rigida	Pitch Pine
strobus	White Pine
sylvestris	Scots Pine

TREES OF RAPID GROWTH

Deciduous

Acer dasycarpum	Silver Maple
Negundo	Box Elder
platanoides	Norway Maple
rubrum	Red Maple
Ailanthus glandulosa	Tree of Heaven
Betula Maximowicziana	Monarch Birch
populifolia	Gray Birch
Catalpa speciosa	Western Catalpa
Fraxinus americana	White Ash
Ginkgo biloba	Ginkgo
Gleditsia triacanthos	Honey Locust
Larix decidua	European Larch
Liriodendron tulipifera	Tulip Tree
Magnolia acuminata	Cucumber Tree
tripetala	Umbrella Magnolia

Deciduous (continued)

Paulownia tomentosa	Empress Tree
Platanus acerifolia	London Plane Tree
Populus alba	White Poplar
nigra italica	Lombardy Poplar
Prunus serotina	Black Cherry
Quercus palustris	Pin Oak
Robinia Pseudoacacia	Black Locust
Salix alba	White Willow
vitellina	Golden Willow
Sorbus aucuparia	European Mountain Ash
Syringa japonica	Japanese Tree Lilac
Tilia americana (T. glabra)	American Linden
Ulmus americana	American Elm
glabra	Scotch Elm

Evergreen

Picea excelsa	Norway Spruce
Pinus resinosa	Red Pine
rigida	Pitch Pine
strobus	White Pine
sylvestris	Scots Pine

TREES FREE FROM INSECT PESTS AND DISEASES
(Seldom attacked, and not seriously affected.)

Deciduous

Ailanthus glandulosa	Tree of Heaven
Cercidiphyllum japonicum	Katsura-Tree
Elæagnus angustifolia	Russian Olive
Ginkgo biloba	Ginkgo
Gleditsia triacanthos	Honey Locust
Gymnocladus dioica	Kentucky Coffee Tree
Halesia carolina	Silverbell Tree
Kœlreuteria paniculata	Goldenrain Tree
Liquidambar styraciflua	Sweet Gum
Magnolia (all species)	Magnolia
Nyssa sylvatica	Sour Gum
Oxydendrum arboreum	Sourwood
Phellodendron (all species)	Cork Tree
Sophora japonica	Chinese Scholar-Tree

Evergreen

Pseudotsuga taxifolia	Douglas Fir
Sciadopitys verticillata	Umbrella Pine
Tsuga (all species)	Hemlock

TREES FOR THE SEASHORE

(Will withstand strong wind.)

Deciduous

Acer pseudoplatanus	Sycamore Maple
rubrum	Red Maple
Betula papyrifera	Paper Birch
Carpinus betulus	European Hornbeam
caroliniana	American Hornbeam
Cratægus oxyacantha	English Hawthorn
Gleditsia triacanthos	Honey Locust
Platanus occidentalis	American Plane Tree
Populus alba	White Poplar
balsamifera	Carolina Cottonwood
tremuloides	Quaking Aspen
Prunus maritima	Beach Plum
serotina	Black Cherry
Quercus borealis (Q. rubra)	Red Oak
laurifolia	Laurel Oak
virginiana	Live Oak
Salix alba	White Willow
Sassafras variifolium	Sassafras

Evergreen

Juniperus horizontalis	Creeping Juniper
virginiana	Red Cedar
Pinus montana	Swiss Mountain Pine
nigra	Austrian Pine
pinaster	Cluster Pine
rigida	Pitch Pine
Thunbergii	Japanese Black Pine

SHADE TREES FOR STREETS

(Will withstand restricted city conditions.)

Acer Ginnala (for Narrow Street)	Amur Maple
platanoides	Norway Maple
pseudoplatanus	Sycamore Maple
saccharum (North)	Sugar Maple
tataricum	Tatarian Maple
Catalpa speciosa	Western Catalpa
Celtis occidentalis (Mid-west)	Hackberry
Cratægus oxyacantha (Narrow Street)	English Hawthorn
cordata (Narrow Street)	Washington Thorn
Crus-galli (Narrow Street)	Cockspur Thorn
Fraxinus americana	White Ash
Ginkgo biloba	Ginkgo
Kœlreuteria paniculata (Narrow Street)	Golden Rain Tree
Liquidambar styraciflua (South)	Sweet Gum
Magnolia grandiflora (South)	Magnolia
Populus alba Bolleana (Narrow Street)	White Poplar
nigra italica (Narrow Street)	Lombardy Poplar
Platanus acerifolia	London Plane Tree
Quercus borealis (Q. rubra)	Red Oak
coccinea	Scarlet Oak
falcata (South)	Spanish Oak
laurifolia (South)	Laurel Oak
macrocarpa	Mossycup Oak
palustris	Pin Oak
Phellos	Willow Oak
velutina	Black Oak
virginiana (South)	Live Oak
Sophora japonica	Scholar-Tree
Syringa japonica (Narrow Street)	Japanese Tree Lilac
Tilia cordata	Littleleaf European Linden
glabra (T. americana)	American Linden, Basswood
vulgaris	European Linden
Ulmus americana	American Elm
glabra	Scotch Elm

TREES WHICH THRIVE IN VERY WET SOIL
Deciduous

Acer dasycarpum	Silver Maple
Negundo	Box Elder
rubrum	Red Maple
Alnus glutinosa	European Alder
Betula lutea	Yellow Birch
nigra	River Birch
populifolia	Gray Birch
Carpinus caroliniana	American Hornbeam
Carya ovata	Shagbark Hickory
Fraxinus caroliniana	Water Ash
lanceolata	Green Ash
Gleditsia aquatica	Water Locust
Liquidambar styraciflua	Sweet Gum
Magnolia glauca	Sweet Bay
Nyssa sylvatica	Sour Gum, Tupelo
Platanus occidentalis	Buttonwood
Populus balsamifera	Carolina Cottonwood
grandidentata	Largetooth Aspen
Quercus bicolor	Swamp White Oak
palustris	Pin Oak
Phellos	Willow Oak
Salix alba	White Willow
babylonica	Weeping Willow
fragilis	Brittle Willow
nigra	Black Willow
pentandra	Laurel Willow
vitellina	Golden Willow
Taxodium distichum	Bald Cypress
Tilia americana (T. glabra)	American Linden

Evergreen

Abies balsamea	Balsam Fir
Chamæcyparis thyoides	White Cedar
Picea mariana	Black Spruce
rubra	Red Spruce
Thuya occidentalis	American Arborvitæ
Tsuga canadensis	Hemlock

For *Trees which will form Good Windbreaks,* see page 269.

253

Scientific Name	Common Name	Height in Feet	Preferred Situation and Soil	Zone of Hardiness*
Acer campestre	Hedge Maple	35 (round, low)		V
dasycarpum (A. saccharinum)	Silver M.	125 (narrow)		IV
Ginnala	Amur Maple	25		IV
japonicum (7–11 lobed)	Japanese Maple	12 (shrubby)	Rich	VI
Negundo	Box-elder	60	Woods or field	II
palmatum (5–9 lobed)	Japanese Maple	25	Rich	V
pennsylvanicum	Moosewood	35 (narrow)	Forest in mt.	IV
platanoides	Norway Maple	90 (round headed)	Rich	IV
pseudoplatanus	Sycamore Maple	90 (round headed)		V
rubrum	Red Maple	125	Low damp soil	III
saccharum	Sugar Maple	125	Forest or pasture	III
spicatum	Mountain Maple	30	Stream bank	II
tataricum	Tatarian Maple	30		IV
Æsculus carnea	Red Horsechestnut	60	Rich moist soil	V
glabra	Ohio Buckeye	30	Rich moist soil	V
Hippocastanum	Horsechestnut	80	Deep rich soil	V
Ailanthus altissima (A. glandulosa)	Tree-of-Heaven	60	Any	V
Alnus glutinosa	Black Alder	70	Moist	IV
incana	Common Alder	30+	Moist	IV
Amelanchier canadensis	Shadbush, Serviceberry	30 (narrow)	Wooded hillsides	IV
Aralia spinosa	Hercules Club	40		V
Betula alba (B. pendula)	European White Birch	60	Poor, sandy	II or III
lenta	Sweet Birch (Black Birch	75	Stony hillside or forest	III
lutea	Yellow Birch	90	Damp, upland forest	III
Maximowicziana		90	Damp	V
nigra	River Birch	90	Wet, rich soil of valleys	III

* See Zone Map of Hardiness, on inside of front and back cover.

DECIDUOUS TREES

Bloom	Season of Bloom	Fruit	Notes
Greenish	May		Beautiful foliage
Greenish	Feb. & March		Branches are brittle
Yellowish white	May		Bright red autumn leaves
Purple	May		Crimson autumn leaves
Yellowish green	March		Rapid growth; excellent windbreak
Purple	June		Many varieties
Yellow	May	2-winged samara	Clear yellow in autumn
Yellow, showy	April & May		Very dense shade
Yellowish green	May		Thrives in exposed place
Red	March & April		Leaves scarlet and yellow
Red	April		Brilliant red or yellow autumn foliage
Greenish yellow	June		Orange and scarlet autumn foliage
Greenish white	May		Red fruit in August
Pink to red	May & June	Shell containing glossy brown nut	
Greenish yellow	May		
White, tinged red	May & June		Very dense shade, superb flowers
Small green	May	Samara	Stands smoke and city conditions
Catkins	March	Cones peduncled	Will thrive in wet places
Yellow catkins	March	Very dark, conelike	Many forms; picturesque
White, nodding	May	Purple, sweet berry	Excellent forest tree
Small white or cream in large panicles	August	Small blue drupe	Very thorny
Powdery yellow		Cylindrical	Short lived, 30–40 years Many varietal forms.
Long catkins			
		Strobiles wide	
Very long yellowish catkins	April	Strobiles large	Catkins 9" long

255

Scientific Name	Common Name	Height in Feet	Preferred Situation and Soil	Zone of Hardiness*
Betula papyrifera	Canoe Birch (White Birch)	90	Mt. or Northern forests	I or II
populifolia	Gray Birch	30	Dry, gravelly soil and old pastures	IV
Broussonetia papyrifera	Paper-mulberry	50		VI
Carpinus Betulus	European Hornbeam	60		V
caroliniana	American Hornbeam Ironwood	40	Forest and stream valley	IV
Carya alba	Mockernut	100	Hillside, poor	IV
glabra	Pignut	130	Hillside, poor	IV
laciniosa	Shellbark Hickory	130	Hillside, poor	V
ovata	Shagbark Hickory	130	Hillside, poor	IV
Catalpa speciosa	Western Catalpa	50 (irregular)		V
Celtis occidentalis	Hackberry	100	Any	II
Cercidiphyllum japonicum	Katsura-Tree	50 (broad with lower branches to the ground)	Rich	IV
Cercis canadensis	Red-bud	35 (broad)	Shade, acid or neutral	V
Cladrastis lutea	Yellow-wood	50	Forest or lawn, rich	V
Cornus florida	Flowering Dogwood	25	Partial shade pH. 6–7	IV
kousa	Japanese Flowering Dogwood	20		V
Cratægus cordata	Washington Thorn	30	Rich soil of meadows	V
Crus-galli	Cockspur Thorn	40	Rich soil of meadows	IV
mollis (C. coccinea)		30	Rich soil of meadows	IV
oxyacantha	English Hawthorn (May tree)	15	Rich soil of meadows	IV
punctata	Dotted Thorn	30	Dry pasture land	IV
Davidia involucrata var. Vilmoriniana	Dove tree	65		V or VI
Diospyros virginiana	Persimmon	60 (irregular)		V
Elæagnus angustifolia	Russian Olive	20	Any well drained	V
Euonymus europæus	European Spindle-tree	30 (broad)		IV
Fagus americana (F. grandifolia)	American Beech	100–125	Forest or lawn	IV

* See Zone Map of Hardiness on inside of front and back cover.

Bloom	Season of Bloom	Fruit	Notes
		Cylindrical	Not happy at coast. Many natural varieties
			Weedy tree
Staminate catkin 3″–diœcious	May	Orange and red in Sept.	Naturalized in Eastern states, Pa. and southward
		Nut held by bract	For hedges; slow grower
		Nut held by bract	Forest undergrowth
		Edible nut	Hard, tough wood
		Edible nut	Gorgeous yellow autumn color
		Edible nut	
		Edible nut	Picturesque and rugged
White, spotted purple	June	Very long pod	Hardy in cities
			For city streets
Inconspicuous		Pod 1″ long	Yellow autumn foliage
Purple bud, deep pink flower	April & May	Pod—Sept.	Irregular rangy growth
Cream	Late June	Clusters of pods	Excellent flowering tree
White	Late April & May	Crimson	Excellent flowering tree
White	Late June	Crimson	Excellent flowering tree
White	May	Scarlet, $\frac{1}{4}''$	Quantities of fruit. Scarlet autumn leaves
White	May	Red, $\frac{1}{3}''$	Long thorns
White, large	April & May	Scarlet, $\frac{1}{2}''$	
Rose	May	Scarlet, $\frac{1}{2}''+$	Several varieties with deeper color
White	May	Dull red and dotted	
Cream white	May	Green, pear-shaped, $\frac{1}{2}''$	Flowers of exquisite beauty
White	May	Orange; edible when fully mature	A magnificent tree with glossy foliage
Fragrant	June	Yellow	Free from disease
Yellow-green	May	Pink or red-orange	Subject to scale
	Inconspicuous	Edible nut	One of most beautiful native trees

Scientific Name	Common Name	Height in Feet	Preferred Situation and Soil	Zone of Hardiness*
Fagus sylvatica	European Beech	80	Lawn as specimen	V
			(low spreading branches)	
Fraxinus americana	White Ash	130	Forest or field. Rich soil	III
caroliniana	Water Ash	50	Swamps	VIII
lanceolata	Green Ash	60	Field	II
Ornus	Flowering Ash	65		V
Ginkgo biloba	Ginkgo tree	130	Rich soil	IV
Gleditsia aquatica	Water Locust	60	Wet	VI
triacanthos	Honey locust	100	Rich	V
			(narrow, irregular)	
Gordonia alatamaha	Franklin tree	30	Rich	VI
Gymnocladus dioica	Kentucky Coffee Tree	100	Rich	V
			(irregular)	
Halesia diptera		30	Rich forest	VI
tetraptera	Silver bell	30	Forest or lawn	V
Hovenia dulcis	Raisin tree	30	Sandy loam	VI
Juglans cinerea	Butternut tree	100	Rich stream banks	II.
nigra	Black Walnut	100	Forest or field	IV
regia	English Walnut	100	Rich	V
Sieboldiana	Japanese Walnut	65	Rich	IV
Kœlreuteria paniculata	Golden Rain tree	40	Rich soil; sheltered	V
Larix americana (L. laricina)	American Larch	80	Damp, swampy land	II
Liquidambar styraciflua	Sweet Gum	60	Damp, rich soil	V
Liriodendron tulipifera	Tulip tree, Tulip Poplar	120	Valley, wood or upland	V
Maclura pomifera (Toxylon pomifera)	Osage Orange	40		VI
Magnolia acuminata	Cucumber tree	100	Gravelly	V
denudata (M. conspicua)	Yulan	50	Rich	V
grandiflora	Bull Bay	100	Rich	VII
Kobus	Kobus Magnolia	30	Rich	V
macrophylla	Bigleaf Magnolia	50	Rich soil of valleys	VI

* See Zone Map of Hardiness on inside of front and back cover.

Bloom	Season of Bloom	Fruit	Notes
	Inconspicuous	Edible nut	Many varieties
Red, diœcious	March	Winged samara	Beautiful pink and purple autumn color
			For wet places
			Will stand wet soil
White, fragrant	May	Winged samara	
Staminate flower. Catkins. Diœcious	May	Nuts 1″ long	Fruit has disagreeable odor
Greenish	May–June	Handsome pods	Will grow in very wet soil
White pea-blossoms in clusters	June	Crooked pods, 12″ long	Picturesque, thorny
Cream white	August	Globose	Highly prized flowering tree
Green-white	June	Brown pods, 10″	Beautiful foliage
White in clusters	May	2-winged dry fruit	Beautiful flowering tree
White	May	4-winged dry fruit	Beautiful flowering tree
Greenish in clusters	June		Elm-like tree
Catkins		Edible nut	Subject to fungus
Catkins		Edible nut	Stately tree but subject to caterpillars
Catkins		Delicious nut	
Catkins		Edible nut	
Yellow panicles	Late June	Hollow pod	Beautiful flowering tree
		Small cone	Exquisite in early spring with young foliage
		Round barbed	Crimson and purple autumn leaves
Cream-green, tulip-shaped	June	Dry, winged	Stately, tall tree; gorgeous yellow autumn foliage
Diœcious,	April	Large green; wrinkled in September	Excellent windbreak
Inconspicuous, yellow-green	May	Red in September	Grows like an oak
White, fragrant	April & May	Brownish	An old favorite
Large, white, fragrant	May & Aug.	Rusty brown	Evergreen
White	April & May	Cylindrical	Quantities of blossoms
Cream-white, fragrant	May & June	Rose-red	Enormous leaves

Scientific Name	Common Name	Height in Feet	Preferred Situation and Soil	Zone of Hardiness*
Magnolia Soulangeana	Saucer Magnolia	25 (spreading)	Rich	V
stellata	Star Magnolia	12	Rich	V
tripetala	Umbrella Tree	40 (wide spreading)	Rich	V
virginiana (M. glauca)	Sweet Bay (Swamp Magnolia)	60 in S. 20 in N.	Damp	V
Malus Arnoldiana	Arnold Crab	30	Rich	V
atrosanguinea	Carmine Crab	15	Rich	V
baccata	Siberian Crab	45	Rich	II
coronaria	Fragrant Crab	30	Rich, moist, but well drained	II
floribunda	Japanese Flowering Crab	30		V
Halliana Parkmanii	Parkman Crab	15		V
ioensis plena	Bechtel's Crab	30		III
Neidzwetzkyana	Redvein Crab	50		IV
Scheideckeri	Scheidecker Crab	25		V
spectabilis	Chinese Flowering	25	Sunny hillside, gravelly soil	V
Morus alba	White Mulberry	50	Any	IV
Nyssa sylvatica	Sour gum (Tupelo)	100 (narrow)	Damp, rich	IV or III
Ostrya virginiana	Hop Hornbeam	65	Gravelly uplands	V
Oxydendron arboreum	Sourwood (Sorrel)	75 (usually 30)	Well drained uplands in forest, or swamp margins. Acid	V
Paulownia tomentosa (P. imperialis)	Empress Tree	50 (wide spreading)	Sun and shelter from wind	VI
Phellodendron amurense	Cork Tree	50	Any	IV
Platanus acerifolia	London Plane Tree	110		V
occidentalis	Buttonwood, Sycamore	165	Damp, rich soil of valleys	IV
Populus alba	White Poplar	100		III ⎫
alba, var. pyramidalis (P. Bolleana)	narrow form of above			III ⎪
balsamifera (deltoides)	Balsam Poplar* Cottonwood	90	Any	II ⎬
candicans	Balm of Gilead	130		IV ⎭

* See Zone Map of Hardiness on inside of front and back cover.

Bloom	Season of Bloom	Fruit	Notes
Purple to white	May		Several varieties
White	March & Apr.	Small	Earliest to bloom
White	May & June	Rose-colored	
White, fragrant	June & July	Dark red	Half evergreen (evergreen in South)
Pink, large		Yellow, 1″	A hybrid
Rose-purple, small		Red	A hybrid
White		Red or yellow	Very hardy Asiatic species
Blush pink, fragrant		Green, 1″	
Rose-pink		Red	
Bright rose		Purplish	
Double rose, fragrant		Green, 1″	
Red		Red	Var. of M. pumila
Large, pale pink semi-double		Yellow	
Deep rose bud, pale pink flowers		Yellow, 1″	
Catkins	Early spring before leaves	Very sweet, variable in color	Forms a good wind-break
Inconspicuous	May & June	Black, small, fleshy	Crimson autumn foliage, turns early
Inconspicuous		Hanging bunches, yellowish strobiles	
White in panicles	July & Aug.	Capsule	Early crimson autumn color
Violet tubular panicles	May	Dark brown capsule	Has run wild in East
Inconspicuous		Black, berry-like	Handsome foliage
Inconspicuous		Usually in pairs. Globose	Hardy street tree in cities
Inconspicuous		Solitary globose	Very massive trunk with shedding outer bark and white inner bark
			White under surface of leaf
In catkins like spikes emitting cottony fluff	Before the leaves	Seeds surrounded by silky hairs	Will grow in wet soil
			Long-lived. Massive trunk

Scientific Name	Common Name	Height in Feet	Preferred Situation and Soil	Zone of Hardiness*
Populus grandidentata	Largetooth Aspen	75	Variety of conditions	III
nigra italica	Lombardy Poplar	75		II
tremuloides		100	Northern forests and uplands	I
Prunus maritima	Beach Plum	8	Sandy	IV
serotina	Black Cherry	100	Rich	V
serrulata	Japanese Cherry	80	Rich	V
Sieboldii		25	Rich	V
subhirtella	Early Japanese Cherry	35	Rich	V
tomentosa	Nankin Cherry	10 (compact)	Rich	IV
yedoensis	Yoshino Cherry	50	Rich	V
Pterostyrax hispida	Epaulette tree	50	Sun or partial shade. Rich	V
Quercus alba	White Oak	150 (wide spreading)	Rich soil. Dry or or moist uplands or valleys	III or IV
bicolor	Swamp White Oak	70	Rich, moist	IV
borealis (Q. rubra)	Red Oak	80	Rich uplands and valleys	IV
coccinea	Scarlet Oak	80	Sandy or gravelly valleys	IV
falcata	Spanish Oak	100	Rich, woods	VI
laurifolia	Laurel Oak	100	Rich, moist	VII
macrocarpa	Burr Oak	90–170	Rich valley lands	II
nigra	Water Oak	80	Rich valley lands	VI
palustris	Pin Oak	80–125	Rich valleys	V
Phellos	Willow Oak	80	Sandy uplands or margins of streams	V
Prinus	Basket Oak	100	Low swamps	V
Robur	English Oak	80–120	Rich	IV
velutina	Black Oak	100–150	Rich hillsides	V
virginiana	Live Oak	65 (spreading)		VIII
Robinia Pseudoacacia	Black Locust	80	Not particular	V

* See Zone Map of Hardiness on inside of front and back cover.

Bloom	Season of Bloom	Fruit	Notes
In catkins like spikes emitting cottony fluff	Before the leaves	Slender, long pedicelled	Will grow in wet soil
			Very rapid grower
			Forms dense thickets
White	April	Red-purple	Will withstand strong winds
White	May & June	Black	Massive tree attaining great age
White	April & May	Black	
Pink double, 1″	May		Short-lived
Light pink	April		Thrives 60 years
White-pinkish	March–April	Light red	
White to pink, fragrant	Late March, April	Black	Several varieties
Cream-white in hanging clusters	June	Dry drupe	Little known, very beautiful tree
		Acorn	Very light bark
			Good for wet places
			Brilliant color in autumn
			Common, Del. southward
		Acorns ½ inch long	Will withstand wind; for the South
		Acorn nearly covered by cup	
Catkins			Avenue tree in South
		Small acorns	Dark bark
			Leaf small
			Beautiful foliage
			Rapid growth, evergreen
White, scented	May–June	Pods	Rapid growth

Scientific Name	Common Name	Height in Feet	Preferred Situation and Soil	Zone of Hardiness*
Salix alba	White Willow	80	Moist	II
babylonica	Weeping willow	30	Moist or stream banks	V
fragilis	Brittle Willow	60	Moist	V
nigra	Black Willow	30–40	Moist	III
pentandra	Bay Willow	65	Moist	IV
vitellina	Yellow Willow	75	Moist	III
Sassafras variifolium		30–60	Light	IV
Sophora japonica	Chinese Scholar-tree	80	Rich, protected from wind	V
Sorbus Aucuparia	Rowan tree	—50	Rich	III
Stewartia Pseudo-Camellia		60	Rich	V
Styrax japonica	Japanese Snowbell	30	Rich	V
Obassia	Fragrant Snowbell	30	Rich	V
Syringa japonica	Japanese Tree Lilac	30	Rich	V
Taxodium distichum	Bald Cypress	150	Wet saturated	V
Tilia glabra (T. americana)	American Linden	130	Rich, moist	IV
cordata	Small-leaved Linden	100	Rich	V
vulgaris	European Linden	130	Rich	V
Ulmus americana	American Elm	130	Rich meadows	II
glabra	Wych Elm	130		IV
pumila	Dwarf Elm	50	Rich lowland	IV

* See Zone Map of Hardiness on inside of front and back cover.

Bloom	Season of Bloom	Fruit	Notes
Catkins			Will thrive in wet soil
			Leaf shining dark green
		Catkins with the leaves	Rapid growth
Yellow	May	Dark blue	Fine autumn color
White in terminal panicles	August	Pods	Compound leaves
White in flat clusters	May	Red pome, Aug.–Sept.	Very beautiful fruit
2″ broad, white	July	5-angled capsule, 1″ long	
White, hanging, bell-shaped	June & July	Dry drupe, $\frac{3}{4}$″ long	Japan
White in racemes	May & June	Dry drupe	Japan, fragrant flowers
White	June		Rapid growth
		Small rounded cone	Beautiful in early spring
Fragrant yellow	July	Pendulous from large bract	Rapid growth
Yellow-white, fragrant	July	Pendulous from large bract	Beautiful shade tree
Flower hanging in clusters	June	Pendulous from large bract	
	April	Elliptic disk	Excellent shade tree
			Many forms
			Leaves small, smooth, dark

TABULAR LIST OF EVERGREEN TREES

Scientific Name	Common Name	Height	Zone of Hardiness*	Notes
Abies balsamea	Balsam Fir	70	III	Will thrive in wet places
concolor	White Fir	130	IV	Best fir for specimen
homolepis	Nikko Fir	100	IV	
Nordmanniana	Nordmann's Fir	165	IV	
Veitchii	Veitch's Fir	80	III	Under side of foliage brilliant white
Cedrus atlantica	Atlas Cedar	130	VI	Beautiful foliage in whorls
Deodara	Indian Cedar	160	VII	Beautiful foliage in whorls
libani	Cedar of Lebanon	200	VI	Beautiful foliage in whorls
Chamaecyparis Lawsoniana	Lawson's Cypress	130	VI	Beautiful foliage
obtusa	Hinoki Cypress	130	III	Beautiful foliage
obtusa compacta		8	III	Dwarf broad conical
o. Crippsii		40	III	Young foliage pale yellow
o. gracilis	Slender Hinoki Cypress	100	III	Compact and slightly pendulous
o. nana	Dwarf Hinoki Cypress	8	III	Very compact and dwarf
pisifera	Sawara Cypress	165	III	Narrow pyramid
pisifera plumosa	Plume Cypress	100	III	Feathery foliage
pisifera squarrosa	Moss Cypress	60	III	Bluish fluffy foliage
thyoides	White Cedar	80	III	Picturesque tree with purple cones
Cryptomeria japonica Lobbii	Temple Cedar	165	VI	Handsome tufted branches
Ilex aquifolium	English Holly	50	VI or VII	Spiny broad leaves and red berries
opaca	American Holly	50	V	Spiny broad leaves and red berries
Juniperus chinensis	Chinese Juniper	65	IV	Leaves sharp needles
chinensis Pfitzeriana	Pfitzer's Juniper	10	IV	Spreading to 20 feet wide
chinensis pyramidalis		30	IV	Very narrow compact shaft
communis	Common Juniper	30	II	Leaves white-marked
communis depressa	Prostrate Juniper	4	II	Spreads to broad patches
communis suecica	Swedish Juniper	25	II	Narrow columnar
excelsa stricta	Greek Juniper	40	VI	Very compact pyramidal form
horizontalis	Creeping Juniper	1½	II	Very low trailing stems
horizontalis Douglasii	Waukegan Juniper	1½	II	Foliage purple in winter

Scientific name	Common name	Height	Zone*	Characteristics
procumbens		1½	V	Stiff ascending branches
Sabina	Savin	15	IV	Spreading low form
Sabina tamariscifolia		10	IV	Similar, with bluish foliage
squamata var. Meyeri		5	V	Dense bright blue foliage
virginiana	Red Cedar	60–90	II	Upright, narrow form, broadening with age
v. Canaertii		30	II	Compact rich green
v. elegantissima		30	II	Tips of twigs yellow
v. glauca		40	II	All foliage glaucous
v. Schottii		30	II	Bright green twigs
Libocedrus decurrens	Incense Cedar	150	VI	Slender tree, long leaf scales
Magnolia grandiflora	Bull Bay	100	VII	Leaves shining dark green, flowers waxy white and fragrant
Picea alba (P. glauca)	White Spruce	100	II	Dense pyramid
Engelmanni	Engelmann's Spruce	165	II	Dense, light blue-green leaves
excelsa	Norway Spruce	165	II	Rapid growth, dark leaves
mariana (P. nigra)		60	II	Rather sparse habit
orientalis	Oriental Spruce	135	IV	Needles glossy, very short
pungens	Colorado Spruce	100	II	Several blue varieties
rubra	Red Spruce	100	II	For cool damp climate
Pinus Bungeana	Lace-bark Pine	80	V	Broad spreading
Cembra	Stone Pine	80	IV	Dense narrow pyramid
densiflora	Japanese Red Pine	115	IV	Bright green foliage
densiflora umbraculifera	Japanese Table Pine	15	IV	Broad flat-topped
excelsa	Himalayan Pine	160	VI	Broad pyramid
flexilis	Limber Pine	80	V	Needles white-lined
koraiensis	Korean Pine	100	III	Dense slow growth
montana	Mountain Pine	35	III	Broad, irregular form
montana Mugo	Dwarf Mountain Pine	10	IV	Dense, compact, broad
nigra	Austrian Pine	100+	V	Dense, dark foliage
parviflora	Japanese White Pine	100	V	Needles short in tufts
Pinaster	Cluster Pine	100	VIII	Will withstand wind in the South and southern California
ponderosa	Western Yellow Pine	160+	V	Narrow pyramid
rigida	Pitch Pine	70	IV	Withstands wind
resinosa	Red Pine	80+	II	Rich green needles

* See Zone Map of Hardiness on inside of front and back cover.

TABULAR LIST OF EVERGREEN TREES—Continued

Scientific Name	Common Name	Height	Zone of Hardiness*	Notes
Pinus Strobus	White Pine	100+	IV	Graceful, vigorous growth
sylvestris	Scots Pine	80	II	Short, bluish needles
Thunbergii	Japanese Black Pine	100	V	Hardy in windy places
Pseudotsuga taxifolia	Douglas Fir	330	IV	Slender, compact, graceful
Sciadopitys verticillata	Umbrella Pine	130	V or VI	Handsome, pyramid, slow
Taxus baccata	English Yew	60	VI	Ascending and spreading
baccata adpressa		12	VI	Dwarf, spreading
baccata fastigiata	Irish Yew	35	VI	Narrow, columnar
baccata repandens		4	VI	Dwarf and drooping
canadensis	Canadian Yew	5	II	Low, spreading shrub
cuspidata	Japanese Yew	15	V	Vigorous, spreading
c. capitata		50	V	Broad pyramid
c. Hicksii		20	V	Broad columnar
c. media		30	V	Cross of C. baccata and C. cuspidata
c. nana	Dwarf Japanese Yew	6	V	Compact, slow growing
Thuya occidentalis	American Arborvitæ	65	II	Rich green, dense column
o. compacta		5	II	Slower and more dense
o. Douglasii pyramidalis		20	II	Narrow pyramid, rich foliage
o. globosa		5	II	Rounded dwarf form
o. Hoveyi		6	II	Rounded dwarf form
o. pyramidalis		30	II	Very narrow dense shaft
o. Vervæneana		12	II	Dense with slender twigs
o. Wareana	Siberian Arborvitæ	15	II	Broad pyramid; slow; dense blue-green
orientalis	Oriental Arborvitæ	30	VI (V)	Foliage in vertical planes
o. compacta (Sieboldii)		30	VI	Compact oval form
o. elegantissima		30	VI	Compact, bronzed in winter
plicata	Giant Arborvitæ	200	V	Rapid growth
Tsuga canadensis	Hemlock	100	IV	Graceful and fine texture
canadensis microphylla		50	IV	Leaves very short
canadensis pendula	Weeping Hemlock	20	IV	Broad weeping form
caroliniana	Carolina Hemlock	70	V	More compact habit
diversifolia	Japanese Hemlock	100	V	Slow growth; difficult to transplant

* See Zone Map of Hardiness on inside of front and back cover.

TREES WHICH WILL FORM GOOD WINDBREAKS

Deciduous

Acer Ginnala	Amur Maple
Negundo	Box Elder
Cratægus mollis	Downy Hawthorn
Maclura pomifera	Osage Orange
Morus alba	White Mulberry
Populus alba	White Poplar
balsamifera	Balsam Poplar
Quercus palustris	Pin Oak

Evergreen

Juniperus virginiana	Red Cedar
Picea alba	Canadian Spruce
excelsa	Norway Spruce
rubra	Red Spruce
Pinus nigra	Austrian Pine
ponderosa	Western Yellow Pine
resinosa	Red Cedar
rigida	Pitch Pine
Strobus	White Pine
sylvestris	Scots Pine
Thunbergii	Japanese Black Pine
Thuya occidentalis	American Arborvitæ
Tsuga canadensis	Hemlock

VIII

Shrubs

Almost every one has respect and veneration for a tree, while flowers have a universal appeal, and our shrubs seem to be a link between the two. Perhaps we do not fully realize, however, how greatly they enhance the beauty of any landscape composition or how many useful purposes they serve.

Think what they do for us! They bound our properties and our gardens with hedges of living green; they soften the harsh lines about our buildings; they screen from our sight objects which are more useful than beautiful; they give us a glorious wealth of bloom during the spring and summer months and provide food and shelter for the birds during the winter; they form priceless backgrounds for other plantings; and they give character and form to the planting in a rock garden. They offer us so much and they ask almost nothing in return. Dependable and sturdy, they demand little in the way of care and attention after they are once well established.

Shrubs form the intermediate furnishing of a home property. They are the great fillers-in, background, barrier, and substance of the enclosure. Most of them are long-lived and, like the trees, are considered a permanent or long-time investment. Unlike the trees, however, they mature in a very few years and thus begin early to pay dividends. Five years after it is planted, a shrub border or boundary screen should look complete, high enough and dense enough to obliterate whatever lies behind, mature enough to bear blossoms and fruit in profusion. In any scheme for planting a home property, shrubs should be given an important place, not merely because they function so well and so economically as a natural screen, but for the sake of their own beauty. In wealth and color of bloom, in range of bloom-

Boundary Planting of Shrubbery and Trees

ing season, in richness and variety of foliage, in vivacity of fruit effect, in individual interest of twig color in winter, there is no other plant group which can surpass the shrubs.

Before winter is really over, some shrubs are already in bloom, followed by others which carry on through the season uninterruptedly until autumn frosts or even later. The great majority of shrubs bloom in spring or early summer. From mid-July on there is only an occasional shrub in flower, but by careful selection a home owner may have some bloom from frost to frost. Shrubs with interesting fruit begin to produce it in late June or July and the succession continues without intermission until mid-winter or early spring. Some of the fruits are pure colors of red, purple, orange, yellow, or blue. Some are but dry capsules, interesting, however, because of their form. Many shrub fruits are used frequently in flower arrangements for the house. Color, form, texture, line; all the essentials of composition are to be found in twigs and fruit as well as in leaves and blossoms of shrubs. The leaves of some shrubs, though not many, turn to brilliant colors in the autumn, some of the Viburnums and Euonymus being as beautiful as any tree.

Like any other type of plant, shrubs should be adapted to the soil and other conditions of the site. Some shrubs thrive in dry soil, others in wet soil, while the majority prefer a medium between. Some respond to cultivation and enrichment of the soil; others prefer a meager diet. Some are hardy on exposed summits; others require protection from the wind. Some like shade, while most prefer plenty of sunshine. And then there is an easily satisfied group of shrubs which seem not to care what their environment is and seem even oblivious to neglect. All of these factors, while they limit in one way the use of shrubs, enlarge the possibilities of their use.

SELECTION OF SHRUBS

Half a century ago the lists of shrubs offered in our nursery catalogs were very limited and the selection of a few reliable kinds offered little difficulty. Within the past few decades, however, plant explorers have discovered many rare and beautiful new species. Consequently, hundreds of new varieties have been recently introduced until the long lists in the catalogs are fairly bewildering.

The subject of selecting shrubs for the site may be approached in either of two ways or a combination of the two. In the first, the existing conditions of the site are (and very often must be) accepted, and only the shrubs which thrive in those conditions are used. In the second, existing conditions are modified to make possible a wider range in the use of shrubs. Sometimes conditions cannot be changed except at great expense. Sometimes it requires time to effect the change. But usually growing conditions may be improved by the application of fertilizer, by cultivation and the removal of grass and weeds, by drainage or by irrigation. If the second method is used shrubs may be selected solely for their quality and for their special contributions to the general composition. In general practice, the more closely we keep to the general conditions as we find them, merely making better what exists, the more satisfactory will be the results. Conditions which require changes are encountered frequently enough.

If on a bare, open ground with alkaline or neutral soil we insist upon having rhododendrons and azaleas, then we will have to make changes in the site, underdrain the soil, plant oak trees for shade and for acidity of soil, add humus and leaf mold to the soil, and mulch every year with a carpet of oak leaves. Only then, when these changed conditions are established, may we plant rhododendrons and laurel with any possibility of success.

If we accept existing conditions without making any changes, we must be content with the shrubs which are happy under such conditions. If conditions are favorable, *i.e.,* ordinary garden soil, some sun, not too much shade, and protection from wind, then the range of selection is very wide and our choice may be made entirely on climatic and æsthetic consideration.

PLANTING AND TRANSPLANTING SHRUBS

Shrubs which have been grown in the nursery should be transplanted either in early spring, which is the more favorable time, or in autumn. Each planting season has its advantages. Except for the early spring flowering shrubs, the spring transplanting is preferred by many plantsmen because it gives the shrubs increasingly good growing weather in which to re-establish themselves. However, spring is a breathlessly busy time for

Photograph by J. Horace McFarland Co.

A Garden of Flowering Shrubs

all gardeners and in apportioning the year's work it often is advisable to plan the transplanting of new shrubs and trees in the autumn when the work may be spread over a longer period of good transplanting weather. In sections of the country from the shores of Chesapeake Bay southward through the coastal plains to Texas, in the central valley of California and on the coast of Oregon, transplanting operations are safely carried on through the winter months, many parts of these regions having six months of continuous good transplanting weather. In northern New York and New England the seasons for transplanting are very short, September and May for evergreens and October and May for deciduous plants.

The best days for transplanting are cloudy, cool days, with a high degree of humidity and no wind. Seldom are we able to pick ideal weather, however, and reasonable precautions against the rapid drying of stems and roots must be taken if satisfactory results are to be expected.

Transplanting is a shock to the plant, even if the man in charge of the job solemnly swears that the "thing will never know it has been moved." Unless the humidity of the air is 90 per cent or more, the plant is losing moisture all the time that it is out of the ground, not only through its stems and leaves, but what is more harmful, through its roots. At best, some of the roots are cut and a proportionate part of the top should be cut off to equalize the loss. Dry roots cause more failures after transplanting than any other factor. Whatever precaution we can take to prevent or retard this loss of moisture will reduce the effect of the shock on the vitality of the plant. As with trees, shrubs may be transplanted with a ball of earth or with bare roots. Most deciduous shrubs and some evergreen shrubs are hardy enough and grow rapidly enough to stand bare-root transplanting perfectly well.

The following exceptions should be handled by the method here recommended for each:

Abelia grandiflora	Ball and Burlap
Ceanothus	" " "
Corylus	" " "
Cotoneaster horizontalis	Potted plants
" adpressa	" "
" microphylla	" "
Exochorda	Ball and Burlap
Hibiscus syriacus	" " "
Ilex serrata	" " "
Magnolia glauca	B. & B. special care. (See p. 232)
Myrica	Ball and Burlap
Pyracantha	Potted plants
Rhamnus	Ball and Burlap
Tamarix	" " "
Viburnum tomentosum plicatum	

Broad-leaved evergreens *all*   Ball and Burlap, except those
                                       noted here for potted plants
                                       and except for collected stock

Nursery-grown plants are usually sold at prices in accordance with their height. While the nurserymen's associations have made every effort in recent years to standardize quality, there is still a marked difference in the general robustness of the plants. This is caused by the various degrees of upkeep in different nurseries, or even in different parts of the same nursery. Where shrubs have grown too large in the nursery row and have become crowded, height is no indication of value; on the contrary it may even be a detriment, the crowding having caused the loss of good form. Likewise, the encroachment of weeds in the nursery rows affects the growth of the plants and sometimes provides the purchaser of the plants with the introduction of a variety of weed he does not yet possess. In selecting plants price certainly should not be the governing factor. Well-grown nursery stock cannot be had at a bargain. As between purchasing medium-sized nursery stock and large shrubs for immediate effect, A. D. Taylor has this to say: "The smaller shrubs will grow rapidly and give a finished effect in four years. The larger shrubs will have to be cut back severely and will require four years to become normal again." Another important consideration in purchasing plants is transportation. Long-distance shipment is not only more expensive but also requires that the plants be out of the ground for a longer period of time. Twenty years ago most nursery stock was moved on the railroads and was rehandled at point of delivery. Now most of it goes by truck, even on long-distance hauling. This has greatly reduced delivery time to the advantage of the plants. Nevertheless, if other considerations are about equal, the best nursery is usually the nearest one.

Transplanting shrubs with bare roots is done by the same method described for tree transplanting. The same general precautions are taken to get the plants into the ground as soon as possible, to water soon after planting and frequently thereafter, to prune back severely, to shade them from sunshine at first, to mulch the ground about the more tender ones. Shrubs will stand even more pruning than seems necessary for trees. It is the roots which count most at first, and healthy roots will send up enough new shoots to balance the intake and evaporation of moisture. If the shrubs are not pruned enough at first, the tops will wilt and gradually die. Much more severe pruning will then be required to save the plants, and in the meantime much vitality has been lost. Shrubs should be moved before the leaves appear in spring or certainly while the leaves are yet very small.

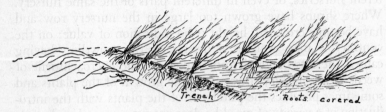

Shrubs "Heeled in"

Some shrubs are much more subject to wilting after transplanting than others. The Honeysuckles are particularly fast wilters and should never be transplanted while in leaf. Forsythias, on the other hand, may be moved while in full flower.

In recent years nurserymen have devised methods of prolonging the planting season to permit the late spring planting of stock. All these methods are dependent on some form of retarding growth such as storing in root cellars or heeling in with loose earth in close formation. Plants thus stored may be planted after leaves are formed, but the plants must be dug up and planted without loss of time.

Normally, shrubs should not be moved while in flower, but Forsythia, which blooms before the leaves come, does not mind it. The Azaleas also may be handled at this time with ball and burlap, and as the root growth is rapid at blooming season, the results are satisfactory. Shrubs which should be moved only in spring include: Buddleia, Abelia, Magnolia (very early). Shrubs which should be moved only in the autumn include: Chæno-meles japonica, Cornus mas, Hamamelis vernalis.

HEELING-IN

So important is it to keep the roots of shrubs and trees from drying out, that when a shipment of plants is received, they should be placed in trenches, and the roots should be covered with soil. This should be done even if the final planting of this material is to be undertaken a few hours later. On cloudy damp days this degree of care is not so essential, but if the planting job will require several days, it should always be done.

PREPARATION OF BEDS FOR PLANTING

Areas to be planted with shrubs should be plowed or dug to a depth of 12 inches, and the soil thoroughly broken up and loosened. Well-rotted manure should be worked into the soil by forking. Heavy soils should be improved by the addition of sandy loam, and sandy soil should have an application of humus or decomposed vegetable matter. The whole planting bed should thus be prepared, not merely little pockets where each shrub is to go. After all, this preparation and improvement of the soil is the last this area is likely to receive for some years and a good soil is essential to the good growth of any plant.

After planting, the top of a shrub should be pruned enough to equalize the loss of roots. With Box bushes, no trimming is necessary because of the dense mat of roots which have remained intact in the ball. The plant should be watered lavishly at first and frequently through the remainder of the season, the foliage being watered as well as the soil, ending with a generous application of water in mid-autumn. Especially is this autumn watering important for Rhododendron, Mountain Laurel, broad-leaved evergreens in general, and Box bushes. These plants all lose moisture through their leaves during the winter. They therefore have to store up a supply of water before winter freezing of the ground about their roots sets in. After freezing the roots cannot replenish the plant's water supply.

The real test of success in transplanting shrubs which have been moved comes the second year after planting. In the first year the new growth comes from the vitality in the plant, stored up from previous years. In the second year its growth is dependent on the nourishment taken in from the new roots made that first year. If the root growth is satisfactory the first year, top growth and general vigor should be good the second year. The importance of good rich soil about the roots of the newly planted shrub cannot be too strongly emphasized.

PRUNING

The best time to prune shrubs depends upon their flowering habits. Those shrubs which bear blossoms on *new* growth in late spring or summer should be pruned in early spring or during the last weeks of winter. In this group are:

Abelia	Hydrangea	Rosa
Acanthopanax	Hypericum	Salix
Berberis	Indigofera	Spiræa
Buddleia	Kerria	Staphylea
Callicarpa	Lagerstrœmia	Stephenandra
Caryopteris	Lespedeza	Tamarix, late-flowering
Ceanothus	Ligustrum	kinds
Clethra	Lonicera	Vitex
Colutea	Neillia	
Hibiscus	Rhus	

The shrubs which bear blossoms on last year's wood should be pruned soon after blooming. This prevents the formation of seed pods and thus conserves the vitality of the plant, and in the case of some plants improves their appearance. In this group are:

Amygdalus	Deutzia	Spiræa
Azalea	Exochorda	Syringa
Caragana	Forsythia	Tamarix, early flower-
Cercis	Magnolia	ing
Chionanthus	Philadelphus	Viburnum Carlesii
Cydonia	Ribes	V. Lantana
Cytisus	Roses (climbers)	

A few shrubs should be pruned lightly after blooming and again lightly in early spring.

Cornus stolonifera	Sambucus	Viburnum tomentosum
C. paniculata	Spiræa Bumalda	V. Opulus
C. alba siberica	Symphoricarpos	Weigela (Diervilla)
Lonicera		

Many jobbing gardeners seem to think that the way to prune shrubbery is to cut off all the branches to an even length. This

Proper cut.

Too slanting.   Too far.   Too close.

Twig Pruning

practice ruins the grace of the shrub and does little to improve its vitality or blooming habits. Branches should be removed by cutting each branch off at its base, and only about ⅕ or ¼ of the branches should be removed. The purpose of this kind of pruning is to give new stems a better opportunity to develop from the bottom, thus improving the whole plant. The pruning of this sort requires less time than cutting a multitude of stems near the tops, and it maintains the natural shape of the shrub.

The primary purpose of pruning most shrubs is to keep them young, and thus maintain their blooming ability. This is done by removing old wood, although it may be perfectly sound, and with it the parts of the stems which have finished bloom-ing. The preponderance of roots will increase the growth of young stems the following year and thus increase the quantity of stems which will bear blossoms. This is particularly effective with the Spiræas, Loniceras, Hydrangeas, and Philadelphus.

If shrubs have to be pruned to keep them from growing too large for their situation, then something is wrong with the planting scheme. Such shrubs should be transplanted to more ample situations and their place taken by smaller sorts.

1. Shrub with an accumulation of crowded stems.
2. Shrub after pruning, surplus stems removed at the base.
3. Wrong—Shrub with flowering parts amputated. This is **not** pruning.

Pruning an Established Shrub

Some kinds of shrubs need annual pruning to keep them in good condition. Those shrubs especially which habitually have dead branches or often are winter killed must have old, mature wood thinned out. Some Deutzias, Hydrangeas, Privets, Mock-orange, Buddleia, Spiræas, Snow-berry, Tamarix, Chaste-tree, Kerria, and Stephanandra, Cornus stolonifera and C. sanguinea are all in this class. Those which winter-kill in the north will need a spring clearing of dead stems. They include some of the preceding list plus Abelia, Callicarpa, Corylopsis pauciflora, Genista germanica, Hypericum Moserianum, English Holly, Kolkwitzia, Meratia præcox, Jasminum nudiflorum, Osman-thus Aquifolium, Mahonia Aquifolium, Pieris japonica, Azalea indica, Azalea pontica, and a few less well known shrubs.

Some shrubs are better for the pruning off of the flower heads after blooming and before seeds are set. These include Lilacs, Azaleas, Rhododendrons, Kalmia, Magnolia, Buddleia, and Stephanandra.

Some shrubs sucker badly and are improved by the periodic removal of the suckers—Lilacs particularly.

Some shrubs may be cut to within a few inches of the ground and will grow again from the root. Such shrubs as Lilac, Sumac, Lycium, Lonicera, Privet, Forsythia, Myrica, Box, are in this group. On the whole, shrubs have great vitality. Many will stand utter neglect and even much abuse, living for years without attention. Those which are particularly self-reliant are Forsythia, Berberis Thunbergii, the Loniceras, Hypericums, the Broad-leaved Evergreens in general, Sumacs, Wild Roses, Viburnums, Elæagnus, and Aronia.

Winter Protection. So many are the hardy shrubs that there seems little justification in trying to maintain shrubs which are not really hardy in the region. Those which may be induced to survive the winters by protecting them and which reward the gardener for this extra care are rare indeed, for an occasional exceptionally cold winter may make the protection of no avail.

Box hedges carefully covered with canvas tents every winter have survived in a garden near Boston for seventy-five years. By carefully bending its branches to the ground and covering the whole plant with a veritable mattress of leaves, a Crape Myrtle has been brought through twenty winters at Philadelphia; but these are exceptions.

The most satisfactory protection for evergreen shrubs and for other half-hardy shrubs is a wind screen. This may be constructed of any material which will remain in place and which will not rot. Mats of straw are often used and are now being manufactured and sold commercially. They may be rolled up and put away at the end of the season and may be used year after year. Cornstalks, flanked against a rough barrier, offer very effective protection, and are usually readily available at a nominal price in country areas. By weaving stout wire in and out among the stalks, a thick, firm matting of any desired width can be made. This may be fastened to a fence made of stakes driven into the ground with two horizontal wires strung between. Burlap, tacked securely onto lath frames, may also be used very satisfactorily.

The winter screen should not be removed in the spring until

all danger of a return to winter has passed. March is one of the most trying months, with much wind and brilliant sunshine, and as the screen is to serve as a protection against these factors, quite as much as against cold, it should remain in place until the weather is springlike and settled.

Straw Mats for Winter Protection

Winter protection is often of great value for newly planted evergreen shrubs, such as Rhododendron, Leucothoë, and Mahonia, and as a general practice it is wise to provide some protection for the two years following transplanting.

Some shrubs suffer seriously from the weight of heavy snow upon their branches. Box is particularly subject to such injury, and suffers also from the action of sunshine on melted snow which has frozen again to ice. In many sections it is therefore wise to cover the bushes with roofs of wood, cornstalks, or heavy canvas in order to prevent the snow from falling on the foliage, and branches. If no covering is provided, careful vigilance should be practiced, and snow should be swept from the branches as soon as it has fallen.

SHRUBS

Aronia arbutifolia (Chokeberry) is a shrub of upright growth, varying in height from 6 to 8 feet. The dense flower clusters which are produced in late May are white with pinkish tints and are followed by bright red fruits, ripening in the early autumn. The foliage turns a glorious and brilliant red in the fall and is very decorative. It is conducive to the production of a more naturalistic and less domesticated type of effect than characterizes the usual small home grounds. It may also be used in the wild garden.

Zone of Hardiness: V.

Soil Requirements: Not particular, but thrives best in rich soil on moist side.

Exposure: Sun or shade.

Propagation: Stratify* seeds in the Fall, removing the pulp first. Suckers. Layers (not considered the best way.) Softwood cuttings under glass.

Culture: Although tall, slender and somewhat irregular growing, this shrub should not be pruned, as it is best used in naturalistic form.

Azalea calendulacea (Flame Azalea) is one of the most beautiful of our native azaleas. The flowers which are borne in such profusion in late May vary in color from yellow to brilliant orange, and a well-grown bush is a gorgeous thing when in full bloom. Under favorable conditions, it will attain a height of 5 or 6 feet. The foliage is deciduous.

Zone of Hardiness: V.

Soil Requirements: Acid, pH. 5.0–6.0. Rich in humus, well drained.

Exposure: Shade or semi-shade. Will withstand considerably more wind and sunshine than its close relative, rhododendron.

Propagation: Seed; cuttings; grafting; layering by low shoots in the spring.

Culture: An oak-leaf or peat moss mulch is of benefit. The uniform moisture conditions of the soil should be maintained in the summer.

A. mucronulata is a Chinese variety of recent introduction and it is particularly valuable because of its early flowering. The flowers appear in early April, coming before the leaves, and are a soft

*See Chapter XXX on Propagation for explanation of term.

pinkish lavender in color. It grows to a height of about 6 feet. It blooms profusely and is a very showy and lovely thing.

Zone of Hardiness: V or IV.

Soil Requirements:
Exposure:
Propagation: ⎱ See *A. calendulacea.*
Culture:

Buddleia Davidi (Orange-eye Butterfly bush) is a welcome addition to any planting as it blooms during the summer months when few other shrubs are in flower. The foliage is a soft gray-green and the tall, slender, wand-like branches are gracefully arched. The beautiful, fragrant flowers are borne in terminal clusters and are violet-purple in color with a small orange eye. The flowering period extends from early July well into the autumn. It often reaches 8 feet in height, and from 6 to 8 feet in diameter. The Butterfly bush is excellent as a source of cut flowers and is considered good for smoky places.

Zone of Hardiness: VI, sometimes V. The wood is not very hardy so that in most northern gardens the plants almost die to the soil each year. See Culture.

Soil Requirements: Rich, well drained.

Exposure: Sunny.

Propagation: Softwood cuttings taken in summer and wintered in coldframes are considered the easiest way. Hardwood cuttings taken in the fall and stored out of danger of frost, also good.

Culture: Given a protection of litter, the rootstock will survive most winters and send up vigorous shoots that flower in late summer. Spring is the best time to cut the plants to the ground. If the plants lack bushy or symmetrical shape, a good practice is to pinch the tips of the branches.

Buxus (Box)—Beloved and cherished in the gardens of our ancestors, Box is as highly appreciated now as it ever has been. Indeed its popularity has so increased within the last two decades that collectors search the countryside for fine old specimens, and nurserymen raise it from cuttings by the thousand.

Box is native to southern Europe, parts of Asia and Japan. It has been in cultivation since the times of the Roman Empire. In ancient gardens it was cut into geometric or fantastic shapes and occupied conspicuous positions in the formal gardens. Through the

Middle Ages it was cultivated in the Cloister garths, in the castle bowers, and in the town yards, and it has played an important part in English garden art. Because of its very general use in England during the seventeenth and eighteenth centuries it was brought to America by the colonists who established gardens here similar to those which they had known and loved in the old country.

The climate of Virginia, Maryland and the Carolinas is particularly favorable for the growing of Box, and in southeastern Pennsylvania, Delaware, New Jersey, Long Island, while its growth is slower, it is hardy. In these regions, many old gardens, such as Westover, Brandon, Hickory Hill, Tuckahoe, Castle Hill, Shirley and Hampden, are famous for their Box gardens, their knot gardens, or Box hedges and even walks overarched and shaded by Box trees. In the region around Philadelphia, many specimens growing since long before the Revolution, have attained great size.

Box is, beyond question, one of the most valuable plants for landscape purposes and it possesses many excellent qualities. Not only is it evergreen, but it retains its deep green color and freshness throughout the year, which is more than can be said of many other evergreen shrubs. When well established, it will thrive for many years, and will endure considerable neglect. It withstands severe pruning and clipping better than almost any other cultivated plant, and some varieties can be kept at any desired height. Box hedges 10 inches high and 75 years old are a matter of record. Broken off one inch above the ground, box will send up new shoots and recover, with surprising vigor.

It is not a voracious feeder and for this reason it is particularly well suited for edging garden beds, as it will not rob the flowers of food and moisture or send its roots out to encroach upon the roots of neighboring plants. The wood is strong, heavy and very enduring, has close, almost indistinguishable grain of a rich yellow hue. It is highly prized for fine cabinet work and is used for the most delicate sculpture tools, and for architects' scales.

The foliage of Box has a delightful odor. As an individual specimen plant it possesses great dignity and beauty, as well as individual character, the billowy foliage masses in some cases taking irregular forms, always expressive of great vitality. Indeed it is this tremendous vitality, this ability to overcome adversity, this marvellous longevity, linking past to present, which is the source of its enduring charm.

Species and Varieties

(For Zones of Hardiness, see map on inside of front and back cover.)

Buxus sempervirens is the type, sometimes referred to as Common Box. The foliage is dark green, the leaves being oval, somewhat tapering toward the outer end, and more thinly set upon the twigs than in most other types. In habit it is rather open and bushy, somewhat pyramidal in form when left unclipped. It makes fairly rapid growth, in favorable conditions 6 inches of new wood per year. It is well suited to clipping into topiary forms, and may be used as specimens and hedges. It is hardy, in Zone VI, but less beautiful in texture and color than some of its varieties.

Buxus sempervirens var. suffruticosa is the True Dwarf Box, most highly prized, most beautiful in form, but slower in growth. The foliage is a deep glossy green, the leaves are small and oval, and in habit of growth it is extremely compact. When left unclipped it is capable of reaching a height of 12 or 15 feet (after many years of growth) and a spread occasionally of 25 feet. In Virginia its rate of growth is 2 or 3 inches a year. Farther north, one inch in two years is normal. It may be clipped annually and kept to a constant height.

In beauty of form, in texture and in rich quality of color, no other variety of box compares with suffruticosa. It is the variety which reached such perfection in the colonial gardens of Virginia. There are several strains varying from one another slightly in leaf form, but the differences are not sufficient to warrant further classification. It is hardy in Zone VI, to Lancaster and York, Bethlehem, Pennsylvania, Long Island, Nantucket, and if given thorough winter protection will survive at Boston, but it is not hardy there.

Buxus sempervirens var. arborescens is the Tree Box. The foliage is very deep green and in habit of growth it is loose, open, irregular, but graceful, the branches being somewhat pendulous. The leaves are larger and longer than those of the type, and taper toward the apex. The growth is rapid, and at maturity it will attain a height of 30 feet. It is at its best when used as a specimen, untrimmed, growing free and natural in picturesque outline. In Virginia, pathways between two rows of tree box are entirely enclosed under its canopy.

Buxus microphylla var. koreana is a compact evergreen shrub with small leaves, reaching a height of 2 feet or more. It is reputed to be the hardiest of all the boxwoods, and has come from the Orient. It is hardy in Zone V.

Buxus japonica, the Japanese Box, has broader leaves than the European form which are borne rather less thickly and on somewhat pendulous twigs. The main stems are stiff and upright. The growth is fairly rapid but the plant lacks the beauty of the other types. It is more hardy than Buxus sempervirens, and is adaptable to Zone V.

Soil Requirements: Deep rich loam with plenty of humus and a porous sub-soil is ideal for Box. A constant supply of moisture is indispensable to good growth. For the transplanting of large specimens a clay loam is preferable to a sandy soil.

Exposure: Partial shade is better than full sunlight in the North, but in the South either sunshine or shade is satisfactory. While these conditions are ideal, box will grow and thrive in a great variety of soil and in many kinds of exposure.

Propagation: Box is most easily propagated by cuttings, and layering is also occasionally practised. Cuttings may be taken at almost any time of the year. Unbranched shoots 4 to 8 inches long are usually selected for cuttings. The leaves of the lower half of the shoot are removed and the cutting is inserted into the soil of the propagating frame, a light, sandy loam or pure sand. A coldframe affords ideal conditions for propagating. The cuttings should be shaded until they have rooted, and the propagating bed should never be allowed to dry out. Cuttings may also be made from branched shoots. These larger shoots do not root as readily as the small ones, but when once rooted they make more rapid growth and soon develop into sturdy bushes.

Culture: Box has a fibrous and extremely compact root system. It may, therefore, be transplanted with ease. Except for small plants up to 12 or 15 inches high, it should be transplanted with ball and burlap; large specimens 3 feet high being moved with a platform.

Where a Box hedge is to be trimmed, the pruning should be done in August. Box bushes which have been recently transplanted, especially in regions north of Philadelphia, should be given winter protection. A fence of cornstalks, or straw matting as shelter from the wind, and even a roof to keep off the weight of snow are reasonable precautions during the first few winters. The barriers should not be removed until late March. If Box bushes are not protected, but are acclimatized, snow should be carefully brushed off of the foliage as soon as it has fallen. Snow damage by breaking and by freezing into ice is the most serious winter hazard for Box.

Calycanthus floridus (Strawberry shrub—Common Sweet shrub) is particularly beloved because of its association with old-time gardens and the delightful and pungent fragrance of its flowers. It is rather coarse and open in its habit of growth and is, therefore, better adapted to mass planting than for specimen purposes. It attains a height of about 8 feet. The flowers which come in June are a dull, reddish brown in color and when crushed give off a very spicy fragrance. The branches also exude a strange, almost camphor-like odor.

Zone of Hardiness: V.

Soil Requirements: Rather rich, moist loam.

Exposure: Shade or open sun.

Propagation: Softwood cuttings taken early root easily; must be protected during the first winter. Root cuttings in early winter. Suckers and division. Layers.

Culture: Mulch in winter.

Carpenteria californica (Californian Mock orange) is a very beautiful evergreen shrub similar in habit of growth to the Mock orange (Philadelphus), to which it is related, and it varies in height from 6 to 10 feet. It flowers from early June on through the summer. The blossoms are white with yellow stamens and are produced in loose terminal clusters of from three to seven flowers. They are delightfully fragrant and resemble an anemone in appearance, the individual flowers being almost 3 inches across. This lovely shrub is not very well known and it should be more extensively planted wherever climatic conditions permit.

Zone of Hardiness: VIII. Needs protection in vicinity of Philadelphia.

Soil Requirements: Well drained.

Exposure: Protected from sun and high winds.

Propagation: Seeds sown in spring. Greenwood cuttings in summer under glass. Suckers.

Caryopteris incana (Mastacanthus) (Common Bluebeard) is an interesting plant of shrubby nature and gives variety and character to a foundation planting. In the vicinity of Philadelphia it seldom attains a height of more than 3 feet, but in warmer climates it grows considerably taller. The gray-green foliage is a bit coarse in texture and the chief beauty of the plant is its bloom, the violet-blue flowers being produced in abundance in late August and early September when few other shrubs are in bloom. Var. candida has white flowers and recently a pink form has been offered.

Zone of Hardiness: VIII. During northern winters, the tops are usually killed back, but the new growth flowers the same summer.

Soil Requirements: Well drained.

Exposure: Open, sunny.

Propagation: Cuttings taken in the spring from stock plants grown indoors during the winter; each of these young plants will bloom the same year. Seed gathered in the fall may be sown in the spring, keeping seedlings in pots. Division.

Culture: Protecting the plants with a light mulch during the winter is advisable. The shrubs should be pruned to the ground each spring and new shoots will bear flowers abundantly.

Chænomeles japonica is a close cousin of the lovely Japanese Quince but is less widely known. It is a low-growing shrub, seldom over 3 feet, and it is of very picturesque outline. The flowers which are borne in great profusion during the month of May are an orange-scarlet in color, a most striking shade. It is a shrub of great beauty and individuality and gives a note of brilliant color when used in a foundation planting.

Zone of Hardiness: V.

Soil Requirements: Any good soil.

Exposure: Sun.

Propagation: Seed, root cuttings and graftings.

Fruit: The fruit, resembling quinces, is hard and green and not edible raw, but is occasionally used in preserving.

Chænomeles lagenaria (Japanese Quince). Blooming in late April, the myriad, brilliant blossoms of the Japanese Quince are very striking. In color they are of various shades, ranging from white to orange-scarlet and are borne close to the stem before the leaves unfold. The shrub is of irregular and rather picturesque growth, varying in height from 4 to 8 feet. As a specimen plant it is a thing of unique and brilliant beauty. It also lends itself well to mass planting and makes a most attractive flowering hedge. Branches may be cut in late winter and readily brought into bloom indoors.

Zone of Hardiness:
Soil Requirements:
Exposure: } See *C. japonica.*
Propagation:
Fruit:

Chionanthus virginica (White Fringe tree) is one of the finest of our native shrubs. It resembles a small tree in its habit of growth and is particularly well suited for specimen purposes or for planting along a fringe of woodland. It usually attains a height of from 10 to 12 feet but occasionally grows considerably taller if conditions are very favorable. In late spring it is a glorious mass of bloom, the cream-white flowers being borne in large, drooping panicles. The fruits are small, blue in color, and are produced in clusters. There are few shrubs more beautiful or more showy than the Fringe tree when it is in flower, and in habit of growth it is also decorative and graceful. A literal interpretation of this name "Chionanthus," coming from the Greek word "chion" meaning snow and "anthos" flower, would give this plant the name "snowflower." Endures smoky and bad atmosphere well.

Zone of Hardiness: V. Native from Pennsylvania to Texas. Farther north, they need protected situations.

Soil Requirements: Sandy, fertile loam. Likes sub-acid, 5.0–6.0.

Exposure: Open, sunny location. Does reasonably well in partial shade.

Propagation: Seeds sown in the fall or stratified, take one year to germinate. Grafting on ash (Fraxinus Ornus) which is a quicker process.

Culture: This shrub should never suffer from lack of moisture.

Colutea arborescens (Common Bladder Senna) is a tall-growing shrub, 10 to 12 feet in height and is excellent when used as a background for lower plantings. The young branches are slightly hairy and the compound leaves are a soft, deep green. Clusters of yellow, pea-shaped flowers are borne intermittently throughout the summer and the fruit is very ornamental, being an inflated, bladder-like pod 2 to 3 inches long. Both fruit and flowers are often found on the shrub at the same time.

Zone of Hardiness: V.

Soil Requirements: Not particular as long as not too wet.

Exposure: Sun or semi-shade.

Propagation: Seeds may be soaked to swell them and then sown in the spring.

Culture: This is a vigorous grower and needs hard pruning in the spring to prevent its becoming loose, open and straggly. Colutea is quite subject to aphids—see Chapter XXXI for control.

Cotoneaster horizontalis (Rock Cotoneaster) is one of the finest of this large and aristocratic family. The branches are horizontal in habit of growth, being almost prostrate, and it seldom reaches a height of much more than 2 feet. The foliage is small, dark green and very glossy. In the North, the leaves turn a brilliant red in the autumn and drop, while in the South they are practically evergreen. The flowers, which are white with a pinkish tinge, are small and are not in the least showy but are followed by myriad bright red fruits which are very decorative.

Zone of Hardness: V. Evergreen in the South.

Soil Requirements: Likes a well-drained soil.

Exposure: Sunny.

Propagation: By seed, stratified at 40 degrees F. for five to six months before sowing. Softwood cuttings taken in August carried through winter in warmth. Layering in the fall.

Deutzia gracilis (Slender Deutzia) is a dainty and lovely thing and as it seldom grows more than 3 feet tall it is particularly desirable for foundation planting. It is of dense, upright growth with gracefully arching branches which, in late May, are festooned with flowers. The pendulous, bell-shaped blossoms are borne in clusters. In the type they are white, but there are numerous varieties with rose, pink, and carmine tints.

Zone of Hardiness: V. Hardy in Michigan and Philadelphia. Needs protected location farther north.

Soil Requirements: Well drained with plenty of humus.

Exposure: Partial shade as well as in full sun.

Propagation: Division. Softwood cuttings in summer (very easy). Hardwood cuttings just before freezing.

Culture: In general, prune as little as possible in order to maintain the grace of the sweeping branches. The wood of the Deutzia is not long-lived; therefore, it must be renewed. This is done by cutting out the old shoots from the base of the plant and allowing new branches to take their places. Shearing should not be practiced on this shrub as it promotes too bushy and top-heavy an appearance. If the new tender growth has been killed by cold in the spring in northern climes, it should be pruned back early in order to allow new growth to take its place.

Deutzia Lemoinei (Lemoine Deutzia) is one of the beautiful hybrid Deutzias and it is particularly desirable as a specimen shrub because of its graceful habit and its profusion of bloom. It seldom attains a height of more than 3 or 4 feet. It blooms about the middle of

May and the masses of white flowers which are borne in thickly clustered panicles are very showy and attractive.

Zone of Hardiness: ⎫
Soil Requirements: ⎪
Exposure: ⎬ See *Deutzia gracilis.*
Propagation: ⎪
Culture: ⎭

Deutzia scabra (Fuzzy Deutzia) is one of the tall-growing members of this family, reaching a height of about 10 feet, and it is well adapted to mass planting. The branches are gracefully arched and the foliage is of rough texture, a dull, soft green in color. The flowers are borne in great profusion during the month of May. There are both single and double varieties, some pure white in color and others tinted with rose and purple. It is a strikingly handsome shrub and gives a most pleasing effect when in full flower.

Zone of Hardiness: ⎫
Soil Requirements: ⎪
Exposure: ⎬ See *D. gracilis.*
Propagation: ⎪
Culture: ⎭

Elæagnus longipes (Cherry Elæagnus) is noted particularly for the silvery sheen of its leaves and for its brilliant fruit. It is a shrub of upright, spreading growth often reaching a height of from 9 to 10 feet. The small, greenish white flowers, which are very fragrant, are borne in the axils of the leaves and are not showy. The fruits, which ripen through the summer, are orange-red and somewhat cherry-like in appearance. They are edible but very tart, and are sometimes used for making jelly.

Zone of Hardiness: V.

Soil Requirements: Well drained. Sandy or clayey. A good drought-resistant shrub.

Exposure: Sunny.

Propagation: Seed, cuttings of mature or half-ripened wood, and by grafting.

Enkianthus subsessilis (Nikko Enkianthus) is a very striking shrub because of its beautiful glossy foliage which is bronze in color through the early part of the season, turning a brilliant red in the autumn. In habit of growth it is compact and upright, reaching a height of about 9 feet. The drooping clusters of white, bell-shaped flowers are borne at the ends of the branches in May and June.

Zone of Hardiness: V.

Soil Requirements: Acid, moist, sandy soil.

Exposure: Sunny.

Propagation: Seed, cuttings or layers.

Euonymus alatus (Winged Euonymus). For either individual or group planting the Winged Euonymus is a lovely thing. It is of regular, rather horizontal growth, 6 to 8 feet in height. The small, delicate flowers are borne in late spring and are followed by purple fruits. The curious corky bark on the branches gives it a winged effect, hence the common name. The leaves are small and finely toothed and in the autumn they turn a deep rose in color, a most beautiful and unusual shade.

Zone of Hardiness: IV.

Soil Requirements: Not particular.

Exposure: Sunny.

Propagation: Hardwood cuttings.

Euonymus japonicus (Evergreen Burning Bush) is a very handsome evergreen shrub. Unfortunately it is not hardy north of the latitude of Philadelphia except in very protected places and commonly fails to set fruit except in warm latitudes. It is of upright growth, reaching a height of 8 to 10 feet and is well adapted for specimen purposes or for hedges. The broad, oval leaves are thick and glossy and it is a shrub of unique character and great dignity.

Zone of Hardiness: VII or VIII.

Soil Requirements:
Exposure: } See *E. alatus.*
Propagation:

Euonymus patens is similar to the preceding but it is hardier and is only half evergreen.

Forsythia intermedia spectabilis (Showy Border Forsythia) is one of the best of this large group. It reaches a height of from 8 to 10 feet and in early April, before the leaves unfold, it is a mass of glorious, golden bloom. The flowers are larger in size and more perfect in form than in some of the other types and it also has the advantage of coming into bloom just late enough to escape any danger from severe frosts.

Zone of Hardiness: V.

Soil Requirements: Any soil.

Exposure: Full sun.

Propagation: Hardwood or softwood cuttings. Layering.

Culture: Forsythias require pruning immediately after blooming, cutting several of the oldest stalks a few inches above ground level in order to allow new growth to take its place. This method allows the shrub to bear its blossoms on gracefully arching branches making a compact appearance of bloom, rather than far out on old heavy branches.

Forsythia ovata, a Korean species, has ascending branches which arch gracefully. The flowers are pale primrose-yellow, borne singly, and are produced ten days to two weeks before any other. Its advantages are in the time of bloom and hardiness.

Zone of Hardiness: V. It is said to be much hardier than the others, the buds withstanding a temperature of zero.

Soil Requirements:
Exposure: ⎫
Propagation: ⎬ See *F. intermedia.*
Culture: ⎭

Forsythia suspensa (Drooping or Weeping Forsythia) grows to 10 feet or more with slender branches often bending to the ground and rooting at the tips. In bloom it forms a golden yellow mound. Var. *Sieboldii* has more slender branches and can be used effectively to clothe a wall or arbor. It is also very effective when trailing over a rock or trained on a wall.

Zone of Hardiness: V.

Soil Requirements:
Exposure: ⎫
Propagation: ⎬ See *F. intermedia.*
Culture: ⎭

Ilex glabra (Inkberry) is one of our native shrubs, a member of the Holly family. It is of open, spreading habit with graceful branches, growing about 4 feet high. The foliage is evergreen, very glossy, and during the winter it becomes an unusually deep, dark green. In spring, the branches are wreathed with tiny white flowers followed by small, shiny black fruits which remain throughout the winter. It is excellent for foundation planting.

Zone Hardiness: V.

Soil Requirements: Naturally, a low, swampy, sandy soil plant but thrives on high ground as well. Mediacid pH. 4.0–5.0.

Exposure: Partial shade.

Propagation: Cuttings made under glass in summer. Seed, which takes a year to germinate, therefore should be stratified.

Culture: All hollies are difficult to transplant. Therefore, they should be ordered from nurserymen who have root-pruned them frequently before delivery. They should be ordered "balled and burlapped." As male and female flowers are borne on separate plants, at least one of each should be planted together.

Ilex serrata (Finetooth Holly) is often called the Japanese Winterberry and it is noted particularly for the beauty of its bright red holly-like berries. It is a shrub of rather graceful habit and lends itself well to either mass or foundation planting. The fruit is smaller, more abundant and shiny, and drops in early winter. Birds eat the red fruit.

Zone of Hardiness: V.

Soil Requirements: Light or heavy, no lime.

Exposure: Partial shade.

Propagation: Seed.

Culture: See *I. glabra.*

Jasminum nudiflorum (Winter Jasmine) is a shrub of trailing, almost vine-like habit. The long, slender stems are green throughout the winter months and in February or very early March, almost before the snows have gone, the small clear yellow flowers begin to open. They are borne very close to the stem and appear well before the leaves. It is a shrub which may be readily trained upon a trellis as a vine and is often very happily used in this way. Its habit of early flowering endears it to the heart of every home-owner, for in its golden cup of bloom it seems to hold the very promise of spring.

Zone of Hardiness: VI. As far north as New York, with protection.

Soil Requirements: Good loam.

Exposure: Sunny position.

Propagation: Cuttings and layers.

Juniperus chinensis Pfitzeriana (Pfitzer Juniper) is one of the larger of the spreading forms, reaching a height of 4 or 5 feet. It is very graceful in its habit of growth, rather open and vase-shaped. The dense foliage is a soft, cool green and retains its fresh coloring throughout the year. It is adaptable to any position where low bulk is required and it is considered one of the best of the spreading Junipers.

Zone of Hardiness: IV. Withstands extremely hard winter conditions.

Exposure: Nearly any exposure. Prefers sun.

Soil Requirements: Thrives in poor soil. Preferably sandy and dry.

Propagation: By seed which germinates second or third year, therefore must be kept moist in sand for over a year.

Culture: Cultivation improves the condition of the plant. If there is evidence of bruise on lower branches which have died, investigate for gnawing mice.

Juniperus Sabina (Savin Juniper) is a graceful, low evergreen with branchlets which ascend at a high angle and flare out at the top, producing a goblet shape. It grows 3 to 4 feet high and is useful on soil which is too light and sandy for some of our more choice things. Yet it is excellent in itself without a suggestion of the coarseness noticeable in some of the other Junipers. The foliage is a soft, light gray-green in color.

Zone of Hardiness: IV.

Soil Requirements: Prefers sandy and dry soil.

Exposure: Sun.

Propagation: Seed.

Culture: The Savin Juniper sometimes shows evidence of a dead branch which may give the entire plant an appearance of weakness. If the dead branch is due to injury of bruise or mice, it may be cut off and the shrub will regain its healthy condition.

Kalmia latifolia (Mountain laurel) is one of the most beautiful of our native evergreens. It is a very valuable shrub for mass planting and is also well adapted for foundation planting under certain conditions, and for underplanting in woodland areas. It has a decided preference for an acid and rather sandy soil and under favorable conditions the plants often attain a height of 8 feet. The handsome foliage is a dark, glossy green and the lovely flower clusters which open in late May and June vary in color from rose to pure white. There are few shrubs more beautiful than our native Mountain laurel.

Zone of Hardiness: V, sometimes IV.

Soil Requirements: Sandy, acid soil.

Exposure: Dense or semi-shade. Or in sun with a mulch.

Propagation: Seed, cuttings, and layers are all slow.

Culture: Transplanting should preferably be done with ball and burlap. If this is not possible, the plants should be cut down to the ground, allowing them to make more bushy growth.

Kerria japonica (Kerria) is a dainty and very useful shrub. The slender, wand-like branches retain their soft, green color throughout the year and are particularly lovely during the winter months after the leaves have fallen. The flowers are a deep golden yellow and there are both single and double forms. It is particularly good for foundation planting because it is not too dense and heavy in texture and rarely grows more than 4 or 5 feet high.

Zone of Hardiness: V. Tops will be killed back if exposed to much below zero temperatures.

Soil Requirements: Well drained.

Exposure: Sheltered, partial shade, to preserve color from bleaching.

Propagation: Softwood cuttings in summer, protected in cold-frames during winter. Hardwood cuttings of good-sized wood.

Culture: Pruning is done for two reasons. One, to prolong the length of bloom by cutting the branches back to various lengths and thus delaying the bloom on some. Two, to cut off any wood that was winter-killed. This last should be done very early in the spring.

Kolkwitzia amabilis (Beauty bush) is of recent introduction and is a very showy and decorative shrub. Of upright habit, with arching branches, it reaches a height of about 6 feet. The flower buds are deep pink in color while the open blooms which are borne in such profusion in May and June are somewhat paler with delicate orange veins in the tubular throat. The flowers are borne in pairs, from twenty-five to fifty in a single cluster.

Zone of Hardiness: V.

Soil Requirements: Soil of poor fertility and good drainage.

Exposure: Full sun and open position for free air circulation. Without free circulation, Beauty bush is apt to winter-kill.

Propagation: Half-ripened wood cuttings in August.

Leucothoë Catesbæi (Drooping Leucothoë) is a low, evergreen shrub with gracefully arching branches. The foliage is a dark, deep green and in winter turns a rich bronze with purple tints. It seldom grows more than 3 feet tall and is often broader than it is high. The flowers, which are borne in late April and May, resemble those of the Lily-of-the-valley, and are very lovely. The little clusters of drooping, bell-shaped waxy flowers appear at the tips of the branches and are quite fragrant. Leucothoë is a very choice thing and is particularly useful as a filler between large evergreen shrubs or for foundation planting.

Zone of Hardiness: V.

Soil Requirements: Rich loam soil of considerable acidity. Subacid, 5.0–6.0.

Exposure: Partial shade.

Propagation: Division. Seed sown in sphagnum moss and sand under glass.

Culture: Set plants in spring 2 to 4 feet apart, moving with a ball.

Lilac (See Syringa).

Lonicera Morrowi (Morrow Honeysuckle) is one of the loveliest of our bush honeysuckles. It is of wide, spreading growth with crooked, angular branches, and it reaches an ultimate height of about 8 feet. The foliage is a soft gray-green and the myriad cream-white flowers which appear in May are followed by brilliant red berries. As the fruits are greatly relished by the birds, it is a particularly desirable shrub for planting in a bird sanctuary.

Zone of Hardiness: V.

Soil Requirements: Not particular providing soil is good. In poor soil, flowers are deficient in size. Circumneutral pH. 6.0–8.0.

Exposure: Open, sunny.

Propagation: Hardwood cuttings. Layers. Stratified seed (pulp removed as soon as ripe).

Culture: New plantings should be made preferably in late fall or very early spring. If medium or late spring deliveries are made and leaf growth has started, the transplanting is somewhat of a shock. In this case, hard pruning should be done to avoid a scraggly appearance the first year. After the shrub is established, pruning should consist of only removing dead branches and sometimes the oldest, thick branches in the spring. This will invigorate the bush and start new growth.

Lonicera tatarica (Tatarian Honeysuckle) is of much more graceful form than L. morrowi. It reaches a height of from 8 to 10 feet and is excellent for mass effect. The flowers which are borne in great profusion are rose, pink or white in color and are followed by bright red fruits which are very decorative and last well into the winter months.

Zone of Hardiness:
Soil Requirements:
Exposure: } See *L. Morrowi.*
Propagation:
Culture:

Mahonia Aquifolium (Oregon Hollygrape) is an evergreen shrub, of rather dwarf habit, seldom attaining a height of more than 3 or 4 feet. The handsome foliage is glossy, rather leathery in texture and prickly. It closely resembles the foliage of our Christmas Holly although it is much more shining. The young growth has a very characteristic bronze tint and the leaves turn a reddish bronze during the winter months. The flowers are yellow and are borne in dense clusters at the ends of the branches in late April and May. The small blue-black fruits ripen in September.

Zone of Hardiness: V.
Soil Requirements: Any soil (Circumneutral pH. 6.0–8.0), even dry and sandy. Likes moisture. Manure or bone meal will keep plants from becoming straggly.
Exposure: In dense or partial shade. Foliage burns in sun.
Propagation: Seed (pulp removed) sown as soon as ripe, takes two years to germinate. Suckers. Layers. Softwood cuttings under glass.
Culture: Better if moved with ball of earth, but not absolutely necessary.

Myrica Gale (Sweet Gale) is a very useful thing for foundation planting and its merits are, perhaps, not fully appreciated. It is of very upright form and grows only 3 to 4 feet tall. The foliage is a medium green, smooth, glossy and very attractive in appearance, having a delicious and pungent fragrance. The flowers are inconspicuous and the small gray-green fruits are clustered close to the stem.

Zone of Hardiness: V.
Soil Requirements: Prefers a moist, peaty soil. Subacid pH. 5.0–6.0.

Exposure: Open, sunny.
Propagation: Suckers freely.
Culture: Rather difficult to establish; therefore, the plants should be balled and burlapped.

Nemopanthus mucronatus (Mountain Holly) is one of our rather rare native shrubs and is related to the true hollies. Growing 6 to 8 feet tall it is of upright habit and its bright green foliage is very attractive. The small white flowers which are produced in May are inconspicuous but are followed by brilliant red fruits which are very ornamental.
Zone of Hardiness: III.
Soil Requirements: Moist, subacid soil, pH. 5.0–6.0.
Exposure: Sheltered and partial shade, as the foliage has a tendency to burn during the summer.
Propagation: Division. Greenwood roots under glass. Seed.

Philadelphus grandiflorus (Big Scentless Mock orange) is very valuable for mass planting because of its substance and its height. It is of large, spreading habit with graceful branches and frequently reaches a height of 12 feet. The large white flowers which are borne in May and June lack almost entirely the fragrance which we associate with most of the other members of the Mock orange family. P. grandiflorus has a tendency to become leggy with age and is, therefore, much better adapted to mass planting than for use as a specimen shrub. Birds like the fruit.
Zone of Hardiness: V.
Soil Requirements: Not particular, as long as it is not soggy.
Exposure: Can stand shade better than most flowering shrubs.
Propagation: Softwood cuttings inserted in summer. Hardwood cuttings taken as soon as leaves fall and stored in a cold pit during winter and planted in the spring.
Culture: Prune after flowering.

Philadelphus virginalis (Virginal Mock orange). This lovely variety of Mock orange was produced by the famous French hybridizer, Victor Lemoine, and it is without doubt one of the most beautiful of the group. The white flowers which are large and semi-double in form are borne in profusion and are very fragrant. It blooms during the month of May and occasional flowers are produced later in the season. The ultimate height varies from 6 to 8 feet. Like many of the other hybrids of this family, it has the advantage of flowering while still quite small.

Zone of Hardiness: V.

Soil Requirements:
Exposure:
Propagation: } See *P. grandiflorus.*
Culture:

Photinia villosa (Christmas berry) is a very desirable thing wherever it can be grown. It is a large, upright shrub reaching a height of 12 to 15 feet. The oval leaves are sharply toothed and are lustrous and glossy in appearance, turning a scarlet or deep red in the autumn. The white flowers which are borne in May in rounded panicles resemble those of the hawthorn, and are followed by bright red berries which last well into the winter.

Zone of Hardiness: V.

Soil Requirements: Light, sandy, loamy soil; requires perfect drainage and likes plenty of leafmold.

Exposure: Prefers sun.

Propagation: Seeds; cuttings of half-ripened wood under glass; hardwood cuttings; layers.

Pieris floribunda (Mountain Andromeda) is a compact, upright evergreen shrub with a considerable spread and rarely more than 4 feet high. In shape and color the foliage resembles that of Mountain laurel. The arrangement is, however, more ascending and the leaves are clustered about the flowers at the ends of the stems. The flowers, which come in early spring, are borne in terminal racemes. These white, bell-shaped blooms are very dainty and lovely and are followed by myriad small fruits of a light green color. The plants should be allowed to develop their naturally graceful habit of growth. They are most valuable for foundation planting.

Zone of Hardiness: V. Native from Virginia to Georgia. In northern sections, these shrubs need a sheltered spot and are fairly hardy in regions around Philadelphia.

Soil Requirements: Acid—well-drained, sandy, peaty soil. Mediacid pH. 4.0–5.0.

Exposure: Partial shade.

Propagation: Propagation is difficult. Seed collected in the fall and sown under heat in January will germinate in two months. Cuttings from forced plants may be taken, but this method is slow.

Culture: The plants should never be crowded. The graceful form of each is too lovely to be marred by crowding.

Pyracantha coccinea Lalandi (Scarlet Firethorn) is a shrub of striking beauty and should be included in every collection. It is of tree-like growth, somewhat resembling the Hawthorns in character, and it reaches a height of 8 to 10 feet. The evergreen foliage is dark and glossy and the branches are thorny. The white flowers are borne in clusters and are followed by brilliant orange-scarlet fruits which last well into the winter. For its beautiful evergreen foliage, its flowers, and its highly ornamental fruits, this is a most desirable and highly prized shrub. It may be used as an individual specimen and in group plantings, or it may be trained against a building or over a doorway, where it creates a very unique and handsome effect.

Zone of Hardiness: VI or VII.

Soil Requirements: Well drained. Likes lime. Circumneutral, pH. 6.0–8.0.

Exposure: Open sun.

Propagation: Seed; cuttings; grafting on Cotoneaster or Cratægus; layers.

Rhododendron carolinianum (Carolina Rhododendron) is of rather dwarf growth, seldom attaining a height of more than 5 or 6 feet. The flowers which are borne in great profusion during the month of May are a pale rose-pink in color and are very decorative and lovely. Although native in the mountains of North Carolina this is a very hardy species and because of its habit of growth, it is one of the best for foundation planting or for facing down large mass plantings. The leaves are evergreen, broad and somewhat blunt at the ends, and are attractive throughout the year.

Zone of Hardiness: V.

Soil Requirements: Acid, peaty, moist soil (not wet), between pH. 4.5 and 5.2.

Exposure: Semi-shade. Resents burning sun. Protection from wind.

Propagation: Seed and layering.

Culture: Pick off seed pods after blooming. Do not cultivate. The roots of the Rhododendron are very shallow and any disturbance may do damage. A year-round mulch of acid tendency—oak leaves, pines needles, or peat moss—is beneficial. Rhododendrons should be transplanted in very early spring before growth begins or else in August and September.

Rhododendron maximum (Rosebay Rhododendron) is one of the best known of our native rhododendrons and is a shrub of great beauty. It is extremely hardy, is of dense growth and although it is generally seen at a height of about 10 feet, under very favorable conditions it will grow considerably taller, sometimes reaching 30 feet. The leaves are larger than in any of the other hardy species and the flowers which vary in color from white to rose-pink are produced in large clusters during June and July. R. maximum is particularly well adapted for large mass plantings, for underplanting in woodlands, and along wooded walks and drives. It is not suitable for foundation planting, or for the small place, as its habit of growth is too bold and vigorous.

Zone of Hardiness: IV.
Soil Requirements: ⎫
Exposure: ⎪
Propagation: ⎬ See R. *carolinianum*.
Culture: ⎭

Rhus canadensis (Fragrant Sumac) is of half trailing habit, varying in height from 2 to 6 feet with a tremendous spread. The leaves are three-parted, slightly downy and have an aromatic fragrance when crushed. The foliage is attractive throughout the season and in the autumn it turns a glorious color. The yellow flowers are not particularly beautiful but are followed by great clusters of dull red fruits which are highly ornamental. It is this sumac which is used so extensively along the drives in the Arnold Arboretum, and it is very valuable when used as a foreground in connection with large shrubbery plantings.

Zone of Hardiness: IV.
Soil Requirements: Will grow in the driest, most barren soil.
Exposure: Full sun or shade.
Propagation: Division.

Rhus Cotinus (Common Smoke tree) is a very decorative and ornamental shrub. It is somewhat tree-like in its habit of growth and reaches a height of about 15 feet. The foliage is a soft, cool green and in July and early August the shrub is a mass of plumy, mistlike bloom, delicately tinted with purple. A few ripening fruits are usually scattered through the panicles of bloom giving a unique and rather striking effect. Rhus Cotinus is a handsome thing either for mass planting or when used as a specimen.

Zone of Hardiness: V.
Soil Requirements: Well drained, not too rich soil.

Exposure: Sun.
Propagation: Seed, root cuttings, and layers.

Rhus typhina (Staghorn Sumac) is of bold, tree-like growth and is native in many sections. It is a very handsome shrub growing 10 to 15 feet high. The branches are covered with velvety hairs and in the autumn the foliage turns a brilliant scarlet. The flowers are not showy but the pointed heads of crimson berries last throughout most of the winter.

Zone of Hardiness: IV.

Soil Requirements: Able to thrive in poor, rocky soil, under most unfavorable conditions.

Exposure: Full sun or shade.

Propagation: Suckers easily. May be propagated from root cuttings. Cut the pieces 3 inches long and plant at a shallow depth in the nursery rows in spring.

Shepherdia (Buffalo berry) is a handsome, native shrub with silvery-gray foliage. It is upright, rather graceful in its habit of growth and reaches a height of about 12 feet. The branches are slightly spiny and the leaves are silvery, both on the upper and undersurface. The small yellow flowers which are produced in April and May are rather inconspicuous but are followed by bright scarlet berries which are borne in great profusion. Although it is not widely known, Shepherdia is a shrub possessing many excellent qualities. It is especially good in natural settings along the banks of streams, as well as in cultivated positions. The flowers are of one sex only; therefore, they must be planted in clumps, making certain to include both male and female plants.

Zone of Hardiness: I. Very hardy; able to withstand extreme cold and dry conditions. Good near the seaside.

Soil Requirements: Prefers cool soil.

Exposure: Prefers some shade.

Propagation: Seed, best sown in fall.

Spiræa prunifolia (Bridal wreath) is a comparatively small shrub, seldom growing more than 4 or 5 feet tall. It is of upright, spreading growth with graceful branches which are wreathed with bloom in early spring. The small white flowers are quite double in form and are borne in great abundance. It has a tendency to become a bit leggy near the ground and is most happily used in mass or foundation plantings. In spite of this fault it is desirable because of its daintiness, and when it is in flower it seems to have about it the very breath of spring.

Zone of Hardiness: VI, sometimes V.

Soil Requirements: Any good soil, but thrives best in a rich, moist loam.

Exposure: Sunny position.

Propagation: Best by softwood cuttings taken in late spring or early summer.

Culture: Pruning is necessary to keep the shrub from becoming too leggy below. Cut out all dead wood from the center which does not bear bloom, allowing new growth to come up. Pruning for this early spring-blooming type should take place after flowering, inasmuch as bloom is borne on previous year's growth.

Spiræa Thunbergii (Thunberg Spirea) is well adapted for the foreground of mass plantings as it grows hardly more than 3 feet tall. It is of bushy habit with very slender, twig-like branches. The leaves are small, being narrow and quite pointed, and they are a slightly yellowish green, turning orange and red in the autumn. It blooms very early in the season, in March or early April, the myriad small white flowers coming before the leaves unfold.

Zone of Hardiness: V.

Soil Requirements: \
Exposure: } See *S. prunifolia.*

Propagation: Seed.

Culture: Prune immediately after blooming.

Spiræa Vanhouttei (Vanhoutte Spirea) is a veritable fountain of bloom when it is in flower and the chief objection to it seems to be that it has been so extensively planted that we have come to look upon it as something rather ordinary. It is a shrub of very graceful form, 5 to 6 feet in height and the finely cut, delicate foliage is attractive throughout the season. The large white flower clusters are borne in the most lavish profusion during the month of May. It may be used as a specimen shrub, for both foundation and mass planting and as a flowering hedge.

Zone of Hardiness: IV.

Soil Requirements: \
Exposure: } See *S. prunifolia.*

Propagation: Hardwood cuttings taken in August, stored in cold pit and inserted in the spring.

Culture: Pruning for this early spring-blooming type should take place after flowering, inasmuch as bloom is borne on previous year's growth.

Stephanandra flexuosa (Cutleaf Stephanandra) is particularly desirable because of the dainty lace-like texture of its foliage. It is of wide, spreading habit and of graceful form. Although it occasionally reaches a height of 6 or 7 feet, it seldom grows more than 4 feet tall. The small white flowers which come in June are inconspicuous but the fern-like foliage, which is a soft green during the summer and a reddish bronze in the autumn, is very attractive.

Zone of Hardiness: V.
Exposure: Sun or shade.
Soil Requirements: Not particular. Likes peat.
Propagation: Cuttings and division.
Culture: If shoots have been killed back in the winter, spring pruning should be done.

Styrax japonica (Japanese Snowbell) is a shrub of tree-like form and attains a height of about 10 feet. The fragrant white flowers are borne in drooping racemes in late May or early June and are very lovely.

Zone of Hardiness: V.
Soil Requirements: Well drained, but moist.
Exposure: Light shade. Particularly good for woodland. Protected location from wind.
Propagation: Seed, layers, grafting.
Culture: Difficult to transplant, therefore should be balled and burlapped when moved.

Symphoricarpos racemosus (Common Snowberry) has slender branches which are drooping in habit and it attains an ultimate height of about 4 feet. The white berries last throughout most of the winter. Its flowers are inconspicuous.

Zone of Hardiness: IV.
Soil Requirements: Not demanding, but likes limestone and clay.
Exposure: Sun or semi-shade.
Propagation: Division, as it suckers easily; seeds grow readily; hardwood cuttings root easily.
Culture: Prune out any dead canes. The bushes need general thinning.

Syringa vulgaris (Lilac), a native of the mountainous regions of Roumania, Jugo-Slavia, Bulgaria and Greece, was highly prized by the Turks, and from Constantinople was introduced into Europe about 1550, first at Vienna, and thence came to Flanders and else-where. It is a vigorous shrub growing to a height of 15 feet or more, bearing large trusses of purplish blossoms. Its ability to naturalize and thrive caused it to run wild throughout western Europe so that by 1780 it was a common hedgerow shrub in parts of Italy and France. When or how it was brought to America is not known but it is likely that it reached the colonies before 1750. It was greatly appreciated by colonists because of its ability to survive severe win-ters and long periods of neglect. By 1823 its name appeared in Ameri-can nursery catalogues. It is hardy in Zone I.

By the early years of the nineteenth century horticulturists were experimenting with lilacs, producing new varieties and discovering sports with distinctive characteristics. Over 400 named varieties have been produced, in France, Belgium, Holland, Germany, Canada, and the United States, and about 200 of these are now offered by American nurseries.

The greatest public collections of lilacs in this country are at the Arnold Arboretum and the Parks of Rochester, New York. In these collections, the following varieties have been greatly admired and have proven to be dependable bloomers.

	Single	Double
White	Reine Elizabeth	Edith Cavell
	Mont Blanc	Jeanne d'Arc
	Marie Le Graye	Mme. Lemoine
		Siebold (cream)
		Miss Ellen Willmott
		Mme. Casimir Perier (cream)

	Single	Double
Violet, Blue, and Bluish lilac	Cavour	Pres. Grevy (Blue)
	Decaisne	Olivier de Serres
	President Lincoln	Pres. Viger
		René Jarry-Desloges

	Single	Double
Lilac	Vulgaris	Victor Lemoine
	Maréchal Foch	Michel Buchner
	Marengo	Hippolyte Maringer
		Thunberg
		Henri Martin

	Single	Double
Pinkish and Rosy-lilac	Clara Cochet (Blush) Lilarosa Lucie Baltet (delicate pink) Macrostachys	Mme. Antoine Buchner Pres. Fallières (pale lav.)

	Single	Double
Red and Magenta	Congo (deep purple-red) Mme. Francisque Morel Ludwig Spaeth Diderot (claret-purple) Mrs. W. E. Marshall	Charles Joly (dark red)

	Single	Double
Purple	Aline Mocqueris (dark reddish purple) Philemon (dark purple) Capitaine Baltet Monge Rochambeau	Archiveque

Soil Requirements and Exposure: Lilacs are not exacting about soil, but they thrive best in rich garden loam with a pH. value of 6.0 to 8.0 (slightly acid or slightly alkaline). Though lilacs endure shade, they should have plenty of sunshine and moisture to bloom well. When well established they withstand wind, deep snows, hard winters and years of neglect.

Propagation—Cuttings: Young softwood cuttings taken during the last part of June root readily, especially if started in frames with bottom heat. Hardwood cuttings are more difficult to root successfully.

Layers: For producing hybrid lilacs on their own roots, layering is a very good method. The bushes must be trained somewhat to produce low branches, and it requires time, so that this method is not used in quantity production.

Budding: The more usual method of nurserymen is to bud lilacs upon the stock of privet in August, Ligustrum vulgare or L. ibota being used as the root stock. This is one of the quickest methods and is particularly preferred for lilacs which are to be forced in pots. It is not so desirable for the propagation of lilac bushes to be used for permanent plantings because plants thus produced are apt to be short-lived. After a year's growth, when the plants are transplanted out, they should be placed so that the union of the graft is 4 or 6 inches beneath the ground surface. This treatment will induce production of roots from above the union and thus the plants will eventually be on their own roots.

Grafts: Grafting lilacs on piece roots of privet or lilac in late winter, placing the grafts in the cellar and planting them in the spring to a depth of 4 inches is one of the best methods. It will require two, three or four years for the bush to develop its own root system from above the graft. The advantage of using privet for root stock is that if suckers develop from below the graft, they may be readily recognized by their leaf, and removed at once. If these suckers are allowed to remain, they will soon ruin the bush by crowding out the grafted hybrid scion.

Culture: Young lilac bushes should be trained to several main stems. The likelihood of loss by the damage of borers is thereby reduced. If borers are detected in one stem, it may be removed and burned and the borers with it, while the other stems carry on. Many lilacs have a habit of suckering. This should be checked by annual pruning. Likewise the central or interior stems tend to become crowded and should be thinned out occasionally. Overgrown lilacs may be cut down to any desired height after blooming; then feed generously with well-rotted cow manure to promote new growth.

Dead flower clusters should be removed to prevent the formation of seed. With abundantly blooming shrubs, the flowering stems may be cut long to include much foliage and may be used in decorating the house. This is one of the best methods of pruning. Failure to bloom regularly may be due to too severe pruning or to no pruning the preceding season, or to the accumulation of suckers.

Lilacs are subject to borers and scales. The borer is most active in June and July, and its presence is evident by piles of sawdust and by dying branches.

Oyster shell scale and San José scale are both damaging to lilacs. Their presence in clusters on the twigs and branches results in the shrivelling of leaves and general lack of vitality. Measures of control for borers and scales are described in Chapter XXXII on Diseases and Insect Pests of Trees and Shrubs.

Syringa Species.

Besides the Syringa vulgaris, there are a number of species native to different parts of Asia and Europe, but none native to America.

S. persica, or Persian Lilac, which for centuries was supposed to have originated in Persia, really comes from Kansu, and was early brought over the great caravan route to Persia where it has been cultivated ever since. The plant is smaller than S. vulgaris, rarely over 10 feet tall, and the leaves are smaller and narrower. The principle difference is in the arrangement of flowers which are borne on lateral leafy branches, in small clusters of pinkish bloom. Its existence in Europe is recorded as early as 1660. Zone V.

S. villosa (China) is a very hardy shrub 11 feet high, with broad leaves often 7 inches long and pale rose or flesh-colored flowers in late May. To some the odor of the bloom is disagreeable. This bush was discovered in China about the middle of the eighteenth century, but was not introduced to Europe until a century and a half later and was offered for sale first by Lemoine in 1890.

S. chinensis, or Rouen Lilac, is not a Chinese species at all but a natural hybrid between S. persica and S. vulgaris. It appeared in the nurseries of a grower at Rouen about 1777 and was first supposed to be an imported species when it was named. Its blossoms are larger, more compact than those of S. persica, reddish purple, dark red, or white. The leaves are larger and broader than those of S. persica. Height 15 feet. Zone V.

Two tree-like forms are *S. japonica,* and *S. pekinensis. S. japonica* is a rapidly growing plant 25 or 30 feet tall with a central stem, low forked branches and cherry-like bark. The cream-white blossoms are borne in enormous, loose panicles in June and July. The odor resembles that of privet, to which it is related. Zone V.

S. pekinensis, though 20 feet tall, has a shrubby form. Its bark is yellowish brown and peels off like birch bark. The flowers are yellowish white in large panicles in June. It was introduced from China about 1880 and is hardy in Zone V.

Tamarix africana (African tamarix) is noted particularly for its light, feathery foliage which forms a pleasant contrast when used in combination with other shrubs of more dense texture. It is slender, graceful, upright in habit, reaching a height of slightly more than 12 feet. The flowers which are a clear warm pink are borne in May in long slender racemes and are very decorative and lovely. It is a shrub of very unusual character and great charm.

Zone of Hardiness: V.

Exposure: Sun. Good for seashore—tolerates salt spray and wind.
Soil Requirements: Light sandy soil, with lime but not too much.
Propagation: Seed, and both softwood and hardwood cuttings.
Culture: For garden use, it is generally best to keep them in bushy form by annually cutting back the long growth. Prune after flowering.

Viburnum Carlesii (Fragrant Viburnum) is a recent introduction from Korea and it is noted particularly for the sweet fragrance of its blossoms. It is a shrub of somewhat rounded form, reaching a height of about 5 feet. The flowers which form a close, compact head are a delicate pink in color when they first open in early April, gradually fading to white, and their fragrance is suggestive of the trailing arbutus.

Zone of Hardiness: V.
Soil Requirements: Not particular, but likes a cool, moist, fertile soil.
Exposure: Full sun.
Propagation: Softwood cuttings, grafting and budding.
Culture: Shrubs of large size do not stand transplanting any too well, so when making a purchase it is wise to choose small specimens.

Viburnum Opulus (European Cranberry bush) is one of the finest members of this large family. It is of upright, rather spreading habit, reaching a height of from 10 to 12 feet. The showy white flower clusters are produced in May and June and are followed by bunches of large, brilliant scarlet berries which remain throughout the winter, as they are too tart in flavor to attract the birds. Unlike most of the other Viburnums, the foliage of V. Opulus does not turn a vivid color in the autumn. It is, however, a most desirable shrub from a standpoint of general form and for both its flowers and its fruits.

Zone of Hardiness: III.
Soil Requirements: }
Exposure: } See *V. Carlesii.*
Propagation: Seed.
Culture: The European Cranberry bush should not be used for foundation plantings about homes, but should be planted farther from the house, as the fruits have a sour odor during the mild days of winter.

Viburnum rhytidophyllum (Leatherleaf Viburnum) is one of the few members of this large family which is evergreen. It is a shrub of vigorous growth with strong, stout branches and it reaches a height of about 10 feet. The yellow-white flowers open in May and June and are borne in broad heads well above the foliage. The fruits are characteristically red, changing to black. The handsome foliage is a deep, dark green, very shining and somewhat wrinkled in texture.

Zone of Hardiness: VI and sometimes in V. Hardy in North, but kills back in below-zero weather. Needs protected position for foliage.

Soil Requirements: } See *V. Carlesii.*
Exposure:

Propagation: Softwood cuttings taken in July, wintered over in the frames.

Viburnum tomentosum (Doublefile Viburnum) (Japanese Snowball) is a strikingly handsome shrub both when in flower and in the autumn when the dark green leaves turn a gorgeous crimson. It is of upright habit, with wide-spreading, horizontal branches. The white flowers which come in May are borne in flat clusters and line the upper side of the branches, producing an unusually interesting effect. The small fruits which are red at first turn gradually to a bluish black. It is a very desirable shrub both for specimen use and for mass planting.

Zone of Hardiness: VI. In V, needs protected position.

Soil Requirements: } See *V. Carlesii.*
Exposure:

Propagation: Easily from seed. As soon as ripe, wash pulp from seed and sow.

Culture: More care should be used when transplanting, as it is moved with difficulty.

Weigela amabilis (Rose Weigela) is a tall, somewhat rank growing shrub, reaching a height of from 6 to 9 feet and it is well adapted to mass planting. The foliage is a soft, cool green and the large tubular flowers which are borne in great profusion in late May and early June are deep rose on the outer side of the petals and paler within. Needs considerable room for its wide spread.

Zone of Hardiness: V.

Soil Requirements: Any good garden soil which is moist.

Exposure: Full sun.

Propagation: Softwood and hardwood cuttings.

Culture: Weigelas will bloom intermittently throughout the summer if pruning is done immediately after flowering and if the stronger shoots are cut back at different times.

A SELECTED LIST OF OUTSTANDING SHRUBS

Name	*Special Features and Advantages*
Abelia grandiflora	Pink flowers bloom from July to October; rich glossy foliage. Persistent. Hardy to Long Island. Small tidy shrub.
Æsculus parviflora	Quantities of white panicles of flowers in July and August. Shrubs spread by layering stems and form very broad thickets. Plant in ample space.
Azalea calendulacea	Orange and yellow blossoms in great quantity.
Hinodegiri	Carmine flowers, April, May.
indica alba	Masses of large, white flowers, May.
Kæmpferi	Orange and red blossoms in great quantity.
mollis	Large, yellow blossoms.
mucronulata	Very early purple-lavender bloom before the leaves. (Do not plant with forsythia.)
pontica hybrids (Ghent azaleas)	Yellow, orange or red flowers.
poukhanensis	Fragrant, lilac-purple flowers.
Schlippenbachii	Early pink, large blossoms.
viscosa (Swamp azalea)	Fragrant, white flowers, July.
Berberis verruculosa	Bronze-purple foliage in autumn.
Caryopteris Mastacantha (C. incana)	Feathery blue flowers in late August and September for six weeks. Low and tidy shrub.
Clethra alnifolia	White spikes of fragrant flowers in July.
Cornus mas	Very early spring bloom; small yellow.
Cotoneaster divaricata	Flowers, fruit.
Francheti	Foliage, flowers, unusual orange fruit.
microphylla	Rich, evergreen foliage (difficult to transplant).
salicifolia	Foliage, flowers.

A SELECTED LIST OF OUTSTANDING SHRUBS—*Continued*

Name	*Special Features and Advantages*
Elæagnus angustifolia	Gray foliage, yellow-orange flowers, red fruit. Very hardy.
argentea	Silvery gray foliage.
longipes	Leaves silvery beneath; orange-vermilion fruit.
Enkianthus campanulatus	Foliage, flowers. Very fine but slow growing.
Euonymus alatus	Autumn color and fruit effect.
Exochorda grandiflora	Dainty foliage. Quantities of white flowers.
Ilex crenata numularia	For hedges or accents. Low, compact.
Jasminum nudiflorum	Very early spring bloom, yellow, in great quantities.
Kolkwitzia amabilis	Flowers and fruit, graceful habit.
Laburnum vulgare	Yellow panicles of pea flowers.
Lonicera Korolkovii	Blue-green foliage; delicate pink flowers.
Maackii	Foliage, flowers, fruit.
Myrica caroliniensis	Fragrant foliage. Gray berries all winter. Thrives in any soil or exposure. (Difficult to transplant.)
Neillia sinensis	Pink, terminal racemes; dark, dense foliage. Low habit.
Photinia villosa	Clustered flowers white. Fruit red. Autumn foliage yellow.
Spiræa Billiardii	Flowers bright rose in terminal panicles.
latifolia	Flowers—white in large panicles.
Staphylea colchica	White panicles of fragrant flowers.
Stewartia pentagyna	White flowers.
Symplocos paniculata	Clear blue fruit like drops of porcelain.
Viburnum cassinoides	Autumn color bright red (wet soil).
dilatatum	Bright red fruit in quantities.
Opulus nanum	Dwarf for deciduous hedge or edging. (Difficult to transplant.)
tomentosum	Fine foliage with rich purple autumn color. Brilliant white flowers.
Vitex Agnus-castus	Spikes of blue flowers in July, beautiful pattern of palmately compound leaves. Dies back to ground in N. but is not killed.

OLD-FASHIONED SHRUBS

(Appropriate for Colonial Gardens)

Origin and Date of Introduction

Buxus sempervirens suffruticosa (Box)	Ancient
Calycanthus floridus (Sweet Shrub)	Va. to Fla., 1726
Chionanthus virginica (White Fringe)	Penn. to Fla. and Texas, 1736
Hibiscus syriacus (Rose of Sharon)	China-India; intro. Europe before 1600.
Ilex glabra (Inkberry)	Nova Scotia to Fla., 1759
Ilex verticillata (Black Alder) (Winterberry)	Canada to Florida, 1736
Lagerstrœmia indica (Crape Myrtle)	China, 1759; hardy to Wilmington, Del.
Ligustrum vulgare (Privet)	Europe and N. Africa, Ancient.
Philadelphus coronarius (Mock Orange)	S. Europe, cult. 1560
Rhus cotinus (Smoke Tree)	S. Europe to C. China, 1656
Rosa alba	1597, origin unknown
Rosa centifolia (Cabbage Rose)	Ancient
Rosa cinnamomea (Cinnamon Rose)	Europe and N. Africa, 1596
Rosa damascena (Damask Rose)	Asia Minor, 1550
Rosa gallica (French Rose)	Cent. and S. Europe, Ancient
Rosa moschata (Musk Rose)	S. Europe, Mediæval
Rosa palustris	E. North America, 1726
Syringa vulgaris (Lilac)	S.E. Europe, 1550
Tamarix gallica (Tamarisk)	Mediterranean, 1596

SHRUBS FOR FINE AUTUMN FOLIAGE

Acanthopanax pentaphyllum	Yellow
Amelanchier canadensis	Red or bright yellow (mid-season)
Aronia arbutifolia	Red
Azalea Kæmpferi	Crimson
" mucronulata	Crimson
Berberis Thunbergii	Red
" (many others)	Red
Cercis canadensis	Yellow (early)
Chionanthus virginica	Yellow
Cornus sanguinea	Red
" paniculata	Purple
Cotoneaster horizontalis	Red
Enkianthus campanulatus	Red or yellow
Euonymus alatus	Deep rose (late)
" radicans, var. coloratus	Blood-red or bronzy in winter
Forsythia viridissima	Purple (late)
Fothergilla	Yellow
Hamamelis	Yellow
Itea virginica	Deep purple
Leucothoë Catesbæi	Bronze (late)
Ligustrum ibota Regelianum	Purple
Mahonia Aquifolium	Bronze (late)
Nandina domestica	Crimson or scarlet
Photinia villosa	Red or yellow
Rhus canadensis	Red (midseason)
" copallina	Red
" typhina	Red
Ribes alpinum	Red
Spiræa prunifolia	Yellow
" Thunbergii	Yellow
Vaccinium corymbosum	Crimson
Viburnum acerifolium	Rose-purple
" affine	Purple-red
" americanum (trilobum)	Red
" cassinoides	Crimson
" dentatum	Yellow
" Lentago	Deep red

SHRUBS FOR FINE AUTUMN FOLIAGE—*Continued*

Viburnum Opulus	Red	
" prunifolium	Purple	
" tomentosum	Purple (late)	
" Wrightii	Red	

SHRUBS WITH FINE FRUIT EFFECTS
(Conspicuous Fruit)

Aronia arbutifolia	Red	Sept.-winter
" " brilliantissima	Red	Sept.-winter
Berberis Thunbergii	Bright red	Winter
" vulgaris, etc.	Red or purple	Winter
Callicarpa purpurea	Purple	Oct.-Nov.
" japonica	Purple	Oct.-Nov.
Chionanthus virginica	Blue	Sept.
Cornus florida	Red	Sept.-Oct.
" mas	Scarlet	August
" paniculata	Blue	Sept.-Oct.
Cotoneaster divaricata	Red	Sept.-Nov.
" horizontalis	Bright red	Sept.-winter
" hupehensis	Bright red	Aug.-Sept.
" Simonsii (and others)	Scarlet	Oct.
Elæagnus longipes	Orange vermilion	July
Euonymus alatus (E. multiflorus)	Red & orange	Sept.-Oct.
" americanus	Light scarlet	Aug.-Oct.
" atropurpureus	Crimson	Oct.
" europæus	Pink or red	Sept.-Oct.
Ilex lævigata	Orange-red	Sept.
" opaca	Red	Winter
" serrata (I. Sieboldii)	Red	Oct.-winter
" verticillata	Bright red	Oct.-winter
Ligustrum ibota	Black	Sept.-Dec.
" vulgare	Black	Sept.-Dec.
Lonicera Maackii	Crimson	Sept.-Nov.
" tatarica	Crimson	July
Mahonia Aquifolium	Blue	Sept.
Myrica caroliniensis	Gray	Sept.-April
Nandina domestica	Bright red or purple-red	Sept.

Shrubs with Fine Fruit Effects—*Continued*

Photinia serrulata	Red	Oct.
" villosa	Bright red	Oct.-Nov.
Pyracantha coccinea	Orange-scarlet	Winter
" " Lalandi	Orange-scarlet	Winter
Rhodotypos kerrioides	Black	Oct.-Nov.
Ròsa multiflora	Red	Winter
" rugosa	Red	Winter
Sambucus canadensis	Black	Sept.
" racemosus	Red	Sept.-Oct.
Symplocos paniculata	Blue	Sept.
Symphoricarpos vulgaris	Red	Oct.-Dec.
" " racemosus (S. albus)	White	Sept.-Nov.
Vaccinium corymbosum	Blue	July-Aug.
Viburnum dilatatum	Red	Nov.
" Lantana	Purple	July-Sept.
" Opulus	Red	Aug.-early winter
" prunifolium	Blue-black	Sept.-Oct.
" Sargenti	Red	Sept.-Oct.
" theiferum	Red	Nov.
" Wrightii	Red	Sept.-Oct.

Reliable Shrubs

(Those which thrive without care, and even in spite of abuse. Rarely attacked by insects.)

Acanthopanax pentaphyllum
Aronia arbutifolia
Azalea calendulacea
"   canadense
"   Kæmpferi
"   nudiflora
"   Vaseyi
"   viscosa
Benzoin æstivale
Berberis Thunbergii
Clethra alnifolia
Corylus americana
Diervilla florida
Elæagnus angustifolia
"   argentea
Forsythia Fortunei
"   intermedia

Hamamelis (all)
Hypericum aureum
Ilex crenata
"   glabra
"   verticillata
Ligustrum ibota
Lonicera fragrantissima
"   tatarica (most of the bush Loniceras)
Lycium chinense
Myrica (var.)
Potentilla fruticosa
Rhododendron maximum
"   carolinianum
"   minus
Viburnum (most)

SHRUBS FOR DRY PLACES

(Survive in poor, sandy soil)

Acanthopanax pentaphyllum
Amorpha fruticosa
Arctostaphylos uva-ursi
Baccharis halimifolia
Berberis Thunbergii
Betula glandulosa
   "   nana
Caragana arborescens
   "   Chamlagu
   "   frutex
Ceanothus americanus
   "   Fendleri
Colutea arborescens
   "   orientalis
Comptonia asplenifolia
Cornus Baileyi
Coronilla Emerus
Cytisus scoparius
   "   supinus
Elæagnus angustifolia
   "   longipes
Gaylussacia baccata
Genista tinctoria
   "   germanica
Hudsonia ericoides
   "   tomentosa
Myrica caroliniensis
Lespedeza bicolor
   "   formosa
Hypericum prolificum
Juniperus communis
   "   horizontalis

Ligustrum vulgare
Lonicera Morrowi
Lycium chinense
Potentilla fruticosa
Prunus Besseyi
   "   maritima
   "   pumila
Rhamnus Frangula
Rhodotypos kerrioides
Rhus canadensis
   "   copallina
   "   glabra
   "   trilobata
   "   typhina
Ribes Cynosbati
Robinia hispida
   "   viscosa
Rosa carolina
   "   gallica
   "   nitida
   "   rugosa
   "   spinosissima
   "   virginiana
Rubus cuneifolius
   "   procumbens
Salix tristis
Shepherdia canadensis
Symphoricarpos vulgaris
Tamarix parviflora
   "   gallica
Viburnum Lantana

SHRUBS FOR WET PLACES

Alnus (various)
Amelanchier canadensis
Aronia arbutifolia
Azalea Vaseyi

Azalea viscosa
Benzoin æstivale
Calycanthus floridus
Cephalanthus occidentalis

SHRUBS FOR WET PLACES—*Continued*

Chamædaphne calyculata
Clethra alnifolia
Cornus stolonifera
Dirca palustris
Hypericum densiflorum
Ilex glabra
" verticillata
Itea virginica
Kalmia angustifolia
Myrica Gale
Pieris floribunda

Rhododendron maximum
Rosa palustris
Salix (various)
Sambucus canadensis
Spiræa tomentosa
Vaccinium canadense
" corymbosum
Viburnum cassinoides
" dentatum
" Lentago
" Sieboldii

SHRUBS FOR CUT FLOWERS

Buddleia
Caryopteris Mastacanthus
Chænomeles
Cornus mas
Corylus maxima
Deutzia
Diervilla
Forsythia
Philadelphus

Physocarpus
Prunus
Salix Caprea
" discolor
Sorbaria
Spiræa
Syringa
Tamarix

TALL SHRUBS OF RAPID GROWTH FOR QUICK SCREEN

	Ht.		Ht.
Acanthopanax pentaphyllum	10′	Ligustrum vulgare	15′
Elæagnus angustifolia	25′	Lonicera fragrantissima	10′
" argentea	12′	" Maackii	15′
Euonymus europæus	25′–30′	Philadelphus coronarius	15′
Forsythia intermedia	10′	Salix pentandra	30′
" suspensa	12′	Viburnum dentatum	15′
" viridissima	10′	" Lentago	20′
Ligustrum amurense	15′	" Opulus	12′
" ovalifolium	15′	" prunifolium	20′

Large Shrubs for Windbreak

(High, dense, very hardy in exposed positions)

Acanthopanax pentaphyllum
Berberis vulgaris
Chænomeles japonica
Cornus mas
Corylus maxima
Elæagnus angustifolia
"   argentea
Euonymus europæus
Kalmia latifolia
Ligustrum amurense
"   ibota
"   vulgare
Lonicera fragrantissima
"   Korolkovii
"   Maackii

Lonicera Morrowi
"   tatarica
Myrica caroliniensis (Seashores)
Rhamnus cathartica
"   Frangula
Rhus Cotinus
Rosa rubiginosa
"   rugosa (good at seashore)
Syringa vulgaris
Viburnum americanum
"   cassinoides
"   dentatum
"   Lantana
"   Lentago
"   Opulus

Low Shrubs of Neat Habit

(Will never grow too tall for a position under windows)

	Ht.		Ht.
Abelia grandiflora	5′	Kerria japonica	6′
Cotoneaster horizontalis	2½′	Leucothoë Catesbæi	3′
" adpressa	3′	Mahonia (var.)	3′
Deutzia gracilis	3′	Myrica Gale	3′
Ilex crenata microphylla	6′	Pieris floribunda	5′
" " nummularia	4′	" japonica	5′
" glabra	6′	Stephanandra flexuosa	6′
Jasminum nudiflorum	4′–5′	Symphoricarpos racemosus	3′
Juniperus communis depressa		Taxus baccata repandens	3′
plumosa	3′	" canadensis	4′
Juniperus horizontalis	1½′	" cuspidata brevifolia	5′
" Sabina tamariscifolia	4′	Viburnum Opulus nanum	2′
" squamata Meyeri	5′		

Low, Spreading Shrubs for Covering a Bank
(Ground Covers)

Arctostaphylos uva-ursi
Callicarpa purpurea
Comptonia asplenifolia (Sweet Fern)
Cotoneaster horizontalis
  " adpressa
Cytisus hirsutus
  " scoparius
Erica carnea
Euonymus radicans kewensis
  " " coloratus
Genista tinctoria
Jasminum nudiflorum (S. exposure)
Lonicera, Hall's Climbing
  " pileata

Lycium chinense
Myrica Gale
Pachysandra terminalis
Pieris floribunda
Rhus canadensis
Rosa Max Graf
  " multiflora
  " spinosissima
  " Wichuraiana
Spiræa arguta
  " Thunbergii
  " tomentosa
Stephanandra flexuosa
Symphoricarpos vulgaris
Vinca minor
Zanthorhiza apiifolia

Shrubs for Shady Places
(Will grow well in dense shade)

Evergreen

Buxus sempervirens, etc.
Euonymus radicans
Ilex crenata
  " glabra
Kalmia latifolia
Leucothoë Catesbæi
Mahonia Aquifolium
  " Bealei
Pieris floribunda
  " japonica
Rhododendron (var.)

Deciduous

Abelia grandiflora
Acanthopanax pentaphyllum
Amelanchier (var.)
Aronia (var.)

Deciduous (Cont.)

Azalea (var.)
Benzoin æstivale (damp)
Calycanthus floridus
Ceanothus americanus
Cephalanthus occidentalis
Chionanthus virginica
Clethra alnifolia (damp)
Cornus alba
  " mas
  " paniculata
Corylopsis spicata
Hamamelis virginiana
Hydrangea arborescens
  " quercifolia
Hypericum (var.)
Ilex verticillata
Myrica (var.)

SHRUBS FOR SHADY PLACES

Deciduous

Rhodotypos kerrioides
Rhus canadensis
Ribes alpinum
"   odoratum
Stephanandra flexuosa
Symphoricarpos racemosus
"   vulgaris

Deciduous (Cont.)

Vaccinium corymbosum
"   pennsylvanicum
Viburnum acerifolium
"   dentatum
"   Lentago
"   Sieboldii

S   Sun.
Sh   Shade.
Part. Sh   Partial Shade.

TABULAR LIST

Scientific Name	Common Name	Height in Feet or Inches	Exposure	Soil
Abelia grandiflora	Abelia	3–6'	S or Sh, Protected	Light, peaty
Acanthopanax pentaphyllum		4–6'	S	Rich, heavy
Æsculus parviflora	Dwarf Horse-chestnut	3–10'	S	Rich, damp loam
Alnus incana	Speckled Alder	20'	S Sh	Wet
rugosa	Hazel Alder	25'	S Sh	Wet
Amelanchier canadensis	Shadbush	30'	S Sh	Limestone, loamy or leaf
lævis	Allegheny Shadblow	36'	S Sh	
Amorpha fruticosa	False Indigo	6–18'	S	
Amygdalus communis	Almond	25'	S	Indifferent
Aralia spinosa	Hercules Club	30'	Sh	
Arctostaphylos uva-ursi	Bearberry	tr. 1"	S or half Sh	Sandy, acid, well-drained
Aronia arbutifolia	Red Chokeberry	9'	S Sh	Moist
var. brilliantissima		10'	S Sh	Moist
melanocarpa	Black Chokeberry	2'	S Sh	Rocky
Azalea arborescens	Sweet Azalea	9–12'	Half Sh	Acid
calendulacea	Flame Azalea	12'	Half Sh	Acid
canadense		3'	Half Sh	Acid
indica	Indian Azalea	6'	Half Sh	Acid
Kæmpferi	Torch Azalea	12'	Half Sh	Acid
mollis	Chinese Azalea	3–4'	Half Sh	Acid
mucronulata		6'	Half Sh	Acid
nudiflora	Pinxter Azalea	6–8'	Half Sh	Acid or lime
pontica hybrids		10'	Half Sh	Acid
rosea	Downy Pinxter A.	9'	Half Sh	Acid or lime
Schlippenbachii		15'	Half Sh	Acid

I to VIII   See Zone Map of Hardiness, inside front and back cover.
(–)   Numeral in ( ) indicates possible hardiness only.
I.   Inconspicuous flower or fruit.

OF SHRUBS

Zone	Color of Flowers	Season of Bloom	Color of Fruit	Remarks
V	White, flush pink	June–Nov.	I.	
V	White	June	I.	
V	White	July–Aug.	I.	
IV	Brown catkin	March	Brown	
IV	Brown catkin	March	Brown	
IV	White	May	Maroon-purple	
IV	White	May	Black	
V	Purple	July	Purple pods	Weedy.
VI	Double, pink	May		
V	White	August	Black	
II	White to pink	April–Aug.	Red	
V	White, pinkish	May	Red	
V	White	April	Red, persistent	
IV (III)	White	May	Black	
V	White	June–July	I.	
V	Yellow to scarlet	June	I.	
IV	Rosy purple	April–May	I.	
VII (VI)	Pink to white	May–June	I.	Evergreen.
V	Orange-red	May	I.	
VI (V)	Yellow	May	I.	
VI	Pale rosy purple	April		Evergreen.
V	Pink	April–May	I.	
VII	Yellow, orange or red brown	May–June		Evergreen.
IV	Pink	April–May	I.	
V	Pink	May	I.	

327

Scientific Name	Common Name	Height in Feet or Inches	Exposure	Soil
Azalea Vaseyi	Pink Shell Azalea	15'	Half Sh	Acid
viscosa	Swamp Azalea	4–7'	Half Sh	Moist
Baccharis halimifolia	Groundsel-Bush	12'	S	Moist, swampy
Benzoin æstivale	Spicebush	6–15'	S Sh	Wet
Berberis buxifolia var. pygmæa	Dwarf Magellan Barberry	3'	S	
Julianæ		5'		Neutral
koreana	Korean Barberry	6'	S	
Sargentiana		6'		Neutral
Thunbergii	Japanese Barberry	3–6'	S Sh	Neutral
var. erecta	Columnberry	6'	Half Sh.	Neutral
var. minor	Dwarf Jap. Barberry	1½'	S	Neutral
Vernæ		5'		Neutral
verruculosa	Warty Barberry	2'	S, Protected spot	Neutral
vulgaris	Common Barberry	10+'	S Sh	Neutral
Wilsonæ	Wilson's Barberry	1½'	S	Neutral
Betula glandulosa	Birch	6'	S, Half Sh	Sandy
nana	Birch	2'	S, Half Sh	Moist, sandy
Buddleia Davidi	Butterflybush	8'	S	Well drained
var. Veitchiana	Veitch's Bush		S	Rich
Buxus microphylla var. japonica	Japanese Box	6'	Half Sh	Rich
microphylla var. koreana	Korean Box	2'	Half Sh	Rich
sempervirens	Common Box	25'	Half Sh	Rich
sempervirens var. suffruticosa	Dwarf Box	10'	Half Sh	Rich in humus
var. arborescens	Tree Box	30'	Half Sh	Rich
Callicarpa japonica	Jap. Beautyberry	4'	S	Well drained for hardiness
purpurea	Chinese Beautyberry	4'	S	
Calluna vulgaris	Heather	3'	S or Part. Sh	Semi-acid

Zone	Color of Flowers	Season of Bloom	Color of Fruit	Remarks
V	Various	April–May	I.	
IV	Pink, white	June–July	I.	
V	White or yellow		Snow-white and showy	Diœcious.
IV	Greenish yellow	March	Red	
VI	Orange-yellow		Dark purple	Evergreen, compact.
(V)	Yellow	April	Bluish black	Evergreen.
V	Yellow		Red, persistent	Deciduous.
VI	Yellow	April	Bluish black	Evergreen.
V	Yellow	April	Red	
V	Yellow	April	Red	
V	Yellow		Red	Very dense.
V	Yellow	April	Red	
VI (V)	Yellow	April	Violet-black	Evergreen.
III	Yellow	April	Red	Host to wheat smut.
VI (V)	Yellow	April	Salmon-red	
II	Catkins		Cones ¾″ long	
I	Catkins		Cones ½″ long	Spreading.
VI (V)	Lilac	July–autumn	I.	
V	Mauve, dense spikes	July		More vigorous than type.
V	Cream, I., axillary		I.	
V	Cream, I., axillary		I.	
VI	I.		I.	Evergreen.
VI	Cream, I., terminal			
VI	I.		I.	Evergreen, grows rapidly.
(V)	Pink	August	Violet	
(V)	Pinkish	August	Lilac-violet	
VI	Rosy pink	July–Sept.		Evergreen.

Scientific Name	Common Name	Height in Feet or Inches	Exposure	Soil
Calycanthus floridus	Sweet-shrub	8'	S	Moist loam
Caragana arborescens	Siberian Pea Tree	20'	S pref.	Sandy
Chamlagu	Pea Shrub	2'	S pref.	Sandy
frutex	Pea Shrub	10'	S pref.	Sandy
Carpenteria californica	California Mock Orange	10'	Protected from sun and high wind	Sandy, well drained
Caryopteris incana (C. Mastacanthus)	Bluebeard	2–6'	S	Well drained
Ceanothus americanus	Jersey Tea	2–4'	Part. S	Dry
Fendleri		1½'	S	Well drained
Cephalanthus occidentalis	Buttonbush	10'	S Sh	Wet, swampy
Cercis canadensis	Redbud, Judas-Tree	40'	S	Sandy loam
Chænomeles japonica (Cydonia Maulei)	Lesser Jap. Flowering Quince	4+'	S	
lagenaria	Jap. Flowering Quince	6+'	S	
Chamædaphne calyculata	Leatherleaf	1–3'	Sh	Wet (peaty or acid)
Chionanthus virginica	Fringetree	10–30'	S	Moist, sandy loam
Citrus trifoliata	Hardy Orange	10+'	S	Neutral
Clethra alnifolia	Sweet Pepperbush	3–8'	Sh	Wet, peaty or acid, sandy
Colutea arborescens	Bladder Senna	12'	S Sh	Dry
orientalis	Oriental Bladder Senna	6'	S Sh	Dry
Comptonia asplenifolia	Sweetfern	2–4'	S Sh	Peaty, sandy or sterile
Cornus alba	Tatarian Dogwood	5–10'	S Sh	Wet
var. sibirica	Coral Dogwood	10'	S Sh	Wet
alternifolia	Alternate-leaf D.	20'	Sh	
Amomum	Silky Dogwood	3–10'	S	Wet
Baileyi		10'	S Sh	Wet
florida	Flowering Dogwood	20'	S Sh	Indifferent
mas	Cornelian Cherry	10+'	S Sh	
paniculata	Gray Dogwood	3–15'	S	

Zone	Color of Flowers	Season of Bloom	Color of Fruit	Remarks
V	Purplish red-brown	June–July	I.	
I or II	Yellow	June		Green pod profuse but not showy.
V	Reddish yellow	May	I.	
V	Bright yellow	May	I.	
VIII	White, fragrant	June–July		Evergreen.
VIII	Violet-blue, rarely white	September	I.	
IV	White	June–Oct.	Silver line cup	
V	White	June		
IV	White, pink pistils	July–Aug.	Globular heads	
V	Rosy pink	April–May	Pods	Fine autumn foliage.
V	Brick red	April	Yellow	
V	Brilliant scarlet	April	Yellowish green	
I	White	April–May	I.	
V	Greenish white	May–June	Blue	
VI	White	April	Orange	Green twigs and thorns.
IV	White, pink tinge	July–Sept.	I.	Flowers fragrant.
V	Yellow	June–Sept.	Bronze-red	
V	Brownish red with yellow spot	June	Pods	
II	I.		I.	
II	Creamy white	May or June	Bluish white	
IV	Creamy white	May–June	Bluish white	Bright coral-red branches.
IV	Pale yellow	May	Bluish black	Usually a tree.
V	White	June	Blue	
V	White	May	White	Reddish branches.
IV	White		Scarlet	Usually a tree.
V	Golden yellow	March	Scarlet	Often treelike.
IV	Creamy white	June	White or pale blue	

Scientific Name	Common Name	Height in Feet or Inches	Exposure	Soil
Cornus sanguinea	Blood-twig D.	10+′	S	Wet
stolonifera	Red Osier	8′	S	Wet
Coronilla Emerus	Scorpion Senna	9′	S	
Corylopsis pauciflora	Winter Hazel	6′		Peaty, sandy
spicata	Winter Hazel	6′	Sh	Peaty, sandy
Corylus americana	American Hazelnut	10′		
Avellana fusco-rubra	Purple Hazel	15′	S	Moist
maxima	Filbert	30′	S	Moist
rostrata	Beaked Hazelnut	9′	S	Moist
Cotinus coggygria (Rhus cotinus)	Smoke-Tree	15′	S	Well drained
Cotoneaster adpressa	Creeping C.	Creep.	S	
apiculata		3′	S	
Dielsiana	Diel's C.	6′	S	
divaricata	Spreading C.	6′	S	
Francheti	Franchet's C.	6′	S	Well-drained soils preferred
horizontalis	Rock Cotoneaster	Trail.	S	
hupehensis	Hapeh Cotoneaster	6′	S	
microphylla		3′	S	
rotundifolia	Round-leaf C.	6″	S	
salicifolia		15′	Part. Sh	
Simonsii	Simon's C.	4′	S	
Cydonia japonica	See Chænomeles japonica			
Cyrilla racemiflora	Leatherwood	–30′		
Cytisus hirsutus	Broom	2′	S	Neutral
scoparius	Scotch Broom	–10′	S	Limy
supinus	Broom	3′	S	Neutral
Daphne Cneorum	Rose Daphne	1–1½′	S	Peaty or sandy alkal.
Genkwa	Lilac Daphne	–3′	S	

Zone	Color of Flowers	Season of Bloom	Color of Fruit	Remarks
V (IV)	White	May–June	Green	
II	Dull white	May	White	Bright red twigs.
V	Yellow	May		
VI	Yellow, fragrant			
VI	Yellow, fragrant			
IV	Drooping catkins			
(III)	Catkins	March	Green	Leaves purple or brown.
V	Catkins	March	Purplish	
V (IV)	Catkins	March	Beaked green	
V	Mist-like	June–July	Small drupe	
V	Pink	June	Red	
V	Pink	June	Red	
VI (V)	Pinkish	June	Scarlet	
V	Pink	June	Red	
(VII)	Pink	June	Orange	
V	Pink	June	Red	
V	White	May	Red	
VI	White	May	Scarlet	
V	White	June	Scarlet	
VI	White	June	Red	Evergreen in the South.
V	White	June–July	Red	
VII (VI)	White	June–July	I.	Beautiful dense foliage.
V	Yellow	May–June		
VI	Yellow	May or June	I.	
V	Yellow	June		
V	Rose	April and Sept.	Yellowish brown	
VI (V)	Violet	April	I.	

333

Scientific Name	Common Name	Height in Feet or Inches	Exposure	Soil
Daphne Mezereum	February Daphne	–3′	S	Alkaline
Deutzia gracilis	Slender Deutzia	3–6′	S	
Lemoinei	Lemoine Deutzia	3′	S	
scabra	Rough Deutzia	4–6′	S	Well drained for greater hardiness
Diervilla hybrida (Weigela)	Collective name for large group of hybrids	10′	S	
rosea (Weigela florida)	Pink Weigela	6–9′	S	
Dirca palustris	Leatherwood	2–4′	S Sh	Moist
Elæagnus angustifolia	Russian Olive	20′	S	Sandy, clay
argentea	Silverberry	6–12′	S	Sandy, clay
longipes (multiflora)	Cherry Elæagnus	9′	S	Sandy, clay
Elsholtzia Stauntoni	Mintshrub	3–5′	S	Well drained
Enkianthus campanulatus	Bellflowertree	6′	S Sh	Acid
subsessilis	Nikko Enkianthus	9′	S	Acid, moist, sandy
Erica carnea	Spring Heath	1′	S	Sandy, acid
Euonymus alatus	Winged E.	6–8′	S	
americanus	Strawberry Bush	5–8′	S Sh	
atropurpureus	Burning-bush	25′		
europæus	Spindletree	20′	S	
japonicus	Evergreen Burning-bush	10–12′	S	Well drained, not particular except E. japonicus which is hardier in dry or sandy soil
patens		9–10′	S Sh	
radicans	Wintercreeper	Climber	S Sh	
var. acutus		Climber	S Sh	
var. Carrierei		Shrubby	S Sh	
var. coloratus		Climber	S	
var. kewensis		Climber	S Sh	
var. vegetus		Climber	S Sh	
Exochorda Giraldii	Pearlbush	10′	S	

Zone	Color of Flowers	Season of Bloom	Color of Fruit	Remarks
IV	Pink, rose, purple	April	Scarlet	
V	Pink, white	May		
V	White	May		
V	Pinkish white	May		
V	Pink	May, June	Capsule	
V	Various (Pinks)	May, June	I.	
IV	Yellow	March–April	Red	
V	Yellow	June	Yellowish	
I	Yellow	June	Silvery	
V	Yellow	June	Red	
V	Red-purple	September	I.	
V	Pink	May	I.	
V	White	May–June		Brilliant autumn coloring.
V	Rose-red	March	I.	Evergreen.
IV	Yellowish	May	Purple	
IV	Greenish purple	June	Light scarlet	
I	Purple		Scarlet	
IV	Yellowish green	May	Pink	
VIII (VII)	I.	June	I.	
VI	White	June–July	Pink	Spreading.
V		June		
V				
V	Greenish	June	Orange	
V				
V				
V	Greenish	June	Orange	
V	White	April–May	I.	

335

Scientific Name	Common Name	Height in Feet or Inches	Exposure	Soil
Exochorda grandiflora	Pearlbush	15'	S Sh	Rich
Forsythia intermedia	Border Goldenbells	9'	S Sh	
var. spectabilis	Showy Border Forsythia	10'	S Sh	
ovata		5'	S Sh	
suspensa	Drooping Golden-bells	9'	S Sh	Indifferent
var. Fortunei		8'	S	
viridissima	Green-stem Golden-bells	9'	S Sh	
Fothergilla Gardeni	Fothergilla	4'	Sh	Light
monticola	Alabama Fothergilla	6'	S	Damp
Gaylussacia baccata	Black Huckleberry	3'	Sh	Dry, sandy
Genista germanica	Broom	2'	S	Dry, sandy
tinctoria	Dyer's Greenweed	3'	S	Dry, sandy
Hamamelis japonica	Jap. Witchhazel	30'	S	
mollis	Chin. Witchhazel	30'	S	
vernalis	Spring Witchhazel	6'	S	Indifferent
virginiana	Common Witchhazel	10–25'	Sh	
Hibiscus syriacus	Rose of Sharon	20'	S Sh	Not too sandy
Hudsonia ericoides	Beach Heather		S	Dry, sandy
tomentosa	Beach Heather		S	Dry, sandy
Hydrangea arborescens		10'		Neutral
macrophylla	House Hydrangea	6'–8'	S	Acid or lime
paniculata	Panicle Hydrangea	25'	S Sh	
quercifolia	Oak-leaf Hydrangea	10'	S Sh	
Hypericum aureum	St. Johnswort	3'	Sh	Sandy
calycinum	Aaronsbeard	1'	Sh	Sandy
densiflorum		6'	Sh	Sandy, rocky
Moserianum	Goldflower	1½'	Sh	Sandy

Zone	Color of Flowers	Season of Bloom	Color of Fruit	Remarks
V	White	April–May	5-ribbed capsule	
V	Yellow	April	I.	
V	Bright yellow	April		
V	Yellow	April	I.	
V	Yellow	April	I.	
V	Yellow	April		Vigorous grower.
VI (V)	Yellow	April	I.	
V or VI	White	April	I.	
V	White	May		Larger flower.
I			Black, shiny	
V	Small	June–July	Pods	Needs protection in winter.
V	Yellow	June–Aug.	Pods	Needs protection in winter.
V	Lemon-yellow	Feb. or Mar.		
V	Golden yellow	Feb. or Mar.		
V	Light yellow	Feb. or Mar.		
IV (III)	Yellow	Oct. or Nov.	Black seeds	
V or VI	White, red, purple	August	Brown	
II	Greenish			Seashore.
II		May–July		Seashore.
III	White	June–July		
VII	Blue or pink	June–July		Flowers of some horticultural forms may be changed from pink to blue by adding iron filings to the soil.
IV	White, pink, greenish bronze	July	I.	
VI(V)	Pinkish white-purplish	July	I.	
V	Yellow	July–August	I.	
VI(V)	Yellow	July–Sept.	I.	
IV	Bright yellow	July–Sept.		Evergreen.
(VII)	Yellow	Aug.–Sept.	I.	

Scientific Name	Common Name	Height in Feet or Inches	Exposure	Soil
Hypericum prolificum		5'	Sh	Sandy, rocky
Ilex Aquifolium	English Holly	40'	Sh	Rich, well drained
cornuta	Chinese Holly	9–15'	S	Well drained
crenata	Japanese Holly	5–10'	Part. Sh	Peaty (acid)
var. microphylla		4'	Sh	Rich, well drained
glabra	Inkberry	8'	Sh	Wet (acid)
lævigata	Smooth Winterberry	8'	S	Damp (acid)
opaca	American Holly	50'	Sh	
serrata	Jap. Winterberry	8'	S	Peaty
verticillata	Winterberry	8'	S	Wet
Indigofera	Indigo	4–6'	Protected	Neutral
Itea virginica	Sweet Spire	3–8'	Sh	Wet
Jasminum nudiflorum	Winter Jasmine	4–6'	S or Part. Sh	Rich
Juniperus chinensis Pfitzeriana	Pfitzer's Juniper	10'	S	Dry, sandy
communis	Common Juniper	30'		
horizontalis	Creeping Juniper	1½'		
Sabina	Savin Juniper	4'	S	Dry, sandy
var. tamariscifolia		10'		
squamata var. Meyeri		5'		
Kalmia angustifolia	Sheep Laurel	6–24"	S Sh	Sandy, acid
latifolia	Mt. Laurel	8'	Sh	Sandy, acid
Kerria japonica	Kerria	4–6'	S Sh	
Koïkwitzia amabilis	Beautybush	6'	S	Good drainage
Laburnum alpinum	Dwarf Golden-chain	10–15'	S, Protect	Well drained, lime
anagyroides	Goldenchain	20'	S, Protect	Well drained, lime
vulgare		30'		
Lagerstrœmia indica	Crape Myrtle	15–20'	S	
Ledum grœnlandicum	Labrador Tea	1–3'	Part. Sh	Wet

Zone	Color of Flowers	Season of Bloom	Color of Fruit	Remarks
II		July–Sept.		Evergreen.
IV		May–June	Red	Diœcious.
VI or VII	White	June	Red	
V or VI	White	June	Black	
IV		May–June		Diœcious.
V	White	July	Black	
IV	White	July	Orange-red	
V			Red	Diœcious.
V	White	July	Red	
IV	White	July	Red	
V	Pink to rosy-purple		Pods	Spring pruning.
V or VI	White	July	I.	
(VI)	Yellow	Feb.–March	I.	Green stems, 3 parted leaves.
V				Pyramidal.
I			Dark blue	
I			Blue	
IV			Brownish blue	Needs protection from severe winter winds.
IV				
V				Upright, dense.
I	Pink, white	June	I.	
V (IV)	White, pink	June	I.	
V	Golden yellow	June–Sept.	I.	
V	Pink and orange	June	I.	
V		May	I.	
(V)	Yellow		Pods 2″ long seeds black	
III	Yellow	May–June	Pods	
VIII	Purple to white	Aug.–Oct.	I.	
I	White	May–June	I.	

Scientific Name	Common Name	Height in Feet or Inches	Exposure	Soil
Leiophyllum buxifolium	Sand Myrtle	1'	S Sh	Acid
Lespedeza bicolor	Shrub Bushclover	3–6'	S	
formosa	Purple Bushclover	3–10'	S	
Leucothoë Catesbæi	Drooping Leucothoë	2–3'	Sh	Acid
Ligustrum amurense	Amur Privet	15'	S Sh	⎫
Ibolium	Ibolium Privet	15'	S Sh	⎬ Indifferent
Ibota (obtusifolium)	Ibota Privet	15'	S Sh	⎭
japonicum	Japanese Privet	15'	S Sh	⎫
lucidum	Glossy Privet	15'	S Sh	⎬ Indifferent
obtusifolium var. Regelianum	Regel's Privet	15'	S Sh	⎭
ovalifolium	California Privet	15'	S Sh	
vulgare	European Privet	15'	S Sh	
Lonicera fragrantissima	Fragrant Honey-suckle	4–5'	S	⎫
Korolkovii	Blueleaf Honeysuckle	12'	S	
Maacki	Amur Honeysuckle	12–15'	S	
Morrowi	Morrow Honeysuckle	8'	S	
nitida	Shiny Honeysuckle	6'	S	⎬ Indifferent
pileata	Privet Honeysuckle	Prostrate	S	
tatarica	Tatarian Honeysuckle	10'	S	
var. lutea		10'	S	⎭
Lycium chinense	Box-thorn	12'	S Sh	Any
Magnolia glauca	Sweet Bay	60'	Part. Sh	Rich. Heavy.
Mahonia Aquifolium	Oregon Hollygrape	2–3'	Sh	Dry, sandy
Bealei	Leather-leaf Holly-grape	2–3'	Sh	Dry, sandy
Meratia præcox	Wintersweet	4'	Part. Sh South	Sandy
Myrica caroliniensis	Northern Bayberry	8–9'	S	Dry
Gale	Sweet Gale	3'	S	Moist

Zone	Color of Flowers	Season of Bloom	Color of Fruit	Remarks
V	White	May–June	I.	
IV	Rose-purple	Sept.–Oct.	I.	
VI (V)	Rose-purple	Sept.	I.	
V	White	April–May	I.	
V	White	June–July	Black	
V	White		Black	
V	White	July	Black	
VII or VIII	White	August	Black	
VIII	White	Aug.–Sept.	Black	Evergreen.
V	White	July	Black	
(V)	White	August		
IV	White	June–July	Black	
(V)	White	March–April		
V	Rose	May		
IV	White	May	Red	
V	White	May, June	Blood red	
VII or VIII	White		Blue, purple	
(V)	Whitish		Purple	
V	Rose, white	May	Red	
V	Rose, white	May	Yellow	
V	Purple	July	Orange-red	
V	White, fragrant	All Summer	Red	Shrubby in North. Tree in South.
V	Yellow	April	Black	
VI (V)	Yellow	April	Black	
VII	Purple-brown	January		
IV	I.		Gray	
I	I.		Gray	

Scientific Name	Common Name	Height in Feet or Inches	Exposure	Soil
Nandina domestica	Nandina	3–6′	S Sh	Peaty loam
Neillia sinensis		5–6′	S	Moist
Nemopanthus mucronatus	Mountain-Holly	8′	Half Sh	Swampy
Osmanthus Aquifolium (O. ilicifolius)	Holly-olive	7–20′	Protected spots	Peaty
Pachistima Canbyi		10″	S, or Part. Sh	
Philadelphus coronarius	Mock Orange	10′	S	Lime to neutral
grandiflorus	Big Scentless Mock Orange	12′	S Half Sh	Dry, neutral
Lemoinei "Avalanche"		6′	S	Lime to neutral
virginalis	Virginal Mock Orange	6′	S	
Photinia serrulata		40′		
villosa	Christmas Berry	15′	S	Light, sandy, well drained
Physocarpus opulifolius	Ninebark	10′	S Sh	Cool, moist
Pieris floribunda	Mt. Andromeda	3–5′	Sh	Acid
japonica	Jap. Andromeda	3–5′	Sh	Acid
Potentilla fruticosa	Shrubby Cinquefoil	3′		Dry or wet
tridentata	Wineleaf Cinquefoil	8–10″	Part. Sh	Dry, acid
Prunus Besseyi	Western Sand Cherry	Prostrate	S	
maritima	Beach Plum	6′	S	Sandy
pumila	Sand Cherry	3–5′	S	Sandy
tomentosa	Nankin Cherry	5′	S	Good, well-drained loam
Pyracantha coccinea Lalandi	Firethorn	6–20′	S	Limestone well drained
Rhamnus cathartica	Buckthorn	12′	S Sh	Sand or clay
Frangula	Alder Buckthorn	12′	S Sh	Sand or clay
Rhododendron carolinianum	Caro. Rhododendron	9′	Sh	Subacid
catawbiense	Catawba Rhododendron	6–18′	Sh	Subacid
maximum	Rosebay Rhododendron	36′	Sh	Subacid

Zone	Color of Flowers	Season of Bloom	Color of Fruit	Remarks
VII or VIII	White	June–July	Red	Evergreen.
V	Pink	June	I.	
III	White	May	Brilliant red	Beautiful autumn foliage.
VI	White	June–July	Bluish	Evergreen.
V	White	April–May		Evergreen.
IV	White	June		
IV	White	May–June		Mass planting.
V	White, fragrant	June		Large flower.
V	Racemes of white semi-double flws.			
V				Evergreen.
V	White	May	Red	
IV	Pinkish-greenish-white	May–June	Reddish	
V	White	April–May	I.	
VI (V)	White	April–May	I.	
I	Yellow and white	June–Oct.	I.	
	White	June, Sept.	I.	
III	White		Black	
IV	White		Red or yellow	Seashore.
IV	White		Purple-black	
IV (III)	White	April	Scarlet	
VI or VII	White	May–June	Orange-scarlet	Evergreen leaves and large bunches of fruit make gorgeous show.
II	Greenish	June	Black	
II	Pale yellow	June, July, August	Black	
V	Pink	May	I.	
V	Red and purple	May	I.	
IV	Pink or white	May	I.	

Scientific Name	Common Name	Height in Feet or Inches	Exposure	Soil
Rhododendron minus		10'	Sh	Acid
Rhodotypos kerrioides	White Kerria	4'	S Sh	Indifferent
Rhus canadensis	Fragrant Sumac	2–6'	S Sh	Dry
copallina	Shining Sumac	3–5'	S	Dry
Cotinus	Common Smoke Tree	15'	S	Well drained
glabra	Smooth Sumac	15–20'	S Sh	Dry
tribolata	Lemonade Sumac	6'		Dry, sandy
typhina	Staghorn Sumac	15'	S Sh	Any
Ribes alpinum	Mountain Currant	8'		
Cynosbati		5'		
odatorum	Flowering Currant	6'	Sh	Moder. fertile
Robinia hispida	Rose Acacia	–3'	S	Limy
viscosa	Clammy Locust	40'		
Rosa alba		6'		
blanda		6'	S	
carolina	Pasture Rose	3'	S	
centifolia	Cabbage Rose	6'		
cinnamomea	Cinnamon Rose	6'		
damascena	Damask Rose	8'		
Eglanteria (rubiginosa)	Eglantine Rose	6'	S	Heavy clay
gallica	French Rose	4'	S	
Harisonii	Harison's Yellow	9'	S	
Hugonis	Father Hugo's R.	8'	S	
moschata	Musk Rose			
multiflora	Japanese Rose		S	
nitida	Bristly Rose	1½'	S	
palustris	Swamp Rose	6'		Swampy

344

Zone	Color of Flowers	Season of Bloom	Color of Fruit	Remarks
V	Pink, spotted with green	June–July		Evergreen.
V	White	May to Fall	Black	
IV	Yellow	March–April	Red	Bank cover.
IV	Yellowish green	August	Red	
V	Mist-like, tinted with purple	July–Aug.		
VI	Greenish	July–August	Red	
V	Greenish		Red and hairy	Ill-smelling.
IV	Greenish	June–July	Crimson and hairy	
III	Greenish-yellow		Scarlet	Diœcious.
IV	Green		Wine-red, prickly	
V	Yellow	April	Purplish brown	
V	Rose-pink	June	I.	
VI	Pink	May–June	Pods	
V	White or pinkish	June		
II	Pink, single	May–June		
IV	Pink	June, July	Red	
V	Pink, very double	June		
IV	Red, fragrant	June		
V	Pale pink to red, fragrant	June		
V (IV)	Pink	June	Red	
V	Pink to crimson, solitary	June		Flower 3″ wide.
V	Orange-yellow	June	Red	
V	Sulphur yellow	May	Red	
VII	White	June		
V	White	June	Red	
V	Pink	Spring	Red	
IV	Pink	June–August		

Scientific Name	Common Name	Height in Feet or Inches	Exposure	Soil
Rosa persica	Persian Yellow	9′	S	
micrantha		6′	S	
rugosa	Rugosa Rose	6′	S	
setigera	Prairie Rose	15′	S	Heavy clay
spinosissima	Scotch Rose	3′	S	
virginiana		6′	S	
Wichuraiana	Memorial Rose	Prostrate		
Rubus cuneifolius	Sand Blackberry	1–3′	S	Dry, sandy
odoratus	Flowering Raspberry	3–6′	Sh	Rich, well drained
procumbens	American Dewberry	Prostrate	S	Dry, sandy
Salix Caprea	Goat Willow	25′		
discolor	Pussy Willow	20′	S	Wet
pentandra	Bay or Laurel Willow	60′		
tristis		1½′		Dry, sandy
Sambucus canadensis	American Elder	5–8′	S Sh	Swampy
racemosus	European Red-berried Elder	6–8′	Sh	Indifferent
Shepherdia argentea	Buffalo Berry	18′	Half Sh	Cool
canadensis		8′	Half Sh	Dry, rocky or sandy
Sorbaria Aitchisonii	Kashmir False-spirea	6–8′	S	Indifferent
sorbifolia	Ural False-spirea	3–5′	S	Indifferent
Spiræa arguta	Garland Spirea	4–5′		
Billiardii	Billiard Spirea	6′		
Bumalda	Bumalda Spirea	3′	Pref. S but most are tolerant of some shade	Neutral
var. Anthony Waterer		2½′		
var. Froebeli		3′		
cantoniensis		4–5′		
latifolia		4–6′		
prunifolia	Bridalwreath	4–6′		

346

Zone	Color of Flowers	Season of Bloom	Color of Fruit	Remarks
(VII)	Yellow	June	Red	
V	Pink or white in clusters of 3 or 4	June		
IV	Pink, white	Spring	Red	
V	Pink	June–August	Red	
V	Yellow, white	June	Black	
	Pink	June, July	Red	
V	White, fragrant	June		Half evergreen.
IV	White or pinkish		Blackish	Useful ground cover on poor land.
III	Rosy purple	June–Sept.	Red	
III	White	May	Black, edible	
V	Catkins	March		
II	Catkins	March	I.	Hardy to Nova Scotia.
IV	Catkins			Leaves lustrous.
III	Catkins	April		
IV	White	June–July	Black	
IV	White	April–May	Red	
II	Yellowish	April–May		Good near seashore.
II	Yellowish	April-May	Red or yellow	Dry soil.
VI (V)	White	June	I.	
II	White	June–August	I.	
IV	White	April	I.	
V	Rose	July–August	I.	
V	Pink	June	I.	
V	Deep rose	June–July	I.	
V	Deep rose	Early June	I.	
VI or VII	White	May	I.	
II (I)	White, pink	June–August	I.	
(V)	White	April	I.	

347

Scientific Name	Common Name	Height in Feet or Inches	Exposure	Soil
Spiræa Thunbergii	Thunberg Spirea	3'	See Spiræa on p. 346	Neutral
tomentosa	Hard Hack	4'		
vanhouttei	Vanhoutte Spirea	3–6'		
Staphylea colchica	Bladdernut	10'	Sh	Moist, rich
Stephanandra incisa (flexuosa)	Cutleaf Steph.	3–6'	S.	Peaty
Stewartia pentagyna		15'		
Styrax japonica	Japanese Snowbell	25'	Half Sh	Moist, but well drained
Symphoricarpos albus (S. racemosus)	Snowberry	–4'	Half Sh	Lime and clay
vulgaris	Coralberry	–4'	Sh	
Symplocos paniculata	Asiatic Sweetleaf	36'		
Syringa chinensis	Rouen Lilac	10–12'	S	Neutral
japonica		30'		
pekinensis		15'		
persica	Persian Lilac	8'	S	
villosa	Himalaya Lilac	15'	S	
vulgaris	Common Lilac	15+'	S	
Tamarix africana	African Tamarisk	12'	S	Light, sandy
gallica	French Tamarisk	30'		
parviflora	Tamarisk	15'	Salt air and wind	Not too much lime
pentandra	Fivestamen T.	15'		
Taxus baccata repandens	English Yew	Nearly prostrate		
canadensis	Ground-Hemlock	6'		
cuspidata brevifolia	Shrubby Japanese Yew			
Vaccinium canadense		1–2'		
corymbosum	Highbush Blueberry	12'	Moist	Acid
pennsylvanicum	Lowbush Blueberry	6–15"	Dry	Acid
Viburnum acerifolium	Dockmackie	5'	Sh	Dry

348

Zone	Color of Flowers	Season of Bloom	Color of Fruit	Remarks
V	White	March–April	I.	
V	Pinkish purple	July–August	I.	
IV	White	May	I.	
VI	Yellow-white	May–June	Green	
V	White	June	I.	
V	White stamens, orange anthers			
V	White, fragrant	May–June		Usually a tree.
IV	Pink	August	White	
V		August	Red	
V	White	May–June	Blue	Very fine fruit cluster.
V	Reddish lilac	June	I.	
V	Yellowish white	June–July		Tree-like.
V	Yellowish white	June		
V	Lav., white	June	I.	
V	Lilac	July	I.	
IV	Various	June	I.	
VIII	Clear pink	May		Seashore.
VII	White or pinkish	June–Aug.		
V	Pink	April	I.	
V	Pink	Aug.–Sept.	I.	
VI				Evergreen.
III				
IV				
IV	Greenish white to reddish		Blue	
IV	White	April	Blue	Edible fruit. Crimson autumn leaves.
III	White	April	Blue	
III or IV	White	June	Black	

349

Scientific Name	Common Name	Height in Feet or Inches	Exposure	Soil
Viburnum affine		6'		
americanum	*See* V. tribolum			
Carlesii	Fragrant Viburnum	4–6'	S	
cassinoides	Withe-rod	6'	S	Wet
dentatum	Arrow-wood	5–15'	S or Sh	
dilatatum	Linden V. or Jap. Bushcranberry	10'	S	
Lantana	Wayfaring Tree	15'	S	
Lentago	Nannyberry	30'	Sh	Wet or moist
molle	Kentucky Viburnum	12'		
Opulus	Highbush Cranberry	10'	S Sh	
var. nanum	Dwarf Cranberry Bush		S Sh	
prunifolium	Blackhaw	30'	S Sh	
rhytidophyllum	Leatherleaf	10'	Shaded in winter	Well drained
Sargenti		12'		
Sieboldii	Siebold V.	10'	S	Damp
theiferum		12'		
tomentosum	Doublefile V.	10'	S	
tomentosum plicatum	Japanese Snowball	10'	S	
trilobum (americanum)	American V.	10'	S Sh	
Wrightii	Wright or Oriental	6–8'	S	
Vitex Agnus-castus	Chaste-tree	10'	S	Slightly acid
Weigela	*See* Diervilla			
Zanthorhiza apiifolia	Yellowroot	1–2'	Sh	Wet or dry
Zenobia pulverulenta	Zenobia	2–3'	Sh	Acid

Zone	Color of Flowers	Season of Bloom	Color of Fruit	Remarks
IV	White	May–June		
V	Pink	April	Black	
III or IV	White	May	Black	Crimson autumn leaves.
IV	White	June	Black	
V	White	June	Red	One of the best red-fruited shrubs.
IV	White	June–July	Black	
II	White	May	Black	
V	White	May	Black	
III	White	May–June	Red	
III	(No flowers)			Good accent plant.
V	White	April	Black	
(V)	White	May	Red to black	Evergreen.
V	White	May–June	Scarlet	
V	White	May–June	Black	
VI	Cream white	May–June	Red	
V	White	May or June	Blue-black	One of the best white-flowering shrubs.
V	White	June		
II	White	May	Red	
V	White		Red	
VII (VI)	Lilac	July–Sept.	I.	Stems winterkill at Phila.
IV	Maroon	April	I.	Excellent ground cover
V	White	June	I.	Glaucous leaves.

351

IX

Hedges

The hedgerow has been a familiar feature of the landscape in Europe since mediæval times. But the hedge antedates the mediæval garden. The ancient Romans used hedges of myrtle, laurel, and box in their gardens. Indeed so important a feature was the hedge in gardens of this period that the gardeners who cared for it and kept it faithfully trimmed to the desired form and height were given the dignity of a special title, being known as "topiarius."

The designers of the Italian villas used hedges of ilex and cypress as great walls of green and made them architecturally important components of the design. The French gave the hedge greater scale to conform to their vast plaisances by using large trees such as elm, linden, hornbeam and beech, trimming them to vertical form. In England hedges played an important part in the design of the "knott" gardens, laid out in geometric patterns. Sometimes the spaces within the hedges were flower beds, but more often they were bits of turf. Herb gardens were frequently designed in this style, each plot being planted to a single herb, and the whole forming a pleasing pattern. In the gardens which surround the Elizabethan manor houses of England, there are magnificent yew hedges which were planted more than four hundred years ago and which have been carefully tended throughout the years.

The primary purpose of a hedge is protection. Another purpose is shelter from the wind, and the third is enclosure. In landscape design, the hedge is one of the best means of enclosing a formal area and separating it from the outer world. But not only does a hedge enclose and frame the garden; it may also be used to frame the vistas within the garden and to provide a background for flowering plants. It would be difficult indeed to find a more satisfactory background for masses of bright flowers than the deep green of an evergreen hedge. The colors of the blossoms are contrasted effectively with the dark green of the background. The hedge is interesting enough in texture, but is not conspicuous or obtrusive.

Furthermore, a hedge has the great attribute of permanence. It fixes the major lines of the design. It establishes the background for the garden, against which the succession of color and mass moves in ever-changing sequence. The hedge is not changeless in itself, but it grows in a slower cycle, and thereby imparts an air of stability to the scene—invites confidence. By its continued existence it links the past with the present. There is the hedge. Season after season the flowers come and go. Generation after generation those who care for the garden come and go—but the hedge remains.

TYPES OF HEDGES

Hedges vary in size from small edging plants hardly a foot in height to towering trees. They may be extremely formal in outline, being trimmed to even surfaces and regular lines, or they may be natural in growth, with billowing masses of foliage and a profusion of flowers. Every kind has its particular adaptation.

The width of a hedge is something not always easy to predict. Theoretically, most hedges can be kept at any desired dimension of height or width. In actual practice it is not possible to do this, for the plants must be allowed to make some growth each year or they will suffer both in vigor and in appearance. It is essential that adequate space be allowed for the eventual spread of the hedge. One occasionally sees box hedges, planted originally beside the garden paths as edgings of the flower beds, which have grown so wide that they entirely close the path.

Hedge materials may be derived from many sources; from deciduous trees of naturally thick growth, branching close to the ground; from evergreen trees which have a fine texture and closely massed foliage; from deciduous shrubs which have dense foliage and which make vigorous growth; from evergreen shrubs; from herbs; and from vines which may be trained to grow on a frame of any desired shape. In order to be satisfactory as a hedge plant a tree or shrub must meet certain very definite requirements. It must possess thick foliage of fine texture, it must be capable of even growth, it must produce branches and foliage close to the ground, and, in the case of trimmed, formal hedges, it must have the ability to withstand cutting.

PLANTING

As the roots of hedge plants are bound to be restricted, it is important to have the soil well prepared before planting is done. To soil of average fertility the addition of manure at the rate of 1 ton to 200 linear feet is recommended. Since hedge plants are to form a dense wall of green, the individual plants should grow so closely that they are not distinguishable in the general mass. The plants are, therefore, set much more closely than they would be in the usual shrubbery border. There should be good light and air on each side of the hedge in order to make up for this deficiency in the interior of the hedge. A hedge which is placed too close to a wall not only looks out of place but seldom does well. Hedges under trees are rarely satisfactory. The root system of a hedge is necessarily crowded. When to this handicap is added the competition of tree roots, it is impossible to obtain vigorous growth and development. We have frequent examples of this in the case of privet hedges which thrive well in the open but which become weak and spindly at the point where they pass under trees. A few hedge plants such as Taxus cuspidata and Ilex glabra are exceptions, and thrive reasonably well under the shade of trees.

In order to increase the density of the growth, hedges are sometimes planted in double rows, the plants being either staggered or paired. The advantages to be gained are somewhat doubtful and a single row is usually adequate.

When planting, the trench should be opened to a depth approximately equal to the depth of the balls of earth, or, in the case of plants which are not balled, to the depth of the root system. After the plants have been spaced in the trench each individual plant should be adjusted for depth and the earth should be filled in about the plants, as in any planting operation. A tape stretching along the side of the trench will aid in the correct spacing of the plants. Care should be taken to see that the plants are in an absolutely vertical position and in line with each other. The usual watering and trimming should follow planting.

PROTECTION AGAINST ENCROACHING ROOTS

Some of the more vigorous hedge plants have root systems which reach out long distances in search of the nourishment they require to maintain their rapid growth and abundant foliage. Privet is one of the most greedy in this respect, and for this reason it is a bad neighbor for the flower border. The bush honeysuckles, the viburnums and the lilacs are also greedy feeders. If close proximity of such hedges to flower beds is unavoidable, then it is wise to interpose a barrier between them. One device is to dig a trench along the garden side of the hedge 18 inches deep and as wide as the spade. Fill the trench with rocks and a lean mixture of cement, about one part cement, three parts sand, and five parts coarse aggregate (gravel or crushed stone). This will keep the roots from intruding into the garden, but it will be necessary to watch for surface roots hurdling over the wall. A modification of this scheme possible on sloping land is to have the garden on ground higher than that outside and in this case the wall becomes a retaining wall, with its foundation below the frost line. The same results could be obtained from burying sheet zinc in a vertical plane parallel to the hedge.

No precaution need be taken against the roots of box, arborvitæ, or red cedar because these roots are confined closely under the tree in a dense mat. Hemlock roots are a little more rangy but are not very damaging to other plants. A separation of 3 feet of space (path or turf), will be enough protection against hemlock roots.

CARE

Untrimmed hedges require no more care than any ordinary planting of the same material. A hedge that is to be trained to a certain form, however, requires periodic care. Formal hedges should have one clipping or more each year, depending upon the type of material which has been used. Yew, arborvitæ and hemlock may be kept in excellent condition with one trimming a year, although two clippings are sometimes given. Privet should have three or four clippings a season, being trimmed whenever it has outgrown its prescribed size. Box and lilacs require but one clipping; beech one clipping—never more. The purpose of trimming is to keep the hedge thick and neat and within bounds. Sometimes an informal hedge may be trimmed lightly to help thicken the mass of foliage. For most evergreen hedges the best season of the year is spring, before new growth starts. But because this is a very busy time for gardeners summer trimming is often resorted to and the results are entirely satisfactory. In this case trimming is done after growth has practically ceased. Lilac hedges should be trimmed in June; box hedges in August. The only tool necessary for the clipping of a small hedge is a pair of shears with long blades and handles. The type with the handles placed at an angle with the blades is the most desirable as it enables the worker to reach the lower parts of the plant without undue bending. There are a number of excellent mechanical hedge trimmers on the market which are of great value if extensive hedges are to be kept trimmed. The blades are set in a series, cutting much as do the blades of a hay mower, and the work can be done rapidly and efficiently. Ladders on wheels are a great aid in clipping high hedges and are used extensively on English estates where the trimming of old yew hedges and trees is one of the important seasonal jobs. The wheel type of ladder is so convenient a piece of equipment for a variety of garden operations that it seems strange that it is so rarely used in this country.

Hedges of regular and geometric outline require more frequent clipping than the more simple forms. Nothing gives a

Hemlock
White Pine
Japanese Yew

Mugo Pine
Japanese Barberry

Beech and
Hornbeam

Spreading form of Japanese Yew

Privet, best form

GOOD FORMS OF HEDGES

Privet, fair form, but it easily becomes the next type with sparse
lower branches

Privet, poor form, because the
lower branches, deprived of light,
become sparse

HEDGE FORMS WHICH ARE NOT SATISFACTORY

garden an appearance of neglect more quickly than a formal hedge in the stages of reverting to the wild. The trimming of hedges into definite forms and shapes requires endless patience and no little practice. Topiary work has never been as popular here in this country as it has been in France and England. Perhaps it is that we have not patience enough, or perhaps it is that even our formal estates are not so formal as to require this extreme expression of the dominance of will power over nature.

The general care of hedge plants does not differ appreciably from the usual routine. An occasional cultivation is beneficial and prevents the intrusions of large weeds or encroaching trees. Nothing spoils the beauty of a hedge more surely than seedling trees which have been allowed to grow up beside it, or within it. At first they are unnoticed. Then by the time they are well above the top of the hedge they are difficult to remove, and their removal leaves an unsightly gap in the hedge.

The yearly application of a complete fertilizer is one of the best means of promoting vigor and growth. A mulch of manure applied in the autumn will not only increase the fertility of the soil but will give protection to the roots during the winter. Box hedges respond remarkably well to an application of humus. This should be worked into the soil along the two sides of the hedge just outside the root ends. In order to rejuvenate an old box hedge which has suffered from neglect, the soil should be trenched along each side of the hedge, at the outer edge of the roots. The soil should be removed to a depth of about 15 inches and the trench should be refilled with a mixture of humus and top-soil. The amount of humus will depend upon the quantity available; any proportion up to one part humus to one part top-soil will be satisfactory—the more humus the better.

If a box hedge has been killed to the ground by an unusually severe winter, do not make the mistake of having it dug up. Cut it back to stubs about 3 inches high and wait. Box has wonderful vitality and often has the power to recuperate, if given a chance. This salvaging job should be done early in the spring before the rush of spring work begins. If it is not done then it will probably be postponed until summer and in the meantime the box, in trying to regain life, will send its sap feebly into all the twigs instead of concentrating its efforts on a few adventitious buds at the end of the stubs. The same treatment will often save a privet hedge which has been injured by severe cold.

HEDGE MATERIAL

EVERGREEN TREES

Scientific Name	Common Name	Suitable for Clipped or Unclipped Hedge	Eventual Height	Minimum Height by Trimming	Spacing
Chamaecyparis obtusa	Hinoki Cypress	C & U	20'	8'	2-3'
obtusa Crippsii	Cripps Golden Cypress	C & U	20'	8'	2-3'
obtusa gracilis	Slender Hinoki Cypress	C & U	12'	6'	2-2½'
pisifera	Sawara Cypress	C & U	30'	6'	2-3'
pisifera plumosa	Plume Cypress	C & U	30'	5'	2-3'
pisifera squarrosa	Moss Cypress	C & U	20'	5'	2-3'
Lawsoniana	Lawson Cypress	U	30'		2-3'
Ilex Aquifolium	English Holly	U	8'		2-2½'
opaca	American Holly	C & U	8'	4'	2-2½'
Juniperus virginiana	Red cedar	C & U	25'	6'	2½-3'
v. Canaertii	Cannart Red Cedar	C & U	25'	6'	2½-3'
v. glauca	Silver Red Cedar	C & U	20'	6'	2½-3'
excelsa stricta	Greek Juniper	U	12'		2½-3'
chinensis Pfitzeriana	Pfitzer's Juniper	C & U	8'	4'	3-4'
chinensis pyramidalis	Columnar Chinese Juniper	U	20'		2-3'
Picea excelsa (P. abies)	Norway Spruce	C & U	30'	6'	3'
alba (P. glauca)	Canadian Spruce	U	30'		3'
Pinus Strobus	White Pine	C & U	40'	10'	3-6'
sylvestris	Scots Pine	U	20'		3-5'
Thunbergii	Japanese Black Pine	U	40'		3-6'
Pseudotsuga Douglasii	Douglas Fir		30'		3-5'
Taxus cuspidata	Japanese Yew	C & U	12'	4'	2½-4'
cus. fastigiata		C & U	12'	5'	2-3'
cus. capitata		C & U	20'	8'	2-3'

baccata	English Yew	C & U	20'	10'	3-5'
baccata adpressa		C & U	20'	10'	3-4'
media Hicksii		U	8'		2-2½'
Thuya occidentalis	American Arborvitæ	C & U	30'	8'	2-3'
occ. Wareana	Siberian Arborvitæ	C & U	30'	8'	2-3'
occ. Douglasii		C & U	20'	8'	2-3'
occ. pyramidalis		C & U	20'	8'	2-2½'
orientalis	Chinese Arborvitæ	C & U	25'	8'	2-3'
orientalis elegantissima		C & U	25'	8'	2-3'
Tsuga canadensis	Canada Hemlock	C & U	30'	10'	3-4'
caroliniana	Carolina Hemlock	C & U	30'	10'	3-4'

HEDGE MATERIAL

EVERGREEN SHRUBS AND DWARF EVERGREEN TREES

Scientific Name	Common Name	Suitable for Clipped or Unclipped Hedges	Eventual Height	Minimum Height by Trimming	Spacing
Berberis Juliane	Barberry	C & U	6'	3'	2'
verruculosa		C & U	3'	2'	1½'
Buxus sempervirens	Box	C & U	8–10'	4'	1–2'
semp. arborescens	Tree Box	U	25'		5–15'
semp. suffruticosa	Dwarf Box Edging	C & U	6–8'	1½'	6"–1½'
Chamaecyparis obtusa nana	Dwarf Cypress	C & U	10'	2½'	1½–2'
obt. compacta		C & U	6'	3'	1½–2'
Euonymus radicans		C & U	4'		2–2½'
rad. minimus (kewensis)		C & U	3'		1½'
rad. vegetus		U	5'		2–2½'
Ilex crenata	Japanese holly	U	8'		2'
c. microphylla		C & U	6'	2½'	1–2'
c. latifolia		U	8'		2–2½'
c. numularia		C & U	4'	2'	1–2½'
Juniperus communis depressa plumosa		C & U	4'		2½–3½'
Lonicera nitida	Evergreen Honeysuckle	U	5'		15–21'
Picea excelsa Maxwellii	Dwarf Norway Spruce	U	2½'	1½'	1', less
Pieris floribunda	Andromeda	C & U	6'		1½–2'
Pinus montana Mugo	Mugo Pine	C & U	10'	4'	2–4'
Pyracantha coccinea	Firethorn	C & U	6'	3'	2–3'
Taxus cuspidata brevifolia	Dwarf Japanese Yew	U	6'	2'	1¼–2'
cuspidata densa		C & U	4'	2'	1¼–2'
baccata repandens	Dwarf English Yew	C & U	3'		
Thuya occidentalis Hoveyi		C & U	6'	4'	2–3'
occidentalis Reidii		C & U	6'	3'	1½–2½'
orientalis Sieboldii (T. orien. compacta)		C & U	5'	3'	2–3'

HEDGE MATERIAL

DECIDUOUS TREES

Scientific Name	Common Name	Suitable for Clipped or Unclipped Hedge	Eventual Height	Minimum Height by Trimming	Spacing
Acer campestre	Hedge Maple	U	25'		3-6'
Ginnala	Amur Maple	U	25'		3-4'
Carpinus Betulus	European Hornbeam	C	20'	6'	2-3'
caroliniana	American Hornbeam	C	20'	6'	2-3'
Crataegus cordata	Washington Thorn	U	20'		3'
Crus-galli	Cockspur Thorn	C & U	20'	10'	3'
Oxyacantha	English Hawthorn	C & U	20'	10'	3'
Elaeagnus angustifolia	Russian Olive	U	25'		4-6'
Fagus sylvatica	European Beech	C	30'	8'	3-4'
Gleditsia triacanthos	Honey Locust	U	40'		3-6'
Maclura pomifera	Osage Orange	U	25'	May be cut to 1' and will sprout again	2-4'
Malus floribunda	Japanese flowering crab	U	20'		4-6'
ioensis	Prairie Crab	U	20'		4-6'
spectabilis	Chinese flowering crab	U	20'		4-6'
Ostrya virginiana	Hop Hornbeam	C	25'		5-10'
Populus Bolleana (P. alba pyramidalis)		U	40'		
nigra italica	Lombardy Poplar	U	50'		5-8'
Quercus imbricaria	Shingle Oak	C	20'	6'	3-5'
Salix pentandra	Shiny Willow	C	25'		3-6'
Tilia cordata	Small-leaved Linden	C	30'	10'	4-6'
Ulmus pumila	Dwarf Elm	C	25'	8'	4'

HEDGE MATERIAL

DECIDUOUS SHRUBS

Scientific Name	Common Name	Suitable for Clipped or Unchipped Hedge	Eventual Height	Minimum Height by Trimming	Spacing
Abelia grandiflora	Glossy Abelia	U	4-5'		2½-3'
Acanthopanax pentaphyllum	Fiveleaf Aralia	C & U	5-6'	3'	2-3'
Berberis Thunbergii	Japanese Barberry	C & U	4-6'	3'	1½-2'
Thunbergii minor	Dwarf Japanese Barberry	C	1½'	1'	9"-1'
Thun. atropurpurea		C & U	4-5'	3'	1½-2'
Caragana arborescens	Pea-tree	U	10'		2½-3'
Cotoneaster adpressa	Rockspray	U	3'		1-2'
microphylla		C & U	3'	2'	1-1¾'
salicifolia		U	12'		2-2½'
Chaenomeles japonica	Japanese Quince	C & U	12'	5'	2-4'
Citrus trifoliata	Hardy Orange	C & U	15'	5'	2½-3'
Deutzia gracilis	Slender Deutzia	U	3'		1½-2'
Lemoinei	Lemoine's Deutzia	U	4-5'		2'
Euonymus alatus	Winged Burningbush	U	6'		3-4'
Hydrangea arborescens grandiflora		U	4'		2'
paniculata grandiflora		U	15'		2½-3'
Ligustrum amurense	Amur Privet	C & U	15'	4'	1-2'
lucidum	Glossy Privet	C & U	25'	4'	2-2½'
ibota Regelianum	Regel's Privet	C & U	6'	3'	1½-2'
ovalifolium	Cal. Privet	C & U	15'	3'	1-1½'
vulgare	European Privet	C & U	15'	3'	1-1½'
Lonicera fragrantissima	Winter Honeysuckle	U	10'		3-6'
tatarica	Tartarian Honeysuckle	U	10'		3-6'
Maackii		U	18'		4-6'
Morrowii			6'		3-5'
Myrica caroliniensis	Bayberry	C & U	6'	4'	2-3'

Botanical name	Common name				
Philadelphus coronarius	Mock Orange	C & U	10'		3-5'
cor. nanus		U	2'	1½'	1'
Lemoinei	Lemoine's Mock Orange	U	6'		2'
Physocarpus opulifolius	Ninebark	C & U	8'		3'
o. nanus		U	3'	2'	1½-2'
Rhamnus Frangula	Buckthorn	U	15'		2½-3'
Rhodotypos kerrioides	Jetbead	U	6'		2-3'
Rosa Harisonii		U	6'		2-3'
Hugonis		U	6'		2½-3'
rubiginosa		U	6'		2½-3'
rugosa		U	8'		2-3'
Ribes alpinum		U	7'		1½-2'
Spirea Bumalda Froebeli		U	3'		1½-2'
arguta		U	5'		2½-3'
Thunbergii		U	4-5'		2-3'
Van Houttei	Van Houtte's Spirea	U	6-8'		3'
prunifolia	Bridal Wreath	U	10'		3-4'
cantoniensis		U	4-5'		2'
Syringa persica		U	6'		2-2½'
vulgaris		U	15-20'		2½-3'
Viburnum Lantana	Wayfaring tree	U	15'		3'
Lentago	Sheepberry	C & U	30'		3-5'
Opulus nanum	Dwarf Highbush Cranberry	C & U	3'	1½'	1-1½'
prunifolium	Black-haw	U	15-18'	8'	3-4'
tomentosum		U	10'		3-4'
Sieboldii		U	15'		3-5'
dilatatum		U	10'		3'

X

Annuals

Plants classed as annuals are those which complete their life cycle within the space of one year and in this group we find some of our most useful garden flowers. We also commonly place in this class a few flowers such as the snapdragons (antirrhinum) and the ageratums which are not true annuals but which are best handled as such.

The annuals have many uses. They are indispensable in the cutting garden, giving a wealth of bloom throughout the summer and early autumn months; they are of value in the herbaceous border, coming into flower after the first riot of spring bloom has passed, and carrying gallantly on through the heat of midsummer when many of the perennials are quiescent; and if a garden is to be but a temporary affair, to be enjoyed for the space of but a single season, the annuals may be used as the only material in the planting scheme. For window boxes and porch boxes, for potted plants on the terrace or on the low coping of a wall, for the indoor window garden, and for winter bloom in the small greenhouse the annuals can hardly be equalled.

In form and coloring they offer us an extraordinarily wide range. As edging plants we have the lobelias, the dainty little Virginia stock, sweet alyssum, phlox drummondi and the low-growing petunias; for border plants of medium height we have a wealth of material from which to choose—the asters, the marigolds, the poppies, salpiglossis, larkspur, zinnias and countless others; and for the background plants we have the tithonia and the exotic castor bean plant.

EXPOSURE

Annuals are essentially sun-loving plants and there are comparatively few members of this group which will thrive in even partial shade. In selecting a site for the annual garden or flower border, it is, therefore, well to choose an open, sunny location where there is a reasonably good circulation of air.

ANNUALS WHICH WILL ENDURE LIGHT SHADE

Basketflower (Centaurea americana)
Chinese Forget-me-not (Cynoglossum amabile)
Clarkia (Clarkia elegans)
Drummond Phlox (Phlox Drummondii)
Lupine (Lupinus Hartwegii)
Pansy (Viola tricolor)
Snapdragon (Antirrhinum majus)
Sweet Alyssum (Alyssum maritimum)
Sweet-sultan (Centaurea suaveolens)
Sweet-sultan, Royal (Centaurea imperialis)

ANNUALS WHICH WILL ENDURE CONSIDERABLE SHADE

Balsam (Impatiens)
Calliopsis (Coreopsis tinctoria)
Cockscomb (Celosia plumosa)
Flowering Tobacco (Nicotiana)
Godetia (Godetia amœna)
Lobelia (Lobelia erinus)
Monkeyflower (Mimulus)
Periwinkle (Vinca rosea)
Stock, Virginia (Malcomia)

SOIL REQUIREMENTS

The majority of annuals will thrive well in a soil of reasonably good fertility which is well supplied with organic matter, a good, mellow garden loam with a reaction varying from pH. 6.5 to pH. 7.5, being considered ideal. A few annuals will grow well on extremely poor soils, some will tolerate a considerable degree of acidity and some seem to be entirely indifferent to soil conditions. For the annual garden, the soil may be prepared in the autumn or in the early spring as soon as the ground is workable. Adequate preparation will bring increased rewards in the way of more vigorous growth and more abundant bloom. If well-rotted manure or good compost is available it may be spread over the surface of the beds and may then be forked or spaded in, or if time and labor do not have to be taken into consideration the beds may be prepared by double digging (see Chap. XXVIII, page 957). If the beds are prepared in the autumn the surface of the soil should be left rough during the winter. If, however, it is prepared in the spring, the surface of the bed should be carefully levelled and raked with an iron rake until the soil is of fine tilth.

If it seems advisable to further increase the fertility of the soil a top-dressing of commercial fertilizer may be applied early in July and again in early August. A 4-12-4 complete fertilizer will give excellent results and it should be applied at the rate of 2 pounds to every 100 square feet. When the application is made, care should be taken not to get any of the fertilizer on the foliage of the plants as it might cause severe burning. It should be sprinkled lightly on the surface of the soil and watered in.

If the soil tests below a pH. of 6.5, lime should be applied. See Chapter I, page 27.

ANNUALS WHICH WILL GROW ON VERY POOR SOIL

Bartonia (Mentzelia aurea)
California Poppy (Eschscholtzia californica)
Calliopsis (Coreopsis tinctoria)
Corn Poppy (Papaver Rhœas)
Feather Cockscomb (Celosia plumosa)
Four-o'clock (Mirabilis jalapa)
Gaillardia (Gaillardia Lorenziana)
Garden Balsam (Impatiens balsamina)
Godetia, Whitney (Godetia grandiflora)
Love-lies-bleeding (Amaranthus caudatus)
Nasturtium (Tropæolum majus)
Petunia (Petunia hybrida)
Rose Moss (Portulaca grandiflora)
Spiderflower (Cleome spinosa)
Sweet Alyssum (Alyssum maritimum)
Sweet-sultan (Centaurea moschata)

ANNUALS WHICH TOLERATE ACIDITY

Calliopsis (Coreopsis tinctoria)
Flowering tobacco (Nicotiana)
Marigold (Tagetes)
Verbena (Verbena)

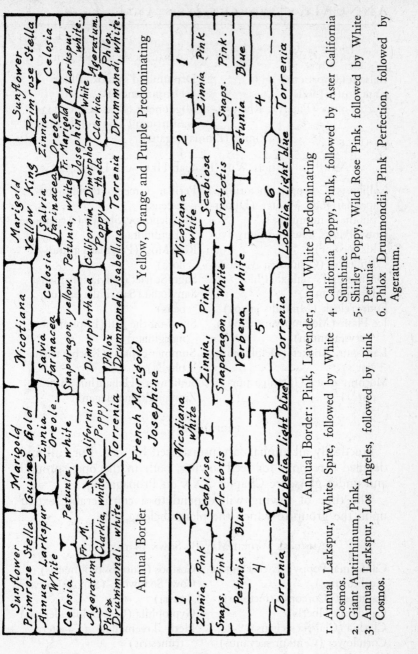

Annual Border — French Marigold Josephine
Yellow, Orange and Purple Predominating

Annual Border: Pink, Lavender, and White Predominating

1. Annual Larkspur, White Spire, followed by White Cosmos.
2. Giant Antirrhinum, Pink.
3. Annual Larkspur, Los Angeles, followed by Pink Cosmos.
4. California Poppy, Pink, followed by Aster California Sunshine.
5. Shirley Poppy, Wild Rose Pink, followed by White Petunia.
6. Phlox Drummondii, Pink Perfection, followed by Ageratum.

ANNUALS WHICH REQUIRE A NEUTRAL OR ALKALINE SOIL

Balsam (Impatiens)
Candytuft (Iberis)
Corn Poppy (Papaver Rhœas)

Drummond's phlox (Phlox Drummondii)
Mignonette (Reseda odorata)
Nasturtium (Tropæolum majus)

Zinnia (Zinnia elegans)

ANNUALS WHICH WILL ENDURE HEAT AND DROUGHT

Calliopsis (Coreopsis tinctoria)
Cape-marigold, Winter (Dimorphotheca aurantiaca)
Convolvulus, Dwarf (Convolvulus tricolor)
Cornflower (Centaurea cyanus)
Drummond's phlox (Phlox Drummondii)
Four-o'clock (Mirabilis jalapa)
Ice Plant (Mesembryanthemum crystallinum)
Larkspur, Rocket (Delphinium ajacis)
Morning-glory (Ipomœa purpurea)

Perilla, Green (Perilla frutescens)
Pricklepoppy, Showy (Argemone grandiflora)
Rose Moss (Portulaca grandiflora)
Sage, Scarlet (Salvia splendens)
Sanvitalia (Sanvitalia procumbens)
Snow-on-the-Mt. (Euphorbia marginata)
Summer-cypress (Kochia trichophylla)
Sunflower (Helianthus annuus)
Zinnia (Zinnia elegans)

PROPAGATION

Practically all annuals are propagated by seed. For full and detailed directions for seed sowing, both in the open ground and under glass, see Chapter XXX on Propagation.

The time of sowing will depend to a considerable extent upon the group to which the plants belong.

ANNUALS WHICH MAY BE SOWN IN THE FALL

California Poppy (Eschscholtzia californica)
Calliopsis (Coreopsis tinctoria)
Candytuft (Iberis)
Clarkia (Clarkia elegans)
Cornflower (Centaurea cyanus)

Cosmos (Cosmos bipinnatus)
Cow Soapwort (Saponaria vaccaria)
Gypsophila (Gypsophila elegans)
Herb Treemallow (Lavatera trimestris)

ANNUALS WHICH MAY BE SOWN IN THE FALL—*Continued*

Larkspur, Rocket (Delphinium Ajacis)

Love-in-a-mist (Nigella damascena)

Pansy (Viola tricolor)

Pink, Chinese (Dianthus chinensis)

Poppy (Papaver)

Pot-marigold (Calendula officinalis)

Snapdragon (Antirrhinum majus)

Sweet Alyssum (Alyssum maritimum)

Sweet Pea (Lathyrus odoratus)

ANNUALS WHICH USUALLY SELF-SOW

Browallia (Browallia)

California Poppy (Eschscholtzia californica)

Calliopsis (Coreopsis tinctoria)

Cornflower (Centaurea cyanus)

Cosmos (Cosmos bipinnatus)

Four-o'clock (Mirabilis jalapa)

Gypsophila (Gypsophila elegans)

Larkspur, Rocket (Delphinium ajacis)

Morning Glory (Ipomæa purpurea)

Petunia (Petunia hybrida)

Pot-marigold (Calendula officinalis)

Rose Moss (Portulaca grandiflora)

Sage, Mealycup (Salvia farinacea)

Snow-on-the-mountain (Euphorbia marginata)

Spiderflower (Cleome spinosa)

Summer-cypress (Kochia trichophylla)

Sweet Alyssum (Alyssum maritimum)

Tobacco (Nicotiana sylvestris)

HALF-HARDY ANNUALS

Arctotis, Bushy (Arctotis grandis)

Cape-marigold, Winter (Dimorphotheca aurantiaca)

Castor-bean (Ricinus communis)

Dusty-miller (Centaurea cineraria)

Gilia, Globe (Gilia capitata)

Lobelia, Edging (Lobelia erinus)

Lupine (Lupinus)

Nemesia, Pouched (Nemesia strumosa)

Painted Tongue (Salpiglossis sinuata)

Penstemon, Gloxinia (Penstemon gloxinioides)

Petunia (Petunia hybrida)

Pink (Dianthus chinensis)

Sage, Mealycup (Salvia farinacea)

Sage, Scarlet (Salvia splendens)

Scabiosa, Sweet (Scabiosa atropurpurea)

Snapdragon (Antirrhinum majus)

Starglory (Quamoclit coccinea)

Statice (Limonium)

Stock (Mathiola incana)

HALF-HARDY ANNUALS—*Continued*

Strawflower (Helichrysum bracteatum)

Tobacco (Nicotiana sylvestris)

Verbena, Garden (Verbena hybrida)

Zinnia (Zinnia)

TENDER ANNUALS

Ageratum (Ageratum houstonianum)

China-aster (Callistephus chinensis)

Cobæa, Purplebell (Cobæa scandens)

Cockscomb (Celosia plumosa)

Honesty (Lunaria biennis)

Laceflower, Blue (Trachymene cærulea)

Lobelia, Edging (Lobelia erinus)

Mignonette (Reseda odorata)

Monkeyflower (Mimulus luteus)

Nasturtium (Tropæolum peregrinum)

Nemophila, Spotted (Nemophila maculata)

Painted Tongue (Salpiglossis sinuata)

Poorman's Orchid (Schizanthus pinnatus)

Scarlet Runner Bean (Phaseolus coccineus)

Tasselflower (Emilia flammea)

ANNUALS WHICH ARE SLOW GROWING
(Requiring a Long Season to Bloom)

China-aster (Callistephus chinensis)

Everlasting, Winged (Ammobium)

Flax (Linum)

Goldencup (Hunnemannia)

Immortelle, Everlasting (Xeranthemum)

Lobelia (Lobelia)

Petunia (Petunia)

Pincushionflower (Scabiosa)

Rhodanthe (Helipterum Humboldtianum)

Salpiglossis (Salpiglossis)

Snapdragon (Antirrhinum)

Strawflower (Helichrysum)

Sweet-sultan, Basketflower (Centaurea)

Verbena (Verbena)

ANNUALS WITH A SHORT SEASON OF BLOOM
(Several Sowings Should Be Made for Succession of Bloom)

Calliopsis (Coreopsis tinctoria)

Candytuft, Purple (Iberis umbellata)

Cape-marigold, Winter (Dimorphotheca aurantiaca)

Cornflower (Centaurea cyanus)

Forget-me-not (Myosotis)

Gypsophila (Gypsophila elegans)

Love-in-a-mist (Nigella damascena)

Mignonette (Reseda odorata)

Drummond's phlox (Phlox Drummondii)

Poppy (Papaver)

Sweet Alyssum (Alyssum maritimum)

ANNUALS DIFFICULT TO TRANSPLANT
(Should Be Sown Where They Are to Flower)

California Poppy (Eschscholtzia californica)
Evening-primrose (Œnothera Drummondii)
Godetia, Whitney (Godetia grandiflora)
Gypsophila (Gypsophila elegans)
Herb Treemallow (Lavatera trimestris)
Laceflower, Blue (Trachymene cærulea)
Love-in-a-mist (Nigella damascena)
Lupine (Lupinus)
Nasturtium (Tropæolum)
Poppy (Papaver)
Prickly Poppy, Showy (Argemone grandiflora)
Rose Moss (Portulaca grandiflora)
Scarlet Runner (Phaseolus coccineus)
Sunflower (Helianthus annuus)
Sweet Pea (Lathyrus odoratus)

THINNING

When annuals have been sown in the open ground the young seedling plants will frequently require thinning, as it is essential that each individual plant be allowed ample space for its full development if good bloom is to be obtained. If the seedlings are not thinned out and are allowed to become overcrowded, the plants will make poor and spindly growth and the quantity and quality of the flowers will suffer seriously in consequence. The ultimate space required by the plants should be determined (see tabular list on page 402) and the thinning should be done before the plants have become in the least overcrowded. In some cases, as with zinnias and marigolds, the plants which are thinned out may be transplanted to some other section of the garden. In the case of seedlings which do not transplant readily (poppies, mignonette, etc.) it is best to discard those which are thinned out. It is advisable to do the thinning out of the young seedlings on a cloudy day when the ground is moist, as those which remain will suffer less shock if their root systems are slightly disturbed, and they will also suffer less from sudden exposure to full sunlight if they have been somewhat shaded by the close proximity of other seedlings.

PINCHING BACK

Some annuals should be allowed to develop their natural habit of growth and will either produce a spire of bloom or will branch quite freely if they are allowed ample space for their full development. There are a number of annuals, however, that are definitely benefited by judicious "pinching back"—as

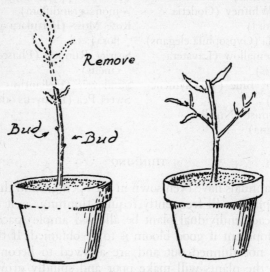

Pinching Back to Induce Branching

the operation is called in common garden parlance. If left entirely to their own devices these seedlings will make rather tall, spindly growth and will produce but scanty bloom. It is, therefore, wise to nip out the terminal bud or the tip of the plant when two or three sets of leaves have developed along the main stem, in order that the plant may have an opportunity to become bushy and well branched. In some cases further pinching may be desirable after the side shoots have developed.

ANNUALS WHICH SHOULD NOT BE PINCHED BACK

Balsam (Impatiens)   Poppies
Cockscomb (Celosia)   Stock
Everlasting (Miscellaneous)

ANNUALS WHICH BENEFIT FROM PINCHING

Ageratum (Ageratum Hous-
tonianum)

Browallia

Calendula (Calendula officinalis)
or Pot-Marigold

Chrysanthemum, Annual

Petunia

Phacelia

Phlox

Pinks (Dianthus chinensis)

Salpiglossis (Salpiglossis sinuata)

Schizanthus (Schizanthus pinnatus)

Snapdragon (Antirrhinum)

Verbena

Zinnia

CULTURE

The cultivation of the soil plays an important part in the success of the annual garden. Frequent, shallow cultivation should be given, the most satisfactory tool for this purpose being the small type of weeder with three flexible prongs. The soil should be kept in excellent tilth throughout the season and a hard crust should never be allowed to form upon the surface of the bed.

Some annuals, such as the poppies, portulaca and phlox Drummondii do not mind a high soil temperature and a minimum supply of moisture in the soil, while many other annuals such as zinnias, marigolds and snapdragons may be greatly benefited by a summer mulch of peat moss or some similar material which will help to conserve the moisture in the soil and will maintain a lower soil temperature.

The period of bloom of most annuals may be greatly prolonged if the fading flowers are removed. This detail of good garden maintenance is of more importance when one is dealing with annuals than it is in the case of any other group of flowers. The chief function of an annual plant is to blossom and produce seed, and having fulfilled this function it has no further reason for existence. In the case of low border plants such as sweet alyssum it is sometimes wise to shear the plants back if they become somewhat shabby, and vigorous new growth will thus be induced.

PESTS AND DISEASES OF ANNUALS

Specific recommendations for the treatment of diseases and pests of annuals are given in Chapter XXXIII on "Diseases and Insect Pests of Common Garden Plants."

SELECTION OF VARIETIES

From the long lists of annuals in the seed catalogues, it is difficult to make wise selections unless one has had an opportunity to become familiar with them. They are all listed there; the dependable ones and the fickle ones; the sturdy ones and the temperamental, sulky ones; the ones with flowers of exquisite daintiness and the ones with flowers of a garish hue. They are all crowded into the long lists, the good with the bad, and since in the space of one brief chapter it is impossible to discuss them all, only those have been selected which are, because of some particular merit, truly worthy of a place in the general garden scheme.

African Daisy (Arctotis grandis). Arctotis is classed among the worthy annuals because of the simple beauty of its flowers, which resemble a white daisy with long pointed petals, lavender on the under side, with a steel blue center. The flowers are borne on long, graceful, almost leafless stems and are excellent for cutting, as they last extremely well. The plants reach a height of 15 to 18 inches and they will continue to bloom throughout the summer if the fading blooms are removed. Arctotis grandis is of value as a plant for the front or middle of the flower border.

Culture: The plants are very tolerant of poor soil and of drought which makes them of particular value for the gardener who must struggle against such handicaps. Arctotis is classed as a half-hardy annual. The seeds may be sown early in the spring indoors, or later in the season either in the frames or directly in the garden where they are to flower. The plants should be spaced from 10 to 12 inches apart. The plants are remarkably free from pests and diseases and since they are so modest in their demands regarding soil and moisture, they may be classed among the most easily grown annuals.

Ageratum, Floss Flower. Ageratum varies in size from the very dwarf, compact type hardly more than 3 inches high, to the tall, branching varieties which often reach a height of from 15 to 18 inches. The pale lavender-blue flowers of the larger types are lovely in the flower border and are also excellent for cutting. White and dark blue varieties are also obtainable but are less satisfactory.

Culture: Ageratum is classed as a tender annual. For early bloom the seed should be sown indoors in March and the young seedlings transplanted to the garden when all danger of frost is over. Sowings made in the open ground after it has become warm and mellow will give later bloom. The plants reseed so abundantly that they will often establish themselves in a garden, new plants appearing year after year. If the faded blooms are removed and the plants are not allowed to reseed, ageratum will remain in bloom over a period of many months, until the plants are killed by the first frost. The dwarf varieties may be used as edging plants and should be spaced from 4 to 6 inches apart. The taller varieties are excellent for the front of the flower border and should be spaced from 10 to 12 inches apart.

Alyssum, Sweet. Sweet Alyssum is one of the most popular of the annual edging plants. Several of the exceedingly dwarf forms attain a height of hardly more than 3 inches, while some of the larger types are fully 9 inches. The plants begin to flower when still very small, and they are covered with a profusion of bloom throughout the summer months. The varieties most commonly used are white, although there is one strain which bears flowers of a deep lavender hue. The plants are very uniform both in height and in habit of growth.

Culture: Being a hardy annual, sweet alyssum may be sown out of doors as soon as the frost is out of the ground, the plants being thinned to stand 6 inches apart. The young seedlings make rapid growth and will begin to bloom in less than 6 weeks from the date of planting. Seeds may also be sown indoors or in the frames, being later transplanted to the garden, and very early bloom may thus be obtained.

Browallia. Blue is a color which is found none too frequently among the annuals and for this reason Browallia is especially prized for its abundant bloom throughout the summer. The small, tubular flowers are a clear violet-blue, and they are excellent for their decorative value in the garden, for cutting, and as potted plants. *Browallia elata* is excellent for bedding purposes, attaining a height of about 1½ feet. *B. speciosa (major)* produces larger flowers, and it is of especial value as a potted plant, for window boxes and for hanging baskets.

Culture: The seeds may be planted early in the season under glass or later in the open ground. The young seedlings should be pinched back when about 6 inches tall to induce a bushy, well-branched plant. The plants prefer a position in full sun and will thrive well in any good garden soil. They should be spaced from 6 to 8 inches apart, and throughout the season they will give a profusion of bloom.

Butterfly Flower (Schizanthus). Schizanthus is sometimes called the poor man's orchid because of the form and color of its dainty flowers and because it may be so easily grown. The foliage is a soft light green, finely cut, and the myriad, delicate flowers form a pyramid of bloom, in tints of lavender, rose, and brown.

Culture: The seed may be sown either out of doors or under glass, and the plants come into bloom in less than six weeks from sowing. They are so profligate with their flowers, however, that the period of bloom is somewhat short. Schizanthus is exceedingly well adapted to pot culture in the greenhouse, and beautiful plants may be produced which are charming for decorative purposes in the house. The taller types which grow from 2–3 feet should be planted from 1 to 1½ feet apart. The more dwarf varieties reach a height of about 1 foot, and 9 inches is sufficient between the plants.

Calendula or **Pot Marigold.** There is a jauntiness about the great golden and orange blooms of the calendulas which is very appealing. The plants are extremely hardy, and in the South they may be grown out of doors during the winter months. In the North, calendulas are popular both as a greenhouse plant to supply flowers for cutting during the winter, and as a summer flowering annual.

Culture: The plants are of easy culture and are not exacting in their demands. The seeds may be sown indoors for early bloom or directly in the garden as soon as the ground can be worked in the spring. The plants reach a height of from 12 to 18 inches, and they should be spaced about 1 foot apart. They offer excellent material for the front of the border and for the cutting garden.

Cape-Marigold (Dimorphotheca). This gay little orange daisy deserves a place both in the cutting garden and in the flower border. It may also be grown very successfully in the greenhouse, and although the flowers are modest in form and size, they are lovely for mixed bouquets. In the garden, the plants seldom reach a height of more than 12 inches. The flowers are daisy-like in form with long, slender, somewhat pointed petals, which seem to shimmer in the sunlight. Several new hybrids have recently been introduced which range in color from pale lemon yellow to deep orange and salmon pink.

Culture: The seed may be sown in the open ground or the young seedlings may be started under glass. The African Daisies prefer an open, sunny location in the garden and will thrive well in very poor soil. They are also more tolerant of drought than some of the other annuals. The plants should be spaced 8 to 10 inches apart.

China-aster (Callistephus). Because of the many diseases and insect pests with which asters may become afflicted, they are classed among the more difficult annuals. It requires considerable skill to bring them to perfection and there are many pitfalls along the way, for if the plants escape the attacks of the yellows and of wilt, they may still succumb to the insidious injury of root aphids or to the devastations of aster beetles. Because of these many afflictions, some gardeners no longer attempt to grow the annual asters and most of the larger commercial growers have accepted the practice of growing them in cloth houses. China-asters may be obtained in widely varied forms and in a wide range of colorings. If early, mid-season and later varieties are selected, the period of bloom may be extended from late June until frost. Among the most decorative varieties are the California Singles, coming in soft pastel shades of pink, lavender and blue, and many of the anemone-flowered types are very lovely.

Culture: Seed may be sown either indoors early in the spring, in hotbeds or in coldframes, or in the open ground later in the season after all danger of frost is over. China-asters may be transplanted with ease and the plants should be spaced from 10 to 12 inches apart. The plants thrive best in a rich soil with an ample supply of moisture.

For the control of insect pests and diseases, see Chapter XXXIII.

Clarkia. Clarkia is a native of our own Northwest and was first discovered at the time of the Lewis and Clark expedition, being named in honor of the explorer. There are two types, Clarkia elegans, which bears its flowers in long, loose sprays, and Clarkia pulchella, which bears its flowers in clusters. The stems are of a coppery tone and the dainty flowers are beautiful both in form and in coloring, ranging from white through salmon pink to purple and crimson. The blooms are excellent for cutting and as the plants do extremely well under greenhouse conditions, they are often grown for cut flowers during the winter months.

Culture: The seeds may be sown in the autumn in the open ground, in the greenhouse or in frames for very early bloom, and directly in the garden as soon as the soil is mellow and workable. The plants reach a height of 15 to 18 inches and they should be spaced from 10 to 12 inches apart.

Cornflower, Bachelor's Button (Centaurea cyanus).

The Cornflowers may be classed in the group of hardy and absolutely dependable annuals. They are of vigorous habit, will thrive on poor, sandy soil and ask almost nothing in the way of care and cultivation.

Culture: If the seed is sown outdoors late in the autumn it will lie dormant during the winter and will germinate with the first warm days of spring. The lusty, vigorous seedlings make rapid growth and will soon come into bloom. Seed may also be sown in the open ground at any time during the spring months. As the period of bloom is rather short, successive sowings should be made. The plants reseed readily and young seedlings will often appear as volunteers year after year. Cornflowers are especially recommended for the cutting garden and for children's gardens. They seem to hold a special delight for children and are so dependable, and of such easy culture that they make failure almost impossible. The plants reach a height of about 18 inches, and as they are of a rather branching habit of growth, they should be spaced at least 1 foot apart.

California Poppy (Eschscholtzia). The California Poppies are among the gayest of our summer-flowering annuals and are beloved by many a gardener. They were named in honor of Doctor Eschscholtz, a Russian ship-surgeon, who found them growing wild on our western coast more than a century ago. While some members of the genus are true perennials in their native habitat, they are not able to survive the extreme cold of northern winters, and they are therefore usually treated as annuals.

Types and Varieties: The plants vary considerably in height, some of the miniature varieties being hardly more than 6 inches, while the larger, more vigorous types often reach a height of from 12 to 15 inches. The foliage is finely cut, a soft grey-green in color, and the lovely flowers are borne on slender, upright stems. During the night and on dull, cloudy days the petals remain closed, but with the magic touch of the sun, they open wide. The flowers are lovely both in the garden and for cutting as they last exceedingly well when cut and require no special attention. The flowers of the true California Poppy (E. californica) vary in color from a soft cream to a deep golden orange. Many of the varieties which we have today, however, are hybrid forms and offer a much wider range of color, being obtainable in shades of ivory, shell pink, salmon, rose, scarlet, crimson and deep tawny orange. Several seed firms offer Eschscholtzias in named varieties which are very beautiful. *Orange Prince* is very fine, the flowers, which measure nearly three inches across, being borne in great profusion. *Flame* is a gorgeous orange-scarlet; *Gaiety* a brilliant cherry-red on the outer side of the petals and pure white within. *Queen of the Buffs* is a lovely, clear apricot-buff in color; *Rosy Queen* a deep rose on the outer side of the petals and a lighter shade within.

Culture: The Eschscholtzias are of very easy culture. Although they prefer a light, sandy soil they will thrive well in soil of almost any type and they will give an abundance of bloom provided that they are planted in full sun. The seeds may be sown in the autumn, shortly before freezing weather sets in, or they may be sown in the open ground in very early spring. The plants make their most rapid growth during the cool, moist days of early spring. The seeds should always be sown where they are to flower, as the Eschscholtzias do not take kindly to transplanting. If the blooms are cut off as soon as the petals have fallen and no seed pods are allowed to form the plants may be kept in flower for many months. The plants should be thinned out so that they are spaced from 8 to 10 inches apart.

Cosmos. Cosmos is of particular value because of its height, the giant varieties often reaching a height of 5 or 6 feet. If both early and late varieties are planted, bloom may be had from July until frost. In habit of growth, cosmos is somewhat spreading and spindly and lacks the grace and charm of many of our other flowers. It is best adapted to the rear of the border and to the cutting garden. There are single, crested, and double forms, coming in tones of pink, mauve, white and crimson. The recently introduced variety, Orange Flare, is a distinct departure from the usual types, the color being an intense golden orange, and the flowers are very decorative.

Culture: Cosmos is classed as a tender annual and the seeds should not be sown until all danger of frost is over. If early bloom is desired the seedlings may be started under glass. As the plants are of a decidedly branching habit of growth, they should be allowed ample room to develop. The dwarf varieties should be spaced 2 feet apart, the tall varieties from $2\frac{1}{2}$ to 3 feet apart. The tall varieties frequently require staking.

Flowering Tobacco (Nicotiana). The flowering tobacco is one of the most valuable of the tall growing annuals and it is so well adapted to a variety of planting compositions that it should be widely grown. In the evening as the lovely white, tubular flowers recede into the twilight, its delicate fragrance pervades the garden and the night moths hover above it in the dusk. The flowers close during the day with the exception of *N. sylvestris*.

Culture: The plants are easily grown, and when once well established in a garden they reseed very readily and the young seedlings will come up year after year. The seed is exceedingly fine and may be sown under glass for early bloom or in the open where the plants are to flower. The plants may be transplanted with ease, and they may be moved into the garden when they are in full flower if they are lifted with ample soil, and if the transplanting is done on a cloudy, moist day. The plants bloom over a long period and may be used very satisfactorily in the herbaceous border after some of the early flowering biennials have been removed. The flowering tobacco is also lovely when used as a house plant during the winter months. Young seedlings may be potted up in the autumn before frost and will give generous bloom throughout the winter.

There are several rather distinct types—*N. affinis* with white, tubular flowers; *N. sylvestris* with drooping tube-shaped flowers, borne on a stout, central stem; and *N. Sanderæ* with flowers of red and carmine hue.

Incarvillea variabilis. Although the annual form of Incarvillea is not widely known, it possesses many delightful qualities, and it has the ability to withstand the intense heat of Southern summers remarkably well. The plants reach a height of about 18 inches and the tubular flowers are produced in great abundance. The colors range through delicate shades of cream, pink, salmon and rose.

Culture: Incarvillea prefers a position in full sun and thrives in widely varying types of soil. The seed may be sown under glass for early bloom, or it may be sown in cold-frames or in the open ground later in the season. The plants should be spaced from 8 to 10 inches apart.

Larkspur. The annual larkspurs are among the loveliest and most decorative of our garden flowers. The stately spires of bloom add their full measure of beauty to any garden composition, and they are highly valued for cutting as well. Several new and greatly improved varieties of annual larkspur have been introduced within recent years. The plants reach a height of from 3 to 4 feet, and the massive spires of bloom are very beautiful, being obtainable in a wide range of colorings—white, shell pink, rose, lavender and purple. The plants should be given ample room to develop. They should be spaced about 18 inches apart.

Culture: The plants are exceedingly hardy, and the seed may be sown in the open ground late in the autumn, germinating with the first warm days of spring; or it may be sown as soon as the ground is workable in March. Autumn sowing and early spring sowing are desirable, as seedlings started later in the season do not thrive as well and the plants do not make as vigorous growth. It is possible to start the seedlings under glass for early transplanting to the open ground.

The annual larkspurs are extremely popular, and deservedly so, for greenhouse culture during the winter months. The lovely spikes of bloom are very decorative as cut flowers and require no special care or attention in the greenhouse benches.

Lobelia. The intensity of the blue found in the lobelia is equalled in almost no other flower. But it has been this very intensity of hue which has made them difficult subjects for the flower border. With the introduction of the lovely *Cambridge Blue* variety, however, and of other varieties of this more delicate tone, the lobelias have gained rapidly in popularity and are now highly valued as edging plants. There are several types, the exceedingly dwarf form suitable only for edgings; the trailing form, which is of particular value for porch and window boxes; and the upright form which reaches a height of almost 15 inches. One of the loveliest of edgings for flower beds during the summer months is a combination of Lobelia, variety Cambridge Blue, with Phlox Drummondii of a clear pink tone.

Culture: The plants are tender and the seeds should be started under glass early in the season, the young seedlings being transplanted into the garden when all danger of frost is over. The plants are of simple culture and will thrive well in any good garden soil. They should be set 4 to 6 inches apart.

Lupine. Although the annual forms are not as large or as decorative as are the perennial types, they possess a certain distinction and charm, and they are well worth growing. The plants do well either in full sun or in partial shade, and if the seed pods are not allowed to form, they will bloom over an exceedingly long period. The tall spikes of bloom are graceful and lovely, coming in tones of clear soft blue, pink, mauve and white. And because of the decorative value of the blooms as cut flowers the annual lupines are frequently grown in greenhouses during the winter months.

Culture: The seeds may be planted in the open ground where they are to flower or they may be started under glass. As they do not bear transplanting as happily as some of the other annuals, an ideal method of growing the plants, if they are to be started indoors for early bloom in the garden, is to sow the seeds in peat moss pots. The plants may then be moved into the garden when they are almost ready to flower. As the roots will be undisturbed, the plants will suffer no set-back. The plants grow from 2 to 2½ feet tall and should be spaced from 12 to 15 inches apart.

Marigold (Tagetes). Although we know them as French and African marigolds, the names are not significant of their origin, as both of these types have come to us from Mexico, where they are found growing in luxuriant abundance.

From mid-summer until frost the marigolds may be counted upon for generous bloom. They may either be used as the dominant note in the late summer garden or they may play a minor role by filling in an occasional gap here and there. In the cutting garden they are indispensable. They are so profligate with their bloom that they may be cut with lavish abandon and great bowls of them will carry the rich yellow and orange tones of late summer into the house, until the first frost has touched the garden.

Culture: The marigolds are of the most simple culture. The seeds are large and germinate readily and the young plants may be transplanted with the greatest ease, it being possible to move them into the garden when they are in full flower. They are tolerant of poor soil, and will thrive under almost any conditions, in full sun or in partial shade, and in wet or dry soil. The seeds may be sown in the open where they are to flower or they may be sown early under glass.

The African marigolds may be obtained in tall and intermediate types, ranging from 18 inches to 4 feet in height. The recently introduced variety, *Guinea Gold,* is one of the most desirable, bearing large double, loosely petalled blossoms of a golden orange hue. The African marigolds should be planted 1½ feet apart.

The French marigolds are more dwarf in habit of growth, about 18 inches in height, and are useful for the front of the border, forming bushy, spreading plants. The colors range from pale lemon-yellow, through deep orange to dull, tawny reds. The variety *Josephine* is excellent. The French marigolds should be planted from 9 to 12 inches apart.

Petunias. In the skillful hands of the hybridizers, petunias have been developed into one of our most useful flowers. Always dependable, demanding almost nothing in the way of care and cultivation, thriving under most adverse conditions of soil and climate, they offer us an abundance of bloom and beauty throughout the long summer season. For porch and window boxes, for gay masses of bloom about a summer cottage, as border plants in the flower garden, they are quite indispensable and there is no other flower that can quite take their place. Single or double, ruffled or fluted, they offer a wider range of color than almost any other flower. Some of the new shades of velvety purple, pale rose, and deep wine-red are exceedingly lovely when used in pleasant color harmonies with other annuals.

Culture: For early bloom the seeds should be sown indoors and the young plants may be transplanted into the garden when they are ready to come into flower. Seed may also be sown in the open ground, being covered very lightly with finely sifted soil, since it is so fine. Petunias have a longer season of bloom than most flowers, and if the plants become spindly at any period in their growth they may be cut back and will soon branch out again. The tall and spreading varieties which reach from 1 to 2 feet should be spaced about 1 foot apart. The dwarf varieties reaching a height of 6 to 8 inches should be spaced about 6 inches apart.

Drummond Phlox (Phlox Drummondii). Phlox Drummondii was found growing wild in Texas. Since its introduction into cultivation it has become one of our most useful edging and low border plants.

Culture: In the South it is often grown as a winter annual, and being extremely hardy it can survive many a sudden cold snap and bloom blithely on. In the North the seeds may be planted in the autumn or in very early spring in the open. Sowings under glass are also frequently made. The plants may readily be transplanted and, if they are not allowed to reseed, will remain in bloom for many months. Seed is now obtainable in a wide range of colors, white, soft buff, shell pink, clear deep pink, lavender, scarlet and deep red. Some varieties have a distinctly marked eye or center and are less attractive than the self-colors. There are low-growing, dwarf types reaching a height of about 6 inches, which should be spaced about 6 inches apart. The larger, more spreading types which attain a height of from 10 to 12 inches should be planted about 9 inches apart. Phlox Drummondii thrives best in an open, sunny position and does exceedingly well on poor sandy soil.

Painted Tongue (Salpiglossis). The trumpet-like flowers of the Painted Tongue come in shades of dusky purple, deep wine-red and ivory, with stencillings of gold, and they are very decorative both in the garden and for cutting, as they last unusually well in water.

Culture: The plants reach an ultimate height of from 2 to 2½ feet and should be given ample space in which to develop, being spaced from 8 to 10 inches apart. Salpiglossis is not of as easy culture as are many of the annuals, and the young seedlings require considerable pampering. The seeds should be sown indoors early in the spring, and the young plants should not be set out until all danger of frost is over. The seedlings should be kept growing on rapidly and should not be allowed to suffer from overcrowding in the seed bed or from lack of moisture. The plants prefer a position in full sun and a deep, rich, loam soil.

Pincushion-Flower—Mourning Bride (Scabiosa). The flowers of the annual scabiosa are borne in profusion from midsummer until frost. The plants are of rather thin growth with but scant foliage, but the flowers are excellent for cutting and they are attractive in the garden as well. The plants reach a height of about 2½ feet and the flowers are borne on long, wiry stems.

Culture: The scabiosas are hardy, and the seeds may be sown in the open where the plants are to flower, or under glass for early bloom. The flowers come in a wide range of colors—white, lavender-blue, flesh-pink, rose, crimson, purple, and deep maroon. They should be planted about 1 foot apart.

Pinks, Annual (Dianthus chinensis). The annual pinks have long been popular. They will produce generous bloom throughout the summer months. Both single and double varieties are obtainable in a wide range of colorings—white, salmon-pink, crimson and deep red. The plants are branching in habit of growth and reach a height of about 1 foot, being useful in the front of the border.

Culture: The seeds may be sown in a coldframe or in the open ground after the soil has become warm and mellow. The plants prefer a sunny location, and they thrive well in a rich, rather moist garden soil. They should be spaced from 8 to 10 inches apart.

Poppies. Of all the annual poppies the Shirley poppies are the most appealing. Their flowers are of exquisite daintiness and they are lovely both in the garden and for cutting. The Shirley poppies are a distinct strain developed from the little corn poppy which is found growing wild throughout Europe, and they owe their origin to that wonderful student of plant life, the Rev. W. Wilks, who, in the year 1880, found a modest little corn poppy with a fine line of white along the edge of the petals, growing in his garden at the Shirley Vicarage in England. He saved the seed from this little poppy, and the following year from the two hundred seedling plants he obtained four or five others with the same fine white line. For many years he worked patiently with these poppies, gradually developing a new and very beautiful strain known as the Shirley Poppies. In habit of growth the plants are somewhat branching, reaching a height of almost two feet, and they bear a profusion of flowers of beautiful form. The single varieties are far more exquisite than the heavy-headed double types, and there is a wide color range—white, salmon pink, apricot, rose and deeper shades of red and crimson. *Wild-rose Pink* is one of the loveliest varieties.

Culture: The Shirley poppies thrive best in full sun in a light, sandy loam soil, and require a free circulation of air. If planted in a damp, poorly drained situation the young plants have a tendency to rot off. The plants are also apt to suffer badly during a rainy season, as the flower buds frequently rot before they open. The flowers of the Shirley poppy are borne on long, slender, hairy stems, and nature endeavors to protect the buds from too much moisture by allowing them to remain in a drooping position until a few hours before they are ready to open. If, however, because of extreme dampness, the calyx which encloses the bud fails to break away, the bud will rot before opening.

The Opium poppies (Papaver somniferum) differ from the Shirley poppies in that the stems are smooth and glaucous and somewhat thicker. The plants attain a greater height and the flowers are larger. There are single and double types, carnation and peony-flowered forms,—and they are all decorative and lovely.

All members of the Poppy family are very hardy. The seeds may be sown either in the autumn or very early in the spring. As it is impossible to transplant the young seedlings with any degree of success, the seeds should be sown in the location where the plants are to flower. As the seed is very fine it should be covered lightly with sifted soil. The young seedling plants should be thinned out to a distance of 6 or 8 inches apart before they become in the least crowded.

Poppies thrive best during the cool, moist, growing weather of spring, and they should, therefore, be sown as early in the season as possible. Particularly is this true in sections of the country where the summer heat is intense.

Snapdragon (Antirrhinum). There are few annuals that are more useful than the antirrhinums. They are indispensable in the flower beds and borders, and are almost equally valuable in the cutting garden. They are lovely in form, and the colors are infinitely varied, ranging from delicate apple-blossom pink through shades of salmon and apricot, to tawny yellow and deep wine-red. The intermediate type, reaching a height of about 18 inches, is the most popular, but for the rear of the flower border the giant types are superbly fine, often reaching a height of 3 feet or more. There are few color compositions in the flower garden more beautiful than the rich tones of apricot antirrhinums massed against the stately spires of the *Giant Primrose* foxgloves. For a border planting of striking color tones, the variety *Bonfire,* a rich tawny red, may be planted in combination with the *Arkwright Ruby* Viola and Delphinium chinense.

Culture: For early spring bloom the seeds may be sown in August and the young plants wintered over in the frames, or the seeds may be sown in the greenhouse in January or February or in hotbeds in March. The young seedlings should be pricked out as soon as they have reached sufficient size, and, as they develop, they should be pinched back in order that they may become well branched. The young seedlings may be transplanted to the garden as soon as the soil has become warm and mellow, being spaced about 1 foot apart.

If the faded flowers are removed and if the plants are given good care and cultivation, they will give generous bloom over a period of many months. Antirrhinums prefer a rich, mellow soil rather high in lime content, but they are tolerant of widely varying conditions. In mild climates, antirrhinums will live through the winter, and they may be regarded as perennials.

Since the introduction of the rust-proof varieties, the gardener need suffer no concern over this disease which formerly took such a heavy toll.

Sunflower (Helianthus). Although many of the members of this family are of such coarse and ungainly growth that they are ill-suited to the flower border, there are a few varieties which are worthy of consideration. The lovely little sunflower, *Primrose Stella,* recently introduced by Sutton's, is a delightful thing. The plants reach a height of about 2 feet and the flowers are of a pale, primrose yellow with dark central discs. It is lovely in the garden, and the flowers are very decorative for cutting.

Culture: The seeds may be sown in the greenhouse or in the frames for early bloom, or they may be sown in the open ground after all danger of frost is over. The plants should be spaced from 15 to 18 inches apart. The sunflowers are among the least exacting of plants and require little in the way of cultivation. They prefer full sun, but will tolerate poor soil and drought to an extraordinary degree.

Stocks (Mathiola). Stocks are beloved for their fragrance and for their association with old-fashioned gardens. When grown in the greenhouse during the winter months the flowers are lovely for mixed bouquets and they are lovely, too, in the garden if the plants are well grown.

Culture: The plants are a bit more temperamental than many of the annuals and sometimes fail to flower well. For most satisfactory results, the seeds should be sown indoors or in frames and the young plants set out in the garden, when danger of frost is over. There are tall-growing types and dwarf-growing types, and both single and double forms, and there is a wide range of color: white, cream, lavender, purple, pink, rose, and a dusky shade of antique copper as well as red and crimson. The tall-growing types, reaching a height of from 2 to 2½ feet, should be planted from 1 to 1½ feet apart, while the dwarf varieties of 1 to 1½ feet in height should be planted from 6 to 9 inches apart.

Swan River Daisy (Brachycome). The Swan River Daisy is a winsome little thing, bearing small, daisylike flowers of a soft blue tone with a brilliant yellow center. The plants are useful near the front of the border or as an edging, as they reach a height of hardly more than 12 inches.

Culture: The seed may be sown either indoors for early bloom or directly in the garden. The plants come into flower within six weeks of the time of sowing. They should be spaced from 6 to 8 inches apart. As the period of bloom of the Swan River Daisy is not long, successive sowings should be made every 4 or 6 weeks if bloom is desired throughout the summer.

Sweet Peas (Lathyrus odoratus). Early sowing is one of the secrets of success with sweet peas. If greenhouse space is available the seeds should be sown in January, in small flowerpots. If seed is to be sown in the open ground, it should be planted as early as possible in the season. In the South autumn sowing is preferred. In order to facilitate early spring sowing it is wise to prepare the trench in the autumn. Sweet peas require a deep, rich soil, and a trench at least 18 inches deep should be prepared with liberal quantities of well-rotted manure and rich compost. A comparatively short trench which has been well prepared will produce vigorous plants and abundant bloom. It is, therefore, wise to prepare a small area thoroughly, rather than to attempt too much. In the spring the trench should be opened to a depth of 6 inches and the seeds placed in the bottom of the furrow, 4 inches apart, being covered with about an inch of soil. If the seeds are either nicked or soaked in water for 24 hours previous to planting, germination will be hastened. As the young plants develop, the trench should be gradually filled until it is almost level, a slight depression being left to conserve moisture. Sweet peas make their best growth during the cool, moist days of early spring and are seriously affected by heat and drought. Wire or brush may be used as a support for the vines.

Torenia (Wishbone flower). The quaint little blossoms of the Torenia are borne in profusion throughout the summer and the plants remain quite undaunted in the face of heat and drought. Attaining hardly more than a foot in height, Torenia is excellent as an edging plant or when planted in drifts along the front of the border. The small flowers are semi-trumpet-like in form and come in shades of lavender and deep violet with a yellow blotch on the lower petal. The plants are admirably adapted to pot culture.

Culture: Torenia is a tender annual. The seed may be sown in the greenhouse or in the frames early in the spring or in the open ground after all danger of frost is over. The seed is very fine and should be covered but lightly. The young seedling plants may be transplanted readily. If they have been started indoors they may be moved to the garden when danger of frost is over, being spaced from 6 to 8 inches apart. Torenia thrives well either in full sun or in partial shade, and the plants will continue to bloom throughout the season, until killed by autumn frosts.

Verbena. Like the petunias, the verbenas are classed among the ever-dependable annuals.

Culture: They are of easy culture and will give generous bloom throughout the long summer season. The seeds may be started under glass or they may be sown in the open where they are to flower. The young seedlings are sturdy and bear transplanting well. Of low, somewhat spreading growth, the verbenas are of particular value as border plants. The parti-colored types with white eyes are far less lovely than the self-colors which come in shades of pink, rose, lavender and deep purple. The dwarf varieties, reaching a height of about 6 inches, should be planted 9 inches apart, while the taller varieties should be planted 1 foot apart.

Zinnias. In spite of their somewhat ungraceful habit of growth, zinnias are one of the most popular of the annuals, and they have much to recommend them. They offer wide variations in form and coloring; they bloom over a long period; they will endure drought and neglect, and will succeed when all else fails; and the brilliantly colored flowers add greatly to the beauty of many a midsummer and early autumn garden. In size, zinnias range from the tiny Lilliput varieties suitable for edgings and borders, to the giant, branching types which reach a height of over three feet. There are single and double forms, crested, curled and quilled forms—and there are few flowers which offer as wide a range of color: white, shell-pink, salmon, rose, scarlet, deep red, mauve, yellow and tawny orange. There are varieties to suit every color planting and they may be had in soft pastel tints or in shades that are fairly vibrant with color.

Culture: Zinnias are of the easiest possible culture and will thrive under widely varying conditions. They are classed as tender annuals, and the seed may be started under glass for early bloom, or sown in the garden where the plants are to flower after all danger of frost is over. Zinnias may be transplanted with ease, as it is possible to move the plants when they are in full flower. Although they thrive best in full sun, they will also endure partial shade. The dwarf varieties, reaching a height of 1 to 1½ feet, should be planted about 9 inches apart, while the taller 3-feet varieties should be spaced about 1 foot apart.

White Annuals

Ageratum Houstonianum (Mexican Ageratum)
Alyssum maritimum (Sweet Alyssum)
Ammobium alatum (Winged Everlasting)
Antirrhinum majus (Snapdragon)
Arctotis grandis (Bushy Arctotis)
Argemone grandiflora (Prickly Poppy)
Brachycome iberidifolia (Swan-river-daisy)
Browallia demissa (elata)
Campanula (Annual Canterbury Bells)
Centaurea (Royal Sweet-sultan, Cornflower, etc.)
Centranthus macrosiphon (Spur-valerian)
Chrysanthemum
Clarkia
Cleome spinosa (Spiderflower)
Clintonia puchella
Collinsia bicolor (Chinese-houses)

White Annuals—*Continued*

Crepis barbata rubra (Hawkweed)
Datura fastuosa (Yellow Floripondio)
Dimorphotheca aurantiaca (Cape-marigold)
Echium plantagineum hybrids
Gilia tricolor
Godetia amœna & grandiflora
Gypsophila elegans
Helichrysum bracteatum (Strawflower)
Iberis amara (Candytuft)
Impatiens (Balsam)
Lathyrus odoratus (Sweet Pea)
Lavatera trimestris (Treemallow)
Limonium sinuatum (Statice or Sea-lavender)
Lobelia erinus & tenuior
Lupinus mutabilis (Lupine)
Malcomia maritima (Virginian-stock)
Mathiola incana (Stock)
Nemesia strumosa
Nemophila maculata
Nicotiana (Flowering Tobacco)
Œnothera americana (Evening Primrose)
Papaver somniferum (Opium Poppy)
Petunia hybrida
Phlox Drummondii
Portulaca grandiflora
Saponaria vaccaria (Soapwort)
Scabiosa atropurpurea
Schizanthus pinnatus (Butterfly-flower)
Senecio elegans (Purple Groundsel)
Verbena erinoides (Moss Vervain)
Vinca rosea (Periwinkle)
Viola tricolor (Pansy)
Xeranthemum annuum (Immortelle)
Zinnia elegans

Red, Rose, and Pink Annuals

Abronia umbellata (Sand-Verbena)	Rose
Adonis	Red
Alonsoa acutifolia (Maskflower)	Scarlet

RED, ROSE, AND PINK ANNUALS—*Continued*

A. Warscewiczii	Orange to scarlet
Amaranthus caudatus (Love-lies-bleeding)	Crimson
Antirrhinum majus (Snapdragon)	Shades red to pink
Calandrinia grandiflora	Rose
C. speciosa	Ruby-red
Callistephus chinensis (China Aster)	Shades red to pink
Campanula (Annual Canterbury Bells)	Pink
Celosia (Cockscomb)	Crimson
Centaurea cyanus	Pink
C. imperialis	Pink
C. moschata	Rose
Centranthus macrosiphon	Rose
Clarkia	Rose, pink
Collinsia bicolor (Chinese-houses)	Pink
Collomia coccinea	Scarlet
Cosmos bipinnatus	Crimson to white
Crepis barbata rubra	Rose
Cuphea ignea (Fiery Cuphea)	Scarlet
Diascia barberæ (Twinspur)	Pink
Echium creticum	Red
E. plantagineum hybrids	Pink
Emilia flammea & sagittata	Scarlet
Eschscholtzia californica (Cal. Poppy)	Red, pink
Gilia	Scarlet
Godetia	Rose to white
Gypsophila muralis	Rose
Helichrysum bracteatum	Red, pink
Helipterum Manglesii & roseum	Rose
Iberis umbellata (Candytuft)	Carmine, pink
Impatiens (Balsam)	Rose, pink
Lathyrus odoratus (Sweet Pea)	Rose, pink
Lavatera trimestris and rosea (Treemallow)	Rose
Leptosiphon hybrida	Rose to carmine
Limonium Suworowi (Statice or Sea-lavendar)	Rose
Linaria bipartita (Toadflax)	Crimson, pink
Linum grandiflorum (Flowering Flax)	Crimson
Lupinus Hartwegii (Hartweg Lupine)	Pink
Lychnis cœli-rosa (Rose-of-heaven)	Flesh

RED, ROSE, AND PINK ANNUALS—*Continued*

Malcomia maritima (Virginian-stock)	Pink
Malope trifida grandiflora (Mallow-wort)	Rose-red
Mathiola (Stock)	Rose, pink
Mimulus (Monkeyflower)	Scarlet
Myosotis dissitiflora (Forget-me-not)	Pink
Nemesia strumosa	Rose, pink
Nicotiana Sanderæ & sylvestris	Crimson to white
Papaver Rhœas (Shirley or Field Poppy)	Crimson to pink
P. somniferum (Opium Poppy)	Red to white
Petunia hybrida	Bright rose to pink
Phlox Drummondii	Rose to white
Portulaca grandiflora (Portulaca)	Purplish-crimson to white
Rehmannia angulata	Rose
Salvia splendens	Scarlet
Saponaria calabrica (Calabrian Soapwort)	Rose
Scabiosa atropurpurea	Rose to white
Schizanthus pinnatus (Butterfly-flower)	Rose to white
Senecio elegans (Purple Groundsel)	Rose to white
Silene Armeria (Sweet-William Campion)	Rose
Tropæolum (Nasturtium)	Scarlet, rose
Vinca rosea (Madasgascar Periwinkle)	Rose to white
Zinnia elegans	Scarlet to white

BLUE, LAVENDER, PURPLE, AND MAUVE ANNUALS

The effect of light and shadow, the difference in varieties, the changing color of the flower itself as it blooms and fades, and personal opinion, often make difficult the drawing of an exact line of demarcation between lavender and blue. The following is a list generally considered correct.

Ageratum Houstonianum	Blue
Anagallis indica (Blue Pimpernel)	Blue
Anchusa var. Blue Bird	Blue
Asperula azurea setosa (Blue Woodruff)	Blue
Brachycome iberidifolia (Swan-river-daisy)	Blue
Browallia demissa (elata)	Lavender
Callistephus (China Aster)	Blue and lavender

Blue, Lavender, Purple, and Mauve Annuals—*Continued*

Campanula (Blue Bellflower or Annual Canterbury Bell)	Blue
Centaurea	Blue and lavender
Clarkia elegans & pulchella	Lavender
Collinsia bicolor (Chinese-houses)	Blue
Cosmos diversifolius	Lilac
Cynoglossum amabile (Houndstongue)	Blue
Datura fastuosa	Purple
Delphinium ajacis (Larkspur)	Blue
Echium plantagineum	Purple to blue
Felicia bergeriana (Kingfisher Daisy)	Blue
Gilia	Purple and blue
Godetia grandiflora	Purple
Heliophila	Blue
Iberis (Candytuft)	Lilac shades
Impatiens (Balsam)	Lilac shades
Lathyrus odoratus (Sweet Pea)	Lilac and purple
Limonium sinuatum (Statice or Sea-lavender)	Lilac
Linaria	Purple
Lobelia	Violet and blue
Lupinus (Lupine)	Purples and lilacs
Malcomia maritima (Virginian Stock)	Purple
Martynia fragrans	Mauve
Mathiola (Stock)	Lilac and purple
Myosotis (Forget-me-not)	Blue
Nemophila insignis (Baby Blue-eyes)	Blue
Nigella damascena (Love-in-a-mist)	Blue
Papaver Rhœas (Shirley or Field Poppy)	Blue
Petunia	Purple, lilac
Phacelia	Lavender and blue
Phlox Drummondii	Purple, lilac
Salpiglossis sinuata	Purple
Salvia (Sage)	Blue
Scabiosa atropurpurea	Purple and blue
Schizanthus pinnatus	Purples and mauve
Senecio elegans	Purple

395

BLUE, LAVENDER, PURPLE, AND MAUVE ANNUALS—*Continued*

Torenia Fournieri	Blue and purple
Trachymene cærulea (Laceflower)	Blue
Viola tricolor (Pansy)	Varied purple & blue
Xeranthemum annuum	Purple

YELLOW AND ORANGE ANNUALS

Alonsoa Warscewiczii	Orange to scarlet
Antirrhinum majus	Orange, yellow
Argemone mexicanum (Mexican Poppy)	Yellow or orange
Calendula officinalis (Pot-marigold)	Gold, sulphur
Callistephus chinensis (China Aster)	Yellow, orange
Celosia (Cockscomb)	Yellow, orange
Chrysanthemum	Yellow, orange, bronze
Coreopsis (Goldenwave and Calliopsis)	Yellow, brown to red
Cosmos sulphureus (Yellow Cosmos)	Yellow
Datura chlorantha (Yellow Floripondio)	Yellow
Diascia Barberæ (Twinspur)	Orange
Dimorphotheca aurantiaca (Cape-marigold)	Orange, lemon
Emilia flammea (Tasselflower)	Orange
Eschscholtzia californica (Cal. Poppy)	Yellow, orange
Gaillardia pulchella (Rose-ring Gaillardia)	Yellow
Gamolepis tagetes	Orange to yellow
Helianthus (Sunflower)	Golden, red to brown
Helichrysum (Strawflower)	Yellow
Hunnemannia fumariæfolia (Tulip Poppy)	Yellow
Lathyrus odoratus (Sweet Pea)	Yellow, orange
Layia elegans (Tidytips)	Yellow
Leptosyne Stillmanii (Stillman Coreopsis)	Yellow
Limonium Bonduellii (Statice or Sea-lavender)	Yellow
Linaria bipartita (Toadflax)	Yellow
Lupinus luteus (European Yellow Lupine)	Yellow
L. mutabilis	Yellow
Mimulus luteus (Monkeyflower)	Yellow
Nemesia strumosa	Orange
Œnothera Drummondii	Yellow
Papaver Rhœas (Shirley or Field Poppy)	Orange

YELLOW AND ORANGE ANNUALS—*Continued*

Portulaca grandiflora	Yellow
Reseda odorata (Mignonette)	Greenish yellow
Rudbeckia bicolor (Pinewoods Coneflower)	Yellow
Salpiglossis sinuata	Variegated yellow
Sanvitalia procumbens	Golden yellow
Sphenogyne speciosa	Yellow
Tagetes (Marigold)	Yellow, tawny
Thunbergia alata (Clock Vine)	Yellow
Tithonia rotundifolia (Mexican Sunflower)	Rich Orange
Tropæolum (Nasturtium)	Yellow, orange
Ursinia anethoides	Orange
Venidium fastuosum	Orange
Viola tricolor	Yellow
Zinnia elegans	Yellow

ANNUALS FOR SEASHORE AND MOUNTAIN
(For Cooler and More Moist Regions)

Alonsoa (Maskflower)
Brachycome (Swan-river-daisy)
Chrysanthemum (Annual sorts)
Clarkia
Collinsia
Cosmos
Eschscholtzia (California Poppy)
Gilia
Godetia (Satinflower)
Hymenoxis
Layia (Tidytips)
Leptosiphon
Lupinus (Lupine)
Mentzelia (Blazing-star)
Mimulus (Monkeyflower)
Nemesia
Nemophila (Love-grove)
Nigella (Love-in-a-mist)
Papaver
Phacelia
Reseda (Mignonette)
Saponaria (Calabrian Soapwort)
Scabiosa (Sweet Scabious)

Edging Annuals

Ageratum (dwarf varieties)
Alyssum maritimum (Sweet Alyssum)
Anagallis Monelli
A. Phillipsii
Antirrhinum, dwarf (Snapdragon)
Asperula azurea setosa
Brachycome (Swan-River-Daisy)
Calendula, dwarf (Pot Marigold)
Centaurea candidissima (Dusty Miller)
Celosia, dwarf
Collinsia bicolor
Coreopsis tinctoria (Calliopsis)
Dianthus sinensis
Eschscholzia californica (California Poppy)
Iberis umbellata (Candytuft)
Kaulfussia amelloides (South African Daisy)
Linum grandiflorum (Scarlet Flax)
Lobelia erinus (dwarf)
Matricaria inodora (a double daisy)
Mesembryanthemum crystallinum (Iceplant)
Nemophila insignis
Phacelia campanularia
Phlox Drummondii
Sanvitalia
Saponaria calabrica
Silene pendula
Tagetes (Marigold)
Torenia (Wishboneflower)
Tropæolum (Nasturtium)
Verbena (Vervain)

Annuals for Window and Porch Boxes

Ageratum
Alyssum
Browallia speciosa
Centaurea (Dusty Miller)
Lobelia erinus
Maurandia
Petunia
Phlox

Annuals for Window and Porch Boxes—*Continued*

Portulaca (Rosemoss)
Tagetes signata var. Pumila
Thunbergia (Clockvine)
Tropæolum majus (Nasturtium)
Verbena
Vinca rosea (Periwinkle)
Zinnia

Annuals for Temporary Hedges

Helianthus debilis (Cucumber Sunflower)
Helichrysum (Strawflower)
Impatiens (Balsam)
Kochia trichophylla
Mirabilis (Four-o'clock)
Pennisetum (Fountain Grass)

Annuals for Moist Places

Ionopsidium (Diamondflower)
Mimulus (Monkeyflower)
Nemophila (Love-grove)

Annuals for Pots in Greenhouse or Conservatory

Browallia speciosa
Campanula (Canterbury Bells)
Celosia
Cobæa
Diascia
Helipterum (Everlastings)
Impatiens (Balsam)
Ipomœa purpurea (Morning Glory)
Nicotiana (Flowering Tobacco)
Penstemon gloxinioides (Beard-tongue)
Reseda odorata (Mignonette)
Schizanthus (Butterfly-flower)
Torenia
Tropæolum (Nasturtium)

Annuals as Everlastings

Acroclinium
Catananche (Cupid's-dart)
Gomphrena (Globe-Amaranth)

ANNUALS AS EVERLASTINGS—*Continued*

Grasses, Ornamental
Helichrysum (Strawflower)
Limonium (Statice) Sea Lavender)
Rhodanthe
Xeranthemum (Immortelle)

ANNUALS FOR COOL OR SHADY PLACES

Anchusa
Campanula (Annual Canterbury Bells)
Impatiens (Balsam)
Nemophila (Love-grove)
Nicotiana (Flowering Tobacco)
Œnothera (Evening Primrose)
Omphalodes
Polygonum

ANNUALS FOR CUT FLOWERS

†Acroclinium (Everlasting)
Amaranthus caudatus (Love-lies-bleeding)
*Antirrhinum (Snapdragon)
Arctotis grandis (Bushy Arctotis)
Argemone (Prickly Poppy)
Browallia demissa
B. speciosa
*Calendula officinalis (Pot Marigold)
*Callistephus (China-aster)
*Centaurea moschata (Sweet Sultan)
Chrysanthemum
Clarkia elegans
Coreopsis tinctoria (Calliopsis)
*Cosmos
*Delphinium ajacis (Rocket Larkspur)
*Dianthus chinensis (China Pink)
Dimorphotheca aurantiaca (Cape-Marigold)
Emilia flammea (Tasselflower)
Eschscholzia californica (California Poppy)
Gaillardia
†Gomphrena globosa (Globe Amaranth)

*Salable cut flowers.
†Everlasting flowers.

ANNUALS FOR CUT FLOWERS—*Continued*

*Gypsophila
Helianthus annuus (Sunflower)
†Helichrysum (Strawflower)
Lathyrus odorata (Sweet Pea)
Lavatera trimestris (Tree-mallow)
Leptosyne Stillmanii (Stillman Coreopsis)
†Limonium sinuatum (Notchleaf Statice)
†L. Suworowi (Suworow Statice)
*Lupinus (Lupine)
Matricaria inodora (a double daisy)
Mathiola bicornis
M. incana
Nicotiana (Flowering Tobacco)
Nigella (Love-in-a-mist)
Papaver glaucum (Tulip Poppy)
P. Rhœas (Corn Poppy)
P. umbrosum (Field Poppy)
Phacelia campanularia
P. tanacetifolia
Phlox Drummondii
Polygonum orientale
Reseda odorata (Mignonette)
Salpiglossis sinuata
Scabiosa atropurpurea (Sweet Scabiosa)
Senecio elegans (Jacobæa)
Tagetes (Marigold)
Verbena erinoides (Moss Vervain)
V. hybrids
Zinnias elegans
Z. Haageana

SCENTED ANNUALS

Ageratum Houstonianum (Mexican Ageratum) delicate
Alyssum maritimum (Sweet Alyssum) delicate
Antirrhinum (Snapdragon) delicate
Calendula (Pot Marigold) pungent
Centaurea moschata (Sweet Sultan) delicate

(*Continued on page 412*)

*Salable cut flowers.
†Everlasting flowers.

TABULAR LIST OF ANNUALS

Scientific Name	Common Name	Height (in In.)	Distance Apart	Color	Dates of Sowing I.=Indoors O.=Outdoors	Remarks
Abronia umbellata	Sand-verbena	6	6	Rose	I. March	Really a perennial but usually treated as an annual
Acroclinium (see Helipterum)						
Adonis aestivalis	Summer Adonis	12	6	Crimson	I. March	Not easy
aleppica		18	6	Red	O. April	
Ageratum Houstonianum	Mexican Ageratum	18–24	12	Blue, white	I. March	Reseeds prolifically and when once established it comes up year after year from self-sown seed.
intermediate		9–12	9	Blue, white	I. March	
dwarf		4–8	6	Blue, white	I. March	
Alonsoa acutifolia	Maskflower	24	9	Scarlet	I. April	Also good as potted plant. Does not endure a hot, humid climate.
Warscewiczii		18	6	Orange-scarlet		
Alyssum maritimum	Sweet Alyssum	3–4	6	White	I. March, O. April	Fine edger
compact varieties		6–10	9	White	I. March, O. April	Fine edger
spreading varieties					O. May	
Amaranthus caudatus	Love-lies-bleeding	48–72	18	Crimson	I. April	
Ammobium alatum	Winged Everlasting	24	12	White	O. April, May	
Anagallis indica	Blue Pimpernel	6	6	Blue	O. May	One of the best of the blue annuals
Anchusa, vr. Blue Bird	Blue Bird Anchusa	18	9	Bright blue	O. May	
Antirrhinum majus	Snapdragon	6	6	Orange, yellow, white, pink, red, purple shades	I. March, O. April	Select rust-proof varieties.
dwarf varieties		18	10		I. March, O. April	
intermediate varieties		36	12–18		I. March, O. April	
tall varieties					I. March, O. April	
Arctotis grandis	Bushy Arctotis	24	10	White, bluish eye	I. March, O. April	Excellent for cutting.
Argemone grandiflora	Prickly Poppy	36	12	White	O. May	Likes warm soil and hottest exposure
mexicana	Mexican Poppy	24–36	12	Yellow or orange	O. May	

Scientific name	Common name	Height	Distance	Color	Time	Remarks
Asperula azurea setosa	Blue Woodruff	9		Gray-blue		Does well in poor soil or light shade.
Aster (see Callistephus)						
Bartonia		36–48	24	White, yellow	O. May	Opens in the evening, fragrant.
Brachycome iberidifolia	Swan-river-daisy	12	6	Blue, pink, white	I. April, O. May	Good edger. Short period of bloom. Sow for succession.
Browallia demissa (elata)		12–18	9	Purple-blue, white	I. April, O. May	
speciosa major		12–24	9	Purple-blue	I. February	Good pot plant for terrace or conservatory
Cacalia (see Emilia)						
Calandrinia grandiflora		18	10	Rose		
speciosa		9	6	Ruby-red		
Calendula officinalis	Pot-marigold	12–24	12–15	Gold, sulphur	O. April	Very hardy. May be grown in South for winter bloom.
Callistephus chinensis	China-aster	18	10	Various (blue, lavender, white, pink, red, yellow)	I. March	
Campanula ramosissima	Bluestar Bellflower	12	6	Blue	I. March	
Annual Canterbury Bells (in variety)		24	12	Blue, pink, white	I. March, O. April	Bloom in late summer and early fall.
drabifolia (attica)		6	6	Blue and white	O. April	
Celosia argentea (plumosa)	Feather Cockscomb	36–48	12–18	Yellow to crimson	O. April	⎫
all var. of argentea argentea, dwarf		12	9	Yellow to crimson	O. April	⎬ The yellow and orange varieties are very effective for autumn bloom in border.
cristata	Cockscomb	24	18	Yellow to crimson	O. April	⎭
Centaurea americana	Basketflower	36–48	15	Lavender	O. April	
Cineraria	Dusty-miller	24	12	Purple-rose	I. March	
Cyanus	Cornflower	36	12	Blue, pink, white	O. Sept. or April	
imperialis	Royal Sweet-sultan	36	12	Blue, pink, white	I. April, O. May	
moschata	Sweet-sultan	36	12	Blue, pink, white	I. April, O. May	Short period of bloom.
Centranthus macrosiphon	Spur-valerian	12	10	Rose, white	O. April	
Chrysanthemum carinatum	Annual Chrysanthemum	24	9	White, marked variously	O. April	

TABULAR LIST OF ANNUALS—Continued

Scientific Name	Common Name	Height (in In.)	Distance Apart	Color	Dates of Sowing I.=Indoors O.=Outdoors	Remarks
Chr. coronarium	Crowndaisy	24	12	Sulphur yellow	O. April	
Parthenium	Feverfew	12–30	9			
segetum	Corn-marigold	24	12	Golden		Excellent for cutting. Prefers cool, growing weather.
Clarkia elegans		12–24	9	Rose to white and purple	I. April	
pulchella		12–24	9	Rose to white and purple	I. April	
Cleome spinosa	Spiderflower	48–60	24	Magenta, white	O. April	Excellent in border because of its height.
Clintonia pulchella		4–6	9	White, marked with blue		
Collinsia bicolor	Chinese-houses	18	6	Blue, pink and white	I. April	
Collomia coccinea		12	6	Scarlet	O. April	
Coreopsis Drummondii	Goldenwave	24	12	Yellow	O. April–June, Sept.	
tinctoria	Calliopsis	36	15	Yellow; brown-red	O. April–June, Sept.	
tinctoria var. Crimson King		8	6	Yellow; brown-red	O. April–June, Sept.	
Cosmos bipinnatus	Cosmos	48–62	18–24	Crimson to white	O. April	Valuable for cutting.
diversifolius	Black Cosmos	36	18	Lilac	O. April	
sulphureus	Yellow Cosmos	48–72	18–24	Yellow	I. March	
Crepis barbata rubra	Hawkweed	12	6	Rose, white (daisy-like)		
Cuphea ignea	Fiery Cuphea	18	12	Scarlet	I. June	
Cynoglossum amabile	Houndstongue	24	9	Blue	I. April, O. May	
Datura chlorantha	Yellow Floripondio	24	18	Yellow	I. April	
fastuosa (D. cornucopia)	Cornucopia Floripondio	18–24	18	White, purple reverse	I. April	
Delphinium Ajacis	Rocket Larkspur	24–36	9	Various blues	O. Sept., March	

Botanical name	Common name	Height		Color	Sowing time	Remarks
Delphinium Consolida	Field Larkspur	18–24	9	Various blues	O. Sept., March	
Dianthus chinensis	China Pink	12–18	6	Various	O. Sept., April, I. March	
Diascia Barberæ	Twinspur	18	6	Pink, orange	I. March	
Didiscus (see Trachymene)						
Dimorphotheca auran-tiaca	Cape-marigold	12–18	9	Orange, lemon to white	I. March	Excellent for hot, dry position
Echium creticum	Viper's Bugloss	12–18	12	Red	I. Jan.	
plantagineum		18–24	15	Purple-blue	I. Jan.	Very effective in border.
plantagineum hybrids		18–24	15	Pale blue, pink, mauve, white	I. Jan.	
Emilia flammea	Tasselflower	18+	9	Scarlet, orange	O. April	
sagittata		18	9	Scarlet	I. March, O. May	
Eschscholtzia californica	California Poppy	12	9	Yellow, pink, red	O. March, Sept.	Do not transplant. Good cut flower.
Euphorbia heterophylla	Painted Spurge	36	12	Red leaves at tips	O. April	
marginata (E. variegata)	Snow-on-the-mountain	36–48	12	Leaves margined white	O. March	Milky juice is poisonous.
Felicia bergeriana	Kingfisher Daisy	6	6	Blue with yellow discs		Daisy-like flower.
Gaillardia amblyodon	Maroon Gaillardia	18–24	9	Brown-red or maroon	O. April	
pulchella	Rose-ring Gaillardia	18–24	9	Yellow and rose-purple	O. April	
Gamolepis tagetes		12	10	Orange-yellow	I. March, O. May	
Gilia capitata	Globe Gilia	24	9	Blue	I. March, O April	
coccinea	Scarlet Gilia	36	12	Scarlet	I. March, O. May	
coronopifolia	Texasplume	36	9	Scarlet	I. March, O May	
tricolor	Birdseye Gilia	24	9	White, purple	O. April	
Godetia amœna	Farewell-to-Spring	24	12	Rose to white	O. April	
grandiflora	Whitney Godetia	18	9	Purple, rose to white	O. April	
Gomphrena globosa	Globe-amaranth	24	12	Magenta, amaranth, salmon-white	I. March, O. May	
Gypsophila elegans	Babysbreath	12–18	6	White	O. April	

TABULAR LIST OF ANNUALS—*Continued*

Scientific Name	Common Name	Height (in In.)	Distance Apart	Color	Dates of Sowing I.=Indoors O.=Outdoors	Remarks
Gypsophila muralis	Cushion Gypsophila	12	6	Rose	O. April	
Helianthus annuus	Sunflower	96–108	3	Golden	O. April	
debilis	Cucumber Sunflower	48	2	Golden, sulphur	O. April	
dwarf varieties		12–36	12	Yellow or red-brown	O. April	
Helichrysum bracteatum	Strawflower	36	9–12	Red, pink, yellow, white	I. March, O. May	Excellent for winter bouquet.
Heliophila		18	10	Blue, white-eyed	I. March, O. May	
Heliotropium	Heliotrope	10	12	Lavender, purple	I. March	
Helipterum Manglesii	Mangles Everlasting Rose E. (Acroclinium)	18	6	Rose	I. March, O. May	Sweet scented.
roseum		12–18	6	Rose	I. March, O. May	
Hunnemannia fumariaefolia	Goldencup or Tulip Poppy	18–24	9–12	Soft yellow	I. April pots	
Iberis affinis	Candytuft	16	16	White, lilac tinge	O. April	
amara		12+	12	White	O. April	
umbellata		16	16	Purple, carmine, pink	O. April	Sometimes fragrant.
Impatiens Balsamina	Garden Balsam	12–18	9	Various—pink, rose, purple, violet, white	O. April	
Sultani	Sultan, Patience	15	9	Rose or white	O. April	
Incarvillea variabilis		18	8–10	Yellow, pink, white	I. March, O. May	
Jacobæa (*see* Senecio)						
Kochia scoparia	Belvidere or Summer Cypress	18–24	12–18		O. May	
trichophila	Summer Cypress	18–24	12–18	White, pink, rose, purple, yellow, peach, orange	O. May	Makes an excellent low hedge.
Lathyrus odoratus	Sweet Pea	48+ (climbing)	6		O. October, April	Prefers cool growing weather.

Lathyrus dwarf varieties		8	6	Same	Same	
Lavatera trimestris	Treemallow	24–60	12–18	Rose, white	O. May	
alba splendens		36	18	White	O. May	
rosea splendens		36	18	Rose	O. May	
Layia elegans	Tidytips	12	10	Yellow, tipped white	O. May	
Leptosiphon hybrida		12	10	Rosy carmine	I. April	
Leptosyne Stillmanii	Stillman Coreopsis	18	15	Large yellow, resembling coreopsis	O. April	
maritima	Sea-lavender or Statice	24–36	12	Yellow	O. April	
Limonium Bonduellii		18–24	15	Yellow	I. March	
sinuatum	Notchleaf Sea-lavender	18–24	15	Violet to white	I. March	
Suworowi	Suworow Sea-lavender	18	15	Rose	I. March	
Linaria bipartita	Toadflax	18–24	15	Yellow to crimson, pink and purple	O. April, May	
maroccana		12	4	Bright purple with yellow spot	O. April, May	
Linum grandiflorum	Flowering Flax	8–12	9	Crimson	O. April	
Lobelia Erinus, dwarf vrs.	Edging Lobelia	4–6	6	Violet, blue, white	I. Feb., March	Excellent as an edger.
Erinus, trailing vrs.		4–6	9	Violet, blue, white	I. Feb., March	
Lobelia tenuior		12–18	6	Bright blue or white	I. March, O May	
Lunaria annua	Honesty	18	12	Magenta	I. March, O. April	Very effective in the border and good for cutting.
Lupinus Hartwegii	Hartweg Lupine	36	12–18	Purple, pink	I. pots March, O. May	
hirsutus	Blue Lupine	24	12	Blue	I. pots March, O. May	
luteus	European Yellow L.	24	12	Yellow	I. pots March, O. May	
mutabilis		24	18	Violet, yellow and white	I. pots March, O. May	
dwarf varieties		12	9	Violet, yellow, pink and white	I. pots March, O. May	
Lychnis Cœli-rosa (Viscaria)	Rose-of-heaven	12	6	Flesh	O. April	

Scientific Name	Common Name	Height (in In.)	Distance Apart	Color	Dates of Sowing I.=Indoors O.=Outdoors	Remarks
Malcomia maritima	Virginian-stock	4-8	3	Purple, pink, white	O. April	
Malope trifida grandiflora	Mallow-wort	30	12	Rose-red	O. April	
Martynia fragrans		24	12	Mauve	O. April	Woolly foliage, sweetly scented.
Mathiola bicornis		12	6	Lilac		Night-blooming, grown for fragrance.
incana dwarf	Stock	12-18	9	Tones of rose and purple, also white	I. March, O. April	
incana tall	Stock	24-30	12-18		I. March, O. April	
Mimulus luteus	Monkeyflower	18	9	Scarlet, crimson, yellow mottled	I. March to April	
tigrinus		12-18	9	Red and yellow	I. March, O. May	
Mirabilis jalapa	Four o'clock	24	12	Pink, white, yellow	O. May	Flowers open at four o'clock.
Myosotis dissitiflora	Forget-me-not	12	6	Blue, pink	I. April	Lovely as an edger.
Nemesia strumosa	Nemesia	18	9	Orange, rose to white	I. March	Prefers cool growing weather.
Nemophila insignis	Baby Blue-eyes	9	12	Clear blue	O. April	
maculata	Spotted Nemophila	10	8	White, black spotted	I. April	
Nicotiana alata (N. affinis)	Winged Tobacco	36-48	12	White	I. March, O. April	Delightfully fragrant.
Sanderæ	Flowering Tobacco	24-36	12	Red	I. March, O. April	
sylvestris		36-48	12	White to crimson	I. March, O. April	
Nigella damascena	Love-in-a-mist	18-24	9	Blue	O. April	Short season of bloom.
Œnothera Americana	Evening-primrose	12	6	White	O. May	
Drummondii	Drummond E.	12	6	Yellow	O. May	
Papaver Rhoeas	Shirley Poppy, Field	18-36	12	Tones of scarlet, orange, pink, blue	O. Nov. or March	Hairy stems and buds.

Papaver somniferum	Opium Poppy	24–36	9	Various (white to red)	O. Sept., March	Source of opium. Smooth stems and buds.
Penstemon gloxinioides	Beard-tongue	24–36	10	Many		For use in pots for the greenhouse.
Petunia hybrida, dwarf	Petunia	6–8	6	White to bright rose and purple	I. March, O. April	Long season of bloom.
tall and trailing		12–24	12	White to bright rose and purple	I. March, O. April	
Phacelia campanularia	Harebell Phacelia	12	9	Blue	I. March, O. April	
ciliata		12	9	Blue	O. April	
viscida		12	9	Blue	O. April	
tanacetifolia		24	12	Light purple	O. April	
Phaseolus	Scarlet runner		8	Red	O. May	Rapid climber.
Phlox Drummondii, dwarf	Drummond Phlox	6	6	White, magenta, rose, tawny and purple	I. March, O. May	Plan for successive plantings.
tall varieties		12–18	9	Purplish-crimson, yellow, white	I. March, O. May	
Portulaca grandiflora	Portulaca	8	6	Rose	O. April	Excellent for hot, dry situations.
Rehmannia angulata		48	18	Rose	I. March	Lovely perennial treated as annual.
Reseda odorata, dwarf	Mignonette	6	12	Greenish-yellow	I. pots April	Lovely fragrance. Does not like transplanting.
tall varieties		12–18	12	Greenish-yellow	I. pots April	
Rudbeckia bicolor	Pinewoods Coneflower	24	18	Yellow, black center	O. April	
Salpiglossis sinuata	Salpiglossis	18–24	9	Purples and yellows variegated	I. March, O. May	Rather tempermental.
Salvia patens	Gentian Sage	18	12	Deep blue	I. March	A most intense and lovely blue.
farinacea	Mealycup Sage	24	9	Blue	I. March, O. May	Half-hardy P. treated as A.
splendens	Scarlet Sage	36	18	Scarlet	I. Feb., March, O. May	Very useful for the border.
splendens vr. Welwyn	Welwyn Sage	36	18	Pink	I. March, O. May	Should be used in moderation.
Sanvitalia procumbens		6, Tr.	9	Golden	I. March, O. May	
procumbens flore pleno		6	9	Golden	I. March, O. May	Double-flowering.
Saponaria calabrica	Calabrian Soapwort	12+	10	Rose	I. March, O. April	
Vaccaria		18	9	Pink, white	I. March, O. April	

TABULAR LIST OF ANNUALS—Continued

Scientific Name	Common Name	Height (in In.)	Distance Apart	Color	Dates of Sowing	Remarks
Scabiosa atropurpurea	Sweet Scabious	36	12	Purple, blue, mahogany, rose, white	I. March, O. April	Attract hummingbirds.
Schizanthus pinnatus dwarf varieties	Butterflyflower	12	9	White, rose, purple spotted	I. June, April, O. May	
tall varieties		24–36	12–18	White, rose, purple spotted	I. June, April, O. May	
Senecio elegans	Purple Groundsel	18	6	Purple, rose to white	I. March	
Silene Armeria	Sweet-William Campion	12	6	Rose	O. April	
Solanum integrifolium		36	24	Inconspicuous	I. March	Grown for orange-red fruit for indoor decoration.
Sphenogyne speciosa		10	6	Yellow, daisy-like		
Statice (see Limonium)						
Stock (see Mathiola)						
Tagetes erecta	Aztec or African Marigold	48	12–18	Gold, lemon	I. March, O. May	Excellent for cutting.
patula	French Marigold	18	9	Gold, spotted maroon	I. March, O. May	Very effective in fall garden.
signata pumila	Mexican Marigold	12	6	Gold	I. March, O. May	
Thunbergia alata	Clock Vine	9	12	Yellow with dark center	I. March, O. May	Trailer.
Tithonia rotundifolia (T. speciosa)	Mexican Sunflower	72–100	36	Rich orange	I. March, O. May	Coarse; spectacular flowers.
Torenia Fournieri	Blue-wings	9–12	6	Blue and velvety purple	I. March, O. May	Sun or partial shade. Endures intense heat well.
Trachymene cerulea	Laceflower	24	9	Soft blue	I. March	
Tropaeolum majus	Nasturtium	48, Cl.	12–15	Scarlet to yellow	O. April	} Pungent odor.
minor	Dwarf Nasturtium	12	6	Scarlet to yellow	O. April	

Ursinia anethoides		12	6	Orange, daisy-like	I. March, O. April	Good for very sunny border.
hybrids		12–24	10	Orange, daisy-like	I. March, O. April	Good for very sunny border.
Venidium fastuosum		24–36	12	Orange with dark centers	I. March, O. April	Spectacular, spiny-looking foliage.
Verbena erinoides	Moss Vervain	8, Tr.	9	Magenta to white	I. March	⎫
hybrida		8, Tr.	9	Magenta to white	I. March	⎬ Long season of bloom.
tall varieties		12	12	Magenta to white	I. March	⎭
Vinca rosea	Madagascar Periwinkle	18	9	Rose, white	I. Jan., Feb.	
Viscaria zerantheum (see Lychnis)						
Viola tricolor	Pansy	8–12	9	Varied purple, blue, yellow, or white	I. Feb., O. April, or O. August	Usually B., but may be treated as an A.
Xeranthemum annuum	Immortelle	24–36	9	Purple, white	I. March	Everlasting.
Zinnia elegans	Giant Zinnia	36	12	Scarlet, rose, white, orange and yellow	I. March, O. April	⎫ Long season of bloom.
dwarf	Dwarf Zinnia	15	9		I. March, O. April	⎬
Haageana	Orange Zinnia	18	9	Yellow, blotched maroon	I. March, O. April	

Scented Annuals—*Continued from page* 401

Heliotropium peruvianum (one of the loveliest)
Iberis coronaria (Candytuft)
I. umbellata (Purple Candytuft)
Lupinus luteus (Yellow Lupine)
*Mathiola bicornis (Night-scented Stock)
M. incana (Ten-weeks Stock)
Mimulus moschata (Muskplant)
*Nicotiana affinis (Flowering Tobacco)
*Œnothera Lamarchiana (Evening Primrose)
Petunia—heavy
Reseda odorata (Mignonette) delightful
Scabiosa—dainty
Tagetes (Marigold) pungent
*Verbascum phlomoides (Tall Mullein)
Verbena erinoides (Moss Vervain)
V. hybrida

  *Night-scented.

XI

Biennials

Botanically, a biennial is a plant which completes its life cycle within the space of two years. During the first year vegetative leaf growth is produced, and during the second year the plant blooms, produces seed, and dies.

In this group we find some of our most beautiful garden flowers, and yet, because they are not permanent residents of the garden, we are inclined to disregard their potentialities. It is true that they are but transients in the flower border—that few, if any of them, may be counted upon for even one full season of bloom, and yet during the space of the few brief weeks when they are in flower they will contribute a full measure of beauty to any planting composition.

Indeed, this transient quality of the biennials may be considered as one of their greatest assets, for it makes it more easily possible to plan for a long succession of bloom. Whereas the perennials, such as the columbines, iris, phlox and peonies, must be left undisturbed in the border throughout the season, even after their period of bloom is over, the biennials may be moved into the garden a few weeks before they are to flower and then, without a qualm, they may be ruthlessly uprooted as soon as their blooming period is over, leaving welcome space for the planting of annuals and autumn flowering bulbs and perennials. Foxgloves may be followed by hardy chrysanthemums, gladioli may be planted as soon as the Canterbury Bells have been removed, and pansies and English daisies, which make such a colorful spring border, may be followed, later in the season, by some of the gay little annuals such as phlox Drummondii, lobelia, and torenia.

So, while we may continue to consider the perennials as

the pièce de résistance of our flower gardens, and while some of the annuals, particularly those which can be counted upon for a long season of bloom, may be considered almost equally invaluable, we must not overlook the possibilities of the biennials, for they have much to offer.

Canterbury Bells (Campanula medium and C. calycanthema).

Propagation: Canterbury Bells may very easily be grown from seed. The seeds should be sown in June, either in frames or in a carefully prepared seed bed. The seed has excellent vitality, and a high percentage of germination is usually secured. The seedlings should be transplanted before they have become in the least crowded. Young Canterbury Bells are not entirely happy if exposed to full summer sunshine and after the first transplanting they will make much more rapid growth if they are protected by a lath frame, through which the mitigated sunlight may filter. A coldframe sloping to the north which does not receive sunlight throughout the entire day, offers a very satisfactory location for the growth of the young plants.

Culture: Canterbury Bells have a very fibrous root system and they may consequently be transplanted with the greatest ease. If the plants are lifted with ample earth about the roots and if the transplanting is done on a damp, cloudy day, Canterbury Bells may be moved into the garden when they are in full flower. As one cannot always be sure of good transplanting weather, however, it is advisable to move them into the garden after growth has started in the spring and before the plants come into bud. They will then have an opportunity to become well established before flowering. In the South, Canterbury Bells come into bloom in March and early April. In the latitude of New York they bloom about the middle of June. Coming as they do just as the foxgloves are over, they are ready to assume a minor role by filling in a gap here and there in the garden border, or they may be used as a dominant June planting. If the fading blooms are pinched off at the base, smaller auxiliary flower buds will develop and the flowering period may be considerably prolonged. In the border, the plants may be set one foot apart.

Canterbury Bells may be obtained in both single (Campanula medium) and double (Campanula calycanthema) forms and in a wide range of color; delicate pink, deep rose, white, pale lavender-blue and a deep bluish-purple.

Soil Requirements: The plants thrive well in almost any soil, pro-

Canterbury Bells and English Daisies

Foxgloves

vided that it is well drained, but they will attain a greater size and will give more abundant bloom if given a soil of high fertility.

Winter Protection: In mild climates, Canterbury Bells may be wintered in the open ground, if the soil is well drained, but where the winters are severe they require the protection of a coldframe. If only a few plants are being grown and if a frame is not available, large inverted flower pots placed over the plants will afford excellent protection. No covering should be used which will mat down over the crowns, as the plants are rather sensitive to crown rot.

English Daisies (Bellis perennis). In England these winsome spring daisies re-seed so prolifically that they are apt to infest the lawns and they are frequently regarded as a pest. Since they do not re-seed abundantly enough in this country to become a nuisance and since they are so gay and charming in the spring border, they have endeared themselves to many gardeners. Coming in shades of pink, deep rose, and white, they may be used in pleasant combination with pansies, violas and forget-me-nots in the planting of a Botticelli border—which is always so colorful and gay.

Culture: English daisies are of very easy culture. The seeds should be sown in July or early August in flats or in frames, and the young seedlings should be transplanted when small, being spaced from 4 to 6 inches apart. In the North they will require some winter protection, in the South they may be wintered in the open ground. In the spring the plants may be transplanted very successfully when in bud or in full flower. They are very accommodating little plants, having no decided soil preferences and no pests or diseases, and yet, modest and humble though they may be, they add their share of bloom and beauty to the spring border.

Forget-me-nots (Myosotis). Some species of forget-me-nots, such as Myosotis palustris, are true perennials, while others are commonly classed as biennials. For spring bloom in the garden the seed should be sown in late July or early August, the seedlings being transplanted and wintered over in the frames or in the open. As the young seedling plants are rather susceptible to damping-off every precaution should be taken to see that the soil in the seed bed is free from contamination. For the control of damping-off, see Chapter XXX.) The plants may be transplanted to the flower border in spring, and they may be moved with great ease. While forget-me-nots prefer a damp, woodsy soil, they will settle down quite happily in any location in the garden. They may be set from 6 to 8 inches apart.

Varieties: The most desirable variety for spring bloom is the large-flowered Myosotis dissitiflora. The flowers are of a more delicate shade of blue than some of the other types and are borne in graceful sprays, the plants reaching a height of from 8 to 9 inches. The plants bloom over a long period, from April well into June, and they sometimes re-seed so abundantly that they seem to be almost perennial in habit, coming up year after year. The pale blue of the forget-me-nots is lovely in combination with other flowers of the spring border. They may be used very delightfully as an under planting in tulip beds.

Foxgloves (Digitalis). Although there are several species of Digitalis which are true perennials, those which are most commonly grown in the flower garden are of a distinctly biennial habit of growth, and they are, perhaps, the most beautiful members of this group.

In England one sees foxgloves everywhere. The steep banks along the country lanes in Devonshire and Cornwall are gay with them in springtime, great drifts of them may be found in the open woodlands, and in the English gardens they are a glory to behold. There is no other flower which can quite take the place of the foxgloves in the spring border. They are among the first flowers of the season to give height and substance to the garden composition, and the stately spires of bloom against a background of hedge or wall add beauty and distinction to any planting. Coming into flower just as the first exultant ecstasy of spring bloom has passed, they may be used as the dominant note in the garden until the delphiniums and roses are ready to claim the stage.

Types and Varieties: Digitalis purpurea is the wild foxglove of England, and it is from this species that most of our improved strains have been developed. *Gloxiniæflora* is an old-fashioned variety which is still popular. It closely resembles the wild type, being more vigorous in habit and bearing longer spikes of bloom. The flowers are always spotted and may be obtained in a variety of colorings —white, rose, purple and mixed. While it is lovely in itself, it cannot compare in size or in beauty of coloring with some of the more recent introductions. The *Giant Shirley Hybrids* were developed by the Reverend W. Wilks at his home in England and bear witness to his skill as a plant breeder. The plants are of extraordinary size and vigor, often reaching a height of 6 feet, and the large, drooping flowers which are clustered closely along the flower spikes range in color from white to dark rose and purple, many of them being blotched and spotted with crimson and maroon. The *Lutz*

Hybrids, which have been recently introduced, offer an entirely new and very charming color range, the flowers varying from a delicate cream pink to a light salmon. *Sutton's Apricot* and *Sutton's Giant Primrose* are two varieties of unusual coloring and great beauty, and may be used in pleasant combination with some of the perennials.

Culture: As the seeds of foxgloves are exceedingly fine, the seed bed should be well prepared. If the seeds are sown in June and if the young seedlings are given good care they will develop into large, vigorous plants by autumn and will give generous bloom the following spring. It is unwise to delay the sowing of the seed until August as the plants will be so small that they will not be capable of giving good bloom the following season. The seed should be sown either in flats or in the frames. The seeds are usually of excellent vitality and germinate within a week or ten days after sowing. Care should be taken to see that the young seedlings are transplanted before they become in the least crowded. The young plants need an abundance of water during the growing season, and they should never be allowed to become stunted. If growth is at any time seriously checked, due to overcrowding, insufficient moisture, or lack of nourishment, the young plants have difficulty in making a full recovery. If conditions are favorable, however, the seedlings make rapid growth. They should be pricked out soon after the first true leaves have formed, and about a month or six weeks later they will again require transplanting, as it is essential that they be given ample room to develop. Where the climate is mild, foxgloves may be wintered over in the open ground, but where the winters are severe it is advisable to give them the protection of a frame, which not only protects them from extreme cold but also from excessive moisture. The thick fleshy leaves and the crown buds rot very easily if the soil remains soggy for any length of time. When the plants are wintered in frames they should be spaced well apart, at least 8 to 10 inches, in order that the air may circulate freely between the plants. In spring the plants may be moved from the frames to their permanent location in the garden. If the plants are lifted with an ample quantity of earth and if the transplanting is done on a cloudy day, they will suffer practically no check and will continue perfectly normal growth. If, however, the soil falls away from the roots or if the plants are exposed to wind and brilliant sunshine at the time of transplanting, they will suffer seriously and will never reach full perfection of bloom. They may be set from 10 to 12 inches apart.

Foxgloves will thrive well in almost any type of good garden soil provided that it is well drained, but they prefer a rich friable loam, and will make good use of a hearty diet of well-rotted manure or rich compost.

Hollyhocks (Althæa rosea). Picturesque and lovely, the hollyhocks are reminiscent of old-time gardens, and they seem equally at home beside a humble cottage doorway or in the long herbaceous borders of a formal garden. There are both single and double forms, and the flowers may be obtained in a wide range of colors—white, rose, salmon, pale primrose yellow, scarlet, crimson, purple and maroon. Hollyhocks are among our most useful background plants, attaining a height of from 6 to 8 feet. They are particularly lovely when planted against an old wall or picket fence. The period of bloom extends through the month of July into early August.

Exposure: Although hollyhocks thrive best in full sun they will also do reasonably well in partial shade, and they may be grown very successfully in a flower border with a northern exposure.

Soil Requirements: Preferring a light, well-drained soil of a neutral or slightly alkaline reaction, hollyhocks will thrive well in almost any garden, provided that the soil does does not remain too saturated with moisture throughout the winter months. The plants respond well to good fertility but they will make fair growth on very poor soil.

Propagation: Hollyhocks may be grown very easily from seed. The seeds may be planted either in a coldframe or in the open ground in late July or early August. The plants will bloom the following season. As hollyhocks produce a strong tap root it is very difficult to move the plants after they have attained any size. It is, therefore, wise to transplant the young seedlings to their permanent position in the garden while they are still quite small. Seedling plants, from seeds sown in July, may be transplanted to the garden in early autumn or early the following spring. Hollyhocks re-seed so readily that after they are once established it is seldom necessary to make additional sowings. If a few flower stalks are allowed to produce seeds, these self-sown seedlings may be transplanted to any desired position in the garden. The chief disadvantage of this method is the fact that these self-sown seedlings will produce a variety of colorings and it is not possible to carry out a definite color planting. However, if only soft, pastel shades are used in the original planting, the colors usually blend harmoniously and mixed seedlings are often very lovely.

Culture: Because of their robust habit of growth, hollyhocks should be given ample space for their development, and should be planted from 2 to 2½ feet apart. As soon as the blooms have

Photograph by J. Horace McFarland Co.

Iceland Poppies

faded, the flower stalks should be cut down unless seed is to be produced.

For the control of insect pests and diseases, refer to Chapter XXXIII.

Iceland Poppies (Papaver nudicaule). Although the Iceland poppies are true perennials in their native habitat, they have assumed all the characteristics of the biennials when grown in our gardens and they are best treated as such. They bloom luxuriantly the year following sowing, and then they usually die out, an occasional plant surviving through another year.

The soft, gray-green leaves form a rosette-like growth just above the ground, and the delicate, lovely flowers are borne on long, slender, leafless stems. The plants vary in height from 12 to 20 inches, and as many as fifty blooms may be produced upon a single plant. The flowers are very lovely in form, being cup-shaped, with delicately crinkled petals.

Varieties: Iceland poppies may be obtained in a wide variety of colorings ranging from pure white to salmon pink and from pale yellow to deep orange. Some of the named varieties which have been recently introduced are very fine. *Gibson's Giant Orange* is one of the best; *Tangerine* bears large flowers of a deep, orange hue, and *Miniatum* is a bright orange scarlet. But perhaps the most beautiful of all is the lovely *Coonara Pink* variety which was originated in Australia. The flowers vary in color from a delicate shell pink to a warm apricot-salmon and are exquisite in their daintiness, being particularly lovely when planted in combination with the blue flax (Linum perenne), that enchanting flower which reflects the blue of the soft spring skies.

The Iceland poppies come into flower in spring, about the time that the late narcissus are in bloom, and if the seed pods are not allowed to develop, the plants will give scattering bloom throughout the season.

Culture: The seeds may be sown in August, or under glass in January or February. If the seed is sown during the summer, the young plants may be wintered over either in the frames or in the open. As the Iceland poppies are natives of the Arctic regions, they are extremely hardy and will withstand the most severe winter cold. The plants may be set a foot apart.

Pansies. No spring garden is quite complete without the piquant blossoms of the pansy, upturned to the sun. Many types and strains are now available and although the giant types have lately come into vogue, the smaller, quainter kinds will probably always be preferred by many gardeners. In planning special color schemes, it is a decided advantage to be able to obtain pansies in separate shades: blue, deep purple, wine red, maroon and yellow.

Culture: Pansy seeds should be sown in August, and the plants may be wintered over in the frames or, if the climate is mild, in the open ground. They may be transplanted with the utmost ease, being moved when in full flower with no apparent set-back to the plant. If the seed pods are not allowed to form, pansies may be kept in flower over a period of several months. When they begin to appear spindly and leggy, the plants may be cut back almost to the ground and a handful of fertilizer may be cultivated into the soil about them, and in reward for one's labor there will be a second blooming.

Pansies may be readily propagated by cuttings as well as by seed, the cuttings being taken in late spring or early summer.

The plants may be set from 6 to 8 inches apart.

Siberian Wallflower (Cheiranthus allioni.) The Siberian wall-flowers are among the most effective of our spring plants for the low border, and their bright orange blooms may be used in pleasant contrast with flowers of a more subtle hue. They may be used very effectively in combination with the Leedsii Narcissus and the lovely, early-blooming tulip, *General De Wet,* with an occasional clump of phlox divaricata and mertensia as a foil for the brilliant tones of the tulips and wallflowers.

Culture: The seeds should be sown in July and the young seedlings should be transplanted when of sufficient size. In mild regions the plants may be wintered in the open very successfully, but in the north the protection of a coldframe is advisable. Being fibrous rooted, the plants may be moved easily in the spring to the desired location in the garden, and as soon as their period of bloom is over the plants may be discarded, making room for other flowers.

Set the plants a foot apart.

English Wallflower (Cheiranthus Cheiri). Throughout England they grow in cracks and crannies in the walls, and in Ireland one sees their tawny yellow blossoms upon the very rooftops of the peasant cottages. They are, indeed, a poignant part of an English spring, and it is to be regretted that they are not more widely grown in our gardens in America.

Culture: The plants may be easily grown from seed sown in July or very early August, and the young seedlings should be twice trans-planted in order that they may develop good, fibrous root systems. The young plants should also be pinched back occasionally in order that they may become stocky and well branched, as they have a tendency to make a rather spindly growth if they are left entirely to their own devices. If the plants are wintered over in frames they will be among the first of the spring flowers to come into bloom, and they may be moved into the garden as soon as the ground is workable. They may be set 10 to 12 inches apart.

When mixed seed is sown many of the flowers are apt to be streaked and blotched, and it is more satisfactory to obtain the seeds in self colors such as pale lemon, buttercup-yellow, deep wine red and mahogany. Both single and double forms are obtainable.

Sweet William (Dianthus barbatus). The Sweet Williams are among the most useful of the biennials and now that they may be obtained in such lovely, pastel shades of pink, salmon and rose as well as in the deeper tones of red and scarlet, they may be given an important part to play in the spring garden. Among the most beautiful of the new varieties are *Newport Pink, Fairy,* and *Sutton's Pink Beauty.*

Culture: The seeds should be sown in June in order that the young plants may reach a good development before winter. If the seeds are not sown until August the plants will be too small to give good bloom the following spring. In the South the plants may be wintered in the open. In the North they should be carried over in frames, being moved into the garden in early spring and set 9 inches apart.

Verbascum phœniceum. Verbascum phœniceum is a member of the Mullein family, and while it is not as well known as many of the other biennials it has distinct character and charm. The leaves form a prim rosette of green upon the surface of the soil, and the flowers, which come in soft shades of rose, mauve, and lavender, are borne on erect flower stalks, which vary from 12 to 15 inches in height.

Culture: The plants should be grown from seed sown in July. Because of the long, fleshy tap root the plants are moved with difficulty and must be handled with extreme care at the time of transplanting. The plant must be lifted from the soil in such a manner that the tap root is not broken, and the soil about the roots must be disturbed as little as possible. The verbascums are reasonably hardy and may be wintered in the open except in locations where the climate is of extreme severity. They may be used as individual accents or massed 18 inches apart.

XII

Herbaceous Perennials

Herbaceous perennials are those plants which die down to the ground during the winter and renew their growth again in the spring. Some herbaceous perennials live on almost indefinitely, while others have a tendency to die out after a few years.

Ever since plants were first grown for the beauty of their flowers, perennials have made an important contribution to the garden scene. The long life of most herbaceous perennials and their relative permanence in the garden have been their principal cultural assets, and in this group we find many of our most beautiful and most dependable garden flowers.

All of these common and familiar garden flowers came originally from wild flowers. They were brought into cultivation because of their beauty, and by selection and hybridization many of them have been developed and improved to such an extent that their relationship to their ancestors is difficult to recognize. Indeed with some flowers it is impossible to determine their place of origin or their line of descent, so dissimilar are they to wild species. In the case of most of these domesticated plants, cultivation has stimulated growth, with the result that the plants are more vigorous, the flowers larger and more varied, and in some instances the blossoms have become so specialized that they no longer set seed. Another result of cultivation is a tendency for plants to be less hardy, and more dependent upon the continual care to which they have become accustomed.

Some perennials have been in cultivation for many centuries, even since ancient times, while others have been introduced more recently, following the era of extensive exploration. Many

425

of them have come from distant lands, and in our gardens we find plants whose original habitats were the bleak shores of Iceland, or the glaciersides of Switzerland; the forests of Mexico, or the mountains of China and Japan; the valleys of India or the veldt of South Africa.

Those plants which have been cultivated in gardens since ancient times were grown first in the countries of their origin and were later introduced into Europe by the returning Crusaders or by travellers and explorers. The flowers thus gathered together in the monastery gardens, and later in the public botanic gardens, gradually became the familiar flowers of the European flower garden.

It is the herbaceous perennials which have made the gardens of England so famous for their abundance of bloom and beauty. Indeed, the long perennial border as developed in the English garden has become one of its most typical features, characteristic of the English style of garden art. Some of these perennial flowers originated in the English countryside and were invited into the gardens, some few were introduced in mediæval times, but the majority were brought into England by botanists and horticultural explorers, beginning in Queen Elizabeth's reign and continuing up to the present time.

The early colonists who established homes in the New World brought with them many of the perennial flowers which they had known and loved in their native lands. Their qualities of hardiness and long life, and their thriftiness under adverse and widely varying conditions, made these perennials particularly welcome to the early settlers of this country, and these same sturdy qualities in the perennials recommend them to us today.

PLANNING THE PERENNIAL BORDER

No planting problem is more diverse and intricate than that of the perennial flower border. No planting plan requires more careful thought, more detailed study, more creative skill. It is the aim of the designer to produce a succession of color harmonies which will merge imperceptibly, one into the other, as the season advances. No other type of plant material offers such

Photograph by *Richard Averill Smith*

Perennial Border Featuring Candidum Lilies

infinite possibilities for color compositions as do the perennials, and the gardener finds in this ever-changing medium wide scope for his artistic skill.

It must be borne in mind, however, that perennials alone will not produce as full an effect of bloom and color throughout the season as will perennials when supplemented with spring and summer flowering bulbs, and with annuals and biennials. Therefore, in planning the border for continuous bloom, it is an advantage to include a few plants of these other valuable groups as well.

In planning the perennial garden the entire life cycle of each plant must be taken into consideration when determining its position—its period of growth, blossoming, and retrogression. In the selection and arrangement of plant material the most important factors are the ultimate height of the plants, the color range, and the season of bloom; but there are other factors which must also be taken into consideration, such as the texture and color of the foliage, the longevity of the plant, and the cultural requirements. All of these considerations may at first seem confusing but they need not be so if the decisions are made in logical sequence.

The usual procedure in preparing a planting plan for a perennial garden is to first draw to scale a plan showing the outline of the various beds or borders. A scale of ½ inch to the foot will usually provide for a plan of workable size, unless the garden is unusually large, in which case the scale may be reduced to ¼ inch to the foot. The next step is to compile a list of the plants and bulbs which one desires to include in the planting plan. On this list they may be jotted down quite at random, as they come to mind, or they may be listed alphabetically, or in some other logical sequence. Such a list, set down at random, might appear as follows:

Narcissus	Linum perenne	Marigolds
Tulips	Veronica	Zinnias
Bleedingheart	Canterbury Bells	Salvia farinacea
Phlox divaricata	Phlox	Nicotiana
Primroses	Gladioli	Asters

Chrysanthemums	Columbines	Lilium regale
Delphinium	Artemisia	Lilium speciosum
Lilium candidum	Anchusa	Heuchera
Foxgloves	Thalictrum	Hollyhocks
Iris	Hardy Asters	Anemone
Violas		

When this tentative list has been completed, it should be broken up into a number of sub-groupings, according to season of bloom, color, and height:

ACCORDING TO SEASON OF BLOOM

May	*June*	*July*
Narcissus	Iris	Hollyhocks
Tulip	Heuchera	Phlox
Bleedingheart	Linum perenne	Veronica
Phlox divaricata	Delphinium	Thalictrum
Primroses	Lilium candidum	aquilegifolium
Columbines	Foxgloves	Thalictrum glaucum
Iris	Canterbury Bells	Gladioli
Linum perenne	Veronica	Marigolds
Heuchera	Anchusa italica	Zinnias
Violas	Thalictrum adian-	Salvia farinacea
	tifolium	Lilium regale

August	*September*	*October*
Phlox	Hardy Asters	Hardy Asters
Artemisia	Annual Asters	Chrysanthemums
Annual Asters	Zinnias	Japanese Anemones.
Zinnias	Marigolds	
Marigolds	Salvia farinacea	
Salvia farinacea	Delphinium	
Delphinium	Gladioli	
Gladioli	Chrysanthemums	
	Jap. Anemones	
	Lilium speciosum	

ACCORDING TO COLOR

White	Blue, Lavender, Purple	Pink, Rose, Salmon	Bronze Yellow, Orange,
Narcissus	Tulips	Tulips	Narcissus
Tulips	Phlox divaricata	Bleedingheart	Tulip
Iris	Columbines	Columbine	Primroses
Violas	Iris	Iris	Columbines
Lilium can-didum	Linum perenne	Heuchera	Iris
	Violas	Foxgloves	Violas
Foxgloves	Delphiniums	Canterbury Bells	Foxgloves
Canterbury Bells	Veronica	Hollyhocks	Hollyhocks
Lilium regale	Anchusa	Zinnias	Thal. glaucum
Hollyhocks	Gladioli	Anemone	Gladioli
Artemisia	Salvia farinacea	Chrysanthe-mums	Marigolds
Nicotiana	Annual Asters		Zinnias
	Hardy Asters	Annual Asters	Chrysanthe-mums
	Phlox	Hardy Asters	
	Thalictrum aquilegifolium	Phlox	
		Gladioli	
		Lilium specio-sum	

ACCORDING TO HEIGHT

Low	Medium	Tall
Primroses	Narcissus	Delphinium
Violas	Tulips	Lilium candidum
Heuchera	Bleedingheart	Foxgloves
Phlox divaricata	Columbines	Anchusa
Pansies	Iris	Thalictrum
English Daisies	Linum perenne	Hardy Asters
	Veronica	Hollyhocks
	Canterbury Bells	Lilium regale
	Phlox	Nicotiana
	Gladioli	Marigolds
	Chrysanthemum	Lilium speciosum
	Zinnias	
	Anemones	
	Salvia farinacea	
	Marigolds	
	Annual Asters	

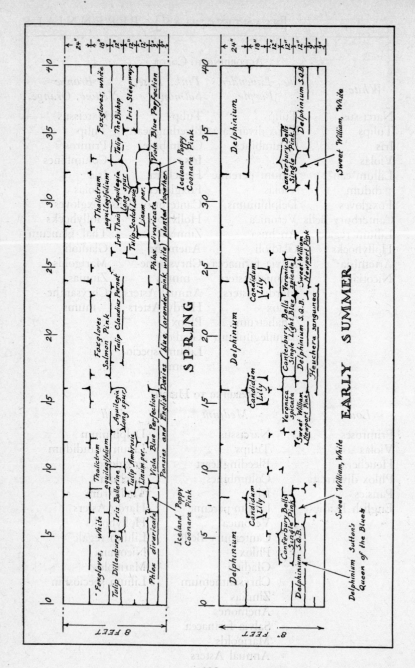

SPRING

EARLY SUMMER

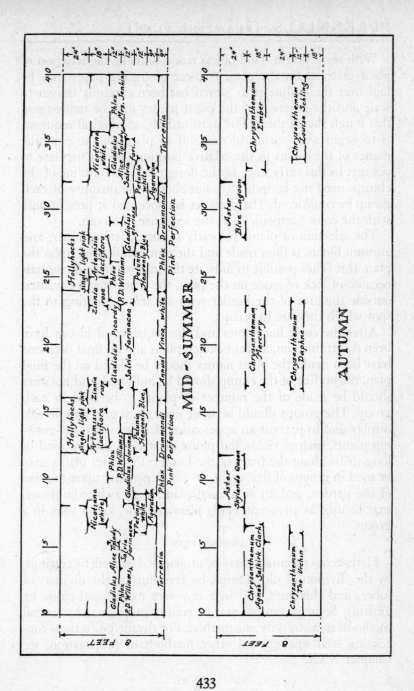

MID-SUMMER

Hollyhocks
Single, light pink

Nicotiana
white

Artemisia
lactiflora

Gladiolus Alice Talady

Phlox
P. D. Williams

Phlox
P.D.Williams

Gladiolus gloriosa

Salvia
farinacea

Petunia
Heavenly Blue

Petunia
Heavenly Blue

Ageratum

Torrenia

Phlox Drummondi
Pink Perfection

Hollyhocks
Single, light pink

Zinnia
rose

Artemisia
lactiflora

Zinnia
rose

Gladiolus Picardy

Salvia farinacea

Nicotiana
white

Gladiolus
Alice Talady

Phlox
Mrs. Jenkins

Phlox
P.D.Williams

Gladiolus
fari...

Salvia

Petunia
white

Ageratum

Phlox Drummondi
Pink Perfection

Annual Vinca, white

Torrenia

24"
18"
12"
12"
12"
9"
9"

AUTUMN

Aster
Skylands Queen

Chrysanthemum
Agnes Selkirk Clark

Chrysanthemum
The Urchin

Chrysanthemum
Mercury

Chrysanthemum
Daphne

Aster
Blue Lagoon

Chrysanthemum
Ember

Chrysanthemum
Louise Schling

24"
18"

24"
12"
18"

8 FEET

8 FEET

With these lists at hand one is ready to make the selection of plant material for the plan. A piece of tracing paper may be laid over the outline plan which has been carefully drawn to scale and the notation of the plant names may be made upon this rough sketch sheet. The most orderly and logical sequence is to begin with spring bloom and to place on the plan the names of the plants in the relative positions which they are to occupy. In this early stage of the design the exact outline of the clumps need not be indicated, nor should the quantity of each group be considered. The designer is concerned at present only with the color harmonies and the sequence of bloom.

The selection of plants for early summer, late summer, and autumn bloom is then made and the names indicated upon the plan. If it is not possible to indicate the interplanting of annuals because of lack of space on the plan, the name may be written outside the area of the border with an arrow pointing to the spot which they are to occupy.

After the color harmonies and the sequence of bloom have been determined on, and the sketch plans and all final decisions have been made, the plant names should be placed on the final plan, the outline of the clump should be indicated, and notation should be made of the number of plants to be used in each group. The groups should be large enough to give an effective display and to prevent an appearance of spottiness. Low-growing plants, such as violas and phlox divaricata, may be used in long drifts along the front of the border, the taller plants may be used in groups of five, eight, or ten, depending upon the size of the garden, and an occasional plant, such as bleedingheart, may be used as an accent, being planted alone, rather than in a group.

PROPAGATION

Herbaceous perennials may be propagated by seed, by cuttings, by the division of old clumps, by layering, by the division of tubers and rhizomes, and in a few very exceptional cases, by grafting. Some perennials may be readily propagated by several methods, some by only one method. For detailed directions concerning seed sowing, and other methods of propagation, see Chapter XXX.

PERENNIALS PROPAGATED BY SEED

Achillea (Yarrow)
Aconitum (Monkshood)
Althea rosea (Hollyhock)
Alyssum saxatile (Goldentuft)
Amsonia
Anchusa (Bugloss)
Aquilegia (Columbine)
Arabis (Rockcress)
Arenaria (Sandwort)
Artemisia (Mugwort)
Asclepias tuberosa (Butterfly-weed)
Aubrietia (Purple Rockcress)
Baptisia (False-indigo)
Bocconia (Plume poppy)
Boltonia
Campanula (Bellflower)
Centaurea
Centranthus (Valerian)
Cerastium tomentosum (Snow in summer)
Chelone (Turtlehead)
Cimicifuga (Bugbane)
Coreopsis
Delphinium (Larkspur)
Dianthus (single types)
Dicentra (Bleedingheart)
Dictamnus (Gas Plant)

Digitalis (Foxglove)
Eupatorium (Mistflower)
Gaillardia (Blanketflower)
Geum
Gypsophila (Babysbreath)
Helenium (Sneezeweed)
Helleborus (Christmas Rose)
Hesperis (Sweet Rocket)
Heuchera (Coral bells)
Iberis (Candytuft)
Linum perenne (Perennial flax)
Lobelia
Lupinus (Lupine)
Monarda (Horsemint)
Myosotis (Forget-me--not)
Œnothera (Evening-primrose)
Penstemon (Beard-tongue)
Physostegia (False dragonhead)
Platycodon (Balloon flower)
Primula (Primrose)
Pyrethrum (Painted Daisy)
Salvia (Sage)
Scabiosa (Pincushion-flower)
Sedum (Stone crop)
Thalictrum (Meadowrue)
Veronica (Speedwell)
Viola

PERENNIALS PROPAGATED BY SOFTWOOD STEM CUTTINGS

Althæa rosea (Hollyhock)
Alyssum saxatile (Golden Tuft)
Amsonia
Arabis (Rock Cress)
Arenaria (Sandwort)
Artemisia (Mugwort)
Asclepias tuberosa (Butterfly-weed)
Aster (all hardy asters)

Aubrietia (Purple Rock cress)
Boltonia
Campanula (Bellflower))
Caryopteris
Centaurea dealbata
Ceratostigma plumbaginoides (Blue Leadwort)
Chrysanthemum
Clematis (herbaceous types)

PERENNIALS PROPAGATED BY SOFTWOOD STEM CUTTINGS—*Continued*

Daphne cneorum (Garland flower)
Delphinium (Larkspur)
Dianthus (Pink)
Dicentra (Bleeding Heart)
Eupatorium cœlestinum (Mistflower)
Epigæa repens (Trailing arbutus)
Gaillardia (Blanket flower)
Geum (Avens)
Gypsophila (Babysbreath)
Helenium (Sneezeweed)
Helianthus (Sunflower)
Heliopsis (Orange Sunflower)
Hesperis (Sweet Rocket)
Heuchera (Coral Bells)
Iberis (Evergreen Candytuft)
Lobelia
Lychnis (Campion)
Lupinus (Lupine)
Lythrum (Loosestrife)
Monarda (Horsemint)
Myosotis (Forget-me-not)
Nepeta
Penstemon (Beard-tongue)
Phlox
Potentilla (Cinquefoil)
Pyrethrum (Painted Daisy)
Rudbeckia (Coneflower)
Salvia (Sage)
Saponaria (Soapwort)
Sedum (Stonecrop)
Silene (Catchfly)
Teucrium (Germander)
Tradescantia (Spiderwort)
Verbascum (Mullein)
Veronica (Speedwell)
Viola

PERENNIALS PROPAGATED BY ROOT CUTTINGS

Anchusa (Bugloss)
Anemone Japonica (Japanese Anemone)
Asclepias (Butterflyweed)
Bocconia (Plumepoppy)
Ceratostigma plumbaginoides (Blue Leadwort)
Dicentra Spectabilis (Bleeding Heart)
Dictamnus (Gas Plant)
Echinops (Globe thistle)
Gypsophila paniculata (Babysbreath)
Œnothera (Evening Primrose)
Papaver orientale (Oriental Poppy)
Phlox
Polygonatum (Solomon's Seal)
Romneya (Canyon Poppy)
Stokesia (Stokes Aster)
Thermopsis
Trollius (Globe flower)
Verbascum (Mullein)
Yucca (Adam's-needle)

PERENNIALS PROPAGATED BY DIVISION OF CLUMPS

Achillea (Yarrow)
Aconitum (Monkshood)
Ajuga (Bugle)
Alyssum saxatile (Goldentuft)
Amsonia
Anchusa (Bugloss)
Aquilegia (Columbine)
Arabis (Rockcress)
Artemisia (Mugwort)
Aster (all hardy types)
Astilbe (Herbaceous Spirea)
Aubrietia (Purple Rockcress)
Baptisia (False-indigo)
Bocconia (Plume Poppy)
Boltonia
Campanula (Bellflower)
Centranthus (Valerian)
Cerastium tomentosum (Snow-in-summer)
Ceratostigma plumbaginoides (Blue Leadwort)
Chelone (Turtlehead)
Chrysanthemum
Cimicifuga (Bugbane)
Clematis (herbaceous types)
Coreopsis
Delphinium (Larkspur)
Dianthus (Pink)
Dicentra (Bleeding Heart)

Doronicum (Leopard's bane)
Echinops (Globethistle)
Eupatorium (Mistflower)
Euphorbia (Spurge)
Filipendula (Meadowsweet)
Gaillardia (Blanket-flower)
Helianthus (Sunflower)
Hemerocallis (Daylily)
Heuchera (Coral Bell)
Iris
Linum perenne (Perennial Flax)
Lupinus (Lupine)
Mertensia (Virginia Bluebells)
Monarda (Horsemint)
Œnothera (Evening-primrose)
Penstemon (Beard-tongue)
Peony
Phlox (all hardy types)
Physostegia (False-dragonhead)
Primula (Primrose)
Pyrethrum (Painted Lady)
Rudbeckia (Coneflower)
Scabiosa
Sedum (Stonecrop)
Statice (Thrift)
Thalictrum (Meadow Rue)
Trollius (Globeflower)
Veronica (Speedwell)

PERENNIALS WHICH MAY BE PROPAGATED BY LAYERING

Daphne cneorum (Garland-flower)
Dianthus (Pink)
Myosotis (Forget-me-not)
Nepeta

Sedum (Stonecrop)
Thymus (Thyme)
Veronica (Speedwell)

PERENNIALS PROPAGATED BY RHIZOMES

Achimenes

Canna

Convallaria majalis (Lily-of-the-Valley)

Helleborus niger (Christmas Rose)

Hosta (Plantain Lily)

Iris—all rhizomatous types

Podophyllum (Mayapple)

Polygonatum (Solomon's Seal)

Primula (Sieboldii)

Sanguinaria (Bloodroot)

Smilacina (False Solomon's Seal)

Trillium (Wake-robin)

PERENNIALS PROPAGATED BY GRAFTING

Gypsophila paniculata florepleno   (Double-flowered Babysbreath)

Tree Peony

PERENNIALS PROPAGATED BY DIVISION OF TUBERS

Dahlias

Liatris (Gayfeather)

PREPARATION OF THE SOIL

Since perennial beds and borders constitute a more or less permanent type of planting, it is a matter of considerable importance that the soil be adequately prepared. Most herbaceous perennials attain their maximum perfection of growth and bloom in a fertile well-drained loam, which is high in organic content, neutral or very nearly neutral in reaction, and which has been deeply and thoroughly prepared previous to planting.

As many perennials are deeply rooted, and as it is well to induce the more shallow rooted types to send their feeding roots downward, the soil should be prepared to a depth of at least 15 inches, preferably to a depth of 24 inches. Trenching and double digging are the most approved methods for the preparation of the soil in perennial beds and borders. For detailed information concerning these practices, consult Chapter XXVIII, page 957. If the soil is poorly drained, this condition should be remedied at the time that the beds are prepared. Refer to Chapter III, page 91.

SOIL REACTIONS

A few perennials definitely prefer a soil that is slightly alkaline in reaction, others are acid tolerant, and some are entirely indifferent. The vast majority, however, prefer a soil which is neutral or very nearly neutral in reaction, with a pH. ranging from 6.5 to 7.5. In preparing the soil for perennial beds, samples should be taken and the soil reaction should be definitely determined. For full and detailed directions, see Chapter I, page 23. If the soil tests show that the reaction is below a pH. of 6.5, an application of lime should be made. The chart on page 27, Chapter I, will indicate the exact amount which should be applied. The application should be made after the beds have been prepared for planting. The lime should be sprinkled over the surface of the bed and should then be cultivated lightly into the soil. In order to meet the needs of those perennials which definitely prefer a slightly alkaline soil, a sufficient quantity of lime should be applied over the area where they are to be planted to bring the reaction up to a pH. of approximately 7.5.

PERENNIALS WHICH PREFER A SLIGHTLY ALKALINE SOIL

Anemone japonica
Gypsophila

Hollyhocks
Iris

PERENNIALS WHICH ARE ACID TOLERANT

Baptisia
Coreopsis

Platycodon
Silene

For perennials preferring distinctly acid soil, see Chapter XVII on the Woodland Garden.

Almost all other perennials may be grouped among those which prefer a neutral or nearly neutral soil, or those which are entirely indifferent to soil conditions.

GENERAL MAINTENANCE

A perennial garden requires faithful care and maintenance throughout the season. After the winter mulch has been removed in the spring (see page 448 for directions regarding the removal of winter mulches) a general inspection of the garden should be made. Any plants which may have been partially heaved out of the soil during the winter should be pressed gently back into place and notations should be made of any plants which have failed to survive the winter. During this first spring survey, the needs of each individual group of plants should be carefully studied, and the plans for spring work should be outlined. Some plants will need to be divided (see section on Renewing Perennial Plants, page 444), other plants will need to be replaced with younger, more vigorous stock, and plans must be made for the spring feeding (see section on Maintenance of Fertility, page 443). It is also wise to make a few soil tests at this time in order to determine whether an application of lime is advisable. During the days of early spring all dead leaves and stalks should be removed and the beds and borders should be edged, in order that the garden may have a neat and trim appearance.

The first cultivation should be given as soon as the soil is warm and mellow and has become sufficiently dry. The soil should never be cultivated when it is too wet as that will seriously injure its physical condition, causing the formation of many hard lumps. An excellent way to test the workability of the soil is to take a small amount and squeeze it tightly in the hand. If it crumbles when it falls to the ground, it is in good condition to be cultivated. If, however, it remains in a firm, compact mold, it contains too much moisture and should not be worked until it has become more thoroughly dry. Subsequent cultivations should be given throughout the season at intervals of every week or ten days. A small weeder of the type which has three flexible prongs is one of the most convenient and efficient tools for the cultivation of perennial beds. It is possible to cultivate very close to the plants without any damage to the roots or crown; the soil is left in excellent tilth, and the work may be done very rapidly, provided that the soil is in good condition for cultivating, being neither too wet nor too dry.

In order that perennials may be kept in vigorous, healthy condition, it is necessary to be constantly alert to detect the first signs of disease or insect infestation, and as soon as any trouble is noticed measures of control should be put into effect immediately. For the control of Pests and Diseases, see Chapter XXXI.

Throughout the season all flower stalks should be cut down as soon as the blooms have faded. Not only will this improve the appearance of the garden, but it will also help to conserve the vigor of the plants, as the production of seed is a heavier drain upon the vitality of a plant than any other function which it is required to perform. There are other advantages to be gained as well: in the case of some plants, it is possible to prolong their blooming season to a considerable extent if seed pods are not allowed to form, and, with other plants such as the Delphiniums, it is possible to induce a second period of bloom.

Included also under the term of general maintenance are the tasks of watering, staking, feeding, and the occasional division and replanting of established plants.

Watering. For their best development most perennials require an adequate but not an over-abundant supply of moisture throughout the season. A few perennials thrive well on very dry soils, and there are others which have the ability to thrive under extremely moist conditions, but the vast majority prefer a moderate and fairly constant supply of moisture. (Reference lists at end of Chapter.) In most sections of the country these requirements are met by normal rainfall. If, however, the rainfall is insufficient at any time during the season to meet the needs of the plants, it is necessary, or at least advisable, to resort to artificial watering. Frequent, light waterings are of little value and usually do far more harm than good as they tend to draw the feeding roots towards the surface. A very thorough watering should be given once in every four or five days and the moisture should penetrate to a depth of at least a foot. Late afternoon and early evening are the most favorable times for watering as there is less evaporation and the soil retains the moisture more readily. There are a number of excellent sprinkling attachments which may be used on an ordinary garden hose and make it possible to cover a considerable area. If the garden is large it is possible to water a section of it each evening and thus to cover the entire area with comparatively little effort.

Staking. Staking appears to be such a very simple and such a purely mechanical operation; yet it is a task which is seldom done in an entirely satisfactory manner. Staking is necessary for two purposes: either to provide support for weak and floppy stems or to protect tall flower spikes from being bent and broken by winds and heavy storms. Whatever the purpose may be, the staking should be done in such a way that the natural form and beauty of the plant are preserved. Some perennials produce a quantity of small stems which have a tendency to be floppy and which consequently need some support. In this group we find Achillea ptarmica, Coreopsis grandiflora, Gypsophila, Platycodon, and the Veronicas; and for such plants twiggy shoots may be used very successfully. While the plants are still young, the twigs may be stuck into the ground close beside them and as the foliage develops the twigs will be entirely concealed. Such twigs offer a very satisfactory framework for the support of weak, floppy stems. Plants such as Delphiniums, Asters, Dahlias, and many others, require fairly tall, strong stakes. Bamboo stakes may be obtained in a variety of sizes and are very satisfactory. Those which are stained a soft green become almost invisible after they are in place. Strong wire stakes are also satisfactory and are obtainable in various styles and sizes. The type with spiral turns is of particular value for supporting individual flower stalks. Wooden stakes are often used, and if they are painted green they are reasonably unobtrusive in appearance. They lack the suppleness of bamboo and wire and unless they are made of suitable wood, such as hickory, ash, or lemonwood, they have a tendency to snap off. It is wise to keep a variety of stakes on hand in order to have one to meet every need. Some plants will require very stout stakes in order that they may be provided with adequate support, while others will require more slender stakes. When staking large clumps it is usually advisable to use more than one stake. When tall flower stalks are to be staked, they should be tied to the stake at several points. The tape should be wound firmly about the stake and should then be wound about the stalk, being brought back and tied to the stake rather loosely. A flower stalk should never be tied tightly to a stake, as the beauty and grace of the plant are impaired. When a large clump is to be staked, the tape may be attached first to one of the stakes and may then be woven through the clump, being wound about each individual stalk until it reaches the far side of the clump where it is attached to the opposite stake. Clumps of Peonies may be supported by special wire hoops which may be placed about the entire plant, the legs resting upon the soil. Care must be taken in the selection of the material to be used in tieing. Stems which are hollow and brittle must be tied with some very soft material which will not cut or bruise the stalk. Asparagus tape is excellent for this purpose. Green in color, soft in texture, strong and durable, it has much to recommend it. There are a number of similar tapes on the market which possess many of the same good qualities but are somewhat more expensive. Raffia is reasonably satisfactory but is more conspicuous if used in the natural shade. The woody stems of such plants as the hardy Asters and Artemisia may be tied with stout, tarred string.

MAINTENANCE OF FERTILITY

In order to maintain the perennial border at its best from year to year, the fertility of the soil must be kept at a constantly high level. Two applications of a good complete fertilizer should be given during the season, one in spring after the plants have started into active growth and one early in the summer. Late summer and fall applications are not advisable as they tend to stimulate a rather succulent growth which would cause the plants to enter the winter in an immature condition. A commercial fertilizer of a 4–12–4 or a 4–8–6 mixture will provide the nutrients required for good growth. This should be applied at the rate of 3 ounces per square yard or 2 pounds per 100 square feet. It should be sprinkled over the surface of the bed, cultivated lightly into the soil, and watered in thoroughly. Fertilizers such as bone meal and cottonseed meal have been used very generally in the past but as they become available very slowly and do not become active until warm weather, they are less efficient than a well-balanced complete fertilizer. During periods of prolonged rain it may be necessary to supply additional amounts of nitrogen as all the available supply of nitrogen in the soil is leached out rapidly under such conditions. This may be applied in the form of a top-dressing of nitrate of soda or sulphate of ammonia.

At the end of every five or six years, it is advisable to entirely remake the perennial garden. If the garden is large, a small section may be renovated each year. The work may be done either in the autumn or in the early spring, autumn being decidedly preferable, because there is usually more leisure to undertake such work and because new bulbs may be planted and old bulbs may be divided at this season. The plants should be lifted from the beds, the soil should be retrenched or double-dug, liberal quantities of well-rotted manure being incorporated, and, where necessary, the plants should be divided before they are reset. Such permanent things as Peonies and Bleedingheart which resent being moved may be left undisturbed during this process of rejuvenation without any serious interference to the work.

RENEWING PERENNIAL PLANTS

Although the term "perennial," when applied to plants, denotes permanence, it cannot be assumed that when perennial plants have once become well established they will bloom on year after year without further thought or care on the part of the gardener. A few of the exceedingly robust types, such as Golden Glow, might measure up to such an expectation, but the vast majority of our more desirable perennials require a reasonable amount of care and attention if they are to make satisfactory growth and give an abundance of bloom.

Some perennials are comparatively short-lived, and new plants should be grown to take the place of those which have served their period of usefulness in the garden. In this group we have the beautiful hybrid Columbines, which have a tendency to die out after several years of luxuriant bloom; the Lupines; the glorious hybrid Delphiniums, which often fail to carry on over a period of many years unless conditions are extremely favorable for their growth; Linum perenne; the lovely but temperamental Daphne cneorum, and Heuchera. As some of our most choice perennials are to be found in this group it is well to recognize the fact that they are more or less transient in the garden and that new plants should be propagated at intervals of every few years.

Other perennials will thrive well for a year or two after they are planted and will then begin to deteriorate rapidly unless the clumps are divided. In this group we have the Chrysanthemums, Physostegia, the hardy Asters, Iris and Phlox. Chrysanthemums should be lifted and divided each year, or new plants should be started from cuttings, as the old clumps produce very inferior blooms. Physostegia should also be lifted and divided each year, not only for the sake of better bloom but also in order to prevent it from encroaching upon its neighbors and becoming a pest. Hardy Asters should be lifted and divided every two or three years. Iris should be divided every three or four years, Phlox every five or six years.

There are a few perennials which will thrive for a period of many years without being divided and replanted; in fact in some cases they seriously resent being disturbed. In this group we find Dicentra spectabilis (Bleedingheart), the Peonies, and the Oriental Poppies.

In maintaining a perennial garden, it is well to know the requirements of each individual group and to meet these needs as adequately as possible.

SUMMER MULCHES

A summer mulch may be used very advantageously in the perennial garden. Peatmoss is the most satisfactory material for this purpose, although other materials such as buckwheat hulls, grass clippings or partially rotted leaves may be used with reasonably good results. A summer mulch fulfills several functions; it reduces to a minimum the labor required for general care and cultivation, it conserves the moisture in the soil, and it maintains a more even soil temperature. When peatmoss is used, a mulch varying in depth from 1 to 2 inches should be applied. If the bales are thoroughly soaked before they are opened, the material may be handled much more easily.

WINTER MULCHES

In the successful maintenance of the perennial garden, the question of the winter mulch plays an important part. Which plants should be mulched and which plants should be left unprotected; what materials should be used and how heavily they should be applied; when the mulch should be put on and when it should be removed—all these points must be taken into consideration.

Purposes of Winter Mulching. A winter mulch serves two important functions. It protects the plants from severe cold, and, in maintaining a more even soil temperature, it prevents the alternate freezing and thawing of the ground, the effect of which is so harmful to plant growth. Winter killing is more often due to the fact that plants have been heaved out of the soil by the action of frost than to the effect of extremely low temperatures. In addition to these two major functions a winter mulch is beneficial in protecting the foliage of certain plants from the effects of drying winds and brilliant winter sunshine which are apt to sear and scorch any tender growth. A mulch is also of value in that it prevents the plants from starting into growth too early in the spring. During an unusually warm spell in late February or March, some perennials start into growth, only to be severely checked later on by a return to severe winter weather. Under such conditions a winter mulch is of great value.

Materials for the Winter Mulch. There are a number of materials which may be used very successfully as winter mulches, such as salt hay, straw, evergreen boughs, glass-wool, strawy manure, leaves from certain hardwood trees, and tobacco stems. Salt hay is one of the most satisfactory of all the materials mentioned. It grows in salt marshes and is cut during the summer and packed in bales for shipment. The hay contained in one bale will cover approximately 1200 square feet. It is not expensive, and the fact that it can be used over a period of several years, provided that it is carefully raked from the beds in the spring and stored away, is a great point in its favor. As a winter covering it is tidy and attractive in appearance, and as it is extraordinarily unabsorptive of moisture, it never mats down or becomes soggy. Wheat or rye straw may be used as a winter covering with reasonably good results, but is not as satisfactory as salt hay as it has a tendency to become soggy before the winter is over and can be used for only one season.

A new material known as glass-wool has recently been developed and is proving very satisfactory as a winter mulch. It is made of very finely spun glass and resembles a covering of snow. In fact it is sometimes spoken of as the non-melting snow. It comes rolled into bales, and it may be spread over the garden beds with the greatest of ease. It is essential that the edges be weighted down in order to make it stable, as it is easily lifted by the wind. A series of stakes or heavy cord may be used to hold it in position. At the end of the season it may be rolled up into a bale again and stored away for future use. This new glass-wool possesses a number of unique advantages as a winter covering. It is light in weight, it admits both light and air, which prevents the plants from becoming yellowish and sickly in color, it permits the evaporation of moisture, it is absolutely sterile, and it discourages field mice and other rodents.

If small evergreen boughs are available, they offer excellent material for winter covering and they are frequently used to hold leaves or straw or other light materials in place. They are light in weight and admit a good circulation of light and air. Fallen leaves are one of nature's own coverings, but if they are to be used as a winter protection on garden beds only those kinds should be selected which will not mat down and which will not become a soggy mass before spring. Leaves from oak trees and beech trees are excellent, while leaves from maples, elms, and many other softwood trees are not desirable and should be avoided. Manure is of somewhat doubtful value as a winter mulch, except around Box bushes and newly planted shrubs, as it has a tendency to hold moisture and also provides an ideal nesting place for field mice. Tobacco stems have recently come into favor as a material for winter mulches and they have much to recommend them. Perhaps the greatest point in their favor is that they act as a direct repellent against rodents. Tobacco stems may be purchased by the bale, and as they rot very slowly they may be used for several seasons.

When to Apply the Mulch. The winter mulch should never be applied until the ground is well frozen and the plants have become completely dormant. If the mulch is put on too early in the autumn it is apt to stimulate a late and rather succulent growth. Particularly is this true when a long spell of Indian summer weather follows a sudden and early cold snap. The consequences are that the plants are not dormant when freezing weather sets in and their chances of coming through the winter in good condition are considerably lessened.

Depth of Mulch. The depth of the mulch will depend upon the type of the material used and the severity of the winter climate. It is quite as disastrous to apply too heavy a mulch and smother the plants to death, as it is to apply too light a covering. Care should be taken not to cover the crowns of such plants as Foxgloves, Canterbury Bells, Hollyhocks, Garden Pinks and Anchusas, which retain their succulent foliage throughout the winter months. The mulch should be worked in about the roots, with perhaps a few wisps of salt hay over the foliage, but the crown of the plant should be left free of all covering. If Foxgloves or other plants which are half-hardy in the North are to be wintered in the open they may be covered with inverted flower pots or berry baskets, which, although somewhat unsightly, afford excellent protection against both cold and dampness, and yet permit a good circulation of air.

Protection from Dampness. Winter killing is sometimes due to an excess of moisture in the soil, which is conducive to rot. Some plants are very sensitive to this condition and if the soil in the garden beds is not naturally well drained, special precautions should be taken. A little mound of sand or, better still, of coal ashes over such plants as Delphiniums and some of the Lilies will facilitate the drainage of surface water from the area about the crown.

Removal of Winter Mulch. The removal of the mulch in the spring is always a matter of concern. It is usually safe, however, to begin the removal of the mulch when the Snowdrops are in bloom. If a heavy mulch has been applied it should be removed gradually, and the final covering should be lifted off on a cloudy day in order that any young plants which have already appeared may not be too suddenly exposed to brilliant sunshine.

PERENNIALS OF MERIT

Aconitum (Monkshood). The Aconites derive their common name of Monkshood from the characteristically hooded or helmet-shaped flowers, and there are a number of varieties which are valued for their rich autumn effect in the garden. The aconites are also well adapted to a semi-naturalistic setting, being suitable for use in the foreground of a shrubbery border or along a fringe of woodland.

A. autumnale reaches a height of from 3 to 4 feet and bears racemes of large, dark blue flowers in late September and October.

A. Fischeri—Although there is considerable confusion regarding this type, the variety as listed in most catalogues is a dwarf type reaching a height of hardly more than 2 feet. It blooms in early autumn and is one of the hardiest of all the aconites.

A. Napellus blooms in July and August and the dark blue flowers are borne on an upright, single spike about $3\frac{1}{2}$ feet in height.

Spark's Variety blooms at the same season as Napellus but is somewhat taller and bears its abundant, deep blue flowers on strongly branching spikes.

A. Wilsonii which blooms in late autumn is distinct both in form and in coloring. The flowers are of a delicate violet-mauve and the tall spikes often reach a height of 6 feet or more.

Exposure: Semi-shade is preferred although the plants will also grow well in full sun.

Soil Requirements: The aconites will thrive in any good garden loam but they prefer a moist soil well supplied with organic matter.

Propagation: The aconites may be propagated by the division of old clumps and by seed. The seed is very slow to germinate, often requiring a month or more, and the viability of the seed is apt to be poor unless fresh seed is secured.

Culture: During dry seasons the aconites should be watered liberally. As the plants are difficult to move they should be left undisturbed for many years after they have once become established. Planting distances vary from 8 to 10 inches.

Anchusa italica (Bugloss). The tall-growing anchusas are useful plants for the perennial border, but being of a robust and somewhat branching habit of growth they require ample space and are not suitable for small garden beds. The small, intensely blue flowers are borne in rather loose clusters on ascending, heavy stems, being produced abundantly in June, and intermittently throughout the summer.

VARIETIES OF MERIT

Dropmore—The flowers are of a deep, gentian-blue. The plants are very vigorous in habit of growth and reach a height of nearly 5 feet.

Opal—The flowers are a clear, pale blue in color and the plants range in height from 3 to 4 feet.

Pride of Dover—One of the most desirable of the recent introductions, the flowers being of a true heavenly-blue shade.

Exposure: Full sun.

Soil Requirements: A fertile garden loam, moist, yet well drained, is considered ideal. Although the plants will make reasonably good growth on soils of moderate fertility they respond remarkably well to liberal feeding.

Propagation: Anchusa italica may be propagated by the division of old clumps, by root cuttings or by seed.

Culture: Transplanting should be done with care as the roots are very brittle. As the plants attain considerable size, they should be spaced from 15 to 18 inches apart. During the growing season, the anchusas require large quantities of water.

Anemone japonica (Japanese Anemone) (Windflower). The Japanese Anemones are among the loveliest of our autumn flowers. The cup-shaped blooms with their brilliant golden stamens are borne on tall, slender stems which rise far above the dense clumps of foliage, often attaining a height of 3 feet or more. The plants are in flower almost continuously from early September until late autumn when they are cut down by heavy frosts. The flowers are exceedingly decorative in the garden and they are also very lovely for cutting.

VARIETIES OF MERIT

Alba—single, pure white.

Alice—large rose-pink flowers, shading to lilac. Robust and vigorous in habit of growth.

Queen Charlotte—Semi-double flowers of a clear pink.

Japanese Anemones in Shade

Aquilegia

Richard Ahrends—Single, shellpink flower; one of the finest of the recent introductions.

Exposure: Full sun or partial shade. The Japanese anemones do exceedingly well at the edge of a shrubbery border where they are protected from strong winds and have the benefit of light shade for a portion of the day.

Soil Requirements: The Japanese anemones thrive best in a cool, moist yet well-drained soil, rich in humus and of a slightly alkaline reaction. The soil should be deeply prepared and liberal quantities of well-rotted cow manure, leafmold or commercial humus should be incorporated previous to planting.

Propagation: Japanese anemones may be propagated by the division of old clumps in the spring, by root cuttings taken at any time during the growing season, or by seed. In purchasing plants from a nursery young, pot-grown plants will usually give the best results.

Culture: The plants should be spaced from 15 to 18 inches apart. They require liberal quantities of moisture throughout the growing season, and they will benefit tremendously from a summer mulch of half-rotted leaves. When once well established the plants should be left undisturbed, as they do not transplant readily and resent intereference. Where the winters are of considerable severity a mulch of leaves or salt hay should be provided.

Aquilegia (Columbine). The columbines are among the most beautiful of our garden flowers. They possess an exquisite daintiness and charm which are equalled by few other perennials, and no spring garden is quite complete without them. Within recent years many new and very beautiful varieties have been introduced and there is a vast difference between the heavy, short-spurred columbines which our grandmothers grew in their gardens and the graceful types which we have today. It is as if the columbines had undergone an almost complete metamorphosis during the past quarter of a century. From dull, uninteresting blooms with but little grace or charm they have been miraculously transformed into flowers as beautiful as butterflies.

There are many species of Aquilegia and they vary considerably in form, in coloring, and in adaptability. Some are definitely perennial in habit and will bloom on year after year, while others are comparatively short lived. Some are particularly well suited to the rock garden, others thrive best in a woodland setting, and some are happily at home in the herbaceous border. Of the many distinct species we find less than a dozen in common cultivation today.

A. alpina—comes to us from the high mountain steeps of Switzerland, and it is one of the most cherished plants in many a rock garden. It seldom reaches a height of more than 9 inches and the flowers which are borne in May and June vary in color from clear blue to white. The spurs are short and stout and distinctly incurved. The plants prefer a light, well drained, rather stony soil which is not too rich, and they thrive in either full sun or partial shade. They may be spaced from 6-8 inches apart.

A. cærulea—which is known as the Rocky Mountain Columbine is one of the most beautiful of all species. It is a native of our mountain regions from Colorado south to Mexico. The lovely, long-spurred flowers are a clear blue with a white cup and golden anthers and they are borne in great profusion. The plants are considered short lived in eastern gardens as they frequently die out after two or three years, but recent experiments tend to show that they will persist considerably longer if given a soil of moderate acidity. Many of our beautiful hybrid strains have been developed from this species.

A. canadensis—is a native of this country east of the Rocky Mountains and is usually found growing on dry, stony ledges. It prefers partial shade and a more or less neutral soil, as it will not tolerate either extreme acidity or extreme alkalinity. It is a modest little flower, seldom growing more than 10 or 12 inches high. The blooms are of a scarlet and yellow hue. It is most happily at home in a woodland setting or in some partially shaded corner of the rock garden. There is also a very dwarf form known as A. canadensis nana.

A. chrysantha—bears flowers of clear yellow, tinted with claret, and the spurs are long, slender and graceful. It comes into flower a little later than some of the other species but has the pleasant habit of blooming intermittently throughout the season. In fact it is sometimes in flower when cut down by frost in the autumn. The foliage is particularly good, being a deep, glossy green and usually retaining its healthy, vigorous appearance through the summer months. The plants reach a height of from 18 to 24 inches and are well adapted either for the woodland or for use in the garden.

A. glandulosa—is a rare and beautiful species which comes to us from the mountain regions of Siberia. The large, pendant, widespreading flowers are a bright, lilac-blue in color, tipped with white, and the spurs, like those of A. alpina, are short and stout, and distinctly incurved. A. glandulosa is one of the first of the columbines to come into flower, blooming from early May until well into June. The foliage is very lovely, having a soft, velvety quality with rich, coppery shadings. The plants vary in height from 12 to 15 inches and are lovely both in the herbaceous border and in the rock garden, thriving either in full sun or in light shade.

A. vulgaris—is th ecommon columbine of Europe and is the one which is so frequently found in old-time gardens. It reaches a height of from 18 to 24 inches and the blooms are heavy, short spurred and decidedly lacking in grace and beauty. There are, however, a number of improved varieties, and some of our lovely hybrid strains have been developed by crossing A. vulgaris with other species.

Hybrid Strains: Many of our most beautiful columbines today are hybrids, and among the most choice of these recent introductions are several distinct strains. The Mrs. Scott Elliott strain bears flowers of large size with long, graceful spurs, the colors varying from deep purple through violet and pink to deep, wine red. The outer petals are often of one color and the corolla of another color, and many of the flowers offer the most subtle and exquisite harmonies and contrasts.

Both Sutton's Pink and Farquhar's Pink are excellent. The plants are hardy and vigorous and the lovely, long-spurred flowers, which vary in color from light to deep pink, are borne in great profusion.

The Rainbow Blend is a strain which was introduced several years ago by one of our Western growers. The flowers are very large with long slender spurs and for brilliancy of color they are quite unsurpassed. Pink, rose, scarlet, deep reds and purples and many other unusual and very beautiful shades are found among them.

Dobbie's Imperial Hybrids is a strain which is offered by the famous Scotch firm whose name it bears. It is the result of many years of careful selection and reselection. The flowers are of beautiful form and the range of color almost defies description.

Propagation: Columbines may be propagated by seed and by the division of old clumps. It is advisable that new plants should be started from seed, as the division of old clumps is not very satisfactory and the results are often disappointing. In order to have plants which will give good bloom the following season, it is essential that the seeds be sown early. If greenhouse space is available they may be sown in frames or in a seed bed in the open later in the season. It is well to have the seed sown before the middle of May in order that the seedlings may have as long a growing season as possible. The seed bed should be carefully prepared and a mixture of equal parts good garden loam, peat moss, and sand provides excellent conditions for germination. The bed should be partially shaded after sowing and the soil should never be allowed to dry out. Growth is rather slow for the first month or so, but after the seedlings have been transplanted they will begin to develop more rapidly. If the young seedlings are protected by a lath shade during the summer months, they will make much more rapid and vigorous growth than they will if exposed to full sunlight. The young plants need a light, mellow soil with excellent drainage. They should be given good cultivation and abundant water throughout the season and they should never be allowed to become stunted, due to over-crowding. If given good care they will develop into thrifty, vigorous plants by autumn, and they may then be moved to their permanent position in the garden or may be wintered over in the nursery beds.

Soil Requirements: Although one or two species among the columbines have decided soil preferences, the long-spurred hybrids, which are those most commonly grown in our gardens, will thrive well in any good garden loam. They appreciate a moderate quantity of well-rotted manure but fresh manure should never be allowed to come into direct contact with the plants. They are, on the whole, most happily at home in a loose, friable soil. In poorly drained locations they are apt to die out during the winter and are also more subject to root rot.

Culture: Most of the hybrid columbines will thrive well either in full sun or in partial shade. As the mature clumps attain considerable size they should be allowed ample room for development and the plants should be spaced from 15 to 18 inches apart in the flower border. During the first year when the plants are small, interplant-ings of Phlox divaricata may be made. Even under the most favor-able conditions many of the new hybrid strains of columbines are comparatively short-lived and will die out after a few years of bloom. It is well, therefore, always to have a few young plants coming on to take the place of those that have failed to survive.

Columbines may be transplanted with the greatest ease and large clumps may be moved when in full flower, provided they are watered well and are taken up with a generous quantity of soil. In fact there are very few other perennials that may be moved with such certainty of success.

Season of Bloom: If each individual bloom is snipped off as it fades, new buds will develop along the stems and columbines may be kept in flower for a month or six weeks. By prolonging their blooming season in this way one greatly increases their value in the spring garden. The bloom of some of the perennials is so fleeting that it hardly seems worth while to grow them, but when plants may be kept continuously in flower for nearly a month and a half, they soon come to be looked upon as indispensables. Columbines are particularly lovely when grown in combination with Lupines, Blue Flax, Nepeta Mussini, and Thalictrum, and the most exquisite color harmonies may be obtained.

Not only are columbines lovely in the garden but they are among the most choice of all our flowers for cutting. They last unusually well and their delightful daintiness and their soft and lovely colorings make possible the most beautiful cut flower arrangements. The pink varieties are lovely when arranged with Nepeta Mussini and those with deep purple tints make a lovely contrast when arranged with sprays of Bleedingheart.

Winter Protection: Columbines are very hardy and need no winter protection except in severe climates. Dry oak leaves which will not mat down over the crowns afford an excellent covering and may be held in place by small evergreen boughs. Salt hay is also good as a winter mulch.

Insect Pests and Diseases: See Chapter XXXIII.

Artemisia lactiflora. With its creamy-white blossoms which are borne on tall, graceful stems, Artemisia lactiflora is one of the most useful background plants for the perennial border. When grown under favorable conditions the plants reach a height of 5 feet or more. The soft tone of the flowers is a pleasant foil for blossoms of a more brilliant hue, and they may be used very effectively in combination with Gladioli, Salvia farinacea and S. azurea. The foliage is somewhat coarse and heavy and forms a dense background mass.

Exposure: Artemisia lactiflora thrives best in full sun.

Soil Requirements: If the plants are to reach maximum development they should be grown in a fertile, deeply prepared, fairly moist soil. On poor soil, and with an inadequate supply of moisture Artemisia will make but poor spindly growth and will produce but little bloom.

Propagation: Usually by the division of old clumps in early spring or in the autumn. The plants may also be propagated by seed or by cuttings.

Culture: Artemisia lactiflora is one of the few tall border plants which usually do not require staking. The plants must, however, be given ample room and they should be spaced at least 15 inches apart.

Asclepias tuberosa (Butterflyweed.) There is hardly a flower of greater decorative value in the garden than the brilliant and beautiful Butterflyweed which blooms during the mid-summer months. The myriad orange flowers are borne in broad, flat umbels of irregular outline, and they are lovely both in the garden and for cutting, being particularly striking when planted in combination with some of the tawny Daylilies and the dwarf Tritomas. The plants reach a height of 12 to 18 inches and remain in flower for many weeks.

Exposure: Full sun is essential.

Soil Requirements: A light, sandy, exceedingly well-drained soil of medium fertility. If soil conditions are favorable the plants will continue to thrive year after year, but in a heavy, poorly drained soil they are short-lived.

Propagation: The plants may be grown very easily from seed which may be sown in the coldframe in early spring or in the open ground later in the season. The young seedlings must be transplanted with care as they suffer seriously if the fleshy tap-root is broken or unduly disturbed. The seedling plants should be placed in their permanent location when still quite small as the transplanting of old, established plants is very difficult and is seldom successful.

Culture: There are no special cultural requirements. The plants should be spaced from 10 to 12 inches apart and when they have once become well established, they will give generous bloom year after year provided that conditions of soil and exposure are favorable. They will withstand long periods of drought better than almost any other perennial.

Asters. There are few perennials which will give such a lavish display of autumn bloom as will the hardy asters. In England one sees them used in gay profusion, and it is in England that many of our most beautiful hybrid varieties have been developed. In the herbaceous garden, as a foreground for a shrubbery border, or along the edge of a woodland, the hardy asters are happily at home. In the rock garden, the dwarf varieties which have recently been introduced are a welcome addition because they bloom at the end of the season and thus bring color in autumn to a garden which has too often been considered only for its springtime effect.

VARIETIES OF MERIT

Name	Color	Ht. in Feet	Blooming Date
Star of Wartburg	Lavender	1	Early June
A. frikarti (Wonder of Stafa)	Lavender	2	August- September
King George	Lavender	2	August
General Pershing	Pink	2	August
Silver Spray	Pale lilac	3	Late September
Mt. Everest	White	3-4	September
Charles Wilson	Ruby-red	3	Late September
Skylands Queen	Lavender	4	Late September
Alderman Vokes	Salmon pink	2½	Mid-September
Barr's Pink	Rose	4-5	Mid-September
Blue Jacket	Blue	3	Mid-September
Blue Lagoon	Blue	3	Mid-September
Blue Eyes	Blue	3	Mid-September
Ivy Logan	Blue	3	Mid-September
Helen Duward	Dark blue	3-4	Late September
Remembrance	Lilac	2	September-October
Burbank's Charming	Shell pink	3-4	Early October

Dwarf Hybrid Asters

Name	Color
Countess of Dudley	Deep pink
Lady Henry Maddocks	Clear, pale pink
Marjorie	Bright rose
Nancy	Flesh pink
Ronald	Lilac pink
Snowsprite	White
Victor	Lavender blue

Exposure: Most of the hardy asters prefer full sun but will thrive reasonably well in light shade.

Soil Requirements: Asters will thrive under almost any soil conditions, provided that the soil is not too saturated with moisture during the winter months. Heavy soil, light soil, moist woodsy soil, dry sandy soil—there are few perennials which are less exacting than the hardy asters. A soil that is exceedingly high in fertility is less desirable than one of moderate fertility as the plants have a tendency to make too rank a growth and become somewhat leggy.

Propagation: Although hardy asters may be propagated very easily from seed this method is seldom used, particularly in the cases of the new hybrids, as they do not come true from seed. The usual method of propagation is by the division of the clumps in early spring, the young vigorous shoots being used. Cuttings may also be made from young shoots in the spring.

Culture: About every three years the clumps should be dug up, divided and replanted. Thus frequently renewed, the plants will not deteriorate. The dwarf varieties may be placed one foot apart in the beds, and the larger growing ones from two to three feet.

To increase the size of the blooms and to restrain the sometimes over-rampant growth, many of the young shoots may be pruned away in spring, leaving only a few stalks, from five to eight, to develop. In the flower garden the taller varieties usually require staking in order to prevent them from encroaching upon other flowers; but in the shrub border or at the edge of the woods the natural growth is preferable. A clever device for keeping tall asters within bounds in a small garden is to stake the shoots while they are still young and pliable in a horizontal position near to the ground, using small wire wickets. The stems will send up short lateral branches and the bloom will thus be spread over a wide area and will remain low.

In England, one frequently sees whole borders devoted entirely to hardy asters and the display of color is magnificent. To attain this effect the cultural procedure is as follows: All of the old clumps are lifted early in the spring as soon as the soil is in suitable condition, and the strong-growing outer shoots are removed. These are planted singly, 1 foot apart, over the entire area, the desired space being allotted to each variety. The ground is well prepared before planting, being enriched with liberal quantities of well-rotted manure. When the plants have reached a height of from 12 to 18 inches a few of the front leading shoots are nipped out. This will greatly improve the form and appearance of the individual plants and will produce a wonderfully fine display of bloom in the border, as each shoot will produce a pyramid of perfect blossoms. One stout stake about two thirds of the height of the plant will be effective in giving the plants the needed support. The opportunities for color harmonies which a planting of this nature offers are almost un-limited, and a most glorious display of autumn bloom may be obtained if this method of planting is followed.

Bocconia cordata (Plumepoppy). Bocconia cordata is a magnificent perennial with large, deeply lobed, glaucous leaves, and with tall, handsome flower spikes which often reach a height of 8 feet or more. The individual flowers, which are cream-white in color, are small, but are borne in large showy terminal panicles. In late sum-mer these panicles bear quantities of small, almost transparent, pale-green pods which become suffused with reddish purple, and these fruits are fully as beautiful as the flowers. Bocconia cordata should be used only where it can have ample space. At the rear of a deep, long border its huge spires of bloom and its gray-green foliage are magnificent. In a small garden it would be entirely out of scale, but when planted in bold masses with a background of evergreens or against a high wall it produces a striking effect. Both the flowers and the seed pods are excellent for bold, decorative arrangements in the house.

Exposure: Full sun or partial shade.

Soil Requirements: A rich, moist, deeply prepared soil is consid-ered ideal although the plants will thrive reasonably well in any garden soil of moderate fertility.

Propagation: By seed, by the division of old clumps and by suck-ers. The plants will attain a height of 3 or 4 feet the first year from seed.

Culture: Bocconia cordata may be planted either in the autumn or in early spring and the plants should be given ample room to develop, being spaced from 2 to 3 feet apart. As the plants produce suckers very freely they are capable of becoming a pest unless they are kept within bounds.

Campanula (Bellflower). The Campanula is a large and varied genus, and its members range in size from the tiny Campanula cæspitosa of the rock garden to Campanula pyramidalis, which grows to a height of 6 feet or more in the border. The flowers of all the species are bell-shaped; in some species they are produced singly, while in others they are borne in clusters. A few campanulas open in May, most of them bloom in June and July, with several lasting into August. Blue is the dominant color among the cam-panulas, with some white forms and pink in a few species. Many are perennial, some are annual or biennial. So varied and adaptable is the genus that few modern gardens are without some form of Campanula.

DWARF KINDS FOR THE ROCK GARDEN OR THE ROCK WALL

C. cæspitosa, Tufted Harebell, 4 to 6 inches high, has bright blue flowers in May and June. Plant about 5 inches apart.

C. rotundifolia, Blue Bells of Scotland, is a compact plant, 6 inches or more high, which sends up thin stems bearing hanging blue, bell-shaped flowers from June to September. Plant from 4 to 6 inches apart.

DWARF KINDS A LITTLE LARGER THAN THOSE FOR THE ROCK WALL

C. carpatica, the Carpathian Harebell, which grows 12 inches tall, is suitable for an edging in the flower border, or along the top of a rock wall. It is graceful, yet compact, with quantities of upturned blue bells. Plant from 8 to 10 inches apart.

C. glomerata has rather stiff stems bearing closely clustered, blue, funnel-form flowers. Plant from 8 to 10 inches apart.

C. garganica is a trailing plant spreading to broad tufts. The flowers are wide blue bells that are divided into five petal-like points. Plant from 8 to 10 inches apart.

LARGER KINDS WELL ADAPTED TO THE HERBACEOUS BORDER

C. persicifolia, the Peach-leaved Harebell, attains a height of 2 to 3 feet and produces lovely, violet-blue, wide, bell-like flowers in June and July. An improved variety with large purple-blue flowers known as *Telham Beauty* is even more beautiful. Variety *Moerheimi* is semi-double, cream-white. The plants should be spaced from 12 to 15 inches apart. The plants should be lifted and divided every second year.

C. pyramidalis is a narrow, columnar form which reaches a height of 5 or 6 feet. The flowers, which open in August, are a clear deep blue and continue in bloom for five or six weeks. Plant from 15 to 18 inches apart.

Exposure: Most of the campanulas prefer a sunny location, although several of the dwarf species will thrive well in partial shade.

Soil Requirements: The campanulas prefer a rich garden loam with a neutral or slightly alkaline reaction. The soil should be well prepared previous to planting and the plants will derive great benefit from the liberal use of well-rotted manure.

Propagation: Almost all campanulas may be raised from seed, by cuttings made from young growth in spring, or by the division of old clumps. Seedlings raised to partial growth by autumn are carried over the winter in coldframes and transplanted to the garden in the spring.

Chrysanthemum. The brilliant tones of the ash and oaks and maples in the woodlands and the deep bronze and golden russets of the chrysanthemums in the garden bring to a close the season's pageantry of color and of bloom. There is no other flower which can take the place of the chrysanthemum in the autumn garden, and from mid-September on they hold the center of the stage. With the introduction of the new Korean hybrids which are noted both for their earliness and for their absolute winter hardiness, the season of bloom has been greatly extended, and it is now possible to grow chrysanthemums in northern gardens with every assurance of success.

Chrysanthemums may be handled very satisfactorily in several ways. They may be grown throughout the season in beds or borders of mixed perennials, or they may be grown in the nursery plots until they are almost ready to come into bloom, and may then be lifted and moved into the garden. If facilities permit, it is wise to follow the latter procedure, as the plants may be grown under more carefully controlled conditions and will consequently make better growth and will give a greater abundance of bloom, which will usually more than compensate for the additional labor involved.

The essentials for the successful culture of hardy chrysanthemums are: vigorous, healthy plants for spring planting, a sunny location, a well-drained soil, enriched with liberal quantities of manure, an adequate supply of moisture throughout the growing season, careful attention to the pinching back of the plants, and protection against insect pests and diseases.

Varieties Recommended for the Home Garden

Early Flowering, Decorative Group: *Ruth Cumming, Tints of Gold, October Gold, Early Bronze,* and *Zelia,* ranging in color from orange-gold to bronze and russet. *Barbara Cumming* is an excellent yellow; *October Dawn* and *Provence* are good pinks and *Jean Cumming* is a pure white.

Korean Hybrids: *Indian Summer* and *Romany,* bronze in color.

Semi-doubles: *Autumn Leaf, Harvest,* and *The Torch,* ranging in color from bronze to old-gold; *Orange Perfection,* and *Mrs. W. E. Buckingham,* an excellent pink.

Single Korean Hybrids: *Orange Wonder, Orion, Apollo, Saturn* and *Fireflame,* ranging from yellow and orange to deep red and bronze.

Small Pompoms: *Adironda* and *Ouray,* a good bronze in color.

Small-flowered Button: *Sunshine,* a good yellow, and *Bronze Button.*

Exposure: Chrysanthemums thrive best in a sunny location. If grown in partial shade the plants have a tendency to become spindly and the lower leaves are apt to shrivel and turn brown.

Soil Requirements: A light, rich, well-drained soil is considered ideal for chrysanthemums. The plants are notoriously rank feeders and require abundant quantities of plant food if they are to attain their maximum development. Liberal quantities of manure should be incorporated in the bed previous to planting and the condition of the soil may be further improved by an application of a 5–8–6 complete fertilizer, applied at the rate of 1 pound to every 30 square feet. The application of fertilizer should be made in early spring at least a week or more before planting. Chrysanthemums thrive best in a soil which is just below the neutral point, and lime should be applied if the soil has a tendency to be acid. During the summer months, from the time of the last pinching back until the time when the buds begin to show color, it is wise to make weekly applications of liquid manure. Although this practice is not followed universally it will greatly stimulate growth and will prove to be of decided benefit to the plants. If liquid manure is not readily available a solution of nitrate of soda may be substituted, one teaspoonful being dissolved in three gallons of water.

Propagation: Well-rooted cuttings, sold as small pot-grown plants, may be purchased in the spring from any reliable nursery, and after a selection of desirable varieties has been obtained it is possible to maintain or increase the stock by propagating new plants each spring. This may be done either by the division of old clumps or by cuttings taken from the young shoots as they start into growth in the spring. (See Chapter XXX on Propagation.)

Culture: Chrysanthemums make their maximum growth during hot weather, and throughout this period they require a liberal supply of moisture. If the plants suffer a serious check at any time during this period of their growth, it will often result in a loss of the lower leaves, which seriously injures the general appearance of the plant.

The pinching back of the plants, which is sometimes spoken of as summer pruning, is a factor of great importance in the culture of garden chrysanthemums. After three or four pairs of leaves have

Delphinium "Wrexham Lady"

formed, the growing tip of the shoot should be pinched back. From three to five side shoots will then develop and these, in turn, should be pinched back to induce further branching. For the early-flowering varieties no pinching should be done after the middle of July; the late-flowering types should not be pinched back after the early part of August. The importance of this summer pruning can hardly be overemphasized. If it is neglected, the plants will assume a spindly habit of growth, sprawling out over the garden in an ungainly fashion, and they will produce but little bloom. If the pinching is done systematically, however, the plants will develop into broad, spreading bushes, bearing many strong, flowering stems.

Hardy varieties may be left in the garden during the winter while the more tender types will need the protection of a coldframe. Many gardeners prefer to dig such clumps as may be needed for propagation as soon as the flowering season is past and to heel them in, in a coldframe. In the spring as soon as the plants start into growth they may be lifted and divided, or cuttings may be taken.

For the control of insect pests and disease on chrysanthemums, see Chapter XXXIII.

Delphinium. June has always been called the month of roses, but within recent years the rose has had to share its honors with the delphiniums. The low-growing types with their starry, single flowers of clear sky-blue are delightful when used in great drifts along the front of the border, and the towering, majestic blooms of the larger types are a veritable glory during the days of early summer. Delphiniums contribute a quality to a garden composition which no other flower can do so completely. The tall spires of bloom hold one's attention by the sheer beauty of their form and the richness of their coloring.

STRAINS OF OUTSTANDING MERIT

Wrexham Hybrids   Vanderbilt Hybrids
Hoodacres Hybrids   Lyondel Strain
Pacific Coast Hybrids   Lancelot Series
Galahad Series

The flower spikes are broad at the base and taper towards the tip, the blooms being clustered closely along the stem. The plants are of extraordinarily vigorous growth and often attain a height of nearly 8 feet. There is considerable variance in the seedlings, both single and double forms being common, and the flowers range in color from deep purple and maroon through the lighter shades, many very beautiful contrasts being found.

NAMED VARIETIES

Pearl Necklace—Large flowers of pure glistening white
Angel's Breath—White with a center of fawn
Organdy—Clear blue, touched with orchid pink
Magnifica—Outer petals blue, inner petals lavender
Summer Skies—Lavender-blue
King Arthur—Royal Violet
Pink Sensation (D. Ruysii)—light rose pink
Queen of the Blues—Clear, light blue
Dwarf Porcelain Blue

There are also several intermediate and low border types which are of great merit and deserve to be more widely grown. *Queen of the Blues* is a delightful variety offered by one of the large English seed firms. The plants are very branching in habit and reach a height of about 18 inches. The pretty, single flowers are a clear, gentian blue in color and are borne in great profusion. The plants remain in bloom for many weeks and are particularly lovely when grown in combination with some of the annuals. *Dwarf Porcelain Blue* is another variety offered by the same English firm, and it is a dainty and choice thing. The plants seldom reach a height of more than 12 inches and are very valuable for use in the front of the border. The flowers are a pure, porcelain blue, and are charming when planted with masses of rose and pink Antirrhinums. If sown early in the spring it will flower the first year.

Climatic Range: Delphiniums thrive best in a moderately cool climate, and they do exceedingly well in high altitudes. They are unable to withstand intense summer heat and are therefore not well adapted to the South.

Propagation: Delphiniums may be propagated by seed, by cuttings, or by the division of old clumps. As the plants seldom come true from seed, unless careful hand pollination is practised, it is necessary to resort to cuttings or to the division of old clumps if one desires to secure new plants of a given variety. It is possible, however, to obtain many exceedingly beautiful plants from carefully selected seed, and it is the most universally employed method of propagation. There are several large firms in this country and in

Delphiniums in the Spring Border

Delphinium	Hollyhocks	Delphinium	Foxgloves	Delphinium	Hollyhocks	Delphinium	Foxgloves	Delphinium
Aquilegia coerulea	Iris Mme. Cheri	Lilium candidum	Phlox Miss Lingard	Papaver Mrs. Perry	Iris Queen Caterina	Lilium candidum	Iris Mme. Cheri	Lilium candidum
Annual Larkspur Exquisite Pink	Delphinium Queen of the Blues	Aquilegia Long spurred Pink	Tulip Le Reve	Tulip Clare Butt	Delphinium Queen of the Blues	Aquilegia Long Spurred Pink	Delphinium Queen of the Blues	Annual Larkspur La France
Nepete mussini	Heuchera sanguinea pink	Antirrhinum Nelrose	Linum perenne	Iris White Queen	Antirrhinum Nelrose	Linum perenne	Antirrhinum Nelrose	Heuchera Sanguinea
Papaver nudicaule Coonara pink	Del. Dwarf Por. Blue	Viola Blue Perfection	Heuchera san.	Viola Blue Perfection		Viola Blue Perfection	Papaver nudicaule Coonara pink	Delphinium Dwarf Porcelain Blue

England which have made a specialty of delphiniums. For years they have maintained extensive trial grounds, and by crossing desirable varieties they have produced some very fine hybrid strains. If seed is obtained from any of these reliable sources one will usually find that a large percentage of the plants are of excellent type and possess great beauty. A few may be disappointing, but these can readily be discarded. It is an excellent practice to allow the young seedling plants to produce one or two blooms during the first season while they are in the nursery rows as it is then possible to select those of outstanding merit and to discard those which are less desirable.

By Seed—Delphinium seeds may be sown at almost any season of the year. They may be sown in mid- or late summer as soon as the seeds are mature; they may be sown in coldframes late in the autumn (Chapter XXII); they may be shown in February or March under glass, either in the greenhouse or indoors; they may be sown in frames as soon as the weather permits; and they may be sown in a seed bed in the open ground if adequate care can be provided. The time of sowing is not as important as the method of sowing.

As delphinium seedlings are very susceptible to damping-off every precaution should be taken to insure protection. The seeds should be dusted lightly with red copper oxide before they are sown, in order to control pre-emergence damping-off, and the medium in which the seeds are sown should be entirely free from infection. (See Chapter XXX for detailed measures of control.) There are many mixtures which have proved satisfactory for the seed bed, one of the most reliable being a mixture of one part finely sifted, pulverized peat moss, one part clean sand, and one part of sterile garden loam. The seed may be sown either broadcast or in drills, being sown at a depth not exceeding ⅛ of an inch. The seed bed should be kept shaded and moist, but not too saturated, until the seeds have germinated. The procedure followed in the handling of the young seedlings is that recommended in the chapter on Propagation. Young seedlings started late in the season should be wintered in frames and should be given a light covering of sand or leaves.

By Cuttings—Within recent years much experimental work has been carried on to determine the most satisfactory methods of propagating delphiniums by means of cuttings, as it is the method most commonly used for the propagation of named varieties and choice hybrids. It has been found that some delphinium plants may be propagated very readily from cuttings, while an attempt to secure rooted cuttings from other plants results only in failure. In the case of occasional individual plants it is possible to secure from 75 to 100 strong, vigorous cuttings in a single season, and from other plants it will be impossible to secure even a single cutting which will strike root. Better results will be secured from plants which are brought into the greenhouse and forced slowly, than from those which are left in the open ground, as more cuttings will be produced, and they will root more readily. Those plants which are to be used for propagation should be lifted in the autumn after the first killing frost and placed in a coldframe where they should be allowed to remain until late in January. When brought into the greenhouse they should be placed in a moderately cool temperature. Cuttings may be taken when the shoots have reached a height of from 2 to 3 inches, each cutting being taken with a very small heel. (See chapter on Propagation.) The cuttings should be soaked in water for an hour before they are placed in the propagating bench. Either pure sand or a mixture of sand and peat moss may be used as the rooting medium, and every precaution should be taken during the first few days to see that the cuttings do not wilt. After the first week watering should preferably be done by sub-irrigation, as it is wise to keep the foliage and stems free from moisture. The shading should be gradually diminished, and as soon as new leaf growth appears, the shade may be entirely removed. When the cuttings have become well rooted they may be lifted with care and planted in pots.

By Division—Old clumps of delphiniums may be lifted and divided in early spring. (See chapter on Propagation.) The work must be done with care if success is to be assured. The soil should be shaken away from the roots and the plants should be gently pulled apart with the fingers. If the clump is cut or torn roughly apart the crown is apt to be badly bruised and various forms of fungus and bacterial rot will gain easy entrance.

Exposure: Delphiniums thrive best in a sunny location where there is sufficient protection from severe wind. Good air circulation is essential. If delphiniums are planted in a shady position, or where the circulation of air is poor, the growth tends to be weak and spindly and the blooms are decidedly inferior.

Soil Requirements: Delphiniums require a mellow, well-drained, deeply prepared soil of a neutral or slightly alkaline reaction. They are not acid-tolerant and if the soil has a pH. lower than 6, an application of lime should be made to bring the soil reaction up to neutral or slightly above neutral. The application should preferably be made several months previous to planting. (See Chapter I, page 25.)

The texture of the soil does not seem to be a matter of great importance, as delphiniums thrive almost equally well in a fairly heavy clay or in a light, sandy loam, provided that the soil is well drained and that other conditions are favorable.

The question of soil fertility is one which is open to great controversy and many theories have been advanced. It is generally agreed, however, that the small-flowered, small-spiked types give the most satisfactory results when grown on a soil of moderate fertility. If such plants are grown on an exceedingly rich soil or if they are fed heavily, they have a tendency to become floppy and leggy and the size and quality of the blooms show little or no improvement. The large-flowered types which normally produce tall, massive spikes of bloom present quite a different problem. If maximum development of the plant, and flower spikes of superior quality are desired, the soil must be of high fertility and heavy annual feeding is necessary. For many years it was the common practice to use manure in liberal quantities in the preparation of delphinium beds but the present consensus of opinion is in favor of commercial fertilizers, as it has been found that manure is conducive to the spread of crown rot and other fungous diseases and that its use is not advisable. Some of the most successful growers of delphiniums of exhibition quality follow the practice of mixing a 12-16-12 complete fertilizer with the soil at the time of planting. A top-dressing of the same fertilizer is applied to established clumps early in the spring and after the first blooming period an application is made of a fertilizer with a lower nitrogen content, a 4-16-20 complete fertilizer being recommended.

Culture: Delphiniums are very dependent upon an adequate supply of moisture during their active period of growth and the soil should receive a thorough soaking at least once a week. In many seasons the natural rainfall will supply the needed moisture but if this is not adequate it is wise to resort to artificial watering.

It is possible to transplant delphinums either in the autumn or in the spring, and since the plants have a fine and fibrous root system they may be moved with comparative ease. As delphiniums are among the first herbaceous plants to start growth in the spring, autumn planting is generally preferred as the plants undoubtedly suffer less shock. If the work is done with extreme care it is possible to move quite large plants when they are just coming into bloom.

The plants must be lifted with a generous quantity of earth in order that the root system may remain practically intact, and the work should preferably be done on a cloudy day, otherwise it will be advisable to provide light shade for a few days. The plants should be kept thoroughly watered until they are well established.

When planting delphiniums it is advisable to use a mixture of sand and charcoal about the crown of each plant as this facilitates drainage and consequently lessens the danger of crown rot.

If blooms of superior exhibition quality are desired, not more than three flower stalks should be allowed to develop on a single plant. The remaining stalks should be cut away before they have had an opportunity to make any growth. When grown for mass effect in the garden, healthy, vigorous plants should be capable of producing from 6 to 8 good spikes of bloom.

The large-flowering types should be given adequate room for development and the plants should be spaced from 18 inches to 2 feet apart. The more dwarf types such as *Porcelain Blue* and *D. chinense* should be spaced from 12 to 15 inches apart.

As soon as the flowering period is over the plants should be given a top-dressing, as recommended under Soil Requirements, and the flower stalks should be partially cut down. A small portion of the stalk and the lower leaves should be left until new growth has appeared at the base of the plant. The old stalks should then be cut down level with the surface of the ground, in order that water may not collect in the hollow tubes projecting above the soil. If new growth has already started at the base of the plant before the flowering period is over, as occasionally happens, the stalks may be cut down to the ground as soon as the blooms have faded. The second bloom will never quite equal the first in size or quality, but through the late summer months the blue of the delphiniums is a very welcome note in the garden and the plants will offer a wealth of material for cutting.

It is becoming a common practice among some of our most expert growers to lift and divide delphinum clumps every second year. If this procedure is followed a stock of young and vigorous plants is constantly maintained and the most desirable types and varieties may be retained.

Staking: The proper staking of delphiniums is a matter of great importance. Unless one is fortunate enough to have an unusually sheltered location, staking is absolutely necessary, and even in positions which may seem very protected the wind will occasionally work havoc. The stems of delphiniums are rather hollow and brittle and as the flower spikes of some of the improved varieties are exceedingly heavy when wet, the plants present little resistance to a combination of rain and wind. An excellent method of staking is to place three light bamboo stakes close to each plant and, at a distance of about 18 inches above the soil, to tie a loop of raffia, winding it securely about each stake. During heavy storms, when there is driving wind and rain, it may be necessary to temporarily protect some of the individual flower spikes by tying them as far up as the very tip to a stout stake.

Winter Protection: Delphiniums are far more sensitive to heat than they are to cold and they are capable of withstanding severe winter weather with very little protection. It is the alternate freezing and thawing of the ground and excessive amounts of surface water which are usually responsible for losses during the winter months. It is, therefore, advisable to provide good drainage about the crown of each plant. A little mound of sand or coal ashes placed over the crown of each plant late in the autumn will facilitate drainage and will afford excellent protection.

For the control of insect pests and diseases, see Chapter XXXIII.

Dicentra spectabilis (Bleedingheart). Bleedingheart is an old favorite associated with gardens of long ago, but its popularity has remained undiminished by the array of new perennials which have been introduced within recent years. It is one of the most beautiful of our spring-flowering perennials and it deserves a place in every garden. Its graceful form, the beauty of its bloom and the quality of its foliage make it one of the most valuable of plants for the spring border. Even in a small garden Bleedingheart does not seem out of place in spite of the wide spread of its arching branches. The foliage is a delicate green in color with a glaucous sheen, and the graceful stems bear hanging, deep pink, heart-shaped flowers which diminish in size towards the tip of the branches. It flowers in May, with the Tulips and the late Narcissus, and it remains in bloom for almost six weeks. By midsummer the foliage begins to die back and gradually disappears entirely. The plants reach a height of from 2 to 4 feet with an almost equal spread.

Exposure: Full sun or partial shade.

Soil Requirements: A deep, rich loam, well supplied with organic matter is desirable, and an adequate supply of moisture is essential.

Propagation: Bleedingheart may be propagated by seed, by division, by root cuttings or by stem cuttings. Cuttings may be taken from the young shoots as they start into growth in the spring or soon after flowering.

Culture: When in flower, the plants need ample room and they should be spaced at least 2 feet apart. They are seldom planted in clumps, being used as accent plants in the general planting scheme. After the leaves have begun to die down, shallow-rooted annuals or chrysanthemums may be planted to fill the vacancy left by the disappearing foliage of the Bleedingheart. The plants resent frequent moving and when once well established they may be left undisturbed for many years. The roots should be planted in an upright position, being placed at a depth of 2 to 3 inches.

Gypsophila (Babysbreath). The wiry, twisted stems of the Gypsophilas bear their narrow, gray-green leaves so sparsely that the plants seem almost transparent. The myriad, small flowers are borne in great profusion and the effect is that of a veil thrown over a portion of the garden, a fairy-like foil for the more colorful flowers of the border.

G. paniculata is the old-fashioned type, forming a symmetrical mass almost 3 feet in height and with an almost equal spread. There are both single-and double-flowered forms, blooming in late summer.

G. Bristol Fairy is one of the finest of the recent introductions, flowering almost continuously throughout the summer. The flowers are much larger than those of the type, being fully double and pure white in color.

G. repens is a dwarf, trailing type suitable for the rock garden, bearing myriads of tiny flowers in July and August.

G. repens, var. Rosy Veil is a new dwarf form bearing double flowers of a clear, soft pink. It comes into bloom fully two weeks earlier than the larger types and flowers almost continuously throughout the summer. It reaches a height of about 2 feet and is excellent for use in the front of the border.

Exposure: Full sun is essential as the plants will not thrive even in light shade.

Soil Requirements: A light, well-drained soil of medium fertility and high in lime content. The very name, Gypsophila, meaning gypsum-loving, denotes the preference which these plants possess for limestone soils. Gypsophilas are noted for their ability to grow well on dry, rather poor soils.

Propagation: By seed, by cuttings, and by the division of old plants. The new double-flowered varieties are usually grafted on the roots of the single-flowering types.

Culture: The Gypsophilas require very little in the way of care and attention. The dwarf types should be spaced from 15 inches to 2 feet apart, the larger types from 2½ to 4 feet, as they form large masses.

Hemerocallis (Daylily). The Hemerocallis is an old-time garden favorite. It was first brought from China to Europe where it was much appreciated, and the English colonists brought it to America. Here it has escaped from cultivation and some forms are so common in the wild, where it forms great masses along the roadsides, that some people suppose it to be a native wild flower. In the flower garden it has a habit of spreading and displacing other plants and so it must be used with discretion. But this ability to form dense clumps of foliage is an asset where a bank or damp piece of ground is to be covered, for it spreads and maintains itself permanently without any care at all. For many years this old-fashioned flower was somewhat neglected and it was seldom seen in cultivated gardens. A few decades ago, however, Doctor A. B. Stout of the New York Botanical Garden began to make crosses of the various species and has developed a race of hybrids which have greatly increased the beauty of its bloom and have extended the color range of the flowers. A number of these are now on the market, and the older species, while they are still used for mass plantings among shrubs or as "ground cover" on banks, are being displaced as garden flowers.

The season of bloom ranges from May to the end of August, and the colors vary from lemon-yellow through deep orange to tawny reds. Although the individual blossoms last but a day, the period of bloom of each species is from three to four weeks.

Species Hemerocallis

Hemerocallis flava, Lemon Daylily, has lemon or canary flowers in May and June which are fragrant, grows about 3 feet high.

Hemerocallis aurantiaca, Orange Daylily, has rich orange flowers shaded to brown in June and July.

Hemerocallis Middendorffii has deep orange flowers in June and July.

Hemerocallis Thunbergii is a late-blooming lemon-yellow sort with fragrant blossoms, blooming in July.

Hemerocallis Dumortierii has flowers of rich yellow inside and bronzy yellow outside, blooming in May.

Hemerocallis fulva, Tawny Daylily, is a deep coppery-orange, darkening to crimson, with flowers in great numbers, in July and August. It is this species which has naturalized itself so much in the eastern states.

Hemerocallis citrina has pale yellow blossoms in June and July, is very fragrant.

Hybrid Hemerocallis

Aureole, Golden yellow, May.

Bay State, Shiny yellow, June.

Dr. Regel, Orange-yellow, May and June.

Florham, Large yellow, fragrant, flowers with Indian yellow markings, June and July.

Kwanso, Large double, bronze-orange blossoms in June, July and August.

Mrs. W. H. Wyman, Lemon-yellow, July and August, tall.

Sovereign, Dark orange, June and July.

The Gem, Deep orange-yellow, tall, June.

Exposure: Hemerocallis thrives well either in full sun or in partial shade.

Soil Requirements: The plants thrive on widely varied types of soil, doing almost equally well on dry banks or in moist situations, and they are among the least exacting of plants in regard to soil fertility.

Propagation: Hemerocallis is very easily propagated by the division of old clumps, either in early spring or after the flowering season is over. The plants should be lifted with a spading fork and the clump should be gently pulled apart.

Culture: The old clumps should be divided every two or three years. Beyond this the plants require no special care. For full development allow each plant two feet of space.

Heuchera (Coral Bells) (Alumroot). The Heucheras are charming, graceful little plants with geranium-like, evergreen foliage which forms a broad mat close to the ground. The graceful, wiry stems, rising above the leaves, bear panicles of tiny, nodding bells. The brilliant hue of the flowers, dispersed as it is into many small particles, makes a delightful sparkle of color and gives life and vivacity to the garden. The Heucheras are excellent border plants, and they are also frequently used in rock gardens with pleasing effect. The flower stems vary in height from 12 to 18 inches.

VARIETIES OF MERIT

Brizoides—The flowers are a pale pink in color and are produced freely in May. The plant is robust in habit of growth, with excellent foliage.

Rosamondii—One of the finest of the newer hybrids. The brilliant coral-pink flowers are borne in profusion over a period of several months. It is strong and robust in habit of growth.

Perry's White—Pure white flowers from June to September.

Sanguinea—The best known of all the Heucheras. The brilliant crimson flowers are lovely for cutting and they are produced in abundance over a period of several months, beginning in June.

Exposure: Full sun, or partial shade.

Soil Requirements: A rich, well-drained loam is considered ideal as the plants will not thrive in a heavy, clay soil. A top-dressing of well-rotted cow manure applied early in the spring will stimulate growth.

Propagation: The most satisfactory method of propagation is the division of established plants. The plants may be lifted and divided either in the spring or in the autumn. If the divisions are made in the autumn, the young plants should be wintered over in a coldframe, and they should be kept well watered until they have become established. Heucheras may also be propagated by seed but the seeds are usually of poor vitality and do not germinate well. Leaf cuttings may also be made. The leaf should be cut at the base of the leaf stalk with a sliver of the main stem attached.

Culture: The Heucheras may be planted in the autumn or in early spring and the plants should be spaced from 6 to 8 inches apart. Spring planting is preferred in sections where the winters are severe.

As Heucheras have a tendency to be heaved out of the soil during the winter, due to the alternate freezing and thawing of the ground, it is well to give them extra attention in the early spring. If the plants have suffered from heaving they should be pressed gently back into the soil and a light mulch of compost should be placed about the crowns.

If plantings of Heuchera are to be maintained in good condition the plants should be lifted and divided every third year, the soil being well enriched before the plants are reset.

Hosta (Funkia) (Plantain Lily). The Plantain Lily is valued both for its foliage and for its flowers. The flower spikes rise above the dense masses of broad, green leaves, reaching a height of $1\frac{1}{2}$ to 2 feet, and bear small tubular flowers in shades of lavender and in white. Funkias will flourish at the foot of a wall or on the north side of a building where little else will grow, and they are, therefore, of particular value for positions in semi-shade.

Exposure: Partial shade.

Soil Requirements: Funkia does well in any ordinary garden soil but prefers a soil with a high moisture content, and makes its most luxuriant growth on a rich, moist loam.

Propagation: The plants may be lifted and divided in early spring.

Culture: The plantain lily requires ample space for its best development and the plants should be spaced from 2 to 3 feet apart. The plants are of exceedingly simple culture, demanding little in the way of care and cultivation.

Iris. Like the roses, the natural habitat of the genus Iris is distributed widely over the world, and, like the roses, they contribute to the garden a quality peculiarly their own. Irises have always been important garden flowers, and by their grace and delicacy of color and form they impart a freshness and joy to the late spring planting not equalled by any other group until the roses open a few weeks later. In mediæval times the Iris was given a special distinction when it became the symbol of the royal house of France and hence the symbol of the realm. It appears in many an illuminated manuscript, and in the heraldry, architecture and jewelry of the early Renaissance in France, where it was affectionately called "Fleur-de-Lis."

Irises are classified into several groups by their root habits and their flower forms. The more commonly cultivated sorts, those originating in Central Europe, have fleshy roots or rhizomes which lie close to the surface of the ground, and they have a bearded tongue on the lower petals of the flowers. They are known as the Pogoniris Group, pogon being the Greek word for beard. The Beardless Iris group, known as Apogons (without a beard) includes the Siberian species, I. orientalis, and I. Kæmpferi (the Japanese Iris).

The first group is divided again into several classes: (1) the modern tall bearded Iris of mixed ancestry; (2) the dwarf, bearded Iris blooming in April; (3) the old species Iris originating in Europe, known by various names, including German Iris, Florentina, and

Dalmatica; and (4) crosses between the dwarf species and the taller groups, known as the intermediate group.

Pogoniris Group

(The Bearded Iris)

Dwarf, Bearded Group. The dwarf bearded irises are useful as edgings and also in the rock gardens where they are most effectively used in rather broad masses because the individual blooms are small. These dwarf irises range in height from 3 to 9 inches and bloom about three weeks earlier than the tall-growing types. Iris pumila, one of the most popular dwarf species, bears flowers of a deep purple hue and there are many hybrid varieties varying in color through yellow, white, blue and reddish purple. One of the most beautiful of these dwarf hybrids is Azurea with flowers of a pure sky blue; Glee is a pale yellow variety; Sckneekuppe, an excellent white.

Intermediate Group. Many of the varieties in this group have been developed by hybridizing some of the dwarf species with the late, tall-growing types. Most of the members of this group attain a height of 12-18 inches and their period of bloom falls between the blooming of the dwarf iris and the blooming of the taller types.

Varieties of Merit

Abelard: rosy fawn	Norma Gage: pink and white
Cosette: white	Papio: violet and purple
Crysoro: orange-yellow	Sir Michael, Jr.: reddish purple
Ingeborg: white	Sundew: yellow

Tall Bearded Group. In this group we find many of our most beautiful garden irises. The plants vary in height from 18 to 42 inches and produce flowers that vary widely in form and coloring. Many new varieties of outstanding merit have been introduced within recent years, and some of the older varieties have maintained their popularity for more than a quarter of a century.

Varieties of Merit

Afterglow: Soft grayish lavender-pink shading to buff; rich yellow at haft.

Alcazar: Standard light bluish violet; Fall deep brilliant purple, bronze veined throat; rich orange beard.

Apache: Standard coppery purple; Fall dark crimson-brown.

Aphrodite: Bright violet-pink self with no veining.

Ballerine: Light blue-violet; Fall a deeper shade; full yellow beard.

B. Y. Morrison: Standard pale lavender-violet; Fall velvety violet-purple.

Candlelight: Pale pinkish buff.

Cinnabar: Standard violet-purple, base shaded copper and veined maroon; Fall flaring, velvety cotinga purple.

Coppersmith: Standard purple; Fall flaring, rich velvety dark red with coppery suffusion.

Glowing Embers: Standard violet on old gold; Fall dahlia purple, hafts netted yellow.

Lent A. Williamson: Standard very broad, lavender-violet, blended with rich yellow; Fall velvety pansy-violet.

Lord of June: Standard light lavender-blue; Fall deeper shade, reticulated brown.

Mary Barnett: A light lavender self.

Mme. Chéri: Standard vinaceous purple, undertone yellow; Fall ageratum violet washed pink, rich yellow undertone; deep orange beard.

Morning Splendor: Standard petunia-violet; Fall rich raisin purple.

Mother of Pearl: Standard glossy light lavender-blue; Fall slightly deeper, rich cream at haft reticulated brown.

Purissima: A pure white.

Santa Barbara: A very light lavender-blue.

Steepway: A smooth purple-tinted flower, slightly flushed peacock-blue, apricot and pale green.

Autumn-Flowering Group. After years of patient effort on the part of plant hybridizers, a new race of iris has been introduced which extends the flowering period through the autumn months. These new irises have two or more distinct flowering periods, blooming in the spring and again in autumn, beginning with September and continuing until growth is checked by heavy frosts. Some varieties also flower intermittently throughout the summer months. Although perfectly hardy in northern gardens, these autumn-flowering irises are specially recommended for the South where the fall-blooming season may extend over many months. The plants vary in height from 15 to 30 inches.

VARIETIES

Autumn Queen: white	Jean Siret: yellow
Black Magic: very deep blue	October Opera: reddish tones
Eleanor Roosevelt: deep violet	September Morn: mauve pink

481

CULTURE OF BEARDED IRIS

Climatic Range: The bearded irises have an extraordinary wide climatic range as they are able to endure the intense heat of southern summers as well as the extreme cold of winters in the Far North.

Exposure: The bearded irises should be planted in a sunny location if they are to be grown at their best. If planted on the north side of a building or in an otherwise shady location they seldom thrive well, the plants being weak and spindly in growth and the flowers being decidedly inferior in size and in quantity of bloom.

Soil Requirements: The bearded irises may be grown successfully on soils of widely varying types, and it has been found that they do almost as well on heavy clay soils as on sandy loam, provided that the soil is well drained. Good drainage is absolutely essential, as the bearded irises cannot thrive on soils which are saturated with moisture. Unless the soil is naturally well drained some provision must be made for artificial drainage. (See Chapter III, page 91.) While it is true that many irises will do reasonably well on rather poor soils, the fact must not be overlooked that the most thrifty plants capable of producing an abundance of bloom are to be found on soils of good fertility. If special beds or borders are to be devoted to irises, the soil should preferably be prepared several months in advance of planting. Well-rotted manure, compost, or some commercial form of humus should be thoroughly incorporated into the soil and the soil should be deeply prepared. Although the bearded irises are generally classed among the more shallow-rooted plants, many of the feeding roots penetrate to a depth of 18 inches or more. At the time of planting an application of a 0–4–1 commercial fertilizer should be made at the rate of ½ pound per square yard. The bearded irises prefer a soil which is very nearly neutral in reaction, although they will tolerate a very mildly acid soil as well as one with a considerable degree of alkalinity. As a general rule, they are classed among lime-loving plants.

Propagation: The bearded irises are propagated by the division of the rhizomes. The clump should be lifted from the soil with a spading fork and the rhizomes either cut or broken apart. Each fan of leaves should have a short, sound piece of rhizome with a number of strong, vigorous feeding roots attached. Any dead or shrivelled leaves should be removed and the foliage should be cut back to within 6-8 inches of the rhizome. The ideal time for the division of bearded irises is the period immediately after flowering. As new root growth is made at this time, new plants will, therefore, have an opportunity to become well established before winter and will usually produce a few blooms the following year. Late autumn planting is not advisable as the plants have had no opportunity to become anchored and are likely to be heaved out of the soil during the winter. Clumps may be divided in the early spring, but the bloom is then sacrificed for that season as they will not flower until the following year.

Planting: The dwarf types of bearded iris may be planted from 5 to 6

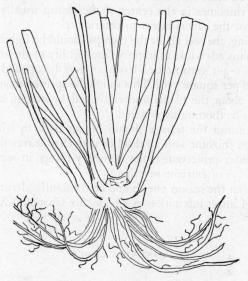

An Iris Division Ready to Transplant

inches apart if the effect of a large clump is desired. The intermediate and tall-growing types should be planted from 15 to 18 inches apart. If immediate mass effect is desired, the rhizomes may be placed as closely as 8–10 inches apart, but this practice is not recommended except as an occasional expedient, as the clumps soon become crowded and growth and vigor are sacrificed. When planting irises, the rhizome should not be covered deeply. The feeding roots should be spread out in a natural position, a hole of sufficient size having been opened, and the upper portion of the rhizome should be barely covered with soil. Deep planting, particularly in heavy soils, makes the rhizomes more susceptible to rot. The newly planted rhizomes should always be well firmed into the soil.

Culture: The cultural requirements of the bearded iris are not exacting. The plants require an abundance of moisture during the blooming season but are able to endure long periods of drought at other periods. The best bloom is usually produced the second, third and fourth years after planting. As soon as the rhizomes show evidences of becoming crowded, the clumps should be lifted and divided. Most iris plantings will continue to bloom well and will remain in good condition for a period of about five years. After this period the rhizomes in the center of the clump usually become so crowded that the plants begin to deteriorate.

Each spring, the soil about the clumps should be lightly cultivated and if it seems advisable to improve the fertility of the soil an application of a 0-4-1 commercial fertilizer may be applied at the rate of ½ pound per square yard. This should be sprinkled on the surface of the soil about the plants and cultivated lightly in, and the soil should then be thoroughly watered.

In the autumn the foliage should be cut back to within 4 or 5 inches of the rhizome and all dead or shrivelled leaves should be removed. Winter protection is not necessary except in sections where the winters are of extreme severity.

Throughout the season one should be constantly alert to detect the first signs of insect infestation or disease. See Chapter XXXIII.

APOGONIRIS GROUP

(The Beardless Iris)

Japanese Iris. The Japanese Irises (I. Kæmpferi) have become increasingly popular within recent years and the plants possess great beauty and dignity. The flowers are characteristically flat and broad, the standards and falls being horizontal rather than ascending and descending. The flowers possess colors dominantly in the red-purple, purple, lavender, blue and white sector of the color scale. Some are even a mahogany red and a few have a gray background tone with deep purple, violet or wine-red markings. The leaves are narrow and grass-like and the blooms, with their broad, crepe-like petals, are borne on tall, erect stems which attain a height of 2½ feet or more. With the exception of the fall-blooming bearded varieties they are among the last of the irises to flower, blooming in late June and throughout July.

Varieties of Merit

Azure: azure blue
Catherine Parry: blue, overlaid
   rosy red
Columbia: blue
Fascination: pink toned

Gold Bound: white
Koko-No-Iro: deep purple
Mahogany
Purple and Gold
Violet Beauty

Exposure: Full sun for at least a portion of the day.
Soil Requirements: The Japanese Irises require an abundance of

Photograph by J. Horace McFarland Co.

Japanese Irises

moisture until after their flowering season is over. They are then able to withstand considerable drought, and during the winter months they prefer a soil which is free from excessive moisture. It is the almost universal custom in Japan to flood the iris plantings during the period when the plants are in bud and in bloom, but during the balance of the year the soil is kept comparatively dry. Japanese Irises should never be planted in a location where the water table rises to the surface of the ground during the winter months as such a condition will usually prove fatal.

Japanese Irises thrive best in a rich, highly fertile soil well supplied with organic matter and with a decidedly acid reaction, since they are unable to tolerate lime. They respond well to liberal feeding and have a particular liking for cow manure, which should be incorporated into the soil previous to planting.

Propagation: Japanese Irises may be readily propagated by the division of old clumps, the ideal time being late August or early September. If the divisions are made at this season the young plants will reestablish themselves quickly and will give some bloom the following summer. Clumps may also be divided early in the spring or immediately after the flowering season, but the results are not as satisfactory. Many of the divisions may fail to grow and only a small percentage will flower the following year. An entire clump may be lifted and divided, being pried apart with two strong spading forks until it is sufficiently loosened to fall into many natural divisions, or large pieces may be removed from established clumps without lifting them. It requires a stout spading fork with considerable pressure behind it to accomplish this feat. The rhizomes should not be allowed to dry out before planting. If immediate effect is desired in the garden, the divisions should consist of three fans of leaves. If, however, rapid increase of stock is desired single fans may be planted. The foliage should be cut back to within 5-6 inches.

Japanese Irises may also be propagated by seeds. If the seeds are sown out of doors in the autumn as soon as they are ripe they will germinate in the spring and will bloom in 2 to 3 years. They do not, however, come true from seed.

Planting: The rhizome of the Japanese Iris is very slender with many fibrous roots. At the time divisions are planted, these roots should be shortened to 5 or 6 inches. The new roots develop from the backs of the leaf fans and the crowns should be planted 2 inches below the surface of the soil in order to make it easy for these new roots to gain anchorage. For mass plantings which will remain undisturbed for many years, the plants should be spaced from 18 inches to 2 feet apart. If clumps of Japanese Irises are to be used in herbaceous borders or in other similar locations more immediate effect may be obtained if three, four or five divisions are planted about 10 inches apart.

Winter Protection: With the exception of newly planted divisions, Japanese Irises require no winter protection. Young plants which have not had an opportunity to become established are liable to suffer severely from the effects of heaving and it is, therefore, wise to protect them during the first winter. Oak leaves are excellent as a mulch if they are held in place by evergreen boughs. Stable manure may also be used. The Japanese Iris is one of the very few members of the Iris family for which a mulch of manure can be used with impunity.

Iris sibirica and **Iris orientalis.** The Siberian Iris, the Oriental Iris and their many hybrids, are of considerable decorative value in the garden and they also offer excellent material for cutting. Although these two species are similar in many respects and are often confused, there are several marked differences between them.

I. sibirica—The flowers are borne well above the leaves on tall, slender stems ranging from 3 to 4 feet in height. The plant grows from a slender rhizome which produces many fine, fibrous roots, and dense tufts of slender, grass-like foliage which is lax and graceful in habit of growth. The flowers are small and from five to ten blooms are carried on long pedicels.

I. orientalis—The flowers are slightly larger than those of I. sibirica, and they are borne three or four on a stem, the flower stems seldom overtopping the foliage. The foliage is broader and the rhizomes slightly more fleshy and heavier.

There are many hybrid forms which are intermediate between the two.

Varieties of Merit

Butterfly: soft blue	Red Emperor: wine red
Gatineau: clear blue	Skylark: soft blue
Kingfisher Blue: bright	Snow Bunting: white
Opal Blue: clear blue	Snowcrest: white
Papillon: soft blue	Snow Queen: white
Perry's Blue: sky blue	Thisbe: soft China blue

Exposure: Full sun or light shade. Both I. sibirica and I. orientalis will thrive reasonably well in positions where they receive several hours of sunlight each day. In dense shade the plants will make some growth but will not flower.

Soil Requirements: For best development, the plants prefer a fairly moist, highly fertile soil. They should not be planted in a location where the crowns would be covered with water during the winter as they cannot survive the effects of a saturated soil during freezing weather. Previous to planting, the soil should be well enriched with rotted cow manure, rich compost, or leaf mold. The plants are acid-tolerant and resent lime.

Propagation: The clumps may be lifted and divided very readily, late August and early September being considered the ideal time. Divisions may be made in spring or immediately after flowering but the percentage of plants which survive is far less than when divisions are made in late summer. The methods of making the divisions and of planting are the same as those for the Japanese Iris, described in detail on page 486. The rhizomes should be planted 2 inches deep and the plants should be spaced from 15 to 18 inches apart.

Both the Siberian and Oriental Iris may be propagated by seed but wide variation is found among the seedlings and it is a method seldom employed except by hybridizers.

Culture: The culture of the Siberian and Oriental Iris is very simple. If the soil is well enriched and thoroughly prepared before planting, the clumps may be left undisturbed for many years and will demand little in the way of care and attention. The plants are almost profligate with their bloom, a well-established clump sometimes producing more than fifty flowering stalks.

Winter Protection: No winter protection is necessary save in the case of young plants which have not had an opportunity to become established.

Louisiana Beardless Species

Of recent introduction are the magnificent beardless species irises which have been discovered in the bayous and marshes of Louisiana. Unique in color and in form, many of these species and their hybrids are startling in beauty and as they become more widely known their popularity will increase. They range in height from 2 to 4 feet and the flowers of many species are most unusual in coloring—deep garnet, Indian red, rosy apricot, rose-petal pink, deep pansy violet, pale lavender and ivory white.

SPECIES AND HYBRID VARIETIES OF MERIT

Carolina: light lavender
Elephantina: ivory white
Fulva: shades of Indian red
Giganticærulea: soft blue
Grapejuice: pansy violet

Moricolor: rich red tones
Regalis: lobelia violet
Rosewood: blood red
Vinicolor: wine red
Viridis: light violet

Exposure: Full sun or semi-shade.

Soil Requirements: Although most members of this group prefer a soil with a high moisture content, they will thrive well in any ordinary garden soil. They respond well to liberal feeding and previous to planting the soil should be well enriched with rotted cow manure. Although they will stand considerable moisture, they should not be planted in a location where the water will freeze about the roots during the winter months.

Propagation: Division of rhizomes in late summer.

Culture: These Louisiana species irises demand little in the way of care and cultivation if they are provided with conditions of soil and moisture which are favorable for growth. The plants should be spaced from 12 to 18 inches apart.

European Beardless Species

Iris pseudacorus. The rich yellow bloom of I. pseudacorus are of striking beauty, being borne on tall, erect stems from 3 to 4 feet in height. There is no finer iris for the watergarden or for naturalization along the banks of a stream.

Exposure: Full sun.

Soil Requirements: I. pseudacorus will thrive in almost any location but prefers a very damp soil.

Propagation: Readily propagated by division of the rhizomes.

Culture: As I. pseudacorus is very hardy it demands little in the way of care and cultivation after it has once become established.

VARIETIES OF MERIT

P. alba: a beautiful pure white form
P. gigantea: a giant-flowered form
P. immaculata: pure yellow without throat markings
P. sulphurea: sulphur-yellow form

American Beardless Species

Iris versicolor. I. versicolor is the beardless marsh iris of our northern states. It is of particular value for the water garden or for naturalization along the banks of streams. The flowers are of a lavender-purple hue.

Exposure: Sun or semi-shade.

Soil Requirements: Rich, very moist soil.

Propagation: The division of the rhizomes.

Culture: As I. versicolor is, perhaps, the most rugged of all the members of the large family of Iris, it requires no special culture. It thrives well in almost any location and is most amazing in its adaptability.

Crested Iris

Iris cristata. The dwarf crested iris, I. cristata, which is a native of our Southeastern States, is a lovely thing for the woodland garden, and sun-splashed patches of it along a forest trail hold joy for all who pass. The flowers, their lavender petals touched with crested gold, spread their bloom above the carpet of soft green leaves in late spring. I. cristata is frequently used very effectively in the rock garden and may also be planted in long, low drifts along the front of a flower border.

Exposure: Partial shade is preferred and I. cristata thrives well in open woodlands. It also does reasonably well in full sun, although it definitely prefers afternoon shade.

Soil Requirements: A gravelly, well-drained soil, rich in humus is ideal, although I. cristata will succeed well in almost any good garden soil.

Propagation: I. cristata is readily propagated by division of the small rhizomes. This may be accomplished with a fair degree of success at almost any time during the growing season, but very early spring is preferred. The roots should be spread out in a natural position and the rhizomes should be barely covered with soil.

Culture: The rhizomes should be planted from 5 to 6 inches apart. When the clumps become too crowded the plants should be lifted and divided. Careful weeding must be done throughout the season in order to prevent more vigorous plants from crowding out the small, delicate rhizomes of I. cristata.

Iris gracilipes (Japanese Crested Iris). In Japan, this dainty little crested iris is found growing in the woodlands and although it is a bit temperamental when transplanted from its native habitat, it may, with a little coaxing, be made to feel quite happily at home with us either in the woodland or in a partially shaded spot in the rock garden. The foliage is slender and grass-like and the miniature flowers, of a pinkish lavender hue, are borne on branching stems hardly more than 8 inches in height.

Exposure: Light shade is essential as it will not thrive in a hot, dry position. Good air circulation is necessary also.

Soil Requirements: A fairly moist but well-drained soil, loose in texture and well supplied with humus, is considered ideal. I. gracilipes is not tolerant of any degree of alkalinity and thrives best in a slightly acid soil.

Propagation: The division of the rhizomes should preferably be done in July when new root growth is active. If attempted at other seasons of the year, it is less apt to be successful.

Culture: As the plants are somewhat frail, careful weeding is necessary throughout the season in order to prevent more vigorous plants from enrcroaching upon the clumps of I. gracilipes. In early spring and again in late June, the plants should be given a top-dressing of domestic humus or well-decayed leaf mold.

Iris tectorum. I. tectorum is the roof iris of China and Japan, so famed in song and story. The flowers are a lavender-blue in color, blotched with purple, and there is a very beautiful white form. The foliage is broad and heavily ribbed, and the flower stalks reach a height of 12 to 15 inches.

Exposure: Full sun or light shade.

Soil Requirements: Rich garden loam, well supplied with humus.

Propagation: I. tectorum should be divided shortly after the flowering period is over. It may also be readily propagated by seed.

Culture: I. tectorum is considered rather temperamental, sometimes thriving in one location and not in another. It is one of the most shallow rooting of all the members of the iris group and it requires frequent division and enrichment of the soil. I. tectorum should be planted in clumps or in drifts, and the rhizomes should be spaced from 6 to 8 inches apart. It should preferably be lifted and divided every second year. It is not very hardy and where the winters are severe it should be given the protection of leaves and brush.

For Bulbous Iris, see Chapter XIII on Bulbs.

Linum perenne (Blue Flax). This lovely flower which reflects the blue of soft spring skies is of particular value in the perennial border because of its airy grace and its long season of bloom. The fine, delicate foliage is a pale bluish green and the lovely, single-petalled flowers of soft azure blue are borne in great profusion on slender, graceful stems. On days of brilliant sunshine the petals fall before evening, but in cloudy weather they remain open throughout the day. The plants vary in height from 12 to 18 inches. Linum perenne is particularly charming when grown in combination with the dainty little Iceland Poppy, Coonara Pink, and with the Columbines.

Exposure: Full sun.

Soil Requirements: A light, sandy, well-drained garden loam of moderate fertility is considered ideal. Linum perenne will not thrive in a heavy soil which becomes saturated with moisture.

Propagation: Linum perenne is readily propagated by seed. The seeds are of excellent vitality, germinate well, and the young seedlings make rapid growth. The seeds may be sown in the coldframes early in the spring or in the open ground later in the season and will produce vigorous flowering plants the following year.

Culture: The plants should be spaced from 8 to 10 inches apart. Being fibrous rooted, Linum perenne may be transplanted with the greatest ease and large, established plants may be moved with a fair degree of success if they are lifted with a sufficient quantity of earth and if the root system remains intact. If half of the flower stalks are cut back early in the season, being allowed to grow up later to take the place of those which are ready to go to seed, the flowering period will be greatly prolonged and the energy of the plant will not be exhausted. Under such treatment the plants will sometimes flower almost continually from May until September.

Winter Protection: No winter protection is required if the plants are grown in light, well-drained soil. Serious losses sometimes occur where the soil is heavy and badly drained.

Lupinus (Lupine). In English gardens, Lupines may be grown to perfection and any one who has seen and admired the beauty of their stately blooms and their glorious colorings comes away with a secret longing to produce lupines in America which are as superbly fine. But, unfortunately, we do not have a combination of English soil and English climate, and in many sections of our country these lovely hybrid lupines will not thrive. In gardens along the New England seacoast and in some sections along the Great Lakes, where the atmosphere is moist, they do exceedingly well, but where the summers are hot and dry and where soil conditions are not to their liking, it is almost useless to attempt to grow them, for in spite of all one's efforts to provide favorable conditions, they will only sicken and die. With the introduction of the magnificent Russell Lupines, there is an increased desire on the part of many gardeners to attain success with these rather temperamental perennials.

Exposure: Full sun and a somewhat sheltered location is considered ideal.

Soil Requirements: A light, moist, yet well-drained soil of good fertility and with a slightly acid reaction is considered ideal. As the lupines belong to the great family of legumes, the Leguminosæ, they will benefit from the activity of the nitrogen-fixing bacteria in the soil if they are inoculated.

Propagation: Lupines may be propagated very readily from seed.

At the time of sowing, the seeds should be inoculated with a specially prepared culture of nitrogen-fixing bacteria. Such a culture may be obtained from most large seed firms and will be accompanied by full directions.

Culture: As lupines are of a somewhat spreading habit of growth the plants should be allowed ample room for development and should be spaced from 12 to 15 inches apart. They require an abundance of moisture throughout the growing season, and they respond well to an annual top-dressing of well-rotted cow manure.

Pæonia (Peony). The Peony has long been a favorite among gardeners, and it is one of the hardiest and most easily grown of any of the perennials. When once established, peonies will continue to flower year after year. Indeed, some of the old-fashioned types are still blooming in gardens where they were planted more than a century ago.

In a small garden peonies are often out of scale. The blooms are so large and the plants themselves require so much room that they should be used but sparingly, if at all. However, in a large garden where quantity of bloom and mass effect are desired peonies may play an important part in the planting composition. They are lovely, also, when planted in small groups along the edge of a shrubbery border, and they may be used very effectively as a low, herbaceous hedge.

There is considerable variability in the flower forms of peonies. The following classification has been drawn up by the American Peony Society:

Single—These consist of a ring of a few broad petals, the center being filled with pollen-bearing stamens and seed-bearing carpels.

Japanese—These show the beginnings of doubling. The outer ring or guard petals are like those in the singles but some of the filaments of the stamens have become petaloid. As long as anthers are present, class as Japanese.

Anemone—The next step in doubling: the anthers have disappeared from the petal-like filaments. The central petaloids still are narrow and short.

Semi-double—Similar to the anemone, except that instead of the petaloids being uniformly wide, they occur in all stages of transformation, the formation being loose.

Crown—The carpels are partly or fully transformed into petaloids which differ from the guard petals and from the petaloids derived from stamens.

Bomb—The next step in doubling finds the petaloids much wider but still differentiated in form from the guard or outer petals, and no anthers are found scattered through the center of the bloom. No collar or crown is in evidence.

Semi-rose—The carpels are fully transformed. The only thing that differentiates this class from the rose is the fact that an occasional pollen-bearing stamen is found.

Rose—This is the fully doubled type, in which the stamens and carpels are completely transformed to more or less evenly arranged petaloids, which are not distinguishable from the guard petals. If the guard petals are distinct, the flower is classed as a bomb, the line of division being arbitrary.

VARIETIES

Among the most desirable varieties are those listed by the American Peony Society with their official ratings. The score is based on a scale of 10 points. Those listed below have received a score of over 9 points.

White		Pink	
Le Cygne	9.9	Therese	9.8
Kelway's Glorious	9.8	Solange	9.7
Mme. Jules Dessert	9.4	Tourangelle	9.4
Festiva Maxima	9.3	Walter Faxon	9.3
Eliz. Barrett Browning	9.2	La Fée	9.2
Frances Willard	9.1	M. Jules Élie	9.2
Baroness Schroeder	9.0	Lady A. Duff	9.1

Dark Red

Philippe Rivoire	9.2
Longfellow	9.0

Exposure: While peonies prefer a position in full sun, they will thrive reasonably well in light shade.

Soil Requirements: Though peonies thrive fairly well in almost any soil, they prefer a rather heavy clay loam which is well drained but which is also retentive of moisture. The soil reaction should be as nearly neutral as possible, as peonies do not grow well in a definitely acid soil. Beds which are to be prepared for new plantings should be enriched with well-rotted manure, and bone meal should be incorporated with the upper 6 inches of soil at the rate of 1 pound of bone meal to every 20 square feet. Fresh manure should never be used immediately prior to planting as it is apt to cause serious injury to the roots.

Although peonies will perform fairly well in a rather poor

soil with comparatively little attention, they respond remarkably to good care and to high soil fertility. Therefore, if blooms of the finest quality are to be produced it is necessary to provide conditions which are most favorable for the development of the plant. Each year in early spring, as soon as the soil is workable, an application of bone meal and hardwood ashes should be cultivated into the soil about the crown of the plants. If wood ashes are not available either sulphate of potash of muriate of potash may be used, a handful being allowed for each plant. Well-rotted manure and leaf-mold worked into the soil about the plants will also help to maintain the fertility of the soil.

Propagation: Peonies are propagated by the division of old clumps. The plants may be lifted during the late summer or early autumn, September and October being considered the ideal months for the planting of peonies, as the young plants will then be able to establish themselves and to make some root growth before winter. The clumps should be divided into small pieces, each piece containing from three to five eyes or buds. In propagating new or very rare varieties only one eye is sometimes allowed. The tubers should be planted so that the top bud is not more than 2 or 3 inches below the surface of the soil. Too deep planting is the cause of many failures. It is wise to allow the plants ample room for full development, and they should be spaced 3 feet apart.

Culture: Peonies resent being moved and when the plants have become well established they may be left undisturbed for many years. It occasionally happens that peonies will fail to bloom, and this may be attributable to any one of several causes. Too deep planting will frequently cause the production of blind buds which fail to open and general lack of vigor, and disease is another contributing cause.

For the control of insect pests and diseases, see Chapter XXXIII.

Oriental Poppies (Papaver Orientale). The Oriental Poppy is a native of Persia and has long been a popular garden flower. In June, the large, flamboyant blooms are borne in profusion above the rough, hairy leaves and there are few perennials which can equal the oriental poppy in intensity of hue. The old-fashioned varieties vary from pure scarlet to deep red in color but many of the newer hybrids offer flowers of more delicate and more pleasing tones. Mrs. Perry is a soft salmon-pink and is particularly striking when grown in combination with Anchusa italica. Princess Ena is of similar coloring and is a very robust and vigorous grower.

Fairy and Princess Victoria Louise are a delicate pink in color and Silver Queen is a pure white. Among the new varieties of more brilliant coloring we have Oriental King, which bears scarlet flowers of marvellous size and substance, Beauty of Livermere, a deep, rich red, and Goliath, a vivid orange-scarlet in tone.

Soil Requirements: Oriental poppies will thrive well in any well-drained garden loam. If they possess any definite preference it is for a sandy, gritty loam rather than for a soil of a heavier type.

Exposure: Full sun.

Culture: There are no special cultural requirements for Oriental poppies, for they do well under average garden conditions. As they have a large, fleshy tap-root they are very difficult to transplant except when they are dormant. This period of dormancy follows the blooming season and if transplanting is necessary it should preferably be done at this time. If spring transplanting is necessary it may be accomplished successfully if great care is taken not to bruise the roots. The plants should not be kept out of the ground for any length of time and they should be shaded for at least a week after being transplanted. It is also essential that they be kept thoroughly watered until they have become well established.

As Oriental poppies require ample room for development during the period when they are in bloom, they should be spaced from 15 to 18 inches apart. Annuals and summer-flowering bulbs may be planted between the poppies in order to carry on a succession of bloom after the poppies have become dormant.

As the Oriental poppies reseed readily, it is important to see that the flower stalks are cut down before the seed pods form. If this is not done the chances are that the following year colonies of sturdy young plants will develop which will bear flowers of every hue, most of them reverting to the brilliant flame of the old-fashioned type.

Propagation: As the Oriental poppies seldom come true from seed, they should be propagated either by the division of old clumps or by root cuttings. After the blooming period is over, the plants die down entirely and remain practically dormant for a month or more. About the middle of August new growth begins and a little tuft of green leaves appears. The plants should be lifted and divided while they are dormant or just after the new growth begins. Root cuttings may also be made at this time and are very easily handled. The roots should be cut into small pieces 1 to 2 inches long, each piece containing at least one joint. These should be placed on a bed of soil, either in a flat or in a coldframe, being laid in a horizontal position. A light covering of sand or sandy loam should be spread over them to a depth of about ½ inch and the bed should be kept well watered and partially shaded until active growth has started. If conditions are favorable roots will develop from each joint and in a short time the leaves will begin to appear. This is undoubtedly the most satisfactory method of propagation. New varieties may be increased very rapidly in this way as a single plant will yield a large number of cuttings.

Phlox. The tall, hardy Phloxes are the pièce de résistance of most midsummer gardens and with the careful selection of varieties the period of bloom may be extended from June until early September. They are among our most useful plants for the perennial garden and give lavish bloom at a time when color and mass effect are most needed.

Like many other herbaceous perennials phlox plants form a definite crown from which a large number of roots arise. New root growth is made in the autumn, shortly after the flowering season is over. Although phlox plants may be transplanted at almost any season of the year, September is considered the ideal time for planting as it is then possible to take full advantage of this new root formation. Phlox is a very shallow-rooted plant, the roots seldom penetrating to a depth of more than 6 or 8 inches. However, the plant more than compensates for this shallow-rooting habit by sending its roots on extensive foraging expeditions, the roots often extending more than 2 feet from the crown.

The two types of hardy phlox most valuable for summer bloom are *Phlox suffruticosa* and *Phlox decussata*. The plants in the suffruticosa group bloom early, have glossy, deep green foliage and are very resistant to disease. *Miss Lingard* is the most outstanding variety in this group, producing large heads of glistening white flowers. In the decussata group some of the most desirable varieties are *Mrs. Jenkins,* a pure white, late-flowering variety of medium height; *P. D. Williams,* producing large flower trusses of a soft rose-pink; *Ethel Pritchard,* a French mauve color; *Rijnstroom,* a bright rose-pink; *Mrs. Scholten,* a midseason variety with deep salmon-pink flowers; and *Caroline Vandenburg,* a pure lavender-blue shade.

Exposure: Phlox plants will tolerate a moderate amount of shade but prefer a position in full sun.

Soil Requirements: Phlox has long been recognized as a voracious feeder. For maximum growth and for a fine quality of bloom phlox requires a rich, well-drained garden loam, high in organic content and very slightly acid. It is important that the fertility be readily available to the plant in the upper 8 inches of top-soil. During the growing season, they require an abundance of moisture and suffer seriously from the effects of drought. However, an extremely wet soil and poor air circulation are quite as injurious as drought and are conducive to poor growth and the spread of various diseases.

Propagation: Phlox may be propagated by the division of old clumps, by root cuttings, and by cuttings made from young, growing shoots. Old clumps may be lifted and divided either in the spring or in the early autumn. The earth should be shaken away from the roots and the clumps should be pulled gently apart into small divisions containing from one to three stems. In replanting the divisions, a hole of sufficient size should be dug and the roots should be carefully spread out, the crown of the plant being covered with not more than 1 inch of soil. The soil should be firmed well about the roots and the plants should be watered thoroughly until they have had an opportunity to become well established. If planting is done in the autumn, a light mulch of strawy manure may be placed over the crowns, being worked into the soil about the plant in the spring. The plants should be spaced from 18 inches to 2 feet apart. The largest flower trusses are usually obtained from newly made divisions. Clumps of phlox are at their best from the second to fourth years after planting. After this period the plants usually begin to lose their vigor and the coloring of the flowers is less brilliant. The clumps should therefore be lifted, divided, and reset every fifth or sixth year.

Culture: If blooms of exhibition quality are desired, not more than three stalks should be allowed to develop from one crown. Under ordinary garden conditions, however, where a mass of bloom is desired, the stems are allowed to develop naturally. As soon as the plants have completed their flowering period, the fading blooms should be cut away in order to prevent the plants from reseeding. Phlox plants reseed prolifically and these young, self-sown seedlings are a great liability in a planting composition, as they seldom come true to color, usually reverting to an ugly magenta shade. If the fading flower stalks are removed promply a second period of bloom will sometimes be induced. Another method of extending the blooming season is to pinch back from one fourth to one half of the stems before the flower buds have begun to form. The remaining stems will produce bloom at the normal time while those which have been cut back will bloom several weeks later.

For insect pests and diseases, see Chapter XXXIII.

Salvia azurea. This hardy perennial is well worth growing. The flowers, which are borne on long spikes, are a clear, azure blue and they are very decorative and lovely both in the garden and for cutting. Salvia azurea is particularly charming when grown in combination with pink gladioli, artemisia lactiflora, white phlox, and pale pink snapdragons, and it may be used in generous quantities for late summer and early autumn bloom.

Exposure: Salvia azurea is very hardy and will withstand long periods of drought with no ill effects. A position in full sun is preferred.

Soil Requirements: Salvia azurea has the happy faculty of doing extremely well on poor soil. Indeed, it seems to reach its best development on soils of medium or low fertility. When it is given an excessively rich diet it attains too great a height and has a tendency to become floppy and untidy.

Propagation: The plants may be propagated either by seed or by cuttings. The seeds are usually of excellent vitality and germinate readily. They may be sown in the greenhouse in February or March or they may be sown later in the season either in a coldframe or in the open ground. If sown before the middle of April, the young plants will give some bloom the first year. The seedlings should be transplanted before they become crowded, and when they reach a height of 6 or 8 inches they should be pinched back in order that they may become bushy and will be well branched.

Culture: After the plants are once well established, they will thrive for many years. Each year they should be cut back severely when they have reached a height of about 8 inches and staking is occasionally necessary in order that the plants may be pleasing and symmetrical in form. The plants vary in height from 2 to 4 feet, and they should be spaced from 12 to 15 inches apart.

Salvia farinacea (Mealycup Sage). There are few flowers that bloom over as long a period as does Salvia farinacea, and it is one of the loveliest members of this group. The flowers are a soft, lavender-blue in color and are borne on slender, graceful spikes. The plants are upright in habit of growth, branching freely, and attaining a height of 3–4 feet. The flower stems are held erect and have no tendency to become floppy. The foliage is a cool, rather light green. From midsummer until frost the plants will give generous bloom and they are lovely both as part of the garden composition and for cutting.

Although a true perennial Salvia farinacea is often treated as an annual in the North, as it is not hardy where the winters are of extreme severity.

Exposure: The plants thrive best in full sun but will make reasonably good growth in partial shade.

Soil Requirements: Salvia farinacea will grow well on almost any type of soil.

Propagation: The plants may be raised very easily from seed. For early bloom the seeds may be sown in the greenhouse or hotbed in March. For later bloom they may be sown either in the coldframe or in the open ground. The seeds germinate readily and the young plants make rapid growth. They should be transplanted or thinned out before they become in the least crowded and when they have reached a height of about 6 inches they should be pinched back, unless very early bloom is desired.

Culture: Salvia farinacea may be transplanted with ease, and the plants should be spaced from 8 to 10 inches apart.

For insect pests and diseases, see Chapter XXXIII.

Thalictrum (Meadow Rue). Light and graceful in form, the Thalictrums contribute to the garden a quality quite their own. Of the many species and varieties there are four which are of particular value in the garden of herbaceous perennials.

T. adiantifolium—The foliage resembles that of the Maidenhair fern and the myriad small, cream-white flowers are produced in abundance in June and early July. The plants attain a height of from 3 to 4 feet, and as they develop into large clumps, they should be spaced from 15 to 18 inches apart.

T. aquilegifolium—The flowers are borne on tall, graceful stems which rise above the foliage to a height of 3 feet or more. They may be obtained in shades of pink, lavender and creamy white, and they are in bloom throughout the month of June. The foliage bears a striking resemblance to that of the Columbines. The plants should be spaced from 12 to 18 inches apart.

T. dipterocarpum is by far the most beautiful of all the Thalictrums and yet it is so temperamental that in many gardens it will not thrive. In English gardens it is so utterly enchanting in its delicacy and beauty that one longs to see it more successfully grown in America. The tiny flowers are a soft shade of lilac-mauve with brilliant yellow stamens and anthers, and they are produced in abundance during July and August. When grown under favorable conditions the plants reach a height of about 4 feet, and they should be spaced about 18 inches apart.

T. glaucum—The glaucous leaves are a soft blue-gray in color and the fragrant yellow flowers are borne on tall, erect stems, varying from 3 to 4 feet in height. The plants are more compact and erect in habit of growth than most of the other Thalictrums and they should be spaced from 12 to 15 inches apart.

Exposure: Full sun or partial shade.
Soil Requirements: A well-drained, moderately fertile garden loam.
Propagation: By seed or by the division of established clumps.
Culture: The Thalictrums may be planted either in the autumn or in the early spring. With the exception of T. dipterocarpum no winter protection is required. In the latitude of Philadelphia and northward it is well to winter this more tender variety in the cold-frame.

Violas. The Violas are invaluable as edging plants and are particularly lovely when used in great drifts along the front of the herbaceous border. Most of the varieties of small violas which are grown today are a cross between the quaint little Horned Viola (Viola cornuta) and the Pansy, and they may be obtained in a wide range of colorings—white, lavender, deep purple, yellow, apricot and deep wine-red.

VARIETIES

Among the many lovely varieties of recent introduction are: V. *Jersey Gem,* of a pure rich violet hue; *White Perfection,* producing an abundance of pure white flowers; *Sutton's Apricot,* one of the most beautiful of all, with flowers of a rich apricot shade; *Blue Perfection,* which is very similar in color to the lovely *Maggie Mott* used so extensively in English gardens, a light lavender-blue shade; and *Arkright Ruby,* a glorious deep wine-red which is very striking when used in combination with Delphinium chinense and Antirrhinum variety Bonfire.

Exposure: Full sun is preferred, although most violas will thrive reasonably well in light shade.
Soil Requirements: Violas will do well in almost any good garden soil but for luxuriant bloom and maximum growth a highly fertile soil is desirable. Previous to planting, well-rotted cow manure should

be worked into the bed. A cool, fairly moist soil, rich in organic matter, is ideal.

Propagation: The plants may be readily propagated either from seed or from cuttings taken soon after the period of spring bloom is over. Some of the named varieties do not come entirely true from seed but the variations in color are usually so slight that it is not a serious matter unless plants of an absolutely uniform shade are desired. Seeds sown in July or August and wintered over in the coldframes will give abundant bloom the following spring.

Culture: Violas may be planted either in the autumn or in the spring, the plants being spaced from 6 to 8 inches apart. If the plants are not allowed to form seed they may be kept in bloom over a long period. Some gardeners follow the practice of cutting the plants back severely after the spring bloom is over, fertilizing the soil about the plants, and giving them an abundant supply of moisture, thus inducing a second period of bloom. Excessive moisture about the plants during the winter is very harmful and is frequently the cause of winter-killing.

PERENNIALS ENDURING SEMI-SHADE

Aconitum Fischeri (Azure Monkshood)
Ajuga (Bugle)
Anemone japonica (Japanese Anemone)
Anemonella thalictroides (Rue Anemone)
Asperula (Woodruff)
Aster, in variety
Campanula (Bellflower)
Convallaria majalis (Lily-of-the-valley)
Cornus canadensis (Bunchberry)
Dicentra eximia (Fringed Bleedingheart)
Dicentra spectabilis (Bleedingheart)
Dictamnus (Dittany or Gas Plant)
Epimedium alpinus (Barrenwort)
Eupatorium (Thoroughwort)
Geranium sanguineum (Blood Red Cranesbill)
Helleborus niger (Christmas-rose)
Hemerocallis flava (Daylily)
Heuchera sanguinea (Coral Bells)
Hibiscus Moscheutos (Swamp Rose-Mallow)
Hosta, in variety (Plaintain Lily)
Hypericum (St John's-Wort)

PERENNIALS ENDURING SEMI-SHADE—*Continued*

Iberis sempervirens (Candytuft)
Lathyrus odoratus (Sweet Pea)
Liatris pycnostachya (Cattail Gayfeather)
Lobelia cardinalis (Cardinal flower)
Lychnis chalcedonica (Maltese Cross)
Mertensia virginica (Virginia Bluebells)
Myosotis palustris semperflorens
    (Dwarf Perpetual Forget-me-not)
Œnothera missouriensis (Missouri Primrose)
Phlox, in variety
Platycodon (Balloon Flower)
Polygonatum biflorum (Smaller Solomonseal)
Primula, in variety (Primrose)
Thalictrum, in variety (Meadow Rue)
Trillium (Trillium)
Trollius europæus (Globeflower)
Veronica rupestris (Creeping Speedwell)
Viola cornuta, in variety

PERENNIALS ENDURING LIGHT SHADE

Althæa rosea (Hollyhock)
Anchusa italica (Bugloss)
Aquilegia hybrids (Columbine)
Campanula rotundifolia (Harebell)
Chelone Lyoni (Pink Turtlehead)
Cimicifuga racemosa (Cohosh Bugbane)
Doronicum plantagineum (Leopardbane)
Linaria (Toadflax)
Lupinus, in variety (Lupine)
Monarda didyma (Beebalm)
Pæonia (Peony)
Physostegia (False Dragonhead)
Polemonium (Valerian)
Pulmonaria saccharata (Bethlehem Lungwort)
Pyrethrum (Chrys. coccineum) (Pink Daisy)
Saxifraga (Saxifrage)
Silene pennsylvanica (Peatpink)

PERENNIALS WHICH WILL GROW IN POOR SOIL

Achillea serrata (Millfoil or Yarrow)
Ajuga genevensis (Geneva Bugle)

PERENNIALS WHICH WILL GROW IN POOR SOIL—*Continued*

Alyssum saxatile (Goldentuft)
Arabis albida (Wallcress)
Cerastium tomentosum (Snow-in-Summer)
Dianthus deltoides (Maiden Pink)
Dianthus plumarius (Grass Pink)
Eryngium campestre (Hundred Thistle)
Euphorbia Myrsinites (Myrsinites-like Spurge)
Geranium sanguineum (Blood Red Cranesbill)
Geranium maculatum (Spotted Cranesbill)
Gypsophila paniculata (Babysbreath)
Helianthemum vulgare (Rock or Sun Rose)
Iberis sempervirens (Evergreen Candytuft)
Linaria vulgaris (Toadflax)
Phlox subulata (Moss Phlox)
Potentilla tridentata (Wineleaf Cinquefoil)
Salvia azurea (Azure Sage)
Saxifraga pennsylvanica (Penn. or Swamp Saxifrage)
Sedum acre (Goldmoss)
Sedum stoloniferum (Running Sedum)
Sempervivum (Roof Houseleek)
Sempervivum arvernense (Auvergne Houseleek)
Verbascum Thapsus
Veronica rupestris (Creeping Speedwell)
Viola cucullata (Blue Marsh Violet)

PERENNIALS FOR DRY, SANDY SOILS

Achillea Ptarmica (Sneezewort)
Ajuga reptans (Carpet Bugle)
Anthemis tinctoria (Yellow Camomile)
Asclepias tuberosa (Butterflyweed)
Aster novæ-angliæ (New England Aster)
· Callirhoë involucrata (Poppymallow)
Cassia marilandica (Wild Senna)
Coreopsis grandiflora (Tickseed)
Dianthus plumarius (Grass Pink)
Echinops Ritro (Steel Globethistle)
Euphorbia corollata (Flowering Spurge)
Helianthus, in variety (Sunflower)
Limonium latifolium (Statice)
Lychnis chalcedonica (Maltese Cross)
Papaver nudicaule (Iceland Poppy)

PERENNIALS FOR DRY, SANDY SOILS—*Continued*

Rudbeckia laciniata (Goldenglow)
Yucca filamentosa (Common Yucca)

PERENNIALS REQUIRING WELL-DRAINED SITUATIONS

Arabis alpina (Alpine Rockcress)
Asclepias tuberosa (Butterflyweed)
Aubrietia deltoides (Purple Rockcress)
Coreopsis grandiflora (Tickseed)
Delphinium hybrids (Delphinium)
Dianthus barbatus (Sweet William)
Digitalis purpurea (Common Foxglove)
Echinops Ritro (Steel Globethistle)
Eryngium maritimum (Seaholly)
Gaillardia aristata (Blanketflower)
Globularia trichosantha (Globedaisy)
Helianthus Maximiliani (Maximilian Sunflower)
Iris germanica (Bearded Iris)
Liatris pycnostachya (Cattail Gayfeather)
Papaver nudicaule (Iceland Poppy)

PERENNIALS FOR WET SITUATIONS

*Arundo Donax (Giant Reed)
Asclepias incarnata (Swamp Milkweed)
Boltonia asteroides (White Boltonia)
*Caltha palustris (Marsh Marigold)
Eupatorium purpureum (Joe-pye-weed)
Helenium autumnale (Sneezeweed)
Hibiscus Moscheutos (Swamp Rose-Mallow)
*Iris pseudacorus (Yellowflag)
Iris versicolor (Blueflag)
Lobelia cardinalis (Cardinal Flower)
Lysimachia clethroides (Clethra Loosestrife)
Lythrum Salicaria (Spiked Loosestrife)
Miscanthus sinensis (Eulalia)
Monarda didyma (Bee Balm)
Myosotis palustris (True Forget-me-not)
Onoclea sensibilis (Sensitive Fern)
Osmunda cinnamomea (Cinnamon Fern)
*Osmunda regalis (Royal Fern)
  *May be grown in water.

Perennials for Wet Situations—*Continued*

Sarracenia purpurea (Pitcherplant)
Saxifraga pennsylvanica (Penn. or Swamp Saxifrage)

Perennials for Borders of Ponds and Streams

(Well-drained soil)
(*Sunny Locations*)

Brunnera macrophylla [Anchusa myosotidiflora] (Siberian Bugloss)
Chrysanthemum uliginosum (Giant Daisy)
Cimicifuga racemosa (Cohosh Bugbane)
Grasses (Ornamental Grasses)
Hemerocallis, in variety (Daylily)
Iris, in variety
Lythrum Salicaria (Spiked Loosestrife)
Myosotis palustris semperflorens (Dwarf Perpetual Forget-me-not)
Tradescantia virginiana (Spiderwort)
Trollius europæus (Globeflower)

(*Semi-Shady Locations*)

Anemone japonica (Jap. Anemone)
Cimicifuga racemosa (Cohosh Bugbane)
Epimedium macranthum (Longspur Epimedium)
Eupatorium purpureum (Joe-pye-weed)
Iris cristata (Crested Iris)
Lythrum Salicaria (Spiked Loosestrife)
Tradescantia virginiana (Spiderwort)

Perennials for Edging

Achillea tomentosa (Woolly Yarrow)
Ægopodium Podagraria (Goutweed)
Ajuga reptans (Carpet Bugle)
Alyssum saxatile compactum (Dwarf Goldentuft)
Arabis alpina (Alpine Rockcress)
Arabis albida (Wallcress)
Bellis perennis (English Daisy)
Aubrietia deltoides (Purple Rockcress)
Campanula carpatica (Carpathian Bellflower)
Cerastium tomentosum (Snow-in-summer)
Dianthus deltoides (Maiden Pink)
Dianthus plumarius (Grass Pink)
Festuca glauca (Blue Fescue)

PERENNIALS FOR EDGING—*Continued*

Heuchera sanguinea (Coralbells)
Iberis sempervirens (Evergreen Candytuft)
Papaver nudicaule (Iceland Poppy)
Phlox subulata (Moss Phlox)
Phlox procumbens (Hairy Phlox)
Primula veris (Cowslip Primrose)
Sedum reflexum (Jenny Stonecrop)
Sedum stoloniferum (Running Stonecrop)
Statice Armeria (Thrift)
Stellaria Holostea (Greater Stitchwort or Starwort)
Tunica Saxifraga (Tunicflower)
Veronica incana (Woolly Speedwell)
Veronica Teucrium (Rock Speedwell)
Viola, in variety (Violas)

PERENNIALS FOR BACKGROUND PLANTING

Althæa rosea (Hollyhock)
Aster novæ-angliæ (New England Aster)
Aster tataricus (Tatarian Aster)
Bocconia cordata (Plumepoppy)
Boltonia asteroides (White Boltonia)
Campanula pyramidalis (Chimney Bellflower)
Cimicifuga racemosa (Cohosh Bugbane)
Delphinium hybrids (Delphinium)
Helenium autumnale (Sneezeweed)
Helianthus Maximiliani (Maximilian Sunflower)
Hibiscus grandiflorus (Great Rosemallow)
Rudbeckia laciniata (Goldenglow)
Solidago altissima (Tall Goldenrod)
Valeriana officinalis (Common Valerian)

FRAGRANT PERENNIALS

Arabis, in variety (Arabis)
Artemisia Abrotanum (Southernwood)
Asperula odorata (Sweet Woodruff)
Centranthus ruber (Jupitersbeard)
Convallaria majalis (Lily-of-the-Valley)
Dianthus plumarius (Grass Pink)
Dictamnus albus (Dittany or Gas Plant)
Hemerocallis flava (Daylily)

FRAGRANT PERENNIALS—*Continued*

Hesperis matronalis (Sweet Rocket)
Hosta plantaginea grandiflora (Funkia or Big Plantain Lily)
Iris, Pallida section
Lathyrus grandiflorus (Everlasting Pea)
Lychnis Viscaria (German Catchfly)
Monarda didyma (Bee Balm)
Œnothera, in variety (Evening Primrose)
Pæonia, in variety (Peony)
Phlox paniculata (Phlox)
Rosa species (Roses—Cabbage and Sweet Briers)
Valeriana officinalis (Common Valerian)
Viola cornuta (Tufted Pansy)
Viola odorata (Sweet Violet)

(Herbs)
Anethum graveolens (Dill)
Thymus, in variety (Thyme)
Lavandula vera (True Lavender)
Origanum Majorana (Sweet Majoram)
Rosmarinus officinalis (Rosemary)

HARDY PLANTS FOR BOLD OR SUBTROPICAL EFFECTS

Acanthus latifolius (Acanthus)
Bocconia cordata (Plume Poppy)
Cimicifuga racemosa (Bugbane)
Dipsacus fullonum (Teasel)
Echinops Ritro and exaltatus (Globe Thistles)
Elymus arenarius (Wild-rye)
Eulalia japonica (Eulalia)
Helianthus orgyalis (Sunflower)
Heracleum giganteum (Cow-parsnip)
Kniphofia Uvaria (Torchlily)
Onopordum Acanthium (Scotch Thistle)
Polygonum sachalinense (Sacaline)
Silphium perfoliatum (Rosinweed)
Spiræa Aruncus (Spirea)
Telekia cordifolia (Telekia)
Verbascum olympicum (Mullein)
Yucca filamentosa (Yucca)

PERENNIALS FOR OLD-FASHIONED GARDENS

Aconitum, in variety (Monkshood)
Althæa rosea (Hollyhock)
Arisæma triphyllum (Jack-in-the-Pulpit)
Asters, not new varieties
Campanula, in variety (Bellflower)
Convallaria majalis (Lily-of-the-Valley)
Delphinium belladonna (Delphinium)
Delphinium formosum (Formosa Delphinium)
Dianthus arenarius (Sand Pink)
Dianthus barbatus (Sweet William)
Dianthus plumarius, Mrs. Sinkins in particular (Grass or Garden
    Pinks)
Dianthus superbus (Lilac Pink)
Dicentra spectabilis (Bleedingheart)
Dictamnus (Dittany or Gas Plant)
Digitalis, in variety (Foxgloves)
Hemerocallis, not new hybrids (Daylily)
Hepatica triloba (Hepatica, or Liverwort)
Hesperis matronalis (Sweet Rocket)
Lilium candidum (Madonna Lily)
Lilium tigrinum (Tiger Lily)
Lunaria (Honesty) (Biennial)
Lupinus, not new varieties (Lupines)
Lychnis chalcedonica (Maltese Cross or Scarlet Lychnis)
Mertensia (Mertensia or Blue Bells)
Myosotis, in variety (Forget-me-nots)
Pæonia officinalis types (Peony)
Primula veris (Primrose)
Trillium, in variety (Trillium or Wake Robin)
Viola odorata (Sweet Violet)
Viola, in variety (Pansies)

PERENNIALS HAVING ESPECIALLY LONG BLOOMING SEASONS

Anchusa italica (Bugloss)
Aquilegia chrysantha (Golden Columbine)
Campanula carpatica (Carpathian Harebell)
Delphinium, if cut back
Heuchera sanguinea (Coral Bells)

PERENNIALS HAVING ESPECIALLY LONG BLOOMING SEASONS—*Cont.*

Iris, fall blooming varieties
Lathyrus latifolius (Perennial Pea)
Lychnis Coronaria (Dusty Miller)
Phlox, if cut back
Scabiosa graminifolia (Pincushion or Mourning Bride)
Scabiosa sylvatica
Verbascums, if cut back (Mullein)
Viola cornuta (Tufted Pansy)
Viola tricolor (Heartsease)

PERENNIALS FLOWERING THE FIRST SEASON FROM SEED SOWN IN THE SPRING

Buphthalmum salicifolium (Willow-leaved Ox-Eye)
Campanula carpatica (Carpathian Harebell)
Campanula carpatica alba
Campanula rotundifolia
Centaurea montana (Mountain Bluet)
Chrysanthemum maximum (Shasta Daisy)
Delphinium formosum (Formosa Delphinium)
Delphinium grandiflorum (Siberian Delphinium)
Dianthus plumarius (Garden Pink)
Erigeron Coulteri (Large White Mountain Daisy)
Erigeron glabellus (Rough Erigeron)
Gaillardia aristata [grandiflora] (Blanketflower)
Geum atrosanguineum (Crimson Avens)
Inula ensifolia (Swordleaf Inula)
Linaria dalmatica (Dalmatian Toadflax)
Papaver nudicaule (Iceland Poppy)
Penstemon campanulatus (Bell-flowered Penstemon)
Salvia farinacea (Mealycup Sage)

PERENNIALS BLOOMING IN APRIL

Adonis amurensis (Amur Adonis)	Yellow
A. vernalis (Spring Adonis)	Yellow
Alyssum saxatile (Goldentuft)	Yellow
A. saxatile compactum	Yellow
Anemone Pulsatilla (Pasqueflower)	Purple
Aquilegia canadensis (American Columbine)	Yellow and Red
A. vulgaris var. alba (White Columbine)	White

Perennials Blooming in April—*Continued*

Arabis alpina (Rockcress)	White
Aubrietia deltoides (Purple Rockcress)	Purple
Bellis perennis (English Daisy)	White, pink, rose
Bergenia cordifolia (Bergenia) (Saxifrage cordifolia)	Pink
Caltha palustris (Marsh Marigold)	Yellow
Daphne cneorum (Rose Daphne)	Rose
Iberis sempervirens (Evergreen Candytuft)	White
Mertensia virginica (Virginia Bluebells)	Blue
Nepeta Mussini (European Catmint)	Lavender
Papaver nudicaule (Iceland Poppy)	White to orange
Phlox divaricata (Blue Phlox)	Blue
P. subulata (Moss Phlox)	Pink, white, lilac
Polemonium reptans (Creeping Polemonium)	Blue
Primula polyantha (Polyanthas)	White, orange, yellow scarlet, purple
P. vulgaris (P. acaulis)	Same
Pulmonaria officinalis (Common Lung-wort)	Pink
Rosmarinus officinalis (Rosemary)	Blue
Trollius europæus (Globeflower)	Yellow

Perennials Blooming in May

Æthionema coridifolium (Lebanon Stonecress)	Pink
Ajuga genevensis (Geneva Bugle)	Blue
A. reptans (Carpet Bugle)	Purple
Alyssum montanum	Yellow
A. spinosum	White
Amsonia Tabernæmontana (Willow Amsonia)	Pale blue
Anchusa Barrelieri (Early Bugloss)	Dark blue
Anemone sylvestris (Snowdrop Wind flower)	White
Aquilegia cærulea (Colorado Columbine)	Blue and white
A. chrysantha (Golden Columbine)	Yellow

PERENNIALS BLOOMING IN MAY—*Continued*

A. glandulosa (Altaian Columbine)	Blue and white
A. sibirica (Siberian Columbine)	Blue
Brunnera macrophylla [Anchusa myosotidiflora] (Siberian Bugloss)	Blue
Centaurea montana (Mountain Bluet)	Blue
Chelidonium majus (Celandine)	Yellow
Dianthus Allwoodii (Allwood Pink)	Various
D. cæsius (Cheddar Pink)	Rose
D. deltoides (Maiden Pink)	Rose-Pink
D. plumarius varieties (Grass Pink)	Various
Dicentra eximia (Fringed Bleedingheart)	Rose-red
D. spectabilis (Bleedingheart)	Rose-red
Doronicum caucasicum (Leopardbane)	Yellow
D. plantagineum	Yellow
Euphorbia epithymoides (Cushion Spurge)	Yellow
Gaillardia aristata [grandiflora] (Blanket-flower)	Red and yellow
Geum montanum Heldreichii (Avens)	Orange
Helenium Hoopesii (Orange Sneezeweed)	Orange
Incarvillea Delavayi (Delavay's Incarvillea)	Purple-rose
I. grandiflora	Crimson
Linum alpinum (Alpine Toadflax)	Violet, orange
L. narbonense (Narbonne Flax)	Blue
Lychnis Flos-cuculi (Ragged-robin)	Red
L. Viscaria (Clammy Cross)	Magenta
Mertensia virginica (Virginia Cowslip)	Blue
M. ciliata (Mountain Bluebells)	Blue
M. lanceolata (Prairie Bluebells)	Blue
Myosotis dissitiflora (Swiss Forget-me-not)	Blue
Nepeta Mussini (Mussin's Catmint)	Lavender
Œnothera cæspitosa (Tufted Evening Primrose)	White
Phlox divaricata (Blue Phlox)	Blue
P. Arendsii (Arend's Phlox)	Mauve
P. subulata (Moss Phlox)	Rose-purple
Platycodon grandiflorum (Balloonflower)	Violet, white
P. Mariesii	Violet, white
Polemonium cæruleum (Greek Valerian)	Blue, white
P. reptans (Creeping Polemonium)	Pale blue

Perennials Blooming in May—*Continued*

Primula cortusoides (Bigleaf Primrose)	Red, purple
P. denticulata (Himalayan Primrose)	Violet
P. denticulata cachemiriana (Kashmir Primrose)	Lilac
P. Sieboldii	White, rose, purple
Pulmonaria saccharata (Bethlehem Lungwort)	Pink to blue
Statice Armeria alba (Thrift)	White
S. Armeria Laucheana	Rosy crimson
Thalictrum aquilegifolium (Meadow Rue)	Pinkish
T. polyganum (Tall Meadow Rue)	White
Trollius asiaticus (Globeflower)	Orange
T. europæus	Yellow
Veronica gentianoides (Speedwell)	Blue
Viola cornuta varieties (Tufted Pansies)	White to violet

Perennials Blooming in June

Achillea filipendulina (Fernleaf Yarrow)	Yellow
A. Millefolium (Yarrow)	White, rose
A. tomentosa (Woolly Yarrow)	Yellow
Alyssum argenteum (Silver Alyssum)	Yellow
A. rostratum (Yellowhead Alyssum)	Yellow
Anaphalis margaritacea (Pearl Everlasting)	White
Anchusa italica (azurea) (Dropmore Bugloss)	Deep blue
Anthemis tinctoria Kelwayi (Yellow Camomile)	Yellow
Aruncus sylvester (Goatsbeard)	Cream
Asphodeline lutea (Jacob's-rod)	Yellow
Aster subcæruleus (Aster)	Blue
Astilbe Davidii (David Astilbe)	Rose
A. grandis (Great Astilbe)	White
A. decandra (A. biternata) False Goatsbeard	Creamy white
A. japonica (Japanese False Goatsbeard)	White
Baptisia australis (Wild-indigo)	Blue
B. tinctoria (Yellow Wild-indigo)	Yellow

PERENNIALS BLOOMING IN JUNE—*Continued*

Campanula alliariæfolia (Spurred Bell-flower)	White
C. barbata	Blue
C. carpatica (Carpathian Harebell)	Blue, white
C. garganica	Light blue
C. persicifolia (Peachleaf Bellflower)	Blue, white
C. rotundifolia (Harebell)	Blue
Centaurea candidissima	Yellow
C. gymnocarpa (Velvet Centaurea)	Pale purple
Centranthus ruber (Red Valerian)	Red
Cephalaria alpina (Yellow Cephalaria)	Sulphur
Cerastium Biebersteinii (Taurus Cerastium)	White
C. tomentosum (Snow-in-summer)	White
Chrysanthemum coccineum (Pyrethrum) (Painted Lady)	Rose
Chrysanthemum leucanthemum (Ox-eye Daisy)	White
Chrysanthemum maximum varieties (Shasta Daisy)	White, pink, lilac
Coreopsis grandiflora (Tickseed)	Yellow
Delphinium Belladona (Delphinium)	Light blue
D. Bellamosum	Deep blue
D. grandiflorum album	White
D. hybrids	Various
D. nudicaule	Orange
D. Zalil (Yellow Delphinium)	Yellow
Dianthus Allwoodii	Various
D. barbatus (Sweet William)	Various
D. cæsius (Cheddar Pink)	Rose
D. plumarius (Grass Pink)	Various
D. latifolius	Red
Digitalis ambigua (Foxgloves)	Yellow
D. ambigua Isabellina	Tawny
Dracocephalum Ruyschiana (Dragonhead)	Purple
Erigeron speciosus (Fleabane)	Pink
Euphorbia cyparissias (Cypress Spurge)	Yellow
Filipendula camtschatica	White
F. hexapetala (Dropwort)	White

PERENNIALS BLOOMING IN JUNE—*Continued*

Gaillardia aristata (Blanketflower)	Red, orange
Galega officinalis (Goatsrue)	Purple-blue
Galium boreale (Bedstraw)	White
G. verum	Yellow
Geranium armenum (Armenian Cranesbill)	Purple
G. Fremontii (Rocky Mountain Cranesbill)	Rose-purple
G. grandiflorum (Lilac Geranium)	Violet
G. ibericum (Iberian Geranium)	Blue, white
Gypsophila paniculata (Babysbreath)	White
G. repens (Creeping Gypsophila)	Blush
G. monstrosa	Pale rose
Helianthemum album	White
Hemerocallis aurantiaca (Orange Daylily)	Orange
H. Dumortierii	Bright orange
H. flava (Lemon Daylily)	Canary
H. fulva (Tawny Daylily)	Bronze
H. Middendorffii (Amur Daylily)	Gold
Heracleum villosum (Cow-parsnip)	White
Hesperis matronalis (Rocket)	Purple
Kniphofia rufa (Early Torchlily)	Yellow
Linum alpinum (Alpine Flax)	Gray Blue
L. flavum (Golden Flax)	Gold
L. perenne (Perennial Flax)	Blue and White
Lychnis Arkwrightii (Campion)	Scarlet
L. Cœli-rosa (Rose-of-Heaven)	Rose
L. Coronaria (Rose Campion)	Rose-purple
L. Viscaria (Clammy Campion)	Magenta
Meconopsis cambrica (Welsh-poppy)	Yellow
Myosotis alpestris (Alpine Forget-me-not)	Blue
Œnothera missouriensis (Ozark Sundrop)	Yellow
O. speciosa	White
Pæonia (Peony)	Various
Papaver nudicaule (Iceland Poppy)	Yellow or white
P. orientale (Oriental Poppy)	Various
P. pilosum (Olympic Poppy)	Brick-red
Penstemon barbatus	Scarlet

PERENNIALS BLOOMING IN JUNE—*Continued*

P. gloxinioides (Gloxinia Penstemon)	Purple
P. lævigatus (Smooth Penstemon)	Rose-lilac
P. Torreyi (Torrey Penstemon)	Scarlet
Phlox Arendsii (Arends Phlox)	Various
P. pilosa (Downy Phlox)	Pink
P. suffruticosa (Smooth Phlox)	Various
Platycodon grandiflorum (Balloonflower)	Violet, white
P. Mariesii	Violet, white
Polemonium cæruleum (Greek Valerian)	Blue, white
Potentilla nepalensis (Nepal Cinquefoil)	Rose
Primula Auricula (Primrose)	Various
P. frondosa	Rose-lilac
P. japonica (Japanese Primrose)	Rose-lilac to crimson
Romneya Coulteri (Canyon-poppy)	White
Rudbeckia maxima (Great Coneflower)	Yellow
Salvia argentea (Silver Sage)	Rose-white
S. pratensis (Meadow Sage)	Blue
Scabiosa caucasica	White, lavender
S. graminifolia	Violet
S. japonica (Japanese Scabiosa)	Lavender
Statice Armeria (Thrift)	Pink
S. Laucheana (Rosalie Thrift)	Rose
S. plantaginea	Pink
Thalictrum aquilegifolium (Columbine Meadow Rue)	White, purple
T. glaucum (Dusty Meadow Rue)	Yellow
T. minus (Low Meadow Rue)	Yellow
T. polygamum (Tall Meadow Rue)	White
Trollius asiaticus (Globeflower)	Orange
T. europæus	Yellow
Verbascum phœniceum (Purple Mullein)	Various
Veronica gentianoides (Gentian Speedwell)	Light blue
V. spicata (Spike Speedwell)	Purple
V. spuria (Bastard Speedwell)	Violet
Viola cornuta (Tufted Pansy)	Various
Yucca baccata (Yucca)	White
Y. filamentosa	White
Y. glauca (Soapweed)	White

Perennials Blooming in July

Acanthus mollis (Bearsbreech)	Lilac, rose
Achillea Clavennæ	White
A. filipendulina (Fernleaf Yarrow)	Yellow
A. Ptarmica (Sneezewort)	White
Aconitum Anthora (Pyrenees Monkshood)	Yellow
A. lycoctonum (Wolfbane)	Pale yellow
A. Napellus	Violet-blue
Alyssum argenteum (Silver Alyssum)	Yellow
Anchusa italica (Dropmore Bugloss)	Deep blue
Anthemis tinctoria (Yellow Camomile)	Yellow
Aruncus sylvester (Goatsbeard)	White
Asclepias tuberosa (Butterflyweed)	Orange
Asperula odorata (Woodruff)	White
Aster Amellus	Purple
Astilbe Davidii (David Astilbe)	Rosy
A. grandis (Great Astilbe)	White
Baptisia australis (Wild-indigo)	Blue
B. tinctoria (Yellow Wild-indigo)	Yellow
Bocconia cordata (Plumepoppy)	Rose
Calimeris incisa	Purple, white
Campanula alliariæfolia (Spurred Bell-flower)	White
C. carpatica (Carpathian Bellflower)	Blue, white
C. glomerata (Danesblood)	Violet
C. lactiflora (Milky Bellflower)	Blue, white
C. persicifolia (Peachleaf Bellflower)	Blue, white
C. rapunculoides	Violet
Cassia marilandica (Wild Senna)	Yellow
Centaurea babylonica (Syrian Centaurea)	Yellow
C. macrocephala (Globe Centaurea)	Yellow
C. montana (Mountain Bluet)	Violet
Centranthus ruber (Jupitersbeard)	Crimson, white
Cephalaria alpina (Yellow Cephalaria)	Sulphur
Chrysanthemum maximum (Shasta Daisy)	White
Clematis integrifolia	Blue
C. recta (Ground Clematis)	White
Coreopsis verticillata (Threadleaf Coreopsis)	Yellow

PERENNIALS BLOOMING IN JULY—*Continued*

Delphinium Belladonna (Delphinium)	Light blue
D. Bellamosum	Deep blue
D. grandiflorum (Siberian Delphinium)	Blue, white
D. hybrids	Various
D. Zalil (Yellow Delphinium)	Yellow
Dianthus Allwoodii	Various
Dicentra eximia (Fringed Bleedingheart)	Rose
Digitalis ambigua (Yellow Foxglove)	Yellow
Dracocephalum Ruyschiana (Dragonhead)	Purple
Echinops humilis (Low Globe Thistle)	Blue
E. Ritro (Steel Globe Thistle)	Blue
E. sphærocephalus (Common Globe Thistle)	White
Epilobium angustifolium (Blooming-sally)	Magenta
Erigeron multiradiatus (Fleabane)	Pink
E. speciosus	Violet
Eryngium alpinum (Bluetop Eryngo)	Amethyst
E. amethystinum (Amethyst Eryngium)	Amethyst
E. maritimum (Sea-Holly)	Pale blue
E. Oliverianum	Blue
E. planum	Steel blue
Eupatorium perfoliatum (Boneset)	White
Euphorbia corollata (Flowering Spurge)	White
Filipendula palmata (Meadowsweet)	Pink, white
Gaillardia aristata (Blanketflower)	Red, orange
Galium boreale (Bedstraw)	White
G. verum	Yellow
Geum chiloense (Avens)	Scarlet
Globularia trichosantha (Globe-daisy)	Blue
Gypsophila acutifolia (Green Gypsophila)	White
G. paniculata (Babysbreath)	White
Helianthemum album	White
Heliopsis Pitcheriana (Pitcher Heliopsis)	Orange
H. scabra var. excelsa	Orange
Hemerocallis, in variety	Yellow, orange
Heuchera sanguinea (Coral Bells)	Crimson
Hypericum Moserianum	Yellow
Lavandula vera (True Lavender)	Lavender

PERENNIALS BLOOMING IN JULY—*Continued*

Linum flavum (Golden Flax)	Yellow
L. perenne (Perennial Flax)	White, blue
Lupinus polyphyllus (Washington Lupine)	Various
Lychnis Cœli-rosa (Rose-of-heaven)	Rose
L. Coronaria (Rose Campion)	Rosy purple
L. Haageana (Haage Campion)	Orange scarlet
Lysimachia clethroides (Clethra Loose-strife)	White
Lythrum Salicaria (Loosestrife)	Rose purple
L. virgatum (Wand Loosestrife)	Rose purple
Meconopsis quintuplinervia (Harebell-poppy)	Lavender
M. Wallichii (Satinpoppy)	Blue
Mentha Requieni (Requien Mint)	Mauve
Mertensia sibirica (Siberian Bluebells)	Blue
Monarda didyma (Bee Balm)	Scarlet
Œnothera fruticosa (Sundrops)	Yellow
O. missouriensis (Ozark Sundrops)	Yellow
Papaver nudicaule (Iceland Poppy)	Yellow, orange, white
P. pilosum (Olympic Poppy)	Brick-red
Penstemon barbatus	Scarlet
P. gloxinioides (Gloxinia Penstemon)	Purple
P. grandiflorus (Shell-leaf Penstemon)	Purple
P. lævigatus (Smooth Penstemon)	Rosy lilac
P. l. digitalis (Foxglove Pen.)	Purple
P. Torreyi (Torrey Penstemon)	Rose, white
Phlox paniculata (Garden Phlox)	Various
Physalis Alkekengi (Strawberry Ground-cherry)	White
Physostegia virginiana (False-dragonhead)	Pink
Platycodon grandiflorum (Balloon-flower)	Violet, white
P. Mariesii	Violet, white
Polemonium cæruleum (Greek-valerian)	Blue, white
Potentilla nepalensis (Nepal Cinquefoil)	Rose
P. Warrensii	Yellow
Rudbeckia laciniata (Golden Glow)	Orange
R. maxima (Great Coneflower)	Yellow
R. speciosa Newmani (Showy Cone-flower)	Golden
R. subtomentosa (Sweet Coneflower)	Yellow

PERENNIALS BLOOMING IN JULY—*Continued*

Salvia farinacea (Mealycup Sage)	Light blue
S. pratensis (Meadow Sage)	Blue
S. turkestanica	White, pale pink
Scabiosa caucasica	White, lavender
S. graminifolia	Violet
S. japonica (Japanese Scabiosa)	Lavender
Scutellaria baicalensis (Baikal Skullcap)	Blue
Sidalcea candida (Prairiemallow)	White
S. malvæflora (Checkerbloom)	Rose pink
S. m. Listeri (Satin Checkerbloom)	Rose pink
Stachys lanata (Woolly Betony)	Purple
Statice Armeria (Thrift)	Pink
S. Laucheana (Rosalie Thrift)	Rose
S. pseudo-Armeria	Crimson
Stenanthium robustum (Featherfleece)	White
Teucrium Chamædrys (Germander)	Rosy purple
Thermopsis caroliniana	Yellow
Trollius chinensis	Orange-yellow
Tunica Saxifraga (Tunicflower)	White, blush
Valeriana officinalis (Valerian)	Blush white
Verbascum phœniceum (Purple Mullein)	Various
Veronica incana (Woolly Speedwell)	Rosy purple
V. spicata (Spike Speedwell)	Purple
V. spuria (Bastard Speedwell)	Violet
V. virginica (Culvers-physic)	White
Viola cornuta (Tufted Pansy)	Various

PERENNIALS BLOOMING IN AUGUST

Achillea Clavennæ	White
A. filipendulina (Fernleaf Yarrow)	Yellow
A. Ptarmica (Sneezewort)	White
Aconitum Napellus	Violet-blue
Alyssum argenteum (Silver Alyssum)	Yellow
Anemone hupehensis	Rosy
Artemisia Abrotanum (Southernwood)	Yellow
A. Absinthium (Common Wormwood)	White, yellow
A. Purshiana (Cudweed Wormwood)	Whitish
A. Stelleriana (Beach Wormwood)	Yellow
Calimeris incis	Purple, white

Perennials Blooming in August—*Continued*

Campanula carpatica (Carpathian Bell-flower)	Blue, white
C. lactiflora (Milky Bellflower)	Blue, white
C. pyramidalis (Chimney Bellflower)	Blue, white
Centaurea babylonica (Syrian Centaurea)	Yellow
Centranthus ruber (Jupitersbeard)	Crimson, white
Cephalaria alpina (Yellow Cephalaria)	Sulphur
Cerastium arvense (Starry Cerastium)	White
Chrysanthemum maximum (Shasta Daisy)	White
Clematis heracleæfolia (Tube Clematis)	Lavender
C. integrifolia	Blue
C. recta (Ground Clematis)	White
Delphinium Belladonna (Delphinium)	Light blue
D. Bellamosum	Deep blue
D. cardinale (Cardinal Larkspur)	Scarlet
D. grandiflorum (Siberian Larkspur)	Blue, white
D. hybrids	Various
Dianthus latifolius (Double Cluster Pink)	Rose
Dicentra eximia (Fringed Bleedingheart)	Rose
Eryngium maritimum (Sea-Holly)	Pale blue
E. Oliverianum	Blue
E. planum	Steel blue
Eupatorium purpureum (Joe-pye-weed)	Purple
Gypsophila monstrosa	Pale rose
Helianthus decapetalus (Thinleaf Sun-flower)	Sulphur
H. mollis (Ashy Sunflower)	Orange
Hypericum calycinum	Yellow
H. Moserianum	Yellow
H. patulum Henryi	Yellow
Liatris graminifolia (Grassleaf Gay-feather)	Rose-purple
L. pycnostachya (Cattail Gayfeather)	Rose-purple
L. scariosa	Purple
L. spicata (Spike Gayfeather)	Purple
Limonium latifolium (Bigleaf Statice)	Lavender
Linum flavum (Golden Flax)	Gold
L. perenne (Perennial Flax)	Blue, white
Lobelia cardinalis (Cardinal flower)	Scarlet

PERENNIALS BLOOMING IN AUGUST—*Continued*

Lythrum Salicaria (Loosestrife)	Rose-purple
Nepeta Mussini	Lavender-blue
Œnothera missouriensis (Ozark Sun-drops)	Yellow
Penstemon gloxinioides (Gloxinia Penstemon)	Purple
Phlox paniculata (Garden Phlox)	Various
P. suffruticosa (Smooth Phlox)	Various
Physostegia virginiana (False-dragonhead)	Pink
P. "Vivid"	Brighter pink
Platycodon grandiflorum (Balloonflower)	Violet, white
P. Mariesii	Violet, white
Potentilla nepalensis (Nepal Cinquefoil)	Rose
Rudbeckia laciniata (Golden Glow)	Orange
R. maxima (Great Coneflower)	Yellow
R. nitida (Autumn Sun)	Primrose
R. speciosa (Showy Coneflower)	Golden
R. subtomentosa (Sweet Coneflower)	Yellow
Salvia azurea grandiflora (Azure Sage)	Light blue
S. farinacea (Mealycup Sage)	Light blue
S. officinalis (Garden Sage)	Purple
S. Pitcheri (Pitcher Sage)	Deep blue
S. pratensis (Meadow Sage)	Blue
S. uliginosa (Bog Sage)	Pale blue
Scabiosa caucasica	White, lavender
S. japonica (Japanese Scabiosa)	Lavender
Scutellaria alpina lupulina (Skullcap)	Yellow solid
Solidago alpestris (Alpine Goldenrod)	Yellow
S. altissima (Tall Goldenrod)	Yellow
S. canadensis (Canada Goldenrod)	Yellow
Stokesia lævis (Stokes-aster)	Lavender, white
Thalictrum dipterocarpum (Yunnan Meadowrue)	Lilac
Tunica Saxifraga (Tunicflower)	White, blush
Veronica incana (Woolly Speedwell)	Rose-purple
V. maritima (Clump Speedwell)	Violet

PERENNIALS BLOOMING IN SEPTEMBER AND OCTOBER

Aconitum Fischeri (Azure Monkshood)	Pale blue
Anemone japonica (Japanese Anemone)	Various

PERENNIALS BLOOMING IN SEPTEMBER AND OCTOBER—*Continued*

Artemisia lactiflora	White
A. montana (Piedmont Wormwood)	White
Aster cordifolius	Lavender
A. "Mauve Cushion"	White tinged with purple
A. novæ-angliæ varieties	Purple
A. novi-belgii varieties	Purple, various
Campanula carpatica (Carpathian Bell-flower)	Blue, white
Caryopteris incana (Bluebeard)	Lavender
Catananche cærulea (Cupids-dart)	Blue
Chrysanthemum morifolium	Various
Cimicifuga fœtida simplex (Kamchatka Bugbane)	White
Delphinium Belladonna (Delphinium)	Light blue
D. Bellamosum	Deep blue
D. grandiflorum (Siberian Larkspur)	Blue, white
D. hybrids	Various
Dianthus latifolius (Double Cluster Pink)	Crimson
Dicentra eximea (Fringed Bleedingheart)	Rose-red
Echinacea purpurea (Purple Coneflower)	Rose-purple
Eryngium maritimum (Sea-Holly)	Pale blue
Eupatorium cœlestinum (Mistflower)	Blue
Helianthus angustifolius (Swamp Sun-flower)	Yellow
H. atrorubens	Yellow
H. scaberrimus (Prairie Sunflower)	Gold
Kniphofia Uvaria (Torch-lily)	Orange
K. Uvaria Pfitzeri (Bonfire Torch-lily)	Orange-scarlet
Lobelia cardinalis (Cardinal flower)	Scarlet
L. siphilitica (Blue Lobelia)	Blue
Lythrum Salicaria (Loosestrife)	Rose-purple
Melissa officinalis (Balm)	White
Penstemon gloxinioides (Gloxinia Penstemon)	Purple
Physostegia virginiana (False Dragon-head)	Pink
P. "Vivid"	Brighter pink

(*Continued on page 535*)

523

TABULAR LIST OF GARDEN PERENNIALS

Scientific Name	Common Name	Height in Inches	Distance Apart	Season	Color	Remarks
Acanthus mollis	Bearsbreech	36		July–Aug.	Lilac, rose	Deeply toothed leaves. Sun. Drainage.
Achillea filipendulina	Fernleaf Yarrow	36		June–Aug.	Yellow	Ferny foliage. Any soil.
Millefolium	Yarrow	18	12	June, July	White, rose	Will thrive in poor soil.
Ptarmica	Sneezewort	24	spreading	July, Aug.	White	Any soil. Cut flower. Profuse.
Aconitum Fischeri	Azure Monkshood	36	9	Sept., Oct.	Pale blue	Shady places.
autumnale	Autumn Monkshood		spreading			(See A. Fischeri.)
lycoctonum	Wolfbane	36	9	July	Pale yellow	
Napellus	Aconite	24	6	June	Blue, white	
Wilsonii	Violet Monkshood	48	12	September	Blue	
Adonis amurensis	Amur Adonis	12		April	Yellow	
vernalis	Spring Adonis	8–12		April	Yellow	
Æthionema coridifolium	Lebanon Stonecress	9	6	April	Pink	
grandiflorum	Persian Stonecress	9	6	May	Pink	
Ayssum argenteum	Silver Alyssum	15	12	June–Aug.	Yellow	Silvery leaves.
montanum		15	12	May	Yellow	
saxatile	Goldentuft	18	12	May	Yellow	Sheets of yellow.
sax. citrinum	"Lemon Queen" Alyssum	12	12	May	Citron	Rarer color.
sax. compactum	Dwarf Goldentuft	8–10	12	May	Yellow	Most popular.
Anaphalis margaritacea	Pearl Everlasting	12	9	June	White	Gray leaves. Dry spots.
Anchusa Barrelieri	Early Bugloss	24	12	May	Dark blue	
italica	Dropmore Bugloss	36–60	36	June, July	Deep blue	Shade tolerant.
myosotidiflora [Brunnera]	Siberian Bugloss	12–18	12	May–June	Blue	
Anemone hupehensis	Anemone	12	12	Aug.–Sept.	Rosy	Resembles A. japonica. Partial shade.
japonica	Japanese Windflower	36	15	Sept.–Oct.	Various	Popular Fall flower. Partial shade.
Anthemis tinctoria	Yellow Camomile	18	12	June	Yellow	Poor soil.

Aquilegia cærulea	Colorado Columbine	18	12	April	Blue and white	Graceful. Good color. Long spur.
canadensis	Amer. Columbine	18	9	April	Red and yellow	Self sows.
chrysantha	Golden Columbine	24	12	May–Aug.	Yellow	Long spur. Blooms longest of any.
glandulosa		12	9	May–June	Blue and white	
sibirica		12	9	May–June	Blue	
Skinneri	Mexican Columbine	12	9	April	Yellow & Red	Short spurs.
vulgaris	European Columbine	18	12	April	Violet	
vul. nivea	Munstead Columbine	18	12	April	White	
Arabis albida	Wallcress	12	9	April	White	Carpet of bloom.
			spreading			
alpina	Alpine Rockcress	12	9	April	White	More tender.
			spreading			
aubrietioides		12	9	April	Pink	
			spreading			
Artemisia Abrotanum	Southernwood	24		August	Yellow	Common in old gardens.
Absinthium	Common Wormwood	24		August	White, yellow	An everlasting. Grown for white foliage.
albula	Silver King	24–36	18	Summer	White	Fragrant cut flower.
lactiflora	Piedmont Wormwood	48–72	24	Aug.–Sept.	White	Tallest herbaceous Spirea.
montana	Cudweed Wormwood	36		September	White	Moist places.
Purshiana	Beach Wormwood	18		August	Whitish	
Stelleriana		18		June–July	White	
Aruncus sylvester	Goatsbeard	60	24	June–July	White	
Asclepias incarnata	Swamp Milkweed	36		July	Pink	Dry, sunny places.
tuberosa	Butterflyweed	24	12	July–Aug.	Orange	Partial shade. Small, fragrant, spreading plant.
Asperula odorata	Woodruff	12	9	July	White	
Aster Amellus		18	12	July–August	Purple	
cordifolius		48	30	Sept.–Oct.	Lavender	
Mauve Cushion		12	12	Sept.–Nov.	White, tinged with purple	
			spreading			
novæ-angliæ var.		48–72	24	Sept.–Oct.	Purple	
novi-belgii var.		12–96	12–36	Sept.–Oct.	Various	
			spreading			
subcæruleus		15	9	June–July	Blue	
			spreading			

Scientific Name	Common Name	Height in Inches	Distance Apart	Season	Color	Remarks
Astilbe Davidii japonica	David's Astilbe	60	18	June–July	Rosy	Like moist soil.
grandis	Great Astilbe	24	12	June–July	Pink or white	
Aubrietia, in variety		60		June–July	White	
						See list of "Rock and Wall Plants" Comparatively Easy to Grow"
Baptisia australis	Wild-indigo	24–48	24–36	June	Indigo	Lupine-like flowers; handsome
tinctoria	Yellow Wild-indigo	24–48	24–36	June–July	Yellow	foliage.
Bocconia cordata	Plumepoppy	72–96	48	July	Cream-white	Among or back of shrubs.
Boltonia asteroides	White Boltonia	60–72	36 spreading	September	Creamy	Useful in back of large border. Like
latisquama	Violet Boltonia	48–72	24 spreading	September	White	Wild Aster, grayish leaves.
nana	Dwarf Pinkray Boltonia	24	12 spreading	September	Pink	Best of all.
Brunnera macrophylla [Anchusa myosotidiflora]	Siberian Bugloss	12–18	12	May–June	Blue	Sun or shade.
Campanula carpatica	Carpathian Bellflower	8	12	June–Oct.	Blue, white	Edging.
glomerata	Danesblood	18	9	July–Aug.	Violet	
lactiflora	Milky Bellflower	36–74	12–36	June–Sept.	Blue, white	
persicifolia	Peachleaf Bellflower	24–36	9	June–July	Blue, white	Good cut flower.
punctata	Spotted Bellflower	18		June	White	
Caryopteris incana	Bluebeard	36		September	Lavender	Often called Blue Spirea.
Cassia marilandica	Wild Senna	60		July	Yellow	Good background.
Catananche cærulea	Cupid's-dart	18		September	Blue	Dry places. Everlasting.
Centaurea babylonica	Syrian Centaurea	36		June–August	Pale purple	Silver leaves.
gymnocarpa	Velvet Centaurea	18		June	Yellow	White leaves. Edging.
macrocephala	Globe Centaurea	18	18	July	Yellow	
montana	Mountain-bluet	48	12	June–July	Violet	Good cut flower.
Centranthus ruber	Jupitersbeard	18	24	June–Aug.	Crimson, white	Needs lime in soil.

526

Cephalaria alpina	Yellow Cephalaria	72	48	June-Aug	Sulphur	Flowers like Scabiosa.
Cerastium Biebersteinii	Taurus Cerastium	8		June	White	Edging.
tomentosum	Snow-in-summer	6		June	White	Edging, ground cover.
Chelidonium majus	Celandine-poppy	24		May	Yellow	Poppy-like.
Chrysanthemum arcti-cum	Arctic Daisy	6		September	White	Good, dark foliage.
coccineum	Painted Lady (Pyrethrum)	24	12	June	Various	Cut flowers. Pyrethrum in catalogs.
Leucanthemum	Oxeye Daisy	24		June	White	Wild Daisy.
maximum	Shasta Daisy	24		June-Sept.	White	Cut flower.
morifolium (hortorum)	Garden Chrysanthemum	12-48	12-18			
nipponicum	Nippon Oxeye Daisy	24		September	White	Background.
uliginosum	Giant Daisy	60	24	September	White	
			spreading			
Cimicifuga cordifolia	Bugbane	60	24	August	White	Graceful, good cut flower.
foetida simplex	Kamchatka Bugbane	36-60	24-36	September	White	
racemosa	Cohosh Bugbane	48-60	24-36	July	White	
Clematis heracleæfolia	Tube Clematis	36-48	36-48	August	Lavender	
integrifolia	Ground Clematis	18-24	12	June-Oct.	Blue	Border.
recta		48	24	June-July	White	Border, needs support.
Coreopsis grandiflora	Tickseed	36	18	May	Yellow	Border, needs support.
rosea	Rose Coreopsis	12		Aug.-Sept.	Pink	Cut flower. ⎫ Valuable for long
verticillata	Threadleaf Coreopsis	18		July-Aug.	Yellow	Fine foliage. ⎬ blooming habit and
Delphinium Belladonna	Larkspur	24	12	June-Sept.	Light blue	Good cut flower. ⎭ for cut flowers.
Bellamosum		24	12	June-Sept.	Dark blue	
cardinale	Cardinal Larkspur	36	12	August	Scarlet	Rather tender.
grandiflorum	Siberian Larkspur	18	9	July-Sept.	Blue, white	Fine foliage.
hybrids		60	18	June-Sept.	Various	Named varieties.
nudicaule	Orange Larkspur	18	9	July	Orange	Rather tender. Not easy in all gardens.
Zalil	Yellow Larkspur	12-24	9	June-July	Yellow	Tuberous.
Dianthus Allwoodii	Allwoods Pink	12-18	9	June-July	Various	Trifle tender in North.
barbatus	Sweet-william	18	9	June	Various	Always popular.
cæsius	Cheddar Pink	8-12	9	June	July	
			spreading			
cruentus	Blood Pink	4-5	6	July	Scarlet	
			spreading			

527

TABULAR LIST OF GARDEN PERENNIALS—Continued

Scientific Name	Common Name	Height in Inches	Distance Apart	Season	Color	Remarks
Dianthus deltoides	Maiden Pink	6–9	9 spreading	June	Rose	Edging.
latifolius	Double Cluster Pink	12–18	9	July–Oct.	Crimson	Edging.
plumarius	Grass Pink	12–18	12 spreading	June	Various	Edging.
Dicentra eximia	Fringed Bleedingheart	18	12	May–Sept.	Rose	Edging. Sun or partial shade.
spectabilis	Bleedingheart	24–36	36	May	Pink	Likes partial shade.
Dictamnus albus	Gasplant	36	24	May	Rose, white	Does not like transplanting.
Digitalis ambigua	Yellow foxglove	36	24	June–July	Yellow	Perennial.
amb. Isabellina		36	12	June–July	Tawny	Perennial.
Doronicum austriacum	Leopard-bane	24	12	May–June	Yellow	Earliest yellow daisies.
caucasicum		24	9	May–June	Yellow	
plantagineum		24	12	June	Yellow	
Dracocephalum Ruyschiana	Dragonhead	24	9	June–July	Purple	Mintlike.
Echinacea purpurea	Purple Coneflower	36	24	September	Rosy purple	Popular.
Echinops humilis	Low Globethistle	12	9	July	Blue	Globular heads. Spiny plants.
Ritro	Steel Globethistle	36	24	July	Blue	Drainage.
sphaerocephalus	Common Globethistle	60	24	July–August	White	
Erigeron multiradiatus	Fleabane	6		July	Pink	Purple daisies.
speciosus		18	12	July–August	Violet	
Eryngium alpinum	Bluetop Eryngo	24	12	July–August	Amethyst	Prickly foliage, teasel-like heads.
amethystinum	Amethyst Eryngium	24	12	July–August	Amethyst	
maritimum	Seaholly	12	12	July–Sept.	Pale blue	
Oliverianum		36	18	July–August	Blue	
planum		24	12	July–August	Steel blue	
Eupatorium coelestinum	Mistflower	24	12	Sept.–Oct.	Blue	Popular in fall.
purpureum	Joe-pye-weed	72	24	August	Purple	Wet places.
urticefolium	Thoroughwort	36	18	August	White	Common wild. Likes shade. Stands dryness.

Botanical name	Common name			Month	Color	Remarks
Euphorbia corollata	Flowering Spurge	36	12	July	White	Cut flowers. Stands dryness.
Cyparissias	Cypress Spurge	12	9	June	Yellow	Fine foliage.
epithymoides	Cushion Spurge	24	12	May	Yellow	Border foliage.
Filipendula hexapetala	Dropwort	12–24	12	June–July	White	Edging.
palmata	Meadowsweet	24–36	18	July	Pink, white	Plumy heads.
Gaillardia aristata	Blanketflower	12–15	12	May–Oct.	Red, orange	Ever popular. Does not mind poor soil.
Galega officinalis	Goatsrue	36	18	June–July	Purplish blue	
Galium boreale	Bedstraw	12	12	June	White	
verum		12– spreading	12	June–August	Yellow	Tiny flowers in sprays good for cutting.
Geranium armenum	Armenian Cranesbill	24	12	May–July	Purple	
Fremontii	Rocky Mountain C.	12	12	June	Rose-purple	
grandiflorum	Lilac Geranium	12	9	June	Violet	Quite evergreen.
ibericum	Iberian Geranium	12	9	June	Blue, White	
pratense	Meadow Cranesbill	24	18	June	Purple, white	
Geum chiloense flore-pleno	Avens	24	12	July–Sept.	Scarlet	
Lady Stratheden		24	12	July–Sept.	Yellow	These varieties do not like poor, dry soil.
Mrs. Bradshaw		24	12	July–Sept.	Scarlet	
montanum Heldreichii		12	9	May–June	Orange	
Gypsophila paniculata	Babysbreath	30	36	June–July	White	
Helenium autumnale	Sneezeweed	48–60	18	Aug.–Sept.	Yellow	
aut. pumilum		30	12	Aug.–Sept.	Yellow	
Hoopesii		30	12	June	Orange	
Helianthus atrorubens	Sunflower	36–72 spreading	36	September	Yellow, reddish	
angustifolius	Swamp Sunflower	36	24	September	Yellow	Background.
decapetalus	Thinleaf Sunflower	72	36	August	Sulphur	Cut flower.
Maximiliani	Maximilian Sunflower	84	36	October	Gold	Cut flower.
orgyalis		84	36	October	Yellow	Graceful foliage.
scaberrimus	Prairie Sunflower	48	24	Sept.–Oct.	Gold	Semi-double usually.
Heliopsis Pitcheriana	Pitcher Heliopsis	36	36	July–August	Orange	
scabra excelsa		36	36	July–August	Orange	

Good for back of a large border but must be watched lest weaker plants are smothered.

529

Scientific Name	Common Name	Height in Inches	Distance Apart	Season	Color	Remarks
Helleborus niger	Christmas Rose	12	12	Winter	White	
Hemerocallis aurantiaca	Orange Daylily	36		June	Orange	Good for border or waterside. Like semi-shade. Narrow, grass-like leaves.
Dumortierii		18		June	Bright orange	
flava	Lemon Daylily	24	24	June	Canary	
fulva	Tawny Daylily	36		July	Bronze	
Middendorffii	Amur Daylily	24		June	Gold	
Thunbergii	Japanese Daylily	48		July	Canary	
Hesperis matronalis	Rocket	36	12	June–July	Purple	
Heuchera sanguinea	Coralbells	12–24	9	July	Crimson	
Hibiscus Moscheutos	Rose Mallow	48–60	36	Aug.–Sept.	Pink, crimson, white	Wet or normal soil.
Iberis sempervirens	Evergreen Candytuft	9–12		March–April	White	
Hosta caerulea	Funkia, Plantainlily	24–36	24	July–August	Blue	Good for edging plant.
japonica		12–24	12	July–August	Pale lavender	
plantaginea		24	24	July–August	White	
Sieboldiana		30	24	June–July	Mauve	
Iris						See descriptive list. Probably the hardiest.
Kniphofia foliosa	Early Torchlily	24–36	18	June–July	Orange and yellow	Showy, popular, needs winter protection.
rufa	Torchlily	18	12	June	Yellow	
Uvaria		36–48	18	Aug.–Sept.	Orange	
U. var. Pfitzeriana	Bonfire Torchlily	36	18	September	Orange-scarlet	Trifle tender.
Lavandula Spica	Spike Lavender	24	24	August	Lavender	
vera	True Lavender	12–24	12	July	Blue	
Liatris graminifolia	Grassleaf Gayfeather	24		August	Rose-purple	Bloom from top of spike downwards. Trying color. Narrow spikes. Needs moisture at root.
pycnostachya	Cattail Gayfeather	48	12	Aug.–Sept.	Rose-purple	
scariosa		24		August	Purple	
spicata	Spike Gayfeather	24–60	9–12	August	Purple	
Limonium Gmelini	Statice			August	Lavender	Everlastings. Dainty flower sprays.
latifolium	Bigleaf Statice	20		August	Lavender	
tataricum	Tartarian Statice			August	Lavender	

Linaria macedonica	Macedonian Linaria	36	9	June	Yellow	Gray leaves.
Linum flavum	Golden Flax	12	12	June–August	Gold	
narbonense	Narbonne Flax	24	12	May	Blue	Evergreen.
perenne	Perennial Flax	18	12	June–August	Blue	Evergreen.
perenne album	White Perennial Flax	18	12	June–August	White	Grows naturally in wet soil but stands ordinary soil.
Lobelia cardinalis	Cardinalflower	24–36	9	Aug.–Oct.	Scarlet	
Lupinus polyphyllus	Washington Lupine	36–48	12–24	June	Various	Very desirable.
Lychnis chalcedonica	Maltese Cross	24–36	12	July–August	Scarlet	Popular. Prolific.
Flos Jovis	Flower-of-jove	18	12	June	Rose	
viscaria	Clammy Campion	12	9	June	Magenta	
Lysimachia clethroides	Clethra Loosestrife	24	1	July–August	White	Excellent.
Meconopsis cambrica	Welsh-poppy	12	9	June	Yellow	Rare. Desirable.
Mertensia virginica	Virginia Bluebells	18	9	May	Blue	Best in shade. Dies to ground.
Monarda didyma	Beebalm	36	12	July	Scarlet	Popular. Stands considerable shade.
Myosotis alpestris	Alpine Forget-me-not	6	spreading	June	Blue	
dissitiflora	Swiss Forget-me-not	9		May	Blue	Always admired.
scorpioides palustris	True Forget-me-not	9		June	Deep blue	
Nepeta Mussini	Mussin Catmint	12		May–Sept.	Lavender blue	Edging.
Œnothera caespitosa	Tufted Sundrops	4		May	White	Leaves like dandelion.
fruticosa	Sundrops	18		June–July	Yellow	
missouriensis	Ozark Sundrops	12		June–Aug.	Yellow	Very large flowers and seed pods. Prostrate with flower 4″ in diameter.
Pæonia	Peony	18–48		May–June	White, pink, red	See descriptive list.
Papaver alpinum	Alpine Poppy	8–10		June	Yellow	
nudicaule	Iceland Poppy	12		June–Oct.	Yellow, orange, white	
orientale	Oriental Poppy	36		June	Various	
pilosum	Olympic Poppy	24		June–Oct.	Orange	Small, but profuse.
Penstemon barbatus	Pink Beauty	36	12	June–July	Scarlet	Long tubular flowers. Popular.
grandiflorus	Shell-leaf Penstemon	24	spreading	July	Purple	
laevigatus	Smooth Penstemon	24		June	Rosy lilac	
digitalis	Foxglove Penstemon	36		June–July	Purple	(All good for cut flowers.)
Torreyi	Torrey Penstemon	36		June–July	Scarlet	Trifle tender.

Scientific Name	Common Name	Height in Inches	Distance Apart	Season	Color	Remarks
Phlox Arendsii	Arends Phlox	24	9	May–June	Various	Wild, but splendid in cultivation.
divaricata	Blue Phlox	12	9	May	Lavender	
paniculata	Garden Phlox	24	12	July–August	Various	Smooth leaves, earlier than standard types of garden Phlox. Disease resistant.
suffruticosa (glaberrima)	Smooth Phlox	24	12	June–Sept.	Various	
Physostegia virginiana var. Vivid	False-dragonhead	36–60	18	July–Sept.	Pink	Good cut flower.
Platycodon grandiflorum Mariesii	Balloonflower	18	12	July–Oct.	Brighter pink	Superior.
		24	12	May–Oct.	Violet, white	
Polemonium ceruleum reptans	Greek-valerian	18	9	June	Blue, white	Flat flowers in spikes.
		9	9 spreading	May	Blue	
Potentilla nepalensis Warrensii	Nepal Cinquefoil	18	9	June–August	Rose	
		24	12	June–August	Yellow	
Primula acaulis auricula	English Primrose	6		April–May	Various	
		12		June	Various	
denticulata	Himalayan Primrose	10		May	Violet	
japonica	Japanese Primrose	24	12	June	White to crimson	Moist soil. Cool places.
polyantha		6–10	9	April–May	Various in combination	
pulverulenta	Silverdust Primrose	30	12	June	Rosy purple	
Sieboldii		10–12	6	May	White, rose, purple	
veris	Cowslip Primrose	9		April–May	Yellow	(See P. acaulis.)
vulgaris		6–12	9	April	Purple	
Pulmonaria officinalis (maculata) saccharata	Bethlehem Sage	6–18	9	April–May	Reddish violet	
Pyrethrum roseum						See Chrysanthemum coccineum.
Romneya Coulteri	Canyon Poppy	48		June	White	Large poppy.

		Height	Spacing	Season	Color	Remarks
Rudbeckia laciniata	Golden Glow	60		July–Sept.	Orange	Cut flower. Double.
maxima	Great Coneflower	60		June–Sept.	Yellow	
nitida	Autumn Sun	60		August–Oct.	Primrose	
purpurea						*See* Echinacea.
speciosa	Showy Coneflower	36	12	July–Oct.	Golden	
subtomentosa	Sweet Coneflower	48	18	July–Aug.	Golden	
Salvia azurea grandiflora	Azure Sage	48	24	Aug.–Sept.	Light blue	Trifle leggy.
argentea	Silver Sage	24–48		June	Rosy white	
farinacea	Mealycup Sage	36	12	Aug.–Sept.	Light blue	Half-hardy.
Pitcheri	Pitcher Sage	48	24	Aug.–Sept.	Deep blue	
pratensis	Meadow Sage	24	12	June–Aug.	Blue	
uliginosa	Bog Salvia	36	18	Aug.–Sept.	Pale blue	Similar to S. azurea.
Scabiosa caucasica		24	12	June–Sept.	White, lavender	Good cut flower.
graminifolia		18	9	June–July	Violet	Silver leaves.
japonica	Japanese Scabiosa	24	12	June–Sept.	Lavender	
Scutellaria alpina lupulina	Skullcap	9	6	August	Yellow	
baicalensis	Baikal Skullcap	12	6	July	Blue	
Sidalcea candida	Prairiemallow	36		July	White	
malvaeflora	Checkerbloom	12–60		June–July	Rose-pink	Fringed petals.
mal. Listeri	Satin Checkerbloom	4–18		June–July	Rose-pink	
Solidago alpestris	Alpine Goldenrod	48–72		August	Yellow	
altissima	Tall Goldenrod	24		September	Yellow	Popular wild flowers worthy of cultivation. Stand drought.
caesia	Wreath Goldenrod	36		August	Yellow	
canadensis	Canada Goldenrod	36		September	Yellow	
rigida	Stiff Goldenrod	60		September	Bright yellow	
Virgaurea	Goldwings					*See* S. grandiflora.
Stachys Betonica grandiflora	Betony	12–36		June	Purple	
lanata	Woolly Betony	12	6	July	Purple	White, silky leaves.
Statice Armeria	Thrift	6	9	June–July	Pink	Good for edgings. Useful for sea-shore planting. *See also* Liminium.
Laucheana		9	9	June–July	Rose	
montana (Alpina)	Rosalie Thrift	8		June	Pale pink	
plantaginea (dianthoides)		18		June	Pink	
Stokesia laevis	Stokes-aster	12–24	12	July–August	Lavender, white	Good cut flower.

Scientific Name	Common Name	Height in Inches	Distance Apart	Season	Color	Remarks
Teucrium Chamædrys	Germander	12		July	Rosy purple	
Thalictrum aquilegi-	Columbine Meadowrue	12–36	18	May–June	White, purple	
folium						Dainty foliage; plumy flowers.
dipterocarpum	Yunnan Meadowrue	48	18	Aug.–Sept.	Lilac	Excellent border plants.
glaucum	Dusty Meadowrue	24	12	June–July	Yellow	
minus	Low Meadowrue	18	12	June–July	Yellow	
polygamum	Tall Meadowrue	36	24	May	White	
Trollius europæus	Globeflower	24	12	April–June	Yellow	Very popular. Excellent cut flow-
asiaticus		24	12	May–June	Orange	ers. Need moist
sinensis		24	12	July	Orange-yellow	soil.
Ledebouri		36	18	June	Golden	Flat flower.
Tunica Saxifraga	Tunicflower	6	6	July–Oct.	White, blush	Edging.
Valeriana officinalis	Valerian	36–60	12	June–July	Blush white	Fragrant, subject to plant lice.
Verbena canadensis		9–12	spreading 12	June–Sept.	Red-purple	
Veronica incana	Woolly Speedwell	12	spreading 6	July–Aug.	Rosy purple	Effective mat of gray foliage.
maritima	Clump Speedwell	24	9	August	Violet	
spicata	Spike Speedwell	12	9	June–July	Purple	
spuria	Bastard Speedwell	18	9	June–July	Violet	
virginica	Culvers-physic	48–60		July	White	
Viola cornuta	Tufted Pansy	6–10	6	April–Oct.	Various	Unexcelled garden sorts.
Yucca filamentosa	Adams-Needle	72	36	June–July	White	Coarse; use as accents in shrub-bery.

534

PERENNIALS BLOOMING IN SEPTEMBER AND OCTOBER

(Continued from page 523)

Platycodon grandiflorum (Balloon Flower)	Blue, white
P. Mariesii	Violet, white
Polygonum affine (Fleeceflower)	Rose
P. sachalinense (Sacaline)	Greenish
Rudbeckia laciniata (Golden Glow)	Orange
R. maxima (Great Coneflower)	Yellow
R. nitida (Autumn Sunflower)	Primrose
R. speciosa (Showy Coneflower)	Golden
Salvia Greggii (Autumn Sage)	Red
S. nemorosa (Violet Sage)	Purple
S. patens (Gentian Sage)	Deep blue
Scabiosa caucasica (Scabiosa)	White, lavender
S. japonica (Japanese Scabiosa)	Lavender
Solidago cæsia (Wreath Goldenrod)	Yellow
S. rigida (Stiff Goldenrod)	Yellow
S. Virgaurea (Goldwings)	Bright yellow
Vernonia noveboracensis (Ironweed)	Purple
Viola cornuta (Tufted Pansy)	Various
V. odorata (Sweet Violet)	Violet

XIII

Bulbs, Corms, and Tubers

SPRING-FLOWERING BULBS

In the pageantry of spring and summer, the bulbs play an important part. From the blooming of the first diminutive snowdrop in early March until the last of the late-blooming lilies has faded, there is an ever-changing succession. The fleeting beauty of the snowdrops, the scillas and the muscari gives way to the far-flung loveliness of the narcissus, and, as the season advances, the tulips, in all their flamboyant beauty, hold the center of the stage.

There are few flowers which give as generously of their bloom and beauty as do the bulbs, and they demand little in the way of care and cultivation. The majority of our spring bulbs will thrive under widely varying conditions of soil and climate, and many of them, when once they have become well established, will increase in beauty from year to year.

NARCISSUS

The Narcissi, with their gay and lovely flowers, usher in the pageantry of spring. Long drifts of them in the garden, masses of them along the edge of the woodland, grassy slopes clothed with them, gay pots of them in the windows, push-carts laden with them on the street corners—one sees them everywhere. And one loves them none the less for the fact that they are to be found in such gay profusion!

Hardy, dependable, completely adaptable, they demand almost nothing in the way of care and cultivation, and they give generously of their bloom and beauty throughout the spring—flowering blithely on, year after year.

Long drifts of Narcissus, piquant little English Daisies, and the myriad golden flowers of Forsythia bordering a flagstone path.

Narcissi are divided into several very definite groups, and with a careful selection of varieties the season of bloom may be extended over a period of many weeks.

Classification of Varieties

(The central tubular part of the flower is called the trumpet, crown or cup. The perianth segments form the corolla from which the trumpet, crown or cup rises.)

Group 1. Narcissus Pseudo-Narcissus—Trumpet Narcissus. In this class the trumpet is longer than the perianth. Coloring all yellow, all white, or bicolor.

Varieties of Merit

Emperor, Empress, King Alfred, Van Waveren's Giant, Mrs. E. H. Krelage, Ærolite, La Vestale.

Group 2. Narcissus incomparabilis—Trumpet is one-third or slightly more than one-third the length of the perianth and is somewhat flaring.

Varieties of Merit

Sir Watkin, Lucifer, Will Scarlet, Dick Welband, John Evelyn, Crœsus, Bernardino, Francisca Drake.

Group 3. Narcissus Barrii—Very short trumpet, less than one-third the length of the perianth. Coloring all yellow or cream with bright orange cup.

Varieties of Merit

Firetail, Mrs. Barclay, Mrs. Walter Brewster, Early Surprise.

Group 4. Narcissus Leedsii—Short trumpet of palest primrose color or white.

Varieties of Merit

Louis Capet, Silver Star, Hera, White Lady, Mrs. Langtry, Lord Kitchener, Evangeline.

Group 5. Triandrus Hybrids—Dwarf in habit, but producing flowers of considerable size with long trumpets.

Varieties of Merit

Thalia, Gertrude, Agnes Harvey, Madonna.

Group 6. Narcissus Jonquilla—Grasslike foliage, small sweet-scented flowers, single or in clusters.

Varieties of Merit

Odorus, Orange Queen, General Pershing, Golden Sceptre, White Wedgewood.

Group 7. Tazetta Hybrids—Bunch-flowered or polyanthus Narcissus. Small, crowned, sweet-scented flowers with broad leaves. Not hardy out of doors, except in the extreme South. Unexcelled for forcing.

Varieties of Merit

Paper-White grandiflora, Grand Soleil d'Or.

Group 8. Narcissus poeticus—Extremely short cup or eye, brilliantly colored; waxy white perianth.

Varieties of Merit

Ornatus, King Edward VII, Glory of Lisse, Horace.

Group 9. Botanical Species—Well suited to the rock garden.

Varieties of Merit

N. Bulbocodium in variety (Hoop-petticoat Narcissus), N. triandrus in variety, N. cyclamineus (Cyclamen-flowered Narcissus).

Time of Planting: When grown under natural conditions narcissi produce their new root growth in the late summer and early autumn, and by the time the ground becomes frozen a strong root system has been developed. The ideal time for planting is during the dormant or rest period which occurs after the foliage has died down and before active root growth commences. If old clumps of narcissi are to be lifted and divided, it should preferably be done at this season. Bulbs which have been purchased from commercial growers are usually shipped early in the autumn and should be planted as soon as possible after their arrival, in order that full advantage may be taken of the good growing weather. If, for some unavoidable reason, planting must be delayed until late in the season, the ground should be kept mulched with fresh manure to prevent it from freezing and the mulch should be replaced again after the bulbs have been planted, in order to give them an opportunity to make as much root growth as possible. Late planting is never very successful. Both the quantity and quality of the spring bloom are dependent to a considerable extent upon the root development which the bulb has made the previous autumn. Good root development means good flowers, other conditions being favorable.

Method of Planting: The depth of planting will vary according to the size of the bulb. A generally accepted rule is to cover each bulb with twice its own depth of soil. The small bulbs of the Jonquil type should, therefore, be planted from 1 to 3 inches deep, while the very large bulbs of some of the Trumpet varieties should be planted at a depth of 6 inches or more. The smaller varieties should be spaced from 3 to 4 inches apart, the larger varieties from 6 to 8 inches apart. If the bulbs are to be planted in well-prepared soil in a garden bed, a trowel or a dibble may be used to open the hole. When using a dibble care must be taken to see that no air space is left below the bulb as it is very easy for the bulb to become hung in the hole. This danger may be avoided by placing a handful of loose earth in the bottom of the hole, making sure that the bulb rests upon it. This precaution is not necessary if a trowel is used for planting. If bulbs are to be planted in an area of sod, or in a woodland, the digging of the holes is often very tedious and difficult. The work can be done more rapidly and efficiently with a mattock than with any other tool. A sharp stroke with the mattock should be used to pry up a piece of sod; it should not be torn entirely loose. The bulb is placed in the hole and the sod is then pressed back into position.

Soil Requirements: Narcissi may be grown successfully in almost any type of soil. A well-drained, sandy loam is considered ideal. An application of well-rotted manure is beneficial in increasing the fertility of the soil and in improving its structure, but fresh manure should never be used as it is apt to cause serious injury. Some varieties of narcissus are more sensitive than others, but it is wise never to use manure in any form until it has become thoroughly rotted. Bone meal is the most satisfactory fertilizer for narcissus and may be applied at the rate of ½ pound to every 25 square feet, being worked into the upper 2 or 3 inches of soil in the autumn.

The foliage of narcissus bulbs should not be removed until it has turned a yellowish brown and has almost completely died down. If the bulbs have been planted in an area of sod, the grass should not be cut until the foliage of the bulbs has matured. If the yellowing foliage becomes unsightly in the garden, the leaves may be braided or rolled into a small mass and tucked under the foliage of neighboring plants.

Narcissus bulbs increase very rapidly, and when the bulbs have become too crowded, they should be lifted, divided and re-planted as soon as the foliage has ripened. In naturalistic plantings, where the size and perfection of the flowers are not matters of great importance, the bulbs may be left undisturbed for a period of many years. In the garden, it is advisable to lift them every 6 or 8 years, as the blooms have a tendency to become smaller, and the bulbs are less thrifty when they have become over-crowded.

TULIP

There are few flowers which offer the gardener a greater opportunity for color harmonies than do the tulips. In the skillful hand of the artist, they may be used to create the most subtle and beautiful compositions. Yet how often do we see them used without any appreciation or feeling for their potential beauty—stiff geometric beds of them, glaring, inharmonious color compositions, long borders of them in marshalled array! In the hands of a gardener who is not an artist and who has no appreciation of form and color they are, indeed, dangerous material.

Tulips are at their best when grown in herbaceous beds or borders in combination with other spring flowers. In such a setting, their stiff, precise formality is mitigated and they add greatly to the charm of the composition. They are lovely when planted with mertensia and columbines, blue flax, phlox divaricata and violas, and they may be used in lavish quantities in the spring garden.

Tulips are divided into several distinct groups:

Duc Van Thol Group

The earliest of all tulips to come into bloom. Flowers small and slightly pointed; both single and double forms; height 6 to 8 inches; colors red, yellow, orange, pink, white, violet, red, and yellow.

Single Early Group

Blooms slightly larger than those of the Duc Van Thol group; flowering period a week to ten days later. Wide color range. The flowers combine well with such low-growing plants as arabis alpina,

Photo. J. Horace McFarland Co.   Thomas W. Sears, Landscape Architect

Tulips in the Formal Garden

Photograph by Walter Beebe Wilder

Snowdrops in Early Spring

myosotis, aubrietia, phlox divaricata, and the Siberian wallflower. An unusually beautiful combination for the spring border is a planting of the single early tulip, General de Wet, with Leedsii narcissus, mertensia, phlox divaricata and the Siberian wallflower.

Varieties of Merit: La Reine; Cottage Maid; Flamingo, in shades of pink; General de Wet, one of the finest of all orange tulips; Diana; White Beauty and White Swan; King of the Yellows and Yellow Queen.

DOUBLE EARLY GROUP

Varieties of Merit: Boule de Neige, Murillo, Electra, Prince of Orange, Tearose.

MENDEL GROUP

The Mendel tulip is the result of a cross between a Duc van Thol tulip and a Darwin tulip, and this new type possesses many of the desirable qualities of both parents. It has the wide color range of the Darwins and the earlier blooming habit of the Duc van Thol, being intermediate between the two. It is excellent for forcing, and some of the recently introduced varieties are lovely in the garden.

Varieties of Merit: Early Beauty, April Queen.

DARWIN GROUP

Among the Darwins we find many of our most beautiful tulips. Tall and stately, lovely in form and exquisite in coloring, the Darwin tulips are held in high esteem by countless gardeners. They were first introduced in 1890 and have gained rapidly in popularity. The Darwins were originated by an amateur gardener in northern France, having been raised from seed of the Bybloem group. The large, globular flowers are of fine substance and are borne on strong, stiff stems, often reaching a height of 2 to 2½ feet.

Varieties of Merit: Pink and Rose: Princess Elizabeth, Aphrodite, Flamingo, Princess Mary, Mermaid, Lyon Rose.

Purple, Violet and Lavender: The Bishop, Anton Mauve, Blue Eagle, Dream, Humming Bird, Gwen Lee.

Carmine to Red: Prince of Wales, King Harold, Feu Brilliant.

White: Zwanenburg.

COTTAGE GROUP

There is wide variance among the members of this group both in height and in the form of the flower, the flowers of some varieties being decidedly pointed and others being globular. The Cottage tulips bloom with the Darwins and they may be used in pleasant combination with them. The bulbs will frequently give good bloom over a period of several years. In this group we find our best late-blooming yellow and orange tulips.

Varieties of Merit: Inglescombe Pink, Mrs. Kerrell, Grenadier, Orange King, Avis Kennicott, Mrs. Moon, Moonlight.

BREEDER GROUP

The beautiful Breeder tulips bring the season to a close. The flowers are of marvelous substance and the colors range from bronze and wine red to dusty purple, mauve, and mahogany.

Varieties of Merit: Apricot, Bacchus, Bronze Queen, Godet Parfait, Louis XIV, Velvet King, and William the Silent.

There are a number of other groups which are of minor importance, such as the Rembrandt, Parrot, Bizarre and Lily-flowered Groups.

SPECIES TULIPS

Among the lovely species tulips, *T. Kaufmanniana* and *T. Clusiana* are the best known.

T. Kaufmanniana, known as the Waterlily tulip, is one of the most exquisite members of this group and it is excellent for naturalization or for use in the rock garden. It is one of the earliest of all tulips to bloom, and the dainty, wide, flaring flowers are a soft primrose yellow, touched with pink. Various hybrids have recently been introduced.

T. Clusiana is also excellent for the rock garden. The delicate, pointed flowers, borne on slender stems, are white, with a dash of crimson on the outer side of each petal. It is a dainty, exquisite thing, excellent for forcing and lovely for cutting.

Culture: Although tulips thrive best in a sunny location they will also do well in very light or partial shade, and in some cases the colors seem to be more permanent when thus protected from the full sun. Heavy shade is not desirable, as the stems have a tendency to bend towards the light and become weak and floppy.

Planting: The depth of planting will vary somewhat according to the type of soil. In a medium-heavy soil the bulbs should be planted so that the tips are approximately 3 inches below the surface; in light sandy soil they may be planted slightly deeper. The bulbs should all be planted at the same depth in order that the flowers may produce uniform bloom. The Early-flowering varieties may be spaced 4 inches apart, the later varieties, such as the Darwins and the Breeders, 6 inches apart. If tulips are to be planted in drifts in the herbaceous border either a trowel or a dibble may be used. If planting is done with a dibble, care must be taken to see that the base of the bulb is resting upon firm soil and that there is no pocket of air beneath it. When a large bed or border is to be planted entirely with tulips, it is a wise plan to remove the upper 4 to 6 inches of top soil. The floor of the bed may then be slightly loosened and raked until the surface is level. The bulbs may be placed in position, being pressed firmly into the soil, and the top soil may then be carefully replaced. This method will assure absolute uniformity of planting, which is necessary if precise regularity is desired.

Tulips should preferably be planted between the middle of October and the middle of November. If the bulbs are planted too early in the autumn, they are apt to start into active growth and will suffer a severe set-back during the winter. Tulips should, therefore, not be planted as early as narcissus. It is important, however, that the bulbs be planted far enough in advance of freezing weather to enable them to make sufficient root growth. A strong vigorous root system produced during the autumn has a very direct effect upon the quality of the bloom the following spring. If planting must be delayed until very late in the season, the same procedure may be followed as that recommended for narcissus.

Soil: The ideal soil for tulips is a light, fertile, well-drained loam. Fresh manure should never be used in the preparation of tulip beds. Well-rotted manure or compost may be used in fairly liberal quantities and bone meal may be applied at the rate of ½ pound per 25 square feet.

Winter Mulch: No covering should be put on the beds until after the ground is frozen. See section on Winter Mulches, page 446.

Care after blooming: Tulips will produce their best bloom the spring following planting. Some varieties will bloom well over a period of several years, while other varieties deteriorate rapidly and show a decided decline in vigor after the first season. If tulips are planted in a bed with herbaceous perennials or as a foreground to a shrubbery border the foliage may be allowed to die down naturally. If quick-growing annuals, such as the Shirley poppies or annual larkspur, are seeded among the tulips early in the season the yellowing of the tulip foliage will hardly be noticed. If tulips are planted in solid beds or borders, and if the space which they occupy is desired for other plantings, the bulbs may be lifted very carefully after blooming, the roots and leaves remaining intact, and they may then be heeled in in a partially shaded spot. They should be left thus, to ripen. When the leaves have turned brown and the bulbs are thoroughly mature they may be placed in storage until planting time in the autumn. The bulbs should be stored in a cool, dark, dry place.

TULIPS FOR SOUTHERN GARDENS

It has always been a matter of great regret to Southern gardeners that tulips were among the flowers which would not thrive in Southern climates, and for generations those who have gardened in the South have had to be content with miserably weak and floppy specimens, or have had to forgo their beauty entirely.

It is only very recently that the discovery has been made that tulips may be grown quite as successfully in the South as in the North, provided that the bulbs are placed in cold storage for a period of several months before they are planted. If they are held in storage at a temperature of 45 degrees for a period of 6 months previous to planting, excellent results may be obtained. The bulbs may be planted during December, January and early February, and in the case of late plantings, active growth will begin almost immediately. If this method is followed an abundance of tall, strong-stemmed bloom may be had.

As soon as the foliage has died down and the bulbs have ripened they should be lifted and placed in storage. Some bulbs will flower well for several seasons if accorded this treatment, while others deteriorate rapidly and must be replaced by new stock, which has been specially prepared for Southern planting.

HYACINTH

Hyacinths lack entirely the grace and charm of the tulips and narcissus and it is difficult to find a place in the garden where they may be used with a truly artistic effect. If planted as a foreground for shrubbery border they sometimes present a striking display of color, and they are more effective in such a location than in the garden.

The bulbs should be planted in the autumn between the middle of September and the middle of October. The depth of

Narcissus in an Old Orchard

planting will vary according to the size of the bulb. The tip of the bulb should be approximately 3 inches below the surface if the soil is of a heavy texture; 5 inches in a light, sandy soil. They may be set from 6 to 8 inches apart.

Hyacinths will produce good bloom in any type of moderately fertile soil provided that it is well drained.

After the bulbs have flowered the foliage should be allowed to ripen. If desired, the same treatment may be accorded the bulbs as that recommended for tulips.

SMALL, SPRING-FLOWERING BULBS

Among the small, spring-flowering bulbs we have the Snowdrops (Galanthus), Winter Aconites (Eranthus) Glory-of-the-Snow (Chionodoxa), Squills (Scilla sibirica), the Grape Hyacinths (Muscari), and the Crocus.

These early harbingers of spring hold a very special place in our affections, and they may be planted in drifts along the edge of the flower borders, or they may be naturalized in great masses. Gay and jaunty, winsome and charming, they usher in the spring. There is no flower more appealing than the Winter Aconite with its little Elizabethan ruff of green leaves; within its golden cup it seems to hold the very promise of spring.

All of these small bulbs should be planted during the early autumn. They may be spaced from 3 to 4 inches apart and the depth of planting will vary from 2 to 3 inches, depending upon the size of the bulb. After they have once become established they will increase rapidly, and they may be left undisturbed for many years. They thrive well in any type of well-drained soil and require no care or attention after they have been planted.

SUMMER-FLOWERING BULBS

Anemones (Anemone coronaria). The anemones are delightful for cutting and may be had in a wide variety of colorings—white, deep purple, lavender, and brilliant scarlet. The cup-shaped flowers are borne on slender, graceful stems which attain a height of from 12 to 15 inches. The St. Brigid strain is considered one of the finest.

Exposure: An eastern exposure is ideal, where they may be protected from afternoon sun.

Soil Requirements: A soil mixture of 1 part loam, 1 part leafmold and 1 part sand is considered ideal.

Propagation: Tubers. Care must be taken to see that the tubers are not planted upside down. The top of the tuber may be recognized by its fuzzy appearance. The bottom of the tuber is usually pointed.

Culture: In warm climates the tubers may be planted in the open ground from August to November. In sections where the climate is severe, anemones may be planted in coldframes or they may be grown in the greenhouse.

Tuberous-rooted Begonias. There are many widely varying types of tuberous-rooted begonias which are decorative and lovely both in the garden and as potted plants. Some types are of a semi-trailing habit and are especially well suited for use in hanging baskets. The flowers are obtainable in a wide variety of colorings—white, salmon, yellow, flame-orange, apricot, and scarlet.

TYPES OF MERIT

Double Hanging Type
New Large-flowered hybrids
Camellia-flowered Type
Double Rosebud Type
Giant Single Type
Single Crested Type
Single Frilled Type
Single Narcissiflora Type
Multiflora Nana

Exposure: Semi-shade and a somewhat sheltered position are essential for success in growing tuberous-rooted begonias. They must be planted where direct sunlight cannot reach them.

Soil Requirements: A coarse, loose, porous soil, perfectly drained and containing a high percentage of leafmold, is considered ideal for tuberous-rooted begonias. Ordinary garden soil may be improved by adding liberal quantities of leafmold or peat, sand and well-rotted cow manure.

Propagation: Tuberous-rooted begonias may be grown either from seed or from tubers. The seed should be sown in the greenhouse during February or March in small seed pans or in flats. A layer of coarse gravelly sand should be placed in the bottom of the flat in order to insure good drainage and above this should be spread a layer

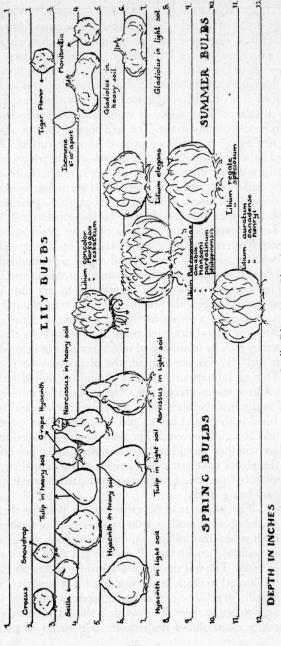

Bulb Planting Chart

1 inch in depth of a fairly coarse mixture of 2 parts leafmold and 1 part peat moss. The same mixture should be put through a very fine sieve to provide a surface layer about ⅛ of an inch deep. This surface layer should be made smooth but it should not be pressed down, as it is desirable that it should be of a spongy character in order that the delicate roots of the young seedlings may penetrate easily. The pans or flats should be placed in water until the surface of the soil has become thoroughly moist. The seed should then be sown, and it should neither be covered nor pressed into the surface. A pane of glass and a sheet of paper should be placed over the pan, which should be kept in a warm, dark place. If the night temperature ranges between 65 and 75 degrees F. the seeds will germinate quickly. If the night temperature drops much below 65 degrees, germination will be much slower and the results will be less satisfactory. The paper should be removed as soon as the seeds have germinated and the glass should be removed 3 or 4 days later. The young seedlings are rather delicate, and their growth and vigor are dependent upon a warm temperature, uniform moisture, and protection from direct sunlight. The seedlings must never be allowed to dry out. When the third leaf has developed, the seedlings may be transplanted into shallow flats containing a somewhat coarse mixture of 2 parts leafmold and 1 part peat. Good drainage must be provided. As the seedlings develop, they may be transplanted into other flats or into pots.

When early flowers are desired, the plants may be grown from tubers. During January or February the tubers should be placed in open flats in a warm greenhouse. They should be moistened occasionally and when the buds begin to sprout, they should be planted in flats filled with peat. They should be spaced about 3 inches apart and should be lightly covered. The flats should be placed in a warm, light place and they should be kept uniformly moist but not too wet. When the plants have attained a height of 3 to 4 inches, they may be transplanted into pots, a potting soil of 2 parts coarse leafmold and 1 part loam being used.

Culture: The plants may be grown on in pots, or they may be shifted to the open ground as soon as all danger of frost is over. In the autumn when the foliage has turned yellow, water should be gradually withheld and when all growth has died down the tubers should be lifted. The soil should be washed from the tubers and they should be allowed to ripen in the sunlight for several days until they are thoroughly dry. Great care must be taken in handling the tubers in order not to bruise them. The old stem should be entirely removed until healthy tissue shows underneath. If particles of stem are left attached to the tuber they are likely to cause decay. During the winter the tubers should be stored in a cool, dry place.

Canna. Perennial herbs, natives of the tropics and sub-tropics. Cannas have in recent years fallen somewhat into disfavor, perhaps because of their use in Victorian times for mass planting in public places. The new hybrids, however, come in striking shades of apricot and watermelon pink, and make excellent strong accents for the back of the large perennial border.

Climatic Range: As they are not hardy in the North, they should not be set out until all danger of frost is past.

Soil Requirements: Of easy cultivation in fertile, moist, deeply-prepared soil.

Culture: Old roots should be divided in the spring with a sharp knife, allowing a bud to each piece. Set 12 to 24 inches apart and from 3 to 5 inches deep. Lift in the fall when the tops have been killed by frost and store like dahlias. For pests and diseases, see Chapter XXXIII.

DAHLIA

There are few flowers which offer us such variety in form and coloring as do the dahlias. All the glorious, translucent tones of a sunset sky, all the warm rosy hues of a summer's dawn are to be found among them, and they bring a richness and a glory to the late summer garden that nothing else can equal. The tall-growing varieties may be used very delightfully at the rear of the herbaceous border, the dwarf sorts are more suitable for bedding purposes, and all types and varieties are invaluable for the cutting garden.

Among the most beautiful of all dahlias both for bloom in the garden and for cutting are the large single varieties such as Newport Wonder and Tango Century. As their decorative value becomes more appreciated they will be more widely grown.

CLASSIFICATION

Dahlias are grouped into several distinct classes according to the form and size of the flower. The classification adopted by the American Dahlia Society is as follows:

Class 1, Incurved Cactus. Fully double flower with the margins of the majority of the floral rays revolute (rolled or quilled) for one-half or more of their length; the floral rays tending to curve toward the center of the flower.

Class 2, Recurved and Straight Cactus. Fully double flowers with the margins of the majority of the floral rays revolute for one-half of their length or more; the floral rays being recurved or straight.

Class 3, Peony. Open-centered flowers with not more than three rows of ray florets regardless of form or number of florets, with the addition of smaller curled or twisted floral rays around the disk.

Class 4, Semi-Cactus. Fully double flowers with the margins of the majority of the floral rays revolute for less than one-half their length.

Class 5, Formal Decorative. Fully double flowers, rays generally broad, either pointed or rounded at tips, with outer floral rays tending to recurve and central floral rays tending to be cupped, all floral rays in somewhat regular arrangement.

Class 6, Informal Decorative. Fully double flower, floral rays generally long, twisted or pointed and usually irregular in arrangement.

Class 7, Ball. Fully double flowers, ball-shaped or slightly flattened, floral rays in spiral arrangement, blunt or rounded at tips and quilled or with markedly involute margins; 2 inches or more in diameter.

Class 8, Anemone. Open-centered flowers with only one row of ray florets regardless of form or number of florets, with the tubular disk florets elongated, forming a pin-cushion effect.

Class 9, Single. Open-centered flowers, with only one row of ray florets regardless of form or number of florets.

Class 10, Duplex. Open-centered flowers, with only two rows of ray florets regardless of form or number of florets.

Class 11, Pompon. Fully double flowers, ball-shaped or slightly flattened, floral rays in spiral arrangement, blunt or rounded and quilled or with markedly involute margins; less than 2 inches in diameter.

Class 12, Collarette. Open-centered flower with only one row of ray florets, with the addition of one or more rows of petal lids, usually of a different color, forming a collar around the disc.

Class 13, Miniature Decorative. All dahlias which normally produce flowers that do not exceed 3 inches in diameter, pompons excluded, to be classified according to the foregoing definition.

VARIETIES OF MERIT

Semi-cactus

Amelia Earhart	Frau O. Bracht	Salmon Giant
Edna Ferber	Roycroft	

VARIETIES OF MERIT—*Continued*

Informal Decorative	*Miniature*	*Orchid-Flowering*
Jane Cowl	Jean	Buttercup
Robert Emmet	Little Jewel	Everest
White Wonder	Pink Pearl	

Pompon	*Single*	*Formal Decorative*
Aimée	Garnet Poinsettia	Avalon
Amber Queen	James Weller	Dahliadel Gold
Anna Lee	Newport Wonder	Jersey's Beauty
Dandy	Scarlet Century	Sagamore
Little David	Tango Century	Snowboy
Morning Mist		

Climatic Range and Exposure: Although dahlias are natives of the mountainous sections of Mexico and thrive luxuriantly in the hot, high, dry climate of that region, they are remarkably adaptable and may be grown in almost every section of America. They prefer an exposure in full sun. If grown in a shady location the plants have a tendency to become spindly and the blooms are poor in quality.

Propagation: Dahlias may be propagated by the division of the tubers, by cuttings and by seed.

(1) *By Tubers.* Dahlia tubers are produced in clumps which are attached very firmly to the parent stems. If the entire clump is planted the results are unsatisfactory, as a mass of thin, weak stems will be produced and the flowers will be poor in quality. The tubers should, therefore, be divided, previous to planting. Dahlias seldom produce buds on the tuber itself, the buds being found only at the neck of the tuber. When dividing the tubers it is essential to include the neck, which will usually produce from one to three buds. Many gardeners find it an advantage to cover the clumps with damp earth, moist peat moss, or sand, and to place them in a warm temperature for a week or ten days previous to planting. Under these favorable conditions the buds or eyes will start into growth and when the tubers are divided those may be selected for planting which have strong, well-developed buds. The clumps should not be kept under these conditions for too long a period as the actual sprouts will begin to develop, which will necessitate very careful handling in order to keep them from being broken off at the time of planting.

(2) *By Cuttings.* If a rapid increase of stock is desired cuttings may be taken from the sprouted shoots produced by the tubers.

Where this method is to be followed, the tubers should be started into growth during February or March. They may be planted in flats in the greenhouse, being given ample light, heat, and moisture in order to induce quick growth. When the shoots have formed two sets of leaves, cuttings may be taken. A clean, sharp cut should be made just below the first set of leaves. These lower leaves should then be carefully cut from the stem and the cutting should be inserted in the propagating case. If conditions are favorable, dahlia cuttings root very readily, and as soon as roots have developed, the cuttings may be potted up in small 2½ or 3-inch pots, a mixture of 2 parts loam, 1 part sand, and 1 part leafmold being used. If the cuttings make

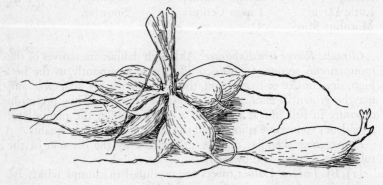

Dahlia clump with buds formed Dahlia tuber cut from clump to include bud

rapid growth and transplanting seems advisable, they may be shifted on to larger pots before they are planted in the open. When planted in the garden, they should be set from 1 to 2 inches deeper than they were when growing in the pot.

(3) *By Seed*. Dahlias do not come true from seed. New varieties are always produced by seed, and some of the small bedding types are frequently grown from seed. A few seed firms offer these bedding types in separate colors, but most of such seed comes in mixed packets and the flowers vary greatly. The seed may be sown under glass early in the season or it may be sown in the coldframe later in the spring. The young seedlings may be transplanted into small pots when the second pair of leaves has developed, and they may be set in the open ground after all danger of frost is over.

Soil Requirements: Dahlias have very definite soil preferences.

They thrive best on a sandy loam with a gravelly sub-soil and they require a soil which is abundantly supplied with organic matter. It is unwise to attempt to grow dahlias on a heavy, clay soil which is poorly drained, as they will make but little growth and will produce blooms of an inferior quality. The texture of a heavy soil may be greatly improved by the addition of liberal quantities of well-rotted manure, rich compost, sand, and in extreme cases the addition of coal ashes may prove beneficial. If the natural drainage is exceedingly poor the entire area upon which the dahlias are to be grown may be underdrained by a tile drain, or the soil where each individual tuber is to be planted may be excavated to a depth of 15 inches and 3 inches of coarse cinders, gravel or some form of rubble may be placed in the bottom.

Dahlias are notoriously heavy feeders and if blooms of superior quality are desired, the plants must have an abundant and well-balanced supply of nutrients throughout the season. An excess of nitrogen should be avoided as it encourages too rank a growth of leaves which are produced at the expense of flower buds. Phosphorus and potash may be supplied in more liberal quantities as they are the nutrients most needed. Unless the soil is naturally fertile and is well supplied with humus and with the necessary nutrients, it is well to prepare it thoroughly previous to the planting of the tubers. The exact location where each tuber is to be planted may be marked off by a stake and the soil may be excavated to a depth of 8 inches. The soil below this depth should be loosened with a spading fork and a shovelful of humus, rich compost or well-rotted manure may be worked into it. The top-soil which was removed should be enriched with a similar amount of humus, and the hole should be refilled until the soil is within 6 inches of the surface.

Planting Tubers: As dahlias are very sensitive to frost, the tubers should not be planted until the ground is warm and mellow and there is no danger of a sudden drop in temperature. In the vicinity of New York, dahlias are usually planted between the middle of May and the middle of June. Little is to be gained from very early planting as the tubers make but slow, unhealthy growth if the soil remains cold and wet. The stakes which are to provide future support for the plants should be driven into the ground at the time the tubers are planted. If this operation is delayed until the plants have made growth enough to actually require staking the tubers may be seriously injured. Dahlias of the large type require ample space for their best development, and they should be planted at least 3 feet apart in the row, the rows being spaced from 3½ to 4 feet apart. The dwarf types require less space, but as they are inclined to be somewhat bushy in habit of growth, they should be allowed a minimum of 15 to 18 inches each way. After the ground has been prepared in accordance with the directions given under the section on *Soil Requirements,* and the stakes have been driven into the ground, the tubers may be planted. The excavation should be approximately 6 inches in depth. The tuber should be placed on the prepared bed, the buds or shoots pointing upward, and it should be covered with 2 inches of earth. It is well to have the neck of the tuber from which the shoots arise near the point where the stake was driven. As the shoots develop, the soil may be filled in about the plant, until the surface of the ground is level. The tuber should be approximately 6 inches below the surface.

Culture: If the finest quality of bloom is desired, only one stalk should be allowed to develop from each tuber. If several shoots have developed the strongest should be selected and the remaining shoots should be discarded. When the main stalk has reached a height of about 1 foot and has formed two or three pairs of leaves, the tiny growing tip may be nipped out. Care must be taken not to cut the stalk back too severely, as the hollow stem will have difficulty in healing,—just the growing tip should be removed. From four to six strong, vigorous stalks will then develop.

If exhibition blooms are to be produced, disbudding is advisable. The lateral or side buds on each terminal branch should be pinched out in order that the middle bud may have every chance to produce a flower of perfect size and substance. The two series of buds below the terminal buds should also be pinched out in order to increase the length of the stem. If the flowers are desired for cutting, severe disbudding is usually not practised.

Frequent, shallow cultivations are advisable throughout the season and at no time should the plants be allowed to suffer from lack of moisture. Early in August an application of a complete fertilizer may be given if flowers of the finest quality are desired. A handful of 2-10-6 commercial fertilizer should be spread in a broad ring about each plant at the rate of 2 to 3 ounces per plant. The soil should then be cultivated and thoroughly soaked. After this application of fertilizer a heavy mulch of partially decayed leaves or some similar material should be spread over the surface of the soil and no further cultivation should be given.

As the plants grow, the stems should be securely fastened to the stakes. Dahlia stems are hollow and pithy and they are easily broken by heavy winds.

Autumn Care: Being extremely sensitive to cold, the plants will be killed with the first heavy frost. The stalks should then be cut off to within 6 inches of the surface of the ground and the tubers should be left in the ground for a week or ten days to become thoroughly ripened. They should then be dug and prepared for storage. A spading fork should be thrust into the ground beside the tubers, and they should be pried loose from the soil with the greatest of care in order that no injury to the tubers may occur. The clump of tubers should be turned upside down in order that any sap or moisture may drain from the stalk and should be exposed to full sunlight for several hours until thoroughly dry.

During the winter dahlia tubers should be stored in a dry, frost-proof place where the temperature ranges between 45 and 55 degrees. Many gardeners prefer to place the tubers in boxes or barrels and to cover them with peat moss or with dry sand to prevent them from becoming badly shriveled. A corner of the cellar will usually prove a very satisfactory place for the storing of dahlia tubers, provided · that it is not too near the furnace.

Insect Pests and Diseases: See Chapter XXXIII.

Eremurus (Foxtail Lily) (Desert Candle). Coming to us from the deserts of Persia, the Himalayas and Turkestan, the giant blooms of the Eremerus are striking indeed when planted against a background of deep green, where they can be viewed from a distance. They are, however, ill suited to planting in a small garden as they are entirely out of scale. The flower spikes often attain a height of 8 feet or more, and the individual, bell-shaped flowers are closely set upon the stalk. The plants flower during June and July and vary in color from cream white through yellow, rose and pink.

SPECIES AND HYBRID VARIETIES

Species	*Hybrids*
Altaicus—yellow, very hardy	Isabellinus—apricot-rose
Bungei—citron yellow	Shelford—tawny yellow and reddish bronze
Himalaicus—pure white	dish bronze
Robustus—rosy pink	Sir Michael—buff yellow

Exposure: A sunny and somewhat sheltered position is desirable. The roots are not particularly hardy and in the latitude of New York and northward, the crowns should be protected with a heavy mulch of straw. An inverted box filled with straw affords an excellent means of protection.

Soil Requirements: The Eremurus prefers a rich, moist but well-drained soil.

Planting: The fleshy roots of the Eremurus should be planted in the autumn. A hole of ample size should be dug in order that the roots may be spread out in a natural position and the plants should be entirely surrounded with sand. The crown of the plant should be only just beneath the surface of the soil. As the roots are very brittle they must be handled with great care. The plants should be spaced from 18 inches to 2 feet apart.

Culture: As growth begins very early in the spring, the winter mulch should be removed as soon as weather conditions permit. The young growth is very subject to injury from frost and during any cold spells which occur after the mulch has been removed, the plants should be protected by a burlap covering or an inverted receptacle of some kind. During the growing season the plants require an abundance of moisture. After flowering the leaves disappear entirely and during this period of dormancy practically no water is required. After the plants are once established, they will thrive for many years, if conditions are favorable. Large plants do not transplant easily and they should be left undisturbed. When the Eremurus is grown in the flower border, great care must be taken not to injure the roots when cultivating after the leaf growth has died down.

Propagation: Eremurus may be propagated either by the division of the root clumps or by seed, the latter process being exceedingly slow and seldom practised.

Galtonia candicans (Summer Hyacinth). The creamy white, bell-shaped flowers of the Galtonia, which is a native of Africa, are decorative and lovely either in the perennial border or against a background of deep green shrubbery. The flowers come into bloom in late August and frequently continue until cut down by frost. The flower stalks usually attain a height of 18 inches, sometimes growing as tall as 3 feet, and the flowers hang suspended from the tall, leafless stems.

Exposure: Full sun.

Soil Requirements: A deep, rich garden loam.

Culture: The bulbs may be planted in the spring at a depth of approximately 6 inches, and they should be spaced from 8 to 12 inches apart. The bulbs are not hardy in the latitude of New York and should be lifted in the autumn and stored in a frost-proof place. As the old bulbs frequently fail to bloom a second season, it is wise to replenish one's stock.

Propagation: Galtonias may be grown very easily from seed as well as from bulbs. It requires two years to produce flowering bulbs from seed and during the winter the small bulblets must be lifted and stored.

Gladiolus. Gladioli are amazing in their adaptability, and because they demand so little in the way of care and cultivation and give so generously of their bloom and beauty they are looked upon as one of our most useful flowers. They are invaluable for cutting and may be had in bloom during every month of the year; and they are equally prized for their decorative value in the garden. They may be planted in great drifts through the garden beds and borders, becoming the dominant note in the planting composition from midsummer on; or they may be used in an incidental way to fill in an occasional gap here and there.

VARIETIES OF MERIT
Large-flowered Type

Apricot Glow—apricot-pink
Berty Snow—clear lavender
Betty Nuthall—orange-pink with yellow throat
Golden Dream—deep yellow
Grand Glory—golden-orange with yellow throat
Harvest Queen—yellow; ruffled petals
Maid of Orleans—white
Marmora—smoky lavender-gray
Mrs. Frank Pendleton—bright rose-pink
Picardy—shrimp-pink
Predominator—salmon-red
Red Splendor—brilliant scarlet

Primulinus Type

Alice Tiplady—saffron orange
Afterglow—deep orange and yellow
Butterboy—buttercup-yellow with red pencilling
Early Orange—bright orange
Orange Butterfly—brilliant orange
Gloriana—golden-salmon
Souvenir—clear yellow
Tawny Gold—salmon gold with coppery sheen
White Butterfly—white with creamy throat

Climatic Range: There are few flowers that have a wider climatic range than do the gladioli, for they may be grown in every section of America. During the winter months one sees them blooming in gay profusion in Southern Florida and in California, and during the summer one finds them in the little dooryard gardens of some remote Canadian village.

Soil Requirements: Gladioli will thrive well on almost any soil of medium fertility. On soils of a slightly heavy texture the flowers are of a superior quality but only a comparatively small number of cormlets are formed. On a light, sandy-loam soil, the flowers are not quite as fine but a large number of cormlets are produced.

Gladioli are moderately acid tolerant and prefer a soil with a pH. of approximately 6. If the soil is extremely acid the condition should be remedied with an application of lime the autumn previous to planting. Gladioli will not thrive well in a soil with a reaction of more than pH. 7, and if the alkalinity runs as high as pH. 7.5, the growth will be decidedly inferior. See Chapter I, page 24.

Superphosphate has proved to be the most effective fertilizer for gladioli as it will increase production and will produce earlier and better bloom. It should be applied in the furrow at the rate of 5 pounds to every 100 feet of row. The fertilizer, which is best applied in the form of 16 per cent superphosphate, should be covered lightly with soil before the corms are planted in the furrow. A complete fertilizer such as a 4–12–4 may be used instead of the superphosphate, but nitrogenous and potassic fertilizers should never be used unless they are liberally supplemented by phosphorus, as the results are definitely detrimental and growth will be seriously checked.

Planting: Gladioli may be planted at any time after danger of frost is over and the soil has become warm and mellow. In order to provide for a succession of bloom, they may be planted at intervals of every 2 weeks until midsummer. The corms come into flower from 8 to 10 weeks after planting. Gladioli corms are graded according to size. The blooming sizes are Nos. 1, 2 and 3. No. 4 will sometimes bloom. The smaller sizes are considerably less expensive than the No. 1 grade and will give equally good results. If grown in rows in the cutting garden, the corms may be planted 4 inches apart in rows 18 inches apart. In garden beds and borders the corms should be spaced about 6 inches apart. The depth of planting will vary somewhat according to the texture of the soil. In light, sandy soil, the corms may be planted 6 inches deep; in heavy, clay soil a depth of 4 inches is preferable. If the corms are planted as deeply as possible, the stalks will be held more firmly in position and less staking will be required.

Culture: Gladioli require no special care. They thrive best in a sunny location, require a moderate amount of moisture, respond to a reasonable amount of cultivation. They will reward one generously for the small amount of time which must be spent upon them.

When gladioli are to be used for decorative purposes in the house, they should be cut as soon as one or two of the blossoms have opened, as the remaining buds will open after the spikes have been placed in water. When cutting gladioli, it is very important to leave two or three of the broadest leaves at the base of the stalk. If all of the foliage is cut away the development of the new corm and the cormlets will be seriously injured. All flower stalks should be cut as soon as the flowers have faded, as the development of the seed pods also affects the vitality of the corm.

Winter Care: As soon as the foliage has turned yellow, which usually occurs about 6 weeks after the period of bloom is over, the corms are ready to be dug. The leaf stalks should be cut off within about 2 inches of the ground. The corms should then be lifted carefully with a spading fork or spade, care being taken to scatter as few of the small cormlets as possible. The corms should be placed in flats and stored in an airy, frost-proof shed for several weeks in order that they become thoroughly mature. If, as sometimes happens in the case of late-planted corms, the foliage has failed to ripen before mid-autumn, the leaf stalks may be allowed to remain on the plant when the corms are dug.

After the period of ripening is over, the leaf stalks should be cut off and the corms should be prepared for winter storage. The old mother corm which was planted in the spring and the roots should be removed from the new corm and the little cormlets should be separated. The corms may be placed on shallow trays and should be stored in a cool, well-ventilated cellar. The temperature should range between 40 and 45 degrees and the air should have a humidity of approximately 80 per cent. If the trays are piled one upon another, a free circulation of air must be provided.

Propagation: Gladioli are propagated by means of the small cormlets which are produced at the base of the corm. These may be separated from the corm at the time of harvest, and they may be stored in paper bags during the winter. In the spring they may be planted in shallow furrows, being lifted in the autumn and stored during the winter. The cormlets will produce flowering-size corms the second or third year.

Insect Pests and Diseases: See Chapter XXXIII.

565

Ismene (Hymenocallis calathina). The funnel-shaped white flowers of the Ismene, with their fringed crown and long, thread-like stamens, are unique in form, and they add a note of interest to a planting composition. The flowers are borne at the top of a stout, leafless stem which often attains a height of 15 inches or more.

Exposure: Full sun.

Soil Requirements: Any ordinary garden soil.

Propagation: By offsets.

Culture: The bulbs should be planted in spring at a depth of approximately 3 inches, being spaced from 8 to 10 inches apart. In the early autumn the bulbs should be lifted, and they should be stored during the winter in a cool, dry, frost-proof place.

Kniphofia (Tritoma) (Red-hot Poker Plant). The decorative value of the Kniphofia is appreciated by the florist and the gardener alike. The brilliant flowers of red and yellow hue are borne on stout, fleshy stems above the sword-shaped leaves and are unique in form and striking in appearance. The dwarf types reaching a height of 18 to 24 inches are of more value as cut flowers in the home than are the larger types, and they combine well with Asclepias tuberosa and the tawny Daylily, Hemerocallis fulva.

Exposure: A sheltered, sunny location.

Soil: A loose, well-drained soil of moderate fertility is considered ideal. A soil which is too rich causes an over-rampant growth.

Propagation: By seed, by the division of the rhizomes, and by offsets. If the seed is sown under glass in January or February, flowering plants may be produced the same season.

Culture: The rhizomes may be planted in the spring after all danger of frost is over, being set from 9 to 12 inches apart. In the North the rhizomes should be dug up in the autumn and stored in dry earth in a cool but frost-proof place.

Tigridia (Tiger Flower) (Mexican Shellflower). The brilliant blooms of the Tigridia, a native of Mexico, Central and South America, are unique in form and coloring and although the individual flowers last only for a day, the blooms are produced in succession over a period of nearly two months.

VARIETIES OF MERIT

Spotted Varieties

Alba grandiflora—white with brilliant carmine spots
Canariense—yellow with purplish-red spots

Varieties of Merit—*Continued*

Lilacea—deep crimson-rose with red spots
Melissa Joan—brilliant scarlet with crimson spots
Mary Gray—apricot-orange with crimson spots

Spotless Varieties

Giant rosea—clear, deep rose
Giant scarlet—rosy scarlet
Lutea—pure yellow

Exposure: Full sun.

Soil Requirements: A light, rich garden loam.

Culture: Tigridias require a warm temperature and abundant moisture during the growing season. The bulbs should be planted in early spring about 2 inches deep, being spaced from 6 to 8 inches apart. In warm regions where there are no heavy frosts the bulbs may be left undisturbed for many years, and they will give generous bloom each season. Where the climate is severe the bulbs should be dug before the ground freezes. It is essential that the bulbs be stored in a cool, airy, dry, frost-proof place. One of the most satisfactory methods of handling them is to tie the dried leaves and stems into small bundles and to hang them up in a cool, dry room. Care must be taken to see that mice cannot reach them. If the top growth is cut off the bulbs may be stored in wire trays. The bulbs are very sensitive to dampness and if they are not kept properly dry, they will decay.

Propagation: Tigridias may be grown very readily from seed, as well as from bulbs. If the seed is sown early in the season about 20 per cent of the plants will bloom the first year.

Tritonia (Montbretia). The brilliant, colorful flowers of the Montbretias, natives of South Africa, are among the most beautiful and most decorative of all the summer-flowering bulbs. The flowers are borne on tall, graceful spikes varying in height from 2 to 4 feet, and they are lovely for cutting, as they last extremely well, often remaining fresh for two weeks or more. Some of the recently introduced varieties of the Earlham Strain are of striking beauty with their wide, flaring flowers in lovely tones of orange and apricot.

Varieties of Merit

His Majesty—deep scarlet, shading to gold
Lady Gwenn—brilliant orange-scarlet

Lady Oxford—apricot overlaid with salmon-rose
Lemon Queen—buds deep orange, flowers cream-yellow
Marjorie—orange-yellow with crimson center
Peter—rich apricot
Pocahontas—coppery scarlet with golden luster
Una—rich apricot with carmine blotch

Exposure: Full sun.

Soil Requirements: Montbretias prefer a rather sandy soil well supplied with rotted manure or some other form of humus.

Planting: In sections of the country where the climate is mild, Montbretias may be planted in the autumn. In sections where the temperature is apt to drop much below 20 degrees above zero it is wise to plant the corms in the spring. The depth of planting is approximately 4 inches and the corms may be spaced from 5 to 6 inches apart.

Culture: Montbretias require an abundance of moisture during the growing and flowering season. After the flowering season is over the foliage will ripen more quickly if moisture is reduced to a minimum. After the first frost, the corms may be lifted and stored for the winter in the same manner as are gladiolus corms.

BULBOUS IRISES

Exquisite in form, varied and lovely in coloring, the bulbous irises are unexcelled as cut flowers and their decorative value in the garden is coming to be more and more appreciated. The erroneous and widespread impression that these lovely bulbous irises are not hardy has meant that they have been used to only a very limited extent for outdoor planting, and it is indeed unfortunate that many of them are known to us only as cut flowers which have been grown in the greenhouse during the winter months.

After a series of extensive trials at the Massachusetts Agricultural Experiment Station, it has been conclusively proven that the bulbous irises are quite as hardy as tulips, that they are able to withstand subzero temperatures with no ill effects, and that they are practically never injured by the most extreme cold.

There are several species and types of bulbous iris belonging to the same botanical sub-genus, Xiphium. Those which are considered the most desirable for garden plantings and for cut flowers are the Spanish Iris, the English Iris, the Dutch Iris, and Iris tingitana.

Spanish Iris (Iris Xiphium). The leaves are narrow and grass-like, about 1 foot in height. The flowers are predominantly blue but vary somewhat in color, and they may be readily distinguished by the characteristic yellow blotch on the falls. Period of flowering, late May and early June.

Varieties of Outstanding Merit

Blanche Fleur	Canary Yellow
Bronze Queen	Prince Henry
Cajanus	Queen Emma

English Iris (Iris xiphioides). The foliage is more abundant than that of the Spanish Iris, and the leaves are somewhat larger. The flowers are produced in various colors, blue predominating, and they are large and showy. The flowering period is slightly later than that of the Spanish Iris.

Varieties of Outstanding Merit

Bleu Amable	Grand Vainqueur
Bleu Celeste	Mont Blanc
Duke of Clarence	Prince of Wales
Emperor	Royal Blue
Grand Lilas	Sunset

Dutch Iris. Most of the varieties listed in the catalogs as Dutch Iris are hybrids which have been originated by crossing I. tingitana with I. Xiphium, I. Boissieri and other species. In general character, they resemble the Spanish Iris, the foliage being somewhat broader and more abundant and the plants more vigorous in their habit of growth, flowering a few days earlier.

Varieties of Outstanding Merit

A. Bloemaard	Early Snow
Abraham Storck	Hart Nibbrig
Anton Mauve	Hobbema
Dirk Daleus	Indian Chief

Iris tingitana. In this group we find the exquisite variety known as Wedgewood which is so familiar as a cut flower during the winter months. It is unexcelled for forcing and is equally lovely in the garden, being fully as hardy as the other bulbous irises. Another meritorious variety is The First.

Exposure: A position in full sun is essential in order that the foliage may become fully ripe after the flowering season is over.

Soil Requirements: A moderately fertile, well-drained soil is desirable, a light, sandy loam being considered ideal. The bulbs are decidedly indifferent to the reaction of the soil and will thrive equally well in slightly acid, neutral, or mildly alkaline soils.

Planting: Shipment of bulbs is usually made in late September or early October. The bulbs should be planted immediately, being spaced from 6 to 8 inches apart and at a depth of 4–5 inches. As the bulbous irises are apparently considered a great delicacy by field mice, some protection should be given if they are planted in an area where rodents are troublesome. (See Chapter XXXIV, page 1167.)

Culture: Active growth begins soon after the bulbs are planted and most varieties will send up several green, spear-like shoots during the autumn. After the flowering period is over in late June the foliage should be allowed to ripen and it is essential that it be exposed to full sun during this period. After the leaves have become brown, the bulbs may be lifted. They should be placed on shallow trays, covered with dry sand, and stored in the hottest attic available, where conditions will approximate as nearly as possible the conditions found in their native habitat. If the bulbs are not lifted, being left undisturbed after the foliage has died down, some few varieties will persist for several years while others will fail to reappear after the first season of bloom. If the flowers are used for cutting it is necessary to reduce the foliage to such an extent that the vigor and vitality of the bulb are seriously impaired, and new bulbs should be planted the following year.

Winter Protection: Little winter protection is required. Salt hay may be used, or small evergreen boughs, placed over the areas where the bulbs have been planted, will be sufficient.

Iris reticulata. This lovely species iris is often in bloom with the Snowdrops and the Crocus, and it may be used very delightfully in the rock garden or in some sheltered spot in the flower garden. The blooms resemble those of the Spanish and Dutch Iris in miniature, the plants being of a decidedly dwarf habit, seldom reaching a height of more than a few inches. The flowers are a rich pansy-violet in color and have the delightful fragrance of violets.

Exposure: A somewhat protected position with a sunny exposure is desirable.

Soil Requirements: A moderately fertile, and very well drained, neutral or slightly alkaline soil is considered ideal.

Planting: The bulbs should be planted in the autumn, in late September or October, being spaced from 4 to 6 inches apart. When once well established, the bulbs will continue to bloom year after year and under favorable conditions will increase rapidly. In exposed situations light winter protection should be given.

—XIV—

Lilies

Few flowers have more decorative value in the garden than the lilies. Their stateliness, their sheer beauty of form, their fragrance and their color harmonies make them one of the most highly prized flowers in a garden composition.

Capricious though they may be as a group, there are some lilies which may be grown in almost every garden. The novice in the art of gardening will find it the part of wisdom to select some of the more easily grown varieties, while the more experienced gardener will find keen interest and joy in growing the more difficult types.

Within recent years there has been a steadily increasing interest in the culture of lilies, and many of our institutions with facilities for plant research have devoted much time and effort to the subject, in an attempt to solve some of the problems involved in the successful growing of lilies. The problem of disease is one of paramount importance, and one which has, in some cases, defied solution.

The essentials of successful lily culture may be outlined as follows: a well-drained soil, abundantly supplied with organic matter; good air circulation; shelter from high winds; disease-free bulbs; the proper time, method and depth of planting; an adequate mulch during the winter and a protective covering for the surface of the bed during the growing season; full sun or partial shade, to meet the requirements of the individual groups; and protection against rodents and disease.

Soil Requirements: Good drainage is an absolutely essential factor, as there is nothing more fatal to the life of a lily bulb than standing water or a soggy, saturated soil. Even those native lilies which are known to prefer a moist situation are unable to endure standing water; they must have their moisture in motion, rapidly trickling through the soil. Therefore, unless the soil is naturally well drained, artificial drainage must be provided. The bed may be drained by the use of 4-inch agricultural tile laid 2 feet below the surface of the soil, or the soil in the

Photograph by Philip B. Wallace   *Agnes Selkirk Clark, Landscape Architect*

Lilies in the Hardy Border

The deep green of the background gives a perfect setting for the stately beauty of the Lilies.

bed may be excavated to a depth of 2½ feet and a 6-inch foundation of crushed stone or coarse hard-coal cinders may be placed in the bottom. If the bed is raised slightly above the surrounding area drainage will also be facilitated.

Lilies thrive best in a good loam soil supplied with an abundance of organic matter. If a new bed is being made, the humus should be incorporated into the soil well in advance of

573

planting, and may be supplied in the form of leafmold, good compost, cultivated peat, or well-rotted cow manure. If the soil is naturally heavy its physical texture will be greatly improved by the addition of liberal quantities of humus, and it will thus be made a more suitable medium for the growing of lilies. Most lilies thrive best in a soil which is nearly neutral, with a pH. ranging between 6.5 and 7.5. There are a few exceptions, as philadelphicum prefers a soil of high acidity, canadense will thrive equally well in either an acid or a neutral soil, and Lilium candidum prefers a slightly alkaline soil. For the majority of lilies, however, a neutral soil will provide conditions which are most favorable.

Exposure: Good air circulation is closely related to the problem of disease control, and it will be found that most lilies, except those which are definitely shade-loving, will thrive best in a sunny, airy situation. Disease is much more apt to be prevalent in a low, badly drained spot where there is poor air circulation than on gently sloping, well-drained ground.

Healthy Bulbs: The importance of obtaining clean, healthy, disease-free bulbs can hardly be over-stressed. The vast majority of failures in the growing of lilies are due to the inroads of disease, and it is a problem which faces every grower. It has been found that lilies grown from seed are more free from disease than those propagated directly from the bulbs. Therefore, many gardeners now make a practice of growing from seed some of the varieties which are particularly subject to disease.

Time of Planting: The time of planting as well as the method and depth of planting will depend to a considerable extent upon the type of lily being grown, although there are a few general rules which apply to practically all members of the lily group. Lily bulbs mature, or ripen, after the flowering period is over. Lilies should be planted as soon as possible after the bulbs have ripened. Most lily bulbs resent being out of the ground, and some varieties deteriorate rapidly during the process of shipment. It is essential, therefore, that the bulbs should be planted without delay as soon as the shipment has been received. The ground should be prepared well in advance, and everything should be ready for immediate planting as soon as the bulbs arrive. The more promptly the shipment can be made after the bulbs have ripened, and the more promptly the bulbs are planted, the greater are the chances of success. Because of long shipments it is sometimes impossible to plant the bulbs at the most favorable time. Candidum lilies should be planted in August as they make a very characteristic growth of basal leaves during the autumn; yet bulbs which are shipped from Northern France or from Russia seldom reach this country before the middle of September and the planting is thus necessarily delayed a month or more. Another problem with which the gardener is faced is that of shipments which arrive late in the autumn when the ground is no longer in suitable condition for planting, being either frozen or soggy. This frequently happens in the case of some of the Japanese bulbs which are late in ripening and must consequently be dug and prepared for shipment late in the season. This situation may be met in either one of two ways.

The bed may be prepared well in advance and the area where these late arrivals are to be planted may be mulched with fresh manure, leaves, or straw, to prevent the ground from freezing and to maintain it in a favorable condition for planting. Even when this is done, however, the bulbs frequently arrive too late to make sufficient autumn root growth to carry them through the winter and they suffer seriously in consequence. In handling bulbs which arrive after the middle of November (in the latitude of Philadelphia) a more favorable procedure seems to be to pot the bulbs in fairly dry soil and to store them during the winter in a root cellar where the temperature will range between 38 and 50 degrees. The pots may be buried in dry sand, being kept without moisture during the winter. In early spring the pots should be set out of doors, being covered with straw, or half-rotted leaves until growth has started. Later in the season, when the ground is in good condition the bulbs may be gently removed from the pots and placed in their permanent position in the garden, care being taken not to disturb the roots. This method of winter storage has given excellent results at the Boyce-Thompson Institute and is far preferable to the use of cold frames for the wintering of bulbs which arrive too late to be planted in the open.

The method and depth of planting are discussed in detail under the cultural requirements of each individual variety. Most growers prefer to set their lily bulbs on a bed of sand, placing an inch or two of sand below the bulb and covering it lightly with sand before the bed or hole is filled with earth. This method will facilitate the drainage of water away from the immediate vicinity of the bulb and will lessen the chances of decay. Some growers also recommend that all lily bulbs be dusted with semesan or formaldehyde dust immediately before planting as a precautionary measure against the inroads of disease.

Winter Mulches: Most lilies, with the exception of a few exceedingly hardy varieties, require the protection of a winter mulch. Well-rotted leaf mold makes an excellent mulch for lilies as it can be left on the ground throughout the year and will aid in increasing the organic content of the soil. Salt hay is also excellent, and glass-wool offers excellent possibilities. (See page 446 on Winter Mulches for time and method of application.)

Summer Mulch: Lilies prefer a cool, moist root-run, and there are but few which will thrive in a soil which becomes hard and parched during the growing season. A soil well supplied with organic matter will naturally be more retentive of moisture than a soil deficient in humus and will, therefore, provide more favorable growing conditions. The surface of the soil, however, should have some form of protective covering. When lilies are grown in the herbaceous border this covering is provided by the natural growth of other plants which, in many cases, will afford sufficient ground cover for the beds. If lilies are grown in beds or borders by themselves, the surface of the soil should be kept mulched throughout the growing season. Peatmoss, well-rotted leafmold, lawn clippings and buckwheat hulls may be used successfully for this purpose.

Protection Against Rodents: Mice are, unfortunately, passionately fond of most varieties of lily bulbs and in gardens where mice are apt to be troublesome it is useless to attempt to grow lilies unless some adequate protection is provided. The most effective protection is afforded by the use of ¼-inch mesh galvanized wire. If the lilies are to be grown in a bed or border by themselves it is the part of wisdom to line the bottom, sides and ends of the entire bed with wire. When the wire is purchased by the roll it is not prohibitively expensive, and it will afford absolute protection from rodents over a period of many years. It may be put in place at the same time that the bed is prepared for planting, and will, therefore, not require much extra labor. If the lilies are to be planted in groups in the border, wire baskets of any desired size may be made of this same ¼-inch mesh wire and the bulbs may be planted within the basket. Although many other means of protection have been tried, such as planting the bulbs in camphor or in medicated peat moss, no method of affording protection has been found which is as entirely dependable as the use of wire. For the control of field mice by the use of poison baits, see Chapter XXXIV.

PROPAGATION

Lilies may be propagated by seed, by scales, by bulbils and by bulblets. Some lilies may be propagated more readily by one method than by another.

Propagation by Seed: Many lilies may be grown very rapidly from seed, and if one does not mind the years of waiting which intervene between the sowing of the seed and the flowering of the plant, the success of this method of propagation will usually far outweigh its disadvantages. Lily seeds may be sown in the autumn as soon as they are ripe, or they may be held over for spring sowing. The seed of most varieties, with the exception of auratum, speciosum, and Henryi, will ripen in time for autumn sowing. A well-drained coldframe with deeply prepared, mellow soil offers ideal conditions for the germination of lily seeds. A soil mixture consisting of one part loam, one part leafmold and one part peatmoss will give excellent results, and the seeds may be sown either broadcast or in rows, being covered with about 1 inch of soil. If the seeds are sown in the autumn the seed bed should be mulched with straw or salt hay during the winter. A lath frame will afford excellent protection for spring-sown seedlings until they have become well established. Some growers prefer to keep their lily seedlings partially shaded throughout the first and second season of growth as it prevents the soil from drying out and promotes more vigorous development. About twelve months after sowing, the young seedlings may be transplanted to another deeply prepared frame in order that they may have more space in which to develop, and the second summer after sowing, the strongest, most vigorous seedlings may be transplanted to their permanent position in the garden or in the nursery. The majority of lilies will flower the third summer after sowing, some will flower considerably sooner, while a few will require a longer period of growth. Philippinense, which is one of the lilies most easily grown from seed, will flower the following summer if it is sown in the autumn and is carried over the winter in a greenhouse. Regale lilies will frequently produce one flower the second season, several flowers the third season; and they are at the height of their glory during the fifth and sixth years. Among the lilies most easily grown from seed are canadense, candidum, concolor, Henryi, philippinense, regale, and speciosum. Of these, canadense and speciosum are of the type which make no growth above ground until the second spring after planting.

Propagation by Scales: Many lilies may be increased very readily by scales. The bulbs should be lifted in early autumn and the scales should be carefully removed from the outside of the bulbs. A shallow trench should be opened in a well-drained, partially shaded spot, and a thin layer of sand should be placed in the bottom of the drill. The scales should be placed in the trench, being spaced several inches apart, and they should be covered with an inch or two of sand. Peatmoss may be substituted for the sand if desired. The young bulbs form about the edges of the scales, and when they have become crowded, they should be transplanted into nursery rows or into coldframes.

Propagation by Bulbils: In some species of lilies small bulbils are produced in the axils of the leaves. Those most frequently propagated by this method are bulbiferum, myriophyllum, Sargentiæ and tigrinum. When the bulbils are ready to be gathered, they will drop from the stem almost at the touch of the fingers. They should be sown in shallow drills in light, well-prepared soil, and they may be handled in very much the same manner as are lily seedlings.

Propagation by Bulblets: Most of the stem-rooting lilies produce bulblets on the underground stem. When these bul-

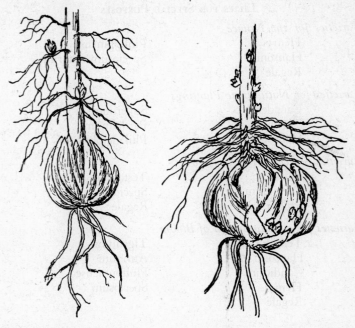

Lilium regale with bulb-
lets forming along under-
ground stem

Lilium auratum with bulblets
forming on stem and scales

blets are left undisturbed, they produce a cluster of small leaves about the base of the main stem and they soon become overcrowded. It is well, therefore, to remove them, even though one does not wish to use them for the purpose of propagation. In the autumn, the earth should be carefully dug away from the main stem with a trowel and the small bulblets should be removed. In some cases the stem may be ripe enough so that it may be gently pulled out without harming the bulbs, in which case the bulblets may be picked off. These bulblets may be planted in shallow drills, being handled in the same manner as are the bulbils.

For Lily Diseases, see Chapter XXXIII.

LILIES FOR SPECIAL PURPOSES

Varieties for the Novice

Henryi	Philippinense
Hansonii	Speciosum rubrum
Regale	

Varieties for Naturalistic Plantings

Canadense	Superbum
Tigrinum	Pardalinum
Hansonii	Philadelphicum

Varieties Suited to Pot Culture

Auratum	Testaceum
Candidum	Speciosum
Philippinense	Regale

Varieties for a Long Season of Bloom

Tenuifolium	Tigrinum
Hansonii	Auratum
Candidum	Philippinense
Henryi	Speciosum
Regale	

LILIES OF SPECIAL MERIT

L. auratum (the Golden-banded Lily of Japan) is considered one of the most beautiful of all lilies, but it is, unfortunately, subject to disease and is short-lived in many gardens, disappearing entirely after the first year or two. The magnificent, heavily-scented flowers, the white petals banded with gold, are borne on stems often reaching a height of more than six feet. It flowers in July and August, prefers a position in full sun, a slightly acid, well-drained soil, rich with leaf mold, and abundant water during the growing season. Being stem-rooting, the bulbs should be planted at a depth of about 10 inches. Of the many varieties listed, platyphyllum is considered one of the best.

L. amabile is one of the finest of the low-growing lilies, seldom reaching a height of more than 2 to 3 feet. It flowers in June and July and the brilliant, waxy, orange-scarlet flowers are very decorative, the reflexed petals being spotted with black. Amabile prefers a sunny position and thrives well when grown among low shrubs. It is stem-rooting and should be planted at a depth of about 6 inches in a well drained, sandy-loam soil.

L. Batemanniæ is a superbly fine lily with flowers of a rich apricot hue. The petals of the upright flowers are gracefully recurving, and the blooms are borne in great profusion, sometimes as many as 20 on a single stem. In height it varies from 3 to 4 feet. Batemanniae thrives well either in full sun or in partial shade, does well under ordinary garden conditions, and blooms during July and August. It is stem-rooting and the bulbs should be planted 6 inches deep.

L. candidum, known as the Madonna Lily, is one of the most beautiful and one of the most beloved of all lilies. A native of Southeastern Europe, it was first introduced into this country many years ago and it is widely grown. It blooms during June and early July, the white glistening flowers being borne on tall, straight stalks from 4 to 6 feet in height. It should be planted in August whenever it is possible to do so. Bulbs produced in this country are available for planting at this season, but imported bulbs, coming from France or Russia, usually do not arrive until late in September. The bulbs are base-rooting and should be planted not more than 2 inches deep. Shallow planting is one of the essentials of success. Candidum lilies prefer a sunny location, and a slightly alkaline, well-drained soil. During the autumn months a growth of basal leaves is produced which remain green throughout the winter. Within recent years Candidum lilies have been very seriously troubled with botrytis, and the bulbs have proved to be extremely short-lived in consequence. The Salonica type which has been introduced within the past few years is proving to be unusually resistant to this disease and is highly recommended by many growers. Candidum lilies are among the few lily bulbs which are not troubled by mice.

L. canadense is the lovely Meadow Lily which is found growing wild in open meadows and along the edge of woodlands throughout the Northeastern part of the United States. It thrives well in either full sun or partial shade, and while in its native haunts it is usually found growing in acid soil, it seems to thrive equally well in neutral soil. The flower stalks range in height from 3 to 6 feet and the lovely, nodding, bell-shaped flowers are golden in color, sometimes shading to orange, being heavily spotted on the inside of

Photograph by J. Horace McFarland Co.

Lilium canadense

the petals with purplish-brown dots. The season of bloom ranges from late June through July. The bulbs produce small stem roots, and they should be planted about 10 inches deep. L. canadense will occasionally fail to thrive under cultivation and in some sections the bulbs have a tendency to disappear after a few years. It is so utterly beautiful, however, both in the garden and in a naturalistic setting, that it is well worth striving for.

L. concolor comes to us from central China and is a semi-dwarf species, varying in height from 12 to 18 inches. The dainty star-like blossoms, borne upright upon the stalk, are a crimson-scarlet in color. L. concolor comes in flower in June and July, following tenuifolium in season of bloom. A sunny position is preferred and the bulbs should be planted at a depth of 3 inches. It is a hardy, adaptable little lily and is frequently grown in rock gardens.

L. elegans is one of the most dependable of all lilies. It is excellent for cutting, is well adapted to pot culture, and thrives well either in a sunny border or in a partially shaded location, provided that it is planted in well-drained soil. The large, upright, cup-shaped flowers are borne two to four on a single stem and range in color from yellow through deep apricot to dark red. The plants vary in height from 3 to 5 feet; the bulbs are stem-rooting and should be planted 5 inches deep. The variety, *Alice Wilson*, is an excellent semi-dwarf form bearing large flowers of a clear lemon yellow; *Leonard Joerg* is a good deep apricot and *Red Star* is a brilliant red, suffused with orange.

L. Hansonii is a native of Korea and is extremely hardy. The nodding, orange-yellow flowers, dotted with brown, are borne on stems 4 to 5 feet in height and possess a curiously waxy appearance. Flowering in June and July, L. Hansonii thrives well either in full sun or in partial shade. The bulbs are stem-rooting and should be planted at a depth of 6 inches. They are fortunately not troubled by field mice, and are more nearly disease-proof than any other lily grown.

L. Henryi comes to us from Central China where it is found growing wild on limestone cliffs. It is often called the "yellow speciosum" as it is somewhat similar in form. The flowers are a soft golden-orange in color with a tinge of green through the center, and the petals are decidedly reflexed. The flowers are borne on stems ranging from 5 to 9 feet in height and are excellent for cutting, opening in water even to the tiniest bud. They bloom late in the season, in August, and the flowers remain in bloom over a period of many weeks. L. Henryi thrives best in partial shade, and as the bulbs are stem-rooting they should be planted at a depth of at least 10 inches. The bulbs are extremely hardy, are seldom troubled by disease, and are usually untouched by field mice.

L. Martagon grows wild throughout many sections of Europe. The type bears flowers of a dull purple and is far less lovely than the variety Martagon album, which is one of the most graceful and beautiful lilies in cultivation. The recurving flowers are of a glistening, waxy white and are faintly scented. A partially shaded location is preferred. The flowers are borne on stalks from 4 to 6 feet in height, from mid June to early July. It is usually the first white lily to bloom. The bulbs are base-rooting and should be planted about 4 inches deep in well-drained soil.

L. pardalinum, the lovely Leopard Lily, is a native of California. In its natural habitat one sometimes comes upon great moist meadows high in the mountains where hundreds of Pardalinum lilies may be seen in bloom. It is hardy and adaptable and increases rapidly. The lovely, recurved flowers are a bright yellow-orange in color, spotted with crimson, and they form a pyramid of nodding bloom upon the graceful stems. Varying in height from 3 to 6 feet, they are lovely when planted in the open border or against a background of shrubbery. Though preferring a sunny location, L. pardalinum thrives fairly well in partial shade. It is one of the few lilies that may be grown successfully in a stiff clay-loam soil. It revels in a moist soil and for its most favorable growth it must have abundant moisture until after it has flowered in late June and early July. It is of the rhizomatous type and should be planted at a depth of not more than 6 inches. It may be readily propagated both by seed and by cutting off a piece of the rhizome with adhering scales.

L. philippinense comes to us from the Philippine Islands and is gaining rapidly in popularity. There are two distinct forms, the early flowering variety which blooms in August and the late flowering type which does not bloom until October. The late-flowering type is sometimes severely injured by frost in the North and is, therefore, particularly recommended for Southern gardens. The flowers are long and trumpet-shaped, pure white, with a tinge of pinkish-purple along the ribs. The early flowering type seldom reaches a height of more than 18 or 20 inches and the stems are slender and wiry. The late-flowering type grows normally to a height of about 3 feet, sometimes attaining a height of almost 6 feet. It is heavily stem-rooting and the bulbs should be planted from 6 to 8 inches deep. It thrives in either full sun or partial shade. L. philippinense is one of the easiest of all lilies to grow from seed, and from seed sown in the greenhouse in March blooms will be produced the following summer. The variety formosanum is hardier, and a better garden subject.

L. regale, the Regal lily, is one of the most popular and most widely grown of all lilies, and it has much to recommend it. It is abso-

Photograph by Walter Beebe Wilder

Lilium regale

lutely dependable under widely varying conditions; it is hardy and vigorous; and it is practically disease-proof. It is undoubtedly one of the most satisfactory of all lilies for the amateur. The large, trumpet-shaped flowers are creamy white, lilac outside, with a golden throat and brilliant golden anthers, and they are very fragrant. The flowers are borne in profusion upon tall, straight stems which often reach a height of from 6 to 8 feet. The Regal lily thrives best in full sun and is one of the few lilies that can be grown successfully in a dry, harsh, unmulched soil. It blooms during late June and well into July. As the Regal lilies are stem-rooting the bulbs should be planted not less than 8 inches deep. At the rear of an herbaceous border,

Photograph by Jessie Tarbox Beals

Lilium auratum

or against a background of shrubbery, the majestic, stately beauty of the Regal lily is superb. They are well adapted for use in parks and in other public places, as well as in the garden. They may be grown easily from seed and will often flower the second summer after sowing. Regal lilies start growth rather early in the spring and it sometimes happens that during a sudden and unexpected cold snap the young shoots are injured by frost. A light protection of straw or an inverted flower-pot placed over the shoots will obviate this danger.

L. speciosum is a native of the Orient and is one of the most beautiful and appealing of all our cultivated lilies. Although it is far less voluptuous and showy than some of its cousins, there is about

Photograph by A. B. Morse Co.

Lilium speciosum

it a grace and charm which make it of distinct value as a cut flower and for the garden. The typical form is white, touched with deep pink and spotted with carmine. There are many varieties, varying in color from pure white to deep carmine. The lovely flowers, with gracefully recurving petals, are borne on stems about 4 feet in height and bloom late in August and on into September. The bulbs are stem-rooting and should be planted from 8 to 10 inches deep. The speciosum lilies thrive equally well either in full sun or in partial shade, but have a tendency to be short-lived in most gardens. All of the speciosums are well adapted to forcing and may be grown very successfully in the small greenhouse.

L. testaceum. The lovely Nankeen lily is one of the few natural hybrids among lilies, and although it is somewhat temperamental, it is so exquisite in form and in coloring that it is well worth striving for. In some gardens it fails to thrive but in gardens where it has once become well established it increases rapidly and blooms on year after year.

The flowers are a most unusual tone of soft apricot, suffused with peach-buff, and the nodding blooms with gracefully reflexed petals are borne on stems about 5 feet in height. The Nankeen lily flowers in June and early July, and it is one of the hardiest of all lilies, being extremely resistant to frost and cold.

The bulbs resent being out of the ground and should be planted as early in the autumn as possible, being set at a depth of 4 inches.

Roses

Since ancient times the rose has held an eminent position
in the hearts of all peoples, a position shared by no other
flower. Because of its significance as a symbol of purity and
faith, because of the many associations, legends, and traditions
surrounding it, because of its sheer loveliness, it has been loved
and revered by generations of gardeners throughout the world.
It personalizes our ideal of beauty. Universal in its appeal to
the spirit of man, it is equally at home over the cottage doorway or within the proud gates of ducal palaces.

The romance of the rose has come down to us in song and
story from mediæval times, and the rose is interwoven into
the very fabric of our history. The symbols of the two factions
contending for supremacy in strife-torn England during the
fourteenth century were the red rose of York and the white
rose of Lancaster. "The War of the Roses" was so called because of these symbols.

One of the first flowers to become domesticated, the rose
has been faithfully protected and treasured, and wherever
civilization has spread, there roses have been planted.

Since the dawn of science, and its application to the study
of plants, no other flower has received so much attention as
has the rose. Botanists have discovered and named two hundred species of the rose in the northern hemisphere. The
natural habitat of members of this genus extends from the
sub-arctic regions to Mexico, Abyssinia, and the Himalayas.
Today, after a century of plant breeding, we have thousands
of varied forms of roses. Indeed, so many are there that it becomes increasingly difficult to make a selection, and personal
taste must be one's guide.

THE ROSE GARDEN—ITS DESIGN

Partly because of the special esteem in which the rose is held, partly because the cultural requirements of the rose differ from those of other flowers, and partly because the rose lacks the fullness of growth of many cultivated plants and so needs special compositional arrangement, a separate garden for roses is the most satisfactory method of planting. A garden devoted entirely to roses may seem to be too great an undertaking but it is not impossible of attainment even on a small place, and where resources are limited. It need not be large in scale or lavish in details of construction. A few well-planted beds of roses within a small enclosure can be a source of pleasure throughout the season, and the satisfactions of such a planting will far outweigh the work involved.

In the planning of a rose garden there are a few essential considerations which should be borne in mind: an enclosure which is not too close and airless but gives shelter from the wind; a background of wall or hedge against which the blooms may be seen to the best advantage; a geometric pattern to give the design definite form, so that the garden will have a beauty of its own, quite independent of the flowers; and, preferably, a location which will provide shade for a portion of the day. Paths made of flagstone or old brick are always pleasing in the rose garden, and they may be edged with dwarf box or with violas. If a ground cover of some shallow-rooted plant such as pansies, forget-me-nots or violas is used, a very lovely effect may be obtained, the flowers being a pleasant foil for the warm tones of the roses.

SOIL REQUIREMENTS

There has been much controversy regarding the soil requirements for roses. On the one hand we have the extremist who is satisfied with nothing short of perfection, and who puts forth the claim that rose beds must be trenched to a depth of at least 3 feet before planting, and that the subsequent care and feeding offer such problems that the knowledge and tech-

Roses in a Latticed Bay

Climbing Roses

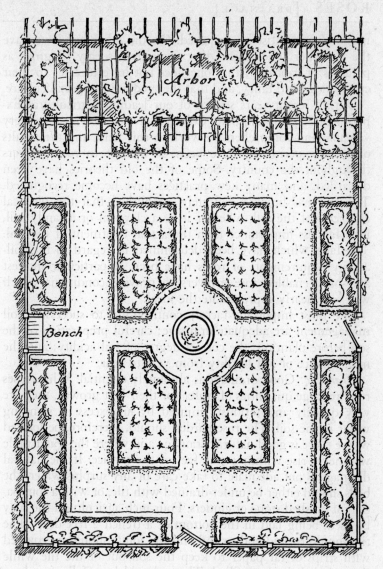

A Rose Garden

Scale 0   10   20   Feet

nique of a scientist are required. On the other hand we have the gardener who claims that roses are as easy to grow as potatoes or cabbages; that one does not have to cater to their every whim and fancy, and that they require no special culture.

During recent years several of our leading Agricultural Experiment Stations and State Colleges have carried on some very valuable and comprehensive work in this field, and the results of these experiments have been of interest to rose growers throughout the country. Some of the old theories have been discarded, and many new practices have become recognized. The fact has become definitely established that the physical character of the soil, whether it be a clay soil or a sandy soil, is of far less importance than the actual treatment of the soil. The facts which have been determined in regard to the soil-acidity requirements of roses have been of particular interest and have enabled rose growers to provide conditions which will very nearly approximate the ideal.

The most important factors contributing to successful soil management are adequate drainage; careful preparation of the soil before planting; the correct degree of soil acidity; and the maintenance of soil fertility from year to year.

Drainage: Good drainage is absolutely essential. While roses require large quantities of water for their best growth, they are very quickly and seriously injured by an excess of standing water in the soil. The rose garden should, therefore, be located where there is good natural drainage and where the water table will never rise within 4 or 5 feet of the surface. If the natural drainage is not adequate to take care of any surplus water, the beds should either be under-drained with tile, or with a foundation of crushed stone or cinders. Four-inch agricultural tile may be used, being laid in the bottom of a trench 2 feet deep. The tile should be laid end to end and the joints should be covered with strips of tar paper to keep the soil out of the tile while the trench is being refilled. There should be a fall of at least 3 inches in every 50 feet. When the beds are being prepared a layer of cinders or crushed stone placed in the bottom of the trench will greatly facilitate the drainage. A 6-inch layer is usually sufficient, unless the natural drainage is excessively bad.

Preparation of the Soil: The soil in the rose beds should be thoroughly prepared to a minimum depth of at least 10 inches, preferably to a depth of 24 inches. The root development of the plants will usually extend to a depth varying from 15 to 24 inches, and if the roots strike deeply into the soil the plants will be more resistant to drought, and the general growth and development will be improved.

If the soil is of a decidedly sandy character its texture may be improved, and its water-holding capacity may be greatly increased, by the admixture of clay-loam, compost, peat moss and other organic materials. In like manner the texture and aërability of extremely heavy clay soils may be improved by the addition of sand, compost, strawy manure, or some similar material.

The method of soil preparation for the rose beds will depend to a considerable extent upon the desires of the owner. If one's means are limited and if labor is not readily available, the old English practice of double-digging will give reasonably satisfactory results. If, however, time, labor and expense do not have to be taken into consideration, and if one wishes to provide conditions which will be as nearly ideal as possible, the beds should be trenched.

Double-digging is a very simple, comparatively rapid, and fairly efficient method of soil preparation. It consists of removing the top spadeful of soil from one end of the bed and placing it at the other end of the bed, ready for later use. A generous layer of well-rotted manure or rich compost should then be worked well into the lower stratum of soil, which has been left exposed after the top spadeful was removed. The next layer of top soil is turned over upon this lower stratum, and the process continues until the end of the bed has been reached. The pile of top soil removed from the first trench is then used to fill in the last trench.

The actual trenching of the bed is a much more laborious and expensive process, but will result in a rose bed which will be a source of satisfaction for years to come. The soil should be removed to a depth of 24 inches. If the natural drainage is poor, an additional 3 to 6 inches should be removed, being replaced with cinders or crushed stone. A 6-inch layer of manure should be placed in the bottom of the trench and the remainder of the trench should be filled with a rich compost, consisting of one part rotted manure and three parts rich loam.

If the roses are to be planted in the spring the beds should, if possible, be prepared the autumn before.

Acidity of the Soil: Recent experiments show that roses prefer a slightly acid soil with a pH. ranging between 5.5 and 6.5*. If the soil is too strongly alkaline, or if it becomes too acid, roses have a tendency to become chlorotic, this condition being indicated by a very characteristic mottling of the leaves, the veins remaining dark green and the leaf areas between the veins becoming yellow, or in extreme cases, almost white. When such a condition becomes evident the soil should be tested to determine whether the trouble is due to too much acidity or to too high a degree of alkalinity, known as lime-induced chlorosis. If the soil tests much above a pH. of 6.5 the trouble is probably due to an excess of lime, and an application of iron sulfate should be made to correct this condition. The iron sulfate should be spread evenly over the surface of the beds at the rate of approximately two pounds per hundred square feet. If the degree of alkalinity is very slight, one pound will be sufficient; whereas if it is more pronounced, as much as three pounds may be required. Ten days after the application has been made the soil should be tested again, and if the pH. has not been lowered to 6.5 another application should be made. If the chlorosis is caused by too high a degree of acidity the condition may be remedied by an application of lime. (See Chart on page 27 for rate of application.) In the preparation of new beds the soil should be tested and a pH. ranging between 5.5 and 6.5 should be definitely established.

Maintenance of Soil Fertility: If the rose beds have been well prepared, no further fertilization will be necessary during the first season of growth. During the second year it will be well to adopt a definite program of fertilization which may be followed from year to year, in order that the soil may not become depleted. Roses are vigorous feeders and require a soil well

*See Chapter I, page 24.

Photograph by Philip B. Wallace

Agnes Selkirk Clark, Landscape Architect

The Change in Levels Adds Interest to this Formal Rose Garden

supplied with the essential elements of fertility. An adequate supply of nitrogen is necessary in order to promote rapid, vigorous growth and good foliage. Phosphorus induces good root development and stimulates flower bud formation, and also increases the size and color of the blooms. Potash is essential in that it gives strength to the cell walls, increases the resistance of the plant to disease, and aids in the ripening and hardening of the wood in the autumn.

Two programs are outlined which have proved satisfactory in maintaining soil fertility under varying conditions. Neither program can be said to be better than the other. An important point which must be heeded, regardless of the program adopted, is that no feeding should be done after the late summer (the first of September in the latitude of New York), as it will tend to stimulate a succulent fall growth which will be subject to winter-killing.

Program No. 1—Apply a good commercial fertilizer with an analysis of 5–10–5 or 4–12–4. Three applications should be made —one in early spring just as growth starts, the second as soon as the first period of bloom is over, and the third early in August to stimulate autumn bloom. The fertilizer should be sprinkled evenly over the surface of the soil about the base of the plant, being applied at the rate of three pounds per hundred square feet, and it should be watered in, in order that it may become more readily available.

Program No. 2—Apply a mulch of cow manure in the autumn and fork it lightly into the soil early in the spring. When growth starts give an application of hard wood ashes at the rate of five pounds per hundred square feet, and follow this with an application of two and one-half pounds of superphosphate per hundred square feet. Early in June make an application of dried blood sprinkled lightly over the soil at the rate of one pound per hundred square feet. After the application has been made the dried blood should be cultivated lightly into the soil about the plants.

It has been known for many years that the soot from chimneys and stoves is of unique value in stimulating the color of the blooms as well as of the foliage, and it should be used whenever it is obtainable. It should preferably be applied in the form of a liquid. A bag containing a peck of soot may be immersed in a barrel of rain water, and this may be poured about the bushes at intervals of every three days during the blooming season.

TIME OF PLANTING

Roses may be planted in the autumn at any time before the ground becomes frozen; they may be planted in early spring while the plants are still dormant; or they may be planted as potted roses after growth is well started. Some growers are enthusiastic over autumn planting, while others prefer very early spring planting. A method which, in some ways, is a combination of both fall and spring planting has been employed very successfully in some cases and is now being highly recommended by rose authorities. The plants are dug and shipped in the autumn, and upon arrival they are placed in a trench, the bushes being completely covered with soil. In the spring, when the soil is in ideal condition, the plants are lifted and placed in their permanent position in the bed. When this method is followed the wood and buds remain plump and firm throughout the winter, and the bushes are in perfect condition for planting in the spring. Planting does not have to be delayed until a spring shipment arrives, but may be done when both soil and weather conditions are most favorable; and one also has the advantage of being able to obtain superior stock. Most of the large commercial rose growers and seed firms dig their plants in the autumn, and store them during the winter in specially constructed storage houses. Consequently orders shipped out in the autumn are filled before the stock has become depleted, and plants of the finest quality may be obtained.

Potted roses should be planted only in exceptional cases. They are almost invariably inferior to roses planted when dormant, seldom attaining as vigorous growth or thriving as well. They serve a very definite purpose, however, in making it possible to replace any bushes which may have failed to survive, or to complete a very much delayed planting program.

Control of Insect Pests and Diseases. See Chapter XXXIII.

(*Roses continued on p.* 601)

Gardens in Color

DIRECT COLOR PHOTOGRAPHS FROM NATURE

Flowers Along a Brick Walk

Viewed from opposite ends of the central path. The varying shapes of the well-trimmed Oriental Arborvitæs provide a definite feature of interest, and lend to the picture the charm of blended and intermingled shades of green. The vivid hues of the flowers have a perfect setting against the evergreens and the Box specimens, which bring the quieter color note into the foreground. A sense of distance and space is given by the walk of brick laid in basket pattern, the color toned down by age and by the moss-grown crevices. The borders show a dramatically beautiful planting of Foxgloves and Snapdragons in warm tones of apricot, orange, and gold.

Photographs by   *Olmsted Brothers, Landscape Architects*
Edward D. Wilson   *Color Planting by Anna Jelinek*

Climbing Roses

In colors blending from deep pink through rose and shell to white, they clothe and soften an old wall of gray fieldstone. Pine trees make a dark background which sets off the gay colors and shelters the Roses from the cold winds of winter. From the south, the sun falls warm upon them, and their roots are grateful for the cool moisture provided by the friendly, supporting wall.

Photographed in natural color
by Mrs. Henry A. Wise Wood

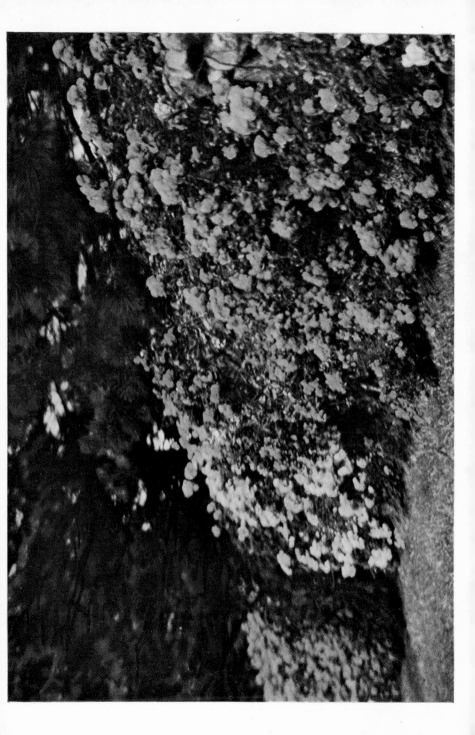

The Intimate Garden

In this small garden, built within the walls of an old barnyard, the color is concentrated in the perennial borders. Here on a June afternoon the spires of the Foxgloves are silhouetted against the warm shadows of the ancient wall. The perennials and annuals in the foreground will continue the succession of bloom throughout the season. Potted plants are grouped about the fountain beneath the Wisteria arbor, and Water-lilies spread their leaves upon the surface of the little pool. Everything is concentrated within a small area, but the details are well proportioned, and harmony of color and of scale have been maintained.

Photograph by Edward D. Wilson

Azalea Gardens of the South

The beauty and color of the blossoms are reflected in still water. Live-oaks draped with picturesque hanging moss frame the planting in quiet grays and greens. Tempered sunlight and varying shadow bring out a wide range of soft pastel tones.

Photographed in natural color
by Mrs. Henry A. Wise Wood

June in the Perennial Border

Any suburban or backyard garden which gets sufficient sunlight can achieve an equally successful effect with a mixed planting of perennials and biennials. Here a clipped Arborvitæ hedge provides the background, with the rigidity of the line broken at intervals by Magnolia glauca and tall shrubs, now past their period of flowering. The border shows Canterbury Bells in purple, lavender, pink, and white; at the far right are the delicate spires of pink Coral Bells. Foxgloves, and Delphiniums just coming into blossom, serve as accents in the rear line, while Newport Pink Sweet Williams and white Candytuft give a profusion of bloom in the foreground. In the center, an Oriental Poppy contributes a controlled and valuable touch of dissident color. Yellow comes into the composition in the clumps of Thalictrum glaucum.

Photograph by
Edward D. Wilson

Perennial Garden at the School of Horticulture
Planting Design by Lois Woodward Paul

METHOD OF PLANTING

Planting distances will depend almost entirely upon the type of rose. Because of their very vigorous habit of growth, the hybrid perpetuals should be planted from 2 feet to 2½ feet apart. For the hybrid teas and the tea roses a distance varying from 18 inches to 2 feet is sufficient except in the case of some of the very vigorous varieties.

Before planting, all injured or broken roots should be carefully pruned away, a clean, slanting cut being made. Any long, straggly roots should be cut back sufficiently so that they will not have to be twisted or bent when the plant is set. A hole of ample size should be dug for each plant. If the loose soil is mounded slightly in the bottom of the hole one will be able to place the roots in a natural position, extending both outward and downward.

The depth of planting is a very important factor. The plant should be placed so that the bud, or crown, which is the point of union between the stock and scion, is between 1 and 2 inches below the surface of the soil. If the bush is planted too deeply, with the point of union more than 3 inches below the surface, the roots will receive an inadequate supply of oxygen from the air and the growth of the plant will be seriously injured in consequence. This factor is of particular importance in heavy clay soils.

After the plant is in place the soil should be packed firmly about the roots. Many failures are caused by loose, careless planting, and if success is to be assured it is necessary that a few simple rules be observed. Packing the soil about the roots with the blunt end of a trowel handle is very effective, care being taken not to bruise the roots. When the hole has been filled almost to the top, the soil may be tramped firmly about the bush with the feet. The plants should then be watered thoroughly, and the beds should not be allowed to dry out until the plants have become well established. This is quite as necessary for roses planted in the autumn, as it is for roses planted in the spring, as the soil about the roots should always be moist when the ground freezes. Immediately after the first watering has been given at the time of planting, the soil should be mounded up about the plants. In the case of roses planted in the autumn this will serve as a winter protection for the plants, and the beds may be mulched in the usual manner. When roses are planted in the spring this hilling up of the soil is equally advisable, as it protects the canes from the drying effects of sun and wind while the new feeding roots are being developed which will, later in the season, supply the moisture which the plant needs. In the spring these temporary mounds of earth should be left about the plants for three or four weeks and the soil may then be gradually worked back into the beds.

Severe pruning is necessary at the time of planting. It is advisable to cut most of the canes back to either two or three buds.

PRUNING

In order to prune roses intelligently it is necessary to understand the requirements of the various classes and types.

Hybrid Perpetuals; Hybrid Teas and Tea Roses; Polyanthas. Roses in this class should be pruned after the dormant season is over, just as the buds are ready to break in the spring. As the hybrid perpetuals usually start into growth several weeks before the teas and hybrid teas they may be pruned somewhat earlier. In the vicinity of New York the hybrid perpetuals may usually be pruned late in March, and the teas and hybrid teas during the early part of April.

The method of pruning will depend to a considerable degree upon the type of flower which is desired. If one wishes to have blooms of exhibition quality with long stems for cutting, it will be necessary to prune vigorously. If, however, one is willing to sacrifice quality for quantity, it is possible to prune more lightly and to have more abundant bloom in consequence. For the gardener who wishes to have lovely roses for cutting and a reasonable display of bloom in the garden, a moderate degree of pruning, between the two extremes, is advisable. To meet these requirements the hybrid perpetuals and some of the more vigorous of the hybrid teas should be pruned back to five or six buds on the stronger canes and from four to five buds on

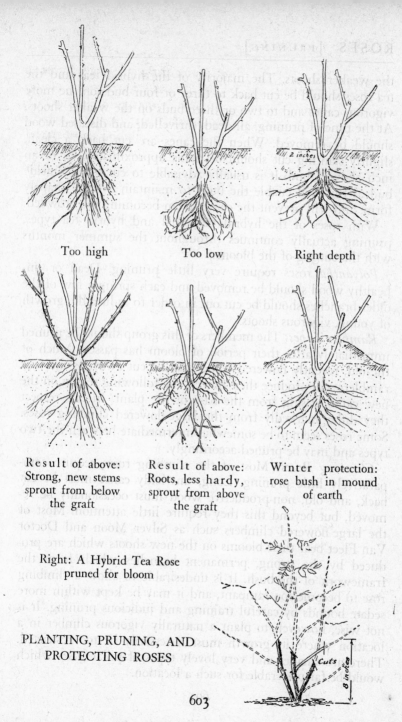

Too high   Too low   Right depth

Result of above:
Strong, new stems
sprout from below
the graft

Result of above:
Roots, less hardy,
sprout from above
the graft

Winter protection:
rose bush in mound
of earth

Right: A Hybrid Tea Rose
pruned for bloom

2 inches

Cuts

8 inches

PLANTING, PRUNING, AND
PROTECTING ROSES

603

the weaker shoots. The majority of the hybrid teas and the tea roses should be cut back to three or four buds on the more vigorous canes and to two or three buds on the weaker shoots. At the time of pruning, all dead, shrivelled, and diseased wood should be removed. When the canes are cut back a clean, slightly slanting cut should be made approximately ¼ of an inch above a bud. It is usually advisable to cut to an outside bud as this will enable the bush to maintain a more shapely form, and will prevent the center from becoming too crowded.

With roses of the hybrid perpetual and hybrid tea types, pruning actually continues throughout the summer months with the cutting of the blooms.

Polyantha roses require very little pruning. Dead or unhealthy wood should be removed and each spring a few of the older branches should be cut out in order to induce the growth of young, vigorous shoots.

Rambler Types: The members of this group should be pruned immediately after their period of bloom has passed. Much of the old, recently flowered wood may be cut away, as the true ramblers will produce their flowers the following season on the new canes arising from the base of the plant. In this respect they differ markedly from the large-flowered climbing roses. Some roses seem to be somewhat intermediate between the two types and may be pruned accordingly.

Climbing Roses: Most of the climbing roses require comparatively little pruning. Long, unwieldy canes must be cut back, and old, non-productive wood must occasionally be removed, but beyond this they require little attention. Most of the large-flowered climbers such as Silver Moon and Doctor Van Fleet bear their blooms on the new shoots which are produced by the strong, permanent branches which form the framework of the bush. It is undesirable to allow a climbing rose to become too rampant, and it may be kept within more sedate bounds by careful training and judicious pruning. It is not wise, however, to plant a naturally vigorous climber in a location where its growth must necessarily be too restricted. There are smaller and very lovely types of pillar roses which would be far preferable for such a location.

WHEN CUTTING ROSES

When roses are cut for decorative purposes, many of the same principles may be applied which are used in the pruning of the plants. A clean, sharp, slightly slanting cut should be made, approximately ¼ of an inch above a leaf-bud. The symmetry of the bush may be maintained by cutting either at an outside or inside bud, it being advisable to direct the growth outward whenever it is possible to do so. The quality and abundance of future bloom will depend upon the number of leaf-buds left on the stem after the flower has been cut. If the shoot is strong and vigorous, three buds may be left—two if the shoot is weak. The length of the stem of the cut flower will, therefore, be determined by the number of buds to be left on the cane. Roses should preferably be cut early in the morning before they have been touched for many hours by the sun.

WATERING

Roses make their best growth during moderately cool weather when the soil is well supplied with moisture. Although roses resent a soil that is too saturated with moisture, or a water table that has risen above the level of the roots, they require an adequate and fairly abundant supply of moisture throughout the growing season. During periods of drought, roses should be watered thoroughly once a week. The bed should be soaked until the water has penetrated into the soil to a depth of at least a foot. Frequent light waterings are of little value and do more harm than good.

SUMMER MULCHES

Throughout the growing season, the surface of the rose beds should either be cultivated or should be kept mulched. Frequent cultivations will maintain a dust mulch, and this has proved to be an entirely satisfactory practice. Some growers prefer to mulch the beds in late spring with a 2-inch layer of peatmoss, and this method has certain advantages. A more even soil temperature is maintained, the moisture in the soil is conserved, subsequent care and cultivation are reduced to a minimum, and the beds present a very trim, tidy appearance. The disadvantages of this practice are that the long-continued use of peatmoss year after year may cause the soil to become too loose in texture, and certain brands of peatmoss tend gradually to increase the acidity of the soil. This may, however, be entirely counteracted by an occasional application of lime. On the whole, the advantages probably more than outweigh the disadvantages. Buckwheat hulls or tobacco stems may be used instead of peatmoss, but they are not as satisfactory and are decidedly less pleasing in appearance.

WINTER PROTECTION

The amount of winter protection which may be necessary depends upon three factors—the severity of the climate; the exposure of the rose garden; and the natural hardiness of the varieties which have been selected.

Winter injury is usually attributable either to the actual freezing of the twigs and roots, which breaks down the cell tissues, or to the loss of moisture from the twigs caused by excessive evaporation. Winter injury is quite as likely to be caused by strong, drying winds and by brilliant sunshine as by extreme cold. Throughout the winter the roots continue to absorb water from the soil and a slow evaporation of moisture continues from the canes. If an undue amount of wind and sunshine increases evaporation beyond the point where the roots can supply sufficient moisture to the twigs, the canes will begin to shrivel, and if the process is prolonged, the plant will die, even though no actual freezing of the plant tissues has taken place. Therefore one of the first preparations for winter should be to see that the soil is well supplied with moisture. The normal autumn rains will often provide for an adequate storage of moisture, but if the autumn season is deficient in rainfall, artificial watering should be done before the ground freezes.

In the South roses require practically no winter protection. In sections of the North, however, where the cold is of such severity that the thermometer will range much below 10 degrees F. it is wise to provide adequate protection for the majority of the hybrid teas, for all the tea roses, for some of the hybrid perpetuals and polyanthas, and for a few of the more tender climbers.

In a normal season the early frosts of autumn will harden and ripen the wood and the plants will gradually become dormant. It is a wise precaution to rake and burn all fallen leaves and bits of twig in order to prevent them from harboring bacterial and fungous diseases. Soil brought into the beds may be mounded up about the bushes to a height of from 10 to 12 inches. This mound of earth will afford considerable protection about the crown of the plant and will also prevent the wood and buds of the lower portion of the stem from drying out. After the ground has frozen, a mulch of salt hay, strawy manure or some similar material may be spread over the beds. It is important that the mulch should not be applied until after the ground has frozen. In the case of the less hardy varieties each individual bush may be protected with a covering of salt hay or dry leaves, and in sections where the winters are of extreme severity a generous covering of salt hay or dry leaves may be heaped over the entire bed until only the tips of the bushes are left exposed. The covering may be held in place by evergreen boughs or by a wire framework. If leaves are used for this purpose, only those should be chosen which do not rot readily, such as oak leaves. Leaves from maples and elms soon form a soggy mat when used for winter covering and usually do more harm than good.

There are various climatic conditions which frequently contribute to the winter-killing of roses, conditions over which one has very little control. If there is a long spell of warm, growing weather in the autumn the plants will not become sufficiently hardened to withstand the rigors of a severe winter. Under such conditions the bushes will have a tendency to continue growth until late in the autumn and the shoots will be so soft and succulent that considerable injury may result. In such cases it is wise to provide careful protection for the bushes, even though it may not usually be necessary.

PROTECTION FOR CLIMBERS

Some of our most beautiful climbers, such as Jacotte and Emily Gray, are not able to survive the extreme severity of a Northern winter unless given sufficient protection.

During the past few years some very interesting experiments have been carried out at Cornell University to determine the most satisfactory method of affording protection for climbing roses. It has been found that cornstalks and evergreen boughs, while affording satisfactory protection, often harbor field mice and rabbits to such an extent that considerable damage may be done. Burlap is not satisfactory, as it holds too much moisture. The most approved method, and one that has given absolute satisfaction, consists of removing the canes from the trellis or support early in October while they are still supple, and allowing them to remain procumbent upon the ground, where the grass will grow up among them and where the falling leaves which are blown in upon them will afford natural protection. Soil is then mounded up about the base of the plant, and after the ground has become frozen a mulch of salt hay or straw is placed over the mound of soil. In order to hold the canes in a procumbent position two strong pieces of wood may be driven into the earth at right angles to each other, forming a wedge to hold the canes in place. This method of protection has proved so satisfactory that even during several winters of extreme severity, when the temperature reached 20 degrees below zero, no injury resulted. Early in the spring, after danger from frost is over, the mounds of soil may be removed from the base of the plant gradually, and the canes may easily be refastened to their supports.

PROTECTION OF STANDARD ROSES

Standard or Tree Roses require careful winter protection. The soil should be removed from the side of the roots, the rose tree should be bent down into an improvised trench and it should then be covered with a heavy layer of soil.

CLASSIFICATION OF ROSES

Roses may be grouped into several classifications, one of the most logical being their adaptability to certain uses.

For the formal pattern of beds and borders in the rose garden the four types which are of the greatest value are the Hybrid Perpetuals, the Tea Roses, the Hybrid Teas and the Polyanthas.

For use on lattices, pergolas and walls, the large-flowered climbing roses, the semi-climbing everblooming types, and the ramblers are the most desirable.

As a ground cover on steep banks some of the species roses are of value, and in this group we also find a number of recent introductions which are of outstanding merit.

For massed shrubbery plantings, for hedges and for beautiful specimens, the lovely Pemberton roses, the Brier roses, the Rugosas and some of the delightful species roses may be used.

And, quite in a class by themselves, we have the old-fashioned roses—the Moss Rose and the Damask Rose; the Bengal and Bourbon roses; the Noisette roses and many others.

ROSES FOR GARDEN BEDS AND BORDERS

Hybrid Perpetuals. The hybrid perpetuals were introduced in 1830 by Laffray, who had succeeded in crossing the lovely old Damask rose with the China rose. The name, hybrid perpetual, is, unfortunately, very misleading, as the members of this group bloom freely during the month of June and yield but occasional, scattered bloom throughout the rest of the season. The term perpetual was originally intended to refer to the hardiness of the plant instead of to its blooming period. The hybrid perpetuals are the "June Roses" which were so cherished by gardeners a half century or more ago, and even today, when they are no longer classed among our favorites, we recognize the fact that they possess many virtues and that they will never be entirely replaced by the newer hybrid teas. The hybrid perpetuals are very hardy, and they are, therefore, able to withstand winters of extreme severity. In habit of growth they are strong and vigorous and require much less coddling than many of their more fastidious descendants. The flowers are large and well formed and are produced on long, strong stems, which makes them of particular value for cutting.

Varieties of Merit

Frau Karl Druschki is considered the best white rose in cultivation and is often called "the White American Beauty." The large, pure white blooms are borne on long, strong stems and are unexcelled for cutting. The flower is of beautiful form and its one failing seems to be that it has no fragrance.

Mme. Albert Barbier bears flowers of a delicate salmon-pink shade and is considered one of the best of this group.

Marguerite Guillard is a sport of Frau Karl Druschki and is very similar in form and color, its distinguishing characteristic being that it is entirely thornless.

Mrs. John Laing is a bush of very vigorous habit, with fragrant flowers, and is a clear pink in color.

General Jacqueminot is a pure crimson and has long been a popular member of this group. It is a very rampant grower and needs vigorous pruning.

TEA ROSES

Tea roses were introduced from China in the year 1810 and they have long been classed among the favorites.

Wherever tea roses can be grown they are greatly prized. The foliage has a coppery tint and the sweetly scented flowers are exquisite in form. Unfortunately tea roses are not hardy in the North unless very elaborate winter protection is provided. They are, therefore, seldom grown except in the lovely rose gardens of the South. They prefer a rich, well-drained soil and require severe pruning.

Varieties of Merit

Lady Hillingdon. Beautifully pointed buds, flowers a clear saffron yellow.

Maman Cochet. Large, fragrant flower of carmine-pink.

William R. Smith. Flowers creamy white, tinged with pink.

Hybrid Tea Roses

The first hybrid tea rose was produced by Guillot in 1867 as the result of crossing the hybrid perpetual rose Mme. Victor Verdies with the tea rose Mme. Bravy. This cross resulted in the lovely hybrid tea rose known as La France, which has maintained its popularity for more than half a century. Many later crosses were made between hybrid perpetuals and tea roses and again between hybrid tea roses and other hybrid teas and as a result of these crosses many strains have been developed.

Our finest and most desirable garden roses are to be found in this group. Most varieties within the group are of a sturdy, vigorous habit of growth and are hardy in the North if given moderate winter protection. Under favorable cultural conditions the hybrid tea roses will give generous bloom from June well into October. During the heat of midsummer the bloom is more scattered and the different varieties vary somewhat in their blooming habits, some giving better autumn bloom than others. There is also considerable variance in habit of growth, some varieties attaining a height of 3 feet or more, while other varieties are somewhat low and spreading in form and produce but scanty foliage. Some varieties are exceptionally vigorous and very long-lived, while other varieties have a tendency to die out after a few years, even when grown under the most favorable cultural conditions. The hybrid teas possess a wide range of color and form, and they are the most desirable type for the average garden.

Varieties of Merit

Ami Quinard. Medium size, semi-double flowers of a deep crimson color and of an unusually velvety texture.

Break O' Day. This lovely rose with orange-apricot flowers was originated by the Brownells and was introduced in 1937. It is a rose which is quite outstanding in its class, being noted for its strong, robust habit of growth, its excellent foliage, its extreme hardiness (it is able to withstand sub-zero temperature) and the exquisite quality of its flowers.

Charles P. Kilham. The large, beautiful flowers are produced on long stems and are exceedingly fine for cutting. In color they are a brilliant red-orange, suffused with scarlet. Rather large and spreading in habit of growth, and the plants need ample room.

Conqueror. One of the most beautiful of all yellow roses. The flowers are a saffron-yellow, the reverse side of the petals flushed with orange. Vigorous in habit of growth.

Duquesa De Penaranda. Large, fragrant flowers of a cinnamon-peach color. Vigorous, upright habit of growth with splendid foliage. Exceedingly fine autumn bloom.

Etoile de Hollande. Considered one of the finest of all red roses. The large, fragrant flowers are of a pure crimson with a velvety sheen, beautiful both in bud and when full blown. A plant of unusual vigor with large, handsome foliage.

La France was the first hybrid tea rose, and it has maintained its popularity for more than half a century because of its many fine qualities. It is considered the most fragrant of all roses and it produces an abundance of bloom, the flowers being a bright silvery pink with slightly curled petals. It is hardy and vigorous in habit of growth and will thrive reasonably well on rather poor soil.

Lady Alice Stanley. A rose which has been a favorite for many years. Long, pointed buds, flowers of fine form, moderately fragrant, pale pink in color with a deep coral-rose tint on the reverse side of the petals.

Lady Margaret Stewart. A rose of striking beauty. In the half-open bud stage, the flowers are a deep yellow, heavily veined and splashed with orange-scarlet, the reverse side of the petals being suffused with carmine. As the flowers open, the colors become more suffused. The buds are long and pointed, flowers fully double and sweetly fragrant.

Margaret McGredy. Noted for its vigorous growth and almost continuous bloom. Flowers large and well formed with remarkable lasting qualities. In color the flowers are an unusual shade of orange-scarlet turning to carmine-rose.

Mme. Edouard Herriot. A rose of exquisite beauty both in bud and in flower. Low and spreading in habit of growth and very thorny. The color of the flowers is one of the most brilliant hues to be found among roses, being an intense coral-red in the bud stage. The flowers are medium in size, semi-double, coral-red shading to bright rosy scarlet and salmon-pink as they fade.

Mme. Cochet-Cochet. One of the most beautiful of the newer roses. Long, pointed buds of coppery pink, flushed with orange. The fragrant flowers are lovely in form and are a soft salmon-pink with the sheen of sateen.

Mme. Henri Guillot. A rose of startling beauty, awarded the Bagatelle Gold Medal. Of a vigorous habit of growth with dark, glossy foliage. The color is a most unusual blending of a deep watermelon shade with raspberry pink, surrounded by a glow of reddish orange.

Mrs. Erskine Pembroke Thom. One of the finest of the yellow hybrid tea roses. Vigorous in habit of growth with fine, dark, bronzy foliage which is very resistant to disease. The buds are long and pointed, the flowers are sweetly scented and of a deep lemon-yellow hue which does not pale with age. Blooms are produced almost continuously throughout the season.

National Flower Guild. A rose of unusual hardiness and of a strong, vigorous habit of growth. The plants are tall and branching, with remarkably fine foliage. The flowers are produced freely throughout the season and are of a handsome scarlet-red tone which does not fade.

Single Hybrid Tea Roses

In this group we find some of our most beautiful hybrid tea roses, exquisite both in form and in coloring. They are decorative and lovely in the garden and offer most delightful possibilities for cut-flower arrangements.

Varieties of Merit

Cecil. Large, single flowers of a soft primrose-yellow. Plants vigorous and bushy in habit of growth, with splendid foliage.

Dainty Bess. A rose of most striking form and color. The flowers are composed of six broad petals of a soft rose-pink with a large cluster of deep wine-colored stamens which give the flower a most unique appearance. The flowers are borne in clusters and vary considerably in size.

Innocence. Large, single, pure white flowers, with a mass of wine-red stamens, tipped with gold.

Irish Elegance. A rose of exquisite beauty, bronze-pink when in bud, the open flowers being a delicate shade of apricot.

Irish Fireflame. The flowers are an orange-crimson shaded with pink and gold and are lovely for cutting. The bush is of vigorous growth and gives generous bloom.

Isobel. Beautiful, large, single flowers of a bronzy tone with shades of flaming orange-pink.

Old Gold. Flowers sweetly fragrant, of a delicate pinkish buff shade.

POLYANTHAS

The dwarf polyantha roses are occasionally used for edgings and, to some extent, for bedding. The plants are very bushy and are of a somewhat dwarf habit of growth, seldom reaching a height of more than 18 inches or 2 feet. The flowers, which are borne in clusters, vary considerably in size and form. Some varieties bear tiny blossoms which resemble miniature tea roses; other varieties bear lovely single blooms, and some bear clusters of double, pompon-like flowers. The polyantha roses are very hardy, and require com-paratively little care and attention.

VARIETIES OF MERIT

(Small-flowering Varieties)

Cameo. The tiny flowers are borne in great profusion and are of a most lovely tone of shell-pink shading to orange salmon.

Cecile Brunner is known also as the Sweetheart rose. The flowers are small and exquisitely formed, being particularly charming when in bud. The color is a delicate shade of pink, tinted with yellow at the base.

Gloria Mundi. The flowers are borne in clusters and are of a most unusual scarlet-orange hue.

Golden Salmon. The small flowers, produced in great abundance, are of a bright scarlet-salmon hue.

(Large-flowering Varieties)

Anne Poulsen. The large, single flowers are of a brilliant scarlet-crimson and are produced abundantly throughout the season.

Bloomfield Abundance. Strong and vigorous in habit of growth with almost perfect foliage. Flowers of light salmon-pink color.

Helen Leenders. The flowers are semi-double in form and are borne in clusters. Bright salmon in bud, shading to light pink as the buds open.

Orange Triumph. One of the outstanding varieties of recent introduction. The large, double flowers are borne in clusters and are of a most striking shade of orange-scarlet.

Springtime. Known as the Appleblossom Rose. One of the most beautiful members of this group. The bushes are well branched, yet compact in habit of growth, and the exquisite single flowers, of a clear, appleblossom pink, are borne in great profusion. There is about them a simplicity and charm which are very appealing and they are a great addition to any rose garden.

ROSES FOR WALLS, PERGOLAS AND TRELLISES

Large-flowered Climbing Roses: In this group we find many of our most beautiful climbing roses. Strong and vigorous in habit of growth, they need ample room to develop, and adequate support. The large-flowered climbers give a profusion of bloom during the month of June and some of the new varieties which have recently been introduced bloom intermittently throughout the season.

VARIETIES OF MERIT

Albertine. The large, fragrant flowers are of a coppery, chamois-yellow, the reverse side of the petals being a bright salmon. As the flowers age they change to a coppery rose hue. A very handsome climber with beautiful, healthy foliage.

Apricot Glow. One of the most beautiful of the new climbers originated by the Brownells. The flowers are borne in large clusters and are of a light, apricot color, shading to yellow at the base.

Emily Gray. An excellent climber with unusually fine glossy foliage. The long, pointed flower buds are deep saffron-yellow, changing to pale orange as they open. Not hardy north of Philadelphia without winter protection.

Golden Orange Climber. Originated by the Brownells and considered one of the finest of their recent introductions. The flowers are large and semi-double in form, the petals being waved and crinkled. In color the flowers range from delicate yellow to orange and they are borne on long stems which make them excellent for cutting. The plants are vigorous in habit of growth and are very hardy.

Jacotte. One of the most beautiful of all climbing roses. The foliage is glossy and holly-like in appearance and the large, semi-double flowers, which are borne in such profusion, are of an exquisite shade of apricot-orange. It is not hardy without protection where the winters are severe.

Mme. Grégoire Staechelin is also known as the Spanish Beauty Rose. It is very vigorous in habit of growth and has excellent foliage. The flower buds are long and shapely and the handsome, semi-double flowers are produced in profusion on long stems. The flowers are most unusual in coloring, being an iridescent, pearly pink, tipped with crimson.

Silver Moon. There is no other climber which possesses the unusual qualities of Silver Moon. The flowers are beautiful in form, being large and semi-double. In color, the flowers are a glistening white, shading to soft cream, and the brilliant golden stamens add greatly to the beauty of the blooms. It is one of the most vigorous of all the climbers.

The New Dawn. One of the few large-flowered climbers with everblooming characteristics. The New Dawn is a sport of Doctor

Van Fleet and possesses all of the fine qualities of the parent. The large, double flowers are of a soft flesh pink and are produced continuously throughout the season.

EVERBLOOMING, SEMI–CLIMBING ROSES

Within the past few decades a new type of semi-climbing rose has been introduced which is worthy of recognition, for it possesses many admirable qualities not found in other climbers. It is of an ever-blooming habit, flowering abundantly in June, and producing scattered blooms throughout the season. The plants attain a height of from 5 to 8 feet and are of particular value for training upon low walls and fences and upon light trellises. These new types were originated by Peter Lambert of Germany and by Captain George C. Thomas, Jr., one of the most outstanding of our American hybridizers.

VARIETIES OF MERIT

Ausonius. One of the finest of the Lambertiana group, producing large, light-yellow flowers on long trusses, and blooming freely throughout the season.

Bloomfield Comet. Vigorous in habit of growth and very persistent in bloom. The buds are of a reddish hue and the large, single flowers are of a coppery yellow, stained with red.

Bloomfield Culmination. One of the most exquisite of this group, producing large, single flowers of a delicate rose-pink with golden stamens.

Bloomfield Dainty. Orange-yellow when in bud, with single flowers of a clear, canary yellow.

Bloomfield Discovery. Buds coppery pink, the large single flowers a soft silvery pink, tinted a darker shade on the reverse side of the petals.

Heideröslein. Single, fragrant flowers, citron-yellow with a pinkish tinge on the reverse side of the petals.

Mrs. George C. Thomas. Flowers semi-double, orange in bud, opening to a light salmon-pink. Blooms throughout the season.

Unique. Flowers orange-salmon and fawn. Blooms continuously throughout the summer and autumn.

RAMBLERS

The rambler roses are particularly well suited for the covering of rough banks. Unfortunately some of the more common sorts such as the Crimson Rambler and Dorothy Perkins have been very much over-planted and it is usually possible to find roses which can be grown under similar conditions and which are far superior both in habit of growth and in quality of bloom. As a group the ramblers are very subject to attacks of mildew and the foliage is apt to become unsightly.

VARIETIES OF MERIT

Aviateur Blériot. Saffron buds and flowers in small clusters, light yellow fading white; magnolia fragrance.

Evangeline. One of the strongest-growing climbers with excellent glossy foliage, and bearing its soft pink, single flowers in enormous clusters. Lovely fragrance.

Phyllis Bide. A graceful rambler with exquisitely formed little buds of pale gold and pink, opening to small buff-yellow flowers.

Sanders' White Rambler. Flowers pure white, double and sweetly fragrant, in huge clusters. A strong grower with good, disease-resistant foliage.

White Dorothy. A pure white counterpart of the common pink Dorothy Perkins.

ROSES FOR SPECIMENS AND AS SHRUBS

Brier Roses: The Brier Roses are native throughout Europe and Caucasia, and we find them divided into several distinct groups.

The *Austrian* and *Scotch Briers* are very lovely and decorative when used as specimens or in the shrubbery border. They prefer a rather dry soil and require very little care and attention.

VARIETIES OF MERIT

Austrian Copper. A lovely brier rose with single flowers of an intense coppery-red hue, the reverse side of the petals being a bright, golden yellow.

Austrian Yellow. The yellow-flowered type of the Austrian Brier Rose.

Harison's Yellow. Originated in 1830 by the Rev. Mr. Harison, this lovely brier rose has maintained its popularity for more than a century. It is hardy and vigorous in habit of growth and the semi-double yellow flowers are produced in great profusion. When it is in flower every branch and twig seems to have blossomed forth, so full is it of starry blooms.

Persian Yellow is a fine, old-fashioned shrub rose producing myriads of small, golden flowers.

The *Sweetbrier or Eglantine Rose* (Rosa Rubiginosa) is a native of England and is famed in song and story. The Eglantine rose, with its hybrids, is the only rose which possesses sweet-scented foliage. Tiny glands on the under surface of the leaves give out a most delightful perfume, and when the plants are wet with dew, or after a warm summer shower, the fragrance is most alluring. The small, single flowers are a bright pink in color.

The *Penzance Sweetbriers* are hybrids of the Eglantine rose and were originated by Lord Penzance. The exquisite beauty of the small, single flowers and the scent of the foliage have endeared them to many gardeners and they are worthy of wider recognition.

Varieties of Merit

Brenda. Fragrant, single flowers of a light peach-pink.

Lady Penzance, with bright, copper-colored flowers and its sweetly-scented foliage, is one of the most desirable of this group.

Lord Penzance bears exquisite single flowers of a delicate fawn tint shading to ecru, and the foliage is sweetly scented.

Meg Merrilies. Very vigorous in habit of growth. Single, fragrant flowers of a rosy crimson.

Minna. Flowers white, opening with the palest tinge of pink.

Rose Bradwardine. Flowers a clear, rose-pink. Foliage heavily scented.

HYBRID MUSK ROSES

In this group we find the many lovely roses originated a few decades ago by the Rev. Joseph H. Pemberton of England, and called, in his honor, the Pemberton Roses. They are hybrids of the Musk Rose, and they are among the most beautiful of our specimen shrub roses. They range in height from 3 to 8 feet, and bloom intermittently throughout the season, flowering both on the old wood and on the wood of the current season's growth. Some varieties may be readily trained as pillar roses.

Varieties of Merit

Clytemnestra. Copper buds; small, ruffled flowers ranging from deep pink through salmon.

Daybreak. Flowers semi-single, produced in clusters, and of a golden-yellow color.

Francesca. Flowers of a bright apricot-yellow.

Pax. Considered one of the finest of this group of ever-blooming shrub roses. Large, creamy buds, opening to beautifully formed white flowers with a delightful fragrance.

Penelope. Flowers shell-pink, shaded saffron, with the characteristic musk fragrance.

Thisbe. Small, semi-double pale-yellow flowers borne in clusters. Vigorous in habit of growth, with gracefully arching branches.

Vanity. Large, semi-single fragrant flowers of a soft rose-pink.

RUGOSA AND RUGOSA HYBRIDS

The name, rugosa, was given to this group because of the very wrinkled appearance of the foliage. The Rugosa roses are natives of Japan, China and Korea and they are noted for their hardiness and their ability to withstand very adverse conditions. They will thrive in almost any type of soil, will endure extreme cold and will withstand neglect better than almost any other rose known. They are of particular value for planting in exposed situations and at the seashore, where they are able to withstand the effects of salt spray. They range in height from 6 to 7 feet and produce numerous erect, very spiny stems. The foliage is a deep green in color, thick and wrinkled in texture, and is practically disease- and insect-proof.

VARIETIES AND HYBRIDS OF MERIT

Agnes. Coppery yellow buds, double flowers pale amber-gold and very fragrant.

Doctor Eckener. Flowers are large, very fragrant, semi-double and of a beautiful coppery-rose shade, blended with yellow.

Polar Bear. Large white flowers with a faint blush, everblooming in habit. Hardy and vigorous.

Rugosa alba. Single, white flowers. Typical in form and habit.

Vanguard. Flowers large, double, orange-salmon, borne on strong erect stems; a very vigorous grower.

SPECIES ROSES

Of the many species roses suitable for specimens the most beautiful of all is the lovely Rosa Hugonis. It was first discovered growing wild in Northern China by Father Hugo, a missionary, and was named in his honor. It is one of the loveliest plants known to cultivation and no rose garden is complete without it. It is the first rose to come into flower, and in late spring the slender, graceful branches are covered with myriad blooms. The flowers are single and exquisite in form, and they are of the softest shade of primrose yellow. It blooms more profusely if not fertilized.

TRAILING ROSES

There are a few roses which are of such low, trailing habit that they are particularly well suited for use as a ground cover on hillsides and embankments. A number of new varieties have recently been introduced which are admirably adapted for this purpose.

VARIETIES OF MERIT

Coral Creeper. Buds deep red, flowers apricot-orange, fading to pink, semi-double in form and of good size.

Little Compton Creeper. Flowers single, deep rose-pink borne in large, open clusters. Foliage dark green and glossy.

Max Graf. Sprays of large, single, clear pink flowers.

Wichuraiana. A species rose of exceedingly rapid growth often producing canes from 12 to 15 feet long in a single season. The foliage is a glossy, pale green and the small white flowers are rather inconspicuous. The Wichuraiana rose is extremely hardy and will grow in almost any type of soil. It is well adapted to washed clay banks and other unfavorable situations.

OLD–FASHIONED ROSES

Beloved by countless generations of gardeners, these old-fashioned roses are seldom seen in gardens of the present day. There are, however, a few rosarians who have made a study of them and have brought together collections which are greatly cherished.

The Provence or Cabbage Rose derives its name from the Provence section of France where it was grown so abundantly. Legends tell us that it was cultivated by the Romans and was later introduced into other sections of Europe. The foliage is deeply wrinkled, broad and heavy, the blooms are large and globular in shape, and sweetly scented. Because of the great number of petals folded upon each other like the leaves of a cabbage it has been called the "Cabbage Rose." It blooms but once during the season. Although the Provence rose will grow in almost any soil and will withstand considerable neglect, it responds remarkably to good care and cultivation, and for best growth it should be heavily pruned.

VARIETIES OF MERIT

Anais Segalas. Flowers a deep tone of almost Tyrian-pink.
Konigin von Danemark. Flowers a delicate flesh-pink.
Unique Blanche. Deeply cupped, pure white flowers.

THE MOSS ROSE

These roses are characterized by the distinctly mossy growth on the outer side of the calyx of the opening buds. As a group they are quite hardy but require severe pruning if good bloom is desired. In order to secure a succession of bloom, half of the canes may be pruned in October and half the following May, the shoots being cut back to 4 or 5 buds.

VARIETIES OF MERIT

Blanche Moreau. Buds heavily mossed, the double flowers being borne in clusters. Color, white tinged with pink. Vigorous and fine-flowering.

Crested Moss. The Crested Moss Rose is an offshoot of the Provence rose and was first discovered in 1827 growing in the crevice of a wall in Fribourg, Switzerland. The large, full flowers are a bright, rose-pink in color.

Gloire De Mousseux. One of the finest of the Moss roses. The flowers are of a carmine-salmon-pink shade and are produced in great abundance.

Old Pink Moss. One of the oldest roses of this type. Buds heavily mossed, flowers pale rose-pink.

THE DAMASK ROSE

This rose is a native of Damascus and Syria and was brought to Europe by the early Crusaders upon their return from the Holy Land. It is known to have been in cultivation in England in 1573. Damask roses are very hardy and vigorous and thrive well in almost any type of soil. The foliage is large and rough and light green in color. The flowers are usually produced in trusses of three or more.

VARIETIES OF MERIT

Damascena officinalis. The original Rose of Damascus, intensely fragrant, and bearing double, rose-pink flowers.

621

Marie Louise. Double flowers of a rich, deep pink. An old variety found growing in the gardens of Malmaison in 1813.

Mme. Hardy. Flowers pure white, occasionally tinged with pink. One of the most beautiful and most fragrant of the Damask roses.

THE BOURBON ROSE

These roses were introduced into France in 1820 from the Isle of Bourbon and are closely related to the China or Bengal Roses. They are moderately hardy and vigorous and bloom freely throughout the early summer, some varieties blooming also in the autumn. The foliage is dark and lustrous.

VARIETIES OF MERIT

Adam Messerich. Fragrant flowers of a clear, rose-red. Bushy in habit of growth.

Louise Odier. Flowers, flesh-pink, of good form, and produced freely throughout the season.

Martha. Flowers a lovely shade of salmon-orange, produced freely on thornless canes.

Souvenir De La Malmaison. Very fragrant flesh-colored flowers. Of dwarf habit—hardly more than 2 feet in height.

THE NOISETTE ROSE

This rose was originated by Mr. Philip Noisette of Charleston, South Carolina, in 1817, as a result of crossing the China Blush Rose with the Musk Rose. Mr. Noisette sent the rose to his father in France and he, in turn, originated from it the beautiful Maréchal Niel rose, so beloved throughout the South.

VARIETIES OF MERIT AMONG THE NOISETTE HYBRIDS

Bouquet D'Or. Flowers large and full, pale yellow, shaded with coppery salmon.

Crépuscule. A beautiful variety with flowers of an orange-pink shade, fading to apricot yellow.

Maréchal Niel. Double, fragrant flowers of a deep, golden yellow. Not hardy in the North, but one of the most beautiful of all roses for Southern gardens.

Rêve D'Or. Fragrant, double flowers of a soft buff-yellow shade. Very vigorous in habit of growth.

CHINA OR BENGAL ROSE

These are noted for their fine, almost evergreen foliage, which is extremely resistant to disease, and for their profuse, everblooming habit.

VARIETIES OF MERIT

Comtesse Du Cayla. Semi-single flowers, buds coppery orange, flowers reddish orange and yellow.

Laurette Messimy. Flowers rose-pink, tinted with yellow.

Old Blush. The original China Rose introduced in 1796. Flowers bright pink, darkening with age.

Rock and Wall Gardens

ROCK GARDENS

Since the time when William Robinson was introducing to England the alpine garden and the possibilities for variety and color in the wild garden, the hybrid of these two garden types, the rock garden, has had a steadily increasing vogue. The efforts of William Robinson in this vivid, naturalistic expression of garden art began about 1870, and his influence continued and increased through his long career. He was one of the strongest partisans and an ardent proponent of the naturalistic school of design, which had been practised in England along very broad, simple lines for about one hundred and fifty years. Before his time nobody had given to naturalistic design that variety and intricate detail which Robinson, with his knowledge of wild flowers and alpine plants, was able to give. Until Robinson brought them to the attention of the public, people did not consider wild flowers worthy of much attention and certainly did not consider them fit material for gardens. One outgrowth of Robinson's early efforts is the present very general appreciation of this type of garden art. Robinson was not alone in this work however. Miss Gertrude Jekyll, Lord Henry Bentinck, Miss Ellen Willmott and many others have contributed their skill and enthusiasm to the development of wild and alpine gardens.

Rock gardens have reached such a degree of perfection in the intervening years, and there are now so many of them, that it is only natural for England to hold the lead in this as well as in so many other specialized fields of gardening.

One of the first rock gardens in this country was planted

A Rock Garden

on the estate of General Weld in Dedham, Massachusetts. At about the same time Professor Charles S. Sargent built his rock garden at Holmlea in Brookline. Professor Agassiz's daughter first introduced alpine plants from Switzerland to Massachusets, and descendants of these early introductions are still to be found in many a rock garden in New England. The enthusiasm for alpine gardens has been greatly stimulated in recent years by the work and writings of Louise Beebe Wilder, Herbert Durand, George D. Aiken, and others. So great has been the demand for rock plants and for native wild flower plants that there are now many nurseries which specialize in such plants. Henry Correvon, who was one of the first to exhibit wild flower collections on the continent, has spent a lifetime in studying and growing alpine plants. His lectures in this country and his book, *Rock Gardens and Alpine Plants,* have greatly increased the enthusiasm in America for this specialized type of gardening.

A rock garden, at its best, is a collection of alpine plants in a soil environment closely approximating the conditions of their native habitat. The true alpine plants grow in stony soil which is moist, but through which the water passes rapidly, and at high altitudes, which gives them a short but active growing season. In less mountainous regions the soil and drainage conditions may be duplicated by careful construction, but the short season with brilliant sunshine is impossible to reproduce. Some authorities hold the theory that a less rich soil will partly compensate for the long growing season and will prevent the plants from growing too abundantly, and thereby losing their natural form, vigor, and blooming habits. All seem to agree that poor soil is best for alpine plants. However, the emphasis which writers have put on "poor soil" has caused many an amateur to starve his plants to death. Alpines need nourishment, but can get it best from a stony soil containing some humus.

Since a rock garden is a paraphrase of natural conditions typical of some other part of the world and not found in the district in which the garden is built, it is not a natural garden at all, but a sort of museum piece, designed and arranged for the sake of the composition and color harmonies *within* its borders. It cannot harmonize with a smooth lawn or a suburban house in a flat and rockless region. Therefore it should be separated from other parts of the place, and thus become an isolated entity within itself. It is as if the owner had a miniature representation of Switzerland or the White Mountains on his place; not a copy of the type of nature as seen in his neighborhood, but a section of some other climate set down where it does not belong but where it can be enjoyed nevertheless. The site for the rock garden may lend itself very agreeably to the subject, as for instance an outcrop of rock in the rocky landscape of New England, an abandoned quarry where the rocky cliffs have had time to mellow, or the craggy sides of a natural ravine. But if the site does not have any such rock structure as a background, the garden builder must exercise the most subtle skill to create a setting which will assume a natural form and seem appropriate. In any case, whether rocks exist on the site or not, the soil must be arranged in such a way that the plants will have moisture, good drainage, acid reaction for some plants, alkaline for others, sunshine for some, shade for others, and all the gradations between these extremes for still others.

The parts of this country which are most favorable to the development of rock gardens are the cooler regions about the Great Lakes, the mountains and hills of the Appalachians, the rugged landscape of New England, the Rocky Mountain states and the Pacific Coast. In the warmer climate and flat land of the Atlantic Coast plain, the lower Mississippi Valley, the prairies and the great southwest desert, such great climatic difficulties are presented that true rock gardens are unattainable in those regions.

An appropriate and favorable location is the first prerequisite to success with a rock garden. Yet this is the one point on which many failures occur. A bank or a sloping piece of ground is favorable, but not every bank is suitable. If it is under trees it is not going to be a true rock garden, but a shady garden composed of rocks. If it is beside a formal house or otherwise in a sophisticated or artificial surrounding, it will fail from the æsthetic standpoint. It will lack harmony with its site.

A place which is surrounded with artificial things is not appropriate for a rock garden. A concrete sidewalk, the porch of a house, the midst of an open lawn make poor settings. Yet often these places are selected for the site. To be in keeping, the whole environment of the garden should harmonize with the informality and casual character of this specialized garden. The open hillside with surrounding trees which frame it and obliterate inharmonious objects is ideal. If the house is visible from the garden, or is necessarily part of the picture, then it should be a most unconventional house, rural, rustic in character, rather than a house whose design obviously has classic ancestry. The small cottage with thick stone walls is one sort of house which can harmonize best with a rock garden.

The best location for a rock garden is on sloping ground falling toward the west or northwest, where the enclosure is made by natural trees that separate it from other areas. Thus the plants will not be exposed too directly to the rays of the winter sun. A north or northeast slope is also favorable, because there will be little winter sunshine. Southern exposures may be used, but in such a case, the plants must be those which tolerate the effect of sunshine and not the more tender specimens from alpine cliffs.

The best treatment of many a bank is not conversion into a rock garden, but simply a carpet of ground cover plants.

GENERAL DESIGN

The general form of the garden, its heights, its slopes, and its valleys, should be sketched in advance. The general location of paths and steps should also be planned in order that they may give adequate access among the plants. The paths may be stepping stones in some parts, gravel in others, or a mat of pine needles or tanbark. In the large rock garden which is likely to attract quantities of visitors at the height of the season, there should be a major system of paths, broad enough to accommodate the crowd. But for the safety of the plants the visitors should be prevented from picking their way among the rocks and herbs of the lesser paths. Little signs are used in some gardens to steer the throng and protect the plants.

While the general ground-form of the garden should be planned in advance, there is no advantage in detailed planning. Indeed the nature of the material is such that the details are determined by the kind of stones available at the moment, and the way in which they may be placed to produce the general masses and slopes. A few conditions should be avoided: pockets with no outlet, where water will collect in pools; slopes so steep that the soil will wash off; overhanging rocks or caverns under which nothing will grow; and, above all, unstable rocks. Soil pockets may be quite large—a square yard in extent—or very restricted. Variety in arrangement of stones and soil is to be sought. The crevices between rocks may be quite narrow in places, only 2 or 3 inches, but the soil in them must run back and be continuous with the soil beneath and behind the rocks. Indeed the soil, every bit of it, should be rammed into place about the rocks with a pick handle or smaller blunt stick. An air pocket left behind the soil will surely cause the soil to dry out, and the plant growing there will die.

Contrary to expectation, rock plants, most of them, want plenty of moisture in the soil but it must be moisture in motion, constantly draining through, and though the soil looks dry and stony on the surface it must be cool and damp below.

The general arrangement of the plants should also be indicated on the sketch plan, and as the stones and soil are put together, special soil conditions should be prepared for the type of plant to occupy each position. This does not mean an exact planting plan similar to a plan for a perennial border, but a general plan which can be followed in arranging for groups of plants requiring definite soil conditions. Many rock plants are self-contained, modest creatures which occupy only a small space, while others have the will to spread and occupy adjacent spaces. These aggressive ones should be placed within rock barriers so that their roots cannot overwhelm their neighbors. Some few rock plants require acid soil, and some demand an alkaline soil. Fortunately most are not fussy and are at home in a soil ranging from pH. 6 to pH. 8. Most rock plants require unmitigated sunshine. Some prefer shade or partial shade, while a few thrive equally well under varying conditions of light and shade. Some plants are happier in a soil more sandy than that generally used for the rock garden. Because of these varying needs of the plants, the spaces which are to be allotted to the more temperamental plants should be designated at the time that the garden is being constructed. Some planning in advance, therefore, is advisable, and some detailed decisions as to the exact position of each plant can be made at the time of planting. The soil preferences of the various groups should be taken into consideration.

GRADING

For methods of grading, removal of top-soil, excavating and filling sub-soil, see the section on Grading, page 83.

To provide proper drainage for the rock garden, the sub-soil should be sufficiently porous to allow a constant flow of water down through it. If the sub-soil is heavy it should be broken up by deep plowing and lightened by mixing into it sand or gravel and sand. Tile drains should be laid along the bottom of this sub-soil mixture at a depth of 18 inches to carry off the water. The tile pipe must be laid with open joints and at a grade of not less than 1 per cent, and it must empty out upon the surface or into a dry well.

CONSTRUCTION

The best stone for the rock garden is that of local origin. Imported stone, no matter how picturesque in shape, will seem out of place. The stone should not be angular and hard, such as trap rock, or flat and sharp, such as slate and shale, but it should be irregular and somewhat soft. The porousness of the stone is a factor of considerable importance because the stones store moisture and thereby become an equalizer of the ground moisture. In this respect the sandstones and the limestones are the best material for rock gardens. Granite is also good, but hard, and gives an acid reaction to the soil. Quartz is too hard and too conspicuous. Freshly quarried stones are not good, stones from old walls or pastures being more desirable. The stones should be large and should hold their place because of their weight. Small stones will move too easily and permit the air to dry the adjacent roots. For the most satisfactory results, both in appearance and in practical stability, large stones are to be preferred. One of the commonest mistakes in rock gardens is the use of small stones. The best size is what might be termed a "two man" stone, the kind which must be jostled into place with crowbars. Such stones are harder to handle, but should be in the majority if one wants to avoid difficulties later.

To the beginner in rock gardening, the rocks are apt to seem an evident major ingredient of the garden. He usually wants to make the most of the rocks by having most of each rock visible.

This is entirely opposed to the real function of the rocks, which is to keep the soil cool and damp, to expose the plant to sunlight increased by the warmth of the exposed surface of the stone, and to prevent the slipping of the soil down steep slopes. Therefore most of the stone should be buried in the ground, only the top surfaces showing. Indeed, to create the proper sub-soil conditions conducive to good drainage, there should be other stones well buried in the ground below the surface stones. The rocks should be partly buried in the sub-soil when they are placed and the final level of the soil kept in mind so that there will be at least 12 inches of prepared soil above the sub-soil.

The rocks should be placed in such a way as to simulate a natural outcropping of ledge, with the strata or grain of the rocks all sloping at about the same pitch. If the rocks are naturally worn boulders, the formation should be that of a glacial moraine with the stones deeply imbedded in the soil.

After the rocks are in place a layer of small stones or gravel should be spread; then the top-soil should be spread to a depth of 6 inches. Above this a 6-inch layer of the specially prepared soil is added, and finally, on the surface, a thin layer of stone chips or coarse sand.

SOIL

The soil requirements of rock plants are quite different from those of garden flowers or vegetables. No fertilizers or manure should ever be used, for they supply too strong a diet. The soil mixture should be one part coarse sand, one part vegetable fibre, one part garden loam. The sand should be coarse, rather than fine, and may contain small gravel. The vegetable fibre should be well-rotted material, such as old sod that has been stacked a year or two, leaf mold, or the rakings from beneath the wood pile. Bog peat, piled and dried for one year, is one of the best of all vegetable fibres, because it breaks into small particles and contains no weed roots or weed seed. Commercial peat may be substituted for bog peat. The garden loam should be any medium loam, low in clay content. As the loam is the only source of fertility for the plants, the sand being for drainage and the fibre for water-holding powers, the loam should be reasonably good in natural quality. If it is sifted, the weed roots may be eliminated and thus much trouble avoided. Weed seeds can only be eliminated when they germinate and grow during the first season of the garden.

PLANTING

Rock gardening is a hobby which demands very special skill. It combines all the virtues of a recreational pursuit and becomes, with practice, a field of endeavor with limitless possibilities for exploration, experimentation, and artistry. There are many stages of attainment in technique and appreciation. It is a wise program for the beginner to become acquainted with the plants which are more easily cultivated, and with them to practise this craftsmanship. As practice develops skill and establishes confidence, then the gardener may prefer to work with the more difficult plants, and attain those great satisfactions derived from accomplishing a difficult task. The higher degrees of rock gardening include establishing conditions in which plants from the high Alps will thrive, collecting plants from distant mountains, and learning by experiment what conditions best suit the individual plant. Rock gardening is a progressive kind of game, and the experiences of each season, the successes and failures, add to one's fund of knowledge of the subject and make possible new delights for the collector-artist.

Considering plants and planting design in the rock garden, one is amazed with the wealth of available material, and intrigued with the infinite variety of possible arrangements. Selection and arrangement is largely a matter of personal taste and judgment.

Good composition with rocks and plants does not differ in principle from good composition in other mediums. It should have balance, harmony, and unity. While colors in a rock garden are apt to be vivid, they must harmonize well together and be well proportioned. For instance, a corner of the garden in which blues and lavenders predominate needs the enlivening of warm colors to compensate for the cool. Pale yellows or pinks may be used in quantity but bright orange and scarlet are better in small spots of color. Deep pinks and oranges are usually an unhappy combination because of the conflict between them, each seeming to spoil the effect of the other.

The lists accompanying this chapter classify the plants according to their soil, cultural requirements, habits, size, color, and season of bloom.

CARE AND MAINTENANCE

Weeds. If the ground has had the prescribed preparation, the weed roots sifted out of the soil and the bare places covered with stone chips, the weeds should be kept in check without much trouble. Seedling weeds should be removed as soon as they appear, while they are still small. Most rock plants are such little fellows, so slow in growing, that they could be easily lost among weeds. Furthermore, nothing could destroy the good appearance of a rock garden more quickly and completely than a crop of weeds.

Watering. Rock plants require a porous but moist soil. The most satisfactory way to keep the soil in this state is to have the water supply from perforated pipes beneath the surface. Such an installation is not always possible. But in any case frequent watering will be necessary to pull the alpine plants through our long, hot summers.

WINTER MULCHES

The winter mulch for the rock garden presents a very special problem and unless one exercises wisdom and good judgment, the results may be most disastrous. Many worthy alpines have been literally smothered to death by well-intentioned but un-enlightened gardeners. We must bear in mind the fact that most of our rock garden plants come from high mountain regions and in these native haunts they are usually buried under a covering of snow from late autumn until spring. Most of these mountain plants are able to withstand extremely low temperatures but suffer sadly from excessive moisture during the winter months. Therefore, in providing winter protection for them, it is really dampness against which we must guard, and the ill effects of alternate freezing and thawing, rather than severe cold. In determining which plants to cover and which to leave unprotected, there are a few general rules which may be followed. Plants with heavy mats of foliage which persist through the winter months need no covering. Their own leaves afford sufficient protection and if a mulch is applied, the plants are very apt to rot. In the second group come those plants which are of an entirely deciduous nature, dying back in the autumn and remaining dormant below the surface of the ground. Plants of this type are usually able to withstand very trying winter conditions without protection. On the other hand, plants that form woolly rosettes of leaves seem to be particularly susceptible to winter ailments and will usually come through in more satisfactory condition if afforded some suitable protection.

Various materials may be used for mulches in the rock garden. It is essential, however, that the material be of such character that it will not form a wet, decaying mat about the plants. For this reason manure should never be used and leaves of such trees as maples and elms are very undesirable. Evergreen boughs form one of the best kinds of winter protection as they permit a free circulation of air. Salt hay is excellent if worked in among twigs so that it will not mat down. Oak leaves are also good as they do not rot easily. If oak twigs are broken in the autumn, the leaves will cling to them throughout the winter, and they make an exceedingly good covering. A method of winter protection very commonly employed in English gardens and one which might well be used here with equal success is that of using glass. Large bell jars, or "cloches" as they are called in England, may be used, or ordinary pieces of flat glass such as are used in the glazing of hotbed sash. The glass should be raised at least 6 inches above the plants in order to allow a free circulation of air, being suported on small stones or wooden pegs. This method offers excellent protection for particularly treasured plants, although it would be rather a tedious and expensive undertaking to employ it on a large scale.

In addition to an actual covering of some sort, there are other precautions which may be taken to make one's rock plants safe during the trying winter months. Where plants are particularly subject to injury from extreme dampness a little collar of stone chips may be built up around the crown in order to facilitate good drainage, and a mixture of sand, peat moss and stone chips may be worked into the soil about the plants to serve the same purpose.

When the first freezing weather of autumn has formed a crust of frozen earth a half inch thick, some of the smaller alpines will have been lifted from the undersoil. At such a time a gentle pressing of the soil back into place will prevent the plants from drying out. The foot is the best means of applying the pressure, but if the space about the plant is small, something smaller must be used. A pick handle or trowel handle will probably be the most useful. After the frost is well into the ground a mulch should be applied to some of the alpines. The crushed fronds of the evergreen fern (Polystichum acrostichoides) make an excellent first covering, because they will not rot or flatten into a dense mat. Above the fronds a layer of autumn leaves may be spread, with a few hemlock branches to keep them in place.

The removal of the mulch in spring should be a gradual process, accompanied by watering. The mulch should not be removed until the frost is out of the bare ground.

Photograph by J. Horace McFarland Co.

A Low Rock Wall

THE WALL GARDEN

The underlying principles of construction of a rock garden apply equally to that special adaptation, the retaining wall garden. The soil mixture is identical in each case and the plants to be used are those rock plants which grow in the crevices of cliffs, Since the wall exists to retain the earth behind it, the construction should be solid enough to withstand the pressure of lateral thrust of frost. The crevices where the plants are to grow must be so tightly filled with soil that there is constant contact with the soil behind the wall. Without this contact the soil in the stones will dry out.

As with the rock garden, large rocks are to be preferred. Since no mortar is used, their sheer weight and the friction of stone on stone are the only factors which will hold them in place. A bulging side or a top row of stones thrust out beyond the others not only spoils the appearance of the wall, but destroys its practical value. It is possible to build retaining walls without mortar 12 or 15 feet high, capable of standing a century, provided the stones are large and well placed. Every device for holding the stones together should be used. The round surface stones should be discarded, and those with reasonably flat surfaces should be placed with the long dimension horizontal. As far as possible stones should be placed in what is called good *bond,* each stone resting on a part of two stones below. Thus, no long vertical crevices are formed and weight is well distributed.

Foundations of the rock-retaining walls need not be below the frost line as in the case of the masonry wall with mortar joints. Here, there is no advantage in avoiding frost heave, because there will be a certain amount of frost action in the wall itself in any case. The footings should be firm and sloping back against the hill, and at the front only 9 or 10 inches beneath the level of the ground at the base of the wall. This depth will be enough to give the wall a hold on the ground and prevent it from sliding on its foundations. The foundations should be constructed of a width equal to the width or thickness of the base of the wall. This is proportioned to the wall's height. A safe rule to follow is to make the width of the base of the wall equal to a third of the height of the wall. Thus a wall 10 feet high will need to be 3 feet, 4 inches thick at the base. Whatever the height may be, the top of the wall needs to be 18 inches across and the wall thickness will thus decrease as the wall goes up. The face of the wall should never be vertical but should slope at an angle, the top face being on a line back of the bottom face. In England the practice is to make the face of the wall slope back as much as 5 inches or 6 inches for every vertical foot. This enables the plants to receive more moisture from rain seeping into the front of the crevices, and tilts the soil pockets back and down so that they will retain the moisture better. Each pocket of earth which is to receive a plant should be so constructed that the stone below is flat, thus holding the soil, and the stones on each side should be placed so that they will bear the weight of the stone above. It is an unnecessary risk to have the soil in the planting pocket actually carry the load of rocks above. With such a construction the action of frost in the wall is much more likely to heave the rocks and plants out of place. Throughout the wall construction, rock should support rock, independent of earth fill, the planting pockets merely representing windows. The soil in the pockets should be continuous back to the earth behind the wall and should be rammed into place so firmly that it cannot possibly separate from the adjacent stones. Air pockets in the wall will serve only to dry the soil and the plants, and these air pockets are difficult to remedy after the wall has been built and planted.

Soil pockets may be very narrow crevices for small plants, but it is easier to get the plant roots properly into place in a pocket 4 inches wide and high.

The shape of the front of the pocket is important. If the pocket is wedge-shaped with the narrow edge down, then the soil as it settles will tend to pack more and more firmly against the sides as well as against the bottom. Also if the pocket and the stone surfaces slope sharply down and back toward the rear of the wall, there will be very little chance for the soil to part from the upper rock.

Plants for the rock wall include all those which form tufts of

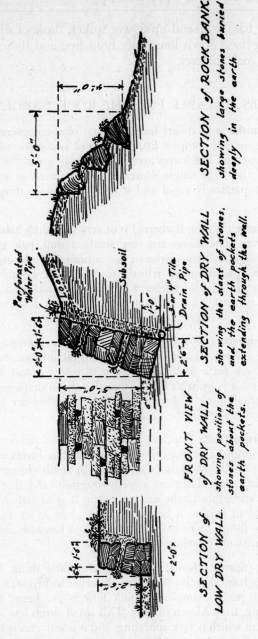

SECTION of ROCK BANK
showing large stones buried
deeply in the earth

SECTION of DRY WALL
showing the slant of stones,
and the earth pockets
extending through the wall.

Subsoil

Perforated Water Pipe

3 or 4" Tile Drain Pipe

FRONT VIEW
of DRY WALL
showing position of
stones about the
earth pockets

SECTION of
LOW DRY WALL.

leaves at the base and send up flower spikes, those of drooping habit, which hang down long leafy branches, and those which cling to the rock surfaces.

SHRUBS SUITABLE FOR THE ROCK GARDEN

Azalea macrantha is of dwarf habit and its foliage is evergreen. It is a rather dense and compact little thing and is considered a gem for the rock garden. The leaves are a deep, glossy green throughout the year and the large single flowers are salmon-red in color. Its growth is comparatively rapid and it is a very showy thing when in flower.

Berberis Wilsonæ (Wilson Barberry) is of very spreading habit, being almost prostrate. The leaves are very small, a dull, pale green in color, becoming a brilliant scarlet in the autumn. The branches are very spiny and the abundant fruits are salmon-red. Because of its low, spreading growth, this Barberry is particularly well suited to the rock garden, and it gives a brilliant note of color at a season when there is little else of interest among the rock plants.

Cotoneaster adpressa (Creeping Cotoneaster) is a low, compact shrub of somewhat creeping habit, with irregular picturesque branches. The small leaves are a deep, shining green, being almost waxy in appearance, and it is from its foliage that this shrub derives its great beauty. The small, pink flowers are inconspicuous but are followed by brilliant red berries in the autumn.

Daphne cneorum (Rose Daphne) is a great favorite and is a dainty and exquisite thing. The fine, somewhat needle-like leaves are evergreen and the shell-pink flowers are borne in small clusters at the ends of the branches. They are sweetly fragrant, and they bloom first in April and again in the early autumn. It is of rather trailing habit and seldom reaches a height of more than 12 or 18 inches. There are few things more lovely than the Rose Daphne, and it is a cherished inhabitant of many a rock garden.

Erica carnea (Spring Heath) is a delightful little thing. It is of low, spreading habit, hardly more than 12 inches in height, with fine evergreen foliage. The small rosy-pink flowers are borne through the early spring, from March to May. This small shrub has a certain sprightly charm which is very appealing, and it is universally beloved.

Juniperus chinensis Sargentii (Sargent Juniper) was introduced by the Arnold Arboretum. It is of low, trailing habit with erect branchlets and it seldom attains a height of more than 6 to 12 inches. The foliage is a silvery, gray-green in tone, and it is a shrub which makes a very beautiful ground cover when allowed to develop its natural habit of growth.

Juniperus communis depressa (Prostrate Juniper) is of low, very spreading growth and forms a dense, green mat. It is hardly more than a foot in height and is admirably adapted to the rock garden. The foliage is a soft, cool green, a pleasant foil for the brilliant colors of the rock plants, and during the winter months it takes on a clear, bronzy tone which is very attractive.

Leiophyllum buxifolium (Box Sandmyrtle) is an evergreen shrub with very small, glossy foliage. It prefers an open, sunny position and a sandy soil of high acidity. The clusters of white flowers which open in May and June are borne at the very ends of the branches and possess a dainty quality. The Sandmyrtle is often found growing wild in the pine barrens of southern New Jersey. It is such a charming little thing and so well suited to the rock garden that it should be more widely grown.

Lonicera nitida (Box Honeysuckle) is a graceful little shrub with very small, oval, glossy leaves which are almost evergreen. The foliage is tinted with rich purple in the autumn and is very decorative and lovely. The flowers, which are very small and inconspicuous, are followed by bluish purple fruits which are borne very sparingly and sometimes not at all. Lonicera nitida is hardy in the latitude of Philadelphia and southward.

Lonicera pileata (Privet Honeysuckle) is an evergreen of low, spreading habit with glossy, box-like foliage. The small white flowers which are borne in profusion in April and May are very fragrant and are followed by purple fruits in July. It rarely attains a height of more than 18 inches and is well adapted for planting in the rock garden or for the foreground of a mass planting of broad-leaved evergreens. It will occasionally prove to be only semi-evergreen in habit.

Ononis fruticosa (Rest Harrow) is a rare gem for the rock garden and is not often seen. It is of dwarf growth, seldom more than 18 inches in height. The bark is a soft, silvery-gray in color and the foliage is three-lobed with long, narrow leaflets. The pink flowers which resemble those of the Pea Family are borne in terminal clusters throughout the summer. It is a dainty little shrub and should be more widely grown.

Pachistima Canbyi (Canby Pachistima) forms a dense, evergreen carpet and is particularly well adapted to the rock garden. The small, dark red flowers are rather inconspicuous and its chief beauty is its deep, green foliage. It prefers an acid soil and a partially shaded location.

Potentilla fruticosa (Shrubby Cinquefoil) is a low shrub of dense, somewhat irregular growth attaining a height of from 1½ to 2½ feet. It comes into bloom in June and from then on through the autumn the bush is starred with pale, lemon-yellow flowers which give a pleasant note of color in the rock garden after the riot of spring bloom has passed.

Potentilla tridentata (Wine-leaf Cinquefoil) grows hardly more than 10 inches tall and has dark, glossy foliage which is almost evergreen. The tiny white flowers are borne in clusters. It makes a very attractive ground cover, as the leaves retain their rich, green coloring throughout many months of the year.

Taxus cuspidata nana (Dwarf Japanese Yew) is a dense, compact shrub of dwarf habit seldom attaining a height of more than 3 feet. It is of irregular and picturesque outline when allowed its free and natural habit of growth, but may be kept symmetrical by occasional shearing. Its great beauty is its evergreen foliage which is a rich, deep color.

ROCK PLANTS FOR ACID SOIL

(Many of these require special care. Those marked with * require strongly acid soil.)

Botanical Name	Common Name
Achillea moschata	Musk Yarrow
Androsace alpina	Alpine Rock-Jasmine
carnea	Pine Rock-Jasmine
Anemone blanda	Greek Anemone
quinquefolia	Wood Anemone
*Arethusa bulbosa	Arethusa
Astilbe simplicifolia	Star Astilbe
Chimaphila maculata	Striped Pipsissewa

ROCK PLANTS FOR ACID SOIL—*Continued*

Botanical Name	Common Name
Chimaphila umbellata	Common Pipsissewa
*Chiogenes hispidula	Creeping Snowberry
Coptis trifolia	Goldthread
Dicentra Cucullaria	Dutchman's Breeches
*Epigæa repens	Trailing Arbutus
*Gaultheria procumbens	Wintergreen
Gentiana alpina	Alpine Gentian
Houstonia cærulea	Bluets
Iris verna	Vernal Iris
*Linnæa borealis	Twinflower
Orchis spectabilis	Showy Orchid
Parnassia caroliniana	Carolina Parnassus
palustris	Marsh Parnassus
Potentilla tridentata	Wineleaf Cinquefoil
Primula elatior	Oxlip Primrose
Pyrola elliptica	Shinleaf
Shortia galacifolia	Oconee-bells
Sibboldia procumbens	Creeping Sibboldia
Silene pennsylvanica	Wild Pink
Soldanella alpina	Moonwort
Thalictrum alpinum	Arctic Meadow Rue
dioicum	Early Meadow Rue
minus	Low Meadow Rue
Tiarella cordifolia	Foamflower
Trillium nivale	Dwarf Trillium
grandiflorum	White Trillium
Trollius chinensis	Chinese Globeflower
laxus	American Globeflower

ROCK PLANTS FOR LIME SOIL

Botanical Name	Common Name
Æthionema (all species)	Stone-Cress
Androsace helvetica	Rock-Jasmine
pubescens	
Anemone alpina	Alpine Anemone
Anthyllis montana	Kidney Vetch
Astragalus hypoglottis	Milk Vetch
Aubrietia deltoidea	Wall cress

Rock Plants for Lime Soil—*Continued*

Botanical Name	Common Name
Dianthus alpinus	Alpine Pink
Draba arabisans	Whitlow Grass
incana	
Erysimum rupestre	Blister-Cress
Gentiana angustifolia	Gentian
acaulis	Stemless Gentian
Clusii	
Heuchera sanguinea	Coral Bells
brizoides	
Hippocrepis comosa	
Hutchinsia alpina	Hutchinsia
Iris pumila	
Lesquerella alpina	
argentea	
Linaria petræa	Toadflax
Lithospermum linearifolium	Gromwell
Opuntia arenaria	Prickly-Pear
humifusa	
vulgaris	
Oxytropis splendens	
Papaver alpinum	Alpine Poppy
Phyllitis Scolopendrium	Harts-Tongue-Fern
Primula (most species)	Primrose
Saxifraga aizoides	Rockfoil, Saxifrage
longifolia	
Sempervivum (all species)	Houseleek

ROCK PLANTS WHICH THRIVE BEST IF AFFORDED WINTER PROTECTION

Botanical Name	Common Name
Acantholimon	Prickly-thrift
Adonis amurensis	Amur adonis
Androsace (all varieties)	Rock Jasmine
Anthyllis montana	Kidney Vetch
Antirrhinum glutinosum	Creeping snapdragon
Arnebia cornuta	Arab primrose
echioides	Prophet flower
Asperula suberosa	Woodruff

Rock Plants Which Thrive Best If Afforded Winter Protection—*Continued*

Botanical Name	Common Name
Calandrinia umbellata	Peruvian Rockpurslane
Campanula Allionii	Bellflower
alpina	
pulla	
Draba, in variety	Whitlow grass
Eritrichium nanum	
Wallichii	
Gentiana verna	Vernal gentian
Leontopodium alpinum	Edelweiss
Lithospermum fruticosum	Gromwell
prostratum	
Lewisia, in variety	Lewisia
Omphalodes Lucilliæ	Navelseed
Onosma, in variety	Borage-wort
Petrocallis pyrenaica	
Phyteuma, in variety	Rampion
Potentilla nitida	Silvery-leaved potentilla
Saxifraga apiculata	Saxifrage
Burseriana	Burser Saxifrage
oppositifolia	Twinleaf Saxifrage
Silene acaulis	Moss campion
Soldanella alpina	Moonwort
pulsilla	

ROCK PLANTS WHICH REQUIRE NO WINTER PROTECTION

Botanical Name	Common Name
Acæna, in variety	New Zealand Burr
Aquilegia, alpina	Alpine Columbine
glandulosa	Altai Columbine
Alyssum saxatile	Goldentuft
Anemone pulsatilla	European pasqueflower
Arabis, in variety	Rock cress
Arenaria, in variety	Sandwort
Armeria, in variety	Thrift
Aster alpinus	Alpine aster
Aubrietia, in variety	Wall cress

ROCK PLANTS WHICH REQUIRE NO WINTER PROTECTION—*Continued*

Botanical Name	*Common Name*
Campanula carpatica	Carpathian bellflower
rotundifolia	Harebell
Cerastium tomentosum	Snow-in-summer
Dianthus, in variety	Garden pinks
Gypsophila repens	Creeping babysbreath
Helianthemum	Rockrose
Heuchera, in variety	Alum-root, Coral Bells
Iberis, in variety	Hardy candytuft
Iris, dwarf rock garden varieties	Iris
Linaria	Toadflax
Linum, in variety	Flax
Nepeta Mussini	Nepeta
Papaver alpinum	Alpine poppy
Phlox amœna	Amœna phlox
divaricata	Blue phlox
subulata	Moss phlox
Primula, in variety	Primrose
Saponaria ocymoides	Soapwort
Saxifraga, most varieties	Saxifrage
Sedum, in variety	Stonecrop
Sempervivum, in variety	Houseleek
Silene, most varieties	Catchfly, Campion
Thalictrum alpinum	Alpine Rue
Thymus, in variety	Thyme
Veronica, in variety	Speedwell
Wahlenbergia	Tufted harebell

PLANTS FOR THE ROCK WALL

(Tufted or Ascending)

Æthionema grandiflorum	Camptosorus rhizophyllus
Alyssum saxatile	Centranthus ruber
Aquilegia cærulea	Cerastium Biebersteinii
canadensis	tomentosum
Arabis alpina	Cheiranthus alpinus
muralis	Cheiri
Campanula carpatica	Dianthus deltoides
glomerata	Heuchera americana
rotundifolia	gracillima

PLANTS FOR THE ROCK WALL—*Continued*

Heuchera sanguinea
Iberis sempervirens
Pellæa atropurpurea
Saponaria ocymoides
Sedum acre
  Ewersii
  sexangulare

Sedum stoloniferum
  ternatum
Veronica repens
  rupestris
Woodsia ilvensis
  obtusa

(Drooping)

Callirhoë involucrata
Campanula muralis
  rotundifolia var. Hostii
Claytonia caroliniana
  virginica
Coronilla varia
Dianthus alpinus
  arenarius
  cæsius
  superbus
Euphorbia Myrsinites

Gypsophila repens
Helianthemum Chamæcistus
Heuchera brizoides
Nierembergia rivularis
Platycodon grandiflorum Mariesii
Polygonum cilinode
  vulgare
Scabiosa graminifolia
Sedum Sieboldii
Solidago cæsia
Tunica Saxifraga

DWARF EVERGREENS, SHRUBS AND VINES FOR THE ROCK GARDEN

Evergreen

Abelia grandiflora
Arctostaphylos uva-ursi
Berberis Gagnepainii
  verruculosa
Calluna vulgaris
Chamæcyparis obtusa nana
  obtusa pygmæa
Chamædaphne calyculata
Cotoneaster horizontalis
  microphylla
  rotundifolia
Daphne cneorum
Erica carnea
Euonymus radicans minimus

Deciduous

Berberis Thunbergii minor
  Wilsonæ
Betula nana
Callicarpa purpurea
Ceanothus Fendleri
Chænomeles Maulei
Comptonia asplenifolia
Cotoneaster adpressa
Cytisus hirsutus
  purpureus
  supinus
Daphne Mezereum
Epigæa repens
Erica Tetralix

(*Continued on page 653*)

ROCK AND WALL PLANTS COMPARATIVELY EASY TO GROW

(SOME WILL SPREAD TOO RAPIDLY)

Scientific Name	Common Name	Season of Bloom	Height in Inches	Color	Soil and Situation. See Key
Achillea Clavennæ	Silver Alpine Yarrow	May–June	4	White	E
tomentosa	Woolly Yarrow	June–Sept.	4	Bright yellow	A
Ajuga reptans	Carpet Bugle	May–June	6	Blue	A
Alyssum saxatile	Goldentuft	April–June	12	Bright yellow	A
sax. compactum	Dwarf Goldentuft	May–Sept.	12	Yellow	A–D
argenteum	Silver Alyssum	May–Sept.	15	Yellow	A
Anemone pulsatilla	European Pasqueflower	March–April	10	Purple	A or B
Antennaria dioica	Common Pussytoes	May–June	4	Pink, white, carmine	A
Aquilegia cærulea	Colorado Columbine	May–June	14	Azure	A or D
canadensis	American Columbine (shade)	May	10	Red	A or D
Arabis albida	Wallcress	March–April	8	White	A–D
alpina	Alpine Wallcress	March–April	6	White	A–D
Arenaria grandiflora	Showy Sandwort	June–Sept.	4	White	A
Aster alpinus	Rock Aster	May–July	10	Purple and yellow	A
Mauve Cushion	Japanese Hardy Aster	September	9	Mauve	A
Aubrietia deltoidea	Aubrietia	May–June	8	Bright purple	A–D
Campanula carpatica	Carpathian Harebell	June–Oct.	8	Lilac blue	A–D
rotundifolia	Harebell, Bluebell	June–Oct.	8	Lilac	A–D
Centaurea montana	Mountain Bluet	May–Sept.	12	Dark blue	A
Cerastium Biebersteinii	Taurus Cerastium (spreads)	May–June	8	White	A–D
tomentosum	Snow-in-Summer (spreads)	June–July	6	White	A–D
Convallaria majalis	Lily-of-the-Valley	May–June	8	White	A–B

EXPLANATION OF SYMBOLS INDICATING SOIL AND SITUATION REQUIREMENTS

A — Plants which do well in garden loam, and need no special soil mixture. They are not particular as to chemical content of soil, and need only ordinary care.

B — Shade-loving plants, preferring a soil rich in humus, porous and well drained. Leaf mold mixed with loam makes the best soil for this group.

C — Plants which thrive in really wet, marshy soil, with sphagnum moss mixed with loam.

D — Plants that will do well in the crevices of the wall.

E — Rock plants which require the mixture of sand, loam and humus. They need perfect drainage, full sunshine, and require very little care. In dry climates, sphagnum with the soil is advisable.

Botanical name	Common name	Bloom time	Height	Color	Zone
Dianthus plumarius	Grass Pink	May–Oct.	8	Rose	A–D
deltoides	Maiden Pink	May–Sept.	4	Bright carmine	A–D
Dicentra eximia	Fringed Bleedingheart	May	10	Rose	A
Doronicum caucasicum	Caucasian Leopardbane	May	10	Yellow	A–B
Geranium macrorrhizum	Bigstem Cranesbill	June–Oct.	12	Bright pink	A
maculatum	Wild Geranium	July	8	Pale pink	A
Gypsophila repens	Creeping Baby's Breath	May–Oct.	4	Pink-white	A–D
Helleborus niger	Christmas Rose	Jan.–March	10	Rose, white	A–B
Heuchera sanguinea	Coral Bells, Alum Root	June–Sept.	12	Coral rose	A
Rosmondi		June		Coral pink	A
Hypericum Moserianum	St. John's-Wort	July–Sept.	10	Yellow and Red	ABD
Iberis sempervirens	Evergreen Candytuft	April–June	8	White	A–D
Tenoreana	Tenore Candytuft	April–May	4	White	A–D
Iris cristata	Crested Iris	May–June	4	Lilac-blue	E
pumila	Dwarf Crimean Iris	May–June	4–8	Lilac-blue, yellow	A–D
verna	Vernal Iris	May	4	Blue-lilac	A
Linum alpinum	Alpine Flax	May–Sept.	6	Light blue	A
perenne	Perennial Flax	May–Sept.	20	Azure blue	A
Lewisii	Prairie Flax	July	10	Blue	A
Myosotis palustris semperflorens	Forget-me-not	May	10	Azure blue	A–C
Nepeta Mussini	Nepeta	July	20	Blue	A
Penstemon alpinus	Alpine Penstemon (Beardtongue)	July	10	Blue and white	A
glaber	Blue Penstemon	July–Oct.	10	Blue	A–C
Phlox amoena	Dwarf magenta Phlox	May	10	Magenta pink	A
divaricata	Blue Phlox	April	8	Lilac-blue	A
pilosa	Downy Phlox (Prairie Phlox)	June	12	Bright pink	A
Stellaria	Mauve Phlox	June	8	Pale blue	A–D
stolonifera	Creeping Phlox	May	6	Carmine	A
subulata	Moss Phlox	April	4	Blue or pink	A–D
s. alba		April	4	White	A–D
Plumbago Larpentæ	Leadwort	Aug.–Sept.	10	Bright blue	A
Potentilla alba	Cinquefoil	April	4	White	A–B
pyrenaica	Pyrenees Cinquefoil	May	4	Bright yellow	A
nitida		May	2	Light rose	D–E
Saponaria ocymoides	Rock Soapwort	April–July	10	Bright pink	A–D

ROCK AND WALL PLANTS COMPARATIVELY EASY TO GROW—*Continued*

Scientific Name	Common Name	Season of Bloom	Height in Inches	Color	Soil and Situation. See Key
Saxifraga caespitosa	Saxifrage	May–June	3	White and pink	A
cordifolia		April–May	12	Flesh-rose. Part shade	A
Sedum acre	Stone Crop	June–Sept.	3	Yellow	A–D
album		June–Oct.	4	White and pink	A–D
altissimum		June–Sept.	10	Pale yellow	A–D
reflexum		June–Sept.	6	Yellow	A–D
rupestre		June	10	Yellow	A–sand
sarmentosum		June–July	4	Yellow	A–D
Sempervivum (many species)	Hen-and-Chickens or Houseleek	May–June	4	Yellow or red	A–sand
Silene maritima	Sea Campion	June	2	White	D–E
Thalictrum dioicum	Early Meadowrue	May	6	Whitish	A
Tunica saxifraga	Saxifrage Tunicflower	May–Nov.	4	Pink or white	A–D
Veronica rupestris	Cliff Speedwell	June–Aug.	8	Blue	A
Viola cornuta	Tufted Pansy	May–Oct.	10	Dark Lilac	A

DWARF EVERGREENS, SHRUBS, VINES—*Continued from page 649*

Evergreen	*Deciduous*
Hedera helix conglomerata	Euonymus nanus
h. gracilis	Fothergilla Gardeni
Ilex crenata nummularia	Gaultheria procumbens
c. microphylla	Genista pilosa
Juniperus chinensis procumbens	Hudsonia tomentosa
communis depressa	Ledum grœnlandicum
horizontalis	Menziesia pilosa
h. Douglasii	Myrica caroliniensis
Sabina	Philadelphus coronarius nanus
S. tamariscifolia	microphyllus
squamata	Rhus canadensis
Leiophyllum buxifolium prostratum (var. Lyoni)	Rosa rugosa Max Graf
	nitida
Lonicera nitida	carolina
pileata	spinosissima
Pachistima Canbyi	Spiræa bullata
Picea excelsa nana	Bumalda
alba albertiana	Vaccinium pennsylvanicum
Pinus densiflora umbraculifera	Viburnum Opulus nanum
montana Mugo	
Potentilla fruticosa	
Taxus cuspidata nana	
Thuya occidentalis Reidii	
Yucca filamentosa	

The Woodland Garden

One of the most beautiful expressions of landscape art is to be found in the woodland garden. Here the ideals are not those of the flower garden, where perfection of bloom or variety in horticultural forms is the desideratum, but rather a representation of unaltered natural forms. Only wild flowers as they grow in nature should be included, and they should be given a setting closely resembling in appearance and physical condition those of their natural habitat. Since such a woodland is fundamentally a garden, it is not a copy or reproduction of nature, but rather a place for growing wild flowers in their accustomed way. It is, in fact, a garden of flowers either in their native habitat, or so recently brought from the wild that they have changed not at all in appearance or in their cultural requirements.

THE SITE

The owner of property containing a mature woodland has the ideal situation for a garden of woodland flowers. Indeed, the development of such a tract into a woodland garden is just as logical and natural as the development of the open sunny spaces into gardens of herbaceous flowers. The very conditions of the sunny site favor its development into a sunny garden, and those of the wooded tract favor development of this other type, the woodland garden. To do anything different with these sites would be to ignore their natural advantages.

During these many centuries, gardeners have been devoting their effort and skill to developing sun-loving plants, but it is only within the last half century that serious effort has been made with the flora of the forest. We now recognize this as a whole new phase of gardening with its own techniques.

A Woodland Pool

THE DESIGN

The limitations of a woodland area should be recognized in the very beginning and every effort should be made to turn into assets those features of the place which might otherwise be regarded as liabilities. A woodland garden must necessarily be developed along naturalistic lines. The informal grouping of the trees themselves determines, to a very large extent, the nature of the design.

There is a very general impression that an informal design is a much more simple and less intricate thing than a formal scheme. On the contrary, quite the opposite is true. There is usually something very straightforward and, in a way, quite obvious about the design of a formal garden, whereas the design of an informal area, if well studied, possesses a subtle quality and charm which it is difficult to define.

Planning the woodland garden does not necessarily require exact plotting of ground areas or the spacing out of plants on a planting plan. But there should be forethought in the planning of major masses of foliage for the sake of good composition and balance, and for the separation of the plants into groups which are congenial and require similar soil conditions. If the site includes areas of varying soil conditions the plants must be assigned to the spaces where they naturally belong. Thus a certain tract might have dry soil on the upper levels, neutral soil in a large area, acid soil where oak trees stand, and wet soil along the stream valley. Whether the plan is actually committed to paper or not, it should be sufficiently definite to keep the plants in the situations where they thrive best and to allot the difficult conditions to those plants which are best able to withstand them.

The person who is a novice in the art of gardening with wild flowers will find that it is possible to develop very attractive groups of plantings by using some of the more easily grown bulbs and perennials which adapt themselves readily to woodland conditions. Masses of pale lavender-blue phlox under a group of white birches in early spring; English primroses and wood hyacinths blooming along a woodland path; foxgloves lifting their stately spires against a background of deep forest green—such delightful pictures may be obtained with a moderate expenditure of time and money.

However, the experienced gardener may not be content to limit his attention to the more easily grown woodland plants. He will want to adventure further and naturalize some of the more fastidious woodland flowers. An adventure of this sort is full of interest and delight.

THE SOIL

It is only within comparatively recent years that there has been much available information on this subject. About 20 years ago Doctor Wherry, Doctor Coville and others began to turn their attention to the growth of woodland plants. They have made some very interesting and helpful discoveries. For years people had tried to grow and to transplant some of our lovely wild flowers such as the trailing arbutus and the pink lady-slipper, but almost invariably they met with failure, no matter how carefully it was done; and we began to accept the fact that these flowers would not survive if moved from their native habitat. On the other hand, such things as the yellow lady-slipper, lily-of-the-valley, and Solomon's seal could be grown and transplanted with the greatest ease and would soon be happily at home in their new surroundings. After many interesting experiments it was discovered that the acidity of the soil plays a very important part in the growth of woodland plants and that it is often the secret of success. Scientists have dispelled the idea that trailing arbutus cannot be grown under cultivation. They tell us that it can be grown quite easily provided we supply it with soil of very high acidity. It should never be transplanted from the wild, but nursery-grown plants are readily available.

It is well, therefore, for anyone who intends to pursue this adventure, to become familiar with the various classifications of soils and to know how to test soil for acidity. (See page 23.)

There are various methods of increasing the acidity of soils. The most simple method is to obtain soil from underneath hemlock or oak trees, as this is usually rich in tannic acid. Aluminum sulphate, which may be obtained from any chemist, is very effec-

A Woodland Garden

A Woodland Glade.

tive in increasing the acidity of soil and is easily applied. A soil may be made properly acid for ericaceous plants by adding aluminum sulphate in various amounts according to the original

Photograph by J. Horace McFarland Co.

Narcissus at the Edge of the Woodland

reaction of the soil. Thus, soils of different reactions should be treated as follows:

Kind of Soil	*Amt. of Aluminum Sulphate*
Medium acid (pH. 5.5 to 6.0)	¼ lb. per sq. yd.
Slightly acid (pH. 6.5 to 7.0)	½ lb. per sq. yd.
Neutral or slightly alkaline (pH. 7.0 to 8.0)	¾ lb. per sq. yd.

Aluminum sulphate is particularly good for rhododendrons and azaleas, and sickly plantings may often be brought back to a healthy condition by an application of it. Commercial tannic acid may also be used for the purpose of increasing the acidity of soils. A solution of one part acid to fifty parts of water should be used and the area to be treated should be thoroughly saturated. A soil station thus treated should be left for two weeks before any planting is done in order that the acid may become thoroughly assimilated. It is also wise to apply a mulch of leaf mold or peat moss.

Making the soil acid is important, but it is not always the only conditioning process necessary. For rhododendrons, azaleas, mountain-laurel and heather, cyprepediums, many of the ferns, and many other woodland plants the soil must be moist, but porous; well drained, and rich in humus. A sandy sub-soil is almost indispensable for some groups of plants.

THE SELECTION OF PLANT MATERIALS

The selection of plant materials for the woodland garden offers fascinating possibilities. There are many rare and lovely flowers that revel in woodland shade, flowers which, for the most part, cannot be grown in the open sunny border. Some of the woodland plants prefer dense shade, others thrive best in partial shade, while still others are indifferent as to the amount of shadow. Some require a neutral, moderately moist soil, others an acid soil, and a few others demand wet soil, either acid or neutral. A study of the relation of soil to the best development of the plant is essential for success with wild flowers.

WOODLAND FLOWERS

Anemone quinquefolia (Wood Anemone) (Wind-flower). The dainty white blossoms of the Wood Anemone are among the most exquisite of the woodland flowers, blooming from early April to late May. The slender, delicate stems are hardly more than 6 inches in height and the deeply lobed leaves are borne in whorls below the flowers.

Distribution: From Canada south to Georgia and west to the Rocky Mountains.

Preferred Habitat: Open woodlands, hillsides; particularly along the borders of moist, open woods.

Soil Requirements: Moist, moderately acid soil.

My dear — We are planning to bring Crowly Home this week ofcourse cant. find out just when will bring Mrs Reed one the night nurse for a wk or Two. Thanks for the Check Rhodes plays Basket Ball tonight — Roberta is coming to spend the night —

Love —
Mother

This one for Lool

address

Mrs E R McClellan
1071 Highland Dr
St Albans
West Va

Culture: The Wood Anemone is somewhat difficult to establish. Plants should be purchased from a nursery.

Period of Bloom: April to June.

Aquilegia canadensis (Canadian Columbine). Unfortunately Aquilegia canadensis is disappearing from many of its native haunts and perhaps only through its cultivation in wild flower sanctuaries will it be spared to future generations. The small flowers are of a scarlet and yellow hue and are borne on slender stems which vary in height from 1 to 2 feet.

Distribution: From Nova Scotia to the Northwest and southward to the Gulf States.

Preferred Habitat: Rather dry, rocky ledges; partial shade.

Soil Requirements: Thrives best in a soil which is very nearly neutral. It can tolerate neither extreme acidity nor pronounced alkalinity.

Culture: Plants should be purchased from a nursery. Despite its long tap roots Aquilegia canadensis may be transplanted readily and it is not difficult to establish, provided that soil conditions are favorable.

Period of Bloom: April to May.

Arisæma triphyllum (Jack-in-the-Pulpit). This jolly wilding is one of the most beloved denizens of our woods and it is particularly lovely when planted among ferns. It is yellow-green in color, with brown-purple stripes, and is quite pale when growing in the sun. Later the berries turn a bright scarlet.

Distribution—From Nova Scotia westward to Minnesota and southward to the Gulf States.

Preferred Habitat: Moist woodlands among underbrush.

Soil Requirements: Thrives best in neutral soil, being able to tolerate neither extreme acidity nor pronounced alkalinity.

Culture: Plants may be purchased from many nurseries. If soil conditions are congenial, the plants are easy to establish, and they spread rapidly. They may be grown readily from seed.

Period of Bloom: April–July.

Cimicifuga racemosa (Black Snakeroot). So many of our woodland flowers come during the spring months that one rejoices to find something for midsummer bloom, and it is during July and August that the tall, stately, white spires of the Snakeroot add their share of beauty to a woodland planting. The plants vary in height from 3 to 8 feet.

Distribution: From Maine to Georgia and westward from Ontario to Missouri.

Preferred Habitat: Deep, moist woods, wooded hillsides, woodland borders.

Soil Requirements: Prefers a rich woodland soil but is indifferent to soil acidity, thriving well in either neutral or acid soil.

Culture: May be transplanted very easily and becomes readily established.

Claytonia virginica (Spring Beauty). Blooming soon after the Hepaticas, the Spring Beauties are among the earliest of our woodland flowers. The dainty fragile blooms are borne in loose terminal racemes and the slender stems seldom reach a height of more than 8 or 10 inches. The flowers vary from white to pale pink.

Distribution: From Nova Scotia to Georgia and westward.

Preferred Habitat: Moist, open woods, low meadows.

Soil Requirements: Thrives best in soil which is very nearly neutral.

Culture: The plants may be transplanted with care from the wild or they may be purchased from a nursery. They are most effective when planted in drifts or masses. The plants should be spaced from 4 to 6 inches apart.

Period of Bloom: March and April.

Cypripedium acaule (Moccasin Flower) (Pink Lady's Slipper). The clear pink blooms of the Moccasin Flower are startling in their beauty when one comes upon them in some deep forest glade, and one feels a sense of triumph when one achieves this beauty in a woodland planting. The orchid-like flowers are borne on stems hardly more than 10 inches in height.

Distribution: From Canada southward to North Carolina, westward to Minnesota and Kentucky.

Preferred Habitat: Deep, rocky or sandy woods. It is found in both dry and moist situations and it has been known to thrive well in full sun, although it definitely prefers partial shade.

Soil Requirements: Intensely acid woodland soil.

Culture: Plants should be purchased from a nursery. No attempt should be made to transplant them from the wild. During the first season after planting they should be kept constantly moist, the plants being mulched with pine needles. Cypripedium acaule is not difficult to establish provided that the soil conditions are congenial, as the acidity of the soil is the secret of success. In planting cypripediums, the crown should never be entirely buried, the tip being approximately ¼ inch above the surface. Cypripediums may be

planted in very early spring while entirely dormant, or in late August and early September, the latter month being preferred.
Period of Bloom: May and June.

Cypripedium pubescens (Yellow Lady's Slipper) (Also C. parviflorum). The Yellow Lady's Slipper is of such rare beauty and of such easy culture that it should be included in every woodland planting. The orchid-like flowers are of a soft luminous yellow hue and are borne on slender stems varying in height from 12 to 18 inches.
Distribution: From Nova Scotia to Alabama, westward to Minnesota and Nebraska.
Preferred Habitat: Rich, moist, stony soil in deciduous woods.
Soil Requirements: Rather indifferent to soil acidity, thriving equally well in neutral or somewhat acid soil.
Culture: The plants should be purchased from a nursery. They are easy to establish and thrive exceedingly well if the surroundings are congenial. Planting directions as for C. acaule.
Period of Bloom: May and June.

Digitalis (Foxglove). All of the foxgloves do exceedingly well in partial shade and they are well adapted to woodland plantings. They are lovely when planted in great masses along a fringe of woodland or when a few plants are grouped together to give accent to a woodland composition. *Digitalis ambigua* and *Digitalis lutea* are true perennials. They bear dainty yellow flowers which cling closely to the tall, slender stems, reaching a height of about 3 feet. The cultivated types are biennial in habit, and they are obtainable in a wide variety of colors,— white, primrose yellow, mauve and apricot—and will often attain a height of 6 to 8 feet.
Preferred Habitat: Open woodlands, along a fringe of wood, light shade.
Soil Requirements: A deep, rich, woodsy soil is preferred.
Culture: Foxgloves are of easy culture and when the perennial forms are once well established, they will bloom on year after year. They may be propagated very readily from seed or by the division of old clumps. Being very fibrous rooted, the foxgloves may be transplanted with the greatest of ease either in the autumn or in very early spring.
Period of Bloom: May and June.

Dodecatheon Meadia (Shooting Star) (American Cowslip). The dainty, cyclamen-like flowers are born on tall, slender, leafless stems, which often reach a height of 20 inches or more. The blossoms vary

665

in color from flesh-white to pink and are as exquisite as tiny butterflies. The leaves form a rosette-like growth close to the ground.

Distribution: Pennsylvania southward to Georgia and westward from Texas to Manitoba.

Preferred Habitat: Moist hillsides, open woods, tops of cliffs. Thrives in full sun or partial shade.

Soil Requirements: Thrives best in soil which is very nearly neutral. It can tolerate neither extreme acidity nor pronounced alkalinity.

Culture: The plants are listed in many catalogues. They are of easy culture and thrive well if supplied with ample moisture, provided soil conditions are congenial.

Period of Bloom: April and May.

Epigæa repens (Trailing Arbutus) (Mayflower). There are few woodland flowers that are more universally beloved than the Trailing Arbutus, and it is tragic, indeed, that where once it flourished so abundantly it is now all but extinct because of thoughtless vandalism. The fragile beauty of its blossoms and their exquisite fragrance have endeared it to many generations, and now at last, we are able to bring it into cultivation in our woodland gardens.

Climatic Range: From Newfoundland to Florida, and west to Kentucky and the Northwest territory.

Preferred Habitat: Wooded hillsides and rocky woods, particularly under or near cone-bearing evergreens.

Soil Requirements: Intensely acid, woodland soil.

Culture: It is advisable to purchase well-established pot-grown plants from some nursery which specializes in the propagation of woodland flowers. It is useless to attempt to grow Trailing Arbutus unless the soil is intensely acid, with a pH. of 4.5 or below. During the first season, the plants should be mulched with a light covering of pine needles and the soil about the plants should never be allowed to dry out.

Period of Bloom: April and May.

Erythronium (Trout Lily) (Dog-tooth Violet). The narrow, lancelike leaves of the dog-tooth violet are a grayish green, being often mottled or streaked with brown, and they are almost as decorative in the woodland garden as are the flowers themselves. The nodding, slightly fragrant blooms are borne on slender stems, varying in height from 4 to 12 inches. The flowers of E. americanum are a pale russet yellow, occasionally tinted with purple. Some of the California varieties which have been recently introduced into eastern gardens are very beautiful, being obtainable in exquisite shades of pale prim-rose, mauve and rose.

Distribution: From Nova Scotia to Florida and westward.

Preferred Habitat: Moist, open woods, along brooksides, and stony banks.

Soil Requirements: Prefers a neutral, or very nearly neutral, soil.

Culture: The bulbs may be purchased from a nursery or a few may be carefully dug from an established woodland planting. In their natural habitat the bulbs are usually found at a depth of from 6 to 15 inches. The bulbs are smooth and egg-shaped, and produce small round offsets from the base. The foliage disappears entirely soon after the flowering season is over.

Period of Bloom: April and May.

Hepatica triloba (Liverwort). The Hepaticas are among the first of the spring flowers to appear, sometimes even blooming under the snow. Hardly more than 3 inches in height, the dainty, cup-shaped flowers, in delicate tints of lilac, deep lavender, and white, are borne above the leathery, bronze-tinted leaves. The foliage is evergreen and the new leaves appear after the flowers.

Distribution: From Canada to northern Florida and westward to Missouri, although more common in the East.

Preferred Habitat: Open woodlands and wooded hillsides.

Soil Requirements: Prefers a woodland soil rich in humus and of a neutral or slightly acid reaction.

Culture: Plants should be purchased from a nursery, and they should be planted in clumps, being spaced from 4 to 6 inches apart. They usually succeed well under cultivation in widely varying situations.

Period of Bloom: March and April.

Mertensia virginica (Virginia Cowslip) is one of the most delightful of all our wild flowers, and it may be used in happy combination with woodland ferns and with some of the spring bulbs. The buds are a lavender-pink in color and the open flowers are a clear and lovely blue. The nodding blooms are borne on stems varying in height from 12 to 15 inches. The foliage disappears entirely after the bloom-ing season is over. Mertensia comes into flower at the same time that the Silver Bell Tree (Halesia carolina) is in bloom, and it is enchant-ingly lovely when planted beneath the spreading branches.

Distribution: Southern New York, southward and westward.

Preferred Habitat: Low meadows, banks of streams, moist hill-sides, thriving in both full sun and partial shade.

Soil Requirements: Thrives most luxuriantly in soil which is very nearly neutral. Does not tolerate pronounced acidity or alkalinity.

Culture: Plants should be purchased from a nursery and when they are once well established, they increase rapidly from self-sown seed. As soon as the seed has ripened, the foliage begins to wither and soon disappears entirely. Mertensia should be planted in an upright position at a depth of approximately 2½ to 3½ inches.

Period of Bloom: May and June.

Phlox divaricata (Wild Blue Phlox) is one of the most easily grown of our woodland plants and has found its way into many a cultivated garden. The dainty flowers are of a soft lavender-blue and are borne in great profusion. While the plants do well in an open, sunny border, they are most happily at home in a woodland setting and one sometimes sees a wooded hillside carpeted with them. Although the plants are somewhat creeping in habit, the flower stalks reach a height of about 12 inches. Phlox divaricata blooms at about the same time as do many of the spring bulbs, and it combines most delightfully with the large-flowered trilliums and scilla campanulata. There are few woodland flowers more completely accommodating than the wild blue phlox. It asks only a chance to establish itself, and will give generously of its bloom and beauty in the spring.

Distribution: From New York, southward and westward.

Preferred Habitat: Open, rocky woods, wooded hillsides. Thrives equally well in full sun or in partial shade.

Soil Requirements: More or less indifferent to soil conditions, but thrives best in a soil which is very nearly neutral in its reaction.

Culture: Phlox divaricata is of exceedingly easy culture, and when it has become well established in a woodland garden it will increase rapidly and will become more luxuriant and more beautiful each year. The plants may be increased by cuttings and also by the division of old clumps.

Period of Bloom: May and June.

Primula (Primroses). Primroses are always associated with the rare beauty of an English spring. There they grow in gay profusion, and during the month of May the woods are fairly carpeted with them. *Primula vulgaris* is the true English primrose, and it is the one which lends itself particularly well to naturalization. It is a lowly little thing, dainty and piquant, the pale lemon-yellow flowers nestling closely among the leaves. The *Polyantha* type grows considerably taller and bears a cluster of flowers on erect stems from 8 to 10 inches in height. The Munstead strain is an excellent one, the flowers ranging in color from pale yellow to deep orange. Some of the more brilliant types with their red, scarlet, and magenta blooms are very difficult to use in combination with other plants and should be avoided.

Preferred Habitat: Open, somewhat moist woods.

Soil Requirements: Rich woodland soil.

Culture: Primroses may be easily grown from seed. One should, however, bear the fact in mind that the seeds germinate very slowly, sometimes requiring six weeks or more. Old clumps may also be lifted and divided shortly after the flowering season. If soil and moisture conditions are favorable, primroses will continue to bloom year after year.

Period of Bloom: May and June.

Sanguinaria canadensis (Bloodroot). Fleeting though the blooms may be, bloodroot contributes its full share of beauty to the spring. The pure white of the petals and the gold of the stamens are lovely in great masses in the filtered sunlight of open woods, though hardly more than a few inches in height.

Climatic Range: Nova Scotia to Florida, and westward to Nebraska.

Preferred Habitat: Low hillsides, rich, stony ground along the borders of woods and along shady roadsides.

Soil Requirements: Entirely indifferent to soil acidity, thriving equally well in neutral or somewhat acid soil.

Culture: Bloodroot may be transplanted successfully at almost any season, and when it has once become well established, it will spread rapidly. It is most effective when used in large clumps. Plants may be purchased from a nursery or they may be transplanted with care from the wild.

Period of Bloom: April and May.

Trillium grandiflorum (Large Flowering Trillium). There are few woodland flowers more exquisite in form than the large flowering trilliums. The beautiful, pure white blossoms are borne on strong, upright stems which often reach a height of 15 inches or more. As in all the trilliums, the parts are in threes: three sepals, three petals, twice three stamens, and a whorl of three leaves—hence the name, trillium.

Distribution: Massachusetts to North Carolina, westward to Minnesota.

Preferred Habitat: Rich, rocky woodlands, and moist but well-drained woodland glades.

Soil Requirements: Prefers a woodland soil which is very nearly neutral in its reaction. Does not tolerate pronounced acidity or alkalinity.

Culture: Trillium grandiflorum is one of the most easily grown members of this family and when the clumps have become well established, they will bloom happily on, year after year. The tubers should be planted in the autumn, being placed at a depth of about 3 to 4 inches. The bud should point upward.

Period of Bloom: May and June.

SOIL REQUIREMENTS FOR HERBACEOUS WOODLAND PLANTS

GROUP 1

Indifferent to Soil Acidity

Actæa rubra (Red Baneberry)
Anemone canadensis (Canada Anemone)
Anemonella thalictroides (Rue Anemone)
Cimicifuga racemosa (Black Snakeroot)
Convallaria majalis (Lily-of-the-Valley)
Cypripedium pubescens (Yellow Lady's Slipper)
Habenaria fimbriata (Purple Fringed Orchis)
Heuchera americana (Alumroot)
Iris cristata (Crested Iris)
Lupinus perennis (Blue Lupin)
Myosotis laxa (Forget-me-not)
Myosotis scorpioides (Forget-me-not)
Podophyllum peltatum (May-Apple)
Polygonatum biflorum (Solomon's Seal)
Polygonatum commutatum (Solomon's Seal)
Sanguinaria canadensis (Bloodroot)
Tiarella cordifolia (Foam-flower)
Trillium erectum (Wake-robin)
Viola conspersa (Dog Violet)
Viola palmata (Common Blue Violet)

GROUP 2

Circumneutral (or very nearly neutral)

Aquilegia canadensis (Canada Columbine)
Arisæma triphyllum (Jack-in-the-Pulpit)

SOIL REQUIREMENTS FOR HERBACEOUS WOODLAND
PLANTS—*Continued*

GROUP 2—*Continued*

Campanula rotundifolia (Bluebell)
Claytonia virginica (Spring Beauty)
Cypripedium hirsutum (Showy Lady's Slipper)
Dicentra Cucullaria (Dutchman's Breeches)
Dodecatheon Meadia (American Cowslip, Shooting Star)
Erythronium americanum (Troutlily, Dog-tooth Violet)
Gentiana Andrewsii (Bottle or Closed Gentian)
Gentiana crinita (Fringed Gentian)
Hepatica acutiloba (Liverwort)
Hepatica triloba (Liverwort)
Mertensia virginica (Virginia Cowslip)
Mitella diphylla (Bishop's Cap)
Orchis spectabilis (Showy Orchis)
Phlox divaricata (Wild Blue Phlox)
Polemonium reptans (Greek Valerian)
Trillium grandiflorum (Large Flowering Trillium)
Trillium stylosum (Southern Pink Trillium)
Viola blanda (Sweet White Violet)
Viola canadensis (Canada Violet)

GROUP 3
Moderately Acid

Anemone quinquefolia (Wood Anemone)
Aquilegia cærulea (Rocky Mt. Columbine)
Galax aphylla (Galax)
Gaultheria procumbens (Wintergreen or Checkerberry)
Habenaria ciliaris (Yellow Fringed Orchis)
Houstonia cærulea (Bluets or Quaker Ladies)
Houstonia purpurea (Bluets or Quaker Ladies)
Mitchella repens (Partridge-berry)
Viola pedata (Bird-foot Violet))

GROUP 4
Very Acid

Clintonia borealis (Clintonia)
Cypripedium acaule (Moccasin Flower)
Epigæa repens (Trailing Arbutus)
Iris verna (Dwarf Iris)

PLANTS FOR THE WOODLAND GARDEN

Botanical Name	Common Name	Height	Color	Season of Bloom	Soil	Habitat
Actaea rubra	Red Baneberry	1–2'	White	April–June	Well-drained, indifferent to acidity	Open woods
Anemone canadensis	Canada Anemone	1–2'	White	May–Aug.	Indifferent to acidity	Low, moist ground
quinquefolia	Wood Anemone	4–8"	White	April–June	Moderately acid	Moist, open woods
Anemonella thalictroides	Rue Anemone	5–9"	White, tinged with pink	March–May	Indifferent to acidity	Thin, moist woodlands
Aquilegia canadensis	Canada Columbine	1–2'	Scarlet and yellow	April–May	Circumneutral	Dry, rocky ledges
caerulea	Rocky Mt. Columbine	2–3'	Blue and white	May–June	Moderately acid	Open woods
Arisæma triphyllum	Jack-in-the-Pulpit	12–30"	Yellowish green	April–July	Circumneutral	Moist woodlands
Campanula rotundifolia	Bluebell	6–18"	Light purple	June–Sept.	Circumneutral	Rocky cliffs, sandy fields. Sun or shade
Cimicifuga racemosa	Black Snakeroot	3–8'	White	June–July	Indifferent	Deep, moist woods
Claytonia virginica	Spring Beauty	6–12"	Pale pink	March–May	Circumneutral	Open, moist woods
Clintonia borealis	Clintonia	8–10"	Buff, sometimes greenish tinge		Very acid	Cool, moist woods
Convallaria majalis	Lily-of-the-Valley	6–8"	White	May–June	Indifferent	Sun or shade; rich, moist
Cypripedium acaule	Moccasin Flower	8–12"	Crimson-pink	April–May	Very acid	Wooded hillsides
hirsutum	Showy Lady's Slipper	18–24"	White, stained crimson	June–July	Circumneutral	Swamps, wet woodlands
pubescens (C. parviflorum)	Yellow Lady's Slipper	12–18"	Yellow	May–June	Indifferent	Moist, rich, stony soil
Dicentra canadensis	Squirrel Corn	8–12"	Greenish white		Indifferent	Fertile, light soil
Cucullaria	Dutchman's Breeches	5–9"	White, yellow tipped	April–May.	Circumneutral	Thin woods, dry rocky slopes
eximia	Wild Bleedingheart	12–18"	Pink	May	Indifferent	Rocky ledges in open woods
Digitalis (see Biennials)						

672

Scientific Name	Common Name	Height	Color	Bloom	Acidity	Habitat
Dodecatheon Meadia	American Cowslip or Shooting Star	8–20"	Flesh white to pink	April–May	Circumneutral	Moist hillsides, open woods
Epigæa repens	Trailing Arbutus	Trail.	Pink	April–May	Very acid	Rocky woods, wooded hillsides under cone-bearing trees
Erythronium americanum	Troutlily, Dog-tooth Violet	4–8"	Yellow	April–May	Circumneutral	Moist woods, along brooks
Galax aphylla	Galax	1–2'	Yellow	April–Oct.	Moderately acid	Open woods and pastures
Gaultheria procumbens	Wintergreen or Checkerberry	2–5"	White	July–Aug.	Moderately acid	Dry, evergreen woods
Gentiana Andrewsii	Bottle or Closed Gentian	1–2'	Violet-blue	Aug.–Oct.	Circumneutral	Borders of woods, banks of streams
crinita	Fringed Gentian	1–3'	Sky blue	Sept.–Oct.	Circumneutral	Low, moist meadows and bogs
Habenaria ciliaris	Yellow Fringed Orchis	18–24"	Orange-yellow	July–Aug.	Moderately acid	Meadows, moist, sandy places
fimbriata	Large Purple Fringed Orchis	To 5'	Lilac or white	June–Aug.	Indifferent to acidity	Wet woods, swampy places
psycodes	Small Purple Fringed Orchis	1–3'	Lilac pink	July–Aug.	Indifferent to acidity	Wet woods, swampy places
Hepatica acutiloba	Liverwort	3"	Brighter than triloba	March–May	Circumneutral	Open, rich woodlands
triloba	Liverwort	3"	Lilac, white, pale lavender	March–May	Circumneutral	Open, rich woodlands
Heuchera americana	Alumroot	18–24"	Whitish green	May–July	Indifferent to acidity	Moist, open
Houstonia cærulea	Bluets or Quaker Ladies	3–6"	White, tinted w. blue-violet	April–Oct.	Moderately acid	Moist, grassy places and sandy fields
purpurea	Bluets or Quaker Ladies	3–8"	Purple or lilac	April–Oct.	Moderately acid	Moist, grassy places and sandy fields
Iris cristata	Crested Iris	3–6"	Violet with orange crest	April–May	Indifferent to acidity	Hillsides and along streams. Needs protected spot in North
verna	Dwarf Iris	4–8"	Violet blue, yellow centers	April–May	Very acid	Wooded hillsides

PLANTS FOR THE WOODLAND GARDEN—*Continued*

Botanical Name	Common Name	Height	Color	Season of Bloom	Soil	Habitat
Lupinus perennis	Blue Lupine	1–2'	Violet-blue	May–June	Indifferent	Barren fields
Mertensia virginica	Virginia Cowslip	1–2'	Sky blue, buds pink	March–May	Circumneutral	Low meadows, banks of streams. Sun or shade
Mitchella repens	Partridge-berry	Trail.	White and pink	June	Moderately acid	Woods and shaded borders of fields
Mitella diphylla	Bishop's Cap	8–12"	White	April–May	Circumneutral	Damp rocks, deep wooded slopes
Myosotis laxa	Forget-me-not	6–12"	Bright blue, but inconspicuous	May–July	Indifferent	Moist, banks of brooks
scorpioides	Forget-me-not	6–12"	Bright blue, larger	May–July	Indifferent	Moist, banks of brooks
Orchis spectabilis	Showy Orchis	5–10"	Rosy lavender and white	May–June	Circumneutral	Moist stony soil
Phlox divaricata	Wild Blue Phlox	9–18"	Lavender-blue	April–June	Circumneutral	Rocky woods
Podophyllum peltatum	May-Apple	12–18"	White	April–May	Indifferent to acidity	Moist, shaded
Polemonium reptans	Greek Valerian	8–12"	Blue-violet	April–May	Circumneutral	Thin, dryish woods
Polygonatum biflorum	Solomon's Seal	18–30"	Greenish white	April–June	Indifferent to acidity	Thickets, dry wooded slopes
commutatum	Solomon's Seal	8'		April–June	Indifferent to acidity	Thickets, dry wooded slopes
Sanguinaria canadensis	Bloodroot	10"	White	April–May	Indifferent to acidity	Borders of woods
Tiarella cordifolia	Foam-flower	6–10"	White	May–June	Indifferent to acidity	Along shaded roadsides. Rich, moist woods
Trillium erectum	Wake-robin	7–12"	Maroon	April–May	Indifferent to acidity	Rich, moist woodlands
grandiflorum	Large Flowering Trillium	10–18"	White, then pink	May–June	Circumneutral	Rich, rocky woods
stylosum	Southern Pink Trillium	12–18"	Rose, pink	May–June	Circumneutral	Rich, rocky woods
Viola blanda	Sweet White Violet	3–5"	White, purple veins	April–May	Circumneutral	Moist or dry situations

canadensis	Canada violet	5–15″	White, tinged purple	May–June	Circumneutral	Well-drained, upland woods
conspersa	Dog Violet	3–5″	Light blue-purple	April–June	Indifferent to acidity	Moist woods, shady borders of roads and fields
palmata	Common Blue Violet	3–7″	Violet-purple	April–June	Indifferent to acidity	Low moist ground
pedata	Bird's-foot Violet	4–8″	Lilac or blue-violet	April–June	Moderately acid, dry sandy	Open banks, thin woods

FERNS FOR THE WOODLAND GARDEN

Botanical Name	Common Name	Type (Deciduous or Evergreen)	Height in Feet or Inches	Habitat
Adiantum pedatum	American Maidenhair Fern	D	2'	Shade
Asplenium platyneuron	Ebony Spleenwort	E	½–1'	Rocky woods
Trichomanes	Maidenhair Spleenwort	E	½'	Clefts in rocks
Athyrium Filix-femina	Lady Fern	D	2–3'	Partial shade or full sun
pycnocarpon	Narrowleaf Spleenwort	D	2–3'	Rich woods
Botrychium virginianum	Rattlesnake Fern	D	1–2'	Open woods
Camptosorus rhizophyllus	Walking Fern	E	4–10"	Limestone cliffs in shade
Cystopteris bulbifera	Berry Bladderfern	D	1–2'	Moist bank or brookside in shade
Dennstaedtia punctilobula	Hayscented Fern	D	2'	Sun or shade
Dryopteris Clintoniana	Clinton Wood Fern	E	2–3'	Moist woods
cristata	Crested Wood Fern	E	1–2'	On hummocks in grassy bogs
dilatata	Mountain Wood Fern	D	2'	Mountain peaks in shade
hexagonoptera	Winged Wood Fern	D	1'	Shade
Linnæana	Oak Fern	D	½'	Shade
marginalis	Leather Wood Fern	E	2–3'	Rocky woods
Phegopteris	Narrow Beech Fern	D	½–1'	Brookside banks
spinulosa	Toothed Wood Fern	E	2–3'	Shade
Lygodium palmatum	Hartford or Climbing Fern	D	4'	
Onoclea sensibilis	Sensitive Fern	D	1–2'	Bogs
Osmunda cinnamomea	Cinnamon Fern	D	3–4'	Roadsides and damp woods
Claytoniana	Interrupted Fern	D	3–4'	Sun or shade
regalis	Royal Fern	D	3'	Sun or shade
Polypodium vulgare	Common Polypody	E	½'	Rocky woods
Polystichum acrostichoides	Christmas Fern	E	1–2'	Rich woods
Pteretis nodulosa	Ostrich Fern	D	4–6'	Banks of streams, sun or shade

Botanical Name	Common Name	Evergreen or Deciduous	Ht.	Color of Bloom
Aronia arbutifolia	Red Chokeberry	D	9'	Pinkish
melanocarpa	Black Chokeberry	D	4'	White
Azalea arborescens	Sweet Azalea	D	9–12'	White
calendulacea	Flame Azalea	D	12'	Yellow-scarlet
canadense	Rhodora	D	3'	Rosy-purple
nudiflora	Pinxter-flower	D	6–8'	Pink
rosea		D	9'	Pink
Vaseyi	Pinkshell Azalea	D	15'	Various
viscosa	Swamp Azalea	D	4–7'	Pink, white
Benzoin æstivale	Spice Bush	D	6–12'	Pale yellow
Clethra alnifolia	White Alder or Sweet Pepperbush	D	4–5'	White
Cornus alba	Coral Dogwood	D	5–10'	Cream
Amomum	Silky Cornel or Kinni-kinnik	D		White
racemosa	Gray Dogwood	D	3–15'	Cream
stolonifera	Golden-twig Dogwood	D	8'	Dull white
Hamamelis virginica	Witch Hazel	D	8–12'	Yellow
Ilex glabra	Inkberry	E	4–8'	White
verticillata	Winterberry, or Black Alder	D	6–15'	Inconspicuous
Kalmia latifolia	Mountain Laurel	E	8'	Pink
Leiophyllum buxifolium	Sand Myrtle	E	1'	White
Leucothoë Catesbæi	Catesby's Leucothoë	E	3–5'	White
Pachistima Canbyi		E	1'	Reddish
Pieris floribunda	Mt. Fetter Bush	E	3–5'	White-pink
Rhamnus cathartica	Buckthorn	D	12'	White
Rhododendron carolinianum	Carolina Rhododendron	E	9'	Pink
catawbiense	Catawba Rhododendron	E	6–18'	Rosy lilac
maximum	Rosebay Rhododendron	E	30'	Pink or white
minus		E	10'	Rosy pink

Season of Bloom	Fruit and Autumn Effect	Soil	Habitat
May	Red fruit and leaves	Moist	
May	Black	Well drained	
June–July	Leaves red	Acid	
June	Inconspicuous	Acid	
April–May	Inconspicuous	Acid	
April–May	Inconspicuous	Acid or lime	
April–May	Inconspicuous	Acid or lime	
April–May	Inconspicuous	Acid	
June–July	Inconspicuous	Moist	
March–April	Gold leaves, scarlet berries	Fertile	Wet woods, swamps
July–August	Inconspicuous	Wet, peaty or acid sandy	Edges of woods and fields
May–June	Bluish white, red twigs		
June	Blue	Wet	
June	White or pale blue	Wet	
May	White	Wet	
Oct. or Nov.	Black seeds	Indifferent	Thickets, edges of woodlands
July	Black berries through winter	Wet	
July	Red	Wet	Swamps, wet thickets
June	Inconspicuous	Slightly acid and moist	Rocky hillsides, woodlands
May–June	Inconspicuous	Acid	
April	Deep red	Acid	Mountains
April–May			
April–May	Flower buds about to burst all winter	Acid	
May–June	Scarlet, good display	Sandy or clay	
May–June	Inconspicuous	Moderately acid	
May–June	Inconspicuous	Moderately acid	
May	Inconspicuous	Moderately acid	
June–July		Moderately acid	

Botanical Name	Common Name	Evergreen or Deciduous	Ht.	Color of Bloom
Sambucus pubens	Elder	D	5–8'	White
Vaccinium corymbosum	High-bush Blueberry	D	4–10'	White
pennsylvanicum	Low-bush Blueberry	D	1½'	White
vacillans	Dwarf Late Blueberry	D	1–3'	Purple
Viburnum acerifolium	Dockmackie	D	5'	White
cassinoides	Withe-rod	D	6'	White
dentatum	Arrow-wood	D	5–15'	White
Lentago	Nannyberry	D	30'	White
prunifolium	Plum-leaved Haw	D	30'	White

Season of Bloom	Fruit and Autumn Effect	Soil	Habitat
June–July	Purple fruit	Swampy	
May–June	Scarlet leaves, blue berries Aug.-Sept.	Acid	Deep swamps, moist woods
May–June	Scarlet leaves, blue berries July–Aug.	Acid	Dry, rocky, sandy hills
May	Crimson leaves, berries last later	Acid	Open woods (dry), shaded thickets
June	Black	Dry	
May	Black	Wet	
June	Blue		
May	Black	Moist	
April	Black		

681

XVIII

Water and Bog Gardens

PLANTS FOR WATER GARDENS

The natural pond or the garden pool may be readily converted into a water garden by the use of water plants. It is often assumed that so exquisite a flower as a water-lily is difficult to grow and that it requires special care. Actually, however, once they are established, the hardy species of *Nymphæa* thrive without much attention. Some of the species are native to this country and are common in the quiet waters of inland ponds. The tender kinds, including *Nelumbium speciosum,* the Egyptian lotus, need more care and are most satisfactorily grown in the greenhouse or removed to the greenhouse for the winter.

It is supposed that water-lilies require abundant space and that one must have a pond of considerable size in which to raise them. While the larger species spread to a circle about 6 feet across, the dwarf species, with small leaves and exquisitely small flowers, are suitable for garden pools hardly more than 3 or 4 feet in diameter.

HARDY WATER-LILIES
Species and Varieties of Merit

Nymphæa odorata, the white, fragrant pond-lily of the Northern States, is hardy and dependable. The leaves are dark green and numerous. The flowers are about 4 inches across, the upcurving white petals encircling yellow stamens.

Many hybrid varieties of *Nymphæa odorata* are on the market.

N. odorata rosea is the pink Cape Cod water-lily.

N. odorata minor is a small plant with tiny flowers. It requires a depth of but 12 inches and spreads to a circle only 3 feet in diameter.

N. odorata caroliniana bears rose-flesh-colored flowers with yellow stamens. The leaves are large, sometimes 12 inches across.

N. odorata Yellow Pigmy has clear yellow flowers. Variety *Helen Fowler* is a good pink. Flowers of *aurora* change color on successive days, yellow the first day, then red-orange and finally red.

N. Marliacea albida and *N. Gladstoniana* are among the best white water-lilies. They are free-growing plants, blooming continuously all season, and they produce large fragrant flowers. Those of *Marliacea albida* have pink sepals. *Gladstoniana* has enormous blooms.

N. Marliacea rosea, similar to *albida* in habit, has deep pink blossoms.

N. alba has large white, floating flowers.

N. alba candidissima has larger flowers than the type and is a vigorous plant with blossoms continuing throughout the season.

Other good pinks are *formosa* and *Pink Opal*.

Attraction, Gloriosa, and *James Brydon* have red flowers. *Comanche* has tones of apricot and red in the petals, and orange stamens. *Sioux* varies from copper yellow to red. *Indian* opens yellow and changes to dark crimson.

N. Marliacea chromatella is still one of the best yellows, bearing blossoms 6 inches across with canary yellow petals and bright yellow stamens in generous numbers. It is a vigorous grower and should be divided every few years to avoid crowding of the leaves in the center of the plant.

All these water-lilies are hardy in Zones V and VI.*

PROPAGATION BY SEED

Sow the seeds in pans of sand. Cover the seeds lightly with screened sand and place the pan in water at a temperature of 70 to 80 degrees F. in such a way that the surface of the sand is above the water, but in contact with it. After soaking them all day, submerge the pans to a depth of 18 inches or more. After the plants have formed the first floating leaf, they may be transplanted to flats with 2 inches of soil containing well-rotted cow manure. Thereafter the young plants should be potted on as they develop and require more space.

CULTURAL REQUIREMENTS

The requirements for culture are quiet water with a trickling inlet and outlet, a depth of 18 inches for the smaller sorts

*See Zone Map of Hardiness on inside of front and back cover.

and 2 or 3 feet for the larger species, full sunshine, and 2 or 3 cubic feet of prepared soil for each plant.

The soil may be a mixture of two parts good garden soil and one part well-rotted cow manure, or, if natural sources are available, a mixture of equal parts garden soil and pond muck. If neither manure nor muck is obtainable, a half quart of bone meal to each plant may be mixed with the soil.

For convenience in keeping the pool neat, the soil is placed in tubs, half barrels, or boxes. Cypress is the best wood for tubs and boxes but the barrels are usually of oak. The soil bed should be almost 12 inches deep and so placed that its surface is 12 to 18 inches below the surface of the water. In planting, the soil is put into the tub, half filling it, the tuber is placed on the soil so that the growing end is upward and about level with the rim of the tub, being held in this position while more soil is filled in around it. The upper inch or two should consist of sand. In planting water-lilies in a natural pond the tubers may be squeezed down into the muck of the bottom. If the muck does not hold them and they float instead, it may be wrapped about them. The best time for planting is April.

WINTER CARE

Once established, hardy water-lilies will require no special care. To carry hardy water-lilies through the winter, the only protection necessary is the muck and water above them. If the ice does not freeze to the bottom where the tubers are, no harm will be done to them.

The pool itself may be protected against ice pressure in several ways. If it is small, it may be covered with a floor of boards, with a mound of leaves and litter heaped above it. This will conserve ground heat and delay and mitigate freezing. The larger pool may be protected by a number of floating logs. As the ice freezes, the logs, being somewhat soft, will absorb the pressure and thus relieve the concrete from a strain which might crack it.

OTHER WATER PLANTS

Other aquatic plants attractive in pools or on pond margins are Floating Heart, which has no roots in the muck; Forget-me-not; Parrot-feather; Primrose Willow; Primrose Creeper; Water-hyacinth; Water Snowflake; Umbrella Palm. Water Snowflake has charming, small white and pale yellow blossoms, which rest on the water like little butterflies.

OXYGENATING PLANTS

Plants which keep the water clear and refreshed by their natural process of charging it with oxygen are known as oxygenating plants. Cabomba and Anacharis are both tiny plants with light green, small leaves—much smaller than those of water cress—floating on the surface, and they grow in shallow water about 4 inches to 12 inches deep. Sagittaria (Arrowhead) is another oxygen plant. It grows from shallow water to a height of 3 feet, and bears arrowhead leaves.

SHORE PLANTS

The shores of a natural pond may be greatly enlivened by groups of Pickerel Rush, Bull Rush, Papyrus, Yellow Flag (Iris pseudacorus), Purple Flag (Iris versicolor), and Arrowhead, most of which grow up from water a few inches deep and stand erect. Such shrubs as Button bush (Cephalanthus occidentalis), Spice bush (Benzoin æstivale), Sweet pepper bush (Clethra alnifolia), are suitable for the larger masses of foliage on the pond side.

INSECT PESTS

Water plants seem to be troubled by only a few enemies.

Aphids sometimes are found on the leaves. The easiest way to be rid of them is to wash them off into the water with the spray of a hose. The goldfish will then dispose of them.

A *leaf miner* occasionally destroys leaves, making tunnels that are easily seen. The only certain method of coping with it is to cut off all affected leaves as soon as the trouble is detected and burn them. The plant should be able to replace the lost leaves with new ones.

A remarkabe insect is the *Leaf-eating Hydrocampa propiralis*, which constructs boats from bits of leaves and cruises about the pond. Picking them off the leaves by hand and catching them in a net while navigating is recommended as the most effective means of control.

Algæ are not damaging but make the pool disagreeable with greenish discoloration. The water can be cleared up by putting copper sulphate in it at the rate of one pound per 500,000 gallons. A pool 3 feet deep and 13 x 30 feet of surface will need only ⅛ of an ounce of copper sulphate. The crystals of copper sulphate should be crushed, put into a cloth bag like a salt bag, and drawn through the water until dissolved.

BOG GARDENS

A true bog is a flat piece of ground composed largely of peat and covered with living sphagnum moss. It retains the moisture throughout the summer season and yet does not have pools of standing water in it. Permanently wet soil of this nature is difficult to recondition or to drain, and the results of such an attempt may not justify the expenditure. A more logical use of such an area is to grow there the many attractive plants which thrive in saturated soil. And because many of these plants cannot be grown in ordinary garden soil, the possession of a natural bog offers an unusual opportunity for a unique type of gardening.

Lacking a bog, but desirous of growing bog plants, the garden owner may create by artificial means the requisite conditions. The two essentials are a continuous supply of water, and a soil which is capable of retaining it. The first may be provided by water pipes in which tiny holes have been bored at intervals of every 2 or 3 feet, the pipes being buried at a depth of approximately 2 inches. The second requisite may be provided by mixing equal portions of sand and peatmoss with generous quantities of humus. The mixture should be deep, 18 inches if possible, and a 1-inch layer of peatmoss should be spread over the surface. The only subsequent care of the bog after the plants have become established is the occasional removal of undesirable plants which may have crept in.

PLANTS FOR THE BOG GARDEN

Cardinal Flower (Lobelia cardinalis)
Closed Gentian (Gentiana Andrewsii)
Fringed Gentian (Gentiana crinita)
Iris (Iris fulva)
    (Iris pseudacorus)
    (Iris versicolor)
Jack-in-the-Pulpit (Arisæma triphyllum)
Lilies (L. canadense)
      (L. superbum)
Marsh Marigold (Caltha palustris)
Pickerel weed (Pontederia cordata)
Pitcher Plant (Sarracenia flava)
          (Sarracenia purpurea)
Primulas (P. Bulleyana)
       (P. Cockburniana)
       (P. helodoxa)
       (P. japonica)
Royal Fern (Osmunda regalis)
Troutlily (Erythronium americanum)
Wake Robin (Trillium erectum)
       (Trillium grandiflorum)

XIX

The Herb Garden

The Herb Garden was one of the earliest expressions of garden art during the period of the Renaissance. Throughout Europe physic gardens were found within the cloistered walls of the monasteries and from these gardens were dispensed a variety of medicinal herbs, in an effort, on the part of the monks, to alleviate the suffering and distress of their people. It was an era when the enjoyment of plants for their beauty alone, while not entirely forgotten, was at least secondary in importance to their more practical uses. People were interested primarily in growing plants which were to be used for medicinal purposes, or as flavorings in cookery, or as a source of color for the dyeing of materials, and in some cases for fragrance alone. An intimate knowledge of such plants was general throughout the countryside, as is evidenced by the wealth of plant names in most European languages; and the superstition and folklore regarding these plants were passed on from generation to generation.

The herb garden of the Middle Ages was usually laid out upon simple, formal lines with quaintly patterned beds, narrow paths, and prim edgings, and in many an old monastery garden the "Mint Pool" was a favorite feature. During the Elizabethan era in England the herb garden was an important feature of the grounds and the patterned beds upon the broad terraces surrounding the manor houses became more and more intricate in design.

The early colonists brought with them to this country a knowledge and understanding of the uses of herbs, and it was not long before many of the old, familiar plants were flourishing in the little dooryard gardens of the towns and villages of New England.

The Herb Garden

The quaintly patterned path of old brick, the bee-skep and the carefully
selected plants, all add to the charm of the garden.

During the 19th century the interest in herbs declined steadily and the herb garden, as it had existed in earlier times, be-

Wattled Fence

An Herb Garden in Tudor Style
Scale 0 2 4 6 8 10 Feet

came an almost forgotten thing of the past. Within the last decade, however, there has been a great reawakening of interest in the culture and the uses of herbs and we have again come to appreciate the quaint beauty and charm of the herb garden.

CLASSIFICATION OF HERBS

Herbs are usually divided into several groups, although there is more or less overlapping. The aromatic herbs are those grown for fragrance; the culinary herbs are those grown to be used as flavorings in cookery; the medicinal herbs still play an important part in modern medicine; and those grown for coloring still give us some of our most beautiful dyes.

CULTURAL REQUIREMENTS

The great majority of our more commonly grown herbs prefer a position in full sun and thrive best in a rather poor, gravelly, well-drained soil. When grown in rich garden beds, they make more luxuriant vegetative growth but lose much of their fragrance and flavor. There are a few herbs which prefer partial or light shade rather than full sun and a few which definitely prefer a moist location.

HARVESTING

If the foliage is to be used either for fragrance or for flavoring, the herbs should be cut just as the flowers are about to open, for with most herbs it is at this stage that the essential oils are the most abundant. The most favorable time for cutting is early in the morning after the dew has dried but before the plants have been touched with hot midday sun. When herbs are to be cut for flowers, as in the case of lavender and chamomile, they should be cut when in full bloom. If the seeds are to be used, the seed heads should be cut when they are no longer green. Those which are harvested for their roots should be dug in the autumn after growth has ceased.

HERBS FOR FLAVORING

Angelica (A. Archangelica)
Anise (Pimpinella Anisum)
Balm (Melissa officinalis)
Basil (Ocimum)
    O. minimum
    O. Basilicum

Borage (Borago officinalis)
Burnet (Sanguisorba officinalis)
    S. minor
Caraway (Carum Carvi)
Catnip (Nepeta Cataria)
Chamomile (Anthemis nobilis)
       (Matricaria Chamomilla)
Chervil (Anthriscus Cerefolium)
Chives (Allium Schœnoprasum)
Coriander (Coriandrum sativum)
Costmary (Chrysanthemum Balsamita)
Cress (Barbarea verna)
Dill (Anethum graveolens)
Fennel (Fœniculum vulgare)
Fennel Flower (Nigella sativa)
Horehound (Marrubium vulgare)
Lovage (Levisticum officinale)
Marjoram (Origanum)
    O. Onites, Pot Marjoram
    O. Majorana, Sweet Marjoram
Mint (Mentha)
    M. rotundifolia variegata, Apple Mint
    M. crispa, Curled Mint
    M. piperita, Peppermint
    M. spicata, Garden Mint or Spearmint
Rue (Ruta graveolens)
Saffron (Crocus sativus)
Sage (Salvia officinalis)
Savory (Satureja)
    S. hortensis, Summer Savory
    S. montana, Winter Savory
Sorrel (Rumex Acetosa)
Sweet Flag (Acorus Càlamus)
Tarragon (Artemisia Dracunculus)
Thyme (Thymus)
    T. vulgaris, Common English Thyme
    T. Serpyllum citriodorus, Lemon Thyme
Watercress (Nasturtium aquaticum)

HERBS FOR FRAGRANCE

Ambrosia (Chenopodium Botrys)
Balm (Melissa officinalis)   (*Continued on page* 700)

Common Name	Botanical Name	Height	Annual, Biennial or Perennial
Ambrosia	Chenopodium Botrys	2'	Annual
Angelica	Angelica Archangelica	2–3'	Biennial
Anise	Pimpinella Anisum	2–3'	Annual
Balm (Lemon Balm)	Melissa officinalis	2½–3'	Perennial
Basil	Ocimum minimum	1'	Annual
Bee Balm	Monarda didyma	2–3'	Perennial
Bergamot	Monarda fistulosa, f. alba	3'	Perennial
Borage	Borago officinalis	1½–2'	Annual
Burnet	Sanguisorba minor	1–1¼'	Perennial
	Sanguisorba officinalis	5'	Perennial
Caraway	Carum Carvi	2'	Biennial
Chamomile	Anthemis nobilis	1'	Perennial
Sweet or false	Matricaria Chamomilla	2'	Annual
Chervil	Anthriscus Cerefolium	½–1'	Annual
Chives	Allium Schœnoprasum	10"	Perennial
Clary	Salvia Sclarea	3'	Biennial
Coriander	Coriandrum sativum	1½'	Annual
Costmary	Chrysanthemum Balsamita	3'	Perennial
Cress	Barbarea verna	2'	Biennial
Cumin	Cuminum Cyminum	4–8"	Annual
Dill	Anethum graveolens	2½–3'	Annual
Fennel Flower	Nigella sativa	1'	Annual
Florence Fennel	Fœniculum vulgare, var. dulce	6–10"	Annual
Geranium, scented, in variety	Pelargonium	1–3'	Tender perennial
Horehound	Marrubium vulgare	3'	Perennial
Horseradish	Armoracia rusticana	18–30"	Perennial
Hyssop	Hyssopus officinalis	18–24"	Perennial

Propagation	Uses	Exposure	Soil Requirements
Seed	Fragrance	Sunny	Any soil
Sow seed as soon as ripe	Food, perfume	Cool climate	Prefers a rather moist soil
Seed	Food, perfume, medicine	Warm, sunny exposure	Moderately rich, well-drained loam
Seed	Medicine, food, perfume	Warm, sheltered position	Poor, light soil
Seed	Seasoning, fragrance	Sunny	Well drained
Seed, division	Medicine, perfume, food	Sun or partial shade	Dry, well-drained soil
Division	Fragrance	Sun or part shade	Any soil
Seed	Food	Sunny exposure	Dry, well-drained soil
Seed, division	Medicine, food	Full sun	Any garden soil, prefers lime
Division, seed	Flavoring	Sunny	Any garden soil
Seed	Medicine, perfume, food	Sunny exposure	Dry, well-drained soil
Seeds, rooting stems	Medicine	Sunny	Dry, well-drained soil
Seed	Flavoring	Full sun	Ordinary soil
Seed	Food, medicine	Sun or partial shade	Any good garden soil
Bulbs, seeds, division of clumps	Flavorings for salads, omelets, sauces	Sunny	Any good garden soil
Seed	Perfumes, food	Full sun	Rocky, dry soil
Seed	Medicine, perfume, food	Sunny exposure	Prefers a warm light soil
Root cuttings	Medicine, food	Sunny exposure	Dry, well-drained soil
Seed	Flavoring for salad	Sun	Any meadow soil
Seed	Medicine, perfume, food	Sunny exposure	Any good garden soil
Seed (do not transplant)	Food, for pickling, for vinegars	Sunny	Any ordinary garden soil
Seed	Condiment, perfume	Full sun	Any garden soil
Seed	Food	Full sun	Light, well-drained soil
Cuttings	Fragrance	Sunny	Any garden soil. Not hardy in North.
Seed	Medicine, as a drink	Full sun	Poor, light, dry soil
Root cuttings	Food, medicine	Sun	Any soil
Seed	Medicine, perfume, food	Sunny exposure	Ordinary garden soil, not too rich. Prefers lime

Common Name	Botanical Name	Height	Annual, Biennial or Perennial
Lavender	Lavandula (vera, officinalis, Spica)	2–3'	Perennial
	Lavandula dentata	2–3'	Perennial
Lavender Cotton	Santolina Chamæcyparissus	2'	Perennial
Lemon Verbena	Lippia citriodora	4–5'	Perennial
Lovage	Levisticum officinale	6'	Perennial
Mint, Apple	Mentha rotundifolia	30"	Perennial
Mint, Curled	Mentha crispa	3'	Perennial
Parsley	Petroselinum hortense	6–10"	Biennial
Peppermint	Mentha piperita	2–3'	Perennial
Pot Marjoram	Origanum vulgare	2'	Perennial
Perennial Marjoram	Origanum (Majorana Onites)	2'	Perennial
Pot Marigold	Calendula officinalis	12–15"	Annual
Rosemary	Rosmarinus officinalis	3–6'	Tender perennial shrub
Rue	Ruta graveolens	2'	Perennial
Saffron	Crocus sativus	4"	Perennial
Sage	Salvia officinalis	2–3'	Perennial
Sesame	Sesamum orientale	2'	Annual
Sorrel	Rumex Acetosa	3'	Perennial
Southernwood	Artemisia Abrotanum	2–3'	Perennial
Spearmint	Mentha spicata	2–3'	Perennial
Sweet Basil	Ocimum Basilicum	1½–2'	Annual
Sweet Cicely	Myrrhis odorata	2–3'	Perennial
Sweet Fennel	Fœniculum officinale	3'	Annual
Sweet Flag	Acorus Calamus	5'	Perennial
Sweet Marjoram	Origanum Majorana hortensis	8–12"	Annual
Sweet Woodruff	Asperula odorata	8"	Perennial
Summer Savory	Satureja hortensis	1–1½'	Annual
Winter Savory	Satureja montana	15"	Perennial

Propagation	Uses	Exposure	Soil Requirements
Cuttings, seed	Fragrance, food	Full sun	Light, well-drained soil high in lime content.
Cuttings, seed	Fragrance	Full sun	Any garden soil
Cuttings	Fragrance	Sunny	Garden soil, not hardy. Winter over in cold frames.
Cuttings of half-ripe wood	Flavor, perfume	Very sensitive to frost. Best grown in pots	Good garden loam
Seed	Medicine, perfume, food	Sunny	Rich, moist soil
Cuttings, divisions	Flavoring, fragrance	Sunny	Good garden soil
Cuttings, divisions	Flavoring, fragrance	Sunny	Good, deep soil
Seed	Medicine, food	Full sun	Prefers a rather moist soil
Cuttings, runners	Medicine, perfume, food	Sunny	Deep, moist soil
Seed, cuttings	Medicine, perfume, food	Sunny	Any garden soil
Seed	Flavoring, fragrance	Sunny	Any garden soil
Seed	Medicine, food	Sunny	Any rich garden soil
Seed, cuttings	Medicine, perfume	Sunny, sheltered position	Dry well-drained soil
Seed, cuttings	Perfume, food	Sunny	Prefers a well-drained yet moist soil
Seed, corms	Perfume, flavoring, coloring	Sunny	Garden soil
Seed, cuttings	Medicine, perfumes, food	Sunny	Any well-drained garden soil
Seed	Medicine, food	Full sun	Any well-drained garden soil
Seed	Salad flavoring	Sunny	Any garden soil not too alkaline
Division	Fragrance, medicine	Sunny exposure	Any garden soil
Cuttings, runners	Perfume, food	Sunny	Deep, moist soil
Seed	Flavoring, medicine, perfume	Sunny	Well-drained soil
Seed, division	Food	Sun or partial shade	Any ordinary garden soil
Seed	Food	Full sun	Well-drained soil
Division	Perfume	Sunny	Moist
Seed	Medicine, perfume, food	Sunny	Dry, well-drained
Division	Fragrance, flavoring	Partial shade	Thrives well in either moist or dry soil
Seed	Medicine, food	Sunny location	Any good garden soil
Seed	Seasoning, fragrance	Sunny	Any garden soil

Common Name	Botanical Name	Height	Annual, Biennial or Perennial
Tansy	Tanacetum vulgare	3'	Perennial
Tarragon	Artemisia Dracunculus	3'	Perennial
Thyme	Thymus, many varieties	6–8"	Perennial sub-shrub
Watercress	Nasturtium aquaticum	5"	Perennial
Wormwood	Artemisia Absinthium	2½–4'	Perennial
Roman Wormwood	Artemisia pontica	4'	Perennial Biennial
Beach Wormwood	Artemisia Stelleriana	2½'	Perennial

Propagation	Uses	Exposure	Soil Requirements
Seed, division	Medicine, perfume	Full sun	Any garden soil
Root cuttings	Perfume, flavoring	Prefers light shade	Any good soil
Seed, cuttings	Medicine, perfume	Sunny	Rocky banks, any well-drained sunny position
Seed or stem cuttings	Salad seasoning	Sunny	Pool or stream margins
Seed, division	Medicine, food	Sunny	Any garden soil
Seed, division	Fragrance	Sunny	Thrives even in poor soil
Seed, division	Fragrance	Sunny	Any soil

HERBS FOR FRAGRANCE—*Continued from page 693*

Basil (Ocimum)
Bergamot (Monarda)
    M. didyma
    M. fistulosa
    M. fistulosa alba
Geranium (Pelargonium)
    P. crispum, Citronella Geranium
    P. denticulatum, Skeleton Geranium
    P. graveolens, Rose Geranium
    P. Limoneum, Lemon Geranium
    P. melissinum, Balm Geranium
    P. odoratissimum, in variety
Lavender (Lavandula)
    L. dentata
    L. spica
    L. vera
Lavender-Cotton (Santolina Chamæcyparissus)
Marjoram (Origanum)
    O. Onites, Pot Marjoram
    O. Majorana, Sweet Marjoram
Mint (Mentha)
    M. citrata, Orange Mint
    M. crispa, Curled Mint
    M. rotundifolia, Apple Mint
    M. piperita, Peppermint
    M. Pulegium, Pennyroyal
    M. Requieni, Creeping Mint
    M. spicata, Garden or Spearmint
Rosemary (Rosmarinus officinalis)
Rue (Ruta graveolens)
Savory (Satureja)
    S. hortensis, Summery Savory
    S. montana, Winter Savory
Southernwood (Artemisia Abrotanum)
Thyme (Thymus) in variety
Verbena, Lemon (Lippia citriodora)
Woodruff, Sweet (Asperula odorata)
Wormwood (Artemisia)
    A. Absinthium, Common Wormwood
    A. pontica, Roman Wormwood
    A. Stelleriana, Beach Wormwood

XX

City Gardens

In spite of cramped quarters within the old fortification walls, the mediæval town had many a small garden. Even in the 16th and 17th centuries, a formal garden was a common adjunct to the larger houses of London, Brussels, and Paris. But cities grew rapidly with the expanding commerce of the 17th century and the discomfort, dirt and disease of city life in London had become so appalling by the time of the great fire (1664), that it was the sincere hope of many of the colonists to do better with their new towns. This natural striving for improved conditions is expressed in some of the important writings of the times, as is evident in the following quotation.

"Let every house be placed, if the Person pleases, in ye middle of its platt as to the breadth way of it, that so there may be ground on each side, for Gardens, or Orchards, or fields, y^t it may be a greene Country Towne, which will never be burnt and will allways be wholesome." Thus William Penn gave instructions to the three commissioners whom he sent to lay out the city of Philadelphia on the banks of the Delaware in 1682. In these words, too, he expressed an ideal of town planning which, if put into practice, can overcome the curse of city congestion. The ideal was heartily accepted by the colonists and they were able to maintain their city as a "greene Country Towne" for more than a century thereafter.

When, about the middle of the nineteenth century, Philadelphia, like many other cities, experienced that phenomenal growth of industrial expansion, houses became crowded together on narrow lots, and at the century's close little remained of Penn's "greene Country Towne." People who cherished the old traditions did one of two things. They moved farther out of town in each succeeding generation, or they remained in the city and preserved what they could of that little oasis, the yard garden, against the increasing odds of meager sunlight, impoverished soil, and stifling summer heat. The custom of the city garden has been greatly stimulated since the beginning of this century. It is remarkable how many tiny yards in residential sections of our great cities have become, during the past twenty-five years, charming gardens of flowers.

No garden is more artificially situated, or beset with greater disadvantages, than the garden in the city. It is cramped for space, for the tremendous increase in land values has made ground space almost unobtainable. Neighboring buildings often deprive it of adequate sunshine and circulation of air. In most cases the soil is impoverished and overlaid by dust and soot. Every ton of loam, every load of manure and humus must be hauled in by truck, and carried to the yard in wheelbarrows.

If, by ingenious designing, the space has been well utilized, and a pleasing composition results, and if, by technical skill, the cultural requirements for healthy plant growth have been provided, then such a garden may bring real satisfaction to the owner. It can be a measure of compensation for much that city life fails to provide.

The crowding of city populations into narrower houses reached absurd extremes, which resulted in an uneconomic use of land and unhealthy, inconvenient homes. The development of steel frame buildings since the last decade of the 19th century has brought about another solution of the city housing problem. Group apartment houses now provide many more families with homes than the single houses did on the same land. When the apartment groups are well planned, as they so often are, space remains in great open courts for gardens, playgrounds and trees; and pleasant views from sunny windows make the interiors delightful.

Even in the crowded sections of great cities, the "set-back" law has brought about new forms of structure and many little flat roofs have become sunny terrace gardens high above the canyoned streets.

A City Garden

Spring Bloom in a City Garden

This new era in city building, made possible by modern methods of construction and by rational designing, has already brought the garden back to the city and it is likely, in the near future, to experience further development in this direction. The garden in the city may reach again that place of importance which it formerly occupied.

DESIGN

The architectural surroundings of the town garden make an architectural approach to its design the most logical one. The backyard site should be enclosed in a beautiful wall or fence, thus securing privacy and framing the composition. Axes should be employed as a framework of the design, giving it strength of form and harmonizing it with the adjoining architecture. However, exact symmetry may not be necessarily important in so small a space. Architectural features such as sculpture, a wall fountain, balustrades, wrought-iron grills, colored tiles, and pavement, all express the formal style and add color and interest of detail to a garden in which flowering plants do not play a dominant part. The design should be simple, straightforward, formal, small in scale and economical of space, but not crowded.

BACKGROUND

As with so many gardens, the background is an important part of the composition. Walls 8 or 9 feet high are an effective means of blocking unsatisfactory views, but in some positions they shut out too much sunshine and air circulation, and they should be used with a careful regard for the points of the compass. Brick, hollow tile with stucco surface, hollow tile with colored-tile surface, or combinations of these, are all satisfactory. The coping on the top of the wall—tile, flagstone or brick—can be made a decorative color note. To mitigate the severity of wall surfaces and the heat radiating from them, vines should be grown on the walls. Such vines as English ivy and Boston ivy cling to brick by rootlets, but clematis, polygonum, and many other vines require lattices upon which to climb. Lattices of white-painted wood can be of simple decorative patterns. Wood frames are good, but wrought iron is preferred for wisteria, which is so strong that it can wreck wooden trellises in a few years.

FENCES

The most satisfactory fence for the city garden is a solid board fence with a lattice top to provide support for vines. Wood fences must be painted frequently, once in two years in some localities. A combination low brick wall and high brick piers with fencing between the piers is satisfactory when designed in good proportions. It is more permanent than a fence with wooden posts and the combination of materials makes it an interesting architectural feature.

PATHS

Paths and pavements present a special problem in the city garden where radiating heat is often one of the severest conditions with which one must contend. Brick and flagstones are necessarily hot materials in full sunshine. Loose pebbles, so appropriate with small French formal schemes, are also hot in the sun and uncomfortable to walk upon with small heels. In the shade of trees, no heat is reflected from those surfaces. A very satisfactory substitute for these hard radiating surfaces is tanbark, which may be spread and rolled on a 6-inch base of cinders. This material has a combination of qualities most valued for walks. It is soft but firm, porous and quickly drying, and it forms a dense mat so that it will not be blown about in the wind. However, the color, a rich reddish brown, may make it difficult to use in certain color schemes. Concrete is permanent and the most practical and economic material for walk pavements, but it is harsh and glaring and its use should be avoided if possible. Its combination with colored pebbles of a fairly uniform size may give pattern to an otherwise monotonous surface. In this type of pavement, the pebbles are pressed into the surface of the concrete while it it still mobile, and protrude above the surface, forming a knobby, rough floor. Such a pavement may be combined with flagstone. In districts where frost action in the soil is not the usual winter condition, "popple" stones may be used. These are small cobble-stones set on edge into the ground and firmed by tamping. The art of laying such a pavement is practised in southern England; and in Spain, where the passion for decoration is so strong, these stones are placed in patterns of varied colors and sizes, especially in the enclosed courts or patios of town houses.

UTILITY BACKYARDS

Many a city-yard garden is also the means of access from delivery truck to kitchen. As a yard it must provide receptacles for wastes, and an area to be used occasionally for drying lines. A cupboard for containing rubbish cans is sometimes concealed behind a low wall, the top of which is a broad shelf for potted plants. If the path to the alley is at a slightly lower level than the rest of the garden, this concealment is all the more easily accomplished.

The wall, with its potted plants, as seen from the garden side, is a very decorative feature, and may be the background of the garden pool or fountain. The cupboard, on the back side of the wall, can be made in two sections, one of which is large enough to accommodate the garden tools. Clothes lines, when in use, may be strung to hooks in the fence or wall or to decorative poles. When not in use they may be rolled up and hung on a peg in the cupboard.

PLANTS

Flower borders, vine-covered walls, potted plants, small trees, turf and ground covers—all the usual components of the flower garden may be used in the city. It is in the selection of the plants that especial care and study must be exercised. Many favorite garden flowers will not endure the severe conditions. On the other hand, some plants which are inhabitants of the wild are surprisingly well suited to resist city hardships, if given the proper soil. As with all planting design, we may use in shaded sections, in pots, and in windy exposures only those plants which tolerate these restrictions. For all city places, the plants must be immune to gas, smoke, and soot.

A city condition which makes a difference in the health and, therefore, the care of the plants is the absence of bees and birds. Those flowers such as fruit trees which are dependent on bees for pollenization will not set fruit in the city. The insect enemies of plants may have an easier existence where birds do not devour them. More than ever must the gardener depend on his sprays to control the pests.

The plants may be arranged in the usual formal beds. But when soil must be brought in, it is practical to have the beds raised above the paving on a little wall. Plants in tubs and flowers in decorative pots are very good devices for producing a variety of effects in the garden composition. The potted plants may be brought in and arranged when they are in bloom, then retired to the conservatory to make space for another set of flowers. In this way new color schemes may be arranged every week or two. Potted plants require more care than perennials in beds, but in so small a garden a little more work makes little difference and adds so much to the gaiety and fullness of the flower display.

Small trees and flowering shrubs, vines and ground cover plants all may be used, wherever there is space. The governing factor, of course, is their hardiness under the special conditions they will meet.

A general list of plants that have been found hardy in extreme city conditions (center of large cities), is appended to this chapter. In general, all will require more care than they would in natural surroundings.

PLANTS WHICH MAY BE GROWN UNDER CITY CONDITIONS
TREES

Deciduous
> American Ash (Fraxinus americana)
> Horse Chestnut (Æsculus Hippocastanum)
> London Plane-tree (Platanus acerifolia)
> Tree of Heaven (Ailanthus glandulosa)
> Tulip Tree (Liriodendron tulipifera)
> Norway Maple (Acer platanoides)
> Sugar Maple (Acer saccharum)

Plants Which May Be Grown Under City Conditions—*Continued*

Trees

Deciduous

European Linden (Tilia vulgaris)
Little-leaf European Linden (Tilia cordata)
Ginkgo Tree (Ginkgo biloba)
American Elm (Ulmus americana)
Wych Elm (Ulmus glabra)
Dwarf Asiatic Elm (Ulmus pumila)
Chinese Elm (Ulmus parvifolia)
Pin Oak (Quercus palustris)
Willow Oak (Quercus Phellos)
Shingle Oak (Quercus imbricaria)
Scarlet Oak (Quercus coccinea)
Black Oak (Quercus velutina)
English Oak (Quercus Robur)
Katsura Tree (Cercidiphyllum japonicum)
Empress Tree (Paulownia tomentosa)
Cork Tree (Phellodendron sachalinense)
Scholar Tree (Sophora japonica)
Keaki (Zelkova serrata)
Catalpa (Catalpa speciosa)
Dogwood (Cornus florida)
European Hornbeam (Carpinus Betulus)
Cockspur Thorn (Cratægus Crus-galli)
English Hawthorn (Cratægus Oxyacantha)
American Holly (Ilex opaca)
Washington Thorn (Cratægus cordata)
Lombardy Poplar (Populus nigra italica)
Carolina Poplar (Populus deltoides)
Star Magnolia (Magnolia stellata)
Saucer Magnolia (Magnolia Soulangeana)
Pekin Lilac (Syringa pekinensis)

Evergreen

Colorado Spruce (Picea pungens)
Austrian Pine (Pinus nigra austriaca)
Mountain Pine (Pinus montana)
Scots Pine (Pinus sylvestris)
Arborvitæ (Thuya occidentalis)
Japanese Yew (Taxus cuspidata)

709

SHRUBS

Deciduous

Five-leaf Aralia (Acanthopanax pentaphyllum)
Hercules Club (Aralia spinosa)
Japanese Barberry (Berberis Thunbergii)
Bladder Senna (Colutea arborescens)
Coral Dogwood (Cornus alba siberica)
Rough Deutzia (Deutzia scabra)
Pearlbush (Exochorda grandiflora)
Forsythia (Forsythia, all species)
Rose-of-Sharon (Hibiscus syriacus)
Ibota Privet (Ligustrum ibota)
California Privet (Ligustrum ovalifolium)
Crape-Myrtle (Lagerstrœmia indica)
Heavenly Bamboo (Nandina domestica)
Bayberry (Myrica caroliniensis)
Mockorange (Philadelphus, most species)
Ninebark (Physocarpus opulifolius)
Glossy Buckthorn (Rhamnus Frangula)
Jetbead (Rhodotypos kerrioides)
Smokebush (Rhus cotinus)
Fragrant Sumac (Rhus canadensis)
Shining Sumac (Rhus copallina)
European Elder (Sambucus nigra)
Vanhoutte's Spiræa (Spiræa Vanhouttei)
Snowberry (Symphoricarpos vulgaris)
Lilac (Syringa vulgaris)
Tamarisk (Tamarix varius)
Viburnum (Viburnum, many species)
Chaste-tree (Vitex Agnus-castus)
Weigela (Weigela hybrids)

Evergreen

Leather-leaf (Chamædaphne calyculata)
Japanese Holly (Ilex crenata and its varieties)
Mountain Laurel (Kalmia latifolia)
Holly-olive (Osmanthus aquifolium)
Lily-of-the-valley-shrub (Pieris japonica)
Rhododendron (Rhododendron Hybrids)

VINES

English Ivy (Hedera helix)
Virginia Creeper (Parthenocissus quinquefolia)
Boston Ivy (Parthenocissus tricuspidata)

FLOWERS FOR THE CITY GARDEN

Perennials

Aquilegia, Columbine
Convallaria majalis, Lily-of-the-Valley
Dicentra spectabilis, Bleeding-heart
Delphinium, Larkspur
Gypsophila paniculata, Babys-breath
Hemerocallis, Daylily
Iris
Phlox divaricata
Phlox paniculata
Viola

Biennials

Sweet William
Foxgloves
English Daisies
Pansies
Canterbury Bells

Annuals

Eupatorium
Larkspur
Lobelia
Marigold
Petunia
Phlox Drummondii
Salvia farinacea
Snapdragon
Sweet Alyssum
Zinnia

Bulbs

Crocus
Chionodoxa
Muscari
Narcissus
Tulips
Lilium auratum
L. candidum
L. regale
L. speciosum

ROOF GARDENS

As the private homes of a few generations ago have gradually been superseded by apartment houses, an entirely new type of gardening has come into vogue, for this present trend of modern city living has led to the development of the roof garden. Such a garden must necessarily have distinct limitations in the use of plant material, and its charm is dependent, to a considerable extent, upon architectural embellishment. A paving of flagstone or patterned brick, decorative tile benches for the growing of plants, ornamental pots, and attractive garden furnishings all contribute to the unique beauty of the roof garden.

PLANT MATERIALS FOR THE ROOF GARDEN

The plant material for the roof garden must be selected with the greatest of care, for there are many plants which are unable to survive the trying conditions of glaring sun and strong winds to which they will be subjected, and as the soil must, of necessity, be shallow, the root system must be considered as well.

There are a few deciduous trees and evergreens which may be grown in large tubs, and although they may not attain their normal size, they lend an air of permanence to the roof garden and are a very definite asset in the landscape composition. Among the trees which are the most suitable for the purpose are the ailanthus, ginkgo, willow, flowering crab, and Chamæcyparis obtusa. Some shrubs are also tolerant of city conditions and have proven satisfactory for the roof garden. In this group we find the ever-dependable Japanese yew (Taxus cuspidata), California privet (Ligustrum ovalifolium), forsythia, oleander, and barberry.

Because of the great expanse of wall adjacent to such gardens, and because a trellis or arbor may be such a distinctive and decorative feature, vines have an important part to play in the development of the roof garden. Wisteria is almost sure to do well, provided it is supplied with a sufficient depth of soil; English ivy (Hedera helix) will usually thrive against a north or west wall but is unable to endure the glare of the sun on a wall with a southern exposure; Japanese honeysuckle (Lonicera japonica) and the Chinese fleece-vine (Polygonum Auberti) will thrive well under almost any conditions, and many of the annual vines, such as the morning glories, will do exceedingly well, although their period of bloom is limited to the summer months.

There are comparatively few perennials which will do well on the roof gardens over a period of years, as the matter of wintering them over presents too great a problem. There are a number, however, such as the hardy chrysanthemums, which may be purchased as young plants and treated as annuals, being retained only for one season. There are also other perennials, such as bleedingheart (Dicentra spectabilis), and the Chimney campanula (Campanula pyramidalis) as well as the biennial forms, the Canterbury Bells, which may be purchased when in bud or in full flower and which will remain in bloom over a period of many weeks, if they are in a position which is sheltered from severe winds. At the end of the flowering period they may be discarded.

For the major portion of the bloom, however, it is wise to depend upon the early spring bulbs, the annuals, and various bedding plants such as the geraniums, begonias, and lantanas. Many of the annuals will do exceedingly well and will give abundant bloom from late spring until autumn. Among the most dependable annuals are sweet alyssum, portulaca, petunias, the African and French marigolds, phlox Drummondii, zinnias, and the delightful little plant known as torenia which is well adapted to pot culture. In most cases it is well to purchase thrifty young plants which are just coming into bloom.

ROUTINE CARE

The routine care of the plants grown on the roof garden differs but little from the care bestowed upon other garden plants, although more attention must be given to such details as watering and periodic feeding. The plants tend to dry out rapidly, due to the effect of wind and sun upon the soil, and it is essential that the watering be done with faithful regularity. And because of the shallow depth of the soil on most roof gardens, care must be taken to see that the plants are adequately supplied with the necessary nutrients. Bi-weekly applications of a good complete fertilizer in liquid form will usually give the most satisfactory results.

WINDOW AND PORCH BOXES

There are a few fundamental principles which should be observed in the preparation and planting of window and porch boxes. Adequate drainage must be provided; a rich, well-composed soil should be used; and the plants should be selected with care. If the boxes are to remain in a permanent position throughout the year it is possible to plan for succession planting. Flowering bulbs, pansies, English daisies, violas, and forget-me-nots will give bloom throughout the spring months, and may be followed by some of the very dependable annuals or by such bedding plants as geraniums, begonias, or lantanas. Among the most satisfactory annuals are ageratum, lobelia, petunias, balsam, phlox Drummondii, and the dwarf marigolds. There are also various trailing vines which are of decorative value, such as the trailing forms of lobelia (Lobelia erinus), Vinca minor and Vinca major, Kenilworth ivy, English ivy, and the black-eyed clock-vine (Thunbergia alata).

In the autumn, after the flowers have been touched by frost, they may be removed and small bushes of dwarf boxwood may be planted, which will retain their lustrous green throughout the winter. Some of the dwarf forms of Japanese yew (Taxus cuspidata) are also satisfactory for window boxes.

CONSTRUCTION

Window and porch boxes of various types are available. Ornamental terra-cotta and concrete have become popular within recent years and have the advantage of permanency. Wood is undoubtedly the most inexpensive material, and if a good quality of cypress is used and if the construction is good, wooden window boxes will last for many years. Screws should be used, rather than nails, in the construction of the boxes and the corners should be reinforced with angle irons. The depth of the boxes should be approximately 8 inches with a width of about 10 inches. Boxes of any desired length may be constructed but if they exceed 3 feet in length the weight becomes something of a problem if they must be moved. Holes for drainage must be provided in the bottom.

XXI

Flower-Pot Gardens

In the gardens of southern France and of Spain and Italy we find potted plants used in gay profusion, but it is only within recent years that we, in America, have begun to appreciate their decorative value. Many a low wall or parapet may be pleasantly adorned with a variety of potted plants. A few pots of bright geraniums placed upon the low coping of a pool will give vivid animation to an otherwise placid scene, and a group of handsome, well-grown Canterbury Bells by the edge of a terrace will add greatly to the charm of the composition.

In very small gardens, and in town gardens, it is often difficult to maintain a succession of bloom throughout the season, and potted plants may be used very successfully to overcome this limitation. With careful planning it is possible to have things follow on in rapid succession, so that as soon as one group has faded another group is ready to take its place. The potted plants may be brought into the garden when they are ready to come into flower and they may be removed as soon as their blooming period is over. In this way it is possible to relieve and mitigate those periods of shabbiness through which many gardens pass, after the first riot of spring bloom is over.

When potted plants are mentioned one is very apt to think of geraniums, for undoubtedly they are the old standby for the flower-pot gardener, and their versatility is truly amazing. They seem quite happily at home by the humble cottage doorway or in the formal garden of the large estate, and they may now be obtained in such lovely and enchanting colors that their popularity is well deserved. But now that the vogue for potted plants has reached this country we are constantly discovering new and delightful things which may be used in this way, and a wealth of material is available.

In order to be of value for pot culture a plant must measure up to certain very definite requirements. It must thrive under the rather trying and very particular conditions which pot culture necessitates; it must be reasonably easy to grow; and it must give bloom over a fairly long period. Some plants adapt themselves very happily to pot culture, while others will sulk away an unwilling existence if such conditions are forced upon them. Among the plants which seem to meet all the requirements we find many of our old-fashioned greenhouse plants, such as the geraniums, fuchsias, heliotropes, lantanas, begonias, and abutilons. We also find that some of our lovely herbaceous perennials and many of our annuals are admirably adapted to pot culture. Among the annuals we have browallia (variety speciosa major) with its dainty flowers of clear blue; torenia, that bewitching little thing with flowers of deep pansy violet and yellow tones; the lovely salpiglossis, with its trumpet-shaped flowers of purple and deep wine red, veined with gold; lobelia (variety tenuior) and ageratum. The flowering tobacco (Nicotiana) is, perhaps, a bit angular and ungainly in appearance, but the individual blooms are so lovely and its fragrance is so utterly delightful that it has much to recommend it, and it thrives exceedingly well as a potted plant. It has a longer blooming season than almost any other potted plant, and with the introduction of the new hybrid forms it may now be obtained in a wide range of color, as it comes in shades of mauve, lavender, rose, and scarlet. Salvia farinacea, although classed as a tender perennial, may be treated as an annual and is extremely well adapted to pot culture. It is of particular value where a plant of considerable height is desired.

Among the biennials and the perennials, the Canterbury Bells, the lovely old-fashioned bleedingheart (Dicentra spectabilis), and the chrysanthemums are the most desirable for pot culture. When Canterbury Bells are well grown they make unusually fine specimen plants and they are very decorative. The chrysanthemums can almost always be depended upon

Ruth Dean, Landscape Architect

A Roof Garden

A Garden Featuring Potted Plants

to do well and, coming as they do in the autumn, they will greatly prolong the season of bloom.

With sufficient forethought and careful planning much may be accomplished in maintaining a succession of bloom throughout the season in the flower-pot garden. The bleedingheart, which is one of the most beautiful of all our perennials, is among the first of the potted plants to come into flower and it will remain in bloom for many weeks. The annuals may be counted upon for early bloom through May and June if the seedlings have been started indoors, and many of them will continue to give generous bloom throughout the summer. The Canterbury Bells are usually at their height about the middle of June, and from late summer until heavy frosts the chrysanthemums will carry on the pageantry of color.

CULTURAL REQUIREMENTS

Greenhouse Plants. The decorative value of well-grown specimens of geraniums, fuchsias, abutilons, oleanders, and lemon verbenas can hardly be over-emphasized, and plants similar to those which bloom so luxuriantly during the winter and spring months in the greenhouse or in the sunroom will give generous bloom during the summer, if accorded the proper treatment. They are admirably adapted to pot culture, and as the plants grow older and increase in size from year to year, cypress tubs may be substituted for the pots, as they are less expensive and there is less danger of breakage. All perennial plants require a period of dormancy, or rest, and if summer bloom is desired, the plants must be given their period of rest during the winter months. During this period they may be kept in a cool cellar or in a pit greenhouse, the amount of moisture which is supplied being appreciably reduced. Early in the spring, the plants should be brought into a warmer temperature, regular watering should be resumed, and active growth will soon start. For details of culture see Chapter XXIV on House Plants.

Annuals. The cultural requirements are very similar for most of the annuals when they are grown as potted plants. If a greenhouse or any other indoor space is available, the seeds should be started early in the season, being sown in late February or early March. If it is not possible to start the young seedlings indoors they may be sown later in the season either in a coldframe or in a carefully prepared seed bed in the open. The seedlings should be transplanted into flats or into small pots before they become in the least crowded in the seed bed, and it is essential that they be allowed to make steady growth without any serious check. If they are allowed to suffer from overcrowding or from lack of sufficient moisture they will be likely to develop into stunted, spindly little plants and they will never be satisfactory as decorative, potted plants. As the plants develop they should be shifted on into larger pots until they are ready to come into flower. For the smaller annuals, such as torenia, browallia, and ageratum, 6-inch pots are amply large. For Nicotiana and Salvia farinacea 8-inch pots are to be preferred. A fairly rich mixture of good garden loam should be used for the final potting soil in order that the plants may have plenty of nourishment. When plants are confined in pots their roots do not have an opportunity to go on foraging expeditions and all the nutrients necessary for growth must be found within the confines of the flower-pot, which is, at best, a somewhat restricted area.

Bleedingheart (Dicentra spectabilis). The roots of the bleeding heart should be potted up in the autumn and should either be carried through the winter in a coldframe or should be buried deeply enough in the ground so that the pots will not be broken by the action of the frost. A soil mixture consisting of 3 parts rich garden loam and 1 part leaf mold is considered ideal. The pots should be of ample size, at least 10 or 12 inches in diameter, in order to allow for root development. In early spring the pots may be brought into the house, or, after danger of severe frost is over, they may be placed in an open sunny area out of doors. Growth is very rapid and the plants will soon reach a height of 3 feet or more. During this period of rapid growth abundant moisture must be supplied. The plants should remain in flower for a period of six to eight weeks, and are among the most beautiful and decorative plants that can be grown. After the blooming period is over the leaves will gradually die down and the roots will become dormant. The plants may be held over for another year, being repotted in fresh soil in the autumn.

Canterbury Bells. Canterbury Bells may be secured in both single (Campanula medium) and double (Campanula calycanthema) forms and they are obtainable in a variety of colors,—white, pale pink, deep rose, lavender, and bluish-purple. The seeds should be sown in June either in a coldframe or in a well-prepared seed bed in the open. The plants usually make sturdy, rapid growth and the young seedlings should be transplanted when they are a few inches high. In the vicinity of Philadelphia and northward the plants should be carried over the winter in a coldframe. In the South they may be safely wintered out of doors. As soon as vigorous growth starts in the spring the plants should be lifted and potted in 8- or 10-inch pots. A rich potting mixture should be used, consisting of 2 parts good loam, 1 part well-rotted cow manure and 1 part leaf mold. When the flower buds begin to develop, it is advisable to give the plants an application of liquid manure. The plants may be kept in flower over an amazingly long period if the individual bells are picked off as they fade. The little axillary buds will then have an opportunity to develop and will form new blossoms. Each set of blooms will be smaller, but lovely, nevertheless. Since Canterbury Bells are true biennials they must be discarded after their flowering period is over.

Chrysanthemums. When chrysanthemums are to be used as potted plants they should preferably be grown from cuttings taken in the spring. Cuttings may easily be taken from plants already established in the garden, or they may be purchased for a very modest sum. The cuttings should be made from the tips of the young, growing shoots, being about 3 inches in length. The lower leaves should be removed and the cuttings should be inserted in clean, sharp sand, being kept moist and partially shaded until they have rooted. Chrysanthemum cuttings root very readily, and after the roots are well formed the plants may be put in small 2-inch pots, the soil mixture consisting of 1 part loam, 1 part sand and 1 part leaf mold. As the plants develop they should be shifted on into larger pots and a richer soil mixture should be used. When the plants have reached a height of about 6 or 8 inches the growing tips should be nipped back in order to induce the lower buds to develop. This will result in a much more bushy plant and in a greater abundance of bloom. In order to promote vigorous growth the plants should be given an application of liquid manure at intervals of every few weeks throughout the summer. If early, mid-season, and late varieties are selected the period of bloom may be extended over several months.

WATERING POTTED PLANTS

The watering of potted plants presents something of a problem as it is almost as disastrous to keep the pots too wet as it is to allow them to become too dry. Since one usually does not wish to bring the pots into the garden until the plants are almost ready to come into flower it is best to keep them in the nursery section during their growing period. As pots dry out in an incredibly short time when they are placed in a hot, sunny location, watering may become quite an arduous undertaking, and during this period the pots may be sunk in the ground. Under these conditions the plants seem to make much more vigorous and sturdy growth, and it is a great saving of labor, as the task of watering is very appreciably lessened. It is often possible to utilize a small plot in the vegetable garden for this purpose. When the plants are ready to make their début in the garden the pots may be lifted and the loose dirt which clings to them may be easily scraped off.

SELECTION OF FLOWER POTS

In the selection of flower pots there are a few points which should be borne in mind. Earthenware pots are, on the whole, considered better than highly glazed pots, as the soil is less likely to become water-logged. But no matter what kind of pot is chosen, it is absolutely essential to the welfare of the plant that some provision be made for drainage. This is usually provided for by a small hole in the bottom of the pot which makes it possible for any surplus water to drain off. If one uses receptacles such as old-fashioned bean pots which are not provided with drainage, it is advisable to place an earthenware pot inside. Where potted plants are to be used in lavish profusion these simple, inexpensive earthenware pots are entirely satisfactory. They make no pretense of being anything more than ordinay, everyday flower-pots, yet the porportions are good and the soft terra cotta coloring blends in pleasantly with its surroundings. If only a few pots are to be used along the coping of a pool or about the rim of a fountain it is pleasant to select some of the lovely hand-made pots which one finds in the shops today. They may be obtained in very graceful shapes, being often moulded with a flare at the top, instead of with the usually heavy band. It is wise to select something simple in design and without much ornamentation, as a highly colored or lavishly decorated pot has a tendency to detract from the beauty of the flowers themselves.

PLANTS SUITABLE FOR POT CULTURE
For the Summer Terrace

Greenhouse Plants
Abutilon
Begonia
Fuchsia
Geranium
Heliotrope
Lantana
Lemon Verbena
Oleander

Annuals
Ageratum
Browallia, var. speciosa major
Lobelia
Nicotiana
Salpiglossis
Salvia farinacea

Biennials and Perennials
Campanula medium (Canterbury Bells)
Campanula pyramidalis (Chimney Campanula)
Chrysanthemum
Dicentra spectabilis (Bleedingheart))
Digitalis

XXII

Coldframes and Hotbeds

COLDFRAMES

A coldframe is an indispensable adjunct, even to the smallest garden. It is, as the name implies, an unheated frame, the plants receiving heat from the penetration of the sun's rays through the glass of the sash.

There seems to be a very general idea that coldframes are useful only for the protection of plants during the winter months and that at other seasons of the year they lie idle. Winter protection, however, is but one of the many uses to which coldframes may be put. Indeed, a really enterprising gardener will find that his frames are in use during every month of the year—that there is never a time from one season's end to another when they lie fallow.

USES OF COLDFRAMES

Early Spring (Hardening-off Plants). During the early spring months, coldframes may be used to harden off seedlings which have been started in the greenhouse or the hotbeds. This hardening-off process is a factor of considerable importance, as young seedlings often suffer a serious setback if moved directly from the greenhouse to the garden. The coldframe provides an ideal transition, as the plants may be protected from sudden drops in temperature and will have an opportunity to become gradually hardened-off. When pots or flats are moved from the greenhouse to the frames, they should be placed on a bed of cinders, in order that drainage may be facilitated. There is also less danger of trouble from slugs, pill-bugs and earthworms if cinders are used.

724

Spring and Summer (Seed Sowing). A coldframe also offers very satisfactory facilities for the starting of young seedling plants throughout the spring and summer months. (See directions for seed sowing, Chapter XXX.) The hardy and half-hardy annuals may be sown in the frames early in the spring, many weeks before seed could be sown in the open ground; perennials may be sown in the spring, and the young transplanted seedlings may be carried on in the frames until they are ready to be moved to the nursery rows or to their permanent place in the garden; biennials may be sown during the summer months, and as many of them, such as the foxgloves, Canterbury Bells and wallflowers, need winter protection, they may be carried on in the frames until spring.

Late Spring and Summer (Propagation by Cuttings). During the late spring and summer months, a portion of the coldframes may be converted into a propagating case, the soil being temporarily replaced with sand or peatmoss or some other medium which is satisfactory for the rooting of cuttings. (See plant propagation, Chapter XXX.)

Autumn (Seed Sowing). Most perennials and a few of the annuals may be sown very successfully in the autumn, and there are many benefits to be gained if such a practice is followed. The object is not to secure germination during the autumn, but to have the seeds remain dormant during the winter months. They will then germinate very early in the spring and the young seedlings will have a vigor and lustiness which usually surpasses that of spring-sown seedlings. Better germination is also frequently secured. A coldframe offers ideal conditions for autumn sowing. The seeds may be sown either in a well-prepared seedbed or in flats. It is essential that good drainage be provided and if flats are used they should be placed on a layer of cinders. The seeds should not be sown until just before the onset of winter, as the ground begins to freeze. There will then be no danger of having the seed germinate before spring. At the time of sowing the soil should be watered so that it is moderately damp, but not excessively wet. If the soil becomes dry during the winter a light watering should be given, preferably during a spell of warm weather. It is a wise practice

725

to inspect the frame every few weeks to check up on the condition of the soil. After the seeds have been sown, the sash should be placed over the frames, being raised slightly to provide adequate ventilation. In order to exclude the winter sunshine and to maintain a more even soil temperature, it is well to place a lath sash over the glass. This slat shade should be removed very early in the spring in order that the soil may warm up as rapidly as possible. As soon as the soil in the frame has begun to thaw out the seeds should be given the usual care. The soil should not be allowed to dry out, adequate ventilation should be provided, the sash should be removed on warm, sunny days, and every effort should be made to hasten early germination.

Winter—(Protection of Less Hardy Plants and Newly Started Perennials; Growing Tender Bulbs). Not only are coldframes useful during the winter months for the protection of the less hardy plants and newly started perennials, but they also make it possible to grow some of the tender bulbs which cannot be grown in the open ground in sections where the winters are of extreme severity. In this group we find the lovely bulbous iris, the dwarf gladioli of the nanus and Colvillei types, which are so decorative as cut flowers, and the St. Brigid anemones. If planted in the autumn in the frames these bulbs will give abundant bloom in the spring.

(Storage of Bulbs and Plants for Forcing). Coldframes may also be used for the storage of bulbs and plants which are later to be forced indoors. Such plants as bleedingheart, astilbe japonica, and mertensia may be handled very successfully in this way. Chrysanthemum plants which are of the less hardy type may be lifted in the autumn and carried over the winter in the frames, and cuttings may be made from these stock plants in the spring.

LOCATION

Coldframes should preferably be located on ground that is very gently sloping in order that good drainage may be assured, a south or southeastern exposure being considered ideal. The frames should be placed with the high end towards the north,

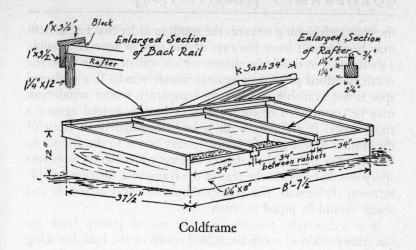

Coldframe

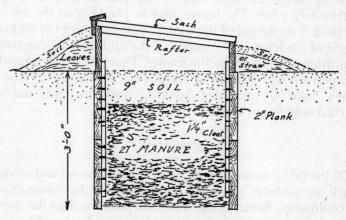

Cross Section of Hot Bed

the glass sash sloping towards the south in order that full benefit
may be obtained from the rays of the sun. Whenever possible
a sheltered spot should be chosen with a wall or hedge upon the
north to afford protection against winter winds. If a sheltered
spot is not available, however, a temporary winter windbreak
may be constructed of corn stalks, or boughs braced against a
snow fence. If a cinder walk is laid immediately in front of
the frames it will greatly facilitate easy access to the frames in
wet weather and will be a matter of great convenience. Sufficient
space should be left at the rear of the frames for the comfortable
removal of the sash. The frames should be easily accessible and
water should be piped to them.

It is occasionally possible to make use of a steep bank for
the construction of coldframes, and much of the back-breaking
work usually associated with the management of coldframes
may be eliminated. A concrete or cinder-block wall should be
built up along the upper side of the path to a level of approximately 3 feet. The frames may be placed upon the top of
the bank if the height of the bank corresponds with the desired
height of the frames, or a section of the bank may be dug back
to provide a level area for the frames. Thus, the frame is raised
to a position where it can be reached as easily as a greenhouse
bench. Sashes of small size should be used, since they can be
reached only from the front.

CONSTRUCTION

Of the many materials which are available, wood and cinder
block are probably the most satisfactory for the construction
of coldframes. Stone, brick, and solid concrete may be used,
and while they are extremely durable materials, the additional
expense is hardly justifiable. Sometimes in old colonial gardens
one will come upon ancient frames of brick, built a century or
more ago and still providing shelter for young seedlings.

Wood is the least expensive material and if a good grade
of cypress is selected, wooden frames will last for many years.
Cypress will resist decay better than almost any other wood and
it is, therefore, particularly well adapted for locations where

it will be exposed to dampness and to the weather. It is an expensive folly to construct frames of cheap lumber which does not possess the ability to resist decay, as the boards will have to be replaced after a few years. Wooden frames are very easily constructed and as they do not require highly skilled workmanship, they may readily be made at home. It is also possible to purchase good cypress frames from some of the large seed firms and greenhouse-construction companies. These are shipped in a "knocked down" state and are easily assembled. These commercial frames are very satisfactory, and they may readily be moved from one section of the garden to another if a change in the general arrangement of the working area should be desired, or if one is moving to a new property.

Frames constructed of cinder blocks are of a more permanent nature than are wooden frames as they cannot be moved from one location to another. The initial cost is considerably higher than for wooden frames, but it is the only cost, as no replacement will be necessary. The cinder blocks should extend into the ground a few inches below the frost line for the locality, and the blocks should be laid with mortar joints. The appearance of the frames will be greatly improved if a cement-sand mortar finish is applied as a surface coat over the cinder blocks.

Regardless of the material used, coldframes should be so constructed that the back is approximately 6 inches higher than the front. This slope will permit the water to drain easily from the sash and will also offer the maximum amount of surface for the penetration of sunlight.

The front of the frame may vary in height from 6 to 12 inches. If the frames are to be used as a seed bed and to winter small plants such as pansies and English daisies a height of 6 inches will be sufficient. If large plants such as foxgloves and Canterbury Bells are to be wintered over in the frames a height of 12 inches will be needed. Crossties usually extend from the back of the frame to the front at intervals of every 3 feet in order to provide additional support for the sash. These ties should be dovetailed into the walls of the sash and a projection in the center of each crosstie will keep the sash from slipping out of position.

The standard size for coldframe sash used by practically all commercial growers and by most private gardeners is 3 feet 6 inches, by 6 feet. For the home garden, where operations are on a limited scale and where convenience is a matter of considerable importance, a smaller size is often more satisfactory. Small sash measuring 2 feet by 4 feet, or 3 feet by 3 feet, may be obtained from several firms, and they have many advantages. They are much lighter and are, therefore, much easier to handle than the standard size sash, and the entire area within the frame may be reached from the front with comparative ease, which greatly facilitates such operations as seed sowing and transplanting.

Most coldframe sash are made of glass, and they may be purchased either as glazed or unglazed sash. The process of glazing is a rather simple one and considerable expense may be saved if this is done at home. A small portion of putty should be worked in the warmth of the hands until it is smoothly pullable without breaking. If the putty is too thick, a little linseed oil may be added to make it of the right consistency. With a putty knife, a thin layer should be spread the entire length of the sash—not too much, but just enough to cover. The first pane is then laid in place at the top, or back, of the sash. The next is then laid underneath, underlapping about ½-inch. The number of panes of glass will depend upon the size of the sash. After all the panes have been evenly spaced the length of the sash, each pane is then snugly fastened in place by several brads, which are tiny pieces of zinc. The triangular shaped brads which measure about ½-inch are most satisfactory. Then a layer of putty is spread along the edge of the pane against the wooden frame which, when dried, keeps out moisture. A layer of green paint, special for coldframe and sash use, may be applied after several days when the putty has become firm but not brittle. This application will both protect the wood from deterioration and the putty from cracking.

Coldframe sash may also be made of celoglass, a glass substitute, which has the advantage of allowing for the penetration of ultra-violet rays. Sash made of celoglass is lighter in weight than glass sash and is, therefore, easier to handle. It is, however, less transparent, and does not provide as much protection against extreme cold as does sash made of glass.

When not in use during the summer months, the sashes should be neatly stacked, preferably under cover where they will not be exposed to the weather. It is a matter of sound economy to keep coldframe sash in good condition. All cracked or broken panes of glass should be replaced and the sashes should be kept well painted. If attention is given to these details, coldframe sash should last for many years.

MANAGEMENT

There are a few general rules which should be followed in the management of coldframes. The most important factors to be considered are ventilation, watering, protection from extreme cold, and protection from extreme heat.

Ventilation. During the late winter and early spring, the sash should be partially raised for a brief period on clear, sunny days, when the temperature ranges above 45 degrees F., the object being to keep an even temperature. As the season advances, the sash may be raised for a longer period each day and on warm days it may be removed entirely during the middle of the day. The sash should be lowered or replaced before the temperature begins to drop in the afternoon, in order to conserve as much heat as possible. On windy days, the sash should be raised on the opposite side from the direction of the wind in order to protect the plants from a direct draft. With the approach of warm weather, the sash may be removed entirely. When sashes are to be raised slightly, small blocks of wood may be placed between the edge of the frame and the sash. A block measuring approximately 1 inch x 4 inches x 6 inches is excellent for this purpose as it enables one to regulate the size of the opening.

Watering. It is an accepted rule among gardeners that plants grown under glass, either in greenhouses or in frames, should be watered when the temperature is rising rather than when it is falling. It is, therefore, advisable, and particularly so early in the season, to water the frames in the morning, in order that the foliage of the plants may be dry at night. In cold, cloudy weather water should be withheld as much as possible in order to avoid trouble from various fungous diseases.

Protection Against Extreme Cold. During periods of extreme cold, additional protection should be given. Straw mats, light frames filled with straw, heavy sisselcraft paper and similar materials may be used for this purpose. In mild climates no protection other than that of the sash is necessary, but in localities where the thermometer reaches zero, it is advisable to provide extra protection.

Summer Shade. In the summer months some provision must be made for protecting the seed beds and the young seedling plants in the frames from intense sunshine. Lath sashes which may be obtained from most seed houses are very satisfactory for this purpose. They are light and easy to handle, they permit a free circulation of air, and a little filtered sunshine reaches the plants. Burlap tacked on lath frames also makes a very satisfactory shade.

HOTBEDS

Hotbeds differ from coldframes in that they are supplied with some form of artificial heat. They may be heated by the old, time-honored method of fermenting manure, or they may be heated by the more modern method of specially devised electric cables. In occasional instances, where hotbeds may be located in close proximity to a greenhouse, they may be heated as a part of the greenhouse unit, which is usually a very satisfactory arrangement. The construction and management of the hotbed will usually be determined by the type of heating which is to be used.

USES OF HOTBEDS

Since the soil in a hotbed is maintained at a warm and fairly constant temperature, it provides excellent facilities for the germination of seeds and for the growing of a wide variety of young seedling plants. Some plants with a short season of growth, such as lettuce, may be carried through to maturity in the hotbed, although the majority of plants started in the hotbed are later transplanted to the garden or field. Seeds may be sown in the hotbed several weeks before it is advisable to make use of the coldframes, and the young seedlings will make much more rapid growth. Later in the season when there is no longer any need for artificial heat the hotbed may serve as a coldframe and may be used to fulfill the same functions.

TYPES OF HOTBEDS

Manure Hotbeds. A pit approximately 2½ feet deep is necessary if manure is to be used, the dimensions for width and length being determined by the size of the frames and the number of frames desired. If the earth walls of the pit are firm, no inside wall need be constructed. If, however, there is any danger that the earth walls may crumble, it will be necessary to construct supporting walls of wood, brick, stone or cinder block. Walls made of wood will be of only temporary value as they will lack durability in such a location, but materials such as cinder block, stone and brick are excellent. The upper part of the frame is similar in construction to a coldframe.

Manure-heated hotbeds should be started in early March and it is necessary to use fresh horse manure obtained from stables where straw has been used for bedding. Approximately four cubic yards of manure will be required for a single sash hotbed. The manure should be piled near the hotbed and every three or four days the heap should be turned, throwing the outside towards the center. When the entire pile has begun to heat evenly, which is evidenced by steam arising from the pile, the manure may be placed in a pit. It should be spread evenly in 6-inch layers, each layer being firmly tramped and packed. After the manure has been placed in the pit to a depth of 2 feet, a thin layer of straw should be placed over it and the soil should then be added. The depth of soil may vary from 4 to 6 inches and it should be of a mixture suitable for a seed bed. A soil thermometer should be placed so that the mercury extends well down into the soil and the sash should be allowed to remain tightly closed. For the first few days the thermometer will register a high degree of heat, ranging well above 90 degrees F. When the soil temperature has cooled down to 75 degrees F. the bed is ready for use and the seeds may be sown.

In extremely cold climates it is well to bank manure about that portion of the bed which extends above the surface of the ground, as this will increase the warmth within the frame to a very appreciable extent.

Electric Hotbeds. There are various types of electric units

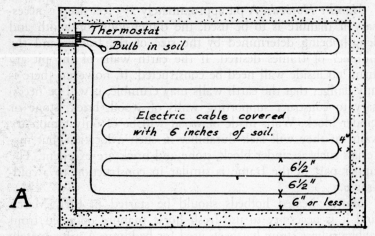

A

Plan of an Electric System of Heating Soil in Hotbed.

which have been especially designed for the heating of hotbeds. One of the most satisfactory types is the insulated electric cable which may be buried in the soil and which will provide uniform heat. The procedure for the construction of such a bed is as follows: A pit approximately 1 foot deep should be excavated and it should be of sufficient size to extend a foot or more beyond the sides and ends of the proposed frame. The pit should be filled with 6 inches of slag or good clinker cinders, free from fine ashes. The frame may be placed directly on the bed of cinders. The outside of the frame should be banked with cinders or soil in order to provide insulation against the penetration of cold air. A layer of burlap or a layer of sphagnum moss should be placed over the cinders and 1 inch of sand should then be spread over the surface of the bed. The electric cable is then laid upon the sand in uniform loops in order that the heat may be evenly distributed. (See diagram A.) No.

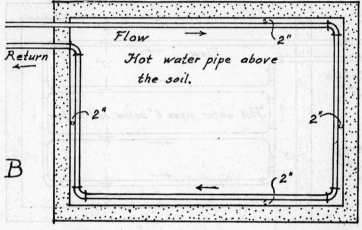

Plan of a Water or Steam System for Hotbed.

19 or No. 20 Nichrome wire protected with a lead sheath having a resistance of one-half ohm per foot is recommended by several authorities as being the best for this purpose. Sixty feet of this flexible, lead-covered cable will be required for a two-sash hotbed, if the voltage is 110–120. This will provide for 10 coils spaced approximately 7 inches apart, the ends of the cable being connected with a thermostat. The thermostat should be installed on the inside of the frame with the switch box on the north side of the bed. The thermostat should be regulated so that a uniform temperature is maintained. Tender plants will require a temperature ranging from 60 to 75 degrees; half-hardy plants will prefer a temperature of 50 to 60 degrees, and those that are truly hardy will thrive well in a temperature ranging from 45 to 60 degrees.

Approximately 400 watts will be required to provide heat for a two-sash hotbed (6 feet x 6 feet) in a moderately cold climate. Operating costs will usually average one kilowatt hour per square yard of hotbed per day.

The soil which is to be used for the seed bed may be placed

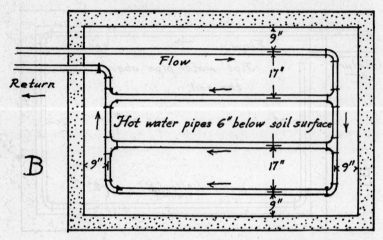

Plan of a Water System of Heating Soil in Hotbed.

over the cable to a depth of 6 inches. If flats are to be used, 3 inches of sand may be spread over the cable and the flats may be placed upon the sand.

The one great disadvantage of an electric hotbed is that the current may go off during a severe storm or because of some other emergency. In such a case the plants are apt to suffer very serious injury, and every effort should be made to protect them, through the use of straw mats or other materials which will provide temporary insulation.

Hot Water or Steam Pipes. One of the most satisfactory and also one of the most economical ways to provide heat for the hotbed is to install a system of pipes which may be connected with the heating system in the dwelling house or the greenhouse. The pipes may be placed around the top of the frame on the inside or they may be placed beneath the soil. (See two diagrams B.) Such a system provides for a very uniform heat which may be maintained at a minimum of expense and labor.

MANAGEMENT

The management of a hotbed is similar in most respects to the management of a coldframe. There is, however, more danger from trouble with damping off, as the plants are somewhat more susceptible to attack, because of the greater degree of heat and humidity. Every precautionary measure should, therefore, be taken to control an outbreak of this disease. (See Chapter XXX for the control of damping-off.)

Since artificial heat is provided, the plants grown in a hotbed are more tender than those grown in a coldframe and are more sensitive to sudden fluctuations in temperature. Ventilation and watering must, therefore, be done with care.

Hotbeds are usually started upon the approach of spring weather. In the latitude of New York and Philadelphia, early March is usually the most favorable time. If severe cold spells occur extra protection for the young plants may be provided by the use of straw mats or other similar materials.

XXIII

The Small Greenhouse

For many of us, gardening is a joyous adventure from the opening of the first winter aconite in the spring until the frosts of autumn have robbed the garden of its beauty and driven us indoors to await the arrival of the first seed catalogs. Fortunate, indeed, are those favored few among gardeners who possess a small greenhouse and can carry on their gardening activities throughout the year.

Small, private greenhouses have always been considered such a luxury that many gardeners have assumed that they were something quite beyond their means and have given the matter little thought. Within recent years, however, new types have been designed along such simple and efficient lines that construction costs have been greatly reduced, and the small greenhouse is now well within the range of many a gardener. It need not be an elaborate or an expensive affair; a small lean-to built against the house may be constructed for only a few hundred dollars and will offer delightful possibilities for winter gardening. The money thus invested will pay big dividends in beauty and in joyous activity. Even the unheated greenhouse offers many opportunities and is a challenge to the skill and ingenuity of the gardener.

LOCATION

If the greenhouse can be attached directly to the house it may usually be operated on the same heating unit, which not only reduces the cost of operation, but also reduces the labor item to a minimum. Such a location also usually has the advantage of providing shelter from strong winds. If a greenhouse is attached to the house, it should preferably have a south or southeastern exposure.

Although there are many advantages to be gained, the greenhouse which is attached to the house presents one very special problem—the maintenance of night temperatures. When the

Photograph by Eric J. Baker   *Courtesy of Lord and Burnham Co.*

A Small Greenhouse

Adjoining the living room, this small greenhouse becomes
an indoor garden.

house furnace is banked for the night it is often difficult, if not impossible, to provide for the maintenance of a uniform night temperature in the greenhouse and there is usually no provision for meeting sudden flunctuations in the outside temperature.

There has recently been put on the market a small portable type of radiator which is thermostatically controlled and which may be operated by merely plugging it in on the electric current. This new type of portable radiator is proving very valuable as a supplementary heating unit for the small greenhouse, as it makes possible the maintenance of a uniform night temperature and eliminates much of the anxiety.

If the greenhouse is not attached to the house, it should be located so that it receives a maximum amount of sunshine and is protected, if possible, from the prevailing winds. If the topography of the ground presents no problem, the greenhouse should preferably be oriented so that the length of the house runs from north to south, as this will provide for a maximum amount of sunlight during the winter months.

THE UNHEATED GREENHOUSE

Although the unheated greenhouse has decided limitations, it offers many delightful opportunities.

In sections of the country where the climate is severe, it is difficult, if not impossible, to obtain any actual bloom in an unheated greenhouse during the midwinter months, but with the first warm days of early spring, such a greenhouse may become a veritable garden, and it will offer a wealth of material for flower arrangements in the house. Bulbs of all kinds may be forced into early bloom, and Astilbe japonica, bleedingheart, mertensia, aquilegia, pansies, and primroses may be brought into flower. Antirrhinums, calendulas, annual larkspur, and wall flowers may be sown in the early autumn and the young plants may be carried over the winter in the benches. Although they will make comparatively little growth during the winter, they will develop into sturdy plants with strong, vigorous root systems and will come into flower months ahead of spring-sown seedlings.

During the spring months, the unheated greenhouse serves the purposes of a somewhat glorified coldframe as it affords ideal conditions for the starting of young seedlings.

It is a decided advantage to have the unheated greenhouse in as protected a location as possible and in some cases it is feasible to have it built so that it is partially below ground. Straw mats, or burlap frames packed with straw, may be used to provide added protection during extremely cold weather.

CONSTRUCTION

In the construction of a greenhouse, even though it be a very simple structure, there are many details which must be taken

Courtesy of Lord and Burnham Co.

A greenhouse of this size offers delightful possibilities
for winter gardening.

into consideration and it is well to have the house erected by a man who is thoroughly conversant with the problems which must be met. It is essential that the house be built of sturdy, durable materials; that satisfactory provisions be made for ventilation; that the benches be designed to meet any special needs which may be designated; and that the heating unit be entirely adequate.

741

The material to be used for the construction of the benches is usually a question for the owner to decide. Wood is the most economical, if only the initial cost is considered, but it is the least satisfactory, for it is not durable and will have to be replaced after a few years. If it is used, the best grade of cypress should be selected, as cypress is more resistant to decay than any other wood which is available. Solid concrete is sometimes used but it is very expensive. One of the most satisfactory types is a combination of metal and tile which is pleasing in appearance, durable, and yet not prohibitive in cost.

Benches which are constructed with pipe legs and an angle-iron frame are the most satisfactory. Benches in which crops for cut flowers are to be grown should be from 6 to 8 inches deep. Adequate provision for drainage must be provided in the form of cracks or narrow openings between the boards or tiles which form the bottom of the bench. Benches upon which potted plants are to be placed need be but 2 or 3 inches deep. Such benches, which resemble shallow trays, should be filled with pebbles or cinders upon which the pots may rest. Such an arrangement will not only facilitate drainage but will aid in maintaining the desired degree of humidity as well.

The greenhouse should be piped with water and a sufficient number of outlets should be provided at convenient points. The faucets should be threaded so that a hose may be easily attached.

Concrete walks are the most satisfactory type for greenhouses, although cinders and gravel are sometimes used where it is necessary to maintain a very high degree of humidity, as in orchid houses. Concrete walks are easy to keep clean, will withstand wear, are impervious to dampness, and are, in general, entirely satisfactory.

It is a matter of great convenience to have a small work room or potting shed attached to the greenhouse, but if space is not available, or if the various items of expense must be kept to a minimum, the north end of the house may be utilized for this purpose. A bench of convenient height and length should be provided for use in the preparation of soil mixtures, and for such operations as seed sowing, transplanting and potting, which are an almost daily part of the greenhouse routine. Bins may be constructed underneath the bench as a storage place for surplus flats and pots and to hold the loam, sand, leaf mold and compost used in the various soil mixtures. Adequate shelf space should also be provided for insecticides, fumigants, labels and other small items.

In the management of a small greenhouse, the most important considerations are the matters of temperature control, ventilation and watering.

HEATING

Hot water is the most satisfactory form of heat for the small greenhouse. The heat is more evenly distributed than in the case of steam heat, there is less danger of a sudden drop in temperature, and the fires require less attention at night. And it is an accepted fact that practically all plants thrive better under a system of hot water heat than under steam heat. It is a more natural kind of heat and is more nearly like the heat of the sun. Hot water heat has the added advantage of being more economical than steam, as it is possible to maintain a very low fire in mild weather.

TEMPERATURE

If the house is of sufficient size it is well to have it divided into at least two sections, and to have the heating system so planned that it is possible to maintain a moderately high temperature in one section and a much lower temperature in the other section. This will make it possible to grow a wide variety of plants, as some will have a preference for a cool temperature, while others will prefer a comparatively high temperature. If, however, the greenhouse is small, and it is not feasible to provide for more than one temperature, it need not be considered a great handicap. The choice of plant materials will, of necessity, be somewhat more limited, but even the smallest greenhouse, maintained at a rather low temperature will offer delightful opportunities for winter gardening. In general commercial practice, greenhouse temperatures range from 40–45 degrees in extremely cool violet houses, to 65–70 degrees in houses where semi-tropical plants are grown. These temperatures refer to night temperatures. During the day the temperatures will naturally rise from 10 to 15 degrees higher. The thermometer in a greenhouse should not be placed where the direct heat of the sun will fall upon it. For a small greenhouse where but one temperature is to be maintained, a range between 50 and 55 degrees at night with a temperature varying from 10 to 15 degrees higher during the day will usually prove to be most satisfactory. Some plants are able to endure severe fluctuations in temperature while other plants are extremely sensitive to changes in temperature, and it is wise for the amateur to choose the less temperamental plants. If one is an experienced gardener and can provide conditions which will very nearly approximate the ideal, it will be possible to grow some of the more exotic greenhouse plants, but if one is a novice it is well to devote one's efforts to the more sturdy types which are less exacting in their demands.

VENTILATION

An abundance of fresh air is essential for the normal, healthy growth of all plants, and at the time of construction adequate provision must be made for ventilation. Some greenhouses are equipped with ventilators on the sides as well as on the glass span which forms the roof, and this is the most desirable type of construction. It requires care, skill, and good judgment to control a ventilating system efficiently. As a general practice the ventilators should be opened in the morning when the temperature is rising. On warm days when there is brilliant sunshine and little wind, the ventilators should be opened to the fullest extent. On very cold days a mere crack may be sufficient. The ventilators should be closed early enough in the afternoon to conserve as much heat as possible. When a strong wind is blowing it is wise to open the ventilators on the opposite side of the house from the direction of the prevailing wind in order to prevent a direct draft of air on the plants. Sudden changes in temperature and sudden shifting from brilliant sunlight to dark clouds mean more or less constant attention to the regulation of the ventilators in a greenhouse if the heating unit is to function at its maximum degree of efficiency.

So important is fresh air to the welfare of the plants that even on days in early autumn and in the spring when it would be possible to maintain the desired temperature within the house, provided that the ventilators were kept closed, it is preferable to admit fresh air even if it necessitates maintaining a low fire.

WATERING

Greenhouse plants vary tremendously in their moisture requirements, and individual plants also vary considerably at different stages of growth. In a program of successful greenhouse management it is, therefore, essential to fully understand the moisture requirements of the plants which one is handling. The moisture requirements of all the important greenhouse plants and plant groups are discussed in detail under the section on Cultural Requirements of greenhouse plants, which is to be found at the end of this chapter.

There are, however, certain general principles which should be observed. Watering should preferably be done when the temperature is rising, and it is, therefore, part of the usual morning routine in the greenhouse. To secure the best results, the temperature of the soil in the beds and benches should be approximately that of the surrounding air in the greenhouse. Water absorption by the plant takes place very slowly in cold soils. Greenhouse plants in ground beds frequently fail to do well because of this factor. Such a condition may be remedied, however, by running heating pipes along the sides of the beds, or placing pipes in tiles underneath the beds. Some plants are so sensitive to the matter of temperature that it is advisable, whenever possible, to supply them with water which has been warmed to a room temperature, approximately 70 degrees F. In this group we find such plants as poinsettias, gardenias, gerberas, lilacs, and roses. Tanks or barrels may be kept in the greenhouse for the storage of sufficient water to supply the needs of such plants.

Most plants will make their best growth, other conditions

being favorable, in soils which are uniformly supplied with a sufficient amount of moisture. In the case of greenhouse plants grown in beds and benches the optimum moisture conditions may best be maintained by heavy watering at rather infrequent intervals. Both the amount of water and the frequency of application will be determined, to a considerable extent, by the age of the plants, the type of root system which the plants possess, and the physical structure of the soil. Large plants which are making active growth will require relatively large amounts of water. Plants with fibrous root systems will require larger amounts than those with tap roots. Heavy soils will require less frequent applications than light, sandy soils. If greenhouse beds and benches are given a fairly heavy watering at rather infrequent intervals, the plants will make a vigorous root growth which will extend deeply into the soil. If frequent, light waterings are given, the plants will have a tendency to become shallow rooted, and will be less vigorous in consequence.

The force with which the water is applied is also a factor which must be taken into consideration. A heavy stream of water should be avoided, as it causes the soil to become more and more compact and thus reduces aëration. An adjustable hose nozzle, or a rose nozzle of a size to permit a moderately fine spray, may be attached to the hose. For the watering of small seedlings and young growing plants a watering can is greatly to be preferred to a hose. The regulation greenhouse watering can with a long spout is ideal for this purpose and a series of rose nozzles of various sizes may be obtained.

Careful attention must always be given to the watering of young seedlings, and on bright, sunny days it is often necessary to water more than once. Seed flats and young transplanted seedlings should never be allowed to dry out.

The watering of potted plants also requires skill and good judgment, and the plants vary tremendously in their moisture requirements. Some plants, such as the azaleas, maidenhair ferns, and certain types of begonias, should never be allowed to dry out. Other plants such as the poinsettias, fuchsias, callas, clivia, and many others, require a definite rest period, during which time the amount of water should be appreciably decreased or, in some cases, entirely withheld. The requirements of the individual plants are discussed at the close of the chapter.

In general, potted plants should be watered only when necessary. Plants which are making active growth and plants which are in full flower will usually require liberal quantities of water. In some cases it may be necessary to water more than once a day. An excellent way to determine a potted plant's need for water is the method used by many old English gardeners—that of tapping the pot with the knuckle. If the tap resounds in a dull thud, it is an indication that the plant does not need water. If, however, the tap resounds with a hollow, ringing sound, additional moisture should be supplied to the plant. The majority of plants with smooth leaves may be watered by the overhead method without any danger of injury to the foliage. Plants with hairy or very fleshy leaves, such as the Saintpaulias, should preferably be watered in such a way that no moisture comes into contact with the foliage. A watering can may be used very successfully for this purpose if the rose nozzle is removed. In some cases it is advisable to place the plants in a pan of water and to allow them to remain thus until the surface of the soil in the pot has become moist.

SYRINGING

There are several very direct advantages to be gained from syringing. It increases the humidity, and very appreciably reduces the evaporation power of the air. Thus the transpiration of water from the leaves is reduced to a point lower than the actual absorption of water by the roots.

Syringing also has a very direct influence upon the control of red spider. (See Chapter XXIV, page 805.)

During the winter, syringing should be done on bright, sunny days when the temperature is rising. It is not advisable to syringe plants late in the afternoon when the temperature is dropping, as the result will be a condensation of moisture on the foliage, which may prove injurious to the plant. During the summer, plants may safely be syringed in the late afternoon.

In general, plants with smooth foliage will benefit from syringing. Plants with fleshy or hairy foliage should not be syringed, as the effects are more harmful than beneficial.

HUMIDITY

The maintenance of a proper degree of humidity in the greenhouse is a matter of vital importance. Plants vary greatly in their optimum humidity requirements, just as they vary greatly in their moisture requirements. The fact that roses require a humidity of 75 per cent or more, while members of the cactus family thrive best where the humidity is less than 50 per cent, means that these two plant groups must be accorded very different treatment. Every gardener should be familiar with the general humidity requirements of the various plant groups. In some cases, the optimum humidity requirements of specific plants have been very definitely determined, and these have been included under the section on culture.

Humidity is closely associated with the respiration of plants and with the manufacture of food within the plant. It is a generally accepted fact that high humidity makes it possible for the leaf stomata to open wider and to remain open longer than is possible under conditions of low humidity. If plants are grown in an atmosphere in which the degree of humidity is far below the optimum, the transpiration from the leaves will be greater than the intake of moisture by the roots and the growth and vigor of the plants will suffer seriously in consequence.

There is a very direct relation between humidity and the factors of light and temperature. During dull, winter days an overabundance of humidity is not to be desired, as it may have a definitely detrimental effect upon the plants, whereas on bright, sunny days when the temperature is comparatively high, the effect will be decidedly beneficial. It is particularly needed on cold, bright days in winter when the fires are being forced to maintain the desired temperature.

There are various ways in which the humidity in a greenhouse may be increased: by syringing the plants, by wetting down the walks, by spraying beneath the benches, particularly on the heating pipes. It is possible to maintain a higher degree of humidity in a house where the walks are made of gravel or cinders than it is in a house where the walks are of concrete. However, most growers prefer concrete because the degree of humidity may be more definitely controlled and the house may be kept dry except when moisture is artificially applied at times when it may seem desirable to increase the humidity. In orchid houses, where a very high degree of humidity is necessary, a sprinkling system is sometimes installed under the benches.

It is advisable to record definitely the degree of humidity in a greenhouse and this may be done by means of a hygrometer, or some similar device designed especially for this purpose.

FUMIGATION

Periodic fumigation of the greenhouse is necessary in order to keep various insect pests under control. The two most satisfactory materials for fumigation purposes are calcium cyanide and nicotine.

In using calcium cyanide certain precautions should be carefully observed. Fumigation with calcium cyanide should be done on a night when there is little wind and when the atmosphere, both outside and within the house, is dry. The plants should not be watered either immediately before or after fumigation. During the period of fumigation the house should be maintained at a temperature ranging between 60 and 70 degrees F. As calcium cyanide gas is a deadly poison, it must be used with great care and the directions, as printed on the container, must be followed implicitly. It is ordinarily used at the rate of ¼ ounce per 1000 cubic feet.

The most satisfactory form of nicotine is a high-grade tobacco powder containing 12 per cent nicotine, used at the rate of 3½ ounces per every 5000 cubic feet of space. The powder is usually placed on the walks and ignited. Fumigation should be done at night and the humidity and temperature of the house are of little importance. Nicotine pressure fumigation is

a recently developed method which is proving very satisfactory.
For the control of diseases of greenhouse plants, see Chapter
XXXIII.

CONTROL OF INSECT PESTS IN THE GREENHOUSE

Insect	Measures of Control	Plants Attacked	
Aphids	Cyanide fumigation	Aster	Roses
	Nicotine fumigation	Cineraria	Snapdragon
	A good contact spray	Calla	Stocks
	such as	Chrysanthemum	Sweet Peas
	Pyrote	Geranium	
	Red Arrow		
Mealy Bug	Cyanide fumigation	Chrysanthemums	Lantana
	Loro	Gardenia	Poinsettia
	Lethane 440 weak	Geranium	Saintpaulia
	dilution	Kalanchoë	
Midge	Pyrethrum dust	Chrysanthemum	
Mites	Nicofume liquid plus soap	Cyclamen	Snapdragon
	Hitox	Kalanchoë	Saintpaulia
Red Spider	Spray with	Bouvardia	Gladiolus
	Pyrote	Buddleia	Lantana
	Hitrox	Carnation	Roses
	Selocide	Cineraria	Snapdragons
	Strong force of water	Calla	Sweet Peas
	Syringing	Gerbera	
Root knot nematodes	Sterilize soil with steam	Sweet Peas	Chrysanthemums
	or hot water		
Scale	Fish Oil Soap plus	Ferns	Palms
	nicotine		
Slugs	Meta	Young seedlings of all types	
Thrips	Loro	Carnations	Rose
	Lethane	Geranium	Snapdragon
		Primula	Sweet Peas
White Fly	Cyanide fumigation	Cineraria	Gerbera
	Black Arrow Dust	Calceolaria	Lantana
	Hitox	Geranium	

SUMMER IN THE GREENHOUSE

With the approach of summer, the intensity of the heat in
a greenhouse would become unbearable both for the plants

and for the gardener if some form of shade were not provided. The ideal device for such a purpose is a roller type of shade made of small strips of wood or thin pieces of bamboo. These may be regulated by means of a pulley and may be rolled up and down at will. It is a decided advantage to be able to lower them on cool, cloudy days and to roll them up on bright, sunny days when the temperature within the house is soaring. If it is not possible to obtain shades of this type the most satisfactory substitute is a coating of some suitable preparation applied to the outside of the glass. The following formula is recommended for this purpose.

MISSOURI BOTANICAL GARDEN PREPARATION

3 gallons of water	6 pounds of cement
5 pounds of whiting	½ pound of powdered glue

Mix all ingredients together with the exception of the glue. Dissolve the glue in hot water and add to the mixture. The mixture must be stirred frequently to keep it well agitated and it should be applied immediately with a brush or sprayer. This preparation has the advantage of gradually wearing off and does not have to be scraped off.

During the summer months when most of the plants have been removed, the greenhouse may be given a thorough cleaning. Any necessary repairs or repainting may be done at this season, the soil from the benches may be removed and fresh soil brought in, and the greenhouse may be made ready for the winter season.

EFFECT OF INCREASING OR DECREASING THE AMOUNT OF LIGHT

During the past decade a number of interesting experiments have been carried on at several of the State Agricultural Experiment Stations to determine the effect on plant growth of increasing or decreasing the amount of light. It has been found that plants vary tremendously in their response to light. In the case of some plants it is possible to hasten the blooming period and to increase the quantity and quality of the bloom by prolonging the day. This is accomplished by means of electric lights placed above the plants. In the case of other plants, the reverse procedure, the shortening of the day, has resulted in the production of early bloom, and this, in turn, is accomplished by shading the plants with black cloth in order to exclude all light for a portion of the day. Extensive experiments have proved that some plants are not affected by either of these treatments, and in other cases the effect has been so slight that the additional labor and expense involved have not been justified.

Increasing the Length of the Day. Additional light may be supplied for a period varying from 4 to 8 hours either at the beginning or the end of the day. The method most commonly employed by commercial growers is to provide additional light for a period of 5 hours, beginning at 5 P.M. and continuing until 10 P.M. The method employed in supplying the light is of considerable importance. The lights should be placed approximately 18 to 24 inches above the plants. For the majority of plants a 40-watt bulb may be used with excellent results. For some plants which are unusually responsive to light a 15 or 24-watt bulb will be sufficient. Either clear or frosted incandescent Mazda lamps may be used. Nitrogen-filled Mazda lamps have, in the majority of cases, proved to be more satisfactory than mercury, neon, or sun lamps. It is absolutely essential that reflectors be used. The most desirable type of reflector is one which is about 8 inches in diameter and which is deep enough so that only the tip of the bulb extends beyond the rim. The plants should be given an opportunity to become well established in the benches before extra light is supplied.

Reducing the Length of the Day. The usual procedure in shortening the length of the day in order to induce early flowering is to drape black cloth or some other dark, opaque material over the plants. Closely woven, black sateen has proved to be one of the most satisfactory materials for this purpose, and if proper care is taken it will give good service for several seasons. In most cases a reduction of 4 or 5 hours in the length of the day is sufficient, and the practice which is most generally followed is to place the cloth over the plants at 5 in the afternoon,

PLANTS WHICH RESPOND PROFITABLY TO ADDITIONAL LIGHT

Common Name	Botanical Name	Intensity of Light	Remarks
Blue Laceflower	Didiscus	40 Watt	Early and more profuse bloom. Stems somewhat shorter when plants are forced early.
Boston Yellow Daisy	Chrysanthemum sp.	25–40 Watt	Earlier and more abundant bloom. Early planting desirable.
Butterfly Flower	Schizanthus	15–40 Watt	Flowers 4–6 weeks earlier. Too rapid growth undesirable.
Calceolaria		40–60 Watt	Flowers 6 weeks earlier. Apply lights when plant is nearly mature. Cool temperature necessary.
Cornflower	Centaurea cyanus	25–40 Watt	Earlier bloom, longer stems.
Corn Marigold	Chrysanthemum segetum	40–60 Watt	Early bloom and an increase in flowers up to 50%.
Clarkia		40 Watt	Earlier bloom, longer stems. Do not apply lights until plants are very well established.
Coreopsis		40 Watt	Earlier flowering and more abundant bloom.
Feverfew	Matricaria capensis	40 Watt	Flowers 6–8 weeks earlier and with more profuse bloom.
Gardenia	G. Veitchii	150 Watt	6 hours of light necessary to produce earlier flowers.
Gaillardia		40 Watt	Earlier and more abundant bloom, longer stems.
Gypsophila	G. elegans	25–40 Watt	4 hours of light will produce earlier bloom.
Iris (bulbous)	I. tingitana	75–100 Watt	Longer stems and almost 50% increase in bloom.
Marigold	Tagetes	40 Watt	Earlier and more abundant bloom.
Nasturtium	Tropæolum majus	40 Watt	Earlier bloom and almost 50% increase.
Pansy	Viola tricolor	40–60 Watt	Flowers 6 to 8 weeks earlier and a tremendous increase in bloom.
Salpiglossis		40 Watt	Earlier bloom and longer stems.
Scabiosa		40 Watt	Earlier bloom, longer stems, more abundant flowering. Not advisable to force too early.
Shasta Daisy		40 Watt	Earlier bloom, longer stems and larger flowers. Increase up to 150%.
Shirley Poppy		40–60 Watt	Long stems and abundant bloom.
Snapdragon	Antirrhinum majus	40 Watt	Earlier and more abundant bloom but stems are short and not heavy. Lights are of doubtful value.
Stock	Mathiola incana	40–60 Watt	Earlier flowers, longer stems.
Violets		40 Watt	Earlier and more abundant bloom.

allowing it to remain until 7 o'clock the following morning. The time when the short-day treatment should be initiated will depend entirely upon the normal bud-forming period of the plants.

Plants Which Respond Profitably to Short-day Treatment

Bouvardia—Treatment should be started from six to eight weeks previous to the date when flowers are desired.

Chrysanthemum—Treatment should be started when standard type plants have reached a height of 18 to 24 inches and pompon types a height of 14 to 18 inches.

Euphorbia fulgens—Plants treated from Sept. 1 to Oct. 20 will flower in December.

Kalanchoë—Short-day treatment: July 20–Sept. 20, flowers Oct. 20; Aug. 1–Oct. 1, flowers Dec. 1–15; Sept. 1–Oct. 20, flowers Dec. 20.

Poinsettia—Late varieties such as Oak Leaf may be brought into flower by Christmas if short-day treatment is given between Oct. 1 and Oct. 20.

Stevia—Plants treated from Sept. 15 to Oct. 10 will flower November 20.

SELECTION OF PLANT MATERIALS

If the potentialities of a small greenhouse are to be realized to the fullest extent, the plant materials which are to be grown must be selected with great care. The usual desideratum is to have as much bloom as possible in the greenhouse from early autumn until late spring and to have a wide variety of flowers which are of particular value for cutting and for decorative purposes in the house.

Annuals, perennials, bulbs and potted plants all have an important part to play, and with careful thought and planning an abundance of bloom may be had throughout the winter months.

Many of the annuals which grow so luxuriantly out-of-doors during the summer months and which are so valuable for cutting will give an equally good account of themselves in the greenhouse. And to this list we are able to add some of the more temperamental annuals which cannot always be grown so successfully under the trying conditions of midsummer temperatures and humidity. This makes it possible for us to introduce into the greenhouse some of the annuals which we greatly admire when we see them growing so luxuriantly in English gardens. Heliophila will not thrive in many sections of the country during the summer months, but it is one of the loveliest flowers we have for greenhouse culture. It will give abundant bloom from October until May and the airy grace of its clear, blue flowers will add charm to many a winter bouquet. Clarkia, schizanthus and many other annuals are also in this group and will give much better bloom under greenhouse culture than out-of-doors.

In order to obtain a succession of bloom from autumn until spring it is necessary to plan one's program of work well in advance and to follow the schedule with exactitude and care.

CALENDAR OF BLOOM

October
Chrysanthemums predominating
Antirrhinums

November
Chrysanthemums
Antirrhinums
Heliotrope

December
Agathæa
Antirrhinums
Bouvardia
Clarkia
Freesias
Gerberas
Larkspur, annual
Lupines

January
Agathæa
Antirrhinums
Bouvardia
Calendulas
California Poppies
Clarkia
Freesias
Gerberas

Heliophila
Larkspur, annual
Lupines
Narcissus
Schizanthus
Stocks

February
Agathæa
Antirrhinum
Bleedingheart
Calendulas
California Poppies
Clarkia
Freesias
Gerberas
Gladiolus
Heliophila
Iris, bulbous
Larkspur, annual
Lupines
Narcissus
Schizanthus
Stocks

March

Agathæa
Antirrhinum
Aquilegia
Bleedingheart
Calendulas
California Poppies
Clarkia
Freesias
Gerberas
Gladiolus, also dwarf
Heliophila
Iris, bulbous

Larkspur, annual
Lupines
Narcissus
Schizanthus
Stocks
Tulips

Agathæa cœlestis (Blue Daisy). Lovely both as a potted plant and for cutting, Agathæa cœlestis is admirably adapted to the small greenhouse. The daisy-like flowers, of a soft powder-blue with golden centers, are borne in profusion throughout the winter and early spring months, and the fact that the plants remain in flower over such a long period of time makes them of particular value as potted plants for house decoration.

Propagation: Agathæa may be raised from seed or from cuttings. In plants grown from seed there is a slight variation in color, and after a stock has been established it is wise to make cuttings from the most desirable plants. Cuttings made during the early spring root readily, and the young plants may be carried on in pots through the summer.

Culture: In early autumn the plants may be transferred to the greenhouse bench if the flowers are to be used only for cutting, or they may be shifted into 6 or 8 inch pots or bulb pans, to be grown on as potted plants. The plants thrive well in a moderately cool house.

Soil Requirements: Agathæa is not particular in regard to soil. A good potting compost is all that is necessary.

Antirrhinum (Snapdragon). The Antirrhinums are among the most satisfactory of all greenhouse plants and will give a wealth of bloom throughout the winter months.

Propagation: If autumn or early winter bloom is desired, the seeds should be sown early in June. The young seedlings should be pricked out before they become in the least crowded, and they may be carried on in flats or in pots until they are ready to be benched in late August or early September.

Soil Requirements: A rather heavy, coarse soil, well supplied with organic matter and of good fertility, is considered ideal, although snapdragons will do well on widely varying types of soil. A soil with a slightly acid reaction is preferred. A soil which is too alkaline in its reaction will cause a yellowing of the leaf margins and veins. An application of superphosphate, 5 pounds per 100 square feet, made at the time of planting will give excellent results, and additional feeding is not necessary.

Culture: When the young seedlings have developed 5 or 6 sets of leaves they should be pinched back. The plants should be spaced 10 inches apart each way in the bench. Antirrhinums prefer a cool temperature and will succeed extremely well if given a night temperature approximating 45 to 48 degrees F. with a rise of 10 to 15 degrees during the day. They are one of the few plants which can be grown successfully in an unheated greenhouse, and will give an abundance of bloom during the late winter and early spring months if grown under such conditions. In the heated greenhouse they are often used to follow chrysanthemums and in this way excellent use is made of all available bench space. For a late planting such as this, the seeds should be sown in late August and the young seedlings carried on in flats or in pots until the chrysanthemums have been removed and bench space is available. These plants will usually not come into flower until late winter but will give luxuriant bloom throughout the early spring months. It is a common practice among commercial growers not to water the foliage of the antirrhinums, watering merely the roots, as a precautionary measure against the spread of rust. Throughout the flowering season the plants should be disbudded, the small shoots appearing at the base of the leaves and in the axils of the flower stalks being removed. Snapdragons prefer a relatively low humidity of approximately 60 per cent.

VARIETIES OF MERIT

Antirrhinums of the forcing type, suitable for growing in the greenhouse, may be obtained in many lovely colors, white, yellow, apple-blossom pink, rose, apricot, scarlet, deep Indian red and wine color. Among the most popular varieties are:

White Rock	Orlando
Cheviot Maid	Judd's Early Light Pink
Afterglow	Sun Tan

Aquilegia (Columbine). It is, perhaps, difficult to think of Aquilegia as a greenhouse plant, yet it can be forced so easily and the flowers are so exquisite for cutting that a few clumps should be included. Plants which have flowered the previous season in the garden or in the nursery should be selected. It is well to mark the clumps at the time that they are in bloom, as it is then possible to choose plants which are unusually beautiful in form or in coloring and which will therefore be of particular value for cut flowers.

Culture: The clumps should be lifted in the autumn and placed in a coldframe where they can be given some slight protection. Late in January or early in February the dormant plants may be brought into the greenhouse, being planted in a bench, or being potted in 10 or 12-inch pots. Growth will start within a few days and by March or early April the plants will be in full flower. A cool temperature, ranging between 45 and 55 degrees, is preferred, as aquilegias will not do well if subjected to too high a degree of heat. After the plants have been forced, they may be replanted in the nursery.

Soil Requirements: Good potting compost.

Azaleas. There are few plants more decorative than the Azaleas when they are in bloom, and there are a number of species and varieties which may be grown very successfully under greenhouse conditions, being forced into bloom either for Christmas or for Easter.

VARIETIES OF MERIT

Mme. Petrick, pink	Prof. Walters, pink
Petrick superba, white	Empress of India, salmon-rose
Vervæneana, salmon-pink	Mme. Vander Cruyssen, pink
Firefly, crimson	Orange Beauty
Lorraine, deep pink	Salmon Beauty
Mrs. Fred Sanders, double cerise	Coral Bells

Propagation: Some varieties may be propagated most successfully from cuttings, while other varieties are usually grafted. As the propagation of azaleas is a highly specialized field, it is advisable for the owner of the small greenhouse to purchase a few plants which have been especially prepared for forcing.

Soil Requirements: Azaleas require a highly acid soil with a pH. between 4.5 and 5.5. The potting soil should consist of a mixture of 2 parts loam and 1 part imported acid peat. Yellowing of the foliage and poor root development are indicative of a soil which is too highly alkaline and of a lack of available iron. A biweekly application of ferrous sulfate, applied at the rate of 4 ounces to 5 gallons of water, will help to correct this condition.

Culture: Azalea plants are shipped with a small ball of earth and as soon as they have been unpacked the ball should be immersed in a bucket of water until it has become thoroughly saturated. It should then be allowed to drain before it is potted. For the first two or three weeks the plants should be placed in a cool greenhouse where the night temperature ranges around 45 degrees. Azaleas require an abundance of water and a moist atmosphere. Frequent syringing of the foliage with warm water is beneficial. If the plants are to be brought into flower by Christmas, they should be kept in a temperature of 45 to 48 degrees until November 5. They should then have a night temperature of 60 degrees with a somewhat higher temperature of 65 degrees during the day. If the plants are desired for Easter bloom they should be kept in a very cool house (45 to 50 degrees) until six weeks before Easter. All new growth which appears at the base of the flower buds should be pinched out. If this is not done the flowers will be small and there will be many blind buds.

After the flowering period is over the plants should be trimmed back lightly, and they should be placed in a warm, moist house in order that vigorous new growth may be encouraged. In June the pots may be sunk in the open ground or the plants may be shifted to the nursery rows. A soil mixture similar to that of the potting mixture should be used. The symmetry of the plant should be maintained by the occasional pinching back of any awkward shoots. No pinching should be done after July 1. In early autumn the plants may be lifted and brought into the greenhouse.

Begonias may be grouped into four general classes: the semi-tuberous-rooted, the tuberous-rooted; the foliage group; and the fibrous-rooted.

(1) *Semituberous Group*

VARIETIES OF MERIT FOR CHRISTMAS FLOWERING

Lady Mac, Melior, Marjorie Gibbs

Propagation: The plants are propagated by petiole leaf cuttings taken from medium sized, well-ripened leaves in November and December. The petioles should be inserted in the propagating case in such a way that the leaves do not come into contact with the sand. The formation of roots requires from four to five weeks but the cuttings should not be potted up until new shoots have begun to develop from the base. A potting mixture of 1 part loam, 1 part sand and 1 part peat moss should be used and the crown of the cutting should be placed as near the surface as possible.

Soil Requirements: A soil with a pH. between 6.8 and 7.2 is preferred. For the final potting soil a mixture of 3 parts loam, 2 parts rotted manure, 1 part peat moss, and 1 part sand is recommended. To each 2½ bushels of soil may be added a 4-inch pot of a 4–12–4 complete fertilizer and a 4-inch pot of horn shavings.

Culture: The young plants may be grown on with a bottom heat of about 70 degrees, and as they develop they may be shifted into larger pots. The final potting in a 6 or 7-inch pot should be done in September. A humid atmosphere and partial shade during the summer are desirable, and pinching should be practised in order to produce stocky, well-developed plants. Staking is advisable, as the stems are very brittle. During the growing period a night temperature of 58 to 60 degrees is desirable, with a slightly higher temperature during the day.

(2) *Tuberous-Rooted Group*
   See Summer-flowering Bulbs and Tubers, page 552.

(3) *Foliage Group*
VARIETIES OF MERIT
   Rex begonia

Propagation: Members of this group are propagated by means of leaf cuttings. Well-matured leaves should be selected. One inch of the margin of the leaf should be cut away and the remaining portion of the leaf should be cut into triangular sections, with a small section of the petiole at the base and a vein running through the middle. The cutting should then be inserted in the propagating case, the section of petiole being well buried.

Soil Requirements: ⎫
Culture: ⎬ See Semituberous Group.

(4) *Fibrous-rooted Group* (Begonia semperflorens)

VARIETIES OF MERIT

Bonfire	Prima Donna
Gloire de Chatelaine	Pride of Newcastle
Luminosa	Westport Beauty

Propagation: The fibrous-rooted begonias may be propagated by seed, by stem-cuttings and in the case of a few varieties, such as Gloire de Chatelaine, by division. Seeds may be sown at any time from November to January. The seeds are exceedingly fine and should be handled with care. (See Chapter XXX on Propagation.) The seedlings should be pricked out as soon as they have developed their second leaf. Cuttings may be taken at any time of the year but will root most readily in March and April.

Soil Requirements: ⎫
Culture: ⎬ See Semituberous Group.

Bleedingheart (Dicentra spectabilis). There are very few perennials which can be forced as successfully as Bleedingheart, and there are few flowers more beautiful or more appealing. After you have once grown them in the greenhouse, you will not want a season to pass without having at least a few plants for decorative purposes in the house or in the conservatory.

Soil Requirements: Good potting compost.

Culture: Two-year-old clumps should be lifted in the autumn and heeled in in a frame. Late in January the plants should be brought into the greenhouse and potted up in ample 10 or 12 inch bulb pans. They should be placed in the coolest temperature available and forced slowly. During this period of growth, the plants will require abundant moisture. By late March or early April the lovely, pendent, heart-shaped flowers will begin to open and the plants will remain in bloom for many weeks if they are kept in a moderately cool temperature. After the flowering period is over, the plants may be replanted out of doors, and will show no ill effects from this gentle process of forcing.

Bouvardia. The waxy, orange-blossom-scented flowers of the Bouvardia are a source of constant joy during the brief months that they are in bloom. The flowers are so lovely for cutting and the fragrance is so delightful that a few clumps should be grown in every small greenhouse.

Propagation: New plants may be started very readily from cuttings made in late winter or early spring, and the young plants may be grown on in pots. Bouvardia may also be propagated by means of root cuttings. The roots may be cut into pieces 1 to 2 inches long and these may be planted horizontally in flats containing a mixture of ½ sand and ½ peat moss.

Soil Requirements: Bouvardia prefers a very fibrous, mellow soil, abundantly supplied with leaf mold or some other form of organic matter. The soil should have a neutral or slightly alkaline reaction, preferably testing between pH. 7 and pH. 7.5. If the soil is too acid in its reaction it will cause a browning of the foliage, and in some cases a complete defoliation.

Culture: During the summer months the young rooted cuttings may be planted in the open, being benched late in August, or they may be planted directly in the greenhouse bed or bench in May, being carried over the summer in their permanent location. The plants should be kept pinched back until the end of August in order that they may become well branched. When the plants are moved from the open ground into the greenhouse they must be lifted with an ample quantity of earth and the roots should be disturbed as little as possible. It is also wise to shade the plants for a few days after transplanting until they have become well established. Bouvardia prefers a moderately cool temperature, a night temperature of 55 degrees F. being considered ideal, with a rise of 10 degrees or so during the day. The plants will usually begin to flower late in September and will continue to give generous bloom throughout November and December. When the plants have finished blooming, they should be cut back, lifted, and placed under the bench, water being withheld gradually. Late in January the soil may be shaken from the roots of the old plants, and they may be potted up in 5 or 6-inch pots. Cuttings may be made from these plants as growth starts, or the old plants may be carried over for another season of bloom. They will often do their best during this second season.

VARIETIES OF MERIT

Bouvardia ternifolia. Red-flowering species
Bouvardia Humboldti. White-flowering species

Calendulas are among the most satisfactory of all plants for the cool greenhouse, and their gay, jaunty blossoms, in shades of orange and gold, are borne in profusion throughout the winter months. The plants are of easy culture, and will repay one generously for the small amount of labor expended upon them.

VARIETIES OF MERIT

Apricot. Rich yellow with contrasting brown center
Gold. Golden yellow, large flowers with long stems

Lemon Queen. Bright yellow
Masterpiece. Deep orange with dark center

Soil Requirements: Calendulas may be grown with a reasonable degree of success in almost any soil, but they thrive best in a rather heavy loam of high fertility. A cool, deep, rich soil is ideal, and in the preparation of the beds 1 part of rotted manure should be used to every 3 parts of soil, and an application of 5 pounds of superphosphate per 100 square feet should be made. The plants are more or less indifferent to soil reaction but, in general, a neutral reaction is considered best. A mulch of peat moss is beneficial in that it helps to maintain a cool soil temperature.

Propagation: The seeds may be sown at any time from mid-July to late October. Seeds sown the last week in July will come into flower about the middle of October. Seeds sown about October 10 will flower early in February. The young seedlings make rapid growth and after being transplanted into pots or flats the plants will be ready for benching about the middle of September.

Culture: The new, improved varieties should be spaced from 12–15 inches apart each way. The size of the flower, the length and stiffness of the stem, and the quality of the foliage will depend to a large extent upon the temperature under which the plants are grown. In order to produce flowers of maximum size with strong, stiff stems, the night temperature should be about 45 degrees. A slightly higher temperature ranging between 50 and 55 degrees, will produce earlier and more abundant bloom but the flowers will be somewhat smaller.

California Poppies. Although California Poppies are seldom thought of as greenhouse flowers, a few plants may well be included if one's aim is to provide a pleasant variety of flowers for cutting. Some of the large-flowering types which have been recently introduced are very decorative and lovely.

VARIETIES OF MERIT

Aurora. A delicate peach-pink in color
Sutton's Buff-pink
Sutton's Rosy Queen

Soil Requirements: A good greenhouse compost.
Propagation: The seeds should be sown in the greenhouse bench where they are to flower, as the young seedlings do not take kindly to transplanting.

Culture: The plants should be thinned out to a distance of 8 to 10 inches. A cool house will provide conditions which are very nearly ideal. The plants will come into flower in about eight to ten weeks from sowing.

Calla (Zantedeschia). Callas are grown for the decorative quality of their blooms when used in cut-flower arrangements.

TYPES

White Calla. (*Zantedeschia æthiopica*)
Yellow Calla. (*Zantedeschia Elliottiana*)

Propagation: The small offsets which form around the parent rhizome may be removed. Several years of growth are required before these young plants will come into bloom.

Soil Requirements: Callas require a very rich soil. A mixture of 2 parts heavy, rich loam and 1 part well-rotted cow manure will give excellent results.

Culture: Callas may be grown either in solid beds, in raised benches, or in pots. A night temperature of 55 degrees and a day temperature ranging between 60 and 65 degrees are preferred. The plants require an abundant supply of moisture throughout their growing period. After the flowering period is over, the plants are gradually dried off and are given a period of rest. Occasional waterings may be given but all active growth is allowed to cease. In August the top soil from the beds may be removed and after the plants have been given a thorough soaking a heavy mulch of stable manure may be applied. Active growth will soon be resumed and the plants will begin to flower late in the autumn.

Carnations (Dianthus). Carnations are among the ever-dependable and ever-popular greenhouse flowers.

Propagation: With the exception of new varieties, carnations are always propagated by means of cuttings. The most accepted practice is to take the cuttings from established plants in November or December. Cuttings may be taken later in the winter season but plants grown from cuttings taken earlier in the season will make more vigorous growth and will produce more abundant bloom the following year. The cuttings should be taken from disease-free plants which are in vigorous growing condition. Cuttings are taken from the axillary shoots, preferably from the lower portion of the flowering stem. Cuttings will range from 3 to 5 inches in length and they should be inserted in the propagating case, clean, sharp sand being the best rooting medium. Although it was formerly a common practice to remove a portion of the foliage, recent experiments have proved that a higher percentage of rootage is obtained if the foliage is not reduced. Under favorable conditions the cuttings should root in about 4 weeks, although some varieties will root more readily than others.

Soil Requirements: Carnations prefer a medium sandy loam, high in organic matter, and the plants are indifferent to soil reaction, thriving equally well in neutral, mildly acid or slightly alkaline soil, within a range of pH. 5.5 to 8. At the time of planting an application of superphosphate, 10 pounds per 100 square feet, may be made. Beginning eight weeks after benching, monthly applications of a 4–12–4 commercial fertilizer may be made at the rate of 4 pounds to every 100 square feet. Planting distances vary from 6 to 12 inches apart according to the variety and, to some extent, to the fertility of the soil in the benches.

Culture: When the cuttings are well rooted, the roots being from ½ to 1 inch long, the cuttings should be removed from the propagating bench and potted up in 2½-inch pots, a mixture of 1 part compost, 1 part sand and 1 part peat moss being used. Before the plants become in the least pot-bound, they should be shifted on to larger pots, as carnations suffer seriously from any check of this sort, the plants becoming hard, yellow, and stunted in appearance. Carnations are one of the few plants which should not be potted very firmly, and care should be taken not to set the plants too deeply. Watering must also be done with care, as overwatering is often fatal to the welfare of the plant.

Soon after the plants have been potted for the first time they should be pinched back to within about 3 inches. The lateral shoots should be pinched back as they develop, in order to produce symmetrical, well-branched plants. Pinching should continue until one desires to let the flower buds mature. If early bloom is desired pinching should cease early in July. If late bloom is desired pinching may be continued until after the plants are benched. It requires from ten to twenty weeks for a newly pinched shoot to produce a flower. The plants may be carried on in pots until they are ready to be benched or, as soon as danger of frost is past, they may be set in the open ground. If field culture is practised a more vigorous growth and greater disease resistance are obtained, while the pot-grown plants will give earlier bloom. The plants should be benched in late summer, and early summer benching is sometimes practised.

Disbudding: The flowering stems of carnations should be kept disbudded, all the axillary buds and shoots being removed from the upper portion.

Watering: Watering must be done with care. Carnation plants thrive best in a soil which is uniformly moist but which is not saturated.

Chrysanthemums. There is no other flower which can take the place of the Chrysanthemums during the autumn months. They are so generous with their bloom, so lovely in form and coloring, so entirely satisfactory, both for cutting and as potted plants, that they should be included in every greenhouse, no matter how limited the space may be. Many exquisite varieties which are not hardy out-of-doors, may be grown successfully in the greenhouse, and with careful planning the period of bloom may be extended over several months.

VARIETIES OF MERIT

	Type	Color
Major Bonnafon	Incurved Regular	Pink and yellow
Sunglow	Incurved Regular	Apricot
Betsy Ross	Incurved Regular	Deep pink
Chieftain	Incurved Regular	Yellow
May Mason	Incurved Irregular	Bronze
Butlers Caprice	Small, Reflexed	White
Maple Leaf	Large Anemone	Bronze
Mrs. Shimmins	Large Anemone	Orange-bronze
Clemencia	Japanese Anemone	White
Gold Corn	Intermediate Pompon	Yellow
Bronze Queen	Intermediate Pompon	Yellow
White Doty	Large Pompon	White
Bronze Doty	Large Pompon	Pink
Frank Wilcox, Jr.	Small Pompon	Bronze
Dainty Maid	Small Pompon	Deep pink

Propagation: Rooted cuttings of many desirable varieties may be purchased from commercial growers and after the first season cuttings may be made from the stock thus obtained. These rooted cuttings should be potted up in March or early April, and they may be carried on in pots, being shifted to larger pots as the plants develop, or they may be transferred to the benches. During the summer the plants should be syringed at least twice a day.

Soil Requirements: The soil in the benches should be carefully prepared. A one-inch layer of rotted sod or coarse, strawy manure should be placed in the bottom of the bench and a soil mixture consisting of 1 part well-decomposed manure and 3 parts good sandy loam is recommended. An application of 20 per cent superphosphate at the rate of 8 pounds per 100 square feet may be made at the time of planting. The soil should be very slightly acid in its reaction.

Culture: If the plants are to be trained to single stems they should be spaced from 8 to 10 inches apart. For the more branching types, 12 inches should be allowed. If large flowers borne on tall single stems are desired, all side shoots and all growth from the base of the plants should be removed. The pompon types should be kept pinched back until the middle of August in order to obtain sturdy, well-branched plants, six or eight flowering branches being allowed to develop. Commercial growers consider it a good practice to bench their chrysanthemums during May, June and July as this enables the young plants to become well established during the summer.

A few weeks after the plants have been benched, a one-inch mulch of domestic peat moss should be applied. Such a mulch has a most startling effect upon the growth and vigor of the plants, sometimes causing as much as a 50 to 100 per cent increase in growth.

When the buds begin to show, weekly applications of ammonium sulphate may be made, 1 ounce dissolved in 2 gallons of water.

Chrysanthemums prefer a night temperature which does not exceed 50 degrees F.

After the flowering season is over the plants may be lifted from the bench and placed in a coldframe, cuttings being taken from these stock plants in the early spring.

Clarkia. The copper-colored stems of the Clarkias, studded with crisp little whorls of bloom, are very lovely for cutting, and a few plants will add welcome variety for flower arrangements. If the flowers are cut just as the buds begin to open, they will last extremely well.

Propagation: For early bloom the seeds should be sown before mid-September; for later bloom, a sowing should be made in October or early November.

Soil Requirements: Clarkia is rather indifferent to soil conditions and will thrive well in any good greenhouse compost.

Culture: The young plants make rapid growth, and they may be grown either in pots or in raised benches, the plants being spaced from 10 to 12 inches apart. Clarkia prefers a decidedly cool temperature of 50 degrees F. at night.

Cyclamen. The blooms of the Cyclamen are like miniature butter-flies poised on slender stems. If the plants are well grown they will flower abundantly during the winter and will add their full share of beauty to the indoor garden.

Exposure and Temperature: When used for decorative purposes in the house, a window with an eastern exposure is ideal. If maximum growth and development are desired, the temperature throughout the growing period should range between 50 and 60 degrees.

Propagation: Cyclamen may be propagated either by seed, or by cutting the corm into sections with one or two leaves attached. The seed should be sown in the early autumn in order to produce flowering plants for the following winter. A mixture of 1 part loam and 1 part German peat may be used for the seed bed and the seeds may be planted about an inch apart. If kept in a temperature ranging between 55 and 60 degrees F. they will germinate in from four to five weeks. After several leaves have developed, the plants should be transplanted into small 2½–inch pots. At the time of this first transplanting, the tiny corm which is forming should be placed so that its top is level with the surface of the soil. At each subsequent repotting the corm should be placed slightly higher until at the time of the last shift it is entirely above the surface of the soil.

Soil Requirements: A slightly acid soil with a pH. between 6.0 and 7.0 is considered ideal. A soil decidedly light in texture should be used for cyclamen plants in the early stages of growth. For plants reaching maturity, the following soil mixture is recommended: 3 parts good loam, 1 part manure, ½ part imported peat, ½ part sand. At the time of the final potting, a 4-inch potful of a 4–12–4 complete fertilizer and a 4-inch potful of horn shavings should be added to each 2½ bushels of soil.

Culture: During the summer months, the young plants should be kept in a cool, semi-shaded spot, a well-ventilated, partially shaded greenhouse being satisfactory. Frequent syringing of the foliage and the maintenance of high humidity is desirable. The shade should be removed in the autumn. If, at this time, the pots are set on a staging or are elevated on overturned flower pots, the development of the plant will be hastened. Cyclamen plants should be grown in clay pots, rather than in glazed containers. Watering must be done with care. The plants should usually be watered twice a day, the pots being set in a saucer or pan until the surface of the soil has become moist. Faded blooms and any yellowing leaves should be removed by giving the stem a quick jerk in order that it may snap off at the base. The plants may be carried over for a second year by resting them after the period of bloom is over.

Euphorbia (Euphorbia fulgens). The brilliant orange-red flowers of the Euphorbias are very decorative and lovely and a few plants are a welcome addition to the stock of a small greenhouse.

Propagation: Euphorbias may be propagated by softwood cuttings taken from the stock plants about the first of May, or by hardwood cuttings taken in January after the parent plants have flowered. The cuttings should consist of 2 or 3 nodes and should be rooted in a medium of half peat and half sand.

Soil Requirements: A rather heavy, slightly acid soil is preferred for Euphorbias.

Culture: The rooted cuttings may be benched or potted up early in July. The plants should be pinched back so that 3 or 4 stems develop from the lower portion of the plant. The plants should be spaced from 10 to 12 inches apart in the bench. A growing temperature of 60 degrees is preferred. Sudden changes in temperature are to be avoided, as they have a very harmful effect upon the plant.

Freesias. Within recent years many new varieties of Freesias have been introduced, and they may now be obtained in a wide range of colors—mauve, lavender, blue, yellow, orange, pink, and carmine-rose. The delicately formed, sweetly scented flowers are lovely for cutting and Freesias are exceedingly well adapted for greenhouse culture.

VARIETIES OF MERIT

Elder's Giant White
Achievement, with flowers of a deep orange color
Golden Daffodil
Orange Glory, a soft buff-orange
Maryon, considered the best blue Freesia
Orchidea, a giant mauve
Isoline, a fusion of rose and amber
Penserosa, a soft carmine-rose

Propagation: If bloom is desired throughout the winter months the bulbs may be planted in succession from August until the middle of December. They may be grown in pots or in flats. For early bloom only large-sized bulbs should be used; for later bloom the smaller sizes will be entirely satisfactory. The bulbs should be spaced approximately 2 inches apart each way.

Soil Requirements: A potting soil consisting of 2 parts loam, 1 part leafmold and 1 part sand is recommended.

Culture: After planting, the bulbs should be placed in a cool, dark place until the leaves appear. In the summer, the pots or flats may be placed in a coldframe, being shaded with lath sash. The pots should be kept moist but not too wet. As soon as leaf growth has started the shade should be removed. The pots should be brought into the greenhouse before there is danger of frost. A night temperature ranging between 55 and 60 degrees is satisfactory. As the flower stems are very delicate, some support is necessary and very small bamboo stakes may be used with a number of strings crisscrossed between them. After the plants have finished flowering, water should be gradually withheld and the bulbs should be allowed to ripen. After the foliage has ripened sufficiently, the bulbs may be removed from the soil and the largest ones may be saved for bloom the following year, being stored during the summer in a cool, dry place.

Geraniums (Pelargonium). The popularity of the Geranium as a house plant has endured over a period of many years. Beloved and cherished by our grandmothers, geraniums were among the few flowering plants which could be grown in the window garden a generation or more ago; and they are still beloved today, their popularity being quite undiminished in spite of the wealth of new material which is available.

Species and Varieties

P. domesticum. Lady Washington Geranium
  Varieties: Easter Greeting
          Lucy Becker
P. graveolens. Rose Geranium
P. odoratissimum. Nutmeg Geranium
P. peltatum. Ivy-leaf Geranium
P. zonale. Horseshoe or Common Geranium

Varieties: Enchantress—light pink
        Improved Poitevine—salmon pink
        Mme. Landry—salmon pink
        Mme. Buchner—white
        Radio Red—red
        Red Fiat—brick red
        Suzanne—cerise

Exposure and Temperature: Full sunlight at all times. A temperature ranging between 65 and 70 degrees during the day and between 60 and 65 degrees at night is considered ideal.

Propagation: Geraniums are propagated by means of softwood stem cuttings. When winter bloom is desired, cuttings should be made in May. (See Chapter XXX on Propagation.)

Soil Requirements: Geraniums require a soil low in nitrogen and relatively high in phosphorus and potash. An excess of nitrogen in the soil induces a rank, vegetative growth and prevents flowering. Geraniums will thrive reasonably well in almost any ordinary garden soil. If, however, maximum growth and abundant bloom are desired, the following soil mixture will give the best results when used in the final potting: 8 parts good garden loam to 1 part well-rotted manure. To $2\frac{1}{2}$ bushels of soil, add one 5-inch flower potful of superphosphate and one 4-inch potful of a 2–10–10 commercial fertilizer. This should be thoroughly mixed with the soil before potting. This same mixture may be used in repotting old plants. If a good potting mixture is used, it is not advisable to make any subsequent application of fertilizer. A soil with a pH. between 6.5 and 7.6 is preferred.

Culture: After the cuttings have rooted, they should be potted up into small 3-inch pots and as the plants develop they may be shifted on into 4 and 5 inch pots. Geraniums require very firm potting, and as they flower more abundantly when they are allowed to become slightly pot-bound they should be carried through the winter in 4 or 5 inch pots. Old plants should be grown in 6 and 8 inch pots. During the first summer of growth the young plants should be pinched back frequently, in order that they may become symmetrical and well branched, and no flower buds should be allowed to develop until early September. The plants should then give ample bloom from October until April. In May these plants which have bloomed through the winter months should be severely pruned back, leaving about 3 strong shoots, 3 or 4 inches long to each plant. During the summer they should be placed in a partially shaded place, and they should be kept fairly dry. It is important not to encourage new growth during this rest period, as the plant is storing up a reserve of strength for winter bloom. In the early autumn, the plants may be repotted in fresh soil and should give abundant bloom during the winter months.

Watering: Geraniums should not be watered too liberally. The plants will give better bloom if they are kept somewhat on the dry side. Overwatering and poor ventilation are frequently the cause of a physiological leaf spot which is very disfiguring to the foliage.

Gerbera (Transvaal Daisy). Coming to us from the fields of the Transvaal in South Africa the Gerbera has gained rapidly in popularity as a greenhouse plant. The flowers are unusually fine for cutting and are obtainable in many exquisite shades of salmon, apricot, orange-pink, and cerise. Gerberas are true perennials in their native habitat but they are too tender to withstand the rigors of our winters north of Virginia and in many sections they are, therefore, best adapted to greenhouse culture.

Propagation: They may be readily propagated both by seed and by the division of old established clumps. As Gerbera seed loses its vitality rapidly, only fresh seed should be used. The seed should be sown in March and as soon as 4 or 5 small leaves have developed the seedlings should be transplanted directly into the beds where they are to flower. Established plants may be divided in June.

Culture: Gerberas should preferably be grown in solid beds. During the summer the plants should be given a light mulch, they should be kept carefully watered, and the house should be well ventilated. The plants should be spaced 12 to 15 inches apart. A moderately cool night temperature of 55 to 60 degrees is preferred, and if given good care the plants will give abundant bloom throughout the winter and early spring months.

Soil Requirements: Gerberas prefer an open, well-drained soil of good fertility, with a pH. value of approximately 7.0 to 7.5. In the fall and spring a weekly application of urea, 1 ounce to 7 gallons, is recommended.

Gladiolus. Both the large-flowered types of gladiolus and the primulinus hybrids, as well as many of the very exquisite dwarf types, may be forced in the greenhouse for early spring bloom. The culture of the latter group is, however, quite distinct from the culture of the large-flowered types; consequently the two groups will be treated separately as regards culture and soil requirements.

VARIETIES AND SPECIES OF MERIT

Large-flowered Type

Mrs. Frank Pendleton—pink with dark blotch
J. E. Shaylor—rose-pink
Morning Glory—yellow

Ming Toy—apricot
Virginian—red

Primulinus Type

Apricot Glow
Gloriana—apricot
Orange Queen
White Butterfly
Butterboy—yellow

Dwarf Type

C. tristis concolor (ranging from pure yellow and citron-white
    to yellow with brown spots)
 Hybrid forms available in shades of orchid, salmon-pink, lavender blue, orange, rose, and scarlet.

G. Colvillei (Baby Gladiolus)
 Peach Blossom—soft peach-pink
 The Bride—white
 February Rose—soft rose-pink
 Ackermani—orange-salmon

Large-flowered and Primulinus Types

Soil Requirements: Any good loam is satisfactory.

Culture: If the large-flowered and primulinus types are to be
grown, corms which have been especially prepared for forcing should
be obtained. These may be planted directly in a bench, the rows
being spaced 12 inches apart and the corms 4 inches apart in the
row, or they may be planted in flats or in pots. The method of
planting will usually be determined by the space which happens to
be available at the time. When pot culture is followed, three corms
may be planted in a 6-inch pot. In flats the corms may be spaced
4 inches apart each way. The corms should be planted at a depth
of approximately an inch, and the soil should be at least an inch
below the rim of the pot or flat in order to allow for watering.
Greenhouse culture is practically identical with outdoor culture.
The plants should be given full sun, they should be watered adequately, and a moderate temperature is preferred. If bench space
is not available at the time of planting, the pots or flats may be placed
beneath the benches for a brief period, until the corms have started
into growth, and the shoots have obtained a height of about 4
inches. They should then be brought into full light. The primulinus hybrids are particularly well adapted to forcing, and as cut
flowers they are far lovelier than the large-flowered types.

Dwarf Types

Soil Requirements: A light, sandy-loam soil is preferred.

Culture: There are few flowers more exquisite in form and coloring than some of the dwarf gladioli and no greenhouse should be without them. Although many of these dwarf types are not hardy enough to be grown out-of-doors in the North, they may be grown to perfection in the small greenhouse. Most of these dwarf species, and their hybrids, have come to us from South Africa and it is to be regretted that they are not hardy enough for general culture out-of-doors, for they are so utterly charming. The corms should be planted in November, either in pots or in flats. The pots should be stored in a coldframe until mid-January, when they may be brought into the greenhouse and forced in a moderately cool temperature. The graceful flower spikes will begin to open in late March, and if a succession of bloom is desired during the spring months, the pots should be brought in from storage at intervals of every ten days.

Heliophila is one of the most charming of that group of South African annuals which has been recently introduced, and as it becomes more widely known its popularity will undoubtedly increase. The long sprays of lovely clear blue flowers, similar in coloring to the flowers of the perennial flax (Linum perenne), are borne in profusion throughout the late winter months, and they are perfectly delightful for cut-flower arrangements. The fact that a few plants will produce such an abundance of bloom, and that they may be cut almost continually over a period of several months, makes them of unique value as a greenhouse flower.

Propagation: The seeds may be sown at any time during the late summer and early autumn months.

Soil Requirements: Good greenhouse compost.

Culture: Heliophila prefers a moderately cool temperature. The plants may be grown either in pots or in raised benches, the latter being preferred. A distance of from 8 to 10 inches between the plants will give ample space for their best development.

Bulbous Iris. Of all the varieties and types of bulbous Iris which may be grown in the greenhouse, the Iris tingitana hybrid, *Wedgewood,* is the most beautiful. It is extremely well adapted to forcing and the lovely, clear blue flowers are of great value for cutting. The Spanish, English, and Dutch Iris may all be forced into early bloom very successfully and they may be had in a wide range of colors. (For a list of varieties, see page 569.)

Soil Requirements: A soil mixture of 1 part compost, 1 part loam and 1 part sand is recommended.

Culture: The bulbs may be planted in September in shallow bulb pans or in flats, being spaced 1½ inches apart. A thorough watering should be given in order to start root action. They should be stored in a coldframe until the middle of November and may then be brought in and placed in a cool house with a night temperature of 45 to 50 degrees F. If a succession of bloom is desired a few pots or flats should be brought in from the frames at intervals of every ten days. When the buds begin to show the temperature may be raised to 55 degrees, but the plants should never be subjected to a high temperature, as the quality of bloom will be seriously affected. The bulbous iris require abundant water during the growing period, but the amount should be reduced when the buds begin to develop. Only the largest-size bulbs should be used for forcing. Bulbs which have been especially prepared for forcing may now be obtained and the variety Wedgewood may be brought into flower by Thanksgiving. This new method of preparing bulbs for early forcing was developed by Doctor David Griffiths of the U. S. Department of Agriculture and consists of subjecting the bulbs to a temperature of 80 degrees F. for three weeks after they are dug in July. From the middle of August to the 25th of September they are held at a temperature of 50 degrees F. and they are then ready for potting.

Larkspur, annual. Some of the new and greatly improved varieties of annual Larkspur are exceedingly lovely and they are well adapted for greenhouse culture. The plants will come into flower several months after sowing and it is possible to plan either for an early winter crop or for a later crop to follow on after the chrysanthemums have been removed from the benches.

Propagation: The annual larkspur is propagated by seed, and the young seedlings may be carried on in pots or in flats until bench space is available.

Soil Requirements: A light, fertile soil, neutral or slightly alkaline, is preferred.

Culture: A decidedly cool temperature, ranging around 50 degrees at night, is most favorable for the development of the annual larkspurs, and the plants are in no way exacting in regard to their soil requirements. The plants should be given ample room in which to develop, being spaced 8 x 10 inches apart. Coming in shades of lavender-blue, rose, white, and pink, the annual larkspurs offer a wealth of bloom, and the tall, stately flower spikes are exceedingly fine for cutting.

Lilies—Easter. There are several species of lilies which are used for forcing, the most popular being Lilium longiflorum giganteum, and Lilium longiflorum erabu.

Propagation: Bulbs are obtainable in three sizes, 5- to 7-inch bulbs, 7- to 9-inch, and 9- to 11-inch. Most commercial growers purchase the 7- to 9-inch size. The larger size, 9- to 11-inch, will give more flowers per stem, but in price they are considerably higher. Northern-grown bulbs will produce shorter plants with more blooms on a plant than Southern-grown bulbs, and they are usually preferred.

Soil Requirements: Easter lilies prefer a somewhat heavy, yet porous, soil with a pH. ranging between 6.0 and 7.0. A soil mixture of 4 parts silt loam, 1 part sand, and 1 part well-rotted, composted manure is recommended.

Culture: Approximately thirteen weeks are required from the time of planting to the time of bloom. The bulbs should be planted in 6-inch pots, being set at a depth of an inch or more, and they should be placed on a bench in a house where the temperature can be maintained between 54 and 56 degrees F. The potting soil should be fairly dry and very little water should be given until root growth has started, at which time the temperature of the house should be increased to 60 degrees F. It is desirable that the plants be watered with warm water of a temperature of approximately 70 degrees F. After active growth has started, and the plants have attained a height of 6 inches, bi-weekly applications of a liquid fertilizer may be given, 1 oz. of ammonium sulphate being dissolved in 2 gals. of water. The time of bloom may be slightly hastened or retarded by raising or lowering the temperature a few degrees.

Lupines, annual. The annual Lupines are well adapted to greenhouse culture.

VARIETIES OF MERIT

The most satisfactory varieties for cutting are Hartwegii; Azure Blue, with flowers of a delicate mist-like hue; and Sutton's Tall Pink, with flowers of a lovely soft shade of pink.

Propagation: The seeds may be sown in the bench where the plants are to flower or they may be sown in flats, being transplanted into small pots.

Soil Requirements: A moderately rich soil, well supplied with organic matter, will produce fine bloom. The soil should be neutral or slightly alkaline in its reaction.

Culture: The plant may be shifted into the benches as soon as space is available, being spaced 12 inches apart. A cool house with a night temperature of 50 to 55 degrees is preferred.

Mignonette (Reseda odorata). Although Mignonette is prized more for its fragrance than for the beauty of its bloom, some of the new and greatly improved forms are valuable for cutting and they are admirably adapted to greenhouse culture.

Propagation: Mignonette is readily propagated by seed. If bloom is desired throughout the winter months, three successive sowings should be made, one early in July, another early in August and the last early in September. The seeds should always be sown where they are to flower as the plants suffer such a check from transplanting and never fully recover. The procedure followed in most commercial greenhouses is to mark the bench area off into rows 6 by 8 inches apart. From 6 to 8 seeds are planted at the intersection of the rows, being covered very lightly. Watering should be done with a very fine spray. After the seeds have germinated and the small seedling plants have developed the third leaf, the three strongest plants should be left and the remaining plants should be thinned out. The young seedling plants should be shaded from intense sunlight during the middle portion of the day until they have become well established.

Soil Requirements: A medium, light, rather turfy loam is preferred. The usual practice is to place an inch of well-rotted stable manure on the bottom of the bench. The remaining portion of the bench is then filled with compost.

Culture: Mignonette prefers a very cool temperature. A night temperature ranging between 45 and 48 degrees and a day temperature between 55 and 65 degrees is considered ideal. Watering must be done with care. As the plants may be seriously injured by an over-abundance of moisture, watering should be done only on bright mornings. If water is allowed to remain on the foliage for any length of time, the leaves become spotted. When the flower spikes begin to form, all side shoots should be removed from around the top of the stem. Three or four vigorous shoots may be left at the base of the plant for later bloom. A top-dressing of one part sheep manure and two parts rich loam may be applied when the plants are ready to come into flower.

Narcissus. All the members of the Narcissus group may be easily forced into early spring bloom in the greenhouse.

VARIETIES OF MERIT

Among the most beautiful varieties for forcing are:

Trumpet Group
  King Alfred
  Van Waveren's Giant
  Tresserve
  Olympia
  Spring Glory

Incomparabilis Group
  Autocrat
  Bernardino
  Dorine
  Crœsus
  John Evelyn
  Will Scarlet
  Lucifer
  Sir Watkin

Barrii Group
  Firetail
  Mrs. Barclay
  Bath's Flame
  Seagull

Leedsii
  Evangeline
  Queen of the North
  White Lady

Poeticus
  Horace
  Glory of Lisse
  Actæa

Soil Requirements: The bulbs should be planted in a good general purpose soil mixture, of two parts loam, one part leaf mold and one part sand.

Culture: The planting should take place in the autumn, either in pots or in flats, and, with the exception of the Polyanthus group, they should be placed in storage for a minimum period of twelve weeks. A coldframe or outdoor pit will provide satisfactory conditions for storage and the pots or flats should be covered with several inches of sand or coal ashes. The pots may be brought in from storage in succession if desired, but if bulbs of the various Narcissus types are planted this will hardly be necessary as there will be considerable variance in the time of bloom and a succession of bloom will automatically be obtained. When the bulbs are first brought in from storage they should not be placed in full light for several days. If forced at a cool temperature, 50 to 55 degrees F. at night, the blooms will be of a superior quality and will last well as cut flowers.

Poinsettias are the most decorative of all plants for the Christmas season, and if conditions are favorable it is possible to have well-grown, specimen plants even in the small greenhouse.

Propagation: Poinsettias are propagated by cuttings taken from mature stock plants. After the flowering season is over, the stock plants are usually lifted and placed under a bench for a period of ten or twelve weeks. The temperature of the house should range between 50 and 60 degrees F. and the plants should be kept very dry—not dry enough, however, to allow the wood to shrivel. About the first of April the plants should be potted up or replanted in the bench, being pruned back heavily. They should be watered thoroughly and the stems should be syringed occasionally. A rich soil should be used for the stock plants consisting of 3 parts loam and 1 part rotted manure with a light application of superphosphate. The first cuttings may be taken early in July. They may be cut at a node or with a slight heel of old wood from the parent stem. As the plants bleed readily, the cuttings should be dropped into cold water for a few moments (not over five minutes). The cuttings should be trimmed so that only the two top leaves remain, and they should be rooted in a medium of moderately fine, sterilized sand, being shaded during the day. The cuttings should be well rooted and ready for potting in about three weeks. A mixture of 2 parts loam, 1 part sand and 1 part well-rotted manure is recommended.

Soil Requirements: Poinsettias thrive best in a soil of medium fertility with a slightly acid reaction, the pH. ranging between 6.0 and 7.0. For the final potting or benching soil, the following mixture is recommended: 2 parts silt loam, 1 part manure, 1 part sand. To each 2½ bushels of soil add a 4-inch flowerpotful of superphosphate and a 4-inch pot of horn shavings. Peat should not be used in any form, as it is detrimental to the best development of the plants.

Culture: The plants may be shifted into larger pots as they develop or they may be benched. If well branched, symmetrical plants are desired poinsettias may be pinched back until early September. The ideal temperature for poinsettias ranges between 60 and 65 degrees F. The temperature should never be allowed to drop below 60 degrees at night. The plants are extremely sensitive to drafts and are very easily injured by chilling or by overwatering. Under such conditions the leaves will turn yellow and drop.

Primroses (Primula) There are several species of Primula which are excellent when grown as potted plants in the greenhouse. They are very decorative when in flower and bloom over a long season. Among the most popular species for greenhouse culture are P. Forbesii, P. kewensis, P. malacoides, P. obconica and P. sinensis.

Propagation: Primroses are propagated by seed which should be sown in February or early March. Germination will be hastened if the seeds are soaked for a few hours previous to sowing. When the young seedlings have attained sufficient size they may be transplanted into flats or into small pots, a soil mixture of 3 parts good loam and 1 part well-rotted manure being used. As the plants develop they may be shifted into larger pots. As the plants have a tendency to wilt badly they should be shaded after each transplanting.

Soil Requirements: Primulas prefer a slightly acid soil with a pH. ranging between 6.0 and 7.0. The final potting mixture should consist of 3 parts good loam, 2 parts well-rotted manure and 1 part sand. To each 2½ bushels of soil a 4-inch pot of a 4–12–4 complete fertilizer should be added. No peat should be used in the potting mixture.

Culture: Primroses require an abundance of moisture, and the pots should never be allowed to dry out. During the summer the pots may be kept in a lightly shaded greenhouse or they may be placed on a bed of ashes in a coldframe under a lath shade. The plants prefer a moderately cool temperature during the winter—a temperature ranging between 50 and 60 degrees being considered ideal.

Roses. There are many varieties of roses which are admirably adapted to greenhouse culture and which will give abundant bloom throughout the winter months. Among the most popular varieties are:

Double White Killarney	Joanna Hill
Briarcliff	President Herbert Hoover
Talisman	Autumn
	Mrs. Paul M. Pierson

Propagation: Greenhouse roses may be propagated by budding, by cuttings or by grafting. Grafting is the most approved method and the one most commonly employed by commercial growers. As the propagation of roses is a highly specialized business it is advisable for the owner of a small greenhouse to purchase strong, healthy potgrown plants which are suitable for forcing.

Soil Requirements: Roses prefer a slightly acid soil with a pH. ranging between 6.0 and 7.0. A rich compost, consisting of 3 parts good loam and 1 part rotted manure will give excellent results.

Culture: A temperature ranging between 58 and 62 degrees F. at night and between 70 and 75 degrees in the daytime is considered ideal for roses. Roses may be grown either in raised benches or in solid beds. Good drainage is essential and beds or benches should be narrow, preferably not over 4 feet wide, as the best blooms are invariably produced on the outside plants. The plants may be set in their permanent position in the greenhouse between the middle of May and the first of July, being spaced from 12 to 14 inches apart. The plants should be set a little deeper than they were when growing in the pots. During this period when the plants are becoming established, they should be watered thoroughly, but at no time should the soil be allowed to become too saturated with moisture; the walks of the house should be kept damp and the foliage should be sprayed several times a day during sunny weather. The temperature should be kept as low as possible and the house should be well ventilated. No flower buds should be allowed to form until early in September. As the plants develop, wire may be stretched along the side of the benches and wire stakes may be placed beside the plants to provide support. During the growing season very shallow cultivation should be given, and at the time of flowering applications of a complete fertilizer, 4–12–4, may be given every three or four weeks, being applied at the rate of 1 pound to every 100 square feet of bench area. Greenhouse roses will usually continue to give good results over a period of three or four years, sometimes longer. Plants which are to be carried over in the benches should be given a period of rest during the summer. Beginning about the middle of June water should be withheld gradually. The plants should not be allowed to become too dry, however. During this period the plants should be pruned vigorously. Weak stems should be pruned more severely than strong ones. The plants should be cut back to within approximately 18 or 20 inches. A few inches of top-soil may be removed and the bed or bench may be refilled with rich compost.

Saintpaulia (African Violet). The Saintpaulia is a native of tropical Africa, and it is a delightfully decorative little plant with its thick, fuzzy leaves and its myriad flowers of a soft violet hue. If grown under favorable conditions, it will remain in flower for many months.

Exposure: Saintpaulias require comparatively little light, and they may be grown very successfully in a north window. The plants should be shaded from intense sunlight during the summer if they are placed out of doors.

Propagation: Usually propagated by means of leaf cuttings, although they may also be grown from seed. The leaf should be cut at the base (without the petiole) and should be inserted in the propagating case. The cuttings root most readily when the bottom temperature ranges between 65 and 70 degrees. The plants will usually root and will be ready for potting in from four to eight weeks. If there is danger of infestation of the cyclamen mite, the leaves should be soaked for five minutes in a solution of colloidal sulphur (3 teaspoonfuls to 1 gal. of water) before being inserted in the propagating case. The plants may be first potted up in 2¼-inch pots and as they develop they may be shifted on into 3-inch pots and later into 4- or 5-inch pots. It requires about 6 months from the time the cuttings are taken to produce a flowering plant.

Soil Requirements: After extensive investigations conducted by the Ohio Experiment Station, it has been found that a mixture of compost soil plus one-fourth leaf mold will give the best results. A small quantity of sand should be used in the first potting mixture but not in later mixtures.

Culture: Saintpaulias prefer a temperature which ranges between 68 and 70 degrees during the day and between 60 and 62 degrees at night. If the plants are grown in too cool a temperature they will develop an affliction known as epinasty, which causes the growth to curve downward. The watering of Saintpaulias is a matter of particular importance. They should be kept moist at all times but they should not be too thoroughly soaked, to the point of saturation. There is, on the whole, more danger from overwatering than from underwatering. The plants should preferably be watered by placing the pots in pans of water until the surface of the soil has become moist. This will avoid any danger of getting water on the leaves, which might cause rotting, due to their fuzzy, hairy surfaces.

Insect Pests: The most common insect pest is the cyclamen mite. Symptoms: plants are dwarfed in appearance; leaves are small and are either cupped upward or rolled downward; the foliage frequently has a dense, whitish pubescence on the upper surface. Flower buds are blighted, flowers are malformed. For measures of control, see page 804.

Stevia. The chief value of Stevia is as a filler-in for mixed bouquets. The small, white flowers are produced in abundance on long stems which are heavily clothed with deep green foliage.

Propagation: Stevia is propagated by stem cuttings taken from the stock plants in January. As soon as the cuttings have rooted they may be potted up in 2½-inch pots.

Soil Requirements: A good rich greenhouse compost will give excellent results. If a light application of superphosphate is made at the time that the plants are brought into the greenhouse the danger of oversucculent, soft-stemmed growth will be reduced.

Culture: As the plants develop, they may be shifted on into 4-inch pots and later into 7-inch pots, being grown in a cool temperature of 40 to 45 degrees F. As soon as all danger of frost is over, the pots may be set on a bed of cinders in a coldframe, or the plants may be transferred to nursery rows. During the summer the plants should be kept pinched back in order that they may become bushy and symmetrical. In the autumn, before the first frost, the plants should be brought into the greenhouse. They may be grown on in pots or they may be planted in beds or benches, being spaced 12 inches apart. Stevia prefers a cool house with a night temperature of approximately 50 degrees. The plants will normally come into flower shortly before the Christmas season. The flowering period may be hastened by shading the plants with black cloth for four hours a day for a period of thirty days, beginning September 1.

Stocks. The delicate fragrance of the Stocks adds greatly to their appeal as a cut flower, and they do extremely well under greenhouse conditions.

Varieties of Merit

Antique Copper—dusky mauve-rose
Beauty of Nice—soft salmon-pink
Giant Perfection—shades of white, ivory, pink, and lavender

Propagation: The seeds should be sown in flats in early August, the young seedlings being transplanted either directly into the benches where they are to flower, or carried on in pots or flats until bench space is available.

Soil Requirements: A light, porous and well-drained soil of good fertility is considered ideal.

Culture: When the young plants are shifted to the benches they should be spaced from 8 to 10 inches apart each way. The plants should be pinched back once in order to induce branching, and they will begin to flower late in the winter. The coolest possible temperature is to be desired, a night temperature of 48 to 50 degrees being considered ideal. Stocks are often used to follow on after the chrysanthemums have been removed from the benches.

Schizanthus (Butterflyflower). Seldom at its best in the garden under the heat of our summer sun, the lovely Schizanthus is one of those annuals admirably adapted to the greenhouse culture. Only indoors does it reach full perfection, and a well-grown pot of Schizanthus is a thing of exquisite beauty. The small, orchid-shaped flowers in tones of luminous pink, lavender, and white, are borne in great profusion and are lovely both for cutting and as potted plants.

Propagation: Seed may be sown in early September and the plants grown on in pots for early spring bloom.

Soil Requirements: A soil composed of 2 parts good, fibrous loam and 1 part well-rotted cow manure will give excellent results.

Culture: The plants may either be grown on in pots, or they may be benched when they have reached sufficient size, being spaced not less than 12 inches apart. They thrive best in a moderately cool temperature of 45 to 50 degrees F. at night. If the plants are allowed to become somewhat potbound, the blooming period will be hastened.

Sweet Peas (Lathyrus odoratus). So delightfully decorative are sweet peas for cut flower arrangements that they are an important crop in the small home greenhouse, even though little space can be allotted to them. Some of the new winter flowering types are exquisite both in form and in coloring, the flowers being borne on long, slender stems.

Varieties of Merit

Pink	*Lavender*
Ball Rose, Improved	Lavender King
Laddie	Orchid
Ophelia	Hawlmark Lavender
Pinkie	
Miss California	*White*
Mary Pickford	Hope
	Snowball
	White Harmony

Propagation: Sweet peas are propagated by seed. As the seeds have a hard outer covering, germination may be hastened by soaking them for 24 hours previous to sowing. The seeds may be sown directly in the beds or benches where they are to flower, or they may be sown in small pots or in flats, being later transplanted to their permanent position in the greenhouse. A light soil mixture should be used, consisting of equal parts of sand and loam. The time of flowering will depend to a considerable extent upon the date when the seed is sown. Seeds of the early or winter-flowering type, which is the type best suited for greenhouse culture, sown about the middle of July will flower from October through January. If sown September 1 the flowering period will extend from February to the middle of March, and if sown late in September the plants will flower in March, April and May. For early bloom it is, therefore, necessary to start the seeds in midsummer.

Soil Requirements: Sweet peas thrive best in a soil which is very nearly neutral in its reaction and which is of an open and porous texture. Good drainage is essential, as the plants are seriously injured by excessive amounts of water in the soil. A good, rich, fibrous compost is considered ideal. To this may be added a 0–10–10 commercial fertilizer, applied at the rate of 4 to 5 pounds per 100 square feet of soil area. An excess of nitrogen in the soil is detrimental to the best development of the plants.

Culture: Sweet peas prefer a cool growing temperature and from the time the young seedlings have begun growth they should be kept as cool as possible in order that they may develop good root systems. During the summer the greenhouse should be well ventilated, and adequate shade should be provided for the seedlings. Throughout the entire growing period low temperatures should be maintained. During the winter the night temperature of the greenhouse should not go above 50 degrees and day temperatures should not range over 55 to 60 degrees, with 65 degrees as a maximum high. Solid beds are preferred, rather than raised benches. The rows may be spaced from 3 to 4 feet apart, double drills being approximately 6 inches apart. The plants are allowed to remain thickly in the rows, being spaced hardly more than a few inches apart. As soon as the plants have become well established they should be provided with adequate support. Wire or stout twine on wire supports may be used. When the plants come into bloom all flowers should be kept picked. If seed pods are allowed to form, subsequent flowering will be seriously checked and the flowers will have a tendency to become short stemmed.

Tulips. Both as potted plants and as cut flowers, Tulips add their share to the galaxy of bloom in the greenhouse during the spring months, and a succession of bloom may be had over a period of many weeks.

VARIETIES OF MERIT

The early varieties force more readily than the Darwin and Breeder types, but under favorable cultural conditions most varieties may be forced with a fair degree of success. Some of the varieties best suited to forcing are:

Single Early
Cottage Maid
General de Wet
Golden Queen
La Reine
Rose Luisante
Le Rêve

Double Early
Murillo
Peach Blossom

Cottage Type
Inglescombe Pink
Moonlight
Dido
Griselde

Darwin Type
Anton Mauve
Faust
Kathryn Watson
Margaret
The Bishop
Venus
Clara Butt
William Copeland

Breeder Type
Cherbourg
Indian Chief
Bronze Queen

Species Tulip
Clusiana

Soil Requirements: A soil mixture consisting of 2 parts good loam, 1 part leaf mold and 1 part sand is recommended.

Culture: The bulbs should be planted in November, either in pots or in flats. Ample drainage should be provided and the tip of the bulb should be from 1 to 2 inches below the surface of the soil. It is absolutely essential that the bulbs be given adequate time for root formation, and they should be kept in storage for a period varying from twelve to fourteen weeks. They may be placed in a coldframe or in an outdoor pit. It is a wise plan to place a light layer of straw or excelsior over the pots or flats to afford protection for any shoots which may push through, and a 6-inch layer of ashes or sand may then be added. Early varieties may be brought in after twelve weeks of storage, late varieties at the end of fourteen weeks. If a succession of bloom is desired, the pots may be brought in at intervals of every 10 days. When first brought in from storage the pots should preferably be placed in a cool, semi-dark place, as it is wise not to expose them to direct sunlight for several days. Tulips should be forced at a comparatively low temperature, 55 to 60 degrees approximating the ideal. A high temperature is conducive to more rapid development, but the quality of the flowers is seriously affected. After the pots have been placed in full sunlight they should be turned every few days in order that the flowers and leaves may develop evenly.

Violets. Violets are admirably suited to the cool greenhouse and if the plants are grown under favorable conditions they will give an abundance of bloom during the winter months.

Propagation: The method of propagation usually preferred by commercial growers is that of cuttings taken from healthy terminal shoots between the middle of January and the middle of March. Violets may also be propagated by the division of the parent plant after the flowering season is over and by root cuttings taken during February and March. After the young plants are well established they may be planted in flats. During the summer the plants may be kept in coldframes or they may be planted in the open ground. Some growers prefer to transplant the young plants into their permanent position in May. If this practice is followed adequate ventilation must be given and the house must be heavily shaded during the summer.

Soil Requirements: Violets prefer a rather heavy, sandy loam soil, well drained, yet retentive of moisture. A good, moderately rich compost is considered ideal.

Culture: Violets may be grown either in solid beds or in raised benches. Most growers prefer solid beds as it is easier to maintain a cool, moist soil. Cool growing conditions are one of the essentials for success. Single-flowering varieties prefer a night temperature of 45 to 50 degrees and a day temperature ranging between 60 and 65 degrees. Double-flowering varieties prefer a temperature of about 5 degrees lower. High temperatures are conducive to an excessive amount of vegetative growth which is produced at the expense of flowers. The plants require an abundance of moisture and an adequate supply of fresh air.

Wallflowers (Cheiranthus Cheiri). The English Wallflowers are prized for their delightful fragrance and for their quaintly decorative quality. They are of comparatively easy culture and they are admirably adapted to the cool greenhouse.

Propagation: Wallflowers are propagated by seed. For bloom during the winter months the seeds should be sown the previous March.

The young seedlings may be pricked out into small pots or into flats as soon as they have made sufficient growth.

Soil Requirements: A good, rich compost will give excellent results.

Culture: During the summer months the young plants may be carried on in pots or they may be planted in nursery beds in the open ground. Wallflowers require a very cool growing temperature. The night temperature should range between 45 and 50 degrees and the day temperature but a few degrees higher. Throughout their growing period, the plants require a liberal amount of water. Wallflowers may be grown in pots, in raised benches, or in solid beds, the plants being spaced approximately 12 inches apart.

Plants Which May Be Grown in Pots for Decoration in the House

Abutilon hybridum
Acacia armata
    Drummondii
Ardisia crenulata
Agathæa cœlestis
Astilbe japonica
Azalea—in great variety
Begonia—in great variety
Bougainvillea glabra
Browallia var. speciosa major
Calceolaria hybrida
    integrifolia
Camellia japonica
Chorizema ilicifolium
Chrysanthemum
Cineraria cruenta
Cyclamen
Cytisus canariensis (Genista)
    racemosus
Dicentra spectabilis
Euphorbia fulgens (jacquiniæflora)
Fuchsia hybrida
Gardenia Veitchii
Geranium
Gloxinia
Kalanchoë

Plants Grown in Pots for Decoration in the House—*Continued*

Lantana Camara
Poinsettia
Primula—in variety
Saintpaulia ionantha
Solanum (Jerusalem Cherry)
Strelitzia reginæ (Bird of Paradise Flower)
Streptosolen Jamesonii
Zygocactus truncatus (Christmas Cactus)

Plants To Be Grown for Cut Flowers

Antirrhinum
Bouvardia
Boston Yellow Daisy
Buddleia
Calendula
Carnation
Clarkia
Chrysanthemum
Cynoglossum amabile
Didiscus cœruleus
   (Bluelace Flower)
Gerbera Jamesonii
Heliophila
Larkspur

Lupine
Mignonette
Myosotis
Nemesia
Orchid
Rose
Salpiglossis
Scabiosa
Schizanthus
Stevia
Stock
Ursinia
Violet
Wallflower

Bulbs, Corms, and Tubers Suitable for Forcing

Achimenes—various species and hybrids
Amaryllis—Hippeastrum vittatum hybrids
Anemone coronaria
Calochortus (Globe Tulip)
Calla
Convallaria majalis (Lily-of-the-Valley)
Freesia
Gladiolus
Hyacinth
Iris (Bulbous)
Ixia—various species
Lilium auratum
   Batemanniæ
   candidum

BULBS, CORMS AND TUBERS SUITABLE FOR FORCING—*Continued*

Lilium elegans
    Krameri
    longiflorum—in variety
    phillipinense
    regale
    speciosum album
    speciosum rubrum
    tenuifolium
    tigrinum
Narcissus—all species and varieties
Ornithogalum lacteum
Ranunculus acris
Tulip—in great variety

CUT BRANCHES OF SHRUBS WHICH MAY BE FORCED

Flowering Dogwood (Cornus florida)
Flowering Quince (Chænomeles japonica)
Forsythia—in great variety
Star Magnolia (Magnolia stellata)
Flowering Crabs—all species and varieties
Flowering Cherries—all species and varieties
Thunberg Spirea (Spiræa Thunbergii)
Viburnums—in great variety

SHRUBS WHICH MAY BE FORCED IN POTS OR TUBS

Astilbe japonica
Azaleas—in great variety
Chænomeles japonica (Japanese Quince)
Clethra alnifolia (Sweet Pepperbush)
Daphne cneorum (Garland Flower)
Deutzia—in great variety
Philadelphus Lemoinei (Lemoine's Mock Orange)
Pieris floribunda (Lily-of-the-Valley Shrub)
Prunus tomentosa (Nankin Cherry)
Rhododendron—in variety
Spiræa prunifolia (Bridalwreath Spirea)
Spiræa Thunbergii (Thunberg Spirea)
Syringa—in variety (Lilac)

VINES FOR THE GREENHOUSE

Allamanda Hendersonii
Antigonon leptopus (Coral-vine)
Asparagus plumosus
Asparagus Sprengeri
Clerodendrum Thompsonæ
Ficus repens (Climbing Fig)
Ficus repens, variety minimus
Hedera helix (English Ivy) in great variety
Jasminum grandiflorum
Passiflora (Passion Flower)
Philodendron cordata
    micens
    pertusum
Senecio mikanioides (German Ivy)
Stigmaphyllon ciliatum
Tradescantia fluminensis (Wandering Jew)
Vinca major

PALMS FOR DECORATIVE PURPOSES

Areca lutescens
Cocos Weddelliana
Kentia Belmoreana
Kentia Forsteriana

Latania borbonica
Livistona rotundifoli?
Phœnix rupicola

FERNS FOR DECORATIVE PURPOSES

Adiantum cuneatum (Maidenhair fern)
    farleyense
Asplenium Nidus (Bird's-Nest fern)
Cyrtomium falcatum
Nephrolepis exaltata (Sword fern)
Pteris cretica

FOLIAGE PLANTS

Araucaria excelsa (Norfolk-Island Pine)
Ardisia
Aspidistra lurida
Caladium bicolor (Fancy-leaved Caladium)
Codlæum variegatum (Croton)
Dieffenbachia Seguine (Dumb-Cane)
Dracæna
Ficus elastica (Rubber Plant)

FOLIAGE PLANTS—*Continued*

Fittonia argyroneura
  Verschaffeltii
Grevillea robusta (Silk Oak)
Pandanus utilis
  Veitchii
Peperomia cordata
  Verschaffeltii
Sansevieria (Bowstring-Hemp, Snake Plant)

PLANTS FOR THE INTERMEDIATE OR WARM GREENHOUSE

For Cut Flowers

Begonia (some varieties)
Cattleya
Cypripedium
Gardenia
Gloxinia

Easter Lily
Lily-of-the-Valley
Poinsettia
Rose

Potted Plants

Azalea—in variety
Bougainvillea
Clerodendrum
Fuchsia

Hydrangea
Kalanchoë
Lantana
Poinsettia

Foliage Plants and Vines

Asparagus plumosus
  Sprengeri
Ficus repens (vine)
Philodendron
Palms—in variety

Ferns—in variety
Aspidistra
Ficus, in variety
Pandanus

Bulbs

Hyacinth

Tulip

PLANTS FOR THE COOL GREENHOUSE

For Cut Flowers

Antirrhinum
Bouvardia
Calendula
Carnation
Centaurea
Chrysanthemum
Clarkia

Cynoglossum
Didiscus
Dimorphotheca
Erlangea
Eupatorium
Euphorbia
Feverfew

Plants for the Cool Greenhouse
For Cut Flowers—Continued

Gerbera
Gypsophila
Larkspur
Lupine
Mignonette
Myosotis
Nemesia
Salpiglossis
Scabiosa

Schizanthus
Statice
Stevia
Stock
Streptosolen
Sweet Pea
Violet
Wallflower

Potted Plants

Acacia
Agathæa
Ardisia
Astilbe japonica
Azalea
Begonia
Browallia
Calceolaria
Camellia japonica
Chorizema ilicifolium

Cineraria cruenta
Cyclamen
Cytisus
Hydrangea
Kalanchoë
Primula
Solanum
Strelitzia
Zygocactus

Foliage Plants and Vines

Asparagus plumosus
  Sprengeri
Cissus rhombifolia
Ficus repens (vine)
Hedera helix
Philodendron
Senecio mikanioides
Vinca major

Palms—in variety
Araucaria
Aspidistra
Dracæna
Ficus, in variety
Grevillea robusta
Pandanus
Peperomia

Bulbs

Anemone coronaria
Calochortus
Calla
Freesia
Gladiolus
Hyacinth
Iris (bulbous)

Ixia
Lilium longiflorum
  speciosum
  candidum
Narcissus
Ranunculus acris
Tulip

XXIV

House Plants and the Window Garden

THE WINDOW GARDEN

In order to attain success with house plants, and to provide a delightful succession of bloom in the window garden throughout the winter months, it is necessary to make plans well in advance, and to have a general knowledge of the cultural requirements of the many bulbs and plants which may be grown indoors. With a little forethought and careful planning, it is surprising how much may be accomplished, and much of the beauty of the garden as we know it in midsummer may be had indoors during the winter months.

Through October and November, the window ledges may be kept gay with potted chrysanthemums and with annuals, brought in from the garden. During the winter there are many plants which may be selected for their decorative value, and by February and March one may have a veritable spring garden indoors. Narcissus, tulips, bleedingheart, mertensia, and many other lovely flowering things may be used in gay profusion.

ANNUALS FOR BLOOM INDOORS

Among the annuals there are several which, if taken up in the autumn and brought indoors, will give generous bloom for several months. Ageratum, browallia, nicotiana, phlox Drummondii, petunias, and torenias are among the most satisfactory. In most cases the period of bloom may be considerably prolonged if some of the little self-sown seedlings are also brought

794

The Window Garden

in, as these will come into flower just as the older plants are beginning to grow shabby. If self-sown seedlings are not available a special sowing may be made early in August and the young plants may be grown on in pots.

POTTING

House plants should be repotted only when they will derive very definite benefit, and it has been found that plants vary greatly in their needs for frequent potting. Most flowering plants will, like the geraniums, give better bloom if they are allowed to become somewhat pot-bound. Such plants as amaryllis, the various palms, and pandanus will also thrive well in very small pots and seem to suffer no ill effects from becoming extremely pot-bound. Many house plants may be grown in comparatively small pots if sufficient nutrients are provided in the form of occasional applications of a complete fertilizer (see page 802 on Feeding).

Young plants, grown either from seed or from cuttings, must be shifted on at frequent intervals from small pots to slightly larger pots. The general practice is to repot such plants as soon as the pots which they occupy have become well filled with roots. Unless this is done, the plants may become stunted, and will be unable to make normal and vigorous growth. A pot from ½ inch to 1 inch larger in size is usually sufficient for the next stage of growth.

When plants are grown in pots it is essential that ample drainage be provided. In small pots a piece of broken crock placed over the hole in the bottom of the pot will usually be sufficient. When large pots are used, and particularly if the plant is to remain in the pot for some time, it is wise to place a layer of broken crock in the bottom, and above the crock a thin layer of sphagnum moss in order to prevent the soil from sifting down and clogging the drainage area.

In potting young seedlings or rooted cuttings the pot may be partially filled with soil. The plant should then be held in place with the roots spread out in a natural position. The remaining soil should be added, and it should be pressed firmly into place with the fingers. In small pots a space of approximately ½-inch should be left between the surface of the soil and the rim of the pot. In potting rooted cuttings a soil mixture consisting of 2 parts sharp sand, 1 part loam, and 1 part leaf mold or peat is recommended. For young seedlings in the early transplanting stages, a mixture of 1 part sand, 1 part loam and 1 part leaf mold or peat moss will give excellent results. The pots should be watered thoroughly and should be shaded from direct sunlight for several days in order that the plants may have an opportunity to become re-established.

In repotting an established plant, the plant may be removed by inverting the pot and tapping the rim on the edge of a firm surface, such as the edge of a potting bench or a work table. The soil in the pot should be fairly moist so that it does not crumble, and while the pot is held in an inverted position the fingers of one hand should be held firmly over the ball of earth. A small quantity of soil should be placed above the drainage material and the plant should be placed in the center of the pot. If the pot is only slightly larger than that previously occupied by the plant it will be necessary to remove some soil from the bottom and sides of the ball of earth surrounding the roots. This should be done with care in order to keep the root system as nearly intact as possible. The space between the old ball of earth and the side of the pot should be filled with the new potting soil, which should be firmed into place with the fingers or with a small potting stick.

POTTING MIXTURES

An excellent general-purpose potting mixture consists of 1 part sand; 2 parts fibrous loam; 1 part humus in the form of compost, leaf mold or peat; ½ part of well-rotted cow manure; to which mixture has been added a 5-inch pot of bone meal per bushel of soil.

Certain groups of plants have very definite soil preferences. The azaleas and all the members of the Heath family prefer an acid soil, and the following potting mixture is recommended: 2 parts sand, 2 parts loam, 2 parts acid peat, 1 part leaf mold, and ⅓ of a part of cow manure.

The succulents, on the other hand, prefer a highly alkaline soil and the following mixture will give excellent results: 2 parts sand, 2 parts loam, ½ part leaf mold—to which mixture there has been added, per bushel of soil, one 5-inch pot of bone meal, and one 5-inch pot of finely ground limestone. The mixture may be further improved by adding a small quantity of finely chipped brick particles or broken crock.

Ferns and begonias thrive best in a soil well supplied with humus, such as a mixture of 2 parts sand, 2 parts loam, 2 parts leaf mold or some other form of humus, and ½ part rotted cow manure.

Further details concerning potting mixtures for individual plant groups may be found under the specific cultural requirements of greenhouse plants.

LIGHT

Light is absolutely essential to the growth of all plants which contain chlorophyll or green coloring matter. The leaves serve as a manufacturing center for plant foods, and this process is carried on under the direct influence of light. If the leaves are entirely deprived of light, they are unable to perform the function of food manufacture, and they gradually turn yellow and die. Plants vary tremendously in the amount of light which they require for their best development. Many of the ferns, which in their native habitat grow in dense woodland shade, require comparatively little light, and there are many house plants, such as the aspidistras and sansevierias, which will thrive well with a minimum of direct light. On the other hand, geraniums, heliotrope, and the majority of our flowering plants require full sunlight for at least a portion of the day. A window with a southern or southeastern exposure will provide most satisfactory conditions for such plants, while ferns, most foliage plants, and some of the begonias may be grown very successfully in a northern window. When house plants are left in one position for any length of time, the leaves and stems will turn towards the light, and the growth of the plant will become very unsymmetrical. In order to avoid this tendency the pots should be turned at occasional intervals so that all portions of the plant may receive an equal amount of light. The growth will then remain symmetrical and well balanced.

Recent experiments have proved that some house plants may be grown very successfully under artificial light, and electric lamps have been devised with carefully constructed brackets to be used for holding potted plants. This makes possible the growing of plants in city offices, in dimly lighted hallways, and in other situations where no direct light is available.

House Plants Which Prefer Full Sunlight

Astilbe japonica
Azalea
Beloperone (Shrimp Plant)
Cactus
Calceolaria
Crassula
Genista (Broom)
Heliotrope
Cineraria
Clivia
Euphorbia (Crown of Thorns)
Kalanchoë
Gardenia
Geranium
Jerusalem Cherry
Impatiens or Balsam
Lantana
Poinsettia
Bulbs of all varieties

House Plants Requiring Partial Sunlight: Two to Three Hours Per Day

Abutilon (Flowering Maple)
Anthericum (Spider Plant)
Anthurium (Flamingo Flower)
Ardisia crenulata (Coral Ardisia)
Asparagus plumosus (Asparagus Fern)
Asparagus Sprengeri
Begonia (in great variety)
Coleus Blumei (Coleus)
Cyclamen
Dracæna
Fuchsia
Peperomia maculosa
Peperomia arifolia
Pothos aureus

Primula malacoides
Primula obconica
Primula sinensis
Many bulbs will also thrive well in partial sunlight.

House Plants Which May Be Grown in North Windows without Sun, or in Partial Sunlight

Aglaonema modestum (Chinese Evergreen)
Araucaria excelsa (Norfolk-Island Pine)
Aspidistra lurida (Iron Plant)
Begonia Rex (Rex Begonia)
Billbergia perringiana (Living-vase Plant)
Crassula arborescens (Chinese Rubber Plant)
Cryptanthus acaulis (Pineapple Plant)
Dieffenbachia Seguine (Dumb-Cane)
Fittonia Verschaffeltii (Fittonia)
Ivies (in great variety)
Monstera deliciosa (Swiss Cheese Plant)
Pandanus Veitchii (Ribbon Plant)
Philodendron cordatum
Saintpaulia (African-violet)
Sansevieria zeylanica (Snake Plant)
Sempervivum Haworthii (Hen and Chickens)
Sedum Adolphi
Sedum dendroideum
Sedum treleasi
Tradescantia (Wandering Jew)
Vitis rhombifolia (Grape Ivy)

HOUSE PLANTS WHICH MAY BE GROWN UNDER ELECTRIC LIGHTS

Begonia	Hyacinth
Coleus	Peperomia
Cyclamen	Philodendron
Fern (Boston and Pteris)	Sansevieria (Snake Plant)
Geranium	Saintpaulia (African Violet)

TEMPERATURE

Most house plants thrive reasonably well in a temperature which ranges between 62 and 70 degrees during the day and which does not drop below 55 degrees at night. Every plant has a definite range of temperature which is desirable for its maximum development, and some plants are able to withstand greater fluctuations of temperature than are others. On very severe nights when there is danger of freezing, a heavy layer of newspaper placed between the plants and the windows will afford excellent protection.

VENTILATION

House plants require an ample supply of fresh air, but every effort must be made to protect them from direct drafts and from being suddenly chilled. Ventilating should, therefore, be done in such a way that they are protected from direct currents of cold air. Either muslin or metal slat ventilators are very satisfactory for use in rooms where house plants are grown, as they provide for an excellent circulation of fresh air without causing a draft. It is wise to plan definitely to provide a change of air at least twice a day in a room where plants are grown. In mild weather the doors or windows of the room may be opened. In severe weather it may be advisable to open the windows in an adjoining room. Ventilation has a very direct influence in mitigating the effect of coal gas and illuminating gas. Some plants, such as the Jerusalem cherry, are extremely sensitive to escaping gas, and even a very minute quantity of gas in the atmosphere, a quantity so minute that it can hardly be detected, will have a very damaging effect, causing a black-.

ening of the buds and a discoloration of the leaves. In the fruiting stage, the fruits will drop prematurely.

HUMIDITY

Closely associated with the problems of ventilation and watering is the problem of humidity. A moist atmosphere is essential to the health, vigor, and well-being of most house plants. There are comparatively few plants which will thrive, or even survive, in the dry, almost desert-like atmosphere of the modern dwelling. It is impossible, therefore, to expect satisfactory growth unless every effort is made to increase the humidity of the atmosphere, and this may be accomplished in several very simple ways. Some of the newer heating systems are equipped with humidifying devices, and special water-holding compartments are attached to some of the more modern types of radiators. If such devices are not already part of the heating system, water pans may be purchased and attached to the radiators. Another excellent method of increasing the humidity is to set the plants on metal trays which have been filled with pebbles and water. The bottom of the pots should rest on dry pebbles which are slightly above the level of the water. This same method may be used with flowerpot saucers, care being taken to make sure that the water does not reach the bottom of the pot, which would cause the soil to be too constantly saturated. A daily syringing of the foliage with a fine spray of clear water will not only greatly increase the humidity but will also help to keep the foliage clean and in healthy condition, as it keeps the stomata or breathing pores open. It is also of benefit in helping to keep insect pests in check. Plants with hairy leaves, such as gloxinias and saintpaulias, should not be syringed, as the effect of moisture upon the leaves is often more harmful than beneficial. A small rubber bulb syringe such as may be procured at any hardware store is excellent for a small number of plants. A glass jar fitted with a small spray attachment is also very satisfactory. It is possible, also, to use a larger type of sprayer, provided that it will throw a fine, mist-like spray. If an adjustable nozzle is used it will be possible to reach the undersurface of the leaves.

WATERING

The watering of house plants is a task which requires good judgment. It is quite as important not to overwater as it is to avoid underwatering. Not only do different species of plants vary tremendously in their moisture requirements, but individual plants also vary considerably according to the stage of growth. When plants are making active growth, forming new shoots and flower buds, they require much more moisture than they do when they are in the resting, non-flowering stage. Although daily watering is not necessary for all house plants it is wise to make a daily survey in order to ascertain their needs. When the surface of the soil in the pot is dry to the point of being crumbly to the touch, or if the pot gives a hollow, ringing sound when it is tapped lightly with the knuckle, the indications are that the plant needs water. Watering should be done in such a way that the entire ball of earth within the pot is thoroughly saturated, and any surplus water should then be allowed to drain off. If water is applied to the surface of the soil by means of a watering can, the surplus water will drain out through the opening in the bottom of the pot. If watering is done by placing the pot in a pan of water it should be allowed to remain in the receptacle until the surface of the soil becomes dark and moist in appearance. It should then be removed and the surplus water should be allowed to drain away. This method of watering is excellent for all potted plants and it is especially recommended for those plants which have dense, fuzzy leaves such as the African violet (Saintpaulia) and gloxinia. Pots should never be allowed to stand in saucers which are filled with water, as the soil in the bottom of the pot will soon become soggy and sour and the growth and vigor of the plant will be seriously affected. It is wise to avoid the use of very cold water. Water which is approximately the same temperature as the room is best.

FEEDING

Many house plants will be benefited by an occasional feeding. Applications of fertilizer should be made when the plants are making active, vigorous growth, preferably after the flower buds have formed but before the flowers have begun to show color. At this period of growth, a light application of fertilizer may be made at intervals of every two weeks. No application should be made when the plants are in a resting stage and are making no new growth. A very satisfactory liquid fertilizer may be made by dissolving 2 ounces of ammonium sulphate in 1 gallon of water. This should be applied to the plant when the soil is reasonably moist.

CULTURE

For the detailed culture of the following plants and bulbs which may be grown successfully in the house, see Chapter XXIII on "The Small Greenhouse."

Azalea	Lily (Easter)
Begonia	Narcissus
Bleedingheart	Poinsettia
Calla	Primrose
Cyclamen	Schizanthus
Euphorbia fulgens	Tulip
Freesia	Wallflower
Geranium	
Gladiolus (particularly the dwarf species)	

INSECTS ON HOUSE PLANTS

Aphis are often very troublesome on house plants. There are various species, some living only on one type of plant while others thrive on many kinds. They are small lice-like insects and they may be either green, black, or brown in color. They are found usually on the tips of the young, growing shoots, both on the leaves, and clustered closely along the stem. Being equipped with delicate, tuber-like mouth-parts they are able to pierce through the outer tissues and suck the juices from the plant, causing a general lack of vigor and stunted growth. All species may be readily controlled by a good contact poison, a poison which will come into direct contact with each insect, causing death by stopping up the breathing pores. Black-leaf 40, which may be purchased from any seed or supply store, is one of the best remedies, being used in a solution of one-fourth teaspoonful to one quart of soapy water. Volck is a commercial preparation which is also excellent for this purpose, being used in the proportion of five level teaspoonfuls to one quart of water. The infested plants may either be sprayed with a small hand sprayer or with a syringe, or they may be dipped for a few moments into a vessel containing the preparation. When the plants are to be dipped special care should be taken to see that the chemicals are thoroughly mixed with the water in order to avoid any danger of burning.

Cyclamen-mites, as the name would imply, are usually found on cyclamen plants but they also attack geraniums, fuchsias, chrysanthemums, and a number of other plants. They are minute little creatures, hardly visible to the naked eye, but if they are present in sufficient numbers they are capable of doing considerable damage. The injury caused by cyclamen-mites is very characteristic. When a plant is attacked, the leaves begin to curl from the outside, taking on a curiously deformed appearance, and if the infestation is severe the plant loses its foliage entirely. The flower buds wither before they open or become badly distorted and drop prematurely. The most satisfactory measure of control is to use a good nicotine spray, one teaspoonful of Black-leaf 40 to one gallon of soapy water. When trouble from cyclamen-mites is noticed the plants should be sprayed or dipped once a week for at least a month.

Mealy-bugs belong to the great group of scale insects and are very often found on plants which have been purchased from a greenhouse or a florist. They are not only very unsightly but they sap the vitality of the plants and every effort should be made to keep them under control. Although found on many kinds of plants they seem to have a particular fondness for abutilon, coleus, and umbrella palms. They may be easily distinguished from other insects by their white waxy covering. At the time the females are ready to deposit their eggs, this covering increases until it resembles a little tuft of cotton. Mealy-bugs are more difficult to control than many other insects. If they are present in only small quantities the leaves of the plant may

be wiped with a soft cloth which has been dipped into dena-
tured alcohol. It is necessary that the body of each individual
insect should be touched with the alcohol. Lemon oil is the
only spray material which has given really satisfactory results.
It is a commercial preparation containing vegetable oil, soap,
and various chemicals. The oil should be mixed with warm
water, and it may be applied as a spray or it may be used as a
dipping solution. As it does not kill the mealy-bugs in the egg
stage it will probably be necessary to repeat the treatment several times during the season. When plants have delicate foliage
the lemon oil should be washed off three or four hours after
the application has been given. In addition to controlling the
mealy-bugs, lemon oil has a very beneficial effect upon the foliage, as it removes all dirt and leaves the plant with a clean,
glossy appearance.

Red Spiders are very minute mites which cause considerable
trouble if they become sufficiently numerous. They collect on
the undersurface of the leaves and suck the juices from the
plant, causing the foliage to become whitish and unhealthy in
appearance. A simple and very effective means of control is to
spray the plant with a strong force of clear water, luke-warm
in temperature. This may be done with a syringe, or the plant
may be held directly under the water faucet. Care should be
taken to see that the water reaches the under-side of all the
leaves.

Scales. House plants are attacked by various forms of scale,
ferns, palms, rubber plants and orange plants being particularly
susceptible. Some scales have soft bodies while others have hard,
shell-like coverings, but they may all be controlled by contact
sprays. Whale-oil soap solution is excellent and lemon oil can
always be depended upon to give satisfactory results. Black-leaf
40 may also be used. In cases where palms or rubber plants are
only slightly infested it is possible to scrub the leaves with a
soft toothbrush, using one of the above solutions. It is more
difficult, however, to destroy scales on ferns and other delicate
plants, and the most satisfactory method is to dip the plant in
a nicotine solution consisting of ½ tablespoonful of Black-leaf
40, 1 tablespoonful of laundry soap and 1 gallon of water. The

soap should be dissolved first in a small amount of hot water and the balance of the ingredients added. After dipping, the plants should be allowed to stand for several hours, and the foliage should then be rinsed or sprayed with clear, lukewarm water.

White-flies seem to have a special fondness for fuchsias, heliotrope, lantana, and geraniums and in some seasons they become very troublesome. They are found usually on the tender new shoots, and as they suck the juices from the plants they cause stunted growth. They are small, whitish flies. Although they are provided with wings they usually settle on the under-side of the leaves and seldom fly unless disturbed by a jolt of some nature. Lemon oil has proved the most satisfactory remedy, although nicotine solution will give fairly satisfactory results if some form of fish oil soap is added. The plants may be either dipped or sprayed, and a few hours later they should be rinsed off with clear water.

VINES SUITABLE FOR THE HOUSE

Common Name	Scientific Name	Remarks
Asparagus Fern	Asparagus plumosus	Perennial. Requires rich soil.
	Asparagus Sprengeri	
Balloon Vine	Cardiospermum Halicacabum	Annual. Sow seeds in pots in May. Do not transplant.
Climbing Fig	Ficus repens	Perennial. Valued for its fine evergreen foliage.
Cup and Saucer Vine	Cobæa scandens	Annual. Sow seeds in pots in March. Place each seed edgewise.
English Ivy	Hedera helix	Perennial. Many varietal forms are obtainable. Prefers a northern exposure.
German Ivy or Parlor I.	Senecio mikanioides	Perennial. Endures difficult conditions well. Grows rapidly.

Common Name	Scientific Name	Remarks
Glory Lily	Gloriosa superba	Perennial. Plant tubers singly in pots in Feb. Require staking. Requires a period of rest after bloom.
Hyacinth Bean	Dolichos Lablab	Annual. Sow seeds in pots in March. Flowers white or purple.
Kenilworth Ivy	Cymbalaria muralis	Perennial. Of trailing habit. Leaves small, light green.
Morning Glory	Ipomœa	Annual. Many lovely varieties. Sow seeds in pots. Before sowing, soak the seeds for two hours in warm water, or notch them. Requires full sun.
Nasturtium	Tropæolum majus	Annual. Sow seeds in pots. Requires full sun and abundant moisture.
Potato Vine	Solanum jasminoides	Annual. Requires staking. Star-shaped, white flowers. Rich soil.
Rosary Pea	Abrus precatorius	Perennial. Requires a warm temperature of 70°. Decorative seed pods.
Star Jasmine	Trachelospermum jasminoides	Perennial. Fragrant, starry, white flowers.
Wax Plant	Hoya carnosa	Perennial. Slow-growing. Evergreen, thick, leathery leaves. Waxy, cream-colored flowers.

FLOWERING PLANTS FOR THE HOUSE

Name	Color	Time of Bloom
African Violet (Saintpaulia)	Lavender	Intermittently
Agathæa cœlestis	Lavender-blue	Throughout the winter months
Azalea (in variety)	Pink, white, cerise	Late winter and early spring
Bauera rubioides	Pink, white	Winter and early spring
Begonia (in great variety)	White, pink, red	Winter and spring
Billbergia nutans	Greenish scarlet bracts	Spring
Bleedingheart (Dicentra spectabilis)	Rose-pink	March, April
Calceolaria	Yellow, spotted brown	Late fall and winter
Chorizema cordatum	Scarlet and purple	Early spring
Chrysanthemums	White, yellow, pink, bronze and russet	Autumn
Cineraria	Blue, lavender, scarlet, cerise	Winter
Coral Ardisia	Reddish	Early summer
Flamingo Flower (Anthurium)	Scarlet, rose, white	Late winter, early spring
Flowering Maple (Abutilon hybridum)	Red, purple, yellow, white	Almost continually
Fuchsia	Red to purple	April to October
Gardenia	White	Winter
Genista	Yellow	March and April
Geranium	White, pink, red, cerise	Autumn to spring
Impatiens Holstii	Bright scarlet	Summer and fall
Japanese Daphne (D. odora)	Rose-purple	March
Lantana	Yellow, orange, red, lavender	Winter and spring

FLOWERING PLANTS FOR THE HOUSE—*Continued*

Name	Color	Time of Bloom
Marica		
Northiana	Violet-tipped	Winter
gracilis	Blue with cream	Winter
cærulea	Blue	Winter
Nicotiana	White, crimson	Winter and spring
Poinsettia	Scarlet bracts	Early winter
Primrose (Primula)		
malacoides	Lilac to pink	Winter
obconica	Lilac to pink	Winter
sinensis	White, pink, rose	Winter
kewensis	Yellow	Winter
Shrimp Plant (Belo-perone)	Purple, spotted white	Late spring
Spiræa (Astilbe japonica)	White, pink	March-April
Stevia	White	Late fall and winter

FOLIAGE PLANTS FOR THE HOUSE

Aspidistra elatior (Cast Iron Plant)
Chinese Evergreen (Aglaonema modestum)
Croton
Dracæna
Dumb-Cane (Dieffenbachia Seguine)
Ferns (in variety)
Norfolk Island Pine (Araucaria excelsa)
Palms (in variety)
Peperomia
Rubber Plant
Screw Pine (Pandanus)
    P. Veitchii
    P. utilis
Silk Oak (Grevillea robusta)
Snake Plant or Bowstring Hemp (Sansevieria)
Threadleaf (Aralia)

HOUSE PLANTS WITH DECORATIVE FRUITS

Jerusalem Cherry (Solanum Pseudo-Capsicum)	Brilliant red berries in early winter
Ornamental Pepper	Attractive bright red fruits resembling miniature peppers
Otaheite Orange (Citrus taitensis)	Branches studded with small orange fruits 1½ inches long.
Skimmia japonica	Berrylike red fruits

BULBS, TUBERS AND CORMS WHICH MAY BE FORCED FOR BLOOM INDOORS

Amaryllis
Amazon Lily
Anemone (St. Brigid)
Babiana
Calla Lily
Calochortus (Butterfly Tulips)
Chionodoxa (Glory-of-the-Snow)
Chlidanthus
Crocus
Fairy Lily (Zephyranthes)
Freesia

Gladiolus (Dwarf varieties)
Bulbous Iris
Hyacinths
Lily-of-the-Valley
Moræa
Muscari (Grape Hyacinth)
Narcissus—all varieties
Ornithogalum
Scilla
Tulip

CACTI SUITABLE FOR HOUSE PLANTS

Bishop's Cap (Astrophytum myriostigma)
Barrel Cacti (in great variety)
Hedge Hog Cacti (Echinopsis), many species
Pincushion Cacti (Neomammillaria), many species
Star Cactus (Astrophytum ornatum)
Strawberry Cactus (Hamatocactus setispinus)
Turk's Cap Cactus (Melocactus)

FERNS SUITABLE FOR HOUSE PLANTS

Bird's-nest Fern (Asplenium nidus)
Boston Fern (Nephrolepis exaltata bostoniensis)
Crested Ferns (Pteris)
    P. cretica
    P. serrulata
Holly Fern (Cyrtomium falcatum)
Maidenhair Fern
    the species—Davallia fejeensis plumosa

THE TERRARIUM

The growing of plants in a terrarium has become an increasingly popular feature of indoor gardening within recent years and offers many delightful possibilities. The principles involved in the growing of plants in glass cases have been known for many years, the discovery being credited to Doctor Nathaniel Ward, a London physician, which explains the use of the term "Wardian" case, so often applied to a terrarium.

TYPES OF TERRARIA

Terraria vary greatly in design and construction. The most simple form is a fish bowl with a pane of glass placed over the top. The large, rectangular type of aquarium may also be very readily converted into a terrarium. Simple wooden boxes or roasting pans may be used, large panes of glass being fitted into the sides and ends, and bound at the corners with adhesive tape. More elaborate and expensive types may be made at home, or may be purchased.

SELECTION OF PLANTS

Some plants are admirably adapted to the conditions under which they must be grown in a terrarium, while other plants suffer seriously from the high degree of humidity and are unable to thrive. Practically all the cacti and other succulents are ill-suited to such conditions and no attempt should be made to grow them in a tightly or even partially closed terrarium. Geraniums and many other plants with soft fleshy leaves also fail to thrive, although some of the begonias and caladiums do reasonably well. Among those plants which seem most happily adapted to such conditions are the small woodland ferns and ground covers and some of the early spring wild flowers. A miniature woodland planting may be created within a terrarium with small maidenhair ferns, partridge berries, hepaticas, and trilliums, with bits of moss and lichen-covered twigs. A slight variation in levels will give added interest.

PLANTS WHICH MAY BE GROWN IN THE TERRARIUM

African Violets
Anemones
Begonias
Bluets
Bloodroot
Caladiums
Hepaticas
Hemlocks—tiny seedlings (for short periods)
Holly fern

Maidenhair ferns
Partridgeberry
Pines—tiny seedlings (for short periods)
Rattlesnake-plantain
Squirrel's-foot fern
Sword fern
Trailing arbutus
Violets
Wintergreen

SOIL PREPARATION

A layer of gravel should be placed in the bottom of the terrarium in order to facilitate good drainage and to prevent the soil from becoming soggy. The soil mixture will depend upon the type of plants which are to be grown. If woodland plants are to be used, their particular soil preferences should be studied (see Chapter XVII on Woodland Gardens) and they should be supplied with the type of soil which will best meet their requirements. Small quantities of such soil may usually be obtained from the forest floor in sections where the plants grow naturally. If plants of a different character are to be grown, such as begonias or caladiums, a good general soil mixture may be used, such as 2 parts garden loam, 1 part leaf mold, and 1 part sand.

ROUTINE CARE

After the planting of the terrarium has been completed, the soil should be thoroughly moistened but not saturated. The soil should not be watered again until it is definitely dry. In most cases it will be necessary to supply water only once in several months. There have been instances where plants have thrived under such conditions over a period of many years without any application of additional moisture. To a considerable extent a very uniform degree of humidity is maintained within the case. The water which is transpired from the leaves of the plant and that which is evaporated from the soil condenses on the glass, from thence returns to the soil, and the cycle is repeated. The amount of ventilation which is desirable will vary considerably. As long as the glass of the terrarium remains clear it may be kept tightly covered or very nearly so. If the glass becomes clouded with the condensation of moisture more ventilation should be given.

XXV

The Culture of Plants in Nutrient Solutions

By Ruth Patrick[*]

I. General Methods

There is probably no phase of horticultural research which has aroused more interest in recent years than has the growing of plants without contact with soil.

Throughout the centuries soil was considered the only natural medium for practically all plant growth. It was known that plants took their mineral nutrients from the soil in solution form, and that certain elements were essential for their normal growth. It is only during the past century, however, that plant physiologists, in their search for knowledge concerning plant nutrition, have developed in their laboratories methods for growing plants without soil, and it was not until ten years ago that any effort was made to shift this interest in growing plants in media other than soil from the laboratory to the layman.

Two general methods are now employed in this work. The one provides for setting the plant in clean quartz sand and watering it at regular intervals with a prescribed mineral nutrient solution; the other places the plant in a supporting medium, such as excelsior or peat, on wire mesh suspended over the nutrient solution.

Growing plants without soil by either of these methods is fundamentally not very different from growing them in soil. It is significant that many of the practices used in good gardening must be observed. Plants, whether in water, sand, or soil, receive their mineral nutrient dissolved in water. Certain defi-

[*]Chairman of the Botany Department, The Pennsylvania School of Horticulture for Women.

nite elements must be supplied in given amounts. In soil, there are many more nutrient substances present in solution than are found in the commonly used experimental nutrient formulas. In either case certain essential elements—the six major elements —must be provided. These are calcium (Ca), magnesium (Mg), sulphur (S), nitrogen (N), phosphorus (P), and potassium (K). They are found in the three so-called salts, calcium nitrate, magnesium sulphate, and potassium phosphate which will be referred to later. In addition, several elements in small amounts referred to as trace elements are needed. Some of these will be present as impurities but the more important ones—manganese (Mn), boron (B), zinc (Zn), iron (Fe)—must be added in very small amounts in making up a solution formula.

In addition to an adequate food supply consideration must be given to good drainage. Roots must have air just as stems and leaves. In well-cultivated soil where the drainage is good there is plenty of air available for the plant roots between the soil particles. In sand culture, air is pulled in between the particles of sand as the nutrient drains off. If grown in sand, plants must not be kept too wet or the effect of good drainage will be destroyed In water culture, air is supplied by continual or frequent changing of the nutrient solution in which the roots are suspended or by placing the plants in a bed of some material such as excelsior. In this latter method the roots extend through the moist excelsior into the nutrient solution beneath.

In well-drained soil, the nutrient solution in contact with the roots changes frequently. Since the laboratory-made solution is apt to become chemically unbalanced by the unequal absorption of its mineral elements by the plant, regular changing of the solution is most important.

Plants grown in nutrient solutions must have plenty of sunlight just as plants grown in soil. Grown in sand or water they may be attacked by fungous or insect diseases but are usually much freer from disease than are soil-grown plants.

The good grower should be able to recognize the symptoms of disease. He should know the symptoms of mineral deficiencies, as these are much more apt to show in sand or water culture than in soil. These are described in Section IV.

II SOLUTIONS

There is no one nutrient solution which is suitable for all plants. In many cases the same solution is not adequate during the whole life of a plant and it is frequently necessary to change the concentration of the nutrient solution used as the plant grows older or, as is often the case, to give the plant more of a given solution than to change the concentration. It has been found, however, that these are problems which the individual grower can best work out for himself as he becomes experienced in the method.

Although, as already stated, there is no one solution suitable for all plants, there are a number of solutions which are practically equally effective. In choosing a solution formula, you must consider the plants which you wish to grow and their requirements under conditions of soil culture. Plants which dislike calcium will naturally not grow well in a solution rich in calcium. Likewise plants which seem to prefer a poor soil will not grow as well in a concentrated nutrient solution as in a more dilute one. For example, it has been found that Arctotis grandis does not grow as well in a concentrated solution as it does when the solution is diluted ¼ strength.

In making up a nutrient solution it is best to use chemically pure salts. This is slightly more expensive, but unless the grower is familar with the chemical composition of the fertilizer salts, he may get into difficulty. Any of the large chemical supply houses can furnish the pure salts.

Glass or stoneware must be used in the making and storing of the solutions, which should not come in contact with metal at any time for more than a brief period, never for more than one half an hour. Metal watering cans may be used for putting on the solution but it should not be allowed to stand in them. All glassware should be perfectly clean before it is used, and rinsed well to remove any soap or other chemical which may have been used in cleansing.

With regard to the kind of water to be used in work other than that of a most careful experimental nature, any spring or well water used for drinking purposes is satisfactory. However, it will be necessary to determine whether the water is acid or alkaline as the solution must have an acidity of an approximate pH. 6 when it is applied to the plant. If the water is alkaline in nature, it may be necessary to add a small amount of dilute sulphuric or acetic acid. Any drug store will supply either of these acids in dilute form.

The acidity or alkalinity may be determined by the use of certain chemicals called indicators, which change color with any variation in acidity. Brom thymol blue is a suitable indicator for this work. It may be obtained from chemical supply houses in solution form or as impregnated strips of paper. It is yellow in a slightly acid solution, green in a neutral one, and blue in an alkaline one.

If the water to be used is alkaline, add the dilute sulphuric or acetic acid drop by drop to a quart of the water until the desired pH. is attained. This is determined by immersing in the water a strip of the paper impregnated with the brom thymol blue. When it is slightly acid, a yellow color will result. Record the number of drops of acid required. Later, when using the same source of water, this given quantity of acid must be put in the water before the salts are added.

It has been found desirable to make up fairly concentrated nutrient solutions, known as stock solutions, from which the solution which is to be applied to the plant is made by dilution. These stock solutions are usually designated "one half molar solutions," meaning that one half the gram molecular weight of a salt is dissolved in a liter of water. The molecular weight of a salt is usually printed on the label of the bottle, as supplied by the manufacturer. Each stock solution should be made with distilled water, and kept separately. Great care should be taken that no contamination occurs.

It is desirable to make up a quart of each stock solution at a time. The ordinary fruit jar used for canning, particularly that with a glass top, is excellent for this purpose. Measure out the exact amount of each salt as indicated in the following formula into separate jars. Fill the jar half full with distilled water and then mix the solution by rotating the jar with a circular motion. By this method, the salt is dissolved. If there is not enough water to completely dissolve the salt, a little more should be added. When dissolved, the jar may be filled with distilled water.

Amounts of salts for stock solutions, in grams and teaspoons for one quart of one half molar solution:

Ammonium Sulphate—(NH_4) $2SO_4$...... 17½ tsp. or 62.5 grams
Potassium Phosphate—KH_2PO_4 .... 13½ tsp. or 64.4 grams
Magnesium Sulphate—$MgSO_4$. $7H_2O$ ..... 27¼ tsp. or 116.6 grams
Calcium Nitrate—$Ca(No_3)_2$. $4H_2O$ ...... 22¼ tsp. or 111.69 grams

In addition to the above elements certain trace elements are necessary. These trace elements or stimulants are, as already stated, required in very small amounts by plants. They are manganese, boron, zinc, and iron. The first three of these are mixed together in a pint of distilled water to form a stimulant solution, as follows:

To one pint of distilled water add

Boric Acid—H_3BO_3 .... ¼ tsp.
Manganese Sulphate—$MnSO_4$. $4H_2O$ .... ¼ tsp.
Zinc Sulphate—$ZnSO_4$. $7H_2O$ .... ¼ tsp.

The iron solution is made up separately, as it deteriorates rapidly. Ferric tartrate is the form in which the iron is supplied. To a cup of water add just enough ferric tartrate to give the solution the color of strong tea. This solution must be carefully watched. If it becomes cloudy or if metallic flakes appear on the surface, it must be thrown out and a fresh solution made. The solution, in time, forms a brown precipitate on the surface of the bottle in which it is kept, which can be removed with hydrochloric acid. The bottle must then be thoroughly cleaned before it is again used.

It is best to make up the solution which is to be applied to the plants one gallon at a time, although larger amounts can be mixed quite easily. The solution has been figured in amounts of one gallon for the convenience of the person who is growing but a few plants, as it is often difficult to store the solution in larger amounts.

The following solution is one which has been tried at the

School of Horticulture. It is a modification of a nutrient solution formula, perfected by Biekart and Connors. Fill a gallon container almost full of water. A wine or vinegar jug will serve excellently for the purpose. If the water is alkaline or neutral in reaction, add the amount of acid which has been determined by the indicator. Using a teaspoon, add the following amounts from each of the four stock solutions already made up:

Potassium Phosphate	4 tsp.
Calcium Nitrate	20 tsp.
Magnesium Sulphate	5 tsp.
Ammonium Sulphate	2 tsp.

These measurements are based on the calculation of 3.7 c. c. (cubic centimeters) to the teaspoon. With an eye dropper, add 40 drops of the stimulant solution containing manganese, boron, and zinc.

Immediately before applying the solution to the plant, add 1 teaspoon of the iron solution to each quart of nutrient solution.

III USES OF NUTRIENT SOLUTIONS
1. House Plants

For the average person the sand-culture method as set forth by Doctors Shive and Robbins of the New Jersey Experiment Station seems to be the most successful. For this method, pots are required which are glazed or which have been well varnished on the inside. Any clear varnish which resists water will do, but the pot will have to be coated several times, as the pores of the clay readily absorb the varnish. A small piece of glass is then placed over the hole in the bottom of the pot. The pieces of crock usually used for this purpose will not serve, as the bottom of the pot must be absolutely flat on the inside to prevent the sand from leaking out. This procedure will not interfere with the drainage of water from the pot.

The sand used for this purpose should be almost pure quartz. Sands high in limestone will not serve. The sand particles should be rather coarse, about 1/8 of an inch in diameter. The ordinary beach sand of our Atlantic coast is in most cases too fine for best results. The sand should be washed in water to which has been added a little hydrochloric acid until it is free from organic matter or clay. Ordinary stonemason's sand is quite clean and requires very little washing.

The plant which is to be grown is then potted up in the sand. The roots should be washed thoroughly, if the plant has been in soil previously. Care should be taken that the tips of the roots and the root hairs are not broken off.

In the sand-culture method, feeding may be carried on in several ways. The plant may be watered from the surface, in which case care should be taken to prevent the sand from being dislodged by the water. A second satisfactory method is to place the pot in a dish containing the nutrient solution, and allow it to stand for several hours. A plant grown in this way should not be left in the solution throughout the day, but should be removed for a given period each day. The solution in the dish should be changed frequently, if it is not all absorbed by the plant, as evaporation from the surface may render the solution more concentrated than is desirable.

Either of these methods is suitable for most house plants. However, the most generally approved method, although a somewhat less convenient one, is that described by Shive and Robbins. This method of Doctor Shive's is the continuous flow method, wherein the nutrient solution is delivered to the plant from a reservoir set at a higher level than the pot containing the plant. (Fig. I). The solution may be drawn from the reservoir through a siphon of thin glass tubing, or by the capillary action of a lamp wick. The latter arrangement is the easier to set up. First fill the quart jar with the solution and lay the end of a six-inch length of candle wick, small lamp wick, or cotton gauze bandage twisted into a loose cord, over its rim. Invert a glass ash tray over the jar so equipped. Then, holding the tray tightly against the mouth of the jar, invert the jar quickly, and set it, with its tray and wick, on a suitable shelf or support a few inches higher than the top of the pot. The wick should then just clear the sand in the pot and should drip the solution slowly, by capillary action, onto the sand. For this setup the pot is not placed in a dish, but the overflow is recovered through the hole in the bottom of the pot which drains into a suitable container beneath the pot.

The amount of nutrient solution which should be applied to a plant varies with the size of the plant. For small plants, a

Fig. 1. Continuous Flow Method

cupful of the solution per day per plant is usually sufficient. Larger plants often consume more than a quart a day. Once a week the sand should be watered well with ordinary water. This is to remove any salts which may have accumulated in the sand. In many cases it is better to give the plants the nutrient solution only three times a week. On the other days the plants are kept moist with ordinary water.

Some of the house plants which have been successfully grown at the School of Horticulture are listed below with comments as to their culture.

Geranium. *Pelargonium tomentosum* (peppermint-scented geranium); *P. peltatum* (ivy-leaf geranium); *P. graveolens* (rose geranium); *P. odoratissimum* (nutmeg geranium); *P. hortorum* (fish geranium); *P. crispum* (lemon-scented geranium). These geraniums have all been raised successfully in mineral nutrient solutions. As in soil, they require plenty of sunlight, and should not be kept too wet; in fact, the sand should be allowed to become quite dry during a part of each day. Quite a variety of solutions have proven satisfactory with geraniums, which are comparatively easy to grow in nutrient solutions. If the young leaves of a plant become a yellowish green color, it is probably due to a deficiency of iron, and indicates that more of the iron solution should be used.

At first, plants in nutrient solution grow rather slowly, but, after about two months, growth is quite rapid and the plants will more than double the size of those grown in soil. The larger plants, quite naturally, need more nutrient solution than the smaller ones, so that it is often necessary not only to increase the amount of nutrient solution applied, but the strength of the solution as well.

Petunia. The petunia requires about the same amount of sun and moisture as the geranium. It, too, is apt to need more iron than the amount prescribed in the formula given. Particularly is this true as the plant grows older. It is wise also to increase the strength of the nutrient solution as the plant gets larger. Doubling the strength of the solution recommended proved satisfactory in some cases.

Begonia and Fuchsia. Begonias and fuchsias have been grown successfully in the solution recommended. However, they do not seem to require as much iron as do geraniums and petunias. Furthermore, it has not been necessary to increase the strength of the solution as the plants increase in size, but rather only the amount of solution applied. Plenty of sunlight is required for the healthy growth of these plants.

Ferns. *Pteris,* the Greenhouse Holly Fern, and the Boston Fern.
These ferns require less sunlight than do geraniums, and the sand in which they are grown should be kept a little more moist. The foliage of ferns which are grown in nutrient solutions is usually a darker green than that of plants grown in soil.

The solution described by Hoagland and Arnon which is given

in "Bench Culture," page 826, seems to be the best of those tried for ferns.

Arctotis grandis. This plant grows well and flowers much more abundantly in mineral nutrient solution than when grown in soil. It requires plenty of sunlight and should be grown in sand which is not too moist. If watered from below, the surface sand should appear quite dry during the middle of the day. Of course, plants should be kept moist enough to prevent wilting, at all times. The best growth was obtained with Arctotis grandis when the nutrient solution was diluted to one fourth the given strength. The stimulant solution, however, should not be diluted but applied as directed.

2. Seeds and Seedlings

There are two methods of germinating seeds and growing seedlings in mineral nutrient solutions which are carried out by the amateur with comparative ease. The one method is used satisfactorily where relatively few seeds are to be germinated, the other where seedlings are wanted in quantity.

In the first method, a small enamelled pan, a deep sauce-dish, or a low jelly glass may be used and the mineral nutrient solution placed in the container chosen. For seed germination, the solution should be one fourth as strong as that used in solution culture, that is, one part of the solution is diluted with three parts of water. A piece of loosely woven cheese cloth of sufficient size to cover the top and extend well over the edges is dipped into melted paraffin and placed at once over the container. The edges should be pressed tightly against the sides of the vessel. When the paraffin cools, the cloth will be relatively stiff and will have formed a mold which can be easily removed. This cover may be held in place more firmly with string or a rubber band. Care should be taken that the paraffin does not completely fill the meshes of the cloth. The container should be filled with the nutrient solution so that it will just come in contact with the cloth.

The seeds are then sown on the cloth. During the middle of the day it is often well to cover the seeds with an inverted pan or dish to prevent drying out. However, this cover must not be left on continuously, as seeds tend to become moldy. Seeds which germinate best in the dark should be kept in a dark place. If the solution in the container used evaporates, it should be filled with ordinary water.

The seedlings may be left in the solution until they are fairly large, when they should be pulled out of the net and planted. Germinating seeds in nutrient solution eliminates the necessity for pricking out the seedlings. Should it seem desirable to leave the seedlings in the solution over a longer period, it is advisable to change the solution once each week.

As previously suggested, a second method is advised where large numbers of seedlings are to be germinated. Flats or pots should be filled with sand which has been cleaned, as already described. This sand should then be saturated with nutrient solution and the seeds sown in the usual manner. The flats should be covered with glass to prevent too rapid evaporation and, if they are to be kept in a greenhouse, or in any place where the light is strong, they should be covered with newspaper. Seed pans and shallow pots may be used to good advantage with this method. However, the inside of the pots should be varnished.

With most seeds which germinate fairly rapidly no watering is required until germination takes place. The seedlings are then watered by means of a fine hand spray with the nutrient solution, diluted one fourth as outlined above. In the case of seeds which take a long time to germinate, it is often well to use the constant drip method which has been described. A single reservoir may be used to supply several dishes (Fig. 2), letting the wicks extend well over the surface of the sand in the containers used.

Seeds of the following plants have been found to germinate quite successfully by this method: ageratum, lupine, marigold, petunia, portulaca, rhododendron, scabiosa, snapdragon, sweet alyssum; also beet, carrot, celery, lettuce, parsnip, radish, and tomato seeds.

3. Cuttings

The use of sand-culture methods for rooting cuttings has proved very advantageous. The root systems of plants treated in this way are much better than those which are put directly into soil when taken from the propagating beds.

As soon as the cuttings show roots, they are transplanted into pots and treated as described in House Plants, page 819. The following cuttings have proven quite successful when

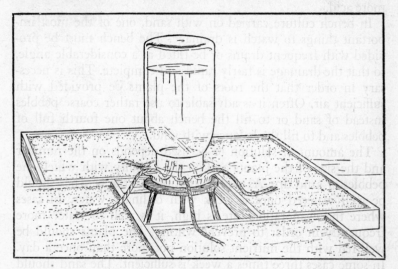

Fig. 2. A Single Reservoir May Be Used to Supply Several Dishes

treated in this manner: arbor-vitæ, cotoneaster, holly, hypericum, ivy, pyrocantha, rambler rose, and taxus.

4. Bench Culture

The two main methods now in use for growing plants in benches are those developed at the University of California, in which the plants are grown in excelsior suspended on wire netting over the mineral nutrient solution, and at the New Jersey Agricultural Experiment Station at New Brunswick, in which the plants are grown in clean sand.

At the School of Horticulture, a bench has been constructed which may be used for either of these two methods. The bench is built of wood and lined with linabestos. This type of bench, which is much cheaper to build than a concrete bench, seems to have all the advantages of the latter and yet, as is the case with concrete benches, tends to make the nutrient solution too alkaline, due to the leaching of lime. This can be overcome by varnishing the inside of the bench or by making the solution more acid.

In bench culture carried on with sand, one of the most important things to watch is drainage. The bench must be provided with frequent drains or be tilted at a considerable angle, so that the drainage is fairly rapid and complete. This is necessary in order that the roots of the plants be provided with sufficient air. Often it is advisable to use rather coarse pebbles instead of sand or to fill the bench about one fourth full of pebbles and to fill the balance with sand.

The amount of solution to be used depends on the number and the size of the plants and on the rapidity with which the pebbles or sand dry. As with potted plants, the benches should be well watered once a week with ordinary water. In cases where the evaporation rate is high, it is well to water more frequently in order to prevent wilting. The plants should be well fed with the nutrient solution not more than once a day. In some cases three times a week is sufficient. The sand should have a moisture content about equal to that of garden soil. If the sand is kept too moist, the roots will be water-logged. If there is not enough solution, the plants will be starved. In cases where the calcium content is high, due to the material used in the construction of the bench or to the lime content of the water, it is often desirable to use a solution of lower calcium content than that generally used. The nutrient solution formula given by Hoagland and Arnon (1938) is suggested.

To make one gallon of this solution, use the following amounts of the half molar stock solutions:

Ammonium Phosphate $NH_4H_2PO_4$ .... ½ tsp. or 1.9 cc.*
Potassium Nitrate KNO_3 .... 3 tsp. or 11.3 cc.
Calcium Nitrate $Ca(NO_3)_2$ .... 2 tsp. or 7.5 cc.
Magnesium Sulphate $MgSO_4$ .... 1 tsp. or 3.8 cc.

*A half molar solution of ammonium phosphate is prepared by dissolving 12¾ teaspoons of the salt in a quart of water. See page 817 for directions for making up half molar solutions of the other salts.

The stimulants and iron are added in amounts as previously directed.

Crops which may be successfully grown in benches are petunias, snapdragons, stocks, lupines, tomatoes, radishes, and lettuce. Some workers have grown carnations and sweet peas quite successfully in this manner.

5. For Plants Grown in Water

The use of mineral nutrient solutions has also been found beneficial in the growing of plants in water, such as ivy and philodendron. The addition of a quarter of a cup of nutrient solution, whenever the water is changed, to a gallon of water gives about the right concentration. This of course varies with the plant. The use of nutrient solution is particularly good when the plants are grown in water which has been variously treated with chemicals to insure purification.

The occasional application of nutrient solutions to dish gardens is also beneficial. A quarter strength nutrient solution should be used. The addition of a half a cup of solution once or twice a month is suggested.

IV SYMPTOMS OF MINERAL DEFICENCY

As a guide to the symptoms of mineral deficiencies, some of the effects as outlined in various publications by Miller, McMurtrey, Hartman and Powers and others, are given below.

Doctor McMurtrey has divided the effects into two main groups; those which affect the older or lower leaves first and those which affect the newer or upper leaves and buds first. Belonging to the first group are effects due to deficiency of nitrogen, phosphorus, potassium and magnesium. In the second group are effects due to deficiency of iron, manganese, sulphur, calcium, and boron.

Nitrogen: Deficiency in nitrogen usually makes the plant appear stunted. The stems are slender and the plant takes on a light green color. The lower leaves are the first to turn yellow or to dry and be shed.

Potassium: Deficiency in potassium shows up first in that the older leaves become mottled. Light yellow spots appear first. The leaf tips and margins become dried and marked with small black spots (necrotic spotting). In some plants, the leaves become crimped, producing a decidedly puckered effect. (Some insect and virus diseases produce a crimped effect, but it is a combination of these characteristics which shows up in potassium deficiency.) The stems of the plant are frequently slender.

Phosphorus: The symptoms of phosphorus deficiency show up in the darker green coloring of the lower leaves and frequently in a reddish coloration of the leaf. This is more clearly seen on the under surface of the leaf. In some cases the roots are a reddish brown color.

Magnesium: The symptoms due to magnesium deficiency seem to vary according to the plant. Generally there is a chlorosis (loss of green color) which attacks the older leaves first. McMurtrey states that chlorosis is characterized by a loss of green color starting at the tip of the leaf and progressing inward along the margins and between the veins. Beaumont and Snell state that chlorosis may occur first at the margin of the leaf, giving a dry shrunken effect. In spinach broad white areas may develop between the veins. As a general rule, the veins remain green longer than the tissue between them.

Iron: This is a deficiency which is very apt to become apparent, particularly when plants are being grown by beginners. Iron is the most difficult of the nutrient elements to keep in solution in sufficient amounts. The amounts of various other elements, such as excess manganese, may affect the availability of iron. If the solution becomes alkaline or neutral, the iron is apt to settle out. Therefore the nutrient solution should be kept slightly acid. The deficiency shows up in yellowing of the new leaves and buds. The tissue between the veins becomes yellow first, while the main veins often remain green for some time.

Manganese: Deficiency of manganese usually shows up in neutral or alkaline conditions. The young leaves become yellow and develop necrotic spots. The tissue between the veins becomes yellow first. The green appearance of the small veins gives the leaf a lacy appearance.

Sulphur: The effects of sulphur deficiency show in a light green appearance of the plant. As compared with a well-nourished plant, it will have a yellow-green cast. Often the veins become lighter than the tissue between them.

Calcium: The deficiency of calcium shows up first in the terminal bud. The young leaves die back at the tips, producing a hooked effect. The leaves become yellow and, if they grow, produce a distorted effect due to the dying of the tips and margins. In severe attacks the terminal part of the stem may die.

Boron: Boron deficiency, like calcium, shows its effects in the dy-

Courtesy U. S. Department of Agriculture   *Technical Bulletin 340*

1. No nitrogen; 2. No phosphorus; 3. No potassium; 4. No calcium; 5. No magnesium; 6. All the essential elements included; 7. No boron; 8. No sulphur; 9. No manganese; 10. No iron

ing of the tissues in the terminal bud. However, in the case of boron deficiency, the bases of the leaves are affected first, while in calcium deficiency the tips of the leaves are the first to die.

SUMMARY

1. Nutrient solution methods are fundamentally not very different from the methods employed in growing plants in soil.

2. They make possible the control of the nutrient solution in contact with the roots of the plant.

3. Good gardening practices are as important in solution and sand culture as they are in soil culture. Sunlight, right temperature and moisture conditions must be provided. An adequate food supply is as necessary as for plants grown in soil. Six major elements and certain trace elements must be present whether solution or soil-growing conditions are provided. Good drainage is also a major consideration in both the solution and sand-culture methods because of the necessity for adequate aëration and the constant demand for water and nutrients by the roots of the plant.

4. In making up a nutrient solution, the requirements of the plant to be grown must be determined.

5. Stock solutions should be made up in clean glass or stoneware containers. Metal vessels should not be used.

6. The mineral salts and acids used should be of good quality.

7. Stock solutions are made with distilled water.

8. For sand culture, a clean, rather coarse, almost pure quartz sand low in lime should be used. It should be washed thoroughly.

9. Pots and flats should be clean. Glazed pots are preferable for this work.

10. It is not possible to give complete directions for adjusting a nutrient solution because of the constantly changing needs of the plant. This adjustment is learned by experience.

11. Nutrient solution methods make it possible to maintain favorable conditions for growth over long periods once the right nutrient solution has been developed. Soil conditions are variable at best.

12. Solution grown plants are usually much freer from disease than are soil grown plants. Insect pests and weeds are practically eliminated and require less consideration than with soil grown plants.

13. By these methods, seeds may be germinated, cuttings rooted, or seedlings grown to maturity and mature plants carried on through years of growth without soil.

14. Nutrient solution methods are far from being perfected and are not yet proof against failure, but they certainly offer an interesting field to the gardener who likes to experiment.

XXVI

The Home Fruit Garden

By John A. Andrew, Jr.*

The small home fruit garden, if it is carefully planned and well maintained, will yield a bountiful and varied supply of fruit throughout the season and will be a constant source of pleasure and of profit. Many choice varieties of fruit, far superior in quality to those grown commercially, may be produced in the home garden. When fruit is to be shipped a great distance it is often necessary to pick it long before it is fully ripe and much of its sweetness and flavor is lost in consequence. Fruit grown in the home garden may be harvested at its finest stage of ripeness and will possess a quality which is unobtainable in the commercial market.

FRUIT TREES FOR ORNAMENTAL PURPOSES

In addition to their purely utilitarian uses, most fruit trees have a decidedly decorative value. There are few things more beautiful than an apple tree when in full bloom, and both pears and apples are often very picturesque in outline. On a place of modest size, fruit trees may play a very important part in the landscape development of the property. They may be used as shade trees upon the terrace or upon the lawn, they may be planted along the driveway, or they may be trained against some supporting structure such as a fence or wall. Espaliered fruit trees are often seen in English gardens and in France, and they are becoming increasingly popular in this country. An "Espalier" is a trellis or open support upon which a vine or a woody plant may be trained. Apple trees, pears, peaches, plums, nectarines and quinces may be very readily used in this way.

*Head of the Department of Fruits and Vegetables, The Pennsylvania School of Horticulture for Women.

Such trees are usually trained to a given number of branches (see illustration), and they should preferably be grown on a wall facing southeast.

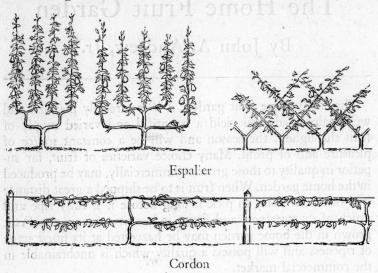

Espalier

Cordon

PURCHASING AND PLANTING NURSERY STOCK

Where to Buy

When one considers the initial cost of nursery stock he may be inclined to shop around for lower prices. One should know that the initial cost is the lowest cost of all. The years of pruning, spraying and general upkeep necessary to bring trees into a successful fruiting period cost much more. Therefore, the reputation of the nurseryman should be your guide, as there are many factors under his control which insure you against getting poor stock. Many people prefer to buy their stock directly from the nurseryman, but this is not necessary provided the firm with whom you are doing business is honest and reputable. Remember that you get what you pay for, and that if the initial cost of a good tree is ten cents more than a second-grade type, the first tree won't have to produce much more in later years to make up for this slight difference.

When to Buy

A large number of trees shipped in the spring months have been dug, sorted and stored the fall before. If stock is ordered before the spring rush begins one may be assured of getting a part of the best selection. If ordering is delayed until planting time or the rush season, certain varieties may be exhausted. Also there may be considerable delay in shipping because of this rush. Therefore, the logical procedure is to place your order early and to let the firm know at least a week in advance of the date you want them shipped to you. Plan to set the stock as soon as the frost is out of the ground.

Grade to Buy

Trees. Trees are graded according to their height and thickness of trunk, and are priced accordingly. Fruit trees are offered in two or three sizes of one- and two-year-old stock. The A, or best, grade costs only a few cents more than a smaller tree. It seems to be a matter of preference as to whether one- or two-year-old stock shall be planted. However, there is no doubt that the best should be purchased, regardless of age.

The main advantages in purchasing one-year trees are as follows:

1. Not as many roots are broken off in transplanting.
2. Easily pruned to desired height.
3. No branches broken in shipping.
4. Better selection of main branches the following year.
5. More quickly handled and planted.

Bush Fruits. Bushes are more easily handled and set out than trees. A well-grown two-year-old bush will give excellent results and possibly produce fruit sooner and in larger quantities than a one-year-old bush. The only reason for buying a one-year-old bush is to be sure that it is of the best grade, as sometimes a two-year-old bush is inferior in size and appearance at the end of its first year's growth.

CARE OF STOCK BEFORE PLANTING

Often the stock is received before planting conditions are satisfactory. The land may not be prepared, or it may be too wet. Other things coming at the same time of year may also necessitate a delay in planting for a short time.

As soon as the stock is received, it should be removed from the package to prevent sweating and possible deterioration. It may be planted temporarily in a trench or kept in a cool damp cellar for several days. The roots should not be permitted to dry out. Plant the stock before the buds begin to open; otherwise, if dry soil conditions exist, watering may be necessary. Also the roots should have a chance to establish themselves before warm weather begins. For this reason the earlier the stock is planted in the spring, the greater the chance it will have to establish its root system before the buds begin to swell. This should result in a greater shoot growth the first season when planted.

See Chapter VII on Trees, pages 228–231.

WHEN TO PLANT

Nursery stock may be planted either in the spring or fall. In some cases fall planting is advisable, especially if the stock is to be planted on heavy land which is apt to be too wet at the proper planting time in the spring. Fall planting also enables a tree to get its root system established so that the period of adjustment after transplanting is long past when conditions are favorable for growth in the spring.

Spring planting also has its advantages:

1. Soil may be in a better physical condition.

2. The stock makes considerable top and root growth before winter.

3. One winter less to control rodents.

4. In a severe winter the stock may winter-kill if set in the fall.

5. Easier to keep the soil cultivated if planting follows plowing.

LAYING OUT THE ORCHARD

Definite planting distances are recommended for each fruit. These should be closely observed. The distances in most cases seem enormous especially after the trees are planted. These distances are the recommendations obtained from many experiments. In many cases, one is puzzled when trees are set next to each other which have different planting distances. This is easily solved at follows. Apples and sour cherries are to be planted in adjacent rows. How far should the sour cherries be planted from the apples? Take the sum of the two planting distances as 35 feet for apples and 20 feet for sour cherries, which equals 55 feet and divide by two. Twenty-seven feet will be about the correct distance to plant the sour cherries from the apples.

Be sure to plant the trees in a straight line, as once they are set they are a picture of your accuracy. Establish a base line along which the first row of trees is to be planted and take all your measurements from it. Wire or coarse string is very practicable to use for this purpose. Then measure off the required distance for each tree on this line and insert a small stake at that point. To lay out the second row, measure the required distance from the base line at each end and set up another line. The formula which is used to insure unquestionable accuracy is: "The square on the hypoteneuse of a right-angled triangle is equal to the sum of the squares of the other two sides."

Therefore, letting y equal the unknown distance,

$$y^2 = A^2 \text{ (or } 40^2) \text{ plus } B^2 \text{ (or } 40^2)$$
$$y^2 = 1600 + 1600$$
$$y^2 = 3200$$
$$y = 56.56 \text{ feet.}$$

If the trees are set out correctly, the line C (See diagram on page 836) will be just 56.56 feet long.

PLANTING THE ORCHARD

The equipment for planting consists of a round pointed shovel and a planting board.

835

To make a planting board, take a board approximately 3 feet long and 6 inches wide. Make a v-shaped notch in each end and one in the middle.

Place the notch in the middle of the board up to the peg which marks the spot where a tree is to be set. Place a peg in

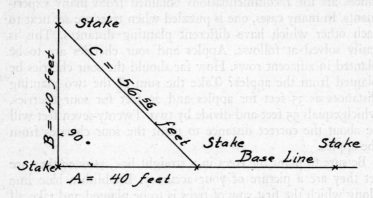

Method of Staking Rows of Trees

the notches at each end of the board and remove the board. Then remove the peg in the middle. Dig a hole between the two pegs which are left. First remove the top-soil and lay it aside. When the sub-soil, which is yellowish in color, appears,

Planting Board

place it in a separate pile. Make the hole just wide enough to receive the roots without crowding. Dig deep enough to allow the tree to be set 2 or 3 inches deeper than in the nursery. Make the two sides of the hole parallel and thus have the bottom as wide as the top. This will allow the soil to be packed uniformly around the roots and avoid any danger of leaving air spaces which would dry them out.

Next, put the planting board back in place so that the two

outside pegs will fit into the v-shaped notch in each end. Then place the tree in the hole with its trunk fitting snugly into the notch in the middle. Have one person hold the tree in place while the other puts in the top-soil first. Move the tree up and down several times with a vertical motion. This will permit the soil to sift in around the roots. When the roots are covered, the soil should be firmed if it is not too wet. Then the sub-soil should be put on top and firmed again. The planting board is removed, the tree is in the correct spot, and the next tree is waiting to be planted.

POLLINATION

Some years ago, between 1820–1830, in a thriving Ohio village called Cincinnati, several farmers noticed that one of their neighbors obtained better and larger yields of strawberries than they did. Their problem was solved when the son of this successful grower told one of his neighbors that practically all of his plants were imperfect or pistillate varieties and that flowers which contain pollen are necessary for pollination. Therefore, a staminate or pollen-bearing variety must be planted with one which has insufficient pollen.

Pollination may be defined as the transfer of pollen from the stamen to the stigma or female part of the blossom. Pollen of many varieties of fruits is not borne in large quantities and is not carried far by the wind. The pollen merely falls on the stigmas or is carried on the bodies of insects that visit the flowers.

In some varieties of fruits the pollen produced is capable of fertilizing the ovules of the same variety, while others must receive pollen from another variety to be successfully cross-fertilized. The causes of self-unfruitfulness are as follows:

1. Viable pollen may be unable to fertilize the ovaries of the same variety.

2. Pollen may be discharged when the pistil is not in a receptive condition.

3. Some varieties produce insufficient viable pollen so that it is necessary that they be interplanted with strong staminate varieties to insure the production of enough pollen.

4. In some fruits and varieties the male flowers and female flowers are borne on separate plants.

These causes of self-unfruitfulness show that plants are somewhat modified in order to avoid self-fertilization and to secure cross-fertilization.

Many years ago, fruit trees were grown from seed. This resulted in the introduction of many worthless varieties. Little was known or done about pollination. However, this was not very important as so many different varieties were interplanted that cross-pollination took place naturally.

As new varieties were developed, fruit growers began to select fewer but better varieties. These varieties were arranged in rows, planted apart at a definite distance, and given proper cultural methods.

However, many trees of a single variety planted on a large acreage were too far away from trees of another variety for cross-pollination to be successful.

Many crosses have been made using the same plant to supply, as well as to receive pollen, from another variety. For example, at an Eastern experiment station the Wealthy variety of apple formed seven fruits from each hundred blossoms pollinated with its own pollen. When the pollen of the Delicious variety was applied to the stigmas of the Wealthy a 31 per cent set was the result.

If a fruit tree fails to set fruit because of lack of proper pollination, this condition may be corrected in several ways:

1. The quickest method is to place bouquets of blossoms of another variety in the tree at blooming time. These bouquets should be placed in a pail of water so that the flowers will last as long as possible, and should be hung in the uppermost part of the tree. This method to be successful depends entirely on the presence of bees or other insects.

2. Another method is to top-graft the tree to a different variety. It usually requires three or four years to get results by this method. Meanwhile bouquets of blossoms may be used in order to keep up production as heretofore described.

Before planting varieties of tree fruits it is well worth the time to write to your state experiment station for further advice.

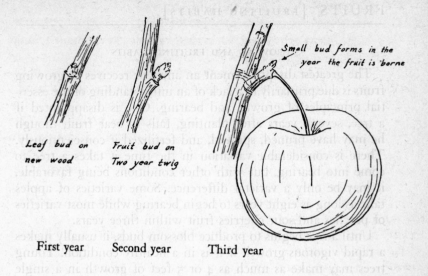

Leaf bud on new wood

Fruit bud on Two year twig

Small bud forms in the year the fruit is borne

First year   Second year   Third year

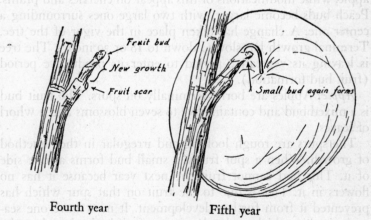

Fruit bud

New growth

Fruit scar

Small bud again forms

Fourth year   Fifth year

Growth of an Apple Fruiting Spur

GROWING AND FRUITING HABITS

The greatest disappointment an amateur receives in growing fruits is due primarily to a lack of an understanding of the essential principles of growth and bearing. One is disappointed if a tree, several years after planting, fails to bear fruit, though he may have pruned, sprayed, and fertilized it conscientiously. There is considerable variation in the time it takes a tree to come into bearing, but with other conditions being favorable, it may be only a varietal difference. Some varieties of apples take as long as eight years to begin bearing while most varieties of peaches and sour cherries fruit within three years.

Until a tree begins to produce blossom buds, it usually makes a rapid vigorous growth if it is in a healthy condition. Young trees may make as much as 4 or 5 feet of growth in a single season. The buds formed are vegetative and contain only leaves. As the tree gets ready to bear fruit, a marked change is noticeable. Fruit buds are larger and more plump, as they have flower parts in them. Short spur-like growths occur on the pear and apple, while modifications of this appear on cherries and plums. Peach buds become larger, with two large ones surrounding a center one. A change has taken place in the vigor of the tree. Terminal growth has slowed down to 18 or 20 inches. The tree is leaving its vegetative period to enter its productive period (fruit bud formation).

Apple. Apples are borne terminally on spurs. The fruit bud is a mixed bud and contains five to seven blossoms and a whorl of leaves.

The spurs are rough looking and irregular in their method of growth. When a spur fruits, a small bud forms at one side of it. This bud cannot fruit the next year because it has no flowers in it. This is due to the fruit on that spur which has prevented it from further development. It must have one season's time in which to develop into a fruit bud other than the year when fruit is borne. Therefore, it is conclusive that a spur will not produce fruit every year but may every other year. When a tree bears a heavy crop one year and none the next, its fruit spurs have all borne at the same time and it is called a biennial bearer. An annual bearing tree has some spurs which bear each year, but no spur bears in successive years.

Fruit spurs are productive until ten or twelve years old, and may not be more than 6 to 10 inches long at that time.

Pear. Very similar to the apple.

Peach. Peaches are borne from lateral buds formed on the previous season's growth. The buds are usually borne in groups of threes. The two outside buds are fruit buds and contain only one blossom each and no leaves, while the center bud is a leaf bud. As this growth on which the fruit is borne each year is

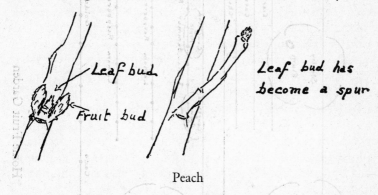

Peach

much longer than that of the apple and pear, pruning is done on a different basis. The terminal bud is always a wood bud.

Plum. Fruit buds are borne axially on spurs. Each fruit bud contains from one to three blossoms. Leaf buds are also on the same spur but are smaller in size. The terminal bud, as in the peach, is always a wood bud.

Cherry. The fruiting habits are very similar to those of the plum. The sour cherry often produces fruit buds on the previous season's growth, the fruits being formed near the lower part of it. Each bud usually contains from two to four flowers.

Quince. Fruit buds are lateral on the previous season's growth. The bud expands as a shoot in the spring, and after making several inches of growth, a single flower blossoms on the end of it. This habit of growth makes the quince a very twiggy bush.

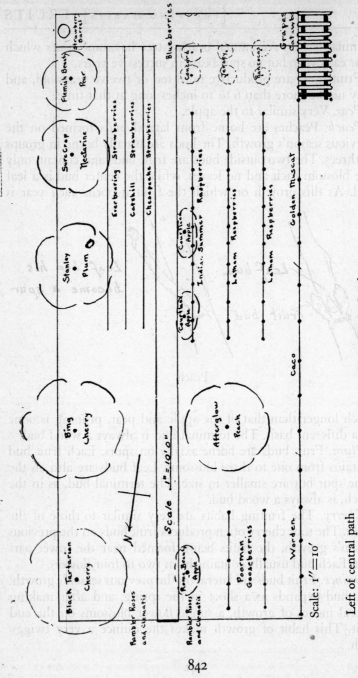

Home Fruit Garden

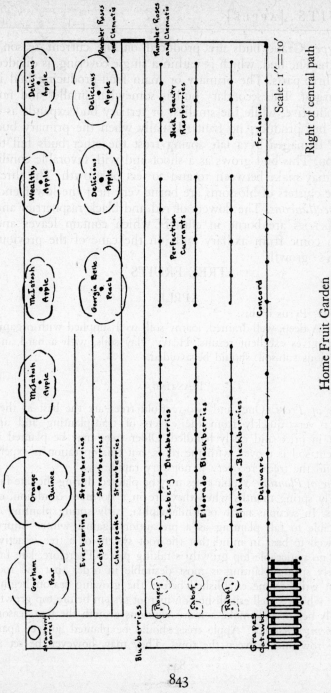

Home Fruit Garden

Planned by Mary Enck and Helen Smith, School of Horticulture for Women, Ambler, Pa.

Scale: 1″=10′

843

Grape. Grape buds are produced on the current season's growth. The bud, which is within a single covering, is divided into three parts. The primary or main fruit-producing bud is the largest. The secondary bud is somewhat smaller and not as productive, while the smallest or tertiary bud expands as a shoot but produces no fruits. Usually when the primary bud is not damaged by a late spring frost the other buds fail to develop. This bud grows as a shoot and with favorable conditions may make between 10 and 20 feet of growth. The three to five clusters of blossoms are borne very near the lower end.

Miscellaneous. The flowers of red and black raspberries and blackberries are borne in clusters which contain leaves and which come from axillary buds on the cane of the previous season's growth.

TREE FRUITS

APPLE

Name: Pyrus malus.

Soil: A deep, well-drained, loamy soil, well supplied with organic matter, gives excellent results. Heavy, clay soils, with a hard and impervious sub-soil, should be avoided.

PLANTING

Age of Trees: One- and two-year-old trees are the best as they recover very quickly from the effects of transplanting and are lowest in price and easily handled. Older trees may be planted if sufficient soil is moved with the roots, but this operation is expensive and the tree's recovery is not very rapid.

Time of Planting: Apple trees may be planted during the late fall or early spring months when they are in a dormant condition, or leafless. In sections north of Philadelphia, early spring planting is preferable to fall planting as a precaution against winter injury. It is well to bear in mind that the root system of a tree is active when no noticeable top growth is taking place. Therefore, late fall or early spring planting is most desirable in order that the root system will become established before the growing season begins. A tree which is well established on its root system before top growth actually begins will make a more vigorous growth the first season.

Planting Distance: Apple trees should be planted 40 feet apart in the row and between the rows. They may, however, be set as close as 30 feet apart each way if space is extremely limited and the varieties are not of the most vigorous types.

Method of Planting: Dig a hole just large enough to receive the roots without crowding and deep enough to set the tree 2 inches deeper than it was formerly growing in the nursery. When removing the soil keep the top and sub-soil separate. Be sure to make the sides of the hole parallel and the bottom as wide as the top.

Trim off any broken, injured or too lengthy roots to within bounds and place the tree in the hole. Put the top-soil in first and firm it around the roots. Then put the sub-soil in last and firm it again. If the soil is quite heavy and has not been prepared previous to planting, a peck of moist peat moss mixed with the soil before setting the tree will give excellent results.

PRUNING

The purpose of pruning and training young trees is to establish a strong framework of branches which will satisfactorily carry the future load of fruit.

One-year Tree: The top of a one-year-old apple tree should be cut back to a height of 36 inches from the ground after it has been set out.

Two-year Tree: Two-year-old trees may contain many branches. In this case it is essential to choose the branches for the framework and remove the others when the tree is planted. Choose three or four branches making at least a 45-degree angle with the trunk, and about 6 inches apart. They, of course, are not on the same plane but are spaced uniformly around the tree for balance. The lowest branch should be at least 18 inches from the ground. These branches should be cut back to approximately 12 to 18 inches, with the exception of No. 3 (see illustration), the leader, which should be 2 inches longer than the others. Trees which are less vigorous than the one just described should be pruned back more severely, but the principle is the same in every case. Crossing, closely parallel, weak, broken, and low branches should be removed. However, it is best to leave branches which are not too thick or which do not directly compete with each other, as they materially aid in increasing the total growth.

Time of Pruning Young Apple Trees: Pruning may be done at any time that the trees are in dormant condition, or leafless. However, as winter-killing begins at the tip of a branch, pruning should not be practised until the coldest part of the winter is past, and not later than the time at which the buds begin to swell.

Pruning Non-Bearing Young Apple Trees: Pruning should be as light as possible until the tree reaches its bearing age. This age varies greatly according to the variety. Remove one of two closely parallel branches; one of two crossing branches, as well as branches which are weak, crowding or diseased. Do not remove any branch which may not be interfering at present just to get rid of it. Such branches are a great help to the tree for several years. Do not allow any of the so-called scaffold branches to grow beyond the leader. This will necessitate some cutting back each year as the leader should be several inches longer than the others. Always cut back to buds on one-year-old wood or to lateral branches on older wood. Permit some branches to fill in the center of the tree without overcrowding.

Pruning Young Bearing Trees: For several years after a tree begins to bear, its crops are not very heavy. Pruning should be light, so as not to cause an over-vegetative condition which will throw it out of bearing.

Pruning Bearing Trees: Pruning is beneficial to a certain point, but it may be overdone if not thoroughly understood. A man who is paid three dollars a day may cause more than fifty dollars' worth of damage if he knows little about it. Therefore, before one prunes or permits others to prune his trees he should be thoroughly informed on the subject and should understand its principles. Less damage is caused by non-pruning than by pruning the wrong way. When a fruit tree reaches the bearing stage it can be kept in a high state of production for many years.

When a tree begins to bear and form fruit-producing points, it becomes less vegetative and vigorous than it was previously. The amount of terminal growth is less, and is made within a period of three to four weeks. Fruit spurs have formed which are to bear the fruit. Severe pruning may throw it out of bearing. The procedure for the amateur, or one not fully experienced, is as follows:

1. Look the tree over at a distance of 15 to 20 feet. Try to visualize how it should look when properly pruned.

2. First remove dead and diseased wood, water sprouts, and suckers.

3. If any large branches must be removed, make your decision on the ground and not up in the tree. They look entirely different from the two points of view. One is justified in removing a large branch if it is:

(*a*) Rubbing against another.

(*b*) Running parallel to another only a few inches away.

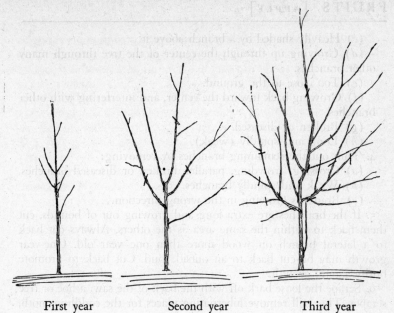

First year   Second year   Third year

How to Prune a Young Apple Tree

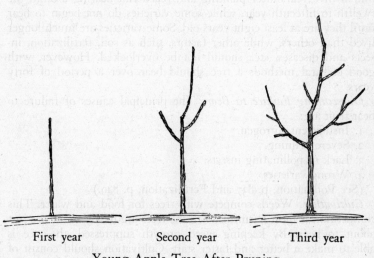

First year   Second year   Third year

Young Apple Tree After Pruning

(*c*) Heavily shaded by a branch above it.

(*d*) Growing up through the center of the tree through many other branches.

(*e*) Too close to the ground.

(*f*) Growing back toward the center, and interfering with other branches.

(*g*) Broken or diseased.

(*h*) Long and spindly (weak).

4. Thin out the remaining branches by removing:

(*a*) Crossing, crowding, parallel, broken or diseased branches.

(*b*) Weak and spindly branches.

(*c*) Branches growing in the wrong direction.

5. If the branches are extra long and growing out of bounds, cut them back to within the same area as the others. Always cut back to a lateral branch on wood more than one year old. One-year growth may be cut back to an outside bud. Cut back to promote bushy, lateral growth.

6. Scrape the loose bark off with the back of the saw, a hoe or tree scraper. This will remove hibernating places for the coddling moth, scale and other insects.

Duration of Bearing: Many varieties of apple trees bear in from four to five years after planting and reach full bearing around the twelfth to fifteenth year, while some varieties do not begin to bear until they are at least eight years old. Some varieties are much longer lived than others, while other factors, such as soil, fertilization, insects and diseases, etc., should not be overlooked. However, with good cultural methods a tree should bear over a period of forty years.

Overcoming Failure to Bear: The principal causes of failure to bear fruit are:

1. Insufficient nitrogen.
2. Severe pruning.
3. Lack of pollinating insects.
4. Wrong varieties.

(See Pollination, p. 837 and Fertilization, p. 849.)

Cultivation: Weeds compete with trees for food and water. This competition is most harmful when the trees are newly set or are just about to bear. By keeping weed growth suppressed, the tree is able to make a better and faster start. Cultivation should consist of removing weeds from around the trees while young and mowing the weeds between the rows, or by frequent disking with a horse or machine disk harrow during the growing season. Cultivation should cease from four to six weeks before fall begins so the trees will be hardened off and be in good condition to withstand the cold winter months. By allowing the weeds to grow at the above late date they actually compete with the tree for favorable results.

If cultivation is not possible, as is the case in some backyards, on lawns or on stony ground, the next best treatment is to keep the weed or grass growth cut. Two cuttings per season is usually sufficient. If possible, these cuttings should be used as a mulch under the tree.

Fertilization:

1. Non-bearing trees.

Non-bearing trees are referred to as trees which have not reached the bearing age. The importance of feeding them to produce a large bearing framework for future years is apparent. If a tree is making from 12 to 18 inches or more of terminal growth each year an application of fertilizer will not be beneficial. If, however, such a tree is making only 1 to 4 inches of growth, fertilization would prove to be extremely valuable and would be justifiable.

A non-bearing tree should be fertilized with particular reference to its age. A two-year-old tree should receive from 4 to 8 ounces, and this amount may be gradually increased as the tree gets older. However, the maximum amount which seems to give best results on a bearing tree is between 5 and 7 pounds.

A high grade complete fertilizer or some form of nitrogen may be used. For best results the nitrogen should be available as soon as spring growth begins. Nitrate of soda can be applied as soon as growth starts as its nitrogen is in a quickly available form. Sulphate of ammonia should be applied a week earlier and cyanamid six weeks earlier.

All fertilizers should be spread under the outer branches around the tree. It is not necessary to spade or rake them into the soil.

When trees are growing on a lawn the best method is to make holes with a stick or bar under the outer branches from 12 to 18 inches apart, 1½ inches in diameter, and about 6 inches deep. Fill them almost to the top with fertilizer. It is not necessary to cover them with soil or other material. This method puts the fertilizer down where the roots will get it, and also prevents an unsightly and uneven lawn which would otherwise be the result.

2. Bearing trees.

Bearing trees should be fertilized regularly in most cases. Besides producing a crop of fruit, a bearing tree should make from 8 to 14 inches of terminal growth each year. Many bearing trees are biennial bearers, which means that they bear a heavy crop one year and few if any fruits the following year. However, fertilization should be just as regular as with an annual bearer, since a fruit spur will not bear two years in succession and each type of tree requires about the same amount of food. Fertilizers help to form fruit buds for the suceeding year's crop and to materially aid in the setting of blossoms which form fruits. Five to seven pounds of a complete fertilizer is sufficient for a full-grown tree.

Thinning: When a tree contains an overabundance of fruits, some should be removed to prevent branches from breaking as well as to increase the size of those left. Thinning should be practised from four to five weeks after the fruits have begun to form. Only one apple should be left in a cluster and individual apples should be from 6 to 8 inches apart on a limb or branch. If one side of a tree has practically no fruits and the other side is heavily laden, good-sized fruits will develop with little thinning. When removing fruits, leave the stem on the spur and use a pair of shears.

With early ripening varieties such as the Early Harvest, Yellow Transparent, and Red Astrachan, thinning may be delayed until six weeks after the blossoms have set. Then the fruits removed are large enough and soft enough to use for pies, applesauce and the like, and come at a time of year when apples are particularly high in price

Harvesting: Apples are mature and ready to be picked when their stems part easily from the spurs on which they are growing. They should be handled very carefully and not be bruised or left in the sun. They will keep longer if put into storage immediately and wrapped or packed with oiled paper. A temperature of 35 to 40 degrees F. is not too low, but a good circulation of moist air is essential for long keeping.

Spraying and Disease and Pest Control: See schedule and table at the end of this chapter.

Varieties of Merit

Apples

Yellow Transparent—An early yellow variety ripening in July. Bears early, heavy annual crops. When the fruits are half mature they may be thinned and used for cooking.

Red Astrachan—An early ripening red variety which bears young, and is excellent for eating and cooking. It ripens unevenly on the tree which makes it possible to get good fruits over a period of three weeks.

Milton—A cross between Yellow Transparent and McIntosh. Very high quality, tree very vigorous and hardy.

Wealthy—One of the best varieties, ripening the last two weeks in August. Fine for culinary and dessert purposes. Comes into bearing young and bears heavy crops. Usually bears every other year.

McIntosh—Ripens in September. One of the finest varieties for general purposes. Tree is very hardy and vigorous. Plant Wealthy with it for pollination purposes. (See section on pollination.)

Delicious—A popular, well-known variety. Bears young and biennially.

Cortland—A cross between Ben Davis and McIntosh to extend the McIntosh season. A good keeper and very high in quality.

McCoun—A variety similar to Cortland but ripening later.

Stayman Winesap—Ripens October 5–10. A very profitable apple for the middle Atlantic and Central states. Good keeper. Bears biennially, usually. Should be planted with Delicious, McIntosh or Grimes Golden for pollination purposes.

Paragon—One of the longest keeping varieties—similar to Winesap.

Crab Apples

Transcendent—Ripens in September, a very good variety. Large size.

CHERRY

Name: Prunus avium—Sweet Cherry.
Prunus Cerasus—Sour Cherry.
Prunus avium x P. Cerasus—hybrids of the sweet and sour varieties, also known as the Dukes.
Soil: A well-drained, loamy soil is suitable for all species.

PLANTING

Age of Trees: Grade A one- or two-year-old trees are preferable as they are, figuratively speaking, the "cream of the crop."
Time of Planting: Same as for Apple.
Planting Distance: Sweet Cherry Trees, 30 feet by 30 feet; Sour or Pie, 20 feet by 20 feet; Dukes or Hybrids, 25 feet by 25 feet.
Method of Planting and Overcoming Failure to Bear: See Apple.
Duration of Bearing: Twenty-five years for the Sour, and up to forty years for the Dukes and Sweet Cherries.

PRUNING

One-year Tree: A one-year-old cherry tree usually contains a few lateral branches. Cut the top back to within 24 to 36 inches from the ground and prune all strong laterals back to 6 or 8 inches. Weak growth should be removed.

Two-year Tree: Select from three to five branches within 15 inches from the ground which are uniformly spaced 3 to 5 inches apart, and which are not on the same plane, but which nevertheless balance the tree. This procedure is very simple to follow if the tree was planted when one year old. If a two-year tree is being pruned at planting time it is best to leave the three to five best branches for the framework and cut back the center branch to the uppermost one which is left. Those branches selected are then cut back to at least 15 to 20 inches if the tree has made a vigorous growth during the first year it was planted. The laterals on a newly set two-year tree should be cut back to 6 or 8 inches in length.

Time of Pruning: Same as Pear or Peach.

Pruning Young Non-Bearing Trees: Most varieties of cherry trees bear in two to five years after setting out. Pruning should be very light and consists of removing only weak, competing, and diseased branches. Slight heading back of the one-year wood is usually necessary in order to promote a bushy habit of growth.

Pruning Bearing Trees: The bearing cherry tree requires but light pruning until it reaches an age of 15 to 20 years, at which time it responds to a heavier pruning which is necessary in order to invigorate it and prolong its life.

Cultivation: See Apple.

Fertilization: Pie or Sour cherries and the hybrids, or Dukes, may be fertilized with the same materials and in the same manner as apple trees, except that the amount should be from one-half to two-thirds as much. Sweet cherry trees, or excessively large pie cherry trees, should receive the same amount as a full-sized bearing apple tree.

Thinning: This is unnecessary with all cherry trees in the home garden.

Harvesting: Sour or Pie cherries may be harvested as soon as they begin to turn red. They may be used for cooking at this stage, but may be left on the tree over a period of approximately three weeks.

Sweet and Duke varieties should not be harvested until they are sweet but firm and ready to eat. Do not allow these varieties to remain on the tree after they once become ripe, as a rain will cause great loss from cracking and possibly brown rot.

All varieties of cherries will keep much longer if picked with the stems attached to the fruit.

Spraying and Disease and Pest Control: See schedule and table at the end of this chapter.

VARIETIES OF MERIT

Sweet Cherries

All varieties described bear in four years:

Bing—One of the largest, black oxheart varieties. Tree is quite small and a slow grower.

Lambert—Very large, purplish red color. Very vigorous.

Napoleon—A yellow-fleshed variety with a red cheek. Known also as Royal Ann.

Black Tartarian—A very large, vigorous growing oxheart. Fine in quality and black in color.

NOTE: The Bing, Lambert, and Napoleon will not bear cherries if planted separately or together. If any one or all of these varieties are planted, a Black Tartarian should also be planted for cross-pollination purposes.

Sour Cherries

All varieties are self-fertile and may be planted alone.

Early Richmond, Montmorency—Both are hardy, vigorous varieties, ripening a week apart. The Montmorency is more highly colored.

PEACH AND NECTARINE

Name: Prunus Persica.

Soil: A sandy loam soil is best. Silt will, however, give fair results.

PLANTING

Age of Trees: See Apple.

Planting Distance: 18 to 20 feet apart each way is the standard distance, although 16 feet apart each way is not too close for the home orchard.

Method of Planting: See Apple.

PRUNING

One-year Tree: The purpose of pruning and training young peach trees is to develop a framework of bowl-shaped branches which will produce the greatest load of fruit close to the ground.

Low-headed peach trees are preferred which branch between 18 and 22 inches from the ground. Oftentimes one-year peach trees contain several small branches. After cutting the main stem back to the height described, the remaining lateral branches should be cut

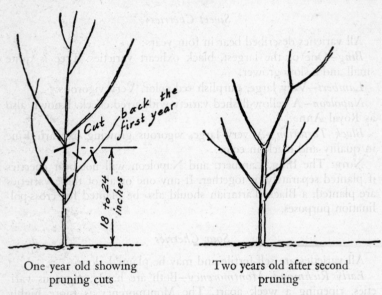

One year old showing
pruning cuts

Two years old after second
pruning

A Young Peach

back to 4 to 6 inches in length. This should be done as soon as the tree is planted.

Two-year Tree: When a two-year-old tree is planted, it is more difficult to prune. In many cases, the trees grew so close together in the nursery that low branches are wanting and higher heading is necessary. Cut the center, or leader, back as close to the 22-inch height as possible, being sure to leave three or four good lateral branches below the cut. The branches selected should come out at a 90-degree angle with the trunk, if possible.

The lateral branches should be 3 to 4 inches apart if it is at all possible to select them that way. If the branches come out at one point the entire tree is in danger of being ruined if one of them breaks at the trunk.

The lateral branches selected should be cut back. The amount of cutting back will vary with their vigor. Under ordinary conditions 12 inches are not too much to leave.

Time of Pruning: Pruning should not be done until all danger of near or below freezing temperatures is past as many varieties are susceptible to these low temperatures.

Pruning Young Non-Bearing Peach Trees: Peach trees come into bearing during their third or fourth year so that their non-bearing period is very short. During this period a vigorous, spreading, bushy framework should be developed. Eighteen to 24 inches of terminal growth is most satisfactory. Pruning should consist of thinning out weak and inferior wood; cutting back several inches on the one-year wood to produce a bushy and stock framework and to remove competing or crossing and too closely parallel branches. The center should be allowed to become filled in but not clogged.

Pruning Bearing Peach Trees: Peaches are borne on growth formed the previous season. The principle involved is to have a good supply of fruiting wood each year which makes cutting back a necessary practice instead of an injury, as would be the result with apple trees. If peach trees were not pruned the fruit would be borne on the terminal ends of the branches at such a height as to cause the limbs to break. Fourteen feet is a good height for a peach tree.

The necessary procedure to prune a peach tree is as follows:

1. Cut out dead, diseased, and broken branches.
2. Thin out weak, crossing, and parallel branches.
3. Keep the center open and allow water sprouts to grow, but thin them out if too many are present.

(A *water sprout* is a type of vigorous, succulent growth which develops on the trunk or limbs of a tree. Severe pruning encourages water sprouts to develop.)

4. Cut back to strong lateral branches to promote vegetative growth.
5. Do not allow the center to become clogged with non-fruiting wood.
6. Cut back one-year growth to 15 inches in length. Lateral growth will be encouraged.
7. Keep the tree within bounds.

If a healthy tree fails to grow vigorously after several years of bearing, the branches should be cut back severely, but always to a lateral branch. This will invigorate new growth better than fertilizers.

Duration of Bearing: A peach tree is an annual bearer of heavy crops over a period of twenty to twenty-five years, although some trees may be productive for as long as forty years.

Overcoming Failure to Bear: Early spring frosts, killing winter temperatures, and lack of food are the main causes of failure to bear. The first two mentioned may be avoided by planting resistant varieties, and the food supply may be given them in the form of commercial fertilizer and organic matter. Very few varieties are self-unfruitful when grown alone, but it is well to look into this matter before planting some of the newer varieties. The J. H. Hale should be planted with another variety.

Cultivation: Peach trees give their best response to cultivation, although results may not be poor if otherwise grown. The soil should be disked or cultivated at frequent intervals during the growing season and cultivation should cease when the varieties begin to ripen. Cultivate at intervals sufficient to prevent weed growth from competing with the trees and to keep a 2-inch soil mulch at all times.

Fertilization: A general rule is to apply from half to two thirds as much fertilizer to a peach tree as to an apple tree, and the application should be made at approximately the same time. See Apple.

Thinning: When about the size of a 25-cent piece, peaches should be thinned to about 4 inches apart. This practice will result in larger and higher quality fruits. When a tree is overcrowded with fruits the stone will be as large in a small fruit as in a larger fruit. Therefore, thinning has the tendency to increase the proportion of flesh to the size of the stone or peach seed.

Harvesting: Peaches should be harvested when they are mature, but firm. If they are left on the tree until fully ripe too many will drop and become inferior in appearance and salability. At the time of maturity the undercolor which changes from green to yellow or white is very apparent. Two or three days after picking, the peaches are in prime condition for eating or preserving. Some varieties first become soft on one side, which is usually the most highly colored side. If picked in this stage the other side will soften up within a short time.

VARIETIES OF MERIT

Peaches

All varieties are freestone and bear in three to four years.

White, 1. *Carman*—A good variety for the home garden, ripens early and has an excellent flavor.

2. *Hiley Belle*—Ripens after Carman.

3. *Georgia Belle*—Flesh has a tendency to be slightly stringy, but its flavor is unsurpassed.

Yellow, 1. *Golden Jubilee*—An early yellow freestone that is without exception the best variety of its season.

2. *Elberta*—The most popular, well-known variety. If allowed to ripen on the tree its flavor is of the best.

3. *Roberta*—Very similar to Elberta but ripens a week later.

Nectarine

Surecrop—Recommended for the home fruit garden.

PEAR

Name: Pyrus.
Soil: A deep, loamy soil with good drainage.

PLANTING

Age of Trees for Planting: See Apple.
Time of Planting: See Apple.
Distance Between Trees: 30 feet by 30 feet.
Method of Planting: See Apple.
Duration of Bearing: Thirty to forty years or more.

PRUNING

One-year Tree: A one-year-old pear tree should be pruned back to a height of 30 to 36 inches. Usually it is a straight whip without any lateral branches. If lateral branches are present, prune them back to 4 to 6 inches in length if they are vigorous. If lateral growth is weak it is best to cut it out entirely.

Two-year Tree: Four or five branches are selected as scaffold branches for the future framework of the tree. The same principles are practised as with apples, which see. The reason for leaving more scaffold branches than with apples is that the pear is quite susceptible to fire blight. If it developed on a limb from which all the main laterals developed, the entire tree would be killed within a short time. By training several branches as described, the removal of one will not seriously injure the tree.

Time of Pruning: The pear is hardier than the peach but not as hardy as the apple. Therefore, do not prune until freezing weather has passed in order to avoid winter-killing.

Pruning Non-Bearing Trees: Light pruning is the answer to this question for reasons discussed in the case of the apple. There are many varietal habits of growth, so allow the tree to grow naturally with a little thinning and heading back when necessary.

Pruning Bearing Trees: See Apple.

Overcoming Failure to Bear: See Apple.

Cultivation: Not entirely necessary, as with the peach, although it is helpful to give young trees a good start when possible. Keep weed growth suppressed as with the apple.

Fertilization: This may vary somewhat according to the variety and its ultimate size. Medium-sized trees may be fertilized like the peach. Large-sized trees should receive the equivalent amounts which are supplied to bearing apple trees.

Harvesting: Pears contain their best flavor if not allowed to fully mature on the tree. Pick them when they begin to turn yellow, or, with green or russet varieties, when they part easily from the spur. They should be juicy and sweet several days later.

Spraying and Disease and Pest Control: See schedule and table at the end of this chapter.

Varieties of Merit

Pears

Varieties listed all bear within four years, except Beurre Bosc.

Bartlett—This variety needs no introduction. It is as well known as the Elberta Peach. It should be planted with another variety as in most cases it is self-sterile.

Clapps Favorite—Resembles the Bartlett, ripening about a week earlier. Has a tendency to become soft when fully ripe more quickly than the Bartlett.

Seckel—One of the highest quality small russet pears. A vigorous grower. Not as subject to fire blight as the Bartlett.

Beurre Bosc—A very large russet yellow color and one of the longest keepers. Does not bear until eight or nine years old.

PLUM

Name: Prunus domestica—European Plum.

Prunus salicina—Japanese Plum.

Prunus insititia—French or Damson Plum.

Soil: A heavy silt or clay loam is most desirable, although some varieties give good results in the lighter soils.

PLANTING

Age of Tree: See Apple.

Time of Planting: See Apple.

858

Planting Distance: 30 feet by 30 feet for domestica and salicina species. Twenty to 25 feet apart each way for the insititia species.

Method of Planting: See Apple.

Overcoming Failure to Bear: See Apple.

Duration of Bearing: Usually twenty to thirty years.

Pruning, Cultivation, Fertilization, and Thinning: See Cherry.

Harvesting: The European types may be harvested when mature but firm. They include the prune plums which will keep for as long as two weeks under ordinary conditions. However, they have the best flavor when allowed to fully mature on the tree. This is indicated by the stem easily parting from the twig.

The Japanese types are much softer and, once they begin to ripen, deteriorate rather soon. They may, however, be picked when firm to prolong their keeping period.

The insititia types keep as well, if not better, than many of the domestica types. They usually ripen several weeks later.

Spraying and Disease and Pest Control: See schedule and table at the end of this chapter.

VARIETIES OF MERIT

Plums

Burbank—A yellow-fleshed variety with a dark red skin. Good for culinary and dessert purposes. Hardy.

Italian Prune—A dark purplish skin with greenish yellow flesh. Very solid and fine for canning or eating.

Green Gage—A yellowish green variety which is very high in quality.

Damson—Not used for eating but an excellent variety for canning in various ways. Very vigorous and prolific.

QUINCE

Name: Cydonia oblonga.

Soil: A well-drained, rich, loamy soil.

PLANTING

Age of Trees for Planting: Two-year-old trees are most desirable as the quince is a comparatively slow grower.

Time of Planting: Early spring planting gives excellent results but fall planting is permissible in regions where the temperature does not go below zero.

Distance Between Trees: Quince bushes are set from 15 to 20 feet apart each way.

Method of Planting: See Apple.

PRUNING

1st Year: The quince is pruned back slightly to stimulate new shoot growth. No definite system is followed.

2nd Year: Thin out the weaker, inferior branches and cut back the remaining shoots from one-third to one-half their length, especially if the tree has been set out that season. Two-year-old trees which have been growing in their permanent position for a year do not require as severe pruning as those just planted.

Pruning the Bearing Quince Bush: Remove a small amount of the twiggy growth each year and cut back any branches which have the tendency to grow out of bounds.

Duration of Bearing: A quince bush will bear for twenty-five years or more.

Overcoming Failure to Bear: There should be no trouble in this respect. See Apple.

Cultivation: See Apple.

Fertilization: See Peach.

Thinning: Fruits will be larger if thinned out from 6 to 8 inches apart. In most cases, however, there is little need of it.

Harvesting: The quince may be harvested when it has attained its fullest development which is around 3 inches in diameter. It is such a hard fruit that it will keep from 4 to 6 months without any special care except careful handling.

Disease and Pest Control: See Spraying Schedule at the end of this chapter.

SMALL BUSH FRUITS

BLACKBERRIES

Name: Rubus (various).

Soil: The Blackberry will grow on any fertile soil where the moisture conditions are satisfactory. As it bears its crop in midsummer, lack of moisture is often the cause of low yields. Once it is established, it will spread rapidly if not kept within bounds.

Planting: The plants are usually set out in the early spring months. Early planting is most favorable for the best results. The tops are cut back to 12 to 18 inches and the plants are set 3 feet apart in the row; 6 to 8 feet between the rows is not too far apart. Suckers may be set out any time after August 1st, but the results are apt to be questionable because of weather conditions at that time of year. Set the plants slightly deeper than they grew in the nursery.

Culture: Vigorous, vegetative suckers grow up one year, fruit the following summer and die. It is, therefore, necessary to permit suckers to grow but they must be kept within bounds. Plants may be trained to wires, or several canes may be tied to a stake. The plants must be kept in rows or hills, which makes it necessary to remove all suckers appearing in the middle of the row. This should be done by pulling up the roots and not by cutting, as new ones will readily sprout from the old stumps. Enough space should be left to allow for cultivation and care in picking.

Cultivation or Mulching: If cultivation is the method chosen to follow, it should be done frequently enough to keep weed growth suppressed. Blackberry roots are close to the surface, so cultivation should be shallow.

A mulch will suppress weed growth and conserve moisture, and if this method is chosen, enough mulch should be applied between the plants and in the row to keep weeds from growing up through it. Grass clippings, hay, leaves, etc., will give satisfactory results.

Fertilizers: Fertilizers should be applied early in the spring when growth begins, to encourage good strong sucker development which is to fruit the following year. A complete fertilizer containing nitrogen, phosphorus, and potash is strongly recommended. The rate of application will depend on the fertility of the soil. Some cases have been known in which blackberries did better without any fertilizer than others did with a heavy application, due to soil and moisture differences. An application of 1 pound to 50 feet of row early in the spring when the plants begin to fruit heavily is a medium application. Manure may also be applied with good results.

Pruning: Fruiting canes may be removed at any time after the crop is harvested until growth begins the following spring. Weak and broken canes should be removed. Thin the others out so that they are at least 6 inches apart. This is not necessary if plants are grown in hills, but never allow more than five or six canes per hill. Cut the tops back to a height between 4 and 5 feet. This varies with the variety and the vigor of growth. Three or four strong laterals may be left per cane if cut back to three or four buds. Cut out the weak ones entirely.

Cutting back should be practised only in the spring as winter killing always starts at the tip. If the canes are cut back in the fall, winter willing will begin at the point of detachment.

If some of the weak suckers are removed during the growing season, those left will have more room in which to develop.

Disease and Pest Control: See table at the end of this chapter.

VARIETIES OF MERIT

Eldorado—The largest and sweetest variety. Very hardy, vigorous, and productive.

Iceberg—A novelty, white-fruited.

BLUEBERRIES

Name: Vaccinium corymbosum.

Blueberry culture is of most recent origin, which is due in part to the increased market demand for a greater supply of large, high-quality berries. The problem is to adapt them to many soils which have been growing other crops with different soil requirements.

Soil: Blueberries produce best results on a soil which is acid in reaction and which is well drained, but retentive of moisture. Soil which has previously grown garden crops is usually not suitable because it is not acid enough. However, the addition of decomposed leaves, peat, woodland turf or sawdust will materially help to make the soil acid. Aluminum sulfate may be applied at the rate of 1 pound to 75 or 100 square feet, but its effect is only temporary. Aluminum sulfate should not supplant the addition of the above materials suggested, but it may be used satisfactorily in conjunction with them if applied each year and worked into the soil.

Land which has not previously been planted to garden or other crops is suitable for growing blueberries, especially if acid-loving plants such as sweet ferns, wild blueberries, white cedar, oak or pines are growing on it.

The land should be plowed after all superfluous growth is removed and allowed to lie fallow for one season. Frequent cultivation or disking during the year will prevent weed growth and also improves its physical condition. If water has the tendency to stand on the surface for a period of several days during the growing season, the plant roots will suffer from lack of oygen. Such places should be drained.

Setting the Plants: Blueberry plants are set during early spring or late fall months. Early spring planting usually gives best results. Do not allow the roots of the plants to dry out before setting in the ground. The plants are set 4 feet apart in the row and from 6 to 8 feet apart between the rows. Dig the holes wide enough to avoid crowding the roots and deep enough to set the plants two inches deeper than they were growing before. Firm the soil around the plants and water if the soil is dry. Several varieties should be planted, as cross-pollination is necessary to produce good yields.

Soil Management: Blueberry plantations may be managed by two methods: clean cultivation and mulching.

If clean cultivation is practised it should be shallow, at intervals of two or three weeks apart from early spring to midsummer to control weeds and thus conserve moisture. Deep cultivation or hoeing to a depth of more than 2 inches will destroy part of the plant's fibrous root system. Do not cultivate within several inches of the base of the plant for this reason.

Plants may be mulched with satisfactory results but cultivation should precede this treatment for at least a year after the plants are set. Shavings, peat moss, pine needles or oak leaves are suitable materials for using as a mulch. Lawn clippings may also be used. The important point is to apply enough of the mulching between the rows and around the plants to prevent weed growth and to conserve moisture. Three or 4 inches are usually necessary.

Fertilization: Fertilizers are applied just as growth begins in the spring and again four to six weeks after the first application. A 4–12–4 fertilizer applied at the rate of 1 pound to 100 square feet will give good results. Cultivate the fertilizer into the soil soon after applying it if the mulch system is not used.

Pruning: Pruning should be done early in the spring before growth begins. During the first three years pruning consists of removing a few of the smaller lateral shoots and thinning out the bushy growth. The plants should not be permitted to bear fruit for the first two years after setting. To prevent bearing, remove the flower clusters when they appear. Pruning after the third year consists in removing from one-fourth to one-third of the old wood, besides removing weak twigs and branches lying on the ground.

Varieties– As many new varieties are being developed, it is strongly recommended that you write to your State Agricultural Experiment Station for their advice on this subject. The Cabot, Pioneer, Rancocas and Rubel are excellent varieties.

CURRANTS AND GOOSEBERRIES

Names: Currant—Ribes, various.
        Gooseberry—(American) R. hirtellum.
               (European) R. Grossularia.

The growing, fruiting and cultural methods are so similar that currants and gooseberries may be discussed together.

Both are very hardy and winter injury is an uncommon occurrence.

Soil and Location: A moist, fertile, well-drained loam soil, supplied with organic matter, is ideal. They should not be planted in low places where late frosts occur, as they bloom early.

Planting: Both fruits may be planted in the fall or spring with equally good results, although in some cases fall planting is preferable.

Good strong one- or two-year-old plants may be set. The planting distance is from 4 to 6 feet apart in the row with 6 feet between the rows.

Broken and extra long roots should be cut back. The tops are cut back to a height of 6 to 8 inches. Cutting back depends to a great extent on the size of the root system and the size of top.

Set the plants slightly deeper than originally growing in the nursery and firm the soil around them.

General Care: Practise shallow cultivation to suppress weed growth. Plants may be mulched with leaves, straw or other material during the growing season but the mulch should be removed in the early fall to discourage rodents.

Fertilizers: Stable manure may be broadcast around the plants early in the spring. Complete fertilizers give most satisfactory results as they contain more readily available plant food. Four ounces per plant as growth begins in the spring is usually sufficient. This is applied in a narrow band 6 to 8 inches away from the main stalk and raked or hoed in.

Pruning: Both bear fruit at the base of the one-year-old wood and on spurs of older wood. The principle of pruning is to maintain a steady supply of new wood and to prevent old, partially fruiting canes from accumulating in any great number so as to interfere with the younger growth. All wood four years or older should be removed at the base of the plant. Remove at the same time spindly and short shoots. Eight or ten strong shoots are sufficient, ranging in age from one to four years. By keeping the old canes going we keep the new canes coming.

A little heading back of the new canes is necessary. In some sections where borers are a pest it is not recommended to any great extent.

Gooseberries are more difficult to propagate than currants. By heaping soil around the plant and covering 3 or 4 inches of the base of the one-year canes, roots will form. This should be done in late June or July. By the middle of September, the soil may be removed and those which have rooted may be severed from the plant and set in another location. Another method is to cut back the one-year growth 6 inches, remove the tips, and plant in the open ground. They will root quite readily. This is best done in the early spring before the growth process is perceptible.

Disease and Pest Control: See table at the end of this chapter.

Varieties of Merit

Gooseberries

American varieties produce twice as many berries as other varieties but they are very small.

European varieties are more susceptible to mildew than American ones.

Downing—Adapted to all conditions in this country. Very productive, high in quality. American.

Poor Man—One of the largest American kinds. Pinkish, sweet, excellent. Produces about 2 quarts when five years old. Berries hang on a long time.

Chautauqua—European. Large. Comparatively free from mildew. Seeds large. Plant hard to propagate.

Houghton—Small. Old, well-known variety. Adapted to a good many soils.

Red Currants

Perfection—Berries large, bright crimson, sprightly sub-acid, mid-season, clusters compact, very long, easy to pick. A heavy yielder. Berries sometimes scald in hot weather if not picked as soon as ripe. Bush more or less spreading, throwing up canes from below the ground; canes break easily.

Wilder—Berries large, dark red, mild sub-acid, hang on bushes well. Mid-season; clusters large, compact, easy to pick. Bush upright and large.

London Market—(London Red)—Berries medium to large, deep red, rather acid, mid-season to late; clusters compact, with short stems. Bush upright, somewhat resistant to borers and diseases; most resistant of any variety to the white pine blister rust. (See Chapter XXXII.)

Red Cross—Berries large, firm, light red, sub-acid, hang on to bushes well; mid-season, but later than the Cherry; clusters of medium length, well filled, easy to pick. Cracks easily. Plant is not long-lived. Fruit ripens unevenly.

Cherry—Berries large, becoming smaller as the bush grows older. Deep red, very acid, mid-season. Bush somewhat spreading. Unproductive. Canes have a tendency to go blind.

White Currants

White Dutch—Earliest and sweetest of white ones. Small berries and not uniform. Good in quality. Sweeter than the red ones.

White Grape—The best. Medium in size, berries fairly large, but not uniform. Rich flavor. Bush very productive.

White Imperial—Berries large, pale yellow, almost sweet; clusters medium length, and loose. Bush spreading, very productive. A desirable variety; considered to have the best dessert quality of all currants.

Black Currants

Champion—Wild flavor. Ripens after the red currants. Mildest of the black varieties. Larger than Perfection (Red). Most susceptible to White Pine Blister Rust.

RED RASPBERRIES

Name: (European) Rubus idæus.
(American) Rubus idæus strigosus.

Soil: A deep loamy soil is most desirable for red raspberries because it is best for the plants and easier to cultivate. Heavy silts and clay soils should be avoided because of poor growth and lower yields. Thorough drainage and an adequate supply of moisture are essential.

The soil should be thoroughly pulverized previous to planting. Sod land should be prepared by growing some vegetable on it at least two years in advance.

Planting: New stock or suckers which developed the previous year should be planted in the following spring, before growth begins. Suckers may also be dug up and planted during the month of August but the first suggestion gives best results under average conditions.

Plants are set 3 to 4 feet apart in the rows, allowing 6 to 8 feet between the rows. Before planting, the tops of the plants, if set in the spring, should be cut back to 12 inches. Set the plants 3 inches deeper than they were formerly growing to protect them from drought.

Cultivation: Tillage should be thorough and more regular than for most other crops. The root system is quite shallow and cultivation should not be deeper than 3 inches.

Fertilizer: The application of commercial fertilizers should be planned with caution since too much nitrogen will cause excessive growth and weak canes which may bend over and touch the ground. A fertile soil is necessary to begin with. Given sufficient cultivation to suppress weed growth, it should be ample under many conditions.

Training and Pruning: Red raspberries fruit on the same principle as do blackberries. Suckers grow one year, fruit the next, and die. The principle of pruning is also the same. Varieties vary greatly in their habit of growth and should be treated accordingly when thinned out. The tops are cut back before growth begins in the spring. Cut the canes back from 6 to 18 inches. Severe cutting will reduce the crop. With some very vigorous varieties more cutting back is practical than with others. The canes should be cut back to a height of 3½ to 4½ feet.

Disease and Pest Control: See table at the end of this chapter.

VARIETIES OF MERIT

Latham—Fruit very large, hardy and resistant to mosaic. Flavor is only fair.

Newburgh—Ripens later than the Latham by a week or ten days. Very hardy, vigorous, and resistant to mosaic. A recent introduction.

Taylor—An outstanding introduction which may surpass the Latham.

Everbearing Variety

St. Regis—A long standing, well-known variety that bears fruit from summer to freezing weather.

PURPLE AND BLACK RASPBERRIES

Name: (Black Raspberries) Rubus occidentalis.
  (Purple Raspberries) R. occidentalis x R. idæus.

Soil: Soil requirements are practically the same as for the red raspberry. Although its water requirements are greater, it may do well on the heavier soils. Its root system is much more fibrous and vigorous.

Planting: Early spring planting is most satisfactory. The plants should be spaced 4 feet in the rows and 6 feet between the rows.

They should be cut back to 6 inches when setting out and the spot should be marked with a stick.

Propagation: Purple and black raspberries do not produce suckers as do red raspberries. All new growth comes from a definite place in the crown of the plant and propagation is done by covering the ends of the new growth with soil during the months of July and August. This is called tip-layering.

Pruning: Three fruiting canes are sufficient for each plant. These

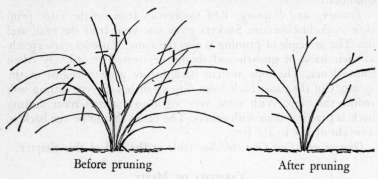

Before pruning   After pruning

A Black Raspberry

are cut back to a height of $3\frac{1}{2}$ to 4 feet. The strong laterals are pruned so as to leave three buds, the weaker ones being cut out.

Other requirements are the same as for the red raspberry.

Disease and Pest Control: See table at the end of this chapter.

VARIETIES OF MERIT

Black Beauty: Resistant to disease, besides being hard and productive. Fruit is large.

Cumberland—Very large and vigorous but is susceptible to disease in many places. It is worth a trial in any garden.

STRAWBERRIES

Name: Fragaria.

Remarks: A large patch of strawberries may be planted at a small cost and will bring quicker returns and high yields sooner than any other fruit crop. It is the first fresh fruit to appear on the markets in early spring.

Soil: Soil is more important than location. A soil for strawberries should contain plenty of organic material, be well drained and fertile. The time of ripening may be extended or delayed several days. A sandy soil warms up most quickly in the spring months. Plant growth will therefore be stimulated sooner than on silt or heavy loam soils which do not warm up as quickly. Too much nitrogen will cause excessive plant development which will result in crowding and lower yields. The soil should be well firmed before planting.

Getting the Plants: Strawberry plants are said to be perfect or imperfect. A perfect blossom has both stamens and pistils while an imperfect blossom has only one or the other. Imperfect varieties should be interplanted with perfect ones so that cross-pollination will insure a good yield of berries. The perfect and imperfect varieties should bloom at the same time. However, over 99 per cent of the varieties sold today are perfect ones.

Time to Plant: Early spring is the best time to plant and the earlier the better. Plants may be set in the fall but this practice is not recommended as the yield is reduced the following year and heaving is very apt to occur during the winter.

The planting distance depends on the variety, method of training, and fertility of the soil. The usual distance is 15 to 20 inches in the row and $3\frac{1}{2}$ to 4 feet between the rows.

Plants are prepared for planting by removing old and decayed leaves and trimming the roots to about three inches. Soak the roots in a pail of water and keep them in the shade.

Setting the Plants: The ideal time to set plants in the garden is on a cloudy day or late in the afternoon. Be sure to keep the roots moist at all times by keeping them in a container which is covered with paper or wet burlap. Do not allow the roots to be exposed to the sun for over two minutes before planting.

Mark out the rows with a tight line. If planting is difficult because of the line a furrow $1\frac{1}{2}$ inches deep may be made with a hoe or other garden implement, using the line as a guide before removing it. The crown center of the plant where the tiny leaves are developing should be just flush or level with the surface of the soil. If set too deeply, it will be covered with soil and will rot; if set too high, the roots will dry out, as they will not be in contact with a sufficient supply of moisture. The plants should be well firmed in the soil to prevent drying out, and to keep the moisture in contact with the roots.

The following method of setting has proven most satisfactory.
1. Have the rows properly marked.
2. Have the plants properly trimmed.

3. Have someone drop the plants on the row 15–18 inches apart.

4. The setter takes a trowel in the right hand, plunges it into the soil and pulls it toward him about 3 inches.

5. The plant which has been dropped is put in the hole in back of the trowel at the proper depth. The roots are spread out. The trowel is removed and the soil firmed around the plant by pressing with both hands. Twenty plants per minute can be set out with excellent results.

Care of Newly Set Plants: Blossoms which will appear after the plants are set out should be removed to allow all the strength to go into the formation of plants instead of fruit the first year.

Keep weed growth suppressed by practising shallow cultivation. About a month to six weeks after planting, runners will appear. The first two plants on each one will develop first and will, therefore, produce more fruit the following year than those rooting late in the season. Four runners per plant is sufficient. Others may be cut off. If these runners are spaced around the plant and a small stone is placed next to where the leaves are appearing, they will take root very easily. On a commercial basis, very little training and pruning is practised and so by the end of the growing season the row has a matted appearance and is called the matted row system. As the new plants form, the row gradually closes in and more hand weeding is necessary as it is impossible to hoe or cultivate between the plants.

However, if plants are not going to be dug up from the middle of the row for planting the following spring, they might just as well be kept hoed out during the first year. Leave a path 12 inches wide which will facilitate harvesting the next summer.

When new runners appear the soil should be slightly mounded 12 inches each side of the parent plant and 2 to 3 inches higher than the level of the field. This will supply soft soil in which the runners will root, besides facilitating better drainage.

The bed should be weeded late in the fall and all weeds, especially clover and chickweed which over-winter, removed.

Manures and Fertilizers: An application of well-rotted manure is a decided advantage. One horse load to a plot 50 feet x 50 feet will bring good results. It should be plowed in at any time previous to planting. A cover crop should be plowed under a year in advance of setting the plants to allow time for decomposition to take place if it is used as a substitute for manure.

Lime is not essential and should not be applied in any great quantity if at all, as the strawberry prefers an acid soil.

A complete fertilizer should be used for best results. It may be applied at the time of setting the plants at the rate of 1 pound to 50 square feet and raked in or applied after the plants are established. In the latter case, it is applied on a dry day by broadcasting it over the plants at the mentioned rate. An old broom or fine brush should be used to remove any of it from the leaves, which will be burned if moisture is present. This application should be raked or cultivated into the soil.

Winter Protection: In sections where winter weather is variable and accompanied by alternate freezing and thawing, the plants should be protected to prevent them from heaving. Coarse material such as straw or hay is best applied after the ground freezes. Cover to a depth of ½ to 1 inch. This material prevents the soil from thawing out very rapidly and thus prevents heaving. Fine material in any quantity, such as pine needles, should be avoided as it may pack too tightly and kill the plants.

Spring Treatment: Winter covering should be removed after all danger is past of a heavy frost which would kill the blossoms. About two-thirds of the straw is removed and placed in the space left between the rows. It serves as a mulch and makes kneeling a pleasure instead of a pain. The plants will grow up through the remaining covering which will settle down around the base of them and keep the berries clean and off the ground.

There has been much discussion as to the feasibility of spring fertilization. It is well to remember at this point that the fruit buds were formed the season before. Nitrogenous fertilizers promote vigorous succulent growth which may result in overcrowding and in soft berries. The main requirement until the fruit is harvested is water. It is the care the plants receive the first season that is so important for the production of the next year's crop.

Harvesting: The picking season for a particular variety ranges from seven to fourteen days. Beds fruiting the second or third time are earlier than those bearing their first crop.

Pick the berries in the coolest part of the day and do not pick when the vines are moist, unless absolutely necessary. Gather the fruit at least every other day, as it becomes soft very quickly after reaching maturity. Put the fruit in the shade and in a cool place immediately after picking. Do not hold more than two berries in the hand at a time.

Renewing or Renovation: After the crop has been harvested, a vigorous treatment is necessary to instigate new life in the patch.

1. Remove all material used for a mulch and burn or compost it.

2. Rake the patch very vigorously. Many plants will be removed but this is unimportant as concerning future yields.

3. Cultivate the rows to a width of 2 feet. This will narrow them considerably but it must be done.

4. Apply a complete fertilizer—1 pound to 50 feet of row.

5. Keep weed growth suppressed.

It is not advisable to keep a patch for more than three years, and two is more generally recommended.

Potted Plants: Some nurserymen sell potted plants which can be set out in August and which will bear fruit the following spring. One hundred such plants cost as much as a thousand dug from the patch in the spring. Also the yield is a comparatively small one.

Pots filled with soil are plunged into the earth next to spring-set plants when the runners are somewhat developed. The first joint on each runner is placed on the soil in the pot. The roots which develop grow into the soil in the pot. Plants from later joints which develop are firmly rooted in the ground by August and need no help from the parent plant. The runner on both sides of the plant growing in the pot is cut and the pot removed with its plant.

Home-grown plants will give excellent results if the bed has received reasonable care. Nurserymen sell excellent plants which are satisfactory, provided they are properly packed and shipped.

Plants may be dug from the patch with a trowel and moved to their new location with soil on the roots. Old and decayed leaves should be removed before planting. Two or three leaves per plant are sufficient to begin with.

If plants are received by mail or express, the package should be opened as soon as received to avoid sweating and deterioration. Set the plants in a trench temporarily, to prevent the roots from drying out.

Disease and Pest Control: See table at the end of this chapter.

VARIETIES OF MERIT

Dorsett—
Fairfax— } Early varieties.

Catskill—Midseason.

Chesapeake—
Gandy— } Late.

The four outstanding Everbearing Varieties are the *Mastodon, Gem, Lucky Strike,* and *Wayzata.*

VINE FRUITS

GRAPES

Name: Vitis Labruscana.

Soil: The grape does well on any fertile soil but shows a preference for the medium to silt-loam types.

PLANTING

Age of Vines for Planting: One- or two-year-old vines.

Time of Planting: Early spring as soon as the frost is out of the ground.

Distance Between Vines: 6 feet x 6 feet, or 6 x 8 feet.

Method of Planting: Set 2 inches deeper than they were originally growing in the nursery.

Pruning and Training: The best time for pruning is in late winter or very early spring before the sap starts to run. There are several systems of training and pruning the grape. They will not be discussed in detail, but the important facts about pruning and training will be stated.

1. The best fruits are borne on pencil-sized canes and between the second and twelfth bud from the base.

2. A vine can supply 40 to 60 buds.

3. Therefore, the best system is one which contains four pencil-sized canes, each cane having from 10 to 15 buds.

Grade A, one- or two-year vines should be planted early in the spring before the buds begin to swell. Cut the vine back to two or three buds at planting time. As the new shoots develop, train them off the ground to a stake or two wires which have been fastened to posts.

Set posts 3 feet in the ground and 4½ feet out of the ground, 15 to 18 feet apart. Attach the first lengthwise wire 18 inches from the ground, the second 18 inches from the first, and the third 18 inches from the second.

The vine should be trained up to the top wire and tied and cut. This is to form the trunk. The following year, growth will appear from all the lateral buds and the system of training will be established when the vine is pruned early the following spring. Select two pencil-sized canes near the middle wire. Train one on each side of the main stem and cut back to 10 to 12 buds. Repeat this process on the top wire, and tie the canes in place with soft string

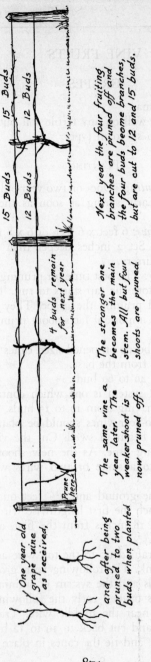

One year old grape vine as received,

and after being pruned to two buds when planted

The same vine a year later. The weaker shoot is now pruned off.

Prune here

The stronger one becomes the main stem. All but four shoots are pruned off.

4 buds remain for next year

Next year the four fruiting branches are pruned off and the four buds beome branches, but are cut to 12 and 15 buds.

15 Buds

12 Buds

15 Buds

12 Buds

Growth and Pruning of a Grape Vine

or binder twine. Tight tying is not necessary as the string serves only as a support for the canes. The other canes should be removed, but be sure to leave two buds on four of them, so that they will be fully developed to produce the crop near each cane the following year.

Oftentimes only two wires are used, as the bottom wire serves mainly for support.

Lateral growths on one-year-old canes are cut back to four buds if pencil-sized.

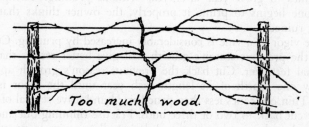

Vine not pruned.

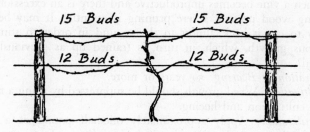

Vine pruned to four branches.

Pruning Grape Vine

The new wood should be kept as close to the head as possible. This is to keep the fruiting wood from growing out of bounds. As a vine gets old, 8 to 10 years, its vigor diminishes, which is well attested to by the shortening of the annual growth. As the vigor decreases it is time to renew the vine. One will notice in most instances that canes are persistent in growing at the base of the trunk. Cut the trunk off so as not to injure these canes and train one up to take the place of the old one removed. The results obtained will be remarkable, with an increase of vigor to a productive result for several years to come.

TRAINING AND PRUNING A GRAPE ARBOR

A grape arbor, besides furnishing shade, should also be productive. As much more space is allowed each vine than when trained to wires the system of training is somewhat different. Vines may be planted 4 feet apart on the sides. The general tendency is to permit the vines to grow year after year without pruning. Then, when someone begins to prune it properly, the owner thinks that it is being ruined.

The vigor of a vine is considerably increased by pruning. Cutting back the previous season's growth will give better results than additional fertilizer. Cut back the previous season's growth approximately one fourth of its length each year until the arbor is covered. Thin out canes less than pencil-sized and leave several of those larger cut back to two or three buds. Practise thinning out and cutting back each year thereafter and do not allow a vine to go without any pruning.

When a vine becomes unproductive and there is an excess of nonfruiting wood present, severe pruning is essential. It may be necessary to cut it back almost to the ground in order to stimulate vigorous growth, which, in turn, is trained up as previously described.

Duration of Bearing: 50 years or more.

Cultivation: Weed growth should be suppressed by using a mulch or by cultivation and hoeing.

Fertilization: Apply approximately one-half pound of a complete fertilizer to a bearing vine in a ring about 2 feet away from the trunk, or broadcast over the surface just as growth begins in the spring. Young non-bearing vines should receive from one half to one third of the above amount and at the same time.

Thinning: Thinning is not necessary if a bearing vine is pruned and trained as suggested, as it can comfortably care for the entire crop.

Harvesting: Grapes should not be harvested until they are fully ripe, at which time they have reached their highest sugar content and flavor. Each bunch should be handled carefully and preferably removed with a pair of scissors to prevent shattering or other injury.

Pest and Disease Control: See the Spray Schedule at the end of this chapter.

VARIETIES OF MERIT

Moore's Early—Black in color, ripens two weeks earlier than the Concord. Not so high in quality. Not such good color. Berries crack easily. Bunch not compact. Shoulders (upper part of grapes) not very good.

Worden—Ripens ten days before the Concord. Berries larger than the Concord. In wet, rainy weather, the berries will crack. When ripening on the bunch, those that ripen first will not wait until the others ripen (tend to shell). Highly recommended, more so than the Concord.

Concord—An old variety. Widely grown except in the warmer sections. Can be depended upon. Still sort of wildish. Will grow without any cultivation. Likes moisture.

Agawam—Large, red. About 2½ times as large as the Concord. Not highly colored. Good flavor. Drawback, hard to swallow. Very vigorous grower.

Caco—Red in color. Yield and quality good. One of the best all-around grapes.

Brighton—Never plant alone. About the only variety that must be cross-pollinated. Recommended for cooler parts. On heavy soil, plant 8 by 8 feet. It is usually planted 6 by 6 feet.

Delaware—About three-sixteenths inches in diameter. Leaves are tiny and many. Must spray thoroughly on account of mildew. Small, red, compact. Late and excellent flavor. Red, small bunches.

Portland—Early white, vigorous and excellent flavor.

Green Mountain—Medium late, white, dark green, sprightly flavored.

SPRAYING OF FRUIT TREES AND BUSH AND VINE FRUITS

Equipment: Any type of hand- or machine-driven sprayer will give satisfactory results from the disease and insect control standpoint, if all parts of the leaves and fruit are covered. One cannot figure on over forty hours of good spraying weather per week. Therefore, the size of the sprayer should be such that complete coverage can be given to all trees to be sprayed within a week.

For a small home orchard consisting of 15 to 20 trees and other small fruit, a five-gallon knapsack sprayer will be sufficient if the trees are not over 15 feet in height. A stepladder will increase efficiency and thoroughness in covering taller trees.

For a small orchard of 25 to 150 trees a hand barrel-pump, 30–60 gallons in capacity, has a pressure capacity of 75–125 pounds and will spray from 1 to 3 gallons per minute.

A small, power sprayer with a capacity of 100 gallons may be purchased in place of the barrel-pump for orchards consisting of 5 to 15 acres. Such a sprayer has a capacity of delivering 3 to 5 gallons of spray per minute at a pressure of 250 pounds.

No machines, even when new, can be depended upon to deliver advertised capacities when placed in service. The average sprayer will not generally deliver over 70 per cent capacity after the newness is worn off. No machine will stand up if operated at full capacity. Therefore, get a machine that need not be operated at full speed in order to get the job done satisfactorily.

Spray Schedules: The spray schedules which follow are not intended to be discussions from the commercial viewpoint, but rather to give the home grower an insight into insect and disease control.

Trees and fruits are attacked by insects and diseases at various stages in their development. Prevention is better than cure, for once an insect or disease attacks a fruit, it decreases in value. Therefore, sprays should be applied to prevent them from gaining a foothold. Certain insects and diseases must be controlled at a definite time or over a definite period. Some materials, especially those which keep fungous diseases under control, may be used in place of others. These substitutions should be closely observed.

SPRAY SCHEDULE FOR PEACHES AND PLUMS

EXPLANATION: On all stone fruits (peaches, plums and cherries) there is a husk which covers the young developing fruit in its early stages of development. As the fruit grows, this outer covering or shuck splits and finally drops off, exposing the young peach.

NOTE: Follow this spray schedule closely and do not use any other form of sulphur than that recommended.

	TYPE OF SPRAY	MATERIALS FOR 100 GAL.	MATERIALS FOR 10 GAL.	INSECTS AND DISEASES CONTROLLED
1.	Dormant or before the buds swell. Note—This is a very important spray and should not be omitted.	10–12 gal. liquid lime sulphur. Dilute to 100 gal. with water	1 gal. liquid lime sulphur. Dilute to 10 gal. with water	Scale and peach leaf curl
2.	When most of the shucks have split or fallen	25 lbs. Jersey dry mix (also called dry mix sulphur lime) 4–8 lbs. hydrated lime 2 lbs. arsenate of lead. Dilute to 100 gal. with water. Note—Wettable sulphur may be substituted for Jersey dry mix at the rate of 6 lbs. plus 16 lbs. of hydrated lime to 100 gal. of water or 2½ cups of wettable sulphur plus 6 cups hydrated lime diluted to 10 gal. with water.	2½ lbs. Jersey dry mix ½–¾ lb. hydrated lime (2–3 cups) 14 level tablespoonfuls (or ¾ cup) arsenate of lead	Scab, brown rot Oriental fruit moth, codling moth and curculio
3.	Two weeks later, shucks have fallen and peach is exposed	25 lbs. Jersey dry mix 4–8 lbs. hydrated lime 2 lbs. arsenate of lead. Dilute to 100 gal. with water	2½ lbs. Jersey dry mix 1¾ lb. hydrated lime (2–3 cups) ¾ cup of arsenate of lead. Dilute to 10 gal. with water	Brown rot Oriental fruit moth, codling moth
4.	Two to three weeks later	25 lbs. Jersey dry mix 4–8 lbs. hydrated lime 2 lbs. arsenate of lead (omit on early ripening varieties)	2½ lbs. Jersey dry mix 2–3 cups hydrated lime ¾ cup arsenate of lead. Dilute to 10 gal. with water	Brown rot Oriental fruit moth, codling moth

SPRAY SCHEDULE FOR APPLES

	TYPE OF SPRAY	MATERIALS FOR 100 GAL.	MATERIALS FOR 10 GAL.	CONTROL
1a.	Dormant or before any growth begins NOTE: Apply either 1a or 1b and not both.	10–12 gal. of liquid lime sulphur Dilute to 100 gal. with water *or* Miscible oil (follow manufacturer's instructions)	1 gal. of liquid lime sulphur Dilute to 10 gal. with water *or* Miscible oil (follow manufacturer's instructions)	Scale insects Aphis eggs, canker worm, leaf-roller eggs
1b.	Delayed dormant—from the time the buds burst until leaves are ½ inch long	10–12 gal. of liquid lime sulphur 1 pint of Black Leaf 40 3 lbs. arsenate of lead Dilute to 100 gal. with water *or* Miscible oil or oil emulsion following manufacturer's instructions	1 gal. of liquid lime sulphur 4 tablespoonfuls of Black Leaf 40 1 cupful of arsenate of lead Dilute to 10 gal. with water *or* Miscible oil or oil emulsion, following manufacturer's instructions	Scale insects Aphis and sucking insects Chewing insects
2.	Prepink—when the whorl of leaves on a bud forms a rosette, the 5–7 buds being in a tight cluster without any pink color showing except a slight pinkish tint to the center bud	2½ gal. of liquid lime sulphur 3 lbs. of arsenate of lead ¾ pint of Black Leaf 40 (if aphis are present) 1 lb. calcium caseinate Dilute to 100 gal. with water	1 quart of liquid lime sulphur 1 cupful of arsenate of lead 4 tablespoonfuls of Black Leaf 40 7 tablespoonfuls of calcium caseinate Dilute to 10 gal. with water	Apple scab Chewing insects Aphis and sucking insects
3.	Pink stage—when blossoms separate from the cluster and turn pink	2½ gal. of liquid lime sulphur 3 lbs. of arsenate of lead ¾ pint of Black Leaf 40 1 lb. of calcium caseinate Dilute to 100 gal. with water	1 quart of liquid lime sulphur 4 tablespoonfuls Black Leaf 40 1 cup arsenate of lead 7 tablespoonfuls calcium caseinate Dilute to 10 gal. with water	Apple scab and other fungous diseases Aphis and sucking insects Red bug, lesser apple worm

No.	Time of Application			Controls
4.	Calyx or petal fall. When 75% or more of the blossoms have fallen	2½ gal. of liquid lime sulphur 4 lbs. arsenate of lead ¾ pint of Black Leaf 40 1 lb. of calcium caseinate Dilute to 100 gal. with water	1 quart liquid lime sulphur 1½ cups of arsenate of lead 4 tablespoonfuls Black Leaf 40 7 tablespoonfuls calcium caseinate Dilute to 10 gal. with water	Apple scab and other fungous diseases Codling moth and chewing insects Aphis and sucking insects
5.	10–14 days after the Calyx Spray	2½ gal. of liquid lime sulphur 3 lbs. of arsenate of lead ¾ pint of Black Leaf 40 1 lb. of calcium caseinate Dilute to 100 gal. with water	1 quart liquid lime sulphur 1 cup of arsenate of lead 4 tablespoonfuls Black Leaf 40 7 tablespoonfuls calcium caseinate Dilute to 10 gal. with water	Scab Chewing insects Aphis and other sucking insects
6.	Two weeks after the 10–14 day spray*	2½ gal. of liquid lime sulphur 3 lbs. of arsenate of lead ¾ pint of Black Leaf 40 1 lb. of calcium caseinate Dilute to 100 gal. with water	1 quart liquid lime sulphur 1 cup of arsenate of lead 4 tablespoonfuls Black Leaf 40 7 tablespoonfuls calcium caseinate Dilute to 10 gal. with water	Scab and other fungous diseases Second brood codling moth and chewing insects Aphis and sucking insects

*The same materials as No. 6 may be applied at two-week intervals after this spray if diseases or insects are still present.

SPRAY SCHEDULE FOR CHERRIES

(See Explanation at top of Spray Schedule for Peaches.)

	TYPE OF SPRAY	MATERIAL FOR 100 GAL.	MATERIAL FOR 10 GAL.	INSECTS AND DISEASES CONTROLLED
1.	Delayed dormant—when ends of buds are green	10–12 gal. liquid lime sulphur 1 pint of Black Leaf 40 Water to make 100 gal.	1 gal. liquid lime sulphur 4 tablespoonfuls Black Leaf 40 Dilute to 10 gal. with water	Leaf spot, scale, red mite Aphis
2a.	When the blossom buds appear but before they open	25 lbs. Jersey dry mix* 3 lbs. arsenate of lead 1 pint Black Leaf 40 (if aphis are present) Dilute to 100 gal. with water	2½ lbs. Jersey dry mix* 1 cup arsenate of lead 4 tablespoonfuls Black Leaf 40 (if aphis are present) Dilute to 10 gal. with water	Brown rot, leaf spot Chewing insects
2b.	When the shucks (outer covering of the immature fruit) split	25 lbs. Jersey dry mix* 3 lbs. arsenate of lead Dilute to 100 gal. with water	2½ lbs. Jersey dry mix* 1 cup arsenate of lead Dilute to 10 gal. with water	Curculio, leaf spot, brown rot Chewing insects
3.	When most of the shucks have fallen	25 lbs. Jersey dry mix* 3 lbs. arsenate of lead Dilute to 100 gal. with water 1 pint of Black Leaf 40 (if aphis are present)	2½ lbs. Jersey dry mix* 1 cup arsenate of lead 4 tablespoonfuls Black Leaf 40 Dilute to 10 gal. with water	Curculio, leaf spot, brown rot Chewing insects
4.	Just before the cherries begin to color	25 lbs. Jersey dry mix* 3 lbs. arsenate of lead Dilute to 100 gal. with water	2½ lbs. Jersey dry mix* 1 cup arsenate of lead Dilute to 10 gal. with water	Brown rot, fruit fly, leaf spot Chewing insects
5.	In sections where leaf spot is serious, it is advisable to spray again after the crop has been harvested			

Note: Bordeaux Mixture: { 4 lbs. copper sulphate crystals / 4–6 lbs. hydrated lime / 1½ lbs. arsenate of lead / Dilute to 50 gal. with water } or { 2½ gal. liquid lime sulphur / 3 lbs. arsenate of lead / 1 lb. calcium caseinate / Dilute to 100 gal. with water } { May be used with good results in place of the Jersey dry mix. }

SPRAY SCHEDULE FOR PEARS

	TYPE OF SPRAY	MATERIALS FOR 100 GAL.	MATERIALS FOR 10 GAL.	INSECTS AND DISEASES CONTROLLED
1.	As blossom buds begin to separate from the cluster	10–12 gal. liquid lime sulphur* Dilute to 100 gal. with water	1 gal. liquid lime sulphur* Dilute to 10 gal. with water	Scale, Psylla eggs, scab, black spot
2.	Just after petals have fallen	2½ gal. liquid lime sulphur* 1 pint black leaf 40 3 lbs. arsenate of lead 1 lb. calcium caseinate Dilute to 100 gal. with water	1 quart liquid lime sulphur* 1 cup arsenate of lead 7 tablespoonfuls calcium caseinate 4 tablespoonfuls black leaf 40 Dilute to 10 gal. with water	Scab, leaf spot, black spot Codling moth Psylla nymphs
3.	Two weeks after the petals have fallen	2½ gal. liquid lime sulphur* 3 lbs. arsenate of lead 1 lb. calcium caseinate Dilute to 100 gal. with water	1 quart of liquid lime sulphur* 1 cup arsenate of lead 7 tablespoonfuls calcium caseinate Dilute to 10 gal. with water	Fungous diseases Codling moth
4.	Two weeks later if necessary	2½ gal. liquid lime sulphur* 3 lbs. arsenate of lead 1 lb. calcium caseinate Dilute to 100 gal. with water	1 quart of liquid lime sulphur* 1 cup arsenate of lead 7 tablespoonfuls calcium caseinate Dilute to 10 gal. with water	

*NOTE: 25 lbs. Jersey dry mix may be substituted for the liquid lime sulphur (2½ gal.). 8 lbs. of copper sulphate crystals, plus 8–12 lbs. hydrated lime may also be substituted for the 2½ gal. liquid lime sulphur.

SPRAY SCHEDULE FOR THE QUINCE

	TYPE OF SPRAY	MATERIALS FOR 100 GAL.	MATERIALS FOR 10 GAL.	INSECTS AND DISEASES CONTROLLED
1.	Dormant (Do not apply unless scale insects are present.)	10–12 gal. liquid lime sulphur Dilute to 100 gal. with water *or* Use Miscible oil (follow manufacturer's instructions.)	1 gal. liquid lime sulphur Dilute to 10 gal. with water *or* Miscible oil (follow manufacturer's instructions.)	Scale
2.	When the blossom buds appear	25 lbs. Jersey dry mix 3 lbs. of arsenate of lead Dilute to 100 gal. with water	2½ lbs. Jersey dry mix 1 cup arsenate of lead Dilute to 10 gal. with water	Scab Chewing insects
3.	When the petals fall	25 lbs. Jersey dry mix 3 lbs. arsenate of lead Dilute to 100 gal. with water	2½ lbs. Jersey dry mix 1 cup arsenate of lead Dilute to 10 gal. with water	Scab Codling moth and chewing insects
4.	Two weeks later	25 lbs. Jersey dry mix 3 lbs. arsenate of lead Dilute to 100 gal. with water	2½ lbs. Jersey dry mix 1 cup arsenate of lead Dilute to 10 gal. with water	Scab and other fungous diseases Codling moth and other chewing insects
5.	Two weeks after No. 4, if necessary	25 lbs. of Jersey dry mix 3 lbs. arsenate of lead Dilute to 100 gal. with water	2½ lbs. Jersey dry mix 1 cup arsenate of lead Dilute to 10 gal. with water	Scab Chewing insects

SPRAY SCHEDULE FOR GRAPES

	TYPE OF SPRAY	MATERIALS FOR 50 GAL.	MATERIALS FOR 10 GAL.	INSECTS AND DISEASES CONTROLLED
1.	When new growth is 12–18″ long	4 lbs. copper sulphate crystals (dissolve in warm water) 4–6 lbs. hydrated lime $1\frac{1}{2}$ lbs. arsenate of lead Dilute to 50 gal. with water	$\frac{3}{4}$ lb. copper sulphate crystals (dissolve in warm water) 1 lb. hydrated lime (4 cups) 1 cup arsenate of lead Dilute to 10 gal. with water	Black rot Chewing insects
2.	Just as the flower buds are opening	4 lbs. copper sulphate crystals (dissolve in warm water) 4–6 lbs. hydrated lime $1\frac{1}{2}$ lbs. arsenate of lead $1\frac{1}{2}$–2 lb. Resin fish oil soap (not absolutely necessary on small vineyards) Dilute to 50 gal. with water	$\frac{3}{4}$ lb. copper sulphate crystals (dissolve in warm water) 1 lb. hydrated lime 1 cup arsenate of lead $\frac{3}{4}$ cup Resin fish oil soap (not absolutely necessary on small vineyard) Dilute to 10 gal. with water	Black rot, mildew Anthracnose Grape berry moth
3.	When the small grapes are evident	4 lbs. copper sulphate crystals 4–6 lbs. hydrated lime $1\frac{1}{2}$ lbs. arsenate of lead $1\frac{1}{2}$–2 lbs. Resin fish oil soap Dilute to 50 gal. with water	$\frac{3}{4}$ lb. copper sulphate crystals 1 lb. hydrated lime 1 cup arsenate of lead $\frac{3}{4}$ cup Resin fish oil soap Dilute to 10 gal. with water	Black rot, mildew Root worm, grape berry moth, chewing insects
4.	Two weeks later	4 lbs. copper sulphate crystals 4–6 lbs. hydrated lime $1\frac{1}{2}$ lbs. arsenate of lead $1\frac{1}{2}$–2 lbs. Resin fish oil soap Dilute to 50 gal. with water	$\frac{3}{4}$ lb. copper sulphate crystals 1 lb. hydrated lime 1 cup arsenate of lead $\frac{3}{4}$ cup Resin fish oil soap Dilute to 10 gal. with water	Black rot, mildew Root worm, grape berry moth
		Note—If leaf hoppers appear, use $\frac{1}{2}$ pint of Black leaf 40 per 50 gal. or 8 tablespoonfuls of Black leaf 40 to 10 gal. of water.		

CONTROL OF FRUIT DISEASES AND PESTS

Not Included in Spray Schedules

(Tree Fruits)

FRUIT	DISEASE	INSECT	DAMAGE	CONTROL
Apple, Pear		Scale insects, codling moth and others		Remove loose bark with a tree scraper so they are exposed on the trunk. Burn the loose bark. Pick up and destroy fruit which drops before it is mature.
		Borers	Large white grubs bore in limbs, thereby weakening them. Presence is noticed by sawdust exuding from their holes.	Dig out with a knife or wire or put a piece of cotton saturated with carbon disulphide into the hole.
	Fireblight		Spreads very rapidly causing the affected parts to turn dark brown in color and also shrink. Leaves turn dark brown to black and hang on very tenaciously.	Remove the infected part and burn it. Cut several inches below its line of demarcation so as not to spread it with pruning tools. Do not fertilize the tree too heavily. Plant resistant varieties.
Peach		Peach tree borer	Larvæ tunnel through tender tissues of trunk feeding on them as they go. Their presence is noticeable by dark brown sawdust stuck together with a gum-like substance exuding from their holes.	On trees 1–4 years old, dig borers out with a sharp knife or wire in August and September. On older trees, from September 1–20, remove trash and grass from base of tree. Spread $\frac{3}{4}$ ounce of paradichlorobenzene in a narrow band 4″ from trunk and around it. Cover the paradichlorobenzene with soil which is mounded around trunk to a height of 12–18 inches. Mound soil high enough to cover any noticeable borer holes on trunk if they are above 18 inches on the trunk. Remove soil in six weeks' time.

Plant	Disease	Symptoms	Treatment
	Brown Rot	Peaches turn brown and shrivel.	Remove brown dried peaches hanging on tree after leaves have fallen and burn them.
Plum	Brown Rot	See Peach	Practise clean cultivation.
(Small Fruits)			
Bramble Fruits (Raspberries, Blackberries, etc.)	Anthracnose	Light to dark colored brownish spots on stem, irregular in size and shape.	Spray just as green tips appear from buds with 1 gallon of liquid lime sulphur diluted to 20 gallons with water. When flower buds appear spray again with 1 quart of liquid lime sulphur diluted to 12 gallons with water.
	Cane Blight	Canes die suddenly and fruit dries up before maturing.	Spraying the plants with the materials as described under Anthracnose will be helpful.
	Orange Rust	Attacks principally the Blackberry. Plant has a dwarfed stunted appearance at first with a slight orange tinge. Later, leaves are covered with an orange-looking powder.	Remove infected plants before these orange spores are mature or can be shaken from the plant, and burn them. Destroy wild brambles as a precautionary measure.
	Virus Diseases	Plant is stunted, dwarfed in appearance. Leaves may be curled inward or mottled with variations.	Remove diseased plants and burn them. Secure plants from a disease-free source. Plant resistant varieties.
	Raspberry Byturus	A tiny white worm which is completely hidden from view in the berry. Several may be present at one time.	Dust plants with rotenone or spray with one-half ounce of arsenate of lead diluted to 2 gallons with water when the flower buds appear and again when the green berries are first formed. Cultivate the soil, remove weeds and other rubbish.

(Small Fruits)

FRUIT	DISEASE	INSECT	DAMAGE	CONTROL
Bramble Fruits (Raspberries, Blackberries, etc.)—*Cont.*		American Raspberry Beetle	A small brownish insect which eats the foliage and also the buds.	Same as for Raspberry Byturus.
		Raspberry Cane Borer	Makes two rows of punctures several inches below the growing tip and lays its eggs between them.	Cut off the infected part and burn.
Currants and Gooseberries		Aphids	Small yellowish insects which congregate in great numbers on the undersides of the leaves causing the leaves to curl and turn reddish.	Apply a nicotine dust at intervals of several days apart until the insect disappears or spray with 1 tablespoonful of Black Leaf 40 diluted to 1 gallon with water to which 4 tablespoonfuls of dissolved soap have been added.
		Currant Worms	Greenish colored worms with black markings or spots, which eat the foliage.	Dust the plants with rotenone when the insect appears or spray with a heaping tablespoonful of lead arsenate diluted to 4 gallons with water.
		Borers	Small grayish white larvæ which bore in the stems causing the infected part to wilt.	Remove the infected part and burn. If borers are very serious in your locality do not cut the plant back too frequently.
Strawberry	Leaf Spot		A fungus which causes circular reddish brown spots on the leaves, thereby impairing their efficiency.	Cultivate sod land with vegetable or other crops for two or three years before setting plants.

XVII

The Home Vegetable Garden

By John A. Anderson

The home garden, when properly planted, and cared for, will supply a variety of vegetables for the home during the entire growing season, and will furnish a surplus for canning and storage. It is also one of the greatest sources of healthful recreation for the city worker. Much depends, however, on careful planning and planting. As vegetables are an important item on one's diet, the necessity of having them fresh and in sufficient amounts is apparent.

One will do well to consider the following:

1. Plan and plant the garden so as to get the greatest yield. Figure out how much of each vegetable will be needed for canning, for eating fresh, or for storage. Some of the root vegetables which will give high yields and melons take up too much space for the yield they give and for this reason should not be planted, where space is limited, can be grown very efficiently with good results.

2. Figure out just how much ground you can profitably care for. It is better to have a small garden properly cared for than to plant so much that you will be disorganized with the summer. A plot 50 feet wide and 100 feet long will furnish an adequate supply of fresh vegetables for a family of six to eight people and enough extra to can and store.

3. If the ground has not been previously plowed, plow it deep in the fall. Freezing and thawing weather will improve its physical condition. Bark in a good application of manure or compost if it is available. Two tons will not be too much for a plot 50 feet by 100 feet.

	Description	Treatment
Virus diseases, yellows, etc.	Plants are stunted and fail to grow or produce.	Plant resistant varieties. Practise rotation.
White Grubs	Larvæ of the so-called May Beetle which live mostly in sod land and injure the plant by chewing the roots.	Remove old and diseased leaves on plants before setting out. Spray with 4 pounds of copper sulphate dissolved in 4 gallons of water plus the addition of 4 pounds of hydrated lime and 1½ pounds of lead arsenate diluted to 50 gallons with water.
Leaf Roller	A small greenish worm which injures the leaves by folding them together.	Just before blossoms open, spray with 1 ounce of lead arsenate diluted to 4 gallons with water.

XXVII

The Home Vegetable Garden

By John A. Andrew, Jr.*

The home garden, when properly planned and planted, will supply a variety of vegetables for home use throughout the entire growing season, and will furnish enough for canning and storing. It is also one of the greatest sources of pleasure and recreation for the city worker. Much satisfaction comes from careful planning and planting. As fresh vegetables are an important item on one's diet, the necessity of having them fresh and in sufficient amounts is apparent.

One will do well to consider the following points:

1. Plan and plant the garden so that it will be a pleasure. Figure out how much of each vegetable you will need for canning, for eating fresh, or for storing, and grow only those vegetables which will give high yields. For example, watermelons take up too much room for the yields they give and for this reason should not be planted, whereas cucumbers can be grown very efficiently with good results.

2. Figure out just how much ground you can properly care for. It is better to have a small garden properly cared for than to plant so much that you will be discouraged with it by midsummer. A plot 50 feet wide and 100 feet long will furnish an adequate supply of fresh vegetables for a family of six grown people and enough extra to can and store.

3. If the ground has not been previously planted, dig it up in the fall. Freezing and thawing weather will improve its physical condition. Fork in a good application of manure or compost if it is available. Two tons will not be too much for a plot 50 feet by 100 feet.

*Head of the Department of Fruits and Vegetables, The Pennsylvania School of Horticulture for Women.

If lime has not been applied for several years, have the soil tested. Lime is best applied after the manure has been dug in. It should be raked in to a depth of 2 inches if possible. If it is not possible to prepare the land in the fall, the same suggestions also hold true for spring preparation.

4. During the early or late winter months before it is possible to plant outside, plan your garden on a piece of paper so that no time will be lost or mistakes made at planting time.

Order your seed from a reputable seedsman at an early date so as to be sure of getting the best varieties. Remember that several varieties of the same vegetable may be planted at the same time which will mature several weeks apart.

5. When planning a garden, the following points should be observed:

(*a*) The earliest and latest planting date. Beets, for example, may be planted as soon as the ground is workable in the spring and planted until midsummer. Most varieties mature in sixty days.

(*b*) The time of year at which each vegetable grows best. The small, quick-maturing varieties of radishes do best when planted in the spring and fall and should not be planted during the hot summer months. They mature in twenty-five to thirty-five days.

(*c*) Period over which the vegetable may be harvested. Sweet corn may be harvested over a period of ten to fourteen days while radishes may last for only several days if the weather is hot and the soil quite dry. Tomatoes are harvested over a period of two months.

(*d*) Those vegetables which mature at the same time should be planted together. Asparagus and rhubarb are two examples and are perennials. They should be planted at one end of the plot, where they will not interfere with soil preparation each year.

(*e*) The planting distances of vegetables in the home garden may be somewhat modified where hand cultivation is to be practised entirely. Cabbage, broccoli, cauliflower are usually set 2½ to 3 feet apart when cultivated with horse-drawn implements; 2 feet is sufficient for hand cultivation.

(*f*) Plant tall-growing crops at one end of the garden and not next to the smaller ones which would be shaded too much. For example, beets should not be planted next to sweet corn but tomatoes or potatoes would give equally good results.

(*g*) Plant those vegetables next to each other which are susceptible to the same insects and diseases so that they may be controlled more easily. Cabbage, broccoli, brussels sprouts, and cauliflower belong to the same group, while eggplant, peppers, potatoes and tomatoes belong to another. Vine crops which include squashes, pumpkins, melons and cucumbers are also in one group.

(*h*) Plan to have the soil producing all the time. As soon as one crop is removed, plant another in its place. Early peas will mature in seventy to eighty days or about July 15. They may be followed by late beets, turnips, lettuce, snap beans, or spinach. This is known as successive cropping.

(*i*) Practise intercropping by planting a quick-maturing crop between those which take a longer time to mature. Radishes or lettuce may be intercropped with peas.

(*j*) Rotation. Some vegetables give better results if not planted in the same place the same year. It is poor practice to plant cabbage or any of its close relations after the early crop has been removed, as the following crop may be very inferior in quality and size.

Other points which might be helpful are as follows:

(1) If parsley is planted, have it on the outside edge next to the house so you won't have to walk through the entire garden to get it.

(2) A path 4 feet wide and 100 feet long through the garden may be bordered with ageratum, zinnias, marigolds, calendulas or other such flowers. This will allow for rows 23 feet long each side of the path which can be easily cared for.

(3) With only a limited amount of time such as evening hours, a garden 50 feet by 50 feet is most practical.

GARDEN EQUIPMENT

A good many garden operations can be done with little effort if the equipment is at hand.

A spade and fork are necessary for preparing the soil as well as for harvesting some of the crops.

A rake is used for smoothing or fining the soil just after it is spaded and also to rake in fertilizers which have been applied.

A hoe is necessary to make rows, cover the seed, move the soil toward some plants, cut off weeds, and make holes for setting plants.

A stout line and stakes are necessary for making rows straight.

Other implements which may be used with a great deal of efficiency are hand weeders, trowels and hand cultivators, which have several attachments for marking rows, cutting weeds, and making furrows.

COMMERCIAL FERTILIZERS

Commercial fertilizers cannot take the place of organic matter in the soil, but do much to supplement it and are especially desirable where land is intensively cropped.

The three elements most essential for garden crops are nitrogen, phosphorus and potash. Generally speaking, nitrogen is used to promote leaf and vegetative growth; phosphorus promotes root growth and hastens maturity, and potash increases general sturdiness and resistance to disease.

A complete fertilizer is one which contains nitrogen, phosphorus and potash. It is usually described by figures giving the percentages of each element, *i.e.,* a fertilizer which contains 4 per cent of nitrogen, 8 per cent of phosphorus, and 4 per cent potash, is called a 4–8–4.

As plants need a well-regulated diet, an understanding of the use of fertilizers and of the reasons for their application will greatly help the gardener.

Every plant has three stages, the germinating and sprouting, the vegetative, and the fruiting. In the germinating stage, the seed absorbs moisture which, when added to heat, changes the concentrated food contained in each seed to a simple form and is sufficient to make a sprout appear through a surface of soil.

From the time the first true leaves begin to turn green, until the fruit begins to form, the plant is in the vegetative state. From the time the fruit first begins to form, the plant is in the fruiting stage.

As plants such as lettuce and spinach are eaten in the vegetative stage, tomatoes, peppers and eggplant in the fruiting stage, it is easy to understand that fertilizer requirements vary greatly. Both phosphorus and potash when placed in the soil are available to plants over a long period, but nitrogen has various forms differing widely in the quickness with which they become available. Nitrogen may be classified into three types: (1) Inorganic, available as soon as dissolved in water; example, nitrate of soda, which is available under all soil conditions. (2) Organic, which must undergo complete decomposition before nitrogen is available; examples, tankage and dried blood, available in about a month if the soil is warm, as the bacteria which promote decay are not otherwise active. (3) Those which are half-way between one and two and must be changed to the nitrate form; example, ammonium sulphate which becomes available in a week or two after being applied. No. 1 is used early in the spring when the soil is cold and at all times for quick results. The effect of an application lasts only two or three weeks and for continuous quick growth over a long period, 1, 2, and 3 should be mixed together as per the following formula. To make one hundred pounds of complete fertilizer, 4–8–4, mix together:

8	pounds	nitrate of soda
4½	"	ammonium sulphate
9½	"	dried blood
50	"	superphosphate
8½	"	sulphate of potash
19½	"	sand or dry soil

Figures for a ton of 4–8–4:

160	pounds	nitrate of soda
133	"	ammonium sulphate
192	"	dried blood
1000	"	superphosphate
167	"	sulphate of potash
348	"	sand or dry soil

The sand is added to make it up to a ton or to one hundred pounds. These ingredients should be thoroughly and evenly mixed. The fertilizer can be stored in a covered tin container. To prevent hardening, which makes it troublesome to use, keep away from moisture; hardening may somewhat impair its efficiency, so pulverize before using. It may be kept indefinitely if properly stored.

The percentages of ingredients used are:

Nitrate of soda contains 15 per cent nitrogen.
Sulphate of ammonia contains 20 per cent nitrogen.

Dried blood contains 14 per cent nitrogen.
Super or acid phosphate contains 16 per cent phosphorus.
Sulphate of potash contains 48 per cent potash.

Many complete fertilizers are on the market, some having fancy trade names, others using the firm name and having the contents described by figures.

As already noted, a one-hundred-pound bag of a good complete fertilizer each season is a great aid in the production of a 50-foot by 50-foot garden.

Where fertilizers have been applied to the first crop, the succeeding crop's requirements are practically satisfied without applying additional fertilizer.

METHODS OF APPLYING FERTILIZER

1. Broadcasting it over the surface and raking it in just previous to planting.
2. Scattering it in the drill or furrow and raking it into the soil just previous to planting.
3. Broadcasting between the rows during the growing season.
4. Drilling it in with an attachment on the seed planter.
5. Applying it in narrow bands, 3 to 4 inches away from the plants and covering it with soil.*

NOTE: Fertilizer will prevent germination if it comes in contact with the seed and will burn the foliage if it is spread on it.

CONTROL OF VEGETABLE DISEASES

Precaution in Use of Frames and Hotbeds. In many cases when vegetables have been started early in coldframes or hotbeds, instead of in the garden, diseases will appear after their transplanting into the open. The cause can often be traced to insufficient care in preparing the seed bed. Many diseases are able to winter-over in old seed beds and gardens, while many of the more damaging ones are also carried over by the seed, such as early and late blights of celery; leaf blights and fruit rots of cucumbers, eggplant, melons, and squashes; black rot

*The most approved method.

VEGETABLE GARDEN PLAN 100 FEET BY 50 FEET WITH CENTRAL PATH 3 FEET WIDE

PLANTING DATES FOR LATITUDE OF PHILADELPHIA

Figures indicate planting distances in feet from row to row

Planting date	Distance	PATH	Distance	Crop
JUNE 15				CELERY (TRENCHED) · GIANT PASCAL
MAY 15	3			LIMA BEANS · KING OF THE GARDEN
MAY 15	4			LIMA BEANS · " "
JUNE 1	4			CORN · STOWELL'S EVERGREEN
JUNE 1	3			CORN · " "
MAY 15	3			CORN · GOLDEN GIANT
WITH PUMPKINS · NEW ENGLAND PIE · JULY 1	3			CORN · GOLDEN SUNSHINE · MAY 1 · INTERPLANT
JULY 1	3			WINTER SQUASH · GOLDEN HUBBARD
MAY 15	5		MAY 15	SUMMER SQUASH · EARLY WHITE BUSH
CUCUMBERS · DAVIS PERFECT · MAY 15	4			CUCUMBERS · WHITE SPINE
JULY 1	5			POTATOES · GREEN MOUNTAIN
JULY 1	3			POTATOES · " "
MAY 1	3			POTATOES · IRISH COBBLER
APRIL 1	2			PEAS · LITTLE MARVEL

Figures indicate planting distances in feet from row to row

PATH

Distance (ft)	Crop & variety	Date(s)
3	PEAS · ALDERMAN	APRIL 15
3	TOMATOES · MARGLOBE	MAY 15
4	TOMATOES · EARLIANNA	MAY 15 · MAY 15
4	EGGPLANT · BLACK BEAUTY MAY 15	PEPPERS · CALIFORNIA WONDER MAY 15
3	CABBAGE · PENN STATE BALL	JUNE 30
3	CABBAGE · EARLY WAKEFIELD	MAY 15
2	CELERY · GOLDEN PLUME	MAY 15
2	KALE · BLUE CURLED DWARF SIBERIAN	MAY 1
2	SPINACH · BLIGHT RESISTANT BLOOMSDALE SAVOY MAY 1 · FOLLOWED BY CARROTS · JULY 1	MAY 15 · JULY 15 · DANVERS HALF LONG
2	LETTUCE · BIG BOSTON MAY 1	MAY 15 FOLLOWED BY RUTABAGA · BLOOMSDALE SWEDE · AUGUST 1
2	LEEK · AMERICAN FLAG	MAY 15
2	ONIONS · AILSA CRAIG PLANTS	MAY 15
2	ONIONS · " "	MAY 15
2	ONION SETS · SILVER SKIN	MAY 1
2	BEETS · DETROIT DARK RED	MAY 20
2	BEETS · EARLY EGYPTIAN · MAY 20 FOLLOWED BY LETTUCE · GRAND RAPIDS · ½ JULY 1, ½ JULY 15	
2	CARROTS · RED CORED CHANTENAY · PLANTED WITH RADISHES, ½ EARLY SCARLET GLOBE, ½ WHITE ICICLE · MAY 1 FOLLOWED BY SPINACH · AUGUST 1 · AUGUST 15	
2	BEANS · GREEN BOUNTIFUL, FOLLOWED BY TURNIPS · WHITE VIENNA JUNE 1	JUNE 15 · AUGUST 1
2	BEANS · SURECROP WAX MAY 1	MAY 20
2	CARROTS · DANVERS HALF LONG PLANTED WITH RADISHES · CRIMSON GIANT JUNE 15 · FOLLOWED BY RADISHES LONG BLACK SPANISH JULY 20	

and black leg of cabbage, turnips and cauliflower; early blight, leaf spot and bacterial canker of tomatoes and others. Therefore, it is highly important to use clean seed and also clean seed bed soil in starting the crop. This may be assured to a large extent by observing the following points:

1. Save seed only from disease-free plants and as early in the season as possible.

2. Purchase seed from reputable seedsmen.

3. Disinfect seed when necessary in order to kill disease germs. (See "Seed Treatment"—page 982.)

4. Change the soil every year in hotbeds, coldframes, benches, etc., or, if practicable, move the site of the hotbeds or coldframes to soil previously used for other crops. Disinfect containers, sides and covers of beds with formaldehyde (1 part F. to 45 parts water).

5. Do not use old seed beds unless soaked with formaldehyde solution. This process kills parasites before sowing the seed. Add formaldehyde dust to the soil, using 8 ounces of 6 per cent dust to each bushel of soil; sow seed and water. Gas will diffuse through the soil, kill the damping-off fungi and disinfect the seeds as well. For full instructions see page 982.

6. Do not use manure or compost under seedlings or transplants if you know it contains old vegetable refuse.

Investment in good seed justifies safeguarding the crop in the seed bed. While the use of disease-free seed and clean seed bed soil are important steps in producing strong healthy plants, so is good seed bed management also. Healthy plants in seed beds usually mean a disease-free crop in the garden.

Precaution Against Infection from Outside Sources. Since many important garden diseases of vegetables secure their start in the seed bed or coldframe, even in spite of precautions already mentioned, we must guard against infection from outside sources. Such sanitary and protective steps consist of the following:

1. Avoid too frequent watering and excess watering of beds; instead, water more heavily at longer intervals; water only in the forenoon and ventilate well to hasten drying as soon as possible. Proper watering, heating and ventilating of beds not only insure

sturdy, vigorous-growing plants, but also provide conditions that are not favorable for damping-off and other diseases.

2. Avoid handling or disturbing the plants while they are wet; otherwise where there are only traces of the disease it might spread in the bed.

3. Discard spotted, wilted and otherwise diseased plants for they are starters of infection.

4. Avoid introducing old plant debris and contaminated soil into seed beds and coldframes.

5. Treat the celery bed at ten- to fourteen-day intervals with copper-lime dust or Bordeaux Mixture when plants are 1 inch high.

6. Dust or spray tomatoes and eggplants twice before setting in the garden with copper-lime-arsenate dust or Bordeaux Mixture with one pound of calcium arsenate added, making the first application fourteen days and the second two days before garden planting.

Remember that thorough protection of the vegetable crop against diseases may be accomplished easily while it occupies so limited a space.

Approximate Seed Quantities

Asparagus	1 oz.—800–1000 plants
Beans	1 lb.—100 feet
Beets	1 oz.—50 feet
Chard	1 oz.—100 feet
Cabbage	
Broccoli	
Brussels Sprouts	¼ oz. will give 700 plants
Cauliflower	
Kale	
Carrots	1 oz.—100 feet
Celery	¼ oz.—500–800 plants
Corn (Sweet)	1 lb. for 125 hills
Cucumbers	½ oz.—25 hills
Endive	¼ oz.—50 feet
Eggplant	¼ oz.—750 plants
Kohlrabi	¼ oz.—100 feet
Leek	1 oz.—100 feet
Lettuce	¼ oz.—750 plants
Muskmelons	1 oz.—35–50 hills

899

APPROXIMATE SEED QUANTITIES—*Continued*

Watermelon	1 oz.—35-50 hills
Parsley	½ oz.—100 feet
Onion Seed	1 oz.—100 feet
Onion sets	1 quart—50 feet
Parsnip	½ oz.—100 feet
Peas	1 lb.—40 feet
Peppers	¼ oz.—600 plants
Pumpkin	1 oz.—20 hills
Rhubarb	1 oz.—75-100 feet
Radishes	1 oz.—75-100 feet
Spinach	1 oz.—100 feet

CAN BE TRANSPLANTED

Asparagus	Celery	Onion
Beets	Endive	Parsley
Swiss Chard	Eggplant	Peppers
Cabbage	Kale	Rhubarb
Cauliflower	Kohlrabi	Tomatoes
Broccoli	Leek	
Brussels Sprouts	Lettuce	

CAN BE GROWN IN POTS AND PLANTED OUTSIDE

Beans, Lima	Cucumbers	Melons
Corn, Sweet	Gourds	Watermelons

STORING HOME-GROWN VEGETABLES

Many people who have vegetable gardens like to grow surplus crops for winter consumption, especially beets, carrots, turnips, onions, cabbage, potatoes, winter squash, parsnips, and salsify. All crops must be matured late in the season for successful storage. Crops maturing earlier will not store successfully. Root crops, including carrots, beets, potatoes, salsify, and parsnips, require cool and fairly moist conditions. Onions and winter squash must be kept warm and dry.

In the House. A cool room in a house cellar should be about 8 by 8 feet to provide sufficient space for a family of five or six from a garden of 5000 square feet. This room should be built so that it will keep the vegetables from freezing and to prevent them from becoming too warm. The floor should be of soil and the walls and ceilings made of 2-inch by 2-inch studs about 3 feet apart and covered on both sides with paper and insulating lumber.

In a Mound of Soil. Root crops including potatoes and cabbage may be piled on level ground, the pile being 3 feet long at the base and tapering to about 2 feet at the top. A 4- to 6-inch layer of straw is put over the vegetables except at the top which is left open about 4 inches to make provision for ventilation. A piece of pipe may be placed on top to allow for ventilation. Then the hay or straw is covered with 12 to 18 inches of soil. In cold weather, a board or stone is placed over the top of the pipe.

The disadvantage of such a pit is that it cannot be opened in cold weather, but serves the purpose of keeping vegetables until the spring months.

A STORAGE PIT

This type of storage pit should be situated in a location which has adequate drainage. It may be built where the ground is level if the soil is well drained and water does not remain on the surface for any length of time.

The pit to be described has been used successfully for several years with the most satisfactory results. Apples, potatoes and other vegetables which will not keep well in a warm, dry cellar have been kept in this pit until May with very little loss.

1. Dig a pit 9 feet long, 6 feet wide and 5 to 6 feet deep.
2. Place three 6-foot posts on each side as close to the soil as possible and set 1 foot into the soil which is firmed around them.
3. Brace these posts with 2 x 4's, one for each side and one across the back and front ends.
4. Place 2 x 4's across the tops of the posts on the sides and also on the ends.
5. Cover the top and sides with rough but strong boards.
6. Remove soil so a door may be used as an entrance in the front end.
7. A door 4 feet high and 2½ feet wide will be very satisfactory and is supported against two 2 x 4 uprights which are used for the framework.

8. Use waterproof paper to cover the top.

9. Fill in with soil the space between the sides of the frame and the earth walls of the pit.

10. Cover the top with 12 to 18 inches of hay when the weather gets cold. Hay is also packed around the door to prevent freezing.

This pit contains approximately 250 cubic feet. It can be built at a cost of twenty dollars and will last for many years with slight repairs. It will more than make up for its cost the first year.

CULTURAL DIRECTIONS

ARTICHOKE—GLOBE

The Globe Artichoke is a tender perennial which must be protected to withstand freezing temperatures.

Botanical Name: Cynara Scolymus.

Soil Preparation: The Globe Artichoke requires large amounts of plant food. The soil should be manured at the rate of 20 tons per acre and should also receive an application of a 4–8–4 or 5–10–5 fertilizer at the rate of 1 pound to 35 square feet. Heavy clay soils should be avoided for best results.

Propagation: Seed is sown in flats during February or the early part of March in a greenhouse or hotbed. When the seedlings are 3 inches high, transplant to 3-inch pots and plant outside after all danger of freezing temperatures has passed. The plants are set 3 feet apart in rows which are 4 feet apart.

During the following year, many suckers will develop at the base of the plant. Remove all but six to eight of them when about 8 inches high. If removed with a knife so as to obtain a root system with them, they may be transplanted to a new location.

As the parent plants are unproductive after the fourth year, constant renewing is necessary to keep up production.

Fertilization and Culture: A complete fertilizer may be applied during the growing season if needed. The plants should receive clean cultivation to suppress weed growth and thereby conserve moisture.

Harvesting: Plants grown from seed do not produce buds the same year. Suckers will in many cases produce a few buds the same year.

ARTICHOKE—JERUSALEM

Botanical Name: Helianthus tuberosus.

Origin: A perennial plant which was known to be cultivated by the Indians. The edible portion is the tuber which develops in the ground. The part above ground closely resembles the sunflower when in bloom.

Soil: Practically any type of soil will give good results if it is in a fair state of productivity. An application of manure plus the use of a 4-8-4 or 5-10-5 commercial fertilizer broadcast at the rate of 1 pound to 50 square feet just previous to planting will be beneficial.

Planting: The tubers may be planted whole or cut like potatoes just previous to planting, which takes place in early spring or fall. The planting distance is 18 to 24 inches in the row and 3½ to 4 feet between the rows; they should be covered with 2 inches of soil.

Harvesting: The tubers may be dug in the fall after top growth ceases, or left in the ground until spring. It is important that all of the tubers be removed; otherwise, those left will become a nuisance if other crops are grown in that place.

Storage: The tubers may be stored by putting them in any type of container with sufficient soil to prevent drying out. They may be left outdoors in this container all winter and even if the temperature falls to 20 degrees below zero they will not be affected; in fact a little frost improves the flavor.

ASPARAGUS

Name: Asparagus officinalis, derived from the Greek word meaning to swell or be ripe.

Origin: Known as food in Europe more than two thousand years ago; grown in this country since colonial days.

Soil: Asparagus will grow on almost any soil, but its growth and development are retarded by too much moisture. A sandy, well-drained soil is best. Also, as a sandy soil warms up quickly in the spring, maturity is hastened. Soil should be plowed or spaded deeply, 10 inches is not too much. Before plowing, well-rotted manure should be spread over the whole area about 2 inches deep; fork or disk the soil until it is very fine.

Planting: Asparagus roots will produce a crop one or two years earlier than if they are grown from seed. One-year-old roots are preferable, because they can stand transplanting much better than the larger ones at two years of age. Plant in trenches 6 to 8 inches deep, 18 inches apart in the rows, with rows 4 feet apart. Cover with 3 inches of soil and as the plants grow, pull more soil around them.

Sowing: Sow the seed as soon as frost is out of the ground in rows

18 inches apart, two seeds to the inch. Germination is slow, but may be hastened by soaking seed in water for two to three days before planting. Germination takes about thirty days, and it is advisable to mix radish seed, ¼ radish to ¾ asparagus, to keep rows marked and the soil from packing. Sow one ounce of asparagus seed to each 40 feet, and cover seed ½ inch.

Transplanting: When the plants are 3 inches high, thin out 4 inches apart. In the latter part of August or in the following spring move to permanent position, setting plants 18 inches apart in trenches 8–10 inches deep and 4–5 feet apart. Cover plants with 2 inches of soil and as they begin to grow, add more soil. Plants must be set in trenches as they have a tendency to rise as they grow old. No crop can be expected for the first two years, as it takes that length of time for the roots to become well established. With good care an asparagus bed should last ten to fifteen years.

Inter-cropping: When first set out, asparagus plants are so small that there is sufficient space between the rows to plant lettuce, radishes, spinach, beets, turnips, carrots, etc.

Cultivation: Keep ground well loosened at all times to a depth of 1 inch to suppress weed growth and to conserve moisture.

Fertilizers: An application of well-rotted manure applied in the late fall or early spring will promote quick, succulent growth. Nitrate of soda, ½ ounce to each plant applied just before growth starts in the spring, will promote good growth and high quality. Stop harvesting as soon as hot weather begins and broadcast a complete fertilizer formula 4–8–4 at the rate of 1 pound to 75 feet between the rows. This application promotes vigorous growth, resulting in a large amount of food being stored in the roots, which will really furnish the next season's crop. The fertilizers which are applied one season as well as the care given that season are materially responsible for next season's crop.

Harvesting: Cut the shoots 1 to 2 inches below the ground, either early in the morning, or late in the afternoon; the best length is 6 to 8 inches. In hot weather, cut twice a day to prevent the shoots from becoming spindly. If not cut immediately before cooking, keep in a cool, moist place. An asparagus bed can be cut over a period of six to eight weeks.

Remarks: If white tips are desired, set the plants in rows 7 to 8 feet apart and ridge plants up in early spring before growth starts. Forty plants are sufficient for a family of six.

Varieties: Mary Washington—rust resistant, produces good shoots, and is not sensitive to hot weather. Martha Washington is very similar, and these are the best varieties.

BEAN

Botanical Name: Phaseolus.

Origin: The American cultivated beans were first known to cultivation only three to four hundred years ago in North and South America. The string bean is the oldest, having been introduced about the last of the fifteenth century. This also applies to the lima bean which came into cultivation soon afterwards. There are two types of beans: those grown for their edible pod as the string or snap bean, and those grown for the seed as the shell, kidney, and lima bean.

SOIL TYPE AND PREPARATION

Bush Snap Beans: For the first and second crop, the soil should be fairly light, but for the summer and fall crops, the soil may be much heavier. The soil does not have to be as fertile as for most of the other crops as too much vine growth, encouraged by rich soil, lessens the productivity. Add a little well-rotted manure or a commercial fertilizer such as a formula 4–8–4 and fork it in to a depth of 6 to 8 inches, but if the soil is not poor, such an application of manure or fertilizer is not advisable.

Bush Limas: These require a much more fertile soil and one which is retentive of moisture during the hot, summer months.

Pole Snap Beans and *Pole Lima Beans:* Require much more fertile soil than either of the bush beans.

WHEN AND HOW TO PLANT

Bush Snap Beans: (String Beans) may be planted after all danger of frost is over until the middle of August, 2 inches apart in the row and 2 feet apart between the rows. Cover with an inch of soil. Seed should germinate in a week, and the plants should be mature in forty-five to sixty days. One pound of seed per 100 feet of row.

Bush Limas: Seed may be sown after all danger of frost is over until the first week in June—4 inches apart in the row and 2 feet apart between the rows. Recent experiments have proven that a much higher percentage of germination results when care is taken to plant lima beans eye-downward. Cover with 1½ inches of soil and they should germinate in ten days. Beans should mature in eighty-five to one hundred days. One pound of seed per 100 feet of row.

Pole Snap Beans: Plant after all danger of frost is over until the first of July in hills 3 feet apart each way. To make hills, remove one or two shovelfuls of soil, put in a shovelful of manure, cover with 4 inches of soil. Use poles about 7 feet long, inserting 1 foot of it into the ground and set before planting the seed. Plant 6 to 8 seeds, cover with 1 inch of soil and when 4 inches high thin out leaving the four best plants. One-half ounce per pole.

Pole Lima Beans: Seed may be planted eye-downward after all danger of frost is over until the third week in May. Prepare hills and plant in the same way as for pole snap beans. One-half ounce of seed per pole.

SUCCESSION AND INTER-CROPPING

Bush Snap Beans: For a succession, plant every ten days to two weeks.

Pole Snap Beans: An early and late planting.

Bush Lima Beans: Two plantings are best.

Pole Lima Beans: Only one planting is necessary, as they bear all season.

Moisture Requirements: When too much moisture is present, excessive vegetative growth reduces the yield. The soil should be kept only slightly moist for the best results. Limas require more moisture than the string beans.

Cultivation: Shallow and frequent to remove weeds.

MANURES AND FERTILIZERS

Pole Snap Beans and *Pole Lima Beans:* A small handful of formula 4-8-4 applied in a ring around each hill when the blossoms first appear, will give good results. When the first crop has been picked, a second application will invigorate the plants to produce a second crop.

Bush Lima Beans: These may also have a complete fertilizer broadcast between the rows, when they are beginning to bloom, at the rate of 1 pound to 75 feet.

HARVESTING

Bush Snap Beans and *Pole Snap Beans:* These beans should be harvested any time before the pods begin to toughen and before the bean itself begins to mature. Both the quality and flavor are superior when the beans are harvested while still young. Do not allow the beans to become overripe as this condition has a tendency to stop plant growth and affects future development. Pick every two or three days, and only when the vines are dry, to prevent Bean Rust. This disease does not harm the vines but impairs the appearance of the pods. Keep the beans in a cool place after harvesting to prevent deterioration by loss of moisture.

Bush Lima Beans and *Pole Lime Beans:* These should not be harvested until the pods are well filled. This may be determined by holding them up to the light. Harvest while the pods still have their attractive green color; do not leave them until they begin to turn yellow. Keep them in a cool, moist place after harvesting. The quality is best if they are eaten as soon after picking as possible.

Remarks: 100-foot row yields 50 pounds Snap, or 20 pecks Pole Snap, or 75 pounds Bush Lima, or 20 pecks Pole Lima.

Varieties

Bush Snap Beans—Green Bountiful, 6 inches long, flat, green, mature in about fifty days. Black Valentine, 6 inches long, round green, mature in fifty days, and for best quality, should be picked when very young. Surecrop Wax, yellow, flat, 6 inches long, matures in sixty days. Round-pod Kidney Wax, yellow, round, 6 inches long, sixty days to maturity.

Pole Snap—Kentucky Wonder, 6 to 8 inches long, round, sixty-five to seventy days to maturity, green. Kentucky Wonder Wax, 6 to 8 inches long, yellow, round, sixty-five to seventy days to maturity.

Bush Lima—Fordhook Bush Lima, seventy-five to eighty days to maturity.

Pole Lima—King of the Garden and Challenger mature in eighty to ninety days.

BEET

Name: Beta vulgaris. Derived from fancied resemblance of the seed to the second letter of the Greek alphabet, beta.

Origin: Originating in the Canary Islands and countries around the Mediterranean Sea, beets have been under cultivation for over two thousand years.

Soil Preparation and Fertilizer: Beets may be grown in practically all types of soil, but one which is friable and well drained gives best results. Plow or fork over soil to a depth of 6 to 8 inches, and then fork or disk in a liberal application of well-rotted manure to a depth of 4 to 6 inches. Pulverize soil thoroughly, rake it over very evenly, broadcast and rake in a complete fertilizer, at the rate of 1 pound to every 50 to 75 square feet.

Sowing: As soon as the frost is out of the ground, sow seed in rows 15 inches apart, 3 seeds to an inch; cover with ½ inch of soil, firmly pressed. These seeds germinate in ten to fourteen days.

Thinning: When the plants are 2 inches high, they should be thinned to 1½ inches apart. These thinnings may be eaten as greens. When the beets are 1¼ inches in diameter, pull up every other one; these will be large enough to eat and those which are left will have room to develop properly.

Succession: For a continuous supply, plant seed every two weeks. One ounce of seed plants 75 feet.

Starting Under Glass: Seed may be started indoors, three weeks before outdoor planting date, in finely pulverized ordinary garden soil. Avoid excess watering. Plants may, if desired, be transplanted while still indoors, 1½ inches apart each way. These plants set out-of-doors the same time as seed is planted will mature two to three weeks earlier. Growth may be further hastened by broadcasting a complete fertilizer formula 4–8–4, at the time of transplanting, at the rate of 1 pound to 50 to 75 square feet.

Cultivation: Beets need shallow cultivation until plants are half grown; after this, it is not necessary as their leaves will shade the ground, control weed growth, and hold moisture in the soil.

Harvesting: Beets are ready for pulling when they are 1½ to 3 inches in diameter; size depending on variety. Keep in a cool moist place until they are used. After they are mature, they can be left in the ground a week or two before they begin to deteriorate.

Storing: Seed should be sown between the first and twentieth of July for the winter-storing crop. Harvest and remove tops early in October; store in moist sand at a temperature between 40 and 50 degrees. In a good root cellar they will keep in boxes or barrels without sand.

Varieties

Early—maturing in forty-five to fifty days: Early Wonder, Eclipse.

Main crop—maturing in fifty-five to sixty days: Crosby's Egyptian and Detroit Dark Red.

Longest keeping variety is the Blood Turnip, which is grown only for winter use, but the two main crop varieties may also be stored with good success.

BROCCOLI

Botanical Name: Brassica oleracea var. italica.

Origin: Known in western Asia for over two thousand years, it has only recently become popular because of its newly discovered food value.

Soil: Any soil is satisfactory, if it is well provided with organic matter and a moderate supply of moisture. As the root system is very shallow and fibrous, proper preparation cannot be over-emphasized. Soil should be well worked to a depth of 6 to 8 inches.

Fertilizer: A good application of well-rotted manure or 4–8–4 fertilizer forked in and then well pulverized.

Sowing: As Broccoli prefers a cool season, it is best to make two plantings, one in the spring (as soon as frost is out of the ground) and the other two months later, both sown at the rate of ⅛-ounce seed to 50 feet of row. Sow seed indoors in flats ¼-inch deep, in rows 2 inches apart. Several hundred seeds should germinate in seven days. When 4 inches high, transplant 18 inches apart in rows 2½– 3 feet apart; transplant only the best plants. Seed may be started in coldframe or hotbed eight weeks before it can be sown in the open.

Moisture: A continuous supply of moisture is necessary for good growth and production; otherwise, the plants will bear prematurely and the quality will be inferior.

Cultivation: Shallow, clean cultivation should be practised frequently to conserve moisture whenever the soil has a tendency to pack.

Harvesting: The first crop looks like heads of green cauliflower and should be about 3 inches in diameter. It should be cut just before the heads begins to separate with 4–6 inches of stem. The second and succeeding crops come as small individual heads from shoots which appear after the first head has been cut. It has the best flavor when cut early in morning. To prevent wilting and to conserve the flavor, keep in a shallow pan of water in a cool place until used.

Fertilizer: Just before the first crop is mature, a good commercial fertilizer (4–8–4) may be applied at the rate of 1 tablespoonful to each plant. Make a ring of fertilizer 6 inches from the stem of the plant and cover with 1 inch of soil.

Varieties: Calabrese: Ninety days to maturity. Italian Green Sprouting is a very similar variety.

BRUSSELS SPROUTS

Botanical Name: Brassica oleracea var. gemmifera.

Remarks: This vegetable is grown for its small buds which mature in the axils of leaves along the main stem.

Soil and Fertilizer: The same as for Broccoli.

Planting: Two crops, the spring and fall ones, are the most satisfactory as the buds are not firm when grown in hot weather. Seed may be sown inside the same as Cabbage and the plants set out when the ground thaws out; or it may be sown inside at the same time the plants are set. Seed for the late crop is sown outside between May 20 and June 15. Cultural requirements are the same as for Cabbage.

Harvesting: The buds are mature when they are hard and from 1-1½ inches in diameter. They may be broken off, trimmed, and stored in a cool, moist place. A well-developed plant will produce from two thirds to a quart of the best grade of buds. The plants may be left outside during freezing weather as they are very hardy.

Varieties: The Long Island Improved is the standard variety. Dobbie's Exhibition Variety from Dobbie Brothers in Edinburgh, Scotland, when planted in the spring, has produced buds all season but those produced in hot weather are not as firm. This variety grows to a height of 4½ feet and should be planted 2½ feet apart in the rows.

CABBAGE

Botanical Name: Brassica oleracea var. capitata.

Origin: Cabbage was known as food more than four thousand years ago in western Asia.

Soil Type and Preparation: May be grown on any fairly fertile soil, but a sandy loam is best for the early crop as well as for the late crop, if the ground is well supplied with manure.

Fertilizer: The same as for Broccoli.

When and How to Plant: For a continuous supply, three crops should be planted. Seed for the first crop should be sown indoors or in a hotbed between the first and the middle of February, six to eight weeks before the date for setting out. Sow the seed in fairly light soil in rows 3 inches apart and cover with ¼ inch of soil. Seed should germinate in a week. When plants are 2 inches high, prick out 2 inches by 2 inches. They should be grown in a temperature of 70 degrees. Plants may be transplanted 3 inches by 3 inches, or in individual 3-inch pots, three weeks later, but this is not necessary.

Plants may be transplanted to the garden as soon as the ground is workable, but the plants must be hardened off beforehand in order to withstand the unfavorable weather conditions. Set out in the garden 18 inches apart in the rows and 2–2½ feet apart between the rows. Set the plants out a little deeper than they were inside.

Succession and Inter-Cropping: Early crop should mature the first week in July. The second crop planted the middle of March to the first of April should be ready to harvest from the last of July till the middle of August. Seed for the late crop may be sown outdoors in the open ground from the middle of June until the first of July. This should mature by October, and it may be stored. Inter-cropping is not practical.

Moisture Requirements: Cabbage requires a liberal supply of moisture for maximum development. Lack of moisture causes the heads to form prematurely. Too much moisture causes improper soil conditions.

Cultivation: The root system of the Cabbage is very fibrous and extremely close to the surface of the ground. For this reason cultivation should be light, but frequent enough to control weeds.

Manures and Fertilizers: Cabbage requires large amounts of nitrogen, phosphorus, and potash. Manures when applied in liberal amounts keep the soil in good physical condition and furnish a part of the nutrients, but unless the soil is very rich commercial fertilizers high in nitrogen, phosphorus, and potash, such as formulas 4–8–4 or 5–8–7, should be used. This should be broadcast at the rate of 1 pound to 25 square feet and raked in just before planting. It may be applied broadcast between the rows when, or just after, the plants are set out.

Harvesting: Do not harvest until the heads are solid, for soft heads are inferior and undeveloped. Cut several of the outer leaves with the head, for these will protect the head and keep it from deteriorating until used. If it is not harvested as soon as the heads are hard, the heads will burst. If the heads become hard, but the cabbage is not to be used for a week or so, simply give the plant a good jerk to break some of the roots, and leave it in the field until the head is wanted.

Storing: The late crop is the one most satisfactorily stored, especially for winter use. Pull plants up by the roots; place in a cellar with a temperature of 40 degrees and a fairly moist atmosphere. Store between the first and middle of November. Although early varieties may be planted so as to mature late, they cannot be stored as satisfactorily.

VARIETIES

Early: Golden Acre, round; Early Jersey Wakefield, pointed head. *Midseason:* Copenhagen Market, round head; Glory of Enkhuizen, round head. *Late:* Penn State Ball, round head; Drumhead Savoy, drum-shaped and crinkly leaves. *Red:* Mammoth Redrock, and a smaller variety, the Red Dutch.

CABBAGE—CHINESE

Botanical Name: Brassica pekinensis.

Origin: Probably a native of China, where it has been under cultivation for fifteen hundred years. Known to the authorities here for some time, but only recently used here in home gardens.

When and How to Plant: Does best on a rich soil, which will retain moisture. Sandy loam or loam soil well enriched with decayed manure before plants are set out is excellent. Seed may be sown outside as soon as the soil is slightly warm, or about May 1, and any time up until July 1. Distances should be 2–2½ feet between the rows and 8–12 inches between plants. For fall crop, seed is sown about July 1; thin out when plants are 3 inches high. For general care and cultivation see Cauliflower. This vegetable cannot be transplanted.

Moisture: Plenty of moisture is required. Should the supply fail, a seed stalk will form before the head has fully developed. For this reason a muck soil, which is also rich in organic matter, will give good results.

Fertilizer: A good commercial fertilizer, such as a 4–8–4 formula, is very beneficial if applied ten days to two weeks after thinning. Apply at the rate of 1 pound to 100 feet between the rows.

Harvesting: Heads should be harvested when fully matured and developed. They should be firm, but the size depends on the variety. Cut from the roots as with Celery. Remove the loose outer leaves, until the bleached interior shows. Keep in a cool moist place; consume as soon as possible. It may, however, be kept several weeks under proper conditions.

VARIETIES

Chihili—18–20 inches, very solid with tapering head.
Pe-tsai—12–14 inches, fairly compact with broad head.
Wong bok—8–12 inches, rather loose, with broad head.

CARROT

Botanical Name: Daucus Carota var. sativa.

Origin: Carrots were known as food in temperate sections of Asia over two thousand years ago.

Soil: The best soil type for this vegetable is a deep, mellow loam, which will not become too compact. Since carrots have a deep-root system and cannot penetrate a hard soil, the soil should by all means be fairly light. A hard, compact soil tends to force the carrots to put forth fibrous roots which are very disfiguring. Never plant this crop on a sod land, but on a land which has been prepared well beforehand by thorough plowing or forking. Apply a liberal amount of well-rotted manure, disk or fork this in, and then rake over the soil, making sure all the lumps are out and the soil is finely pulverized. If sod land is to be used, plant two or three deep-rooted crops over the area first, such as corn or potatoes.

When and How to Plant: The seed should be planted in early spring, as soon as the ground is workable. There are usually two crops: the spring one, for summer consumption, and the fall one, sown in June or July, depending on the locality, and harvested in November. Those harvested late are usually stored for winter use. Since both crops are treated alike, they can be discussed together, except for dates. Sow the seed at the rate of 1 ounce per 100 feet. Allow 1 foot between the rows, and since the seed is usually a long time in germinating, lettuce seed may be mixed with it. The lettuce seed will quickly germinate and mark the rows, so that cultivation will be easier until the carrots appear. Plant the seed as soon before or after a rain as possible, for they require a good deal of moisture in order to germinate. In a month's time, the carrots should be from 3 to 4 inches in height. At that time they should be thinned, and the lettuce should be removed. Thin the carrots ¾ inch to 1½ inches apart. The lettuce may be transplanted if desired. These thinnings are very young and tender and are delicious when served whole.

Succession: The early crop is followed by a fall crop which should be planted about the first of June. This receives the same treatment as the first one.

Moisture Requirements: Carrots need plenty of moisture, particularly when the seeds are germinating. However, they should receive only a moderate supply when they really begin to grow, for too much moisture will make the roots crack, especially when they are reaching full size.

Cultivation: Cultivate to keep all the weeds out. However, the cultivation should be fairly shallow to prevent the formation of adventitious side roots which disfigure the main root so much. After the plants are 8 inches high, the tops will begin to fall over a bit, thereby making a natural mulch or ground cover which will prevent the weeds from coming up, and will conserve all the moisture necessary for the proper maturity of the crop.

Fertilizers: Three to four days after thinning, it is advisable to apply a good commercial fertilizer such as a formula 5–10–5, scattered over the area on a dry day. See Beet for rate of application.

Harvesting: The early crop is harvested about the first of July, depending on the date planted, and the nature of the weather of the locality. They should be pulled only as they are needed, for the fresher they are when cooked, the better they will be. The late crop is harvested about November and is usually stored.

Storing: Carrots should be stored in slightly moist sand if they are to be put in an ordinary cellar. This sand keeps them from drying out too much while in storage. However, if they can be stored in a good root cellar, they need only be put in bags. The natural dampness of a root cellar makes the damp sand unnecessary. Pull the carrots and let them dry out in the field for at least half a day before storing them either in sand or in a root cellar.

Varieties: The best varieties are the Red-cored Chantenay and Guerande, which are early and of the 3-inch stump-rooted size; the Danver's Half-long is the finest midseason carrot, being long, slender, and pointed. It usually is from 6–8 inches long, and it always pulls easily. For the late planting the best variety is the Long Orange, which is about 12 inches long, pointed, and large-cored. This is a good variety for storing. It should always be thinned to the width of three fingers and no more in order to encourage the root to be long and slender, as it should be.

CAULIFLOWER

Botanical Name: Brassica oleracea botrytis.

Origin: Known as food in western Asia over two thousand years ago.

Soil: Same as for Cabbage, Brussels Sprouts, and Broccoli.

When and How to Plant: Being a cool season crop, seed should be sown indoors about February 15. Sow in a sandy loam soil, 3 inches between rows; cover with ¼ inch of soil. When the plants are 1½ inches high, transplant to 2 inches apart each way. Keep at 55–60 degrees to develop a good root system and stocky tops. One more transplanting is advisable, but not usually practised. Harden off plants a week before setting out, about April 15, 18 inches apart in rows 2½-3 feet apart.

Seed for the second or fall crop may be sown in the open ground between the middle of June and the first of July. One-eighth ounce of seed should produce at least 100 plants. Germination takes one week.

Moisture: Soil should be well supplied with moisture, especially when heads are beginning to form.

Cultivation: Keep weed growth suppressed at all times, but cultivation should be shallow to avoid root injury. For best results, cauliflower should be grown as quickly as possible.

Manures and Fertilizers: Manure is most effective if applied when the ground is being prepared. A complete fertilizer, 4–8–4, will hasten growth and may be applied at the rate of a good tablespoonful to each plant, two weeks after the plants have been set out. A second application at the same rate may be applied just as the tiny heads appear.

Shading: As the heads begin to form, the outside leaves should be brought together and tied at the top to keep heads completely shaded.

Harvesting: In two weeks to a month after the head has been tied up, depending on the variety and weather, it should be ready to harvest. Properly matured heads should be firm and show no signs of discoloration or breaking. Cut the head off at the junction of head and leaves; trim off any discolored leaves, leaving a few trimmed to within 1 inch of the top of the head. These will give protection until the head is ready for use. Store in a cool, moist place.

Storing: If the plants mature too quickly for consumption, as they may in hot weather, the entire plant may be pulled up by the roots and stored in a cool, moist place for about two weeks.

Varieties: Dwarf Erfurt and Snowball. These mature in from one hundred to one hundred and twenty days, depending on growing conditions.

CELERIAC

Botanical Name: Apium graveolens var. rapaceum.

Origin: Probably first grown in Europe although the date is not known. Same family as the celery and like it in many ways. The thick tuberous underground stem is the edible portion; the leaves resemble those of celery, but they are a darker green and smaller. Celeriac has a hollow stem.

Soil: The soil requirements are the same as for celery. Celeriac is a much slower growing plant.

Planting: The seeds may be started in the open ground, but there may be two crops, the first one started indoors and the second one in the open ground. The first crop should be sown indoors not later than the first of March, since it is slow to germinate and to grow, and it should be transplanted once about the first of April. Plants should be ready to set out in the open ground the middle of April, but this depends mainly on the locality and the seasons. This crop is set out in the open ground as celery is, but the distance between the rows may be lessened, for this vegetable is not hilled up more than 2 inches to be bleached. The leaves and stems are never used, only the enlarged root stem.

Harvesting: This first crop should be harvested on or before the first of September; the second or late crop will provide the succession. Pull up, clean off side roots and top, and use as soon as convenient.

Succession: The second crop should be started in the open ground from the middle to the last of May, with the same distance between the rows. When the plants are 2 inches high, they should be thinned to 6 inches apart.

After thinning or transplanting, from a week to ten days later, an application of a good commercial fertilizer should be put on at the rate of 1 pound to 35 square feet. Put it down the rows as close to the plants as possible and then cultivate it in. If the soil was not very rich with manure to begin with, another application equal to the first may be made a month later.

Cultivation: Shallow cultivation is necessary. The leaves should eventually grow so that no weed growth will be possible. Then cultivation need be done only occasionally.

Storing: Pull up, clean off the side roots, twist off the tops, and then store in moist sand at a temperature of 40–50 degrees.

Varieties: Giant Prague is the best.

CELERY

Botanical Name: Apium graveolens. Derivation is speculative. Possibly from the Greek word for parsley—selinon.

Origin: In its wild state, celery has a wide range. It was not used for food until the sixteenth century.

Soil: Celery does best on soils which are well supplied with organic matter and which do not contain an overabundance of clay. Land which has not previously been planted for several years should be manured and dug or plowed the fall previous to planting and these operations should be repeated in the spring. If manure is not available, any organic matter such as leaf mold may be used with good results. A complete fertilizer, such as a 4–8–4, 5–10–5, or 4–12–4, should be broadcast at the rate of 1 pound to 50 square feet and raked in just before setting out the plants.

When and How to Plant: Celery does best in the cooler parts of the year, and the spring and fall crops are most practical. All varieties do not mature at the same time; so it is possible to plant several at the same time and have a continuous supply for home use.

(1) *Early Crop:* For the first crop, sow seed in a hotbed or cold-frame about ten weeks before planting in the open ground, which may be done as soon as danger from heavy frost is past. Broadcast the seed after watering the soil and cover very lightly with fine sand. The temperature should be between 60 and 75 degrees F. Four to five weeks after planting the seed, the plants will be large enough to transplant, though this is not necessary, as a little thinning in the seed bed will prove to be more satisfactory and faster growth will be made if transplanting is not practised. Ten days before the plants are set in the field, withhold all water to harden them off. The plants are set 6 inches in the row and 2–3 feet between the rows. *Cultivation:* Shallow cultivation will control weeds and thereby conserve moisture. The root system is very fibrous and shallow, so cultivation should not be more than 1 inch deep. *Bleaching:* Celery must be bleached in order to get rid of the green coloring which gives it a bitter taste, and to cause the rapid growth of the undeveloped stalks in the crown. Boards 8 inches wide may be placed on both sides of the plants as close as is possible without injury, and kept in place by stakes 18 inches long, driven 6–10 inches into the ground at sufficient intervals to hold the boards upright. The distance between the boards at the top should be 3–4 inches. Be sure to have all leaves in a vertical position to protect the center leaves during bleaching. These small undeveloped leaves receive a stimulus when light is withheld, and in two weeks they should be the same height as the outside leaves. Then it is ready to be harvested. By bleaching only a few plants at a time, the early crop will last at least six weeks. There are numerous other methods of bleaching, but the principle is to exclude light from the leaves, make the plant compact, and force the heart to respond to the stimulus of light.

Waterproof bleaching paper and cardboard collars are some of the other materials used for this purpose. Soil should not be used for the early crop as there are too many injurious organisms in soil when it is warm. *Harvesting:* The early crop is harvested by cutting off the stalk 2 inches below the ground. Trim off outside leaves, which are usually tough in warm weather. Store in a cool place.

(2) *Late Crop:* Seed is planted in a prepared seed bed, in a coldframe or in the garden from April 10 to May 10. Plants should be set in the garden between June 20 and July 20. Transplant 6 inches apart in the row and leave 4 feet between the rows. Inter-cropping with radishes, beets, lettuce or any other quick-maturing crop is practical. *Bleaching:* The late crop is of the highest quality when bleached with soil. It can remain in the ground and survive a heavy freeze if the tops are adequately protected. About two months after the plants have been set in the field, begin to hill them up by pulling the soil toward them. Keep it even with the center of the plant but do not allow the soil to reach the center, or growth will be inhibited. Hill up ten days later and repeat if necessary until the plants are 12–18 inches in height.

Fertilizers: 1 pound of a high grade complete fertilizer containing nitrogen, phosphorus, and potash is applied to every 25–50 square feet at planting time. A quick-acting nitrogenous fertilizer such as nitrate of soda or Cal-Nitro, applied just before the bleaching process, will hasten the development of tender succulent stalks. One pound to 100 feet of row is sufficient.

Storing the Late Crop: If the crop has not been bleached with soil it may be trenched to prevent it from freezing. Dig a trench 2 feet wide and deep enough to allow the leaves to be on the same level as the ground and pack the celery, roots and all, in a close, upright position. Decayed or broken stalks should be removed before trenching. Mulch with hay in cold weather. It will keep outside until Thanksgiving. When bleached with soil, it may be dug with roots intact, put in boxes in a cool damp place, and kept for a much longer period.

Varieties: The Easy Blanching and Golden Self-Blanching types are the earliest to mature, requiring about 120 days. The Golden Plume type matures 2 weeks later and is excellent for an early or late crop. Many prefer the large Giant Pascal which is entirely a late, green variety, blanching creamy-white.

SWISS CHARD

Botanical Name: Beta vulgaris, var. Cicla.

Origin: Of garden origin, but the date is unknown.

Soil: Fairly rich soil is good, and an application of well-decayed manure turned under before planting is beneficial.

Sowing: Sow seed as early in spring as the ground can be worked, in rows 18–30 inches apart, and when plants are 3 inches high, thin 3 inches apart. Thinnings may be used as greens. When plants are 7–9 inches high, thin to 9 inches apart. A crop matures in sixty days, but careful cutting before that time does no harm. One sowing will last until the crop is killed by autumn frost.

Cultivation: Cultivate shallowly and sufficiently often to keep down weeds.

Fertilizers: Two weeks after the last thinning, an application of 4–8–4 at the rate of ¾ of a pound to 75 feet will be beneficial, but it is not absolutely necessary. Spread in rows between plants and cultivate in shallowly. A second application, same method and amount, about the middle of August, will help insure the crop for the rest of the season, but it is not necessary unless poor growth is being made.

Harvesting: Harvest by removing the outer leaves with a sharp twist, taking care not to injure the small, undeveloped leaves in the center. Keep in a cool moist place, and use as soon as possible.

Varieties: A good variety is the Lucullus.

Remarks: May be overwintered if protected with salt hay. Will produce a good early crop, but will not last very long. Also may be started indoors in pots and transplanted out.

CHICORY

Botanical Name: Cichorium Intybus.

Origin: Also known as French Endive and Witloof Chicory; the origin and date of introduction are doubtful, but it is definitely known not to have been cultivated by the ancients.

Soil: Will give good results on any soil which will grow root crops, such as carrots, etc.

Planting: Started outside the first of June, for the crop will mature and go to seed if started earlier. Top of plant is of no value. The roots are used as a substitute for coffee and they may be forced at any time during the winter. Seed is sown in rows, 18 inches to 2 feet apart, covered with ½ inch of soil. When plants are 2–3 inches high, thin 6–8 inches apart.

Moisture: A constant and well-regulated supply of moisture is necessary to make good plants and to prevent the plants from sending up a seed stalk.

Inter-Cropping: One crop is sufficient, and inter-cropping is not practicable.

Cultivation. Cultivation is the same as for any root crop.

Fertilizers: Thorough preparation in the beginning, before putting in the crop, is best for good results. No additional feeding should be really necessary. The addition of manure or a complete fertilizer after this crop has been planted will do very little toward producing good results. Nothing can make up for a lack of complete soil preparation in the beginning.

Harvesting: Roots should be harvested late in the fall before the ground freezes; they should be removed with a fork or a spade so completely and carefully as not to injure them in any way. Tops should be removed and the roots stored in a cool, moist place. They may be stored in sand kept slightly moist. Injured or diseased roots should never be stored. The roots store best at a temperature of 40 degrees.

Forcing: The main use of Chicory is for forcing during the winter months, using the tender bleached shoots for salad. To force the roots properly, they may be taken out of storage at any time, using only a few for each forcing, so that the supply will last all winter. They should be started at intervals of every two weeks, for one crop will last about a month, and the next crop may be coming on to take its place when it is exhausted. The roots should be placed upright in sand; if there is no sand, ashes may be used; all light should be excluded, and they should be kept moist at a temperature of 50–55 degrees. As they sprout, they should be covered with the sand until the shoots are 3 inches long. Then they should be cut and used as soon as possible. Each crop may be cut on the average of three times during the month they are forced, and much better shoots are obtained from the good strong roots.

Variety: The Witloof is the only variety.

SWEET CORN

Botanical Name: Zea Mays, var. saccharata.

Origin: Grown by the Indians in Mexico and eastern North America before this continent was discovered.

Soil: Corn requires a well-drained soil, high in organic matter. A good application of well-decayed manure is the best source of organic material. Early crops do best on a sandy loam soil which warms quickly in the spring, but later crops prefer a heavier soil which retains moisture.

When and How to Plant: Seed may be sown as soon as the soil has warmed up, or about May 1 to 10. Plant 3–4 seeds in hills from 2–3 feet apart each way. Mix a small handful of commercial fertilizer with the soil in the bottom of each hill and cover the seeds with 1–1½ inches of soil. Seed germinates in one week to ten days. Thin to three plants to each hill, when plants are from 3–6 inches high.

Inter-Cropping: May be practised with squash, melons, or pumpkins, string beans, lettuce, and other quick-maturing crops. Plant every ten to fourteen days for a continuous supply.

Cultivation: Should be frequent, beginning when plants first appear. Practise shallow cultivation, pulling the soil toward the hills each time. Three to four cultivations are all that are necessary. Cultivation should cease as soon as the tassel shows.

Manures and Fertilizers: When plants are 4–8 inches high, broadcast 4–8–4 between the rows at the rate of 1 pound to 50–75 feet and cultivate in carefully and shallowly. Another application is sometimes made just before the tassels appear, but is not necessary in every case, being advisable when satisfactory growth is not being made. The above applications are optional.

Harvesting: Harvest when the silk has begun to turn brown. Corn should be used just as soon as picked, as the sugar content is higher at that time. If it cannot be used at that time, husk and keep in a cool place, but the quality deteriorates very quickly.

VARIETIES

Golden Bantam—Yellow, sweet, seventy days to maturity.

Golden Sunshine—Larger than the Golden Bantam; matures in seventy to seventy-five days.

Golden Cross Bantam—Matures in ninety days.

Spanish Gold—Matures in seventy to eighty days.

Country Gentleman Shoe-Peg—Matures in ninety days; white.

Stowell's Evergreen—Matures in ninety-five to one hundred days.

Remarks: Too much emphasis cannot be placed on the fact that corn should be eaten as soon as picked. Husking immediately after picking is an aid in preventing deterioration. Corn may be picked early in the morning, or late in the afternoon, husked and kept cool and shaded. In this way, it will keep in good condition for twelve hours, but is at its best if picked immediately before using.

CRESS

Botanical Name: Lepidium sativum—Garden Cress.
    Nasturtium officinale—Water Cress.

Origin: Probably of Persian origin; its cultivation dates from a very early period.

When and How to Sow: Garden cress is a cool season crop, the leaves being used for salad or for garnishing. Goes quickly to seed in hot weather. Sow seed in any garden soil as weather conditions permit. Sow in rows 12 inches apart and thin as needed for use.

If leaves are cut without injuring the crown, the plant will keep bearing for several weeks. It should be ready for use four to six weeks after planting.

Water cress may be grown in any stream where the water is pure and fresh. Once established in a good stream, it will last indefinitely. It is a perennial which will throw out roots from the joints and which may also be propagated from seed or pieces of stem. It may also be grown in the garden in well-prepared, very moist soil, by starting the seed indoors and transplanting to the garden. If given plenty of moisture, plants should last some time. If grown like ordinary vegetables it will be a failure.

CUCUMBER

Botanical Name: Cucumis sativus.

Origin: Native of southern Asia, in cultivation for over four thousand years.

Soil: Heavy soil is best because it tends to be more fertile and retentive of moisture. If well-decayed manure is available, it should be used in liberal quantities and should be well forked in before planting.

Sowing: When ground has become thoroughly warm (May 1 to 15), plant in hills 4 feet apart each way. If available, a forkful of well-rotted manure placed at the bottom of each hill and covered with 4 inches of soil gives excellent results. In each hill plant 12 seeds, ½ inch deep. Seeds germinate in ten days and plants should be thinned out gradually, so that when they are 4 inches high there should be 4 plants to each hill. A less satisfactory method is to sow seeds in rows 4–6 feet apart, 6 or 8 seeds to 1 foot, and thin plants to 1 foot apart after they are 2–4 inches high. Cucumber plants cannot be satisfactorily transplanted. Four to six hills is enough for a family planting.

Succession: For a continuous supply, there must be at least two plantings between May 1 and July 10. If a few radish seeds are sown in each hill, they will germinate quickly and attract all the insects. As soon as the cucumbers appear, pull up the radishes and destroy them, insects and all.

Moisture: Vines will not develop properly and fruit will be small without a continuous supply of moisture. Heavy land, well prepared, is an excellent method of insuring moisture.

Cultivation: Should be shallow and constant until vines cover the ground. Do not step on the vines—it will kill them, as they cannot put out new shoots below the injury.

Fertilizer: Cucumbers must have a maximum amount of nitrogen; if the soil is rich, a complete fertilizer, applied when plants are 4 inches high, will promote satisfactory growth. If it was impossible to put manure in the hills before planting, complete fertilizer should be applied, a small handful to each hill, when the plants are about 3 inches high. Applied to plants grown in rows, 1 pound is sufficient for 50 feet.

Harvesting: Do not pick cucumbers until leaves are dry in the morning, as disease is easily spread by disturbance of damp foliage. Harvest fruit before it begins to turn yellow; in a cool moist place, it will keep a week.

Varieties: Longfellow, Davis' Perfect, White Spine, Early Fortune, Straight Eight, and Stokes Windermoor Wonder.

Remarks: The Gherkin used for pickling is planted July 1 and given the same treatment as the Cucumber. As the plants are somewhat smaller, they need only be thinned to 6–7 plants per hill. There are two varieties: West India Gherkin is round, and the Boston Pickling is long, from 2 to 4 inches.

EGGPLANT

Botanical Name: Solanum Melongena.

Origin: Known as food in India several thousand years ago. The varieties cultivated in America are long and ovate in shape, while those cultivated in India are even longer, slender and slightly curved.

Soil: A sandy loam soil yields the best crop. It should have plenty of well-decayed manure forked in to a depth of 6 inches and it should be finely pulverized, at any time before the plants are set.

Sowing: Eggplant requires warm soil conditions and a long period in which to mature, and north of Virginia it must be started indoors. Seed may be sown in flats from February 15 to March 15, in soil with a high percentage of sand. Seed germinates in ten days to two weeks. When plants are 1½ inches high, transplant 2 inches each way. The temperature should be 75 degrees at all times; when plants begin to crowd, transplant to individual 3-inch pots, transplanting to larger pots as the plants grow. They should be in 6-inch pots one month after they are in 3-inch pots. If plants show any tendency to turn yellow, water with nitrate of soda (1 ounce dissolved in 1 gallon of water). Plants should not be set out before June 1, and later if the ground is not thoroughly warm; if set out earlier they are checked by cool nights and cool soil conditions. When set out, plants should be 4–6 inches high. Planting distance should be 3 feet between rows, 2 feet between plants.

Moisture: Eggplant is distinctly fussy about moisture; if it has too little, leaves turn yellow, become spotted and drop; if too much, flowers will not set fruit.

Cultivation: Should be exceedingly shallow as roots are very near the surface. Cultivate just enough to keep down weeds.

Fertilizer: A small handful of a complete fertilizer, 4–8–4, should be placed in a ring around each plant when it is set out. This should be cultivated in lightly. At any time satisfactory growth is not being made, a second application is advisable.

Harvesting: Always cut the fruit from the plant. It is best when about 4 inches in diameter. Keep in a cool place until ready to use; do not keep more than 4 days.

Varieties: Black Beauty and New York Purple are the two main varieties, both high in quality. Black Beauty is usually preferred because of its attractive appearance.

ENDIVE

Botanical Name: Chicorium Endivia.

Origin: In very early times endive was cultivated in Egypt.

Soil: Should be rich and heavy. Prepare with plenty of organic matter (compost or well-decayed manure) to a depth of 6 inches before planting. Ground at the base of a slope is advisable because of the greater supply of moisture available.

Sowing: Sow seed from June 1 to August 1 in rows 18 inches apart.

When plants are 2 inches high, thin to 1 foot apart. Thinned plants may be transplanted. One-fourth ounce of seed will plant 50 feet of row. An early sowing may be made as soon as the ground can be worked in spring, but is not as satisfactory as the later one, for the ground warms up too quickly.

Moisture: A continuous supply is essential for good endive.

Cultivation: Three weeks before crop is harvested, plants must be bleached to make them more tender and less bitter. Draw outside leaves over the heart and center leaves until they come together at the top. Put a piece of waterproof paper around them to hold them in place and tie with string or an elastic band. This must be done on a dry day as the inside leaves rot quickly if tied when wet. When the endive is bleached, the plants should be cut as close to the ground as possible and stored in a cool, moist place.

Varieties: Broad-leaved Batavian or Escarole is mainly used for culinary purposes and is hardier, but of poorer quality than French Green Curled, which is the best salad variety; when properly raised and bleached the latter is of excellent quality.

KALE

Botanical Name: Brassica oleracea var. acephala.

Origin: First known in Europe, and cultivated for several thousand years.

Soil: A well-drained, sandy loam, well prepared with plenty of decayed manure or other organic matter is ideal for Kale. Prepare to a depth of 6–8 inches and dig in manure any time before planting. Kale will, however, grow on any soil which is fairly rich.

Sowing: Sow in place, ⅛ ounce seed to 50 feet in rows 18 inches to 2 feet apart, as soon as the soil can be worked in the spring. Seed germinates in seven to ten days, and when plants are 3 inches high, they should be thinned to one plant to 8–10 inches. Sow again in midsummer for fall and winter crop. Plan on sixty to eighty days to maturity.

Cultivation: Should be frequent and shallow. All weed growth must be suppressed.

Fertilizer: A complete fertilizer, 4–8–4, applied to plants a month after thinning, will prove beneficial. Apply at the rate of ½ pound to 25 feet of row.

Harvesting: When leaves are sufficiently mature, they should be bright green and of an attractive appearance. When old, they become dark green and tough. Cut and keep in a cool, damp place and use as soon as possible. If allowed to remain on the plant too long, they become tough. The fall or winter crop may be left in the field, covered lightly with salt hay or straw, and the leaves cut when desired. They will keep until late into the winter.

VARIETIES

First crop—Dwarf Green Curled or Dwarf Curled Scotch.

Fall and Winter crop—Dwarf Siberian or Bloomsdale Double Extra Curled.

Scotch types are usually used for the early crop, while Siberian is more hardy and is used for the late crop.

KOHLRABI

Botanical Name: Brassica caulorapa.

Origin: Date of introduction uncertain, for there are no wild types. Known as an extreme varietal form of Wild Cabbage.

Soil: Any well-prepared soil is satisfactory. After first working, an application of manure should be well turned under and the soil should be pulverized. Soil should be prepared to a depth of 6 inches.

Sowing: No advantage is gained by early or by indoor sowing. First crop should be sown as soon as the frost is out of the ground; then sow every two weeks until August 1. Sow in rows 18 inches apart at the rate of ¼ ounce seed to 75 feet. Cover lightly with soil, and when plants are 3–4 inches high, thin to 6–8 inches apart. The thinnings may be transplanted to another row and will take about an extra week to develop. Leave and transplant only the best seedlings. Days to maturity, 50–60.

Cultivation: Keep soil loose at all times, but do not cultivate deeply near plants.

Fertilizer: About five days after thinning, plants will be in condition to benefit by additional fertilizer, and a small amount (¾ pound to row of 50 feet) of nitrate of soda or ammonium sulphate may be broadcast between rows and lightly raked in. If fertilizer remains on the leaves, it will burn the plants.

Harvesting: Kohlrabi is a member of the Cabbage family and is peculiar because the edible portion is a swollen stem which develops just at the level of the ground; it should be used when this is the size of a silver dollar. It becomes tough and flavorless as it grows larger. Pull up the entire plant to avoid disease from rotting roots and leaves.

Varieties: Early Purple Vienna, Early White Vienna, and Smooth White Vienna, which is short-leaved.

LEEK

Botanical Name: Allium Porrum.

Origin: First known in Mediterranean countries, leeks have been grown since prehistoric times.

Soil: Leeks prefer a soil which is very rich, supplied with plenty of decayed vegetable and animal matter. Prepare as early as weather will permit by plowing or digging and then pulverizing.

Sowing: About February 15, seed should be sown indoors in any good garden soil in a temperature of 60–70 degrees. Will germinate in about ten days. When plants are 2–4 inches high, transplant 2 inches apart each way. First week in May, set plants out 6 inches apart in rows 2–3 feet apart.

Seed sown in open ground does not give leeks of large size and highest quality, but does give satisfactory results. Seed should be sown ¼ inch deep at the rate of 1 ounce to 100 feet, in rows 2–3 feet apart, as soon as ground is in workable condition. As the root system is meager, leek plants take at least two weeks to become established before noticeable growth takes place. Since the plants do not all mature at the same time, only one planting is necessary. Leeks may be left in the ground until the soil freezes.

Cultivation: Keep the soil friable at all times; as the plants begin to grow, hoe the soil toward them.

Fertilization: When the plants are from 4–6 inches high, apply a complete fertilizer, about one teaspoonful to each plant; put over each plant a paper collar made of waterproof paper. Collar should be 3 inches high and 2 inches in diameter. This hastens upward growth; they should grow 3–4 inches in three weeks. Move collar up 3 inches, hilling the soil about the plants; continue to do so until plant grows, always keeping soil hilled up to the collar. Some of the plants will be mature about August 15, but will not deteriorate if left in the ground until late fall.

Another method of planting: set the plants in trenches 6 inches deep, 4 feet apart, and, as they grow, fill in soil to bleach them.

Moisture: Plants must have a continuous and liberal supply of moisture in order to make maximum growth.

Harvesting: Plants may be dug before freezing weather and stored in a trench as celery is, where they will keep from four to six weeks.

Varieties

American Flag attains a diameter of 1–1½ inches and a white stalk 8–12 inches high when properly bleached.

Prizetaker and Musselburg attain a diameter of 1½–2 inches and do not grow quite as tall.

LETTUCE

Botanical Name: Lactuca sativa.

Remarks: Lettuce is best if grown in the cooler parts of the year. Only the Cos, or Romaine, type is adapted to warmer conditions.

Soil Preparation: Lettuce likes an abundance of decayed organic matter and just as good results may be obtained with it as with commercial fertilizers, on soils of a fine structure. The soil should be spaded to a depth of 6 inches or more and plenty of well-rotted manure worked in. A complete fertilizer may be added at this time if deemed necessary.

Planting: April to May 15, then again in August. Seed may be sown in flats in a greenhouse or hotbed for transplanting outside. Seed should be sown six to seven weeks before transplanting outside. The young plants grow most satisfactorily at a temperature between 50 and 60 degrees. Too high a temperature makes the plants spindly and non-heading. At high temperatures the sugar changes rapidly to starch which results in a disagreeable and bitter flavor. When the plants are about 2 inches high they are pricked into other flats, 2 inches apart each way. They are kept in these flats until set in the garden, which should be preceded by a hardening-off period. The plants are set 8 inches apart in rows 15 inches apart.

Lettuce seed may be planted in the open ground as soon as the frost has disappeared, the plants being thinned out to 8 inches apart when crowding begins to occur. These plants may be set out and will mature a week or so later than those which have not been moved. One ounce of seed is sufficient for 3000 plants.

Cultivation: Shallow, and frequent enough to control weeds.

Succession: For a continuous supply sow seed every two weeks or plant varieties that mature at different dates.

Fertilizers: Lettuce responds to nitrogen very quickly which, with plenty of moisture available, will promote a rapid, succulent, crisp growth. Nitrate of soda, Cal-Nitro, or sulphate of ammonia, applied at the rate of 1 pound to 100 feet of row two weeks before harvesting, may be used to hasten maturity.

Harvesting: Loose-leaf varieties may be harvested in any stage of development before they become tough. Heading varieties should be allowed to mature. As only a few heads mature at a time, it will not be a case of a feast or a famine if seed is sown every two weeks. The root may be cut close to the ground, removing all leaves with it. If the heads are pulled up some of the leaves may be injured.

Storing: Lettuce may be stored in a cold place such as an ice chest for a period of ten to fourteen days if the humidity is relatively high.

Varieties: Grand Rapids is a loose-leaved, non-heading, early variety. May King is a very early variety with a very small head. Big Boston is a standard heading, commercial variety, as are the New York or Iceberg types. The Cos (Romaine) varieties are able to mature in hot weather.

MUSKMELON

Botanical Name: Cucumis Melo.

Origin: Origin doubtful; presumably they were first known either in Africa or Asia. Not cultivated before the Christian era.

Soil Type and Preparation: Melons grow well in many soils which are either sandy or slightly sandy in character. Heavy clay soils should be avoided. The more sand the soil contains, the earlier a crop may be planted. An application of well-rotted manure is advisable before planting, or it may be somewhat supplemented by a complete fertilizer broadcast at the rate of 1 pound to 35 square feet and raked in before planting.

When and How to Plant: Melons are very tender, and must not be planted until the soil is thoroughly warm, from the tenth of May until the middle of June. For best results, sow seeds in hills 4 feet apart each way, and for large varieties, 4–6 feet apart. This is for hand cultivation. For horse cultivation, they should be planted 6–8 feet apart. To make a hill, remove 2 shovelfuls of soil, insert 1 shovelful of well-rotted manure, and cover with 6 inches of well-firmed soil. Plant 6–8 seeds per hill and cover with ½ inch of soil. Hills should be at least 12 inches in diameter, and the seeds placed 2 inches apart in the hill. One ounce of seed is enough for 20 hills. Seed should germinate and appear above the ground in about two weeks; when plants are 3–4 inches high, thin out to the three best plants. Seed may also be sown indoors in pots a month previous to setting out of doors. Two plants may be grown in each pot and two pots set out in each hill.

Succession: By one planting of two or more varieties, early and late, a continuous supply may be obtained, without successive plantings.

Moisture: A continuous supply of moisture is very necessary to insure proper vine development and maximum fruit production. Plants require much more moisture when fruit begins to mature than they do in the growing stage.

Cultivation: Keep soil lightly cultivated between rows at all times, but do not cultivate too close to the plants; weeds near the plants should be carefully pulled out to avoid disturbing roots of vines. As the vines give shade, they conserve the moisture near the plants, and cultivation is most needed where ground is exposed to sun.

Fertilizers: A commercial fertilizer is needed for good growth and production. Apply 4-8-4, at the rate of ½ ounce per hill in a ring around each hill, 4-6 inches away from the plants, and cover with 1 inch of soil taken from between the rows. Apply after thinning.

Harvesting: Yield: 10-15 melons per hill. Melons are ready for harvesting when the stems part easily from the fruit with a very slight pull. They are not mature until the stems begins to separate and should never be cut if highest quality is desired. If not picked at this stage, they will become overripe and too soft for use. In four or five days after reaching this state, they will completely detach themselves. If picked when stems part easily, flesh is firm, but will mellow if kept in a cool place, 60-70 degrees. Vines will continue producing fruits from three weeks to a month.

VARIETIES

Hearts of Gold—Eighty to ninety days, high in quality, deep orange flesh.

Rocky Ford—One hundred days, flesh light green, weight 2-3 pounds.

Hale's Best, four to six pounds yellow flesh, and *Bender's Surprise,* same weight, golden fleshed, are two of the best larger varieties.

OKRA

Botanical Name: Hibiscus esculentus.

Origin: Asiatic in origin, but not cultivated during ancient times. Grown in the warmer parts of the United States since the eighteenth century.

Soil Type and Preparation: Any good garden soil will give good results if enriched before planting with manure or commercial fertilizer.

When and How to Plant: Okra is a tender plant, giving good results only in hot weather. Sow seeds from the middle of May to the middle of June, in rows 2½–3 feet apart. When plants are 3–4 inches high, thin the dwarf varieties 12–18 inches apart, and the larger varieties 18–30 inches apart. Not easily transplanted unless enough soil is moved to prevent root disturbance.

Cultivation: Keep soil well stirred and weeds suppressed.

Fertilizers: A liberal application of manure or complete fertilizer should be well worked in when the soil is prepared. If plants do not grow steadily, apply one teaspoonful of fertilizer to each plant as a side dressing.

Harvesting: Pods should be gathered while young—1–2 inches long. For continuous growth, do not allow pods to mature. Two plantings are often made in the South, but only one is possible in the North.

VARIETIES

White Velvet—3½–5 feet high, white and smooth.
Dwarf Green—15–18 inches high, green and furrowed.

ONION

Botanical Name: Allium Cepa.

Origin: Probably first known in parts of Asia. Grown by the ancient Egyptians, it is one of the oldest of cultivated vegetables.

The onion is one of the hardiest vegetables and may be sown as soon as the frost is out of the ground in the spring. Onion sets may also be planted at the same time.

Onion Sets are immature onions which have been produced by close seeding the season before. Those best suited for planting range from ½ to ¾ inches in diameter. The seed may also be sown in flats in a hotbed or greenhouse and the plants transplanted to the garden at any time soil and weather conditions permit.

Soil Preparation: Thorough preparation cannot be over-emphasized. The organic and nutrient and water content should be high. The onion plants feed within a limited range, due to their sparse root system. Heavy applications of commercial fertilizers are often necessary, at the rate of 1 pound to 20 or 25 square feet, being worked into the soil before planting.

Planting: Seed may be sown in flats in a greenhouse two months before the earliest planting date in the field. Four to five seeds are sown per inch. Before setting in the field the tops are cut back to a height of 3 or 4 inches. They are set 4–6 inches in rows 15–18 inches apart. Seed may be sown in rows, planting three or four seeds per inch. The plants are thinned to 4–6 inches apart when well established but before the onion begins to swell.

Onion sets are planted the same distance apart, in and between the rows, as transplanted plants. One pound of small onion sets will plant 100 feet.

Succession: If sets are planted early and followed by plants from seed, either indoors or out, there should be a steady supply, as sets mature in ninety to one hundred days, and seed onions in one hundred fifty to one hundred eighty days. Plants started from seed should be put in the open ground when sets are put out.

Moisture: A continuous, well-regulated supply of moisture is absolutely necessary. In experiments conducted at the School of Horticulture, onions at the lower end of a 100-foot row on a slight slope were twice as large as those at the top, due to the greater amount of moisture.

Cultivation: Should be shallow and constant and should begin as soon as the plants appear. Wait until tops straighten out, about one week, before weeding between the seedlings, to avoid disturbing plants. Keep rows free from weeds.

Harvesting: Tops are practically dead before plants are mature. Pull or dig and leave in sun for a few days to dry out and to toughen skins. This will improve the keeping quality.

Storing: Onions should be thoroughly cured by being exposed to sun for several days. Do not try to remove the soil until onions are thoroughly cured; then it will come off easily without washing. Only the onions grown from seed will keep for any length of time. Store in a cool, dry place spread out on a flat, dry surface. They do not need moisture and should keep five to six months.

Varieties: Yellow Glove Danvers, Yellow Strassburg, Southport Red Globe, and Southport White Globe are the best varieties for the main crop. Prizetaker and Ailsa Craig are two very large varieties, often weighing a pound or more. One variety of sets is as good as another.

PARSLEY

Botanical Name: Petroselinum hortense.

Origin: Indigenous to southern Europe. Known to the Greeks only as a wild plant. Mentioned in a list of plants for Charlemagne's garden, and introduced into England in 1548.

Soil: Variety used for leaves may be grown in any soil, but requires ample food material; that which is grown for its root system needs a deep, 6–8 inch, well-drained soil.

Sowing: Seed requires about 3 weeks to germinate and may be sown in the open ground at any time after soil can be easily worked until August 1. Sow in rows 18 inches apart; barely cover with soil. One packet of seed is sufficient for a family. Seed may also be started in hotbeds two months before it can be sown outside. Transplant when 1 inch high, 2 inches each way, and later move into the garden when the ground is workable. Transplant 8 inches apart in rows 18 inches apart.

Parsley may also be sown in coldframes about August 1. Keep plants covered with hay in the frames all winter and transplant to garden in early spring.

Cultivation: Keep soil lightly cultivated and free from weeds.

Moisture: In dry weather parsley is greatly benefited by thorough watering two or three times a week.

Fertilizer: Plants will thrive without fertilization, but will be much larger if commercial fertilizer, 4–8–4, or well-rotted manure, is applied just before planting. A little nitrate of soda applied after planting out in the field is often beneficial.

Harvesting: First leaves may be picked about 75 days after seed is sown. Kept in water, they will remain fresh for several days. Never pick plant clean; some leaves should be left around the center of the crown to insure continuous growth.

Varieties: Champion Moss Curled is a good leaf variety. Hamburg (Turnip-Rooted) is grown mainly for its roots, which are used for flavoring.

Remarks: Plants may be taken up before ground freezes and kept in a coldframe where they will produce in early spring, or they may be potted and kept in the house in a sunny window.

PARSNIP

Botanical Name: Pastinaca sativa.

Origin: Grown since the beginning of the Christian era. Native of Europe and Asia.

Soil: Parsnips need a very fertile, but fairly heavy soil, deep and well drained. If too heavy, roots become distorted; if too sandy, superfluous fibrous roots form.

Fertilizers: To get long, straight roots, apply all manures and fertilizers, such as a 4–8–4, before the land is plowed, and turn under to a depth of at least 8 inches. The long tap root forms before the parsnip begins to develop, and if fertilizer is too close to the surface, roots will not be encouraged to grow down.

Sowing: Sow seed as early as possible in spring, 1 inch deep, at the rate of ⅛ ounce to 50 feet. They should be in rows 18 inches to 2½ feet apart. They germinate in 12–18 days and rows may be marked by radish seed mixed with parsnip seed. When plants are 2–4 inches high, thin 4–6 inches apart.

Inter-Cropping: Parsnips, being a long-season crop, may be inter-cropped with any quick-maturing crop such as beets, lettuce, radishes, or spinach.

Cultivation: Should be constant, but not deep.

Moisture: A constant supply of moisture is essential for smooth, long, well-developed roots.

Harvesting: Parsnips may be harvested before the ground freezes, or may remain in the ground, protected by coarse hay or straw, until spring. Freezing tends to reduce the bitter flavor present in the fall. Dig parsnips out, never try to pull them.

Storing: Store in moist sand or in root cellar like carrots at a temperature of 40–50 degrees.

Varieties: Guernsey and Improved Hollow Crown.

PEA

Botanical Name: Pisum sativum.

Origin: This vegetable is a native of Europe, and has been cultivated since antiquity.

Soil: Peas should be grown in a sandy loam which is rich in organic matter. The soil should be well prepared the fall previous to planting, for the crop is planted early in the spring, often before the frost is all out of the ground. If the soil is well worked over in the fall, very little work is necessary in the spring. Plenty of well-rotted manure well mixed in with the soil will give the best results.

Planting: Peas are divided into two groups, smooth-seeded and wrinkled. The smooth varieties may be planted two weeks before the wrinkled sort, because they can stand moister and cooler soil conditions—as soon as enough of the frost is out of the ground to make it easily workable. The wrinkled sorts should be put in two weeks later, for by that time the soil is drier and warmer, which is essential for this type. The seed for both types should be sown in rows $2\frac{1}{2}$ feet apart and $1\frac{1}{2}$–2 inches in the row. Thin them if it seems necessary. Make a trench 4 inches deep, and cover the seed to the depth of an inch, filling in the trench as the plants grow. One pound of seed is sufficient for 50 feet of garden row. The plants cannot be transplanted successfully.

Succession: For a continuous supply, seed should be sown every ten days. They should not be planted after hot weather sets in, for they will not mature nor thrive properly. A fall crop may be sown about August 1, but it is not nearly as productive as the spring crop. They should be mature in from 60–80 days, depending on the variety.

Moisture: Peas do not require an abundance of moisture, but they do need a continuous supply. Practice clean, shallow cultivation for the best results.

Training: Peas do not need a definite system of training unless they grow to a height of more than 2 feet. Training is then necessary to keep them off the ground and to facilitate harvesting.

Birch brush or any twiggy brush is the best for training the taller growing varieties. The brush should be put from 6–10 inches apart in the row any time before the peas begin to spread.

Fertilizer: An additional application of a complete fertilizer may be given during the blooming period, if the land is not very fertile. Use the fertilizer at the rate of 1 pound for every 75 feet, broadcast between the rows, and lightly cultivated in.

Harvesting: The wrinkled varieties should be harvested when the pods are well filled out, while the smooth-seeded sorts are best when the pods are only about half full, for the peas lose their flavor as they grow larger and more mature. Both varieties are best when harvested either early in the morning or late in the evening, never during the hot part of the day. The quality becomes inferior in a very short time, if, after picking, they are not kept in a very cool place.

VARIETIES

Smooth-seeded sort—Alaska, 2–2$\frac{1}{2}$ feet high. Plant for the first crop only.

Wrinkled-seeded—Blue Bantam, 65 days to maturity, 18 inches high and very productive, with large pods. Little Marvel, 2 feet high, small podded, high in quality, mature in 65 days. Laxtonian, 18 inches high, large podded, high in quality, and mature in 65 days. Potlatch, 2 feet in height, pods from 4–5 inches in length, 75 days to maturity. Telephone, from 4–5 feet high, 80–85 days to maturity. Prince Edward, 4–5 feet in height, and 80–85 days to maturity.

PEPPER

Botanical Name: Capsicum fruticosum.

Origin: Native of South America, and cultivated for a number of centuries.

Soil Type and Preparation: Sandy loam is best, though any type will give fair results. For preparation, see Eggplant.

When and How to Plant: Should be started indoors from the first of February to the first of March. Sow in soil composed of two parts garden loam to one part sand. Put in rows 3 inches apart, and cover seed with ¼ inch of soil. Seed will sprout in 10 days to 2 weeks, and when plants are 1½ inches high transplant 2 inches by 2 inches. The temperature should not be lower than 70 degrees. A month to six weeks later, transplant again to 3 inches by 3 inches or 4 inches by 4 inches. Set out of doors as soon as the ground has warmed up and all danger of frost is over. Set 18 inches in the row and 2½ feet between the rows.

Moisture Requirements: Continuous moisture supply is necessary for proper development; too much will promote excessive leaf growth and less fruit.

Cultivation: Practise shallow cultivation. The plants may be slightly hilled up, as they grow. When the first peppers are ready to harvest, cultivation should cease. Keep all weeds out even when the time for cultivation has ended.

Fertilizers: A complete fertilizer such as 4–8–4 or 5–8–7 should be used, as the average soil is usually deficient in nitrogen, phosphorus, and potash. If the soil is not very fertile, fertilizer should be applied just before or when the plants are set out. If applied when setting out, mix about two tablespoonfuls with the soil at the bottom of the hole into which the plants are to be set. Another application may be made when the fruits are just beginning to form, to hasten growth and maturity. This is applied in the form of a circle around each plant 3 inches to 4 inches away from the stem of the plant, and covered with soil. Two tablespoonfuls per plant is enough.

Harvesting: All sweet peppers are green until they reach a stage where they no longer increase in size, and at that time they turn red. They are usually harvested in the green stage. Red sweet peppers are usually used only for their color. They may be picked at any time after they have reached the desired size, being kept in a cool place to prevent them from wilting. They may be kept this way for as long as two weeks.

Storing: If the entire plant is pulled up and hung upside down in a cellar, the peppers will remain in good condition for as long as three weeks.

Varieties: Ruby King, Ruby Giant, and California Wonder are good. These will mature in 150 days. The California Wonder is thick-fleshed, very solid, and a rather late-bearing variety unless started early and given proper care. Hungarian Wax, Long Red Cayenne, the Red Cayenne, and Red Chili are the best pungent varieties.

POTATO

Botanical Name: Solanum tuberosum.

Origin: Native of South America; found here in the latter part of the sixteenth century.

Soil Type and Preparation: A light, well-drained, loamy soil is best. Potatoes are very heavy feeders, so the soil should be plowed or forked as deeply as possible and a liberal amount of well-decayed manure incorporated. Fresh manure should never be used unless it is applied the fall previous to planting. If fresh manure is applied in the spring it will make a good deal of nitrogen available to the plants right away, which will cause them to make an excessive amount of top growth, and little root growth. Lime should never be applied to the soil as it activates organisms which cause potato diseases. All manure which is applied should be turned under as deeply as possible.

When and How to Plant: Early crop may be planted as soon as the frost is out of the ground, and succeeding crops may be planted until the first week in July. Make the trenches from 4–6 inches deep and 2½–3 feet apart. Plant the potatoes 15–18 inches apart in the trench and cover with 2 inches of soil. Use only disease-free or certified seed. Potatoes should be prepared for planting 10 days beforehand, being cut so there are at least two eyes for each section, with a small piece of the potato attached. Spread the pieces in a box not more than two layers deep, and sprinkle them with sulphur. The sulphur should come in contact with all the cut surfaces, causing them to dry out and to toughen up. This is known as suberization, for it prevents the potato from becoming diseased before the plant gets a good start. Potatoes are sometimes planted without this treatment. Potato skins are also planted, but the results in both cases are variable. They should be planted at the rate of 3–4 pounds every 50 feet. Sprouts should appear above the ground in two weeks. The later crops are all treated in the same way.

Cultivation: Keep the soil loose and friable at all times. When the plants are from 4–6 inches high, begin to hoe the soil toward them. Kill all weeds before they have a chance to develop enough to compete with the potatoes. Hoe the soil around the plants gradually at intervals of ten days to two weeks, taking the soil from between the rows. Continue until the plants have grown so that working between the rows is impossible.

Manures and Fertilizers: An application of a complete commercial fertilizer, 4–8–4, at the rate of 1 pound to 50 feet may be broadcast between the rows one month after the plants have sprouted, if the soil was not very fertile to begin with.

Harvesting: The early crop may be dug from the time vines begin to die until they are actually dead. Leaving the potatoes outside on the ground in the sun for a day to toughen up the skin makes them easier to handle, and prevents them from bruising so easily. The late crop should not be dug until the vines are dead. Leave outside for a day in the sun, as with the early crop.

Storing: Requirements for storing potatoes are: temperature of 50 degrees, medium amount of humidity, uniform conditions. They may be stored in bags, boxes, or in piles, provided there is an allowance for proper air circulation. Will keep for five months or more.

Yield: 1–2 bushels per 100 feet for early crop.

Larger yield for late crop.

Varieties: Best early variety is the Irish Cobbler. Midseason varieties: Katahdin, Green Mountain, Rural New Yorker, Gold Coin, Rose. These varieties are also good used for the late crops. Jersey Redskins may be planted around the first of July, and because of their resistance to disease and freedom from insects, the crop is seldom a failure. Early crops mature in 90–115 days. Late crops mature in 150 days.

PUMPKIN

Botanical Name: Cucurbita Pepo.

Origin: Grown for thousands of years, for rinds have been found in the Swiss lake dwellings.

Soil, Sowing, Cultivation, Etc.: See Squash.

Varieties: Connecticut Field Pumpkin, chiefly used for decoration, indifferent for cooking. Small Sugar Pumpkin, 3–5 pounds, is the best cooking variety, being sweet and of fine texture.

Remarks: The chief difference between Squash and Pumpkin

is in the stems. Squash stems are round and tender, Pumpkin stems are hard, square and woody. Pumpkins cannot stand freezing, so they should be picked before a heavy frost.

RADISH

Botanical Name: Rhaphanus sativus. The name is derived from the Latin, *radix,* meaning root.

Origin: The radish is probably native to western Asia, but it has been under cultivation for so long that it is impossible to know its origin. The turnip, the onion, and the radish are the oldest vegetables known.

Sowing: Sow as early as possible. The seeds need a cool moist period in which to germinate. Sow 4 seeds to the inch at the rate of 1 ounce to 100 feet, rows 12 inches apart. Thin when plants are 2 inches high to ¾ inch apart, or 12 plants to a foot. Sow seed every two weeks to provide a continuous supply. Seed of the early spring varieties may be sown April 15 to June 1. Seeds of summer types may be sown from June 1 until July 15. Seed for the early spring varieties may be sown from the first of August until the first of September, as they will not mature in hot weather. A sowing may also be made in the hotbed, where they will come to maturity for an early delicacy.

Cultivation: Cultivate at least once a week; or four times before harvesting.

Moisture: Plenty of moisture is needed for germination and for growing. If too moist when they mature, they will crack; if too dry, they will become pithy and pungent much sooner than otherwise.

Harvesting: If roots remain in the ground too long, they become woody and crack. Pull as soon as mature. The large summer or fall varieties may be stored in moist sand at a temperature of 40–50 degrees.

Varieties: The best quick-growing varieties are Scarlet Globe, Crimson Giant, French Breakfast, White Icicle, which mature in 25–35 days. The best summer or storing varieties are Long Black Spanish and China Rose.

RHUBARB

Botanical Name: Rheum Rhaponticum.

Origin: Discovered after the Christian era in the desert and sub-alpine regions of southern Siberia and the Volga River.

Soil: Any soil is satisfactory; if it is well prepared before plants are set out, they should last for eight or nine years. Work in a liberal application of well-decayed manure as deeply as possible and cultivate until it is finely pulverized.

Planting: As seed does not always come true to type, it is best to buy good one- or two-year-old plants. Set them out as early as possible in the spring, 18 inches apart in rows 30–36 inches for hand cultivation. The advantage of spring planting is that the soil is in the best condition, but Rhubarb can easily be transplanted whenever the tops are dead.

Cultivation: Cultivate regularly, but not deeply. Keep all weed growth out, as the weeds compete with the plants, lessen the productivity of the bed, and reduce the quality of the stalks.

Harvesting: Always pull the stalks, never cut them. Do not harvest the first year the plants are set out and only lightly the second year, but from the third year on, heavy harvesting does not hurt the roots. Do not allow the plants to go to seed.

Remarks: Plants may be forced very early in the spring by putting boxes or barrels, with the top and bottom knocked out, over them, and heaping fresh horse manure 18 inches high around the barrel. If the top can be covered with glass, heat is kept in and sunlight is allowed to enter. Even without manure, a glass-covered box or barrel over the plant gives protection from cold and causes shoots to grow up for light. If glass and manure are both used, forcing may be started in really cold weather, at least two weeks earlier than if only boxes are used.

Varieties: Victoria and Linnæus.

RUTABAGA

(See Turnip)

SALSIFY

Botanical Name: Tragopogon porrifolius.

Origin: Salsify is also known as the Oyster-plant, for its flavor is said to slightly resemble that of the oyster. It was known as food less than two thousand years ago in Algeria and southern Europe.

Soil: The soil should be like that for the Parsnip—deep, rich and sandy, and easily worked. If the soil is too heavy, fibrous roots will form, and the roots will be distorted. All fertilizers should be applied before the ground is worked at all, and turned in to a depth of at least 8 inches. This will cause the roots to grow downward in search of nutrients.

Punch holes in the ground a foot in depth. Put manure in the bottom, then add garden soil with a teaspoonful of commercial fertilizer. Leave the level about 2 inches below that of the ground. Put in four to five seeds per hole, and when they are up, thin to one seed per hole. The rows should be 15–18 inches apart, and the holes should be 6 inches apart.

Planting: Since Salsify is a long-season crop, it should be planted as early in the spring as possible, or as soon as the ground can be worked. One-eighth ounce of seed to 50 feet of row is sufficient.

Inter-Cropping: This crop may be inter-cropped with any quick-maturing vegetable such as spinach, lettuce, or radishes. Practise clean cultivation.

Harvesting: Salsify roots may be harvested in the late fall and stored in a cellar in damp sand, or they may be covered with hay and left out in the field until spring. Never try to pull them out, for, as in the case of Parsnips, the tap root may be broken. Dig them out with a spade or fork.

Variety: Mammoth Sandwich Island is the best variety to plant.

SPINACH

Botanical Name: Spinacia oleracea.

Origin: Probably Persian in origin, introduced into Europe in the fifteenth century. The New Zealand type has very recently been introduced from that country.

Soil Preparation and Type: For both the cool season or broad-leaved type and the warm-season or trailing type (New Zealand), the soil should be rich and well prepared by spading to a depth of 6 inches, with well-rotted manure disked or forked in. Soil should be finely pulverized. Both types give a high response to lime, which should not be applied in direct contact with the manure, but after the manure has been spaded in, at the rate of 1 pound to 35 square feet. Lime should be used if the soil has not been limed for several years previously.

When and How to Plant:

(1) *Cool-season type*—Plant in the open ground as early in the spring as possible. Can be planted during a February or March thaw; sow seed at the rate of 1 ounce to 50 feet in rows 12 inches apart. The plants are not usually thinned. Mature in 40–50 days. May also be sown in late September or October, and protected by a covering of salt hay before the ground freezes. This crop is ready to use very early the following spring.

(2) *Warm-season type*—New Zealand Spinach seed germinates slowly, and should be soaked in water 24–48 hours before planting. May be sown in the open ground from May 1 to June 1. Plant in rows 3 feet apart, 6–8 seeds to each foot, and thin 12 inches apart when plants are 3–4 inches high. Seed may also be started indoors about April 1 in flats or in pots. If started in flats, plants when 2 inches high should be transplanted to pots, one plant to a pot containing good garden soil. About May 15, they may be transplanted into the open ground, same distance as above.

Cultivation:

(1) *Cool-season type*—Keep soil well loosened, keep weeds down.

(2) *Warm-season type*—Cultivate carefully and shallowly until plants begin to run; after that pull weeds, do not cultivate.

System of Training: For New Zealand Spinach, or warm-season type, plants grow quickly when well established. Rapid growth usually takes place 3–4 weeks after the seeds have germinated. As crop is dependent on well-established plants, nothing should be picked until growth is well established, about June 15. All yellow leaves should be removed.

Manures and Fertilizers:

(1) *Cool-season crop*—When plants are half grown, top-dress with nitrate of soda or ammonium sulphate at the rate of 1 pound to 100 square feet applied as for beets, and cultivated in.

(2) *Warm-season crop*—Will be benefited by an application of either a complete fertilizer or nitrate of soda, if applied just as cultivation is stopped.

Harvesting:

(1) *Cool-season type*—Can be picked only once. Best method is to cut individual plants by the roots, and wash.

(2) *Warm-season type*—Harvested by breaking off the tips, 3–4 inches long. Plant continues to send out new shoots until killed by frost.

VARIETIES

Cool-season type—King of Denmark, smooth-leaved, slow to bloom, long standing.

Bloomsdale Savoy, mosaic resistant, an excellent variety, savoy-leaved, which should be cut when 3–4 inches high.

Warm-season type—New Zealand is the only variety. This is not really spinach, but Tetragonia expansa, which resembles spinach in flavor.

SQUASH

Botanical Name: Cucurbita, various species.

Origin: Tropical America, about 1490.

Types: Squash is of three types, summer, fall and winter. The summer or bush type will mature in 60–70 days and should be used before it reaches maturity and while the skin is still soft. The fall type matures more quickly and does not store as well as the winter type, which it otherwise resembles. The winter type will take 90–130 days and should be thoroughly mature before harvesting.

Soil: Squash likes a fairly light soil, containing plenty of organic matter. Work the soil to a depth of 6–8 inches and spade in a liberal quantity of well-rotted manure, as the squash plant is a heavy feeder. Summer squash should be planted in hills 4 feet apart each way; fall and winter squash in hills 6–8 feet apart each way.

Sowing: For summer types, it is advisable to make at least two plantings for a continuous supply. For the fall and winter types one planting is sufficient. Except in regard to distance of hills, planting, cultivating, and fertilizing are the same for all types. Sow seed as soon as the frost is out of the ground in hills prepared by removing one or two shovelfuls of earth and putting in a shovelful of manure; this should be packed firmly and covered with 4 inches of soil. A good squash hill should be about 1½ feet in diameter and about 3 inches above ground level. If commercial fertilizer such as 4–8–4 is substituted for manure, mix one handful with at least one shovelful of soil before planting the seed. Plant 6 seeds to the hill, 2 inches apart; cover with 1 inch of soil and pack down firmly. Seed should germinate in about 10 days. When the plants are about 3 inches high, thin out to the three best plants. If more are left, the size and the quality of the fruit will be inferior.

Plants may also be started indoors in small containers about three weeks before seed is sown in the open ground. Use any good garden soil, and sow several seeds in each container. Thin out to two and set out when all danger of frost is past, being careful not to disturb the soil about the roots.

Moisture: Squash requires a continuous but not a heavy supply of moisture to insure steady growth and maximum production.

Cultivation: Practise shallow cultivation from the time the plants begin to grow until they have extended into the rows so far that cultivation would injure them. Do not cultivate within 6 inches of the plant, to avoid injury to the fibrous roots which are very close to the surface. After cultivation is impracticable, plants should be weeded to prevent the weeds from taking nourishment needed by the plants. To avoid disturbing the roots of the squash plants, cut large weeds growing close to them rather than pull them out.

Fertilizer: If soil has not been thoroughly enriched before seeds were planted, a good commercial fertilizer may be added, just after thinning the plants. Another application is made just before the vines begin to run, at the rate of ½ ounce to 1 ounce per hill, applied in a ring 6 inches away from the plants and covered with 1 inch of soil, taken from between the rows.

Harvesting: Summer squash may be harvested any time before the skin hardens; they should be used immediately, or kept in a cool place to prevent evaporation. Pick all fruits before the skin hardens. If fruit is allowed to ripen, the vines will stop growing.

Fall or winter types are mature when the stems turn to a light greenish yellow. They may then be cut and exposed to the sun for two weeks until the stem turns grayish and shrivels, or they may be left on the vines until the same condition is reached. Do not pull the fruit; cut it. Winter squash should remain in the sun two weeks after reaching maturity, as evaporation reduces the high water content, making the fruit more edible and in better condition for storing.

Storing: Many vegetables prefer a damp atmosphere, but Squash must have a dry one. Handle each fruit so carefully that the skin is not broken or bruised in any way. Do not pile in more than two layers, to prevent bruising. Storing temperatures should be 45–55 degrees.

VARIETIES

Summer types—Golden Straight Neck, an improved strain of the old-fashioned Crooked-Neck.

Early White Bush, Patty pan types.

Early Yellow Bush.

Cocozelle and Zucchini are Italian Vegetable Marrows which are greenish in color at the edible stage.

Fall types—Boston Marrow, 5–20 pounds when mature.

Des Moines, Table Queen, or Acorn Squash, 1–1½ pounds when mature. Suitable for fall use, but will also keep during the winter.

Winter types—Golden Hubbard, 4–8 pounds when mature, very hard skin, bright orange in color.

Blue Hubbard, 10–30 pounds when mature, one of the best keepers.

Remarks: Squash and pumpkins may be inter-planted in corn

when the corn is about 3 inches high. Plant 2-3 seeds in every fourth row to every four to five hills of corn.

TOMATO

Botanical Name: Lycopersicon esculentum.

Origin: First known as food in Peru. Until comparatively recently tomatoes were cultivated for ornamental purposes only. Even in colonial days, the fruit was considered deadly poisonous to eat, and was known as the ornamental Love Apple.

Soil: The soil should not be very acid in reaction, nor should it re-act as alkaline. It should be well drained; a sandy loam is the best. Early tomatoes particularly require a light soil and do best with a southeastern exposure. Land which has grown corn or potatoes the previous year is good for tomatoes, especially if it is plowed or forked over in the autumn. Just before setting out the plants, fork in a very liberal supply of well-decayed manure and work the soil well to a 6-inch depth, being certain that the texture is very fine.

When and How to Plant: North of the latitude of Philadelphia the season is too short to insure fruit from seed planted in the open ground for the first crop; therefore, people buy their tomato plants, which should be set out when all danger from frost is past. Plants 6-10 inches in height, set 2 inches deeper than they were growing in the seed bed, are the best size to set out.

Seed may, however, be sown indoors in March in a light loam soil. Sow in rows 3 inches apart, four seeds to the inch, and cover with ½ inch of soil. In a temperature of 75 degrees, they should germinate in about 10 days. The best plants for transplanting come from the seeds which germinate first. When plants are a week old, about 2 inches high, with true leaves showing, transplant 2 inches apart each way into flats of the same soil as that in which they were sown; 2-3 weeks later, transplant 4 inches apart each way into the same soil and at the same temperature. Should the seedlings turn yellow, let them dry out slightly and then water with 1 ounce of nitrate of soda to 1 gallon of water. As with the purchased plants, the best plants should be 6-10 inches high. Set out deeper than they were in the flats indoors. Set out when all danger of frost is past. If the plants are not to be staked, set out 4 feet apart each way. When the fruit begins to ripen, dry hay beneath the plants will prevent rotting due to moisture.

Staking is, however, a much more satisfactory method for the early crop, although it does not give as large a crop. Set out 3 feet between rows and 1½ feet between plants. Put stakes 3 inches away from the plants a week after they have been set out, or put them in before planting. Stakes should be 6 feet high, and driven 18 inches into the ground. Plants should be tied to stakes in three or four places; use raffia or soft rope and a figure-8 knot to prevent the plants' coming too close to the stake or being cut. A second method is to fasten three wire hoops, 2 feet in diameter, to three stakes and to slip these over the plants, so that the plant can spread inside the hoops but cannot touch the ground.

Pruning: All suckers should be pruned off until the fruiting period is well advanced, as they sap the strength of the good fruit and will set fruit of poor quality and size. The suckers grow in the joints of the stems, between the leaf and the main stalk. True fruiting spurs come directly from the stem. Unstaked plants are practically impossible to prune.

Cultivation: Cultivate carefully and shallowly until plants are established and really begin to grow. In any case, cultivate sufficiently often to keep soil stirred and to suppress weed growth. When they are well started begin to hill them very slightly. Cultivate until plants have so grown together that it is impossible to get through the rows without disturbing the plants. By this time they should be covering the ground enough to prevent weed growth and to conserve moisture.

Fertilizing: When plants are set out, put a small handful of good fertilizer, preferably 4–8–4, in each hole and thoroughly mix with the soil. Or scatter a handful in a ring, 6 inches in diameter, around each plant one week after they are set out. This should be covered with soil. At the last cultivation, apply a 4–8–4 or a 5–8–7, 2 pounds to 100 feet, broadcast lightly down the row and hoed in.

Harvesting: Allow tomatoes to ripen on the vines and do not pick them when the foliage is wet. They may also be picked when the first tinge of red shows and stored in a warm, dark place, where they will take about a week to ripen. Well-grown plants should each yield 12 pounds of tomatoes.

Storing: Tomatoes may be picked while green, before frost has touched them, and buried in hay in coldframes under glass where they will keep warm and ripen slowly. It is essential that they be picked while firm, and kept dry. The whole vine may also be pulled and hung up in a frost-proof, dry place, and the fruit will ripen for some time. Tomatoes which show white on the blossom end will ripen.

VARIETIES

Earliana—good for home garden, but fruit is not very uniform.
Valiant—a large, round, early maturing variety.
Break o' Day—also good, coming one week later.
Bonny Best—standard midseason variety. Can always be depended on.
Pritchard's Marglobe—standard midseason to late variety, and also dependable.
Rutger's—the most widely planted variety for eating and canning.
Queen Anne and *Tangerine*—yellow varieties.

TURNIP

Botanical Name: Brassica Rapa.
Origin: Native of southern Europe, and under cultivation for more than 4000 years.
Soil: Any good garden soil is satisfactory. Should be prepared to a depth of 6–8 inches.
Sowing: Sow in open ground as soon as soil can be worked, at the rate of ¼ ounce to 50 feet, in rows 18 inches apart. Cover seed with ¼ inch of soil, and when plants begin to crowd, thin to 3 inches apart. For fall crop, maturing in 60 days, sow from July 15 to August 10.
Cultivation: Should be shallow and sufficiently frequent to prevent soil packing.
Fertilizer: Complete fertilizer, applied before the spring crop is planted. Late crop does not need any, as fertilizers are not all used up by preceding crop.
Harvesting: Spring crop should be harvested when 1½–2½ inches in diameter. Fall crop any time before ground freezes.
Storing: Fall crop may be stored like Carrots.

VARIETIES

White Egg, Purple Top, White Globe and Golden Ball are all good for either early or late crop.
Remarks: The spring crop is a quick-maturing crop which is good only in cool weather. Fall crop much superior to spring crop.

Rutabaga, Golden Neckless, is given the same treatment as Turnip, but should be planted only from July 10 to 20, for winter use.

947

VEGETABLE INSECTS AND DISEASES AND THEIR CONTROL

VEGETABLE	DISEASE	INSECT	DESCRIPTION	DAMAGE	CONTROL
Asparagus	Rust		Yellowish brown	Needle-like leaves.	Plant resistant varieties.
		12-spotted Asparagus Beetle	Dark orange, $\frac{1}{4}$" long with 12 black spots.	Chews the newly developing shoots from spring to summer.	Dust plants in early morning while dew is on them with rotenone or a mixture of 1 part of lead arsenate or calcium arsenate mixed with hydrated lime.
		Asparagus Beetle	Same size as the 12-spotted beetle but diversified in color.	Chews the needle-like leaves.	Same as above.
Bean	Anthracnose		Circular black sunken areas with a pinkish center.	Leaves, stems, and fruits.	Plant resistant varieties. Secure disease-free seed and practise rotation of crops.
	Bacterial Blight		Irregular large brownish areas on leaves, smaller irregular spots on the pods, with a reddish brown margin.	All parts of the plant and seed.	Plant disease-free seed. Do not pick the beans when wet.
		Mexican Bean Beetle	Adult: Roundish oval in shape with copper-colored wings each containing 8 black spots. Larvae: Lemon yellow with many spines of the same color.	Larvae feed on undersides of the leaves, skeletonizing them.	Dust undersides of leaves with rotenone when dew is on them or apply a mixture of 1 part of magnesium arsenate and 7 parts of hydrated lime at frequent intervals.

Crop	Pest / Disease	Description	Part Affected	Treatment
	Bean Weevil	Small and grayish.	Eats round holes in dried beans especially after they have been harvested or stored.	Fumigate the seed with carbon bisulphide or paradichlorobenzene.
Beet	Leaf Spot	Brownish circular spots which dry up and fall out, leaving holes.	Leaves.	Treat seed with red copper oxide.
	Aphids	Small greenish soft-bodied lice.	Dwarf leaves by sucking juice from them	Apply a nicotine dust to the leaves. *or* Spray with any good nicotine solution.
Broccoli Brussels Sprouts Cabbage Cauliflower	Blackleg	A depressed brownish canker which girdles the stem and in late stages is covered with black dots. Leaves have same characteristics of this disease on the stem.	Stems, leaves and seed pods.	Dissolve 1 tablet of bichloride of mercury in a pint of water, using a glass or earthenware container. Put seed in a cheesecloth bag and soak for 25 minutes, after which time soak in fresh water for 5 minutes. Dry in sun or a warm room for future use or sow immediately while moist.
	Clubfoot or Finger-and-Toe Disease	Club-like swellings on the roots which cause a derangement of their function and prevent normal growth and development of the above-ground parts. Plants may wilt during hot part of the day but appear normal in early forenoon.	Root.	Practise rotation of crops. Keep the soil pH. between 6 and 7. Do not plant these crops on the same land less than three years apart.

VEGETABLE	DISEASE	INSECT	DESCRIPTION	DAMAGE	CONTROL
Broccoli Brussels Sprouts Cabbage Cauliflower —*Cont.*		Cabbage Worms	A greenish caterpillar from one-half to over an inch in length with yellow spots along its sides.	Foliage is devoured.	See Asparagus Beetle.
		Cutworms	Caterpillar 1–2 inches in length, pale brown with variegations.	Chew stems of newly set plants close to the ground. May also eat roots and leaves.	Mix the following together: 1 lb. bran, ½ orange ground up, 2 tablesp. molasses, 1 tablesp. white arsenic. Add water to moisten and stir thoroughly. Spread this mixture on the ground late in the afternoon a day or so before plants are set out. Prepared bait may be bought at seed stores.
		Maggots	Small white larvæ, ¼–⅓ inch long.	Burrow in roots, preventing the plant from functioning properly.	Add 1 oz. of bichloride of mercury to 7½ gal. of water. Apply ½ cupful around the base of each plant soon after setting in field and make two more applications at ten-day intervals.
Cabbage	Yellows		In seedling stage, the whole plant dies. Partly matured plants have a dwarfed yellow appearance. The lower leaves drop in succession.	Stems and leaves.	Plant newly developed resistant varieties where this disease is serious.
(Cabbage aphids also attack Brussels Sprouts)		Aphids	See Beet.	See Beet.	See Beet.

Crop	Disease	Symptoms	Part affected	Control
Carrot	Bacterial Soft Rot	A water-soaked appearance followed by decay.	Carrot root.	Place only healthy roots in storage at temp. around 40° F. in sand.
	Phoma Root Rot	A brown canker on or near the top of the root with black dots on it.	Carrot root.	Plant seed in a good loam soil. Select best roots for storing purposes.
Celery	Early Blight	At first, minute yellowish spots which enlarge and darken, changing from a yellow to a gray color with a thin papery texture.	Leaves.	Dusting or spraying the plants at intervals of 10–14 days with Bordeaux mixture from the time plants have sprouted in the seed bed until harvested will give excellent results. Bordeaux dust: 1 part of powdered copper sulphate mixed with 4 lbs. hydrated lime. If chewing insects are present, add ½ oz. lead arsenate to each gal. Bordeaux. If sucking insects, 1 level tablesp. Black Leaf 40 to each gal.
	Late Blight	Circular yellowish spots which turn black and have minute black dots on them.	Leaves and stems.	Soak the seed in calomel, 1 oz. to 1 gal. water, for 3 min. and dry for future use, or sow immediately.
Cucumber	Bacterial Wilt	Entire plant wilts and finally dies.	Leaves and stems.	See Celery Early Blight for field control.
	Leaf Spot	Leaves develop water-soaked areas which later become gray.	Leaves.	Apply Bordeaux mixture in dust or liquid form at intervals of 10–14 days.

VEGETABLE INSECTS AND DISEASES AND THEIR CONTROL—*Continued*

VEGETABLE	DISEASE	INSECT	DESCRIPTION	DAMAGE	CONTROL
Cucumber —*Cont.*		Striped Cucumber Beetle	Dark yellow in color, $\frac{1}{4}''$ long with 3 black stripes.	Eats foliage of young tender plants. Spreads Bacterial Wilt.	Use tobacco dust as a repellent. Dust plants with rotenone. A copper-lime dust mixture is also a good repellent. Clean up all refuse in fall and burn.
Eggplant	Phomopsis Blight		Stems of seedlings next to ground turn brown and shrivel, causing plant to fall over. Circular, defined gray to brown area on the leaves with black dots, causing leaf to yellow and finally die. On fruit, spots are pale sunken areas with numerous black dots on them.	Stems, leaves and fruit.	Seed: See Blackleg of cabbage. Apply Bordeaux mixture (see Celery Early Blight).
		Flea Beetle	Tiny shiny black beetles.	Make tiny holes in the leaves, giving them the appearance of a sieve.	See Striped Cucumber Beetle.
		Colorado Potato Beetle	Medium-sized reddish larvae. Beetles are striped with brown markings.	Eats the foliage.	Dust plants with rotenone *or* Spray with arsenate of lead, $\frac{1}{2}$ oz. to 1 gal. of water *or* Dust with arsenate of lead 1 lb. to 7 lbs. hydrated lime.

Crop	Disease	Symptoms	Part Affected	Treatment
Melon	See Cucumber	See Cucumber		
Onion	Neck Rot	Dark sunken spots on the neck of the onion which rots the entire bulb.	Bulb.	Well dried before storing and stored at a temperature of 50–60° F. should reduce this disease to a minimum.
Parsley	Crown Rot	A soft rot which gradually spreads, rotting off the roots from the leaves.	At junction of leaves and roots.	Rotation.
Pea	Root Rot	Stems decay, causing above-ground parts to die.	Roots.	Rotation, resistant varieties and treating the seed with red copper oxide.
	Aphids	See Beet.	See Beet.	See Beet.
	Ascochyta Blight	Pods: Grayish areas covered with brown dots. Stems: Sunken cankers which may surround the stem and cause death. Leaves: Poorly defined circular grayish areas with black dots.	Pods, stems and leaves.	Rotation and planting resistant varieties.
Pepper	Bacterial Spot	Leaf: Upper side of leaf is slightly sunken in small spots with a corresponding bulge on the lower side. Fruit: Spots very visible, brownish black in color with a roughened surface.	Leaves and fruit.	Place seed in small glass container. Add a pinch of red copper oxide and shake vigorously until all the seeds are coated with a thin layer of the dust. or Spray plants with Bordeaux mixture. (See Celery.)

953

VEGETABLE	DISEASE	INSECT	DESCRIPTION	DAMAGE	CONTROL
Pepper—*Cont.*	Phoma Rot		Small, water-soaked areas which enlarge and turn black.	Fruit.	Rotation of crops. Careful handling of the fruit.
Potato	Early Blight		Dark brown circular spots on the foliage which enlarge as the disease spreads.	Leaves.	When plants are 4–6″ high and at intervals of 10–14 days thereafter, spray with a mixture of 12 oz. of copper sulphate crystals, 1 lb. hydrated lime. Dilute to 12 gal. with water.
	Late Blight		Water-soaked areas with no definite margins.	Leaves.	Same.
	Rhizoctonia		Tiny dark fungous bodies on the tuber. Sprouts are attacked when growth begins. Sprouts are only partially affected, which causes many small tubers to form in a hill.	Tubers.	Use disease-free seed for planting.
	Scab		Small swollen or depressed areas on the surface with a corky ridge.	Tuber.	Treat cut pieces with inoculated sulphur, prior to planting. Plant seed on soil that is slightly acid in reaction.
		Potato Beetle	See Eggplant.	See Eggplant.	See Eggplant.
		Flea Beetle	See Eggplant.	See Eggplant.	See Eggplant.
		Aphids	See Beet.	See Beet.	See Beet.

Crop	Disease/Pest	Description	Part Affected	Control
Pumpkin	See Cucumber.			
Spinach	Yellows	A dwarfing and yellowing of the leaves.	Leaves.	Plant resistant varieties.
Squash	See Cucumber.			
	Squash Bug	Grayish to dark brown hard-shell insects.	Sucks juices from the plant, stunting it.	See Cucumber. Hand picking in early spring is also effective.
Sweet Corn	Bacterial Wilt	Wilting of plant before mature.	Leaves and stalk.	Plant crossbred varieties.
	Smut	Large black powdery substance.	Ear and tassel	Cut and burn as soon as noticed.
	Corn Borer	Grayish caterpillar.	Bores into ears.	Plow corn-planted land in fall. Destroy all stubble.
	Corn Ear Worm	Very similar.	Bores into ears and develops.	Cut silk to within half inch of husk when it appears. This will prevent larvae from crawling into ear.
Tomato	Anthracnose	Small water-soaked areas which enlarge, shrink and and turn dark. Larger areas show a distinct zonation or circling.	Ripening fruits.	Spray at 10–14 day intervals with Bordeaux mixture until fruits begin to color. See Potato Blight.
	Early Blight	See Potato.	See Potato.	See Potato.
	Late Blight	See Potato.	See Potato.	See Potato.
	Phoma Rot	See Pepper.	See Pepper.	See Pepper.

VEGETABLE INSECTS AND DISEASES AND THEIR CONTROL—*Continued*

VEGETABLE	DISEASE	INSECT	DESCRIPTION	DAMAGE	CONTROL
Tomato—*Cont.*	Blossom End Rot		A physiological disease which causes a breakdown of the rapidly growing tissues. Appears as a water-soaked area at first, gradually turning black and sunken in appearance.	Fruit.	Good cultural methods will prevent it to a great extent. However, as it may be caused by too much or too little water, weather conditions may play an important part.
		Potato Beetle	See Eggplant.	See Eggplant.	See Eggplant.
		Flea Beetle	See Eggplant.	See Eggplant.	See Eggplant.
		Aphids	See Beet.	See Beet.	See Beet.
		Tobacco Worm	A long greenish caterpillar with white stripes, yellowish spots and a spine protruding from the posterior end.	Eats the leaves and green fruits.	Hand pick. Dust with rotenone.

XXVIII

Garden Practices

A good program of gardening includes seven essential practices—deep digging, cultivation, watering, feeding, pruning, control of pests and diseases, and winter protection.

The application of these garden practices to various types of gardens and to special plant groups has been discussed in the various chapters, but it is well to understand some of the underlying principles involved.

DIGGING

Double Digging. Dig an initial trench two feet in width, one foot deep, across the end of the bed. This soil is moved to the farther end of the bed to be used in filling the final trench. Spread manure in the trench and fork it into the ground as deeply as possible. Dig the next trench two feet wide and one foot deep, turning the soil into the first trench and enriching it with a layer of manure, when half the soil has been moved in. Break up and enrich the bottom of the second trench and continue across the bed in this manner.

Trenching. This operation is the same as double digging except that two feet of soil are removed in each trench. The top soil of the second trench is placed in the bottom of the first and the lower foot of soil becomes the top soil of the first trench. This is only practical when the garden soil is a very deep loam. Where the top soil is only one foot in depth, fresh soil can be hauled in for the fill and the lower foot of sub-soil discarded.

Bastard Trenching. This is a modification of trenching and is done by having three trenches open at a time instead of two. Trench number one receives the top foot of soil from trench number three and the lower foot of soil from trench number two, manure being put in between the layers. At the start it is necessary to haul to the other end of the bed for the final fill the soil from the top foot of trench number two, as well as all that from trench number one in order to proceed with the mixing of soils from trenches two and three.

Trenching and bastard trenching are expensive and arduous, but where the soil is poor or the drainage bad they will repay the added cost. For well-drained locations with good deep soil double digging should be sufficient.

CULTIVATION

The cultivation of the soil serves several important functions. It destroys weeds; breaks the crust which forms on heavy soils after a rain; aërates the soil, thus permitting air to reach the roots of the plants; and establishes a dust mulch on the surface which helps to conserve the moisture in the soil.

Under normal conditions the ground should be cultivated as soon as possible after a rain. If the soil is extremely sandy it may be cultivated almost immediately. In the case of heavy, clay soils it is necessary to wait until they have dried out sufficiently, as it is imperative that such soils should not be worked when they are too wet, as it will cause the formation of many hard little lumps and will seriously injure the physical condition of the soil. There are occasional instances when it is unwise to cultivate the soil after a rain. Such a situation occurs during a period of drought when but a light rain has fallen. Under such circumstances it is wiser to allow the plants to derive what refreshment they can from the meager supply of surface moisture, which would be almost entirely dissipated and lost if the surface were stirred.

Certainly one of the most important functions of cultivation in the garden is the destruction of weeds, and it is essential that cultivations be given so frequently that the weeds never have an opportunity to gain headway. If the weeds are very small, less than an inch in height, at the time that the cultivation is given, it will not be necessary to remove them, as they will wilt as soon as they have been uprooted and will disappear entirely within a very short time.

For the cultivation of flower beds and borders and nursery plots various types of small hand weeders are available. A small inexpensive type with three flexible wire prongs is one of the most efficient. For more extensive areas, such as shrubbery borders and the vegetable garden, there are the long-handled prong cultivators, hoes of many and varied types—the small half-moon type being one of the most satisfactory—, and the wheel hoes, which are exceedingly useful in the cultivation of long rows.

WATERING

As all plants derive their nutrients from the soil in the form of a solution, it may readily be understood what an important part water plays in the maintenance and welfare of the garden.

In order to be fully effective very thorough watering is necessary. Frequent, light waterings tend to do infinitely more harm than good. If only the few surface inches of soil are moist, and if there is not enough water to allow for a sufficient depth of penetration, the plant roots, in their search for moisture, will be drawn upward toward the surface, and if this process continues the plants will become more and more shallow rooted. And it is a well-established fact that shallow-rooted plants are less vigorous than those which are deeply rooted, as they can derive their nutrients from only a very limited soil area, and suffer seriously during periods of drought. It is therefore the wise practice to water thoroughly, even if less frequently.

The most favorable times for watering are late afternoon and evening, or very early in the morning, evening being preferable. The evaporation of moisture is considerably less at such times, and the plants are consequently able to derive more lasting benefit from the application. It is not wise to water during the heat of the day, except in the case of young seedling plants which must never be allowed to suffer for lack of moisture.

The method of watering, or of supplying constant moisture, will vary considerably, being dependent upon the type of plants which is being handled and, to some degree, upon the extent of one's gardening operations. One of the most satisfactory ways of maintaining a constant and uniform supply of moisture in the soil is to sink pieces of 4-inch drain tile in the ground, one open end being level with the surface of the soil. If these pieces of tile are kept filled with water there will be a gentle and very gradual seepage of moisture through the soil. Such a method is of particular value in providing moisture for trees and shrubs. It may also be used in flower beds and borders of ample size, as the tile openings are inconspicuous and are seldom noticed. English primroses, which are extremely dependent upon moisture, will usually thrive well when water is supplied by this method.

The usual method of supplying water to plants is through the use of a sprinkling can or a garden hose. There are various attachments which are available for the hose. An adjustable nozzle which is capable of throwing both a fine, mist-like spray and a comparatively heavy stream of water is one of the most useful. Rose attachments similar to those used on a watering can may also be obtained and are very useful for certain types of watering where a gentle, steady spray is desired. There are also various types of automatic sprinklers which are very satisfactory and which will relieve the tedium of hand watering. Sprinklers should be left in place until an area is thoroughly soaked, and should then be moved on to another section of the garden or lawn. A new device has recently been put on the market, known as a water sword, which may be attached to a hose and plunged deeply into the ground, being of special benefit in the watering of trees and shrubs.

There is comparatively little danger of too liberal applications of water when watering is done artificially, but during prolonged periods of excessively heavy rains the soil may become so saturated with moisture that plant growth suffers seriously in consequence. Under such conditions much of the available nitrogen in the soil is leached away and plants are unable to make normal growth. The ground also becomes so densely saturated with water that the aëration of the soil is seriously checked and plants fail to thrive, due to the fact that their roots are unable to obtain sufficient air. Large trees sometimes die as a result of such a condition. Under such circumstances it is well to apply additional nitrogen to the soil in order to stimulate plant growth, and to make up for the deficiency in nitrogen due to leaching. In areas where trees are beginning to show ill effects from such a condition, evidenced by a browning of the leaves and a generally unthrifty appearance, it is wise to bore holes in the soil beneath the spread of the branches, in order to increase the supply of oxygen and to permit air to reach the roots.

FEEDING

As all plants are dependent upon mineral nutrients for their growth and development, it is essential that an adequate supply of those elements which are necessary be maintained in the soil. A detailed discussion of the value of soil tests, the mineral nutrients needed for plant growth, and the form in which these nutrients may be applied, will be found in Chapter I on Soils and in various other chapters dealing with special plant groups.

There are, however, a few fundamental principles which should be observed in the application of all fertilizers.

Under no conditions should commercial fertilizers be allowed to come into contact with seeds at the time that they are sown, or into direct contact with the roots of trees, shrubs, or herbaceous plants at the time of planting. The germination of most seeds will be seriously affected if commercial fertilizers are used in the drill at the time of sowing. The most approved method of supplying nutrients to young plants is to place the fertilizer in drills 3 or 4 inches away on each side of the row. The drills should be from 2 to 3 inches in depth and the fertilizer should be covered with a small quantity of soil. This method is especially recommended for vegetables and for flowers in the cutting garden which are grown in rows.

The most satisfactory way to apply fertilizer to garden beds and borders is to broadcast it over the surface of the soil at the prescribed rate and to cultivate it in very lightly. The soil should then be thoroughly watered in order that the fertilizer may become more readily available to the plants. If individual plants within the border are to be fertilized a shallow furrow in the form of a ring may be made several inches from the

crown of the plant and the fertilizer may be placed in the furrow. Care must be taken not to allow the fertilizer to come
into contact with the foliage, as it may cause severe burning.

When fertilizers are to be applied in the form of a solution
they may be dissolved in the desired quantity of water and
applied with a watering can from which the rose or sprinkler
has been removed.

PRUNING

It is important that every gardener should have a knowledge
of the fundamental principles of pruning. One should know
why pruning is necessary, and at what season of the year it
should be done. And one should also be familiar with the most
approved pruning practices.

These are the primary purposes of pruning: to restore a proper
balance between root and top growth at the time of transplanting; to remove injured, diseased or dead wood; to increase both
the quantity and quality of flowers and fruit; to control the
structure of a tree or shrub and to guide its growth; to improve
the appearance and symmetry of a plant; and to aid in the
rejuvenation of old trees, shrubs or vines.

To be able to prune a tree or shrub intelligently it is necessary
to understand that there is always a very definite relation in all
plants between root growth and top growth. If there is a reduction in normal root growth there must be a compensating reduction in top growth. It is for this reason that the judicious
pruning of trees and shrubs at the time of transplanting is a
matter of such paramount importance. In bare-root transplanting it is almost inevitable that some of the roots will be severed
entirely or severely injured. Therefore, in order to compensate
for this reduction in root growth, the top must be pruned; moreover, because the plant has suffered more or less shock and will
require some time to re-establish itself, it is not able to sustain
its usual amount of top growth; consequently severe pruning is
recommended.

Although each tree and shrub has a natural form, its symmetry and appearance may be controlled to a considerable de-

gree by judicious pruning. No attempt should be made, however, to radically change the shape or form of a plant. Pruning should serve merely as an aid in building a strong framework, and in guiding the natural growth. After ornamental trees have attained their full development, and have been trained to the desired form, comparatively little pruning is necessary. Sys-

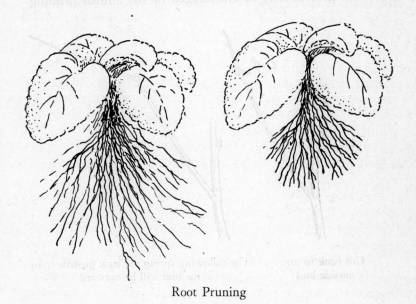

Root Pruning

tematic yearly care includes the removal of broken branches and of any dead or diseased wood, and the cutting away of any branch which may be interfering with the development of other branches. In the case of shrubs the same general principles hold true, with the exception of the fact that in many cases some of the old wood should be cut away entirely in order to stimulate the production of vigorous new growth. The pruning requirements of the various groups of shrubs are discussed fully in Chapter VIII.

Just as the removal of roots necessitates the reduction in top growth, so does the severe pruning of top growth disturb the equilibrium of the normal function of the roots, and nature tends to restore the balance by the production of new shoots and branches. In many cases this is what is desired, as with fruit trees and with flowering shrubs, where the production of vigorous, young, flowering and fruiting wood is the desideratum. Some plants bear flowers and fruit on new growth, and such growth may be encouraged by the annual pruning-

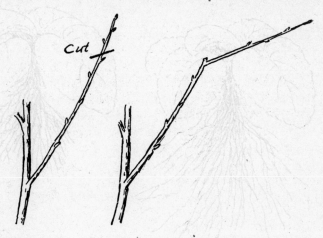

Cut back to an
outside bud

The following spring the new growth from
the bud will be outward

out of old wood. Many of our flowering shrubs, most roses, the small bush fruits, and the grapevines may be found in this group.

Such pruning is also associated with the rejuvenation of old trees and shrubs which have become weak and unthrifty through age or neglect. Invariably, vigorous pruning is followed by an increase in top growth, but moderation must be practised. Particularly is this true in the rejuvenation of old trees. If very severe pruning of large trees seems necessary or advisable, the process should be extended over a period of several years. If excessively heavy pruning of top growth is attempted at one time it will usually cause the formation of much undesirable growth in the nature of water sprouts and suckers. These rampant, upright shoots are entirely unproductive, injure the form and appearance of the tree, and rob the more desirable growth of nourishment. Not only should they be removed if they occur, but their production should be controlled by judicious pruning.

Pruning Equipment. Elaborate pruning equipment is not necessary. Practically all of the pruning on a place of average size may be accomplished efficiently with three or four tools—a pair of good pruning shears, a pair of lopping shears with

Proper Method and Improper Method
of Cutting Branches

extended handles, one or two pruning saws, and a pair of pole pruners are the only tools necessary. It is essential that the shears be sharp, as much damage may be done with dull tools. Pruning shears should always be kept well sharpened and properly tightened, and they should be oiled at frequent intervals.

Pruning Practices. To make a close, clean cut, and to avoid injury to the bark, the shears should be held with the blade next to the portion of the twig or branch which is to remain upon the plant. A ragged cut, with torn and mutilated bark, reflects only discredit upon the one who is responsible for the pruning. In cutting back small branches the cut should be made at a slight angle, just above a bud (see sketches). If the cut is made above an outside bud the growth will be directed outward, and the form will be open and spreading. If a more compact, upright growth is desired the cut should be made above an inside bud.

When branches have opposite rather than alternate buds, one of the buds may be removed, and the growth may thus be guided in any desired direction.

If large branches are to be removed the final cut should be made as close to the main trunk as possible, in order that the wound may heal rapidly and that there may be no disfiguring stump. If the limb is of any size, more than one cut may be advisable. The first cut should be made from below, about a foot from the main trunk, and it should extend but half way through the branch. The second cut should be made from above, at a distance 3 or 4 inches further out on the branch, and it should sever the limb entirely. The final cut should consist of the removal of the stub as close to the trunk as possible. (See sketches.)

CONTROL OF PESTS AND DISEASES

It requires constant vigilance on the part of the gardener to keep insect pests and diseases under control, and it is necessary to be able to recognize the first symptoms of disease, or the first manifestation of the presence of injurious insects. The effectiveness of any treatment depends upon the promptness and the frequency with which it is applied and the thoroughness of the application.

The identification and full description of all the more common insect pests and diseases are given in Chapters XXXI to XXXIV. The most approved measures of control and the methods of application are also given in detail.

WINTER PROTECTION

The problem of providing adequate winter protection for trees, shrubs and flowers is one which all gardeners in northern climes must face. The amount of protection necessary depends upon the natural hardiness of the plants, upon the severity of the climate, and upon the exposure.

Winter injury to plants is usually attributable to two factors: either to severe cold or to the loss of moisture from shoots and branches. Extreme cold will cause the twigs, stems and roots to freeze, with a consequent breaking down of the cell tissues. Excessive loss of moisture, which is quite as frequently a cause of winter-killing as is severe cold, is due largely to the effect of strong, drying winds during periods of brilliant winter sunshine. It is a well-known fact that the evaporation of moisture from the twigs, branches, canes, and, in the case of evergreens, from the leaves, continues at a slow rate throughout the winter, and that in order to supply this moisture the roots of the plant must continue to absorb water. When the evaporation is unduly accelerated by prolonged periods of winter wind and sunshine, the roots are unable to supply moisture rapidly enough, and the branches and canes become shrivelled in consequence. If this condition becomes sufficiently aggravated it frequently results in the dying back of a large portion of the plant, or in its death.

Therefore, one of the most important preparations for winter in the case of all woody plants, and most particularly in the case of broadleaved evergreens, is to see that the soil is adequately supplied with moisture. If rainfall has been light during the autumn months, it will be necessary to see that the ground is thoroughly soaked before it freezes. Many trees and shrubs may be saved from winter injury if this precaution is taken, and for many plants a winter protection against wind and sun is quite as important as a protection against extreme cold.

The most approved practices for providing winter protection for herbaceous perennials, rock plants, roses, trees, and shrubs have been discussed in detail in the various chapters.

XXIX

Tools and Garden Equipment

For the greatest efficiency in practically all gardening operations, good tools are an essential factor. Not only should the gardener know how to select tools which are strong and durable and which will give service over a period of many years, but he should also know how to care for tools properly in order that they may be kept in good condition at all times. A well-organized tool room where the tools may be kept in good order and where supplies, such as insecticides, labels, and other garden accessories may be kept readily at hand, will be a source of constant satisfaction. If a small building or a room adjoining a greenhouse may be devoted to such a purpose, it will greatly facilitate the general arrangements, but if such space is not available, a closet or a corner of the garage may be converted into a very efficient storage place.

The type of tools selected and the number and variety required will depend to a considerable degree upon the extent of one's gardening operations. Two lists are appended herewith, one listing such tools and equipment as are an absolute necessity, even in a very small garden; the other listing those which are desirable, although not always necessary.

The Essentials	Supplementary List
Spade	Turf edger
Spading fork	Grass edging shears
Hoe	Hedge shears
Iron rake	Pruning saw
Bamboo lawn rake	Long-handled pruning shears
Trowel	Lawn roller
Hand weeder	Lawn spiker
Garden line	Lawn fertilizer distributer

THE ESSENTIALS	SUPPLEMENTARY LIST
Hand sprayer	Knapsack or bucket sprayer
Hand duster	Sickle
Measuring cup	Mattock
Set of measuring spoons	Crowbar
Light bamboo stakes	Kneeling pad
Tape or raffia	Baskets
Pruning shears	Asparagus knife
Knife	Asparagus buncher
Labels	Dibber
Lawn mower	Pushcart for leaves, etc.
Garden hose	Long-handled shovel
Extra washers	Manure fork
Putty knife	Wheel-hoe cultivator
Wheelbarrow	
Watering can	
Yardstick	
Pots	
Flats	

It is a matter of sound economy to buy good tools. A good tool differs from a poor one in the materials used in its manufacture and in its type of construction. Good tools are more durable than cheap tools and they are usually more efficient. Particularly is this true in the case of tools used for cutting purposes such as lawn mowers, pruning shears, grass shears, and hedge trimmers, as they may be sharpened more readily and will retain a better edge.

The most satisfactory type of spade is that with a metal shank which extends part way up the handle, as this makes for additional strength. The same type of construction is desirable for spading forks and for long-handled shovels. Trowels made from a single sheet of metal pressed into shape are not so strong or so durable as trowels with wooden handles driven into a metal shank.

The most satisfactory type of small hand cultivator for use in flower borders is the weeder with three claw-like prongs which are not rigid. It is capable of doing very rapid and efficient work and it leaves the soil in excellent tilth. It is also possible to work with it among very small seedling plants. There are a number of other types on the market which are reasonably satisfactory.

The garden hoe has been designed in a great variety of sizes and shapes. A hoe that is too large and heavy is cumbersome and is better fitted for the mixing of cement than for garden work. The 6-inch draw hoe, the 6-inch scuffle hoe and the light-weight pointed type of hoe are all satisfactory for general garden cultivation. The pointed type is of particular value for opening seed drills in the vegetable garden. If the broad-bladed type of hoe is used, its efficiency will be greatly increased if it is kept well sharpened.

CARE OF TOOLS

Tools should be cleaned immediately after use and before they are returned to their place. It is far easier to remove soil from a spade or hoe when it is still moist than when it is hard and dry and has become encrusted onto the metal. A blunt stick of the type used to mix paint is a very convenient thing to use in removing the soil from spades and hoes. If the soil has been allowed to become badly encrusted, it may be removed by rubbing the surface vigorously with a rag soaked in kerosene.

When tools are to be put away for the winter, they should first be thoroughly cleaned and they should then be covered with a coating of grease in order to protect them from rust. Almost any type of grease which happens to be available will be satisfactory—a cheap grade of vaseline is excellent, cup grease is entirely satisfactory, or lard may be used. It is a wise plan to see that such tools as pruning shears, lawn mowers, knives and hoes are sharpened before they are put away in order that they may be ready for use when the rush of spring work begins.

The Garden Hose is one of the most indispensable pieces of equipment on any country or suburban place. If a hose of good quality is purchased, and if it is well cared for, it should last for fifteen or twenty years, whereas a cheap hose, or one which does not receive the proper care, will need to be replaced within a comparatively short time. A one-ply hose has the advantage of being light and is therefore easily handled, and if it is of good quality rubber it will give excellent service over a period of many years. A two-ply hose will give longer wear, however, as it is built for heavy service, and it has the added advantage that it will not kink. In determining the quality of a hose it is well to remember that a hose which is made of red rubber is invariably one of superior quality. A hose of black rubber may also be excellent quality, or it may be of very inferior quality. But as red rubber can only be built into a hose of superior grade, it would seem to be a definite indication of good quality. It is a matter of sound economy to purchase a hose reel, and the hose should be kept upon it at all times when it is not in use. Nothing shortens the life of a hose more rapidly than to allow it to lie out in the sun day after day. When a hose is put away for the winter, care should be taken to see that it is clean and that it has been properly drained.

Propagation

There are few subjects of more vital interest to the gardener than that of propagation.

Many of the old and established practices may still be followed, but within recent years certain new discoveries have been made which have revolutionized some of the techniques of the propagator. It is rapidly becoming an accepted practice to start young seedlings in sand which is watered with a mineral nutrient solution, and with the discovery of the hormone-like substances which are now available to the gardener as well as to the scientist in his laboratory it has been possible to stimulate the rooting of cuttings to a remarkable degree, thus making possible the propagation of hitherto difficult species. The newly discovered uses of colchicine, that substance derived from lily bulbs which, in some mysterious way, has the ability to upset the normal behavior of the chromosomes, holds much of interest for the plant breeder. Although the art of propagation dates back to time immemorial, more progress has been made by scientists within the past few decades than had occurred in many previous centuries.

REPRODUCTION BY SEED

GROWING ANNUALS FROM SEED

Practically all annual flowers and vegetables may be grown very readily from seed. They may be grouped into three general classifications: those which are extremely hardy and may be sown in the open ground early in the spring as soon as the ground is in condition for planting; those which are half-hardy and may be sown in the open ground after all danger of frost is over; and those which are either extremely tender and delicate, or which make such slow growth that it is advisable to sow them in either the greenhouse or hotbed where they may be kept under carefully controlled conditions until they are well started. For lists of hardy, half-hardy, tender and slow-growing annuals, refer to Chapter X, pages 370 to 372.

If early bloom is desired many of the hardy and half-hardy annuals may also be started under glass. The rapidly growing kinds such as the zinnias and marigolds should not be sown more than six weeks before time for transplanting to the garden as they will become spindly and leggy if held too long indoors. The slow-growing annuals such as lobelia, petunia, snapdragon, salpiglossis and verbena may be sown from eight to ten weeks before the time for transplanting to the open.

RAISING BIENNIALS FROM SEED

Practically all biennial flowers may be grown very easily from seed. The seeds are usually sown in coldframes during the summer months. When the seedlings have reached sufficient size they are transplanted, being carried on in the frames until autumn. Those that are tender are wintered in the frames, while those that are hardy may be transplanted to the open ground. For details regarding time of sowing and method of handling, see Chapter XI on Biennials.

RAISING PERENNIALS FROM SEED

There are many perennials which may be raised very successfully from seed. It must be borne in mind, however, that this method of propagation is not suitable for all perennials, as there are some which have become so highly developed that they do not produce seed, and many hybrid types such as the iris and phlox do not come true from seed. There are others which develop so slowly when grown from seed that it is far more practicable to resort to the division of old clumps or to some other means of vegetative reproduction.

For the list of perennials which may be grown from seed, see Chapter XII, page 435.

SEED SOWING

In order to raise plants successfully from seed, it is necessary to provide conditions which are as nearly ideal as possible. The essential considerations are: good seed; favorable temperature; correct degree of moisture; and a medium suitable for seed germination which provides for sufficient oxygen.

Good Seed. Some seeds retain their vitality for many years whereas others must be planted as soon as they are ripe if good germination is to be secured. The seeds of most of our commonly grown annual and perennial flowers retain their vitality for at least a year and some of them for two years or even longer. Weed seeds are notoriously hardy in this respect, and records show that seeds of some of our common weeds will germinate readily after fifty years of dormancy. One of the most outstanding examples of longevity in seeds is to be found in the case of the Lotus. Recent experiments have proved that Lotus seeds still retain their viability after a period of four hundred years.

With the majority of our garden flowers we can expect a percentage of germination ranging from 75 to 85 per cent, and in some cases an even higher percentage may be obtained if conditions are extremely favorable. If seed has been carried over from one season to another, or if there is any reason to doubt its viability, it is wise to run a test for germination before the seed is sown. There are a number of methods which may be used in testing seed, one of the very simplest being the blotting paper method. The seeds should be placed between two sheets of blotting paper which are kept constantly moist and at a temperature ranging between 65 and 70 degrees. If several varieties of seed are to be tested, the paper may be marked off into small squares. The percentage of germination may be determined by dividing the number of seeds which have sprouted by the total number tested.

When seeds are to be held for any length of time they should be stored in a dry place with a range of temperature varying from 45 to 50 degrees.

LONGEVITY OF FLOWER SEEDS

Name	Period of Germination (Days)	Approximate Longevity (Years)
Achillea, the Pearl	14	4
Acroclinium	14–20	3
Ageratum	14	4
Agrostemma	10–14	4
Alyssum	10–20	4
Amaranthus	6–10	4–5
Ammobium	14	1–2
Anagallis	21	4–5
Anchusa italica	14–20	3
Anemone	28–40	2
Anthemis	14	2
Antirrhinum	10–14	3–4
Aquilegia	30–50	2
Arabis	21	2–3
Armeria	14	2
Aster	8–12	1–2
Aubrietia	25	2
Balsam	10–14	5–6
Bartonia	5–10	1–2
Bellis (English Daisy)	10–14	2–3
Boltonia	20	5
Brachycome	10	3–4
Browallia	28–40	2–3
Calendula	14	5–6
Calliopsis	14	2–3
Candytuft	14	2–3
Canna	14	3
Canterbury bells	14	3
Carnation	10	4–5
Celosia	6–10	4
Centaurea americana	20–13	1–2
Centaurea gymnocarpa	14–30	1–2
Centaurea imperialis	15	1–2
Centaurea moschata	12–14	1–2
Cheiranthus Allionii	14	2–3
Chelone	20–30	1–2

LONGEVITY OF FLOWER SEEDS—*Continued*

Name	Period of Germination (Days)	Approximate Longevity (Years)
Chrysanthemum, annual	11–18	4–5
Cineraria	15	3–4
Clarkia	14	2–3
Cobæa	21	2
Coleus	14	2
Coreopsis	21	2
Cosmos, Mammoth	10–14	3–4
Cosmos, Orange Flare	14	
Cyclamen	21	4–6
Cynoglossum	10	2–3
Dahlia	10	2–3
Datura	15–21	3–4
Delphinium	15–21	1
Dianthus	6–10	4–5
Didiscus	12–14	2–3
Digitalis	15	2
Dimorphotheca (African orange daisy)	15–21	1
Erigeron	14	2
Eschscholtzia	10	2
Euphorbia heterophylla	7	2–3
Euphorbia marginata	19	3–4
Gaillardia grandiflora	15–20	4
Gaillardia picta	15–20	2
Geranium	30–40	1
Gerbera	14	1
Geum	21	2
Godetia	15	3
Gourds, small mixed	14	3–4
Gourds, large mixed	14	3–4
Gypsophila elegans	10–14	2
Gypsophila paniculata	10–14	4
Helianthus cucumerifolius	10–14	2–3
Helianthus, double chrysanthemum flwd.	10–14	2–3
Helichrysum	14	1–2
Heliotrope	21	1–2
Hesperis	18	3–4

LONGEVITY OF FLOWER SEEDS—*Continued*

Name	Period of Germination (Days)	Approximate Longevity (Years)
Hibiscus	15–30	3–4
Hollyhock	21	2–3
Hunnemannia	14	2
Impatiens Holstii	15	2
Ipomœa, Cardinal Climber	10	5
Ipomœa, Cypress Vine	10	4–5
Ipomœa, Japanese selected	21	2–3
Ipomœa noctiflora	40–60	2–3
Larkspur, annual	20–28	1–2
Lathyrus latifolius	21	3–4
Lavatera	14–35	4–5
Lilium regale	21	1
Linaria	15	2–3
Linum perenne	21–30	1–2
Linum (Scarlet Flax)	14	5
Lobelia	10–15	3–4
Lunaria (Honesty)	14–21	1–2
Lupinus Hartwegii	10	2
Lupinus nanus	10	2
Lupinus polyphyllus	21–30	2
Lychnis	21–30	2–3
Marigold, African	8	2–3
Marigold, French	8	2–3
Marvel of Peru	14	2–3
Matricaria	11–14	2–3
Mesembryanthemum	14	3–4
Mignonette	11–14	2–4
Myosotis	14	2
Nasturtium, Golden Gleam	12–14	6–7
Nasturtium, tall single mixed	12–14	6–7
Nemesia	18–21	2–3
Nepeta	17	2–3
Nicotiana	10	3–4
Nigella	14	1–2
Œnothera	31	2
Pansy	14	1–2

LONGEVITY OF FLOWER SEEDS—*Continued*

Name	Period of Germination (Days)	Approximate Longevity (Years)
Penstemon	17	2
Petunia hybrids, mixed	10	2–3
Phlox	10–15	1–2
Physostegia	25	2–3
Platycodon	12–15	2–3
Polemonium	20	2
Poppy, carnation flowered	10–14	4–5
Poppy, glaucum	10–14	4–5
Poppy, nudicaule	10–14	3–4
Poppy, oriental	10–14	5
Poppy, Shirley	10–14	5–6
Portulaca	14	3
Pueraria (Kudzu Vine)	30–50	4
Pyrethrum aureum	21	1
Pyrethrum roseum	21	1
Ranunculus	30–40	6–7
Salpiglossis	14	6–7
Salvia (Scarlet Sage)	14	1
Saponaria Vaccaria	10	2
Scabiosa, annual	14–21	2–3
Schizanthus	21–30	4–5
Shasta Daisy	10–14	1–2
Smilax	32	1
Statice sinuata	14–21	2–3
Stocks	6–10	5–6
Stokesia	28	2
Sweet Peas	10	2–3
Sweet William	6	2
Thalictrum	30	1
Thunbergia alata	21	2
Thunbergia Gibsoni	10–14	2
Tithonia	25	2
Torenia	14	1–2
Tritoma	21	2
Verbena	14	1
Vinca rosea	14	1–2

LONGEVITY OF FLOWER SEEDS—*Continued*

Name	Period of Germination (Days)	Approximate Longevity (Years)
Viola	14	1
Virginian Stock	12	1–2
Wallflower	10–14	5
Wisteria	7	2
Zinnia, dahlia-flowered, mixed	5–10	6–7
Zinnia, Lilliput, mixed	5–10	6–7

SEED SOWING IN THE OPEN

Many of our annual flowers may be sown directly in the garden where they are to bloom. Some of the perennials and biennials, as well as many annuals, may be sown in out-of-door seed beds, being transplanted to their permanent position in the garden after they have made some growth in the nursery plots. The disadvantages of sowing seeds in the open ground are that one is unable to control conditions of temperature and moisture, and it is more difficult to provide an ideal seed bed. Heavy rains often cause the soil to become too firmly compacted before the seeds germinate and may also seriously injure the delicate young seedlings. Long hours of hot sunshine may cause the soil to dry out too rapidly and to form a hard crust unless constant attention is given to watering, but in spite of all these handicaps, seed sowing in the open can be done successfully in the majority of cases if careful attention is given to a few essential details. A well-prepared seed bed will do much to offset the vagaries of nature.

The time of sowing will depend, to a large extent, upon the variety of seed. A few of the very hardy annuals such as the California poppies, the Shirley poppies, larkspur, cornflowers and Nigella may be sown in the autumn where they are to flower. The secret of success in autumn sowing lies in the fact that the seeds should not be sown until late in the season. They will then lie dormant in the soil throughout the winter and will germinate with the first warm days of spring, many weeks before the soil is in condition for the sowing of spring seeds. These autumn-sown seedlings are unusually sturdy and vigorous and will give an abundance of early bloom. For the more tender annuals spring sowing is preferable and it is wise to wait until the soil is mellow and warm and workable. It is a sad error to attempt the sowing of seed when the soil is wet and heavy and sticky, for all one's efforts will be in vain. Unless the soil will crumble readily after it has been pressed firmly in the hand, it is best to wait.

If the garden soil is a mellow loam one need not be greatly concerned about the preparation of a special seed bed, particularly in the case of the more sturdy plants such as the lupines, zinnias, and marigolds. If, however, one is dealing with a heavy soil which will have a tendency to form a hard, baked crust, it is necessary to prepare a special seed bed. This may easily be done by working finely pulverized peat moss, compost and sand into the upper 3 inches of soil. This will make the soil more retentive of moisture and, most important of all, will prevent it from forming a hard crust through which the young seedlings cannot penetrate. In the case of very fine seeds, such as petunias, nicotiana, and ageratum it is advisable to sift the top inch of soil and the final light covering. With larger seeds this precaution is not necessary. The depth of sowing will depend upon the size of the seed. In general, seeds should be sown at a depth corresponding to twice the diameter of the seed. Large seeds such as lupines and sweet peas are planted about ¾ of an inch deep; zinnias and marigolds about ¼ to ½ inch; while petunia, nicotiana and ageratum seeds are so fine that they need only be barely covered with a light sprinkling of sand or mellow soil.

After the seeds have been sown, the soil should be watered with a fine spray and should not be allowed to dry out until the seeds have germinated and the young plants have become well established. It is advisable to provide some light shade. If the seeds have been sown in the garden where they are to flower this is usually not feasible, but in an outdoor seed bed in the nursery it is readily possible. A lath frame forms a very satisfactory shade as it permits free circulation of air and admits a small amount of direct sunshine. Inexpensive shades may be easily made by tacking pieces of burlap on plasterer's lath.

In preparing a seed bed in the nursery it is essential to select a well-drained location, and the natural drainage will be augmented if the bed is raised a few inches above the surrounding ground.

SEED SOWING INDOORS

In Soil. When sowing seeds indoors it is well to realize that the texture of the soil is of far greater importance than the fertility of the soil. In order to provide a good medium for seed germination the soil must be loose and mellow. An excellent soil mixture for the seed bed consists of one part good garden loam, one part coarse sand, and one part peat moss or fine leaf mold. The necessary equipment for sowing seeds indoors is very simple. Flower pots may be used; small square clay seed pans are very satisfactory; and, for larger quantities, shallow boxes or greenhouse flats may be used.

Damping-off. One of the greatest handicaps in sowing seeds in soil is the prevalence of the fungi which cause the damping-off of the young seedlings.

These soil microbes attack the young seedlings at the ground level, causing the stem to rot away until it can no longer provide support for the plant. The loss of one or two plants may not seem serious, but it is the danger signal, as the fungus spreads rapidly, and hundreds of plants may become affected in a very short time. Unfortunately, the very conditions which are the most favorable for the germination and growth of young seedlings are also favorable for the growth and spread of the fungi which cause damping-off. These fungi cannot grow in absolutely dry soil, but under conditions of warmth and moisture they develop rapidly. Consequently the disease is apt to be more serious in damp, cloudy weather than it is in bright, sunny weather; and it is more serious where there is inadequate ventilation than it is where there is a good circulation of air. Weak plants are invariably more susceptible to attack than strong ones, and the overcrowding of young seedlings tends to aggravate the spread of the disease.

In order to insure complete control of damping-off, the seed, the soil and the containers (if old ones are used) should be sterilized.

Seed Treatment. The treatment of the seed is very simple, and will insure the pre-emergence control of damping-off. This protection of the seeds and tiny plants has become an accepted practice in many commercial greenhouses and it should be quite as generally adopted by home gardeners, as it is a very important factor in the successful control of the disease. The most effective means of protecting the seeds is to dust them with red copper oxide or zinc oxide powder, immediately before sowing.

Soil Sterilization. It is now possible to purchase sterilized soil suitable for seed boxes, and if one's gardening operations are done on a very small scale the additional expense involved is more than justified. There are, however, a number of simple and yet very effective methods of soil sterilization which may be employed at home.

Method No. 1—Soil Sterilization with heat.

Place the flats of soil in a hot oven where the temperature can be maintained at 400 to 475 degrees for a period of two hours.

Method No. 2—Soil Sterilization with red copper oxide spray.

A method of control which has recently been perfected by the New York State Agricultural Experiment Station at Geneva is extremely simple and has been remarkably effective.

As soon as the seeds have been sown the soil should be thoroughly sprayed with the following solution:

Three ounces of red copper oxide to 1 gallon of water. Subsequent applications should be made every week or ten days until the seedlings have passed the danger stage. The material should be sprayed heavily onto the surface of the soil and onto the plants until it runs down the stems into the soil. When the damping-off fungus comes into contact with the red copper oxide spray, it is immediately killed. Fortunately the spray, if it is used in the proportions which are recommended, has no toxic effect upon the young seedlings.

Method No. 3—Soil Sterilization with formaldehyde.

Use ½ cup of formaldehyde to 1½ gallons of water. Soak the soil thoroughly and allow it to stand undisturbed for twenty-four hours. Then turn it over once daily for three days with a spade or trowel and aërate it well. The seed should not be sown until this process of aëration has been completed.

If old pots or flats are used, they should also be sterilized as they are very apt to harbor the damping-off fungi.

PROCEDURE

After the soil mixture has been prepared and the seed, soil, and containers have been sterilized, preparations for the sowing of the seed may be made.

As it is essential that adequate drainage be provided, broken

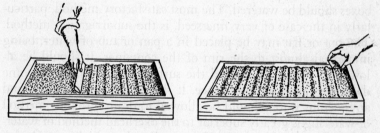

Seed Sowing

pieces of crock, small stones or other forms of rubble should be placed in the bottom of the pot or flat. A layer of sphagnum moss or coarse leaf mold will facilitate drainage and will aid in preventing the fine soil from sifting out through the cracks in the bottom of the flat. The flat or pot should then be filled practically level with prepared, sterilized soil. The soil should be fine enough in texture to pass through a ¼-inch mesh screen. If it is of coarse texture it may be sifted or, if a sifter is not available, it may be easily pulverized with one's hands. The soil should be levelled off, and it should then be firmed slightly with a brick, the bottom of a glass, or some flat piece of wood. This will bring the surface of the soil about ⅜ of an inch below the rim of the pot or flat.

When pots or seed pans are used, the seeds are usually sown

broadcast over the surface of the soil. Every effort should be made to sow the seed as evenly as possible over the surface, and it is wise not to attempt to plant too many seeds in a small area. The seedlings will soon become overcrowded and will suffer in consequence. After sowing, the seeds may be covered with finely sifted soil or with sand. The depth of the covering will depend entirely upon the size of the seed. Large seeds should be covered to a depth of ½ inch or more while very fine seeds require only a light sifting of soil. When boxes or flats are used, the seeds may be sown either broadcast or in drills, the rows being spaced from 1½ to 2 inches apart. The soil should be firmed lightly after the seeds have been sown.

As soon as the process of sowing has been completed, the seed boxes should be watered. The most satisfactory method, particularly in the case of very fine seed, is the sub-irrigation method. The pot or flat may be placed in a pan or tub of water, being immersed almost to the rim of the container. It should be allowed to remain thus until the surface of the soil has become dark and moist in appearance. It should then be removed and any surplus water should be allowed to drain off. This method of watering is greatly superior to the overhead method of watering with a sprinkling can. If the overhead method is employed, a very fine spray should be used. A clothes sprinkler or a rubber bulb sprinkler is very useful for this purpose if only a small number of pots are being handled. The seed boxes should never be allowed to dry out.

The seed boxes or pots should be kept carefully shaded until the seeds have germinated. Such a covering will greatly facilitate the conservation of moisture and will consequently hasten germination. A pane of glass may be used, a small burlap frame or newspapers. It is essential that some provision be made for the circulation of air, and the covering should be raised very slightly above the rim. One or two small sticks placed across the flat or pot will be sufficient to permit the circulation of air.

Germination will be hastened if the pots or flats are placed in a warm, dark place, the ideal temperature ranging from 60 to 70 degrees. In a greenhouse the seed boxes are usually placed along the heat pipes underneath the benches. In the house, however, this is not usually possible, and fortunately it is not essential, although it is a desirable practice.

As soon as the seeds have germinated, the covering should be removed and they should be placed in full light. If the seedlings are placed in a sunny window the pots should be turned every two or three days as the seedlings will have a tendency to lean towards the light. Watering must be continued with faithfulness as young seedlings have very little reserve upon which they can draw and suffer seriously if they do not have a sufficient supply of moisture.

SOWING VERY FINE SEEDS

When very fine seeds are sown, such as seeds of begonias, gloxinias, petunias and various other plants, they should not be covered with soil. The most satisfactory results will be obtained if the seeds are scattered over the surface of the finely prepared seed bed in the pot or flat, and then pressed gently into the soil with a float or small tamper. This will bring the seeds into contact with the soil and will alleviate any danger of having them covered too deeply. A pane of glass should be placed over the rim of the seed pan until after germination has taken place. Overhead watering should not be practised when handling very fine seeds. The seed pan should be placed in a vessel of water until the surface of the soil becomes dark; it should then be removed.

SOWING SEEDS IN SAND WITH CHEMICALS

As a result of recent experimental work, it has been found that seeds may be germinated very successfully in pure sand, watered with a mineral nutrient solution. This new method of seed sowing has so many points in its favor that it is being widely adopted both by commercial growers and by home gardeners. The procedure is extremely simple and there are many advantages.

Advantages. The materials are clean and easy to handle; excellent germination is usually secured; the root development of the young seedlings is strong and vigorous; in some cases the seedlings may be transplanted directly from the sand to their permanent location in the garden because of this superior root development; and, most important of all, the seedlings are entirely free from all soil-borne diseases, such as damping-off.

Materials Required. Fresh clean sand of a slightly coarse grade; suitable receptacles, such as greenhouse flats, flower pots, seed pans, or tin cans. Any container which is used should be waterproof and should be provided with holes in the bottom for drainage. If flowerpots are used they should preferably be painted, glazed or varnished. All containers, unless they are new, should be thoroughly cleaned and sterilized before they are used, as there is serious danger that old pots or flats might harbor harmful fungi or bacteria.

The necessary chemicals consist of a small quantity of a well-balanced complete fertilizer or a small amount of saltpeter and superphosphate.

Procedure. The sand should be washed before it is used. An effective method is to place the sand in a bucket or tub, filling it not more than half full. Hot water may then be poured into the receptacle and the sand thoroughly washed. This procedure should be repeated two or three times until the sand is clean and contains no particles of foreign matter. Boiling water should then be poured over the sand in order to sterilize it.

A half inch layer of sphagnum moss placed in the bottom of the flat or pot will greatly facilitate drainage. The receptacle may then be filled with the warm sand to within ½ inch of the top. An application of the mineral nutrient solution should be made before the seeds are sown.

The following solutions are recommended:

No. 1: 1 teaspoonful of a well-balanced complete commercial fertilizer (5–8–5 analysis or 6–8–5 analysis) to 1 quart of water.
No. 2: ¼ teaspoonful of saltpeter.
    ¼ teaspoonful of superphosphate.
    1 quart of water.

Apply either of the above solutions at the rate of one cupful of the solution to each quart of sand. In mixing the solutions, some of the material may be found to be insoluble, and after the mixture has been stirred for several minutes any particles of fertilizer which have not dissolved may be discarded.

There are various methods by which the solution may be applied, one of the most satisfactory being with the use of a clothes sprinkler or a rubber bulb plant sprinkler. The sand should be moist when the solution is applied in order that the nutrients may remain in the sand and not be washed out. After the solution has been applied, the seeds should be sown on the moist sand, and they should be covered lightly with clean, sifted, dry sand. In order to hasten germination the pot or container should be covered with a piece of glass, burlap or heavy paper, and should be placed in a dark, warm place. At no time should the sand be allowed to dry out. The pots may be watered with a fine bulb sprinkler or they may be placed in a pan of water. The moisture will then rise by capillary action and the pots should be allowed to stand in the water until the surface of the sand becomes dark and moist.

As soon as the seeds have begun to germinate the covering should be removed and the pots should be placed in full light.

Subsequent applications of the mineral nutrient solution will depend upon the growth of the seedlings. If they are to be held for some time before transplanting or if they begin to show a slightly yellowish color, additional applications should be made, not oftener than once or twice a week, however. These applications may be made with a sprinkler, or the pot may be placed in a pan containing the solution, in which case there is less danger of the nutrients being washed away.

It is important to bear in mind that the sand should be kept moist at all times.

When the plants have reached sufficient size they may be transplanted from the sand into a soil medium.

So successful have been these experiments in germinating seeds in sand cultures that, once it has been tried, one will be loath to return to the old methods.

HASTENING GERMINATION

Most seeds germinate readily under average conditions. There are, however, some seeds which, because of an unusually hard outer coating, require special treatment if a good percentage of germination is to be secured. In this group we find such seeds as canna, moonflower, morning glory, sweet peas (particularly in the case of old seed), honey locust, Kentucky coffee tree, beets, parsley, carrot, celery, parsnip, blackberry, raspberry, sweet clover, burr clover and a few others. In some instances, as in the case of apple and peach seeds, special treatment of the seed may take the place of stratification, if desired.

Various methods are employed as outlined below:

Method No.1—Soaking. The length of time will vary considerably, some seeds requiring only twenty-four hours, other seeds requiring several weeks. As a general rule the seeds should be soaked until they begin to swell. After the seeds have been soaked, they should not be allowed to dry out before sowing and the soil should be moist but not excessively wet at the time that they are sown. During the process of soaking, the seeds should be kept uniformly damp but not too wet, and if the process is continued for more than a few days the mass of seed should be stirred and aërated occasionally.

Method No. 2—Scalding. In the case of some very dry, hard-shelled seeds, such as seeds of the Kentucky coffee tree, scalding water may be used with considerable success. Boiling water should be poured over the seeds and they should be allowed to cool gradually.

Method No. 3—Mechanical Aids. There are also a number of mechanical aids which may be employed very successfully, such as filing and clipping. In the cases of some extremely large seeds a very minute hole may be bored. The germination of some seeds is greatly increased if they are scarified previous to sowing. Scarification is usually done by a machine, designed especially for this purpose, which scratches the surface of the hard seed coat, making it more permeable to water.

RAISING TREES AND SHRUBS FROM SEED

The fact has long been known that the seeds of many trees and shrubs require very special care, and within recent years the technique of handling some of the more difficult species has been greatly improved. As a result of extensive scientific research, many new methods have been adopted which have proved to be of great benefit to all those who are interested in the propagation of trees and shrubs from seed.

In order to meet with success in this field it is necessary to know the needs of each individual species, as there is wide variance in their requirements. The seeds of some species are exceedingly short-lived and must be planted almost immediately after they are ripe. Other seeds must be stratified or held at a low temperature over a period of several months if successful germination is to be secured. In some cases it is necessary to remove the fleshy outer covering or pulp before the seeds are planted; in other cases it is necessary to soak the seeds in warm water or in some acid in order to soften the hard, impervious coating.

TREE SEEDS WHICH SHOULD BE PLANTED AS SOON AS RIPE

Elm

Maple (all species that ripen in the spring)

Poplar

Willow

SEEDS WHICH MAY BE KEPT DRY AND PLANTED IN THE SPRING

Althea (Hibiscus syriacus)

Amer. Arborvitæ (Thuya occidentalis)

Bald Cypress (Taxodium distichum)

Bluebeard (Caryopteris)

Catalpa

Cedar (Cedrus)

Chaste-tree (Vitex)

Crape Myrtle (Lagerstrœmia)

Cryptomeria

Cypress (Cupressus and Chamæcyparis)

Hemlock (Tsuga)

Larch (Larix)

Mock Orange (Philadelphus)

Mulberry (Morus)

Oriental Arborvitæ (Thuya orientalis)

Pear, oriental species (Pyrus Calleryana and P. ussuriensis)

Plane tree (Platanus)

Redbud (Cercis)

Sophora

Spruce (Picea)

Sweetshrub (Calycanthus)

Umbrella pine (Sciadopitys)

Wisteria

SEEDS WHICH SHOULD BE STRATIFIED

Apple (Malus)

Ash (Fraxinus)

Barberry (Berberis)

Beech (Fagus)

Bittersweet (Celastrus)

Box (Buxus)

SEEDS WHICH SHOULD BE STRATIFIED—*Continued*

Chestnut (Castanea)
Cherry (Prunus)
Cork tree (Phellodendron)
Cotoneaster
Cranberry bush (Viburnum)
Dogwood (Cornus)
False Indigo (Amorpha)
Firethorn (Pyracantha)
Flowering Quince (Chænom-
   eles japonica)
Fringe tree (Chionanthus)
Hackberry (Celtis)
Hawthorn (Cratægus)
Holly (Ilex)
Honeysuckle (Lonicera)
Hornbeam (Carpinus)
Horse Chestnut (Æsculus)
Juniper, Red Cedar (Juniperus)
Linden (Tillia)
Locust (Robinia and Gleditsia)
Magnolia

Maidenhair tree (Ginkgo)
Maple (Acer), species that ripen
   in the fall
Nandina
Oak (Quercus)
Papaw (Asimina)
Peach (Amygdalus)
Pear, French (Pyrus communis)
Pearlbush (Exochorda)
Persimmon (Diospyros)
Plum (Prunus)
Privet (Ligustrum)
Russian Olive (Elæagnus)
Shadblow (Amelanchier)
Siberian Pea-tree (Caragana)
Silver-bell (Halesia)
Snowbell (Styrax)
Sweet Gum (Liquidambar)
Tulip tree (Liriodendron)
Yellow-wood (Cladrastis)
Yew (Taxus)

Stratification of Seeds. The most outstanding research work
to be done within recent years relative to the stratification of
seeds has been carried on at the Boyce Thompson Institute. As
a result of this extensive experimental work data are now available regarding the most effective temperature and the length of
time required for the stratification of a wide variety of seeds.
(See Table on page 992.)

The method formerly employed for the stratification of seeds
consisted of placing the seeds between layers of moist sand and
subjecting them to freezing conditions or to alternate freezing
and thawing. Although this method has been used with a reasonable degree of success for many years, the more recently developed techniques are definitely preferable, as the results obtained are far more satisfactory.

Medium for Stratification. Granulated peat moss has proved to be the most efficient medium for the stratification of seeds, being far more satisfactory than sand because it not only prevents the seeds from drying out, but also provides for a sufficient supply of air. In order to obtain the best results there must be a properly regulated supply of water and air throughout the period of stratification. The peat moss should be thoroughly moist, but not water-logged, and the seeds should be mixed with peat, rather than being placed in definite layers. At the end of every three or four weeks during the process of stratification the material should be shifted from one box to another. Water should be added if the peat moss has become dry, and if the mass of seeds and peat has become too compact it should be loosened in order to provide for a more adequate supply of air.

Temperature. The theory has long been held that freezing temperatures, or alternate freezing and thawing, were essential for the successful stratification of seeds, but it has now been proven that temperatures just above freezing, varying from 32 to 50 degrees, are the most effective, and that no benefits are to be gained from freezing. In some cases lower temperatures have actually retarded the process of stratification. For the most effective temperatures for the stratification of seeds refer to Table on page 992.

Time. The length of time required for the stratification of different varieties and species is a matter of considerable importance. If this requirement is known, the desired planting date may be determined in advance and the seeds may be stratified for the necessary period. If some seeds are stratified for too long a period, germination may actually take place, with unfortunate results. As an example, apple seeds require from 60 to 70 days at a temperature of approximately 40 degrees and after this period they will germinate in the stratification medium. They should, therefore, be removed at the proper time and sown promptly. Some seeds do not germinate at a low temperature and may be carried in the stratification medium for some time after they are ready to germinate without detrimental results, but it is wise to schedule one's program with care.

EFFECTIVE PRE-TREATMENT FOR SEEDS REQUIRING PERIOD OF LOW TEMPERATURE BEFORE GREENHOUSE PLANTING

SPECIES	BEST TEMP. °F.	EFFECTIVE RANGE, °F.	DAYS AT BEST TEMP.
Abies arizonica	33	33–41	30
Alisma Plantago-aquatica	41	33–50	30–60
Amelanchier canadensis	41	33–41	90
Aralia hispida	41	33–50	90–120
Asimina triloba	50	33–50	100
Belamçanda chinensis	41	41–50	120
Benzoin æstivale	41	41–50	120
Betula lenta*	41	33–50	60–75
Betula lutea,* Betula papyrifera*	41	33–50	60–75
Butomus umbellatus	41	33–50	30–60
Carya ovata	41	37–50	30–120
Celastrus scandens	41	33–50	90
Celtis occidentalis	41	33–50	60–90
Cornus florida	41	33–50	60–90
Cornus Kousa	41	33–50	120
Cratægus coccinea	41	41	135
Cratægus mollis	41	41	180
Cratægus phænopyrum	41	41	135
Cupressus macrocarpa	33	33–50	60
Dictamnus albus	41	41–50	60
Diospyros virginiana	50	41–50	60
Gaultheria procumbens	41	33–50	30–75
Gentiana acaulis	33	33–41	60–90
Gentiana Andrewsii	41	33–50	60–90
Gentiana crinita	33	33–41	30–60
Impatiens biflora	41	33–41	60–90
Iris versicolor	41	33–50	75
Juglans cinerea, Juglans nigra	37	33–50	60–120
Libocedrus decurrens	33–41	33–50	30–60
Liriodendron Tulipifera	33–50	33–50	70
Mitchella repens	41	33–41	150–180
Myrica caroliniensis	41	33–50	90
Nyssa sylvatica	50	41–50	60–90
Picea canadensis, Picea excelsa	33	33–41	30–60
Picea Omorika	41	33–50	30
Picea pungens	41	33–50	42–60
Picea sitchensis	33	33–50	30–60
Pinus austriaca	41	33–50	30–60
Pinus Banksiana	33	33–41	30–60
Pinus caribæa	41	33–59	30–60
Pinus contorta	41	33–50	30–60
Pinus Coulteri	41	33–50	30
Pinus densiflora	50	33–50	30
Pinus echinata	41	33–59	30–60
Pinus flexilis, Pinus insignis	41	33–50	30–60

Courtesy of the Boyce Thompson Institute.

* Transferred to higher temperature ovens instead of greenhouse.

SPECIES	BEST TEMP. °F.	EFFECTIVE RANGE, °F.	DAYS AT BEST TEMP.
Pinus koraiensis	50	33–50	30–60
Pinus Lambertiana	41	33–50	90
Pinus Laricio	33–41	33–50	30–60
Pinus monticola	33	33–50	60–90
Pinus ponderosa	33–41	33–50	30–60
Pinus resinosa	33–50	33–50	30
Pinus rigida	41	33–50	30
Pinus Strobus	50	33–50	60
Pinus tæda	41	33–59	30–60
Pinus Thunbergii	41	33–50	30
Polygonum acre	33–50	33–50	30–60
Polygonum arifolium	41	33–41	90–120
Polygonum lapathifolium	50	33–50	30
P. pennsylvanicum, P. virginianum	50	33–50	60–90
Prunus americana	41	33–41	150
Prunus persica	41	41–50	60–90
Ptelea isophylla	33	33–41	60–120
Ptelea serrata	33	33–41	150
Ptelea trifoliata	41	41	60–90
Ptelea trifoliata var. mollis	41	41	30–90
Pyrus arbutifolia	33	33–41	90
Pyrus arbutifolia var. atropurpurea	50	33–50	60
Pyrus (French pear)	41	33–41	60–90
Ribes Grossularia	41	33–50	90–120
Rosa multiflora	41	41–46	50
Scirpus campestris var. paludosus	41	33–50	90–120
Sequoia gigantea	41	33–41	30–60
Smilacina trifolia	41	33–50	90–120
Sorbus aucuparia	33	33–41	60–120
Taxodium distichum	41	33–50	30
Thuya gigantea	41	33–50	30–60
Thuya occidentalis	41	33–50	30
Thuya orientalis	41	33–50	60
Typha latifolia	41	33–50	30
Vitis æstivalis	41	33–50	90
Vitis bicolor	41	41	90–120
Vitis (Concord grape)	41	41–50	90
Vitis (Delaware grape)	41	41	90
Zizania aquatica	41	33–50	30

Courtesy of the Boyce Thompson Institute.

EFFECTIVE PRE-TREATMENT FOR SEEDS REQUIRING PERIODS AT BOTH HIGH AND LOW TEMPERATURES BEFORE PLANTING IN THE GREENHOUSE

SPECIES	BEST TEMPS. °F.		EFFECTIVE RANGE OF TEMPS °F.		DAYS AT BEST TEMPS.		EFFECTIVE H_2SO_4 TIME TREATMENT
	High	Low	High	Low	High	Low	
Aralia racemosa*	77	41	58–77	33–50	30–60	90–120	10 min.
Arctostaphylos Uva-ursi†	77	50	68–77	41–50	60–90	120–240	2–4 hr.‡
Cornus canadensis*	77	33	77	33–41	30–60	120–150	10–30 m.
Cotoneaster divaricata	58–77	41	58–77	33–41	90–120	90–120	2.5 hr.
Cotoneaster horizontalis*	58–77	41	58–77	33–41	90–120	90–120	1.5 hr.
Cratægus Crus-galli	77	41	77	41	120	180	2 hr.
Cratægus flava	77	41	77	41	120	180	2 hr.
Cratægus Oxyacantha	77	41	77	41	90	180	2 hr.
Cratægus punctata	77	41	77	41	120	180	2 hr.
Cratægus rotundifolia	77	41	77	41	120	180	2.5 hr.
Halesia carolina*	68	41	58–80	33–41	30–90	60–90	—
Rhodotypos kerrioides*	77	41	77–86	33–50	30	90	—
Symphoricarpos racemosus	77	41	77–86	41	90–120	180	75 min.
Taxus cuspidata	68	41	68–77	33–41	90	120	—
Tilia americana*	68	41	58–68	33–41	120	90–150	20 min.

Courtesy of the Boyce Thompson Institute.

 * Give some germination with pre-treatment at low temperature only but much better with high + low.

 † Neither high temperature nor H_2SO_4 alone sufficient to overcome coat effect. Best results when these two treatments were used together.

 ‡ Effective length of treatment depends on whether entire nutlet stones, stone pieces, or single seeds are used.

EFFECTIVE TREATMENT FOR PRODUCING PLANTS FROM SEEDS WITH DORMANT EPICOTYLS

SPECIES	REQUIREMENT FOR ROOT PRODUCTION		PRE-TREATMENT FOR SHOOT PRODUCTION	
	Temp. °F.	Time (mos.)	Temp. °F.	Time (mos.)
Lilium auratum	68	3–6	33–50	2–3
Lilium canadense	68	3–6	33–50	2–3
Lilium japonicum	68	3–6	41–50	3–4
Lilium rubellum	68	3–6	33–50	3
Lilium superbum	68	3–6	41–50	2–3
Lilium szovitsianum	68	3–6	50	3–4
Pæonia suffruticosa	59–86*	2–4	41–50	2–3
Viburnum acerifolium	68 or 68–86*	6–17	41	2–3
Viburnum dentatum	"	6–17	41–50	½–2
Viburnum dilatatum	"	7–9	41–50	3–4
Viburnum opulus	"	2–3	38–59	1–2
Viburnum prunifolium	"	7–9	38–59	1–2

Courtesy of the Boyce Thompson Institute.

 * Daily alternation.

TRANSPLANTING

When the first or second pair of true leaves has developed young seedlings should be transplanted, in order to prevent over-crowding and to induce better root development. They may be transplanted into other flats, or they may be transplanted singly into small, 2½-inch pots. If the young seedlings are strong and vigorous and if weather conditions are favorable, they may be transplanted into the coldframes, and in some exceptional cases, they may be transplanted directly into the open ground.

The soil should be a slightly richer mixture than that prepared for the seed bed, the following mixture being recommended: one part sand, one part leaf mold, two parts loam, one part well-rotted, sifted cow manure or good compost. It is essential to see that good drainage is provided. The soil should be neither too wet nor too dry at the time of transplanting. If it is moist enough to form a fairly firm ball when pressed together in one's hand, yet dry enough to crumble when the ball falls to the ground, it is of excellent consistency for transplanting. After the soil has been made level it should be firmed and marked off into rows from 2 to 3 inches apart. The young plants should be spaced from 2 to 3 inches apart in the row, depending upon their size and vigor.

In order that the roots may receive as little injury as possible, the seedlings should be very carefully removed from the seed bed. The pointed end of a small label is excellent for this purpose. If the small seedling plants are massed together in a clump, as so often happens when the seeds have been sown thickly, the soil should be shaken gently from the roots and the individual plants should be carefully separated from the group. Only a small number of seedlings should be removed at a time, as only a few moments should elapse between the time when the young plants are lifted from the seed bed and when the operation of transplanting is completed. If the roots are exposed for any length of time the plants may suffer a serious check. The roots should be kept covered with soil as much as possible and under no condition should the young plants be exposed to direct sunlight.

Long, straggly roots should be pinched back in order to induce a vigorous, well-branched, fibrous root system. A hole large enough to receive the roots without crowding should be made with a dibber or with the pointed end of a label or small stick. The roots of the plant should be placed in the hole and the soil should be pressed firmly about the roots and stem. Most seedling plants should be set a little deeper than they were when growing in the seed flat. In the case of very spindly plants, which have suffered as a result of overcrowding or because of other unfavorable conditions, it is advisable to set them quite deeply. In transplanting delphinium seedlings, care must be taken not to cover the crown with soil as the plants are very apt to rot unless the crown is slightly above the surface of the soil.

Most seedlings may be very easily handled, being picked up by the leaves with the thumb and forefinger. In the case of very tiny seedlings, such as begonias and primroses, it is sometimes a matter of convenience to use a small pair of forceps.

In transplanting seedlings into small pots, place sufficient quantity of rubble in the bottom of the pot to provide good drainage, and then fill the pot with the prepared soil mixture without packing it down. Make a hole in the center, place the seedling so that it will be at the desired depth and firm the soil about it with both thumbs. The surface of the soil should be about three-quarters of an inch below the rim of the pot.

As soon as the transplanting has been completed, the flats, pots or frames, whichever the case may be, should be watered with a fine spray and the plants should then be shaded until they have had an opportunity to re-establish themselves. Transplanting is a severe shock to young seedling plants, as many of the tiny root hairs which supply moisture and nutrients to the plant are injured or destroyed. It is, therefore, necessary to provide conditions which are as nearly ideal as possible during this critical period when the plant is re-establshing itself.

REPRODUCTION BY SPORES

Spores are the asexual reproductive bodies produced by non-flowering plants such as ferns and mosses. They are usually one-celled, and they are differentiated from seeds in that they contain no embryo. In ferns the spore cases, which appear as small brown spots, are to be found on the undersurface of the leaves.

In the propagation of ferns it is essential that the spores be harvested when they are ripe. The following table indicates the usual time of spore collection.

Name	Date
Adiantum pedatum (Maidenhair fern)	August–September
Aspidium cristatum (Crested shield fern)	June–September
Aspidium Filix-mas (Male fern)	June–September
Aspidium marginale (Marginal shield fern)	June–October
Aspidium noveboracense (New York fern)	June–September
Aspidium spinulosum (Spinulose wood fern)	June–August
Aspidium Thelypteris (Marsh fern)	August–September
Asplenium acrostichoides (Spleenwort)	July–September
Asplenium Filix-femina (Lady fern)	June–September
Asplenium platyneuron (Ebony spleenwort)	July–September
Asplenium Ruta-muraria (Wall rue)	July–September
Asplenium Trichomanes (Spleenwort)	July–September
Camptosorus rhizophyllus (Walking leaf)	June–September
Cystopteris bulbifera (Bladder fern)	June–August
Cystopteris fragilis (Brittle fern)	June–July
Dicksonia punctilobula (Hay-scented fern)	June–August
Lygodium palmatum (Climbing fern)	July–August
Onoclea sensibilis (Sensitive fern)	July–September
Onoclea Struthiopteris (Ostrich fern)	June–August
Osmunda cinnamomea (Cinnamon fern)	April–June
Osmunda Claytoniana (Interrupted fern)	April–June
Osmunda regalis (Royal fern)	April–June
Pellæa atropurpurea (Cliff brake)	April–July
Phegopteris Dryopteris (Oak fern)	May–July
Phegopteris hexagonoptera (Winged woodfern)	June–August
Phegopteris polypodioides (Beech fern)	May–July
Polypodium vulgare (Polypody)	May–July
Polystichum acrostichoides (Christmas fern)	June–September
Pteris aquilina (Brake)	June–September
Scolopendrium vulgare (Hart's tongue)	August–September
Woodsia ilvensis (Rusty Woodsia)	August
Woodsia obtusa (Woodsia)	May–July
Woodwardia virginica (Chain fern)	May–September

When fern fronds are collected for the purpose of propagation they must be carefully handled. If the spores are not to be sown immediately, the fronds should be wrapped in sheets of smooth paper (rough paper should not be used as the spores have a tendency to cling to it) and they should be stored in a cool, dry place.

METHODS OF PROPAGATION

There are a number of methods which may be used in the propagation of ferns by spores.

Method No. 1—A method very commonly employed is to sow the spores in shallow seed pans which have been filled with finely pulverized, sterilized soil. Portions of the fern-frond bearing ripe spore-cases may be laid on the surface of the soil, or the spores which have been discharged from the spore cases may be sown in the same way that exceptionally fine seeds are sown. After the spores have been sown, the seed pans should be covered with a pane of glass. Overhead watering should not be practised. After the fertilization of the egg cells has taken place and the young sporophyte plants have produced a few leaves, they may be pricked out into flats.

Method No. 2—A method of propagation which has recently been developed and which has proved very successful is that of growing fern spores on nutrient solution. The plants develop more rapidly when grown by this method than when grown in soil.

The method of germinating fern spores on nutrient solution as described by Doctor Lewis Knudson has been used successfully at the School of Horticulture during the last several years. To one liter of distilled water the following salts are added in the order listed. Be sure that each salt is dissolved before the next one is added.

Calcium nitrate	1.00 gram
Magnesium sulphate	.25 gram
Potassium phosphate	.25 gram
Ammonium sulphate	.5 gram
Iron phosphate	.01 gram

To this solution 17 grams of agar are added, and dissolved by heat. Care should be taken that the agar does not stick to the bottom of the container and burn. After the agar is completely melted, the pH. of the solution should be determined. It should be about pH. 5. It may be made more acid by the addition of a few drops of hydrochloric acid. It can be made more alkaline by the addition of a few drops of sodium hydroxide solution. These solutions should be very weak and should be added carefully in order to prevent a too rapid change in pH.

While the solution is still warm and in liquid form it should be poured into test tubes. Test tubes which are about an inch in diameter are best. They should be filled about one-fourth full. Cotton plugs are then placed in the tops of the tubes. The tubes must then be sterilized. This can best be done by placing them in a pressure cooker or in an autoclave for twenty minutes at fifteen pounds pressure. At the end of this period the tubes are removed and laid on a table or fairly flat surface. Care must be taken that the top is slightly raised so that the agar will not reach the cotton plug. After the contents have formed a hard jelly the tubes are ready for use. By means of a small blade which has been sterilized by passing it through a flame, the spores can be sown on the agar. Care should be taken when the cotton plug is removed that it does not come in contact with anything which may contaminate it. It is best to hold it by one end between the fingers.

These tubes will contain enough food so that the ferns can remain in them until they fill the tube with their foliage.

Another method which seems just as practicable has been suggested by Doctor Alma Stokey. Ordinary sphagnum peat moss is sterilized by boiling. It is then placed in small glass dishes. They should have a glass top. The peat is spread in a layer which is about one-quarter of an inch thick. When the peat is cool, the spores are sown on it as described above. The dish is then closed and is not opened until the small filaments are well established. If fungi develop, the dish should be opened and the contents watered with a deep pink solution of potassium permanganate. Of course, the young plants should not be allowed to become dry. When the upright leaves begin to form, the plants should be removed and planted in proper soil mixture.

VEGETATIVE REPRODUCTION

PROPAGATION BY CUTTINGS

Many of our greenhouse and garden plants, the majority of our shrubs, and a few perennials may be successfully propagated by cuttings. The term "cutting" is applied when a small portion of a plant is removed and is treated in such a way that root growth is induced, a new plant being formed which is similar in every respect to the parent plant. Cuttings may be made from various portions of a plant, some plants being propagated more readily by one type than by another. In general garden practice, cuttings are usually made from a portion of the stem, from leaves, from tubers, and from roots.

Rooting Medium

The best rooting medium for softwood cuttings is either sand or a mixture of sand and peat moss. Cuttings of some plants may be rooted very easily in water, in moist sphagnum moss, or in a light sandy loam soil, but in general practice sand, or the sand and peat moss mixture, will prove the most satisfactory. If pure sand is used, it should preferably be of a moderately coarse grade, known as mason's sand.

Propagating Cases

Flowerpots, small shallow boxes, greenhouse flats and old fish aquariums may all be converted into very satisfactory propagating cases, if a greenhouse propagating bench is not available. The receptacle should have a depth of at least 4 inches and some provision should be made for shading the cuttings. When only a few cuttings are to be rooted the double flowerpot is one of the most satisfactory devices. A small 3- or 4-inch pot is placed within a larger pot, the hole in the bottom of the small pot being tightly closed with a cork. The rim of the small pot should be level with the area of sand in the large pot. (The intervening space below and about the sides should be filled with sand or with sand-peatmoss mixture.) The small pot should be kept filled with water and there will be a gradual seepage through the porous clay of the pot which will keep the sand uniformly moist. If a large glass jar, such as a bell jar, is inverted over the pot, it will prevent an excessive evaporation of moisture and will provide very favorable conditions for the

Propagating Pot

rooting of the cuttings. A shallow box may also be easily converted into a very satisfactory propagating case if a pane of glass is placed at each end and on each side with a large pane on top. It is not necessary for the glass to fit closely at the corners, as a small amount of ventilation is desirable. An old aquarium makes an ideal small propagation case if adequate provision is made for drainage. In greenhouses special benches are usually provided for propagating. The lower portion of the bench is enclosed to conserve the bottom heat and the bench is usually provided with a hinged sash which may be raised or lowered to any desired height. A hotbed or coldframe may also be used very successfully during the more mild seasons of the year if shaded and protected from drafts.

Stem Cuttings

Stem cuttings may be grouped into three separate classes: softwood cuttings; cuttings made from half-ripened wood; and those made from hard or dormant wood, known as hardwood cuttings. Practically all greenhouse plants and all herbaceous perennials as well as some shrubs may be propagated by softwood cuttings. Many shrubs, vines, and some trees are propa-

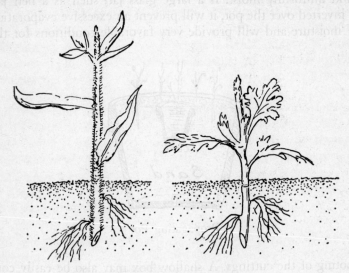

Softwood Stem Cuttings

gated by cuttings made from half-ripened wood, while others are most successfully propagated by hardwood cuttings.

Softwood Stem Cuttings

Stem cuttings are sometimes referred to as "slips," the term being frequently applied to small shoots which are pulled or slipped from a plant for the purpose of propagation.

Time of Making Cuttings. Softwood stem cuttings of herbaceous perennials such as delphiniums, phlox and chrysanthemums should preferably be taken in the spring just as the plants are starting into growth, although they may be taken at any time during the growing season when young, non-flowering shoots are obtainable. Cuttings of violas and of the majority of rock plants such as phlox divaricata, phlox subulata, arabis, and iberis are most successful when taken during June and July after the flowering season is over. Softwood cuttings of ornamental shrubs and other woody plants should be taken between the middle of May and the middle of July before the wood has begun to ripen.

Making the Cutting. The parent plants from which the cuttings are taken should be vigorous, healthy and preferably well branched. The cuttings should usually be taken from the terminal growth, preferably from non-flowering shoots. Growth that is too soft and succulent should be avoided as cuttings taken from such shoots are apt to rot before root formation has taken place. Shoots that are somewhat older and are brittle enough to snap when bent double should be selected. Old fibrous stems are also unsatisfactory as they root very slowly and have a tendency to produce inferior plants. In some cases old plants can be headed back in order to induce a growth of new lateral shoots suitable for cuttings.

Softwood cuttings vary in length from 2 to 4 inches; 2 inches being sufficient in the case of small plants such as arabis, alyssum saxatile, and many of the rock plants, while geranium cuttings and softwood cuttings of shrubs are usually at least 4 inches in length. A sharp, clean, slightly diagonal cut should be made a short distance below a node or joint, a node being the point at which the leaf is attached to the stem. There are occasional exceptions to this generally accepted rule of cutting slightly below a joint, as a few plants have been found to root more readily if the cut is made midway between the nodes or slightly above a node. After the cuttings have been taken, it is advisable to plunge them in cold water or to wrap them in damp newspaper for a brief time, a half hour or more, as it will prevent them from wilting. This practice does not apply to geraniums or to other plants which exude a milky juice. Cuttings from such plants should be sprinkled lightly with water and spread out on a surface where they will be exposed to the air for several hours. This will give the bleeding cells an opportunity to become sealed and there will be less danger of rot after the cutting is placed in the propagating case.

In preparing the cutting, all flower buds should be removed and the leaf surface should be slightly reduced. The leaves should be removed from one or two nodes at the base of the cutting, being cut with a sharp knife, not pulled or stripped off, but the leaf area at the top should not be reduced unless there is an excessive amount. In the case of coleus and a few other plants with large, succulent foliage a portion of the leaves may be removed, but as a general practice it is well to leave as much leaf area at the top of the cutting as possible. The leaves of a softwood cutting aid in the manufacture of food for the plant and they consequently have an important part to play in the development of the new root system.

Planting the Cutting. After the cuttings have been prepared, they should be inserted in the propagating case. The depth will vary somewhat with the type of cutting but, in general, the depth should be such that one or two nodes are buried. The sand or other rooting medium should be pressed firmly about the cuttings and a thorough watering should be given after the cuttings are in place. Shade should be provided for the first few days at least, and in some cases for a much longer period. One may be guided by the condition of the foliage. The leaves should be firm and should never be allowed to show any appearance of wilting. Plants differ greatly in this respect. As the roots begin to form it is important that full sunlight be provided.

Temperature. The matter of temperature is of considerable importance. For the majority of plants a temperature ranging between 65 and 75 degrees is ideal, although some plants require a somewhat lower or a much higher degree of heat. Root formation is usually greatly stimulated if bottom heat is provided. If possible, the temperature of the sand should be 5 to 10 degrees warmer than the surrounding air. In greenhouses the bottom heat is supplied by the hot water or steam pipes which comprise the regular heating system. In a hotbed it may be supplied by manure or by an electric heating cable, while in the house it may be supplied by radiator pipes, if they are accessible.

Moisture. An adequate supply of moisture and sufficient circulation of air are also important factors. For the majority of plants a moderate degree of moisture is desirable. The sand or rooting medium should never be allowed to dry out completely, nor should it be allowed to become wet to the point of being soggy. Cacti and other succulents require a rather dry environment, while a few of our large-foliaged greenhouse plants prefer a very high degree of humidity.

Air Conditions. There should be a sufficient circulation of air so that moisture does not remain on the leaves constantly or for too long a time, and direct drafts should always be avoided, as the effects are usually very harmful.

Potting-up. From three to four weeks will be required for the rooting of most softwood cuttings. Evidence of root formation will usually be indicated by the beginning of new top growth. When the roots are well developed, having reached a length of ½-inch or more, the cuttings should be removed from the sand. They may then be potted up in small pots or planted in flats or frames. A sandy loam with a small proportion of leaf mold is ideal for this first potting, and after the young plants have become well established they may be allowed a richer diet.

Half-ripened Stem Cuttings

The majority of shrubs may be readily propagated by half-ripened stem cuttings. The cuttings may be taken during the summer months, the exact time depending upon the growth of the plant. The cuttings should be taken from the tip end of the shoots and the wood should be just brittle enough to snap off when bent double. The cuttings will vary in length from 4 to 6 inches and a clean cut should be made below a node. The leaves should be removed from the lower portion of the stems and the cuttings should be inserted in the propagating case. At this season of the year a coldframe offers a most satisfactory place for the rooting of cuttings. It should be provided with a sash which may be kept tightly closed when desired, and a lath or burlap frame may be used to provide shade. The sand or the sand and peat moss mixture should be kept damp, but not too damp, and a daily sprinkling will keep the foliage from wilting. From four to six weeks will be required for the rooting of most half-ripened wood cuttings. After rooting they may be transplanted into flats or pots, or directly into the nursery beds. If space is available it is advisable to carry them over the winter in the frames, but if they must be wintered in the open ground they should be provided with a protective mulch.

Hardwood or Dormant Stem Cuttings

Many deciduous trees and shrubs may be propagated very readily by means of dormant or hardwood cuttings. These cut-

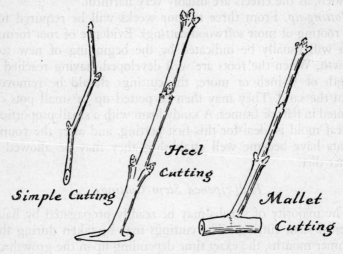

Simple Cutting   *Heel Cutting*   *Mallet Cutting*

Hardwood Stem Cuttings

tings should be taken in the autumn after the leaves have fallen. In the case of a few shrubs, such as Althea and Diervilla, only the tips of the branches should be used. With the majority of shrubs and trees, however, the branches may be cut into sections varying from 6 to 10 inches in length. The cuttings should be made from healthy wood of the current season's growth. In most cases there should be at least three or four buds on each section of stem used as a cutting. A clean, slightly diagonal cut should be made just above a bud at the top and just below a bud at the bottom of each cutting. After the cuttings have been made, they should be tied in bundles of convenient size with the lower or butt ends even and the cuttings facing in the same direction. A label should be attached to each group and the bundles should then be buried in slightly moist sand, soil, peat moss or sawdust. A cool cellar with a temperature ranging between 40 and 45 degrees Fahrenheit provides an ideal storage place for hardwood cuttings during the winter months. If such a place is not available, however, the bundles of cuttings may be buried out of doors in sand or in light, sandy soil, a well-drained spot being selected, and the bundles should be buried below the frost line. During this period of storage, a callous will form over the butt ends of the cuttings. In the spring when the ground is workable the cuttings may be removed from storage and may be planted out in nursery rows. The depth of planting will vary somewhat according to the type of cutting. The general practice is to set the cutting so that only the tip shows above the surface of the ground. In the case of cuttings containing a large number of buds, one third of the stem may protrude above the surface of the soil, thus allowing several buds to develop into new shoots. By autumn the cuttings should be well rooted and the young plants may be shifted to more ample quarters in the nursery.

Evergreen Cuttings—Coniferous. Many evergreens may be readily propagated by cuttings. The usual practice is to take cuttings during October and November from growth of the current season. In the case of some of the rather slow-rooting evergreens, the heel or mallet type of cutting is preferred. (See illustrations.) The cuttings should be inserted in a propagating case and kept at a moderately cool temperature of approximately 60 degrees F. with mild bottom heat. The cuttings should be protected from strong sunshine and, for best results, there should be a reasonably high degree of humidity. Some evergreens will root readily in any medium such as sand, peat moss, or a combination of the two, while other types of evergreens such as yews prefer sand as a rooting medium. Some of the very quick-rooting evergreens such as the arborvitæs and the retino-sporas may also be propagated by cuttings taken in August. These late summer cuttings may be inserted in an outdoor propagating frame and will root readily.

Substances Which Promote Root-forming

Within the past decade the research scientists have made several very important discoveries which have led to the development of various root-forming substances. These chemical compounds, which are known as plant hormones, have a very direct influence upon plant growth, and hasten the root development of both succulent and hardwood cuttings.

There are a number of excellent commercial preparations on the market. Detailed instructions are given for the use of these various substances and the directions should be followed with great care.

The method of treatment consists of immersing the basal ends of the cuttings in a solution of designated strength for a given period of time. Some plants are very sensitive, while others are very tolerant of the action of these root-forming substances, and the success of the treatment depends upon the strength of the solution and the duration of the treatment. Overtreatment of the cuttings will cause a characteristic discoloration of the lower portion of the stem, and in some cases will result in the death of the cutting. In other cases it may cause the production of an excessive number of roots, or the development of roots for too great a distance up the stem.

These plant hormone substances may be used with a wide variety of cuttings and they mark a distinct advance in the technique of propagation. Root formation can be stimulated on many plants which have formerly been difficult to propagate, and this new method is of particular value with such plants as Holly, Magnolia, Blueberry, Rhododendron, Azalea, Taxus, Dogwood, Dahlia and many others.

Leaf Cuttings

Among our more commonly grown house plants there are several which may be very easily propagated by leaf cuttings, various methods being used to meet the requirements of the individual plant. In general, plants with thick, fleshy leaves may be most readily propagated in this manner as the leaves contain a sufficient supply of reserve food.

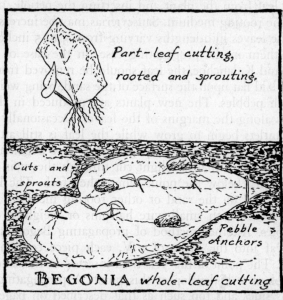

Part-leaf cutting, rooted and sprouting.

Cuts and sprouts

Pebble Anchors

BEGONIA *whole-leaf cutting*

Sprouted

ST. PAULIA LEAF CUTTINGS

The Saintpaulia, Gloxinia, Peperomia, and the Begonias of the Gloire de Lorraine group may be propagated by removing an entire leaf from the plant and inserting the petiole, or leaf stem, in the rooting medium. Sansevierias may be increased by cutting the leaves into lengths varying from 3 to 5 inches and inserting them in the propagating case. In the case of Bryophyllum and Kalanchoë, the leaf should be removed from the plant and laid flat upon the surface of the sand, being weighted down with pebbles. The new plants are produced in the indentations along the margins of the leaves. Occasionally these young plantlets begin to grow while the leaf is still attached to the parent plant. In the propagation of Rex Begonias, the usual practice is to make a slight cut through the main veins of the leaf just below the point where they fork. The leaf is then placed flat on the sand or other rooting medium, being pinned in place with small wire hairpins or weighted down with pebbles. Another method of propagating Begonias is to cut the leaf into the shape of a V, each piece containing a large vein. The point of the V is then inserted in the sand and the new plant will develop at this point. A propagating case with glass sides and top such as that described on page 1001 is ideal for the rooting of leaf cuttings if a greenhouse propagating frame is not available.

Root Cuttings

The Japanese Anemones, Bleedingheart, Oriental Poppies, Phlox, Verbascums and a few other herbaceous perennials may be propagated by root cuttings and this method is also used for a number of woody plants.

After the plants have been lifted, the roots may be cut into lengths varying from 2 to 3 inches. These small pieces of root should then be planted in greenhouse flats or in frames, being placed in a horizontal position at a depth of approximately an inch. Pure sand, sand and peat moss in mixture, or a light sandy soil will all give satisfactory results as a rooting medium.

If the cuttings are taken in the autumn, they may be carried over the winter in the coldframe, and by spring the new plants will be ready to set out in the nursery. If the cuttings are given mild bottom heat in the greenhouse propagating bench, the development of new root and top growth will be very rapid. Root cuttings may be taken at almost any season of the year, but the most favorable time will usually be indicated by the natural habit of growth of the plant. Anemone Japonica, which flowers in the autumn, may be propagated most successfully if lifted late in the season after the blooming period is over. The Oriental Poppies and Bleedingheart become dormant soon after flowering, and root cuttings should preferably be made during this period. Phlox may be successfully propagated by this method at almost any season and the root cuttings develop new plants so readily that they may even be planted in small shallow drills in the open ground.

PROPAGATION BY DIVISION

Clumps

The division of old clumps is one of the most simple of all methods or propagation. A few shrubs and many of the herbaceous perennials may be propagated very successfully in this way, among them—the hardy Asters, Phlox, Bleedingheart, Peonies, Daylilies, Plantain-lily, Astilbe, Blazing Star, Chrysanthemums, and a large variety of rock plants.

The plants should be lifted from the soil and pulled apart with care in order that the roots and crown may be injured as little as possible. In cases where the crowns have become tough and hard, two spading forks or hand forks may be used to loosen them. In occasional instances where no alternative seems possible, a clean, sharp cut can be made with a strong butcher's knife or with a spade.

In the case of certain herbaceous perennials, the frequent division of the clumps is desirable from the standpoint of good cultural methods; in other cases it is employed only when there is a desire to increase the stock. Hardy Asters and Chrysanthemums deteriorate rapidly if left undisturbed over a period of many years, and they should, therefore, be systematically lifted and divided every two or three years, whether new plants are desired or not. Peonies should preferably not be divided

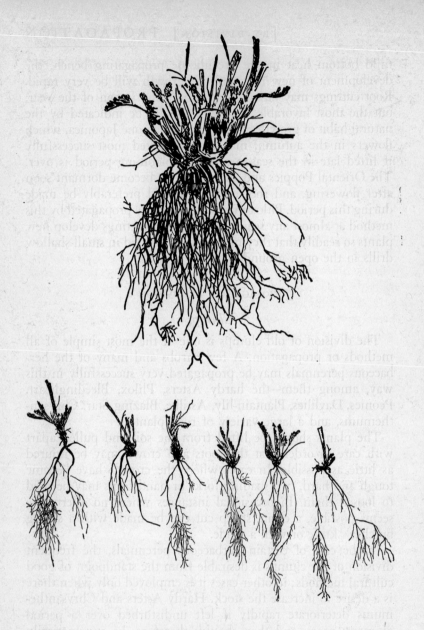

Pyrethrum Divisions

more frequently than once in seven or eight years and they may often be left undisturbed for many years with no apparent injury to the plant. Bleedingheart should never be disturbed unless an increase of stock is desired as the plants will increase in beauty as the years pass.

The season of the year most favorable for the division of old clumps will vary with the natural habit of growth of the plant. Hardy asters and chrysanthemums should be divided in very early spring just as growth starts. Phlox should preferably be divided in the early autumn after the period of bloom has passed, although it may be divided at almost any season of the year with reasonable success. Bleedingheart should always be divided in the autumn, never in the spring if one wishes to have bloom the same season. Peonies should be lifted and divided early in September.

In cases where the plant grows from a definite crown, the hard, woody center should be discarded and the vigorous outside growth should be selected for purposes of propagation. After the divisions have been reset, they should be kept watered until new root growth has started and they have become well established.

Rhizomes

Botanically a rhizome is an underground, or partially underground stem which, in most cases, produces roots, shoots, and leaves. A rhizome may be distinguished from a root by the presence of nodes. A true root has no nodes. The rhizomes of some plants penetrate quite deeply into the soil, while in the case of certain Irises, the rhizomes rest upon the surface of the ground, being only partially subterranean. Plants of this type may be readily propagated by a division of the rhizomes. In the case of the Bearded iris, the plant may be lifted from the soil and the rhizomes gently separated, each rhizome having two or three sprouts for new growth. The rhizomes of some plants bear no prominent shoots and in such cases the rhizome should be cut into short pieces. These sections should then be planted in sand until they have rooted. The majority of rhizomatous plants should be propagated when dormant. In the case of the

Bearded iris, however, the most favorable time is the season immediately following the blooming period. Among the plants which may be propagated by a division of the rhizomes we have the rhizomatous types of Iris, Lily-of-the-valley, Hellebore, May apple, Solomon's-seal, Bloodroot, Trillium and many others.

Tubers

Tubers are thickened underground stems bearing conspicuous buds or eyes. Among our flowering plants, the Dahlia is the most prominent member of this group while the Irish potato and the Jerusalem artichoke are well known among the vegetables. The tubers may be cut into sections, as in the case of the Potato, or they may be planted whole, as in the case of the Dahlia. It is essential that each tuber have at least one healthy bud. When Dahlias are propagated by tubers, a small portion of stem should be attached to each tuber.

"BULBOUS" PROPAGATION

Bulbs and Bulbils

There are numerous bulb-like structures, commonly called "bulbs," but which in reality may be tubers or rhizomes (as described above) or corms. Bulbs are, botanically, modified leaves and stems which occur usually underground. They are composed largely of fleshy, scale-like leaves and they contain large quantities of stored plant food. There are two general types of bulbs, the tunicated type composed of close-fitting layers of leaf tissue covered with a dry husk, such as the hyacinth and tulip; and the scaly type which is composed of thick, loose, overlapping scales, such as the lily.

Many bulbs are readily increased by natural separation. A fully matured bulb, known as a "mother bulb" will, under favorable conditions, produce one or more bulbs of flowering size and a number of small bulbils. These small bulbils should be removed when the mother bulb is dug and should be planted in flats or in nursery plots, as they will usually require several years to reach blooming size.

Lilies may be propagated by the separation of the bulbs, by bulblets produced in the axils of the leaves, and by the fleshy scales. The bulblets produced in the axils of the leaves should be planted in the same way as the bulbils from the base of the bulb. After the flowering period, the bulbs should be lifted and three or four of the outer scales may be removed. These scales should be placed in damp sphagnum moss in a warm greenhouse. Tiny bulbils will develop at the base of the scales and will reach flowering size in from two to four years. Another method of propagation which has proved successful with some lilies is to remove the scales and plant them in the nursery during the summer. They should be set about 2 inches deep and they will usually produce flowering bulbs in about three years.

Madonna lilies may be propagated by removing the lower portion of the flower stems from the bulb. After the blooming season is over and the flower stalk has been cut off, the base of the stem may be pulled out and may be planted in sand, being placed in a horizontal position. Small bulbs will be produced along the stem and will flower in from two to three years.

Hyacinths may be increased very rapidly by notching or scooping the bulbs. The usual practice is to dig the bulbs in late spring or early summer. In notching, a transverse cut is made through the base of the bulb. In scooping, the entire basal section of the bulb is removed in such a manner that the various layers of scales are slightly severed. In order to hasten the production of new bulbils, the notched or scooped bulbs are dusted with slaked lime and are then placed, bottom up, in a moist atmosphere where a high temperature, ranging around 80 degrees F., can be maintained. If this procedure is followed, the new bulbils will begin to form within a few weeks and in the autumn the mother bulbs with the small bulbils still attached should be planted in the nursery. When the bulbils have reached maturity they may be separated from the mother bulb. Notched bulbs will produce a small number of large bulbils which will reach blooming size in from three to four years. Scooped bulbs will produce a larger number of small bulbils which require from four to five years to reach blooming size.

Tulip bulbs, when they have reached maximum size, usually

split up into a number of smaller bulbs. These may be lifted and planted in nursery rows, and, if conditions of soil and climate are favorable, they will reach bloming size in from two to four years.

Narcissus, Scilla, Muscari and many other bulbs may be easily increased by division or separation as the bulbs multiply very rapidly under natural conditions.

Corms and Cormels

A corm is a fleshy, underground base of a stem, rounded in shape. It is solid, being composed almost entirely of stem tissue, and is unlike a bulb in this respect. A bulb consists largely of leaf tissue, and when a crosswise section is cut from it a number of concentric scaly rings are revealed, whereas a corm thus cut reveals only solid tissue. Among the most familiar examples of plants grown from corms are the Calochortus, Crocus, Cyclamen, Gladiolus, Ixia, and Tritonia. Each year one, and in some cases several, new corms of flowering size are formed on top of the mother corm which deteriorates at the end of the growing season. Many small cormels are also usually formed at the base of the new corm. When the plants are dug in the autumn, the new, flowering-size corms may be separated and stored away for spring planting. In general practice these corms are planted the following season to produce bloom. If, however, a very rapid increase of stock is desired, as in the case of a new or very expensive variety, these large corms may be cut into sections in order that more plants may be produced. The tiny cormels should be stored until planting time in the spring. They may then be planted in rows, being treated very much like seed, and they will reach bloming size in from one to three years.

PROPAGATION BY SPECIALIZED SHOOTS

Layering

Layering is one of the simplest and most dependable methods of propagation although it is adapted only to those plants which possess a characteristic habit of growth and which root readily when their branches come into contact with the soil. It is a method which is of especial value in the propagation of some of the broad-leaved evergreens such as certain varieties of Rhododendrons and Magnolias.

There are several different types of layering: tip-layering, simple layering, serpentine layering, mound layering, and air layering.

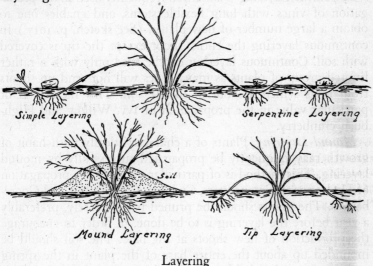

Layering

Tip-Layering is the method commonly used in the propagation of Black Raspberries and plants of a similar habit of growth. In late summer the supple canes are bent over, the tip being anchored in the soil. A new plant will soon form which may be severed from the parent plant and transplanted to any desired position.

Simple Layering is usually done during the spring and summer months. If the branch is woody in character, a notch should be cut in it about 18 inches from the tip. The notch should be propped open with a match or some very small piece of wood. The branch should then be bent over to the ground, the portion where the notch occurs being covered with soil. The leaves should be removed from that portion of the stem which is to be buried. The tip end of the branch should be left exposed. If necessary the branch may be pegged down with a forked stick, or it may be held in place by the weight of a small stone. After the layer has rooted, it may be severed from the parent plant and when the new plant is well established, it may be transplanted the following spring.

Serpentine Layering is a method frequently used in the propagation of vines with long flexible stems, and enables one to obtain a large number of new plants. (See sketch, p. 1017.) In continuous layering the entire shoot except the tip is covered with soil. Continuous layering can be used only with a rather limited group of plants as many types will not send up shoots from buds which are buried in the soil. This method is of particular value in the propagation of Ivy, Willow and High-bush cranberry.

Mound Layering. Plants of a characteristically bush habit of growth may frequently be propagated successfully by mound layering. This method is of particular value in the propagation of Hydrangeas, Cotoneasters, Cydonia, Calycanthus and Goose-berries. The plants should be pruned back severely, preferably a year before the layering is to be done, in order to encourage the production of new shoots at the base. The soil should be mounded up about the entire base of the plant in the spring and these new basal shoots will strike root at the nodes. This method of propagation is somewhat slow, as it will frequently require from one to two years for the new plants to become well established.

Air Layering is a method occasionally employed with greenhouse plants possessing rigid woody stems, such as Rubber plants and certain Dracænas. The usual practice is to make a slanting cut through one or more nodes on the stem, propping the cut open with a toothpick. A mass of moist sphagnum moss is then bound about the stem at the point where the cuts have been made. The moss should be kept damp and the temperature should be moderately warm in order to induce rooting. After the roots have formed, the new plant may be severed from the parent plant and potted up. This method may also be used with trees and shrubs with stiff upright branches which cannot be bent to the ground. The notch on the branch is usually made about 18 inches from the tip and a specially constructed layering pot is used which is filled with moist soil. The pot is kept in place until the stem has rooted.

Suckers

Some plants may be propagated by means of suckers which are leafy shoots produced from adventitious buds on the underground parts of a plant. Certain varieties of Cherries and Plums produce suckers very rapidly, and Lilacs may be propagated by this method. If the tree or shrub which is to be thus propagated has been grafted it is important to make certain that the sucker has been produced from a bud above the graft. If it happens to have come from a bud below the graft it will be similar to the stock upon which the tree or shrub was grafted and will not possess the desirable characteristics of the grafted plant. Willows, Poplars, Black locust and Sassafras may be very readily propagated by means of suckers.

Runners

Some plants, such as the Strawberry, the Boston Fern and the Strawberry Saxifrage, may be readily propagated by means of runners. In plants of this type the stems creep along the surface of the ground and strike root at the nodes, producing new plants which continue to receive nourishment from the parent plant until they are well established. The connecting stem may be severed at any point between the old plant and the new plant, and the new plant may then be moved to its new location.

Stolons

A stolon is a slender branch which, under favorable conditions, will take root. Stolons may be produced either above ground or below ground, the new plant being produced from the bud at the end of the stolon. Some of the bent grasses may be very readily increased by the planting of stolons. The sod is broken into small pieces and the stolons are strewn upon the surface of the well-prepared seed bed, being covered with approximately ½-inch of soil. The soil should be kept moist until growth has started, and at no time should the stolons be allowed to dry out.

Some shrubby plants also take root very naturally by means of stolons and may be readily propagated in this way. In this group we find Forsythia, the red-twigged Dogwood, Matrimony-vine, many of the Willows and the Red raspberries.

GRAFTING

Fruits trees do not come true from seed, as most of our garden varieties are hybrids. In order to perpetuate a variety, vegetative propagation or a vegetative union is necessary.

Grafting and budding are the two common methods of propagating fruit trees. An undesirable variety may be changed to a more desirable one by grafting. Pollination troubles can be solved by grafting the proper variety on part of an unproductive tree, because the presence of another or pollinating variety will result in cross-fertilization, causing fruits to form on the heretofore non-productive variety. When the trunk of a tree has been girdled by mice, grafting will save the tree.

Bridge Grafting

This is the only method to save trees girdled by mice.

1. Remove soil from around the trunk of the tree until the live bark on the roots is exposed.

2. Trim off rough edges of the bark with a sharp knife at the base of the tree and also on the root.

3. Take a piece of dormant one-year-old wood (previous season's growth) and measure the distance to be bridged over. Allow 1¼ inches on the bark and also on the root, and cut with a sharp knife.

4. Cut out a piece of bark above and below the girdled area, into which the ends of the scion should fit snugly. (Def.—A *scion* is a young shoot used for grafting.)

5. Make a slanting cut, 1¼ inches long on each end of the scion and place each end in the part where the bark was removed.

6. Place the scions 2 inches apart around the trunk.

7. Two small brads without heads should be used to hold the scion firmly in place at each end. They should be nailed through the middle two-thirds of each scion, each end of which is properly fitted above and below the girdled area.

8. Apply grafting wax over the united areas to keep them airtight.

Whip Grafting

This graft is used to propagate nursery stock and may be done in midwinter when most orchard operations are at a standstill.

One-year-old root stocks should be used. (Def.—*Stock* is that

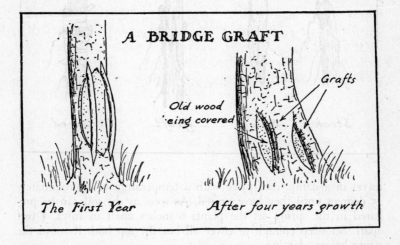

A BRIDGE GRAFT

Grafts

Old wood being covered

The First Year

After four years' growth

part which is to receive the scion.) They may be grown from seed or purchased from firms in mid- and far-western states which make a specialty of this. The procedure is as follows:

1. Cut the root from the one-year whip and below any green tissue.

2. Cut the root into 3–inch lengths.

3. Make a clean slanting cut about 1½–2 inches in length. The next cut on the root is made parallel to the edge of the root and should be 1¼–1½ inches long.

4. Select a piece of scion wood from the middle of one-year

terminal growth with three buds on it. Cut it 1¼ inches below the third bud and proceed as in No. 3.

5. Join the two tongues together and be sure that the cambium layer of one side of the root is in contact with one side of the scion. (Def.—*Cambium* is a layer of cells which is between the bark and the wood; these cells grow and multiply rapidly.)

6. Wrap tightly with waxed string and store in moist sand or

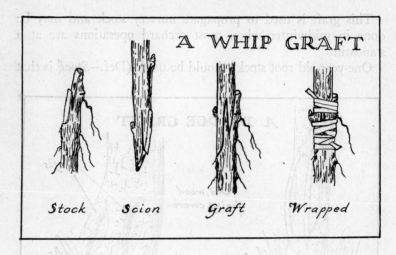

A WHIP GRAFT

Stock   Scion   Graft   Wrapped

leaves in a damp, cool place with a temperature of approximately 45 degrees until they have united. As soon as the soil can be prepared in the spring set the plants 6 inches apart in rows, 3 feet apart. Set deep enough to cover all but the top bud. Remove the string before planting.

This method may also be practised on young trees in the nursery row which are not over one year old. If older, the smaller branches may be successfully grafted in this manner.

Cleft Grafting

Cleft grafting is a method used to top-work trees, especially when the limb to be grafted is somewhat larger than the one-year scion to be grafted. A limb may vary from more than ½ to 2 inches in diameter. This type of grafting is most successful if done early in the spring when the bark is slipping, or loose, or before growth has made much progress. It may be done after that, however, if the scions are dormant. The procedure is as follows:

1. Saw the limb off at the desired point where the limb is to be grafted.

2. With a sharp knife smooth the edges so the cambium layer may be easily seen.

3. A grafting chisel is placed on the center of the stump and

A brace graft after one year.   A brace graft after six years.

Sometimes used to strengthen forked branches. The illustration
is self-explanatory.

driven into the stock to a depth of 3 to 4 inches with a wooden mallet or club.

4. The scion of the desired variety should have been taken from the terminal growth of a bearing tree which should be the previous season's growth.

5. The tip of the scion should be cut off, and the second cut is made 1½ inches below the third bud.

6. That part of the scion below the third bud is cut to make a wedge. The side with the bud should be slightly thicker than the side which will be in toward the center of the stump. This wedge should be 1¼ inches in length.

7. The cleft is opened with the end of the chisel which is wedge-shaped and the scion inserted so that its cambium layer is in direct contact with that of the stock. One scion is inserted on each side of the stock if it is more than an inch in diameter, and the chisel is removed. The pressure from the sides of the split stock holds the scions firmly in place. It is well to remember that the scions should be uniform in size to fit well and have equal pressure from both sides of the stock.

8. Cover the exposed area immediately with grafting wax to prevent drying out, the entrance of disease organisms, and the entrance of excess moisture.

An extra large branch may be cleft grafted by making two clefts at right angles to each other. In this case four scions are necessary. A small piece of wood, or a wedge, must be put in the center to prevent the scion from being crushed, as the larger the limb, the greater the pressure.

When the grafting of an individual limb is finished, the entire exposed area should be waxed over to prevent the entrance of moisture, disease organisms or drying out. The grafts should be checked occasionally to make sure that the wax is properly protecting it. When grafting is done after considerable growth has been made, it is best to cover the entire scion with wax, which keeps it in a dormant state a little longer while the scion is uniting with the stock.

Cleft grafting is very satisfactory on Apples and Pears but more difficult on Plums and Cherries and almost impossible with Peaches.

Bark Grafting

Bark grafting must be done in the spring after the sap starts to flow, or the bark will not easily separate from the cambium layer. This graft is most practicable on limbs which are too large to be cleft grafted. The limb is removed at the desired place and a smooth area is selected where the graft is to be placed.

There are three ways of bark grafting which will be described after directions for preparing the scion are first stated.

1. The scion should contain three buds and be cut from the terminal growth 1½ inches below the third bud for all three types.

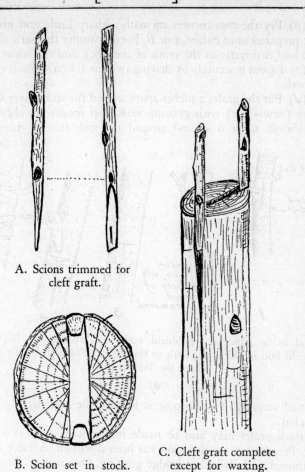

A. Scions trimmed for
cleft graft.

B. Scion set in stock.

C. Cleft graft complete
except for waxing.

Figure 9. Cleft Graft

2. *A.* Directly opposite the lower bud make an abrupt cut to the center and then straight down to the end; *or*

B. Make a sloping cut on the side opposite the lowest bud to the end of the scion, or 1½ inches.

The three methods of bark grafting are as follows:

1. (*a*) Make a cut 1¼ inches in length on the stock and at right angles to the stub which is to receive the graft.

(*b*) Pry the two corners up with a sharp knife and insert the scion prepared as in either *A* or *B*. Force it under the bark until the outer bud is directly at the point of the stock and the scion.

(*c*) Fasten it securely by driving two small brads into it through the bark.

(*d*) Put the grafts 2 inches apart around the stub, cover exposed tissues (newly cut) with grafting wax. Best results are obtained if, in addition, raffia is wound around the stub two to three times

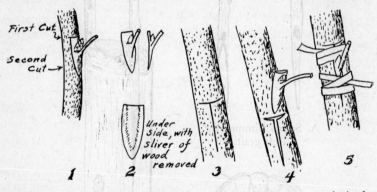

1. Bud to be removed. 2. Shield bud. 3. Two cuts in stock bark. 4. Shield bud is slid under bark in the cut. 5. Raffia closes the opening about the bud in place.

and tied securely. The purpose is to hold the bark tightly against the scion.

2. Bark grafts may also be made in the same way as a bridge graft. Preparation for the scion has been discussed. A piece of bark is removed as described in bridge grafting. One side of the scion is cut as described in *A* or *B*, inserted, fastened with brads and waxed over. This is the easiest method for the amateur to follow.

3. Budding. This type of grafting is done during the month of August or in the early part of September when the bark slips easily. Its main use is to propagate young trees of the desired variety.

(*a*) At the point where the budding is to be done, that is, as close to the ground as possible, make a cut in the shape of a T. Its vertical distance is ¾ of an inch long and the horizontal distance, ½ inch.

(*b*) The bud to be used is selected from the terminal growth on the current season's growth. Be sure that the bud is well developed. Remove the leaf next to the bud, but leave on part of its stem.

(c) Using a sharp knife remove the bud with some of the wood and bark attached to it. When properly removed it looks like a shield.

(d) Loosen carefully the corners of the T-shaped cut in the stock and slip the bud in under the corners.

(e) Use raffia, rubber bands or waxed string to wind above and below the bud.

(f) Two weeks later the bud should be united. The bud remains dormant until the following spring. The stock is cut back to the bud which develops into the desired limb.

Pruning and Training of Grafts

Grafts, especially those on large limbs which have been cleft or bark grafted, must be properly understood. If two or more grafts are made on a stub only one should be allowed to fully develop. The best one should be selected before next season's growth starts. It is cut back to promote lateral branches. The other is cut back to two or three buds. The purpose is to keep it alive so that it will help to heal over the stump but not to compete with the one selected. The principle used to train them until maturity or bearing is the same as with young trees planted in the ground.

It is best to graft one side of a tree at a time if it is more than eight years old. The side not grafted can be grafted the follow-ing year.

XXXI

Plant Diseases and Insect Pests

PLANT DISEASES

Plant diseases may be grouped into three general classes—those brought about by unfavorable environment or by some physiological disturbance, those caused by fungi and by bacteria, and those caused by a virus.

In the first group we find plants suffering from malnutrition, from an improper balance of food elements in the soil, from an excess of one or more food nutrients, from extreme soil acidity, or from extreme alkalinity as is the case in lime-induced chlorosis. The symptoms are very much the same in most cases. Growth is retarded, the foliage becomes a sickly, yellowish green, and the root systems are poorly developed. For the control of such physiological diseases, refer to Chapter I on Soils and Soil Management.

In the second group we find the majority of our common plant diseases, those caused by fungi. Fungi are minute forms of plant life, too small, for the most part, to be seen with the naked eye. They differ primarily from other plants in that they possess no green coloring matter, which is known as chlorophyll. All fungi are classed as parasites as they cannot live except on some other plant or animal. Some forms, such as the rust fungi, can exist only on living plants; other forms can live only on dead plants, and a few forms can live on either living or dead plant tissue. Some fungi attack many different plants, while other forms can live on but one kind. Some forms are very short lived, while others live on in the soil for many years. Most fungi produce small seed-like bodies which are called spores. These tiny spores are very easily carried from one plant to another by the wind and other agencies, and the spread of fungous diseases is therefore often very rapid. When supplied with sufficient moisture these spores germinate and produce new fungus plants. Since they require a certain amount of moisture in order to germinate, it may be readily understood why fungous diseases are apt to be much more prevalent in wet seasons than in dry seasons.

Bacteria are also a form of plant life, being even more minute in size than the fungi. There are many different kinds of bacteria but those that attack plants do not usually produce spores. They differ from fungi in this respect, and since they cannot be blown about by the wind they do not spread as rapidly from plant to plant. They must depend upon some mechanical means such as human hands, insects, garden tools and things of this nature, or upon the splashing of rain drops from leaf to leaf, or the spattering caused by heavy rains upon the surface of the soil. It is in just this way that the dreaded Leaf Spot of delphiniums is spread. The bacteria winter over in the soil, and with the spring rains they are spattered up onto the lower leaves.

VIRUSES

The infections due to viruses seem to be an increasing group of plant diseases. As yet it is not known just what viruses are. The virus which causes tobacco mosaic has been found to be a complex protein molecule. But we do not know if this is generally the case. Viruses are spread by dirty pruning instruments, insects, and in some cases they seem to be transmitted in the seed. Some of the commonest symptoms of virus infection are curling of leaf tissue, yellowing of leaves, a mottled effect due to the alternating of green and yellow patches, and a bushy type of growth.

INSECT PESTS

Many scientists have devoted their lives to the study of insects and, as a result of their patient investigations, information is now available regarding the habits and life histories of practically all our common insect pests. Nearly seven hundred thousand species of insects have already been classified, nor is this figure astonishing when we realize that insects constitute the largest group in the animal kingdom. It has been estimated that 75 per cent of all known kinds of living animals belong to the insect world, and there are probably many species in remote sections of the earth that have not, as yet, been discovered.

Continual warfare has been waged between man and insects since the dawn of history, and from present indications it would seem as if we who inherit the earth today would have to continue the struggle. It is disheartening to learn that in spite of all that modern science has done no insect species has ever been known to be completely exterminated. So probably the best that we can hope for in our gardens is to keep them under control, and this can be done only by prompt and concerted effort. We will have to resign ourselves to the fact that the struggle will continue year after year. In order to give our gardens intelligent care, however, there are certain things which we should know regarding the common insect pests that disturb our peace. We should know something about the way in which insects grow, something about their life histories, their feeding habits, and the various factors of control.

Insects, in common with all other animals, begin life from a single cell known as the egg. In most cases the eggs are fertilized by the male and are then deposited in some suitable place by the adult female. In some cases, however, fertilization does not seem to be necessary and the females produce living young without mating. This remarkable phenomenon is known as parthenogenesis and the most common example is the aphid. Throughout the summer months generation after generation is produced, consisting entirely of females which have developed from unfertilized eggs. As many as 98 generations have been produced in this manner. In the autumn males suddenly appear and the eggs which are to carry the species over the winter are fertilized.

Insect eggs vary greatly in size, shape, and coloring, most of them being very small. The number laid by one female varies from a single egg, which is exceptional, to as many as one million. The average number is probably about one hundred. The eggs of some species are laid all at one time; in the case of other species they are laid in successive batches. Instinct almost invariably guides the female to lay her eggs where the newly-hatched young will be able to find suitable food. After the eggs are laid the mother's responsibility usually comes to an end and she gives them no further heed. From the moment of hatching the young insects are thrown entirely upon their own resources. There are a few cases where the adult insects prepare elaborate nests and provision them with food for the young, but this is the exception rather than the rule. The time spent within the egg varies considerably. In the majority of cases it is about two weeks. In the case of the house fly it is only 8 hours, and in other cases the period is decidedly prolonged, the winter frequently being passed in the egg stage. The life cycle of most insects is completed within the year. A few species such as the ants, the honey bees and wire worms live longer than a year. The shortest life cycle as yet known among insects is ten days.

In studying the life histories of insects we find that they are grouped into three classes, those without a metamorphosis, those with a simple, or gradual metamorphosis, and those with a complete or complex metamorphosis. A metamorphosis may be defined as a noticeable change in the form of an animal between the time of hatching, or birth, and the time of maturity.

Those insects which do not undergo a metamorphosis constitute a relatively small group and include such species as spring tails and fish moths which are of little or no importance to the gardener. When the young are hatched they are perfectly formed and resemble the adults in every respect except in size.

In the second group, those having a simple or gradual metamorphosis, we find many of our old acquaintances such as the grasshoppers, squash bugs, the scale insects and the aphids. In the case of many species in this group the newly-hatched young are very similar to the adults except for the absence of wings. In some species, however, the difference is more widely marked. The young insects in this group are spoken of as nymphs. In general they have the same feeding habits as their parents and are often found together. As they grow, their wings develop and they become more and more like the adults.

We find the largest number of insect species in the last group, those which pass through a complete metamorphosis, having four distinct life stages: the egg stage, the larva stage, the pupa stage and the adult stage. In most cases the newly-hatched young in no way resemble the adults and have totally different habits. The young are known as larvæ (singular larva). When the larvæ become full grown they pass into the pupa stage and later the adult form emerges. All growth is made in the larva stage. No growth ever occurs in the adult stage. Little beetles never grow into big beetles or little butterflies into big butterflies.

The way in which insects make their growth is very interesting. They do not grow gradually, almost imperceptibly, as do the young of most other animals. The body wall is incapable of expanding, and increase in size can take place only through a series of molts. An entirely new skin is created within the old skin and when this is ready a fluid known as the molting fluid is poured forth by certain specialized cells in the body. This loosens the outer skin and the insect crawls forth. Ordinarily four or five molts occur before the nymphs or larvæ become full grown. In some species an insect passes through as many as 20 molts. In the case of a nymph the final molt results in a fully developed adult, whereas in the case of a larva the final molt carries the insect into the pupa stage.

The pupa stage is one of the most important in the life of an insect for it is during this period that it undergoes the wonderful transformation from a sluggish, stupid larva into an alert, highly developed adult,—a bee, a moth, a beetle, a fly—according to the species. Most larvæ make very careful provision for the safeguarding of the pupa, protecting it under bark or rubbish of some kind, hiding it in the long grass, enfolding it within a leaf or burying it in the soil. In a few species, such as the lady beetles, the pupa is found exposed, with the tip of the body merely fastened to a leaf. The protection about the pupa varies considerably with the different species. In the case of many of the flies the larva retains its own mottled skin and pupates within it. The skin undergoes something of a change, however, becoming hard and forming a waterproof and in most cases a completely airtight case. In some species the larva spins a cocoon for the protection of the pupa and in other species it constructs intricate little cells within the soil. The period of pupation varies greatly. Many species pass the winter in the pupa stage while others spend only a few days within the pupa case.

The Control of Insect Pests

There are various natural factors which enter into the control of insect pests. Weather conditions have a considerable influence upon the prevalence of some species. For example, most of the eggs of the gypsy moth are killed during a cold, open winter, whereas they will survive a snowy winter. If heavy rains occur during the time that the eggs are hatching other species suffer severe losses. This may help to explain the reason why certain insects are much more numerous in some seasons than in others.

On farms we use crop rotations to control certain insects and resort to deep plowing in order to expose the larvæ of other species at a critical time in their development. But here the farmer has a decided advantage over the gardener, for it would be neither practicable nor possible to use these methods in the flower garden.

Probably few realize what staunch allies we have in the birds, when it comes to the control of insects. But when we stop to consider the fact that the number of insects eaten in a day by certain birds is equal to the weight of the bird itself, we begin to appreciate the extent of their usefulness. Some birds are, of course, much more valuable as insect destroyers than others. Many of the smaller mammals are also useful. Moles, skunks, toads, and some species of snakes depend almost entirely upon insects for their food. Predatory parasites also play an important part in insect control. These are insects which are harmless in themselves from the viewpoint of the gardener but which prey upon other insects. In most sections of the country natural parasites exist and are a constant source of help. When new insects are brought into the country—and more than one half of our pests are of foreign origin—one of the most effective means of control is the introduction of these predatory parasites. When the gypsy moths were working such havoc in New England a decade or so ago insect parasites were imported from Europe and Asia, and were of inestimable value. The Australian lady beetle was imported into California to help control the Cottony cushion scale on the citrus fruits, and one of the most interesting recent examples is found in the case of the Japanese beetles. The beetle has existed for many years in Japan but has never become a serious pest because it has been kept practically under control by its natural enemies. Some years ago a few beetles were brought into this country on a shipment of plants from Japan. For a year or so they escaped notice and then, too late, we woke up to the fact that they were increasing in alarming numbers and that they threatened to become a very serious pest. It is doubtful whether, in the history of this country, any pest has increased so rapidly or proved so destructive. The Government has appropriated millions of dollars to aid the fight against the Japanese beetles and to prevent their spread into uninfested territory. And one of the most important measures of control has been the importation of some of the natural parasites which have so successfully kept the beetle in check in its native home. The two that have proved most valuable are a parasitic fly which lays its eggs upon the adult beetle, the larvæ boring their way into the body of the beetle, and a parasitic wasp which attacks the beetle in the larva stage.

In spite of the fact, however, that these natural factors are constantly at work to prevent the increase and spread of insect pests, the gardener will find that he cannot depend upon them for entire control, save in rare instances. It is necessary, therefore, to resort to other means, such as chemical control through the use of poison sprays, dusts and fumigants; or to mechanical control through the use of traps, tree bands, and hand picking. In controlling insect pests by these means it is necessary to determine the type of pest which one is fighting, to decide upon the remedy to be used, and to apply it promptly and thoroughly.

Insects are grouped into two distinct classes: those with chewing mouth parts and those with sucking mouth parts. In the first group we have caterpillars and beetles, of every kind and description, and other less important insects such as grubs, grasshoppers and some "slugs." These feed largely upon the foliage of growing plants and in the case of grubs and borers upon the roots; and among them we find some of our worst enemies, such as the aster beetles, the iris borer, the rose beetle, the yellow wooly-bear caterpillar, the cabbage looper and many others. The insects in this group chew and swallow solid plant tissues and they may, with very few exceptions, be controlled by stomach poisons.

In the second group, those insects having sucking mouth parts, we find such familiar enemies as the aphids, the various scale insects and the leaf-hoppers. Instead of being equipped with jaws with which they can tear off and chew their food, these insects have delicate tube-like mouth parts with which they are able to pierce through the outer layer of plant tissue and suck the juices from within. These long, needle-like beaks are usually jointed and they may point forward, upward or downward. When not in use they are generally laid back on the breast between the front legs. It is not possible to control the insects in this group by coating the outer surface of the plant with poison dusts or sprays, as they are able to pierce through the poisoned layer and can then draw their nourishment from the plant, quite un-harmed. It has been found, however, that these sucking insects can be controlled by what we call contact poisons,—poisons which come into direct contact with the body, either clogging up the little pores through which the insects breathe and thereby suffocating them, or coating the body with some corrosive sub-stance. When using a contact poison it is, of course, necessary that each insect be reached, and the spraying or dusting must be done very thoroughly.

The Garden Medicine Shelf

It is wise for every gardener to become familiar with some of the standard and reliable remedies which are used in con-trolling insect pests and diseases and to keep a sufficient quan-tity on hand for ordinary use. An orderly, well-stocked medicine shelf for the garden is not only a great source of satisfaction in itself but also means that in an emergency you will find yourself prepared, and you will not have to send forth a frantic order at the last minute.

For the average flower garden comparatively little is needed in the way of equipment. A quart measure, a measuring spoon (the kind that comes in little sets is very useful), a sprayer, and a dust gun are really all that are necessary. The size of the sprayer and dusting outfit will depend largely upon the extent of one's gardening operations. In a very small garden a hand sprayer such as may be purchased from any hardware store for fifty or seventy-five cents will probably be entirely adequate. For a larger garden a sprayer of the knapsack or bucket type would be more satisfactory.

INSECTICIDES

All insecticides may be grouped into three classes; stomach poisons, contact poisons and fumigants.

Stomach Poisons

In order to be satisfactory for general use in the garden it is necessary that stomach poisons measure up to certain definite requirements. A good stomach poison must not repel the insects against which it is to be used; it must give reasonably quick results; it must not burn the foliage of tender plants; it must spread uniformly when applied and adhere well to the foliage of the plant; it must keep its strength during periods of storage; and it must be reasonable in price. Of all the poisons which have been put on the market, arsenate of lead more nearly meets these requirements than any other. It is a by-product in the mining and smelting of metals and was developed by the Government Bureau of Entomology in 1892 when they were working on the control of the gypsy moth. It comes in both powder and paste form and it may be applied either as a dust or as a spray. It may also be used in combination with other materials such as sulphur and Bordeaux. It has only a very slight tendency to burn tender foliage, it is readily eaten by the majority of chewing insects, it adheres well and gives quick results—so altogether it is very satisfactory and should always be kept on hand.

There are a few insects, however, against which arsenate of lead is not entirely effective. This is true in the case of the aster beetle, and for this particular pest sodium fluosilicate is recommended.

Contact Insecticides

Contact insecticides are used for all insects with sucking mouth parts and they are also occasionally used against insects with chewing mouth parts. In order to be effective they must come into direct contact with the body of the insect, therefore the spraying or dusting must be done with great care. These contact insecticides kill the insect either by clogging up the breathing tubes or by entering the body and causing a chemical action upon the body tissues. There are various types of contact insecticides on the market, some forms being more effective against certain insects than others. For aphids and other insects of this type a good nicotine dust or spray is usually the most effective, while for the various forms of scale, oil or soap emulsions are the most satisfactory.

Nicotine is a yellowish, oily liquid which is extracted from tobacco. It is put on the market under a number of trade names, most brands containing 40 per cent nicotine. Black Leaf 40 is an old stand-by and is very reliable. When mixing any of these nicotine sprays, soap should be added not only to serve as a spreader but also to aid in liberating the nicotine. One cubic inch of soap per gallon is sufficient. This should be dissolved in hot water and added to the spray. Nicotine is also available in dust form, being mixed with sulphur, hydrated lime, or some other substance. These nicotine dusts should be applied when the plants are perfectly dry as they are not as effective in their action if the plants are wet. Nicotine, in all its forms, should be stored in air-tight containers, as it readily loses its strength when exposed to the air. The liquid forms should not be allowed to freeze as they lose their effectiveness.

Fish-oil or whale-oil soap and some good oil emulsion should be kept on hand for use against the various forms of scale.

Combination Insecticide

Rotenone is an insecticide which is toxic to both chewing and sucking insects and which has the advantage of being non-toxic to man and animals. It is derived from the roots of certain tropical plants such as derris and cube. It is on the market in various commercial forms and may be used either as a dust or as a spray. Its chief disadvantage is that when it is used as a stomach poison it loses its toxic properties within a few days, as it decomposes rapidly.

FUNGICIDES

Bordeaux mixture is probably more generally used than any other fungicide. Not only is it an effective control for many plant diseases; it is also useful as a repellent against flea beetles, leaf-hoppers and various other insects. There are various brands of Bordeaux on the market which are reasonably satisfactory, but it is an accepted fact that these commercial brands are not quite as effective as material which is freshly mixed. It is a fairly simple matter to make one's own mixture at home, and in order to obtain the best results it is often wise to undertake the extra work involved.

Formula for garden use:

Cold water	3 gallons
Hydrated lime	5 ounces
Copper sulphate	3 ounces

The copper sulphate should be dissolved in a small quantity of hot water and to this two gallons of cold water should be added. The lime should be slaked in a small quantity of water and the remaining cold water added to it. The lime water should then be poured into the copper sulphate solution and stirred vigorously. For best results Bordeaux mixture should be used within a few hours after mixing. When handling Bordeaux it must be remembered that it is highly corrosive, and it should consequently never be left standing for any length of time in a metal container. It should be mixed, if possible, in a wooden or earthenware receptacle.

It is rather interesting to know something about the origin of Bordeaux, for it was rather an amusing and entirely accidental discovery. In a section of France near the town of Bordeaux there are many acres devoted to vineyards, and years ago some of the owners whose grapes grew along the highways suffered sadly from vandalism. In an effort to discourage people from taking their fruit, they coated their vines with a mixture of lime and copper sulphate. This, as we know all too well, disfigures the foliage and the boys, assuming that the grapes had been poisoned, let them alone from then on. And the story might have ended there had it not been for the fact that about this time a serious epidemic of disease swept over the vineyards in that section of France, and the only vines that showed no trace of infection were those along the roadsides which had been sprayed with lime and copper sulphate. And it was in this way that the great fungicidal value of Bordeaux came to be known.

Copper lime dust is a commercial preparation which has been put on the market within recent years and is gaining rapidly in favor. It is a mixture of non-hydrated copper sulphate and hydrated lime and it practically makes Bordeaux mixture when it comes into contact with moisture on the plant. For best results it should be applied when the plants are wet with dew or rain.

Sulphur should always be kept on hand as it is indispensable in controlling mildew and many other diseases. Fine, dusting sulphur should be purchased, as it adheres to the foliage very much better than the ordinary flowers of sulphur. Sulphur may be used in combination with many other chemicals such as arsenate of lead and nicotine. It should preferably be applied in the late afternoon or evening as it has a slight tendency to burn very tender foliage when exposed to brilliant sunshine. This precaution does not need to be heeded unless the plants which are being dusted have very tender, delicate foliage.

Mercuric Compounds. Within recent years we have begun to appreciate the value of the various organic mercury compounds in fighting plant diseases and it is well to keep something of the sort on hand. Semesan and Uspulun are two commercial compounds recently put on the market and they are both excellent. Corrosive sublimate in tablet form may also be used.

WISE PRECAUTIONS

It is fortunate that under normal conditions plants are subject to the attack of only a small number of the various pests and diseases to which they are susceptible. Sad, indeed, would be the life of a gardener if this were not true. There are, for example, some 14 insect pests and diseases which attack dahlias and yet practically never would the plants be attacked by all of these in a single season. A few will probably make their appearance every year, some will be prevalent in some sections of the country and give little or no trouble in other sections, while others may suddenly appear one season and not be seen again for a number of years.

It is well, however, to take certain precautions in order to protect one's plants as far as possible from the various pests and diseases to which they are subject. One should become familiar with the common sources of infection and infestation and should use every possible precaution in guarding against them. There are, of course, some pests and diseases against which it is almost impossible to protect one's plants, no matter how careful one may be. If your neighbor's plants are attacked by certain fungous diseases you will probably get them sooner or later, as the spores are very easily blown about by the wind and nothing that you can do will prevent them from lodging upon your plants when the wind is in the right direction.

On the other hand, we find that many diseases are carried on the seed, on rhizomes, on bulbs and tubers, and on the foliage of newly-purchased plants, and in cases of this sort every precaution should be taken to guard against bringing infection into the garden. When making new purchases it would, therefore, be wise to observe the following rules.

CHRYSANTHEMUMS

Examine the foliage of newly purchased plants with care in order to detect any of the following signs of infection:

Dark spots or blotches on the foliage, indicative of Blight and Leaf Spot.

Small, rust-colored pustules on the under surface of the leaves, indicative of Chrysanthemum Rust.

Tiny galls on the upper surface of the leaves indicative of Chrysanthemum Midge.

If only a few leaves show signs of infection they may be removed and burned but if the plants are seriously affected they should be rejected or destroyed.

DAHLIAS

Examine tubers carefully for any signs of Rot. If the tubers have a soft, spongy feeling it is wise to reject them.

DELPHINIUMS

Examine the foliage and discard any plants that have small dark spots upon the leaves in order to avoid bringing the dreaded Bacterial Leaf-Spot into your garden.

GLADIOLUS

Remove the outer husk and reject or destroy corms that show any of the following signs of infection. As a precautionary measure against introducing disease it is wise to soak the corms for seven hours before planting in a solution of Semesan, one tablespoonful to one gallon of water.

Dark, reddish-brown spots on the lower portion of the corm near the old bulb scar—indicative of Dry Rot.

Dark brown spots with a water-soaked margin found on both the upper and lower surfaces of the corms—indicative of Hard Rot.

Dark sunken spots on the corms. Husks stuck to the corms with a peculiar varnish-like secretion—indicative of Neck Rot or Scab.

Corm a mass of dark, porous, rotting tissue—indicative of Penicillium Rot.

HOLLYHOCKS

Examine leaves, particularly on the lower surface, for small brown pustules which are a sign of Hollyhock Rust.

HYACINTHS

If bulbs show any signs of unsoundness, being discolored, light in weight, or soft and spongy, they should be rejected.

IRIS

Examine rhizomes for signs of rot. If badly affected they should be rejected. If only slightly affected the rotted portion may be carefully scraped out and the rhizome may then be treated as follows.

Dust thoroughly with sulphur, *or*

Soak for a few minutes in a pink solution of potassium permanganate, *or*

Soak in Semesan solution, one tablespoonful to one gallon of water.

If small holes and tunnels are found in the rhizomes it means that borers are or have been present. If the rhizomes are badly riddled they should be discarded. If only one or two holes are found the point of a small knife should be inserted up into the tunnel and the borers should be cut out if they are still there. By the early part of August the borers have usually passed into the pupa stage and although the holes may be found the borers will have departed.

LILIES

Examine the bulb for the following sign of infection.

Flesh of the bulb near the roots dark in appearance, bulb soft at the base, heart rotten—indicative of Bulb Rot.

Discard bulbs if seriously affected. If only very slightly affected, scrape away rotten portion and soak bulb for 1½ hours in a solution of carbolic acid, one part to forty parts of water. Then dust bulbs with powdered charcoal. Many gardeners consider it wise to maintain quarantine quarters for their lily bulbs in order to determine whether mosaic is present. (See Lily Diseases, Chapter XXXIII.)

NARCISSUS

Reject bulbs that show any of the following signs of infection or infestation:

Tissues soft and rotted—indicative of either Botrytis Bulb Rot or Gray Bulb Rot.

Bulbs soft and very light in weight. When cut open small maggots are found feeding upon the tissues—indicative of infestation from the Bulb Fly.

Bulbs soft and spongy. Tiny, reddish-brown spots found on the outer bulb scales—indicative of injury from the Bulb Mite.

Healthy bulbs are firm and solid and only such bulbs should be planted.

ROSES

In order to avoid bringing any of the dreaded forms of canker into your garden it is wise to be on the alert to detect signs of infection on newly purchased roses. Since roses are seldom in leaf when purchased it is not possible to detect the fungus spores of Black Spot and Mildew.

Purplish-red areas on the stems, indicative of Brown Canker.

Dark, swollen area at or just above the point of union of the stock and scion, bark cracked, wood somewhat lifeless in appearance—indicative of Crown Canker.

Brown, dry sunken areas on the stem—indicative of Stem Canker.

If the plants are seriously affected they should be rejected. If only an occasional branch is affected it may be cut back to well below the point of attack. When cutting back diseased canes it is well to dip the shears in some good disinfectant such as corrosive sublimate solution before passing from one bush to another.

TULIPS

Bulbs that show any of the following signs of infection should be rejected. Remove the outer husk when examining.

Deep, yellowish-brown lesions found on the outer bulb scales indicative of Botrytis Blight.

Top of the bulb soft and spongy, flesh a reddish-gray—indicative of Gray Bulb Rot.

Very small, reddish spots found on the bulb—indicative of the infestation of the Bulb Mite.

INSECTICIDE	TYPE	CONTROL FOR	HOW APPLIED	REMARKS
Arsenate of Lead	Stomach Poison	Standard control for most chewing insects.	As a spray. A spreader should be used to insure good coverage. May also be applied as a dust.	A good spray formula: 2 tblsp. arsenate of lead 2 tblsp. casein or 1 cup skim milk 1 gal. water
(Coated) Arsenate of Lead	Stomach Poison	Japanese beetles.	As a spray—4 lbs. to 50 gal. of water.	More effective against Japanese beetles than any other form of arsenate of lead.
Hellebore	Contact and Stomach Poison	Sawfly larvae.	As a spray.	1–2 oz. to 1 gal. water.
Lemon Oil	Contact	Various forms of scale.	As a spray.	
Lime-sulphur	Contact	Various forms of scale. Also a fungicide.	Usually as a dormant spray.	Follow manufacturer's instructions.
Magnesium Arsenate	Stomach Poison	Mexican bean beetles.	As a spray: 1 lb. to 50 gal. water or as a dust	
Miscible Oils	Contact	Various forms of scale.	As a spray when plants are dormant. Temperature must be above 45° F.	Used on trees, shrubs—both deciduous and evergreens.
Nicotine Dust	Contact	Aphids, leaf-hoppers, thrips, etc.	Apply with dust gun. Most effective when temperature is over 70° F. and when plants are dry.	Store in an airtight container.

Nicotine Soap Solution	Contact	Aphids, leaf-hoppers and most soft-bodied insects.	As a spray: 1 tsp. 40% nicotine 1 cu. in. soap 1 gal. water	Dissolve soap in hot water and add to the spray. Do not allow liquid nicotine to freeze.
Pyrethrum	Contact and Stomach Poison	Aphids, leaf-hoppers, young caterpillars.	As a dust and also as a spray.	Has the advantage of being non-poisonous to human beings and animals.
Rotenone	Contact and Stomach Poison	Flea beetle, cucumber beetles, cabbage worm and many caterpillars.	As a dust and also in the form of a spray.	Does not discolor the foliage.
Sodium Fluosilicate	Stomach Poison	Aster beetles, Mexican bean beetles.	As a dust: 1 part s.f. 9 parts hydrated lime	

FUNGICIDES

FUNGICIDE	CONTROL FOR	HOW APPLIED	REMARKS
Ammoniacal Copper Carbonate	Leaf spot on phlox.	As a spray.	Does not stain foliage. In most cases much less effective than Bordeaux.
Bordeaux	Leaf spot on asters, delphinium and digitalis; Botrytis Rot of lily; Peony Bud Blight; Anthracnose and Blight on snapdragons.	As a spray.	May be combined with lead arsenate and with nicotine sulphate to make a combination spray.
Copper-lime Dust	Leaf spot on chrysanthemums. Also other forms of leaf spot as above.	As a dust. Plants should be wet when application is made.	Store in airtight container. May be combined with arsenate of lead.
Corrosive Sublimate	Root rot of aquilegia, delphinium; Scab and Dry Rot of gladiolus corms; Bacterial Rot of iris.	As a solution to soak bulbs, corms, etc., or to drench the soil about the plant. Do not get on foliage.	Very corrosive to metal. Use wooden or earthenware container.
Formaldehyde Drench	Damping off, nematodes.	Dilute 1 gal. commercial formalin with 50 gal. water. Apply at rate of ½ to 1 gal. to each sq. ft. of soil. Cover soil for 24 hrs. with boards or paper. Do no planting until all odor of f. has disappeared. This may require 10 days to 2 weeks.	This method is injurious to some soils because of puddling.

Material	Uses	Directions
Formaldehyde Dust	Damping off, nematodes.	Mix 8 oz. of 6% f. dust with each bu. of soil or 6 oz. with each cu. ft. Shovel over thoroughly. Do not use soil except for sowing seeds until odor has disappeared. Usually about 72 hours. One of the most effective means of sterilizing the soil.
Red Copper Oxide	Damping off; seed- and soil-borne diseases.	As a dust for disinfecting seeds. As a drench for damping off. Full directions in Chapter on Propagation under Seed Sowing Indoors.
Sulphur	Mildew on chrysanthemums, delphiniums, phlox, roses. Partially effective against rust.	As a fine dust (300 mesh). The effectiveness of the sulphur depends upon the fineness of the particles. May be combined with arsenate of lead.

TABLE OF MEASUREMENTS

4 tablespoonfuls = ¼ cupful
16 tablespoonfuls = 1 cupful
4 cupfuls = 1 quart
4 quarts = 1 gallon

TABLE OF DILUTIONS

(No. of tablespoonfuls to 1 gallon of water)

Tablespoonfuls	Dilution
¼	1 to 1000
½	1 to 500
1	1 to 250
1¼	1 to 200
2½	1 to 100
5	1 to 50
10	1 to 25

FORMULAS

Arsenate of Lead
(Usual strength)

½ ounce or 2 tablespoonfuls to 1 gallon of water
3 pounds to 100 gallons water

SPRAYING PRECAUTIONS

As many spray materials are deadly poisonous, they must be handled with care and every precaution should be taken to protect children, birds, dogs and other animals.

PLANTS SELDOM ATTACKED BY PESTS
AND DISEASES

ANNUALS

Acrolinium (Everlasting)
Ageratum
Alyssum
Arctotis grandis
Balsam
Brachycome (Swan River Daisy)
Browallia
Calliopsis (Coreopsis)
Candytuft
Celosia (Cockscomb)
Clarkia
Cynoglossum (Houndstongue)
Didiscus (Blue lace flower)
Dimorphotheca (African orange daisy)
Eschscholtzia (California poppy)
Euphorbia marginata (Snow-on-the-mountain)
Gilia (Thimble flower)
Godetia
Gypsophila (Babysbreath)
Helichrysum (Straw flower)
Hunnemannia (Goldencup)
Incarvillea
Larkspur
Lupin
Mirabilis
Nemesia
Nemophila
Nierembergia
Nigella (Love-in-the-mist)
Nicotiana (Flowering tobacco)
Portulaca
Salpiglossis
Salvia splendens (Scarlet sage)
Scabiosa
Schizanthus
Shirley poppy
Stocks

PLANTS SELDOM ATTACKED BY PESTS AND DISEASES—*Continued*
PERENNIALS

Achillea (Yarrow)
Aconitum (Monkshood)
Adonis
Ajuga (Bugle)
Alyssum
Anchusa
Anemone
Arabis (Rock cress)
Artemisia
Asclepias tuberosa (Butterflyweed)
Aubrietia
Baptisia australis
Boltonia
Cerastium tomentosum (Snow-in-summer)
Cimicifuga (Black snake root)
Coreopsis
Crucianella (Crosswort)
Dicentra eximea (Fringed bleedingheart)
Dicentra spectabilis (Bleedingheart)
Echinops (Globethistle)
Erigeron (Fleabane)
Eupatorium
Geum
Gypsophila (Babysbreath)
Helenium (Sneezewort)
Helianthemum (Sunrose)
Helianthus (Hardy sunflower)
Hemerocallis (Daylily)
Hesperis (Sweet rocket)
Heuchera (Coral Bells)
Hibiscus
Iberis sempervirens (Hardy candytuft)
Liatris
Linum perenne (Perennial flax)
Lupin
Lychnis (Campion)
Mertensia (Virginia bluebells)
Myosotis (Forget-me-nots)
Nepeta Mussini

Plants Seldom Attacked by Pests and Diseases

PERENNIALS—*Continued*

Papaver nudicaule (Iceland poppy)
Papaver orientale (Oriental poppy)
Papaver pilosum (Olympic poppy)
Penstemon
Physostegia (False-dragonhead)
Platycodon (Balloonflower)
Plumbago larpentæ (Leadwort)
Potentilla (Cinquefoil)
Rudbeckia (Coneflower)
Salvia azurea (Azure sage)
Saponaria ocymoides (Rock soapwort)
Scabiosa
Sedum (Stonecrop)
Sempervivum (Houseleek)
Silene (Catchfly)
Spiræa Filipendula
Statice (Thrift)
Stokesia cyanea (Stoke's aster)
Thalictrum (Meadowrue)
Thermopsis
Tritoma (Red hot poker)
Trollius (Globe flower)
Verbascum (Mullein)
Veronica (Speedwell)

BIENNIALS

Bellis perennis (English Daisy)

XXXII

Diseases and Insect Pests of Trees and Shrubs

DISEASES AND PESTS

Anthracnose of Sycamore and Oak—Leaf and Twig Blight

Symptoms: The usual type of lesion appears as elongated brown spots along the main veins of the leaf. The infected tissue causes the death of the surrounding leaf tissue, and two or more lesions may involve an entire leaf. A tree so infected may appear from a distance to be scorched. The leaves soon drop after they are dead, and the tree may become completely defoliated by early summer. Sometimes the young twigs become infected and turn brown as they start to grow. This symptom is often confused with frost injury. Cankers may also appear on the twigs. The center of the canker is usually sunken with a slightly raised margin. The repeated killing of the young branches often produces a gnarled type of growth.

Nature of the Disease: The disease is caused by the fungus, Gnomonia veneta (Sacc. and Speg.) Klebahn. Of the oaks, those belonging to the red and white groups are most commonly affected. Frequent rains and a humid atmosphere promote the spread of the disease.

Control: All infected leaves should be raked up after they have fallen, and burned. Twigs bearing cankers should be carefully pruned out. Spray by means of a power spray with Bordeaux mixture (4–4–50 or 5–5–50). Be careful that all leaves are covered. The first application should be made after the buds have burst and before the leaves are half grown. A second application should be made about a week later. Three or four applications should be made if the season is a rainy, humid one.

Cedar-Apple Rust.

Symptoms: This fungus, like many rusts, has to have two different plants as hosts in order to complete its life history. In this case the two hosts are the ordinary cedar, Juniperus virginiana, and the crab or ordinary domestic apple. On the leaves of apples, the infection first appears as small yellow spots which enlarge, deepen in color, and frequently have reddish borders. On the under-surface of the leaf the tissue develops a cushion or blister on which small tubular projections appear. Likewise on the twigs small swollen areas develop, bearing many tubular projections. In the case of the cedar, galls, commonly called apples, are produced. On the surface of the gall, small round indentations are produced. In the spring, from these indentations arise gelatinous raylike processes. In this stage, the infection is sometimes called a cedar flower.

Nature of the Disease: The fungus, Gymnosporangium Juniperi-virginianæ Schw., causes the disease. The life history is as follows. The fungus winters over in the galls or cedar apples. In the spring, the gelatinous rays are produced which bear many spores. These spores infect the apple. Several stages of the life history are completed on the apple. In June, reinfection of the cedar may occur.

Control: If possible remove either the apples or the cedars as the fungus must have both plants to complete its life history. Spraying or dusting may also help to control the disease. Spray cedars with 6-6-48 Bordeaux, plus three pounds of soap in late July or early August. Apples should be dusted with 1–40 lime-sulphur when the blossoms show good color, within one or two days after the first blossom opens, when one-half to two-thirds of the petals have dropped, then four successive times at four- to five-day intervals.

Blister-Rusts of Pines

There are many forms of blister-rust which attack various species of pine, the most common being the fungus *Cronartium ribicola,* which causes the stem blister-rust of the white pine and of other five-needle pines. Young trees are the most susceptible, and on older trees it is the young branches which are first attacked.

As is true with practically all of the blister-rusts, part of the life-cycle of the fungus must be passed on an alternating host plant. In the case of the white pine blister-rust, currant and gooseberry bushes are the alternating hosts, and the only way in which the disease may be brought under complete control is by the destruction of all such bushes within a radius of 500 feet of any white pine plantings.

The injury caused by the white pine blister-rust is very characteristic. The young twigs are the first portion of the tree to become affected. When infection first takes place the bark becomes somewhat swollen, but it is not until the spring of the second or third year that the orange-colored fruiting bodies appear. When the covering of these blisterlike pustules has broken, the fine, powdery spores are liberated and are blown in every direction. These spores cannot infect other pine trees, however, for in order to complete their cycle they must find lodgement on the leaves of the currant or gooseberry.

At the point where the fruiting pustules appeared on the pine, a cankerous scar is left, and in many cases the branch becomes completely girdled and dies. If the infection extends into the trunk of the tree the growth becomes characteristically stunted and compact and there is a decidedly yellowish cast to the foliage. All affected branches and cankerous growths should be cut out as soon as infection is detected.

Fire Blight

This disease attacks the pome fruits such as apples, pears, and quinces, and to a lesser extent the stone fruits.

Symptoms: The flowers, leaves and twigs may be attacked. Blossoms begin to turn brown soon after they open. The infection may spread down the pedicels and into the adjacent leaves causing them to become dark and appear as if fired. The leaves may be directly affected in which case the infection starts at the margin of the leaf causing a darkened triangular area with its apex toward the midrib. Viscid drops of bacterial exudations may appear on the petioles or at the base of the leaf blades. The first evidence of twig infection may be the blackening or browning of the tip which soon wilts and dies. Cankers may appear on the branches. In active cankers the bark is darker in color and appears to be water soaked. The gummy exudation characteristic of bacterial ooze may be found.

Nature of the Disease: The disease is caused by the bacterium, Bacillus amylovorus. One of the most important disseminators of the disease is insects which transmit the bacteria to the various plants which they visit. The disease is also transmitted by dirty pruning instruments.

Control: Care should be taken that the plant makes a good sturdy growth. Spraying the trees with Bordeaux mixture (1–3–50) when the trees are in full bloom has been found very effective. Pruning instruments should be sterilized and cut surfaces should be painted with the following solution: mercuric chloride 1 ounce, mercuric cyanide 1 ounce, glycerine 3 gallons and water 1 gallon. Diseased twigs should be pruned out.

LEAF-CAST OF CONIFERS

This name refers to several similar diseases of pine, larch, fir, spruce, and juniper. Several other common names such as leaf-browning, leaf-reddening, and cracking-scurf have been applied to these diseases.

Symptoms: The general symptoms are similar to those of sun-scorch in that the needles die and turn brown. However, the first symptoms of leaf scorch differ in that yellow or brown bands or spots appear on the needle. Also in leaf-cast all the needles of a bunch are usually not affected simultaneously. The fruiting bodies of the fungus appear as roundish or elongated black pustules on the surface of the leaf. If the twigs are affected they either die or produce a witches broom type of growth.

Nature of the Disease: The diseases are caused by several fungi of the genera Lophodermium, Hypoderma, and Hypodermella.

Control: Spraying the trees with Bordeaux mixture before the rainy periods will help to control the disease.

LEAF SPOTS

Symptoms: There are many kinds of leaf spots on the various types of deciduous trees. Usually they are not fatal, but they may spoil the looks of the tree. The disease is characterized by the formation of dead areas in the tissue of the leaf. The areas may be large or small, round, angular or irregular. The spots may vary in color from yellow to black. In the case of more or less rounded spots the dead tissue often drops out and gives the leaf a shot hole appearance. In severe cases the trees may lose their leaves. As the season progresses, minute dark specks, which are the fruiting bodies, appear in the center of the spots.

Nature of the Disease: The fungi which cause these diseases belong to the following genera: Phyllostictia, Septoria, Cylindrosporium, Cercospora, Marssonia, and Glœosporium. Wet summers are particularly favorable to the development of these diseases.

Control: Remove and burn the fallen affected leaves. In cases where twigs have been infected, they should be pruned out. Sometimes it is advisable to spray or dust the leaves as they unfold and are still growing, using Bordeaux as for Anthracnose.

ROOT ROT

One of the commonest root rots is caused by the honey mushroom. It attacks a great variety of hosts. Among the evergreens it may attack cedars, firs, hemlocks, larch, and pine. Among broad-leaf trees it has been found on alder, beech, birch, walnut, almond, chestnut, locust, maple, mulberry, oak, sycamore, and poplar.

Symptoms: In conifers the trees exude an abnormal amount of resin. The needles turn brown and drop off. In broad-leaf trees the branches die back. The leaves may wilt rather suddenly and drop off prematurely. Root rot may also be due to poor soil conditions, but in such cases the tree seems to die more slowly, showing a gradual decrease from year to year. The final proof of the disease in both conifers and broad-leaf trees is the appearance of honey-colored mushrooms around the base of the tree.

Nature of the Disease: The disease is caused by the mushroom, Armillaria mellea (Vahl.) Sacc. The fungus usually enters through some injury in the root. If the soil is dug away, brown or black cord-like structures will be found associated with the roots or base of the trunk.

Control: This is one of the hardest diseases to control as it spreads so easily through the soil from tree to tree. Diseased trees should be removed at once. Replanting should not be done for at least three years. To prevent the spread of the disease it is often wise to dig a trench 1 foot wide and 2 feet deep about the diseased tree.

PROTECTING DOGWOOD FROM BORERS

Dogwood trees which have been transplanted are susceptible to borers because of their reduced vitality. Various repellent agencies have been developed to prevent borers from starting their excavations. One of the safest is a formula developed by the Michigan Experiment Station which contains naphthalene. It is non-toxic and can be painted on the trunk and branches by brush.

Another good repellent for borers is a mixture of one gallon of boiled linseed oil and one pound of Paradichlorobenzene crystals painted on the bark of trunk and larger branches in February and September. This is very effective when applied just before or just after a tree has been transplanted, and should be repeated twice a year for the first two years after transplanting.

Borers are the most difficult insects to reach and to destroy, once they have started, and anything which will prevent their entry is welcomed by the owner of valuable trees.

DUTCH ELM DISEASE

Symptoms: In the case of acute attacks the foliage of the entire tree may wilt rather quickly. The leaves may or may not turn yellow before wilting. Soon afterwards the tree may drop its leaves. However, the disease usually presents a more chronic condition, and only a few branches at a time are attacked. For this reason it is often difficult to distinguish from other diseases. The presence of branches bearing wilted or yellow branches should be investigated at once. A diagonal section through the twig will show, if the disease is present, a whole or partial brown ring. Sometimes the ring consists of a series of brown spots. The symptoms of the disease are so similar to other diseases that it is often difficult in the case of minor infections to recognize it.

Nature of the Disease: The disease is caused by the fungus, Ceratostomella ulmi (Schwarz) Buisman. The elm-bark beetle seems to be one of the principal carriers.

Control: The best control method now known is to destroy the tree as soon as infection is apparent. Pruning is usually not sufficient as the disease spreads rapidly through the tree. Surface spraying is not effective as the fungus develops beneath the surface.

TENT-CATERPILLARS

Tent-caterpillars are a serious pest of orchard and roadside trees in many sections of the country. They are particularly prevalent on wild cherry, apple, peach, and plum, and they occasionally attack beech, birch, oak, and willow trees. Unless measures of control are undertaken promptly, tent-caterpillars may entirely defoliate a tree in a comparatively short time.

The caterpillars pass the winter in the egg stage, the shiny, dark-brown egg-masses being attached to the twigs and small branches in a collar-like form. One of the most effective measures of control is the removal of these egg masses during the winter months when they are readily discernible upon the bare branches.

The eggs hatch in the spring about the time that the apple leaves begin to unfold, and the young caterpillars construct their weblike nests in the forks and crotches. They feed during the day upon the foliage of near-by branches, returning to the nest at night, and remaining in the nest during periods of rain. They are voracious feeders and become full grown in about a month. They then spin a cocoon upon the tree trunk and emerge from the pupa stage as a light brown moth.

As a means of protection, trees may be sprayed with arsenate of lead, 1½ pounds to fifty gallons of water. The nests may be destroyed by dipping a swab (a cloth tied to the end of a stick) into a can of discarded crank-case oil and then poking it into the web. This should be done in the evening after all the caterpillars have returned to the nest.

PESTS AND DISEASES OF ORNAMENTAL TREES AND SHRUBS

PLANT	PEST	DISEASE	INJURY	CONTROL	REMARKS
Arbor-vitæ	Leaf-miner		Foliage tips appear white or brownish. Tunnelled with small mines.	Spray early in July with nicotine and arsenate of lead.	
	Bagworm		Feeds on the foliage.	Spray with arsenate of lead in early spring.	Remove and burn all cases and bags.
	Red Spider		Foliage appears unhealthy. Upon close observation, minute pale spots may be found.	Dormant spray of miscible oil, 1 gal. to 30 gal. water, will destroy many winter eggs. Summer spray of Dritomic sulphur, 5 lbs. to 50 gal. water.	
		Twig Blight	Tips of the twigs are killed back.	Spray with Bordeaux in early spring.	Remove and burn all affected twigs.
		Leaf Blight or Black Leaf Spot	Lower branches appear as if scorched by fire.	Spray with Bordeaux as soon as disease is detected.	
Ash (Fraxinus)	Oyster-shell Scale See also p. 1079		Scales suck the juices from the tree and reduce its vigor.	Dormant spray of miscible oil, 1 gal. to 15 gals. water.	Scale may be observed clustered along twigs and branches.
Azalea	Lace-bug		Upper surface of foliage becomes spotted and grayish in appearance. In severe infestations foliage dries up and falls.	Spray with nicotine-soap solution as eggs are hatching. Mid to late May in latitude of New York.	The Lace-bug causes serious injury in many sections.

Beech (Fagus)	Woolly Beech Aphid	Foliage is unhealthy in appearance. Presence of aphids easily detected.	Spray with nicotine as soon as infestation is noted.	Purple beech particularly subject to infestation.
	Beech Scale	Vigor of tree reduced.	Dormant spray—miscible oil, 1 gal. to 15 gal. water.	
Birch (Betula)	Birch Leaf-miner	The miners feed upon the tissues between the upper and lower leaf surfaces, causing a browning of the foliage.	Spray in spring just after the eggs have been laid, with a nicotine-oil solution.	
	Birch Aphid	Sucks the juices from the foliage.	Spray with nicotine-soap solution as soon as infestation is noted.	
	Bronze Birch Borer	Indicated by dying tops. Smaller branches show ring-like ridges.	Cut and burn dying trees. In the beetle stage the insects feed to some extent upon the foliage. Spray in early June with arsenate of lead.	Feeding the trees to keep them in vigorous growing condition will often enable them to overcome injury from borers.
Box (See page 1078)				
Dogwood (Cornus)	Twig Blight	Tips of twigs die back.	Prune the affected twigs well below the point of injury.	Feed the trees to increase their vigor.
	Borers (several species infest the dogwood)	The borers tunnel under the bark causing the branches to die back and frequently causing the death of the tree.	Remove and burn all infested branches just after the leaves start. Spraying the foliage in May with arsenate of lead will destroy the adult beetles of certain species.	Keep trees in vigorous condition.

PLANT	PEST	DISEASE	INJURY	CONTROL	REMARKS
Elm (Ulmus)		Dutch Elm Disease	See page 1056 for full description.		
	Cankerworm		Foliage devoured and in the case of extreme infestations trees may become completely defoliated.	Spray with arsenate of lead just as the first green of the foliage appears in spring.	Sticky bands about the trunk of the tree from October to May will greatly lessen the chances of infestation.
	Bagworm (See Arbor-vitæ)				
	Brown-tail Moth		Feeds on foliage of many deciduous trees.	Spray with arsenate of lead, 4 lbs. to 100 gals.	Remove winter webs from ends of bare branches.
	White-marked Tussock-moth		The young caterpillars feed upon the under surface of the leaves, leaving only the veins.	Spray with arsenate of lead as soon as the presence of the caterpillars is detected.	There are many natural parasites, which help to keep the moth under control.
	Elm-leaf Beetle		The beetles eat oval holes in the foliage in early spring and will almost completely defoliate a tree.	Spray the under surface of the leaves with arsenate of lead as soon as injury is noted.	Particularly troublesome where trees are situated near old walls, or sheds, as the beetles winter in such shelters.
	Oyster-shell Scale		See Ash.	See Ash.	See Ash.

Plant	Pest	Description	Treatment	
Euonymus	Euonymus Scale	The scales feed upon the foliage as well as upon the woody parts.	Dormant spray of miscible oil: 1 gal. of oil 30 gal. of water Late summer spray: 1 gal. oil 50 gal. water.	
Horse-chestnut (Æsculus)	White-marked Tussock-moth	See Elm.	See Elm.	See Elm.
	Bagworm	See Arbor-vitæ.	See Arbor-vitæ.	See Arbor-vitæ.
Ivy (Boston) (Parthenocissus tricuspidata)	Caterpillar of 8-spotted Forester	The caterpillars feed upon the foliage.	Spray with arsenate of lead as soon as infestation is noticed.	
	Japanese Beetles	The beetles feed upon the foliage.	Spray with coated arsenate of lead.	
Japanese Quince (Chaenomeles lagenaria)	Scurfy Scale and San José Scale	Vigor of the plant is seriously diminished.	Dormant spray of miscible oil: 1 gal. of oil to 15 gal. of water.	
Juniper (Juniperus)	Bagworm and Red Spider	See Arbor-vitæ.	See Arbor-vitæ.	See Arbor-vitæ.
	Juniper Webworm	The larvæ feed within the web.	Pyrethrum spray. Use a strong force in order to penetrate the web.	
	Juniper Scale	Injures the vitality of the plant.	Dormant spray of miscible oil: 1 gal. oil to 30 gal. water.	

PESTS AND DISEASES OF ORNAMENTAL TREES AND SHRUBS—*Continued*

PLANT	PEST	DISEASE	INJURY	CONTROL	REMARKS
Juniper (Juniperus) —*Cont.*	Red-cedar Aphid		Feeds upon the smaller twigs and branches and sometimes causes the death of the tree.	Spray thoroughly with nicotine-soap solution in early spring.	
	Cedar-Apple Rust		See page 1052 for full description.		
Larch (Larix)	Japanese Beetle		See Ivy.	See Ivy.	
	Larch Case-bearer		The caterpillars cause a yellowing or browning of the foliage.	Spray with arsenate of lead in early spring.	
	Woolly Larch Aphid		Foliage has a white, powdery appearance.	Dormant spray of miscible oil: 1 gal. oil to 15 gal. water *or* a nicotine-soap solution in May.	
Laurel	Laurel Psylla		Growth stunted. Leaves become curled and thickened and have a smutty appearance. Leaf-galls are produced.	Spraying with miscible oil kills all stages except those which are protected by the galls.	
	Mulberry White-fly		The insects are found on the under surface of the leaves.	Spray the under surface of the leaves with a nicotine-miscible oil combination spray.	

Plant	Pest	Injury	Treatment	
Lilac (Syringa)	Leaf-spot	In early stage, the spots are small and reddish. Later they become larger with a light center and reddish border.	Spray with Bordeaux as soon as injury is detected.	
	Lilac Leaf-miner	Foliage seriously injured and may become completely skeletonized.	Spray with nicotine-soap solution when presence of miners is first detected.	
	Mildew	Foliage becomes covered with powdery mildew.	Dust or spray with sulphur.	
	Oyster-shell Scale	See Ash.	See Ash.	See Ash.
	Euonymus Scale	See Euonymus.	See Euonymus.	
Locust (Robinia)	Locust Leaf-miner	Feeds upon the foliage and often skeletonizes the upper surface of the leaves.	As soon as the leaves are fully developed spray with arsenate of lead, using casein as a spreader.	
Magnolia	Magnolia Scale	Decreases the vigor of the plant by sucking the juices.	Dormant spray of miscible oil: 1 gal. oil to 15 gal. water.	
Maple (Acer)	Cankerworm	See Elm.	See Elm.	See Elm.
	White-marked Tussock-moth	See Elm.	See Elm.	See Elm.
	Bagworm	See Arbor-vite.	See Arbor-vite.	See Arbor-vite.

PLANT	PEST	DISEASE	INJURY	CONTROL	REMARKS
Maple (Acer) —*Cont.*	Forest Tent-caterpillar		Feeds upon the foliage and may entirely defoliate the tree.	Spray with arsenate of lead as soon as the presence of the caterpillars is noted.	
	Maple Aphid		Leaves become wrinkled and blackened and dwarfed in size. May drop prematurely.	Spray the under surface of the leaves thoroughly with nicotine-soap solution.	Norway Maple is the species usually affected by aphids.
	Cottony Maple Scale		Reduces the vigor of the tree.	Spray with miscible oil in the early spring.	
Oak (Quercus)	Cankerworm		See Elm.	See Elm.	See Elm.
	Gipsy Moth		The caterpillars feed upon the foliage, often completely defoliating a tree.	Spray thoroughly with arsenate of lead as soon as infestation is noted. Destroy all egg cases during the winter.	
	Brown-tail Moth		See Elm.	See Elm.	See Elm.
	Oak Leaf-miner		Feeds upon the foliage.	Spray with nicotine-soap solution. Burn all infested leaves.	
		Anthracnose	See page 1051.		
	Golden Oak Scale		Vigor of the tree seriously affected. Twigs and branches killed.	Dormant spray of miscible oil.	

Plant	Pest	Symptoms	Treatment	
Pine (Pinus)	Pine Sawflies (several species)	The small caterpillar-like insects feed in clusters near the tips of the branches and they may defoliate an entire tree.	Spray with arsenate of lead as soon as infestation is noted.	
	Imperial Moth	The caterpillars feed upon the foliage, appearing in August and September.	Spray with arsenate of lead as soon as infestation is noticed.	
	Pine Leaf-miner	Begins feeding at the tips, causing them to turn yellow and dry up.	Spray in early spring with nicotine oil.	
Plane-tree (Platanus)	Bagworm	See Arbor-vitæ.	See Arbor-vitæ.	See Arbor-vitæ.
	Leaf and Twig Blight	See page 1051.	See Oak.	
Poplar	Gipsy Moth	See Oak.	See Oak.	
	Poplar Borer	Large, black, swollen scars on trunk and limbs.	Inject carbon disulphide in the openings and seal immediately with wax or putty.	
Rhododendron	Lace-bug	Causes a yellowish or brown spotting of the leaves.	Spray thoroughly with nicotine-soap solution as soon as infestation is noticed.	
	R. Clear-wing	Causes leaves to wilt. Small plants most frequently affected.	Prune away and burn all dead or infected wood.	

PESTS AND DISEASES OF ORNAMENTAL TREES AND SHRUBS—*Continued*

PLANT	PEST	DISEASE	INJURY	CONTROL	REMARKS
Spruce (Picea)	Spruce Leaf-miner		Foliage seriously affected. Leaves mined and webbed together.	Spray with arsenate of lead in early June.	
Tulip-tree (Liriodendron)	Tulip-tree Scale		Vigor of tree seriously affected. Twigs may become completely covered with the scales.	Dormant spray of miscible oil: 1 gal. oil to 15 gal. water.	
Viburnum	Viburnum Aphid		Leaves become curled and badly deformed. Sooty, black fungus appears.	Spray thoroughly with nicotine-soap solution just as leaves begin to develop.	
Walnut (Juglans)	Walnut Caterpillar		Very destructive and may completely defoliate a tree. Feeds in clusters.	Spray with arsenate of lead as soon as infestation is noted.	

Diseases and Insect Pests of Common Garden Plants

—————————————————————————

ANTIRRHINUM

(Snapdragon)

DISEASES

Anthracnose.

Symptoms: Small, brownish spots with a dark, narrow margin appear on the leaves. Cankerous formations develop on the stems, frequently girdling them. Growth is seriously affected and badly diseased plants may succumb entirely.

Nature of the Disease: A fungous disease caused by Colletotrichum antirrhini Stew. It is rather common on greenhouse plants and is frequently found on outdoor plants which have been started under glass.

Control: Thorough and systematic spraying with Bordeaux will keep anthracnose under control. Spray every 10 days to 2 weeks.

Blight.

Symptoms: Yellowish, somewhat circular spots appear on the foliage. Stems brownish. Occasionally dark shrunken areas resembling cankers are found on the stems. In the center of each leaf spot there is a minute black pimple which readily distinguishes Blight from other diseases attacking antirrhinums. Young seedlings die off rapidly when affected with Blight, apparently rotting off at the ground line. Older plants are more resistant but will succumb in time unless the disease is checked.

Nature of the Disease: A fungous disease caused by Phyllostictia antirrhini Sydow which is very prevalent in some sections.

Control: Spray thoroughly with Bordeaux.

Flower Spike Disease.

Symptoms: Flowers die prematurely. The lower blossoms at the base of the spike die first and the disease extends upward to the tip.

Nature of the Disease: A fungous disease caused by Sclerotinia sclerotiorum (Lib.) Mass. The fungus is carried to the stigma of the flower by bees and it is spread rapidly from plant to plant in this manner.

Control: All diseased flowers should be cut off and burned in order to remove sources of infection. Aside from this no effective measure of control is known.

Rust.

Symptoms: Stems and leaves become covered with rusty, brown pustules. If rust is allowed to gain headway the plants will be killed in a comparatively short time.

Nature of the Disease: A fungous disease caused by Puccinia antirrhini Diet. and Holw. The spores of the fungus are readily blown about by the wind and the disease spreads rapidly from plant to plant. As the spores require a certain amount of moisture for germination the disease is more prevalent during a rainy season than during a dry season.

Control: Dust thoroughly with superfine dusting sulphur. This is more in the nature of a preventive rather than a cure. When rust has once gained headway it is very difficult to control. As soon as the disease is first detected the infected plants should be pulled up and burned and all the other antirrhinums in the garden should be given a thorough dusting. It is well to be constantly on the alert to detect the first signs of trouble and if you have been troubled with rust in the past it will be wise to give the plants an occasional dusting just on general principles.

Rust resistant varieties are now obtainable in a variety of colorings.

Wilt.

Symptoms: Plants suddenly wilt and die as if from lack of water. When the stem is split open the sap tubes will be found to be dark and discolored.

Nature of the Disease: A fungous disease which attacks the plant through the roots. It is usually first introduced on infected seed and the fungus lives over in the soil for many years. Extremely moist conditions favor its spread.

Control: Pull up and burn all diseased plants. Disinfect the soil thoroughly before planting other antirrhinums.

Method No. 1—Soak the soil thoroughly with a solution of Semesan used at the strength of 1 tablespoon to 1 gallon of water.

Method No. 2—Use 1 pint of 40 per cent formaldehyde to 12½ gallons of water. Apply at the rate of one gallon of the solution to every square foot of soil. Let stand for twenty-four hours, then fork the soil over and aërate it well. Do not plant any seed or set out plants for several days.

AQUILEGIA

(Columbine)

DISEASES

Root Rot or Crown Rot.

Symptoms: Plants show general lack of vigor and rot off at the crown. They may be attacked at any time during the growing season or they may fail to winter over.

Nature of the Disease: A fungous disease caused by certain fungi known as Sclerotinia sclerotiorum (Lib.) Mass. It is becoming more and more prevalent and causes serious losses in some sections. The long-spurred types seem to be more susceptible than the old fashioned short-spurred varieties.

Control: Water the soil about the plants with either of the following solutions as soon as trouble is detected. As a safeguard against the disease it is well to make an occasional application through the growing season.

Semesan, 1 tablespoonful to 1 gallon of water, *or*

Corrosive sublimate solution, 1 oz. to 20 gallons of water. (When using the corrosive sublimate be sure that the soil about the plants is moist before it is applied.)

INSECT PESTS

Aphids.

Identification: Soft-bodied, lice-like insects which are usually found clustered near the tips of the young, growing shoots. They are light green in color and vary in size, the newly hatched young being considerably smaller than the adults.

Injury: Aphids suck the juices from the plant and cause a general lack of vigor and stunted growth.

Life History: In the North aphids pass the winter in the egg stage, while in the South where the winters are mild they continue to breed throughout the year. The eggs which are small, black and glossy in appearance hatch early in the spring and the young aphids begin feeding immediately. This first brood becomes mature in about two weeks and from then on, until autumn, living young are produced from unfertilized eggs. These are all females and reproduction takes place with startling rapidity as each mature female gives birth daily to several young and nearly one hundred generations are sometimes produced in a single season. In the autumn males appear and the eggs which carry the aphids over the winter are fertilized. The life history of the aphids is one of the most remarkable in the entire animal kingdom.

Control: Spray or dust with nicotine in some form. The first application should be made as soon as any infestation is noticed and it should be repeated every four or five days for several weeks. As it is necessary to reach each individual insect the spraying or dusting must be done with the utmost thoroughness.

Spray Formula

Black Leaf 40 .... 1 teaspoonful
Soap .... 1 cubic inch
Water .... 1 gallon

Leaf Miner (Phytomyza aquilegiæ Hardy).

Identification: Small worms which feed within the tissues of the leaf making a white serpentine trail. The trail usually crosses itself several times and ends in a small spot about ⅛ of an inch in diameter. Eight to ten larvæ sometimes develop within a single leaf.

Injury: The foliage becomes badly disfigured and the vitality of the plant is lowered.

Life History: The adult flies which are small and dark brown in color appear early in May. They feed for a short time, doing no noticeable damage, and then deposit their eggs on the under side of the leaves. The eggs hatch within a few weeks and the larvæ immediately tunnel their way into the leaves where they feed for about 10 days. They then pass into the pupa state, the tiny pupa being attached to the leaf. A short time later the adult flies emerge and the life cycle begins again. There are several generations during the summer, the last appearing about the middle of September. The winter is passed in the pupa state, the pupa case being buried in the soil close to the plants.

Control: Cultivate the ground thoroughly about the plants as early as possible in the spring in order to destroy the pupa cases before the flies emerge.

Remove and burn all infested leaves during the growing season.

Rose Beetles.

Identification: Long-legged beetles, grayish-fawn in color and about ½ inch in length.

Injury: The adult beetles feed upon the flowers, completely destroying them in a very short time.

Life History: Refer to page 1151.

Control: Picking the beetles off by hand and dropping them in a receptacle of water with a thin film of kerosene over it seems to be the one satisfactory measure of control. Any spray strong enough to control the beetles would ruin the fragile flowers of the columbines.

Clean cultivation in and about the garden is also advisable.

White Fly.

While white flies are generally regarded as greenhouse pests, they occasionally attack plants in the open. This is particularly apt to happen if the garden is located near a greenhouse or conservatory.

Identification: Very small, whitish flies about 1/16 of an inch long with four wings. They are found usually on the under surface of the leaves.

Injury: White flies suck the juices from the plant, causing a general lack of vigor. The leaves turn yellow and if the infestation is severe the plant eventually dies.

Life History: The females deposit their minute, yellow eggs on the under side of the leaves upon which they are feeding. The young nymphs which hatch from the eggs are very small and almost flat, being a pale green, somewhat transparent color. The nymphs feed for about four weeks and pass through four molts before they become full grown. The average life of an adult fly is between 30 and 40 days and many generations are produced during the year.

Control: Spray thoroughly with a nicotine solution, making sure to reach the under surface of the leaves. Several applications should be made 3 or 4 days apart.

Spray Formula

Black Leaf 40	1 teaspoonful
Water	1 gallon
Soap	1 cubic inch

ASTER (ANNUAL)

(Callistephus)

DISEASES

Leaf Spot.

Symptoms: Small dark spots appear on the leaves, gradually becoming larger.

Nature of the Disease: A fungous disease which is prevalent in some sections. It is caused by Septoria callistephi Gloyer, ascochyta asteris Gloyer, Botrytis sp.

Control: Spray with Bordeaux as soon as the disease is detected. Occasional applications throughout the balance of the season are also advisable.

As the disease is carried on the seed it is a wise precaution to disinfect all aster seed before planting. This may be done by soaking them for 1½ hours in a 3 per cent solution of hydrogen peroxide.

Rust.

Symptoms: Orange-colored patches of rust appear on the leaves and unless the disease is checked the leaves turn yellow and die.

Nature of the Disease: A fungous disease caused by Caleosporium Solidaginis (Schw.) Thum., one stage of which is passed on asters or closely related plants, the other stage being passed on pine trees.

Control: Occasional dusting with fine sulphur will, to a large extent, prevent attacks of rust. It is not, however, an effective remedy after the disease has gained headway. All infected plants should be pulled up and burned in order to prevent the spread of the spores. Some varieties seem to be much more susceptible to rust than others.

Wilt.

Symptoms: Young plants in the seed bed are frequently attacked and rot off at the ground line. The time of transplanting and of blossoming seem to be susceptible periods for older plants. The lower leaves are usually affected first, turning a yellowish green in the early stages, later becoming withered and black. Occasionally only one side of the plant is affected. Dark streaks develop in the cortext of the stem and in severe cases the stems and roots rot away entirely. Plants sometimes die quickly when attacked and sometimes linger on for months, producing a few small blooms.

Nature of the Disease: Wilt is a fungous disease caused by Fusarium conglutinans vr. callistephi Beach. which attacks the plant through the roots. It is usually first introduced on infected seed and the fungus lives over in the soil for many years. Extremely moist conditions favor its spread.

Control: Use clean seed and be sure that the soil both in the seed bed and in the garden is free from infection. If there is danger of infection treat the seed and soil as follows:

Soak seed for 1½ hours in a 3 per cent solution of hydrogen peroxide.

Disinfect soil with a Semesan solution, 1 tablespoon to 1 gallon of water.

Yellows.

Symptoms: Plants become dwarfed if attacked when young. Older plants have a curiously bushy and erect habit of growth, the young branches which arise from the axils of the leaves being thin and yellowish in color. Leaves that are not mature at the time infection takes place turn bright yellow. This is first evidenced by a slight yellowing along the veins. Occasionally only one side of a plant is affected. The injury to the flowers is very characteristic of the disease, the blossoms becoming dwarfed and distorted and frequently developing only on one side. Plants are practically never killed outright, usually living on until cut down by frost.

Nature of the Disease: The Yellows is caused by a virus in the sap of the plant. A leaf-hopper (Cicadula sexnotata Fall.) is the principal and probably only carrier. The disease apparently cannot be spread in any other way. One can handle badly diseased plants without any fear of spreading the infection. Many other closely related plants are attacked by the Yellows and the disease is carried over the winter by perennial hosts.

Control: In order to control the Yellows it is first necessary to control the leaf-hoppers which spread the infection by injecting the virus into the plant when they feed. This may be done by spraying or dusting every week or ten days with some form of nicotine. It is also a wise precaution to destroy diseased plants in order to remove sources of infection from the path of the leaf-hoppers.

Spray Formula

Black Leaf 40	1 teaspoonful
Soap	1 cubic inch
Water	1 gallon

Black Blister Beetle, also known as **Aster Beetle.**

Identification: A slender, jet-black beetle about ½ inch in length with prominent head and neck.

Injury: The beetles feed voraciously upon the flowers, completely destroying them in a short time.

Life History: The winter is passed in the larva stage, the grubs pupating early in the spring. The adult beetles appear about the middle of June.

Control: Dust the plants thoroughly with sodium fluosilicate. This should be applied when the foliage is absolutely dry.

The following spray has also been found effective:

Nicotine oleate .... 1 oz.
Water .... 1 gal.

Buffalo Tree Hopper.

Identification: A small, green insect about ⅜ of an inch long, triangular in shape with a two-horned enlargement at the front.

Injury: The nymphs and adult insects feed upon the plants and do considerable damage if they become numerous.

Life History: The eggs are deposited in slits in the bark of trees and occasionally in the bark of rose bushes. The winter is passed in the egg stage and late in the spring the small, green nymphs hatch out and begin feeding on the sap of various plants. They become full grown by August and the adult females die as soon as they have deposited their eggs.

Control: The only satisfactory measure of control for the Buffalo Tree Hopper seems to be clean cultivation in and about the garden. Hand picking may also be resorted to on small areas.

Leaf Miner.

Identification: Small worms which feed within the tissues of the leaf, making a white serpentine trail. The trail usually crosses itself several times and ends in a small spot about ⅛ of an inch in diameter. Eight to ten larvæ sometimes develop within a single leaf.

Injury: The foliage becomes badly disfigured and the vitality of the plant is lowered.

Life History: See page 1070.

Control: Cultivate the ground about the plants as early as possible in the spring in order to destroy the pupæ cases before the flies emerge.

Remove and burn all infested leaves.

Leaf Roller.

Identification: Small caterpillars about ¾ of an inch in length when full grown. They vary in color from yellow to light green.

Injury: The caterpillars feed upon the flower buds and the foliage, rolling and tying the leaves in a very characteristic manner with fine silken threads.

Life History: The moths deposit their eggs in tiny masses upon the foliage of the host plants. The young caterpillars hatch out a few weeks later and begin feeding. They become full grown in about a month and pupate within the rolled leaves. The pupa stage extends over a period of about two weeks. The adult moths then emerge and the life cycle begins again. Two broods are generally produced during the season.

Control: Spray or dust with arsenate of lead. Open the leaves which have already been rolled and destroy the caterpillars or pupæ found within.

Spray formula: 3 teaspoonfuls arsenate of lead powder
                1 gallon of water

Root Aphids.

Identification: Soft-bodied, whitish-gray insects found clustered along the roots or near the crown of the plant.

Injury: Root aphids suck the juices from the plant causing it to become dwarfed and stunted. The foliage frequently turns yellow, indicating general lack of vigor.

Control: Pour ½ cupful of nicotine solution (¼ teaspoonful of Black Leaf 40 to 1 quart of water) about the base of each plant, making sure that the soil is cupped out about the crown in order that the solution may reach the roots and not run off the surface.

Keep the ground about the plants well cultivated.

Where there is danger of infestation it is advisable to use a handful of tobacco dust in each hole as the seedlings are transplanted.

Stalk Borer (Common).

Identification: Slender caterpillars about an inch or two in length. The young caterpillars are brown with white stripes. When full grown they lose their stripes and become a solid, dirty gray in color.

Injury: The stalk borer makes a small, round hole in the stem and tunnels up through the stalk causing the injured shoot to suddenly wilt and break over.

Life History: The Common Stalk Borer passes the winter in the egg stage, the eggs being laid on grasses and weeds in the autumn. The larvæ hatch very early in the spring and when small they attack the stems of grasses but as they grow they become more ambitious and attack larger plants. They change frequently from the stem of one plant to that of another, seldom remaining for any length of time in one place. The caterpillars become full grown about the first of August and pass into the pupa stage within the stem of the plant upon which they happen to be feeding at the time. Late in September the adult moths emerge and the females deposit their eggs.

Control: Clean cultivation about the garden in order to destroy breeding places is one of the most important measures of control.

Cut off and burn infested shoots or insert a small wire with a hook on the end of it into the tunnel and drag the culprit out. If this is done as soon as trouble is detected the shoot may sometimes be saved.

Tarnished Plant Bug.

Identification: A small, very active bug about ¼ inch in length. The body is oval in shape, being somewhat triangular in front. Coppery-brown in color with dark brown and yellow flecks on the back.

Injury: The bugs puncture the shoots just below the flower heads, causing the buds to droop and die. The injury completely destroys any chance of bloom. It is thought that while feeding the Tarnished Plant Bug injects some substance into the sap that is highly injurious to the plant and has the effect of a poison.

Life History: The adults live over the winter in the shelter of long grasses and with the first warm days of spring they become very active and begin feeding. The eggs are usually laid in the stems of herbaceous plants, occasionally in growing fruit such as peaches. Two generations are produced during the season.

Control: A good nicotine dust or spray is usually effective against the young nymphs. Application should be made early in the morning. Spraying is not a satisfactory measure of control for the adults, however. Bordeaux acts as a repellent but hand picking seems to be the only sure method of getting rid of them. This should be done in the evening or early in the morning when they are less active and may be shaken off into a pan of water covered with a thin film of kerosene.

Clean cultivation both in and about the garden will destroy breeding places and will aid in keeping the Tarnished Plant Bug under control.

White Fly.

Identification: Very small whitish flies, about 1/16 of an inch in length. Four wings. Found usually on the under surface of the leaves.

Injury: White flies suck the juices from the plant causing a general lack of vigor. Leaves turn yellow and if the infestation is severe the plant will eventually die.

Life History: See page 1071.

Control: Spray thoroughly with a nicotine solution, making sure to reach the under surface of the leaves.

Spray Formula

Black Leaf 40	1 teaspoonful
Water	1 gallon
Soap	1 cubic inch

White Grubs.

Identification: Large, fleshy grub worm, grayish-white in color with a brown head and six prominent legs. They are usually found in a curled position, buried in the soil.

Injury: The grubs feed upon the roots causing the plant to become stunted and weakened. If the infestation is severe the plants may die.

Life History: Both the larvæ and the adult beetles, known as June Beetles, winter over in the soil. In the spring the adults emerge from the soil at night, feeding while it is dark and returning to the soil at daybreak. The females deposit their eggs several inches below the surface of the soil, generally selecting grassy fields or weedy areas. The eggs hatch in two to three weeks and the young grubs begin feeding on the roots of nearby plants. Some species complete their growth in 1 year while others require from 2 to 4 years. The most common species requires 3 years and the grubs cause the greatest damage during the second feeding season. During the winter they burrow down below the frost line. Grub worms are particularly troublesome on grassy or weedy ground.

Control: Use either of the following remedies:

Make a round, diagonal hole about an inch in diameter and deep enough so that the bottom is below the base of the plant. Insert a funnel into the hole and pour in one teaspoonful of carbon bisulphide. Plug up the opening of the hole and leave undisturbed for several days. *Or* pour one half cupful of carbon bisulphide emulsion about the base of each plant.

BOX

Box Leaf Miner.

Identification: The adult form of the box leaf miner is a yellowish fly, slightly smaller than a mosquito. These flies may readily be distinguished by their very definite yellow coloring. The larvæ are small, being only about 1/10 of an inch long when full grown, and they are a muddy white in color.

Injury: The lower, more protected branches are usually the first to become infested. Leaves in which the miners are at work gradually turn yellow and drop prematurely. Bushes that are badly infested present a scraggly, unthrifty appearance.

Life History: The adult flies emerge from the pupa stage in late April or early May. The emerging period for the entire brood extends over several weeks. The average life of the adult fly is about 2 days and soon after emerging the females deposit their eggs within the leaf tissues, piercing through the epidermis on the under surface. The eggs hatch during the next 2 or 3 weeks and the tiny larvæ feed within the tissues of the leaves throughout the summer and autumn and the early spring of the following year. In late March or early April the larvæ pass into the pupa stage and 3 or 4 weeks later the adult flies emerge and the life cycle begins again.

Control: The most effective measure of control consists of coating the foliage with some substance which is both poisonous and sticky in order to kill the adult flies as they emerge or as they alight to deposit their eggs. It is therefore imperative that the spray be applied at the proper time. The exact date when the first adult flies emerge varies somewhat with the season. As a general rule they appear about 10 days after the dogwoods have come into bloom and at this time the foliage should be well coated. The spray should be applied with a compressed air sprayer and care should be taken to see that all parts of the bush are covered, particularly the lower branches, the innermost shoots and the under side of the leaves. Subsequent applications should be given every 6 or 7 days for a period of at least 3 weeks. If heavy showers occur in the interim additional applications should be given. It is possible to keep the spray from being washed off by spreading muslin or canvas over the bushes during the time when it is raining. In addition to killing the adult flies the spray will destroy a large number of eggs and will also kill some of the flies before they emerge from the pupa stage. If spraying is done systematically and thoroughly the box leaf miner may be kept under absolute control.

Spray Formula

Cheap molasses	1 gallon
Black Leaf 40	5 teaspoonfuls
Water	4 gallons

Box Psylla.

Identification: Small, greenish insects about ⅛ of an inch in length, the body being covered with a white, waxy secretion. They are usually found at the tips of the young terminal shoots.

Injury: The young nymphs feed upon the young, growing shoots, sucking the juices from the plant and causing a very characteristic curling of the leaves at the tips of the branches. The damage done by the box Psylla is usually not very serious unless the bushes are heavily infested.

Life History: The adults emerge in late April or early May and the females lay their eggs upon the tips of the young shoots. Several weeks later the nymphs hatch out and begin feeding.

Control: The control is practically the same as for the box leaf miner. Most of the box Psylla nymphs are killed at the time the application of the molasses-nicotine spray is made.

Oyster Shell Scale.

Identification: Small, grayish-white scales, resembling an oyster shell in shape. They are usually found clustered in masses along the lower branches and the innermost twigs.

Injury: The scales suck the juices from the bush greatly lowering its vigor and vitality. If the infestation is not checked they will in time cause its death.

Life History: During the winter the eggs are protected by the hard, shell-like covering of the old scales. The young hatch out about the end of May or early in June. At this stage they are soft-bodied and look like small, yellowish-white specks crawling about on the branches. Soon after hatching they select a place to feed and pierce through the outer bark. As the season advances the hard, shell-like covering is formed.

Control: It is possible to destroy the young scales while they are are in the soft-bodied stage, and the spraying should be done at this time. It is wise to spray about June 1st and again on June fifteenth.

Spray Formula

Fish-oil soap .... 1 pound
Black Leaf 40 .... 1 ounce
Water .... 4 gallons

Spider Mites.

Identification: Minute animals hardly visible to the naked eye. Their presence may usually be detected by their characteristic injury.

Injury: The mites suck the juices from the young, tender leaves of the new growth, causing the foliage to lose its fresh, bright green color. The infested leaves at first become mottled, later taking on a dull, grayish-brown appearance and dropping prematurely.

Life History: The winter is passed in the egg stage, the eggs being infinitesimal, round, pinkish dots. The first brood hatches in April and as they breed rapidly four or five generations are produced during a single season.

Control: A thorough dusting with sulphur is the most effective measure of control as the fumes kill both the mites and the eggs. The number of applications will depend to a large extent upon the severity of the infestation.

CALENDULA

DISEASES

Mosaic.

Symptoms: The foliage has a curiously mottled appearance, being blotched and streaked with yellow. In some cases the leaves become distorted in shape.

Nature of the Disease: Aphids and leaf hoppers are probable carriers of the disease in very much the same way as mosquitos carry malaria to human beings. In sucking the juices of a diseased plant these insects pick up the infectious virus, later transmitting it to healthy plants.

Control: When once injected the virus penetrates to every portion of the plant and there is no known cure for the disease.

All diseased plants should be pulled up and burned in order to lessen sources of infection.

Nicotine dusts and sprays may be used to keep both the aphids and leaf hoppers in check.

Soft Rot.

Symptoms: Plants rot away. The rotted tissues are frequently covered with a white mold.

Nature of the Disease: A fungous disease which is apt to be prevalent during damp seasons. The resting bodies of the fungus, known as sclerotia, resemble little hard, black balls.

Control: Remove and destroy all infected plants.

Do not let young seedlings become too crowded.

Water plants and soak the ground about them with some organic mercury solution such as

Semesan, 1 tablespoonful to 1 gallon of water

INSECT PESTS

Aphids.

Identification: Soft-bodied, louse-like insects which are usually found clustered near the tips of the young shoots. They are light green in color and vary in size, the newly hatched young being considerably smaller than the adults.

Injury: Aphids suck the juices of the plant and cause a general lack of vigor and stunted growth.

Life History: See page 1069.

Control: Spray or dust with nicotine in some form. The first application should be made as soon as any infestation is noticed and it should be repeated every 4 or 5 days for several weeks. As it is necessary to reach each individual insect the spraying or dusting must be done with the utmost thoroughness.

Spray Formula

Black Leaf 40	1 teaspoonful
Soap	1 cubic inch
Water	1 gallon

Black Blister Beetle also known as **Aster Beetle.**

Identification: A slender, jet black beetle about ½ inch in length with prominent head and neck.

Injury: The beetles feed upon the flowers, completely destroying them in a short time.

Life History: See page 1074.

Control: Dust the plants thoroughly with sodium fluosilicate. This should be applied when the foliage is absolutely dry.

The following spray has also been found effective

Nicotine oleate	1 oz.
Water	1 gallon

Cabbage Worm.

Identification: Small, velvety, green caterpillars, somewhat more than an inch in length when full grown.

Injury: Large, irregular holes eaten in the foliage.

Life History: The winter is passed in the pupa stage and the adult butterflies which are white with three or four black spots on the wings emerge early in the spring. The females lay their small, yellow eggs one at a time upon the under surface of the leaves of the various host plants. Several hundred eggs are laid by each female. The very small, green caterpillars hatch out in about a week and begin feeding immediately. They develop rapidly, becoming full grown within a few weeks, and they then pass into the pupa stage. Several weeks later the adult butterflies emerge and one generation swiftly succeeds another throughout the summer until sometimes as many as five or six broods are produced.

Control: Spray or dust with arsenate of lead as soon as infestation is noticed.

Spray Formula

Arsenate of lead ....½ oz.
Fish oil soap ....1 cubic inch
          (dissolved in boiling water)
Water ....1 gallon

Dust Formula

Arsenate of lead ....1 part
Sulphur ....3 parts

Stalk Borer.

Identification: Slender, caterpillars about 2 inches in length when full grown. The young caterpillars are brown with white stripes. When full grown they lose their stripes and become a solid, dirty gray in color.

Injury: The stalk borer makes a small round hole in the stem and tunnels up through the stalk, causing the injured shoot to suddenly wilt and break over.

Life History: See page 1076.

Control: Clean cultivation about the garden in order to destroy breeding places is important.

Cut off and burn infested shoots or insert a small wire with a hook on the end of it into the tunnel and drag the borer out.

White Fly.

Identification: Very small, whitish flies about 1/16 of an inch in length. Four wings. Found usually on the under surface of the leaves on plants near greenhouses.

Injury: White flies suck the juices from the plant causing a general lack of vigor.

Life History: See page 1071.

Control: Spray thoroughly with a nicotine solution.

Spray Formula

Black Leaf 40 .... 1 teaspoonful
Soap .... 1 cubic inch
Water .... 1 gallon

CALLA LILY

DISEASES

Root Rot.

Symptoms: The plants appear normal for a time, then the outer leaves begin to yellow along the margins, and gradually the whole leaf yellows and droops. Other leaves are affected progressively inward. However, new leaves continue to develop. If flowers are developed the spathe usually does not open properly. The tip of the spathe may turn brown.

Nature of the Disease: The disease is caused by the fungus, Phytophthora richardia. If the roots are examined, they are found to be infected. The feeder roots start rotting at the tips, and the infection sometimes spreads through the root to the corm. The rot in the corm is more or less dry and spongy.

Control: The fungus is carried on the corms; therefore it is wise to sort them carefully and discard the infected ones. Corms may be treated by soaking for 2 hours in 1 to 1000 solution of corrosive sublimate or for 1 hour in 2 per cent formaldehyde solution. As the infection lives over in the soil, it is best to change or sterilize the soil before replanting.

Soft Rot.

Symptoms: The leaf stalks are often attacked near the base. Water-soaked areas develop which later become dark and slimy. The leaf blade yellows at the tip and along the margins, and as the infection spreads, becomes entirely yellow, shrivels and dies. If the flower is attacked, the flower turns yellow and the stalk eventually falls over.

1083

Nature of the Disease: The disease is caused by the bacterium, Bacillus carotovorus. The top of the corm at or just below the top of the soil is usually attacked first. The plant may rot off at this point. Sometimes it spreads downward through the corm producing a soft, mushy rot with a foul odor.

Control: See Calla Root Rot.

CARNATION

DISEASES

Rust.

Symptoms: The rust is first characterized by yellow swollen areas on the leaves and stem. These soon break open and expose the brown spores. The whitish ruptured edges of the epidermis give the pustules a ragged appearance.

Nature of the Disease: The disease is caused by the fungus Uromyces caryophyllinus. The infection usually extends throughout the entire plant.

Control: Cuttings should be taken only from healthy plants. Both field and pot-grown plants should be sprayed at 2- to 3-week intervals. This same spray schedule should continue after the crop is benched until it is finally taken out. Either Bordeaux mixture or lime-sulphur is a satisfactory spray. However, a good spreader should be used, as carnation leaves are coated with a waxy material which is very difficult to wet. The plants should not be syringed any more than necessary. Care should be taken in watering to wet the foliage as little as possible.

Stem Rot.

Symptoms: This is a very common disease of carnations. It may attack cuttings or older plants. In the case of cuttings and plants which have recently been potted, the plants may appear to damp-off. On older plants, the rot usually starts at an injury in the cortex of the stem. As the infection spreads it girdles the stem and the plant then wilts and dies. In this type of infection, the rot is more or less dry and corky.

Nature of the Disease: The disease is caused by the fungus, Rhizoctonia solani.

Control: See Carnation Rust.

Leaf Spot.

Symptoms: Circular or oblong spots which are blanched or pinkish with purple borders develop on the leaves. In the center of the spot are small black dots. Sometimes the stem may also become infected.

Nature of the Disease: The disease is caused by the fungus, Septoria dianthi. The disease is most abundant on the lower part of the leaves. The diseased part often becomes contracted, causing the leaves to be bent and curled.

Control: See Carnation Rust.

Alternaria Leaf Spot.

Symptoms: The disease appears as spots on the leaves, which become infected near the tip and die back, and sometimes on the stems, especially at the nodes. The spots are white with the center occupied by a black fungous growth.

Nature of the Disease: The disease is caused by the fungus, Alternaria dianthi. The lower leaves are usually more seriously infected than those at the top of the plant. When the stem becomes infected, the part of the plant above the infection dies.

Control: See Carnation Rust.

Bud Rot.

Symptoms: This disease affects only the flowers of the plant. In some cases the buds do not open, others fail to expand perfectly while others are only slightly abnormal. The petals are first infected, then the sepals. The entire flower may rot and turn brown.

Nature of the Disease: The disease is caused by the fungus, Sporotrichum anthophilum. Mites are usually found associated with the disease and are believed to carry the spores. The fungus can sometimes be seen with the naked eye.

Control: Clean cultivation.

CAMPANULA

DISEASE

Root Rot.

Symptoms: Plants show signs of wilting; tips of the branches dry up, foliage turns a pale, yellowish green, roots become rotted. Occasionally only a single branch is affected.

Nature of the Disease: The Root Rot of the Campanula is caused by the fungus, Sclerotium Rolfsii Sacc., and it is particularly troublesome during hot, wet weather. The fungus produces small, brown, resting bodies resembling mustard seed.

Control: Remove and burn badly infected plants.

Water plants thoroughly with an organic mercury solution such as
Semesan, 1 tablespoonful to 1 gallon of water

INSECT PEST

Rose Beetle.

Identification: Long-legged beetles, grayish-fawn in color and
about ½ inch in length.

Injury: The beetles feed upon the flowers.

Life History: See page 1151.

Control: Pick the beetles off by hand and drop them into a can
of water with a thin film of kerosene over it.

CANNA

DISEASE

Bud Rot.

Symptoms: The young buds become a mass of rotted tissue and
the foliage becomes spotted. The disease is seldom fatal and vigorous plants will often entirely outgrow it. When plants are severely
attacked, however, it causes considerable loss of bloom.

Nature of the Disease: A bacterial disease caused by Bacterium
cannæ Bryan. Some varieties seem to be much more susceptible to it
than others.

Control: Root stocks should be selected from clean, healthy plants.

INSECT PESTS

Corn Ear Worm.

Identification: Large striped worms about two inches in length
when full grown. They vary in color from light green to brown and
the stripes, which run lengthwise with the body, are alternating
light and dark. The head is yellow, the legs almost black.

Injury: The caterpillars feed upon both the foliage and the flower
buds, causing considerable damage.

Life History: The adult female moths deposit their eggs upon the
host plants, flying only in the evening or on dark, cloudy days. The
eggs are laid singly and an individual moth will deposit anywhere
from 500 to 2,000 during her lifetime. The eggs hatch in from 3 to
5 days and the larvæ feed ravenously for about 3 weeks. At this time
they have reached their full growth and drop to the ground where
they burrow into the soil and form a small cell-like structure in
which the pupa stage is passed. Two to three weeks later the adult
moths emerge and the life cycle begins again. From two to three
generations are produced each year and the winter is passed in the

pupa stage 4 to 5 inches beow the surface of the soil. Before entering the pupa stage the larva carefully prepares a small exit tunnel through which the moths may crawl when they are ready to emerge. The moths vary in color from light gray to brown.

Control: Dust or spray with arsenate of lead.

Greenhouse Leaf Tyer. Although primarily a greenhouse insect the leaf tyer is often troublesome on garden flowers.

Identification: Slender, yellowish green caterpillars having a broad white stripe running lengthwise down the back with a dark green band in the center of the stripe. When full grown they are about ¾ of an inch in length.

Injury: The caterpillars feed upon the leaves, often completely skeletonizing them. They also form a light web which draws the edges of the leaves together in a very characteristic way.

Life History: The adult moths, which are of a brownish color, fly usually at night and the females lay their eggs upon the underside of the leaves of the host plants. The eggs hatch in about 2 weeks and the larvæ begin feeding. When the caterpillars are full grown and ready to pupate they roll the edge of the leaf over and fasten it with a delicate web. Within this shelter they spin their silken cocoons and 10 days later the adult moths emerge. The life cycle takes about 40 days and several generations are produced each season.

Control: Spray or dust with arsenate of lead, making sure to reach the undersurface of the leaves.

Leaf Rollers. Cannas are attacked by two distinct species of leaf rollers. These are both very prevalent in some sections of the South but are seldom seen in the North.

Lesser Canna Leaf roller.

Larger Canna Leaf roller.

Injury: The caterpillars feed upon both the foliage and the blossoms, rolling and tying the leaves together with fine silken threads.

Control: Spray or dust with arsenate of lead, taking care to reach the undersurface of the leaves. Open the leaves which have already been rolled and destroy the caterpillars or pupæ found within.

Rose Weevil.

Identification: Dull, brownish gray beetles slightly over ¼ inch in length with a white line running diagonally across each wing.

Injury: The beetles feed upon the foliage, unopened buds and flowers. Most of their feeding is done at night.

Control: The beetles may be trapped under boards placed on the surface of the soil beneath the plants in the daytime. The plants may also be protected by banding them with little strips of fly paper or other sticky material. If the infestation is very severe carbon bisulphide may be used. Make a round diagonal hole about an inch in diameter and about four inches deep. Insert a funnel into the hole and pour in one teaspoonful of carbon bisulphide. Plug up the opening and leave undisturbed for several days.

Saddle-back Caterpillar.

Identification: A caterpillar about an inch in length and of very striking appearance. It is brown at each end, the main part of the body being light green with a little purple saddle over the back. It also possesses stinging, poisonous hairs.

Injury: The caterpillars feed upon the foliage and the flowers.

Control: Spray or dust with arsenate of lead.

Be careful not to touch the caterpillars with the bare hands as certain hairs on the body inject a poison into the skin which causes a very unpleasant, stinging sensation.

Spotted Cucumber Beetle.

Identification: A yellowish green beetle about ¼ inch in length with twelve very conspicuous black spots on its back. The head and antennæ, which are almost two thirds as long as the body, are black.

Injury: The beetles feed upon the leaves, buds and flowers.

Life History: The adult beetles hibernate during the winter in long grass and about the base of woody plants. They become active very early in the spring and begin feeding. The females deposit their eggs in the ground and upon hatching the young larvæ bore into the roots of near-by plants where they feed until they become full grown. Early in July they pass into the pupa stage which lasts for about a week and the adult beetles then emerge. Two generations are produced each season in the South and one or two in the North.

Control: Spray or dust with arsenate of lead. Bordeaux added to the arsenate acts as an additional repellent.

CENTAUREA

DISEASES

Root Rot.

Symptoms: Plants become sickly and rot off near the crown and a growth of white mold is often found on the lower portion of the stem.

Control: Space plants well apart to permit a good circulation of air. Water thoroughly with some organic mercury solution such as: Semesan, 1 tablespoonful to 1 gallon of water .

Rust.

Symptoms: Rusty spots appear on the leaves and stems.

Control: Destroy all diseased plants. Dust thoroughly with sulphur as a preventive.

INSECT PESTS

Root Aphids.

Identification: Soft-bodied white or grayish green insects found clustered along the roots or near the crown of the plant.

Injury: Root aphids suck the juices from the plant causing it to become dwarfed and stunted. Foliage turns yellow.

Control: Pour ½ cupful of nicotine solution (¼ teasp. of Black Leaf 40 to 1 qt. of water) about the base of each plant. Make sure that the soil is cupped out about the crown.

For additional precautionary measures see page 1075.

CHRYSANTHEMUM

DISEASES

Blight.

Symptoms: Dark blotches about ½ inch in diameter appear on the foliage. The disease spreads rapidly. The leaves turn yellow, become somewhat shrivelled and drop. Severely infected plants die in a comparatively short time.

Nature of the Disease: A disease caused by the fungus, Cylindrosporium chrysanthemi.

Control: Destroy all badly infected plants.

Spray thoroughly with Bordeaux mixture.

Leaf Spot.

Symptoms: Dark brownish black spots of circular or somewhat irregular outline appear on the leaves. The spots enlarge until they merge together and the entire leaf becomes involved. The lower leaves are usually the first to be affected. The vitality of diseased plants is seriously affected and growth is stunted. The diseased leaves become black and shrivelled and drop prematurely. In severe cases the plant may become entirely defoliated.

Nature of the Disease: A fungous disease caused by Spetoria chrysanthemi Cav. It is becoming very prevalent in some sections and causes severe losses.

Control: Pick off and burn all affected leaves.

Spray with Bordeaux mixture to which soap has been added in order to make it adhere. Five or six applications are advisable during the growing season. Or dust with copper lime dust. Use only healthy plants which are known to be absolutely free from disease for propagating purposes.

Mildew.

Symptoms: Leaves become covered with a white, powdery growth. In the most advanced stages the affected areas turn black.

Nature of the Disease: A fungous disease caused by Erysiphe cichoracearum D. C. It is particularly prevalent in damp, rainy weather.

Control: Dust thoroughly with fine dusting sulphur.

Root Rot.

Symptoms: Plants show signs of wilting—the tips of the branches dry up and the foliage turns a pale, yellowish green, roots become rotted. Occasionally only a single branch is affected.

Nature of the Disease: A fungous disease caused by Sclerotium Rolfsii Sacc. The resting bodies of the fungus resemble small, brown mustard seed. The disease is particularly troublesome during hot, wet weather.

Control: Remove and destroy badly infected plants.

Water plants thoroughly with an organic mercury compound such as:

Semesan, 1 tablespoonful to 1 gallon of water

Rust.

Symptoms: In the early stages small, rusty blisters about the size of a pinhead are found on the lower surface of the leaves. Very occasionally they occur on the upper surface. At this stage the blister is covered by the epidermis of the leaf. As the disease progresses the epidermis breaks away, exposing a mass of dark, brownish spores. When plants are badly affected the undersurface of the leaves may be almost entirely covered with these rust spores. The leaves gradually shrivel and die, and the plants become stunted and fail to produce good bloom.

Nature of the Disease: Rust is a fungous disease caused by Puccinia chrysanthemi Roze. It is thought to be a native of Japan and was introduced into this country in 1896 by way of Europe. It has spread very rapidly until it is now prevalent in almost every section where chrysanthemums are grown. It attacks only the chrysanthe-mum, as yet having been found on no other host plant. The fungus is comparatively short lived and soon dies out unless it is continually transmitted from one living plant to another. Some varieties seem to be more susceptible than others.

Control: Pick off and burn all diseased leaves as soon as trouble is detected. Use only healthy, disease-free plants for propagating purposes. Inspect all newly purchased stock with great care in order to avoid bringing infection into the garden. Reject or destroy any plants which show the least sign of infection.

The use of fine dusting sulphur is advocated not as a control after the plants are attacked but as a preventive measure. It is of great value in keeping healthy plants free from infection.

Wilt.

Symptoms: Plants wilt suddenly and die, the lower portion of the stem becoming black.

Nature of the Disease: A fungous disease caused by Verticillium alboatrum McA. The fungus lives for some time in the soil. The disease is more prevalent on greenhouse plants than on plants grown in the open, although it sometimes causes considerable trouble in the garden.

Control: Destroy diseased plants. Use fresh soil which is known to be free from infection.

Yellows.

Symptoms: Leaves turn yellow. Plants become stunted and fail to produce normal bloom, the blossoms being distorted and fre-quently developing only on one side. The plants are seldom killed.

Nature of the Disease: See page 1073.

Control: In order to control the Yellows it is first necessary to control the leaf hoppers which spread the infection by injecting the virus into the plant when they feed. This may be done by spraying or dusting every week or 10 days with some form of nicotine. It is also a wise precaution to destroy all diseased plants in order to re-move sources of infection from the path of the leaf hoppers.

Spray Formula

Black Leaf 40	1 teaspoonful
Soap	1 cubic inch
Water	1 gallon

Aphids.

Identification: Soft-bodied, louse-like insects which are usually found clustered near the tips of the young shoots or on the underside of the leaves. Chrysanthemums are attacked by several different species, some being pale green in color while others are brown and black.

Injury: Aphids suck the juices from the plant, causing a general lack of vigor and stunted growth.

Life History: See page 1069.

Control: Spray or dust with nicotine in some form. The first application should be made as soon as any infestation is noticed and it should be repeated every 4 or 5 days for several weeks. As it is necessary to reach each individual insect the spraying or dusting must be done with the utmost thoroughness.

Spray Formula

Black Leaf 40 . . . . 1 teaspoonful
Soap . . . . 1 cubic inch
Water . . . . 1 gallon

Greenhouse Leaf Tyer. Although primarily a greenhouse insect the leaf tyer is often troublesome on outdoor chrysanthemums.

Identification: Slender, yellowish green caterpillars having a broad white stripe running lengthwise with the body with a dark green band in the center of the stripe. When full grown they are about ¾ of an inch in length.

Injury: The caterpillars feed upon the leaves, often completely skeletonizing them. They also form a light web which draws the edges of the leaves together in a very characteristic way.

Life History: See page 1087.

Control: Dust or spray with arsenate of lead, making sure to reach the undersurface of the leaves. Open the rolled leaves and destroy the caterpillars or pupæ found within.

Midge.

Identification: Small, cone-shaped galls about ½ inch in length are found on the leaves, stems and flower buds. When on the leaves they are almost always on the upper surface. Within the galls small maggot-like larvæ are found.

Injury: The foliage becomes disfigured and the flowers are badly distorted. If the infestation is very severe the tips of the stems become dwarfed and curiously gnarled, and no flower buds develop.

Life History: The adult midge is a tiny, two-winged fly and the females deposit their bright, orange-colored eggs on the tips of the young tender shoots. The larvæ hatch within from 1 to 2 weeks, depending upon temperature conditions, and for several days after hatching they move about upon the surface of the plant. They then bore into the tissues and as a result of the irritation the little galls are formed. The larvæ feed until they reach full development and then pupate within the gall. When the pupa is fully developed and while it is still enclosed in the pupal skin, it pushes itself out of the gall and the adult flies emerge. It is a peculiar fact that the flies always emerge shortly after midnight and the females lay their eggs very early in the morning about dawn. Frequently the discarded pupal skin may be seen protruding from the opening of the empty gall. The period from the time the larvæ penetrate the tissues of the plant until the adults emerge from the pupa stage varies from 21 to 46 days.

Control: If the infestation is light pick off and destroy all infested leaves. Pull up and burn all heavily infested plants. Examine all newly purchased plants with care in order to make sure that they are free from galls. Cut plants close to the ground in the autumn and burn all refuse.

Spray late in the afternoon every alternate day for 4 to 6 weeks. This will destroy most of the eggs and will also kill many of the adult flies as they emerge.

Spray Formula

Black Leaf 40	1¼ teaspoonful
Soap	1 cubic inch
Water	1 gallon

Tarnished Plant Bug.

Identification: A small, very active bug about ¼ inch in length. The body is oval in shape, being somewhat triangular in front. Coppery-brown in color with dark brown and yellow flecks on the back.

Injury: The bugs puncture the shoots just below the flower heads, causing the buds to droop and die. The injury completely destroys any chance of bloom. It is thought that while feeding, the Tarnished

Plant Bug injects some substance into the sap that is highly injurious to the plant and has the effect of a poison.

Life History: See page 1076.

Control: See page 1076.

Nematodes. For complete description and control, see Narcissus, page 1130.

CLEOME

(*Spider-Flower*)

INSECT PEST

Harlequin Bug (Harlequin Cabbage Beetle).

Identification: The body is flat, shield-shaped and about ⅜ of an inch in length, the back being gaily decorated with red and black markings.

Injury: Both the young nymphs and the adults suck the sap from the plant tissues and if the infestation is severe it will cause the death of the plants.

Life History: The Harlequin bug is a distinctly Southern insect as it is incapable of surviving the cold of Northern winters. In the extreme South it feeds and breeds during the entire year. In the more northerly part of its range the adults find shelter in long grass or under piles of rubbish in the winter, emerging with the first warm days of spring. The eggs are usually laid on the underside of the leaves of host plants, and they are very amusing in appearance, as they resemble tiny white kegs. They are set on end, about a dozen being glued together, and each one is bound with two black bands which look like miniature barrel hoops. There is even a black dot set in the very place for a bung hole. The time of hatching varies from 4 to 25 days, according to weather conditions. The young nymphs begin feeding as soon as they have hatched and at the end of 8 weeks, after passing through five molts, they become full grown. Three and sometimes four generations are produced during the season.

Control: The Harlequin bug is rather difficult to control. On large commercial areas where it is troublesome, hand torches are used and trap crops are grown during the winter months, but such methods are hardly practicable for the small garden.

A nicotine spray will prove effective against the young nymphs and if a generous quantity of soap is added to this it will prevent most of the eggs from hatching as they will slide to the ground as soon as they are deposited. Spraying should be done every few days until the beetles are under control. The adult beetles should be picked off by hand.

Spray Formula

Black Leaf 40 .... 2 teaspoonfuls
Soap .... 2 cubic inches
Water .... 1 gallon

COLEUS

INSECT PESTS

Orthezia.

Identification: The young nymphs are very tiny, dark green in color and wingless, with a row of waxy plates extending back over the body. The adult females have a very conspicuous white, fluted egg sack which extends back from the body for a distance of two or more times the diameter of the body.

Injury: Although primarily a greenhouse insect the orthezias frequently infest bedding plants when grown in the open and cause considerable trouble. They are closely related to the scales and mealy bugs and suck the juices from the plant tissues.

Control: Spray with lemon oil. Wash the foliage thoroughly several hours after the application has been made.

Spray Formula

Lemon Oil .... ½ pint
Warm water .... 6 quarts

White Fly.

Identification: Small, whitish flies about 1/16 of an inch long with four wings. They are usually found on the undersurface of the leaves.

Injury: White flies suck the juices from the plant causing a general lack of vigor and if the infestation is severe the plant eventually dies.

Life History: See page 1071.

Control: Spray thoroughly with a nicotine solution, making sure to reach the undersurface of the leaves. Several applications should be made 3 or 4 days apart.

Spray Formula

Black Leaf 40 .... 1 teaspoonful
Water .... 1 gallon
Soap .... 1 cubic inch

Yellow Woolly-bear Caterpillar.

Identification: A caterpillar about 2 inches in length when full grown. The body is completely covered with long hairs which vary in color from pale yellow to reddish brown.

Injury: The caterpillars feed upon the foliage.

Life History: The winter is passed in a cocoon made from the woolly coat of the caterpillar and silk which it spins. These pupa cases are usually found under piles of dead leaves or loose brush. The adult moths which emerge early in the spring are pure white with a few black spots on each wing. The females deposit their eggs in small patches on the leaves of the host plants. The larvæ hatch out within a few days and begin feeding, attaining full size in about two months. There are usually two generations during the season.

Control: Spray or dust with arsenate of lead.

COSMOS

DISEASES

Botrytis Rot.

Symptoms: Attacks foliage, stems and flower buds. The affected parts appear to be covered with a greenish mold.

Nature of the Disease: A fungous disease which is seldom prevalent except in very wet seasons.

Control: Pull up and burn badly infected plants.

Spray with Bordeaux mixture or dust with copper-lime dust.

Wilt.

Symptoms: Leaves turn a sickly yellow. Plants wilt and die.

Nature of the Disease: A bacterial disease caused by Bacillus solanacearum E. F. S. which also causes the wilt of potatoes and tomatoes.

Control: No remedy has as yet been discovered.

All diseased plants should be destroyed.

INSECT PESTS

Aphids.

Identification: Soft-bodied, louse-like insects which are usually found clustered near the tips of the young shoots. They are light green in color and vary in size, the newly hatched young being considerably smaller than the adults.

Injury: Aphids suck the juices from the plant and cause a general lack of vigor and stunted growth.

Life History: See page 1069.

Control: See page 1070.

Spotted Cucumber Beetle.

Identification: A yellowish green beetle about ¼ inch in length with twelve very conspicuous black spots on its back. The head and antennæ, which are about ⅔ as long as the body, are black.

Injury: The beetles feed upon the leaves, buds and flowers.

Life History: See page 1088.

Control: Spray or dust with arsenate of lead. Bordeaux added to the arsenate acts as an additional repellent.

Stalk Borer.

Identification: Slender caterpillars about an inch or two in length. The young caterpillars are brown with white stripes. When full grown they lose their stripes and become a solid, dirty gray in color.

Injury: The stalk borer makes a small round hole in the stem and tunnels up through the stalk, causing the injured shoot to suddenly wilt and break over.

Life History: See page 1076.

Control: See page 1076.

DAHLIA
DISEASES

Mildew.

Symptoms: Leaves become covered with a powdery, white growth. In the most advanced stages the affected areas turn black.

Nature of the Disease: A fungous disease caused by Erysiphe polyoni D. C. which is apt to be prevalent in damp, rainy weather.

Control: Dust thoroughly with fine dusting sulphur.

Root Rot.

Symptoms: Affected tubers rot during storage, becoming soft in the center and having a spongy, water-soaked appearance.

Nature of the Disease: A fungous disease caused by Botrytis sp. which always gains entrance through bruised areas on the surface of the tubers.

Control: Handle tubers with care in order to avoid bruising. Store in a cool and dry place. Dust any scarred places with fine dusting sulphur.

Stunt.

Symptoms: Plants become a yellowish green in color, leaves are small, flowers poor and malformed. The growth of the plant is curiously bushy and stunted and the flower buds do not show until very late in the season.

Nature of the Disease: A disease closely resembling mosaic. It is transmitted through the roots.

Control: Pull up and burn all diseased plants. Use tubers from healthy plants for propagating.

Dahlias are subject to various physiological disorders caused by lack of water at time of blossoming, hot weather and intense sunshine, too much shade, too rich soil, etc. Such conditions are apt to cause stunted growth, distorted blossoms, and burning along the tips of the leaves. Such troubles can usually be overcome by good cultural methods.

INSECT PESTS

Corn Ear Worm.

Identification: Large, striped worms about two inches in length when full grown. They vary in color from light green to brown and the stripes which run lengthwise with the body are alternating light and dark. The head is yellow, the legs almost black.

Injury: The caterpillars feed upon the foliage and the flower buds, causing considerable damage.

Life History: See page 1086.

Control: Spray or dust with arsenate of lead.

European Hornet.

Identification: A small hornet with a dark body and two, gauzy wings.

Injury: European hornets cause serious trouble in some sections by gnawing or peeling off the tender bark on the stems of dahlia plants. In some cases the stem becomes completely girdled and the plant dies.

Control: Locate the nest and destroy it. This should be done at night when all the hornets are in and it may be speedily accomplished with a kerosene torch.

Cutworms.

Identification: Smooth, plump little caterpillars, about an inch in length when full grown and varying in color from greenish gray to muddy brown.

Injury: Cutworms are exceedingly destructive as they sever the stem at or near the ground line, causing the immediate death of the plant attacked. Young plants are most susceptible to attack but older plants are frequently injured.

Life History: There are numerous species of cutworms which are injurious to flowering plants. In the case of most species the adult moths deposit their eggs on the stems of weeds and grasses. The larvæ conceal themselves in the ground during the day, emerging to feed only at night. They start feeding early in the spring and continue until midsummer when they pass into the pupa stage. Most species produce only one generation a year, the winter being passed in the larval stage in little cell-like structures in the soil.

Control: Cutworms may be very readily controlled by the use of a poisoned bait. This should be placed in little piles on the surface of the soil near the spot where the worms have been troublesome.

Formula for Poison Bait

Arsenate of lead..............1 tablespoonful
Molasses ....1 tablespoonful
Wheat bran ....1 cupful

Greenhouse Leaf Tyer. Although primarily a greenhouse insect the leaf tyer is often troublesome on dahlias.

Identification: Slender, yellowish green caterpillars having a broad white stripe running lengthwise down the back with a dark green band in the center of the stripe. When full grown they are about ¾ of an inch in length.

Injury: The caterpillars feed upon the leaves, often completely skeletonizing them. They also form a light web which draws the edges of the leaves together in a very characteristic way.

Life History: See page 1087.

Control: Spray or dust with arsenate of lead, making sure to reach the undersurface of the leaves. Open the leaves which have been webbed together and destroy the larvæ or pupa found within.

Leaf-cutter Bee.

Injury: The bees first make a tunnel in the stem and then construct their nest within it. In most cases they cause the death of the shoot.

Life History: The bees cut a neat circular piece out of some growing leaf, usually preferring roses, and with this they build a nest composed of thimble-shaped cells within the tunnel which has already been prepared in the stem of some half-woody plant. The cells are arranged one above another and when they are completed each contains a single egg, some nectar and some pollen. The young bees develop within the nest until ready for flight.

Control: Remove and burn infested shoots.

Spotted Cucumber Beetle.

Identification: A yellowish green beetle about ¼ inch in length with twelve very conspicuous black spots on its back. The head and antennæ, which are almost ⅔ as long as the body, are black.

Injury: The beetles feed upon the leaves, buds and flowers and do considerable damage if they become numerous.

Life History: See page 1088.

Control: Spray or dust with arsenate of lead. Bordeaux added to the arsenate acts as an additional repellent.

Stalk Borer.

Identification: Slender caterpillars about an inch or two in length. The young caterpillars are brown with white stripes. When full grown they loose their stripes and become a solid, dirty gray in color.

Injury: The stalk borer makes a small round hole in the stem and tunnels up through the stalk, causing the injured shoot to suddenly wilt and break over.

Life History: See page 1076.

Control: See page 1076.

Tarnished Plant Bug.

Identification: A small, very active bug about ¼ inch in length. The body is oval in shape, being somewhat triangular in front. Coppery-brown in color with dark brown and yellow flecks on the back.

Injury: The bugs puncture the shoots just below the flower heads, causing the buds to droop and die. The injury completely destroys any chance of bloom. It is thought that while feeding the Tarnished Plant Bug injects some substance into the sap which is highly injurious to the plant and has the effect of a poison.

Life History: See page 1076.

Control: See page 1076.

DELPHINIUM

DISEASES

Bacterial Leaf Spot.

Symptoms: Dark spots of irregular outline appear upon the leaves. The lower leaves are usually the first to be affected. The spots occasionally appear on the stems and flower buds and in some cases the leaves become distorted.

Nature of the Disease: A bacterial disease of an insidious nature caused by Bacterium delphinii (E. F. S.) Bryan. The bacteria remain alive in the soil during the winter and are spattered up onto the leaves with the early spring rains. The disease spreads rapidly and the entire plant is soon affected. The original source of infection may usually be traced to the purchase of diseased plants. In rare instances it has been found that infection was carried on the seed.

Control: Pick off and burn all affected leaves in order to prevent the spread of the disease.

In early spring before growth starts drench the soil about the plants with Bordeaux. Repeat this operation several times during the season and spray the foliage thoroughly at the same time.

In severe cases cut the plants back to the ground in late July and drench the soil with corrosive sublimate solution.

1 tablet to 1 quart of water, or
1 ounce to 14 gallons of water.

Be sure that the ground about the plant is moist before this application is made.

Black Rot, also known as Root Rot and Crown Rot.

Symptoms: Plants wilt and die suddenly, rotting off at the crown, or plants fail to come through the winter. The crown and roots sometimes become covered with a yellowish, moldy growth which has a characteristically strong odor of decay.

Nature of the Disease: A fungous disease caused by Sclerotium delphinii (Welch). The fungus spreads rapidly through the soil and is particularly prevalent on low, poorly drained land. It is also favored by damp, rainy weather.

There is also a form of crown rot which is caused by a bacterium. This organism enters the plant through wounded surfaces and causes the crown to decay. In appearance it is very characteristic, being wet and shiny, and it possesses a very strong and unpleasant odor.

Control: There is no known remedy; infected plants should be dug up and burned, and the adjacent soil should be removed and subjected to fire. In order to lessen the danger of infection to other plants it is well to scrape away the soil from around the crown of each plant, replacing the soil with sand or coal ashes. Do not allow animal manures of any kind to come into direct contact with the crown of the plant.

If the disease is prevalent, water the crown of the plants with a corrosive sublimate solution:

1 tablet to 1 quart of water, or
1 ounce to 14 gallons of water.

Be sure that the ground about the plants is moist before this application is made, and care should be taken not to water the foliage with the solution as it is liable to cause injury.

Mildew.

Symptoms: Foliage becomes covered with a white, powdery growth. In the most advanced stages the affected areas turn black.

Nature of the Disease: A fungous disease caused by Erysiphe polygoni D. C. It is particularly prevalent in damp, rainy weather. It is very disfiguring to the appearance of a plant but seldom causes its death.

Control: Dust thoroughly with fine dusting sulphur (300 mesh) upon the first sign of mildew. Burn all leaves and stems in the autumn.

Burning of the Leaves.

Symptoms: Leaves have a curious metallic sheen on the under-surface and in some cases the edges begin to dry and curl up.

Nature of the Disease: Although this condition may appear alarming it is not in the true sense a disease. It is a physiological condition caused by intense summer sunshine and it seldom results in any permanent injury to the plant.

INSECT PESTS

Aphids.

Identification: Soft-bodied, louse-like insects which are usually found clustered near the tips of the young shoots. The species that infest delphiniums are usually black in color and they vary considerably in size, the newly hatched young being smaller than the adults. .

Injury: Aphids suck the juices from the plant, causing a general lack of vigor and stunted growth.

Life History: See page 1069.

Control: See page 1070.

Cyclamen Mite (Pallid Mite).

Identification: A very minute creature hardly visible to the naked eye. The adult mites are pale brown in color, somewhat glossy and have four pairs of legs. The presence of cyclamen mites is usually detected by their very characteristic injury.

Injury: Both the leaves and flower spikes become blackened and very much distorted. Stems become twisted and flower buds fail to open. Injury usually is evident on young, succulent growth.

Life History: The eggs, which are infinitesimal in size, are laid either about the base of the plant or on the leaves. The young begin feeding as soon as they have hatched.

Control: The only completely successful control for the pallid mite on delphiniums is the immersion of the plants in hot water. Although this treatment entails a considerable expenditure of time and effort on the part of the gardener, it is so entirely successful that the extra work is more than justified. It is fortunate that the plants are able to withstand a temperature which proves fatal to the mites in all stages of their development. Any convenient receptacle may be used for the treatment, provided it is of sufficient size to permit a complete immersion of the plants. A laundry tub, an old-fashioned wash-boiler, an ash can or a bucket may be used. The water should be heated to a temperature of 110 degrees F. and it should be maintained within 1 degree of this temperature throughout the treatment. A small quantity of hot water may be added occasionally during the treatment to prevent the temperature from dropping. Young seedling plants, or plants which have been lifted from the open ground, should have all soil washed off the roots. They may then be placed on trays or within a loose roll of small-meshed wire. They should never be tied in tight bundles. The plants should be entirely immersed in the hot water (110° F.) and should be held for a period of 10 minutes. If the plants are potted it is not necessary to remove them from the pots, as the pot and plant may be immersed together. It is necessary to immerse potted plants for a period of 25 minutes in order to kill all the mites below the surface of the soil. When the plants are removed, the pots should be tilted, in order to allow the water to drain off. Plants with bare roots should be spread out and allowed to cool off and dry slightly before they are replanted. It is advisable to shade the plants for several days after they have been replanted in order to reduce the danger of shock, and to give them an opportunity to become re-established as promptly as possible. As little time as possible should elapse between the digging of the plants, the treatment, and the replanting.

There are several other measures of control which are reasonably effective against mites, but none is so efficaceous as the hot water treatment.

Dusting the plants at intervals of every week or ten days with very finely ground sulphur dust (300 mesh) will help to keep the mites under control as it is fairly effective against those which are actually exposed.

Regular applications of a rotenone spray at the rate of 1 table-spoonful to 1 gallon of water is also effective to some extent against mites which are exposed. The plants should be sprayed at weekly or ten-day intervals from April until the time of bloom. Spraying should be resumed after the flower stalks have been cut down and new growth has started.

As a matter of general precaution, all infected shoots and flower stalks should be removed and burned.

The importance of keeping a garden free from infestation in the beginning can hardly be overemphasized.

In bringing new plants into the garden, it is a wise precaution to give them the hot water treatment in order to avoid any possibility of introducing mites. It is far easier to thus prevent the introduction of mites than it is to control them after they have once gained headway and have caused a serious infestation.

Stalk Borer (Common).

Identification: Slender caterpillars about two inches in length when full grown. The young caterpillars are brown with white stripes. When full grown they lose their stripes and become a solid dirty gray in color.

Injury: The stalk borer makes a small round hole in the stem and tunnels up through the stalk, causing the injured shoot to suddenly wilt and break over.

Life History: See page 1076.

Control: See page 1076.

DIANTHUS

(Pink)

DISEASES

Anthracnose.

Symptoms: Leaves turn yellow and the plant gradually dies.

Nature of the Disease: A fungous disease caused by Volutella dianthi (Hal.) Atk.

Control: Spray with Bordeaux, or dust with copper-lime dust.

Root Rot.

Symptoms: Leaves wither and die. Plants rot off at the crown.

Nature of the Disease: Caused by the same fungus which attacks many other plants, Sclerotium Rolfsii Sacc.

Control: The most satisfactory measure of control seems to be the use of gypsum. Several handfuls should be cultivated in about the plants early in the season

DIGITALIS
(Foxglove)
DISEASE

Leaf Spot.

Symptoms: Leaves have an unhealthy, rusty-brown appearance. Young seedlings are very subject to attack and older plants are also susceptible.

Nature of the Disease: A fungous disease caused by Phyllostictia digitalidis. Very prevalent in some sections.

Control: Leaf spot may be readily controlled by spraying with Bordeaux as soon as trouble is detected.

INSECT PEST

Red Spider.

Identification: Minute mites, some red in color, others greenish, yellow and black.

Injury: Red spiders feed usually on the undersurface of the leaves, puncturing the outer tissues and sucking the juices of the plant. The foliage has an unhealthy, white, curiously glazed appearance and frequently drops prematurely. Fine silken threads will be found, spun across the undersurface of the leaves.

Life History: The very minute eggs are laid on the undersurface of the leaves, usually being attached to the web. Each female lays from two to six eggs per day, depositing about seventy in all. The eggs hatch in four or five days and the young mites begin feeding. The females pass through three molts, the males through only two. The life cycle covers a period of from 35 to 40 days.

Control: The following measures of control are recommended.

Syringe the plants frequently with a strong force of luke warm water, making sure to reach the undersurface of the leaves. This will destroy the webs and kill many of the mites. Frequent dusting with super-fine sulphur is very effective in keeping red spiders in check.

Any of the following sprays will also give good results.

Lemon Oil, ½ pint in 4 quarts of warm water.

Volck, 5 teaspoonfuls to 1 quart of water.

FRITILLARIA IMPERIALIS

(Crown Imperial)

DISEASE

Gray Bulb Rot.

Symptoms: Dry rot begins at the nose of the bulb. The flesh of the bulb becomes a reddish-gray in color. In the advanced stages of the disease the bulbs rot away entirely.

Nature of the Disease: Caused by the same fungus that attacks tulips and various other bulbs, Rhizoctonia tuliparum (Kleb.) Whetzel and Arthur.

Control: Dig up and burn all diseased bulbs. Disinfect the soil with formaldehyde before planting any of the following bulbs: narcissus, hyacinths, tulips, scilla sibirica.

GAILLARDIA

DISEASE

Yellows.

Symptoms: Plants become dwarfed if attacked when young. Older plants have a curiously bushy habit of growth. Leaves that are not mature at the time that infection takes place turn a bright yellow. Occasionally only one side of the plant is affected. The blossoms become dwarfed and distorted. Plants are practically never killed outright, living on until frost.

Nature of the Disease: See page 1073.

Control: See page 1073.

GALTONIA

(Hyacinthus Candicans)

INSECT PEST

Bulb Fly (Merodon equestris Fab.)

Identification: Small, brown scars are sometimes found upon the outer scales. Bulbs are suspiciously soft and light in weight. Upon cutting the bulb open, large, fat, grayish to yellowish-white maggots are found, ½ to ¾ of an inch in length.

Injury: The maggots feed upon the tissues and render the bulbs practically worthless.

Life History: See page 1118.

Control: Discard and burn badly infested bulbs that have become light and soft.

If there is danger of infestation it is wise to treat the bulbs as follows:

Submerge bulbs for 2½ hours in hot water which is held at a temperature of 110 to 111½ degrees F. Then plunge immediately in cold water. This will destroy the larvæ in all stages of their development and will not harm the bulbs if they are sound.

GERANIUM
DISEASES
Bacterial Leaf Spot.

Symptoms: The affected area first shows as a water-soaked dot which can be seen only in transmitted light. As the spots become older they are brown in color and usually irregular though sometimes circular in shape. Several spots may appear on a single leaf. The tissue between the spots may turn brown and die, but the original spots show up clearly in the dead area.

Nature of the Disease: The disease is caused by Bacterium pelargoni Brown. It may be present on young as well as old leaves.

Control: Out-of-doors the plants should be planted so that they will get plenty of sunlight and air. In the greenhouse, plants should be kept in a well-ventilated house and care should be taken that the tops are not splashed in watering. Plants may be sprayed with Bordeaux mixture or colloidal sulphur.

Bacterial Spot.

Symptoms: The soft leaf tissue is invaded between the veins which give rise to a rather large elongated area which converges toward the base of the leaf. Occasionally the infected areas are more or less round. The affected area may retain the original color or become brownish or pinkish in color.

Nature of the Disease: The disease is caused by the Bacterium erodii Lewis. The disease may start at the margin of the leaf and give rise to the angular areas or it may start by a small translucent spot.

Control: See Bacterial Leaf Spot.

Cercospora Leaf Spot.

Symptoms: The spots are small, light brown or pale brick-red in color, more or less circular in shape, and have a narrow, slightly raised and darker border. It can be differentiated from bacterial spot in that the borders of the spots are raised and darker in color than in the center of the spot, while in bacterial spot the borders are colorless.

Nature of the Disease: The disease is caused by the fungus, Cercospora brunkii Ell. and Hall.

Control: See Bacterial Leaf Spot.

Dropsy.

Symptoms: The leaves develop water-soaked areas which later become brown and corky. The leaf yellows first around the spot, and later becomes entirely yellow and drops off. The stems and petioles develop corky ridges.

Nature of the Disease: Dropsy is believed to be caused by a warm, damp soil which stimulates root growth and a moist, cool air which inhibits transpiration. The disease is more common in late winter.

Control: Give the plant plenty of light and good ventilation. Avoid over-watering.

GLADIOLUS

DISEASES

Bacterial Blight.

Symptoms: In the early stages, dark, water-soaked spots appear on the leaves. The diseased areas spread gradually until the entire leaf is affected. There is usually a very characteristic, somewhat sticky, exudation of the infected areas which gradually dries until it becomes a thin film. The corms are seldom affected.

Nature of the Disease: A bacterial disease caused by Bacterium gummisudans McCulloch. Some varieties seem very susceptible while others are quite resistant.

Control: Cut off and burn all infected leaves in order to prevent the spread of the disease.

Soak the corms before planting in any of the following:

Corrosive sublimate.........1 tablet to 1 pint of water	
1½ hours...........1 ounce to 7 gallons of water	
Formaldehyde...........1 cup in 15 gallons of water	
1½ hours	
Semesan..........1 tablespoonful to 1 gallon of water	
7 hours	

Dry Rot.

Symptoms: Dark, reddish-brown spots are found on the corms. These spots are sunken with raised margins and are usually most numerous on the lower part of the corm near the old bulb scar. When corms which are badly diseased are planted the growing plants may become affected later in the season, the leaves turning yellow and rotting off at the ground level. In advanced stages the roots and the corm itself rot away. When diseased corms are lifted and stored in the autumn the dry rot continues and frequently the corms become entirely mummified before spring.

Nature of the Disease: Dry Rot is a fungous disease caused by Sclerotium gladioli Mass. which is becoming more and more prevalent and causes severe losses. The Primulinus varieties seem to be particularly susceptible. The fungus lives over the winter in the soil in the form of minute resting bodies known as sclerotia which are found on the base of decayed leaves.

Control: After the corms have been harvested in the autumn any of the following treatments are recommended:

Always remove the husks before treatment.

(1) Soak corms for 7 hours in Semesan solution
    1 tablespoonful to 1 gallon of water

(2) Soak corms in water for 15 minutes. Place corms between pieces of moist blotting paper for several hours. Then soak for twenty minutes in a corrosive sublimate solution, one tablet to one pint of water or one ounce to seven gallons. Rinse immediately in clear water after treatment. Allow corms to dry thoroughly before storing away.

(3) Soak corms in water for 15 minutes. Keep moist as above for several hours. Soak in formaldehyde, one cupful to fifteen gallons of water for thirty minutes. Allow corms to dry thoroughly.

Hard Rot.

Symptoms: Reddish-brown spots appear on the leaves, producing a rusty caste. As the disease advances minute black specks appear in the center of the leaf spots. These are the fruiting bodies of the fungus and later on this center frequently drops out, giving the leaves a shot-hole appearance. The corms are also affected, dark brown spots with a water-soaked margin being found on both the upper surface and the base. In severe cases the corm becomes a hard, shrivelled mummy. When badly diseased corms are planted spindly, unthrifty growth results and the plants eventually die.

Nature of the Disease: Hard Rot is a fungous disease caused by Septoria gladioli Pass. It is particularly prevalent on young plants grown from seed or from small cormels. It may spread directly from the old corm to the new corm and cormels, or it may first attack the leaves. In an apparent endeavor to resist the disease and to check its spread on the corm a layer of cork-like tissue is frequently built up around the infected area.

Control: Destroy all infected plants as soon as the disease is detected.

Give the corms the same treatment as recommended for Dry Rot.

Neck Rot or Scab.

Symptoms: This disease usually first manifests itself by the appearance of light-brown streaks on the lower leaves near the ground line. Upon close observation minute brown spots are apparent which, as they enlarge, become black and merge into one another. The blackened leaves rot off at the base and frequently the entire plant is killed.

The corms are also affected. Dark, burnt-looking streaks are found on the bulb scales and the corms are covered with brownish or blackened sunken spots having a slightly raised margin. In the advanced stages of the disease the entire corm presents a rough, scabby appearance and is covered with a varnish-like secretion. The outer husk is frequently stuck to the corm with this sticky exudation. In some cases the husk is entirely destroyed.

Nature of the Disease: A bacterial disease caused by Bacterium marginatum. The bacteria are carried on infected corms.

Control: The same as for Dry Rot. See page 1109.

Penicillium Rot.

Symptoms: The entire corm becomes a mass of dark, porous, rotted tissue.

Nature of the Disease: A fungous disease caused by Penicillium gladioli Machk. It always gains entrance through wounded tissues. Small, light brown sclerotia or resting bodies are found in the infected corms.

Control: Since rot fungi live in the soil, rotation is essential in controlling disease. Spray small plants from seed or cormels with Bordeaux mixture at 10-day intervals. Potash fish-oil soap should be added to spray for a spreader at the rate of 1 ounce to 1 gallon of spray. Handle the corms carefully.

INSECT PESTS

Black Blister Beetle.

Identification: A slender, jet-black beetle about ½ inch in length with prominent head and neck. Its best means of identification is a yellow exudate.

Injury: The beetles feed upon the flowers.
Life History: See page 1074.
Control: See page 1074.

Corn Ear Worm.

Identification: Large striped worms about two inches in length. They vary in color from light green to brown and the stripes which run lengthwise with the body are alternating light and dark. The head is yellow, the legs almost black.
Injury: The caterpillars feed upon the foliage and the flowers.
Life History: See page 1086.
Control: Spray or dust with arsenate of lead.

Stalk Borer.

Identification: Slender caterpillars about two inches in length. The young caterpillars are brown with white stripes. When full grown they lose their stripes and become a solid, dirty gray in color.
Injury: The stalk borer makes a small, round hole in the stem and tunnels up through the stalk causing the injured shoot to suddenly wilt and break over.
Life History: See page 1076.
Control: See page 1076.

Gladiolus Thrips.

Life History: The adults appear early in the spring and feed within the tissues of the leaf, where the eggs are laid. The eggs hatch into small, wingless insects that continue feeding until they are full grown when they pass into a quiescent stage and emerge as adults.
Identification: The adult thrips are black-winged insects about 1/16 of an inch in length. In the immature stage they are wingless, pale yellow in color and very active.
Injury: The thrips feed upon the leaves, buds and flowers of the gladioli, causing a very characteristic injury. Affected flowers open imperfectly, the flower spike is apt to nod, and small, silvery-white streaks may be found on both the flowers and the leaves.
Control: After the corms have been harvested all the tops should be burned as soon as they are dry. The corms should then be treated in order to destroy any thrips which may be present. One of the most simple and yet one of the most effective treatments is the use of naphthalene flakes. These should be used at the rate of one ounce per 100 corms or one pound per 2000 corms. After the flakes

have been sprinkled over the corms the trays should be covered with a light canvas or with paper. For small quantities of corms paper bags make very satisfactory containers. Air-tight containers should never be used. The naphthalene flakes should be allowed to remain on the corms for a period of four weeks. This treatment should be applied in the autumn shortly after the corms have been harvested. If applied in the spring it will seriously affect the growth of the corms, causing delayed and very uneven development.

If gladiolus corms are stored at a temperature ranging between 30 and 40 degrees F. thrips may be kept almost entirely under control and no other treatment is necessary.

Another measure of control which is frequently practised is to dip the corms shortly before planting in a corrosive sublimate solution, 1 tablet to 1 pint of water (1 to 1000).

It is very difficult to control the gladiolus thrips during the growing season but several sprays have given fairly satisfactory results. Spraying should be done at weekly intervals and it is essential that all parts of the plant be covered. The spray should preferably be applied on cloudy days, or early in the morning or in the evening when the thrips are most active.

Spray Formulas

(1)	1 tablespoonful	Paris Green
	2 pounds	Brown Sugar
	3 gallons	Water
(2)	3 tablespoonfuls	Nicotine sulphate
	4½ tablespoonfuls	Bindex
	2½ ounces	Lead Arsenate
	5 gallons	Water

The first application should be made when the foliage is about 6 inches high and weekly applications should be made for a period of 6 weeks, being discontinued about 2 weeks before blooming.

Woolly Aphids. Gladiolus corms are occasionally attacked by woolly aphids during storage. This is particularly true if they are stored in or near a conservatory or greenhouse.

Identification: Small, soft-bodied insects with a whitish woolly covering are found clustered on the corms.

Injury: The insects suck the juices from the tissues of the corms and weaken their vitality.

Control: Soak corms in a solution of Nicotine sulphate, 1 teaspoonful to 1 gallon of water. Allow the corms to dry thoroughly before replacing them in storage.

GOLDEN GLOW

DISEASES

Mildew.

Symptoms: Foliage becomes covered with a white, powdery growth. In the most advanced stages the affected areas turn black.

Nature of the Disease: Caused by the fungus Erysiphe cichoracearum D. C.

Control: Dust thoroughly with fine dusting sulphur.

Root Rot.

Symptoms: Plants show signs of wilting, the tips of the branches dry up and the foliage turns a pale yellowish green, roots become rotted.

Nature of the Disease: See page 1090.

Control: See page 1090.

INSECT PESTS

Aphids.

Identification: Soft-bodied, louse-like insects, usually found clustered along the tips of the growing shoots. The species that attacks golden glow is a dark reddish-brown in color.

Injury: Aphids suck the juices of the plant, causing general lack of vigor and stunted growth.

Life History: See page 1069.

Control: See page 1070.

Stalk Borer.

Identification: Slender caterpillars about two inches in length. The young caterpillars are brown with white stripes. When full grown they lose their stripes and become a solid, dirty gray in color.

Injury: The stalk borer makes a small, round hole in the stem and tunnels up through the stalk, causing the injured shoot to suddenly wilt and die.

Life History: See page 1076.

Control: See page 1076.

GRAPE HYACINTH
(*Muscari*)

DISEASES

Rot.

Symptoms: A white, moldy growth appears on the surface of the ground about the plants. Bulbs become rotten.

Control: Water the ground about infected plants with an organic mercury solution.

Semesan, 1 tablespoonful to 1 gallon of water

Also soak bulbs in the same solution for two hours before planting.

Smut.

Symptoms: The flowers are imperfect and become covered with a greenish-brown smut. The smut spores replace the ovaries and anthers of the flowers and utterly ruin their beauty.

Control: Pick off and burn all infected flowers as soon as the disease is detected in order to prevent the spread of the smut spores.

Before planting soak the bulbs for three hours in water kept at a temperature of 110 degrees F. Plunge in cold water immediately after the hot bath.

HELIOTROPE

INSECT PESTS

Greenhouse Leaf Tyer.

Identification: Slender, yellowish-green caterpillars having a broad white stripe running lengthwise down the back with a dark green band in the center of the stripe. When full grown they are about ¾ of an inch in length.

Injury: The caterpillars feed upon the leaves, often completely skeletonizing them. They also form a light web which draws the edges of the leaves together in a very characteristic way.

Life History: See page 1087.

Control: See page 1087.

Orthezia.

Identification: The young nymphs are very tiny, dark green in color and wingless, with a row of waxy plates extending back over the body. The adult females have a very conspicuous white, fluted egg sack which extends back for a distance of two or more times the diameter of the body.

Injury: The orthezias are closely related to the scales and suck the juices from the plant tissues.

Control: See page 1095.

HOLLYHOCK

DISEASES

Anthracnose.

Symptoms: The foliage becomes covered with irregular, dark brown spots and the leaves wither and fall. Sunken spots varying in color from pale yellow to black appear on the stems and petioles of the leaves. When young plants in the seed bed are attacked the stems usually collapse.

Nature of the Disease: A fungous disease, Colletotrichum malvarum (Br. & Casp.) South., which causes severe losses in some sections.

Control: Spray thoroughly with Bordeaux mixture. If one is troubled with this disease in the seed bed, spraying should begin as soon as the first true leaves appear and subsequent applications should be given every few days until the seedlings are well started.

Dusting with superfine sulphur is also recommended as a measure of control.

Rust.

Symptoms: Leaves and stems become covered with raised pustules, a light, rusty-brown in color. If the infection is severe the whole plant may wither and die. In mild cases however, the lower leaves are killed but the plant continues to grow and flower.

Nature of the Disease: A fungous disease caused by Puccinia malvacearum Bert. It was first discovered in Chili and from thence it was introduced into France. It was brought into this country in 1886 upon some infected seed and has spread with alarming rapidity to almost every section of the United States where hollyhocks are grown. It renders the plants extremely unsightly and is a very insidious disease.

Control: As soon as the leaves appear in the spring dust the plants thoroughly with superfine sulphur. Make subsequent applications every week or 10 days throughout the season. This is more in the nature of a preventive than a cure. When rust has once gained headway it is very difficult to control.

Cut all hollyhock plants down to the ground in the autumn and burn the stalks, leaves, and all other refuse.

Cercosporose.

Symptoms: Large, dark, angular spots appear on the leaves. The spots are surrounded by darker margins and as the disease progresses the center becomes a light, ashen gray in color. Upon this light center small black dots may be distinguished. When the infection is severe the plants lose nearly all of their foliage.

Nature of the Disease: A rather uncommon fungous disease caused by Cercospora althæina Sacc.

Control: Spray every 10 days with Bordeaux or with ammoniacal copper carbonate.

INSECT PESTS

Japanese Beetles.

Identification: Large, handsome beetles, a metallic, greenish-bronze in color, with two conspicuous and several small white spots near the tip of the abdomen. During the middle of the day they are very active, making rapid flight when disturbed.

Injury: The beetles feed upon both the foliage and the flowers and will completely demolish a plant in a very short time.

Life History: See page 1149.

Control: Spray with coated arsenate of lead or with the commercial preparation Insectrogen, used double strength.

Leaf Roller.

Identification: Small, active caterpillars about ¾ of an inch long, olive-green in color.

Injury: The caterpillars feed upon the foliage, their work being very characteristic as they roll and tie the leaves together with fine silken threads.

Life History: See page 1075.

Control: Spray or dust thoroughly with arsenate of lead. Open any leaves which have already been rolled and destroy the caterpillars or pupa cases found within.

Stalk Borer.

Identification: Slender caterpillars about two inches in length. The young caterpillars are brown with white stripes. When full grown they lose their stripes and become a solid, dirty gray in color.

Injury: The stalk borer makes a small, round hole in the stem and tunnels up through the stalk, causing the injured shoot to suddenly wilt and die.

Life History: See page 1076.

Control: See page 1076.

Yellow Woolly-bear Caterpillar.

Identification: A caterpillar about two inches in length when full grown. The body is completely covered with long hairs which vary in color from pale yellow to reddish-brown.

Injury: The caterpillars feed upon the leaves.

Life History: See page 1096.

Control: Spray or dust with arsenate of lead.

HYACINTH

DISEASES

Black Rot.

Symptoms: Bulbs become a mass of black, rotted tissue. Small black resting bodies of the fungus known as Sclerotia are frequently found within the bulb.

Control: Bulbs which are badly affected should be destroyed. If only very slightly affected the rotted portion may be cut away and the bulbs soaked in an organic mercury solution.

Semesan, 1 tablespoonful to 1 gallon of water. Soak for two hours.

Gray Bulb Rot.

Symptoms: Dry rot begins at the nose of the bulb, and the flesh of the bulb becomes a reddish-gray in color. In the advanced stages of the disease the bulbs rot away entirely.

Nature of the Disease: See page 1106.

Control: See page 1106.

Soft Rot.

Symptoms: Flower stalks rot off at the base. Bulbs come "blind," failing to form flower buds, or the flower head becomes distorted.

Nature of the Disease: A bacterial disease caused by Bacillus caratovorous. Jones.

Control: The treatment is preventive rather than curative. Avoid excessive watering and also avoid too high a temperature when the bulbs are being forced.

Yellow Rot.

Symptoms: The tip of the leaf is usually affected first and a characteristically yellow or brownish stripe appears down the mid-rib, causing the leaf to die. The sap tubes of the bulb become filled with a yellowish, slimy substance and in time the entire bulb is destroyed.

Nature of the Disease: Caused by the Pseudomonus hyacinthi

(Walker) E. F. S. Some varieties seem much more susceptible to Yellow Rot than others.

Control: No measure of control has as yet been discovered. All diseased bulbs should be dug up and destroyed.

INSECT PESTS

Bulb Mite.

Identification: Minute, whitish mites, bead-like in form. These are found in large numbers within the bulb scales. Reddish-brown spots appear at the point of injury.

Injury: The mites suck the juices from the plant tissues and the bulbs become soft and mushy. The vitality of the bulb is weakened and as a result growth is generally stunted—the leaves turn a sickly yellow and the flower buds either fail to develop or produce distorted flowers.

Life History: The eggs are laid inside the bulb scales and hatch out into six legged nymphs. After passing through a molt these change to an eight-legged form and it is in this stage that they are the most destructive. They molt again before becoming adults and several generations are produced each year. The mites frequently migrate through the soil from decaying bulbs to healthy ones.

Control: Discard and burn all badly infested bulbs. If the infestation is not severe treat the bulbs as follows:

Submerge bulbs for 3 hours in water which is kept at a temperature of 110 degrees F. This will kill all the mites but will not injure sound healthy bulbs in which root growth has not started.

Or: Soak bulbs for ten minutes in a solution of nicotine sulphate held at a temperature of 122 degrees F.

Nicotine sulphate—$2\frac{1}{2}$ teaspoonfuls to 1 gallon of water

Bulb Fly (Merodon equestris Fab.)

Identification: Bulbs are suspiciously soft and light in weight and small, brown scars are sometimes found upon the outer scales. Upon cutting the bulb open large fat maggots, grayish to yellowish-white in color, are found.

Injury: The maggots feed upon the tissues and render the bulbs practically worthless.

Life History: The adult fly is yellow and black in color and very hairy, resembling a bumble bee in appearance although it is considerably smaller. The female lays her eggs either in the neck of the bulb or at the base of the leaves. Upon hatching the young maggots bore their way into the bulb and begin feeding. They are equipped with strong, slightly hooked mouth parts which are admirably adapted for this purpose. The pupa stage is passed sometimes within the bulb, sometimes in the soil.

Control: Discard and burn badly infested bulbs that have become light in weight and soft.

If there is serious danger of infestation the following treatment is recommended.

Submerge bulbs for 2½ hours in hot water which is held at a temperature of 110 degrees F. Immerse in cold water as soon as they are removed. This will kill the larvæ in all stages of development and will not harm the bulbs if they are sound and have not started root growth.

Lesser Bulb Fly (Eumerus strigatus Fall).

Identification: Bulbs become soft and light in weight and upon examination maggots will be found feeding within the tissues. The maggots are grayish to yellowish-white in color, about ½ inch in length when full grown, and the body is decidedly wrinkled in appearance. They may be distinguished from the larvæ of the Bulb Fly (Merodon equestris) by this characteristic.

Injury: The maggots feed upon the tissues and ruin the bulbs.

Life History: The adult fly is blackish-green in color with white markings on the sides of the abdomen. It is about 1/3 of an inch long with an almost hairless body, and in general appearance it resembles a small wasp. The eggs are laid at the base of the leaves or in the neck of the bulb and the larvæ tunnel down into the bulb as soon as they have hatched. Two generations are usually produced during the season.

Control: Same as for Bulb Fly (Merodon equestris).

White Grubs.

Identification: Large, fleshy grub worms, grayish-white in color, with a brown head and six prominent legs. They are usually found buried in the soil in a curled position.

Injury: The grubs feed upon the roots, causing the plant to become stunted and weakened.

Life History: See page 1077.

Control: See page 1077.

IRIS

DISEASES

Leaf Spot.

Symptoms: In the early stages small brown spots appear on the leaves. The spots enlarge as the disease progresses, the center becoming lighter and the margin decidedly darker. The foliage gradually turns brown and is killed entirely.

Nature of the Disease: A fungous disease caused by Didymellinia Iridis (Desm.) Hoehn. It is becoming more and more prevalent in many sections and causes severe losses. The fungus lives over the winter on the dead leaves and infection on the new growth usually becomes apparent about the middle of June. Some varieties seem to be very much more susceptible than others.

Control: Leaf Spot on Iris may be controlled to a very large extent by destroying all foliage during the winter months.

During the growing season infected leaves should be cut back as soon as trouble is detected. If the disease has gained headway it may be advisable to cut back the entire clump to within five or six inches of the ground and allow it to make new growth.

Lime and superphosphate worked into the soil about the plants are both considered helpful in keeping the disease in check.

Sclerotial Rot.

Symptoms: Leaves turn a yellowish-brown. Leaf stalks and flower stalks rot off at the base.

Nature of the Disease: Sclerotial rot of iris is caused by the fungus Sclerotium delphinii Welch., the same fungus which attacks many other plants. It is particularly prevalent during damp weather and where irises are planted on low, poorly drained land.

Control: 1. Sprinkle copper salt powder over the rhizomes. 2. Work several handfuls of gypsum into the soil about the plant.

Soft Rot.

Symptoms: The affected leaves and stems have a yellowish, unhealthy appearance, and at the base they become a mass of ill-smelling, rotting pulp. This disagreeable odor is very characteristic of the disease and readily distinguishes it from Sclerotial Rot, which is far less serious.

Nature of the Disease: A bacterial disease caused by Bacillus caratovorus. It is very prevalent in some sections and causes very severe losses.

Control: Dig up and burn all seriously affected plants. If the infection is slight apply any of the following treatments:

1. Sprinkle copper salt powder over the rhizomes, liberally.

2. Lift the rhizomes, scrape away all rotted portions and dip them in a pink solution of potassium permanganate, *or* dip in a solution of Semesan, 1 tablespoonful to 1 gal. water.

3. Dust the rhizomes thoroughly with fine sulphur. If the disease is prevalent it is well to take precautionary measures and to occasionally water all iris clumps with either the Semesan or permanganate solution.

Lime and superphosphate worked in about the plants are also effective in keeping Soft Rot under control.

INSECT PESTS

Iris Borer.

Identification: The borers are a pinkish-white in color with a row of dark spots on each side of the body. When full grown they measure about two inches in length. In spring the presence of the borers may be detected by the characteristic "bleeding" of the leaves at the point where they enter.

Injury: The borers tunnel down through the leaf into the rhizome, feeding upon the plant tissues as they continue their peregrinations. They weaken the vitality of the plant to a very serious extent and cause sickly, stunted growth.

Life History: The winter is passed in the egg stage and the young larvæ hatch out late in March or early in April. The tiny caterpillars crawl up the leaves, make a small hole in the outer surface, and as soon as they are safely within the tissues of the leaf they begin tunnelling their way down into the rhizome, feeding as they go. They become full grown about the first of August and pass into the pupa stage. At the end of three weeks the adult moths emerge, and early in the autumn they lay their eggs near the base of the leaves or on the roots which appear above the surface of the ground. The moths fly only at night.

Control: As a precautionary measure rake off and burn all dead leaves during the winter months. If great care is taken the entire bed may be burned over. This should be done early in March before the eggs hatch. The leaves should be loosened with a rake and a quick fire run through them. Unless the fire passes over the bed very quickly there is danger of injuring the rhizomes.

It is also frequently possible to detect some of the borers at work in the leaves early in the spring; they may be killed by squeezing them within the leaf. This is not a very agreeable way to annihilate them but it is very effective.

The following measures of control are also recommended.

Spray every ten days from the middle of April until the middle of June with:

Arsenate of lead 1 ounce, Casein 1 ounce, water 1 gallon. Use good pressure in order to obtain a fine mist which will adhere well. If this spraying is done thoroughly and systematically it should give about 90 per cent control.

After the borer has tunnelled its way down into the rhizome spraying is no longer effective and it is necessary to resort to more drastic measures of control.

The clumps may be lifted and the borers cut out of the rhizomes or the following treatment may be given:

Place a rounded teaspoonful of paradichlorobenzene (which may be secured from any seed and supply firm) in a small saucer and set it in the middle of the clump or as near to the plant as possible. Cover the plant with a bucket or a large air-tight container of some kind, piling up the earth around the bottom to prevent any passage of air. After twenty-four hours remove the can and the chemical. This treatment should be done when the temperature of the soil is between 75 and 85 degrees F. as the fumes of the chemical are not volatile enough to be effective when the temperature is below 70. The soil should be neither very wet nor very dry. The leaves of the plant may turn white from the heat but fresh growth will soon start and no ill effects will be seen the following season. Badly infected clumps may be absolutely freed of iris borers by this treatment.

Another measure of control which is recommended is the use of Calcium Cyanide. The rhizomes should be covered with dry sand before the application is made in order to prevent burning, and another layer of sand should be spread over the surface of the soil as soon as the calcium cyanide has been applied. The calcium cyanide should be applied at the rate of one ounce per square foot. If smaller quantities are used the results are not satisfactory.

The Lesser Bulb Fly which occasionally infests iris may also be entirely controlled by this treatment.

LANTANA

INSECT PESTS

Orange Tortrix.

Injury: The caterpillars roll and tie the leaves upon which they feed. They are a distinctly southern pest and sometimes cause considerable injury.

Control: Spray or dust with arsenate of lead.

Orthezia.

Identification: The young nymphs are very tiny, dark green in color, and wingless, with a row of waxy plates extending back over the body. The adult females have a very conspicuous white, fluted egg sack which extends back for a distance of two or more times the diameter of the body.

Injury: The orthezias are closely related to the scales and suck the juices from the plant.

Control: See page 1095.

White Fly.

Identification: Very small, whitish flies about 1/16 of an inch in length. They are usually found on the undersurface of the leaves.

Injury: White flies suck the juices from the plant causing a general lack of vigor. Leaves turn yellow and if the infestation is severe the plant will eventually die.

Life History: See page 1071.

Control: See page 1071.

LILIES
DISEASES

Botrytis Rot.

Symptoms: Spots which range in color from orange to brown appear on the leaves, stems and flower buds. A small dark area will be found in the center of each lesion. The spots gradually increase in size and in the latter stages of the disease, when the spores of the fungus begin to develop, the affected areas appear to be covered with a grayish mold. In severe cases the stem of the plant rots off, the flower buds fail to develop and the disease spreads down into the bulb.

Nature of the Disease: A fungous disease, Botrytis illiptica (Berk.) Cooke., which is very prevalent in some sections. Its spread is particularly favored by cool, wet weather. The spores are carried from one plant to another by wind and other agencies. The fungus lives over the winter on dead and decaying leaves and other garden refuse.

Control: Botrytis Rot can be almost entirely controlled by thorough and systematic spraying.

Spray with Bordeaux every week or ten days during the growing season; *or* Spray with livers of sulphur,* 2 ounces to 3 gallons of

---

*Potassium sulphide.

water. When the disease is first detected pick off and burn all affected leaves. If the disease has gained considerable headway cut off and burn all portions of the plant above the ground, lift the bulbs, and either dust them thoroughly with super-fine sulphur before replanting them or soak them in Semesan, 1 tablespoonful to 1 gallon of water, for several hours. They should be replanted in fresh soil.

It is also a wise precaution to practise clean cultivation and to rake up and burn all dead leaves and other refuse in the autumn.

Bulb Rot.

Symptoms: In the early stages a slightly darkened appearance is noted in the flesh of the bulb about the roots. As the disease progresses the bulb softens at the base and the entire heart may become rotten. The rotted portion is brown and cheesy. When bulbs are seriously affected the flower stalks are usually dwarfed and frequently break over and if any blooms are borne they are distorted and malformed.

Nature of the Disease: A fungous disease caused by Rhizopus necans Mass. It is frequently present on bulbs shipped from Japan and causes severe losses.

Control: If the bulbs are badly rotted discard them entirely. If, however, they are of considerable value and are only slightly affected it may prove worth while to treat them. The rotted portions should be carefully scraped out and the bulbs may then be given the following treatment:

Soak bulbs for 1½ hours in a solution of 1 part carbolic acid to 40 parts of water. After this treatment dust the bulbs thoroughly with powdered charcoal.

Leaf Spot.

Symptoms: Brown spots appear on the foliage and as the disease progresses the spores of the fungus form a powdery, mildew-like substance on the surface of the leaves.

Nature of the Disease: A fungous disease caused by Cercospora richardiæcola Ptk.

Control: Dust thoroughly with sulphur every week or ten days or spray with livers of sulphur, 2 ounces to 3 gallons of water.

Mosaic.

Symptoms: In the early stages the leaves have a curiously mottled appearance, being blotched and streaked with yellow. The disease usually progresses slowly. The second year the leaves and stems become twisted and distorted and no flowers are formed. Eventually the plant succumbs entirely but it will usually linger on for a number of years.

Nature of the Disease: Mosaic disease is becoming more and more serious and in some sections it is entirely wiping out large colonies of Lilies. The disease is carried from one plant to another by aphids in very much the same way that mosquitos carry malaria to human beings. In sucking the juices of a diseased plant the aphids pick up the infectious virus, later transmitting it to healthy plants. The virus penetrates to every portion of the plant. If infection occurs late in the summer the disease may not become active until the following season. Therefore apparently healthy bulbs may be carriers of the disease.

Control: At present no effective cure for mosaic disease is known. Pull up and burn all diseased plants in order to reduce sources of infection.

Frequent dusting with nicotine will help to keep the aphids under control and will thus lessen the chances of infection. Some gardeners prefer to grow newly purchased bulbs in a quarantine area until it is known that they are free from disease.

Rust.

Symptoms: Small, brown, rusty patches appear both on the upper and undersurface of the leaves.

Nature of the Disease: A fungous disease. Some varieties are much more susceptible than others. Regal and Bermuda lilies are seldom attacked. Candidum lilies are very susceptible, particularly so when planted in shady places.

Control: Dust thoroughly with super-fine sulphur or spray with livers of sulphur, 2 ounces to 3 gallons of water. After rust has once gained headway it is very difficult to control and this treatment is more in the nature of a preventive rather than a cure.

INSECT PESTS

Aphids.

Identification: Soft-bodied, louse-like insects which are usually found clustered near the tips of the young, growing shoots. They vary in size, the newly hatched young being considerably smaller than the adults.

Injury: Aphids suck the juices from the plant, causing a general lack of vigor and stunted growth. They are also carriers of the

1125

Mosaic disease on lilies and every effort should therefore be made to keep them under control.

Life History: See page 1069.

Control: See page 1070.

Stalk Borer.

Identification: Slender caterpillars from one to two inches in length. The young caterpillars are brown with white stripes. When full grown they lose their stripes and become a solid, dirty gray in color.

Injury: The stalk borer makes a small, round hole in the stem and tunnels up through the stalk causing the injured shoot to suddenly wilt and break over.

Life History: See page 1076.

Control: See page 1076.

LOBELIA

INSECT PEST

Red-Banded Leaf Roller.

Identification: Small, active caterpillars, about ¾ of an inch in length. Greenish in color with a distinctive red band from which they derive their name.

Injury: The caterpillars feed upon the leaves, rolling them together in a very characteristic fashion.

Life History: See page 1150.

Control: Dust or spray with arsenate of lead.

LUNARIA

(Honesty)

INSECT PEST

Harlequin Bug (Harlequin Cabbage Beetle).

Identification: The body is flat, shield-shaped and about ⅜ of an inch long, the back being gaily decorated with red-and-black markings.

Injury: Both the young nymphs and the adults suck the sap from the plant tissues and if the infestation is severe it may cause the death of the plant.

Life History: See page 1094.

Control: See page 1094.

MARIGOLD

DISEASES

Wilt.

Symptoms: The lower leaves turn yellow in the early stages and this condition gradually spreads over the entire plant. The sap tubes become brown and the plants eventually wilt and die.

Nature of the Disease: The wilt of marigolds is caused by the same bacteria that affect tomatoes and various other vegetables.

Control: At present no remedy is known. Diseased plants should be pulled up and burned.

Yellows.

Symptoms: Leaves turn yellow. Plants become stunted and fail to produce normal bloom. The plants are seldom killed outright, usually lingering on until frost.

Nature of the Disease: See page 1073.

Control: See page 1073.

INSECT PESTS

Tarnished Plant Bug.

Identification: A small, very active bug about ¼ inch in length. The body is oval in shape, being somewhat triangular in front. Coppery-brown in color with dark brown and yellow flecks on the back.

Injury: The bugs puncture the shoots just below the flower buds, causing the buds to droop and die. The injury completely destroys any chance of bloom. It is thought that while feeding the Tarnished Plant Bug injects some substance into the plant which is highly injurious and has the effect of a poison.

Life History: See page 1076.

Control: See page 1076.

MIGNONETTE

DISEASES

Leaf Spot or **Blight.**

Symptoms: Small, slightly sunken spots with pale yellowish-brown margins appear on the leaves. As the disease progresses dark specks which are the fruiting bodies of the fungus develop in the center of the spots and the leaves gradually wither and die.

Nature of the Disease: A fungous disease caused by Cercospora resedæ. Fckl.

Control: Spray with Bordeaux every week or ten days during the growing season.

INSECT PESTS

Cabbage Looper.

Identification: Greenish caterpillars with a white line along each side of the body and two lines near the middle of the back. The middle half of the body is without legs, and when resting or moving the caterpillar is usually in a very characteristic humped position.

Injury: The caterpillars feed upon the leaves.

Life History: The winter is passed in the pupa stage, the delicate, white pupa cases being attached to a leaf of some host plant. The small, grayish-brown moths emerge in spring and the females lay their eggs singly upon the upper surface of the leaves of the host plants. The moths fly only at night. After hatching the larvæ feed for three to four weeks and then pass into the pupa stage. During the summer the pupa stage covers a period of only two weeks and there are usually three or four generations during the season.

Control: Spray or dust as soon as infestation is noticed.

Spray Formula

Arsenate of lead .....½ ounce
Fish oil soap ....1 cu. in. dissolved in boiling water
Water ....1 gallon

Dust Formula

Arsenate of lead ...1 part
Sulphur...........3 parts

Cabbage Worm.

Identification: Small, velvety-green caterpillars somewhat more than an inch in length when full grown.

Injury: Large irregular holes eaten in the foliage.

Life History: See page 1082.

Control: Same as for Cabbage looper. (See above.)

MORNING GLORY

INSECT PEST

Golden Tortoise Beetle or **Gold Bug.**

Identification: A small, golden-colored beetle about ¼ of an inch long. Occasionally black stripes or dots are found on the body. The beetle is turtle-shaped, being flat on the underside with the head and legs partially hidden.

Injury: The beetles feed upon the foliage.

Life History: The adult beetles hibernate during the winter in dry, sheltered places, and they usually do not come out of hiding until late in the spring. The eggs, which are laid on the leaves of the host plants, hatch in about a week or ten days and the larvæ begin feeding. Their feeding is confined largely to the underside of the leaves. After feeding for a short time they pass into the pupa stage and a few weeks later the adults emerge.

Control: Spray or dust thoroughly with arsenate of lead.

NARCISSUS

DISEASES

Botrytis Bulb Rot.

Symptoms: Leaves and stems become covered with unsightly spots. Small, black, resting bodies known as sclerotia are frequently found in the rotting tissues of the bulbs.

Nature of the Disease: A fungous disease similar to that which affects tulips.

Control: Dig up and burn badly infected bulbs. Soak bulbs for two hours before planting in
> Semesan—1 tablespoonful to 1 gallon of water

Gray Bulb Rot.

Symptoms: Dry rot begins at the tip of the bulb. The flesh of the bulb becomes a reddish gray in color and the diseased portions are often covered with dark brown sclerotia or resting bodies. The bulbs finally rot away entirely.

Control: Dig up and burn all diseased bulbs. Disinfect the soil with formaldehyde before planting any other bulbs in the same area.

INSECT PESTS

Bulb Fly (Merodon equestris Fab.).

Identification: Small brown scars are sometimes found upon the outer scales. Bulbs are suspiciously soft and light in weight. Upon cutting the bulb open large, fat maggots are found. The color varies from grayish to yellowish white and when full grown they are about ¾ of an inch in length.

Injury: The maggots feed upon the tissues and render the bulbs practically worthless.

Life History: See page 1118.

Control: See page 1119.

Lesser Bulb Fly (Eumerus strigatus Fall.).

Identification: Bulbs become soft and light in weight and upon examination maggots will be found feeding upon the tissues. The maggots are grayish to yellowish white, about ½ inch in length when full grown and the body is very much wrinkled. They may be readily distinguished from the larvæ of Merodon equestris by this characteristic wrinkled appearance.

Injury: Same as that of the Bulb Fly.

Life History: See page 1119.

Control: See page 1119.

Bulb Mite.

Identification: Minute whitish mites, bead-like in form, found in large numbers within the bulb scales. Reddish brown spots appear at the point of injury.

Injury: The mites suck the juices from the plant tissues and the bulbs become soft and mushy. The vitality of the bulb is weakened and as a result growth is stunted. The leaves turn a sickly yellow and the flower buds either fail to develop or produce distorted blooms.

Life History: See page 1118.

Control: See page 1118.

Nematodes.

Identification: Upon cutting open an infested bulb a brown ring will be found, and with the use of a hand lens one may detect the nematodes, which are minute worms of a transparent color and hardly more than 1/25 of an inch in length.

Injury: Plants make stunted growth. The leaves become curiously twisted and distorted and lie prostrate on the ground, turning yellow and dying prematurely. Thickened specks or speckles are produced upon the leaves and are very characteristic of infestation.

Life History: The eggs, four to five hundred being laid by a single female, are deposited within the tissues of the plant. Upon hatching, the larvæ usually remain within the plant but occasionally they migrate through the soil to other hosts. It is during this stage that they so often find their way into the greenhouse or into the garden when fresh soil is brought in. Located in the mouth of each worm is a sharply pointed, spear-like apparatus which is used to bore through the root tissues when a new host plant is attacked, and it is also used while feeding. During the first two to three weeks after hatching the male and female larvæ are identical in size and shape. During the molting period, however, when the old skin is shed, the female undergoes a distinct change and becomes pear-shaped, being pearly white in color. The male remains spindle-shaped.

In the South the worms winter over in the open. In the North they are usually killed by the cold unless harbored in frames or in greenhouses.

Control: Destroy all badly infested bulbs. Bulbs which are only lightly infested or of which one may be suspicious may be given the following treatment:

Submerge bulbs for three hours in water kept at a temperature of 110 degrees F. Plunge immediately in cold water after treatment.

NASTURTIUM

DISEASE

Wilt. The lower leaves turn yellow in the early stages and this condition gradually spreads over the entire plant. The sap tubes become brown and the plants eventually wilt and die.

Nature of the Disease: The wilt of nasturtiums is caused by Bacterium solanacearum E. F. S., the same bacteria that causes the wilt of potatoes.

Control: At present no remedy is known. Diseased plants should be pulled up and burned.

INSECT PESTS

Aphids. Soft-bodied, louse-like insects usually found clustered on the tips of the young, growing shoots. The species that infests nasturtiums is black in color.

Injury: Aphids suck the juices from the plant, causing the leaves and stems to become curled and distorted.

Life History: See page 1069.

Control: See page 1070.

Cabbage Looper.

Identification: Greenish caterpillars with a white line along each side of the body and two lines near the middle of the back. The middle half of the body is without legs, and both when resting and when moving the caterpillar is in a very characteristic humped position.

Injury: The caterpillars feed upon the leaves.

Life History: See page 1128.

Control: See page 1128.

Cabbage Worm.

Identification: Small, velvety-green caterpillars somewhat more than an inch in length when full grown.

Injury: The caterpillars feed upon the foliage.

Life History: See page 1082.

Control: See page 1082.

ŒNOTHERA
(Evening Primrose)

INSECT PEST

Primrose Flea Beetle.

Identification: A small, very active beetle, a metallic blue in color.

Injury: Both the larvæ and the adult beetles feed upon the foliage. If the infestation is severe the leaves may become completely skeletonized.

Life History: The adult beetles usually appear early in June and the females deposit their eggs upon the leaves of the host plant. Upon hatching, the larvæ feed for a short time and then pass into the pupa stage, the second generation emerging late in July. The winter is passed either in the pupa or adult stage.

Control: Spray or dust thoroughly with arsenate of lead as soon as infestation is first noticed. Bordeaux mixture acts as a repellent.

PANSY

DISEASES

Anthracnose.

Symptoms: Small brown spots with a narrow, dark border appear on the foliage and the petals. The flowers are usually malformed and fail to produce seed. If the disease is not checked the plants eventually die.

Nature of the Disease: A fungous disease caused by Colletotrichum violæ-tricoloris Smith. The spores of the fungus are carried on the seed and infection may usually be traced to this source.

Control: Spray thoroughly with Bordeaux as soon as trouble is detected. It is also wise to pull up and burn all badly infected plants in order to check the spread of the ripened spores.

Leaf Spot.

Symptoms: Dead-looking spots appear on the leaves. In the very early stages the spots are small with dark margins but they rapidly become larger until the whole leaf is involved. The petals of the flowers also become blotched and spotted; flower buds fail to open or produce distorted bloom.

Nature of the Disease: A fungous disease caused by Cercospora violæ Sacc.

Control: Spray every few weeks with Bordeaux or with ammoniacal-copper carbonate. Destroy badly diseased plants.

Rust.

Symptoms: Small, reddish-brown pustules found upon the leaves and stems.

Nature of the Disease: A fungous disease caused by Puccinia violæ.

Control: Pull up and burn all infected plants. Dust remaining plants with super-fine sulphur as a precautionary measure.

Yellows.

Symptoms: Plants become dwarfed and stunted. Foliage turns a greenish yellow.

Control: At present no effective control is known. Pull up and burn all diseased plants.

INSECT PESTS

Aphids.

Identification: Soft-bodied, louse-like insects usually found clustered along the tips of the young growing shoots. The species that most commonly infests pansy plants is pale green.

Injury: Aphids suck the juices from the plant, causing it to have a sickly, unhealthy appearance.

Life History: See page 1069.

Control: See page 1070.

Violet Sawfly.

Identification: Small, slug-like larvæ, bluish black in color with conspicuous white spots on the back and sides. When full grown they are about ½ inch in length.

Injury: The larvæ are usually found close to the ground, feeding upon the lower leaves, but if the infestation is severe the entire plant may be eaten.

Control: Spray or dust thoroughly with arsenate of lead, making sure to reach the lower leaves.

PEONY

DISEASES

Anthracnose.

Symptoms: Spots appear on the stems and leaves. In the early stages the center is almost white with a dark, reddish border. Later in the season, the spots become sunken with a small black pimple in the center.

Nature of the Disease: A fungous disease which occasionally attacks peonies.

Control: Spray frequently with Bordeaux mixture. Remove and burn diseased portions of the plant.

Botrytis.

Symptoms: Young shoots rot off at the ground line when 5 to 8 inches tall, the stems having a water-soaked, cankerous appearance. The rotted portion later becomes covered with a soft brown mass of spores. The flower buds turn brown and fail to open and the flower stalk is usually affected for several inches below the bud. During a severe outbreak of the disease 90 per cent of the flower buds may fail to develop. Open flowers also occasionally become affected, turning dark brown and becoming a mass of rotting petals. The leaves are usually the last part of the plant to show any trace of infection, being attacked first at the tips. Large, irregular spots appear, being dark in the early stages, later fading to light brown. There are dark concentric rings within the lesions on both the leaves and the stems which are very characteristic of the disease.

Nature of the Disease: A fungous disease caused by Botrytis pæoniæ Oud. which is very destructive in many sections of the country. It is particularly prevalent in damp, rainy seasons. Small, black resting bodies, known as sclerotia, are formed in the diseased stems and the fungus is carried over the winter in this manner.

Control: Partial control may be obtained by spraying with Bordeaux. The first application should be given as soon as growth begins in the spring and subsequent application should be given every few weeks throughout the season. Bordeaux is not entirely satisfactory as the sugary exudation from the buds seems to neutralize the effect of the spray to some extent. This is extremely unfortunate since this very exudation provides ideal conditions for the germination of the spores. The spores are carried by wind and by insects and the disease spreads rapidly from one plant to another. It is thought that the ants play an important part in carrying the spores from the base of the diseased plants to the buds.

One of the most effective measures of control consists in the removal of all dead stubble. The soil should be scraped away from the base of the plant and the old stalks should be cut as close to the crown as possible.

During the growing season any shoots, leaves or flower buds that show the least sign of infection should be immediately removed and burned. It is important that the disease be detected in the early stages as the spores are produced very rapidly and in great abundance.

Leaf Blotch.

Symptoms: Large spots, 2 to 3 inches in diameter, appear on the leaves late in the season. The spots are very characteristic, being purple on the upper surface and dull brown on the lower surface. In damp weather the spots on the lower surface appear to be covered with a felt-like substance, olive-green in color.

Nature of the Disease: A fungous disease caused by Cladosporium pæoniæ Pass.

Control: As the fungus lives over the winter on the old leaves the disease may be kept almost entirely under control by cutting off and burning all top growth after the plants have become dormant in the autumn.

Mosaic Disease.

Symptoms: Leaves become blotched with alternating rings of light and dark green. The spots vary considerably in size, some being small with narrow margins and others being large with much wider margins. Frequently only one or two stalks in the clump are affected

Nature of the Disease: See page 1125.

Control: See page 1125.

Phytophthora Blight.

Symptoms: Large, dark brown spots appear on the leaves resembling those of Botrytis but lacking the concentric markings. The buds are usually blighted and fail to open and the crown of the plant may become rotted.

Nature of the Disease: The disease is caused by the fungus Phytophthora pæoniæ Coop. and Port.

Control: Spray with Bordeaux as soon as growth begins in the spring and every few weeks during the growing season. Destroy all top growth in the autumn.

Stem Rot.

Symptoms: Stalks suddenly wilt, due to rotting at the base. Large black resting bodies or sclerotia are found in the pith at the base of the plant and readily distinguish this disease from any other.

Nature of the Disease: A fungous disease caused by Sclerotiorum (Lib.) Mass. Damp, rainy weather is particularly favorable to its spread.

Control: As soon as the disease is detected, the infected stalks should be cut away close to the crown. As the fungus spreads from stalk to stalk through the soil it is well to remove the soil from about the crown, replacing it with clean sand. Manure should never be allowed to come into direct contact with the crowns. All growth above ground should be burned in the autumn.

Wilt.

Symptoms: Plants show signs of wilt and gradually die. The sap tubes become clogged and when the stem is split open they appear as greenish streaks.

Nature of the Disease: The disease is caused by the fungus Verticillium albo-atrum Reinke and Berth.

Control: See page 1069.

INSECT PESTS

Ants. Ants are frequently found on peonies, being attracted by the sweetish, sticky substance which is exuded from the buds. While they do no direct harm themselves, it is very probable that they carry the spores of fungous diseases from one plant to another, provided such spores are present. For control see Chapter XXXIV.

Rose Beetle.

Identification: Long-legged beetles, grayish fawn in color and about ½ inch in length.

Injury: The beetles feed upon the flowers, completely destroying them in a very short time.

Life History: See page 1151.

Control: See page 1151.

Rose Cucurlio.

Identification: Bright red beetles with black legs and snout, about ¼ inch in length.

Injury: The beetles eat holes in the unopened buds and also feed to some extent upon the leaves. Buds either fail to open or produce flowers riddled with holes.

Life History: See page 1152.

Control: See page 1152.

Nematodes causing *Root Gall.*

Identification: Swollen places are found on the roots which are caused by microscopic worms. The roots are often short and stubby, the fine rootlets being covered with galls. The crown of the plant is also occasionally swollen.

Injury: The growth of the plant is very seriously affected if the infestation is severe.

Life History: See page 1130.

Control: If the infested plants are of considerable value they may be lifted and the affected portions of the roots may be cut away. The remaining roots should then be soaked for several minutes in a 1 per cent solution of formaldehyde. When the roots are replanted sulphur may be mixed with the soil which acts as a repellent.

Infestation is less likely to be serious on heavy soils than on sandy soils.

Oyster Shell Scale.

Identification: Small, grayish white scales, resembling an oyster shell in shape, are found clustered in masses along the stems.

Injury: The scales suck the juices from the plant causing general lack of vigor and the eventual death of the infested shoots.

Life History: During the winter the eggs are protected by the hard, shell-like covering of the old scales. The young hatch out about the end of May or early in June. At this stage they are soft-bodied and look like small, yellowish white specks on the stems. Later in the season the hard, shell-like covering is formed.

Control: About June 1 and again about June 15 spray the plants thoroughly with the following solution:

Spray Formula

Black Leaf 40	2 teaspoonfuls
Fish-oil soap	¼ pound
Water	1 gallon

It is possible to destroy the scales at this time while they are in the soft-bodied stage. Later in the season after the hard scale-like covering has formed it is practically impossible to reach them as any spray strong enough to be effective would be injurious to a growing plant.

As a means of destroying wintering places, all growth above ground should be cut down and burned in the autumn after the plants have become dormant.

Stalk Borer.

Identification: Slender caterpillars about 2 inches in length. The young caterpillars are brown with white stripes. When full grown they loose their stripes and become a solid, dirty gray in color.

Injury: The stalk borer makes a small round hole in the stem and tunnels up through the stalk, causing the injured shoot to suddenly wilt and break over.

Life History: See page 1076.

Control: See page 1076.

PETUNIA

DISEASE

Mosaic.

Symptoms: The foliage becomes a mottled yellow and green in color. The leaves are frequently distorted and the growth of the plant is stunted.

Nature of the Disease: See page 1125.

Control: See page 1125.

INSECT PESTS

Orthezia.

Identification: The young nymphs are very tiny, dark green in color and wingless with a row of waxy plates extending back over the body. The adult females have a very conspicuous white, fluted egg sack which extends back for a distance of two or more times the diameter of the body.

Injury: The orthezias are closely related to the scales and suck the juices from the plant tissues.

Control: See page 1095.

Potato Flea Beetle.

Identification: Small, very active beetle about 1/16 of an inch long, black in color. The hind legs are longer than the front legs and enable the beetle to jump like a flea when disturbed.

Injury: The beetles feed upon the foliage, making many small holes either round or irregular in shape. The leaves have the appearance of being peppered with fine shot. The foliage becomes badly disfigured and if the infestation is very serious it may cause the death of the plant.

Life History: The adults hibernate during the winter under leaves or trash and emerge early in the spring. The eggs, which are minute in size, are laid in the soil about the plants. The larvæ are small, slender whitish worms. They feed to some extent upon the roots and underground stems of weeds and cultivated plants but do comparatively little damage. After feeding for a few weeks they pass into the pupa stage in the soil and a short time later the adult flea beetles emerge. There are usually two generations a year.

Control: Spray every ten days with a mixture of arsenate of lead and Bordeaux.

Yellow Woolly-bear Caterpillar.

Identification: A caterpillar about 2 inches in length when full grown. The body is completely covered with long hairs which vary in color from pale yellow to reddish brown.

Injury: The caterpillars feed upon the foliage.

Life History: See page 1096.

Control: See page 1096.

PHLOX

DISEASES

Leaf Spot.

Symptoms: Dark spots, ranging in color from brown to black, appear on the leaves and in time the plant may become almost completely defoliated.

Nature of the Disease: A fungous disease caused by Septoria divaricata Ell. and Ev. The fungus lives over the winter on the fallen leaves and is ready to reinfect the new growth in the spring.

Control: Dust with copper-lime dust when the plants are wet with dew. Or spray with ammoniacal-copper carbonate. Rake up and burn all dead leaves and rubbish in the autumn.

Mildew.

Symptoms: The foliage becomes covered with a white, powdery substance. In the most advanced stages the affected areas turn black. Mildew is very disfiguring to the plant and is injurious to its growth. Especially prevalent in damp seasons.

Nature of the Disease: The disease is caused by the fungus Erysiphe cichoracearum D. C.

Control: Dust thoroughly with superfine sulphur or spray with livers of sulphur at the rate of 1 oz. to 3½ gal. of water. In the autumn remove the tops and rake up and burn fallen leaves. It is well to divide the clumps and give the plants plenty of space.

Phlox Blight.

Symptoms: The lower leaves of the plant become spotted and gradually turn brown and die. In the majority of cases only the lower portion of the plant is affected. The upper portion of the plant continues to make good growth, appears healthy and vigorous, and produces normal bloom. In occasional instances the disease progresses slowly upward, eventually killing the entire stem.

Nature of the Disease: In the past it has been thought that Phlox Blight was caused either by a fungus or by injury from some insect or mite, but recent investigations carried on at Cornell and at the New Jersey Agricultural Experiment Station tend to prove that the trouble is attributable to the peculiar growth habits of certain types of phlox. In the paniculata types the new shoots in the spring are borne on the stem of the previous season's growth, and these new shoots obtain their water and nutrients through the old stems. As growth advances the old stems begin to decay and there is an apparent disturbance in the flow of nutrients into the young and vigorously growing shoots, causing the characteristic symptoms of phlox blight, the theory being that the growing tips draw the moisture from the lower leaves. Some varieties appear to be much more susceptible than others, and when phlox plants are grown in a very moist climate the trouble is less severe. The suffruticosa types of phlox seldom suffer from blight, due to the fact that the new shoots start from a much lower point on the old stems or directly from the crown, and they soon become established on their own roots.

Measures of Control: Various measures of control are recommended. The removal of the first shoots in early spring will induce the formatioin of new bud growth, either directly from the crown of the plant or at a point lower down on the old stem, and it has been found that such growth is comparatively free from blight. Another measure of control which is proving very satisfactory is to prune back the old stalks to sound wood and to paint them with Bordeaux paste.

INSECT PESTS

Black Blister Beetle.

Identification: Slender jet black beetles about ½ inch in length with very prominent head and neck. It exudes a yellow oily fluid from joints of legs when disturbed.

Injury: The beetles feed upon the flowers, completely destroying them in a very short time.
Life History: See page 1074.
Control: See page 1074.

Corn Ear Worm.

Identification: Large striped worms about 2 inches in length when full grown. They vary in color from light green to brown and the stripes which run lengthwise with the body are alternating light and dark. The head is yellow, the legs almost black.
Injury: The caterpillars feed upon the plants.
Life History: See page 1086.
Control: See page 1087.

Nematodes.

Identification: Minute, microscopic worms. Their presence is usually detected by their characteristic injury to the plant.
Injury: Plants are dwarfed and stunted. Few flowers develop. Foliage frequently becomes spotted and distorted. Small, swollen, knotty growths are found upon the roots.
Life History: See page 1130.
Control: See page 1131.

PHYSALIS FRANCHETI
(Japanese Lantern Plant)

INSECT PEST

Tortoise Beetle or Gold Bug.

Identification: A small golden beetle about ¼ inch in length. Occasionally black spots or stripes are found on the body. The beetle is turtle-shaped, being flat on the underside with the head and legs partially hidden.
Injury: The beetles feed upon the foliage.
Life History: See page 1129.
Control: See page 1129.

PRIMROSE
DISEASES

Chlorosis.

Symptoms: Leaves become somewhat mottled in appearance, yellow and white. Plants fail to make vigorous growth.

Nature of the Disease: A physiological disease which is thought to be due to intense acidity in the soil.

Control: An application of the following is recommended. Three applications should be made, one week apart.

> 1 oz. sulphate of iron
> 1 oz. nitrate of soda
> 15 gal. water

Rot.

Symptoms: Plants rot off at the crown, becoming covered with a gray mold.

Nature of the Disease: The disease is caused by Botrytis vulgaris Fr. which is very prevalent under conditions of extreme dampness.

Control: Spray with Bordeaux or dust with copper-lime dust.

INSECT PEST

Potato Flea Beetle.

Identification: A small, very active beetle, metallic blue in color. The hind legs are longer than the front legs and enable the beetle to jump like a flea.

Injury: The beetles feed upon the foliage, making many small holes, either round or irregular in shape. The leaves have the appearance of being peppered with fine shot.

Life History: See page 1139.

Control: Spray frequently with a mixture of arsenate of lead and Bordeaux.

PYRETHRUM

DISEASE

Yellows.

Symptoms: Plants become dwarfed if attacked when young. Leaves that are not mature at the time infection takes place turn bright yellow. Blossoms become dwarfed and distorted, frequently developing only on one side. Plants are seldom killed outright, usually living on until cut down by frost.

Control: See page 1091.

ROSE

DISEASES

Black Spot.

Symptoms: Black spots appear on the foliage. Leaves turn yellow and drop prematurely. The spots are somewhat circular in shape, having irregular margins, and they occasionally reach a diameter of half an inch or more. They are confined entirely to the upper surface of the leaf. The disease first makes its appearance early in the summer and becomes particularly virulent later in the season. It saps the vitality of the plant to a great extent and in severe cases causes complete defoliation.

Nature of the Disease: Black Spot is caused by a fungus known as Diplocarpon rosæ Wolf. The winter spores, which are protected during the cold months by minute sacs, mature at about the time that roses begin their growth in the spring. These spores are carried to the leaves by wind, splashing rain, and other agencies and when conditions of temperature and moisture are favorable they germinate, sending out tiny germ-tubes which penetrate the outer covering or cuticle of the leaf. When safely within the leaf these germ-tubes develop a vegetative, thread-like structure which is known as mycelium. About two weeks after infection has taken place these mycelium produce millions of spores which are spoken of as secondary or summer spores. These are readily blown about by the wind, finding lodgement on near-by plants. If conditions happen to be extremely favorable they germinate within a few hours. Thus successive crops of these summer spores are produced throughout the season at intervals of from two to three weeks and the disease gains tremendous headway as the season advances unless proper measure of control are taken. The fungus lives over the winter on dead and decaying leaves, special winter spores being produced.

Control: Black Spot cannot be cured but it *can* be kept under control. After a leaf is once attacked, after the minute germ-tubes have once penetrated through the outer tissues, there is no chemical known which will kill the fungus and not be injurious to the growing plant. The problem, therefore, is to prevent infection, and fortunately, with a reasonable amount of care, this is possible. However, the importance of prompt and systematic attention cannot be over-emphasized. If the foliage is coated with an effective fungicide the spores will fail to germinate, and will be unable to start new centers of infection. As a matter of further precaution all leaves which drop to the ground should be immediately raked up and burned.

Fungicides

As the spores require a certain amount of moisture in order to germinate it is essential that the foliage be protected particularly well during rainy weather. The following controls are recommended:

1. Massey Dust is one of the most efficient fungicides to be used in the control of Black Spot. It is a very finely ground mixture consisting of nine parts of sulphur and one part arsenate of lead. This should be applied with a dust gun or bellows either in the evening, or early in the morning when the foliage is wet with dew. The first application should be made as soon as the bushes are well leafed out, and from then on, through the balance of the season it is advisable to make weekly applications.

2. There are various commercial preparations on the market which are similar to Massey Dust in analysis and most of these are equally efficient. One large chemical company puts out a dust which is green in color and is consequently less disfiguring to the foliage than most dusts containing a large percentage of sulphur. This is on the market as Pomo-Green.

3. One of the most effective commercial sprays on the market is put out under the trade name of Triogen. It is effective against aphids, Japanese beetles, and numerous other pests as well as against Black Spot. If roses are sprayed systematically every week or ten days throughout the season with Triogen, the foliage may be kept in vigorous, healthy condition and Black Spot may be kept under perfect control.

4. A very effective spray material may be mixed as follows:

> 2 tablespoonfuls of Magnetic Wettable Sulphur
> 2 tablespoonfuls of Powdered Arsenate of Lead
> 2 teaspoonfuls of Nicotine Sulphate (40% solution)
> 1 gallon of water

Each of the ingredients should be mixed separately with a small quantity of water, a pint or slightly more. The balance of the required amount of water should then be put in the spray tank or bucket. The sulphur which has been mixed with water should be added and stirred thoroughly, being strained through a fine screen. The arsenate of lead mixture should then be added, also being strained. The nicotine should be added and the entire mixture stirred thoroughly.

Brown Canker

Symptoms: In the early stages small, purplish-red areas appear on the stems and the petioles of the leaves. As the disease progresses the spots develop a lighter center with a definite purple margin. When the leaves and flowers are affected the same characteristic spots appear, being more or less cinnamon-buff in color. Usually only the outer, more exposed petals of the flowers are affected. When the flower buds are attacked they either fail to open or produce distorted, malformed blooms. In some cases a branch becomes completely girdled by Brown Canker and occasionally an entire plant will succumb to the disease if it is not checked.

Nature of the Disease: Brown Canker is caused by Diaporthe umbrina (Jenk.). It is a disease which has gained much headway during the past decade and it causes severe losses in many sections.

Control: Recent experiments have proved that thorough and systematic spraying with Bordeaux mixture will keep Brown Canker pretty well under control. Spraying should begin early in the spring and continue throughout the growing season.

Crown Canker.

Symptoms: Crown Canker usually attacks roses at the point of union between the stock and the scion and it frequently extends up the stem for a short distance above the ground. The affected area appears blackened and water-soaked. The stem above the canker becomes swollen, the bark cracks and the wood becomes lifeless. The roots may also be affected and become rotten.

Nature of the Disease: Crown Canker is caused by Cylindrocladium scoparium Morg. While it seldom kills the plants outright their vigor and vitality is greatly reduced and they become more susceptible to attacks from other diseases. They lack the healthy, green color of a normal plant and are not as floriferous.

Control: Rose bushes which are seriously attacked by Crown Canker should be dug up and destroyed. As a precautionary measure sand or coal ashes should be placed about the crown of the plant in order to provide better drainage.

Stem Canker.

Symptoms: In the early stages Stem Canker appears as a slender, purple stripe on the branches. As the disease progresses the affected area becomes dry and brown and somewhat sunken and the stem may become partially or entirely girdled. It reduces the vigor of the plant, causing sickly, weakened growth above the point of attack.

Nature of the Disease: Stem Canker is caused by Coniothyrium frickelii Sacc., the same fungus which causes the cane blight of raspberries.

Control: Cut out and burn all branches attacked by Stem Canker. It is a wise precaution to dip the shears in a corrosive sublimate solution each time they are used in order to lessen the danger of carrying the spores of the fungus from one branch to another.

Leaf Rust.

Symptoms: In the early stages bright orange-colored pustules are found on the undersurface of the leaves. As the disease progresses the pustules become brick-red in color.

Nature of the Disease: Leaf Rust is a fungous disease caused by Phragmidium sp. It causes the foliage to become unhealthy in appearance and if the infection is severe the vitality of the plant is seriously affected.

Control: Frequent dusting with super-fine sulphur will keep the disease under control to a considerable extent.

Affected leaves should be picked off and burned. All fallen leaves should be raked up and burned in the autumn.

A dormant spray of lime-sulphur or Bordeaux mixture followed by weekly applications of sulphur dust during the growing season will control the disease.

Mildew.

Symptoms: In the early stages grayish or whitish spots are found on the young leaves and shoots. These spots gradually enlarge and the stems, foliage and unopened buds become almost completely covered with a white, powdery substance. In the most advanced stages the affected areas turn black. Not only is mildew very disfiguring but it also seriously affects the vigor and growth of the plants. If it is not checked the foliage and flower buds become dwarfed and mal-formed and many of the leaves drop prematurely.

Nature of the Disease: Mildew is a fungous disease caused by Sphærotheca pannosa (Walk.) Lev. It is a mold-like growth, the greater portion being confined to the outer surface of the leaves. The minute white threads form a network with their numerous strands and at frequent intervals chains of egg-shaped spores are borne on upright branches. When mature these spores are blown about by the wind and find lodgement on nearby plants. As soon as temperature and moisture conditions are favorable they germinate and establish new centers of infection. The individual spores are comparatively short-lived but new ones are constantly being produced. Special spores are produced to carry the fungus over the winter months and these are ready to start trouble as soon as spring comes.

The original source of infection may usually be traced to spores which were brought into the garden when new plants were purchased. Pot grown roses are very apt to be infected. Greenhouse roses may also prove another source of infection. Mildew is often very troublesome on roses grown under glass, and as the spores are blown about by the slightest wind it is probable that roses growing in a garden some distance away might become infected in this manner.

Mildew is especially prevalent during damp, rainy seasons as the spores are then provided with ideal conditions for germination. Some varieties are much more susceptible to mildew than others. The Crimson Ramblers and closely related forms are highly susceptible.

Control: Since mildew is one of the most common of our rose diseases it is fortunate that it is a comparatively easy thing to control. Frequent and thorough dustings with fine sulphur will keep roses free from mildew throughout the season.

Stem Rust.

Symptoms: Canker-like spots, bright orange in color, appear on the petioles of the leaves and the stems of the young shoots. The affected shoots frequently become distorted.

Nature of the Disease: A fungous disease caused by Earlea speciosa.

Control: All infected shoots should be cut off and burned.

Bronzing of Leaves.

Symptoms: A single leaf or several leaves on the same shoot become a mottled bronze in color, turn yellow and drop prematurely.

Nature of the Disease: A physiological disease due to some functional disturbance in the growth of the plant. It may sometimes be due to very rapid growth caused by the drastic pruning of some particular shoot.

INSECT PESTS

Aphids. There are two species of aphids that attack roses, the Rose Aphid (Macrosiphum rosæ L.) and the Small Green Rose Aphid (Francoa Myzaphis rosarum) (Kalt.). The latter is usually the most troublesome in greenhouses but it is also frequently found on outdoor roses in the South and in California. The identification, injury and control of the two species is practically the same.

Identification: Soft-bodied, louse-like insects. Body globular or pear-shaped, green in color. Usually found clustered along the tips of the young growing shoots.

Injury: Aphids suck the juices from the plant, reducing its vigor and vitality and in many cases causing the leaves and flowers to become unsightly and distorted.

Life History: In the North the Rose Aphids pass the winter in the egg stage. The eggs are small, glossy black in color and are attached to the bark near the buds. The eggs hatch early in the spring, as soon as plant growth begins, and the young aphids begin feeding. The first brood which hatches out from the eggs becomes mature in about two weeks and from then on, through the balance of the season, living young are produced. As each female gives birth daily to several young they multiply with startling rapidity. These living young are produced from unfertilized eggs and are all females. In the autumn males appear and fertilize the eggs which are to carry the species over the winter. In the South they do not pass through an egg stage as the winters are mild and they breed throughout the year.

Control: A good nicotine spray or dust is the most effective remedy. Spraying should begin as soon as infestation is first noticed and it should be repeated at intervals of every few days for several weeks. As it is necessary to reach each individual insect the spraying should be done with the utmost thoroughness. Even so, it will usually take several applications before the aphids are well under control as some are usually concealed within the folds of the tender, unopened leaves at the tip of the young shoots. If great care is taken these tips may be bent over very gently and dipped in the spray solution. It is not an easy thing to do, however, as one or two will almost invariably break off no matter how careful one may be.

Spray Formula

Black Leaf 40 . . . . 1 teaspoonful
Soap . . . . 1 cubic inch
Water . . . . 1 gallon

As a repellent, tobacco dust or ground-up tobacco stems may be used as a mulch on the rose beds.

Japanese Beetles.

Identification: Large, handsome beetles, a metallic, greenish-bronze in color with two conspicuous and several small white spots near the tip of the abdomen. During the middle of the day they are very active, making rapid flight when disturbed. During the evening they are more sluggish.

Injury: The Japanese beetles are among the most destructive of any of our garden pests. They feed voraciously upon the foliage, buds, and open flowers, and will completely sekletonize a bush in a very short time. They are gregarious in habit and sometimes as many as twenty or thirty beetles will be found clustered on a single flower bud.

Life History: The adult beetles appear early in July and for a period of about six weeks they ravage the entire countryside, feeding upon fruit and shade trees, field crops and vegetables and many ornamentals. The female beetles deposit their eggs in the soil, usually selecting an open, sunny area where the grass is short. The larvæ hatch in several weeks and begin feeding on decaying vegetable matter in the soil and also to a considerable extent upon the roots of grasses and other plants. At this stage they do considerable damage to lawns and golf courses. At the approach of cold weather the grubs burrow down into the soil to a depth of six to twelve inches and construct a little earthen cell in which they pass the winter. In the spring the grubs work their way towards the surface again and feed for several weeks before passing into the pupa stage. The pupa stage extends over a period of about six weeks and the adult beetles then emerge.

Control: The foliage may be entirely protected from the ravages of the Japanese beetle by coating it with some effective spray material but it seems almost impossible to protect the flower buds. However, if the foliage is sprayed the beetles do not seem to be attracted to the rose garden in such numbers and it is possible to pick them off the buds by hand. Fortunately the beetles do not put in an appearance until the roses have passed the height of their bloom, and in sections which are heavily infested with Japanese beetles it would almost seem the part of wisdom to disbud the roses during July and early August. This would in no way interfere with the vigor of the plant and in fact would tend to conserve its energies for more abundant autumn bloom after the beetles have departed.

Spray Formulas

Coated arsenate of lead, *or*
Insectrogen, used double strength.

Leaf Rollers. There are a number of caterpillars of this type which attack roses. The life history, injury and control is practically the same in all cases.

Identification: Rose Leaf Roller (Archips rosaceana Harr.). Small, active caterpillar, about ¾ of an inch long. Olive-green in color with a black head.

Rose Leaf Tyer (Archips [Cacœcia] rosaceana Harr.). Small caterpillar varying in color from yellow to light green and distinguished by an oblique band running across the body.

Red-banded Leaf Roller (Eulia velutinana Wlk.). Small caterpillar, similar to the above but readily distinguished by the red band on the body.

Injury: The caterpillars feed upon the foliage and the blossoms, their work being very characteristic, as they roll the leaves together and web them with fine, silken threads.

Life History: The moths vary somewhat in appearance according to the species. They deposit their eggs in tiny masses on the foliage and within a few weeks the caterpillars hatch and begin feeding. They become full grown in about a month and pupate within the rolled leaves. Several weeks later the moths emerge and the life cycle begins again. Two broods are usually produced during the summer.

Control: Spray or dust thoroughly with arsenate of lead. Open any leaves which have already been rolled and destroy the caterpillars or pupa found within.

Rose Beetle, also known as **Rose Chafer** or **Rose Bug.**

Identification: Long-legged beetles, grayish fawn in color and about ¼ inch in length.

Injury: The beetles feed chiefly upon the flowers. Sometimes a dozen or more will be found clustered upon a single bloom which will be completely demolished. Rose beetles are, beyond any doubt, the most destructive of our rose pests. They appear in hordes just as the first roses are coming into bloom and their depredations continue throughout the height of the rose season.

In closely built, suburban areas rose bugs are seldom seen and cause little damage, due probably to the fact that conditions are not so favorable for them, as the land is too intensively cultivated. In open country districts, however, where open fields abound, and particularly where the soil is of a sandy texture, conditions are ideal for them and they make the most of their opportunities by increasing in alarming numbers. They are not apt to be so numerous in sections where the soil is of a heavy clay texture, as it is almost impossible for the females to deposit their eggs, and consequently they never gain much headway.

Life History: The adult rose beetles appear early in June and feed for about six weeks. Towards the end of this period the females deposit their eggs. Under normal conditions each female deposits three sets of eggs, about twelve being laid at one time. The beetle selects a rough, grassy place where the soil is somewhat sandy, burrows into the ground for a depth of three to six inches and lays her eggs singly in tiny soil pockets. The eggs, which are oval, white and smooth in appearance, hatch in about two weeks. The larvæ feed both on decaying vegetable matter and upon the roots of weeds and grasses, reaching maturity about the latter part of October. They then burrow down into the soil to a depth of about twelve inches and curl themselves up in little earthen cells for the winter. In the spring the grubs work their way up towards the surface again and usually feed for a short time before they pupate. The pupa stage varies from three to four weeks and the adult beetles then emerge just as the first roses are coming into bloom.

Control: Rose beetles are one of the most difficult of all insects to control.

Repellents: Tobacco dust or ground tobacco stems may be used as a mulch on the rose beds and will keep rose beetles away to some extent.

Sprays: No spray has as yet been found which is entirely effective. Arsenate of lead to which cheap molasses has been added has proved fairly successful when used on grape vines which have been attacked by rose beetles, but if used in any quantity on roses it would ruin the delicate petals of the opening blooms and little would be gained.

Hand Picking: Tedious though it may be, hand picking is probably the most effective means of control. It must, however, be done early in the season if any lasting results are to be secured. The female beetles usually begin to deposit their eggs during the last week in June and in order to have any effect upon next year's generation the beetles must be annihilated before the eggs are laid. When the beetles are picked off by hand they should be dropped into a receptacle of water upon which a thin film of kerosene has been poured.

Protection: As a means of protection against rose beetles the beds may be covered by mosquito netting or a cheap grade of tobacco cloth tacked onto a light frame. In sections where rose beetles are very numerous—and no one can possibly appreciate what a curse they are unless one has lived through an epidemic of them—this seems to be the only way to insure absolute protection and to obtain unmutilated blooms.

Rose Cucurlio.

Identification: Bright red beetles with black legs and snout. Small in size, measuring only about ¼ inch in length.

Injury: The beetles eat holes in the unopened buds and in the fruits and they also feed upon the leaves and flower stems to some extent. Many of the injured buds fail to open and the petals of those that do expand are usually riddled with holes.

Life History: The beetles appear early in June. The eggs, which are oval in shape, are deposited in the holes which the beetles bore in the buds and young fruits. Within a week or 10 days the eggs hatch and the small, white, legless larvæ feed upon the seeds and flower petals until they are full grown. In late summer the grubs migrate down to the ground near the base of the plant where they enter the pupa stage and pass the winter.

Control: If the infestation is light the beetles may be picked off by hand. All dried up buds and fruits should be cut off and burned as they are likely to contain eggs or larvæ. Wild roses growing in the vicinity may become a serious source of infestation and if so they should be destroyed.

Spraying with arsenate of lead, 1 oz. to 1½ gal. of water, will help to keep the beetles under control.

Rose Leafhopper.

Identification: Small, narrow, yellowish-white insects. Very active, hopping quickly from one leaf to another when disturbed.

Injury: The nymphs and adults feed usually from the under-surface of the leaves, sucking the juices from the plant. The leaves at first appear yellow and somewhat faded and if the infestation is severe they later turn brown and die.

Life History: The adult females deposit their eggs in late summer under the bark of the rose bushes. The winter is passed in the egg stage and the young nymphs hatch out early in May. They begin feeding immediately and pass through several molts before reaching the adult stage.

Control: The adults are somewhat difficult to control but the young nymphs may readily be destroyed by spraying with a nicotine-soap solution. Care should be taken to reach the under-surface of the leaves.

Spray Formula

Black Leaf 40	1 teaspoonful
Soap	1 cubic inch
Water	1 gallon

Rose Scale.

Identification: Small scale insects, snow-white in color, usually found clustered thickly along the branches and twigs. The female scales are circular in shape, being about 1/10 of an inch in diameter. The male scales are considerably smaller, being long and narrow in shape.

Injury: The scales feed upon the plant juices, causing weakened growth and general lack of vigor. If they become sufficiently numerous they cause the death of the plant.

Life History: The young scales emerge from beneath the scale of the female parent and for the first few days they crawl about actively upon the plant. They find a favorable location and then insert their thread-like mouth parts into the bark and begin feeding. After a short time they pass through the first molt and at this stage they lose their legs, and the scale-like covering forms over the body. The scale is composed of fine threads of wax which have exuded from the wall of the body and have become practically welded together. The female scales molt twice, remaining under the scale for the period of their entire life. The males pass through four molts, and at the end of this period they become minute, two-winged, yellowish insects with three pairs of legs, and with eyes and antennæ. They do not feed in this stage but move about actively, mating with the female scales. The female scales continue to feed for a short time after mating.

Control: During the winter or in very early spring while the plants are still dormant spray with commercial lime sulphur when the temperature is above 45° F., using it at the strength of

> Lime sulphur .... 1 part
> Water .... 8 parts

Miscible oils, such as Sunoco, are also very effective against Rose Scales when used as a dormant spray.

Rose Slugs. There are three distinct species which are apt to be troublesome on roses:

American Rose Slug.

Identification: Greenish when young, becoming more yellow as they grow older. ½ to ¾ of an inch in length.

Injury: The slugs do most of their feeding at night, skeletonizing the upper surface of the leaves. The foliage becomes unsightly and eventually dries up and drops off.

Life History: The adult flies are black in color, about 1/5 of an inch long, and they possess four wings. They appear at about the time that the rose bushes start growth in the spring, and the females deposit their eggs between the tissues of the leaves. The eggs hatch about 10 days later and the slugs begin feeding, attaining full growth in from two to three weeks. When mature they burrow into the soil to a depth of an inch or two and construct a cocoon in which to pupate during the winter. The following spring the flies emerge and the life cycle begins again.

Control: Various measures of control are recommended. A strong spray of water from a hose will usually dislodge and kill most of the slugs.

Arsenate of lead, used either as a spray or as a dust, is also very effective.

Nicotine sulphate may be used with good success provided each individual slug is reached.

Bristly Rose Slug.

Identification: Yellowish-green in color, about ⅜ of an inch in length, the body being covered with little bristly hairs.

Injury: When young the slugs merely skeletonize the leaves, feeding upon the under-surface, but as they grow older they eat large, irregular holes along the edge of the leaves.

Life History: The adult is a black, four-winged fly, slightly larger than that of the American Rose Slug. The female deposits her eggs just under the surface of the leaf petiole. The eggs, which are small, white and round, hatch in from 7 to 10 days and the young slugs make rapid growth. Six or more generations are produced during the season and the winter is passed in the pupa stage, the cocoons, which are very thin and transparent, being protected by rubbish and old leaves.

Control: Same as for American Rose Slug.

Coiled Rose Slug.

Identification: The upper surface of the body is green with a metallic sheen. There are numerous white spots on the body and a wide band runs across the middle of the abdomen. The slug is about ¾ of an inch in length.

Injury: The slugs feed along the edge of the leaves with the tip of the body usually coiled beneath the leaf. The entire leaf surface will, in time, be destroyed by them.

Life History: The adult flies appear in early spring and the females deposit their eggs, singly, upon the under-surface of the leaves. The larvæ hatch out within a few days and begin feeding. When full grown they bore into the pith of a dead or decaying branch and pass into the pupa stage. Two broods are produced each season, the winter being passed in the pupa case.

Control: Same as for American Rose Slug.

Rose Stem Borer.

Identification: The larvæ, which are seldom seen unless an infested shoot is slit open, are small, whitish caterpillars.

Injury: The larvæ feed within the shoots, making small tunnels which weaken the branches and eventually cause their death.

Life History: The adult of the Rose Stem Borer is a wasp-like insect which appears early in the summer. The females puncture the shoots and deposit their eggs within the tissues. A short time later the larvæ hatch out and begin feeding within the stem.

Control: Infested shoots should be cut off and burned.

Rose Stem Girdler.

Identification: Small, whitish caterpillars. Their presence may be detected by the characteristic swelling of the shoot.

Injury: The larvæ tunnel their way into the stem, making short, spiral mines. The shoots swell over the affected area.

Life History: The adult beetles appear in June and July and the females deposit their eggs on the bark of the branches. Upon hatching the larvæ tunnel their way into the shoots and begin feeding. When full grown they construct little cells in the pith of the plant and pass into the pupa stage.

Control: Cut off and burn all infested shoots.

Rose Weevil, also known as Fuller's Rose Beetle.

Identification: Dull, brownish-gray beetle, slightly over ¼ inch in length with a white line running diagonally across each wing.

Injury: The larvæ feed upon the roots to some extent and the adult beetles feed upon the foliage, buds, and open blooms. They are most commonly found on greenhouse roses but occasionally they become a serious menace to roses grown in the open. Most of their feeding is done at night.

Control: See page 1088.

SALVIA FARINACEA
(Mealycup Sage)

INSECT PEST

Aphids.

Identification: Soft-bodied, louse-like insects, usually found clustered near the tips of the young, growing shoots and along the flower stems. The species that attacks Salvia farinacea is black in color.

Injury: Aphids suck the juices from the plant, causing a general lack of vigor and stunted growth. The leaves at the tips of the growing shoots become curled and distorted and the flower heads are stunted and malformed.

Life History: See page 1069.

Control: See page 1070.

SWEET PEA

DISEASES

Anthracnose.

Symptoms: The growing tips of the plant wilt and die, becoming white and brittle. As the disease progresses the entire plant becomes affected and the flower buds dry up and fail to open. When an infected leaf is examined under a hand lens it is found to be covered with very small pustules of a peculiar salmon-pink color. These pustules are also prominent on the seed pods. Small cankers are sometimes produced on the stems and leaf petioles.

Nature of the Disease: The anthracnose of the sweet pea is caused by Glomerella rufomaculans (B.) V. Sch. and Sp., the same fungus which produces the bitter rot of the apple and the ripe rot of the grape. It is confined almost entirely to sweet peas grown in the open. Only in rare instances has it been found on greenhouse plants. The spores of the fungus are carried on the seed and the disease is usually transmitted in this way.

Control: Remove and destroy all diseased plants and near-by refuse. Soak the seed for five minutes, just before planting, in a 5 per cent solution of formaldehyde. Spray occasionally with Bordeaux as a preventive.

Collar Rot, also known as **Stem Rot.**

Symptoms: Young seedlings are particularly susceptible to this disease although older plants are occasionally attacked. The plants wilt at the tip, the leaves show a peculiar flagging, and the stem rots off at the ground line. The roots are practically never affected.

The disease spreads quickly from plant to plant and is always fatal.

Nature of the Disease: Collar rot is caused by Sclerotinia libertiana Fckl., the same fungus which attacks a number of different plants. The fungus penetrates the stem at the ground level, clogging up the vessels and preventing the flow of sap from the roots to the upper portion of the plant. After a plant has succumbed it soon becomes covered with a white, moldy growth which is the mycelium of the fungus. The small black sclerotia or resting bodies of the fungus are later found both on and within the affected parts of the plant. The fungus lives over in the soil from year to year.

Control: If Collar Rot has proved troublesome it will be advisable to use fresh soil which is known to be free from the disease, or the soil may be sterilized with formaldehyde. Use one pint of 40 per cent formaldehyde to twelve and one-half gallons of water at the rate of one gallon to every square foot. Let the soil stand for 24 hours. Fork over and aërate well and do not plant seed for several days.

Mildew.

Symptoms: Leaves turn yellow and drop prematurely. The white, powdery growth so typical of mildew is more apt to be found on the dead and fallen leaves than on the growing plant.

Nature of the Disease: This disease is caused by the fungus, microsphæra alni (Walk.) Wint.

Control: Dust thoroughly with fine dusting sulphur or spray with livers of sulphur used at the rate of 3 oz. to 10 gal. of water.

Mosaic.

Symptoms: Leaves become a mottled yellow and green in color and have a tendency to curl. Flower stalks become twisted and fail to make normal growth. If the plants are affected when young they frequently remain dwarfed and stunted.

Nature of the Disease: See page 1125.

Control: See page 1125.

Root Rot. Sweet Peas are attacked by several forms of Root Rot. The control is practically the same in all cases:

Black Root Rot (Thielavia basicola [B. and Br.] Zopf.).

Symptoms: Plants affected with Thielavia Root Rot have practically no root system except a dark, charred-looking stub. The new roots are destroyed as soon as they are formed. The disease occasionally spreads up the stem for some two or three inches above the ground. The affected plants seldom die but remain dwarfed and stunted, being a sickly color and producing no bloom.

Rhizoctonia Root Rot (Rhizoctonia solani Kuhn).

Symptoms: Roots become rotted, plants wilt and finally collapse entirely. Stems frequently become affected, being covered with reddish, sunken spots. Young seedlings seem to be more susceptible to attack than older plants.

Shredded Root Rot (Aphonomyces entiches).

Symptoms: The underground portion of the stem becomes rotted and the tissues have the appearance of being shredded. The roots usually rot away entirely.

Control: Destroy all diseased plants. Disinfect the soil thoroughly with formaldehyde. Use one pint 40 per cent formaldehyde to twelve and one-half gallons of water at the rate of one gallon to every square foot. Let the soil stand for twenty-four hours, then fork it over and aërate it well. Do not plant the seed for several days.

Streak.

Symptoms: The disease usually makes its appearance just as the plants are coming into bloom. Peculiar spots or streaks, varying in color from light reddish brown to dark brown, appear on the stems. This condition is usually first apparent near the ground line but spreads gradually to other portions of the plant. In some cases the streaks merge and the stem becomes entirely girdled, the plant being killed. In the advanced stages of the disease, water-soaked spots are found on the leaves, petioles and flowers.

Nature of the Disease: Streak is a bacterial disease caused by Bacillus lathyri Manns and Taub. The bacteria are carried on the seed and are spattered up on to the plant by heavy rains. The bacteria gradually destroy the tissues of the plant.

Control: Root up and burn all diseased plants. Little can be done after the disease has once gained headway, the only satisfactory measure of control being the treatment of seed before planting.

Soak seed for five minutes in a 5 per cent solution of formaldehyde.

INSECTS

Aphids.

Identification: Soft-bodied, louse-like insects usually found clustered along the tips of the young growing shoots. The species that most commonly infests sweet peas is pale green in color.

Life History: See page 1069.

Control: See page 1070.

Nematodes causing *Root Knot.*

Identification: Swellings are found on the roots, singly, in pairs or in strings, often giving the root a beaded appearance. The swellings are sometimes very small, and sometimes almost as large as the root nodules, with which they must not be confused. The root nodules which are peculiar to sweet peas and all other members of the legume family are lobed outgrowths which are attached to the root at one end, whereas the galls or swellings caused by nematodes produce a swelling of the entire affected portion of the root. Upon cutting open a swelling the minute worms may frequently be seen with a hand lens.

Injury: Infested plants become sickly and fail to make normal growth. Leaves turn yellow and flower production is seriously affected. The plants usually linger on for a long time before dying.

Life History: See page 1130.

Control: Root up and burn infested plants.

Sterilizing the soil with formaldehyde as recommended for the various forms of Root Rot will aid in keeping nematodes under control, but it is not entirely dependable.

Calcium cyanide used at the rate of one pound per 12 square feet is also recommended. This should be mixed thoroughly with the soil.

Root Aphids.

Identification: Soft-bodied, grayish white insects found clustered along the roots or near the crown of the plant.

Injury: Root aphids suck the juices from the plants, causing them to become dwarfed and stunted. The foliage frequently turns yellow, indicating a general lack of vigor.

Control: See page 1075.

TULIP

DISEASES

Blossom Blight.

Symptoms: The flower stalks turn white and gradually shrivel just below the flower buds. Buds drop over and fail to develop.

Nature of the Disease: A fungous disease caused by Phytophthora cactorum (Leb. & Cohn) Schröt. It seems to be particularly prevalent when tulips are planted in wet locations.

Control: Pick off and burn all diseased flower stems. Very little is as yet known about Blossom Blight and no satisfactory measure of control has been found.

Botrytis Blight, also known as **Fire Disease.**

Symptoms: The leaves, stems and flowers become covered with unsightly spots. In the early stages the spots appear as small, yellowish areas with a dark, water-soaked margin. As the lesions enlarge they become covered with a moldy growth and appear a light gray in color. The bulbs are also frequently affected, deep, yellowish brown lesions being found in the fleshy scales. Black sclerotia or resting bodies develop on the dead stalks and are also found within the outer scales of the bulbs. When plants are severely affected the stalks rot and break over; the leaves become twisted and distorted and the flower buds are blighted.

Nature of the Disease: A fungous disease caused by Botrytis tulipæ (Lib.) Hopk. It is causing severe losses in many sections of the country and every effort should be made to keep it under control.

Control: Remove and destroy infected plants in order to prevent the spread of the disease.

· Thorough spraying with Bordeaux will keep the disease under control to a considerable extent, but it is so disfiguring to both the foliage and flowers that it is hardly practicable.

Every precaution should be taken to see that newly purchased bulbs are free from disease. It is far easier to keep the disease out of one's garden than to try to control it after it has gained entrance. The outer scales of the bulbs should be removed in order to make sure that they are healthy and absolutely free from infection. As an additional measure of precaution the bulbs may be soaked in some organic mercury solution before planting.

Soak for two hours in a solution of Semesan, 1 tablespoonful to 1 gallon of water.

Gray Bulb Rot.

Symptoms: Dry rot begins at the tip of the bulb. The flesh of the bulb becomes a reddish gray in color and the diseased portions are often covered with dark brown sclerotia or resting bodies. The bulbs finally rot away entirely.

Nature of the Disease: A fungous disease caused by Rhizoctonia tuliparum (Kleb.) Whetzel and Arthur, which affects tulips and various other bulbs.

Control: Dig up and burn all diseased bulbs. Disinfect the soil with formaldehyde before new bulbs are planted. Use one pint of 40 per cent formaldehyde to twelve and one-half gallons of water at the rate of one gallon to every square foot. Let the soil stand for twenty-four hours. Then fork it over and aërate it well before planting.

INSECTS

Bulb Mite.

Identification: Minute, whitish mites, bead-like in form, are found in large numbers within the bulb scales. Small, reddish brown spots appear at the point of injury.

Injury: The mites suck the juices from the plant tissues and the bulbs become soft and mushy. The vitality of the bulb is weakened and as a result growth is stunted. The leaves turn a sickly yellow and the flower buds either fail to develop or produce distorted blooms.

Life History: See page 1118.

Control: See page 1118.

SWEET ALYSSUM

INSECT PESTS

Cabbage Worm.

Identification: Small, velvety-green caterpillars, somewhat more than an inch in length when full grown.

Injury: The caterpillars feed upon the foliage.

Life History: See page 1082.

Control: See page 1082.

Diamond-Back Moth Caterpillar.

Identification: Small, slender caterpillars, about 2/5 of an inch long, light green in color. The caterpillars are very active and when disturbed they usually drop from the plant, suspending themselves by a fine silken thread.

Injury: The caterpillars feed upon the foliage.

Control: Spray or dust thoroughly with arsenate of lead.

VERBENA

INSECT PESTS

Leaf Roller (oblique-banded).

Indentification: Small caterpillar varying in color from yellow to light green and distinguished by an oblique band running across the body.

Injury: The caterpillars feed upon the foliage and the flowers, their work being very characteristic as they roll the leaves together and web them with fine silken threads.

1161

Life History: The female moths deposit their eggs in tiny masses on the foliage and within a few weeks the caterpillars hatch out and begin feeding. They become full grown in about a month and pupate within the rolled leaves. Several weeks later the moths emerge and the life cycle begins again. Two broods are usually produced during the season.

Control: Spray or dust thoroughly with arsenate of lead. Open any leaves which have already been rolled, and destroy the caterpillars or pupæ found within.

Red Spider.

Identification: Minute mites, some red in color, others greenish, yellow or black.

Injury: Red spiders feed usually on the under-surface of the leaves, puncturing the outer tissues and sucking the juices of the plant. The foliage has an unhealthy, whitish, and curiously glazed appearance. Fine silken threads are sometimes found, spun across the under-surface of the leaves.

Life History: See page 1105.

Control: See page 1105.

Yellow Woolly-Bear Caterpillar

Identification: A caterpillar about two inches in length when full grown. The body is completely covered with long hairs which vary in color from pale yellow to reddish brown.

Injury: The caterpillars feed upon the foliage.

Life History: See page 1096.

Control: Spray or dust with arsenate of lead.

WALLFLOWER

INSECT PESTS

Diamond-Back Moth Caterpillar.

Identification: Small, slender caterpillars about 2/5 of an inch in length, light green in color. The caterpillars are very active and when disturbed they usually drop from the plant, suspending themselves by a fine silken thread.

Injury: The caterpillars feed upon the foliage, often completely skeletonizing it.

Control: Spray or dust thoroughly with arsenate of lead.

Potato Flea Beetle.

Identification: Small, very active beetles about 1/16 of an inch long, of a dark, somewhat metallic color. The hind legs are longer than the front legs and enable the beetle to jump like a flea when disturbed.

Injury: The beetles feed upon the foliage, making many small holes either round or irregular in shape. The leaves have the appearance of being peppered with fine shot. The foliage becomes badly disfigured and the vitality of the plant is greatly weakened.

Life History: See page 1139.

Control: Spray with a mixture of arsenate of lead and Bordeaux as soon as infestation is noticed.

ZINNIA
DISEASES

Leaf Spot.

Symptoms: Large, dark spots appear on the leaves. Usually not troublesome except in very wet weather.

Nature of the Disesae: A fungous disease caused by Cercospora atricinata.

Control: Spray with Bordeaux, or dust with copper-lime dust as soon as trouble is detected.

Mildew.

Symptoms: Foliage becomes covered with a white, powdery growth. In the most advanced stages the affected areas turn black.

Nature of the Disease: This disease is caused by Erysiphe cichoracearum D. C.

Control: Dust thoroughly with fine dusting sulphur.

Sclerotium Disease of Zinnia.

Symptoms: The disease attacks the plant at ground level and works upward. The stems become blackened and the leaves turn yellow and wilt. The stem finally collapses. The reproductive bodies may be seen as small bumps on the surface of the stem. Sometimes they become quite large.

Nature of the Disease: The disease is caused by the fungus, Scleroinia sclerotiorum Mass. It attacks the plant at ground level. The vegetative growth of the fungus completely fills the vessels of the plant and thus deprives the leaves of water.

Control: Diseased stems should be burned. In flower beds where the disease has been, the top-soil to a depth of two inches should be removed. New soil which has been mixed with a little quicklime should be added. Green manure favors the development of the disease.

Black Blister Beetle.

Identification: A slender jet-black beetle about ½ inch in length with prominent head and neck. The best identification is the yellow oily, blistering fluid exuded when handled.

Injury: The beetles feed upon the flowers.

Life History: See page 1074.

Control: See page 1074.

Japanese Beetles.

Indentification: Large, handsome beetles of a metallic, greenish bronze color. There are two conspicuous and several small white spots near the tip of the abdomen. During the middle of the day they are very active, making rapid flight when disturbed. During the evening they are more sluggish.

Injury: The beetles feed upon both the foliage and the flowers, completely demolishing a plant in a very short time.

Life History: See page 1149.

Control: Spray with coated arsenate of lead or with Insectrogen, used double strength.

Leaf Roller (Red-banded).

Identification: Small caterpillar varying in color from yellow to light green, readily distinguished by the red band on the body.

Injury: The caterpillars feed upon the foliage, their work being very characteristic, as they roll and tie the leaves together with fine silken threads.

Life History: See page 1150.

Control: Dust or spray with arsenate of lead. Open any leaves which have been rolled and destroy the caterpillar or pupa found within.

Stalk Borer.

Identification: Slender caterpillars about two inches in length when full grown. The young caterpillars are brown with white stripes. When full grown they lose their stripes and become a solid, dirty gray in color.

Injury: The stalk borer makes a small, round hole in the stem and tunnels up through the stalk, causing the injured shoot to suddenly wilt and break over.

Life History: See page 1076.

Control: See page 1076.

Tarnished Plant Bug.

Identification: A small, very active bug about ¼ inch in length. The body is oval in shape, being somewhat triangular in front; coppery brown in color with dark, brown and yellow flecks on the back.

Injury: The bugs puncture the shoots just below the flower heads, causing the buds to droop and die. The injury completely destroys any chance of bloom. It is thought that while feeding, the Tarnished Plant Bug injects some substance into the sap which is highly injurious to the plant and has the effects of a poison.

Life History: See page 1076.

Control: See page 1076.

Miscellaneous Insect Pests, Rodents, and Animals

MICE

Meadow Mouse.

Identification: Small, dark brown mouse with coarse fur. The ears are almost entirely concealed and the tail is much shorter than that of our common house mouse. The meadow mice make little runs readily visible just under the surface of the soil.

Injury: The meadow mouse does most of its feeding at the surface of the ground, nibbling at the roots and crowns of many herbaceous plants and gnawing the bark of trees, shrubs and vines at or just above the ground level, in many cases completely girdling them and causing their death.

Pine Mouse.

Identification: The pine mouse is smaller than the meadow mouse, it is a reddish brown in color and has an exceedingly short tail, the tail being about the same length as the hind foot. The burrows of the pine mouse are well below the ground level with occasional small openings upon the surface.

Injury: The pine mouse does all of its feeding below the surface of the ground. It has a particular fondness for tulip and lily bulbs, and it feeds also upon the roots of herbaceous plants, trees and vines. In sections that are severely infested with pine mice the destruction is often alarming. Literally thousands of bulbs may be destroyed in a single season and fruit trees forty or fifty years of age have been known to be killed outright by the work of pine mice. One of the greatest tragedies is that one is seldom aware of their presence until considerable damage has been done.

Control: The use of poison bait is probably the most satisfactory measure of control for these field mice, and the following baits are recommended.

1. Sweet potato bait.

Cut the sweet potatoes into small cubes. Mix together equal parts of powdered strychnine and baking soda. Sift this over the potatoes, making sure that each cube is thoroughly coated. The bait should be used immediately, while it is fresh, and it should be dropped directly into the runs or placed in crevices in dry stone walls known to be infested with mice.

2. Poison grain bait.

Mix 1 tablespoonful of gloss starch in ¼ cup of cold water until it makes a thin paste. Stir slowly into ¾ of a pint of boiling water. Into this starch stir 1 ounce of powdered strychnine and 1 ounce of baking soda which have been thoroughly mixed together. Add to this ¼ pint of heavy corn syrup and 1 tablespoonful of either glycerine or petrolatum. The mixture may then be poured over the grain, using about 12 pounds of steamed, crushed oats or wheat, or a mixture of the two. The grain should be stirred until every kernel is coated.

Great care should be taken to see that this poisoned grain is not placed where birds, dogs or other animals will be able to get at it. A convenient method of placing it about the garden is to use wide-mouthed glass jars, the jars being laid upon their sides, pressed firmly into the soil and a piece of board tilted over the opening. A few spoonfuls of the grain may be spread upon the floor of the jar, and the mice will have easy access to it while it will not be accessible to birds. Small pieces of drain tile open at both ends may be used in much the same way, or stations may be constructed by bending a piece of tin over a board.

Protection of Trees, Plants and Bulbs: Field mice seldom trouble narcissus and hyacinth bulbs, but they seem to have a particular fondness for tulips and lilies and in sections that are badly infested with mice it is quite useless to attempt to grow them unless some protection is given them. One of the surest and most satisfactory means of protection is to plant them in wire baskets with open tops. They may be made of quarter-inch mesh wire and will do duty for a number of years. Camphor flakes may also be placed about the bulbs at the time of planting and will afford some protection, although in time the effects will wear off.

As a protection for trees, shrubbery, and vines, sulphonated oil has proved remarkably satisfactory. It may be applied to the lower part of the trunk or to the stems with an ordinary paint brush, or a sprayer may be used if preferred. The mixture consists of one part flowers of sulphur to nine parts of linseed oil by weight. In preparing the mixture the linseed oil should be heated to a temperature of about 470 degrees F. It should then be placed out of doors and the flowers of sulphur should be sifted slowly into the hot oil, the mixture being stirred constantly. The heat will increase until all the sulphur has been dissolved. When cool it is ready for use. Where application of this sulphonated oil has been made, trees will practically never be touched by field mice.

MOLES

While moles feed entirely upon worms, grubs and other insect forms and do not eat anything in the way of plant materials, they are often very destructive in a garden because of their tunnelling propensities. They cause the death of many plants by practically uprooting them, and they work havoc on newly planted lawns. In sections where they are prevalent they are classed among the most troublesome of our garden pests.

Control: Poison gas is often very effective. A commercial preparation known as Cyanogas is probably the most satisfactory thing for this purpose. A small opening should be made in the run and a teaspoonful of the material should be placed upon the bottom. The opening should then be covered over with an inverted saucer or something of this nature. Care must be taken not to use too much Cyanogas in the garden as large quantities of it are liable to prove injurious to the growth of plants in surrounding areas.

Traps: There are several types of strong, steel mole traps on the market and some of them are very satisfactory if properly handled. It is well to handle the traps with rubber gloves, and the results will be better if several traps are set at the same time. One trap should be set at the point where the main tunnel divides and one or two others along the branch tunnels. The soil should be pressed down very firmly at the spot where the trap is set.

ANTS

Injury: Although ants seldom cause any direct injury to plants, they can be a source of great annoyance in the flower garden. They are often found on peony buds, where they feed on the sweet secretions which are exuded by the opening flowers, and they are very frequently found on plants which are infested with plant lice as they are fond of the honey dew which is given off by the aphids. In some sections of the South, ants are very troublesome, as they carry off newly sown seed before it has had time to germinate.

Control: The most effective means of control is to destroy ants in their nest through the use of carbon bisulphide. The treatment should be applied in the early evening after the ants have returned to their nest for the night. A tablespoonful of carbon bisulphide should be poured into the opening in the center of the nest and the hole should then be immediately covered with a stone or a clod of earth. If the nest is large is it wise to make several holes near the outer rim and to apply the carbon bisulphide in a similar manner. No holes should be made within 6 or 8 inches of the roots of near-by plants.

There are various commercial preparations on the market which are very effective in controlling ants. Some of these poison baits may be secured in very small glass jars which may be placed at unobtrusive yet strategic points about the garden or greenhouse.

CUT-WORMS

Many plants, particularly when in the young seedling stage, are subject to the attack of cut-worms. In most cases the plants are cut off just above the surface of the ground, occasionally just below the surface. The plants are not eaten by the cut-worm, being left to wilt and die after the worm has nibbled the end of the stem at the point where it was severed from the plant. In very exceptional instances a cut-worm will climb up the stem and eat the leaves. The damage usually occurs at night, and during the day the worms may be found in the soil about the roots of the plants.

Control: The most effective measure of control is the use of a poison-bran bait which may be placed upon the surface of the soil near the point of attack. An excellent formula consists of one tablespoonful of arsenate of lead, one tablespoonful of molasses, and one cupful of wheat bran.

RABBITS

A good shotgun seems to be the most effective control for rabbits. The use of poisoned feed is successful to some extent. Chopped alfalfa hay may be soaked in water and then sprinkled with a poison such as strychnine or white arsenic. If one prefers to spare the rabbits as well as to protect one's plants, a plot of soybeans may be planted adjacent to the garden, or, in the case of a vegetable garden, a double row of soybeans may be planted around the entire garden. Rabbits are so passionately fond of soybeans that they will eat them in preference to almost anything else and the chances are that the more choice plants in the garden will therefore be spared.

Measures of Control: Powdered aloes have proved to be one of the most satisfactory repellents. The material may be kept in a salt or flour shaker and dusted lightly over the plants, the application being repeated after heavy rains. It has been found that rabbits will seldom bother plants which have been thus treated.

NEMATODES

Identification: Nematodes are small eel-worms of microscopic size which live in the soil and within the tissues of certain host plants. They bore into the roots of these plants, causing the formation of very characteristic knots or galls.

Injury: Plants which are infested with nematodes become stunted in growth, and, in some extreme cases, they may succumb entirely. The roots become malformed and are unable to carry on their normal functions. Although most species of nematodes confine their activities to the roots, there are some species which affect other portions of the plant, causing small, thickened areas on the leaves, and in some cases the foliage becomes badly deformed.

Control: In the South, nematodes winter over in the soil and often become a serious pest in the garden. In the North, they are more commonly regarded as a greenhouse pest. The only really satisfactory means of control is a complete sterilization of the soil. In the greenhouse, steam will prove to be the most satisfactory agent for sterilization. If, however, steam is not available, reasonably good results may be obtained with the use of a 6 per cent formaldehyde dust. This should be mixed thoroughly with the soil at the rate of 1 pound of dust per bushel of soil, or 6 ounces with each cubic foot of soil. No plants should be set in the soil for at least 72 hours, or until there is no longer any odor of formaldehyde. Flats, pots, or greenhouse benches which have held plants known to be infested with nematodes should be thoroughly scalded with boiling water or flushed out with a formaldehyde solution of 1 part F. to 50 parts of water.

It is extremely difficult to control nematodes in the open ground. All affected plants should be lifted with their root system intact and with as much soil as possible and should be burned or otherwise destroyed. The remaining soil in the beds may be given the formaldehyde dust treatment if it seems practicable. The drench method may be used but is less satisfactory on the whole, as it causes a severe puddling of some soils and a consequent condition which is unfavorable to plant growth. The soil should be lightly forked over, and it should then be thoroughly saturated with the solution, 1 gallon of commercial formalin being added to 50 gallons of water.

Garden Calendar

SPRING GARDEN CALENDAR

(Pages for full instructions are listed after some of the topics.)

THE FLOWER GARDEN

Mulch—The mulch on flower borders may be gradually removed or, if composed of manure, it should be lightly forked in. (Page 448.)

Lime—Lime may be broadcast *after* manure is forked in (if considered necessary). (Page 439.)

Edging—Edge the garden beds, and as soon as the soil is warm and mellow give the first cultivation. (Page 440.)

Fertilizer—Apply a top-dressing of a good complete fertilizer to the perennial beds. (Page 443.)

Hotbeds—Start manure-heated hotbeds in very early spring. (Page 733.)

Roses—New roses should be planted as soon as the ground is workable. Prune the bush roses before growth starts. Remove hills and the winter mulch. Top-dress the rosebeds with a good commercial fertilizer. Later, after leaf growth begins, keep up a regular spray or dust schedule. (Pages 602, 603.)

Lily Pool—Drain and clean pool before growth begins. Plant new hardy water lilies early.

Wood Ashes—Wood ashes from winter fireplaces may be spread at the rate of 1 pound to 200 square feet and cultivated in.

Division of Perennials—Lift and divide such perennials as the hardy asters, chrysanthemums, phlox, and physostegia, which have a tendency to become overcrowded.

Hardening-off—Seedlings started in the greenhouse or indoors should be hardened off by use of coldframes.

Coldframes—Lift sash on coldframes when temperature rises above 45°. (Page 731.)

1171

Seed Sowing—1. In very early spring, start seeds indoors or in the greenhouse in flats, pots, or nutrient solution. (Pages 833, 981, 985.)

2. Start spring-sown perennials and hardy and half-hardy annuals early in frames. (Page 725.)

3. Sow lily seed (or in fall). (Page 577.)

4. Sow very hardy annual seeds in open ground as soon as the ground is workable. (Page 979.)

5. Sow half-hardy annual seeds in open as soon as frost is over. (Page 979.)

Cuttings—Take softwood stem cuttings of such perennials as delphinium, phlox, chrysanthemum—when new growth is tender.

Dahlias—Divide dahlias, and plant after all danger of frost is over.

Gladioli—Treat gladiolus corms with bichloride of mercury, and make several plantings for succession of bloom.

Tender Bulbs—Plant tender summer-flowering "bulbs"—galtonia, tritonia, tigridias, gladioli, anemones, kniphofia, ismene. (Page 551.)

Tuberous-rooted Begonias may be planted out of doors after all danger of frost is over. (Page 552.)

House Plants—Remove house plants to shady place in garden in late spring when night temperatures do not drop too low.

Peonies—In late spring an application of complete fertilizer or liquid manure may be made. Pinch off any side buds to encourage larger bloom.

Pinching Back—Pinch back annuals which need to be trained for bushiness when 4 to 6 inches high—zinnias, petunias, salvia, etc. (Page 374.)

Weeding—Keep ahead of the weeds with cultivator or hoe.

Staking—Place garden stakes as plants reach medium height.

THE VEGETABLE GARDEN

Preparation of Soil—If fall cultivation with strawy manure was done, spread lime in very early spring, several weeks before seeding. If fall cultivation was not done, then fork in strawy manure as early as possible.

Rhubarb—An early crop may be had by covering the plants with tall baskets and mounding manure about them in very early spring. (Page 940.)

Hotbed—Make a sowing of melon and cucumber seeds for an early crop as soon as there is room after transplanting other seedlings into the open ground.

Weeds—Keep ahead of the weeds with cultivator or hoe.

LAWN

Fertilizer—Make an early application of commercial fertilizer. (Page 180.)

Mowing—Do not mow the lawn until the grass has reached a height of about 2 inches. It is at this season that the roots are renewed and it is essential that the plants have an opportunity to make vigorous top growth.

Rolling—Rake and roll in order to level any mounds caused by freezing action.

Seeding—Bare spots on lawn may be seeded when the soil is not soggy. New lawns may be started at this time, but a better time is the fall. (Page 184.)

TREES AND SHRUBS

Transplanting—When transplanting trees and shrubs, place several shovelfuls of damp peat moss in the hole. The great benefits to be gained in following this practice are explained on page 231.

Wax Spray—If trees and shrubs are sprayed with a specially prepared wax at the time of transplanting, they will suffer comparatively little shock. (Page 226.)

Pruning—Spring-flowering shrubs should be pruned after bloom. (Page 280.)

Evergreens—Prune evergreens just before growth starts.

Fertilizers—Fertilize trees and shrubs before growth begins. (Page 245.)

Spraying—If there is any evidence of scale, spray with dormant spray early, before buds open, and again in the fall.

FRUIT

Strawberries—Set strawberry plants in early spring. Gradually remove straw mulch from strawberry plants wintered over and place in between rows when danger of frost is over.

New Stock—Plant blueberries, blackberries, currants, and gooseberries very early in spring.

SUMMER GARDEN CALENDAR

THE FLOWER GARDEN

Mulch—Mulch lily borders or bulb clumps. Mulch perennials where soil is clayey and inclined to bake hard into a crust. (Page 445.)

Propagating Case—Use part of frames for propagating case, replacing soil with sand and peat moss, for cuttings. (Page 1004.)

Cuttings—Take cuttings of violas, phlox divaricata, phlox subulata, arabis, iberis and other rock plants. Take softwood and half-ripened cuttings of woody plants and shrubs before wood ripens. In late summer, take cuttings of garden-flowering plants for house-plant use.

Lilies—Propagation of lilies by scales after flowering period. Any transplanting may be done after the foliage dies back, toward the end of the summer.

Division—Divide Bearded iris. Divide old clumps of narcissus, hyacinths and other spring-flowering bulbs in early summer after blooming.

Insect Control—Watch for insects now and keep to spray schedule on those plants which need it throughout the summer.

Tropical Water-Lilies—Plant tropical water-lilies early in summer.

Roses—Ramblers and climbers should be pruned immediately after blooming. (Page 604.)

Hollyhocks—Gather and sow hollyhock seed where plants are to bloom.

Annuals—Keep faded blooms of annuals cut off so that seed will not set, if longer blooming period is desired.

Weed Control—Toward late summer, weed killers may be applied to poison ivy and any other rank growers.

Delphiniums—Cut delphiniums back after blooming to prevent seeding. A second bloom will thus be encouraged late in summer.

Everlastings—Cut, dry and store everlastings in paper bags toward the end of the summer.

Seed Sowing—Many perennial seeds may be sown now. (Page 974.)

VEGETABLE GARDEN

Succession—Make replantings as soon as early crops are harvested.

Cultivation—Keep ahead of the weeds with hoe or cultivator, which at the same time forms a dust mulch beneficial to the plants. (Page 957.)

Insect Control—Watch for insects on each crop and apply proper controls.

Late Crops—A late crop of beans, beets, lettuce, peas, and spinach may be planted toward the end of summer (as late as the middle of August in the vicinity of Philadelphia).

LAWN

Crab-Grass—If crab-grass is troublesome, make an application of sodium chlorate in late July or early August in order to prevent seed formation. (Page 192.)

Cutting—Lawns should not be cut as closely during the summer as during the faster growing periods. Therefore, raise the cutting blades of mower.

New Lawn—Make plans and preparations for any new lawn areas toward the end of the summer, in order to do the seeding in early fall. (Page 176.)

TREES AND SHRUBS

Box—Trim box in late summer after new growth is made.

Lilacs—When cutting branches of bloom for indoor bouquets, it is best to keep in mind the shape of the shrub at the same time. Often this is all the pruning lilacs need. However, if the shrub is inclined to be leggy, this may be remedied by cutting off dead heads after blooming, with somewhat long branches.

Mulch—A mulch of humus on box increases the vigor and protects the roots from summer heat.

Dead Heads—Remove dead flower-heads from rhododendrons and azaleas for neatness and strength of the plant.

Wisteria—A light pruning should be made during the summer to shorten lengthy vegetative strands and to promote better bloom the following year.

Hedges—Early in the summer, trim sheared deciduous hedges before the new growth hardens, which makes it difficult to prune. Late in the summer, evergreen formal hedges can be clipped. Deciduous hedges may have a second light trimming.

Evergreen Plantings—Evergreens should be planted toward the end of the summer.

FRUIT

Layering—Many plants may be propagated during the summer by layering. Black Raspberries, and plants similiar in habit of growth, may be tip-layered in late summer.

Raspberries—Plant suckers of raspberries in late summer.

Thinning—The fruit of apples, pears, peaches, plums, etc., need thinning if they are too thick on the branches.

Pruning—Cut out blackberry and raspberry canes which have fruited.

AUTUMN GARDEN CALENDAR
THE FLOWER GARDEN

Seed Sowing—Most perennial and some annual seeds may be planted in the fall in frames, late enough to leave them dormant during the winter without germinating until very early spring. Sow certain annuals very late in the autumn in the open ground. For list, see page 370. Sow lily seed as soon as ripe (or in the spring). See page 577.

Lilies—Plant lily bulbs as soon as received and mulch over winter in northern regions. (Page 574.)

Tender Bulbs—Lift certain tender summer-flowering "bulbs"— tritonia, galtonia, tigridias, gladioli. Lift tuberous-rooted begonia, tender anemones, kniphofia, ismene.

Peonies—Plant new peonies and fertilize established plants in early fall. (Page 495.)

House Plants—Pot up any garden plants which are to be used indoors, and bring house plants in early in the fall. (Page 794.)

Roses—Order bushes early in fall for late planting. Hill up earth around roses in late fall while the soil is still workable, and put on a mulch of strawy manure. (Page 606.) Make certain climbers and ramblers are fastened securely against winter blasts.

Dahlias—Dahlia tubers may be lifted after the first killing frost and may be placed in storage for the winter. (Page 560.)

Planting of Bulbs—Plant certain hardy summer-flowering "bulbs" such as Eremurus.

Plant tulips and small spring-flowering bulbs in middle to late autumn. Plant hyacinths in early to mid-autumn.

Division of Perennials—If necessary, divide lilies, oriental poppies, bleedingheart, Japanese iris, phlox, peonies. (Page 1012.)

Temporary Protection—Have on hand some heavy paper, boxes, etc. to cover tender garden plants on first nights of frost. Often if the tender plants can be protected from the first early frost, they will bloom for several more weeks.

Transplanting—Any changes in perennial borders should be made in mid-autumn. New perennials may be planted at this time.

Plants and Bulbs for Forcing—Pot up in late fall, for forcing, narcissus, hyacinths, lily-of-the-valley, mertensia, bleedingheart, astilbe japonica, and store in coldframes for the required period.

Cuttings—Make root cuttings of phlox, Japanese anemones, and other plants.

Soil—Bring a supply of soil into the house for potting purposes during the winter and for seeding indoors in early spring.

Sweet Peas—Prepare trench and sow sweet peas in late fall for seeds to lie dormant for spring germination. (Page 389.)

Pools—Protect any pools by covering, or by floating logs in the water in late autumn. (Page 146.)

Clean Cultivation—Clean up and burn all refuse which may harbor insects.

Insects—Gather and burn insect cocoons, nests, and webs.

THE VEGETABLE GARDEN

Harvesting—Harvest and store the late vegetable crops such as carrots, winter squash and cabbage.

Celery—Bank celery plants with earth.

Spinach—Prepare a plot of ground for a late winter sowing of spinach seed. Spade or fork it over lightly and leave a roughly raked surface.

Fall Preparation of Soil—Prepare the ground in the fall preferably, by digging and leaving the soil in large clods for the winter action of freezing and thawing to work it into good physical condition. If manure is available, it may be dug in also at the same time. An alternate plan is to work in the lime in the fall, spreading the manure in the spring. The first plan is preferred in order to give the strawy manure a longer time to decay.

Cover Crops—Any free area may be planted with a cover crop to be turned under for green manure the following spring.

Storage—Gather winter squashes and pumpkins after the first frost and store in a pit or mound. Gather any late summer squashes and green tomatoes before frost. The tomatoes can be ripened indoors and will last for several weeks. Harvest the root crops (except parsnips and salsify which are improved by freezing).

Clean Cultivation—Gather any garden refuse—vegetable roots, stalks or leaves—and burn, to avoid harboring insects over the winter.

LAWN

Seeding—Early autumn is the best season of the year for the sowing of grass seed. (Page 176.)

TREES AND SHRUBS

Planting—Many trees and shrubs may be planted very successfully in the autumn. The few which are the exception to this rule are listed in the chapters on trees and shrubs.

Fertilizer—Trees may be given an application of commercial fertilizer late in the fall to be used for the growth made the following spring.

Evergreens—Be sure that the area surrounding broad-leaved evergreens is well supplied with moisture. Such plants suffer seriously during the winter if the ground is dry, as the transpiration of moisture from the leaves continues, and the roots must be able to absorb sufficient moisture to meet this demand.

Cuttings—Take hardwood and dormant cuttings of deciduous trees and shrubs after the leaves fall. Take evergreen cuttings.

Manure Mulch—A mulch of manure on small trees and shrubs will add fertility to the soil as well as protect them during the winter.

Spraying—If there is any evidence of scale, spray in late fall with dormant spray and again in early spring.

FRUIT

Planting—Plant blueberries, currants, gooseberries in late fall.

Borers—Apply paradichlorobenzene to peaches and other trees attacked by borers in early fall. (Page 886.)

WINTER GARDEN CALENDAR

FLOWER GARDEN

Mulch—The winter mulch should not be applied until after the ground is well frozen. (Page 446.)

Coldframes—On days when the temperature rises above 45° F., raise the coldframe sash a few inches in order that the plants may have the benefit of good ventilation. Protect frames with straw mats or similar coverings during extreme cold.

Seeds—Water the seeds which have been sown in the frames if the soil becomes too dry.

Tender Plants—Half-hardy plants, newly started perennials, and tender bulbs may be stored in the frames.

Plants for Forcing—The potted plants and bulbs placed in the cold-frames in late autumn may be brought indoors after the necessary period for root development has elapsed.

Cuttings—Take cuttings of Saintpaulia, begonia and other house plants.

Tools—Clean tools and rub rusty places with grease or oil before putting away. (Page 970.)

Wood Ashes—Save all wood ashes from the fireplace to be incorporated into the soil in the spring.

Storage—1. Inspect tubers of dahlias to make certain of right moisture conditions. Sprinkle with water if too dry.

2. Inspect all bulbs, corms, etc. Cut off portions which show decay, and dust with sulphur.

Seed Catalogs—Study seed catalogs and place orders for spring plantings.

Hardy Plants for Forcing—Bring into greenhouse plants which have been stored dormant in frames.

THE VEGETABLE GARDEN

Seed Sowing Outdoors—In January or early February sow spinach seed on the ground which was prepared for it in the autumn. Cover lightly with strawy manure. The seed will germinate in very early spring and an excellent crop may be obtained.

Seed Sowing Indoors—Celery, cabbage, and onion seed may be sown in late winter for an early crop.

Rhubarb Forcing—Rhubarb dug up in the fall may be forced in the cellar.

Seed Catalogs—Study seed catalogs and place orders for spring planting.

TREES AND SHRUBS

Protection—Protect young evergreens and newly planted trees and shrubs from wind and severe cold. Corn stalks, burlap tacked onto wooden frames, and straw mats may be used to advantage. Shake snow off evergreen branches to avoid bending and breaking.

Pruning—During the late winter months, prune the shrubs which bear their flowers on the current year's growth. (Page 280.)
Ornamental trees and fruit trees may be pruned during the late winter months (Page 247). Burn any parts with disease or insects.

Spraying—Late winter is the most advisable time to apply the dormant spray for various scale insects and other pests and diseases. The chart on page 1058 will give full details. Do not use a miscible oil spray when the temperature is below 40° F. as it is liable to cause considerable damage.

Insects—Watch for nests, webs, and tents of various insects. Burn, and use proper spray.

Wisteria—Prune wisteria during its dormant period. (Page 216.)

Mice and Rabbits—Protect trees and shrubs from mice and rabbits by baiting. (Pages 1166, 1169.)

Shrub Branches for Forcing—Cut sprays of early-flowering shrubs—forsythia, quince, etc.—in late winter for indoor bloom.

FRUIT

Strawberries—Cover strawberry plants with straw ½ to 1 inch deep. (Page 871.)

Maps of the United States Showing Regions of
Approximately Similar Growing Conditions
and Frost Dates for Spring and Autumn

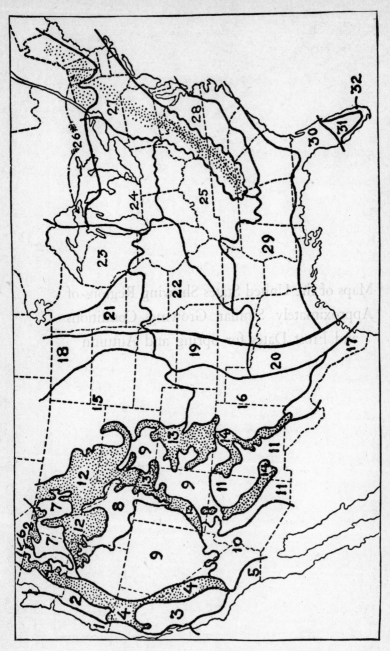

FIG. 1. A map of the United States showing, by numbers within the heavy border lines, the regions having approximately similar growing conditions for the same elevation. The stippled areas are mountain regions. *Reproduced through the courtesy of the United States Department of Agriculture.*

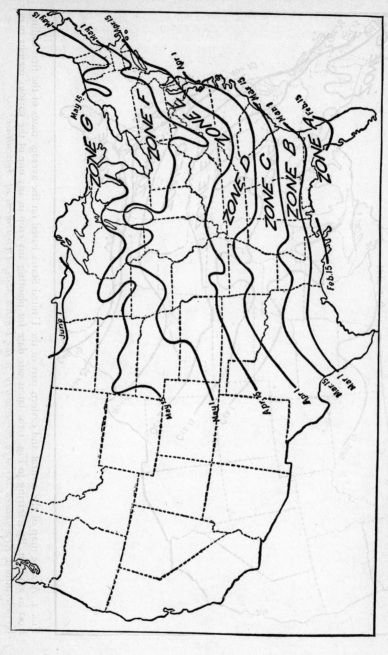

Fig. 2. A zone map of the United States based on the average dates of the latest killing frost in spring east of the Rocky Mountains. *Reproduced through the courtesy of the United States Department of Agriculture.*

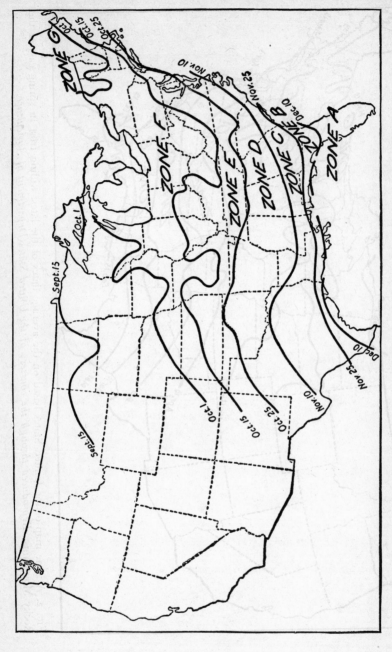

FIG. 3. A zone map of the central and eastern part of the United States based on the average dates of the first killing frost in autumn. By referring to Fig. 1 the latest safe date for planting any crop in any one of the various regions may be determined. *Reproduced through the courtesy of the United States Department of Agriculture.*

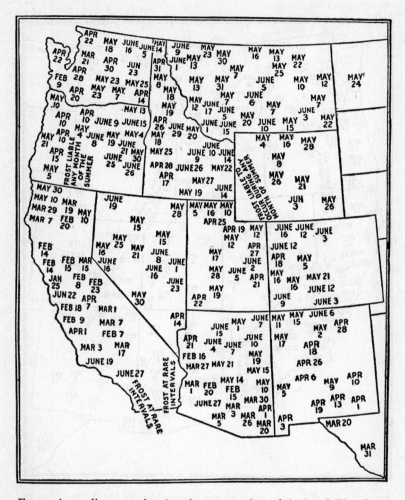

Fig. 4. An outline map showing the average date of the last killing frost in spring in the western portion of the United States. *Reproduced through the courtesy of the United States Department of Agriculture.*

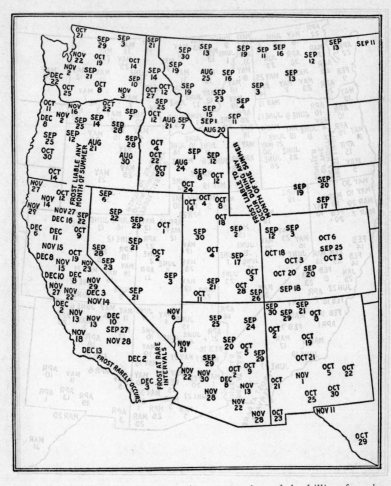

FIG. 5. An outline map showing the average date of the killing frost in the autumn in the western portion of the United States. *Reproduced through the courtesy of the United States Department of Agriculture.*

Glossary

Anther—The terminal part of the reproductive organ or pollen-disseminating part of the "male" flowering plant.

Broadcast—To scatter seed, rather than to sow it in rows or drills.

Cambium—The layer of growing cells just under the bark and outside the wood.

Casein—A substance contained in milk which, when added to sprays and dusts, adds to their adhesive and spreading qualities.

Coniferous—Pertaining to a tree which bears woody cones containing naked seeds.

Crop Rotation—The practice of alternating crops in a garden or field to avoid (1) the plant's taking the same food elements out of the soil year after year which are necessary to the plant's growth, and (2) the increase of the insects and diseases characteristic of one plant.

Cultivation—The practice of stirring the surface of the soil (1) to aërate the soil, (2) to break the crust which sometimes forms after the wet soil has dried in the sun, (3) to discourage weed growth, (4) to form a dust mulch.

Deciduous—A term applied to trees which drop their leaves annually, in contrast to "evergreen."

Decomposition—Decay, usually of strawy manure, compost, or some similar substances.

Diœcious—A term applied to plants which bear staminate and pistillate flowers.

Dormant—The period during which a plant makes no active growth. Most plants are completely dormant during the winter season. The rest period of a plant is not identical, but is controlled by internal factors, characteristic of the plant itself.

Drying-off—A method of preparing bulbs for ripening or plants for resting between periods of forcing. It may be done by gradually reducing the amount of water or by laying the pots on their sides in a spot protected from the sun.

Emulsion—A liquid mixture in which a fatty substance is suspended in minute globules, usually appearing like milk.

Erosion—The washing away of soil or rock. Often it is advantageous. More often it is destructive, as when rainfall starts gullies in a field which grow to the proportions of a deep ditch, washing away the valuable top-soil and sometimes even sub-soil.

Everlastings—Flowers which are grown for their winter effects, as they hold their shape and color.

Fertilization—(1) the application of fertilizer, (2) the union of the "male" reproductive body (pollen) with the "female" reproductive body (egg) to produce offspring (seeds).

Flats—Shallow boxes, usually 16 x 22½ inches and varying in depth from 2 to 4 inches. The young stages of plant growth may be carried on in flats, thus eliminating the back-breaking work of planting and transplanting tiny seedlings in nursery rows indoors or out of doors.

Forcing—A process (1) of making plants or bulbs bloom at a time that is not natural for them to do so, or (2) of making them bloom in a shorter length of time than is normal. In the first case, only duplication of their normal growing conditions may be necessary, while in the second excess heat and moisture are necessary.

Fumigation (Plant)—The control of injurious infestation by the use of toxic fumes given off by chemical substances.

Grafting—A process whereby a part of one plant, usually tree or shrub (scion), is made to unite with a part of another plant (stock). There are many ways of performing this process, for which see page 1020.

Habitat—The region in which a plant is found growing wild.

Hardening-off—The process of gradually reducing the amount of water and lowering the temperature for plants grown indoors or under glass, in order to toughen their tissues, making it possible for them to withstand colder conditions.

Heaving—The lifting of plants out of the ground, produced by alternate freezing and thawing during the winter. In some cases, roots may be left exposed, which may prove injurious if they are not pressed back into the soil. A light, porous texture of the soil, or a mulch will help to prevent this injury.

Heel—A small piece of two-year-old wood left on a cutting of one-year-old wood, for a certain method of propagation.

Heeling-in—A method of storing plants in the ground until conditions are favorable for planting. They are usually laid on their sides in trenches and covered with soil until only a small part of their top growth is left exposed.

Hilling-up—A practice of mounding the earth about a plant, performed for various purposes (1) protecting half-hardy plants during the winter, (2) bleaching celery, (3) strengthening the stand of aerial-rooted plants, as corn, (4) to protect shallow roots or tubers from sun-scorch.

Hybrid—A variety or individual resulting from the crossing of two species. The result of cross-fertilization; a cross.

Insecticide—A substance which kills insects by poisoning, suffocation, or paralysis. There are stomach poisons, contact poisons, and fumigants.

A repellent is not really an insecticide as it does not kill, but repels insects by its disagreeable properties.

Mat (Hotbed)—A straw or fabric covering used to protect plants in cold-frames and hotbeds against excessive cold.

Monœcious—A term applied to plants which bear flowers of different "sexes," that is, staminate and pistillate, on the same individual plant.

Naturalizing—The planting of trees, shrubs, flowering plants, bulbs, mosses, etc., in such a way as to bring about the effect of natural wild growth.

Nitrification—The change of crude forms of nitrogen first into ammonia, then into nitrites and finally into nitrates, in which form the nitrogen is available to the plant.

pH.—A term which represents the hydrogen ion concentration by which scientists measure soil acidity. The pH. acidity scale measures from 1 (acid) to 14 (alkaline) with 7 as neutral.

Pinching Back—The shortening of young shoots either to achieve bushy plant form, to encourage the development of a greater quantity of buds, or to enhance flower or fruit development.

Pistil—The central organ or reproductive part of a pistillate flower.

Pistillate—Often referred to as "female" flowers because they contain cells which, when fertilized, become seeds.

Pollen—The dusty substance found on the anther or terminal part of the reproductive organ of the opening "male sex" flowers.

Pollination—The transfer of pollen from the anther of the "male" flower to the stigma of the "female" flower, accomplished by wind, insects, or man.

Pot-bound—A stage of potted plant growth when the roots become a mass of fibers and no longer can reach out freely to make growth. Normally potted plants should be transplanted before they become pot-bound, but some prefer to be slightly so.

Potting-on—A term applied to the repeated transplantings of a plant from seedling stage to maturity in graduating sizes of flowerpots, each transplanting taking place as soon as the roots have filled the pot.

Potting-up—The transplanting of seedling plants from flats or seed pans into flower pots; the transplanting of mature plants from outdoor positions into pots, usually for the purpose of winter or ornamental effects.

Pricking-out (Pricking-off)—The process of transplanting tiny seedlings from the seed pans, pots, or other containers, into flats. The purpose is to give the seedlings more room to develop leaf and branch growth, and to help them develop more compact masses of roots by the breaking off of the tiny tips of rootlets.

Propagation—The increase or multiplication of plants. For different methods, *see* chapter on Propagation.

Repellents—Substances which, when used alone or in combination with other substances, protect plants by warding off, without killing, insects or animals.

Respiration—The process by which a plant takes in oxygen, oxidizes matter, and gives off the product.

Scabrous—Rough or gritty to the touch, as leaves.

Scarification—(1) A process of loosening the soil without turning it over, (2) a method of scratching hard-coated seeds to hasten germination.

Scion (Cion)—A term given to a bud or cutting of an improved variety which is to be inserted into the rooted "stock" in the process of grafting.

Seedlings—A term usually applied to very young plants. It is also sometimes applied to mature plants which have been produced from seed, in order to distinguish them from similar plants grown from cuttings, grafts, budding, etc.

Species—A group of individuals forming a subdivision of a genus with similar characteristics, but differing from the genus too slightly to form another genus. In "Anchusa italica" "Anchusa" is the genus, and "italica" is the species.

Stamen—The reproductive organ of the "male," pollen-bearing flower, the top part of which is the anther.

Staminate—A term used to describe a flower containing only stamens, or male reproductive organs.

Sterilization (Soil)—A term commonly given to the process of making a soil, or similar material, free from all harmful organisms before it is used for sowing seed, or for transplanting purposes.

Stigma—The terminal part of the reproductive organ, or pollen-receiving part, of the "female" flowering plant.

Stock—In grafting, the plant into which the scion is to be inserted, and which will assume the rooting function of the new plant. Any leaf or stem growth from the stock should be cut back close to the root or branch, as only new growth from the scion is desired.

Stomata—Minute openings on the under-surface of a leaf through which transpiration of moisture takes place.

Stratification—An artificial method of reproducing Nature's way of preparing seeds for germination. Some seeds require a longer period of storage than others before germination will take place, and this is usually done by placing them between layers of peat moss, soil, or similar materials which are kept moist to prevent them from drying out. Stratification is usually done in the winter so that frost action will help split hard-shelled seeds.

Sub-soil—A stratum of soil lying beneath that commonly referred to as top-soil. It is less fertile. Since it contains practically no humus and no micro-organisms essential to plant growth, roots do not penetrate it, except those of very large vigorous plants.

Sucker—Vegetative growth which comes from the roots of a tree near the base or at a short distance.

Tamping—The process of lightly firming down freshly loosened soil, either in the open or in containers, with a flat surface such as a block of wood or a board.

Top-dressing—Any material such as manure, compost, fertilizer, etc., which is placed on the surface of the ground, and which may in some cases be cultivated in. It differs from a mulch in that its primary function is to feed the plant, while the primary purpose of a mulch is to hinder weed growth and to protect from heat or cold, although a mulch may have some food value.

Transpiration—The process by which excess water is given off by the leaves of a plant, through *stomata,* or minute openings, primarily on the undersurface of the leaf. The greatest amount of moisture is given off when the heat rays of the sun reach the plant.

Transplanting—The process of moving seedlings or mature plants from one location to another. The first transplanting process out of the seed pan or pot is referred to as "pricking out."

Variety—A group of individuals forming a subdivision of a species with similar characteristics, but differing from the species too slightly to form another species. In "Anchusa italica Dropmore," "Dropmore" is the variety.

Water Sprout—A quick, succulent shoot growth which may appear on the trunk, or limbs.

Index

Important descriptive references are indicated in bold face numerals.

INDEX

INDEX

INDEX

INDEX

INDEX

INDEX

INDEX

INDEX

INDEX

INDEX

Notes

Notes

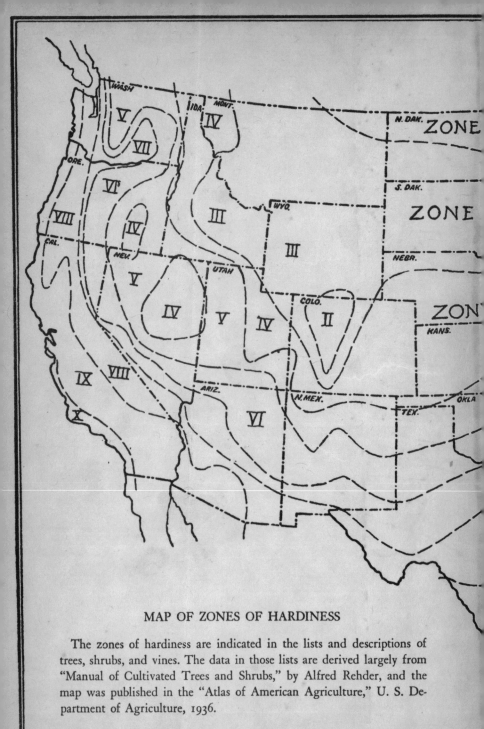

MAP OF ZONES OF HARDINESS

The zones of hardiness are indicated in the lists and descriptions of trees, shrubs, and vines. The data in those lists are derived largely from "Manual of Cultivated Trees and Shrubs," by Alfred Rehder, and the map was published in the "Atlas of American Agriculture," U. S. Department of Agriculture, 1936.